The Thiselton Companion to Christian Theology

The Thiselton Companion to Christian Theology

Anthony C. Thiselton

WILLIAM B. EERDMANS PUBLISHING COMPANY
GRAND RAPIDS, MICHIGAN

© 2015 Anthony C. Thiselton
All rights reserved

Wm. B. Eerdmans Publishing Co.
4035 Park East Court SE, Grand Rapids, MI 49546

Hardcover edition 2015
Paperback edition 2022

Library of Congress Cataloging-in-Publication Data

Thiselton, Anthony C.
    The Thiselton companion to Christian theology / Anthony C. Thiselton.
        pages   cm
    ISBN 978-0-8028-8301-8 (pbk.: alk. paper)
    1. Christianity — Dictionaries.   2. Theology — Dictionaries.   I. Title.

BR95.T54   2015
230.03 — dc23

                                                      2014035864

www.eerdmans.com

Contents

Preface	vi
Abbreviations	viii
Time Chart	xi
List of Entries	xvii
Entries, A-Z	1

Preface

Several features of this *Companion to Christian Theology* are distinctive. First, a single author has written the 600-plus articles in this book. This has the advantage of coherence, and avoids the danger of presenting an uneven work, which often becomes the fate invited by a multiauthored volume. A single author provides a single judgment, in this case gained from fifty years of teaching and research. It also ensures that the entries receive the word length that each subject or thinker genuinely needs, rather than one imposed in advance by a general editor or format.

Second, a judicious balance between research material and a tool for teaching has been reached in the work. I originally conceived of this work as a teaching tool comparable to my *Concise Encyclopedia of the Philosophy of Religion* (Oxford: OneWorld, 2002; Grand Rapids: Baker Academic, 2005). As I wrote, however, it became clear that many topics deserved long, thoughtful essays, which drew on research, evaluation, and careful judgment. The articles on God, Christology, and the Holy Spirit, for example, vary between 20,000 words and 28,000 words apiece. Similarly, the entry on the atonement merits 16,000 words. These are all subdivided into biblical and historical sections, and are often divided topically, for the sake of convenience and readability. Each section has its separate bibliography. Hence this work combines some shorter articles, which sometimes constitute explanatory teaching tools of 50-100 words, with longer articles that embody reflection and research. Some 122 articles exceed 1,000 words; over 480 are shorter articles.

I must bear full responsibility for the length and selection of each article, and I readily confess to the difficulty of choosing some subjects over others among 600 articles. There are bound to be mistakes. The length accorded to specific theologians varies enormously, depending on their creative originality and influence, and the confines of space. Wolfhart Pannenberg, for example, receives more than 8,000 words, and Karl Barth and Martin Luther some 6,000 words each. Augustine, Bultmann, Balthasar, Calvin, Küng, Moltmann, and Rahner receive 5,000, or a little less. On the other hand, numerous theologians receive less than 100 words, to explain their date and significance as briefly as possible.

Third, although I have made every effort to be scrupulously fair and accurate, I have often added my own value judgment or comment. This may be reflected even in some of the recommended reading. The average length of article is 700 words. Hence I have listed reading suggestions for entries that exceed 700 words, and usually restricted these to six or occasionally seven books, or sometimes articles.

Fourth, this is specifically a companion to *Christian* theology. I have avoided exploring other faiths, and only marginally touched on ethics and liturgy. However, I have been careful to document sources (including publisher, place, date), and where possible to quote the actual language of theologians, rather than rely on loose paraphrase. For me, this exemplifies "Do as you would be done by" for reference books. I have also added a time chart after this preface, in response to requests to do so in reviews of my *Concise Encyclopedia of the Philosophy of Religion*. This allows for a comparison between the different dates of the thinkers listed.

Finally, I thank my patient wife, Rosemary, for endless meticulous typing and proofreading, when she would rather have maintained our overlarge garden. She also alerted me when sentences seemed obscure or convoluted, and the thought needed to be expressed in several shorter, simpler sentences. I also thank my four other typists, especially Miss Rowan Gillam-Hull and Miss Rachael Brough, without whom this work would never have been finished, and Mr. Jon Pott of Eerdmans for his friendship and encouragement for this work and over many years, and allowing space for over 600 entries. I am also very grateful to Mr. Tom Raabe, who meticulously subedited the manuscript at a later stage, and smoothed out several infelicities.

ANTHONY C. THISELTON, FBA
Emeritus Professor of Christian Theology
University of Nottingham, U.K.

Abbreviations

AB	Anchor Bible
ABD	*Anchor Bible Dictionary.* Edited by D. N. Freedman. 6 vols. New York and London: Doubleday, 1992
ANF	*Ante-Nicene Fathers.* Edited by A. Roberts and J. Donaldson. 10 vols. Grand Rapids: Eerdmans, 1993
BAR	*Biblical Archaeology Review*
BDAG	W. Bauer, F. W. Danker, A. F. Arndt, and F. W. Gingrich. *A Greek-English Lexicon of the New Testament and Other Early Christian Literature.* 3rd ed. Chicago: University of Chicago Press, 2000
BDB	F. Brown, S. R. Driver, and C. A. Briggs. *The New Hebrew and English Lexicon.* Lafayette, Ind.: Associated Publishers, 1980
Beveridge	John Calvin. *Institutes of the Christian Religion.* Translated by Henry Beveridge. 2 vols. Grand Rapids: Eerdmans, 1989
BJRL	*Bulletin of the John Rylands University Library of Manchester*
BQT	*Basic Questions in Theology.* By W. Pannenberg. 3 vols. London: SCM, 1970-1973
CD	*Church Dogmatics.* By Karl Barth. Edited by G. W. Bromiley and T. F. Torrance. 14 vols. Edinburgh: T. & T. Clark, 1957-1975
CSEL	Corpus scriptorum ecclesiaticorum latinorum
CUP	Cambridge University Press
DOTT	*Documents from Old Testament Times.* Edited by D. W. Thomas. London, 1958
DTIB	*Dictionary for Theological Interpretation of the Bible.* Edited by Kevin J. Vanhoozer. Grand Rapids: Baker Academic, 2005
EDNT	*Exegetical Dictionary of the New Testament.* Edited by H. Balz and G. Schneider. 3 vols. Grand Rapids: Eerdmans, 1990
ExpTim	*Expository Times*
FCF	*Foundations of Christian Faith.* By Karl Rahner. New York: Seabury Press; London: Darton, Longman, and Todd, 1978
GL	*The Glory of the Lord.* By Hans Urs von Balthasar. 7 vols. San Francisco: Ignatius; Edinburgh: T. & T. Clark, 1982-1990. Vol. 1, 1982; vol. 2, 1984; vol. 3, 1986; vol. 4, 1989; vol. 5, 1991; vol. 6, 1991; vol. 7, 1990
Grimm-Th	C. L. W. Grimm and J. H. Thayer. *A Greek-English Lexicon of the New Testament.* 4th ed. Edinburgh: T. & T. Clark, 1901

H-R	Edwin Hatch and Henry A. Redpath. *A Concordance to the Septuagint and Other Greek Versions of the Old Testament*. 2 vols. Athens: Beneficial Books, facsimile of 1897 edition
HTR	*Harvard Theological Review*
IB	*Interpreter's Bible*. 12 vols. Nashville: Abington-Cokesbury, 1952
JBL	*Journal of Biblical Literature*
JGM	*Jesus — God and Man*. By W. Pannenberg. Philadelphia: Westminster; London: SCM, 1968
JPT	*Journal of Pentecostal Theology*
JR	*Journal of Religion*
JSNT	*Journal for the Study of the New Testament*
JTS	*Journal of Theological Studies*
Lampe	G. W. H. Lampe. *A Patristic Greek Lexicon*. Oxford: OUP, 1961
LCC	Library of Christian Classics
LSJ	H. G. Liddell, R. Scott, and H. S. Jones, with R. McKenzie. *A Greek-English Lexicon*. Oxford: Clarendon, 1996
LW	*Luther's Works*. American ed. 55 vols. Philadelphia: Fortress; St. Louis: Concordia, 1955-1986
MG	W. F. Moulton and A. S. Geden. *A Concordance to the Greek Testament*. 2nd ed. Edinburgh: T. & T. Clark, 1899
MM	J. H. Moulton and G. Milligan. *The Vocabulary of the Greek Testament Illustrated from the Papyri and Other Non-Literary Sources*. London: Hodder and Stoughton, 1952
NIDB	*New International Dictionary of the Bible*. Edited by J. D. Douglas and M. C. Tenney. Grand Rapids: Zondervan, 1987
NIDOTTE	*New International Dictionary of Old Testament Theology and Exegesis*. Edited by W. A. Vangemeren. 5 vols. Carlisle: Paternoster, 1996
NIDPCM	*New International Dictionary of Pentecostal and Charismatic Movements*. Edited by S. M. Burgess. Grand Rapids: Zondervan, 2002
NIGTC	New International Greek Testament Commentary
NPNF	*Nicene and Post-Nicene Fathers*. Series 1, edited by P. Schaff. Series 2, edited by P. Schaff and H. Wace. 14 vols. Grand Rapids Eerdmans, 1991, 1993
NTS	*New Testament Studies*
OUP	Oxford University Press
PG	Patrologia Graeca. Edited by J.-P. Migne
PL	Patrologia Latina. Edited by J.-P. Migne
REB	Revised English Bible
SBL	Society of Biblical Literature
SJT	*Scottish Journal of Theology*
ST	*Systematic Theology*. By W. Pannenberg. 3 vols. Grand Rapids: Eerdmans, 1992-1998

Abbreviations

Su Th	*Summa Theologiae.* By Thomas Aquinas. 60 vols. New York: McGraw-Hill, 1963
TDNT	*Theological Dictionary of the New Testament*
TDOT	*Theological Dictionary of the Old Testament*
Theol	*Theology*
TI	*Theological Investigations.* By Karl Rahner. 23 vols. New York: Seabury Press; London: Darton, Longman, and Todd, 1961-1993
TKG	*The Trinity and the Kingdom of God: The Doctrine of God.* By J. Moltmann. London: SCM, 1981
TLG	*Thesaurus linguae graecae*
VT	*Vetus Testamentum*
WA	Weimarer Ausgabe, of Luther's *Works*
ZNW	*Zeitschrift für die neutestamentliche Wissenschaft und die Kunde der älteren Kirche*
ZTK	*Zeitschrift für Theologie und Kirche*

Time Chart

First Century
c. 30	Crucifixion and Resurrection of Christ
c. 33	Conversion of Paul
c. 50-64(?)	Pauline Epistles
c. 64-70(?)	Gospel of Mark
70	Fall of Jerusalem
c. 70-85(?)	Gospels of Matthew and Luke
c. 85-95(?)	Gospel of John
c. 96	*1 Clement*

Second Century
c. 35–c. 108	Ignatius of Antioch
c. 100	*Didachē*
c. 100–c. 165	Justin
c. 130–c. 200	Irenaeus
c. 150–c. 215	Clement of Alexandria
c. 150–c. 225	Tertullian
d. c. 160	Marcion

Third Century
c. 170–c. 236	Hippolytus
c. 185–c. 254	Origen
c. 200-258	Novatian of Rome
c. 205-270	Plotinus
c. 232-303	Porphyry
d. 258	Cyprian of Carthage

Fourth Century
c. 250–c. 325	Lactantius
c. 250-336	Arius
c. 296-373	Athanasius
313	"Conversion" of Constantine
c. 315-368	Hilary of Poitiers
c. 315-387	Cyril of Jerusalem

Time Chart

323	Eusebius's *Ecclesiastical History*
325	Council of Nicaea
c. 330-379	Basil of Caesarea
c. 330-390	Gregory of Nazianzus
c. 330-395	Gregory of Nyssa
c. 339-397	Ambrose of Milan
c. 347-407	John Chrysostom
381	Council of Constantinople

Fifth Century

c. 345-420	Jerome
350-428	Theodore of Mopsuestia
354-430	Augustine (*City of God* 426)
c. 355-420	Pelagius
c. 360–c. 435	John Cassian
384-404	Approximate origins of the Vulgate
393-458	Theodoret
431	Council of Ephesus
451	Council of Chalcedon

Sixth Century

c. 480-525	Boethius
c. 480-547	Benedict of Nursia
c. 500	Dionysius (Pseudo-Dionysius)
c. 540-604	Gregory of Rome

Seventh-Eighth Centuries

664	Synod of Whitby
c. 673-735	Bede (*Ecclesiastical History* 731)
c. 675-754	Boniface
c. 740-804	Alcuin

Ninth Century

c. 810–c. 895	Photius of Constantinople

Eleventh-Twelfth Centuries

c. 1033-1109	Anselm
c. 1075-1129	Rupert of Deutz
1079-1142	Peter Abelard
1090-1153	Bernard of Clairvaux
1098-1179	Hildegard of Bingen
c. 1100-1160	Peter Lombard
1135-1202	Joachim of Fiore

Time Chart

Thirteenth Century
c. 1209	Franciscan Order founded
c. 1217-1274	Bonaventura
1220	Dominican Order founded
1225-1274	Thomas Aquinas
c. 1266-1308	John Duns Scotus

Fourteenth Century
1265-1321	Dante (*Divine Comedy* 1321)
1270-1349	Nicholas of Lyra
c. 1285-1349	William of Ockham
c. 1330-1384	John Wycliffe (Wycliffe's Bible 1388)
1342-1416	Julian of Norwich
c. 1343-1396	Walter Hilton
c. 1347-1380	Catherine of Siena
c. 1372-1415	John Huss

Sixteenth Century
c. 1466-1536	Desiderius Erasmus
1483-1546	Martin Luther (Ninety-five Theses 1517)
1484-1531	Ulrich Zwingli
1489-1556	Thomas Cranmer
1491-1551	Martin Bucer
c. 1494-1536	William Tyndale
1497-1560	Philip Melanchthon
1504-1575	Heinrich Bullinger
1509-1564	John Calvin (*Institutes:* 1st ed. 1536; 3rd ed. 1559)
1542-1591	John of the Cross
1545-1563	Council of Trent
1549	First Prayer Book of Edward VI
1552	Second Prayer Book of Edward VI
1554-1600	Richard Hooker
1582	Douai-Reims Bible

Seventeenth Century
1583-1645	Hugo Grotius
1593-1633	George Herbert
1596-1650	René Descartes
1613-1667	Jeremy Taylor
1615-1691	Richard Baxter
1618-1619	Synod of Dort
1623-1662	Blaise Pascal
1624-1691	George Fox

Time Chart

1632-1677	Baruch Spinoza
1632-1704	John Locke
1635-1705	Philipp Jakob Spener
1646-1716	Gottfried Wilhelm Leibniz
1648	Westminster Confession (final approval)
1662	*Book of Common Prayer*

Eighteenth Century

1687-1752	Johannes Albrecht Bengel
1692-1752	Joseph Butler
1703-1758	Jonathan Edwards
1703-1791	John Wesley (Origins of Methodism 1738)
1711-1776	David Hume
1724-1804	Immanuel Kant
1729-1781	Gotthold Ephraim Lessing
1743-1805	William Paley
1762-1814	Johann G. Fichte

Nineteenth Century

1768-1834	Friedrich D. E. Schleiermacher
1770-1831	Georg Wilhelm Friedrich Hegel
1772-1834	Samuel Taylor Coleridge
1775-1854	Friedrich W. J. von Schelling
1792-1834	Edward Irving
1792-1860	Ferdinand Christian Baur
1797-1878	Charles Hodge
1800-1882	John Nelson Darby
1801-1890	John Henry Newman (conversion to Rome 1845)
1802-1876	Horace Bushnell
1804-1872	Ludwig A. Feuerbach
1805-1872	F. D. Maurice
1808-1874	David F. Strauss
1809-1882	Charles R. Darwin
1810-1871	Henry Alford
1813-1855	Søren Kierkegaard
1817-1893	Benjamin Jowett
1818-1883	Karl Marx
1819-1875	Charles Kingsley
1822-1889	Albrecht Ritschl
1825-1901	Brooke Foss Westcott
1828-1889	Joseph Barber Lightfoot
1837-1920	Abraham Kuyper
1844-1900	Friedrich Wilhelm Nietzsche

1846-1922   Wilhelm Herrmann
1848-1921   Peter T. Forsyth
1851-1930   Adolf von Harnack
1856-1917   James Denney
1870   First Vatican Council

Twentieth Century
1879-1977   Gustaf Aulén
1881-1955   Pierre Teilhard de Chardin
1884-1973   Charles H. Dodd
1884-1976   Rudolf Bultmann
1884-1978   Étienne Gilson
1886-1965   Paul Tillich
1886-1968   Karl Barth
1889-1966   Emil Brunner
1889-1976   Martin Heidegger
1890-1978   Anders T. S. Nygren
1892-1971   Reinhold Niebuhr
1894-1962   H. Richard Niebuhr
1896-1991   Henri de Lubac
1900-2002   Hans-Georg Gadamer
1902-1999   Oscar Cullmann
1903-1958   Vladimir Lossky
1904-1984   Bernard Lonergan
1904-1984   Karl Rahner
1904-1995   Yves M. J. Congar
1905-1988   Hans Urs von Balthasar
1906-1945   Dietrich Bonhoeffer
1912-1980   Geoffrey W. H. Lampe
1913-2003   Carl F. H. Henry
1913-2005   Paul Ricoeur
1913-2007   Thomas Forsyth Torrance
1914-2009   Edward Schillebeeckx
1915-1972   Ian T. Ramsey
1917-1984   George Caird
1917-2011   C. Kingsley Barrett
1919-1983   John A. T. Robinson
1922-1988   Hans W. Frei
1923-2007   Brevard Childs
1924-2006   James Barr
1926-2009   Martin Hengel
1928-2014   Wolfhart Pannenberg
1930-2004   Jacques Derrida

Time Chart

1941-2003   Colin Gunton
1962-1965   Second Vatican Council

Into the Twenty-first Century

b. 1923   George Lindbeck
b. 1926   Jürgen Moltmann
b. 1927   Benedict XVI (Joseph Ratzinger)
b. 1928   Hans Küng
b. 1929   Harvey Cox
b. 1931   John D. Zizioulas
b. 1932   Walter Brueggemann
b. 1932   David H. Kelsey
b. 1932   Alvin Plantinga
b. 1932   Nicholas Wolterstorff
b. 1934   John Dominic Crossan
b. 1934   Eberhard Jüngel
b. 1939   James D. G. Dunn
b. 1939   David Tracy
b. 1939   Frances W. Young
b. 1940   Stanley Hauerwas
b. 1945   Oliver O'Donovan
b. 1946   Richard J. Bauckham
b. 1947   Michael Welker
b. 1948   N. Thomas Wright
b. 1950   Peter Ochs
b. 1950   Rowan D. Williams
b. 1951   Sarah Coakley
b. 1955   John Webster
b. 1956   David Fergusson
b. 1956   Miroslav Volf
b. 1957   Kathryn Tanner

List of Entries

Abba
Abelard, Peter
Absolute
Absolute Idealism
Accident
Adam
Adiaphora
Adoption, Adoptionism, Adoptianism
A Fortiori
Aggiornamento
Agnosticism
Alcuin
Alford, Henry
Allegory, Allegorical Interpretation
Ambrose of Milan
Ambrosiaster
Amen
Anabaptists
Analogy
Analytic
Anamnēsis
Anaphora
Anathema
Anchorites
Angel
Anglican Theology
Anglo-Catholic
Angst
Anhypostasia
Annunciation
Anselm
Anthropology
Antichrist
Apocalyptic
Apocrypha
Apollinarianism
Apologetics
Apologists
Apophatic Theology

Apostasy
A Posteriori
Apostle, Apostolicity
Apostles' Creed
Apostolic Constitutions
Apostolic Fathers
Apostolic Succession
Apotheosis
Appropriation
A Priori
Aquinas, Thomas
Aristotle
Arius, Arianism
Arminius, James
Ascension of Christ
Asceticism
Aseity
Assumption
Assurance
Athanasian Creed
Athanasius
Atheism
Atonement: Biblical
Atonement: Historical
Attributes
Augustine
Aulén, Gustaf
Austin, John L.
Authority of the Bible
Azazel

Bacon, Francis
Bakhtin, Mikhail
Balthasar, Hans Urs von
Baptism
Baptism in the Holy Spirit
Baptist Theology
Barmen Declaration
Barr, James

xvii

List of Entries

Barrett, C. Kingsley
Barth, Karl
Base Communities
Basil of Caesarea
Bauckham, Richard J.
Baur, Ferdinand Christian
Baxter, Richard
Beatific Vision
Bede
Benedict XVI
Benedict of Nursia
Bengel, Johannes Albrecht
Bernard of Clairvaux
Biblical Criticism
Biblical Theology
Bioethics
Bishop
Black Theology
Blake, William
Blessing and Cursing
Blood
Body
Boethius
Bonaventura
Bonhoeffer, Dietrich
Boniface
Book of Common Prayer
Bousset, Wilhelm
Brueggemann, Walter
Brunner, Emil
Buber, Martin
Bucer, Martin
Bulgakov, Sergei Nikolaevich
Bullinger, Heinrich
Bultmann, Rudolf
Bushnell, Horace
Butler, Joseph

Caird, George B.
Calendar
Calvin, John
Cambridge Platonists
Canon
Canon Criticism
Cappadocian Fathers
Carthusian Order
Cassian, John
Casuistry
Catechism

Cathars
Catherine of Siena
Catholicity
Cause, Causality
Celsus
Celtic Christianity
Cessationalism
Chalcedon, Council of
Chester Beatty Papyri
Childs, Brevard
Christology: Jesus of History
Christology: Ministry of Jesus
Christology: Christ's Resurrection and
    Lordship
Christology: History of Thought
Chronology
Chrysostom, John
Clapham Sect
Clement of Alexandria
Clement of Rome
Cloud of Unknowing, The
Coakley, Sarah
Codex Bezae
Codex Sinaiticus
Coleridge, Samuel Taylor
Communion of Saints
Comte, Auguste
Concept
Conditional Immortality
Confirmation
Congar, Yves M. J.
Conscience
Constantinople, Council of
Contingent
Cosmological Argument
Counter-Reformation
Covenant
Cox, Harvey
Cranmer, Thomas
Creation
Creationism
Critical Realism
Critical Theory
Cross
Crossan, John Dominic
Cullmann, Oscar
Curia
Cyril of Alexandria
Cyril of Jerusalem

List of Entries

Dante
Darby, John Nelson
Darwin, Charles R.
Day of Atonement
Dead Sea Scrolls
Death and Mourning
Death of God Theology
Deconstruction, Deconstructionism
Deification
Deism
Denney, James
Deontology
Depravity
Derrida, Jacques
Descartes, René
Descent into Hell
Desert Fathers
Dialectic, Dialectical Theology
Dilthey, Wilhelm
Dionysius, Pseudo-
Disciples of Christ
Dispensationalism
Dodd, Charles H.
Dogma, Dogmatics
Dominicans
Donatism
Dort, Synod of
Douai
Double Procession
Dove
Dualism
Dunn, James D. G.
Duns Scotus, John
Dysteleology

Ebionites
Ecclesiology
Eckhart, Meister
Edwards, Jonathan
Election and Predestination
Emanation
Empiricism
Encounter
Enlightenment, The
Enthusiasm
Ephesus, Council of
Epistemology
Erastianism
Eristics

Eschatology
Eternity
Ethics
Eusebius of Caesarea
Evangelical, Evangelicalism
Evidentialism
Evil, Problem of
Evolution
Exegesis
Existentialism
Existentiell
Expiation

Faith, Faithfulness
Father, God as
Feminist Theology
Fergusson, David
Feuerbach, Ludwig A.
Fichte, Johann G.
Fideism
Filioque
Forgive, Forgiveness
Form Criticism
Forsyth, Peter T.
Fox, George
Franciscans
Francis de Sales
Frankfurt School
Freedom, Free Will
Frei, Hans W.
Freud, Sigmund
Fundamentalism

Gadamer, Hans-Georg
Gilson, Étienne
Glory
Glossolalia
Gnosticism
God, Trinity: God Creates, Speaks, or Reveals; Acts in Transcendence and Immanence
God, Trinity: Almighty, Omniscient, Omnipresent
God, Trinity: Historical Development
God, Trinity: The Holy Trinity
Grace
Gregory of Nazianzus
Gregory of Nyssa
Gregory of Rome

xix

List of Entries

Grotius, Hugo
Gunton, Colin

Habermas, Jürgen
Harnack, Adolf von
Hauerwas, Stanley
Healing
Heart
Heaven
Hegel, Georg Wilhelm Friedrich
Heidegger, Martin
Heilsgeschichte
Hell
Hengel, Martin
Henry, Carl F. H.
Herbert, George
Hermeneutical Circle
Hermeneutics
Herrmann, Wilhelm
Hilary of Poitiers
Hildegard of Bingen
Hilton, Walter
Hippolytus
Historicality
Historical Theology
Historicism
History of Religions School
Hodge, Charles
Hollenweger, Walter J.
Holy, Holiness
Holy Spirit: The Spirit of God in the Old Testament and in Judaism
Holy Spirit: The Spirit in the New Testament
Holy Spirit: The Spirit in Historical Theology
Homiletics
Hooker, Richard
Hope
Horizon
Hume, David
Huss, John
Husserl, Edmund
Hypostasis

Iconoclasm, Icons
Idealism
Ignatius of Antioch
Image of God

Immaculate Conception
Immanence
Imminence of the End
Impassibility of God
Incarnational Theology
Incommensurability
Indirect Communication
Inspiration
Intention
Intermediate State
Intersubjectivity
Irenaeus
Irresistible Grace
Irving, Edward
Irwin, Benjamin H.
Iser, Wolfgang

Jansenism
Jaspers, Karl Theodor
Jerome
Jesuits
Joachim of Fiore
John of Damascus
John of the Cross
Jowett, Benjamin
Judaism in the Time of Jesus
Julian of Norwich
Jung, Carl Gustav
Jüngel, Eberhard
Justification

Kairos
Kant, Immanuel
Kelsey, David H.
Kenotic Theology
Kerygma
Kierkegaard, Søren
Kingdom of God
Kingsley, Charles
Küng, Hans
Kuyper, Abraham

Lactantius
Lampe, Geoffrey W. H.
Language, Religious
Last Judgment
Latimer, Hugh
Latitudinarians
Laud, William

Law
Lectionary
Leibniz, Gottfried Wilhelm
Lessing, Gotthold Ephraim
Lexicography
Liberalism
Liberation Hermeneutics and Theology
Life, Eternal Life
Lightfoot, Joseph Barber
Lindbeck, George
Liturgy, Liturgical Movement
Locke, John
Logical Positivism
Lombard, Peter
Lonergan, Bernard
Lord's Supper
Lossky, Vladimir
Love
Lubac, Henri de
Luther, Martin

Marcel, Gabriel
Marcion
Marx, Karl
Materialism
Maurice, F. D.
Maximus the Confessor
Mediator, Mediation
Melanchthon, Philip
Mennonites
Metaphor
Metaphysics
Methodist, Methodism
Millennium
Ministry
Miracles
Modalism
Moltmann, Jürgen
Monasticism
Montanism
Moral Argument
Moravians
Mysticism
Myth

Narcissism
Narrative
Natural Law
Natural Theology

Necessary
Negative Theology
Neoplatonism
Neo-Thomism
New Hermeneutic
Newman, John Henry
Nicaea, Creed and Council of
Nicholas of Lyra
Niebuhr, H. Richard
Niebuhr, Reinhold
Nietzsche, Friedrich Wilhelm
Nominalism
Novatian of Rome
Nygren, Anders T. S.

Occasionalism
Ochs, Peter
O'Donovan, Oliver
Ontological Argument
Ontology
Open Theism
Opus Operatum
Origen
Original Righteousness
Other, Otherness
Otto, Rudolf

Panentheism
Pannenberg, Wolfhart
Pantheism
Parables of Jesus
Paradox
Parousia
Pascal, Blaise
Pastoral Theology
Patriarchate
Patripassianism
Patristic/Patristics
Pelagius
Pentecostals, Pentecostalism
Perichoresis
Perseverance
Phenomenology
Philo of Alexandria
Photius of Constantinople
Pietism
Pilgrimage
Plantinga, Alvin
Plato

List of Entries

Plotinus
Pluralism
Pneumatomachi
Political Theology
Polyphonic Discourse
Porphyry
Positivism
Postcolonial Theology
Postliberalism
Postmodernism, Postmodernity
Pragmatism
Prayer
Presbyterian, Presbyterianism
Preunderstanding
Prevenient Grace
Process Thought
Promise
Providence
Purgatory
Puritanism

Quakers, or Society of Friends
Queer Theology

Radical Orthodoxy
Rahner, Karl
Ramsey, Ian T.
Rapture
Rationalism
Realism
Reason
Recapitulation
Reception Theory and Reception History
Reconciliation, Reconcile
Redeem, Redemption
Reformation
Reformed Theology
Religion
Renewal Movement
Repentance, Repent
Restorationism
Resurrection of the Dead
Revelation
Richard of St. Victor
Ricoeur, Paul
Righteousness
Risk
Ritschl, Albrecht
Robinson, John A. T.

Romanticism
Rupert of Deutz

Sachkritik
Sacraments
Sacrifice
Sanctification
Sartre, Jean-Paul
Scapegoat
Schelling, Friedrich W. J. von
Schillebeeckx, Edward
Schleiermacher, Friedrich D. E.
Scholasticism
Science and Religion
Scofield Reference Bible
Scotus of Erigena
Scriptural Reasoning
Self-Involvement
Silence
Sin: Biblical
Sin: Historical
Sinless Perfection
Skepticism
Sobornost
Social Gospel
Socinianism
Soteriology
Soul
Speech Act Theory
Spener, Philipp Jakob
Spinoza, Baruch
Spirituality
Stoics, Stoicism
Strauss, David F.
Strawson, Peter F.
Structuralism
Subjectivity, Subject-Object Relation
Subordinationism
Substitution
Supralapsarianism
Symbol
Synergism
Systematic Theology

Tanner, Kathryn
Taylor, Jeremy
Teilhard de Chardin, Pierre
Teleological Argument
Temptation

Teresa of Ávila
Tertullian
Theism
Theodore of Mopsuestia
Theodoret
Theological Positivism
Theology of Crisis
Tillich, Paul
Time
Torrance, Thomas Forsyth
Tractarianism
Tracy, David
Tradition
Traducianism
Transcendence
Transcendental
Trent, Council of
Trinity, the Holy
Troeltsch, Ernst
Tutu, Desmond
Tyconius
Tyndale, William
Typology

Ultramontanism
Unitarianism
Universalism
Universals

Vatican I
Vatican II
Virgin Birth
Volf, Miroslav
Vulgate

Warfield, Benjamin B.
Webster, John
Weil, Simone
Welker, Michael
Wesley, John
Westcott, Brooke Foss
Westminster Confession
William of Ockham
Williams, Rowan D.
Wisdom
Wittgenstein, Ludwig J. J.
Wolterstorff, Nicholas
Womanism
Word of God
Wrath of God
Wright, N. Thomas
Wycliffe, John

Young, Frances M.

Zizioulas, John
Zwingli, Ulrich

A

Abba
This is the Aramaic word for "father" used by Jesus in Mark 14:36, and reproduced in the heart of Christians by the Holy Spirit in Rom. 8:15 and Gal. 4:6. In a wider sense God is honored as Father by virtue of creation (Deut. 32:6; Mal. 2:10), and also as One who pities and cares for his children (Ps. 103:13; Jer. 3:19-20; Hos. 11:3). In 1955 J. Jeremias argued that Palestinian Jews were reluctant to call God "Father" (although the word could be used in the whole phrase "Our Father, Our King"). He therefore concluded that Jesus used "Abba" as an intimate word, and as "something new, something unique and unheard of. . . . Jesus dared to take this step" ("Abba," in *The Central Message of the New Testament* [London: SCM, 1955], 21). Today it is widely recognized that Jeremias may have pressed his case too far, but that in a more moderate form this claim may be largely true. Clearly Paul singles out the term in Christian address to God as indicating Christlike intimacy with God and a sonship derived from Christ's unique Sonship.

Abelard, Peter
A French philosopher and theologian, Peter Abelard (also Abailard) (1079-1142) contributed to Christian thought in the main areas of philosophy and logic; the doctrine of the Holy Trinity; biblical exegesis; theories of the atonement; and ethics. He was indebted mainly to three teachers: he began his studies in the French school under Roscelin, an advocate of nominalism; he studied further under William of Champeaux, who advocated realism, regarded as the opposite to nominalism; finally his teacher became Anselm of Laon.

(i) On logic and philosophy, it is not unduly surprising that after study with the nominalist Roscelin and the realist William of Champeaux, Abelard attempted to mediate between both sides, affirming what is best in each. At this time France was the home of heated philosophical and logical debate, and this issue was central for many. Nominalism sees "universals" as human inventions, in opposition to Plato's theory of the reality of "forms" or universal "ideas." Abelard agreed that universals represented "names" *(voces, nomina)* and were not "things" *(res)*. But he also argued that they served to establish knowledge, and were *more* than mere "names." His view is sometimes described as moderate realism; universals are not simple constructions of the mind. He set up his own school in Paris, where he was recognized as a competent teacher of logic and theology. Indeed, he was bitterly opposed by Bernard of Clairvaux for putting reason in the place of faith. He argued, contrary to Anselm of Canterbury's famous dictum, that faith was impossible without understanding.

(ii) Abelard's work on the Trinity was initiated by his reply to Roscelin's philosophy. Roscelin saw the Trinity as a diversity of three Beings, bordering on tritheism. Abelard stressed the unity of the one substance, yet also the individuality of the three persons, in *Theologia Summi Boni*. But Bernard nevertheless attacked him for viewing the persons as abstractions, as power, wisdom, and goodness. Hence the Council of Soissons condemned his work (1121) and required him to recite the Athanasian Creed.

(iii) Abelard was regarded as a good biblical exegete. But his best work, on Ezekiel, was lost. He wrote a commentary on Romans, of which the section on Rom. 3:19-26 has been endlessly scrutinized because of its influence on shaping a theology of the atonement. Of itself, many would regard this as poor exegesis, in which he seems to equate God's righteousness with God's love, and to advocate what many call a moral influence theory of the atonement, or a subjective theory, in opposition to Anselm's objective account. However, it can be argued that this work is so short that it cannot include everything that he thought about the subject.

(iv) Abelard's publication on ethics is thought to be related to his tragic love affair with Heloise. The affair was discovered, and Abelard was vilified and even castrated. Heloise had argued that she was guilty for encouraging the affair, but innocent in as far as her *intentions* and love for Abelard were concerned. It can scarcely be accidental, therefore, that Abelard's *Ethics* argued that ethically good deeds rest on *intention*, not consequences.

Reading: M. T. Clancy, *Abelard* (Oxford: OUP, 1997); D. E. Luscombe, *The School of Peter Abelard* (Cambridge: CUP, 1969); D. E. Luscombe, *Peter Abelard* (London: Historical Association, 1979).

Absolute

"Absolute" popularly denotes that which is unconditioned and complete, characterized by aseity, in contrast to all that is relative. However, the term has different resonances in different philosophical contexts or traditions. Kant uses the term to denote what is unconditionally valid, including the categorical imperative, or moral obligation. Schelling sees the Absolute as the prior ground of selfhood, its self-awareness, and its perception of the world. Similarly Tillich sees it as "being-itself" prior to any distinction between subject and object in human knowledge. Hegel identifies the Absolute as Spirit, which finds expression in the world through dialectic in history and logical necessity. Spirit is Absolute but self-differentiating. Hence God may be Absolute, but also Trinity. F. H. Bradley argues that only the Absolute in its wholeness is *real;* diversity is mere *appearance.* The Absolute is unconditioned by time or change. The American J. Royce identifies the Absolute not only with God, but also with a projected "final community of persons" (1897). This partly reflects Nicholas of Cusa, to the effect that God is "absolutely infinite," but as Absolute holds together a "coincidence of opposites." However, the usual meaning of "Absolute" remains that which is independent, and unconditioned. Hence, today, especially in view of fresh debate about divine impassibility, it is often debated whether God can be both "absolute" and "personal," even if we exclude a human sense of "personal." This is better formulated as: Can God be both Absolute and Suprapersonal?

Absolute Idealism
In practice this often denotes the philosophical approach of Fichte, Schelling, and especially Hegel. But the simple term "idealism" conveys a wide range of meanings. It may denote "immaterialism," of which Berkeley is a well-known advocate. Berkeley did not use the term "idealist," preferring to use "immaterialist." He argued that nothing could be known to exist except ideas in the mind. In Greek philosophy Plato used the term differently to denote a belief in forms or ideas, which were universals (e.g., *whiteness* in contrast to white *things*). Kant described his philosophy as transcendental idealism, in which he saw space, time, and the categories as conditions for the possibility of knowledge. Hence, absolute idealism distinguishes the thought of Fichte, Schelling, and Hegel from Berkeley's immaterialism, Plato's ideas or forms, and Kant's transcendental thought.

Fichte's philosophy was mind-dependent and more radical than that of Kant. Schelling's philosophy was always developing into a fresh stage, as he moved from transcendental idealism (1800) to absolute idealism, arguing that "aesthetic idealism" made people aware of the Absolute. Hegel is the most influential of this group, arguing that "every genuine philosophy is . . . Idealism." In essence, he argues that *the finite is "not genuinely real."* He rejects Berkeley's idealism as subjective idealism. He sees the Absolute disclosing itself in history. As infinite Spirit God may take finite form in the incarnation of Christ, but reveals its true nature as infinite and absolute at the resurrection. His thought is akin to F. H. Bradley's, that "only the whole is real" in his *Appearance and Reality*.

Accident
Accident denotes a contingent quality, object, or event, which might or might not exist, and happens to inhere in some underlying substance. Depending on the mind and the eye, an orange may appear to possess the accidents of roundness and orange color, while its substance is the fruit itself. It is a technical term found in Aristotle and Aquinas. In transubstantiation, the traditional Roman Catholic teaching based on Aquinas is that the "accidents," or bread and wine, may still *appear* as such to the worshipers, but the underlying substance of the elements of the communion, or Eucharist, or Lord's Supper, becomes the body and blood of Christ. Aquinas writes, "The accidents of the bread and wine remain, when the substance of the bread *(substantia panis)* is no longer there" (*Su Th* 3, qu. 75, art. 5).

Adam

Adam (Heb. *'ādām*) is used either as a personal name (Gen. 4:1) or as denoting humankind (probably Gen. 1:26, translated as "humankind in his image" in the NRSV, *'ādām* in Hebrew). It also denotes *the first man*, or *primal humankind*, leaving open the question of a named individual. In the NT the term does not occur in the Gospels, but Paul uses Adam-Christ typology in 1 Cor. 15:22 and Rom. 5:14. Even this reference may be ambivalent, referring either to Christ as the last Adam or to Christ as the representative of the corporate new creation of humankind. James Dunn argues that, in these passages, "When Paul speaks of or alludes to 'Adam' he speaks of humankind as a whole. . . . We should probably see the figure of Adam, the archetypal human. . . . We may note at once, therefore, Paul's awareness that Adam *(adam)* denotes humankind" (*The Theology of Paul the Apostle* [Grand Rapids: Eerdmans, 1998], 83, 91). But he admits that this may not exclude the notion of a historical individual: "Whether Paul also thought of Adam as a historical individual and of a historical act of disobedience is less clear" (94). Dunn carefully discusses the background in Genesis 1–5; postbiblical tradition in Judaism, including Philo; *4 Ezra* and *2 Baruch* (although they postdate Paul). He also considers C. K. Barrett's *From First Adam to Last* (London: Black, 1962) and J. R. Levison, *Portraits of Adam in Early Judaism* (Sheffield: Sheffield Academic Press, 1988).

R. W. L. Moberly provides a fascinating history of interpretation of Genesis 1–11 (*The Theology of the Book of Genesis* [Cambridge: CUP, 2009], 21-41). He points out that in the third century Origen argued the need for "spiritual" interpretation of (i) God's walking in the evening; (ii) Adam's hiding from God under a tree; (iii) Cain's going from the presence of God; (iv) the origin of Cain's wife; and so on. Augustine explained this last in terms of narrative omissions; Adam had many children. Moberly suggests that "tillers of the ground" and "keepers of sheep" presuppose divisions of labor when there are more than a handful of people. The narrative remains important, Moberly urges, but not always as it stands at face value. As Gary Anderson argues, Hebrew readers and speakers would know that *'ādām* could equally refer to humankind and to an individual person, and would assume that normally it referred to the former as representative of all humankind. The most cogent example is 1:26 about the image of God; this is clearly not restricted to a single human person. Barth and P. Trible argue convincingly that at the very least the term includes both genders.

In this *representative* capacity, the logic of Paul's argument in Romans 5 and 1 Corinthians 15 remains intact, and some pressure is removed from not very edifying debates in some institutions about whether Adam is an individual person. One of those who maintain that Adam carries a double reference is J. Wenham. He argues, "*'ādām*,' 'man,' in Gen. 1–4 is usually preceded by the definite article 'the man,' except when it is preceded by an inseparable preposition. . . . In chap. 5 *'ādām* is used without the article as a personal name 'Adam,'" although "Adam" is possible in 4:1, 25 (*Genesis 1–15* [Waco, Tex.: Word, 1987], 32). E. A. Speiser sees the reference in 4:23 and 5:2 as a personal name, which is common in the so-called P sources, in contrast to "humankind" in the J sources, but he adds: "The documentary source is not clear-cut" (*Genesis* [New York: Doubleday Anchor Bible, 1964], 40). B. Vawter also discusses editorial sources. In historical theology there has been much discussion about Adam's "original righteousness" before the Fall. But most exegetes and an increasing number of theologians regard this as speculation often imposed on the text. Barth points out, "Adam is mentioned relatively seldom both in the Old Testament and the New. . . . The meaning of Adam is simply man, and as the bearer of this name . . . denotes the being and essence of all other men" (*CD* IV/1, 507-8).

Reading: G. W. Anderson, *The Genesis of Perfection* (Louisville: Westminster John Knox, 2002); Peter Enns, *The Evolution of Adam* (Grand Rapids: Brazos, 2011); R. W. L. Moberly, *The Theology of the Book of Genesis* (Cambridge: CUP, 2009).

Adiaphora

This word denotes "things indifferent," or things not essential to the Christian faith. But such things could be allowed if they helped "the weaker brother." Melanchthon, for example, placed the veneration of saints in this category for the sake of Catholic consciences.

Adoption, Adoptionism, Adoptianism

These terms are used in four different senses. (i) The word "adoption" occurs in the NT only in Paul (Rom. 8:15, 23; 9:4; Gal. 4:5; Gk. *huiothesia*). The Spirit of adoption enables Christians to enjoy a sonship derived from Christ's "natural" Sonship, whereby, like him, "we cry, 'Abba! Father!'" (Rom. 8:15). Hence Christians are "joint heirs with Christ" (v. 17). (ii) At the end of the second century "dynamic Monarchianism," more accurately called adoptionism, emerged as the theory that Christ was a "mere man" *(psilos anthrōpos)* upon whom the Spirit had descended (J. N. D. Kelly, *Early Christian Doctrine* [London: Black, 1977], 115). Theodotus is said to have originated this in c. 190 to stress the oneness of God; it was attacked by Novatian (c. 250). Later the most notorious advocate of adoptionism was Paul of Samosata in c. 250 as well as the Ebionites, but it was condemned as heretical at the Synod of Antioch in 268. A few NT scholars misinterpret Rom. 1:4, "declared to be Son of God . . . by resurrection," in this way. (iii) Adoptianism (often spelled with an *a* rather than an *o*) broke out in Spain in the eighth century, and was condemned by Pope Leo III at a synod in Rome in 799. In the Middle Ages a more moderate version was revived by Abelard. (iv) Harnack identified adoptionism as a distinct stream of thought in Greek theology. If it is defined in a weak, overbroad manner, some count Theodore of Mopsuestia and Nestorius as adoptionists.

A Fortiori

This Latin term denotes an argument that applies "all the more," or "with greater force." It is centuries old, and found its way into Rabbi Hillel's seven "rules" of interpretation.

Aggiornamento

From the Italian, an "updating" or a "renewal," aggiornamento is associated with Vatican II and especially Pope John XXIII, and denotes a fresh presentation of the faith. Continuity with the past is not rejected, but the emphasis lies on the need to rejuvenate a living past that can move forward.

Agnosticism

Agnosticism must be distinguished carefully from atheism. Agnosticism holds that to affirm or deny the existence of God is impossible because of the limitations of human knowledge. T. H. Huxley is generally thought to have coined the term to affirm a value-neutral approach to belief in God. In practice, however, it has become in some quarters a reason for putting aside the whole question of God as impossible to resolve. The limits of reason were emphasized by the ancient Greek philosophers, and at the dawn of the modern era by Immanuel Kant, especially in his *Critique of Pure Reason* (1781). Before Kant, David Hume was noted for his skepticism. In the twentieth century A. J. Ayer and his logical positivism regarded God, and the question of God, as without meaning, and as "non-sense."

On the other hand, many regard the admission that one does not know as a first step toward truth. God is not to be "discovered," but (in Karl Barth's language) "reveals himself where and when he pleases." Henry Mansel wrote *The Limits of Religious Thought* (1858). As an Anglican, he argued that truths of God and religion could not be grasped by speculation. God is in himself unknowable, and can only be revealed. The unknowability of God is also a theme of much medieval mysticism, especially *The Cloud of Unknowing* and St. John of the Cross. More frequently and more popularly, however, the term is used of nontheists and religious skeptics, in the traditions of David Hume and W. K. Clifford.

Reading: B. Lightman, *The Origins of Agnosticism* (Baltimore: Johns Hopkins University Press, 1987); S. R. White, *A Space for Unknowing* (Dublin: Columba Press, 2006).

Alcuin

Educated in the Cathedral School of York, Alcuin (c. 740-804) later joined the court of Charlemagne. He contributed works on biblical exegesis and a theological treatise on the Trinity. He adapted the Gregorian Sacramentary for use in Gaul.

Alford, Henry

Henry Alford (1810-1871) was a talented NT commentator, artist, and hymn writer, and is best known for his four-volume classic, *The Greek Testament* (1841-1861). He became dean of Canterbury in 1857.

Allegory, Allegorical Interpretation

This is derived from the Greek *allos*, "other," signifying a meaning "other" than the straightforward historical and grammatical meaning of a word or a text. Plato preferred to speak of *huponoia,* an "undermeaning." In the first century Heraclitus Stoicus defined it as "saying one thing and meaning something other than what it says" (*hetera de ōn legei sēmainōn epōumōs allēgoria kateitai; Quaestiones Homericae* 22). A. Louth firmly argues that the assumption that such a procedure is dishonest is mistaken. It is not a matter only of smuggling in the interpreter's own ideas, which can then be "read" from the text. Louth argues that it is a way of advancing the *corporate* horizon of interpretation on the part of the community, as theology, or as what Origen called "God's symphony." It is a way of plumbing "the depth of its signification" (*Discerning the Mystery* [Oxford: Clarendon, 1983], 112-13; cf. 96-131).

The origins of allegorical interpretation go back to the Greeks, to Theagenes of Rhegium (c. 525 B.C.). He interpreted passages in Homer allegorically to defend the "sacred" status of the text, when many of these stories depicted jealousies or immoral acts among Greek deities. He interpreted these as allegories representing natural forces. Thus Apollo and Hephaestus represented fire; Poseidon stood for water; Hera signified air; and so on. In the fifth century B.C. Metrodorus of Lampsacus interpreted these tales of deities as parts of the human body: Apollo stood for bile; Demeter represented liver. Zeno (c. 334-262), founder of the Stoic school, interpreted Hesiod allegorically, followed by Cleanthes (c. 331-232). However, Plato expressed reservations about the procedure in many cases. Sometimes a "myth" may convey a meaning that is deeper than the descriptive, referential, or normal meaning. But allegorical interpretation should not in general be unrestrained. In other cases allegory can emerge from a "rustic sort of wisdom," or sheer fancy. In the first century A.D. Heraclitus and Cornutus debated the status of allegory, generally encouraging readers to look "below the surface." Plutarch recommended caution but admitted particular cases.

The OT recognizes some examples of allegory. Ezek. 17:1-10, for example, expounds an allegory of the king of Babylon, the king of Judah, and relations between them. Verse 2 calls it an allegory, and typically it is not a coherent narrative-world, as would be set out in a parable of Jesus. The "mighty eagle" represents Nebuchadnezzar of Babylon, who comes to "Lebanon," which represents Jerusalem. The topmost branch of the "cedar" represents Jehoiachin. Unlike parables, which are coherent stories usually addressed to "outsiders," allegories are addressed to "insiders" or those "in the know." E. Linnemann states, "An allegory cannot therefore be understood unless one knows . . . the state of affairs to which it refers" (*The Parables of Jesus* [London: SPCK, 1966], 7). It is like encoded information, for which the key is needed. Perhaps the most widely known example of allegory in English is John Bunyan's *Pilgrim's Progress.* This assumes knowledge of the Bible. Mr. Worldly Wiseman is not a genuine character, any more than the Slough of Despond is a genuine geographical location. On the other hand, the woman who looks for the lost coin genuinely sweeps the room in the parable (Luke 15:8-10), while the Holy Spirit does *not* literally use a brush and dustpan in Bunyan's House of the Interpreter.

The NT, therefore, usually uses parables rather than allegories, but it does include important allegories also. The most fascinating example is the parable of the great supper. In Luke 14:16-24 Luke treats this as a parable, by expounding a coherent narrative that implies a practical application. He recounts, "They all alike began to make excuses" (14:18). So the host of the great supper extends his invitation to "the poor, the crippled, the blind, and the lame" (v. 21). Something very different happens in the parallel in Matt. 22:1-10. As in Luke, Matthew recounts, "They would not come" (22:3). But the result is different: "The king was enraged. He sent his troops, destroyed those murderers, and burned their city" (22:7). The tale becomes a thinly veiled allegory of God's wrath upon the Jews; no host in real life would react to rejected invitations by sending an army to wreak destruction on the intended guests. In any case, as J. Jeremias argues, the Hebrew word for parable, *māshāl,* and the Aramaic *mathla* embrace the meaning "parable, similitude, allegory, fable, proverb, apocalyptic revelation, riddle, symbol . . . jest" (*The Parables of Jesus* [London: SCM, 1963], 20). Furthermore, allegories occur more frequently in the Fourth Gospel. Jesus declares: "I am the gate for the sheep" (John 10:7), and "I am the good shepherd" (10:11).

One of the more controversial examples in the NT concerns Paul's comment "This is an allegory *(allēgoroumena)*" in Gal. 4:24. L. Goppelt declares, "Only certain features of the exposition [about Sarah and Hagar] come close to being an allegorical interpretation as we conceive it. His exposition is entirely confined to a *typological* comparison of the historical facts" (*Typos* [Grand Rapids: Eerdmans, 1982], 139, italics mine). Typology concerns *historical* correspondence between *events;* allegorical correspondence concerns *conceptual* correspondence between *ideas.* On the other hand, Origen appealed to Gal. 4:24-31 as a precedent for his own allegorizing. While O. Michel opts for typology here, C. K. Barrett, F. F. Bruce, and others accept a use of allegory in Gal. 4:24-31, and J. W. Aageson prefers to use the term "correspondence." The Reformers were divided over Gal. 4:24. Paul does appear to use allegory in 1 Cor. 10:1-4 and perhaps in 1 Cor. 9:9-10. In 1 Cor. 10:4, "the rock was Christ" historically referred to the "following rock" of Moses in the wilderness.

Meanwhile Philo of Alexandria notoriously uses allegory in his interpretation of Genesis and the OT. Philo (c. 20 B.C.–A.D. 50) wishes to present the OT as acceptable to Roman readers. Hence the rivers of the Garden of Eden are to be understood not as geographical locations but as Platonic virtues: "Gihon" (Gen. 2:13) represents courage; "Pishon" (Gen. 2:11) stands for prudence. Cain and Abel represent types of character; Lot stands for sensuality, and Rachel represents innocence (Philo, *De congressu quaerendae eruditionis gratia* 1-6; *De plantatione* 8; *De ebrictate* 36). R. P. C. Hanson distinguishes Paul's more "historical" intention from that of Philo: "Paul is not trying to emancipate the meaning . . . from its historical context. . . . He is envisaging a critical situation which took place under the Old Covenant . . . as repeated by a situation under the New Covenant" (*Allegory and Event* [London: SCM, 1959], 82).

Allegory, Allegorical Interpretation

Nevertheless, the Church Fathers frequently used allegorical method. Clement of Rome (A.D. 96) suggests that the scarlet thread placed in the window of Rahab's house alludes to "the blood of the Lord" (*1 Clem.* 13.7). *The Epistle of Barnabas* provides an allegorical interpretation of the Levitical laws (*Barn.* 10.1-12) and of the men of Abraham (9.8). On the other hand, the other Apostolic Fathers use allegory rarely or sparingly. The Valentinian Gnostics use allegory plentifully, believing in three "levels" of interpretation. Clement of Alexandria (c. 200) argues that Christian truth is conveyed especially in the OT "in enigmas and symbols, in allegories and metaphors" (*Stromata* 5.21.4). Clement, like the Gnostics, understood revelation as often "secret," whereas Irenaeus insisted that it was public and open to rational scrutiny. Clement's successor, Origen, explicitly commends "spiritual" interpretation. He is probably the best-known exponent of it.

Thereafter the issue became more controversial. It is a popular maxim to suggest that the school of Alexandria from Clement onward practiced allegorical interpretation, whereas the school of Antioch, including Chrysostom, practiced a much more historical and grammatical exegesis. This has only general truth; it requires careful qualification. Origen discusses biblical inspiration in *De principiis* 4.1-3, and clearly respects the historical or "bodily" meaning as the starting point, even if he proposes three "levels" of meaning. Harnack's charge of "biblical alchemy" is not entirely fair. He does aim at *reader-effect* as well as unfolding the *original situation*. His allegorical interpretation takes a variety of forms, with "safeguards" against excessive allegory. Similarly, while Chrysostom declares that "we must mark the mind of the writer" (*Chrysostom* 10.675A), in his *Homilies* he sometimes uses allegorical interpretation in his pastoral application, often in the second part of the homily.

The Reformation marks a similar ambivalence, even if Calvin called allegories "idle fooleries." Luther used allegorical interpretation liberally in his earlier writings. Only when it became clear that the Roman tradition could read its own views *into* the Bible so that it could become "a nose of wax" did Luther and Calvin vigorously attack this use of allegory. Luther declared in this context, "The Christian reader should make it his first task to seek out the literal sense, as they call it" (*LW* 9:24). The Radical Reformers also used allegory. Calvin was stricter than Luther about the historical and grammatical meaning. This was partly due to the excesses of the medieval and Gregorian tradition, which had used allegorical interpretation in many cases (but not all) without due restraint. At best, allegorical interpretation can be seen as a step toward the role of the reader in hermeneutics, as well as the corporate faith of the church, and its theology. Its legitimacy will often depend on whether it is engaging with historical, or allegorical and symbolic, texts. Those engaged in hermeneutics often distinguish between "open" and "closed" texts, also called "poetic" and "transmissive" or even "engineering" texts, as Umberto Eco and J. Lotman do with some justice. Allegorical interpretation might be more appropriate for the former than the latter.

Reading: J. W. Aagerson, *Written Also for Our Sake* (Louisville: Westminster John Knox, 1993); L. Goppelt, *Typos* (Grand Rapids: Eerdmans, 1982); R. P. C. Hanson, *Allegory and Event* (London: SCM, 1959); A. Louth, *Discerning the Mystery* (Oxford: Clarendon, 1983); H. de Lubac, *Medieval Exegesis,* 3 vols. (Grand Rapids: Eerdmans, 1998, 2000, 2002); J. O'Keefe and R. Reno, *Sanctified Vision* (Baltimore: Johns Hopkins University Press, 2005).

Ambrose of Milan

Ambrose (c. 339-397) was governor of a Roman province and had a well-respected Roman administrative career. But on the death of Auxentius, bishop of Milan, he succeeded him as bishop by popular acclaim. Although brought up in a Christian family, he had not yet been baptized, and it is said that he rose through the ranks of laity and clergy in eight days. As bishop he became an effective and popular preacher, and robustly defended Christian orthodoxy against Arianism. He also defended church order and church unity. His learning, competence, wisdom, and energy became proverbial. As a major theologian of the Western Church, he nevertheless drew on the works of Basil in the East, and produced the three-volume work *On the Holy Spirit.* In 381 Milan became the governmental center of Italy. His preaching was instrumental in the conversion of Augustine.

Ambrosiaster

This was the name given in later years to the author of commentaries on thirteen letters attributed to Paul. The name originated from the Benedictine editors of the works of Ambrose. The Pauline texts are in Latin, and until the sixteenth century Ambrose was wrongly thought to have written these commentaries.

Amen

This word means "truly" in Hebrew, and was transliterated into Greek. It is used as a term of assent, agreement, or ratification. Each of the twelve Mosaic "curses" in Deut. 27:15-26 concludes with "Amen." Jesus often uses "Amen" to introduce especially solemn sayings, for example, in Matt. 5:26 and Luke 23:43: "Truly I tell you . . ." (Gk. *amēn, legō soi* . . .). In Rev. 3:14 Christ is "the Amen," which denotes that his witness is true and faithful. A twice-repeated "Amen" occurs in John 1:51. Patristic writings witness to the liturgical use of "Amen" in ancient prayers (e.g., Justin, *First Apology* 65.3; Eusebius, *Commentary on the Psalms* 105.48).

Anabaptists

Anabaptists refused to have their children baptized, originally in opposition to the major Reformers of the sixteenth century. The term "Anabaptist" was coined by their opponents from Greek *ana,* "again," and *baptizō,* "I baptize." The main group was the Radical Reformers, led by Thomas Müntzer (c. 1489-1525), and later Baptists and Quakers. Luther, Calvin, and Zwingli denounced them.

Analogy

"Way of." Analogy provides a way of understanding God and speaking of God that does not attribute to him an exact match with people, things, or qualities in the world. In this respect analogy stands in contrast with univocal meaning (a supposed exact match) and equivocal meaning (a relation of ambivalence). Alongside symbol, model, and metaphor, it provides a vital resource for speaking of God. The analogy of being *(analogia entis)* constituted a major concept in medieval Scholasticism, and was expounded especially by Thomas Aquinas. Nature is said to exhibit "traces" of God. Karl Barth is uncompromising in expressing his disapproval of this approach, preferring to speak of the analogy of *faith*. He writes, "I regard the *analogia entis* as the invention of the Antichrist, and I believe that because of it, it is impossible ever to become a Roman Catholic; all other reasons . . . being to my mind . . . trivial" (*CD* I/1, xiii). Most Protestant theologians, however, including Emil Brunner, do not share Barth's position so strongly, if at all. Brunner points to the image of God, among other factors. "Way of Analogy" often refers to one of Aquinas's Five Ways.

Aquinas expounds his doctrine of analogy mainly in *Summa Theologiae* 1a, question 13, on theological language. In question 13, article 1 he writes, "we come to know God from creatures" (Eng. 3:49). In article 2 he contrasts analogy with the *via negativa:* it is not true that we can say *only* what God is *not*. In article 3 he quotes Ambrose: "There are some ways of referring to God which show forth clearly what is proper to divinity . . . others . . . are used of God metaphorically." In article 5 he distinguishes analogy from univocal and equivocal language. He writes, "Some words are used neither univocally nor purely equivocally of God and creatures, but analogically, for we cannot speak of God at all except in the language we use of creatures" (Eng. 3:65). Aquinas prepares to introduce "image of God" with the initial statement: "The divine nature can be communicated to others only in the sense that they can share in likeness to God" (qu. 13, art. 9). Does Barth make too much of this? The editor of the Blackfriars edition comments in appendix 4, "Analogy is not a way of getting to know about God, nor is it a theory about the structure of the universe; it is a comment on the use of certain words" ([New York: McGraw-Hill, 1963], 3:108). It is usual to argue that Thomas's exposition of analogy also implies a "trace of God" *(vestigium Dei)* in human persons. But Alan Torrance has shown that this owes more to Cardinal Thomas Cajetan's attempt to systematize the thought of Aquinas (*Persons in Communion* [Edinburgh: T. & T. Clark, 1996], 127-41).

The reason for Barth's attack is his belief that it compromises God's sovereign *freedom to reveal himself "where and when he wills."* If human beings can bring their own "preunderstanding" as a key to unlock analogy, revelation appears not to be wholly on God's initiative. By contrast Brian Davies insists that it is not, for Aquinas, "a self-contained method for constructing a language in which to talk of God" (*The Thought of Thomas Aquinas* [Oxford: Clarendon, 1992], 73). Even Barth asserts, "Our reply to the Roman Catholic doctrine of *analogia entis* is not, then, a denial of the concept of analogy. . . . According to Rom. 12:6 the *analogia tēs pisteōs,* the likeness of the known in the knowing, ... [is] the word that is thought and spoken by man" (*CD* I/1, 243-44). Rom. 12:6 simply asserts that the gift of prophecy (i.e., speech concerning God) is "in proportion to faith." Here he also insists on "the knowability of God" (246). Here it is difficult to distinguish Barth's examples from a traditional use of analogy. The relationship of analogy is one of "partial correspondence" (*CD* II/1, 227). While Barth rejects a *doctrine* of the analogy of being, he approves the *use* of analogy. Many argue that this is also true of Aquinas, rather than Cajetan.

Brunner defends the use of analogy, although he recognizes that it may be misused and perverted. He bases this on God's role as Creator. "Whatever the Creator makes bears the imprint of His Creator-Spirit ... and is therefore a parable or analogy" (*Dogmatics 2: The Christian Doctrine of Creation and Redemption* [London: Lutterworth, 1952], 22-23; cf. 21-24). He then appeals to the image of God in humankind. P. Tillich prefers symbol to analogy, not least because it requires participation and self-involvement rather than purely cognitive aspects. But he respects analogy insomuch as we can speak of the Ultimate or Infinite by using finite beings (people and objects) to point beyond themselves to their Ground. In general, modern theologians agree that analogy, or the analogy of proportionality, as it is sometimes called, serves to guarantee the incomparability or difference between God and his creatures at a purely "literal" level. More explicitly, the analogy of proportionality means that particular qualities of God relate to God's nature in exactly the same way as particular qualities of a created being relate to the nature of that being. In one respect Barth and critics of the analogy of proportionality are right: this use of analogy hardly brings *fresh* knowledge of God of itself, even if it functions as an explanatory model. Some uses of analogy rest on theories about likeness of cause and effect; this is sometimes called an analogy of attribution. Simply as an explanatory theory of language, however, analogy is widely used in Christian theology.

Reading: Aquinas, *Su Th* 1a, qu. 13; V. Brümmer, *Speaking of a Personal God* (Cambridge: CUP, 1992), 43-52; E. L. Mascall, *Existence and Analogy* (New York and London: Longmans, Green, 1949); A. Torrance, *Persons in Communion* (Edinburgh: T. & T. Clark, 1996).

Analytic

Analytic statements are true by definition, or true a priori. Typical philosophical examples include "All bachelors are unmarried" or "Water boils at 100° Centigrade." Kant called statements analytic when their predicate is already presupposed by their subject, for example, "six is a number." Wittgenstein treated analytical propositions as purely formal ones, or as logical tautologies.

Anamnēsis

Normal Greek for "remembrance," or in Heb. 10:3, "reminder." Its most significant function is in the words of institution of the Lord's Supper (1 Cor. 11:24-25; Luke 22:19) where the English translates, "Do this in remembrance of me." However, although the Greek verb *mimnēskomai* means "to call to mind" or "to remember," in the eucharistic tradition it almost certainly reflects the Hebrew term for "remembrance," which is *zākar*. The Hebrew suggests not simply "calling to mind," but something more objective. Some even suggest "reenactment," but any sense of repetition goes too far, and contradicts the unrepeatable "once-for-all" *(ephapax)* emphasis of the NT and especially Hebrews. The "objective" emphasis became distorted by the myth and ritual school of Bentzen and others. Many Catholics and Protestants opt for a more cautious notion of *dramatic representation.* In the seder or haggadah of the Passover, the Passover is *not repeated,* but every individual participant is urged to regard the celebration *"as if he were there."* At the Reformation Zwingli tended to regard the Lord's Supper as a purely subjective intellectual remembrance; for Luther and Calvin it was something more, though not a "repetition." We consider the NT, Luther, Calvin, and Zwingli in more detail in the entry **Lord's Supper.**

Anaphora

This is the name sometimes given to the central core of the Lord's Supper or Eucharist, which contains the account of the sacrament's institution (1 Cor. 11:23b-26) and the prayer of "consecration" of the bread and wine. Usually or technically it also includes the greetings of the president and congregation, "Lift up your hearts," the Sanctus, and the Doxology. The term is used in the Orthodox Church, whereas the Western churches normally use the term "Canon" of the Holy Communion or of the Lord's Supper.

Anathema

In the LXX the Greek *anathema* is a translation of the Hebrew *chērem,* which has the double meaning of a thing devoted to God and a curse or that which has been cursed or is accursed (BDAG, 63). It occurs in the OT in Deut. 7:26, Josh. 6:17, 7:12, Judg. 1:17, Zech. 14:11. NRSV translates it an "abhorrent" thing in Deut. 7:26; "devoted to the LORD for destruction" in Josh. 6:17 and "a thing devoted for destruction" in 7:12; and "devoted . . . to destruction" in Judg. 1:17. Zech. 14:11 has simply "doomed to destruction." The main OT contexts are war and extermination (N. Lohfink, *chāram, chērem,* in *TDOT* 5:180-99). In the NT the Greek *anathema* occurs six times, usually with the English translation "accursed." In Rom. 9:3 Paul is willing to be accursed for the sake of the salvation of the Jews. This self-sacrifice is parallel to that of Moses when he prays, "But if not, blot me out of the book that you have written" (Exod. 32:32). In Gal. 1:8-9 those who have seduced Christians in Galatia to proclaim a different gospel twice invite God's curse. In 1 Cor. 16:22 "anathema" represents the alternative to loving the Lord. In Acts 23:14 the word relates to a dire oath. The most interesting and debatable use is in 1 Cor. 12:3: "no one speaking by the Spirit of God ever says, *'Anathema Iēsous.'"*

If we accept a traditional interpretation, various explanations for the translation "Jesus be accursed" have been offered. (i) O. Cullmann and others suggest the context of a *confession* formula, where the confession "*Caesar* is Lord" is expected. A double Roman safeguard would be to expect "Jesus is accursed" as the corollary of this, but Paul insists that this could never be prompted by the Holy Spirit. (ii) W. Schmithals, J. Weiss, and M. Thrall suggest that these words might be uttered in uncontrolled ecstasy, and even J. D. G. Dunn thinks this "quite likely." (iii) J. Bassler argues that the cry may reflect preconversion days, or be simply a hypothetical utterance. (iv) J. D. M. Derrett presses the context of a Jewish pronouncement, perhaps on the basis of Deut. 18:17-22. (v) U. Wilckens postulates a Gnostic background that devalues the earthly Jesus. (vi) J. Héring argues for a "charismatic" who is open to the influence of the demons. (vii) Perhaps more ingenious and plausible than most explanations, W. C. van Unnik proposes that some Christians pronounced a curse on a Jesus who was preached merely as a *crucified* Christ who stood under God's curse in Deuteronomy in the atonement but with *no* reference to his resurrection and exaltation. (viii) The most persuasive explanation of all, however, is that of Bruce Winter, who appeals to the discovery of so-called curse tablets near Corinth that record prayers to a pagan deity to "curse" a rival in love, sport, or business. On this basis Paul declares that the *Holy Spirit* would *never inspire a prayer for God's curse upon a rival* or another person. The fact that there is no verb governing *Anathema Iēsous* reinforces the argument for a possible *active* "May Jesus curse" or "May Jesus speak a curse," rather than the *passive* "Jesus be accursed."

Within the NT a number of confessions of truth occur. But as the church developed over the centuries, the term began to identify generally false confessions that were regarded as heresies, and outside the tradition of the church. The specific term "anathema" was not always used. The Council of Elvira (c. 306) appears to have used it, and then the Synod of Gangra (c. 340), applying "anathema" to Manichaeism. By the fifth century it was more commonly used. Cyril of Alexandria issued twelve anathemas against Nestorius in 431. Among the Eastern Orthodox churches "anathema" does not mean damnation, but is a warning about what the church condemns. In the Roman Catholic Church the pope may declare an anathema. Pope Silverius declared anathema on any who seriously deceived a bishop (c. 538). Benedict XIV used the declaration in the eighteenth century, and the Council of Trent declared anathema on those who denied the teachings of the Roman Church. A stronger meaning in the OT and NT is replaced by the notion of a ban by a particular church, but those who use it regard it as more serious than excommunication.

Reading: A. C. Thiselton, *The First Epistle to the Corinthians* (Grand Rapids: Eerdmans, 2000), 917-25; B. W. Winter, *After Paul Left Corinth* (Grand Rapids: Eerdmans, 2001), 164-83.

Anchorites
From Greek *anachōreō*, "I withdraw," the term denotes those who withdraw from the world to live a solitary life of silence and prayer. The feminine form, "anchoress," is also used.

Angel

The word "angel" (Heb. *mal'ākh*; Gk. *angelos*) normally denotes "a messenger," whether heavenly or earthly. In the OT angels are prominent in Genesis, Judges, Ezekiel, and Zechariah. About half of the 200-plus OT occurrences of the word are used of human beings and half of heavenly beings. On the rare occasion in which the Hebrew uses "Sons of God," the LXX translates the phrase by using *angelos*. Angels are also called the host of heaven (1 Kings 22:19) or God's hosts (Josh. 5:14; Ps. 103:21), which probably refers to God's armies. Sometimes heavenly angels are called seraphim (Isa. 6:2, 6, 7) who fly; or cherubim (Exod. 25:20; Ezek. 10:2, 15). Cherubim (Heb. *cherubim*) are mentioned ninety times in the Hebrew Bible (and only once in the NT, at Heb. 9:5). The term denotes awesome winged creatures that adorn the Holy of Holies (Exod. 26:1, 31; 36:8, 35), and cover the ark of the covenant (1 Kings 8:6-7). In Ezekiel 10 they represent God's glory. When he flees from Jezebel, Elijah is given food by an angel. In Gen. 18:2 Abraham saw "three men," who were intermediaries from God. Angels are clearly created beings (Ps. 148:1-6), and first and foremost messengers.

In the NT, in Matt. 11:10 the Greek for "messenger" is *angelos*, when this clearly refers to John the Baptist. Similarly the Greek *angeloi* represents human messengers in James 2:25 where the word denotes human spies sent by Joshua to Rahab. But angels are also "holy ones" in Jude 14 and more than human in Rev. 1:20, 2:1, 3:1, Luke 2:13, and Acts 7:42. In Rev. 1:20 "the seven stars ... are the angels of the seven churches." Here "angels" are probably "guardians" of the churches, just as in Matt. 18:10 angels appear as guardians of children. Acts 12:15 may depict an angel as Peter's guardian. But in Rev. 19:10 the seer is *forbidden to worship* angels: "You must not do that! I am a fellow servant." The sentence is repeated in Rev. 22:9. In Matt. 4:6 (and par. Luke 4:10-11) angels guard Jesus from a fatal event, and minister to him after the messianic temptations (Matt. 4:11; Mark 1:13). Twelve legions of angels could be readied for Jesus' defense at his arrest (Matt. 26:53). They roll away the stone at the resurrection (Matt. 28:2). According to Acts 7:38, 53; Gal. 3:19; and Heb. 2:2, Moses received the law from an angel. Angels proclaim the birth of Jesus to the shepherds (Luke 2:8-14), and warn Joseph to flee to Egypt (Matt. 2:13). The archangel announces the return of Christ (1 Thess. 4:16), and will appear with him (Matt. 16:27; 25:31; Mark 8:38). There is no biblical precedent for praying directly to angels.

Angels appear frequently in the intertestamental literature. They receive personal names in Daniel, Tobit, *1 Enoch*, and the Dead Sea Scrolls. The four most often mentioned are Michael, Gabriel, Raphael, and Uriel (Dan. 9:21; 10:13; Tob. 12:15; *1 En.* 9.1; 21.10; *4 Ezra* 4.1; 1QM 9.15-16). Philo and Josephus mention angels. In addition to their function as messengers and intermediaries, the War Scroll and other literature depict them as a heavenly army. *2 En.* 20 depicts ten classes of angels in the seventh heaven. "Heavenly host" appears in Luke 2:13, and the angel of the annunciation is named Gabriel in Luke 1:19 and 26, where he is also an angel of the presence. The term "archangel" occurs in the NT only as "the archangel

Michael" in Jude 9 and in an allusion to "the archangel's call" in 1 Thess. 4:16. In Matt. 12:24, according to the Pharisees, Beelzebul is "the ruler of the demons." Evil and good angels receive mention in *Jub.* 11.4-5 and 12.20. In 1 Cor. 4:9 Paul depicts angels as watching his apostolic ministry. In 1 Pet. 1:12 the angels become aware that they serve Christians, yet also long to look into the gospel. In Col. 2:18 Paul urges the avoidance of "worship of angels."

Speculation about angels grew in the patristic era. They were often thought to have existed before the creation of the world, perhaps being created along with "the heavens." Augustine speculated about an angelic fall (*City of God* 11.9). Medieval traditions speculated about angels as immaterial; they had minds but not bodies. Anselm and Aquinas both speak of fallen angels, and medieval tradition speculated about ranks of angels as a hierarchy. The Reformers reinstated their primary role as messengers, usually on behalf of God.

Reading: C. Auffarth and L. Stuckenbruck, eds., *The Fall of the Angels* (Leiden: Brill, 2004); P. R. Carrell, *Jesus and the Angels* (Cambridge: CUP, 1997); S. F. Noll, *Angels of Light, Powers of Darkness* (Downers Grove, Ill.: IVP, 1998).

Anglican Theology

Anglican theology denotes the belief and practice of churches formally in communion with the archbishop and province of Canterbury, although the "being in communion" is at present under discussion. In practice it may be defined negatively as "Anglican theology" in contrast to that of Roman Catholics, Eastern Orthodox, Methodists, Baptists, Pentecostals, and other Protestant traditions. Again in practice, it includes a spectrum ranging from Reformed to Anglo-Catholic. "Reformed" is manifested in the second *Book of Common Prayer* under Edward VI, which Cranmer and Bucer shaped; Anglo-Catholic is manifested in the first 1549 prayer book of Henry VIII (which was only partially "Reformed") and in the Tractarians or Oxford Movement. In theory the Thirty-nine Articles of the 1662 (fourth) prayer book under Charles II provides the basis of Anglican doctrine, although many Anglicans would probably not assent to all thirty-nine articles. It is an irenic convention to say that Anglicanism is both "Reformed and Catholic." This diversity is also reflected in Anglicanism as manifested in different parts of the world. There are about thirty provinces and 300 dioceses in about 170 countries. Starting in 1957, most Anglican provinces have revised their liturgies to reflect local needs. To cite some examples, in Africa those dioceses and provinces that still reflect the ethos of the Church Missionary Society and Bible Churchmen's Missionary Society (now Crosslinks) are firmly evangelical and Reformed. Those founded by the Society for the Promotion of Christian Knowledge and the United Society for the Propagation of the Gospel may be largely Anglo-Catholic. In Australia the Sydney Province is Reformed; other dioceses vary. Anglicanism has no equivalent to the pope. Formally its doctrine is that agreed up to the Council of Chalcedon, before the division of the church.

Although the 1662 prayer book remains the decisive source for the Church of

England, a succession of revised liturgies may have led in practice to certain local or more modern emphases. Queen Elizabeth II, as head, informed the Church's General Synod that she saw the prayer book of 1662 as legally irreplaceable, but capable of supplementation. Over the last ten years the worldwide primates (senior archbishops) of the world Anglican Church appointed a panel for the Theological Education of Anglican Churches, to draw up advice for the appointment and qualifications of bishops, priests, and deacons of the church. This largely accorded with biblical teaching in the Pastoral Epistles, and the ordination services of the prayer book. The Church of England published seven Doctrine Commission Reports, in 1922, 1938, 1976, 1981, 1987, 1995, and 2003. Although commissioned by the archbishop of Canterbury, these reports are not mandatory for doctrine, but advisory guides. Similarly, commissions work on liturgy and the Bible, but their reports, too, are advisory, even if also influential.

In principle, the Anglican view of the Bible still adheres to the principles expounded by Richard Hooker in the settlement of Elizabeth I. Anglicans of different subtraditions, including the Anglo-Catholic John Keble, have happily promoted Hooker's view of the Bible and of ecclesiology. Today, however, many from the southern provinces of the world are asking for more representation in what they perceive to be a "northern"-dominated church, with possible hints of outworn "imperialism" and "colonialism" from England. From 1786 until 1841 or the end of the nineteenth century, it was legally possible for the British monarch and archbishops to appoint overseas bishops, but this responsibility was passed to local provinces long ago. One current source of debate is the freedom of local provinces to formulate their own theology and ethical practice. At the time of writing, for example, the English bishops are troubled by a need to hear, and accord with, opposite ethical beliefs in Nigeria, with its huge number of Anglicans, and the United States, with its record of financial generosity.

Meanwhile the Thirty-nine Articles and Prayer Book Ordinal retain a unique place in Anglican theology. Ten articles were produced in 1536, and thirteen were compiled in 1538 with the agreement of Lutheran theologians. In 1553 forty-two articles were produced, and described as "Reformed Catholic." But after the death of Mary Tudor and accession of Elizabeth I in 1558, Archbishop Parker had a leading role in the formulation of the Thirty-nine Articles, which were approved by convocation and Parliament. Cranmer and Parker saw these as apostolic doctrine, which would serve to guide the clergy and protect the laity from unorthodox or Roman Catholic doctrine. They were also to ensure the unity of the church. It has been suggested that articles 1-5 define the substance of faith; 6-8 the rule of faith; 9-18 the life of faith; and 19-39 the corporate nature of faith, or the household of faith. The homilies were published in 1547 with a requirement that every parish church have a copy of the whole Bible in English. A second Book of Homilies was approved in 1563, edited by Bishop John Jewel. The Declaration of Assent constituted a declaration from all Church of England clergy of agreement with the faith "revealed in the Holy Scripture and set forth in the catholic (i.e. ecumenical) creeds and to which the historic formularies of the Church of England bear witness." The churches of Ireland, Scotland, Wales, Australia, Canada, New Zealand, Uganda, Rwanda, Zaire, Nigeria, and West Africa retain the Articles (or at the very least have done so until very recently). The Episcopal Church in the United States revised the *Book of Common Prayer* for their own use in 1789, 1892, 1928-1929, and 1979. The introduction of the *Alternative Service Book* in 1980 by the Church of England was an attempt to modernize the *Book of Common Prayer,* but many believed that its prayers of confession and some other prayers were shallow and that its style and tone lacked dignity, weight, and sometimes seriousness in theology. Although it purported to make no *doctrinal* changes, the *Alternative Service Book* introduced All Souls' Day, which had been excluded at the Reformation. *Common Worship,* introduced in 2005, restored some of the dignity and depth of the prayer book, but it is meant to supplement rather than *replace* it.

Reading: P. Avis, *Anglicanism and the Christian Church* (New York: T. & T. Clark, 2002); A. Middleton, *Restoring the Anglican Mind* (Leominster, U.K.: Gracewing, 2008); S. Neill, *Anglicanism* (Harmondsworth: Penguin, 1958); S. W. Sykes, *The Integrity of Anglicanism* (London: Mowbray, 1978); S. W. Sykes and J. Booty, eds., *The Study of Anglicanism* (Philadelphia: Fortress, 1988).

Anglo-Catholic

The tradition or party within the Anglican Church that has its roots in the Tractarians or Oxford Movement of the 1830s. The popular term is often "High Church" because of its special regard for the sacraments, elaborate religious ceremony, and the church. Traditionally it has also attached importance to apostolic succession, although this is now widely understood not in mechanical ways (nicknamed "the pipeline theory"). But some Anglo-Catholic versions of apostolic succession still cause much misgiving regarding the admission of women to the episcopate. One of the most positive contributions of Anglo-Catholics is their insistence on doctrinal continuity, especially with the early church and its councils and creeds; another is their emphasis on devotion and social concern. Respect for doctrine represents a common feature between Anglo-Catholics and most evangelicals, in contrast to classical liberals.

"The swing towards high churchmanship," as Owen Chadwick calls it, is evident from J. H. Newman, J. Keble, H. Froude, and E. B. Pusey. Both Newman and R. W. Church located the beginning of Tractarianism with Keble's sermon "National Apostasy" in 1833, when Keble attacked the government's decision to suppress ten Irish bishoprics. Keble, Froude, and others saw this as an attempt by politicians to shape the church of the apostles. This initiated a series of tracts, the first written by Newman, who argued that "We encroach not upon the rights of the successors of the apostles." The Tractarians appealed to the collective witness of the Church Fathers. Strictly, the Tractarian Movement lasted from 1833 to 1845, at which point Newman converted to Roman Catholicism. But the

Anglo-Catholic tradition was now firmly embedded in the Anglican Church. The movement now developed and made its impact on parishes.

Anglo-Catholics urged personal discipline, prayer, fasting, and often confession. Pusey, H. P. Liddon, and in some ways Charles Gore joined Newman in attacking liberalism. On the controversial side, they were often seen as "ritualists" who delighted in externals. Later, vestments and Mariolatry became a divisive issue for the rest of the church. In the twentieth century they flourished from the end of the First World War (1918) to well after the end of the second (1945). They held five Anglo-Catholic congresses between 1920 and 1933. After 1945, although they held "Catholic Renewal" conferences in 1978 and 1983, the movement was showing signs of decline. Their earlier dominance was challenged both by liberals and by evangelicals. Between 1970 and 1990 the General Synod tended to operate largely as three "parties" (Anglo-Catholics, liberals, and evangelicals), held together by a common allegiance to Anglican theology and to the House of Bishops. After representing about a third of the synod, the Anglo-Catholic numbers began to decline. One of many blows against them, though not the only one, was the issue of the appointment of women bishops. Over the years this was repeatedly considered in synod and by bishops and various committees. The Anglo-Catholic group was itself divided on the issue, for example, between Affirming Catholicism (founded in 1990) and Forward in Faith (founded in 1992). A small number of Anglo-Catholics were received into the Roman Catholic Church, which did not help their argument that they were to be regarded as loyal Anglicans. The more "Catholic" vestments were declared to be of no doctrinal significance, while some, perhaps many, evangelicals began to pay higher priority to the service of Holy Communion than to "Services of the Word." The new movement known as Radical Orthodoxy, largely in the Anglo-Catholic tradition, might have helped matters, but it was largely academic, and most speeches in synod were not notable for their erudition and theological learning. It would be premature to call Anglo-Catholicism a spent force, especially since it flourishes in other parts of the world. The Church of England is still often called "Reformed and Catholic." Affirming Catholicism works for "the wider Anglican Communion, as held by those professing to stand within the catholic tradition." There is still an Anglo-Catholic Ordination Candidates' Fund, while Forward in Faith exists "to support all who in conscience are unable to accept the ordination of women to the priesthood or the episcopate." In 2014 the General Synod finally approved the ordination of women bishops.

Reading: W. S. F. Pickering, *Anglo-Catholicism* (London: Lutterworth, 2008); G. Rowell, *The Vision Glorious* (Oxford: OUP, 1983); R. Williams, *Anglican Identities* (London: Darton, Longman, Todd, 2004).

Angst
The nearest English translation for this word is "anxiety" or "dread." It plays a significant role in the thought of S. Kierkegaard, M. Heidegger, Reinhold Niebuhr,

P. Tillich, and to a lesser extent in R. Bultmann. Kierkegaard provides a classic treatment in *The Concept of Dread* (*Angst;* 1844) and *The Sickness unto Death.* Anxiety or dread is not caused by some contingent event, he argues, such as the death of a loved one, but by an undefined dread of emptiness or nothingness, which is partly caused by the finite human gazing into infinite possibility before God. Anxiety may provide a creative moment, or a sense of guilt, for the experience of anxiety is bound up with a sense of responsibility. In his *Being and Time* (1926; Eng. 1973), Heidegger examines anxiety in chapter 6, especially in section 40. He writes, "The turning-away of falling is grounded in anxiety.... That in the face of which one has anxiety *(der Angst)* is Being-in-the-world as such.... What oppresses us is not this or that . . . it is the possibility of the ready-to-hand in general" (Eng. 230-31; Ger. 186-87). Anxiety stems from "the uncanny" *(unheimlich);* or not "being-at-home." On the other hand, this can deliver the self from its absorption in the "world."

Like Kierkegaard, Niebuhr sees anxiety as arising from the paradox of "freedom and finiteness" (*The Nature and Destiny of Man,* vol. 1 [1941], 195). But anxiety about insecurity can lead to trust in God on one side, or to temptation on the other. Bultmann's analysis is along these lines. Tillich follows a similar approach. He writes, "Man is not only finite . . . he is aware of his finitude. And this awareness is 'anxiety' . . . associated with the German and Danish word *'Angst,'* which is itself derived from the Latin *angustiae,* 'narrows'" (*Systematic Theology,* vol. 2 [1957], 39). Anxiety relates to an "awareness of existential estrangement" (35). Jesus partly anticipates the view of Kierkegaard and later existentialists not to be anxious about *things:* "Do not worry about your life, what you will eat or . . . drink, or . . . what you will wear. Is not life more than food . . . more than clothing?" (Matt. 6:25). As Bultmann comments, the Christian "lets care [for himself] go, yielding himself entirely to the grace of God" (cf. 1 Cor. 6:19; *Theology of the New Testament* [London: SCM, 1952], 331).

Anhypostasia

This term denotes the human nature of Christ when considered in abstraction from his hypostatic union as the God-man. Post-Chalcedonian Christology does not consider that Christ's human nature has independent existence apart from its union with the divine nature. *Anhypostasia* would be a presupposition of adoptionism or adoptianism.

Annunciation

Angel Gabriel's announcement to Mary of the birth of Jesus by the power of the Holy Spirit as recorded in Luke 1:26-38. Traditionally Christians celebrate the Feast of the Annunciation, often popularly called "Lady Day," on 25 March, nine months ahead of Christmas Day. In the West the first reference to the feast seems to be in the Gelasian Sacramentary (seventh or eighth century). The child Jesus would be great, and called the Son of the Most High (Luke 1:32). Mary responded: "Here am I, the servant of the Lord; let it be with me according to your word." The NRSV translation of the greeting, "Greetings, favored one! The Lord is with you" (1:28; Gk. *chaire kecharitōmenē, ho kurios meta sou*), was mistranslated from the Greek by the Vulgate Latin as "Hail, Mary, full of grace," the devotional use of which began only in the eleventh century. Mary *receives* grace; it is not a natural quality she could dispense to others.

Anselm
Anselm of Canterbury (c. 1033-1109) entered the monastery at Bec, Normandy, where Lanfranc was abbot. Lanfranc became archbishop of Canterbury in 1070, and Anselm became his successor in 1093. Augustine and Boethius were two main influences upon his thought. É. Gilson has called Anselm "the Father of Scholasticism." His work went beyond biblical exegesis, and he explored the two areas of philosophy and systematic theology. This marked a new stage in medieval Christian thought. In 1076 he composed his *Monologion*, or a meditation on the grounds of faith, and in 1077-1078 he wrote the *Proslogion*, which E. Fairweather calls "the great charter of mediaeval Christian philosophy" (*A Scholastic Miscellany* [Philadelphia: Westminster, 1956], 49). He suggests that this book might be called "faith seeking understanding." As we see in the entry **Ontological Argument**, many readers regard this as a philosophical or logical argument, while Barth and others view it as a theological confession. Some even regard it as mystical theology. To treat the existence of God as an a priori argument may seem to exclude natural theology.

As decisive and great as his *Proslogion* may be, Anselm's *Cur Deus Homo* (1098) classically shows how mutually dependent the doctrines of the person and work of Christ truly are (*see* **Atonement; Christology**). As these other entries show, Anselm is concerned to take account of the glory of and majesty of God (*see* **God, Trinity: Historical Development**), which leads to his interpretation of the atonement by Jesus Christ as the God-man, which some criticize for a medieval theory of law. Abelard was among those who criticized and opposed it. But Anselm worked in other areas as well. In 1098 he attended the Council of Bari, where he defended the double procession of the Spirit in the West (the doctrine that the Holy Spirit proceeded from the Father and the Son; i.e., the *filioque* clause). Earlier he wrote *On Truth* and *Freedom of the Will*, and an introduction to dialectic called *De grammatico*. In 1095 he published *On the Incarnation of the Word*.

Reading: E. R. Fairweather, *A Scholastic Miscellany* (Philadelphia: Westminster, 1956); J. McIntyre, *St. Anselm and His Critics* (Edinburgh: Oliver and Boyd, 1954); R. W. Southern, *Anselm* (Cambridge: CUP, 1990); S. N. Vaughn, *Archbishop Anselm* (Aldershot: Ashgate, 2012).

Anthropology
This concerns the theology of being human, humanity, or what used to be called, before inclusive-gender language, the doctrine of man. Calvin declares: "The

knowledge of God and the knowledge of ourselves are bound together by a mutual tie" (*Institutes* 1.1.3; Beveridge, 1:39). He adds: "It is evident that man never attains to a true self-knowledge until he has previously contemplated the face of God" (1.1.2; 1:38). Many studies begin with humankind's being made in the image of God (Gen. 1:26; Ps. 8:4-7; 1 Cor. 11:7; Col. 1:15; James 3:9). As we see under that entry, God intended that humankind should represent him to the world. Images in pagan religions often constituted ways of representing deities. The peril of idolatry is seen especially in constructing alternative "images" by the people of God, to escape from the task of representing God, as D. A. Clines and J. Moltmann argue (*see* **Image of God**, with which this entry originally overlaps). This means more than revealing those qualities that distinguish humans from animals, which are traditionally reason or mind; dominion over nature, or stewardship of the world; freedom; and especially relationality, or the capacity to enter into relationships with the other or another. Although most theologians stress the importance of these qualities, V. Lossky stresses the importance of understanding the image of God as a whole, while Heb. 2:6-9 makes it plain that only Christ fulfilled what it is to represent God as his image in every respect. Humankind, Hebrews argues, has lost or forfeited its role as steward or "lord" of creation.

Plato and Aristotle see *nous*, "mind," as directing human or bodily capacities and affairs in a responsible way (*Phaedrus* 247C; *Republic* 6.508D). Augustine, Aquinas, and Reinhold Niebuhr see reason or mind as an important control over the self, as against passion, greed, or pride. Paul does not devalue reason. As G. Bornkamm and W. Pannenberg argue, he uses persuasion and rational argument, not "revelation speech," that is, such pronouncements as "Thus says the Lord" (Bornkamm, "Faith and Reason in Paul," in *Early Christian Experience* [London: SCM, 1969], 29-46; Pannenberg, "Insight and Faith," in *BQT* 2:28-45, esp. 34-35; S. K. Stowers, "Paul on the Use and Abuse of Reason," in D. Balch et al., *Greeks, Romans, and Christians* [Minneapolis: Augsburg, 1990], 253-88).

Biblical tradition and patristic tradition also view "dominion" over nature as part of bearing the image of God (Ps. 8:4-7; Heb. 2:6-9). This does not, however, imply "mastery" of nature, let alone its exploitation. Hebrews states, "We do not yet see everything in subjection to them"; only Christ is "crowned with glory and honor." Humankind can learn from Christ what it means to represent God's sovereign kingship by being stewards who care for, and husband, the resources of the earth. Paul speaks of being conformed to the image of Christ (Rom. 8:29). 1 Cor. 15:49 looks forward to the future of bearing the image of the man from heaven. Although H. Gunkel complains of the space given to "image of God" in Christian theology, Gerhard von Rad defends it as "highly significant." Irenaeus draws a distinction between "image" and "likeness," but most scholars see the terms as an example of Hebrew parallelism (Heb. *dĕmuth* and *tselem*). While Aquinas stresses human dominion over the animal order (*Su Th* 1a, qu. 93, art. 2), Niebuhr and Moltmann stress human responsibility and stewardship, and Moltmann subtitles his *God in Creation* "An Ecological Doctrine of Creation" (Eng. 1985). Niebuhr attributes human mastery of nature to "lust for power" and "exploitation" (*The Nature and Destiny of Man* [1941]). Responsible stewardship, for Pannenberg, may be "sharing in the creative force that comes from God" (*ST* 2:131). This may have huge implications for pharmacology, medicine, and generic developments.

Most of all, the capacity to relate to others seems even more important, especially since it includes the capacity or potentiality to relate to God. Barth argues that in creation God willed the existence of a being who "can be a real partner ... capable of action and responsibility in relation to Him" (*CD* III/1, 184-85). This involves the genuine *encounter* stressed by E. Brunner, and the subject-to-subject confrontation and reciprocity expounded by M. Buber in his classic work *I and Thou*. Among the Church Fathers, Lactantius argued at the beginning of the fourth century that being made in the image of God means to hold fellow humans in respect, giving them "what is due to other people." Fundamental "God-likeness" emerges in true reciprocity and mutuality, "a free co-existence and co-operation, an open confrontation and reciprocity" (Barth, 185). Barth expounds this especially in terms of "the differentiation and relationship of man and woman, the relation of sex" (186). He argues that masculine and feminine should not be blurred, for the important gift is that of *relationality in difference*. The genders "must not be confused and interchanged" (*CD* III/4, 168). Barth, followed by Phyllis Trible, argues that both male and female bear the image of God (*God and the Rhetoric Of Sexuality* [Philadelphia: Fortress, 1978], 12-30). Migliore insists that human beings *"find their true identity in coexistence with each other and with all other creatures"* (*Faith and Understanding* [Grand Rapids: Eerdmans, 1991], 125). Human existence, he argues, is "not individualist, but communal.... We live in dialogue" (125-26). Pannenberg also argues that "being with others as others is central to bearing the image of God" (*ST* 2:193). This is fundamental in S. Grenz's social Trinity. Moltmann, too, warns us of the danger of a "culture of narcissism" that surrounds the self only with self-affirmations (*The Trinity and the Kingdom of God* [London: SCM, 1981], 5). P. Ricoeur also argues that true self-identity arises only when we are accountable to others (in *Oneself as Another* [Chicago: University of Chicago Press, 1992]).

We now pass to a different question. Is the biblical view of humankind dualistic and partitive or holistic? The biblical tradition is that of an *aspective* or *psychosomatic self*, in striking contrast to Gnostic or Greek dualism. Pannenberg explicitly defends "the biblical idea of psychosomatic unity" (*ST* 2:181-202). The Hebrew word *nephesh*, often translated as "soul," can sometimes mean a dead body or animal flesh. Athenagoras argued that the soul did not represent the whole person. But rapidly many of the Greek Fathers fell under the influence of Greek or Hellenistic thought (*see* **Soul**). The climax of this trend can be seen in Aquinas, when he sees *mens* (Latin for "mind") as "the essence *(essentia)* of the soul *(animae),*" and understanding *(intellectus)* as the soul's very essence (*Su Th* 1a, qu. 79, 1, 1). Thus Plato speaks of the "liberation of the soul from bondage to the body of death" (*Republic* 611E). Tertullian holds a dualistic view, for which he seeks biblical support from Gen. 2:7, when God breathes spirit into a vessel of clay. In the NT *psuchē,* sometimes translated "soul," is more often translated "life." In Paul the adjective *psuchikos* denotes humankind as *not* open to the Holy Spirit. J. D. G. Dunn comments, "Paul uses *psychē* just 13 times, 4 of them in Romans. This itself is in striking contrast to the regular use of the term in classical Greek and of *nephesh* in the OT (756 times)" (*The Theology of Paul the Apostle* [Grand Rapids: Eerdmans, 1998], 76). He adds, "*Nephesh* denotes the whole person" (76). D. E. H. Whiteley similarly presses for an "aspective" understanding of "body" and "soul" in Paul. Dunn concludes: "The gospel is not about an innate spirituality awaiting release, but about the divine Spirit acting upon and in a person from without" (77). The old nineteenth-century debate about "dichotomy" and "trichotomy" on the basis of 1 Thess. 5:23 now seems bizarre and preposterous. Its reference to "spirit and soul and body" is no more partitive than the English "put your heart and soul into it"!

This does not imply that humankind is isolated from nature. It concedes that humans are partly biological in nature, and recognizes that mental attitudes can influence bodily life, just as bodily disease may affect mental life. H. Thielicke makes this point in his *Man in God's World* (1967). Indeed, this is what the term "psychosomatic" primarily indicates. Pannenberg discusses the materialist views of humankind in Feuerbach, Nietzsche, and Freud, and the significance of psychoanalysis, and shows the inadequacy of behavioralism for establishing self-identity (*Anthropology in Theological Perspective* [New York: Continuum, 1985], 191-242). Clearly in the NT Christ is the paradigm case of humanism. Barth asserts that Jesus is man as God willed and created him. What constitutes human nature in us depends upon what it is in him (see *CD* III/2, §§43, 50). D. Bonhoeffer calls Jesus the "man for others." It is odd to ask whether Jesus was truly human; in the light of his human life as God-man, we need to ask: "Are we truly human?" J. Murphy O'Connor says that for Paul Jesus was normative humanity; he did not first look at other people (*Being Human Together* [Wilmington, Del.: Glazier, 1982], 33-57). Jesus accepted the constraints of the time and place, but regarded bodiliness as a gift from God. Nowadays we might say that Jesus Christ accepted the constraints of his historicality or historicity. Paul asserts: "The body is meant . . . for the Lord, and the Lord for the body" (1 Cor. 6:13).

E. Käsemann describes God's gift of *the body* (Gk. *to sōma*) particularly well. "Body" denotes, for Paul, "that piece of the *world* which we ourselves are and for which we bear responsibility because it was the earliest gift of our Creator to us. 'Body' is not primarily to be regarded . . . from the standpoint of the individual. For the apostle it signifies man in his worldliness and therefore in his *ability to communicate.* . . . In the *bodily* obedience of the Christian . . . in the world of everyday, the *lordship of Christ finds visible expression,* and only when this visible expression takes personal shape in us does the whole thing become *credible* as Gospel message" (*New Testament Questions of Today* [London: SCM, 1969], 135, italics mine). The corporate or communal aspects of "body" are also expounded by J. A. T. Robinson in *The Body* (London: SCM, 1952).

"Flesh" (Gk. *sarx*) is carefully distinguished from "body," as Robinson argues. He declares, "While *sarx* stands for man in the solidarity of creation in his distance from God, *sōma* stands for man, in the solidarity of creation, as made for God" (*The Body*, 31). But within this category "flesh" can denote many things. Robinson writes, "Flesh represents . . . man in his weakness and mortality" (19). The more "theological" uses of "flesh" are expounded by Bultmann and by R. Jewett. Jewett shows how, in Galatians, sensual libertines and hyperconservatives on the law could *both* be called "fleshly" by Paul. Both parties, Jewett maintains, are "shifting [their] boasting from the cross of Christ to the circumcised flesh"; this provides "the key to the interpretation" (*Paul's Anthropological Terms* [Leiden: Brill, 1971], 95). "The opposition between flesh and spirit rests not on a thoroughgoing dualism between the material and the pneumatic worlds, such as one might find in Gnosticism," but in a situation where "there was a danger of replacing the boast of the cross with a boast in the circumcised flesh" (100). Jewett shows how the situation in Romans is parallel (135-66). Bultmann reaches similar conclusions. After considering less "theological" uses of "flesh" in Paul, he states, "Living out of 'flesh' is the self-reliant attitude of the man who puts his trust in his own strengths" (*Theology of the New Testament*, vol. 1 [London: SCM, 1952], 240). It is "trust in one's self as being able to procure life by the use of the earthly and through one's own strength" (239).

"Heart" *(kardia)* is also important in Paul (Heb. *lēbh*). It may denote depths of feeling, firmness of will, or the center or core of the whole personality. Calvin stresses the importance of "heart" in this sense. Human beings are not simply unfeeling minds or unthinking bodies. They can decide, resolve, or even be obstinate. But perhaps the most significant aspect for today is the arguments of Bultmann and G. Theissen that "heart" also denotes subconscious or unconscious depths of a human being. Paul says regarding his own ministry: "I do not even judge myself" (1 Cor. 4:1-5), for some things remain hidden in the heart. In Rom. 2:12-16 Paul speaks of the secrets of the heart, and in 1 Cor. 14:21-25 he refers to the disclosure of the secrets of the heart, perhaps denoting suppressed consciousness (Theissen, *Psychological Aspects of Pauline Theology* [Edinburgh: T. & T. Clark, 1987], 59-80 and throughout).

On "conscience" *(suneidēsis)*, we refer to our separate entry, since interpretations have been debated and are perhaps controversial. Paul does not use the term as do the Stoics, but mainly, although not entirely, he uses it to signify pain consequent upon acts believed to be wrong. The roles of *pneuma, psuchē,* and *esō anthrōpos* are noteworthy, but not of decisive significance. At all events, we know that Paul and the NT did not hold a dualist view of human beings, and this is confirmed by most current theologians, including Pannenberg. Admittedly, from Augustine to Aquinas we see the influence of Greek thought. But there is a broad consensus today between biblical interpreters and modern systematic theologians. The anthropological vocabulary that is applied to human beings or to humankind functions mainly to convey modes of being, not "parts." This is not true of every single passage, as Robert Gundry reminds us in his *Sōma in Biblical Theology* (Cambridge: CUP, 1976).

Reading: J. D. G. Dunn, *The Theology of Paul the Apostle* (Grand Rapids: Eerdmans, 1998), 51-79; R. Jewett, *Paul's Anthropological Terms* (Brill: Leiden, 1971); J. Murphy-O'Connor, *Becoming Human Together* (Wilmington, Del.: Glazier, 1982); W. Pannenberg, *Anthropology in Theological Perspectives* (New York: T. & T. Clark/Continuum, 1985); Pannenberg, *Systematic Theology*, vol. 2 (Grand Rapids: Eerdmans, 1994), 161-230 and 297-324; G. Theissen, *Psychological Aspects of Pauline Theology* (Edinburgh: T. & T. Clark, 1987); The Church of England Doctrine Commission Report, *Being Human* (London: Church Publishing House, 2003).

Antichrist

It is important to appreciate the contrast between the occasional occurrence of the word in the NT (only four references) and its more frequent occurrence in the Church Fathers and in Reformation and post-Reformation thought. In the NT the term is restricted to 1 and 2 John. 1 John 2:18 refers to an oral tradition that the "antichrist is coming" in the last days, and also states that "many antichrists have come," presumably in the shape of false teachers or false prophets, especially "one who denies the Father and the Son" (2:22). Second, in 1 John 4:3 "the spirit of the antichrist" does not confess that Jesus is from God. Third, and finally, in 2 John 7 the antichrist is a "deceiver" who denies Christ. The term is not used in 2 Thessalonians, but is associated by later writers with "the man of sin" or "lawless one" in 2 Thess. 2:3-4, and the "lawless one" in 2:7-10.

The first explicit reference in the early church comes in Irenaeus, *Against Heresies* 3.16.5-6, which refers to 1 John 2:18 (*ANF* 1:442), and 30.1 (*ANF* 1:558-59). Thereafter, in about 200 Hippolytus writes *On Christ and the Antichrist*, in which the antichrist apes the qualities of Christ as an inverted parallel. For example, Christ is the Lamb; the antichrist appears to be a lamb, but is a wolf in sheep's clothing (*On Christ and the Antichrist* 6; *ANF* 5:206). Tertullian refers the term to 2 Thess. 2:1-10 (*On the Resurrection of the Flesh* 24; *ANF* 3:563). Origen refers to Daniel and 2 Thess. 2:1-12. Commodianus refers the figure to "Nero ... raised from hell" (*Instructions* 41-45; *ANF* 4:211-12). Lactantius also reflects an apocalyptic perspective (*Divine Institutes* 7.14-16; *ANF* 7:211-13). Cyril of Jerusalem stresses the figure's magician-like qualities; he also seeks to rebuild the Jewish temple (*Catechetical Lectures* 15.14, 17; *NPNF*, ser. 2, 7:108). Tyconius and Augustine see the antichrist as present evil in the church.

In the Middle Ages Joachim of Fiore (1135-1202) associates the antichrist with a triumphal pope. John Wycliffe develops this further (*Pastoral Office* 11-17), and John Huss identifies this figure with a specific pope (*On Simony* 2.4, 5). Martin Luther identifies the antichrist with the papacy as an institution (*LW* 51:311; *Against the Execrable Bull of Antichrist;* WA 6:596). John Calvin also implies that the papacy is antichrist (*Institutes* 4.2.11 and 4.7.24-25), but with less polemic. A Roman Catholic writer, Estius, responded that the antichrist was the "secessionist" church (*Commentarii* 2.604-11). Some Puritan writers were ferociously polemical. Obbe Philips writes, "The whole Papacy is a Sodom, a Babylon . . . the work of Antichrist" (*A Confession* 121). Arminius follows the Protestant tradition: the pope, as antichrist, professes himself to be the vice-regent of Christ (*Disputation* 22.11). By the time of Bengel this had been softened (*Gnomon* 806). In the nineteenth century only a minority of writers refer to the figure, but often as an oppressive figure or regime, who or which sought to rule the world in place of God. Hence Napoleon, and in the twentieth century Hitler and Stalin, are seen as embodiments of the antichrist.

Reading: Kevin L. Hughes, *Constructing Antichrist* (Washington, D.C.: Catholic University of America, 2005); Bernard McGinn, *Antichrist: Two Thousand Years of the Human Fascination with Evil* (San Francisco: Harper, 1994).

Apocalyptic
The significance and relevance of apocalyptic for Christian theology must not be confused with questions about its literary sources. In theological terms apocalyptic denotes six themes: (i) an emphasis upon new creation by God, rather than upon merely human aspirations; (ii) the decisive place of divine judgment and resurrection in the transformation of history and the world; (iii) the notion that since the present age is too evil to be reformed, God himself will intervene in history to inaugurate a new age; (iv) this pattern concerns the whole world, and not merely the history of Israel or the church; (v) trust in God's interventions and new creation with special relevance to the poor, the oppressed, and the persecuted, to those who have no hope in human agencies or rulers; and (vi) since the term strictly denotes *revelation* or *disclosure,* there is a further contrast between merely human discovery and God's choice to reveal (or to reveal in advance) what is hitherto hidden from human eyes. In the nineteenth century the term "apocalyptic" covered a wider range of issues, but these six are of special relevance to Christian thought. Sometimes the fourth point above (its universal or cosmic scope) leads it to be associated with such cosmic signs as the falling of stars, changes to the moon, and dramatic world events. These features color the more popular use of the term.

In terms of literary sources, we find the roots of apocalyptic in the OT. Some cite Amos 5:18-20, which begins, "Alas for you who desire the day of the LORD! . . . It is darkness, not light." Joel continues the promise of the Spirit in the new age (Joel 2:28–3:21). In Isaiah 24–27, according to S. B. Frost, "apocalyptic first achieves its characteristic form" (*Old Testament Apocalyptic* [London: Epworth, 1952], 143). Certainly Isaiah 24 conveys cosmic judgment ("The earth is utterly broken . . . shaken . . . staggers like a drunkard" [vv. 19-20]). Chapter 25 praises God for his acts, and sees him as "a refuge to the poor" (25:4). 26:1 and 27:12 speak of "that day." Various parts of Ezekiel are involved, especially 37:1-4 and chapters 38 and 39 (Gog and Magog in 38:2, 14; 39:1, and "on that day" in 38:10). Much of Zechariah 12-14 includes apocalyptic elements, and parts of Daniel, including chapter 7, with its vision of the four beasts (7:3-8), of the Ancient One (7:9-12), and of the Son of Man or "one like a human being" (7:13-14) and a succession of empires (7:23-27). In the intertestamental period, apocalyptic is found in *1 Enoch, Jubilees, Testament of Abraham,* 2 Esdras, and *Psalms of Solomon,* as well as in parts of the War Scroll and other Dead Sea Scrolls. Within the NT, Jesus gives an apocalyptic discourse (Mark 13:24-27, 32-37, and parallels in Matthew 24, especially vv. 36-44). Here the apocalyptic themes concerning the end of the world remain distinct from Jesus' predictions of the fall of Jerusalem. Paul has an apocalyptic discourse in 2 Thess. 2:1-12 (assuming that it is Pauline), and perhaps in 1 Cor. 15:23-28. The book of Revelation contains much apocalyptic, including the vision of the four horsemen, who represent conquest, violence, famine, and death (Rev. 6:2-8). But apocalyptic is not confined to this vision. The heavenly perspective (Rev. 4:1-11), the Lion opening the scroll of history (5:1-10), the sealing of the elect (7:2-14), and many other passages may be included as apocalyptic.

In the early church Augustine engaged with the divine control of political history in *The City of God,* which largely constituted a reply to pagan objections that the collapse of the Roman Empire owed much to the rise of Christianity. Book 20 addresses the theme of the Last Judgment, and 20.20 the theme of resurrection. 20.19 speaks of the Day of the Lord. But for the most part Tyconius and Augustine offer a "spiritual" (rather than historical) interpretation of apocalyptic, although we find traces of apocalyptic themes in Tertullian, Lactantius, and perhaps John Chrysostom. In the Middle Ages, there are traces in Bede, Haimo of Auxerre, Thietland of Einsiedeln, the Exeter Book, and especially Joachim of Fiore. John Calvin stresses apocalyptic elements in relation to the sovereignty of God, especially in history, new creation, knowledge, and life. Among the Puritans, John Owen and Thomas Vincent are prominent, especially in the latter's *Fire and Brimstone in Hell* (seventeenth century).

Interest in apocalyptic declined from the eighteenth to the early twentieth century. But, Klaus Koch comments, after the early 1960s "Unexpectedly... the term apocalyptic re-emerged from the depths, and became a hotly disputed slogan" (*The Rediscovery of Apocalyptic* [London: SCM, 1972], 13). In the 1960s Ernst Käsemann called apocalyptic "the mother of Christian Theology" (*New Testament Questions of Today* [London: SCM, 1969], 137). Wolfhart Pannenberg introduced the apocalyptic concept of history to systematic theology. Although O. Plöger and D. Rössler deemed apocalyptic important, Pannenberg's intervention was decisive. In NT studies J. Christiaan Beker argued the significance of apocalyptic for Paul and for "the triumph of God" in *Paul the Apostle* (Edinburgh: T. & T. Clark, 1980). Alexandra Brown followed him in *The Cross and Human Transformation: Paul's Apocalyptic Word in 1 Corinthians* (Minneapolis: Fortress, 1989). Jürgen Moltmann returns a cosmic perspective in *The Coming of God* (London: SCM, 1996). We may once more recapture the permanent theological relevance of apocalyptic by citing some words from H. H. Rowley, even if they were written long ago: "The apocalyptists . . . did not believe in the power of the evil present to generate the longed-for morrow. . . . Their spring of hope was in God alone. . . . They knew nothing of the idea that man would steadily work his way upward on the stepping-stones of his sins to the goal of his being. They . . . could only rise by the power of God. . . . The unseen world was very real to them" (*The Relevance of Apocalyptic* [London: Lutterworth, 1944], 153).

Reading: Ernst Käsemann, "Primitive Christian Apocalyptic," in *New Testament Questions of Today* (London: SCM, 1969), 108-37; Klaus Koch, *The Rediscovery of Apocalyptic* (London: SCM, 1972); D. S. Russell, *The Method and Message of Jewish Apocalyptic* (London: SCM, 1964).

Apocrypha

The Apocrypha denotes in general certain books (around thirteen) accepted alongside the OT within the LXX, or Greek translation, but excluded from the canon of the Hebrew Bible. These are considered canonical by the Eastern Orthodox Church and, with a proviso, by the Roman Catholic Church, but are excluded as noncanonical by Protestant Christians and Jews. This remains only a generalized verdict. The Council of Trent accepted the books, with the exceptions of 1 and 2 Esdras. Luther in 1534 regarded them as noncanonical, but placed them at the end of his translation of the Bible. The Church of England (art. 6) rejects the Apocrypha as a source of doctrine, but commends it "for example of life and instruction of manners"; the Westminster Confession (1647) prohibited it as not to be "approved or made use of" except as purely human writings. Probably the most familiar and widely used books are the Wisdom of Solomon and Ecclesiasticus, or the Wisdom of Ben Sirach. Ecclus. 44:1 contains the speech: "Let us now praise famous men . . ." (KJV) or "Let us now sing the praises of famous men . . ." (NRSV). Wis. 7:25-26 calls personified Wisdom

> a breath of the power of God,
> and a pure emanation of the glory of the Almighty. . . .
> She is a reflection of eternal light,
> a spotless mirror of the working of God.

Many NT scholars understand this as the background to Col. 1:15 and Heb. 1:3. Paul calls Christ "the image of the invisible God" (Col. 1:15), and the writer to the Hebrews says, "[Christ] is the reflection *(apaugasma)* of God's glory and the exact imprint of God's very being" (Heb 1:3). The NT claims for Christ what Wisdom of Solomon claims for Wisdom, and more. But the NT never speaks of "emanation," and does not explicitly quote from the Apocrypha as Scripture.

On one side it is argued that the LXX primarily became the Bible of the Greek-speaking church. Its books cover the intertestamental period from c. 300 B.C. to c. A.D. 100. It expounds God's choice of Israel, sees the Law as a gift of God's grace, and recounts the persecution and martyrdom of loyal Jews under the oppression of Antiochus Epiphanes, especially in Maccabees. It is indeed useful as "instruction" on NT background, and perhaps for the Christian life. On the other hand, the NT does not seem to regard it as Scripture, and a number of its doctrines were rejected by the Reformers. There are suggestions that human martyrdom can provide atonement for others (2 Macc. 7:37-38); perhaps the intercession of saints for God's people (2 Macc. 15:12-14); the treasuring up of "virtuous deeds" for time in need (Tob. 4:8-11); and hints of immortality rather than resurrection. Again, it can be argued that in the history of the church *1 Clement* (c. 95-96) and Polycarp (c. 156) quoted from Wisdom and Tobit respectively, Irenaeus and Tertullian cited certain passages, and Clement of Alexandria and Origen cited the Apocrypha freely. On the other hand, Jerome excluded the Apocrypha, and indeed seemed to have coined the word, while Augustine initially accepted it as canonical but later thought it contained "outside books," that is, books not for the church.

The Apocrypha is to be distinguished from the Pseudepigrapha, a large body of intertestamental writings. It is also distinguished from apocryphal NT books and writings, and from legendary or fictitious accounts of Jesus and the church, which were intended to supplement the NT. Even then, however, the precise boundaries of the Apocrypha are disputed in various traditions. Normally it includes 1 Esdras (largely parallel to Chronicles, Ezra, and Nehemiah, with the addition of some non-Jewish folklore); 2 Esdras (called 4 Esdras in the Vulgate, which is a Palestinian-Jewish apocalypse); Tobit (a popular intertestamental story, albeit with some errors); Judith (another popular story); the Rest of Esther; the Wisdom of Solomon (written in Greek, in the first century B.C., which sees wisdom as a hypostasis of God and uses largely Greek categories of thought); Ecclesiasticus, or Wisdom of Ben Sirach, written in the second century B.C. in the style of Proverbs; Baruch, once attributed to the scribe of Jeremiah; the Letter of Jeremiah, which includes a typical attack on idolatry; Additions to Daniel, which includes the Song of the Three Holy Children or "Benedicite," Susanna, and Bel and the Dragon. 1 Maccabees recounts events under Antiochus Epiphanes in 175-134 B.C.; and 2 Maccabees also relates to history more loosely, often using theological interpretation. Given the content and history of the Apocrypha, it is thoroughly understandable why its status is so strongly contested, and why it became an issue at the Reformation. (*See also* **Canon; Judaism in the Time of Jesus.**)

Reading: B. Metzger, *An Introduction to the Apocrypha* (Oxford: OUP, 1957); D. de Silva, *Introducing the Apocrypha* (Grand Rapids: Baker, 2002).

Apollinarianism

Apollinarius (c. 310–c. 390) is said to have denied the presence of a human mind in Christ. He seceded from the church c. 375, and was condemned by the Synod at Rome in 374-380. Apollinarian worship was forbidden in 381. But most of his writings have been lost, and it is difficult to reconstruct the fragments that remain. For most of his life he vigorously defended Christian orthodoxy against the Arians, and became a close friend of Athanasius, whose views on Christology he largely shared. He stressed the deity of Christ, but at the expense of denying his complete and full humanness.

Apologetics

From the Greek *apologia,* "a defense," apologetics traditionally denotes the defense of Christian belief, doctrine, and practice against criticism and attack from those outside the church. Scholars usually locate the earliest example in Paul's defense of Christian belief in Athens (Acts 17:17-31), in which "he argued *(dielegeto)* in the synagogue ... and also in the marketplace every day with those who happened to be there" (17:17). In the second century a series of apologists addressed "defenses" of Christian belief to the emperor and the Senate, among others, in which they made much of rational or reasonable argument, and the rationality of Christian belief. Many of the Church Fathers continued this tradition. Origen addressed the attack from Celsus, and Augustine addressed criticisms from non-Christians in his *City of God.* In the Middle Ages Aquinas produced his *Summa contra Gentiles* (c. 1259) to help missionaries answer non-Christian doubts, as well as his *Summa Theologiae* for Christians. In the nineteenth century Schleiermacher defined apologetics as seeking "to ward off hostility towards the [Christian] community" (*Brief Outline on the Study of Theology* [1811]).

Karl Barth rejected apologetics (*CD* I/1) as natural theology, which he saw as seeking to climb up to God by reason, rather than appropriating revelation. But E. Brunner retained this discipline, although he preferred to use the term "eristics" for it. He recognized that faith cannot be "proved," but accepted the need for "disputation" and replies to attacks or criticisms. Paul Tillich described all his theology as "answering theology." His *Systematic Theology* attempts to reply to five questions from "outsiders," and in effect constitutes apologetics. Bultmann did not explicitly attempt apologetics, but attempted to lay bare the kerygma, even if some doubt his success. Among current or recent Protestant theologians, the work of W. Pannenberg emphatically includes apologetics, while among Roman Catholics K. Rahner and especially H. Küng are robust advocates of it, in the tradition of Aquinas. Today a number of philosophers or exponents of philosophy of religion take on this role. Such names as A. Plantinga, N. Wolterstorff, R. Swinburne, and V. Brümmer come to mind.

Apologists

This collective name groups together Christian writers mainly from the second century who addressed the emperor or educated Romans in defense of the Christian faith. They generally used rational or reasonable argumentation, often engaging either with Greek philosophy or with Jewish objections, from about A.D. 120 or 130 to around 200 or 220. (i) Aristides and Quadratus are thought to represent the first of the apologists (c. 124 or 138), perhaps addressing the emperor Hadrian if the earlier date is correct, or more probably addressing Antoninus Pius. Before the nineteenth century their work was known only through Eusebius and Jerome, but in 1878 Armenian and Syrian translations came to light.

(ii) Probably the most widely known is Justin Martyr (c. 100–c. 165), who in his *Dialogue with Trypho* (c. 135) debated the claims of Judaism. He later produced his *First Apology* (c. 155) to the emperor Antoninus Pius, and his *Second Apology* (c. 161) to the Roman Senate. His early work was written in Ephesus, and later work in Rome, where he opened a Christian school of instruction. Justin's *Dialogue with Trypho* (PG 6; *ANF* 1:194-274) begins by describing his studies in philosophy and subsequent conversion, and the limitations of the knowledge of God by "the soul." Knowledge of God does indeed come from the prophets (*Dialogue* 7). But the Law has been abrogated, and the new covenant, promised by God, has been given (11). Righteousness comes not by Jewish rites but through conversion and Christian baptism (14). Jews boast of the sonship of Abraham, but salvation comes through Christ (25, 26). Many OT ceremonies and rites prefigure Christ. Trypho demands that Christ be shown to be God (55), and Justin responds (56, 63). He cites the birth of a messianic figure from a virgin (66), and reinterprets prophecies (77-78). He acknowledges that to Trypho the cross is an "offense" (89); indeed, the one who hangs on a tree is cursed (94-95; Deut. 21:23). But "the Father of all wished His Christ . . . to take upon Him the curses of all, knowing that after He had been crucified and was dead, He would raise Him up" (95; *ANF* 1:247). All these are predicted in various parts of the OT (106-129). Those Gentiles who have become converted to Christ prove that they are more faithful than unconverted Jews (131). He exhorts the Jews to be converted (137), and Trypho concludes that he has been "particularly pleased" with this consultation (142).

The *First Apology* of Justin (PG 6) is in English translation in *ANF* 1:163-86. After the address, Justin protests that Christians are unjustly accused (1.3, 4). Especially the charge of atheism is unjust (1.5, 6). They desire "the eternal and pure life, and seek the abode which is with God" (1:8). They reject idolatry, which is folly (9). Christians offer hymns of thanks for our creation, health, and life. "Our teacher of things is Jesus Christ, who was . . . crucified under Pontius Pilate. . . . We reasonably worship him, having learned that he is the Son of the true God himself" (1.13; *ANF* 1:166-67). Christ taught prayer for enemies, kindness and mercy, patience, and civil obedience, namely, to "render to Caesar the things that are Caesar's" (1.15-19; *ANF* 1:168). Next he argues for the possibility of the resurrection (1.19), and that Christ was predicted by Moses (32). Prophecy is authentically from God (1.36). There are affinities with Plato (1.59-60). Christians worship God weekly "on the day called Sunday . . . [and] gather in one place" (1.67; *ANF* 1:186).

In his *Second Apology* (PG 6; translation in *ANF* 1:188-93), Justin more briefly replies to unjust accusations against Christians. Punishments have been imposed unfairly, and some critics love bravado and prejudice. "When we are examined, we make no denial, because we are not conscious of any evil, but count it impious not to speak the truth" (2.4; *ANF* 1:189). As it is, God preserves the world for the sake of Christians; it is not simply a matter of "fate," as Stoics claim (2.7). "Christ ... was partially known even by Socrates" (2.10; *ANF* 1:191); "Socrates ... was accused of the very same crimes as ourselves" (10). Christians (like Justin) are "fearless of death" (2.12). "Our doctrines are ... more lofty than all human philosophy" (22.15; *ANF* 1:193).

(iii) Tatian was Justin's pupil between 150 and 165, but thereafter adopted views of his own, which were different from most apologists. Apart from writing his apologia *Oration against the Greeks* in 172, he traveled to the East, where he founded the ascetic sect of the Encratites, who held to a rigorous lifestyle. His attack on Greek civilization was so violent and extreme that much of the church regarded him a heretic. He argues that only those who live righteously and obey wisdom are armed with the breastplate of the heavenly Spirit (*Against the Greeks* 16).

(iv) Athenagoras of Athens addresses his *Legatio, Embassy on Behalf of Christians*, to the emperor Marcus Aurelius and his son Commodus (c. 176-180). He rejects the popular charge against Christians of atheism, arguing that Christians believe in God, who created all things by his Word, and holds them together by his Spirit (*Embassy* 6). Broadly, *Embassy* 4-30 reject current accusations against Christians, while 31-36 address charges of Oedipean incest and Thyestian banquets. To believe in the Son of God, he argues, is not unreasonable or irrational (10). He even argues that the Father, the Son, and the Holy Spirit are *one* "by the unity and power of the Spirit *(henotēti kai dunamei pneumatos)*. . . . God is no more 'separate from the Holy Spirit' than the sun's rays from the sun" (10.3; PG 6:909B). God's Word and Wisdom flow from God, "as light from fire" *(Embassy* 12, *hōs phōs apo puros)*. A second treatise, *The Resurrection,* has often been attributed to Athenagoras, but we cannot be certain about its authorship. He holds together *Trinitarian theology with rational, philosophical inquiry.*

(v) Theophilus, bishop of Antioch, argues for the rationality of the doctrine of creation, as against the immorality of the myths of the Greco-Roman pantheon. God has embodied *logos,* or intelligibility, in the created order. Through his Word, the Son, and his Wisdom (the Spirit), God has created all things in accordance with Ps. 33:6 (*Autolycus* 1.7). In Gen. 1:2 the movement of the Spirit on the waters shows his life-giving and effective power (*Autolycus* 2.13). He also believes in the divine inspiration of the prophets (*Autolycus* 2.9; PG 6:1064A).

Reading: *ANF* 1:159-271; Henry Chadwick, "Justin Martyr's Defence of Christianity," *BJRL* 47 (1965): 275-97; R. M. Grant, *Greek Apologists of the Second Century* (London: SCM, 1988); Michael W. Holmes, ed., *Apostolic Fathers: Greek Texts and English Translations* (Grand Rapids: Baker Academic, 1992, 2007); Kirsopp Lake, ed., *Apostolic Fathers,* 2 vols., Loeb Classical Library (Cambridge: Harvard University Press; London: Heinemann, 1955, Eng. and Gk.); J. B. Lightfoot, ed., *The Apostolic Fathers* (London: Macmillan, 1891).

Apophatic Theology

This emphasizes that the transcendence and mystery of God surpass human speech and all conceptual or logical expression. He is beyond the logic of predication. The apophatic is sometimes called the way of negation and complements its opposite, namely, cataphatic theology. In certain strands of mysticism, paradoxically knowledge of God entails "unknowing." The thinker and mystic Dionysius, or more accurately Pseudo-Dionysius, is especially associated with this approach.

Apostasy

Apostasy denotes the abandonment of Christianity. The Greek *apostasia* may mean "rebellion" (2 Thess. 2:3) or "abandonment" (1 Macc. 2:15-19; Justin, *Dialogue* 110.2), but is not used in the technical sense in the NT. The Greek word *apostasis* usually meant "renunciation" in a more general sense. Heb. 6:6 speaks of those who "have fallen away," and 2 Pet. 2:21 of turning back from the commandment. In the early church apostasy was regarded as so serious a sin that it was classified with murder and fornication. The Donatist controversy discussed its status and the possibility of restoration. The term "heresy," by contrast, refers to deviation into unacceptable doctrine within the church. In 1983 the Roman Catholic Church officially defined apostasy as total renunciation of the Christian faith.

A Posteriori

A posteriori arguments are drawn from everyday or universal experience, and observation of the world. They depend on empirical evidence, in contrast to logical or rational principles furnished by the mind or reflection alone. These are analytical arguments.

Apostle, Apostolicity

From the Greek *apostolos,* an apostle is one *sent as an envoy on behalf of another;* usually in the NT it denotes one sent by and on behalf of *God* or *Christ.* Paul frequently calls himself an apostle (Rom. 1:1; 11:13; 1 Cor. 1:1; 9:1-2; 2 Cor. 1:1; Gal. 1:1; Eph. 1:1; Col. 1:1; 1 Tim. 1:1). He is especially an "apostle to the Gentiles" (Rom. 11:13). Although, as F. Danker states, it can be used in the NT of "a group of highly honoured believers with a special function" (BDAG 122), the Gospels and Acts use the term to denote "twelve, whom he [Jesus] also named apostles, to be with him, and to be sent out to proclaim the message" (Mark 3:14); or in Matt. 10:2, "These are the names of the twelve apostles." Some suggest that Paul did not know of this usage. But at all events it may not *primarily* suggest "authority," although this may be included. Chrysostom proposed that it was a term of humility: "Of him that calleth is everything; of him that is called, nothing . . . but only to obey" *(Homily 1 on 1 Corinthians).*

J. A. Crafton understands apostles as transparent "windows" through which people can see Christ who called them (*The Agency of the Apostle* [Sheffield: Sheffield University Press, 1991], 53-103). After the betrayal of Judas, Acts 1:15-26 recounts the choice of Matthias to make up the number "twelve." Paul regards the primary qualification for apostleship as having "seen Jesus our Lord" (1 Cor. 9:1; 15:5-6). In his group of "highly honored believers," he includes "Junia . . . prominent among the apostles" (Rom. 16:7), which E. J. Epp has recently argued is without doubt a feminine name (*Junia: The First Woman Apostle* [Minneapolis: Fortress, 2005]). The "twelve" is not restricted to the Gospels and Acts: Rev. 21:14 speaks of "the twelve names of the twelve apostles of the Lamb." Crafton's work suggests caution about a "division" between Paul and Luke. 1 Cor. 12:28-29 implies that not all Christians are called to be apostles. In Eph. 2:20 the church is built "upon the foundation of the apostles and prophets." They clearly have a foundation ministry for the whole church and for apostolic tradition.

Modern research on apostleship has passed through several phases, ranging from institutional or quasi-mechanical to kerygmatic or christocentric approaches. (i) In the 1930s K. L. Rengstorf appealed to the analogy of the rabbinic background, in which an official representative or delegate was "sent" *(shaliach)* on behalf of another. He quoted the rabbinic saying "A man's *shaliach* is like himself" *(Berakhot* 3:5). This could be interpreted in such a way as to give grounds for a rigid notion of apostolic succession, as promoted in the 1940s by Gregory Dix and A. G. Hebert (Rengstorf, *"Apostolos,"* in *TDNT* 1:398-447; and G. Dix, in K. Kirk, ed., *The Apostolic Ministry* [London: Hodder and Stoughton, 1946], 183-303, and Hebert, 493-533). (ii) Rengstorf was criticized by H. von Campenhausen, H. Mosbeck, B. Rigaux, and C. K. Barrett, following a long essay by E. Käsemann, "The Legitimacy of Apostleship," in 1942 (*ZNW* 41 [1942]: 33-71; H. von Campenhausen, *Ecclesiastical Authority and Spiritual Power* [London: Black, 1969], 30-54; C. K. Barrett, *The Signs of an Apostle* [London: Epworth, 1970], 12-16). Käsemann declared, "The signs of apostleship are not ecclesiastical or 'miraculous,' but Christological." Apostleship is defined in terms of exhibiting the mindset of Christ (1 Cor. 2:16). It is "service which lives out the cross" (61). Thus the first two phases set out the two basic ways of viewing apostleship.

(iii) Käsemann's former pupil, J. H. Schütz, took up Käsemann's approach in 1975 with the addition of Max Weber's sociological distinction between institutional and charismatic authority. He continued Käsemann's approach of seeing apostleship as centered on the cross, but also understood both Paul and his opponents to appeal to the work of the Holy Spirit. In *Paul and the Anatomy of Apostolic Authority* (Cambridge: CUP, 1975), he discusses authority, and then rehearses the history of research on apostleship beginning with J. B. Lightfoot's essay in his *Galatians* in 1865, which traced the roots of apostleship to the ministry of Jesus. Schütz then assesses Rengstorf on the *shaliach* in later Judaism, where "the case against Rengstorf's argument is serious" (27). He concludes that this does not apply to missionaries, or to events that occurred earlier than the second century (28), and then examines Hans von Campenhausen and "the glory of evangelical service" (29). He approves his warnings about "reducing authority to . . . 'office'" (31). He notes, rightly, that most subsequent studies are being undertaken within this framework. He includes G. Klein and W. Schmithals. Schütz examines passages in Paul that bear on apostleship, not least 1 Corinthians 15, Gal. 1:1-12, and 2 Corinthians. The task of the apostle, he declares, is to be "in Christ" as both witness and messenger, to share Christ's sufferings, and to build up the church. Power becomes "an authenticating sign" (239), but in effective speech and within a power-weakness dialectic (244-48). The Holy Spirit is both an empowering and a regulating gift (253). *Charisma* becomes a key concept, which also involves the appropriation of tradition (263). He concludes: Paul's authority "has its starting point in the call to preach." But to what extent his drawing on the sociology of Max Weber genuinely takes discussion forward perhaps remains open to question. His study leaves us with the question: Would not some of Paul's opponents claim the same apostolic criteria as Paul?

(iv) Bengt Holmberg takes us a step forward with his book *Paul and Power* (Lund: Gleerup, 1978). His new thesis is the *collaborative* nature of apostleship. This was diffused in networks of transcontextual oversight (204-7). This coheres convincingly with A. Eriksson's *Traditions as Rhetorical Proof* (1998) on the role of *shared, common, apostolic traditions*. "Shared leadership" becomes a major theme. Not surprisingly, this matches some concerns of the Congregationalist P. T. Forsyth, in his older work *Lectures on the Church and Sacraments* (1917).

(v) E. Best (1986) partly draws on the work of C. K. Barrett in "Paul's Apostolic Authority" (*JSNT* 27 [1986]: 3-25). Apostles, he argues, are "founders" of communities, who become translocal overseers. Their call is a source of humility, not of pride.

(vi) J. A. Crafton, as we noted, argues for the transparency of apostles as a means of seeing Christ, especially in 2 Corinthians (*Agency of the Apostle,* 53-103). Rather than focus on the personalities or qualities of *agents,* Paul focuses on *agency,* that is, on the apostolic task. This also coheres with J. Roloff's study of 1965, which stresses Christ's Lordship and commission as finding visible expression in apostleship. Paul certainly attacks self-selecting and self-promoting "superapostles" in 1 and 2 Corinthians.

In spite of the importance of "apostle" in Paul, the word occurs nearly thirty times in Acts. 1 Tim. 2:7 closely associates it with preachers; Titus 1:1 with servants. It is used as a title in 1 Pet. 1:1, and Rev. 18:20 parallels apostles and prophets. In the subapostolic church we come across the idea of transmitting the gift or office. Timothy and Titus are often seen as apostolic delegates. *1 Clem. 44.1-2* (c. A.D. 96) narrates that the apostles appointed "approved men *(dedokimasmenoi)* [to] succeed to their ministry." Some argue that as "foundation" apostles, their ministry cannot be repeated, but is unique to the first generation. Others argue that since their ministry is to the whole church, not only to a specific time and place, their work continues through duly appointed successors, usually regarded as bishops (*see* **Apostolic Succession**). Outside the NT, the term "apostle" becomes used distinctively in the Catholic Apostolic Church, which was inspired by E. Irving and H. Drummond, in the belief that offices of the primitive church could be replicated after eighteen centuries (*see* **Holy Spirit: The Spirit in Historical Theology**).

Pannenberg comments, "In the first beginnings of the church the authority of the apostles kept the churches in their faith in the crucified and risen Lord" (*ST* 3:377). After the death of the apostles this function seemed to face uncertainty. Itinerant charismatics could not achieve it. Pannenberg declares, "The Pastorals certainly suggest that the apostles themselves appointed bishops as their successors" (378). Yet, he adds, we should be cautious about such passages as *1 Clem.* 42.4, which do not suggest a "straight line" of development. "Nevertheless . . . uniting teaching authority and leadership in the episcopate still corresponds materially to one aspect of the apostolate . . . preserving the churches in evangelical teaching" (379). This was linked with presiding at the Eucharist or Lord's Supper in Catholic, Orthodox, and Reformation teaching. It guarantees continuity in the public world (386-89).

Reading: Pope Benedict XVI, *The Apostles* (Rome: Sunday Visitors Publishing, 2007); E. Best, "Paul's Apostolic Authority," *JSNT* 27 (1986): 3-25; H. von Campenhausen, *Ecclesiastical Authority and Spiritual Power* (Stanford: Stanford University Press, 1969); B. Holmberg, *Paul and Power* (Lund: Gleerup, 1978); J. H. Schütz, *Paul and the Anatomy of Apostolic Authority* (Cambridge: CUP, 1975).

Apostles' Creed
The creed did not originate until the late sixth or early seventh century, after the close of the patristic era. But it constitutes a version of the old Roman creed, which does date from the third century. In this earlier form it became a model for various Latin creeds; its final form emerged in southwestern France, and was used by Charlemagne to establish uniformity within his empire in the early ninth century.

Apostolic Constitutions
A body of ecclesiastical law, which dates from c. 350 to 380, and probably of Syrian origin, the Apostolic Constitutions embody Arian tendencies, and have probable roots in the *Didachē* and perhaps in Hippolytus.

Apostolic Fathers
Since the eighteenth century, this term has denoted those documents or writers spanning roughly between the close of the NT and the early Christian apologists. These include Clement of Rome (c. 96), the *Didachē* (c. 90-120), Ignatius (c. 112), Polycarp of Smyrna (d. 155), *Shepherd of Hermas*, Papias, and the *Epistle of Barnabas*. (See also individual writings or writers.)

Apostolic Succession
Apostolic succession denotes an unbroken continuity of doctrine, tradition, and church order from the original apostles. Usually this is said to be preserved by an

unbroken succession of bishops. Thus the Roman Catholic Church traces bishops of Rome from Peter up to the contemporary pope, and even the *Church of England Year Book* traces an unbroken line from Augustine of Canterbury in 597 (commissioned by Pope Gregory) to the present holder of the office. Reformed theology and many Protestants, however, regard this continuity as a continuity of the church's doctrine, preaching, and message. This difference of outlook depends partly on what view of apostle and apostleship is held. The more institutional view is adopted by K. Rengstorf, G. Dix, and mostly Roman Catholic or "High Church" Anglicans (*see* **Anglo-Catholic**). The more christocentric or kerygmatic view is reflected in the more recent work of H. von Campenhausen, E. Käsemann, J. H. Schütz, B. Holmberg, and others.

The Roman Catholic Church denies the institutional apostolic succession of Anglicans, even though it acknowledges their historical closeness to Rome. Because at the Reformation Anglicans rejected the jurisdiction of the papacy and the Mass, it is claimed that it thereby lost its structural continuity with Rome. This is contested by Anglo-Catholics. More Reformed and Protestant Anglicans hold entirely to a doctrinal or "gospel" understanding of succession. Before the days of ecumenical dialogue, they would dismissively call the institutional approach "the pipeline," or mechanical, theory of apostolic succession. Traditionally the Roman Catholic Church considered Anglican and Lutheran orders of ministry "absolutely null and void." But after Vatican II, this polarization softened, to embrace the notion of *degrees* of apostolicity. In 1973 the International Theological Commission declared that Anglican and Lutheran churches possessed "some degree" of apostolicity. Recently Thomas Kocik has examined changing Roman Catholic attitudes in *Apostolic Succession in an Ecumenical Context* (London: Alba House, 1996), with reference to Rahner, Congar, and Balthasar, as well as earlier history. The Eastern Orthodox Church takes apostolic succession very seriously in both the institutional and the doctrinal sense. However, its claims and those of Rome seem incompatible.

Apotheosis

This term denotes the elevation of a person to the status of a deity, normally to be sharply distinguished from deification. Greeks and Romans regularly assimilated emperors or heroes as gods, often after their deaths, while Christians rigidly contrasted God from created persons and objects. Deification, on the other hand, is the equivalent in Eastern Orthodox Churches to what the West would call sanctification. Humans may become "like" God in deification, but apotheosis normally denotes *pagan* assimilation of humans into deity.

Appropriation

Appropriation, or making one's own, has three distinct uses in theology and the history of the church. (i) Luther and Kierkegaard apply the term "making my own" to faith or knowledge. Luther believed that the Christian believer can and should appropriate the work and righteousness of Christ as "his or her own" in trust and faith. Kierkegaard believed that truth became a matter of "making it my own" when knowledge was subjective or participated in subjectivity. We can receive truth, he urged, only by making it our own, not simply by assenting to objective propositions objectively. There remain echoes of this approach in Gadamer.

(ii) A different use of the term refers to understanding God as Trinity in patristic thought. Many of the Fathers argued that in external relations with the world, all persons of the Trinity share in the same work as one, but that in internal terms the Father as "begetting" could be distinguished from the Son as begotten, and from the Holy Spirit as proceeding from the Father. *In this context,* "appropriation" would denote ascribing given divine actions to specific persons of the Trinity.

(iii) The third sense of the term belongs to the medieval history of the church. A monastery and perhaps its dean, chapter, and college could be annexed or *appropriated,* and a vicar appointed in its place as, in effect, a substitute or "vice" cleric. The third meaning concerns history rather than theology.

A Priori

This Latin term denotes what is prior to, or independent of, observation of the world or human experience. One example is the analytical statement, which is true, in effect, by definition. The premises of the ontological argument are truly a priori.

Aquinas, Thomas

Thomas Aquinas (1225-1274) marks a turning point between the earlier and later Middle Ages. During the earlier era, thinkers were educated in monastic foundations; during the later years they were trained increasingly in universities. Thomas, born near Naples, began his education in a Benedictine monastery, and then moved to the newly founded Dominican Order, in which monks lived in the world. But in 1245 he entered the University of Paris to study under Albert the Great. Albert urged him to study the works of Aristotle, which had recently been translated into Latin and made available, after their study by the Arab philosophers Averroes, al-Ghazali, and Avicenna. In about 1248 he followed Albert to Cologne. Around 1252 he returned to Paris to teach, and wrote his commentary on the *Sentences* of Peter Lombard. From c. 1256 he taught and preached on Scripture and its interpretation. His two major works were *Summa contra Gentiles,* written for missionaries carrying the gospel to unbelievers, and his magisterial *Summa Theologiae,* which was still unfinished at his death. This became, in effect, the classic theological textbook, alongside the Bible and Augustine, for the Roman Catholic Church. Pope Pius V named him a doctor of the church in 1567. He is often called "the Angelic Doctor."

In 1256 Thomas became master in theology at Paris, and wrote several volumes that today might be called apologetics. His first in this period was *Against Those Who Assail the Worship of God,* followed by *Disputed Questions on Truth.* In accordance with the method of Scholasticism, also reflected in the *Summa Theologiae,* these answered questions on aspects of faith in dialectical form. He then wrote a commentary on the doctrine of the Trinity in Boethius. By 1259 he had begun work on *Summa contra Gentiles.* In 1260 he returned to Naples, and in 1261 became responsible for the pastoral and theological formation of friars in his order. He completed *Summa contra Gentiles* and produced further material for Pope Urban IV. In 1265 the pope's successor, Clement IV, summoned Thomas to Rome as papal theologian, and he began to write *Summa Theologiae* as a textbook for his students, especially for those beginning the study of theology. Most of this was written either at Santa Sabina in Rome or during a further term in Paris, where he became Dominican regent master and served until 1272. Here he also wrote other works attacking the extreme Aristotelians and Averroists. These held, for example, that the world was without a beginning. He also disputed with some Franciscans, including Bonaventura. In 1272 he returned to the Naples area, but for whatever reason became disillusioned with work on the *Summa,* which he said "seems like straw to me." Some attribute this change of outlook to some kind of mystical or "supernatural" experience. Within two years he had died of poor health. In 1879 Pope Leo XIII declared that Thomas's theology was a definitive exposition of Roman Catholic doctrine, and that Catholic universities and seminaries should teach it.

In popular thought Aquinas is often thought of as a philosopher or philosophical theologian who has rethought the philosophical tradition of Aristotle. He also uses commentators on Aristotle. But although he quotes Aristotle frequently and regularly, he also supports most of his claims or statements on the basis of biblical passages and references. Indeed, it is said that currently there is a reaction against emphasizing his indebtedness to Aristotle in favor of recovering his status as a theologian.

The *Summa Theologiae* is arranged in three parts with a subdivision making effectively four. Part 1 contains 119 "questions," first about the nature of Christian theology; 4 about the existence of God, his names, knowledge of God, and God's will and power; then questions about the Trinity, creation, angels, cosmogony, man, and divine providence. Each "question" is divided into articles, which often voice objections and replies in Scholastic style. For example, question 2, on the existence of God, contains the Five Ways, which include the cosmological argument. Conventionally the first part is called 1a, and covers fifteen volumes, or a quarter, of the Blackfriars edition, which totals sixty volumes in Latin and English. The prologue implies that the *Summa* is only the "milk" of the word (1 Cor. 3:1-2). *Summa* denotes a systematic summary, which replaced *sententiae* (sentences), or judgments.

Question 1 (with ten articles) concerns the nature of theology. From the first, Aquinas cites Scripture, quoting Isa. 64:4. He states: "We stood in need of being instructed by divine revelation, even in religious matters the human reason is able to investigate.... Rational truth about God would have appeared only to few... mixed with many mistakes" (1a, qu. 1, art. 1, reply). Revelation and reason are not in conflict, but *revelation is needed.* Similarly, we need faith, but "Christian theology should be pronounced to be a science" (art. 2, reply). Science, in the thirteenth century, denoted an ordered and coherent body of knowledge, even if its first principles were derived from a "higher" knowledge. "Science" *(scientia)* embraces the whole of life, including the natural world. Yet God's truth is one. He writes, "Holy teaching should be declared a single science" *(unam scientiam;* art. 3, reply). It includes theory and practice (art. 4, reply), and is "wisdom highest above all human wisdoms" (art. 6, reply). God must remain the subject of this science (art. 7). As Scripture witnesses, the truth of theology may be stated metaphorically or poetically, or as pointers from literal statements (art. 9, reply). God is the author of Scripture, but, as Gregory declared, "the literal sense is what the author intends *(auctor intendit),*" but a spiritual sense may also be implied (art. 10, reply).

Question 2 discusses "whether there is a God." According to É. Gilson's interpretation of article 1, God is a necessary being "who cannot not be." He is a subsistent Being. What this means and entails Aquinas expounds in question 2, articles 2-3, and questions 3-11. Article 3 contains the famous "five ways in which one can prove that there is a God" (Eng. and Lat. vol. 2, 13). The first is an argument from change (Lat. *motus*) and potentiality *(potentia)*. He writes, "A thing in process of change cannot itself cause that same change" (qu. 2, art. 3, reply). In the end "one is bound to arrive at some first cause of the change.... This is what everyone understands by God." The second way "is based on the nature of causation"; this again arrives at a first cause. The third way depends on the contrast between a necessary and a contingent Being (*see* **Cosmological Argument**). The fourth is on degrees of Being, and the fifth, in effect, formulates the teleological argument, or "the guidedness of nature." Thomas appeals to Augustine. The remaining questions expound God's simpleness *(de Dei simplicitate),* in which "God is his own essence" (qu. 3, art. 4); "nothing is prior to God.... God does not belong to a genus" (art. 5). He urges, "Accidents cannot exist in God" (art. 6). Question 4 considers "God's perfection." He agrees with Dionysius that "God does not exist in any qualified way, but possesses primordially in himself all being without qualification" (qu. 4, art. 2). He quotes Matt. 5:48, Ps. 85(86):8, Gen. 1:26, and 1 John 3:2.

Aquinas then turns to goodness in general, and to the goodness of God (qu. 6). He declares, "God alone is good by nature" (art. 3, reply). In question 7 he considers "God's limitlessness" *(infinites).* He writes, "God's existence subsists without being acquired by anything, and as such is limitless" (art. 1, reply). This distinguishes him from everything else. He appeals here to Aristotle (art. 2). In question 8 he expounds God's omnipresence, citing Jer. 23:24, "I fill heaven and earth" (art. 2). God exists in everything both as "operative cause" and "within the acting subject" (art. 3, reply). In question 9 Aquinas expounds one of the most controversial claims about God today. He argues that God is "unchangeable" *(immutabilis)*. He cites Mal. 3:6, "I change not," but his main argument concerns actuality and potentiality, from which "it clearly follows that God cannot change in any way" (qu. 9, art. 1, reply). He adds: "Only God is altogether unchangeable; creatures can all change" (*Solus Deus est omnino immutabilis;* art. 2, reply). It is also related to accidents, which change, and to underlying substance, which does not. This at once ties his doctrine to philosophy: "change" belongs to accidents, which might or might not be. As B. Davies expresses it, "God can undergo no accidental or substantial change. He cannot be modified and he cannot perish" (*The Thought of Thomas Aquinas* [Oxford: Clarendon, 1992], 102). But many theologians today would claim that self-willed change is possible for God, as in biblical literature "he repents" of an earlier action. It is correct, however, that change cannot be imposed on him from without, by some external agency or causes.

We are on less controversial ground when in question 10 Aquinas addresses the eternity of God. He follows Boethius, after considering objections to his notion of eternity. We do need to begin with our experience of duration in time to appreciate what "unending" can mean, but "eternity itself exists as an *instantaneous whole* lacking successiveness" (art. 1, reply). Eternity, he concludes, derives from the unchangeableness of God (art. 2, reply). He appeals to Augustine's notion of God as the source of eternity, which can be shared: "Eternity in the true and proper sense belongs to God alone" (art. 3, reply). Question 11 deals with the "oneness" of God, which "adds nothing real . . . but denies division of it" (art. 11). It is simply the opposite of "many" (art. 2).

After this fundamental beginning, Aquinas moves on to knowing God in questions 12-18, to the will and power of God in 19-26, and to the Holy Trinity in 27-43 (Eng. vols. 3-7). Thomas declares, "It is impossible that any created mind should see the essence of God by its own natural powers" (qu. 12, art. 4, reply). Almost anticipating Barth, he quotes Ps. 35(36):9, "In Thy light we shall see light"; Rev. 21:23, "The brightness of God will illuminate her"; and 1 Cor. 2:8, 10, "God has revealed to us through his Spirit . . . a wisdom which none of this world's rulers know" (art. 13). Question 13 looks again at theological language, including the theology of negation. Sometimes a word is used in a quite different sense from its usual meaning (art. 2, reply). Words are not univocally of God and creatures (art. 5): "Some words are used neither univocally nor purely equivocally of God and creatures but analogically" (art. 5, reply; *see* **Analogy**). He also discusses metaphor, of which he approves (art. 6, reply). Question 16 discusses truth. He notes that Augustine defines truth as "showing forth what is" (art. 1), and Aristotle distinguishes truth from opinion. Thomas asserts, "Truth is defined as conformity between intellect and thing" (*conformitatem intellectus et rei veritas definitur;* art. 2, reply). He cites John 14:6, "I am the way, and the truth, and the life."

Thomas discusses the Holy Trinity in questions 27-43. Like W. Pannenberg today, he argues: "The name 'Father' signifying his [God's] fatherhood, is the name proper to the person of the Father" (qu. 33, art. 2, reply). Similarly he appeals to Augustine for the statement "The Son alone is taken to be the Word" (qu. 34, art. 2). In question 36, article 1, he defends the double procession of the Holy Spirit from the Father and the Son. If this is not true, the Spirit could not be distinct from the Son (art. 2, reply). He appeals here to Hilary of Poitiers (*see* **Holy Spirit: The Spirit in Historical Theology**). He concludes, "The Father loves the Son by the Holy Spirit" (qu. 37, art. 2, reply). Finally, the gift conveys what is "givable," that is, what is at the disposal of a donor and recipient (qu. 38, art. 1, reply). In question 42 Thomas establishes the coequality of the three persons of the Godhead (art. 1). Questions 44-49 consider creation and evil. In question 45, article 5, Thomas states: "Creation is the proper activity of God alone." In 47 he expounds the multiplicity and plurality of creation, and this "inequality" *(inequalitas)* of things is the first step toward envy and *evil* (art. 2). He comments, "Divine wisdom causes the distinction and inequality of things for the perfection of the universe" (qu. 47, art. 2, reply). *Evil is an absence of good.* Even Aristotle speaks of the difference between black and white (qu. 48, art. 2). Hence evil may arise from the lack of such a quality: "The absence of good taken deprivately is what we call evil, thus blindness... is the privation of sight" (art. 3). Evil then proceeds from a bad character: "The Lord calls an evil will a bad tree" (qu. 49, art. 1, reply).

Questions 75-83 concern humankind, including Thomas's view of the nature of the soul, its union with the body, and its intellectual powers. Questions 84-110 discuss human intelligence, the image of God, divine government, and world order. This concludes part 1, and the heart of the *Summa Theologiae*. The second part (2.1) deals with happiness, moral virtues, sin and the effects of sin, and the gospel of grace. Part 2.2 discusses faith, hope, and love, and the Platonic and Aristotelian virtues of prudence, justice, courage, and temperance. Part 3 then considers Christ, his incarnation, mediation, passion, and resurrection, and the sacraments. (*See* **Baptism; Christology; Lord's Supper; Sacraments**.)

Aquinas's questions in part 3 about the Eucharist and sacraments greatly influenced the history of the church, and formulated what is still the official Roman Catholic doctrine of transubstantiation and the Lord's Supper (part 3, qu. 60-83). He addresses transubstantiation in question 75, "The change of the bread and wine into the body and blood of Christ" (Blackfriars ed., 58:53-91). In articles 4 and 5 he sums up transubstantiation in terms of Aristotle's substance and accidents. "The complete substance of the bread is converted into the complete substance of Christ's body, and the complete substance of the wine into the complete substance of Christ's blood" (art. 4, reply). However, the *appearance* of the bread and wine remains the same: "The substance of the bread departs but leaves its accidents behind... under the appearance of things in common use. Namely bread and wine" (art. 5), but "the substantial form of the bread no longer remains" (art. 6).

Whereas the *Summa Theologiae* was for the instruction of Christian friars in the Dominican Order, *Summa contra Gentiles* addresses the problem of evil and other objections to Christian faith. Thomas anticipates his later work, expounding similar themes. He argues that evil is "the privation" of what is good, and is "the non-existence of something in a substance" (chap. 7). Although evil may injure, it is ultimately a good (chap. 11). All things are directed to one end, namely, God (chap. 17). To know God is the end of every mind (chap. 25). Human happiness does not consist in wealth (chap. 30), but ultimately in contemplating God (chap. 37). Aquinas's sheer volume of writings is quite astonishing, especially when we recall that he died about age forty-nine. In the sixteenth century there was a revival of his theology under Cajetan, and in the modern era Thomism embraces a variety of interpretations of his work. His significance for Roman Catholic theology cannot be overestimated.

Reading: Thomas Aquinas, *Summa Theologiae*, 60 vols. (New York: McGraw-Hill, 1963); B. Davies, *The Thought of Thomas Aquinas* (Oxford: OUP, 1992); N. M. Healy, *Thomas Aquinas* (Burlington, Vt.: Ashgate, 2003); N. Kretzmann and E. Stump, eds., *The Cambridge Companion to Aquinas* (Cambridge: CUP, 1993); A. C. Pegis, ed., *The Basic Writings of Thomas Aquinas*, 2 vols. (New York: Random House, 1945).

Aristotle

Aristotle (384-322 B.C.) is one of the two most important and influential philosophers of the ancient world. The other is Plato (428-348 B.C.), who developed and went beyond what he had learned from Socrates. Whereas Plato held to a dualism of appearance and reality, or of copies and forms or ideas, Aristotle sought to provide a *unified* view of truth and reality, based on a hierarchy that began with *everyday things in the world*. His remarkable achievement was to produce a view of reality, or an ontology, that dealt with virtually every branch of philosophy. (i) He formulated principles of logic, which he called analytics, including deductive logic and the syllogism, especially in his *Prior Analytics, On Interpretation*, and *Categories*. (ii) He produced a view of ontology or reality that included a close study of causality, distinguishing between four kinds of cause. This remains relevant to the cosmological argument for the existence of God. (iii) His ontology included a study of attributes and "elements," such as earth, water, air, and fire, and of possibility and actuality, which again relates to the cosmological argument. (iv) He explored metaphysics, including teleology, proposing a graduated scale of forms, and this relates to the teleological argument for the existence of God. In his *Physics* 7-8 and *Metaphysics* 2 he saw God as changeless and immaterial (*The Heavens* 279A.18, and *Metaphysics* 1072B). (v) He wrote on ethics and politics, in which writings he discussed both his doctrine of the mean and his concept of virtue.

Aristotle was born at Stagira, the son of a court physician to the king of Macedon. After his father's death his guardian sent him to study in Plato's academy at Athens c. 367 B.C., where he remained for some twenty years, until Plato's death. At first he moved to Assos and Mytilene, but in 342 Philip of Macedon invited him to become tutor for the thirteen-year-old Alexander, later to become Alexander the Great, for some three years. He returned to Stagira for five years, and in 335 returned to Athens, where he founded his own school in the Lyceum. He died at age sixty-two. His works are probably based on his lectures at the Lyceum, and are of great subtlety, scope, complexity, and innovation. The timing of his gradual departure from the ideas of Plato is still a matter of debate.

(i) Aristotle's influence on *logic* is fundamental. (a) His greatest contribution is the first formulation of the syllogism in formal, deductive, logic. In his *Prior Analytics* 25B.32-37 he formulates the threefold scheme of major premise, minor premise, and conclusion in which the "middle term" (shared by two or more premises or conclusions) could not in any sense change in meaning. If we draw an example from the cosmological argument, the major premise might be: "Every event (or state of affairs) has a cause." The minor premise would then be: "The world is an event (or is a state of affairs)." The conclusion would be: "Therefore the world has a cause." But this syllogism would not match up to Aristotle's criteria of validity. In this argument "cause" in the minor premise denotes "caused cause," while "cause" in the conclusion (if it refers to God) denotes "*uncaused* cause." (b) In his attempt to verify meanings Aristotle also explores the problem of *defining* a word. He proposes to define words by examining their genus, their class or category, and their distinctive function (definition through *genus et differentiam*). (c) He also examines the nature of propositions. His scheme or logical symbolism of propositions still remains today: S (subject) relates to P (a predicate). (d) This, in turn, implies some kind of correspondence theory of truth. The conditions for truth are expounded in his *On Interpretation*.

(ii) Aristotle's careful distinctions between *types of cause* feature as part of his *ontology*, or study of being or reality. A cause *(aitia)*, he argues, may be material, efficient, formal, or final. If we consider the standard example of a statue, (a) the *material cause* would normally be marble or bronze; the material is the matter *(hulē)* out of which the statue is made. (b) The *efficient cause* would be the blows of the hammer and chisel *(archē tēs kineseōs)*. This is the movement that shapes the statue. (c) The *formal cause* is the pattern and shape *(ousia)* which the sculptor is aiming to achieve. (d) The *final cause* (*telos*, "end") is the purpose for which the statue is eventually to be produced. Is it to remember a particular person, or to honor the person, or to glorify him or her?

(iii) Aristotle's ontology also includes his view of *nature*. He examines and classifies attributes in terms of quality, quantity, and location in time and space, and as acting on other things or being acted upon by other things. Especially he is concerned with the question of order or of finding unity in diversity, a question that later concerned Augustine, al-Farabi, and Aquinas. Order and unity were implied by nature, not merely imposed by the mind, as Kant later argued. Hence, "elements" of the universe such as earth, water, air, and fire, and hot or cold, wet or dry, are part of a more extensive hierarchy and not merely bare, raw "facts."

(iv) This can be seen in Aristotle's *Metaphysics*, namely, what *underlies ontological investigations*. His inquiries about the everyday world as it is cannot stop there. He proposes a teleology of a graduated scale of forms. Humankind is not a mere "thing," like stone and trees. Aristotle even postulates a changeless and immaterial First Cause or God (*Metaphysics* 1072B.4). He is "mind" *(nous)*, and perfect: the Prime Unmoved mover *(prōton kinoun akinēton)*.

(v) Aristotle elaborates his thoughts on *ethics and politics*. In his *Nichomachean Ethics,* the *Eudemian Ethics,* and *Politics,* he considers *practical wisdom (phronēsis)* in contrast to theoretical wisdom *(sophia)*. Both together constitute an intellectual "virtue" *(aretē)*. *Eudaimonia* transcends happiness, honor, and wealth; it is a fulfillment of a goal *(telos)* of humankind. It requires reason and patience. Virtue is usually situated between two extremes; for example, *courage* is situated between *timidity* or *cowardice* and *rashness*. *Virtue* constitutes the *habitual* making of good choices. The rational control of desires is essential. In his later work, *Politics,* he addresses ethics in social groups. Good political ends match the good of human life, in which humankind is viewed as "a political animal." Books 2-6 of *Politics* consider political constitutions, and 7-8 consider possible forms of the *polis*, or city.

After Aristotle's death, many formulated versions of Aristotelianism, from the Middle Ages until today. Al-Kindi (c. 813–c. 871), al-Farabi (875-950), Ibn Sina (Avicenna, 980-1037), and Ibn-Rushd (Averroēs, 1126-1198) formulated an Islamic or initially Arabian version of Aristotelianism in diverse ways. In the thirteenth century Aristotle was translated into Latin, often through Islamic thinkers in Spain or Sicily. Some regarded Aristotle as heavily indebted to Plato. Aquinas, however, was an accurate interpreter of Aristotle's texts, and in turn used him greatly in the formulation of the *Summa Theologiae,* especially in his notion of substance and accidents in transubstantiation.

Reading: J. L. Ackrill, *Aristotle the Philosopher* (Oxford: OUP, 1981); D. J. Allan, *The Philosophy of Aristotle* (Oxford: OUP, 1981); J. Barnes, *The Cambridge Companion to Aristotle* (Cambridge: CUP, 1995); J. Barnes, ed., *The Complete Works of Aristotle,* 2 vols. (Princeton: Princeton University Press, 1984); M. Jordan, *The Alleged Aristotelianism of Thomas Aquinas* (Rome: Pontifical Institute of Mediaeval Studies, 1992); K. Knight, *Aristotelian Philosophy* (Oxford: Polity Press, 2007).

Arius, Arianism

Arius (c. 250-336), a priest of Alexandria, came into conflict with his bishop in c. 318-320 in his effort to extol and honor God the Father, even at the expense of devaluing the status of Jesus, the Son. His bishop, Alexander, argued that God the Son was eternally generated by God the Father. Arius, by contrast, defended subordinationism. God is transcendent and unique, he argued, and an unoriginate source *(agennētos archē)* of all reality, alone without beginning *(anarchon)*, and alone sovereign and judge of all. On the other hand, God the Son is a creature *(ktisma)*, even if the one perfect creature. He declared, "The Son has a beginning, whereas God is without beginning." Admittedly Christ was "born outside time" *(achronōs gennētheis)*, but prior to his generation he did not exist. Arius denied the orthodox doctrine that God the Father and the Son are coeternal. The Son, he argued, is liable to change. In principle Christ could have sinned. In words that Athanasius attributes to him, "He is not God truly, but by participation in grace.... He, too, is called God in name only (Athanasius, *Orations against the Arians* 1.5). Arius cited various biblical texts. Christ is Wisdom, but Prov. 8:22 (LXX) states, concerning Wisdom, "The Lord created me." In Acts 2:36, "God made him both Lord and Christ." In Rom. 8:29 and Col. 1:15 Christ is "the firstborn." In John 14:28, "the Father is greater than I." J. N. D. Kelly comments, "The net result of his teaching was to reduce the Son to a demigod" (*Early Christian Doctrines*, 5th ed. [London: Black, 1977], 230). Arius shared many of these views with Eusebius of Nicomedia and believed they were earlier inspired by Lucian of Antioch (d. 312), a pupil of Paul of Samosata. He traced some ideas to Origen, also of Alexandria.

Arius was condemned at the Council of Nicaea in 325. Rowan Williams comments that "Arianism" has often been regarded as "the archetypal Christian deviation" (*Arius*, 2nd ed. [Grand Rapids: Eerdmans, 2001], 1). Newman saw his work as derogating "the honour due to Christ"; Harnack thought it was influenced by "Aristotelian rationalism"; H. Gwatkin interpreted it as a kind of adoptionism; and G. L. Prestige saw Arianism as "crypto-pagan." But more recently T. Barnes (1976 and 1993), M. Simonetti (1971 and 1975), and G. C. Stead (1976-1997) have done much to redress a one-sided imbalance, and especially a simplistic Alexandria versus Antioch dichotomy. Even so, some, like R. Gregg and D. Groh, tend to maintain the older polarization, seeing Arius as "adoptionist." Williams points out that we have only a handful of texts to give us Arius's own thinking, rather than a version mediated by Athanasius and others. Primary sources include the letter of Arius to Eusebius and his confession submitted to the emperor Constantine in 327. In his letter to Eusebius, Arius does write that God must preexist the Son. The Son is firstborn and only-begotten. Only God preexists him. God was not eternally a Father; there was a time when God was all alone. But Williams shows that when we seek to go beyond this, the thought of Arius becomes exceedingly complex (*Arius*, 98-116). His aim "is to develop a biblically-based *and* rationally consistent catechesis" (111). He is certainly aware of issues of metaphor and genre, which some underrate.

At the Council of Nicaea Arius was exiled, but the tension within the church remained. The term *homoousios*, "of the same being" or "same substance," served to distinguish Athanasius and the orthodox from Arius. This became a catalyst for further controversy. The pro-Nicaean Eustathius of Antioch and Marcellus of Ancyra were also exiled. Eusebius of Caesarea and Eusebius of Nicomedia retained a broadly Arian tradition, and the emperor Constantius supported a subordinationist theology, urging that the Son is only "like" *(homoios)* the Father. Eunomius argued that the Father and Son were "unlike" in *ousia*. Nevertheless, the Cappadocian Fathers, Basil of Caesarea, Gregory of Nyssa, and Gregory of Nazianzus, together with Hilary and Ambrose in the West, developed Nicene theology with sufficient nuancing to facilitate the *homoousios* clause at the Council of Constantinople in 385.

Reading: R. P. C. Hanson, *The Search for the Christian Doctrine of God* (Edinburgh: T. & T. Clark, 1988); J. N. D. Kelly, *Early Christian Doctrines* (London: Black, 1977), 223-52; R. D. Williams, *Arius: Heresy and Tradition* (Grand Rapids: Eerdmans, 2001).

Arminius, James

In popular thought, James Arminius (1559-1609) is chiefly known for his opposition to Calvin and Reformed theology on the doctrine of election and predestination. "Predestination" arises, Arminius argued, only on the basis of *divine foreknowledge* concerning the free choice of human beings about how to respond to the gospel. This is largely true of Arminianism, which indeed distanced itself from the Synod of Dort. But this is not the first impression the actual text of the works of Arminius as a whole may make upon the reader, since he addresses a range of theological themes, of which election and predestination constitute one, mainly in his *Declaration of Sentiments*. It is understandable that while some regard Arminius as an opponent of Reformed theology, many insist that in a very broad sense he robustly upholds the tradition of the Reformation, even if he departs from mainstream Reformed theology on free will. Some argue that Melanchthon (1497-1560) largely anticipates him, although this is debated. He certainly emphasizes divine grace, and shows a robust and uncompromising hostility to Roman Catholicism. His views developed during his lifetime, but his most important text on predestination, as R. Müller argues, is his *Declaration of Sentiments* (1608). On the basis of his *Declaration,* he is certainly not a Reformed theologian.

Arminius was born near Rotterdam, the Netherlands, and on the death of his father left home to study at Marburg with the philosopher R. Snellius. In 1576 he returned to Holland to study theology at Leiden, and six years later at Geneva. At Leiden he focused on the Bible and Church Fathers, and at Geneva (1582-1587) he studied especially Reformed confessions and Reformed theology. Although he was influenced by T. Beza, it is likely that Calvin and H. Bullinger were even more influential. In 1588 he returned to Amsterdam to take up a pastoral post, and to immerse himself in the study of Romans. He argued that the struggle depicted in Romans 7 was "preconversion" (although today the vast majority of biblical scholars do not understand this chapter as autobiographical at all). Most Reformers would probably, like Luther, have interpreted it as the Christian's conflict with the powers of the old aeon. He then studied the issues of election and predestination in Romans 9–11, arguing that Romans 9 did *not* refer to *individual* predestination. In 1598 he encountered W. Perkins's treatise on predestination, and strongly reacted against it. Finally in 1602 he returned to Leiden as professor of theology. During these final seven years his views became more explicit, and were met with hostility and criticism from his Leiden colleagues, F. Gomar and L. Trelcatius. His *Declaration* constitutes a reply to them. Here he compares the "supralapsarian" doctrine of Calvin, namely, that God decreed the election of individual human beings *before* the fall of Adam, with the "infralapsarian" (or sublapsarian) doctrine that God predestined or decreed the election of human beings only *after* the fall of Adam.

Since the most influential picture of Arminius concerns his arguments in the *Declaration,* we shall consider these next, but bear in mind that the larger part of his writings reflects views that the Reformers as a whole would have held. For example, he wrote the treatises *The Divinity of Scripture, The Agreement of Doctrine, Prophecy, Miracles and the Witness of the Holy Spirit.* These alone occupy over 100 pages of the three volumes of his works. We cannot judge Arminius's theology *solely* from his *Declarations.* He discusses various Reformed confessions (*The Works of Arminius* [Bible Truth Forum, e-books]). Declaration 1 expresses his dissent from the Dutch Confessions and Heidelberg Catechism, and a desire for their revision (1603). In response to requests, he sets out his views, first, in *On Predestination and Election.* He writes, "The first opinion, which I reject, is espoused by those [supralapsarians] who assume the very highest ground of this Predestination" (sect. 1). This concerns God's "eternal and immutable decree" that "predestinated from among men ... certain individuals to everlasting life, and others to eternal destruction, without any regard whatever to righteousness or sin" (1.1, Eng. 106). Second, in section 2 Arminius writes, "For my own part [I prefer] to speak my sentiments with freedom.... This doctrine contains many things that are both false and impertinent" (1.2; 109). This is not, he says, the decrees by which God appointed Christ as Savior (1.3; 109). It is "not the foundation of certainty of salvation" (1.3; 110). He argues that this doctrine was not discussed in the councils. They would not even have endorsed the Belgic Confession and Heidelberg Catechism. These doctrines are "repugnant to the nature of God" (1.2.7; 112), and "inconsistent with the freedom of the will" (114). In that this entails destruction, "it is repugnant to the nature of Divine Grace" (prop. 13; 115). It also extinguishes zeal for prayer (117). There are twenty propositions in all.

The second part considers "A Second Kind of Predestination." In one form "by an eternal and immutable decree" God determined within himself to save a portion of humanity, but left the rest to suffer the consequences of their own sin (2.1; 123). Predestination may also rest upon "the *prescience* of God, by which he foreknew those whom he had predestinated" (2.2, italics mine). These believers he prepared for salvation, through Christ. Arminius next considers "A Third Kind of Predestination." Here God "considered the human race not only as created but as fallen and corrupt" (3.1; 124) (i.e., infralapsarianism). Out of that state God determined "to liberate certain individuals and freely to save them by his grace." In the fourth part Arminius repeats that election does not begin until *after* the fall of humankind.

Arminius finds that this third view escapes the self-contradiction of the first two. The third allows the concept of "Divine permission, by which God permits sin" (4.2; 125). He states, "Permission is the withdrawing of Divine grace" (4.2). In the fifth part Arminius gives his own view of predestination. He argues, (i) the first absolute decree of God appoints his Son for "the salvation of sinful men" (5.1; 126). Christ is Mediator, Redeemer, Savior, Priest, and King. (ii) God's second decree is "to receive into favour those who repent and believe," for Christ's sake and through him (5.2). (iii) God's third decree is to supply what is needed for repentance and faith; (iv) "God decreed to save and damn certain particular persons because he *foreknew* who would repent and believe 'through his Preventing Grace'" (5.4; 127; *see* **Prevenient Grace**). Predestination, therefore, remains "the foundation of Christianity, and of salvation and its certainty" (prop. 1, 127).

In part 2 Arminius moves to related topics. He considers the providence of God; the free will of human beings, which stands in need of grace; and the doctrine of grace itself. Grace is "a gratuitous affection by which God is kindly affected towards a miserable sinner" as well as "an infusion" of the gifts of the Holy Spirit (130). The fifth section is entitled "The Perseverance of the Saints." God, Arminius believed, will give sufficient powers by his Holy Spirit for believers successfully to battle against temptations, the flesh, the world, and sin. Jesus affords them "ready aid." But it requires "diligent enquiry of the Scriptures" to determine "whether it is not possible for some individuals through negligence to desert the commencement of their existence in Christ" (130). But Arminius nevertheless adds that he has *never* taught that "a true believer can either totally or finally fall away from the faith, and perish" (131). He is also entirely positive about "the assurance of salvation." Finally, he neither asserts nor denies the possibility of the "sinless perfection" of believers in this life. This shows his closeness to much in Reformed theology, as well as his differences from it.

As for more general doctrines, Arminius stands foursquare with the Reformers. He affirms Christ's divinity, as do the Catholics and the Orthodox. He holds to justification before God, in accordance with beliefs "held unanimously by the Reformed and Protestant Churches" (135). But he repeats his reservations about the Dutch Confession and the Heidelberg Catechism. Yet he begins his writings with a ringing declaration that many might have expected to hear from Calvin: "To Almighty God alone belong the inherent and absolute right, will, and power, of determining, concerning us" (*Oration* 1; 2); "God is the first and chief good, and goodness itself; he alone is good"; "Nothing can be added to him" (4). God and Christ are the substance of Christian theology (Col. 1:15, 19; Heb. 1:3). God is "the Author and End of Theology" (*Oration* 2; 18). He then expounds "the certainty of Sacred Theology" (*Oration* 3; 34). Certainty is different from optimism. Scripture asserts "its own Divinity" (3.1; 39), and speaks with harmony. Miracles provide confirmation of faith. The church is "the pillar of truth" (1 Tim. 3:15); but it is "the Papists" who appeal to "the authority of the Church" (48). With many Protestants, Arminius speaks more readily of "The Internal Witness of the Holy Spirit" (art. 9; 49). Like other Reformers, he expounds the priesthood of Christ, as Hebrews teaches it, and attacks the sacerdotal priesthood of the Roman Church (64-70).

The second volume of the works of Arminius tends to recapitulate the same ground. Arminius again expounds the nature of theology, the authority and certainty of Scripture, the perspicuity and interpretation of Scripture, the will and attributes of God, his providence and his covenant. Then he proceeds to consider the restoration of humankind, and the person and work of Christ. Like Calvin, he sees Christ especially as prophet, priest, and king. He turns to the church and sacraments, where he has sections entitled "The Popish Mass" and "The Five False Sacraments" (vol. 2, 80-83). Finally, he considers the Decalogue, Church Fathers, and the doctors of the church. Volume 3 contains a varied collection of theses and propositions.

After the death of Arminius, Simon Episcopius (1583-1644) took up the Arminian position as his successor at Leiden, together with J. Uitenbognert (1557-1644). They rewrote Arminius's *Declarations,* with perhaps a greater emphasis on human freedom, synergism, and human choice. Conflict raged in the Netherlands and a colloquium was held in Delft in 1613. Eventually the Synod of Dort met in 1618-1619, which constituted, in effect, an international statement of Reformed theology. There were representations from England, including the bishops of Salisbury and Chichester. The followers of Arminianism became known as Remonstrants, after the name of one of their documents, *The Remonstrance.* The Synod of Dort regarded them as heretics, but their main tenets emerged in many quarters in England and America. J. Wesley was a passionate Arminian.

Reading: James Arminius, *The Works of Arminius,* 3 vols. (Bible Truth Forum, e-book); C. Bangs, *Arminius* (Nashville: Abingdon, 1971); A. H. W. Harrison, *Arminianism* (London: Duckworth, 1937); R. A. Müller, *God, Creation, and Providence in the Thought of James Arminius* (Grand Rapids: Eerdmans, 1991); R. E. Olson, *Arminian Theology* (Downers Grove, Ill.: IVP, 2006).

Ascension of Christ

The most extended account of the ascension is in Acts 1:6-11, especially verse 9: "As they were watching, he was lifted up (Gk. *epērthē*), and a cloud *(nephelē)* took him out of their sight." Luke also gives us the other main NT reference: "While he was blessing them, he withdrew from them and was carried up into heaven" (Gk. *anephereto eis ton ouranon;* Luke 24:51). The reference in Mark 16:19 to how the Lord was "taken up (Gk. *anelēmphthē*) into heaven and sat down at the right hand of God" comes from the textually doubtful "Longer Ending" of Mark. If this represents an earlier tradition, it may reflect the Epistle to the Hebrews. Heb. 4:14 declares that Jesus "has passed through the heavens" *(dielēluthota tous ouranous)* as Son of God and high priest. As high priest he intercedes in heaven for us (Heb. 7:24-25), and in 8:1 is "seated at the right hand of the throne of the Majesty in the heavens." Heb. 10:12 repeats, "He sat down at the right hand of God," reflecting the prologue of Heb. 1:13. Paul prefers to speak of the resurrection, but he also expects "the Son from heaven" (1 Thess. 1:10), and asserts that Christ will "descend from heaven" (4:16), and is now "at the right hand of God," making intercession for us (Rom. 8:34). Christ is "from heaven" (1 Cor. 15:47); he is "the man of heaven" (15:49). Paul certainly speaks of Christ's *exaltation.* In the hymn of Phil. 2:5-11 (which may be pre-Pauline in origin, but is Pauline in use), Paul asserts: "God also highly exalted him (Gk. *huperupsōsen*)" (v. 9).

The ascension in the sense of *exaltation to heaven* cannot be doubted. As the Nicene Creed declares: Jesus Christ "ascended into heaven, and is seated at the right hand of the Father" *(ascendit in coelum, sedet ad dexteram Patris)*. However, the precise *mode* of the ascension has been questioned, especially as the actual event is recorded only by Luke, in contrast to the multiply-attested exaltation and heavenly session. Already in the early third century Origen asked how a raised, spiritual Christ could be said "to ascend" in *spatial* categories. Clearly much of the accompanying imagery is metaphorical, for example, the right hand of God denotes exertive authority and honor; and being "seated" clearly has nothing to do with posture, but announces the *completion* of Christ's ministry on earth (so important in Hebrews), and his status of cohonor with God the Father. Even the "cloud" is not a meteorological feature in the atmosphere, but an indication of God's presence, as in the transfiguration. In Acts and Hebrews "sitting" at the right hand of God is drawn from Ps. 110:1.

There seems to be no direct evidence to indicate that Luke wants to allude to the ascensions of Enoch (Gen. 5:24), of Moses (Deut. 34:6), or of Elijah (2 Kings 2:11), although OT allusions to "ascensions" cannot be excluded. Apart from issues about an alleged localized heaven, the main biblical problem concerns the location of Bethany in Luke 24:50, whereas the same author, Luke, seems to imply an ascension from Jerusalem in Acts 1:4 ("ordered them not to leave Jerusalem"), leading to verse 9 ("he was lifted up"). Acts 1:12 refers to the Mount of Olives ("they returned to Jerusalem from the mount called Olivet"). But the text seems to exclude an overt contradiction. The disciples waited in Jerusalem, as they were commanded. Luke 24:50 begins: "Then he [*Jesus*] led them out (Gk. *exagō*) as far as Bethany, and . . . blessed them." Acts 1:12 simply records that after the ascension "they returned to Jerusalem from the mount called Olivet" (i.e., the Mount of Olives). As Howard Marshall points out, Bethany lay on the eastern slope of the Mount of Olives (*The Gospel of Luke* [Grand Rapids: Eerdmans, 1978], 908). Olivet often seems to be a place of private prayer, and a natural place for prayer.

Many NT scholars expect Luke to "objectify" and to make visible the parting of Jesus Christ to dwell with God out of human sight. But if so, what was he "objectifying"? Without professional NT scholarship, but with characteristic common sense, C. S. Lewis observes: "Perhaps mere instantaneous vanishing would make us feel more comfortable. . . . But if spectators saw a short vertical movement and then a vague luminosity ('cloud' . . . in the account of the Transfiguration) and then nothing — have we any reason to object?" (*Miracles* [London: Collins/Fontana, 1947; Geoffrey Bles, 1960], 166). Writers might have ascribed the descent of the Spirit at the baptism of Jesus to Luke's "objectifying" a "spiritual" event, had not Matthew (Matt. 3:16) and Mark (Mark 1:10) recounted this visible event also. The only question must be: Is this Luke's editorially *constructed metaphor* or God's *acted metaphor*? As Pannenberg argues, "Metaphor is . . . unavoidable if we are dealing with a transformation into a reality which is entirely unknown to us" (*The Apostles' Creed* [London: SCM, 1972], 98). The whole "point" of the event is not a movement of location, but the completion of forty days after the resurrection, and *transformation into a new mode of being with God*. This is why many scholars merge resurrection and ascension together. But Luke, probably Hebrews, and certainly the creeds see the two as distinct events. In the NT, including John, "going to the Father" becomes a precondition of sending the Holy Spirit. Indeed, in one of Paul's rare references to the ascension he (or his disciple) exclaims, "When he [Christ] ascended on high ... he gave gifts to his people." The "gifts" turn out to be "gifts of the Spirit" (Eph. 4:8-11). Although some allude to "gone into heaven" in 1 Pet. 3:22, the primary reference there seems to be to the resurrection, or perhaps to resurrection-ascension as the single event of exaltation.

The patristic church expressed its belief in the ascension from at least the second century. Irenaeus distinguishes between Christ's "resurrection from the dead" and "the ascension into heaven in the flesh of the beloved Christ Jesus" (*Against Heresies* 1.10.1; *ANF* 1:330). This may be anti-Docetic polemic against the Gnostics. In the fourth century the Feast of the Ascension entered the liturgical calendar. Augustine regarded it as the festival that "confirms the grace of all the Festivals together." Luther maintained belief in the ascension, but rightly disputed any spatial concept, especially any spatial interpretation of sitting at the right hand of God. Calvin asserts that, by his ascension, Christ fulfilled what he promised (*Institutes* 2.16.14). He observes, "Scripture ... carefully narrate[s] the ascension of Christ, by which he withdrew his bodily presence" (4.17.36; Beveridge, 2:594). The Westminster Confession of Faith declares: "He ascended into heaven, and there sits at the right hand of His Father, making intercession, and shall return" (chap. 8, art. 4). Eastern Orthodoxy sees the ascension as a culminating indicator of the two natures of Christology. Bultmann argues that it is mythological, but for H. Küng it means "going into reality" (*Does God Exist?* [London: Collins/Fount, 1979/1980], 678).

Reading: J. G. Davies, *He Ascended into Heaven* (London: Lutterworth, 1958); D. Farrow, *Ascension Theology* (Edinburgh: T. & T. Clark, 2011).

Asceticism

The word is derived from the Greek noun *askēsis*, which simply means "practice," especially of athletes in training. In 1 Cor. 9:25 Paul writes, "Athletes exercise self-control *(enkrateuetai)* in all things." A verse later he says he does not "box as though beating the air; but I punish *(hupōpiazō)* my body and enslave it *(doulagōgō)*, so that ... I myself should not be disqualified" (9:26-27). Paul does not use the word *askēsis*, nor is it used in the NT (although the verb occurs in Acts 24:16 in a different sense). But he does stress self-discipline and training. In 1 Tim. 4:7-8, he (or the writer) declares, "Train yourself (Gk. *gumnaze seauton*) in godliness *(pros eusebeian)*, for, while physical training *(sōmatikē gumnasia)* is of some value, godliness is valuable in every way." V. C. Pfitzer has a section on

Timothy's "*gumnasia* in godliness" in *Paul and the Agōn Motif* ([Leiden: Brill, 1967], 171-77). He writes: "1 Cor. 9:25 pictures Paul himself as practising self-control in all things.... But the scope of his *'enkrateia'* is ... not the narrow negative dualism between the soul ... and the body." In Col. 1:29 Paul does use the word "struggle" *(agōnizomenos)*, but warns the Colossian Christians against self-abasement (*tapeinophrosunē,* 2:18) and against such regulations as "Do not taste. Do not touch," which promote "self-imposed piety, humility, and severe treatment of the body" (2:21-23).

This double attitude places a question mark as well as an affirmation on what the Church Fathers and monastic orders have often prized so highly, but about which Luther and the Reformers had reservations, namely, a world-denying self-discipline and renunciation of things that may be good in themselves. On one side, the NT and the church in general affirm the need for self-discipline and self-control, which is sometimes furthered by asceticism, that is, practices of renunciation of otherwise good things, for the sake of training in self-discipline and self-control. But Paul and the NT do not regard it as a "higher" spiritual life as such, nor as rectifying sin or the deeds that are effects of the fall of humankind. Many of the standard practices of asceticism, celibacy or singleness, chastity, self-mortification, poverty, vigils, voluntary manual labor, and abstinence from wine and certain foods, may be valuable as means to self-control. "Mortification" may be seen not only as the deadening of lusts, but also as the outworking of Paul's words, "Put to death the deeds of the body" (Rom. 8:13). Theologically it may be an expression of "having died with Christ." R. Tannehill declares, "Paul ... is speaking of the destruction of the dominion of sin, of which all believers were a part" (*Dying and Rising with Christ* [Berlin: Töpelmann, 1967], 30; cf. 84-129). Rom. 8:17 speaks of suffering with Christ (112-14). Jesus suggests this in the saying: "If any want to become my followers, let them deny themselves and take up their cross and follow me" (Mark 8:34). Luther, however, was cautious in believing that such actions could genuinely put the old nature to death, even though he also insisted on struggle *(agōn)* and discipline. Yet if asceticism is simply understood as self-denial, it clearly has a role in Christian discipleship.

In the early church some practiced the renunciation of marriage, property, and food and drink, not simply as self-denial but as a substitute for martyrdom. Clement of Alexandria and Origen hinted at the notion of purification of the soul by ascetic practices, as many of the Stoics believed. It becomes an elitist sign of spiritual advancement. The Desert Fathers of the late third century and much of the monastic tradition favor asceticism as a special mark of discipleship. This becomes evident in the *Conferences* and *Institutes* of John Cassian. John speaks of "untiring perseverance, humility and subjection ... humility and patience ... not being contaminated by a single coin from his former possessions ... the discipline of the monastery ... the poverty and difficult life of the monastery" (*Institutes* 4.2 and 3). In the medieval period this practice flourished, and the world-denying attitude came to be regarded as an aspect of penance. During the Reformation period, a division arose between Reformers who feared that it compromised justification and grace, and those who practiced it as a discipline of life, as John of the Cross did. In modern times the Trappist monks of the Cistercian Order (c. 1890) represent an extreme example of the practice.

Aseity

Aseity denotes an order of being that is "from itself" (Lat. *a se esse*). In philosophical terms its being is necessary (but not only logically necessary), and not contingent. In practice it denotes the uniqueness of God, in contrast to all that God has created. Thus in the cosmological argument God is not simply "cause" but *first* cause. The term can apply to the fourth-century debates about the Holy Spirit: there are two orders of being, created and uncreated. The persons of the Trinity belong to the *uncreated* order. By contrast, everything in the universe depends on God, and does not possess aseity.

Assumption

Of the Virgin Mary. In 1950 Pope Pius XII promulgated a papal bull in which he proclaimed that Mary was taken up (assumed) bodily into heaven at the end of her life on earth. No scriptural support for this belief exists, and indeed there is no evidence for the rise of the tradition until the sixth and seventh centuries. The notion was defended by Albert the Great, Aquinas, and Bonaventura. Many Roman Catholics, though formally committed to the doctrine, regard it as devotionally acceptable, but do not hold this belief primarily as doctrine. Appeals to such biblical passages as "a woman clothed with the sun" (Rev. 12:1) are irrelevant as far as exegesis and hermeneutics are concerned.

Assurance

In the biblical writings the most relevant terms include Hebrew *bāṭach* and Greek *plērophoria* and *pistis*. The Hebrew verb *bāṭach* denotes "trust, trust in, rely upon," or "be confident," while the noun *beṭach* denotes "security" (BDB 105). Isa. 12:2 declares,

> God is my salvation;
> I will trust *(bātach)*, and will not be afraid.

In 2 Kings 18:5 the king "trusted in the LORD the God of Israel." Ps. 31:14-15 exclaims,

> I trust in you, O LORD; ...
> My times are in your hand.

The Greek noun *plērophoria* denotes "a state of complete certainty, full assurance" (BDAG 827), while a second meaning of the verb *plērophoreō* is "to convince fully." In 1 Thess. 1:5, Paul's converts, in the power of the Holy Spirit, believed the gospel "with full conviction." Paul says, "Let all be fully convinced in their own minds" (Rom. 14:5). Trust and confidence are usually born in response to a divine promise, and rest on the faithfulness of God to perform them. The biblical writings regard such trust as an essential part of the life of faith. Rom. 4:20 observes, concerning Abraham, "No distrust made him waver concerning the promise of God, but he grew strong in his faith." In 2 Cor. 5:7-8 Paul asserts: "We walk by faith, not by sight. Yes, we do have confidence."

In historical theology this became a central theme of the Reformers, Reformed theology, and most Protestants. They believe that their salvation is secure. In medieval Catholicism the doctrine often seemed to be presumptuous. But for Luther the doctrine was vital. He did not see this, however, as a static deposit, but as that which the believers renewed moment by moment. It was closely connected with justification by grace through faith and its appropriation. In his *Preface to the Epistle to the Romans* (1522) Luther writes, "Faith is a living, daring confidence in God's grace, so sure and certain that a man would stake his life on it a thousand times. This confidence . . . makes men glad and bold and happy in dealing with God. . . . This is the work of the Holy Spirit in faith. Hence a man is ready and glad, without compulsion, to do good to everyone, to serve everyone, to suffer everything, in love and praise of God." There is nothing here that suggests presumption, or lack of ethical action and response. Luther reiterates this in *The Bondage of the Will* (1525). He writes, "God has taken my salvation out of the control of my own will, and put it under the control of his. . . . 'No one,' he says, 'shall pluck them out of my hand' . . . (Jn. 10:28-29). . . . This is the glorying of all the saints in their God" ([London: James Clarke, 1957], 314).

Calvin gave "a full definition of faith. . . . It is a firm and sure knowledge of the divine favour toward us, founded on the truth of a free promise in Christ, and revealed to our minds, and sealed on our hearts, by the Holy Spirit" (*Institutes* 3.2.7; Beveridge, 1:475). He saw ethical action as motivated not by uncertainty and self-justification, but simply by gratitude. The problem, however, for succeeding generations was caused initially by heart-searching or introspection, which unwittingly shifted the focus from God's grace to measuring response. The doctrine of assurance reached its climax in the biblical writings and the classical Reformers. Luther accused the very concern for "spirituality" among the Radical Reformers as undermining the doctrine of pure grace and effective justification. Some contemporary theologians, including Barth, have sought to restore the confidence stressed by Luther and Calvin. Introspection may sometimes lead to an unintended legalism. John Bunyan in his *Pilgrim's Progress* provided a magnificent picture of the Celestial City of which "all the bells in the City began to ring again for joy" (169); yet he recounts that in his dream, "I saw that there was a way to hell, even from the gates of heaven" ([London: Religious Tract Society, n.d.], 170). R. C. Zachman presents a positive picture of Luther and Calvin in *The Assurance of Faith* (Louisville: John Knox, 2005).

Athanasian Creed

This document is to be dated later than Athanasius. It appears to have been composed in Latin, not in Greek, and its date is disputed. It is found officially in the Catholic daily office, in the Lutheran *Book of Concord,* in documents of the Reformed Synod of Dort, and in the Anglican *Book of Common Prayer,* to be said on thirteen holy days. But it is not always used, and embodies negative anathemas. It does not rank in authority with the Nicene Creed and the Apostles' Creed.

Athanasius

Bishop of Alexandria from 328, Athanasius (c. 296-373) is best known for his resistance to Arius and Arianism, and for his insistence that the Holy Spirit is not a creature or created being. He is associated with the Nicene term *homoousios.* In the language of the creeds he insisted that Christ is "very God," and is "eternally begotten." In his *Epistle to Serapion* Athanasius replied to the "Tropici" or "Pneumatomachi" that the Holy Spirit is not a created thing or person *(ktisma).* On the basis of 1 Cor. 2:12, Athanasius insisted that the Holy Spirit comes forth from God (*Ep. Serapion* 1.22). The Spirit raised Christ from the dead (Rom. 8:11; *Ep. Serapion* 1.23). He attacked the exegesis of those who called the Spirit a creature. Christ is the image of God (*On the Incarnation* 12), and died for all (20). Appeal is often made to his statement that Christ or the Word "was made human that we might be made divine" (*On the Incarnation* 54), especially for the Eastern Orthodox notion of deification. Athanasius was frequently involved in polemic and controversy; he suffered exile five times between 335 and 366. He did not originate the Athanasian Creed, which is to be dated later. For more detail and other sources see P. J. Leithart, *Athanasius* (Grand Rapids: Baker Academic, 2011), and T. G. Weinandy, *Athanasius* (Aldershot: Ashgate, 2007).

Atheism

Atheism boldly affirms the nonexistence of God. It must be distinguished from agnosticism, which asserts that human reason cannot justify either belief that God exists or belief that God does not exist. Atheism may also be either theoretical, making the nonexistence of God an ontological affirmation, or practical, asserting that if God were to exist, it would make no difference to the world or to human life. The "fool" in the Psalms probably asserts practical atheism in the statement, "The fool says in his heart, 'There is no God'" (Ps. 14:1 RSV). A similar distinction may be made between "avowed" atheists, who are making a universal statement, and implicit atheists, as when Epicurus challenged the notion that "God" might exist anywhere, except strictly in "spaces" between things in the world, perhaps in the form of atoms. There are also many examples of "marginal" atheism, as when Socrates denied the conventional deities of the Greek pantheon as "superstition." Within these margins, there can be degrees, or types, of atheism. In one sense, for example, Kant affirmed the existence of God; but in a different sense, "God" for Kant was merely the presupposition of a moral universe or moral imperative, not the personal, living God of the biblical writings. On the theist side of the border, clearly Paul Tillich did believe in God, and was a Christian theologian, but also made statements about God as "Being-itself," and denied his "existence" in the technical sense, thereby inviting some writers to describe him as "atheist."

Avowed or explicit atheism occurs in popular belief from the mid–seventeenth century onward. T. Hobbes attributed the cause of religious belief to "ignorance of second causes." Hence, he argued, people believe in ghosts and other superearthly phenomena. He states in *Leviathan* (1651) that such ignorance is "The Naturall seed of Religion." Yet Hobbes also asserts later in *Leviathan* that the manipulative abuse of religion by Catholics and Protestants in England hid the God who is "the first and eternal cause of all things." Hobbes cannot therefore be called a fully avowed atheist. Similarly Voltaire may be popularly regarded as an atheist. But in fact, he attacked claims to religious authority, including Leibniz's theodicy. He respected the teleological argument for the existence of God, and attacked the atheism of Paul von Holbach.

Two decisive steps toward atheism were taken in the eighteenth century. One was a *mechanistic* picture of the world as self-sufficient. In the nineteenth century Ludwig Feuerbach and Friedrich Nietzsche gave this their own formulation and development. The French Enlightenment gave a privileged place to human *autonomy*. Hence while Isaac Newton remained very broadly a theist, Paul von Holbach proposed a fully mechanistic account of the causes in the world as a self-contained and autonomous system (*Système de la nature* [1770]). This cleared the path for the French mathematician and astronomer Pierre de Laplace, who explored probability, to see a self-contained world, which allowed him, if the story is correct, to say to Napoleon about God, "Sir, I have no need of that hypothesis." The *mechanistic method* of science had been extended to become a *mechanistic worldview*.

The next decisive step, as W. Pannenberg urges, is the explicit atheism of Feuerbach and Nietzsche ("Types of Atheism," in *BQT* 2:184-200). Feuerbach wrote, "The divine being is nothing else than the human being, or rather the human being purified . . . made objective — . . . revered as another, a distinct being" (*The Essence of Christianity* [New York: Harper, 1957], 14). As we note under Feuerbach, God is a *projection of humankind*. Feuerbach's teacher, Hegel, would have said that God transcends human nature, but in that context sees the infinite as an extension of the finite. The most seminal atheist, however, is Nietzsche. He sees God as a mythical projection of human consciousness. Both in his work *The Gay Science* (or *Joyful Wisdom* [1882]) and in *Thus Spoke Zarathustra* (1883-1885), it is announced that "God is dead." "Religion" consists of "fictions." As Pannenberg notes, this is transplanted "into the ground of his metaphysics of the will to power" (*BQT* 2:192). If "God is dead," as Nietzsche asserts, everything is permitted, and this brings the "greatest elevation of men's consciousness of *strength*, as that which creates superman" (Nietzsche, *Complete Works*, ed. O. Levy, 18 vols. [Eng. London: Allen and Unwin, 1909-1913], 15:425). All this is part of Nietzsche's translation of all values. Yet, although he declares avowed atheism, his definition of "God" as a projection of the infinite in humankind or our highest aspirations comes dangerously close to Don Cupitt's "non-realist" God. Yet, while others might call him an atheist, Cupitt was ordained priest in 1959, became dean of a Cambridge college, and at the time of writing is still a priest in the Church of England. Clearly his "atheism" belongs to a very gray area.

The two other towering figures of atheism are Karl Marx and Sigmund Freud. Marx also viewed "God" as a human construct, at least in his later writings. "God" is an *instrumental device* used by the capitalist establishment to promote submissive contentment on the part of the masses or proletariat. Religion, he claimed, was "the opium of the people." It never seems to have occurred to him that if sometimes religion *can* be used manipulatively, *all* religion is *necessarily* manipulative. Freud attributes virtually everything to biophysical and neurological "forces," as if the self were merely an expression of such forces, often in tension. Aspirations of self-worth and conflicts with guilt are "objectified" into a fatherly God, who offers both grace and judgment. God, he argues, is an infantile illusion. His use of the Oedipus complex probably comes from sociological theories about totemism: he writes, "The totem animal . . . became the prototype for God." More specifically, "infantile wishes" arising from "the father-complex" became a source of religion (*The Future of an Illusion* [1928; reprint, London: Hogarth, 1962], 30). Hans Küng has devoted many pages to a study and critique of Freud (*Does God Exist?* [London: Collins, 1978], 262-339, and *Freud and the Problem of God* [New Haven: Yale University Press, 1990]). Küng writes, "Freud took over from Feuerbach and his successors the essential arguments for his personal atheism" (*Does God Exist?* 299). But, he adds, "this turns out to be a pure hypothesis, an unproved postulate" (302).

Much twentieth-century atheism derived from Feuerbach, Marx, and Freud, or even the French mechanistic worldview. The latest end-of-the-century phase, which has now entered the twenty-first century, is largely based in the field of genetics. C. Richard Dawkins was professor of the Public Understanding of Science at Oxford, and an evolutionary biologist. In 1976 he published *The Selfish Gene*, and in 1982 *The Extended Phenotype*. He is an avowed atheist, and in 2006 wrote *The God Delusion*. In *The Selfish Gene* he argued that all life evolves by the differential survival of all replicating entities. He seems to dismiss altruism as a paradox, unless it rests on a reciprocal expectation of a favorable return. Critics, however, suggest that genes must *cooperate with* other genes to build an individual. Dawkins coined the word "meme" to denote the behavioral equivalent of a gene. In response to *The God Delusion,* Terry Eagleton, Alister McGrath, and others have accused Dawkins of ignorance about Christian theology. Dawkins, for example, attacks the teleological argument for the existence of God, and most other defenses of theism. He is associated with A. C. Grayling and Daniel C. Dennett, in forming a "New Atheism," which argues that religion should not simply be tolerated, but countered, criticized, and exposed. Among the younger members are the American authors Sam Harris, who wrote *The End of Faith* (2004) and *The Moral Landscape* (2010). But Christians have not been silent. John Bowker challenged Dawkins's notion that religious belief was like a form of mental virus, and published *Is God a Virus?* (1995), while Alister McGrath has published *The Twilight of Atheism* (2004), *The Dawkins Delusion* (2002), *Dawkins' God* (2005), and, earlier, *A Scientific Theology* (2003).

Reading: C. Richard Dawkins, *The God Delusion* (Boston: Houghton Mifflin, 2008); Ludwig Feuerbach, *Essence of Christianity* (New York: Harper and Row, 1957); Sigmund Freud, *The Future of an Illusion* (London: Hogarth, 1962); Hans Küng, *Does God Exist?* (London: Collins, 1978), 188-424; Hans Küng, *Freud and the Problem of God* (New Haven: Yale University Press, 1990); A. E. McGrath, *Dawkins' God* (Oxford: Blackwell, 2005); A. E. McGrath, *A Scientific Theology* (Edinburgh: T. & T. Clark and Continuum, 2002); Friedrich Nietzsche, *The Antichrist* (London: Penguin, 1969).

Atonement

Biblical

"Atonement" is one of the few theological terms derived not from Greek or Latin, but from the old English term *at-one-ment,* or reconciliation. This involves reconciliation with God through the work of Christ. Although the creeds and ecumenical councils offer precise definitions of the person of Christ (*see* **Christology**), such specification is largely absent for the work of Christ, even if a variety of themes are employed, including sacrifice, expiation, propitiation, and mediation. The usual form in the creeds is "and was crucified for us under Pontius Pilate. He suffered and was buried and on the third day he rose again according to the Scripture" (Nicene Creed). The main point is that he was crucified at a point in history "for us." To understand more, this is amplified as being "according to the Scripture," that is, it is to be understood and interpreted within an OT framework. To understand more details of the biblical and historical understanding of atonement, its intelligibility today has largely to be rescued by examining at least four presuppositions about atonement and salvation, which are central to the OT. Broadly, however, the atonement of Jesus Christ is understood as reconciliation with God, through Christ's doing what we cannot do for ourselves at the initiative of the grace of God. "Substitution," for example, constitutes one theological term for "doing what we cannot do for ourselves."

(i) **Four Presuppositions Inherited from the OT.** (a) *Redemption.* There are two main Hebrew words for "redemption" or "redeem": first, *gā'al* (verb) and *gō'el* (noun), and second, *pādāh*. The NT uses the Greek *agorazō* for "redeem," or "buy." Redemption virtually always contains *three* aspects: redemption *from* a state of bondage or jeopardy; redemption *by* a costly act; and redemption *to* a state of freedom, new life, or ownership by a different "lord." Redemption *by* does not always involve the payment of a price *to* someone. This mistake becomes a distraction if or when it leads to spurious questions that ask: To whom is the ransom price paid? In the ancient world Gregory of Nyssa made this mistake (*see* **Atonement: Historical**). In modern times A. Deissmann distracted many scholars by overpressing the example of a slave who was freed by the payment of a price. D. Martin, among others, has convincingly shown how and why Deissmann's work is seriously misleading. Redemption denotes *not* the status of an autonomous free person, but transfer *from* ownership by evil forces *to* becoming the purchased property of a *new* Lord, Jesus Christ. A classic example concerns the exodus, when Israel was redeemed *from* bondage in Egypt *by* God's mighty arm, *to* a state of security and safety in the Promised Land (Exod. 6:6; 15:13; Pss. 74:2; 77:15). Similarly the Passover celebrates redemption *from* the death of the firstborn son, *by* the splashing of blood on the lintel, *to* the journey transfer to the Promised Land.

The term *gō'el* often has a special meaning, which occurs mainly in Deuteronomy. If a person commits a trespass unintentionally against a neighbor, a near relative may act as that person's "redeemer" *(gō'el)* to deliver him from the penalty incurred. If the person is subject to "blood revenge," the redeemer is called *gō'el-ha-dām*, a redeemer of blood (cf. Job 19:25; Isa. 43:1). On the basis of these two terms, the NT can interpret the atonement as redemption by the costly act of Jesus' sacrifice.

(b) *Salvation.* The Hebrew terms *yᵉshû'ah* and *shālōm* denote liberation from oppression to salvation, which brings peace and prosperity. The earliest and classic example comes in the book of Judges. The book repeats a cycle of salvation from bondage, in five acts, as follows: Israel sins against the Lord; God sells Israel into the hands of the Philistines, who oppress them; Israel cries to the Lord in their distress; God raises up a "savior" to deliver Israel from this oppression; and Israel again dwells in peace, security, and safety. Israel then sets this cycle in motion once again. The cycle is first expounded in general terms (Judg. 2:13-14, 16, 19). The cycles are then focused, respectively, among others, on Othniel (3:7, 9-10), on Ehud (3:15, 21, 28), on Deborah and Jael (4:4, 9, 13, 21-22), on Gideon (6:1-2, 7, 12-13; 7:4-22), on Jephthah (11:4–12:7), and on Samson (13:1–16:20).

(c) *Agents of Salvation.* These agents were often judges, prophets, kings, and priests. In spite of doubts expressed by some, Calvin saw Jesus Christ as fulfilling the role of prophet, priest, and king, in the power of the Holy Spirit. It is notable that in Judges each of the judges had a weakness, which thereby directed attention to the anointing and equipping by God. Some of these supposed "weaknesses" were perceived to be such only in the ancient world. Ehud, for example, was left-handed; Deborah and Jael were women; Gideon nurtured doubts and wanted tests; Jephthah made a rash vow, which cost his daughter her life; and Samson frittered away his energies on self-gratification. But the judges were regularly equipped by the Spirit of God, as Jesus was in the NT, who turned their efforts into success. The prophets and priests were essentially mediators, as Christ would be. In general, the prophets were "descending" mediators, representing God to humankind, often through commandments. The priests were usually "ascending" mediators, representing humankind to God, often through prayer.

Moses was already a mediator, passing on the commandments of God, and interceding on behalf of the people. Moses takes this role so seriously that he asks God to "blot him out of his book" if he does not heed his intercession. Because he faces both God and Israel as mediator, Ryder Smith calls him "like a man torn in two." He stands in solidarity with Israel, pleading to God for Israel; but he also stands alongside God, communicating God's commands to Israel. The climax of this mediating role can probably be seen in the Suffering Servant of God in Isa. 42:1-4, 49:1-6, 50:4-11, and 53:1-12. Sometimes it seems as if the Servant *is* Israel, a corporate entity. At other times, God chastises the Servant as an apparent substitute for, or representative of, Israel. On one side,

> He made my mouth like a sharp sword,
> in the shadow of his hand he hid me. (49:2)

On the other hand,

> He has borne our infirmities
> and carried our diseases;
> yet we accounted him stricken,
> struck down by God. (53:4)

All this is an explicit presupposition for interpreting the life and death of Jesus Christ in terms of mediation, sacrifice, substitution, and representation.

(d) *Sacrifice.* This constitutes the fourth presupposition that serves to interpret the atonement won by Jesus Christ. As Pannenberg observes, we cannot abandon these terms simply because they require some knowledge of the history of the biblical tradition that lies behind them. Indeed, the whole sacrificial system needs to be understood in the light of its distinctions. Sacrifices in Israel embraced two main kinds: the "gift" sacrifices, which were emphatically not to win God's favor but usually to express thanksgiving and homage; and "expiatory," "propitiatory," or "guilt" sacrifices, which were to cover sin, to acknowledge guilt, and to make atonement for sin.

These two types represented two distinct words in Hebrew. In earlier passages Hebrew *minchāh*, "offering," could cover both types, but in later thought (Lev. 2:1) it more specifically denoted "meal offering." It could even be translated as "gift" or "present," and directly led to *qorban* (Mark 7:11) in the NT. Within this general "gift" category the Hebrew *'olāh*, "burnt offering," could be made as an expression of sheer devotion or dedication. Further, the Hebrew *shelem* or *sh^elāmim*, "peace offering," denoted not so much peace after alienation but *communion with God* (*see* **Sacrifice**). All these differed from the second general category of Hebrew *'āshām*, "guilt offering," typically used in the so-called P literature to express compensation, confession of sin, recognition of guilt, and expiation or atonement (*see* **Day of Atonement**). It is associated with Hebrew *kippûr,* "to cover" or "to expiate." The Hebrew *chaṭṭā'th* could also be used to denote "sin offering" or "expiation." It is taken up in Heb. 10:26-31, and the accompanying ritual described in Lev. 4:1–5:13. Both *'āshām* and *chaṭṭā'th* became prominent in postexilic times.

(ii) **Atonement in the NT.** In 1 Cor. 1:18 Paul sums up the thrust of his preaching as "the message about the cross." In Gal. 1:4 he interrupts his usual greetings form by inserting "Christ, who gave himself for our sins to set us free from the present evil age." It is "anathema" to preach any other gospel (Gal. 1:8-9). In Rom. 8:3 Paul again asserts, "God has done what the law . . . could not do: by sending his own Son in the likeness of sinful flesh, and to deal with sin," but Greek *peri hamartias* "is frequently used in the LXX to denote a sin offering (e.g. Lev. 14:31, *chaṭṭā'th*; Ps. 40:6 [LXX, Ps. 39:7]; Isa. 53:10, *'āshām*). . . . It has quite often been understood here to mean 'as an offering for sin'" (Cranfield, *The Epistle to the Romans* [Edinburgh: T. & T. Clark, 1973], 1:382). Nevertheless, in the end Cranfield opts for sin as "having to do" with Christ's mission. At all events, Paul defines the gospel as Christ's dealing with sin "for us."

Paul and other NT writers see the cross not only as the work of Jesus Christ, but also as flowing from the grace of God. In 2 Cor. 5:19 Paul declares, "In Christ God was reconciling the world to himself," and Donald Bailey entitled his book on the atonement *God Was in Christ* (London: Faber and Faber, 1948). There is *no* sense in which God "sent" Jesus to do a task that he himself was not prepared to undertake. J. Moltmann speaks of the suffering of God no less than Christ in the event of the cross. Moreover, it is wholly incorrect to suggest that the cross "*awakened*" God's love; the cross is *the fruit of God's love*. In Bailey's words, the cross is "not simply of the love of Jesus, but of the love of God." A popular critic of this approach, Steve Chalke, who says it suggests appeasing an angry God, or even hints of child abuse, seems to have ignored this point, or at least not given it adequate attention. One of the most conservative writers of the last hundred years, Leon Morris, observes, "Sometimes, in their anxiety to give due emphasis to what Christ has done for us, Evangelicals have unwittingly introduced a division into the Godhead. . . . Emphatically this is not the position taken up in the Bible" (*Glory in the Cross* [London: Hodder and Stoughton, 1966], 46-47). Moltmann declares, "Was not God present in Jesus' sufferings 'seriously'?" (*Experiences of God* [London: SCM, 1985], 16). Moltmann rejects the notion that this is Patripassianism.

If we examine the multitude of NT writings that speak of the cross, it is clear that writers use diverse imagery to convey the meaning and significance of the atonement of Christ. J. Jeremias asserts, "By an increasing number of comparisons and images, Paul tries to make his hearers and readers understand the meaning of . . . 'for us'" (*The Central Message of the New Testament* [London: SCM, 1965], 36). Colin Gunton makes a similar point. He first urges that metaphors may be creative, and lead us to insights that prosaic literalism might never reach (*The Actuality of Atonement* [Edinburgh: T. & T. Clark, 1988], 27-52), and then comments, "As we move from one family of metaphors to another, we must be aware that they do not operate in self-contained worlds" (83). Both Jeremias and Gunton draw on a similar variety of language or images from the NT. Jeremias sees at least six diverse fields to explore.

(a) One area concerns *sacrificial* language. Jeremias cites 1 Cor. 5:7: "Our paschal lamb, Christ, has been sacrificed *(etuthē)*"; and Rom. 3:25, Christ, "whom God put forward as a *sacrifice of atonement* by his blood." (Some translate this as "expiation or propitiation (Gk. *hilastērion*) for us"; *see* **Expiation**.) Groups of NT scholars interpret *hilastērion* differently. The NRSV avoids the propitiation/expiation debate by translating "*a sacrifice of atonement* by his blood." The REB and NEB translate *hilastērion* as the "means of expiating sin"; the NJB translates it as "propitiation." The Greek term regularly translates the Hebrew *kappōreth*, "mercy seat," in the LXX (Cranfield notes, in twenty-one of its twenty-seven occurrences). It occurs elsewhere in the NT only once, in Heb. 9:5. Hence A. Nygren and T. W. Manson understand it as the antitype of mercy seat, and Cranfield considers this a strong possibility. Morris, however, urges the meaning "propitiation," along with J. Klausner and D. Hill, while C. K. Barrett and many others opt for "expiation," or "means of dealing with sin." C. H. Dodd emphatically insists on this, since, he argues, Paul does not say that God is "appeased." However, Morris excludes this when God is the subject of the action. At all events, it underlines the atoning and redemptive efficacy of the work of Christ. There are advantages and disadvantages to each proposed translation, as we set out under **Expiation**.

The concept and role of sacrifice are central in the Epistle to the Hebrews. The problem, as Gunton recognizes, is that while metaphors of victory and justice can appeal to the modern mind, the modern world often understands sacrifice merely as a figure of speech (*Actuality,* 115). "In the ancient world sacrifice was no figure of speech, but a stark fact; the solemn taking and surrendering of the warm blood of life itself. . . . It asserted the powerful efficacy of shed blood" (115). In Christianity we depend for the concept on its OT Jewish basis. Sacrifice is also used in an extended way in the OT, as in "The sacrifice acceptable to God is a broken spirit" (Ps. 51:17). Gunton quotes Caird's words, "The New Testament . . . constantly employs the language of sacrifice to declare the benefits of the Cross"; this is bound up with "the imperative need of those whom sin has defiled . . . which can cleanse the conscience from dead works" (G. B. Caird, *The Language and Imagery of the Bible* [London: Duckworth, 1980], 17; and Gunton, *Actuality,* 127). Gunton recognizes also that sacrifice may be regarded in legal, commercial, or "external" transactional terms. But this is "a crude parody of the tradition" (128). Sacrifice may be equally understood in inner, personal terms, as in the second-century *Letter to Diognetus,* "O sweetest exchange! O unfathomable work of God! . . . The sinfulness of many is hidden within the Righteous One, while the righteousness of the One justifies the many that are sinners" (9.5). E. Irving, for all his work in other directions, nevertheless defends the biblical theme, "He himself bore our sins in his body on the cross" (1 Pet. 2:24), in terms other than that of "a debtor and creditor account" or a "stock-exchange" understanding. In Hebrews this constitutes part of Christ's priestly work. To quote Gunton again, "It seems unlikely that any conception that remains true to the Bible can avoid" what he has just called "a substitutionary understanding of the atonement" (130).

The logic of Hebrews is inescapable. Jesus Christ is our great high priest. This has been established by his divine appointment as high priest, his oneness with humankind and with God, his appointment by God, his sinlessness, and his perfect offering and permanence (Heb. 4:14–8:2). But "every high priest is appointed to offer gifts and sacrifices; hence it is necessary for this priest also to have something to offer" (8:3). Christ is Mediator (8:6), and "entered once for all into the Holy Place, not with the blood of goats and calves, but with his own blood, thus obtaining eternal redemption" (9:12). For if the blood of bulls and goats is effective for the purpose of expiation, "how much more will the blood of Christ, who . . . offered himself without blemish to God, purify our conscience from dead works to worship the living God" (9:14). Whereas the Aaronic priests had to repeat their task again and again, Christ "has appeared once for all at the end of the age to remove sin by the sacrifice of himself" (9:26). Christ has "been offered once to bear the sins of many" (9:28a). (*See also* **Day of Atonement**.)

(b) The greatest danger to understanding sacrificial language correctly is to isolate it from what Jeremias and others have called "the variety" of comparisons and images that the NT uses to convey the truth of the atonement of Christ. A second image or metaphor is *purchase* or *redemption*. 1 Cor. 6:20, 7:23, Gal. 3:13, 4:5 say "you were bought (Gk. *ēgorasthēte*) with a price" (Gk. *timēs*; genitive of "price"). Gal. 3:13 uses the intensive compound *exēgorasen ek tēs kataras tou nomou . . . huper hēmōn*. As Jeremias comments, "Christ redeemed us from slavery through his death" (*Central Message*, 37). This is the second of his diverse images. We need not discuss *apolutrōsis* and related terms here, since we explain these under the entry **Redeem, Redemption**, and have introduced the concept as a presupposition drawn from the OT above.

(c) The third theme of Jeremias is borrowed from criminal law, and called the *forensic* theme. Like sacrifice, this can be misunderstood if taken by itself. Ian Ramsey showed that a plurality of models guards us against overnarrow and overliteral understanding, which lacks all qualifiers. It is, however, deeply embedded in the theology of Jesus and Paul that God has erased "the record that stood against us with its legal demands. He set this aside, nailing it to the cross" (Col. 2:14). Jesus declares, "The Son of Man came . . . to give his life a ransom (Gk. *lutron*) for many" (Mark 10:45). Danker translates *lutron* as "price of release, ransom," and *lutroō* as "to free by paying a ransom, to redeem," or "to rescue" (BDAG 605-6). This occurs not only in the parallel Matt. 20:28, but also in the LXX, Philo, and Josephus. However, what Jeremias calls a forensic category overlaps substantially with the *victory* theme (as in Gunton, *Actuality*, 64-70), and with the so-called *commercial* theme of buying and selling. Under the "forensic" subheading Jeremias includes Rom. 4:25, "[He] was handed over to death for our trespasses and was raised for our justification," although this may also be called a substitutionary and sacrificial theme (*Central Message*, 37). Indeed, he places "to buy" in 1 Cor. 6:20 under cultic and legal themes.

(d) Jeremias adds as a fourth theme *"ethical substitution consisting in Christ's vicarious obedience"* (38, italics mine). Here he cites Rom. 5:18-19, "Just as one man's trespass led to condemnation for all, so one man's act of righteousness leads to justification and life for all.... By the one man's obedience the many will be made righteous." He also cites Gal. 4:4-5: Christ was "born under the law, in order to redeem those who were under the law."

(e) This language is supplemented by what many term *transference language*. Paul declares, God "has rescued us from the power of darkness and transferred us (Gk. *metestēsen*) into the kingdom of his beloved Son, in whom we have redemption, the forgiveness of sins" (Col. 1:13-14). Danker suggests for *methistēmi* the meaning "transfer from one place to another" or "remove." It is arguable that John's language about birth from above (Gk. *anōthen;* John 3:3; cf. 3:6-10) entails transference from one domain to another. Indeed, most of the "signs" in John involve transformation, for example, water to wine, the gift of life and light, and raising to life.

(f) *Reconciliation*. We need not repeat our material under **Reconciliation** here. The Greek is *katallassō* (verb) and *katallagē* (noun). The gospel is described as "the word of [or message about] reconciliation" (2 Cor. 5:19; cf. Rom. 5:11). This word has a wide currency in secular society, whether in marriage, business, or politics. It is largely due to the genius of Paul to coin this readily understandable word for atonement (in Old English *at-one-ment*). In 2 Cor. 5:18, Paul comments, "All this is from God, who reconciled us to himself through Christ." It presupposes a "change" (Gk. *allos,* "other") from a previous state of hostility or alienation. In Ephesians Christians who were once "far off" are "brought near by the blood of Christ. For he [Christ] is our peace" (2:13-14). Paul insists, "While we were enemies *(echthroi)*, we were reconciled to God through the death of his Son ... saved by his life" (Rom. 5:10). Gunton includes a chapter that applies the term in the NT to the whole Christian community (*Actuality,* 173-203), and that transforms the world as well as the church. One reason why "reconciliation" is so important is that it is above all a *personal* word canceling rebellion and alienation, and restoring an uninterrupted *relationship* with God. In addition to its use by Paul, it can be found in 1 Pet. 1:2, 18, 19, and 2:21-24.

(g) *Other Themes*. The six themes above represent the main NT ones. They are not exclusive to Paul. Sayings and actions in the Gospels, Acts, Hebrews, the General Epistles, and Revelation share the same contours. However, these documents also use some distinctive themes. Hebrews, for example, stresses the ascension and heavenly intercession of Jesus Christ. In Heb. 7:25 Christ "always lives to make intercession for them [Christians]." Cullmann comments that Christ continues his high priestly office and work of mediation. Mediation includes intercession (Gk. *entunchanein*), while in 9:24 Christ "appear[s] in the presence of

God on our behalf." Cullmann's words are explicit, and not without disagreement. He writes, "Christ intercedes for us no longer simply in a collective sense.... Now he intercedes in every moment for each individual" (*Christology of the New Testament* [London: SCM, 1963], 102). This is an active dimension of reconciliation, which should not be excluded among other aspects of the work of Christ. Cullmann insists that this stands in continuity with "the same Christ who was on earth" (102). He also includes the eschatological return of Christ, which is usually described as the parousia, but Hebrews alone calls it "appear[ing] a second time" (Heb. 9:28; Gk. *ek deuterou*).

In an older book (1940) Vincent Taylor combs through numerous passages in the four Gospels, Acts, and the rest of the NT, including the dereliction on the cross (Mark 15:34, "My God, my God, why have you forsaken me?"); Gethsemane (Mark 14:36); probable allusions to the Suffering Servant (Mark 9:31; 10:45); and the Lord's Supper (also in 1 Cor. 11:25). He concludes, "The New Testament clearly implies that the Atonement is a work of God upon the greatest and grandest scale: It is nothing less than the doctrine of how man . . . separated from God by his sins, can be brought into a relationship of true and abiding fellowship with Him, and thus be enabled to fulfil his divine destiny. . . . From beginning to end it is a doctrine of reconciliation" (*The Atonement in New Testament Teaching* [London: Epworth, 1940], 245-46).

Reading: D. M. Bailey, *God Was in Christ* (London: Faber and Faber, 1948); J. D. G. Dunn, *The Theology of Paul the Apostle* (Grand Rapids: Eerdmans, 1998), 207-33; Colin Gunton, *The Actuality of Atonement* (Edinburgh: T. & T. Clark, 1988), 27-52; J. Jeremias, *The Central Message of the New Testament* (London: SCM, 1965); Leon Morris, *The Cross in the New Testament* (Grand Rapids: Eerdmans, 1965); Vincent Taylor, *Atonement in New Testament Teaching* (London: Epworth, 1940).

Historical

(i) **The Subapostolic Writings.** *1 Clement* (c. 96) is primarily concerned about church order and unity, but also expounds the love of God in action (13.6-7). It concludes, "For the sake of the love that He had towards us, Jesus Christ our Lord gave His blood by the will of God for us, His flesh for our flesh, and His life for our lives" (Gk. *huper tōn psuchōn hēmōn*; *1 Clem.* 49.6; see K. Lake, *The Apostolic Fathers*, vol. 1 [London: Heinemann, 1912]), for quotations from 1 Clement). Clement of Rome also exhorts his readers, "Let us gaze steadfastly upon the blood of Christ, and know that it is precious to His Father, since it was shed for our salvation" (*1 Clem.* 7.4). He also speaks of "redemption through His blood" (Gk. *lutrōsis*; 12.7).

Ignatius (30-107), on his way to martyrdom in Rome, identifies with the sufferings of Christ and repeats Paul's declaration in 1 Cor. 1:18-25: "The cross is an affront (Gk. *skandalon*) to unbelievers, but to us salvation and eternal life" (*To the Ephesians* 18.1; see Lake, *The Apostolic Fathers*, vol. 1, for Ignatius quotations). By Jesus Christ "the old kingdom was destroyed" (18.2; 19.3). Christian faith urges that we be "nailed to the cross of Christ" (*To the Smyrnaeans* 1.1). Christ is our physician (*To the Ephesians* 7.2). Christians may be "drawn up to the heights by the engine of Jesus Christ, that is the cross, using the Holy Spirit as a rope" (9.1). He declares, Christ died "for our sake, so that believing in his death you may escape death" (*To the Trallians* 2.2). Perhaps the most celebrated words are those concerning his martyrdom: "I am God's wheat, and I am ground by the teeth of the wild beasts that I may be found pure bread of Christ.... Then I shall be truly a disciple of Christ" (*To the Romans* 4.1-2). The atonement constitutes a regular theme with practical implications for life.

Polycarp of Smyrna (c. 69-155), if Irenaeus is right, represents a direct link between John and church leaders in Asia. He quotes 1 Pet. 2:22 and 24: "In pledge of our righteousness... Christ Jesus, 'who bore our sins in his own body on the tree, who did no sin, neither was guile found in his mouth, endured all for our sake, that we might live in him'" (*To the Philippians* 8.1, in Lake, 1:293; Gk. *anēnenken hēmōn tas hamartias tō idiō sōmati epi to xulon*). In 1.2 Christ suffered, died, and was raised "for our sins" (Gk. *huper tōn hamartiōn*).

The *Epistle of Barnabas* cannot be dated with certainty. It may range from A.D. 70 to 150. It uses a quantity of sacrificial imagery with reference to the fulfillment of the OT, and attacks animal sacrifice on the grounds of its fulfillment in Christ. It directly quotes Isa. 53:5-7 in the context of the substitutionary death of Christ. "The Lord endured to give his flesh to utter destruction in order that we may be made holy through the forgiveness of sins, which is by the sprinkling of his blood (Gk. *en tō haimati rhantismatos autou*)" (5.1; see Lake for *Barnabas* quotations). In the next verse Barnabas quotes Isa. 53:5-7. He adds: "The Lord endured to suffer for our life" (Gk. *peri tēs psuchēs*; 5.5). Other passages portray Christ "as a sacrifice for our sins" and as an antitype of the sacrifice of Isaac in Gen. 22:1-14 (*Barnabas* 7.3).

After the virtual close of the NT canon, there is an unbroken line of the NT tradition from c. 96 to nearly the middle of the second century. The doctrine seems to assume no controversy. The constant theme of "for us" accompanies virtually every reference to Christ's death. This solid tradition then reaches the apologists and Justin, and then Irenaeus and Tertullian.

(ii) **Justin and the Ante-Nicene Fathers.** Justin Martyr (c. 100–c. 165) argues for the reasonableness of the Christian faith. Hence his language about the cross is all the more striking. He explains Paul's argument in Gal. 3:13: "Although a curse lies in the law against persons who are crucified, yet no curse lies on the Christ of God, by whom all that have committed things worthy of a curse are saved" (*Dialogue with Trypho* 94; see *ANF* 1 for Justin quotations). He continues, "The whole human race will be found to be under a curse" (Gk. *hupo kataran*; *Dialogue* 95). Justin explains the role of Deut. 27:26 and Deut. 21:23 in the NT. He also formulates symbolic and metaphorical language to express the "for us" of atonement. He alludes to Moses' casting a "tree" into the bitter waters of Marah, so that they became sweet (Exod. 15:25), and to the righteous person who is like a "tree" that flourishes by the waters (Ps. 1:3). It was Justin who allegorized the biblical account of Elisha's casting a wooden stick into the Jordan to recover the sunken axe-blade, "just as Christ, by being crucified on a 'tree'... has redeemed us" (*Dialogue* 86). Yet he also uses straightforward propositions: "By his blood Christ cleanses those who believe in him" (*First Apology* 32). The passion is the mystery "by means of which humankind is saved by God" (*Dialogue* 74).

Irenaeus (c. 130–c. 200) placed a high value on "the rule of faith," which transmitted apostolic tradition. His most distinctive language about the atonement concerns "recapitulation." In Christ, he declares, "All things are gathered up together by God in Christ" (*Against Heresies* 1.3.4; see *ANF* 1 for Irenaeus quotations), or, he declares, "To the glory of God the Father to gather all things in one, and to raise up anew... the whole human race" (1.10.1). The Latin *recapitulatio* translates the Greek *anakephalaiōsis*, denoting "summary," "gathering up," or "summing up," as in Eph. 1:10, where God sums up "all things in [Christ]," or NRSV, "gather[s] up all things" in Christ. Danker suggests "sum up" or "recapitulate" (BDAG 65). Elsewhere Irenaeus speaks of "summing up in Himself all things which are in heaven and which are on earth" (*Against Heresies* 5.20.2). Irenaeus has four references to Eph. 1:10 and several more to recapitulation. For him this "recapitulation" denotes restoration of all things, especially the image of God. He writes: Christ "commenced afresh the long line of human beings and furnished us, in a brief comprehensive manner with salvation... to be according to the image and likeness of God — that we might recover in Christ Jesus" (3.18.1). Irenaeus also refers to Christ's "descent into the regions beneath the earth" (4.27.2), although at the Reformation "descent into hell" was at first interpreted differently by Lutherans and Calvinists. Irenaeus also uses more traditional ways of describing the atonement, such as victory over evil powers (5.21.2).

Tertullian (c. 150–c. 225) closely follows Irenaeus. In *Against Marcion* 2.27 he speaks of God as "prostrating the supreme disparity of his majesty" in undergoing "death, even the death of the cross." In *On the Resurrection of the Flesh* 63 he asserts that Christ the Mediator "shall reconcile both God to man and man to God." In this passage Tertullian uses the Latin *reddet*, which normally means "to restore, to return," or "to give back," as Irenaeus stresses. In a fundamental statement where he affirms the real body of Jesus against Marcion, Tertullian writes, "Christ's death, wherein lies the whole weight and fruit of the Christian name," would be denied if Marcion were right (*Against Marcion* 3.8; see *ANF* 3 for Tertullian quotations). Tertullian, like Irenaeus, stressed "the rule of faith" or apostolic tradition (*Prescription against Heretics* 16). He even introduced the postbiblical term "satisfaction" into the process of dealing with sin.

Origen associates the work of Christ and the cross with the destruction of evil and evil forces. More broadly, he writes: Christ "suffered as one who was wise and perfect... for the good of the human race, even for the good of all intelligent beings" (*Against Celsus* 7.17; see *ANF* 4 for Origen quotations). The first blow in the conflict "is to overthrow the power of that evil spirit, the devil, who had obtained dominion over the whole world" (7.16). He refers to "the rulers of this age ... [who] crucified the Lord of glory" (1 Cor. 2:6-8; *On First Principles* 3.3.1, 2; 4.1.13; *Against Celsus* 3.19). According to R. S. Franks, "Origen says that sin necessarily requires a propitiation" (*The Work of Christ* [London: Nelson, 1962], 41).

From the time of Origen to the Council of Nicaea, Cyprian of Carthage (d. 258), Hippolytus of Rome (c. 170–c. 236), and Novatian of Rome (c. 210-280) were occupied with ecclesiastical issues, and wrote less on the atonement of Christ, and Lactantius (c. 250–c. 325) wrote primarily as an apologist. None, however, deviated from tradition on this subject.

(iii) **The Post-Nicene Fathers.** Athanasius (c. 296-373) is best known for his consistent opposition to Arianism, but he wrote the treatise *On the Incarnation of the Word of God* (Eng. London: Mowbray, 1953) when he was little more than twenty, a few years before the Council of Nicaea. One major theme of the book is the celebration of the victory and triumph of Christ over evil. In *On the Incarnation* 3 he presupposes that without the work of Christ humankind would "remain in the state of death and corruption." We are "by nature subject to corruption" (5). But God in his goodness saved humankind from being "brought to nothing through the deceit wrought upon man by the devil" (6). God ensured that death did not have dominion over him (7). Hence Jesus Christ "surrendered his body to *death in place of all, and offered it to the Father*" (8, italics mine). Christ, Athanasius argues, "became in dying a sufficient exchange for all" (9). Later in the treatise Athanasius concludes, "The Lord offered for our sakes the one death. ... He had come to bear the curse that lay on us; and how could he 'become a curse' otherwise than by accepting the accursed death" (25; Gal. 3:13). Again, he argues, "The death of the Lord is the ransom of all, and by it 'the middle wall of partition' is broken down" (25; Eph. 2:14). In John he foretold his death: "I, if I be lifted up, will draw all people to myself" (25; John 12:32). He adds, "The Lord came to overthrow the devil," who is "the prince of the power of the air" (25; Eph. 2:2). The resurrection of Christ is "a very strong proof of this destruction of death" (27).

Athanasius uses further images and comparisons in sections 28-57. He calls not upon one single theme, as Aulén might seem to suggest, but on all the themes and imagery we have considered in our survey of the NT. In his last few sections he utters the sentence that the Eastern Orthodox Church often cites as the foundation theme of *theōsis,* or divinization: "He (Christ) assumed humanity that we might become God" (54), often popularly rendered "He was made man that we might be made God."

Gregory of Nyssa (c. 330-395) has material on the atonement especially in his work *The Great Catechism.* His most notorious analogy was based on Paul's statement in 1 Cor. 2:8, where Paul says that the "rulers of this age" did not understand the atonement, "for if they had, they would not have crucified the Lord of glory." Gregory uses what S. Cave calls a "grotesque" parallel. He urges that "the opposing power" would shrink from "the undiluted presence of God." Thus: "In order to secure the ransom on our behalf ... the Deity was hidden under the veil of our nature so that, as with ravenous fish, the hook of the Deity might be gulped down along with the bait of flesh, and thus, life being introduced into the house of death . . . that which is diametrically opposed to light and life might vanish" (*Catechism* 24; *NPNF*, ser. 2, 5:494). This "grotesque" simile is repeated in John of Damascus in the eighth century, and qualified by Gregory of Nazianzus. However, its place in the thought of Gregory is less than popular tradition might suggest. His main theme, like that of Clement of Alexandria, is that the diseases and plight of humankind needed a physician, Jesus. "Our diseased nature needed a healer. Man in his fall needed one to set him upright" (*Catechism* 15). If we are puzzled about the lengths to which God goes to save us, "the sick do not dictate to their physicians the measures for their recovery" (17); indeed, chapters 26 and 27 refer constantly to the physician's ability to turn sickness to health, even if he uses fire to restore purity, or "for their cure makes them subject to the knife and cautery" (26). In the same group of chapters Gregory declares that Jesus Christ underwent every aspect of human life, so that through this identification with all human experience, redemption and atonement might be complete.

Gregory of Nazianzus (c. 330-390) provides a less detailed and less comprehensive view of atonement than Gregory of Nyssa, or even than Athanasius. He accepts the notion of Christ's costly redemption or ransom, but he rejects the notion in Gregory of Nyssa that the ransom should be "paid" either to the devil or to God. He asks, "To whom was that blood offered that was shed for us, and why was it shed? . . . If it is to the Evil One, fie upon the outrage (Gk. *pheu tēs hubreōs*)!" But it cannot be to God, "for it was not by him that we were oppressed" (*Oration 45: The Second Oration on Easter* 22; *NPNF*, ser. 2, 7:431). All that we say with certainty is that the "ransom" achieved the restoration of humankind. Gregory also repeats the dictum of Athanasius that the Eastern Orthodox quote as the basis of divinization: "The Deity being made man, and the manhood deified" (*Letter 101 to Cledonius against Apollinarius*; *NPNF*, ser. 2, 7:439-40). This is the famous letter in which he defends "Holy Mary [as] the Mother of God," of which the context makes clear that it concerns the genuine nature of Jesus Christ to redeem, not the status of Mary as such. Apollinarius had denied that the Son of God possessed a genuinely human mind.

Meanwhile among the Western Fathers, Hilary of Poitiers and Ambrose of Milan largely follow the Greeks, and reproduce the apostolic tradition on the work of Christ. Augustine of Hippo (354-430) teaches so much about grace that the atonement is almost eclipsed within this subject. Both grace and the atonement confirm that life and salvation are not a reward for human achievement. Augustine declares, "For what good work can a lost man perform, except so far as he has been delivered from perdition?" (*Enchiridion* 30). Hence Christ comes as Mediator and Reconciler who offers the one sacrifice, of which those under the Law are simply "types." Franks comments, "Not only does he (Augustine) sum up in himself what has gone before, but he incorporates with it new and original elements of the greatest importance" (*The Work of Christ*, 87). Original sin, grace, and predestination form the frame into which fits the traditional teaching on the atonement. Justification and merit also play a part. Kelly suggests a similar verdict: "It was his special role . . . to sum up the theological insights of the West, and pass them on, with the impress of his genius . . . to the Middle Ages" (*Early Christian Doctrines* [London: Black, 1977], 390).

Augustine stressed, first, Christ's work as Mediator. "He is the one true mediator, reconciling us to God by the sacrifice of peace," both one with God and one with humankind (*On the Trinity* 4.14, 19). Mediation is coupled with sacrifice, reconciliation, and oneness with God and humankind. He repeats the theme in *Confessions* 10.68. Christ represents, and is both God and humankind (*Enchiridion* 108). Second, he speaks often of atonement in a variety of images, which include reconciliation (*Epistle* 187.20), and occasionally of Christ's becoming human so that humans might be made divine. The atonement is also understood as redemption or release from bondage to Satan (*On the Trinity* 13.19), although he would agree with Gregory of Nazianzus and Hilary that the ransom price is not paid to Satan. Kelly argues, in contrast to Aulén, that the theme of release from the devil is *not* "the pivot of Augustine's soteriology" (*Early Christian Doctrines*, 392).

Augustine also asserts, "By his death, that one true sacrifice offered on our behalf, he purged, abolished and extinguished . . . whatever guilt we had" (*On the Trinity* 4.13.17; *NPNF*, ser. 1, 3:78). This section includes a variety of metaphors, themes, and passages, including principalities and powers in Col. 2:15; predestination to new life in Rom. 8:30; an act of selfless love in John 15:13; and leading captivity captive in Eph. 4:8. Elsewhere he speaks of Christ's bearing the "curse pronounced on sin," although he was sinless (*Reply to Faustus the Manichaean* 14.4; *NPNF*, ser. 1, 4:208). He adds, "He was made a curse for us," and "an old self is crucified with him" (14.4). Augustine stresses the life and death of Christ as an example, although not simply or solely as an example. Christ demonstrates God's wisdom and love, and breaks our pride: "God became incarnate . . . that an example might be set to disobedient humankind in the life of the God-man" (*Enchiridion* 108; *NPNF*, ser. 1, 3:172). But this short chapter contains a variety of language on the atonement.

(iv) **Anselm (1033-1109) and Abelard (1079-1142)**. The patristic writers, including Augustine, like the NT, used a variety of images to convey the "for us" aspect of the work of Christ, and the medieval period up to 1100 largely followed Augustine. But in subsequent years Anselm and Abelard tended to give prominence to a particular aspect; the former highlighted "objective satisfaction" and the latter, the subjective theory of "moral influence." It is often argued that in the Reformation era John Calvin gave special importance to penal substitution, and in the modern era G. Aulén placed special emphasis on redemption and victory in his book *Christus Victor*.

Anselm's account of the atonement, like Moltmann's work in another direction, paid particular attention to God as well as Christ, and contrary to later liberalism, emphasized its objective character, not merely human awareness. He argued rightly that atonement is bound up with Christology, and with governance of the world. Only Christ, he urged, who is both God and human, can atone for sin as an act and state against God. He expounds his thesis in his classic work *Why God Became Man* (in E. R. Fairweather, ed., *A Scholastic Miscellany* [London: SCM; Philadelphia: Westminster, 1956], 100-193). The book is easy to read.

In part 1, chapters 1–25 (pp. 101-46), Anselm argues that *only God* can put right the damage that sin has done. Sin concerns not just humankind as if it were a domestic or internal matter, but God and our relationship with God (esp. 105-6). Humankind stands under bondage and in need of redemption (chaps. 6 and 7, pp. 106-10). When Jesus became incarnate, "the will of God" was sufficient reason (110). He became "obedient unto death" (111). Jesus said, "Not as I will, but as Thou wilt" (112). Sin, meanwhile, constitutes "an infinite debt" to God (chaps. 11-15, pp. 118-24). Anselm borrows what for him is a contemporary analogy from the eleventh century. He writes, "To sin is . . . not to render his due to God. . . . It is not enough for someone who violates another's honour to restore the honour, unless he makes some kind of *restitution* . . . according to the extent of the inquiry and dishonour. . . . Everyone who sins must repay to God the honour that he has taken away, and this is the *satisfaction* that every sinner ought to make to God" (119, italics mine). This is based on the law in feudal society that compensation is owed to the person who has been offended, and in a feudal society, the more esteemed the person injured, the greater should be the compensation or satisfaction.

From chapter 12 onward Anselm offers an explanation of this state of affairs. First, he addresses the popular and even biblical notion that Christ "must" die, and that sin "must" be punished. "Must" is misleading or clumsy shorthand for God's governance of the world in terms of "what is fitting." The "must" arises from the presupposition of God's spirit and wise governance of the world. Anselm explains, "It is not fitting for God to do anything unjustly or without due order" (121). Moreover, "God maintains nothing more justly than the honour of his dignity. . . . Otherwise God will be . . . unjust to himself" (121 and 122). Humans cannot be saved without this satisfaction (134). Whatever its problems (and there are several), Anselm's approach is at least centered in the majesty and glory of God, and in sin as a matter between humans and God, not mere mortality.

Part 2 concerns another twenty-two chapters (pp. 146-83). After looking again at "necessity" (149), Anselm argues, "No one but God can make this satisfaction" and "Only a God-Man can make the satisfaction by which man is saved" (150-51). Humankind alone would not be capable of making an "infinite" satisfaction. Jesus Christ then transfers this satisfaction to humankind's benefit, and offers it to God on our behalf. In a penetrating response to one of today's greatest problems, Anselm declares, "If the Son willed to give to another what is owing . . . , could the Father rightly forbid him?" (180). It all redounds to God's great mercy (181-82).

Many criticize the relative inattention to grace and love, the commercial language of medieval law, and the almost "external" language of a contract. Nevertheless, Anselm pays attention to what is often lacking today: the seriousness of sin as a transgression against God; the atonement as part of God's governance of the world; the integral interaction between the person and work of Christ; and the clarification of "must." Two different points need to be made in evaluating Anselm on the atonement. On one side, as Franks comments, "All histories of doctrine recognize the epoch-making character of Anselm's theory of satisfaction and merit" (*The Work of Christ*, 135). In S. Cave's language, "the influence of [Anselm on the atonement] would be difficult to exaggerate" (*Doctrine of the Work of Christ* [London: University of London Press, 1937], 130). On the other hand, Franks comments, "The Anselmic conception of satisfaction is derived not from Scripture but from ecclesiastical penance" (135). To quote Cave, "It was essentially Catholic in its conception of sin and penance" (131), even if it found a place in Protestant thought. Anselm did consider, and reject, other theories of the atonement. He argued that "recapitulation" in Irenaeus was a beautiful analogy but lacked solid evidence. He rejected "redemption from the devil" as a half-truth. He even anticipated theories of love as "moral influence," but claimed these had insufficient grounding in Scripture. In the end, he combined some brilliant insights with some serious defects.

Abelard, with his "moral influence" theory, was no doubt influenced by his personal life and his experience of love, in his tragic love affair with Héloise. He was drawn to such passages as "No one has greater love than this, to lay down one's life for one's friends" (John 15:13). Abelard knew that no one should underestimate the *power of love* to invite love in return. He also wrote not only on the atonement, but in his book *Christian Theology* raised wider theological questions, laying the foundation for a scientific treatment of theology. Here his purpose was primarily apologetic, for which he used dialectic method. On the atonement, he rejects Anselm's view. The central point was that the loving example of self-sacrifice undertaken by Jesus Christ leads us to reconciliation with God. Franks comments, "He has reduced the whole process of redemption to one single, clear principle, namely the manifestation of God's love to us in Christ, which awakens an answering love in us. Out of this principle Abelard endeavours to explain all other points of view" (*The Work of Christ*, 146).

On the basis of Abelard's *Exposition of the Epistle to the Romans*, this view might be plausible (*A Scholastic Miscellany*, 276-87). Rom. 3:20 states, "'No human being will be justified in his sight' by deeds prescribed by the law," and 3:24 states, "They are now justified by his grace as a gift, through the redemption that is in Christ Jesus." Abelard comments, "'To the showing of his justice' — that is, his love — which, as has been said, justifies us in his sight" (279). He further comments, "How cruel and wicked it seems that anyone should demand the blood of an innocent person as the price for anything . . . still less that God should consider the death of his Son so agreeable that by it he should be reconciled to the whole world" (283). He has simply bound us to himself by love that kindles our hearts with love. Abelard's exegesis seems questionable, but some have argued that if we consider his thought as a whole, it is inconceivable that he should aim to expound his doctrine of the atonement through a few odd comments on Romans. Certainly Abelard influenced many who came after him. We might mention Faustus Socinus (1509-1604), F. Schleiermacher (1768-1834), A. Ritschl (1822-1889), many during the Enlightenment, and those afterward who were of a liberal persuasion. Many in the contemporary world would follow him.

Yet even in the Middle Ages many criticized this view of the atonement. Bernard of Clairvaux, for example, attacked Abelard, in spite of his stress on the love of God, citing the need for a fuller understanding of Rom. 3:26. To quote Franks again, "Bernard argues that Abelard's theory implies the denial of original sin" (*The Work of Christ,* 153). Peter Lombard shares Abelard's emphasis on the love of God, but seeks a more "objective" account of the atonement; by his sacrifice, he says, Christ blotted out our guilt. Thomas Aquinas (1225-1274) was closer to Augustine and Anselm than to Abelard, stressing the necessity of Christ's work, and his work as satisfaction for sin. "Satisfaction for the sin of another has as its matter the penalties which one undergoes for the sin of another" (*Su Th* 3, qu. 14, art. 1, reply).

(v) **The Major Reformers: Luther and Calvin.** Martin Luther (1483-1546) never found anything contrary to Scripture in the ancient creeds. In his very early works of 1517-1518, that is, his *Commentary on Hebrews* and the Heidelberg Disputation, we see a fully rounded doctrine of the atonement both in terms of a sacrifice that God accepts and as redemption from the law to righteousness. On Heb. 4:14 Luther commented, "We have Christ himself as our high Priest . . . the greatest of all priests . . . for he is great and able to save us" (J. Atkinson, *Luther: Early Theological Works* [London: SCM; Philadelphia: Westminster, 1962], 99). On 5:1 Luther wrote, "When Christ cried out for us on the cross, it was then in that atoning work, where all human values are reversed, that his priesthood reached its moment of highest perfection" (102). On 5:7 he declared, "In the hour of his passion . . . he was forsaken by the Father and suffered in the flesh" (109). In 8:3 he interpreted "the offering" as one of "expiation for sins" (149). In 9:14, "dead works" are what "defile the conscience" and from which "a man is cleansed through the blood of Christ" (171). On the next verse he quoted Rom. 5:20, "The law entered that offence might abound," and Gal. 3:19, "The law was added because of transgressions" (175). Luther concluded, "This sacrifice of the New Testament has been perfected and absolutely ended" (185). On Heb. 9:27, Christ has died "but once" (187). On 10:4 he urged, "A body is offered in some unique way" (191). The result is freedom and confidence (10:19).

These themes also occur in a different context in the Heidelberg Disputation (1518). By 1518 Luther had clarified much of the relation between the work of Christ, and "works" and faith respectively. In this work he wrote, "The works of man appear beautiful but inwardly they are loathsome" (*Luther: Early Theological Works,* 282, art. 3). He commented, "The theologian of glory says bad is good and good is bad. The theologian of the cross calls them by their proper name" (291, art. 21). As in 1 Cor. 1:18-25, the cross, or the atonement, reverses human values.

Luther then quoted Gal. 3:13, "Christ has freed us from the curse of the law" (292, art. 23). He declared, "The righteousness which comes from faith in Christ is sufficient for him" (294, art. 25), Grace is not a response of love, but a *cause* of it (art. 28). On "sinless perfection" Luther replied, "A righteous man sins even when he is doing good" (297, art. 28).

Luther returns to this emphasis in a variety of his writings. In the *Larger Catechism* he exclaims, "Christ has delivered me by his blood, from sins, the devil, death, and all destruction" (2.2). In this catechism he also alludes to the wrath of God at our "open and rebellious disobedience to God," until Christ descended from heaven to bring us help, and liberated us from all captivity of sin and death, and the devil, into the freedom of his adoption (in Franks, *The Work of Christ*, 287). Luther continues, "He suffered, died, and was buried to 'satisfy for me and pay my debt *(culpa)* . . . with his own precious blood'" (*Larger Catechism* 2; in Franks, 288). It is clear that G. Aulén is right in claiming that "victory over evil powers" plays a prominent role in Luther, but wrong to claim that it eclipses other theories or models, or becomes the chief model. Interpretations of Luther vary because he wrote prodigiously, yet gave no systematic treatise such as we find in Calvin. Harnack's verdict seems valid, namely, that Luther treated all the schemata of traditional theology, but "found in each of them, rightly understood, the whole doctrine" (*History of Dogma,* vol. 3 [Boston: Little, Brown, 1901], 835).

John Calvin (1509-1564) reflects Luther's influence, but in *The Institutes* sets out a *systematic* doctrine, which leaves him free to offer more contextual and exegetical comments in his numerous commentaries on the Bible. Book 2 of the *Institutes* expounds sin, the Fall, and bondage in its first eleven chapters. Then chapters 12 to 17 expound Christ's work as Mediator, as participating in human nature, and the offices of prophet, king, and priest. In chapters 16 and 17 he expounds "How Christ performed the office of Redeemer in procuring our salvation." Calvin begins chapter 16 by asserting, "Neither is there salvation in any other" than Christ (Acts 4:12; *Institutes* 2.16.1; Beveridge, 1:434). Everything needful for us exists in Christ. There appears to be a contradiction between God's justice and his mercy. But this is because our position is "miserable and calamitous . . . without Christ" (2.16.2; 1:435). Indeed, we earn God's wrath, and are "estranged from God by sin." Calvin continues: "Then Christ interposed, took the punishment upon himself, and bore what by the just judgment of God was impending over sinners; with his own blood expiated the sins which rendered them hateful to God, by this expiation satisfied and duly propitiated God the Father . . . on this basis founded peace between God and men" (2.16.2; 1:435). Calvin also stresses that grace initiates the atonement: "God the Father, by his love, prevents and anticipates our reconciliation in Christ" (2.16.3; 1:436). He then quotes Rom. 5:10, "If we were enemies, we were reconciled to God" (2.16.4).

It is important to Calvin to see the whole of the life of Jesus, and not simply his death alone, as grounds of redemption. He comments, Paul "extends the ground of pardon which exempts from the curse of the law to the whole life of Christ"

(Gal. 4:4-5; *Institutes* 2.16.5; 1:437). Nevertheless, "Scripture ... ascribes it peculiarly and specially to the death of Christ." Jesus declared that he gave his life "a ransom for many" (Matt. 20:28; 2.16.5). Calvin then cites the classic verse in Paul: "Christ Jesus, whom God put forward as a sacrifice of atonement [NRSV; Calvin has 'to be a propitiation'; Gk. *hilastērion*) by his blood, effective through faith" (Rom 3:25; 2.16.5; 1:437). The second classic passage in Paul follows: 2 Cor. 5:21, "For our sake he [God] made him [Christ] to be sin who knew no sin, so that in him we might become the righteousness of God." Calvin believes that the Apostles' Creed and Phil. 2:7 share this perspective as well as sayings in John; prophecies in Isa. 53:5, 7, and 12; and Heb. 10:5. Sections 5-7 summarize "why Christ died." In 2.16.6 Calvin appeals to the sacrificial system in Leviticus and, again, to the Servant Songs, according to which "the guilt and penalty ... ceases to be imputed to us." Christ is "a propitiatory victim." Turning from Paul to Peter, Calvin urges: "He himself bore our sins in his body on the cross, so that, free from sins, we might live for righteousness; by his wounds you have been healed" (1 Pet. 2:24; *Institutes* 2.16.6). Calvin's extensive quotations of biblical passages in 2.16.6, 7 show his allusion to a variety of models, although chiefly to *"our substitute-ransom and propitiation"* (2.16.6).

Sections 8-18 of 2.16 discuss Christ's descent into hell, the inadequacy of Abelard's approach, the resurrection of Christ, his ascension, exaltation, intercession, and return. "He descended into hell" stands in the creed, and is important for the atonement. "The omission of it greatly detracts from the benefit of Christ's death" (2.16.8; 1:441). Calvin rejects the notion that *Infernis* merely denotes "sepulchre" here. He also rejects the interpretation that Christ descended to announce to the patriarchs Christ's "accomplished redemption, and bring them out of ... prison" (2.16.9; 1:442). This application of 1 Pet. 3:19 is, he insists, "not perfectly definite." There is a "surer" exposition. Christ not only had to endure physical or bodily death, but he also had to "engage, as it were, at close quarters with the powers of hell and the horrors of eternal death" (2.16.10; 1:443). Hence "He descended into hell" is "nothing strange," for "not only was the body of Christ given up as the price of redemption ... but ... the tortures of condemned and ruined man" (2.16.10). Otherwise, the allusion to his "fearing" death in Heb. 5:7 would be to physical death, which others experience (2.16.11).

This is the full meaning of "My God, my God, why hast thou forsaken me?" Calvin cites Hilary of Poitiers: "The cross, death, hell, are our life," and "The Son of God is in hell, but man is brought up to heaven" (2.16.11; 1:444). Luther had held the "victory" view of this clause, and Calvin recognizes that some oppose him (2.16.12). In 2.16.13 he turns to the resurrection through which we are born again to a living hope (1 Pet. 1:3), and of which Paul asserts, "If Christ has not been raised, your faith is futile and you are still in your sins" (1 Cor. 15:17; 2.16.13). His exaltation and triumphs "made captivity itself a captive; / he gave gifts to his people" (Eph. 4:8; 2.16.16). Further, "Christ will descend from heaven in visible form" (2.16.17) and "judgment is vested in him" (2.16.18). In Christ we see "the whole sum of our salvation" (2.16.19). The exposition of the atonement is not confined to *Institutes* 2.16.1-19, but this chapter provides the essence and heart of Calvin's thinking. Substitutionary sacrifice or "penal substitution" carries the main emphasis, but other aspects of Christ's atoning work are included from the NT.

Criticisms of Calvin's theology have abounded since his time. Even Cave, in his older textbook *The Doctrine of the Work of Christ*, claims: "This penal theory of the Atonement, to which Calvin here gives vigorous expression, has tended to make God appear not loving but vindictive" (167). Currently in popular theology Steve Chalke has berated evangelicals for making too much of penal substitution, especially, he says, in days when the abuse of children is so prominent. But this is to misunderstand Calvin's emphasis on God's initiative of love and grace. The primary cause of salvation, he urged, was God's decree. God's grace means that "God was in Christ, reconciling the world to himself." Calvin urged, "The first step . . . is, to acknowledge that God is a Father, to defend, govern, and cherish us, until he brings us to the eternal inheritance of his kingdom" (*Institutes* 2.6.4; 1:297). Calvin argues that God himself was "in" the sufferings of the cross. "God, in his infinite mercy, having determined to redeem us, became himself our Redeemer *in* the person of his only-begotten Son" (2.12.2; 1:402, italics mine). Further, the major patristic witness is that the *whole* Trinity participates in *all* acts of creation and redemption. Calvin would not disagree. Even Ritschl recognizes that the *Institutes* remains "the masterpiece of Protestant theology." In his own time Calvin was attacked by Socinus (1539-1604), who held no doctrine of original sin and, like Abelard, saw the will of God only as the source of atonement and pardon. He rejected any notion of "satisfaction." Others, however, have maintained the tradition of Reformed theology. Calvin led to "Calvinism," which many distinguish from the theology of its master.

(vi) **Modern Views of the Atonement.** The thinkers of the Enlightenment tended to regard much of traditional church doctrine from Irenaeus to Calvin as irrational. English Deism began the new direction, and German liberalism became the general expression of it. (a) *Kant* (1724-1804) brought a new era into being, especially in his *Critique of Pure Reason* (1781). Jesus Christ, he believed, constituted perfect humanity, which pleases God. But in the end, the absolute realm is that of the moral imperative, and humankind can follow Christ's moral perfection only through its own exertions. Humanity's moral struggle is only *symbolized* by the cross, and the switch of emphasis from God to humankind "is a transmogrification of Christianity into its opposite. . . . God is [only] to be found in human moral reason and action, not encountered as a personal creator and redeemer" (C. E. Gunton, *The Actuality of Atonement* [Edinburgh: T. & T. Clark, 1988], 7). Kant's work ushers in the era of Schleiermacher (1768-1834) and Hegel (1770-1831).

(b) *Schleiermacher's* attitude to Kant combined affirmation and denial. As he moved from his early years in Pietism and the Moravian school at a seminary at Barby to the very different, now rationalist University of Halle, he assimilated many of the assumptions of the Enlightenment. Yet he utterly rejected any notion of autonomy or "self-help," insisting on humankind's "feeling of absolute dependence on God" (*see* **Christology: History of Thought; Schleiermacher, Friedrich D. E.**).

Schleiermacher sought to hold together the person and work of Christ. He wrote, first, "The peculiar activity and the exclusive dignity of the Redeemer imply each other, and are inseparably one in the self-consciousness of believers" (*The Christian Faith* [1821; Edinburgh: T. & T. Clark, 1989], 374). Second, he stressed Christ's solidarity with humankind, but bequeathed the question of whether he saw Christ as *different in kind* from human beings or merely *different in degree*. J. Macquarrie and A. McGrath offer different answers to this question. Schleiermacher wrote, "The Redeemer, then is like all men in virtue of the identity of human nature, but is distinguished from them all by the constant potency of his God-consciousness, which was a veritable existence of God in him" (385). On the same page he asserts that sin in humans is a mere "disturbance of nature." Third, Jesus Christ somehow draws humankind into his unclouded blessedness and relationship with God. In sum, Schleiermacher rejects "substitution" and "expiation" in favor of an *exemplarist* account of the cross, not dissimilar to the tradition of Abelard.

Schleiermacher retains from church tradition, found especially in Calvin, the three roles of prophet, priest, and king. As a prophet, Christ is mediator of revelation, which in Christ is "inexhaustible," and can never be surpassed. But kingship tends to be concerned with society, rather than with the reign of God. Priesthood includes Christ's fulfillment of the Law (451). But Christ's priesthood was not "for our advantage" (456). His suffering is not an offering or satisfaction to God, but "an absolutely self-denying love" (458). Traditional language offers "artificial constructions" (459). The key is "Christ's representation of us before God" (463). This priesthood is then passed over to Christians, who are called "a priestly nation" (465; cf. 1 Pet. 2:9). He rejects a notion of substitutionary atonement. On the other hand, he regularly calls Christ "the Redeemer" (425). Most critics insist that in the end his doctrine of God remains subjective, always related to human consciousness; more controversially, while a few suggest his understanding of the Trinity forms a climax to his work, most insist that to give only about a dozen pages out of 750 to the subject shows his treatment of it is seriously inadequate. He wants to stress Christian experience, but it is not surprising that he dismisses much of the traditional doctrine when he considers the doctrine of the Trinity so little.

(c) *Albrecht Ritschl* (1822-1889) has often been associated with the nineteenth-century liberalism that reached its climax in Harnack. But James Richmond and others have more recently protested that this categorization is an oversimplification. Pannenberg's work on Ritschl's Christology, for example, shows that "those who have been taught to regard him as a 'typical' nineteenth century 'liberal Protestant' . . . would be severely shocked if they open-mindedly examined his christological texts" (Richmond, *Ritschl* [London and New York: Collins, 1978], 168). This may be correct, but R. S. Franks rightly comments, "Ritschl here occupies a middle position between Schleiermacher and older Protestant theology" (*The Work of Christ*, 630). Like Schleiermacher's, his theology is immanental, in contrast, for example, to that of I. A. Dorner (1809-1884). On the other side, he more clearly takes account of biblical material than Schleiermacher. But in the end, his conclusions are closer to those of Abelard than to those of Anselm. That all these points are correct can be seen by examining his work on the kingdom of God, especially in the light of N. Perrin's comments. On one side, Perrin argues, the kingdom of God is central in Ritschl's theology. On the other hand, he conceives of the kingdom "in purely ethical terms . . . [as] the moral task to be carried out by the human race," and, like Schleiermacher, understands it in communal terms (*The Kingdom of God in the Teaching of Jesus* [London: SCM, 1963], 15-16).

Ritschl's theology of the work of Christ finds expression in the third volume of his *Christian Doctrine of Justification and Reconciliation* (Clifton, N.J.: Reference Book Publishers, 1966; Ger. 1870-1874). He first states that Christ is the perfect revealer of God, who also manifests his Lordship over the world. Next, he sees Christ's atoning work as part of his vocation. Thus the person and work of Christ are rightly interrelated. Christ's vocation is to establish the kingdom of God, which finds expression in his prophetic, priestly, and especially kingly work (428-29). His sufferings are part of his vocation, but his work is fundamentally ethical. His violent death occurred in the service of his ethical work (448-49). The sufferings of Christ are not "punishment," but a result of his faithfulness to his vocation. As priest, the role of Christ is mainly as representative of the community. Christ is founder of God's kingdom, not the bearer of vicarious punishment. Like Abelard, Ritschl sees forgiveness as springing primarily from God's will as an expression of his love. The primary object of forgiveness is the community.

(d) *From Ritschl to Barth.* In very general terms, historical theology provided no striking or creative breakthrough until the recent era of Gunton, Moltmann, and "nonviolent" theories of the atonement. Yet the controversies of modernity are not surprising. Already in the eighteenth century, Joseph Butler, bishop of Durham (1692-1752), had accepted the sacrificial notion of the atonement but also believed that the biblical writers offered no clear explanation of it, certainly not one acceptable to the rationalistic eighteenth century. The American Congregational minister *Horace Bushnell* (1802-1876) stood broadly in the liberal tradition, and advocated what he called "progressive orthodoxy." He aimed to transcend both rationalism and orthodoxy, and was influenced by Schleiermacher and S. T. Coleridge. In his work *The Vicarious Sacrifice* (1866), he in effect reproduced the theory of moral influence in Abelard, but through metaphor and analogy explored the capacity of love to suffer vicariously on behalf of the loved one. A mother, for example, may often suffer for the sake of her child. He excluded any notion of legal language. The incarnation and suffering of Christ bring about a new kind of power in the world. God, he argued, also suffers on account of evil. He rejected the notion of God's "abhorrence" of sin, asking, "To what in the transaction of the cross can God's abhorrence, by any possibility, fasten itself?" (399). The sacrifices of the OT constitute only figures or analogies for what are mysteries. In some ways he anticipated Bultmann's later objections to "objectification."

Robert W. Dale (1829-1895), the English Congregationalist, engaged with Bushnell in his book *The Atonement* (1875). He argued that Bushnell had not been "objective" enough, but also wrote in the more liberal tradition of Coleridge and F. D. Maurice. He nevertheless argued that the wrath of God is real. Yet, like Bushnell, he saw ransom, vicarious suffering, and propitiation as metaphors. Like Butler, he did not doubt the objective fact of the atonement, but showed caution about precise explanations.

By contrast, *James Denney* (1856-1917) was educated in the Free Church of Scotland at Glasgow, and in his book *The Death of Christ* (London: Hodder and Stoughton, 1911; rev. ed. 1951 and 1997) expounds an orthodox doctrine of the atonement, which focuses on the NT. In effect, it constitutes an exegetical survey of the Synoptic Gospels (11-59), the earliest preaching (61-107), the Pauline Epistles (108-203), and Hebrews and John (204-80). He writes, "Christ is not an instrument, but the agent, of the Father in all that he does" (125). The death of Christ springs from the love of God, and Paul "relates it essentially to sin" (126). Explicitly he states, "Something is done which enables God to justify the ungodly who believe in Jesus and at the same time to appear signally and conspicuously a righteous God" (167). He admits, "This is not the way in which St. Paul's gospel is usually presented now" (179). But he insists that the death of Christ was both penal and substitutionary.

Meanwhile, however, even the notion of "sacrifice" became less widely acceptable, except in traditional Roman Catholicism, where it was integral to eucharistic theology. Some confessed to skepticism about sacrifice in the light of the slaughter in the First World War, while Adolf Hitler later extensively used sacrificial imagery to prepare for the Second World War. Strictly in terms of chronology, we ought next to mention Gustaf Aulén, but we allocate him to the next section (e) for his distinctive work.

Karl Barth (1886-1968) remained forthright in his orthodoxy on this subject. In his *Church Dogmatics* IV/1, section 59, 2, he speaks of "the judge judged in our place" (211-83). He discusses here how God is "for us" (214). "The Son of God exists with man and as man in this fallen and perishing state" (215). We see the "self-humiliation of God in His Son." This is through his solidarity with us. A key moment is the cry of Jesus on the cross: "My God, my God, why have you forsaken me?" (Mark 15:34). "'Jesus Christ for us' means that . . . this one true man Jesus Christ has taken the place of us men . . . in order to act in our name . . . in all matters of reconciliation with God and . . . our redemption and salvation, representing us without any co-operation on our part" (230). He is "our Representative and Substitute" (230). Christ "took our place" (231). "In this suffering and dying of God Himself in His Son, there took place reconciliation with God. . . . The world is not itself capable of this reconciliation. Man cannot convert himself. . . . He fulfils His judgment on us all, but fulfils it in this way — God Himself is for us" (250-51).

Emil Brunner (1889-1966), Barth's Swiss associate, published his main work on the atonement in *The Mediator* (London: Lutterworth, 1934; Ger. 1927 and 1932). He repeats the basic position of Calvin and Reformed theology. He refuses to regard legal and forensic terms as optional explanations. He writes, "The law is the backbone, the skeleton; the granite foundation of the world of thought" (458). Sin includes the violation of the law, and this is the presupposition of the atonement. This is not dispensable, he urges, because it is part of God's revelation. The atonement overcomes "a wholly personal wrong relationship between God and man" (515). He adds: "Reconciliation presupposes enmity between two parties" (516). Without the work of Christ, this enmity would remain two-sided, both on God's part and on humankind's; it includes "enmity on the side of God" (518). The atonement has an "objective character," but also a subjective one (522). Objectively "sin is covered"; subjectively this is appropriated by faith; both "set things right" (522-35).

(e) The Swedish theologian *Gustaf Aulén* (1879-1977) produced what has become a classic work on the atonement entitled *Christus Victor* (London: SPCK, 1931), based on lectures delivered in Uppsala in 1930. He subtitled his book *A Historical Study of the Three Main Types of the Idea of the Atonement*. The three main types are the tradition of Anselm, "the objective" approach; that of Abelard, the "subjective" view; and what Aulén calls "the classic view" of the Church Fathers and the NT, namely, the idea of Christ as victor over evil forces and reconciliation with God. This has as its central theme, he writes, "the Atonement as a Divine conflict and victory" (20). In this "dramatic" view, reconciliation is "from first to last a work of God Himself, a *continuous* Divine work" (21). He claims that theologians have confused this "classic" and "dramatic" idea of the atonement with Anselm's "Latin" view. Admittedly these two views share some common imagery, such as "substitution" and "sacrifice," and both oppose the subjective and exemplarist view of Abelard. But he claims that the two views are not the same, and claims that Luther mainly held the "classic" view.

Aulén rejects both a conservative obsession with Anselm and a liberal reductionist view of the classic imagery as mythology. The eighteenth- and nineteenth-century liberals, he urged, overreacted against dualism. He approved of the "deification" formula: "Christ became man that we might be made divine" (34). But this is an insufficient explanation of the atonement. As Irenaeus also declared, Christ came "that He might destroy sin, overcome death, and give life to men" (35; and Irenaeus, *Against Heresies* 3.18.7). Divine victory over evil "stands in the centre of Irenaeus' thought" (37), and is part of his idea of "recapitulation" and restoration. The Eastern Orthodox Church has consistently held this view. But the victory is "not by violence," and "without any infringement of justice" (43). Aulén does affirm the centrality of sacrifice, which has relation "both to God and the powers of evil" (47). In Christ, God "overcomes the tyrants which hold man in bondage" (50). God is both Reconciler and the Reconciled.

Aulén claims that as well as Irenaeus, the Church Fathers Origen, Athanasius, Basil, Gregory of Nyssa, Gregory of Nazianzus, Cyril of Alexandria, Cyril of Jerusalem, and Chrysostom all held fast to this approach. He also argues that, among the Western Fathers, Ambrose, Augustine, and Leo the Great shared this same view. Although he sees Anselm as offering a "Latin" approach, he credits him with "having overcome the idea of a transaction with the devil, as well as the grotesque idea of a deception of the devil" (63). He then points out that in the NT Paul describes "objective powers of evil, namely . . . 'flesh,' sin, the Law, death" (81). He also alludes to demonic powers (1 Cor. 2:6; cf. Col. 2:15). "Ransom" certainly appears in the Synoptic Gospels (Mark 10:45), as well as in the Epistles (Eph. 1:7; 1 Tim. 2:6; Heb. 9:12; 1 Pet. 1:18).

In his survey of the Middle Ages and the Reformation, Aulén sees issues of value in Anselm and Abelard, but his main point is to claim the dominance of the "classic" approach in Luther. He writes, "Though Luther returns to the classic type, and teaches it with unique power, post-Reformation theology goes back to the Latin type" (160). Nowadays, he writes, the classic approach has "dropped almost out of sight" (161). Again, Aulén laments the perhaps unintended consequence of the Enlightenment and the more deliberate consequences of liberalism.

Aulén has done much to restore the emphasis of the atonement as an act of God, which is both objective and subjective. The OT often depicts God and his hosts with the image of a victorious warrior. Luther certainly included much of the emphasis discussed by Aulén, but whether Aulén has overstated this, others must judge. Some would say that he has overpressed his case both about Luther and about the supposedly exclusive alternative of two of the approaches (see on Gunton, below). His exegesis is also open to question. But he has succeeded in other ways in bringing to view the liberal peril of simply making the sensibilities of the modern age the criterion of truth.

(vii) **Recent and Current Modern Writers.** We select here mainly Gunton in England and Moltmann in Germany, but we note other writers more briefly.

(a) *Leon Morris* (1914-2006) is a conservative evangelical Anglican writer in Melbourne, Australia, who produced three books on the atonement between 1955 and 1966. The first was *The Apostolic Preaching of the Cross* (London: Tyndale, 1955). This focused on redemption, covenant, propitiation, and reconciliation. Second, *The Cross in the New Testament* (Grand Rapids: Eerdmans, 1965) examines the Gospels, Paul, and other parts of the NT. Third, his brief *Glory in the Cross* (London: Hodder and Stoughton, 1966) offers a more popular account of the atonement. In effect, this re-presents a conservative and orthodox view. But he also seeks to guard against an overcrude exposition of this view. Following Donald Baillie and anticipated by Jürgen Moltmann, he insists that the initiative of this work is God's and laments that some conservatives "have unwittingly introduced division into the Godhead" as if Christ sought to "change the mind" of

God (*Glory in the Cross,* 46). In his more scholarly *Apostolic Preaching of the Cross,* he carefully traces the covenant background in the OT, including the theme that "the sprinkling of the blood had a purifying effect" (71). He firmly retains the meaning of the Greek *hilastērion* as "propitiation," arguing, "More than expiation is required, for to speak of expiation is to deal in sub-personal categories" (169).

(b) **Colin Gunton** (1941-2003) was professor of Christian doctrine at King's College, London, and a minister of the United Reformed Church. He was awarded honorary doctorates from London, Aberdeen, and Oxford. He published *The Actuality of Atonement* (Edinburgh: T. & T. Clark, 1988), with the subtitle *A Study of Metaphor, Rationality, and the Christian Tradition,* among about seventeen other books. His book achieves two goals: it shows that the various theories of, or approaches to, the atonement are complementary, not exclusive alternatives; and it traces the power, function, value, and limitations of metaphor among images of the atonement. He laments "the intellectual and cultural poverty that remains so much a feature of our age" (*Actuality,* 1). He sees Kant, Schleiermacher, and Hegel as indirectly largely responsible for this in theology, in spite of some definite insights. He blames the Enlightenment more generally. In particular he laments the effect of Hegel's distinction between "concepts" *(Begriffe),* which convey tested cognitive truth, especially in philosophy, and "images" *(Vorstellungen),* which convey largely precognitive "pictures" especially in religion. Gunton's book "is designed to demonstrate the opposite: that metaphor above all is an indispensable means for the advance of cognitive knowledge and understanding" (17). Nevertheless, Hegel does convey elements of Christian tradition, for example, that the atonement involves "the removal of opposition and estrangement between God and humankind" (19).

The second chapter of Gunton's *Actuality of Atonement* addresses the role of metaphor. He cites P. Ricoeur as lamenting "the view of metaphor as an abuse of language" in the Age of Reason (29). On the contrary, advances in physics occurred partly through the use of metaphor, for example, in the metaphorical use of "field" and even "machine," and he cites the work of Ingolf Dalferth on linguistic change through metaphor in his *Religiöse Rede von Gott* (1981). Further, he appeals to Richard Boyd and his "Metaphor and Theory Change" (1979) for the view that "new language and discovery happen together, with metaphor serving as the *vehicle* of discovery" (31). He also appeals to the work of Janet Martin Soskice, Eberhard Jüngel, and Ricoeur (and later, G. B. Caird) for the use of metaphor to convey truth in theology. He also cites Coleridge for the claims that metaphor is necessary for creative thought, even though the relation between thought and language is sometimes "indirect" (37). He concludes this second chapter with the claim that "atonement metaphor is particularly well suited to show that language takes shape in a kind of conversation" (48). This is no confrontation between two or three exclusive alternative views, but a conversation in which each party conveys an insight. Indeed, "metaphor" can have "a revelatory function" (51).

In his third chapter Gunton looks especially at Aulén's "victory" theme, even though it was formulated around 1930. Is Aulén correct in juxtaposing "legal" imagery against his "dramatic" image of conflict and victory? Gunton challenged the notion that Aulén's approach is as comprehensive and decisive as Aulén believed. He also advocated "too triumphalist a view of the atonement" (58). What is correct is that "There is, then, in the Bible, much encouragement for those who wish to see the metaphor of victory used in connexion with God's saving activity." Nevertheless, "we do not find the basis for a *theory* of the atonement, particularly if such a theory is opposed to other supposed alternatives" (61). One of several problems was "an increasing tendency to personify the devil as an individual being defeated by Christ on the cross" (62), as we see in Gregory of Nyssa. Caird rightly speaks of "political, social, economic, and religious structures of power" (65), and "the language of possession by demonic forces, then, is used to express the helplessness of human agents in the face of psychological, social, and cosmic forces in various combinations" (70). To speak of the victory of the cross is "to use metaphor in a bold way" (77).

Gunton's fourth chapter turns to the justice of God, and to Anselm's account of atonement. Whereas many simply criticize Anselm for borrowing an inadequate image from medieval feudal law, the opposite, Gunton suggests, is the case. In his time, "It was the duty of the feudal ruler to maintain the order of rights and obligations without which society would collapse. Anselm's God is understood to operate *analogously* for the *universe as a whole;* as upholder of universal justice" (89, second italics added). Anselm sees the atonement not only as a matter of God's love, but also as "some objective righting of the balance" in the universe (91). The concept of justice and divine government cannot simply be brushed aside. Gunton appeals to Hans Urs von Balthasar for support, and earlier to P. T. Forsyth in England. Forsyth argued for "the conceptual compatibility of God's omnipotence and goodness, which demonstrates his justice" (106). Then he refers to the section in Barth's *Church Dogmatics* that we considered above. Gunton writes: "Barth argues that God exercises his function of judgment by taking to himself 'the lost cause of man'" (110). We might see some parallels with Isaiah's legal concern for the cause of Israel. Gunton convincingly concludes, "Anselm, Luther, Forsyth and Barth have in common" this general approach, despite differences in how "they 'cash' the central metaphor" (112).

Gunton rightly attempts to rescue "sacrifice" from being regarded as an outworn "dead" metaphor in his fifth chapter. He addresses various arguments about sacrifice from Frances Young and Mary Douglas, and examines the roles of sacrifice in the OT. He describes the notion of Jesus and his death as a sacrifice as "the dominant" NT metaphor (123). It concerns the heart of the human condition and signals "a real change in human relationship to God" (127). Admittedly the theme can be crudely expressed, and Edward Irving showed how it need not involve a "profit-and-loss" or "stock-exchange" theology (133). In Calvin, too, it is bound up with the high priesthood of Christ, as it is in Hebrews. Gunton concludes this chapter with a quotation from the very early *Epistle to Diognetus* that begins, "O sweetest exchange! . . . The sinfulness of many is hidden within the Righteous One, while the righteousness of the One justifies the many who are sinners" (9.5; *Actuality*, 140).

Finally, Gunton examines the themes in relation to the Holy Trinity (chap. 6) and the church as the community of reconciliation (chap. 7). The three major personal metaphors of the atonement are complementary, not exclusive alternatives. This is *not* to deny that the "subjective" theories, in Donald MacKinnon's words, "trivialize evil" (159). Nor should we reduce atonement to mere "legal fiction." But representation and substitution, Gunton urges, "form the basis and framework of an account of the divine initiative" (160). The victory theme has its place, for there is nothing intractable in the way of liberation. Further, "the metaphor of justice derives . . . from a broader conception of life . . . than the merely legal or forensic" (161). Again P. T. Forsyth, Gunton urges, was correct to argue that the atonement is the fruit not only of God's love, but of his *holy* love. The Son of God "allows the consequences of human evil to fall upon his head" (161). In sum, Jesus is "our substitute because he does for us what we cannot do for ourselves" (165). This is precisely the starting point that I suggested. Finally, as D. Baillie has urged, the atonement springs from the love of *God* in Christ, and it remains a word that concerns not only the individual but also the community, or the world. It is difficult to find better or saner expositions than Gunton's.

(c) *Jürgen Moltmann* (b. 1926) writes on the atonement in many of his numerous and impressive works. However, the three most directly relevant are probably *The Crucified God* (London: SCM, 1974), *The Trinity and the Kingdom of God* (London: SCM, 1981), and *The Way of Jesus Christ* (London: SCM, 1990). In *The Crucified God* Moltmann laments that "we have surrounded the scandal of the cross with roses," whereas in fact it relates to humiliation, contradiction, and nothingness (36). He urges, "The 'religion' of the cross is a contradiction in itself" suggesting leaving behind "religious traditions" (40). In this earlier work there is some continuity with liberation theology. Moltmann writes that "the poor . . . find in him [Christ] the brother who put off his divine form and took on the form of a slave (Phil. 2:6-11) to be with them and to love them" (49). To suffer and to be rejected signified the cross. As many liberation theologians urge, "The assimilation of Christianity to bourgeois society always means that the cross is forgotten and hope is lost" (58). Moltmann explicitly states, "Jesus died, whether rightly or wrongly, a political death as a rebel, on the cross" (69). The cross is no different from his life, which involved hostility and opposition.

Perhaps Moltmann's most distinctive contribution is to ask: *"What does the cross of Jesus mean for God himself?"* (201). He considers Barth and Jüngel on "the death of the living God." In particular Moltmann appeals to Luther's concept of "the cross of the outcast and forsaken Christ" as "the visible revelation of God's being for man" (208), and refers to his *theologia crucis* in the Heidelberg Disputation of 1518. For Luther, "this visible being of God is the passion and cross of Christ" (212). He also follows Bonhoeffer. He writes, "God allows himself to be forced out. God suffers, God allows himself to be crucified and is crucified, and in this consummates his unconditional love" (248). Finally he quotes Hegel: "The death of Christ is the death of this death itself, the negation of the negation"; he adds that God's forsakenness "is lifted away from him in the forsakenness of Christ" (254).

This is developed and amplified in *The Trinity and the Kingdom of God*. At its heart stands the principle "A God who cannot suffer cannot love either; A God who cannot suffer is a dead God" (38). The cross becomes God's deliverance of himself. Post-Enlightenment liberal Protestantism can hardly conceive of such supposedly mythological language. It is utterly anthropocentric. By contrast Moltmann declares, "The New Testament talks about God by proclaiming in narrative the relationship of the Father, the Son and the Spirit" (64; *see* **God, Trinity**). On the cross and in Gethsemane Jesus faces "fear of separation from the Father, horror in the face of 'the death of God' " (76). Moltmann adds, "Abandonment by God is 'the cup.' . . . The Father withdraws; God is silent" (77). Hence: "the Father suffers the death of the Son; so the pain of the Father corresponds to the death of the Son. . . . The innermost life of the Trinity is at stake" (81). As in creation, all persons of the Trinity are actively involved. Even the incarnation is "an intra-Trinitarian process" (118). Much of the rest of this book is concerned with developing formulations of the Holy Trinity.

The Way of Jesus Christ traces the growth of the messianic hope in the OT and in Jewish-Christian dialogue. Again Moltmann rejects "the turn to anthropology" (38). Christology presupposes faith in Christ. But anthropological Christology is "simply Jesusology" (55; *see* **Christology: History of Thought**). We need, he argues, to trace Jesus' history with God or "the Trinitarian history of the Father, the Son, and the Spirit" (17). Moltmann takes up again the theme of the new creation of "the poor . . . the hungry, the unemployed, the sick, the discouraged . . . oppressed and humiliated people" (99). Jesus dies "the death of God's child" (165). The Gethsemane narrative includes "the frightening eclipse of God." Again, we find here echoes of Luther. Yet the modern theme also finds a place: "Jesus died the death of a poor man" (168). It was both his own death and a death for others. Moltmann insists on the unique character of faith in the resurrection of Christ. What is "historically provable" emerges "from the assertion of the women . . . at his empty tomb" (216). On the basis of the whole redeeming event, we enter a new age of the "free history of the Spirit" (208). Clearly within the modern era both Colin Gunton and Jürgen Moltmann have produced distinctive and solid reinterpretations of the atonement that deserve to be considered very seriously. We might suggest other theologians also, but a line must be drawn somewhere. As a postscript, we may note an approach that has emerged only in the early twenty-first century.

(d) *"Nonviolent" Approaches to the Atonement: J. D. Weaver.* J. Denny Weaver published *The Nonviolent Atonement* (Grand Rapids: Eerdmans, 2001, 2011). He is a Mennonite who teaches religion at Bluffton College, Ohio. As a Mennonite he draws some inspiration from J. H. Yoder, but also admits that his concern has been sparked by feminist and womanist writers and by African American and contextual theologies. His main targets are Anselm's "satisfaction" theory and the Reformers' emphasis on penal substitution. Instead he seeks to present a "narrative" version of Aulén's "victory" approach in a nonviolent way (7). He seems to avoid discussion with Catholics by regarding the Eucharist as the Catholic route to grace, reconciliation, and atonement (2). But this overlooks the approach to the atonement in which the sacraments are believed to be based. The further target, especially in America, is "retributive" justice, that is, the idea that "to do justice" means primarily to punish the criminal perpetrator (2-3). Weaver cites other "nonviolent" approaches, including those of René Girard and the feminists Joanne Carlson Brown and Rebecca Parker. His general appeal is to "black, feminist, and womanist theologies" (5).

Weaver points to Jesus' life and teaching on nonviolence as "generally, if not universally, accepted" (13). The church, it is claimed, tends to marginalize this, as Yoder's *Politics of Jesus* (2nd ed. 1993) argued. We need not repeat Aulén's contentions, considered above. We may note, however, that Gunton's trenchant criticisms seem to be ignored. The "classic" theory is primarily seen as one that achieved freedom. Weaver attacks "penal suffering" as he finds it in Anselm, Luther, and Calvin. Abelard's theory receives much attention, and the history of the theology of the atonement is seen largely as a debate between the traditions of Anselm and Abelard in theology (19-20). Indeed, one of the strongest sections of the book traces the "victory" motif in the book of Revelation. Weaver is correct to claim that "victory" in Revelation often denotes martyrdom, and that this is often by faithful witness, never by violence. The conqueror is "the slaughtered lamb, signifying the (non-violent) manner of the victory" (21). The victory song celebrates a kingdom and priests from people of all ethnic backgrounds, including the vignette of the 144,000 in chapter 7, which constitutes a symbolic number (21-22).

After examining Revelation, Weaver returns to the Gospels. Here, it is argued, "worldly rule" is contrasted with the reign of God, which is "not accomplished by violence" (37). In Matt. 26:55 Jesus rejects a sword, and in John 18:36 he stresses, "My kingdom is not from this world." Jesus shows the true nature of power. Weaver again cites the approach of Girard (48-51), before moving on to Paul. In Paul the defeat of the powers is "an apocalyptic event" (55). Here he especially appeals to Raymund Schwager and David Brondos. Predictably he rejects the notion of *hilastērion* as "propitiation" (67), before proceeding to consider sacrifice in the OT and in Hebrews. His conclusion is "how *completely outside history* satisfaction atonement is" (85, italics mine). In the following chapter Weaver rejects the notion that Jesus' violent death was caused or sanctioned by God. By contrast, in the traditional approach, he argues, "the divine economy has a need for a death penalty to balance the sin of humankind as a basis for restoring justice" (91). The rest of the book compares black, feminist, and womanist theology, with reference to specific writers.

The general reception of Weaver's book is broadly similar to how admirers and critics view liberation theology. On the positive side it is agreed that attention to narrative, apocalyptic, and other themes in biblical studies is helpful. Moreover, in an era when much child abuse seems to have surfaced, the book may address some contemporary problems. But the customary criticisms of some liberation theology are twofold: namely, that of generalization and selectivity. Some may query, for example, whether the traditional approaches move the atonement "completely outside history" (85). It cannot be said that Weaver presents the traditional approach with accuracy or with due concern to avoid crudities or to employ sensitivity. Worst of all, I cannot find significant references to such major modern exponents of more traditional theories as Gunton and Moltmann, while those known for "popular" critiques of traditional theories, such as Steve Chalke, seem to enjoy dedicated sections (305-6). Weaver largely repeats his argument in John Sanders, ed., *Atonement and Violence* (Nashville: Abingdon, 2006). Hans Boersma's "Response to J. Denny Weaver" in Sanders's book is noteworthy. (Boersma is the J. I. Packer Professor of Theology at Regent College, Vancouver.) Boersma laments the way in which allegedly "the entire Christian tradition has failed in its appropriation of the biblical witness," while Weaver solves "all the errors and problems" of a doctrine of the atonement (33). Classic atonement doctrine almost becomes "child abuse," while Moltmann's moving work on the suffering of God the Father seems to be completely ignored, as is Gunton's on complementary metaphors. The traditional approaches, Boersma replies, do not speak of "an abusive God who punishes his child as an innocent third party" (35). The status of Weaver's work is hardly decisive, with its exaggerated claims, and its failure to engage with much careful, current scholarship, even if it should be noted for many of its warnings.

Reading: Gustaf Aulén, *Christus Victor* (London: SPCK, 1931); D. M. Baillie, *God Was in Christ* (London: Faber, 1956); John Calvin, *Institutes of the Christian Religion*, trans. Henry Beveridge, 2 vols. (Grand Rapids: Eerdmans, 1989); R. S. Franks, *The Work of Christ* (London: Nelson, 1962); Colin E. Gunton, *The Actuality of Atonement* (Edinburgh: T. & T. Clark, 1988); Jürgen Moltmann, *The Crucified God* (London: SCM, 1974); Jürgen Moltmann, *The Way of Jesus Christ* (London: SCM, 1990); Adonis Vidu, *Atonement, Law, and Justice* (Grand Rapids: Baker Academic, 2014).

Atonement, Day of; see Day of Atonement

Attributes

At its broadest, an attribute simply constitutes a characteristic, feature, or trait, often ascribed to a person or object. In traditional theology people have long spoken of the attributes of God. But the term derives from Aristotle, who defined attributes as what characterize a substance, usually in terms of time, place, and relation. Hence, at one level we may speak of the holiness, wisdom, sovereignty, or omnipresence of God as his attributes. But at another level, an increasing number of modern theologians are reluctant to use the term of God. First, it appears to reduce God's transcendence or "otherness"; second, it may also seem to imply that God is a static object rather than an active, dynamic, ongoing presence, as the "living God" of the OT. Many maintain that it seems presumptuous to assign properties or attributes to the living, transcendent God. On the other hand, God remains God of the covenant, who is faithful to what he has revealed himself to be. In general, the term is not downright "wrong" but is ill-advised, and not the happiest term to use of God.

Augustine

Augustine of Hippo (354-430) remains probably the most influential of all patristic writers, at least in the Western Church. Not least because he has bequeathed to history more writings than any of the Church Fathers, including three hundred letters, five hundred sermons, and numerous doctrinal treatises. He drew on many, if not most, of the Church Fathers, especially on Gregory of Nazianzus, as well as thinkers in Latin Christianity from Tertullian to Ambrose, and transmitted these traditions to the medieval church, together with a central focus on Christ and the Scriptures. A. C. Outler comments, "A succinct characterisation of Augustine is impossible; mostly because his theology is so complex, partly because it is 'incurably digressive,' and partly because 'lively tensions' occur within it" (Introduction to *Augustine: Confessions and Enchiridion* [Philadelphia: Westminster; London, SCM, 1955], 14). He had no "system" except Scripture (13). Hence we shall follow J. McWilliam in dividing his writings into five types: (i) the anti-Manichaean writings; (ii) the anti-Donatist writings; (iii) the anti-Pelagian writings; (iv) the *City of God;* and (v) the less polemical writings, namely, *The Confessions, The Enchiridion,* and *On the Trinity*. This very broadly follows the scheme of P. Schaff, *NPNF*, ser. 1, vols. 1-5 (vols. 6-8 are biblical expositions).

Augustine's *Confessions* constitutes his spiritual autobiography seen from specific viewpoints. He was born in Thagaste, a small town in North Africa, the son of a devout Christian mother, Monica, but in his early years believed that Christianity was rationally unacceptable. He studied rhetoric in Carthage, and became a Manichaean. At first he thought that the Manichees were rationally acceptable, but became gradually disillusioned with their system. He taught rhetoric in Carthage and Rome, and was appointed to the imperial court in Milan. There he was greatly influenced by Ambrose, bishop of Milan, especially by his preaching. He tells us of his regard for Ambrose in *Confessions* 5.13.23, where he comments that Ambrose was "famed through the whole world as one of the best of men, thy devoted servant," and "his eloquent discourse" led him to God (H. Chadwick's translation). In *Confessions* 8.12.28-29, Augustine tells us also how, while crying in tears before God, he heard "the voice of a boy or girl . . . chanting over and over again, pick it up and read it" *(Tolle, lege)*. He found a Bible and opened it at Rom. 13:13: "Not in reveling and drunkenness . . . instead put on the Lord Jesus Christ, and make no provision for the flesh." Later convinced that three means of God's grace, namely, Ambrose, Paul in Rom. 13:13, and Monica's prayers, had been decisive for him, he came to Christian faith. He was baptized by Ambrose on Easter Eve 387. In 388-389 he returned to North Africa, and was ordained in 391 in a small coastal town. In 397 Augustine was ordained assistant bishop, and in 398 became bishop of Hippo, where he remained until his death.

(i) **The Anti-Manichaean Writings.** Augustine began to write his critique of the Manichaeans about six years after his conversion in August 392, and produced seven treatises over the years. Manichaeism seems to have arisen nearly 500 years before Christ in connection with Buddhism and Zoroastrianism. Much later Mani (c. A.D. 216-276) was born in Persia, and began teaching in 240. Opposition from Zoroastrians forced his initial flight to India before his return in 242. His teaching was fundamentally Gnostic and dualist based on a primeval conflict between light and darkness. Asceticism, he thought, could help facilitate a resolution. The influence of Manichaeism became great, and Augustine was held captive by it for nearly nine years. In *Confessions* 5.3 he speaks of Faustus the Manichaean teacher, who came to Carthage when Augustine was twenty-nine (5.3.3). "Many were entangled by him through the charm of his eloquence.... Even though I found this eloquence admirable, I was beginning to distinguish the charm of words from the truth of things" (5.3.3). Later he wrote of "two tricks: . . . one, that of finding fault with the scriptures . . . , the other, making 'show of chastity and of notable abstinence'" (*On the Morals of the Catholic Church* 1.2 [written in 388]).

From the beginning Augustine adressed Manichaean errors. He argued for the integrity of the OT and the NT (*On the Morals of the Catholic Church* 9.14), attacked the notion of "two Gods" (10.16 and 16.26), and urged the goal of love (11.18; 26.48; 16.29). Again, he returned to the authority of Scripture (29.59). He argued that the church is not to be blamed if some Christians have strayed (34.74). His second treatise (also written in 388) is *The Morals of the Manichaeans*. In chapter 8 he wrote, "Evil was not a substance" (8.11). In chapter 15 he described their asceticism as "superstition," in contrast to the Christian use of restrictions "to check indulgence" and "help the weak" (14.35; 15.36, 37). Again he appealed to "the authority of Scripture" (12.55). At Rome, he observed, many thought the Manichaean rule "intolerable, and left; not a few felt ashamed and stayed" (20.74). In his third treatise, *On Two Souls* (391), he argued that every soul derives its existence from God (1.1). Sin is "only from the will" (10.14). The fourth, *Against Fortunatus the Manichaean* (392), addressed the recipient's dualism. The fifth, *Against the Epistle of Manichaeus, Called "Foundations"* (397); sixth, *Reply to Faustus* (400); and seventh, *On the Nature of God* (403), continue in the same vein. *Reply to Faustus* is the most substantial (*NPNF*, ser. 1, 4:151-345). Faustus claims to be a Christian but rejects the incarnation of God and the OT. Augustine replied, "Had you read the Gospel with care . . . instead of rashly condemning [it], you would have seen that the recognition of the authority of the evangelists by so many learned men . . . proves that there is more in it than appears at first sight" (3.2). The main works, then, are early (388-400), but the Manichees never remained entirely in the past.

(ii) **The Anti-Donatist Writings** consist primarily of *On Baptism* (c. 400), but also include other letters, especially the *Correction of the Donatists* (also c. 400). The Donatist "pure church" movement not only held a rigorist view about the status of those who had "lapsed" under persecution, but also held a "pure" view of the status of ministers of the sacraments. They not only looked for "a pure church," like some of the more conservative Puritans and Pietists, but also questioned the validity of sacraments administered by clergy who themselves had lapsed and returned. In *On Baptism* Augustine envisaged an extreme case. "If Marcion consecrated the sacrament of baptism with the words of the gospel, 'In the name of the Father, and of the Son, and of the Holy Ghost' [Matt. 28:19], the sacrament was complete" (3.15; *NPNF*, ser. 1, 4:442). The same would apply to "Valentinius, Arius, or Eunomius." This had always been the case, since the earliest days of the church (chap. 16). What is important, Augustine argued, "is the especial gift of the Catholic unity" (chap. 16). In practice both Donatists and Catholics tried to appeal to Cyprian. Augustine points out that for Cyprian unity could not be disrupted. The Donatist rigorists had become especially influential in Carthage and North Africa, and had received support from Tyconius and Novatian. But Augustine's work on the validity of sacraments, whoever the minister, became decisive for the church. The one problem Augustine left, however, was whether this might imply an *opus operatum* view of the sacraments (*see* **Donatism**).

(iii) **The Anti-Pelagian Writings** occupy a full volume in *NPNF* (ser. 1, vol. 5). The best known include *On the Spirit and the Letter* (c. 412), *On Nature and Grace* (c. 415), *On Grace and Free Will* (c. 427), and *On the Predestination of the Saints* (c. 428). Augustine first intervened with a sermon, stressing that grace must *precede* all good desires or good acts in human beings. He coined the term "prevenient grace" or "preventing grace." He wrote "[The Lord] anticipates us that we may be healed. . . . He anticipates us that we may be called. . . . He anticipates us that we may lead godly lives" (*On Nature and Grace* 35.31; *NPNF*, ser. 1, 5:133; *see also* **Pelagius**). His friend at Rome, the tribune Marcellinus, who was then secretary of state, wrote to him to express his concern about Pelagius in Rome. In reply Augustine wrote *On the Merits and Remission of Sins*, and *On the Baptism of Infants* (412) in three books, the first of the "anti-Pelagian" writings. He first attacks Pelagius's view that Adam would have died even if he had never sinned, and that his sin is not transmitted to his posterity. He cites Gen. 2:17, "In the day that you eat of it you shall die" (chap. 2), and a range of scriptural passages. He distinguishes between *mortale*, "capable of death"; *mortuum*, "dead"; and *moriturus*, "destined to die" (chap. 5). In chapter 10 he quotes Rom 5:12, with the notorious Latin *in quo*, "in whom," in place of the Greek *eph' hō*, "in that all die" (*NPNF*, 5:19; although few defend his meaning today). A climax comes in chapter 19: "All" are sinners through Adam, but "all" are just through Christ (Rom. 5:18). He explains, "As none partakes of carnal generation except through Adam, so no one shares in the spiritual except through Christ" (19.15).

The next section of the three books addresses infant baptism. Pelagius argued that if baptism effaced "original sin," the children of baptized parents could not be born in sin. Augustine argued that "death reigns" since Adam, since all share in Adam's sin. This is not simply by example, as Caelestius claimed, and infant baptism, Augustine insisted, is the practice of the Catholic Church (chaps. 22–23). Infants "in a certain sense profess faith by the words of their parents" (chap. 25; *NPNF,* 5:24). Why some are saved and others are not is "inscrutable" (chap. 29): "O the depth of the riches and wisdom and knowledge of God!" (Rom. 11:33; chap. 29). Augustine then cites numerous passages from Romans, 1 Corinthians, Galatians, Ephesians, and Colossians on the universality of sin (chaps. 43–51). Against excessive asceticism, he also argues for the good of marriage (chap. 57), and returns again to the baptism of infants (chap. 58). Books 2 and 3 develop the same themes.

Augustine continues to reply to Marcellinus the same year (412) in *On the Spirit and the Letter.* Without the Spirit, he argues, the Law is simply "the letter [that] kills" (2 Cor. 3:6; *On the Spirit* 6.4; *NPNF,* 5:85). Augustine's chief point is that the Law is unable to check or conquer sin. On the contrary, through the Law sin "has abounded," even though "grace did much more abound" (9.6; Rom. 5:20-21). He compares the "law of works" and "the law of faith" (21.13). He concludes that no person is justified by works (chap. 22). The Law can be fulfilled only in the promise of Christ: "grace was given, in order that the law might be fulfilled" (chap. 34). Augustine expounds, in effect, Paul on faith and works, or on grace and Law. Under the Law "each has discovered his own weakness ... not by his own strength ... but by faith the Justifier" gives life (chap. 51; *NPNF,* 5:105). The treatise *On Nature and Grace* sharpens the contrast further and mentions Pelagius explicitly. If a person can choose to live righteously, Augustine argues, "faith in Christ" becomes unnecessary (chap. 2). A person's sin is his own, but such a one needs grace and Christ for his care (chap. 34). The epoch making of Augustine's claims and the fallenness and bondage to sin of humankind are difficult to overstate. W. Pannenberg comments, "The classical significance for the Christian doctrine of sin consists in the fact that he viewed and analyzed the Pauline link between sin and desire more deeply than Christian theology had hitherto managed to do. The many aspects of his teaching that call for criticism should not blind us to this extraordinary achievement" (*ST* 2:241).

(iv) ***The City of God*** **(413-426) gives us Augustine's philosophy of history.** It was occasioned by the fall of Rome to the Goths in 410. Pelagius was one of many who fled Rome, and many fled to North Africa. The two "cities" are the city of God and that of humankind. Augustine did not identify the city of God with the earthly, visible church. Further, many pagans were blaming the tragedy on Christian denials of the deities of Rome. Augustine's work constitutes partly an answer to this, but is much more. P. Schaff calls it "the first attempt at a philosophy of history under the aspect of ... the eternal city of God and the perishing city of the world," and a "masterpiece of great genius ... most read of all his works except the 'Confessions'" (*NPNF,* ser. 1, 2:v).

Augustine begins *City of God* by considering pagan charges of causing the fall of Rome as "a stranger in the midst of the ungodly" (preface). The cruelties imposed upon Rome by the Goths accorded with the customs of war (1.7). Yet we cannot explain every human action: "No one knows the things of man, save the spirit of man in him" (1.25; cf. 1 Cor. 2:11). Christianity offers some restraint (1.30). Indeed, it is because of Christ that some sanctuaries were safe (2.2). The life of the Roman Republic was often corrupt, and its deities even worse (2.5-15). Whatever life brings depends on the will of the true God (2.23). Roman history involves cruelty and suffering (3.15-31); yet the long history of Rome depends on God (books 4-5). Moreover, many in the empire, such as Constantine, chose to pursue good (5.25). The Roman deities cannot give eternal life (book 7). To Christ alone belongs the gift of eternal blessedness (book 9). Augustine attacks Porphyry's modifications of Platonism (10.26-32). Book 11 reaches the heart of the matter: the history of destiny of each of the two cities is compared, like light and darkness (11.19-21). Book 12 considers the nature of good and bad angels. Books 13 and 14 explore Adam's sin, including "eternal and everlasting punishment" (13.2). Books 15, 16, and 17 look at biblical history, while 18 traces the parallel but different causes of the two cities, and 19 portrays the end of the two cities. 20.17 expounds the endless glory of the church; book 20 concerns the Last Judgment and resurrection. Augustine describes the end of "the city of the devil" (book 21) and the end of "the city of God" (22).

(v) **The *Confessions*, the *Enchiridion*, and *On the Trinity*.** Terence Tilly's contention that Augustine's works are largely polemical tends to break down in at least three or more cases (*see* **Evil, Problem of**). We could add to this nonpolemical section *On Christian Doctrine* and other works. *The Confessions* constitutes Augustine's spiritual autobiography, albeit from given perspectives, although A. C. Outler emphasizes its theological selectivity. Book 1 recounts how Augustine owes his life to God, and tells of his failure in his early years to love God. Indeed, as a young child, he writes, "I used to be indignant with my seniors for their disobedience . . . to my interests" (1.8; H. Chadwick's translation). As he grew older, "I in my misery seethed and followed the driving force of my impulses" (2.4), and at sixteen, "I stole something which I had in plenty . . . merely for the excitement of thieving and doing what was wrong" (2.4.9). The allusion is to the famous theft of pears, but the deeper purpose is to show human depths of sin. Book 4 recalls his seduction by Manichaeism, and his search for sexual gratification. By 5.2.2 he has come to Milan and heard Ambrose. Book 8 tells of his conversion. 8.2 tells of his inquiries to Simplicianus, "the spiritual father of Ambrose," and 8.12 tells the story of *Tolle, lege,* which brought him to examine Rom. 13:13. 9.11.28 and 12.28 tell of the death of his mother Monica. Book 11 reflects on time and eternity. But none of this can indicate the yearning and passion of Augustine's prayers or his deep communion with God, which mark every page.

The *Enchiridion* (c. 421) is a brief handbook to theology, which majors on the grace of God. Augustine wrote it in response to a request from Laurentius for a "handbook" that would sum up Christian doctrine. The framework is broadly that of the creed and the Lord's Prayer. Thus chapter 3 concerns God the creator of all; 4 digresses into the problem of evil; 7 concerns the limits of knowledge; 8, the plight of humankind after the Fall; 11, the incarnation; 12, the Holy Spirit; 13, baptism and "original sin"; 14, justification; 16 and 17 concern the church; 18, faith and works; and 23, the resurrection.

It is often said that Augustine's deepest thought can be found in *On the Trinity* (c. 400-424). In the West Hilary and Ambrose had laid out the ground, and in the East Athanasius and the Cappadocian Fathers had done the same. Augustine drew especially on Gregory of Nazianzus, but his anthropological analogy of memory, understanding, and the will (*On the Trinity* 10) remains distinctively his. Whether it is constructive remains open to question, for it rests on anthropological analogy, even if Augustine would claim more. He is more convincing on the rationality of "one" and "three," and on the mutuality of Father, Son, and Spirit (*see* **God, Trinity**).

Augustine also wrote numerous commentaries, not least on John and the Psalms, and much of his distinctive theology can also be found here. For example, he appreciates the christological focus of John. These, together with his letters, must be included as sources for his theology.

Reading: Augustine, *Confessions*, trans. H. Chadwick (Oxford: OUP, 1991); L. Ayres, *Augustine and the Trinity* (Cambridge: CUP, 2010); P. Brown, *Augustine: A Biography* (Berkeley: University of California Press, 2000); M. T. Clark, *Augustine* (London: Chapman, 1994); C. Harrison, *Augustine* (Oxford: OUP, 2000); *NPNF*, ser. 1, vols. 1-8; J. van Cort, ed., *Augustine and Manichaean Christianity* (Leiden: Brill, 2013).

Aulén, Gustaf

Gustaf Aulén (1879-1977) was professor in the University of Lund in 1913, and from 1933 to 1952 was bishop of Strängnäs in the Swedish Lutheran Church. He wrote *The Faith of the Christian Church* (1923; Eng. 1948), *Jesus in Contemporary Historical Research* (Eng. 1976), and other works, but his most famous and influential book was *Christus Victor* (Swedish 1930; Eng. 1931). He subtitled this: *A Historical Study of the Three Main Types of the Idea of the Atonement*.

Aulén begins his book with the argument that the last two centuries have, in effect, reduced three types of atonement theory to two, namely, the "objective" account of Anselm and the medieval West (the "Latin" view) and the "subjective" view, represented by Abelard, Socinianism, Schleiermacher, and the period of the Enlightenment. He proposes that his own view, the "dramatic," which stresses divine conflict and victory, should be regarded as the "classic" view of the Church Fathers. Humankind is under bondage to, and suffering at the hands of, "tyrants" or "powers," but God overcomes this bondage by an act of atonement, which is his own work (*Christus Victor*, 17-23). In the course of history, theologians confuse this "classic" view with the "Latin" view; both orthodox and liberal theologians have tended to ignore this classic view. In particular, liberal theologians have dismissed what they regard as grotesque imagery of Christ's victory over the devil as mythological. Moreover, in the eighteenth and nineteenth centuries, liberal theology regarded it as "dualist," and a "sidetrack" (23-31).

Aulén's next move is to recover the dramatic doctrine as he finds it in Irenaeus. He stresses that in the incarnation "Christ became man that we might be made divine" (34). The purpose of the incarnation was to destroy sin, overcome death, and give life to men (Irenaeus, *Against Heresies* 3.18.7; *Christus Victor,* 35). In addition to the theme of "recapitulation," which stresses restoration, Irenaeus emphasizes the victory of God over enemies that had held humanity in bondage, especially to sin and death. Hostile powers used violence to gain dominion, but they cannot be granted "rights over men" (43). God himself makes the sacrifice, but the sacrifice of Christ is also offered to God. God is both active and passive (47). Aulén finds similar themes in Origen, Athanasius, Basil the Great, Gregory of Nyssa, Gregory of Nazianzus, Cyril of Jerusalem, and Chrysostom. He also claims to find them in Ambrose and Augustine (52-76). On the other hand, he criticizes Gregory of Nyssa for implying that "the devil had acquired rights over mankind through the Fall" (64). The basic intention behind the imagery is to establish the guilt of humankind.

In Paul, the "powers of evil" take the form of the flesh, sin, the Law, and death (Romans 5–8). Sometimes Paul speaks of demons, and of principalities and powers, as in 1 Cor. 2:6, 15:26, and Gal. 1:4. "Christ's victory over the demonic powers is of primary importance" (*Christus Victor,* 85-86; cf. Col. 1:15). In the Synoptic Gospels "the Son of Man came ... to give his life a ransom for many" (Mark 10:45; *Christus Victor,* 89). "Redemption" occurs in 1 Tim. 2:6, Eph. 1:7, Heb. 9:12, and 1 Pet. 1:18 (*see* **Redeem, Redemption**). Aulén might have included the references to God as victorious warrior in the OT (Isaiah 59), where "redeem" (Heb. *pādāh* and *gā'al*) frequently occurs. Similarly in the NT, Greek *apolutrōsis* occurs in Rom. 8:23, 1 Cor. 1:30, Col. 1:14, and elsewhere, as does "purchase" (*agorazō;* 1 Cor. 6:20).

Colin Gunton, however, questions whether Aulén's exegesis supports all his claims, including his use of Col. 1:15 (*The Actuality of Atonement* [Edinburgh: T. & T. Clark, 1988], 55-58). He shares his concern for an "objective" account of the atonement, but does not wholly share Aulén's enthusiasm for "recapitulation" in Irenaeus. Just as seriously, we may question his claim that Luther shared Aulén's "classic" view. Indeed, Aulén admits that Luther is ambiguous about "merit," rejecting the notion in the context of justification but still inclined to use the term in the context of atonement. Christ has "merit" in a way that humankind does not, however, and in *this* sense Luther's theology is not contradictory. Moreover, in his chapter on Luther (117-38) Aulén expounds atonement and salvation so widely that it comes as no surprise to find Luther included in his interpretation. Certainly there are passages in Luther that address "Christ's conflict with the tyrants" (119); but Luther's language about the "curse" (121) applies no less to a substitutionary interpretation, as, for example, Calvin understands this. While he criticizes others for merging Anselm's theory with the ransom approach, Aulén might be accused of merging his approach with the "substitutionary" one. Nevertheless, his criticisms of the "subjective" view still stand. The theology of the atonement is perhaps wider, and the approaches more complementary, than he seems at times to recognize.

In *Jesus in Contemporary Historical Research* (London: SPCK, 1976), Aulén first discusses briefly Schweitzer, Bultmann, Dibelius, and Dodd, but his main interest concerns the period after 1960. He establishes the "Jewish" approach of W. D. Davies and Birger Gerhardsson, and sees them and Herbert Braun as acknowledging the place of Jewish apocalyptic in the thought and background of Jesus, in accord with his Jewish heritage. He then discusses Jesus and the Pharisees; his relation to his disciples; his lifestyle; and his proclamation of the kingdom of God, including the enigma of his identity. The center of his teaching is "the radical love commandment"; "the Old Testament was Jesus' Bible" (136). Loving God is to be realized in loving one's neighbor (138). The kingdom of God "is about to break forth in a new deal" (143). Compared with the excesses of the later Jesus Seminar of the 1980s and 1990s, this book is a judicious model of restraint.

Reading: G. Aulén, *Christus Victor* (London: SPCK, 1931); G. Aulén, *Jesus in Contemporary Historical Research* (London: SPCK, 1976); C. Gunton, *The Actuality of Atonement* (Edinburgh: T. & T. Clark, 1988).

Austin, John L.

John L. Austin (1911-1960) was a pioneer of what was later called speech-act theory. During the Second World War he served in military intelligence at a high level, earning the O.B.E. and the Croix de Guerre. In 1952 he became White's Professor of Moral Philosophy at Oxford; he also visited Harvard and Berkeley. In his distinguished career he published only a few papers. His Harvard lectures, put together as *How to Do Things with Words* (Oxford: Clarendon, 1962), and *Sense and Sensibilia* (1962) were compiled from lecture notes. He paid minute attention to "ordinary language" and dictionaries. His central thesis was that "An 'illocutionary' act" is the "performance of an act *in* saying something as opposed to the performance of an act *of* saying something" (*How to Do Things*, 99). An act *of* saying is defended as a "locution"; performing an act *by* saying something is defined as a "perlocution"; an act performed *in* saying something is an "illocutionary" act (100-107). Basic examples of "speech acts" (as these were later called) are the utterance of "I do" in a marriage service; "I promise," if it is a sincere commitment; or "I open" (a fête or a library): these utterances *do* something. A fact constantly overlooked by European theologians is his comment, "For a certain performative utterance to be happy (i.e. effective), certain statements *have to be true*" (45). Many of Austin's illustrations are very witty, especially on borderline cases: "Can I baptize a dog, if it is admittedly rational?" (31); and "I baptize this infant 2704" (35). (*See* **Speech Act Theory** for more examples.) I have tried to set out some theological applications of Austin's approach in *Thiselton on Hermeneutics* (Grand Rapids: Eerdmans; Aldershot: Ashgate, 2006), 52-150, and *New Horizons in Hermeneutics* (Grand Rapids: Zondervan, 1992, 2013), 283-307. Promises constitute an outstanding example, as the Reformer W. Tyndale saw centuries ago. "Acts" of forgiveness and "acts" of blessing constitute only two of many more possibilities. Philosophical issues in Austin are explored in K. T. Fann, ed., *Symposium on J. L. Austin* (New York: Humanities Press; London: Routledge, 1969).

Authority of the Bible

Before the seventeenth century Christians simply presupposed the authority of the Bible for doctrine and life. This consensus was weakened by the Deists, by the effects of the Enlightenment, and by the rise of biblical criticism. It is unnecessary to recapitulate the years of consensus, but for the sake of completeness and evidence we may briefly select some examples.

(i) **The Biblical and Patristic Periods.** Critics of biblical authority might perceive any evidence from Scripture as providing only a circular argument. But we are concerned not with "proof" but with evidence of a universally held presupposition. Admittedly some have appealed to the biblical material as "proof of the doctrine" (Charles Hodge, *Systematic Theology* [1871; Grand Rapids: Eerdmans, 1946], 1:157-58; cf. 151-88). Hodge immediately cites 1 Thess. 2:13, "You accepted it not as a human word but as what it really is, God's word." This is evidence that the converts regarded Paul's preaching as "God's word," but the term hardly alludes to the whole Bible.

It remains true, however, that the biblical material speaks of the Holy Spirit as speaking *through* prophets, Jesus, and other biblical agents with the utmost regularity. The two well-known texts are 2 Tim. 3:16, which declares: "The Scriptures" or "writings" are "God-breathed" (Gk. *graphē theopneustos*), and 2 Pet. 1:21, which speaks of "prophecy" as not coming by human will but "by the Holy Spirit" and "spoken" from "God." Hodge appeals to the Greek for inspiration in Josephus and others (158). In the OT, as G. Montague comments, the Spirit is understood "as the instigation and the animation of prophecy" (*The Holy Spirit* [Eugene, Ore.: Wipf and Stock, 1976], 45). He inspires Balaam (Numbers 22–24), the messianic figure (Isa. 11:1-2), Micaiah (1 Kings 22:14), and others. The whole issue of true and false prophecy brings this to the fore (R. W. L. Moberly, *Prophecy and Discernment* [Cambridge: CUP, 2006]). In the NT Peter appeals from the earliest days to the Psalms as spoken by the Holy Spirit (Acts 1:12-21; 4:25-26). Heb. 4:12 declares that "the word of God is living and active . . . piercing until it divides soul from spirit," but we have to be sure that "the word of God" denotes Scripture, although in this context it probably does.

Belief among the early subapostolic writers, the apologists, and the Church Fathers is unanimous. *1 Clement* (c. 96) ascribes Isa. 53:1-12 to the Holy Spirit (16.2-5). The Scriptures, Clement of Rome declares, "are true and given by the

Holy Spirit" (Gk. *dia tou pneumatos tou hagiou; 1 Clem.* 45.2). Ignatius (c. 110) shares this view. The *Didachē* quotes the Sermon on the Mount (1.3-5) as the rule for the church. *The Epistle of Barnabas* (c. 98–c. 150) associates the inspiration of the Spirit with the narratives of Abraham, Moses, and the prophets (9.1-2-7; 10.2, 9). Among the second-century apologists, Athenagoras speaks of the Holy Spirit as inspiring the Scriptures like a flute player playing the flute, and Theophilus also speaks of the inspiration of the Spirit (*Ad Autolycum* 2.9.22).

The Church Fathers also begin from the first moment to presuppose this doctrine. Clement of Alexandria declares, "The Spirit, by the mouth of Isaiah," is witness to what Jesus teaches (*The Instructor* 1.5.13; cf. *Stromata* 6.14). Irenaeus similarly includes Scripture and tradition in his "rule of faith" for the church. The reactions to the heretic Marcion (c. 150) were decisive. The Fathers responded by affirming that one God had inspired both Testaments. This became so widely accepted without question that, in general, references to the subject became relatively rare in later centuries. This is not uniformly the case. Origen states, "The sacred books are not the compositions of men. . . . They were composed by inspiration of the Holy Spirit, agreeable to the will of the Father" (*De principiis* 4.1.9). There are also plentiful references in Cyril of Jerusalem (*Catechism* 4.2, 16; 16.1, 2; 17.3), in Gregory of Nazianzus (*Theological Orations* 5.1, 18, 24), and in Basil of Caesarea. Basil warns us that to reject Scripture is to grieve the Holy Spirit *(Letter 22).*

(ii) **The Medieval and Reformation Periods.** This unbroken line of testimony continues through the Middle Ages and Reformation. Thomas Aquinas quotes the classic verse 2 Tim. 3:16 as the very basis of human inquiry (*Su Th* 1.1, art. 1), from which he infers that Scripture conveys God's revelation, not humanly derived thoughts. In 2.2, question 4, article 8 he quotes 1 Thess. 2:13: "You accepted it . . . as God's word," and Rom. 10:15-17, "Faith comes from what is heard, and what is heard comes through the word of God" (*see* **Word of God**). There is no effective difference in the following centuries between Catholic and Protestant thought. Before the Reformation itself, John Wycliffe declared, "A Christian should speak Scripture's words as Scripture's authority in the form Scripture displays" (*On the Truth of Holy Scripture* 1.2).

Martin Luther regarded the Bible as bringing about a living relationship between God and human beings. The Bible chiefly addresses us from God through divine promise (*LW* 31:357). The Word of God may address us also as our adversary or judge, to correct and to change us. But Luther also begins the path that eventually leads to biblical criticism. He admits that there are errors in the prophets; evaluates 1 and 2 Kings as more accurate than 1 and 2 Chronicles; and claims that the Epistle of James "mangles Scripture" and is "an epistle of straw." He begins to see the authority more in terms of its *effect* than in terms of its *origins.* In this respect he begins a tendency that ends closer to Orr and "progressive" evangelicals than to Hodge and Warfield. By definition he would not have endorsed full "inerrancy."

Hugh Latimer, in his famous "Sermon of the Plough," analogizes on the Bible breaking up the soil of the hard heart and "producing a right faith" (*Sermons* [Cambridge: CUP, 1844], 70). William Tyndale also writes in the tradition of Luther and Latimer. They all wanted every person to have access to the Bible in his or her own tongue. Tyndale also appreciated the power of the Bible, not only to *say* something, but also to *do* something in the saying of it. Today we call this speech act theory. Tyndale insisted, like Luther (and, later, Barth), that it conveyed God's *promises*. Hence "It makes a man's heart glad, it proclaims joyful tidings; it names some as heirs" ("A Pathway into the Holy Scripture," in *Doctrinal Treatises* [Cambridge: CUP, 1848], 8-9). Tyndale cites no fewer than eighteen "speech acts": Scripture promises, names, appoints, declares, gives, condemns, curses, binds, kills, drives to despair, delivers, forbids, ministers to life, wounds, blesses, heals, cures, and wakes (8-12 and 18-23). Tyndale insisted that Scripture did not simply "convey thoughts" but changed lives, especially when it was "unlocked and opened."

John Calvin wrote carefully on the authority of Scripture, both in the *Institutes* and in his commentaries. In the *Institutes* he writes: "Aided by glasses, [people] begin to read distinctly, so Scripture . . . dissipates the darkness, and shows us the true God clearly" (1.6.1; Beveridge, 1:64). He insists that the Bible beautifully "harmonises in all its parts" (1.8.1). He adds that the Scriptures are too mighty to need rhetorical art. Only Scripture can "suffice to give a saving knowledge of God when its certainty is founded on the inward persuasion of the Holy Spirit" (1.8.13; 1:83). John, he declares, "strikes down more powerfully than any thunderbolt the petulance of those who refuse to submit to the obedience of faith" (1.8.11; 1:81). J. K. S. Reid has devoted a whole volume to the authority of the Bible in Calvin and in Reformed theology. He stresses Calvin's appeal to the Holy Spirit, and writes, "The authority which Scripture possesses is proper to itself, and not conceded to it by some quite external agent. In this case the testimony of the Holy Spirit is an internal witness" (*The Authority of Scripture* [London: Methuen, 1957], 49). Reid also insists that Calvin regards the inspiration of Scripture as belonging through the Holy Spirit to the *writers* and the *purpose* of Scripture, not to its *words* and *language* (48-49). Paul Achtemeier strongly argues that Calvin "does not delegate it (inspiration) to the *words* of Scripture, but rather *uses* these words to convince people of the *content* of the message to which Scripture bears witness" (*The Inspiration of Scripture* [Philadelphia: Fortress, 1980], 140).

This is significant in relation to later doctrine and theories. For it separates the later views of A. A. Hodge and B. B. Warfield, who stressed the inerrancy of the words or text, from those of James Orr and many others who still defend biblical authority, but not in terms of words. Reid calls this "no longer an authority of testimony, but an authority of petrifaction" (49). The interpretation of Calvin, however, is complex and controversial. A. M. Hunter concedes that for Calvin "It is not the words but the doctrine that is of prime concern" (*The Teaching of Calvin*, 2nd ed. [London: James Clarke, 1950], 75). However, even Hunter argues that Calvin rejected any notion of "evolution of thought or belief exhibited in the Bible" (78). Thus, a majority would probably follow Reid and Achtemeier in distancing Calvin from Warfield, although some would resist this view.

For almost a century Luther's and Calvin's view held sway among Protestant thinkers. In the 1662 *Book of Common Prayer,* article 7 of its Thirty-nine Articles states that the creeds are supported by "warrant of Scripture," and article 20 states that Scripture is "sufficient for salvation," and no one has to believe anything that is contrary to Scripture. R. Prenter argues that from the first the authority of the Bible in the Lutheran church was "not the authority of the book, nor of its author, but the authority of the content of its message" (Prenter, "A Lutheran Contribution," in *Biblical Authority for Today,* ed. A. Richardson and W. Schweitzer [London: SCM, 1951], 100). Barnabas Nagy argues that Reformed theology continued to urge Calvin's emphasis on "the witness of the Spirit" ("A Reformed Contribution," in *Biblical Authority for Today,* 89-92). The Westminster Confession (1649) declared that the Hebrew OT and the Greek NT are "immediately inspired by God," and that they appeal to "the Holy Spirit speaking in Scripture." Reid comments, "The Calvinistic tradition gives Holy Scripture a more explicitly prominent place" than does the Lutheran tradition (*The Authority of Scripture,* 76). But he adds that we should not make too much of this. As a summary we could ascribe *sola fide* to Luther and *sola Scriptura* to Calvin (100).

Nevertheless, Reid claims that in later generations Protestant orthodoxy hardened. "It is found easier to credit authority with an external and autocratic authoritarianism than to live permanently under the authority of a more persuasive ... kind" (101). The living authority of the Word becomes "the armoured strength of verbal infallibility" (101). Yet this is no "harder" than the Roman Catholic view of the times. The Douai Bible asserts, "All the books which the Church receives as sacred and canonical are written wholly and entirely ... at the dictation of the Holy Ghost ... essentially incompatible with error" (*Providentissimus Deus* 23). Reid comments, "Inerrancy and infallibility is, then, the form in which the Roman Church represents and maintains the authority of the Scriptures" (104).

The real or supposed "hardening" of post-Reformation orthodoxy reached its climax in the nineteenth century with Hodge and Warfield. But Charles Hodge is a little more "progressive" than Warfield. At the conservative end of the spectrum, he insists, "Inspiration extends equally to all parts of Scripture" (*Systematic Theology,* 1:163). This is known as the plenary "inspiration" of the Bible. Second, "inspiration ... extends to words" (164). Hodge appeals to Jer. 1:9, "I have put my words in your mouth," and to Paul's argument about the singular of "seed" in Gal. 3:16. He calls the two points "the doctrine of plenary inspiration" (165). On the standard objection about "discrepancies," he replies that these are "for the most part trivial" (169), or can be "ascribed to transcribers" (169). On the "progressive" side, he argues that, on scientific objections, the biblical writers use the "language of common life" (170) and often do not "teach" what looks questionable. Hodge acknowledges that views of the time are assumed by biblical writers (171-72). In the end, the argument turns on "supernatural" inspiration, rather than the naturalistic view of Schleiermacher and others.

(iii) **Deism, the Enlightenment, and the Rise of Biblical Criticism.** One of the most important books on the change of intellectual climate is Henning Graf Reventlow, *The Authority of the Bible and the Modern World* (London: SCM, 1984). He begins with John Wycliffe, Erasmus, and Bucer, and struggles with Puritanism. Some Puritans followed Luther and Melanchthon on adiaphora; others followed Calvin and Hooker; still others pursued "a clear shift of stress compared with the Reformers" (122). The seventeenth century was "the century of transition" (147). Reventlow discusses William Chillingworth and others. The first Deists entered the stage with Edward Herbert, Lord Cherbury. Reventlow writes, "He emerges in modern accounts as the founder of English Deism" (185), in spite of his diplomatic activity. But in this century Deism was felt as an "undercurrent" rather than a more explicit influence. Nevertheless, his criticism of the Bible achieved a wide readership, and his work was "characteristic of the later Enlightenment and its criticism of the Bible . . . ahead of its time" (193).

Reventlow finds ambiguity or perhaps "two levels" in Thomas Hobbes. On one level Holy Scripture is the only criterion for judging any doctrine. On a different level he urges "rational matter-of-factness" (222). He is followed after the Restoration by the growing influence of Latitudinarians. They urged rationalism and moralism. Then John Toland provided a more serious or influential impact of Deism, especially through his book *Christianity Not Mysterious,* in which he claimed that the Christian faith was not contrary to unaided natural reason. He said, "Reason is the foundation of all Certitude," and revelation becomes unnecessary (297). Toland was followed by Matthew Tindal and his book *Christianity as Old as Creation* (1730). He also attacked the "High Church" piety. Reventlow claimed that these Deists were less isolated than many think, and their criticism of the Bible matched the method of Richard Simon in France (329). Many of the theistic defenses were also rational, as in Samuel Clarke and Joseph Butler. Then Anthony Collins spoke of revelation whose "literal meaning is false, but whose real meaning is consistent with reason" (355). Free thinking must remain independent of all authority. This fully accords with Kant's definition of the Enlightenment as freedom to think for oneself, free from all external authorities. Collins published the *Philosophical Inquiry concerning Human Liberty* and *Discourse of Free Thinking* (1713).

Reventlow concludes with some subtlety that the Deists tried to demonstrate the parallel between the religion of nature and Christian revelation, but "in fact demonstrated precisely the opposite" (388). This conclusion was that "revealed religion is superfluous" (383). The spirit of the age would now offer little help to many thinkers who wished to defend the authority of the Bible. We have set out the effects of the Enlightenment under the entry **The Enlightenment.** The other distinctive context is explored in the entry **Biblical Criticism.** However, some comments may be offered here in briefer form.

Richard Simon was in many ways a loyal Catholic, but aimed to undermine Protestant confidence in the Bible. He argued that the Pentateuch contained two incompatible traditions. Jean Astruc took this further, distinguishing between the "J" (Yahweh) and "E" (Elohim) traditions in Genesis. But the real founder of biblical criticism was J. S. Semler. In his book *A Treatise on the Free Investigation of the Canon* (1771-1775), he argued that the canon was formed by strictly *historical* factors, not *theological* ones. This began the serious blight of a "history versus theology" choice, which has plagued much (but not all) biblical criticism ever since. We may compare his work with a more recent comment from F. F. Bruce: "We are not dealing so much with the recognition of the Biblical oracles as authoritative, as with the formation of those writings which had *already* the [theological] stamp of authority upon them" (*The Books and the Parchments* [London: Revell, 1953], 95).

The work of many other biblical critics was less radical than Semler's and less of a challenge to biblical authority. J. A. Ernesti retained a theistic faith and stressed historical and grammatical exegesis. But J. D. Michaelis gave emphasis to comparative studies as well as languages, and abandoned a pietist faith. G. E. Lessing was also a radical exponent of biblical criticism, arguing that history could produce only "accidental" truths, in contrast to the necessary truths of reason. His dichotomy was less "history versus theology" (although this was included) than "reason versus faith." J. G. Eichhorn remained a theist, but argued for the mythical nature of the early chapters in Genesis. Finally, in this era, W. M. L. De Wette reconstructed Israel's history, regarding Chronicles as secondary, Numbers as largely mythological, and the traditional dating old-fashioned and wrong. In the NT he identified very different traditions in Paul, John, and Hebrews. His whole approach blazed a trail for J. Wellhausen, who largely popularized his ideas.

It would be a mistake, however, to view biblical criticism as a uniform movement with a uniform method. In Germany E. W. Hengstenberg's work was constructively exegetical. On the other hand, the work of F. C. Baur on the NT challenged all but the major four epistles as genuinely Pauline, and David Strauss produced an idiosyncratic "life" of Jesus, in which he defined myth as ideas set out in the form of narrative (*see* **Biblical Criticism**). In England, however, the nineteenth-century emphasis was very different. B. F. Westcott, J. B. Lightfoot, and J. A. Hort (sometimes called the Cambridge triumvirate) were professors at Cambridge, but also loyal churchmen, who placed their biblical criticism in the service of theology and the church. Two of them became bishops of Durham.

By the twentieth century it became clearer than before that there were multiform types of biblical criticism. There are simply too many to select examples. But it became apparent that many aim at research that will enrich the church; on the other hand, others either have little interest in the church or even theism, or go as far as to enjoy taking up an iconoclastic posture against orthodox belief. In America, John Bright, for example, wrote, "The Bible provides us with the primary, and thus normative, documents of the Christian faith. To ask, as we continually do, is this teaching truly Christian? . . . is to be driven initially back to the Bible" (*The Authority of the Old Testament* [London: SCM, 1967], 30). Another OT scholar, Norman H. Snaith, wrote, "The authority of the Bible, thus, for me, rests in the inner witness of the Holy Spirit" (*The Inspiration and Authority of the Bible* [London: Epworth, 1956], 45). C. H. Dodd speaks of the community that produced the Bible as having "delivered us from the tyranny of private impressions . . . and helped us to true objectivity of judgement" (*The Authority of the Bible* [London: Nisbet, 1928], 299). Clearly, biblical criticism as such represents both positive and negative perspectives on the authority of the Bible. These largely depend on a diversity of aims, methods, and attitudes of life.

(iv) **The Debate in the Late Twentieth Century and Early Twenty-First Century.** Whatever biblical critics may think and say, many philosophers and theologians have utterly different attitudes about authority and freedom than were once fashionable among the Deists or the Enlightenment. Thus Gerhard Ebeling reminds us: "According to Luther, the word of God comes as *adversarius noster,* our adversary. It does not simply confirm and strengthen us in what we think" (*Introduction to a Theological Theory of Language* [London: Collins, 1973], 17). James Smart warns us, "Let the Scriptures cease to be heard, and soon the remembered Christ becomes an imagined Christ, shaped by the religiosity and unconscious desires of the worshippers" (*The Strange Silence of the Bible in the Church* [London: SCM, 1970], 25). On the principle of authority, the humanist philosopher Hans-Georg Gadamer firmly rejects any contrast between authority and freedom. "Authority . . . rests on acknowledgement, and hence on an act of reason itself, which, aware of its limitations, trusts to the better insight of others" (*Truth and Method,* 2nd ed. [London: Sheed and Ward, 1989], 279). Gadamer, in fact, dismisses the mood of the Enlightenment as simplistic. "The fundamental prejudice of the Enlightenment is the prejudice against prejudice (or pre-judgement) itself, which denies tradition its power" (270). He consistently and convincingly attacks Enlightenment thought.

One of the most recent ways in which the authority of Scripture has been undermined is an exaggeration of biblical diversity, perhaps partly in reaction to the biblical theology movement. One such advocate of theological diversity is Heikki Räisänen of the University of Helsinki and the Academy of Finland. In *Beyond New Testament Theology* (Leiden: Brill, 2000) he stresses theological diversity within the biblical canon. One of several responses has been to take up Bakhtin's notion of polyvalent discourse. This can often do better justice to a complex reality than monologic discourse or a "unity" of propositions. Bakhtin prefers to speak of "concordance" and "harmony" rather than of a flat monochrome unity.

A second way forward in the debate about the Bible is to call on speech act theory. Jesus' utterance "Your sins are forgiven" is a speech act because it rests on the God-given authority to forgive sins. As Tyndale had argued, acts of promise, acts of commissioning, acts of appointing, acts of liberating, and acts of saving all derive from the authority of the one who conveys the speech act, and in the very utterance brings about a change in situations and circumstances. The basic example of a bequest in a will can illustrate this. The words "I give and bequeath" can revolutionize someone's life, by conveying property, money, or some other means.

A third and quite different way forward is to stress the reliability of oral traditions and eyewitnesses in the Gospels. Richard Bauckham, *Jesus and the Eyewitnesses* (Grand Rapids: Eerdmans, 2006), has in effect demolished much of the earlier skepticism about oral tradition and reliable eyewitnesses. He considers the testimony of Papias, considers names in the Gospel traditions, examines the Petrine perspectives on Mark, and so forth. At the turn of the twenty-first century various publications by Joel Green in the USA and N. T. Wright and J. D. G. Dunn in England indirectly contributed to a constructive defense of biblical authority. Meanwhile, few doubt that the Bible remains "essential to devotion and discipleship as well as to doctrine" (N. T. Wright, *Scripture* [London: SPCK, 2005], 2). Further, the authority of the Bible is clearly asserted in many, if not all, of the church's traditions. Writing on behalf of Reformed dogmatics, G. C. Berkouwer asserts it in *Holy Scripture* (Grand Rapids: Eerdmans, 1975). At the other end of a spectrum, the Roman Catholic Church has produced *The Interpretation of the Bible in the Church*. This was produced by the Pontifical Biblical Commission in 1993. Pope Benedict (then Cardinal Joseph Ratzinger) summed up its wide breadth of hermeneutical resources as inquiring "how the meaning of Scripture might be known" (preface). There is also a growing recognition that, in John Webster's words, "Scripture's authority is not exercised apart from the work performed in the text by its readers... the interaction between God's self-revelation and its hearers" ("Scripture, Authority of," in *DTIB* 727). Reader-response theory and reception theory may contribute in ensuring that the authority of the Bible is seen as a corporate or communal process, in which scholars and pastors, clergy and laity, and men and women all have an active part to play.

Reading: W. Abraham, *The Divine Inspiration of Holy Scripture* (Oxford: OUP, 1981); G. C. Berkouwer, *Holy Scripture* (Grand Rapids: Eerdmans, 1975); John Goldingay, *Models for Scripture* (Grand Rapids: Eerdmans, 1994); Henning Graf Reventlow, *The Authority of the Bible and the Rise of the Modern World* (London: SCM, 1980); J. B. Rogers and D. K. McKim, *The Authority and Interpretation of the Bible* (New York: Harper and Row, 1979); J. Webster, *Holy Scripture* (Cambridge: CUP, 2003); J. Webster, *The Domain of the Word: Scripture and Theological Reason* (New York and London: T. & T. Clark, 2012); N. T. Wright, *Scripture and the Authority of God* (London: SPCK, 2003).

Azazel

Azazel (Heb. $^{ca}zā'zēl$) occurs in the OT in the ritual of the Day of Atonement in Lev. 16:8, 10, and 26. Three interpretations of the meaning are possible. It is usually applied to one of the two goats that Aaron uses. The word can represent a combination of "goat" (Heb. $'ēz$) and "to go away" (Heb. $'āzal$), that is, the scapegoat. Aaron first lays his hands on it, and then sends it out into the wilderness as the bearer of Israel's sins. Second, it may simply denote the rocky place or rugged cliff to which the scapegoat is sent, and over which it plunges. *Targum Pseudo-Jonathan* may imply this. Third, some relate the word to a demon of the wilderness. This last meaning occurs in *1 En.* 8.1-4, 10.4-6. (*See also* **Day of Atonement; Expiation; Sacrifice; Scapegoat.**)

B

Bacon, Francis
Francis Bacon (1561-1626) was primarily a philosopher, but also a lawyer and politician. He has been described as the most profound philosopher of the sixteenth and seventeenth centuries, and as the first English philosopher of importance since William of Ockham. He argued that natural philosophy should be founded on empirical experiment, and should serve to promote human welfare. As against the mere replication of tradition, he urged the importance of cumulative knowledge. He attacked Scholasticism and "dilettante" learning as misleading avenues to truth. He had much in common with Deism, but some of his leanings were toward theism.

Bakhtin, Mikhail
Mikhail Bakhtin (1895-1975) is a theorist of polyphonic discourse, which has become increasingly valuable in hermeneutics. Perhaps we should explain why his influence in the Western world peaked after he had died. He read classics and philosophy at the University of Petrograd (1913-1918), and then kept a low profile in the 1919 civil war. In the 1920s many intellectuals were arrested under Stalin's regime, and he was accused of links with the Russian Orthodox Church. He was arrested and sent to the far north. He wrote on the nature of the novel during the 1930s, and in 1941 returned to Moscow. Only in the 1950s, after Stalin's death, was his work "discovered" in Russia; then in Paris in the 1970s; and finally in America in the 1980s.

Bakhtin recognized that monologic discourse conveys thoughts, assertions, or propositions that can be separated from a text. Reality, he claimed, was often too complex to state simply as a packaged truth. Like Gadamer and others, he argued that a *dialogue* between two or more standpoints can convey more. Dialogue "is born between people collectively searching for the truth" (Bakhtin, *Problems of Dostoevsky's Poetics* [Minneapolis: University of Minnesota Press, 1984], 110). Dialogic or polyphonic discourse is *"owned" by a collective, intersubjective, mutually responsible community*. In *Horizons in Hermeneutics* (ed. S. E. Porter and M. Malcolm [Grand Rapids: Eerdmans, 2013]), John Thomson follows Bakhtin by writing of the importance of basing hermeneutics on the community. If Emilio Betti is right to regard hermeneutics as fostering tolerance and respect for the other, Thomson and Tom Greggs add that *love and respect for the other* demand listening to the "other" especially in polyphonic discourse. In the Russian Orthodox Church this relates to *sobernost,* togetherness in solidarity. As Kierkegaard also insisted, dialectical communication invites participation. This may be applied to Christian doctrine within the church or congregation. Genuinely *multiple voices* arise from polyphonic discourse. While Bakhtin is the great theorist of polyphonic discourse, F. Dostoevsky is the great practitioner and exponent of it. Dostoevsky uses it in *The Brothers Karamazov;* in the biblical writings it is used in Job, and in various books of the canon. For more detail see K. Clark and M. Holquist, *Mikhail Bakhtin* (Cambridge: Harvard University Press, 1984). (*See also* **Polyphonic Discourse.**)

Balthasar, Hans Urs von

Hans Urs von Balthasar (1905-1988) has enjoyed varied esteem in the Roman Catholic Church. Until the late 1960s he was marginalized in the Catholic Church, not being invited along with Küng, Rahner, and Congar to participate in Vatican II (1962-1965). But immediately thereafter he rapidly gained esteem and entered the public eye. He was said to be the favorite theologian of Pope John Paul II. He was held in high esteem by Benedict XVI, and was due to be appointed cardinal when he died before the ceremony in 1988. He has produced a vast quantity of theological literature. The most famous and illustrious of his many published works is his trilogy, the first part of which, *The Glory of the Lord: A Theological Aesthetics (GL),* was written in seven volumes between 1961 and 1969 ([San Francisco: Ignatius; Edinburgh: T. & T. Clark], vol. 1, 1982; vol. 2, 1984; vol. 3, 1986; vol. 4, 1989; vol. 5, 1991; vol. 6, 1991; vol. 7, 1981). The second part of the trilogy, five volumes, carries the title *Theo-Drama: Theological Dramatic Theory,* written between 1973 and 1983 ([San Francisco: Ignatius; Edinburgh: T. & T. Clark], vol. 1, 1988; vol. 2, 1990; vol. 3, 1992; vol. 4, 1994; vol. 5, 1998). The third set of the trilogy, entitled *Theo-Logic,* was written on truth, in three volumes between 1985 and 1987 ([San Francisco: Ignatius; Edinburgh: T. & T. Clark], vol. 1, 2000; vol. 2, 2004; vol. 3, 2005). These are far from all that Balthasar published. He has produced a huge amount of material, which at least matches the output of Karl Barth, including many smaller works on particular subjects.

Yet Balthasar held no teaching position in a university. He was born into a patrician family in Lucerne, and completed his doctrinal studies in German and philosophy in 1929, but experienced a clear call from God in the same year in the Black Forest near Basel, which led him to join the Jesuits (1929). His Jesuit training took place largely in the context of neo-scholasticism, which he found dreary and dull at that time. A breakthrough came when he became friends with Henri de Lubac, whose motto in the study of the Church Fathers was "back to the sources." With de Lubac's encouragement, he translated and edited an anthology from Origen (1957); *Homily on the Song of Songs* by Gregory of Nyssa (1942); and texts from Irenaeus, Basil of Caesarea, Augustine, and Maximus the Confessor (1941). He was ordained in 1936, and in 1940 became university chaplain at Basel.

In 1940 he began a lifelong association with Adrienne von Speyr, a Protestant Swiss doctor and laywoman, whom he welcomed into the Catholic Church that year or the next year. He became her spiritual director. Thereafter she underwent a number of mystical experiences. In 1943-1944 they jointly founded the Community of St. John, initially for laywomen, and then for laymen, with a branch for priests. This "secular institute" was thought to be inappropriate for a Jesuit, and after a difficult period Balthasar left the Jesuits in 1950. In 1950 he also set up his own publishing house.

Meanwhile, with his arrival in Basel in 1940, Balthasar was in a position to attend seminars by Karl Barth. A friendship emerged between the two thinkers, and in 1949 Balthasar gave a series of lectures on Barth's theology, which Barth sometimes attended. This resulted in the publication of *The Theology of Karl Barth* in 1951 (Eng. San Francisco: Ignatius, 1992). Balthasar showed respect and admiration for Barth's thought. He firmly agreed with Barth's emphasis on prevenient grace and divine sovereignty, and his critique of the Enlightenment and emphasis on revelation. But although he agreed about the importance of the Trinity and Christology, Balthasar maintained that they held disproportionate attention and prominence in Barth at the expense of other doctrines. Before 1956 Balthasar did not enjoy good standing with his local bishop. But this was reversed after 1956. Throughout this period and in later life, Balthasar could name Adrienne von Speyr, Karl Barth, and Henri de Lubac as the three major influences on his life and thought.

Even up to the midsixties, however, many found him puzzling and obscure, and theologians tended to make too much of his departure from the Jesuits. Rodney Howsare asserts that "Balthasar's theology does not fit easily into the modern university setting" (quoted in Karen Kilby, *Balthasar* [Grand Rapids: Eerdmans, 2012], 6). But with the publication of his major works, in the midsixties, estimates of his work began to change. He was increasingly seen as fresh, original, creative, and after Vatican II, Kilby observes, "For those within Roman-Catholicism who worried that the Church was conceding too much to the world . . . Balthasar became a very important figure" (37). Cardinal Ratzinger (Pope Benedict XVI) saw him as a powerful force for *correct* renewal.

Balthasar's massive major works concern the three transcendental themes of beauty (in *GL*), goodness (in *Theo-Drama*), and truth (in *Theo-Logic*). Balthasar sums up succinctly the purpose of the first of the seven volumes of *Glory of the Lord* at the beginning of volume 2, as follows: "The first volume attempted to show that one both can and must consider the revelation of the living God, as the Christian understands it, not only from the point of view of its truth and goodness, but also from that of its ineffable beauty" (2:11). The beauty of the Lord is *epiphaneia*, a manifestation or revelation, a "radiance and splendour which breaks forth . . . from a veiled and yet mighty depth of being . . . an event of self-revelation of the free and sovereign God" (2:11). But since it is "ineffable," Balthasar nowhere actually defines beauty. It is contemplative, rather than critical or conceptual.

The first volume especially concerns light and the light of faith, and is subtitled *Seeing the Form.* He speaks of form *(Gestalt)* and figure *(Gebilde),* both of which can mediate splendor, radiance, or luminosity. Balthasar speaks of "great radiance from within" (1:20). The light shines forth from the form's interior. This is not chaotic or shapeless. Kilby observes, "We do not meet beauty in general, beauty as an abstraction, but always a particular beautiful thing" (*Balthasar,* 44). But the term *Gestalt* points to its totality or wholeness. Ben Quash comments, "This form . . . is self-disclosing and enrapturing, and the conditions for the perception of this form (which is *Gestalt Christi*) are given with and in it" ("Hans Urs von Balthasar," in *The Modern Theologians,* ed. D. F. Ford, 3rd ed. [Oxford: Blackwell, 2005], 110).

This, as Quash points out, takes us far from Platonism or Plato's eternal ideas. In the history of theology Balthasar regards Irenaeus as certainly not Platonizing, but as extolling "the creation of God" (*GL* 2:17). Although I am not aware that others have made this comparison explicitly, when Karen Kilby speaks of "standing transformed before the beauty of a work of art" in Balthasar, I cannot help comparing the role of art in the later thought of Heidegger and in H.-G. Gadamer. Be that as it may, music was important to Balthasar. He and Barth shared a common appreciation of Mozart, and Balthasar refers to "Vivaldi, Bach, Haydn, or Mozart, Mahler or Schoenberg" and the theme of beauty (2:16). Augustine "praises the beauty ever ancient and ever new of the love of God" (2:17). Balthasar continues, "Anselm's Benedictine, contemplative reason is aesthetic in a new and original way" (2:18). He sees "the glorious form of order," which God has placed in the world through his love. He appeals to Dante, John of the Cross, Pascal, and others. Sometimes, he declares, "The divine glory . . . has taken on increasingly a kenotic colouring," and "the true depth of the divine is only manifest in suffering love" (23).

In volume 2 Balthasar makes a special study of Irenaeus (2:31-94), Augustine (2:95-143), Anselm (2:211-39), and Bonaventura (2:260-362). In *Against Heresies* 1, Irenaeus expresses the "internal contradictions" of largely Gnostic thought. But in book 2 he "comes to the unity of reality" (*GL* 2:42). Things are arbitrary in the Gnostic system, but "in Catholic unity everything is internally plain and bright, and can be made clear to anyone who wishes to see within the enduring mystery of God" (43). To see is to stand before the clear message (45). Irenaeus shows "the principle of clarity" (49), which overcomes Gnostic "secret tradition," and the adaptation and destruction of Scripture in Gnosticism. Irenaeus's "central concept . . . of recapitulation" constitutes "a formative element in the world and in history" (51), and provides the "interpreting power of Christ" (53). He does not build by hypothesis, but "places his trust in the logos of being" (55). Nothing can transcend God: "he who encloses the earth with his fist" and "cannot be measured" (59). Balthasar quotes Irenaeus: "The glory of God is the living man, but the life of man is seeing God" (75). He concludes, "Irenaeus' consciousness of the dazzling rightness of the dimension he has revealed gives him a self-confidence and exhilaration similar to Paul's" (90). This is in part due to his "great fidelity to the Bible" (93).

Balthasar begins his study of Augustine with the comment, "No one has praised God so assiduously as the supreme beauty, or attempted so consistently to capture the true and good with the categories of aesthetics" (2:95). He quotes Augustine as declaring: "God is the true light without any darkness" (98). To Augustine God is "the good and beautiful God, in whom and from whom and through whom everything is good and beautiful" (99). Balthasar expounds his concept of illumination, commenting, "The only way in which finite mind can make judgements is in the 'light' of absolute mind" (109). Augustine rejects Plato's "Dualism of world and God, sense and mind" (123). He goes back instead to Irenaeus, and sees that "all beauty derives from the supreme beauty which is God," even if each stage of life has its particular beauty (141).

An intermediate chapter is devoted to Denys, whom Balthasar calls "a unique case in theology, indeed in all intellectual history" (144). He argues that he has been grossly underrated. He asserts that "such radiance of holiness streams forth from this unity of person and work — as the Middle Ages sensed immediately — that he can in no case be regarded as a 'forger,' not even as a clever 'apologist'" (147). Indeed, Denys rejects the term "apologetic." Balthasar argues that the content of his *Theological Outlines* concerns "the unknowability of God" (157). He concludes, "Theology is exhausted in the act of wondering adoration before the unsearchable beauty in every manifestation" (170). It would be tempting here to refer to K. Kilby's distinction between contemplative theology and critical theology, or between "lyric" and "epic" theology (*Balthasar*, 61-63), but this perhaps relates more directly to volume 3.

Anselm is the next figure to receive attention in volume 2. Since Anselm is Benedictine, his work is "communal and dialogic" as well as "contemplative, beholding, transparent" (*GL* 2:211). He contemplates revelation in creation and redemption. Balthasar recalls Anselm's prayer, "Grant me to behold your light, even if only from afar, from the depths" (217). Anselm, as many argue, aims at understanding. Balthasar comments, "To think means to make something visible spiritually" (220). The *Proslogion,* with its ontological argument for the existence of God, is a "condensation of the *Monologion*" (231). The end of the process is "joy at the 'utmost beauty' of God" (233-34). Finally, Balthasar turns to Bonaventura, who "of all the great scholastics . . . offers the widest scope to the beautiful in his theology" (260). In his work, "The Trinity is truly revealed in its overflow into the world" (261). Jesus Christ is "the sum of all the ideas of the world," but "he alone [is] the total expression of God" (295).

The subtitle of volume 3, *Lay Styles,* stands in contrast to the subtitle of volume 2, *Clerical Styles.* But this should not mislead us. It is not about "clericalism," or even about "lay leadership." The "clerical" figures, as we have seen, are Irenaeus, Augustine, Denys, Anselm, and Bonaventura. The "lay" theologians, among whom are poets and philosophers, are Dante, John of the Cross, Pascal, Hamann, Soloviev, Hopkins, and Péguy. Quash suggests that much may be inspired here by Adrienne von Speyr. Dante represents the painful experience of the collapse of monastic and clerical theology into a lay theology, Balthasar observes. John of the Cross is partly a response to Luther's reforms, and expresses the glory of heaven through the "dark night" of hell. Yet he still unveils "the dazzling love of God." Pascal, according to Balthasar, provides a second Catholic answer to the Reformation, fashioning a bridge between faith, metaphysics, and natural science. His bridge, however, is still centered in the crucified Christ. Hamann refers to the *kenosis* of Christ and the Holy Spirit, although they become unsurpassable bearers of *Logos* and *Pneuma*. Hopkins is an English Jesuit and a poet "of the highest caliber," who apprehends God in nature and in the history of salvation.

Volumes 4 and 5 together address metaphysics. Volume 4 considers the ancient metaphysical tradition of the contemplation of Being, in Homer, Plato, Plotinus, and the Middle Ages. Balthasar asks how this relates to the Christian tradition of the glory of the Lord as revealed through and in the Trinity. Volume 5 considers later metaphysical tradition. One tradition is traced through Eckhart, Julian of Norwich, and Ignatius. A second is traced through Nicholas of Cusa, Hölderlin, Goethe, and Heidegger. A third is that of the rationalists: Descartes, Leibniz, Spinoza, and idealism. The strengths and weaknesses of each are considered and evaluated.

Volumes 6 and 7 of *Glory of the Lord* explicitly turn to Scripture. Volume 6 concerns the OT; volume 7 concerns the NT. *Glory* is "a constant biblical theme" (6:17), beginning with the epiphany in Sinai. Again, in the time of Elijah we see "the luminous splendour" of God's glory (18). Ezekiel contains much about God's glory, and in 2 Corinthians 3 Paul refers to it in relation to Moses (19). As volume 7 will elucidate, in Jesus Christ "We have seen his glory, the glory as of the Father's only Son, full of grace and truth" (John 1:14). Balthasar follows OT scholars when he connects the Hebrew *kābōd*, "glory," with "heavy or weighty," and also with "renown, fame, or honour" (6:33). Yet Moses knew God "face to face" (Deut. 34:10). Balthasar explores the imagery of "a consuming fire" and "dazzling darkness" (6:41-44). The statement "the LORD your God is a devouring fire" (Deut. 4:24) can be explored only as dialectic. Balthasar then considers "The Divine 'I'" with particular reference to power, Word, holiness, and face. The sensory signs of God's presence are 'overwhelming'" (6:55). These may include storms, overcoming darkness, the growling voice of thunder, and lightning that blindingly flares out of the darkness. It also relates to the notion of the warrior-hero (Exod. 15:3), or to the processional hymn of Psalm 24: "Who is this King of Glory? The LORD, strong and mighty, . . . mighty in battle" (*GL* 6:56). Balthasar comments, "All sensory revelation of glory is directly united to the word of God" (57); "God's word always undergirds its hearer's whole existence" (58). What the holiness of God might be comes to light very slowly. But like his word, God's holiness is active; it imposes itself and has an effect. He writes, "God's face always gives forth light. . . . God's glances and his face are grace, but God's face can be either . . . turned towards one or averted" (69). If God hides his face, everything created dies. Man may live if the light of God's face shines on him (Pss. 31:16; 44:3; 67:1; 80:3, 19; 119:135). Finding

God's face can be called "taking shelter in God's shadow, in the shadow of his wings or of his hand" (*GL* 6:73; cf. Pss. 17:8; 57:1; 63:7; Hos. 14:7; Isa. 49:2; 51:16).

The rest of volume 6 focuses largely on the graciousness of God in the covenant between God and Israel. It looks forward to the final volume, on the NT, which expounds God's revelation of his glory in Christ. But even before he turns to the covenant, Balthasar explores the significance of the image of God (6:87-139). A fashioned "image" *(tselem)* is derived from the skills of handicraft, and "likeness" *(d^emûth)* shows man's "similarity to" God himself (89). The image of God signifies God's "special relationship" to man (91). Humankind is "crowned with glory" (Ps. 8:3-9; *GL* 6:93-103). Like V. Lossky and others, Balthasar argues, "The existence-for-one-another of the man and the woman . . . is what constitutes the human subject . . . [and] the fact that man can be addressed by God and that God does indeed speak to him" (99).

Yet the image of God remains provisional. The era of the kings shows successes and failures in the "great theatre of the world" (109). Solomon may show "the splendour of power," but there are setbacks. The treatment of the covenant, however, also exhibits the grace of God (144-211). Balthasar quotes from N. Glueck, "*Chesed,* grace, loving-kindness, constitutes the new substance of the covenant" (159). The covenant points to interpersonal relationship, which is both ethical, legal, and personal. From Hosea onward, God offers "grace" like a gift to a bride. *Chesed* is supplemented by *chen* and *charis* (161). But issues arise of judgment *(mishpāt)* and righteousness *(tsedeq).* Hence Balthasar moves to consider "the obedience of the prophecy" (225-98). He traces a variable history from the early prophets through Amos, Hosea, Isaiah, and Jeremiah, to those who look forward to the new age. He writes, "God will deal with Israel: so much is implied, too, in the promises of unconditional forgiveness of sins" (Isa. 1:18, 25; 6:7; *GL* 6:254). A precious cornerstone will be set in place. Balthasar then argues, "Without Messianism, apocalyptic, and wisdom theology, there would be no New Testament" (363). There emerges a tragic but dynamic hope for the future. There is "glory ahead" (305-20), and God's great "speech event" will be renewed.

Volume 7 concerns the NT vision of God's revelation of his glory in Jesus Christ. Christ is God's manifestation or appearing. Christ both represents God and is God. But this entails the incarnation, the cross, and the descent into hell before the resurrection. But as B. Quash observes, "The Glory of the Lord gives birth to Theo-Drama" ("Hans Urs von Balthasar," 112). Indeed, much of Balthasar's thought on Christology appears in volume 2 of *Theo-Drama* (59-261), and much on the work of Christ, the cross, and descent into hell occurs in volume 4 of *Theo-Drama.* Because of limits of space, we turn now to *Theo-Drama.*

The five-volume *Theo-Drama* owes much to Karl Barth's emphasis on God's purposive and dynamic action through the grand theater of history from creation to the end. Balthasar shares Barth's Trinitarian and christological perspective, although, as we have seen, with certain reservations. In the first volume he observes, "The shortcomings of the theology that has come down to us over the centuries have called forth new approaches and methods in recent decades" (1:25). The key is Balthasar's comment, "All see theology stuck fast on the sandbank of rational abstraction, and want to get it moving again" (25). This undoubtedly reflects a "mood," as can be seen from two Protestant writers, among others, Kevin Vanhoozer, *The Drama of Doctrine* (2005), and Samuel Wells, *Improvisation: The Drama of Christian Ethics* (2004). Balthasar wants to focus on "events" rather than abstract ideas or concepts, and the "dramatic tension" inherent in Christian doctrine.

Volume 1 presents what its subtitle says: it is "prolegomena." The mere term "history," Balthasar explains, is not adequate: "the horizontal absorbs the vertical" (1:29). Humankind has a transcendental-historical destiny. More than this, we need *dialogue*. He comments, "Nowhere is this clearer than in the life of Jesus as the Fourth Evangelist describes it: there are many dialogues" (35). The action that takes place between God and the world required more than monologic discourse: it prepares for a new level. Balthasar also comments positively on "orthopraxy." He admits that it may encourage the tendency to dilute doctrine into ethics, but, understood rightly, it "fastens on action, embodiment, and the dimension of everyday human life." Political theology should not degenerate into liberal utopianism; such comments would encourage those who thought that Vatican II had gone too far. All these, however, if rightly understood, should promote communal theology. Balthasar's profound model is that of drama. "Narrative theology," by contrast, tends to assign predetermined fixed roles. Drama promotes the idea of a "world stage" (135), which some of the ancient Greek writers already anticipated. Pindar and Aristotle offer two of many examples (136-44). This is closely parallel with salvation history (155-77). Balthasar does not advocate the assimilation of this to idealism. Genuine drama presents "the illumination of existence," and a conjoint production of creativity by the author, the actor, and the director. They aim together at presentation, situation, and perhaps the theme of death. He endorses Goethe's comment, "The spectator's senses should be in a continual state of tension" (309), and the drama should be "shown" to him.

Volume 2 of *Theo-Drama* majors on the problem of hermeneutics, although it also speaks of humankind. Balthasar writes, "All theology is an interpretation of divine revelation. Thus, in its totality, it can only be hermeneutics . . . God interprets himself." This includes "his plan for the world — and this, too, is hermeneutics" (2:91). There occurs "the transposition of horizons" as horizons expand and change. Scripture is thus "a Word that journeys with us" (102). It is "precarious" to distinguish several "senses of Scripture" (113). The contrast between "letter" and "Spirit" should not be overpressed. But, like Pannenberg, he seeks a hermeneutic that will disclose a "totality." The remainder of the volume in part gathers themes and characters that may apply to the "world stage." Volume 3 is subtitled *The Dramatis Personae: Persons in Christ*. The first half of the volume again looks at problems of method, considering *Historie* and *Geschichte*, and historical-critical methods. Balthasar takes issue with both Strauss and Bultmann, seeing a hiatus between "the 'neutral,' historical Jesus and the existentially committed, bi-polar kerygma-faith" (3:68). Can this hiatus be overcome? The nineteenth-century thinkers largely failed to overcome it, as do also Fuchs and the New Quest, W. Marxsen, and many others. The "consistent eschatology" of Schweitzer and Werner cannot be revived. In the end we need both "dogmatic overlay" and an "exegetical overlay" for our Christology (110). The upshot of the discussion is to see dramatic "tension within the Christ-event itself" (117). It may resist an "epic" theological account, but will allow a "lyric," or contemplative, one. The goal is to reinstate a concrete invitation to discipleship. The way forward is to stress the role of *mission,* both that of Jesus and that of disciples (149-261).

In the second half of volume 3 of *Theo-Drama,* Balthasar finds the defining feature of the life of Jesus in his sense of mission. Jesus fully identifies himself with his mission. John, as we noted, gives this particular prominence. Karen Kilby rightly calls this "central" to Balthasar (*Balthasar,* 95). This is Balthasar's response to offering an "exegetical" and "dogmatic overlay" in his Christology. Jesus "was to complete his task, which embraced the whole of creation" (*Theo-Drama,* 3:149). This is "Christology from below," but with an eye to the possibility of "a Christology from above." "The concept of Jesus' mission appears linked with his highest qualification as 'Son of God'" (150). The idea of mission is "at the centre of John's Christology and expresses both the Trinitarian and soteriological dimensions of the mind of Jesus" (151). It is also part of the witness of the Synoptic Gospels. The notion of "sending" is related to that of "coming." He declares, "We see identity being given along with mission" (155). The person and work of Christ are rightly indissolubly tied together. Jesus was guided and "driven" in this mission by the Holy Spirit. This also finds expression in Jesus' relation to God as "Abba"; Balthasar comments, "Prayer is essential to the One who is sent" (170). This relates to Jesus' consciousness of God and consciousness of his mission (173-83). For Balthasar, this opens up a fruitful approach to the Trinity; "as Son, in the Holy Spirit, he obeys the Father" (227). Balthasar concludes this section with a discussion of woman as somehow "completing" man, although Kilby regards this as "ambiguous" (*Balthasar,* 127-36). Meanwhile, Balthasar comments, "The primary needs a partner of equal rank and dignity for its own fulfilment" (*Theo-Drama,* 3:284). Kilby finds this section troubling. In the remainder of the volume Balthasar explores Christology, Mariology, ecclesiology, and Trinitarian doctrine.

Volumes 4 and 5 explore "the action" and "the last act" of the drama. God's decisive action appears most of all in the cross. Volume 4 sets forth Balthasar's soteriology, and places time, freedom, victory, power, sin, and conflict in the light of the cross. It opens with the vision of the sovereign God in the book of Revelation. A. von Speyr sees this as pointing to its visionary and contemplative character, and Balthasar quotes her. In Christ, they urge, we receive "ever greater understanding of God" (4:18). The seer is lifted up to perceive the whole, and Christ's victory on the cross enables him to "open the book" of revelation. Christ's work has both substitutionary and participatory aspects. In volume 5 Balthasar develops this further, exploring "the Trinity and the mystery of God." The cross and the resurrection are above all "for us." This is the "the last act" of what Quash calls "the supra-drama of the Trinitarian God of love" ("Hans Urs von Balthasar," 114). A number of passages from von Speyr are quoted. God the Father, Balthasar has said in volume 4, "strips himself, without remainder, of his Godhead and hands it over to the Son" (4:323). He writes that he "lets go of his divinity" (325). This has echoes of the Protestant theologian Jürgen Moltmann. Balthasar emphasizes otherness and separation. *Kenosis* begins not in the incarnation or even the cross, "but in the Father's generation of the Son" (Kilby, *Balthasar*, 100).

Balthasar has also written about "Holy Saturday," or Christ's descent into hell. Whereas most theologians follow Luther in seeing this as a moment of Christ's victory in the realm of the dead, Balthasar sees it as the experience of solidarity with the dead in utter passivity. This is close to Calvin's idea of Christ's suffering that fate of the lost. Self-emptying, suffering, and *kenosis* receive the kind of attention that Moltmann gives to these themes.

Balthasar concludes his sixteen-volume masterpiece with three volumes entitled *Theo-Logic,* the first of which considers the role of theological logic within divine self-revelation. *Truth of the World* considers finite Being. The second volume inquires about norms of truth, and the third considers the work of the Holy Spirit. Balthasar's work is not so much argument as "showing" and contemplation. It may remind some in this respect of what both Heidegger and Wittgenstein have said about "saying" and "showing." It is certainly "contemplative" or "lyrical" rather than argumentative and critical. He has also introduced polyphonic discourse in his *Truth Is Symphonic,* and many other ideas. He is a cautious, but not dogmatic, Universalist. Like Barth, Balthasar often repeats the same themes in different contexts. His work, however, is simply too vast and too complicated to pick out simplistic points for endorsement or question, even if many Protestants would have reservations about his work on the Virgin Mary. Its strength seems to lie in its originality. To try to assess this monumental work in a closing page would simply be cheap and inadequate.

Reading: Hans Urs von Balthasar, *The Glory of the Lord,* 7 vols. (San Francisco: Ignatius; Edinburgh: T. & T. Clark, 1982-1991); Hans Urs von Balthasar, *Truth Is Symphonic* (San Francisco: Ignatius, 1987); Hans Urs von Balthasar, *Dare We Hope "That All Men Be Saved"?* (San Francisco: Ignatius, 1988); Hans Urs von Balthasar, *Theo-Drama,* 5 vols. (San Francisco: Ignatius; Edinburgh: T. & T. Clark, 1988-1998); Hans Urs von Balthasar, *Theo-Logic,* 3 vols. and epilogue (San Francisco: Ignatius; Edinburgh: T. & T. Clark, 2000-2005); Karen Kilby, *Balthasar* (Grand Rapids: Eerdmans, 2012); Ben Quash, "Hans Urs von Balthasar," in *The Modern Theologians,* ed. D. F. Ford, 3rd ed. (Oxford: Blackwell, 2005), 106-24.

Baptism

Infant baptism is treated in the entry **Baptist Theology,** although the arguments on both sides of that issue relate to the very nature and purpose of baptism, rather than only to subordinate questions about administration of this sacrament.

The main block of biblical material on baptism is found in Rom. 6:3-11, where it represents sharing in Christ's death and resurrection. Paul asserts, "All of us who have been baptized into Christ Jesus were baptized into his death. . . . We have been buried with him . . . just as Christ was raised from the dead . . . we too might walk in newness of life" (vv. 3-4). In Paul, therefore, it is symbolically and sacramentally (*see* **Sacraments**) dying out of the life in this world, and being created anew in the new world to the life that shares in Christ's resurrection. Paul speaks of new creation through death-and-resurrection, where John speaks of new birth.

The classic study of baptism in Paul, Rudolf Schnackenburg, *Baptism in the Thought of St. Paul* (New York: Herder and Herder, 1964), distinguishes between (i) baptism as cleansing (Gk. *apolouesthai*; *Baptism*, 3-17); (ii) baptism as incorporation into the body of Christ (*baptizein eis Christon*; 18-29); and (iii) baptism as sharing with Christ in a "salvation event" such as death and resurrection (*sun Christō*; 30-61). Schnackenburg's striking claim is that "cleansing" is the *least* prominent. Indeed, whether the supposed allusions of 1 Cor. 6:11, Eph. 5:26, and Titus 3:5 explicitly refer to baptism is open to question, as J. D. G. Dunn argues. This may be simply interpretative tradition or assumption. Dunn prefers to use the term "conversion-initiation" (*Baptism in the Holy Spirit* [London: SCM, 1970, 2010], 104, 120-23, 116-31).

The other two meanings remain prominent in Paul's thought, and Rom. 6:3-11 provides a *locus classicus* for the notion of baptism as sharing in the death and resurrection of Christ. The translation of *baptizein eis Christon* as "baptism *into* Christ" remains controversial. Certainly F. Danker in his third edition of Bauer's *Lexicon* renders the phrase "involvement in Christ's death and its implications for the believer" (BDAG 164). But whether *eis* denotes motion or movement here remains debated. If it denotes "into," it probably denotes "into the body of Jesus Christ." But it may signify simply allegiance to Christ ("baptized into Moses" in 1 Cor. 10:2). Whatever we conclude, Rom. 6:5 speaks of being "united with [Christ] in a death like his," for which the Greek is *sumphutoi*, "planted with." Grafting begins the process of union with Christ, but becomes an increasingly inextricable union. Gal. 3:27 offers a parallel: "As many of you as were baptized into Christ have clothed yourselves with Christ" (NRSV); (AV/KJV, "have put on Christ"; Gk. *Christon enedusasthe*). If movement is not implied, the use of *eis* in "believe in" *(pisteuein eis)* may offer a parallel. But the Greek for "put on" implies "dressed in new clothes," as the NRSV spells out. Baptism endows the candidate with a new public identity, which corresponds with the new life. In baptism the candidate "strips off" the old, to "put on" the new.

Schnackenburg comments, "Christ is not a 'sphere' into which we are plunged, but the personal Christ, with all that happened to Him; our baptism 'to Christ' has the goal of uniting us with this Christ" (*Baptism*, 25). (Schnackenburg is a Roman Catholic scholar but his book was translated into English by a Baptist, George Beasley-Murray.) Schnackenburg, too, sees baptism in Paul as an issue of a new *identity* (26-29). The notion of *pledging allegiance* to Christ naturally arises in this context. This is confirmed by baptism "in the name of Christ," and the parallel of allegiance to Moses in 1 Cor. 10:2. Schnackenburg sums this up: "Dying to the ruin wrought by the power of sin, with the goal of walking in a new life for God, is something different from the 'new birth' of the mystery religions" (59).

The most decisive and convincing work on supposed parallels with, or dependence on, Greek or Oriental mystery religions has been provided by G. Wagner, *Pauline Baptism and the Pagan Mysteries* (Edinburgh: Oliver and Boyd, 1967). Such theories date back to R. Reitzenstein and H. Wendland in the first decades of the twentieth century. But Wagner shows that both the alleged dating and the content offer insuperable problems. Most allegedly "parallel" rites in the mystery religions actually postdate Paul, making Paul's "dependence" on them impossible. Further, Paul prefers the term "new creation," as against rebirth in John, and centers his baptismal theology in Christ, the cross, and the resurrection (2 Cor. 5:14; Col. 3:3-4), and also death to the Law (Rom. 7:4).

C. F. D. Moule and Alan Richardson have drawn attention to baptism as an anticipation of the Last Judgment. Moule writes: "If Baptism is a voluntary death, it is also a pleading guilty, and acceptance of the sentence" ("The Judgment Theme in the Sacraments," in *The Background to the New Testament and Its Eschatology in Honour of C. H. Dodd,* ed. W. D. Davies and D. Daube [Cambridge: CUP, 1956], 465; cf. 464-81). Likewise, Richardson declares: "To be baptized is to accept God's verdict of 'guilty,' and so to be brought past the great assize and final 'judgment'" (*Introduction to the Theology of the New Testament* [London: SCM, 1958], 341). Finally, Tom Holland (and Arie Zwiep) also urges that in Paul baptism is not an individualist concept, especially in the light of Rom. 6:3-11, 1 Cor. 12:13, and Eph. 5:25-27. Christian baptism is "modelled on the baptism of Israel.... Paul has stayed within the corporate categories of the Old Testament" (Holland, *Contours of Pauline Theology* [Fearn: Mentor, 2004], 152-53).

All four Gospels underline the eschatological significance of baptism. John the Baptist baptizes those prepared for the Last Judgment (Matt. 3:1-12; Mark 1:4-8; Luke 3:1-17; John 1:19-27). The baptism of Jesus occurs in this context, to enable him to be "one of the prepared people of God" (C. K. Barrett). In Oscar Cullmann's words, "Jesus must unite himself in solidarity with his whole people, and go down himself to Jordan.... The baptism of Jesus points forward to ... the Cross" (*Baptism in the New Testament* [London: SCM, 1950], 18-19). Hence Jesus asks, "Are you able to ... be baptized with the baptism that I am baptized with?" (Mark 10:38). In John 3:22, Jesus is said to have baptized (cf. v. 26), and this is corroborated in John 4:1-2, which says the disciples of Jesus were baptizing. The meaning of John 3:5 is debated, though most refer "born of water" to baptism, unless it is natural birth. In Acts baptism includes remission of sins, but also the beginning of a new life (Acts 16:15; cf. 2:38; 8:36-38; 22:16). Peter's sermon in Acts 2 continues the theme by referring to God's promise (*see* **Sacraments**). Whereas the Lord's Supper is explicitly described as a covenant ritual, the covenantal significance of baptism remains often implicit in the biblical writings (Acts 3:25; 7:8;

Rom. 11:27; 2 Cor. 3:6; Gal. 4:24; Heb. 7:22; 8:6). This rightly became explicit in the Reformers and others. Baptism sets forth God's covenantal promise. Matt. 28:19 presents the commission to baptize in the threefold name of the Trinity as an explicit command of the risen Jesus Christ.

In the *Didachē* (probably the end of the first century or beginning of the second), chapters 7 and 8 give instructions about baptism. The *Didachē* declares: "Baptize in the Name of the Father and of the Son and of the Holy Spirit, in running water; but if you have no running water, baptize in other water" (7.1-2). The minister and candidates are bidden first to fast (7.4), and to pray the Lord's Prayer (8.1-3). Justin Martyr (early second century) refers briefly to baptism and the Lord's Supper (*First Apology* 65; *ANF* 1:185). Tertullian includes the treatise *On Baptism* among his writings, in which he calls it "our sacrament of water" (1.1). It washes away sins, and points, he argues, to the creative capacity of water to bring life (chap. 3; *ANF* 3:670). He relates water to the Spirit in Gen. 1:2 (chap. 4). Water may also prepare us to receive the Spirit (chap. 6). The laying on of hands may be used (chap. 8). Jesus Christ did baptize (chap. 11). But baptism must not be "rashly administered" (18.1; *ANF* 3:677). Hippolytus is often regarded as the most important third-century theologian, and was a rival bishop of Rome to Callistus. His treatise *Apostolic Tradition* recounts a period of three years before baptism for catechetical instruction in Scripture, morals, and prayers; prayer over the water of baptism; anointing and/or laying on of hands; renunciation of evil and the devil; and confession of belief. In postbaptismal clothes the candidate(s) would enter the congregation. Many argue that this reflects third-century practice at Rome.

In the post-Nicene church, the Syrian church included both turning from Satan *(apotaxis)* and adherence to Christ and the Trinity *(syntaxis)*. There is also a "second stage" of anointing (*Apostolic Constitutions* 7.22; *ANF* 7:469). But the stage of the anointing may be "beforehand," and "afterwards baptize," then "seal him with the ointment . . . the seal of the covenant." This is "dying together with Christ." In the late fourth century a postbaptismal anointing often occurred, which many compare with confirmation. After the fourth century, baptismal rites and ceremonies sometimes became more elaborate, especially later in the medieval West, when such additions as salt (representing wisdom) came to be involved.

Thomas Aquinas insisted on the one hand that God, not a human rite, brought forgiveness and new birth, but on the other hand that "every sin is taken away by baptism" (*Su Th* 3, qu. 69, art. 1, reply). In baptism a person "is incorporated in the Passion and death of Christ, according to Rom. 6:8. . . . He who is baptized is free from the debt of all punishment due to him for his sins" (art. 2, reply). Thomas quotes Augustine as declaring: "The fullness of grace and virtue flows from Christ, the Head of all His members" (art. 4, reply). He also cites Augustine as saying that children "die to that sin which they contracted at birth" (art. 6, reply). "Baptism opens the gates of the heavenly Kingdom to the baptized" (art. 7, reply to obj. 1). But to approach baptism with insincerity is "a mortal sin" (art. 10, reply).

John Calvin considers baptism in the *Institutes* 4.15. "Baptism is the initiatory sign by which we are admitted to the fellowship of the Church, that being ingrafted into Christ we may be accounted children of God" (4.15.1; Beveridge, 2:513). Like justification, it is independent of renewed forgiveness, bestowed "not . . . only with reference to the past" (4.15.3; 2:514). Baptism especially represents dying-with-Christ "and new life in him" (4.15.5; 2:515). "In baptism the Lord promises forgiveness of sins: receive it and be secure . . . God works by external means. But from this sacrament . . . we gain nothing unless in so far as we receive in faith" (4.15.15; 2:521). Even if the administration is faulty, Calvin resists "rebaptism": "This confutes the error of the Donatists, who measured the efficacy and worth of the sacrament by the dignity of the minister" (4.15.16; 2:521). Calvin then attacks the medieval embellishments of the rite: "the taper and chrism . . . exorcism . . . and other follies, to the open disgrace of baptism" (4.15.19; 2:523-24).

We treat infant baptism in the entry **Baptist Theology**, but we conclude by noting some broad trends. The "magisterial" Reformers advocated infant baptism, but in general in modern times Lutherans and Anglicans have stressed the importance of proxy sponsors in relation to vows and faith, while Calvinists or those in the Reformed churches tend not to require sponsors to speak for the child, on the analogy of circumcision under the old covenant. Hence confirmation became important, although recent rules about admission to Holy Communion have weakened this traditional emphasis. Roman Catholics tend to baptize infants, with an earlier date for confirmation and first communion, and the Roman Catholic *Ordo baptismi parvulorum* (1969) puts direct questions to the parents and godparents. However, the "radical" Reformers, who plagued Luther, pressed for baptism to be administered only to believers, along with the abolition of clerical robes and other "ceremonial" items. Thomas Müntzer is typical of this reaction. Zwingli initially argued for believer's baptism, but changed his mind, in line with Luther and Calvin. Some twentieth-century theologians have expressed sympathy for "believer's baptism," including Karl Barth, Emil Brunner, Eberhard Jüngel, and Jürgen Moltmann. In the modern ecumenical movement, many stress baptism as a focus of unity of all the churches.

Reading: O. Cullmann, *Baptism in the New Testament* (London: SCM, 1950); J. D. G. Dunn, "Baptism," in *The Theology of Paul the Apostle* (Edinburgh: T. & T. Clark, 1998), 442-59; L. Hartman, *"Into the Name of the Lord Jesus"* (Edinburgh: T. & T. Clark, 1997); R. Schnackenburg, *Baptism in the Thought of St. Paul* (New York: Herder and Herder; Oxford: Blackwell, 1964); G. Wagner, *Pauline Baptism and the Pagan Mysteries* (Edinburgh: Oliver and Boyd, 1967); G. Wainwright, *Christian Initiation* (London: Lutterworth, 1969).

Baptism in the Holy Spirit

Baptism in the Holy Spirit is decisively important in most Pentecostal and many Renewal Movement churches. The Pentecostal and Charismatic Churches of North America states: "We believe that the full gospel includes holiness of heart and life, healing for the body, and baptism in the Holy Spirit with the evidence of speaking in other tongues." M. P. Hamilton asserts: "The term *charismatic* applies to those who have experienced a 'baptism of the Holy Spirit'" (Hamilton, ed., *The Charismatic Movement* [Grand Rapids: Eerdmans, 1975], 7). It is often said to be rooted in Pentecost (Acts 2:1-4), but this is a *corporate* event for the apostles, not primarily an *individual* event. The promise that Jesus will baptize with the Holy Spirit (Mark 1:8) is also invoked, and most appeal to the further references in Acts 11:16 (Cornelius and Gentiles are baptized) and 10:44-46 (Gentiles are baptized). Frank D. Macchia broadens the concept to include "empowerment for ministry distinct from regeneration" (*Baptized in the Spirit* [Grand Rapids: Zondervan, 2006], 20), and insists that it is "a powerful experience received with or at a moment distinct from Christian initiation" (153). But he still views this as an "identity marker" for Pentecostals, although his fellow Pentecostal Gordon Fee calls it simply "the identity marker of the converted" (*Paul, the Spirit, and the People of God* [Peabody, Mass.: Hendrickson, 1996], 88). Yet Fee represents a minority view among Pentecostals.

The classic Pentecostal book edited by G. B. McGee, *Initial Evidence* (Eugene, Ore.: Wipf and Stock, 1991), argues that tongues-speech and "Holy Spirit baptism" are together "initial evidence" of the Pentecostal life (see C. M. Robeck, "William J. Seymour and 'the Bible Evidence,'" in *Initial Evidence*, 88). Veli-Matti Kärkkäinen has in fact shown that, whatever the theory, some 40 percent of Pentecostals do not speak in tongues. F. D. Bruner and A. W. Zwiep, among many others, argue, on the other hand, that the supposed experiences in Acts are all, first, *corporate* ones, not individual experiences; and second, whether they relate to Cornelius or the Samaritans, they are *"barrier-breaking"* events. A third serious problem lies in the *"event"* concept of sanctification, which is normally understood as a process that involves struggle, as Luther insisted. Macchia and Kärkkäinen, while remaining loyal Pentecostals, admit that the Holiness Movement in the past has left behind it controversial issues. Many "mainline" Christians may endorse the validity of the *experiences* of baptism in the Spirit while denying that Pentecostals use the appropriate biblical *terminology* for it.

Baptist Theology

For part of this article I am indebted to Stephen R. Holmes, *Baptist Theology* (London: T. & T. Clark and Continuum, 2012), as well as to many other Baptist writers, including especially H. W. Robinson, Paul Fiddes, George Beasley-Murray, and R. Torbet. Holmes begins his book by making three points. First, he declares, "Baptists form the largest Protestant denomination in the world today, numbering 100 million members spread across each continent" (1). Second, the influence of Baptist thinkers may be disproportionate to these numbers, because, since the emphasis falls so much on the local congregation, there are no catechisms, ordinals, or confessional statements that can be compared with those of "Reformed theology" or the Anglican Thirty-nine Articles or *Book of Common*

Prayer. Third, in spite of popular belief to the contrary, the practice of baptizing Christian believers only does not constitute the very most central doctrine of Baptists. It is the primacy of the individual and of the local congregation that is the deepest characteristic, and believer's baptism flows from this. In harmony with this conviction about the individual and the local congregation, they recognize no external constraint on these, whether in the form of state control or of centralized church control, such as bishops. Hence, historically they belong to the "separatist tradition," which may be traced back, according to Holmes, to the Radical Reformers, although Paul Fiddes argues that their roots lie with the mainline or magisterial Reformers. In addition to these three fundamental features, Holmes and others note a difference of emphasis between many Baptists in America and Baptists in Britain, Sweden, Germany, and other European countries. For example, Holmes claims that in American Southern Baptist thought, to be Baptist is often thought of as being "the purest evangelical" (4). They may also be unwilling to accept the proposals of such British Baptists as Paul Fiddes and George Beasley-Murray about structures for the ministry.

The earliest Baptists reacted against the brutal persecution of Protestants by Queen Mary (1553-1558) by escaping to exile in the Netherlands, where they formed local congregations. Under Elizabeth I (1558-1603) many returned, but because of Elizabeth's policy of moderate uniformity, some suffered imprisonment. A Baptist church was first founded in London between 1612 and 1616. Some joined the "Pilgrim Fathers" who sailed to Massachusetts in 1620, when James I was king. Meanwhile in England, a confession of faith was drawn up by several local Calvinist Baptist churches in 1644, who were known as "Particular Baptists." Further crises emerged with the 1662 Act of Uniformity under Charles II, which imposed the *Book of Common Prayer* on all clergymen, under oath. Meanwhile British Baptists had divided into "Particular Baptists" and "General Baptists." Particular Baptists limited the effects of the atonement to the elect and were usually Calvinist, while the General Baptists believed in a wider application of the atonement and were often Arminian. By around 1700, there were about 120 General Baptist congregations, who were largely in the Arminian tradition, and about 206 Particular Baptist congregations, in the Calvinist tradition. Holmes declares that by 1700 "Baptist life . . . was reasonably extensive and varied" in America (29), and in 1707 the first Baptist association was formed, composed of five Calvinist congregations. The first Baptist church in Boston was founded in 1663. The nineteenth century witnessed enormous growth, from 100,000 adherents in 1800 to three million in 1900. During this period a major split emerged in America, which was mainly regional. The Southern Baptist Convention was established in 1845. But in Britain the General Baptists and Particular Baptists came together in 1891 to form the Baptist Union of Great Britain.

Some of the American seminaries seemed to become more open to German biblical criticism and liberalism than their British counterparts. In the late 1820s, I. Chase modeled the curriculum of Newton Theological Institute to accord with that of German universities, while E. G. Robinson sought a mediating theology at Rochester Seminary. Nevertheless, others, such as, notably, Augustus H. Strong, maintained a strong conservative approach at Rochester from 1862 to 1912. In the 1890s the University of Chicago was founded by Baptists, and stressed the historical contingency and context in biblical studies, and theology took seriously Rauschenbusch's Social Gospel. Inevitably, a reaction set in against liberal theology, and from 1910 to 1915 some ninety essays were written and compiled in a work called *The Fundamentals,* edited by A. C. Dixon and R. A. Torrey. Dixon was an admirer of the leading English Baptist preacher C. H. Spurgeon. The Northern Baptist Convention declared in 1922 that the NT alone provided its basis of belief and practice. In turn, this led to a split between some seminaries: Northern Baptist Seminary, Chicago; Eastern Baptist Seminary, Philadelphia; and Boston Missionary Training School (which later became Gordon-Conwell Seminary) became rivals, in effect, to Chicago and Newton. In 1946 they formed the Conservative Baptist Fellowship. There were equivalent moves in the South. Meanwhile, from 1834 Baptists began to flourish in Germany.

Apart from the conservative-liberal division, which also affected other denominations, Holmes comments, "On most central doctrines — Trinity, Christology, eschatology and so forth — there is no distinctive Baptist theology" (8). Later he adds, "Fundamentalism is not the holding of particular doctrines, but a particular posture and attitude towards the wider world" (44). The movement was basically reactive and defensive. Nevertheless, it is "perhaps the most significant event for a theological history of Baptists in America in the twentieth century" (45). Yet later in the century there was a wide divergence in attitudes toward social issues, and from 1950 to 1970 "the public face of Baptist life in North America was theologically moderate" (45). Yet, since 1970 there has been a "resurgence of much more conservative tradition" under such theologians as Carl F. Henry (45). The Southern Baptist Convention is said to have been especially watchful about seminary teaching positions. Northern Baptist life and American Baptists in general, Holmes comments, seem "more generous" in recent years (49). On the other hand, Southern Baptists are also noted for their active involvement in politics and in social concern.

Meanwhile in Britain, at a grassroots level, many converts from the Billy Graham crusades became members of Baptist churches. Baptist biblical scholars from the 1960s to the 1980s included H. H. Rowley, H. Wheeler Robinson, George Beasley-Murray, and Ron Clements, and currently include Paul Fiddes, although Fiddes increasingly moved from NT to Christian doctrine. Many, such as Nigel Wright, retained links with Spurgeon's College, London.

Numerous arguments have been proposed about baptismal *practice,* but the issue of believer's baptism depends less on arguments about early practice than on fundamental theological convictions about the nature of baptism. Some writers trace a difference between "symbolic" and "sacramental" views within the Baptist tradition. The "symbolic" view understood baptism as broadly an "enacted sermon" (Holmes, 93) through the medium of personal witness and obedience that testified to God's grace in the life of the candidate. In the "sacramental" view, it is believed that baptism may bring about change in the believer as a "means of grace." Fiddes argues that the "symbolic" view derives ultimately from Zwingli on the Lord's Supper, and reflects especially the approach of the earlier General Baptists. The so-called sacramental view, he urges, goes back to Calvin on the sacraments, and is reflected especially in the earlier Particular Baptists. Further, in Germany, the classic debate between K. Aland and J. Jeremias emerged in the 1960s. Aland argues, "Because children are innocent they do not need baptism, they need it only when sinfulness awakens" (*Did the Early Church Baptize Infants?* [London: SCM, 1963], 106).

The heart of the problem, as H. Wheeler Robinson expresses it, is that "believers' baptism . . . is a simple return to primitive Christian custom," and it "emphasizes the necessity and the individuality of *conversion;* it is a *conscious* acceptance of his (Christ's) authority" (*Baptist Principles,* 4th ed. [London: Carey Kingsgate, 1960], 11, 13, 17, and 23). Both Wheeler Robinson and Karl Barth emphasize the place of consciousness. A well-known debate took place in Germany about baptismal practice in the earliest churches. First, J. Jeremias wrote *Infant Baptism in the First Four Centuries* (Eng. London: SCM, 1960; Ger. 1958). K. Aland offered a reply from the point of view of believer's baptism in *Did the Early Church Baptize Infants?* (London: SCM, 1963). Then Jeremias gave a counterreply in *The Origins of Infant Baptism* (London: SCM, 1963, 1971), and Aland responded again in an enlarged edition of his earlier book. In 1971 Aland noted Karl Barth's contribution. Jeremias examined proselyte baptism and "household" baptisms, which included Lydia (Acts 16:15), the jailer at Philippi (Acts 16:31-33), and Stephanas (1 Cor. 1:16; 16:15). He then traced the rise of infant baptism up to the end of the third century (*Infant Baptism,* 19-87). Aland replied that "households" did not necessarily include children, but may have included slaves and other adults. He identifies infant baptism as beginning not earlier than 200-203. Both sides tend to use the same data, and many regard this debate as inconclusive. O. Cullmann insists, "Those who dispute the Biblical character of infant Baptism have therefore to reckon with the fact that adult Baptism for sons and daughters of Christian parents . . . is even worse attested by the New Testament than infant Baptism" (*Baptism in the New Testament* [London: SCM, 1950], 26).

Nevertheless, many Baptists would argue that this is not the distinctive point about Baptist theology. Cullmann bases the case for infant baptism, in addition to arguments about divine promise and covenant, on the faith of the congregation as a *corporate* response, whereas the whole ethos of Baptist theology involves the *individual,* and the key role of *conscious* commitment. Indeed, the restriction of the age of baptism has not always been an issue, as long as baptism was by *immersion* and involved a *conscious* confession of faith. For Baptists there are prior questions about the church as the *gathered* community of the *local* church. The faithful believers are the "invisible" church. Normally baptism is essential for church membership. But in common with all Christian traditions, Baptists see baptism as unrepeatable, and an anchorage of the Christian life in the death and resurrection of Christ (Rom. 6:1-11). But even such baptism is only "normal." John Bunyan regarded only a confession of faith as necessary for belonging to the church, even if baptism was lacking. A more central issue under ongoing debate is the status of the ordained ministry. If ordination is through the call of a local church, does this mean that local ministers can have "universal" authority? P. Fiddes argues for a more-than-local significance for ordained ministry. But this view is still hotly debated.

Reading: G. R. Beasley-Murray, *Baptism in the New Testament* (New York and London: Macmillan, 1963); Paul S. Fiddes, *Tracks and Traces: Baptist Identity in Church and Theology* (Carlisle: Paternoster, 2003); Stephen R. Holmes, *Baptist Theology* (London: T. & T. Clark and Continuum, 2012); H. W. Robinson, *Baptist Principles* (London: Carey Kingsgate, 1960); R. G. Torbet, *A History of the Baptists*, 2 vols. (Valley Forge, Pa: Judson, 1973).

Barmen Declaration

This statement was drawn up by the Confessing Church of Germany at Barmen in May 1934 in the face of trends to make the church an instrument of Nazi policy. It stressed the sole Lordship of Christ, and defined the church's belief in the mission of the gospel in the face of liberalizing tendencies. It was influenced by the Swiss theologian Karl Barth.

Barr, James

James Barr (1924-2006) was born in Glasgow, and ordained to the Church of Scotland ministry in 1951. He was appointed professor successively at the University of Edinburgh, the University of Manchester, Vanderbilt University, and Oxford University, where he was first appointed Oriel Professor of Biblical Interpretation (1976-1978) and later Regius Professor of Hebrew (1978-1989). His most influential and remarkable book is *The Semantics of Biblical Language* (Oxford: OUP, 1961). In this book he draws on accepted principles in linguistics and semantics, especially those of Ferdinand de Saussure, to reappraise and criticize many examples of the neglect or misuse of linguistics in biblical interpretation. One such error is the regular tendency in some earlier volumes of G. Kittel, *Theological Dictionary of the New Testament*, to draw inferences about *concepts* from the use of *words* and their *etymologies*. On this basis some contributors put forward invalid claims about "Hebrew" and "Greek" thought forms. Another target is T. Boman's *Hebrew Thought Compared with Greek* (Eng. 1960). Barr attacks such generalizations as the contrast between supposedly static Greek thought and "dynamic" Hebrew thought, and between "abstract" Greek thought and "concrete" Hebrew thought (10-11). He declares, "The idea that the grammatical structure of a language reflects the thought-structure of those speaking it" is false (39). Saussure stresses the *conventional* character of grammar. In particular Barr attacks what he calls "the illegitimate totality transfer," namely, "adding up the semantic effects of various contexts... and from this you get a general picture" (71). Some scholars and preachers are notorious for adding up a multitude of contextual meanings, and then expounding the "total" cumulative "concept," as if the whole weight could be transferred to any context.

Barr next attacks confusion between etymology and meaning. He rightly declares, "The etymology of a word is not a statement about its meaning but about its history" (109). This can become "a kind of opportunist homiletic trick" (113). One mistake is to call etymology "the root meaning," as if it were essential to later meanings (114). Barr then looks more closely at Kittel. He asks, "Is there one concept for each word or not? Does the lexical stock correspond to the 'concept' stock?" (209). In practice Barr suggests at least five different meanings of "concept" (211). He then summarizes another principle. It is also an example of "illegitimate totality transfer" (217-18). A particular passage is used to bring together "the whole conception" in a theme (217). A clear example is "an adding or compounding of different statements about the *ekklēsia* made in various passages," and then pronouncing on "the New Testament conception of the church" (218). The seminal cause of all these errors is to regard the single isolated *word* as the bearer of meaning, rather than the *sentence* or speech act. The whole book has numerous practical outcomes, for example, the ascription of gender on the basis of accidental or conventional features of grammar. For example, do the Turks, he asks, have no concept of sexual difference because they do not assign gender in language, or have the French "extended their legendary erotic interests" by "forcing every noun to be masculine or feminine" (39)?

Barr's book is a classic landmark. Nothing else has had quite the same influence. Nevertheless, in *Biblical Words for Time* (London: SCM, 1962; rev. 1969) Barr calls for more careful study of the biblical vocabulary for time, for example, than may be found in Cullmann or Marsh. In *Fundamentalism* (London: SCM, 1977) he attacks a conservative evangelical view of Scripture. He especially attacks B. Ramm, J. I. Packer (226-29), R. K. Harrison, C. Hodge, and perhaps most of all B. Warfield (261-79). On the other hand, D. Guthrie and F. F. Bruce are commended for taking NT criticism seriously. Barr then published *The Scope and Authority of the Bible* (1980), *Beyond Fundamentalism* (1984), *Biblical Faith and Natural Theology* (1992), *The Concept of Biblical Theology* (1999), *History and Theology in the Old Testament* (2005), and *History and Theology at the End of a Millennium* (2005). Although he is often polemical and controversial, Barr is always provocative and sometimes creative, and nothing can detract from his work on semantics. It is unfortunate that this work is not more widely known and read, not least for his comments on gender.

Barrett, C. Kingsley

C. Kingsley Barrett (1917-2011) was professor of divinity in the University of Durham (1958-1982), a fellow of the British Academy (from 1961), president of

Studiorum Novi Testament Societas (1973), and a lifelong Methodist minister and preacher. He wrote numerous commentaries and other books on NT issues. His *Gospel according to St. John* appeared in 1955 and 1978, then his *Epistle to the Romans* (1957, 2nd ed. 1991); *The First Epistle to the Corinthians* (1968 and 1971); *The Second Epistle to the Corinthians* (1973); and *The Acts of the Apostles*, 2 vols. (1996 and 1998). Other works included *Essays on Paul* (1982); *Freedom and Obligation* (on Galatians, 1985); *From First Adam to Last* (1962); *The Gospel of John and Judaism* (1970 and 1975); *The Holy Spirit and the Gospel Tradition* (1967); and *New Testament Essays* (1972). He combined a lifelong interest in NT exegesis with issues in theology and the church.

Barth, Karl

Karl Barth (1886-1968) was born at Basel in Switzerland. His home background anchored him to a love of the Bible, and his confirmation class (1901-1902) also engaged positively with philosophical objections to Christianity. He studied initially at Bern, all the while wondering whether historical critical questions in biblical studies touched the central nerve of the gospel. His attitude to philosophy was mixed. He then moved to the University of Berlin, where Adolf von Harnack taught the "simple" truths of the Gospels in contrast to the supposedly "Greek" history of dogma. Wilhelm Herrmann shared Harnack's liberalism in theology, but Barth at least admired his characteristic notion of faith as relationship to Christ. The gospel, Herrmann stressed, was not simply *about* Christ. Neither Harnack nor Herrmann saw faith primarily as belief in doctrine but, Barth declared, Herrmann "was not ashamed of the Gospel," and he "soaked Herrmann in through all [his] pores." In spite of the influence of Kant, he was uncompromisingly church-centered.

Barth became ordained in 1909, and from 1911 to 1921 was pastor at Safenwil. There he saw his primary task as preaching, and began a constructive dialogue and correspondence with Eduard Thurneysen, pastor in a neighboring parish. Barth believed, however, that he "failed" as pastor at Safenwil. He thought he was too much under the spell of liberal theology. In 1914 a bombshell occurred. Germany invaded Belgium, and ninety-three German intellectuals signed a manifesto supporting Germany and the kaiser. The shock was that, in Barth's words, the signatories included "almost all my German teachers." Harnack and Herrmann had supported a hopeless cause. Barth recalls: "A whole world of exegesis, dogmatics, and preaching was shaken to the foundations." His diagnosis of liberalism included the following: (i) the confusion between Christian truth and "religion," when the latter might well justify Feuerbach's criticism of "God" as no more than a human projection; (ii) Kantian ethics that ignored sin's damage to human nature; (iii) human self-assertion, pride, and tendency to independence; and (iv) the reduction of Jesus to the status of a mere "teacher," in contrast to his demand for new creation and a radical "no" on human sin.

Barth declared, "The whole of human independence is weighed in the balance and found wanting." He could no longer share the legacy of Scheiermacher and Ritschl, but turned to the biblical message of "the living God." He began to mark out his distinctive alternative from 1917 onward. In February 1917 he wrote "The Strange New World within the Bible." This "new world" requires "not right human thoughts about God, but right divine thoughts about persons" (in Barth, *The Word of God and the Word of Man* [London: Hodder and Stoughton, 1928], 43). He writes: "A new world projects itself into an old ordinary world.... There is only 'the other,' new, greater world" (37, 42; cf. 28-50).

Barth's early work made a worldwide impact, especially *The Epistle to the Romans* (1919; 2nd rev. ed. 1922). He drew heavily on the nineteenth-century Dane, Søren Kierkegaard, to stress the shallowness of nominal Christianity, the hiddenness of God's grace, and the critical turning point required by our new creation. God remains transcendent, "Other," and sovereign. Christian experience arises not from latent capacities in human aspirations, but in the possibility of new God-given life. Barth rejects human religiosity, discovery, and a self-generated approach to a projected "God"; he stresses divine sovereignty, grace, freedom, decree, and choice. The second edition of 521 pages expanded these themes, as well as a dialectic of "no" upon the old life and "yes" upon the new. The influence of Kierkegaard became more prominent, especially his dialectic of either/or. The "no" to law was coupled with the "yes" to grace. Light blinds and brings judgment; or dispels darkness. All human groups and strivings are relativized before the message of grace. A "stone fell into the pool," it was commented, and the ripples extended throughout theology.

The Resurrection of the Dead was published in 1921 (London: Hodder and Stoughton, 1933). The Corinthians to whom Paul wrote believed, Barth argues, "not in God, but in their own belief in God, and in particular leaders.... Against this the clarion call of Paul rings out: 'Let no man glory in men' (1 Cor. 3:21).... 'Let him glory in the Lord' (1 Cor. 1:31).... 'Then shall everyone receive praise of God' (4:5). This 'of God' is clearly the secret nerve of the whole ... section" (17-18). In 1924 Barth published *Come Holy Spirit,* in which he stressed the priority of revelation over human discovery.

The transition or "hinge" that led to Barth's magisterial lifework, *Church Dogmatics* (Eng., 14 vols. with index), was his book *Anselm Fides Quaerens Intellectum* (1930), which he described as the "key" to the *Church Dogmatics.* Belief is a process initiated by God and ending in God, not a human construct. He makes this clear in the preface to the second edition of volume 1 of 1958, when he calls it "a vital key" to the *Dogmatics.* Belief is not a human striving toward God, but a participation in processes initiated by God. He writes: "It is only God himself who has a conception of God" (cf. 1 Cor. 2:7-16).

One of the last events before the appearance of the monumental *Church Dogmatics* came in 1933-1934, with the rise of Adolf Hitler and the Nazis. Barth took the lead in May 1934 in formulating the Barmen Declaration, the confessional document of the "Confessing Church," which called for the unity and renewal of the church and asserted the exclusive sovereignty of God with the Lordship of Christ. Officers of the state deserve respect, but do not "fulfil the Church's vocation, and the Church is not an organ of the State." Many Lutheran and Reformed pastors signed this confession. It constituted a clear challenge to the claims of Hitler and the Nazis. Later in 1934 Barth was in Rome when he formulated his famous dialogue and disagreement with his Swiss colleague Emil Brunner on natural theology. Barth associated the apparent willingness of the Roman Church to acquiesce to Hitler's demands with an overdependence on natural theology. He produced a rebuttal of Brunner entitled simply *No!* and denied any supposed "natural" point of contact between God and man. In 1933 the Nazis expelled him from his chair at Bonn for failing to take the oath of loyalty to Hitler, and he became professor at Basel until retirement in 1962.

The German edition of the *Church Dogmatics* ran from 1932 to 1967 (Eng. 1956-1975), but Barth was not entirely satisfied with the first volume, and subsequently revised it. The story of the earlier years has been recounted especially by E. Busch. In the first volume Barth asks: "Does Christian utterance derive from God? Does it lead to Him? Is it conformable to Him?" (*CD* I/1, 4). In sections 1-3 he sees the nature of theology as involving critical reflection on the limits of human knowledge, and on the basis for any possibility of talk concerning God. If God is the "object" of inquiry, "objectivity" entails not value-neutral inquiry, but inquiry in accordance with God, its "object." The Word of God comes to us as his *gift,* and as his *address* and his *act.* Yet this approach is far from "narrow." He declares: "God may speak to us through Russian Communism, a flute concerto, a blossoming shrub, or a dead dog.... God may speak to us through a pagan or an atheist" (p. 55). Section 3 also urges that the Word of God is revelation. Barth writes, "The Bible is the concrete means by which the Church recollects God's past revelation, is called to expectation of His future revelation, and is thus summoned and guided to proclamation and empowered for it" (111). "God speaks," but also where and when he chooses (120).

Section 4 expounds the Word of God in its threefold form: "the Word of God preached ... the Word of God written ... and the Word of God revealed" (88-124). Barth continues: "The Word of God is itself the act of God" (sect. 5, p. 143). The act may take the form of "a promise, a judgment, a claim" (150). This comes to a focus in Jesus Christ: "Jesus Christ, the Word of God, meets us as no other than God" (sect. 11, p. 435). Barth adds, "We believe in Jesus Christ as being 'of one substance (or essence) with the Father,'" and what God speaks in Christ is God himself (438). God is both Speaker and the Word. Barth adds that the works of the Trinity outside us are indivisible: *"opera trinitatis ad extra sunt indivisa"* (442), in accordance with patristic and Reformation doctrine.

In the second English volume (*CD* I/2) Barth continues to consider the Word of God. In sections 13-15 Barth considers the incarnation of the Word and revelation. The expectation and hope of Christ appear in the OT; and Jesus Christ is "very God and very man" (sect. 15, pp. 132-71). The phrase "born of the Virgin

Mary" shows that "Jesus Christ is the real son of a real mother" (185). Section 16 concerns the Holy Spirit, who is the subjective reality of revelation (203).

From 1955 onward Barth held special informal seminars for those English-speaking students who found his arguments in German not always easy to follow closely. These are published in Karl Barth's *Table Talk,* edited and verified by J. D. Godsey, SJT Occasional Papers 10 (Edinburgh: Oliver and Boyd, 1963). Commenting on I/1 and I/2, Godsey explains, "The Doctrine of God ... purposely *follows* the exposition of the Trinity, a reversal of the usual procedure in dogmatics" (5). In retrospect, Barth calls the term "dialectical" "unfortunate" when it functions partly as a contrast to "positivist" or "mystical" (24). In I/1 section 6, 4.2, he explains, "For me, the Word of God is a *happening,* not a thing ... the Bible must *become* the Word of God ... through the work of the Spirit" (*Table Talk,* 26). The church did not ultimately "choose" what constitutes the canon of Scripture; through the Holy Spirit the canon "forced" itself upon the church, and the church "recognised" this (27). In section 13 (I/2) Barth defends a polemic tone: "Liberalism is coming back.... Look at Rudolf Bultmann: he stems from Father Schleiermacher" (*Table Talk,* 41). He mentions Martin Werner and Fritz Buri in Switzerland. He reaffirms the last point: "The Church exists only as an *event* of the Word ... Word is a *living* reality" (42). Nevertheless, "we must begin with Christ.... It is Christ who assembles the Church." The Roman Catholic Church, in Barth's view, imprisons God (43).

In II/1 Barth turns explicitly to the doctrine of God. In a crucial sentence he urges, "God is known by God and by God alone" (179). He anticipates E. Jüngel by speaking of the "possibility" of knowing God, or of thinking and speaking of him. Barth stresses that God is always an *active* God, not an abstraction, or the static Being of Aristotle and perhaps Aquinas. Hence in section 26, "The Knowability of God," the theme is the readiness of God to be known (63). Knowledge of God depends on "His good pleasure" (74). But humankind must also become "ready" (sect. 26, pt. 2). Sin and the Fall express a high degree of human "closedness" in relation to God. This is why the problem of natural theology, he urges, is "grounded mischievously deep" (p. 135): humankind "finds God in Jesus Christ and in him alone" (149). "The victory of grace ... is called Jesus Christ: the crucified Jesus Christ, very God and very man.... In this the enmity of man against the grace of God is overcome, and therefore man is no more outside, where God must be unknowable to him" (153).

CD II/1, section 27, concerns the limits of the knowledge of God. Apart from his grace and decree, God remains hidden, as Luther declared. But even God's hiddenness can be perceived through faith alone. By God's grace and revelation, the ineffable, incomprehensible, and inexplicable can become manifest (186). Jüngel will later begin much of his work on the basis of Barth's axiom: "The hiddenness of God is the inconceivability of the Father, the Son and the Holy Spirit" (197). Hence in the following part (II/1, sect. 27, pt. 2) Barth considers the *truth* of God's revelation.

In the second half of II/1 Barth considers the reality of God, not as an abstraction, but through his actions: "God is who He is in the act of His revelation. God seeks and creates fellowship between Himself and us" (257). Most especially God "loves in freedom." God is "event, act, and life" (265). Essentially, God is "the One who loves" (272). This love entails a seeking and creation of fellowship (278). This love is lavished as a free and sovereign choice. The Lord loved you because he loved you (cf. Deut. 7:7-8); "God loves because He loves" (279). He loves to eternity. God's loving is his being and essence. In section 28, part 3 Barth writes: "His act is His own" (297). He loves in a unique way. God is "free from all origination, conditioning or determination from without" (307). God is the One who loves in the very act of his existence (321).

In the next sections (II/1, sects. 29 and 30) Barth writes of the perfections of God. These include God's grace and holiness (Heb. *chēn, chesed;* Gk. *charis*) and election. Typically this involves divine choice: "I will ... show mercy on whom I will show mercy" (Exod. 33:19; p. 353). Grace involves further that the one who receives it from God is "not only not worthy of it but utterly unworthy ... God is gracious to sinners ... [His] goodwill and favour ... remains unimpeded even by sin" (355). Further: "the holiness of God consists in the unity of His judgement with His grace. God is holy because His grace judges and His judgement is gracious" (363). In section 30, part 2, Barth includes among God's perfections his mercy and righteousness, and in part 3, his patience and wisdom. Section 31 considers God's unity and omnipresence, constancy and omnipotence, and eternity and glory, but is very closely associated with sections 28-29. Rightly he concludes: "Eternity is the living God Himself; it is impossible to look on eternity as a uniform grey sea" (sect. 31, p. 639).

In *CD* II/2 Barth considers the *God who elects and the God who commands* (chaps. 7 and 8). In his *Karl Barth's Table Talk,* Godsey comments, "In chapter 7 we came to an architectural positioning of decisive importance ... what Barth asserts to be the heart of the Gospel; the Dictum of God's Gracious Election" (6). He continues: "Election is not some hidden and horrible decree, but the decree revealed in Jesus Christ, who is the electing God and the elected man" (6). This volume explores the election of Jesus Christ, the election of the community, and the election of the individual. Indeed, Barth explicitly repeats much of *CD* II/2, section 33: "The Election of Jesus Christ." He repeats for the second time: "The election of grace is the sum of the Gospel" (II/2, p. 13). This theme relates to the mystery of God, the freedom of God, and the righteousness of God: "He rescues the creature from condemnation and ordains it to blessedness" (29). The freedom of this election confirms the sovereignty of God. In section 32, part 2, Barth recognizes that much of this is "apparently self-evident" from Scripture, but "not generally recognized today" (35). We have only to compare most German theology in the first half or middle of the twentieth century to appreciate the epoch-making orientation of Barth's theology.

Election is not a *decretum absolutum,* which might suggest *arbitrariness.* It is not just an inscrutable decree. It is part of God's involvement with us in Christ Jesus. Barth asserts: "Our own election by the grace of God directed towards us is revealed in the election of Jesus Christ" (107). "Jesus Christ reveals to us our election as an election which is made by Him" (115). As Paul said, and Jüngel would say again, "The *crucified* Jesus is the 'image of the invisible God'" (123; cf. Col. 1:15). This election expresses "the eternal will of God" (sect. 33, pt. 1). The election of the community includes Israel and the church (sect. 34, pt. 1) and is in accord with the promise of God, as heard and believed (pt. 3). The election of the individual ensures security: "He may let go of God, but God does not let go of him" (sect. 35, pt. 1, p. 317). An elected person has a special relation with God (pt. 2). Election expresses itself as Christ-like behavior (pt. 3). A "rejected" man isolates himself from God by resisting his election, but "God is for him . . . God is precious to him . . . God receives him" (pt. 4, p. 449). God refuses "to deal with the ungodly as the ungodly deserves" (319). For the cost was borne by Christ. When accused of universalism, Barth responded, "I do not teach it, and I do not *not* teach it."

The second half of II/2 is entitled "The Command of God." At one level "ethics interprets the Law as the form of the Gospel," but in a deeper light this encounters humankind "as sanctification" (chap. 8, sect. 36, p. 509). The context of God's command is the covenant. Hence ethics belongs to the doctrine of God. Barth writes: "It is only in this concept of covenant that the concept of God can itself find completion" (509). He argues that obedience to God is entailed when God is understood as the Lord of man (535). To that extent he asserts "dogmatics coincides with the ethical problem" (535). Ethics concerns right conduct, but dogmatics no less so. Hence Barth does not wish to build on "philosophical ethics" or "general ethics" (543). He will not follow either Roman Catholic or liberal Protestant ethics here. Theological ethics follows *from the doctrine of God as Lord and King,* not from some human ethical construction. He states: "The goodness of human action consists in the goodness with which God acts towards man. . . . God deals with man through His Word" (546). This is plausible and valuable, but does pose a dilemma. Diverse thinkers from Emil Brunner to C. S. Lewis have asked how human beings can "repent" if these standards are entirely and exhaustively given from without.

Barth now devotes no fewer than four of the fourteen English volumes to the doctrine of creation (III/1-4). The British editors make the point that while in volume II God cannot be known in abstraction, but "only in the outflow of his life and love to the creature," so in III/1-4, "*creation* cannot be known or interpreted . . . apart from the knowledge of divine election and salvation in Jesus Christ" (III/1, editors' preface, p. vii). Similarly, in Godsey's words, "The Doctrine of Creation can properly come only *after* the Doctrine of God, the heart of which is God's Gracious Election" (*Table Talk,* 7). *The eyes of faith transform "cosmos" into "creation."* Creation is understood on the basis of "the analogy of faith," not Roman Catholicism's "analogy of being." This theme occurs throughout the four

English parts of volume III. At the beginning of III/1, section 40, Barth expounds faith in God as the Creator. Creation itself is *not divine*. The belief in God as Creator is bold, and is an "appeal to faith . . . accepted only in faith" (p. 11). Creation is "an absolute gift of God" (15), and includes heaven and earth. Barth declares: "It is not enough to say that it [creation] occurs at the very beginning of the Bible. . . . It is plainly recalled and explained in many subsequent passages" (23).

In section 41 Barth explains the relation between *creation and covenant*. In 41, part 2, the distinctive existence of humankind emerges, he declares, "in the true confrontation and reciprocity which are actualised in the reality of an 'I' and a 'Thou'"; God "'created them male and female.' . . . He would not be man if he were not the image of God. . . . He willed the existence of a being which in all its non-deity and therefore its differentiation can be a real partner; which is capable of action and responsibility in *relation* to Him [God]" (184-85, italics mine). "It is in the *differentiation and relationship* of man and woman, the relation of sex, that there is . . . an indication of the creatureliness of man. . . . It is in this form of life and this alone, as man and woman, that he will continually stand before God" (186, italics mine). This capacity for entering with a relationship, or "relationality," becomes the condition or basis for entering into a covenant between two persons. However, in section 41, part 3, Barth also approaches this from the opposite angle. He declares: "Creation is the road to covenant" because the creature is in no position to act alone as the partner of God (231).

CD III/2, as G. W. Bromiley and T. F. Torrance suggest, "should finally destroy the charge that Karl Barth has nothing to say about man. Here under the title 'The Creature' he has in fact given us the most massive account of the doctrine of man in our times" (preface, p. vii). This volume exceeds 650 pages, and expounds human creatureliness; humankind as God's covenant partner; the unity of mind and body; and human beings and time. The *most striking feature of this volume is that the uniqueness of the human relation to God is summed up in Christ*. Barth declares: *"Jesus is man as God willed and created him"* (III/2, sect. 43, p. 50, italics mine). This is because, among other things: "What man is, is determined by God's immediate presence and action in this man." *Jesus Christ is* "the ground and goal of man's creation: *man as God willed him to be*" (50, italics mine). We should *not* ask in theology "Was Jesus truly human?" but "Are *we* truly human, in the light of Christ's perfect humanness?" To be a human being is to be with God. III/2, section 44, part 1 expands the theme of "Jesus, man for God." Part 2 explains "the phenomenon of the human." In part 3, Barth states: "We are condemned to abstractions so long as our attention is riveted as it were on other men, or . . . on man in general [rather than] that one man among all others . . . the man Jesus" (132).

In section 45 Barth anticipates D. Bonhoeffer's aphorism that Jesus is "the man for others." As covenant partner of God, we see "Jesus, Man for other men" (203-22). Real man is responsible before God, and in the case of Jesus Christ "other men are the object of [His] saving work" (208). In section 46 Barth affirms that humankind also belongs to the visible, natural, earthly world of bodies (349), a theme Ernst Käsemann will later take up. Finally, in this volume (III/2), "Man lives in the allotted span of his present, past, and future life" (sect. 47, p. 437). Man lives as he has time (438).

Church Dogmatics III/3 largely concerns the *providence and care of God*, God as Father, and the *threat of "nothingness."* "Nothingness," for Barth, denotes anything evil that threatens to thwart the will and love of God. In providence, God "has associated Himself with it [his creation] in faithfulness and constancy as this sovereign and living Lord, . . . preserving, co-operating and overruling" (14). The doctrine of providence and divine "ruling" is part of the biblical and Christian theme "that the idea of divine world-governance becomes a practical idea: an idea which illuminates both individual life and the life-process generally. . . . [Life is] more than a mere mass of things and events" (191; *see* **Kingdom of God**). Evil emanates from chaos, which is the absence of God's creative and re-creative activity. In this sense, evil becomes "nothingness," an absence of God's action, which is unnatural, absurd, and without order. For "God . . . alone, can deal with it and has already done so. . . . We cannot and must not include it in the creaturely world" (303). Yet it has an objective reality for the creature, as Paul expounds in 1 Corinthians 8 (350). Thus: "The character of nothingness derives from its ontic peculiarity." ("Ontic" concerns "entities," in contrast to "ontological," which concerns Being-itself.) Barth then discusses angels, who are God's messengers or authentic witnesses, and "victoriously ward off the opposing forms and forces of chaos" (369).

In *CD* III/4 Barth again rejects the notion of an *independent ethical system*. Ethics arises *as obedience to God*. A variety of practical issues emerge: the Sabbath, confession, and prayer (sect. 53); man and woman, parents and children, and neighbors (sect. 54); and respect for life, and protection of life (sect. 55). God gives freedom to humankind to keep God's holy day as a day of worship, freedom, and joy, to confess to him, and to bring his own requests for prayer (sect. 53, p. 47). The Sabbath commandment is central because "it points him [man] away from everything that he himself can will and achieve and back to what God is for him and will do for him" (53). *Confession* constitutes part of humankind's responsibility to bear witness to God, and "not [be] ashamed of the gospel" (Rom. 1:16). Barth urges: "Prayer is continually described in the Bible as the content of particular moments in the history of biblical man" (89). The basis of prayer is human freedom before God. Prayer states both need and desire in the form of petition. "Freedom" also excludes "mechanical" prayer (113).

In section 54 Barth expounds the difference between men and women. "Man never exists as such, but always as the human male or the human female. . . . Normative for all other relationships, is . . . the relationship in this differentiation. . . . In all that characterises him as man he will be thrown back upon woman, or as woman upon man" (117-18). He appeals to Eph. 5:22-23 and other passages for the cooperation and complementarity of the genders. Barth attacks what he calls "flight from one's own sex," which he finds in Simone de Beauvoir's *Second Sex*

(1949) and in the atheistic existentialist influence of Jean-Paul Sartre. Admittedly, he says, her book has merits, but she reinstates one mythology in place of another (161-62). Certainly "there is no longer male and female . . . in Christ Jesus" (Gal. 3:28), "but each sex has also to realise that it is questioned by the other. . . . As man and woman [they] are human in their co-existence and mutual confrontation" (167). Hence: "Marriage as a life-partnership is in itself a highly significant work" (189). Barth further argues that fatherhood and motherhood confer an indelible character and "irrevocable turning-point" in the life of an individual (277). This status and role bestow both honor and obligation. Parents themselves must be disciplined people. The challenge to children to honor parents is balanced by the challenge to parents to love and care for their children, until they no longer need parental discipline.

CD IV/1-4 concerns the doctrine of reconciliation. This includes Christology, soteriology, justification, sanctification through the Holy Spirit, and related themes. Barth begins with Christology and the phrase "God with us," which is "at the heart of the Christian message" (IV/1, sect. 57, p. 6). God's being with us constitutes an *event*, not a state, which is part of God's *act*. It is "the entry of God for us in becoming man as the making of peace between Himself and us" (13). It initiates our "restoration" after the loss caused by our own transgression. This is "the fulfilment of the covenant between God and man . . . the resumption of a fellowship which once existed" (22). The fulfillment of the covenant "has the character of atonement" (67). Reconciliation begins with the grace and initiative of God, or as Barth explains in section 58, God reestablishes and continues his covenant.

Reconciliation is unfolded in section 58, part 2, in terms of faith, hope, and love. In the course of explaining the role of faith, Barth declares, "God's justifying sentence is His all-powerful decision what man really is and is not. In Jesus Christ he is not a rebel" (p. 99). On love, he asserts, "The love of God in Jesus Christ is decisively, fundamentally and comprehensively His coming together with all men" (103). On hope, Barth writes, "Jesus Christ is the divine pledge as such" (115).

In part 3 Barth expounds Jesus Christ as Mediator. The Mediator stands between "the reconciling God above and reconciled man below" (122). (Even in industrial, political, international, and marital disputes, "mediation" has become a familiar term, and certainly remains very important to John Calvin.) Barth reiterates that "in Jesus Christ we have to do with very God" (pt. 4, p. 128). He represents, and is, God to us (as in descending mediation). But he is also man in this process of mediation, representing us to God (as in ascending mediation). Hence Jesus is both Servant, as man, and Lord, as God: "the Servant is Lord" (135). As Mediator, Jesus Christ is also Guarantor of reconciliation (157).

In sections 59-63 Barth expounds the work of Christ as man (the obedience of the Son of God), the fall of man, his justification, and the work of the Holy Spirit in the gathering of the Christian community. Barth writes in section 59:

"The eternal Son of the eternal Father became obedient by offering and humbling Himself to be the brother of man, to take His place with the transgressor, to judge him by judging Himself and *dying in his place*. But God the Father raised Him from the dead, and in so doing recognised and gave *effect to His death and passion as a satisfaction made for us*" (p. 157, italics mine). It is often claimed that "vicarious substitution" is simplistic, but to accuse Barth of being simplistic is to be either overbold or rash. Barth places all this work under the category of "history." He adds, "There can be no doubt about the full and genuine and individual humanity of the man Jesus of Nazareth" (159-60).

Barth does not quite establish a *narrative* of the Trinity in the way taken by Moltmann, Pannenberg, and Rogers, but the christological part of IV/1 increasingly turns to narrative, and thus partly anticipates this. Barth compares the work of Christ with taking the way of the Son of God "into the far country." At this time Barth was also writing *The Humanity of God*. It is *as God* that Christ emptied himself and took the form of a servant (Phil. 2:5-11). The incarnation means "not only God's becoming a creature . . . but it means His giving Himself up to the contradiction of man against Him, His placing Himself under the judgement under which man has fallen . . . under the cause of death. . . . The meaning of the incarnation is plainly revealed in the question of Jesus on the cross: 'My God, my God, why hast thou forsaken me?' (Mk. 15:34)" (185). But "He does not cease to be God. . . . He mingles with sinners and takes their place" (185). Section 59, part 2, repeats the theme: "The Judge Judged in Our Place" (211-83). "The far country" in Barth is "the loneliness of creaturely being" (211). Part 3 continues the theme with "the verdict of the Father." Faith demands "trusting and obeying the divine verdict" (323).

In section 60 Barth considers "the pride and fall of man." He has postponed the subject until now because "the knowledge of God alone includes within itself the knowledge of sin" (363). *It is when we are confronted with the holiness of God that knowledge of sin emerges.* This ensures that sin, as Athanasius and Anselm insist, is to do with our attitude to God, and not mere moralism. Sin is also exposed in our knowledge of the obedience of Christ: "It is again Jesus Christ in whose existence sin is revealed" (403). In section 60, part 2, Barth sees sin as especially pride: "the sin of man is the pride of man" (413). It is a loss of being-open to God, in contrast to the humble obedience of Jesus. There are points of affinity with Reinhold Niebuhr here, especially in Barth's language about "the concealment of human pride." Barth cites: "The chastisement of our peace was upon him" (453). The concept of "the fall of man" (part 3) underlines the essence of sin as the pride of man (478). Sin is that under which "all men stand" (Rom. 3:23; 5:12; 11:32; p. 501).

Section 61 considers the justification of the sinner by grace alone. Barth asserts: "Promised to man in Jesus Christ, hidden in Him and only to be revealed in Him, it cannot be attained by any thought or effort or achievement on the part of man" (514). The judgment and sentence of God were executed in the death of Christ. It concerns not only status, but the transition of man "without God and dead" into man "living from God" (520). Although in Barth justification is not the "central dogma," he finds it "understandable" that at times it has to assume this position (521). But "pardon by God ... unconditionally pronounced and unconditionally valid — that is man's justification" (568). This is by "faith alone" (sect. 61, pt. 3). But, as he has said before, this does not contradict obedience or ethics. He declares, "The Holy Spirit is the awakening power in which Jesus Christ has formed and constantly renews His body" (sect. 62, p. 643). This is the "catholic and apostolic Church" (643).

CD IV/2 and IV/3 continue what was promised in IV/1. Barth considers the exaltation of Christ. He also uses the phrase "misery of man" (sect. 65), as Wolfhart Pannenberg does for humankind separated from God, and then considers justification (sect. 66) and the Holy Spirit in the church. To those who have been justified "the call to discipleship . . . has come," and this awakening to conversion and obedience (IV/2, sect. 66, p. 499). Sanctification is sometimes called "renewal." In practice, justification and sanctification are "two different aspects of the one event of salvation" (503). The relation of one of "connexion, not identity" (503), although "they do belong inseparably together" (*see* **Sanctification**). IV/3.2 includes "The Vocation of Man" (sect. 71). This signifies primarily vocation to be a Christian, and to be united with Christ. This carries with it the command to be a witness to Christ. Since "witness" is related to (Gk.) *martus* and martyrdom, witness often involves affliction (pt. 5). Barth then turns to the sending of the Christian community by the Holy Spirit.

CD IV/4 is only partially complete. Barth was aware that, in his words, "I have gradually begun to lose the physical energy and mental drive necessary to continue and to complete the work" (vii). In 1967 he was in his seventies, and when the British editors were checking the proofs, Barth died in December 1968. The existing text considers the Holy Spirit and obedience or ethical conduct. Barth regards "Christ" as true baptism, but uses the term "baptism with the Spirit" to distinguish the Spirit-led life from water baptism. Baptism with the Spirit is bearing the fruit of the Holy Spirit, as in Galatians 5 (39). Water baptism is "an act of hope" (206). Baptism, prayer, and the Lord's Supper are pivotal in importance, but in each we must distinguish between God's work of grace and man's work.

After years of the dominance in Europe of liberal theology, Barth shattered the theological world with a strong and detailed presentation of orthodox (largely evangelical) truth. The way of Kant, Schleiermacher, and Harnack had been rejected. He re-presented the text as Reformed theology for the twentieth century. His influence can be seen in Britain in T. F. Torrance, John Webster, and Alan Torrance, in America in George Hunsinger and in part Hans Frei, and in Germany in Eberhard Jüngel. Barth has also been an important influence on Dietrich Bonhoeffer, Jürgen Moltmann, and Wolfhart Pannenberg. He has influenced the Roman Catholic theologians Hans Küng and Hans Urs von Balthasar. Necessarily he remains controversial. We conclude by noting again that his most important contributions are in the two areas of the Holy Trinity and Christology. He sees Jesus Christ as "the man of God as God willed Him to be" (*CD* III/2). Many dissent from him on the Trinity, accusing him of a tendency toward modalism. Many also criticize his dismissal of natural theology and of general ethics, rejecting the implication that humankind has no moral sense independent of knowledge of God. Even his colleague Emil Brunner took issue with this: How could "repentance" be possible if this is the case? Yet his belief that ethics derives from the doctrine of God is a valuable defense against mere moralism and anthropocentric ethics. He remains one of the half dozen key theologians of the twentieth century, probably the greatest of the first half of the twentieth century. It is a pity that many seem to write him off on the basis of short summaries, which can never do justice to Barth's complex and nuanced thought. (*See also* **Barmen Declaration; Brunner, Emil; Dialectic; Harnack, Adolf von; Natural Theology.**)

Reading: Karl Barth, *The Word of God and the Word of Man* (London: Hodder and Stoughton, 1928); Karl Barth, *The Epistle to the Romans* (Oxford: OUP, 1933); Karl Barth, *The Resurrection of the Dead* (London: Hodder and Stoughton, 1933); Karl Barth, *Church Dogmatics,* 14 vols. (Edinburgh: T. & T. Clark, 1957-1969); E. Busch, *Karl Barth: His Life from Letters and Autobiographical Texts* (Philadelphia: Fortress, 1976); J. Webster, *The Cambridge Companion to Karl Barth* (Cambridge: CUP, 2000).

Base Communities

These emerged especially in the late 1960s and 1970s and in the context of Latin American liberation theology. The movement as a whole insisted that grassroots church members should not be overshadowed by "academic" leaders. Carlos Mestos and Rubem Alves urged that "base communities" comprise lay-led groups. Often they range in number from about a dozen to thirty or more. Tape-recorded transcripts of their discussions are available in *The Gospel of Solentiname,* ed. Ernesto Cardenal (Maryknoll, N.Y.: Orbis, 1982). These communities suggest freedom from academic constraints and from church hierarchy. But some of the "lay-led" ideas betray lack of necessary competence or knowledge, as when Mary is called a "Marxist." They at least stimulate thought and commitment at the most basic grassroots level.

Basil of Caesarea

Also known as Basil the Great, Basil (c. 330-379) was the brother of Gregory of Nyssa and friend of Gregory of Nazianzus. The three are known as the Cappadocian Fathers. In 364 Eusebius of Caesarea called him to defend orthodoxy, and he succeeded Eusebius as bishop of Caesarea in 370. He defended an orthodox doctrine of Christology against Eunomius and the Arians, and the deity of the Holy Spirit against the "Pneumatomachi." It is said that he was exceptionally learned, eloquent, and devout. Most of his work *On the Holy Spirit* was written during his episcopate. One primary theme was to give honor to the Holy Spirit in the use of the threefold Trinitarian Gloria (1.3). He urged that the Spirit is holy without qualification. Hence, two years after his death, the Council of Constantinople confessed, "The Holy Spirit is worshipped and glorified together with the Father and the Son." In *On the Holy Spirit* 2-8 he carefully examines biblical passages that relate to the Spirit, arguing in 6-8 for the coequality of the Three; in 17-22 he reemphasizes the Spirit's coequality with the Father and the Son, his deity, and his coglorification.

Bauckham, Richard J.

Richard J. Bauckham was born in London in 1946, and has numerous publications in theology, the history of doctrine, and the NT. This gives him a distinctive command of three fields. After a doctorate and fellowship at Cambridge, he taught the history of Christian thought at the University of Manchester for fifteen years and then was professor of NT at St. Andrews from 1992 to 2007. He is emeritus professor and a fellow of the British Academy. His exceptional book *Jesus and the Eyewitnesses* (Grand Rapids: Eerdmans, 2007) won both the Book Award from *Christianity Today* and the Michael Ramsey Prize for its careful argument that established the importance of eyewitnesses for the life and teaching of Jesus. He followed this with *The Testimony of the Beloved Disciple,* on John. He also wrote *The Theology of the Book of Revelation* (1993), *The Theology of Jürgen Moltmann* (1995), and *Jesus and the God of Israel* (2008).

Baur, Ferdinand Christian

Ferdinand Christian Baur (1792-1860) was educated at the University of Tübingen and taught NT there from 1826 to his death. He became the founder of the so-called Tübingen School. He famously denied the authenticity of all the Pauline epistles except Galatians, 1 and 2 Corinthians, and Romans, and attributed the date of Acts to the later second century. Technically he was professor of church history and dogmatics. His criteria for Pauline authenticity were arguably circular, assuming that Paul was dominated by the controversy of Judaism and the Law, and that the absence of this theme invalidated claims to Pauline authorship. He saw the beginning of church history in terms of the "parties" at Corinth: a "Pauline" party was supposedly opposed by a "Petrine" or Matthean Judaizing party, which led to a third stage of early "Catholicism" represented by the latest NT writings, especially John and Acts. J. Munck has since argued that the splits at Corinth were not "parties" at all, let alone theological parties, and D. R. Hall argued recently that the leaders' names were fictitious or artificial devices used for pastoral reasons. Baur's supposed dependence on Hegel's view of history and dialectic remains controversial, and depends on the careful dating of his writings in comparison with Hegel's.

Baxter, Richard

Richard Baxter (1615-1691) represents the Puritan tradition, but he was also a loyal priest of the Church of England. He was known for his literary output, his pastoral sensitivity, his concern for the unity of the church, and his evangelistic concern and outreach. He served as a Church of England minister from 1638 to 1642, when he became chaplain in the Parliamentarian Army. After the Restoration he was appointed a royal chaplain. He declined an appointment as bishop in 1662. He wrote some eighty-seven books, of which *The Saints' Everlasting Rest* (1650) is probably the most widely known. In this he argues that no Christian should expect to "rest" in the present. But he also considers "the glorious appearing of Christ," the resurrection of the dead, the Last Judgment, and "the saints' coronation." If the heavenly host of angels praised God at the birth of Jesus, he writes, "with what shouting will saints and angels at the Day proclaim glory to God" (*Saints' Everlasting Rest* 2.1). The resurrection of the dead will equally be a cause of praise. Baxter was also an accomplished hymn writer, writing, for example, "Ye Holy Angels Bright" (*Hymns Ancient and Modern,* 546). In the church he struggled tirelessly against separation and on behalf of unity. He is also very well known for his book *The Reformed Pastor* (1656). This encouraged his colleagues to see the privileged and stupendous nature of their office, and to be diligent in pastoral care.

Beatific Vision

This is the term used to denote the final face-to-face vision of God that is granted to the Christian at the end of the earthly pilgrimage. It is often said, "It is not in heaven that we find God, but in God that we find heaven," that is, eternal blessedness. This does not imply transposition into some "timeless" state, such as we find in Platonism. Christians will behold God in all his living, purposive, ever-fresh action.

To see God entails enjoying his presence and his glory. Paul writes, "For now we see in a mirror, dimly, but then we will see face to face" (1 Cor. 13:12). God's glory also involves the climax of a process: we "are being transformed . . . from one degree of glory to another" (2 Cor. 3:18), and Christians will see "the light of the knowledge of the glory of God in the face of Jesus Christ" (2 Cor. 4:6). The writer to the Hebrews also sees Christ as "the reflection of God's glory and the exact imprint of God's very being" (Gk. *apaugasma tēs doxēs kai charactēr tēs hypostaseōs autou;* Heb. 1:3). Similarly in Luke-Acts Stephen "gazed into heaven and saw the glory of God and Jesus standing at the right hand of God" (Acts 7:55). Jude affirms that God will "make you stand without blemish in the presence of his glory with rejoicing" (Jude 24). In the Revelation of John the martyrs enter the open heaven and acknowledge, "Just and true are your ways," and see the manifestation of the glory of God (Rev. 15:3, 8), while heaven is permeated with "the glory of God and radiance like a very rare jewel" (21:11). The "city" has no need of the sun, "for the glory of God is the light, and its lamp is the Lamb" (21:23). "Glory" is articulated by the symbol of light, but this merely scratches the surface of what is meant by "glory."

Glory denotes the visible manifestation of God's presence. In the OT the phrase "the glory of God" occurs some forty times, often in the context of seeing God's glory as an encouragement to be fearless and strong (Isa. 35:2, 4). Ezekiel uses the symbol of a rainbow on a cloud as "the appearance of the likeness of the glory of the LORD" (1:28). The glory of the Lord in Ezekiel can move. In Hebrew the word for glory *(kābōdh)* denotes "what weighs heavily" or is "weighty," as when we might speak of a "weighty" person. In the LXX and NT the Greek *doxa* and the verb *doxazō* are associated with honor, splendor, and reputation. God's glory includes the reputation of his faithful goodness to Israel over the generations. In secular Greek "glory" often denotes people's ground of confidence or special gift, as when Odysseus glories in his cunning and guile, or Agamemnon or Achilles in his strength. God's glory, however, is especially the *cross,* a glory that points to his grace even through humiliation and self-emptying. Hence the beatific vision includes seeing God not only in majesty, but also in the crucified Christ. Indeed, one writer uses the phrase "the Christlikeness of God." To glorify God, as J. Moltmann asserts, also means to love him for his own sake. The glory of God is not the means to something else; it is the sheer joy of celebration.

It is important to understand the *Trinitarian* nature of the beatific vision. God is God-in-Christ, who suffered and died for us, and has been raised and exalted in glory. But God-as-Holy-Spirit offers no timeless, abstract, or static portrait of God (which some may fear could put a limit to "eternal" joy). The Holy Spirit is ever fresh, ever new, ever moving, and the beatific vision will be a vision of the *living, sovereign, purposive God,* who will do *new* things. Thomas Aquinas speaks of the beatific vision, but this tends to be abstract and timeless. The beatific vision will immerse Christians in the Being and Life of God, for which *purely visual* imagery is symbolic of something that is beyond earthly things. Its particular climax lies in *face-to-face* meeting. A face sums up a whole history of a relationship. God's face will not only be splendiferous and overwhelming in majesty and holiness, but also, through God in Christ, *welcoming.* In biblical language, the Christian shall "see" a shining, radiant face, which will in turn cause the "face" of the Christian to shine and be radiant. (*See also* **Time**.)

Bede

Known as "the Venerable," Bede (c. 673-735) may be especially famous for his *Ecclesiastical History of the English People* (731), but he was above all a biblical scholar. He wrote the *Commentary on the Acts of the Apostles* (c. 709); *Homilies on the Gospels; A Commentary on Luke* (c. 709-716); *Excerpts from Augustine on the Letters of Paul;* and numerous other works. He entered the monasteries of Wearmouth and Jarrow at the age of seven, and at thirty was ordained priest. "Venerable" refers not to a title as archdeacon, but most probably to the veneration of his bones, moved from Jarrow to Durham Cathedral for safety. He describes the first duty of his life as "applying myself entirely to the study of Scripture" (*Ecclesiastical History* 567). He learned Latin, Greek, and Hebrew, and his commentaries drew upon traditions from Augustine, Ambrose, Jerome, and Gregory.

Benedict XVI

Formerly Cardinal Joseph Ratzinger (b. 1927), Benedict XVI served as pope from 2005 to 2013, following Pope John Paul II. He was born in Bavaria, Germany, and his family was hostile to the Nazis. At fourteen he was compelled to join the Hitler Youth, and in 1943 was called up as a "child soldier," and then drafted into the infantry. In 1945, as the Allies advanced, he deserted. After the war he studied in the Catholic Faculty at Munich, and was ordained a priest in 1951. In 1953 he submitted a doctoral dissertation on Augustine, and completed his "Habilitation" thesis on Bonaventura. He became professor at the University of Bonn in 1959, and professor at Münster in 1963. Like Rahner, he served as *peritus*, or theological adviser, for Vatican II (1962-1965). Like Küng, Schillebeeckx, and Rahner, whom he greatly admired, he was regarded as a reformer. In 1966 he became professor of dogmatic theology in the University of Tübingen. In 1977 Pope Paul VI appointed him archbishop of Munich, and the same year he became cardinal. Pope John Paul II elected him as prefect of the Congregation of the Faith in 1981. He became subdean of the College of Cardinals in 1998, and dean in 2002.

Although up to and including Vatican II Ratzinger was regarded as a firm "progressive," he steadily became disillusioned with some of the reforms. It is possible that the rebellion against authority on the part of many students, together with their trends toward Marxism, contributed to a growing moderate conservatism, and he and Küng drifted apart in their theology. On the other hand, he still supported ecumenical dialogue. In the 1970s he worked with Balthasar, de Lubac, and Walter Kasper. As prefect of the Congregation of the Faith he promoted Catholic doctrines, and suspended Leonardo Boff, one of the leaders of liberation theology. The withdrawal of Küng's teaching license occurred in 1979, before Ratzinger was in his post. He supported Roman Catholic theology on homosexuality and relations with other churches, calling Protestant churches "ecclesial communities."

As pope, Benedict issued encyclicals on hope (2002), "charity in truth" (2002), and love (2005). He stressed the "eternal reason" of God, the power of the Word, and the need for faith. He was open to various tools of biblical exegesis and hermeneutics. He was clearly much more "conservative" than Küng and Rahner.

Benedict of Nursia

Benedict of Nursia (c. 480-547) was educated in Rome and is often called "the father of Western monasticism." Around 500 he left Rome to become a hermit, but in c. 529 he moved to Monte Cassino with a small band of monks. He appears to have planned a reform of monasticism and composed his Rule there. This drew on material from Basil of Caesarea, John Cassian, Augustine, and the Desert Fathers, and was elaborated into a thorough Rule for the life of a monastery. The monks would renounce private ownership and vow obedience to the abbot, whom they elected. The seventy-three chapters of the Rule combine doctrine with practical conduct for the monastic community. The community's "daily office" began with matins or lauds at about 2 A.M. After prime, tierce, sext, none, and vespers, it concluded with compline.

Bengel, Johannes Albrecht

Johannes Albrecht Bengel (1687-1752) was both a Lutheran NT scholar and a Pietist. His main significance is as an expositor and textual critic of the NT. In 1742 he published his famous *Gnomon Novi Testamenti*, which combined exegesis, textual criticism, and practical edification. It remains a classic masterpiece of sane, pithy aphorisms and brevity. J. Wesley used and appreciated this work, and many use it today.

Bernard of Clairvaux

Bernard of Clairvaux (1090-1153) founded the monastery of Clairvaux, of which he became abbot. Clairvaux became the motherhouse of the Cistercian Order. He urged contemplation and the mystical life. In his work *On the Love of God* he stresses "four degrees" of love *(caritas)*. In the first degree, "A person begins by loving God, not for God's sake, but for his own." In the second degree he loves without self-interest, and tastes "how sweet is the Lord." In the third degree he loves God for himself. The fourth degree is perfection beyond words (chaps. 8, 9, and 10). His work *On the Steps of Humility and Pride* summarizes the Rule of Benedict. He composed many sermons and hymns, including probably "O Sacred Head, Sore Wounded." In his sermons on the Song of Songs he urges, "Let the Lord Jesus be your heart sweet and pleasant" (20.4). Bernard opposed the teaching of Peter Abelard and Anselm, and supported the Second Crusade. His mysticism stands in contrast with Scholasticism.

Biblical Criticism

H. Reventlow traces the roots of biblical criticism to the intellectual climate of the Deists and the Enlightenment. More narrowly and specifically, however, modern biblical criticism can be anticipated in Richard Simon (1638-1712), who was a loyal Catholic but argued that the Pentateuch contained two incompatible traditions, neither of which went back as far as Moses. He aimed to undermine Protestant dependence on the Bible, but was expelled from his French oratory for his views. Jean Astruc (1684-1766) had been influenced by Spinoza, and argued for different traditions within Genesis, based on the use of different names for God (Elōhim in the "E" tradition, and Jahweh [Yahweh] in the "J" tradition). The genuine founder of modern biblical criticism proper, however, was J. S. Semler (1725-1791), whom W. G. Kümmel calls "the actual father of the new critical theology." He was professor of theology at Halle, where he reacted against the Pietist legacy of Zinzendorf and others. His key book was *A Treatise on the Free Investigation of the Canon* (4 vols., 1771-1775). He argued that the canon was formed by *strictly historical* factors, and he excluded all theological considerations. He was less extreme than G. E. Lessing and H. S. Reimarus, but he excluded all theological factors in his exegesis.

He came close to what we today would call the "history of religions" approach. Although he remained a Lutheran, he argued against a Lutheran "leveling down" of the Bible to uniformity rather than diversity. His method of approach was always strictly *historical* only, and resisted the "imposition" of doctrinal theology on the Bible.

J. A. Ernesti became professor at Leipzig in 1756. He stressed historical and grammatical exegesis, and argued for the "objectivity" of biblical studies, even if he himself retained a theistic faith. J. D. Michaelis studied Hebrew, Aramaic, Arabic, and Ethiopic at Halle, and his contacts in England with English Deism led him to abandon a Pietist faith. In OT studies he set great store on comparative sources outside the Bible. But he still defended Mosaic authorship of Genesis, and argued for the apostolocity of Matthew and John. G. E. Lessing was very different. He oversaw the publication of Reimarus's *Wolfenbüttel Fragments,* in which Reimarus argued that the simple teaching of Jesus was corrupted by doctrine, and he denied both miracles and the resurrection. Lessing is notorious for his dictum: "The accidental truths of history can never become the proof of necessary truths of reason," that is, rational truth is eternal, but historical truth is temporal and relative. He wrote on the Gospels in 1778, but his work was published only posthumously. He argued that the three Synoptic Gospels went back to an Aramaic gospel of the Nazarenes, a departure at the time in source criticism.

J. G. Eichhorn became professor at Göttingen in 1788, and was one of the earliest writers to produce an "introduction" to the Bible, which discussed problems of the authorship, date, genre, and historical situation of individual books. Eichhorn was a "neologist," that is to say, he broadly accepted the divine inspiration of the Bible but viewed plain reason as adequate for interpreting it. He argued for a mythological genre in the early chapters of Genesis. The flight from Eden was due to a thunderstorm, and a talking snake was a naïve picture, or a myth. J. J. Griesbach was primarily a textual critic. On the NT he distinguished between an Alexandrian, Western, and Byzantine tradition. As a result of his work, the domination of the sixteenth-century *Textus Receptus* was largely abandoned. J. P. Gabler concludes the mainly eighteenth-century series of biblical critics. He was professor at Altdorf, and sought to establish "biblical theology" as a purely historical discipline. If we consider theology in its time and place, we have a "true" *(wahr)* biblical theology; a "pure" *(rein)* biblical theology is not conditioned by its time and place.

Many see a later or second "founder" of biblical criticism in W. M. L. De Wette (1780-1849), who taught at Berlin and was the first to formulate a critical account of the development of Israel's history. He did this by reconstructing Samuel and Kings, regarding Chronicles as secondary, and understanding Leviticus as a projection back from the postexilic period. He viewed Numbers as largely mythological. He dated Deuteronomy in 621 B.C., at the time of Josiah's reforms. He saw most of the priestly themes after the exile as a so-called decline from pure prophetic religion. On the NT, he distinguished between three very different traditions consisting of John, Paul, and Hebrews. Probably more than any other, he changed the face of biblical criticism. W. Vatke sought to sharpen De Wette's conclusions, and later J. Wellhausen followed them. Wellhausen is sometimes inaccurately regarded as originating them. K. Lachmann published two editions of the Greek Testament, and followed Griesbach in rejecting the *Textus Receptus*.

Until the mid–nineteenth century biblical criticism was almost entirely a German movement. But even within Germany more conservative scholars resisted much in the movement. One example is E. W. Hengstenberg (1802-1869), professor of biblical exegesis at Berlin. He wrote a number of OT commentaries, still often used today, and opposed what he regarded as liberal or rational claims. Ironically, the translation of his works into English alerted many outside Germany to the claims of biblical criticism. In the nineteenth century biblical criticism had made relatively little impact in America and Britain. In America Andrews Norton (1786-1853) argued that the doctrine of the Trinity was irrational and a two-natures Christology was contradictory. But this reflected Unitarianism rather than NT criticism. He argued for the traditional authorship of the four Gospels. Theodore Parker, however, read the major German scholars, including De Wette, whom he translated in 1843. In practice, his views reflected earlier Deism, especially the views of M. Tindal. Moses Stuart stressed linguistic and historical exegesis, and read Eichhorn's *Introduction to the Old Testament*. W. Baird suggests that he accepted critical method "without submitting to its conclusions" (*History of New Testament Research*, vol. 2 [Minneapolis: Fortress, 2003], 27). Edward Robinson maintained an orthodox theology while making advances in biblical geography.

Meanwhile the critical works of F. C. Baur (1792-1860) and David Strauss (1808-1874) were about to burst on the scene. Baur was the founder of what used to be known as the Tübingen School. He studied in the University of Tübingen, and after ten years of teaching became professor of NT at the school in 1826. He postulated a major struggle in the NT church between a party led by Peter and another led by Paul. Eventually, he argued, these became subsumed under a third movement represented by John and "early Catholicism." Baur also argued that only the "major" epistles were authentically Pauline: Romans, 1 and 2 Corinthians, and Galatians. This was largely because he had already defined Paul as anti-Judaistic, and these issues were largely explicitly confined to these four epistles. Many have assumed that Baur borrowed his thesis-antithesis-synthesis from Hegel, but others also argue that his affinities with Hegel became apparent only after his main thesis was formulated. The Tübingen School flourished roughly from 1835 to 1860. Baur and the Tübingen School had significant influence in Germany, but were largely ignored in Britain. Baird records, "When in the early 1870s a Fellow of an Oxford college was asked if the Tübingen School was much read, he replied, 'No. No theology of any school is much read at Oxford'" (*History*, 55; cited from C. K. Barrett). English or British theology has seldom been inspired or troubled by "schools."

David F. Strauss was originally Baur's pupil, and an avid disciple of Hegel. In 1835 he published his notorious *Life of Jesus*. He drew on Hegel's contrast between "representations" *(Vorstellungen)* in religion and the critical concept *(Begriff)* in philosophy. He then argued that the Gospels were largely myth: in his terms, ideas presented in the form of narrative. He regarded miracles and the supernatural as secondary additions by the church. He published the first edition of the work as a young man (barely twenty-seven), and produced five editions in all. The third appeared in 1838-1839; the fourth in 1840; and the fifth in 1864. George Eliot translated the 1840 edition into English (to which a possible allusion may appear in *Middlemarch* [1869]). Strauss eventually abandoned all "churchly" theology. His book was criticized even by Baur and Nietzsche. Jesus, according to his book, was an apocalyptic fanatic who cannot have been the Christ of orthodox Christian faith.

In England, Benjamin Jowett and Charles Gore are often regarded as moderate biblical critics. Jowett, Regius Professor of Greek at Oxford, wrote an essay on biblical interpretation in *Essays and Reviews* (1860) in which he famously, or notoriously, declared that the Bible should be interpreted like any other book. Charles Gore represented liberal Anglo-Catholicism. He saw the patriarchs as "idealized," and believed that there were mistakes in some of the teaching of Jesus. In Germany, Wellhausen became widely known for attempting to refine De Witte's recasting of the chronology of biblical sources. In addition to De Wette's proposal to contrast the Jahwist tradition from the Elōhim tradition, Wellhausen also postulated the Deuteronomist tradition, "D," and the priestly tradition, "P." Many think of him as the originator of the J, E, D, P division of the OT, but, as we noted, he is dependent on De Wette for this basic scheme. Today this hypothesis has largely lost favor in detail, but not necessarily in its basic approach to development in Israel's history.

The outstanding example of moderate, believing, theistic biblical critics in England at the end of the nineteenth century is "the Cambridge triumvirate" of B. F. Westcott, J. B. Lightfoot, and F. J. A. Hort. The three became lifelong friends. From 1870 to 1890 Westcott was Regius Professor of Divinity at Cambridge, and in 1890 he succeeded Lightfoot as bishop of Durham (the Church of England's traditionally "most academic or theological" bishopric). Lightfoot had been Hulsean Professor of Divinity at Cambridge in 1861, and Lady Margaret's Professor of Divinity at Cambridge in 1875, until his consecration as bishop in 1879. Hort became professor at Cambridge in 1878. The three men wrote magnificent commentaries on the Greek text. Westcott wrote on John and Hebrews; Lightfoot wrote on the Pauline Epistles; Hort wrote on 1 Peter, James, and Revelation, but was hampered by poor health. Hort wrote a judicious theology of the church, *The Christian Ecclesia;* Lightfoot wrote an influential essay on the Christian ministry in an extended appendix to his *Commentary on Philippians;* and Westcott wrote over twenty books, including *The History of the Canon* (1853), *Characteristics of the Gospel Miracles* (1859), *The Gospel of the Resurrection* (1866), *Commentary of the*

Gospel of St. John (1881), and *The Incarnation and Common Life* (1893). The three were clearly Christian theologians as well as NT critics. Baird compares them favorably with the best of the Germans, calling them "giants."

The pattern and nature of biblical criticism have now been set for the twentieth century and onward. Clearly there is no such thing as *the* critical method, but only a variety of very *different methods*. *Dictionary of Biblical Criticism and Interpretation,* edited by Stanley Porter (New York: Routledge, 2007), lists not only those discussed in the eighteenth and nineteenth centuries but also, in Germany, Bultmann, Deissmann, Eichrodt, Fuchs, Harnack, Hengel, Jeremias, Kümmel, von Rad, Schweitzer, and Wrede. In America it lists R. E. Brown, Brueggemann, Childs, Cadbury, Fitzmyer, Kaiser, Ladd, Perrin, and Torrey. In Britain it discusses Barr, Dodd, Dunn, Moule, Moulton, Ramsey, and Thiselton. This is far from a comprehensive sample: in Britain, for example, Bruce, Marshall, Bauckham, and Wright should be added. However, it shows the wide variety of those who go under the name "biblical critics." Some stress the exclusive use of *history* as against theology. Others regard biblical criticism as *serving* the Christian church and Christian theology. Writers such as Dodd, Moule, and Wright stand in the tradition of Westcott, Lightfoot, and Hort. Others may promote *antitheological* tradition. The term "biblical criticism" is as varied as its practitioners. (*See also* **Baur, Ferdinand Christian; Deism; Enlightenment; Exegesis; Liberalism; Lightfoot, Joseph Barber; Myth; Rationalism; Strauss, David F.; Westcott, Brooke Foss.**)

Reading: W. Baird, *History of New Testament Research* (Minneapolis: Augsburg, 1992), vol. 1; (Minneapolis: Fortress, 2003, 2013), vols. 2 and 3; D. K. McKim, ed., *Dictionary of Major Biblical Interpreters* (Downers Grove, Ill.: IVP Academic, 2007); S. E. Porter, ed., *Dictionary of Biblical Criticism and Interpretation* (New York: Routledge, 2007); J. W. Rogerson and J. M. Lieu, eds., *The Oxford Handbook of Biblical Studies* (Oxford: OUP, 2006).

Biblical Theology

Biblical theology attempts to use biblical exegesis and interpretation to provide a coherent and constructive account of biblical data, which often interacts with systematic theology. It perhaps reached its heyday from about 1950 to 1965 with the work of such scholars as O. Cullmann and A. Richardson. Critics of the movement were quick to diagnose three of several problems. First, they argued for a relative lack of attention to the distinctive nature of different theologies within the biblical writings; second, they attacked the frequent claim that biblical "concepts" were *sui generis* or unique; and third, they criticized the tendency to separate OT theologies from NT theologies. These were associated with both the rise and rapid decline of the biblical theology movement.

The emergence of biblical theology as a distinctive discipline was regularly traced to John P. Gabler (1753-1826). In his inaugural lecture at Altdorf (1787), he proposed a distinction between "a true biblical theology," which gave a historical account of the theologies of different biblical writers, and a "pure" biblical theology. This attempted to identify concepts in the Bible that provided lasting truths, rather than those that were merely historically conditioned or relative to their context alone. "Pure" biblical theology provided a direct source for dogmatic theology. "True" biblical theology remained descriptive, historical, grammatical, and time-bound. "Pure" biblical theology was evaluative, and was concerned with ideas and more general themes. Gabler cited as an acceptable example the work of his colleague at Altdorf, G. L. Bauer, *Biblical Theology* (1796, 1802), although Bauer already began to separate OT and NT theology. "Pure" biblical theology faced a difficulty because of the rationalism of the time. For example, W. M. L. De Wette, in spite of his recasting of the chronology of OT writings, tried to liberate "the moral idea of a god" from "mythological" trappings around it (*Biblische Dogmatik* [1813]). On the other hand, F. C. Baur, in 1818, virtually reduced theology to history. D. G. C. von Cöllin tried to carry Gabler's beginnings through, but also published OT theology and NT theology separately (1836). W. Vatke wrote a historical development of Israel's religion in 1835, but was heavily influenced by Hegel's philosophy. Hengstenberg produced a conservative work on the unity of the two Testaments, but this swam against the stream in Germany (*Christology* [1829-1835]). In general, biblical theologies became the history of OT or NT religion.

An inevitable reaction arose on the OT side in 1933 with the first volume of Walther Eichrodt's two-volume *Theology of the Old Testament* (London: SCM, 1961, 1967; Ger. 3 vols., 1933, 1935, 1939). Eichrodt sought to steer between two "misconstructions" of biblical theology. One mistake was "historicism," or "developmentalism," a simplistic quasi-mechanical and causal conception of events and their relation to faith. The other mistake was "naïve orthodoxy," which treated the Bible as a source of timeless proof texts for Christian doctrine. Eichrodt argued that historical and theological disciplines properly converged. In the preface to his English edition, he appealed also to the work Gerhard von Rad did in this respect, as well as that of Vriezen and Jacob (1:18). He aimed "to *have the historical principle operating side by side with the systematic in a complementary role*" (1:32). His fundamental category is "God and the People," and seen in this light it should not surprise us that covenant becomes a major organizing key. The criticism of his attention to "covenant" was perhaps disproportionate.

The covenant, Eichrodt argues, gives "definitive expression to the binding of the people to God" (1:36). The covenant "was thought of as Yahweh's pledging of himself," but it was a two-sided relationship (1:37). It had a special place in the theology of Deuteronomy, in which it also presented "Israel's past in the form of 'Salvation History'" (1:53). Its most profound exposition emerged in Deutero-Isaiah, which spoke "of the deliverance from Egypt" (1:61). The Law is therefore seen as a "covenant statute" (1:70-177). This includes the cultus, under which Eichrodt considers several types of sacrifice. Some are gift sacrifices, but a fourth category of sacrifice is *"the idea of atonement or expiation"* in a personal relationship with God (1:158). This leads to an exposition of the covenant God. He is transcendent, and his "existence" denotes "active existence" or effective presence (1:190). He is King and Lord, and the prophets warn of *"the danger of approximating him too closely to the human"* (1:211). In volume 2, Eichrodt considers God's self-manifestation, the cosmic powers of God, creation and providence, sin and forgiveness. Enough has been said to demonstrate that this weaving together of history and theology can be successful.

With varying emphases, this approach was developed by Gerhard von Rad, *Old Testament Theology*, 2 vols. (Edinburgh: Oliver and Boyd, 1962, 1963); Th. C. Vriezen, *An Outline of Old Testament Theology* (Oxford: Blackwell, 1962); and E. Jacob, *Theology of the Old Testament* (London: Hodder and Stoughton, 1958). Meanwhile, in the same era, we may note O. Cullmann, *Christ and Time* (London: SCM, 1951); *The Christology of the New Testament* (London: SCM, 1963); and *Salvation in History* (London: SCM, 1967); R. Bultmann, *Theology of the New Testament*, 2 vols. (London: SCM, 1952, 1955); A. Richardson, *An Introduction to the Theology of the New Testament* (London: SCM, 1958); and E. Stauffer, *New Testament Theology* (London: SCM, 1955). Cullmann clearly intertwines history and theology. Each new interpretation, he urges, is itself a reinterpretation of an integrated past event. God is active in history, especially in the tension between "now" and "not yet." Christ stands at the "midpoint" of history in theological terms, not chronological ones.

Bultmann has a distinctive and complex attitude to history. But our separate entry on Bultmann is extensive; hence we refer the reader to this entry. A. Richardson seeks coherence in his work, and pays due attention to the apostolic faith. Faith comes as a gift from God. God discloses himself through his action. Reconciliation is a right relation with God (*Introduction*, 215-17). Such issues as the kingdom of God, the Holy Spirit, Christology, the resurrection, the atonement, the church, and the ministry are fully explored. The frame is historical, but nevertheless the differentiation between various writings and traditions within the NT could be clearer. E. Stauffer considers such contextual phenomena as the apocalyptic and the Jewish background, and shows how the NT themes lead to the "creeds of the primitive church." He rejects a purely "genetic" approach in favor of a "performatory" one (*New Testament Theology*, 255). The meaning of history is the revelation of God's glory (55). He declares, "God's action in history is a conversation with mankind" (56). He concludes, "The final revelation of the *gloria dei* begins with the personal activity of God in the ordering of history" (229).

Theologies of the New Testament continue to be written. Hans Conzelmann published his *Theology of the New Testament* in 1968, although he may be less committed to the historical aspect than some. J. Jeremias argued that the proclamation of Jesus is a constitutive element of NT theology (1971), although only volume 1 of his projected *Theology* is complete. He accepts the validity and authenticity of Jesus' announcement of his suffering and death. In general, many writers became suspicious of holistic works, and it would be tempting to say that little emerged in the 1970s and 1980s. But J. L. McKenzie wrote on the OT in 1974; W. Zimmerli in 1978; and C. Westermann in 1982. On the NT, E. Lohse wrote in 1974; L. Goppelt in 1975-1976; and G. E. Ladd in 1975. G. B. Caird began his work before his untimely death in 1984; it was completed later by others. The lesson about differences among the biblical writings has been heeded, and the twenty-first century now witnesses a renewal of biblical theology.

I. Howard Marshall published *New Testament Theology* (Downers Grove, Ill.; InterVarsity, 2004). In its nearly 800 pages separate chapters are offered on each Gospel writer, the different Pauline letters, Hebrews, the Catholic Epistles, and the Johannine writings. It may be "conservative," but it avoids the classic mistakes of the biblical theology movement. J. D. G. Dunn has written two distinct volumes on NT theology: *Jesus Remembered* (Grand Rapids: Eerdmans, 2003) and *The Theology of Paul the Apostle* (Edinburgh: T. & T. Clark, 1998). Brevard Childs not only warned of dangers in his *Biblical Theology in Crisis* (1970), but published *Old Testament Theology in a Canonical Context* in 1985, and *Biblical Theology of the Old and New Testaments* (Philadelphia: Fortress, 1992). This includes a history of biblical theology, models of biblical theology, and a canonical approach. Like all biblical theologies today, it distinguishes carefully between different traditions and genres within the Bible. Currently N. T. Wright is working on a five-volume series that contains history with the theology of the NT. The series, called Christian Origins and the Question of God, so far includes the following: volume 1, *The New Testament and the People of God* (1992); volume 2, *Jesus and the Victory of God* (1996); volume 3, *The Resurrection of the Son of God* (2003); and volume 4, *Paul and the Faithfulness of God* (2013); all published by Fortress and SPCK. At least one further volume is projected. (*See also* **Bultmann, Rudolf; Cullmann, Oscar; Exegesis; Systematic Theology; Wright, N. Thomas.**)

Reading: O. Cullmann, *Salvation in History* (London: SCM, 1967); W. Eichrodt, *Theology of the Old Testament*, 2 vols. (London: SCM, 1961, 1967); A. Richardson, *An Introduction to the Theology of the New Testament* (London: SCM, 1963); and volumes by G. B. Caird, N. T. Wright, J. D. G. Dunn, and other primary sources. For secondary literature, see P. Balla, *Challenges to New Testament Theology* (Peabody, Mass.: Hendrickson, 1998); W. J. Harrington, *The Path of Biblical Theology* (Dublin: Gill and Macmillan, 1973).

Bioethics

This term was coined in 1971 to denote ethical reflections on issues in biological and medical sciences. From 1990 onward the most pressing issues have been in vitro fertilization, artificial insemination, the gene pool, and genetic research. At the opposite end of life, problems have arisen with equal urgency about death and its definition, and self-chosen death in the face of terminal illness, as well as the transplant of body parts. Meanwhile, such complex issues as defining the beginning of life often determine issues in abortion. Nowadays it has become impossible to draw a clear line between medical ethics and genetic or biological studies. (*See also* **Ethics.**)

Bishop

In Episcopal churches the bishop (Gk. *episkopos*) is the chief pastor within a diocese, just as an archbishop is the chief pastor within a province. But the Greek also means more widely one who is responsible for "safeguarding or seeing to it that something is done in the correct way, guardian" (BDAG 379-80). *Episkopē* may simply mean "oversight" or "watching over." Hence many (including Lightfoot and Lampe) regard *episkopos* as interchangeable with *presbuteros*. In 1 Tim. 3:1-13 the writer distinguishes between qualifications or characteristics for bishops (3:1-7) and qualifications or characteristics for deacons (3:8-13). But Titus 1:5-9 also considers elders, and it is possible to draw up lists that relate to bishop, priests or presbyters, and deacons respectively (W. D. Mounce, *Pastoral Epistles* [Nashville: Nelson, 2000], 156-58). Clearly by the time of Ignatius (c. 108), bishops and elders could be distinguished at least in some parts of the church. The lists do not necessarily prescribe "qualifications" but describe "the right type of person" (159).

The characteristics bear on the task. A bishop (for many, elder) should be "skilled in teaching" (*didaktikos;* BDAG 241), level-headed or clear-minded (*nēphalion;* BDAG 672); thoughtful and prudent, and with good personal discipline (*sōphrōn;* BDAG 987); gracious, tolerant, courteous (*epieikēs;* BDAG 371); able to win people's respect (*kosmios;* BDAG 561); and not least, able to manage, to lead, or to direct (*proïstanai,* from *proïstēmi;* BDAG 870). The most presupposed qualities are to be a leader in mission, to have a pastoral heart, and to be a guardian. In the history of the church, a bishop is increasingly a focus of unity.

As the history of the concept developed, and especially in recent times, Roman Catholic and Anglican documents emphasize the bishop's role not as an isolated figure, but as a member of the college of bishops. Indeed, in NT times, as A. T. Hanson has urged, the nature of ministry emerges by seeing how NT figures *do* ministry in practice. Paul, for example, was no individualist. He was surrounded by a host of "fellow workers" *(synergoi):* Barnabas, Silvanus, Apollos, Timothy, Titus, Epaphras, Luke, Priscilla, and Aquila. Collaborative ministry has been stressed by J. Schütz, B. Holmberg, W. H. Ollrog, and many others. Appeal is also made to a common pre-Pauline tradition.

After the Reformation, bishops continued to be elected or appointed in England, and in the Lutheran churches in Denmark, Norway, Sweden, Finland, and certain German provinces. Otherwise the German Lutheran churches and Methodists in England appoint "superintendents," although American and African Methodists usually, or often, appoint bishops. In many countries the bishop is elected by diocese. In England a Crown Nominations Commission recommends two names to the prime minister in order of preference, who submits one name for appointment by the Queen. The traditional *insignia* of a bishop are a pastoral staff, pectoral cross, ring, and in most cases a mitre. A few evangelical bishops prefer the canonical rochet and chimere to a cope and mitre. Before the eleventh century the mitre was associated with a crown in the East and with the pope in the West. Officially most see no doctrinal significance in the mitre today.

Black Theology

Black theology first appeared in J. H. Cone's *Black Theology and Black Power* (1969). He also wrote *A Black Theology of Liberation* (1970) and *God of the Oppressed* (1975). Black theology articulates what is distinctive in the black church, and from roots in the American civil rights movement, became active in liberation theology. Black experience became a lens in hermeneutics. Like other liberation theologies, it constantly returns to favorite biblical "liberation" passages such as the exodus and the teaching of Jesus on liberating the captives. Cone argues that God identifies himself especially with "blackness." He writes, "Either God is identified within the oppressed to the point where experience becomes God's experience or God is a God of racism. The blackness of God means that God has made the oppressed condition God's own condition" (*A Black Theology of Liberation* [New York: Orbis, 1970], 63-64). In addition to its links with the civil rights movement and Martin Luther King Jr., in origin it was also linked with "black power" and Malcolm X.

Black theology also called for an exchange of some traditional Christian symbols. I. J. Mosala urged, "All major black theological studies in South Africa draw in some way on the work of James Cone. . . . The black experience of oppression . . . provides the epistemological lens through which to perceive the God of the Bible as the God of liberation" (*Biblical Hermeneutics and Black Theology in South Africa* [Grand Rapids: Eerdmans, 1989], 14, 15). The black American story is recorded in tales, songs, and narratives of African slaves and their descendants. For Cone "black" denotes not primarily skin color but the psychosocial experience of being "defined" by others, and by inequality and oppression. Hence "the black Christ" is not black in a literal sense, but at least "not white," that is, not part of the ruling class. In South Africa a range of approaches is represented by Mosala, who veers toward Marxism, and Desmond Tutu, Allan Boesak, and Manas Buthelezi, who take a more traditional stance. B. Gobo urges people to take sides with marginalized, oppressed people. In the 1980s African theologians stressed contextual theology, and in the 1990s a distinctive "womanist" theology emerged. Currently there is concern also with postcolonial theology. (*See also* **Feminist Theology; Liberation Hermeneutics and Theology; Postcolonial Theology; Womanism.**)

Blake, William

William Blake (1757-1827), poet, artist, and romantic, is best known by most Christians for part of his poem *Milton* entitled "Jerusalem." This longs for the reversal of the Industrial Revolution and the supposed restoration of an idealized rustic or rural life. Similarly, Blake rejected Enlightenment rationalism and a mechanistic rather than organic worldview. His work marked the early beginnings of romanticism. He urged simplicity in his *Songs of Innocence* (1789). Many consider his greatest work to be *Illustrations to the Book of Job* (1826). According to one's viewpoint, Blake is either a creative visionary or a nostalgic maverick. (*See also* **Romanticism.**)

Blessing and Cursing

The Hebrew uses the feminine plural *berākōth* for "blessings," and the verb only in the passive, *bārûk*, for "blessed be." The Niphal form *nibʽrʽku* means "to bless oneself" and the Piel form *bērak*, "to bless." There is no working Qal form. Characteristically the verb means "to bless God" (Gen. 24:48; Deut. 8:10; 1 Chron. 29:10, 20) or "to bless the name of God" (Neh. 9:5; Pss. 96:2; 100:4; 145:21). But God is at least as often the one "who blesses" (Num. 23:20; 24:1; Ps. 109:28; Exod. 20:24; see BDB 138-39). Humans may bless fellow humans, whether this is a priest (Deut. 10:8; 21:5; 2 Sam. 6:18), Moses (Deut. 33:1; Exod. 12:32; 39:43), David (2 Sam. 6:20), or Melchizedek (Gen. 14:19). The NT uses the Greek verb *eulogeō*, "to bless," and the noun *eulogia*, "blessing," or sometimes "gift." Heb. 7:1 takes up Gen. 14:19 to recall that Melchizedek blessed Abraham, while Heb. 11:20-21 takes up Gen. 27:28-29 to recall that Isaac blessed Jacob. Nevertheless, H. W. Beyer points out that this simple noun-verb-noun construction may hide its deeper meaning. He rightly comments, "When Jacob blesses his son Joseph he does so in the form of a *prayer to God:* 'May he bless thee with the blessings of heaven'" (Gen. 49:25). This is the sacred knowledge underlying all OT statements concerning blessing (*"eulogēs," TDNT* 2:756, italics mine). Similarly in the NT, "the one who blesses confidently gives those blessed by him into God's protection" (2:761).

This provides a radical reinterpretation of Jesus' supposed "blessing" of the bread and wine at the Last Supper and in the tradition of the Lord's Supper. In Mark 14:22 the KJV/AV translates, "Jesus took bread, and blessed, and brake it," leaving the object open, even if implied. But the KJV/AV most unfortunately, if not tragically, translates Matt. 26:26, "Jesus took bread, and blessed *it,* and brake it." Yet the Jewish haggadah of the passion meal explicitly states that the host blesses *God for* the bread. "Bless" applies to God in praise and thanks, not to the bread, still less to some supposed "consecration," as this has passed into much of church tradition. This is not to deny that inanimate objects may sometimes be "blessed" in the sense of thanking God for them and praying that they may be used for a sacred purpose. But such a use is rare, if not absent, in the biblical writings. Again some versions are misleading. In Mark 6:41, we read, "Jesus blessed, and broke the loaves." Even the NRSV leaves the Greek unexplained — "and blessed and broke the loaves" — when "blessed God" would have been understood by Jewish readers. A Jew of the time would know that Jesus said "grace," that is, blessed *God* for the loaves, as no doubt he would have done at every meal. A common Jewish grace was "Blessed be Thou, King of the earth, who gives bread to the eater." Again versions may mislead us in the OT. The KJV/AV has in 2 Sam. 6:12, "The LORD hath blessed the *house* of Obed-edom"; the NRSV has "The LORD has blessed the *household* of Obed-edom."

A second fallacy has further bedeviled our understanding of both blessing and cursing. The most characteristic Hebrew word for "curse" is 'rr, which occurs some forty times as a Qal passive participle, *'arur,* to mean "cursed be . . ." (Gen.

3:14, of the serpent; 4:11; Deut. 27:15-26, the twelve curses). Another Hebrew term is *'ālāh* (Jer. 23:10-11). This latter term merges into the notion of the *effects* that a curse may bring, often represented by Hebrew *ch-r-m*, "disaster." The NT and LXX may use *anathema* and *anathematizō*. The fallacy that is often promoted is the reliance of *blessing* and *cursing* on appeals to primitive word-magic. This view was promulgated by Hempel in 1915, drawing on analogies from the ancient Near East, and compared to a magical incantation. Curiously scholars as eminent as S. Mowinckel (1923), O. Grether (1934), L. Dürr (1938), H. Ringgren (1947), and W. Zimmerli (1962) followed Hempel and Pedersen. But in the 1960s H. Brichto, in *The Problem of "Curse" in the Hebrew Bible* (1963), and R. Gordon in 1996 took a more careful approach including the status of the speaker. Grether, Dürr, and others appealed to the supposedly irrevocable nature of a curse as evidence in the two narratives of Isaac and Jacob, and Balaam and Balak. Jacob has tricked blind Isaac into believing that he is Esau (Gen. 27:1-20). Isaac then gives him his blessing (27:21-29). Esau then enters and asks for his father's blessing (27:30-32). Isaac is distraught when the trick is exposed, and with trembling exclaims: "I have blessed him — yes, and blessed he shall be" (27:33). The blessing *cannot be recalled.* The same pattern occurs in the case of Balaam's blessing and curse. Balak pleads with him, "Curse Jacob for me" (Num. 23:7). But Balaam can only curse or bless as God has directed him. He exclaims, "He has blessed, and I cannot revoke it" (23:20). Grether and Dürr argue that this is because it is like "a missile with a time-fuse"!

We need not resort, however, to such mechanistic and primitive explanations. We argue in our entry for speech acts, as do Austin and Searle, that some forms of language constitute *acts* that *do* something. "Illocutions," as Austin calls them, rest on conventional procedures that must be performed by an appropriate person in an appropriate situation. What, then, can be done if no recognized procedure exists for "unblessing" or "uncursing"? This can no more be intelligible than a service of "unbaptism." Once the commitment has been undertaken with sincerity, God honors it in appropriate circumstances.

We also suggest a third example of possible misunderstanding, although we cannot claim absolute certainty for it. In 1 Cor. 12:3 Paul's statement: "No one speaking by the Spirit of God ever says 'Let Jesus be cursed!'" Who could imagine such a thing? Several theories have been put forward. Was the speaker influenced by an ecstatic frenzy? Was he a Jewish critic? Was it a quasi-Gnostic devaluing of the earthly Jesus? Was it a Christian who affirmed the "curse" of Gal. 3:13 but stopped short of the resurrection? I have assessed these theories in my commentary on 1 Corinthians ([Grand Rapids: Eerdmans, 2000], 917-27). B. Winter points out that the Greek *anathema 'Iēsous* occurs without a verb, and therefore could be understood as passive, meaning "be cursed," *or* as *active,* meaning "Jesus, grant a curse." Near to Corinth several "curse tablets" have recently been discovered, which plead for pagan deities to curse rivals in love, business, or sport. The most probable explanation of 1 Cor. 12:3 seems to be that no Christian can ask

Jesus "to curse" a rival, if he or she is genuinely led by the Holy Spirit. The verses are discussing criteria for being "of the Spirit."

Lastly, in the NT Paul declares that Christ has redeemed us from the "curse" of the Law by becoming a "curse" *(katara)* for us, as it is written, "Cursed is everyone who hangs on a tree" (Gal. 3:13, referring to Deut. 21:23 LXX, with Deut. 27:26 as part of the frame of reference). This has long been a traditional part of the theology of the atonement together with sacrifice and substitution. C. Westermann writes, "The bestowal of blessing in today's church is a responsible practice only if it is based on a comprehensive knowledge of the biblical data" (*Blessing in the Bible and the Life of the Church* [Philadelphia: Fortress, 1978], 103). Even if it is human person-to-person, it remains primarily *prayer to God* for his blessing on that person. He adds, "It became impossible to regard blessing any longer as a magical act or a magical transfer of power" (104). It is also combined with the work of Christ, and characteristically *concludes* congregational worship. It also *introduces* worship, and may occur as a blessing or act of praise to God in hymns. Three other standard practices in the tradition of the church concern blessing, or more accurately, a prayer for *God's* blessing, namely, at baptism, at the Lord's Supper, and at mealtimes, as a "grace." (*See also* **Austin, John L.; Speech Act Theory.**)

Reading: Herbert C. Brichto, *The Problem of "Curse" in the Hebrew Bible* (Philadelphia: SBL, 1963, 1968); A. C. Thiselton, "The Supposed Power of Words in the Biblical Writings," *JTS* 25 (1974): 283-99, reprinted in *Thiselton on Hermeneutics* (Grand Rapids: Eerdmans, 2006), 53-68; Claus Westermann, *Blessing in the Bible and the Life of the Church* (Philadelphia: Fortress, 1978); Bruce Winter, "Religious Curses and Christian Vindictiveness," in his *After Paul Left Corinth* (Grand Rapids: Eerdmans, 2001), 164-83.

Blood

The phrase "the blood of Christ" is used in the NT much more frequently than either "the death of Christ" or "the cross of Christ" to indicate his death or his atonement. Three OT passages, Gen. 9:4, Lev. 17:11, and Deut. 12:23, do assert that "the blood is the life," but they assert this to show that "the very life of the body ... is ended when the blood is shed" (F. J. Taylor). The term is often used to denote a violent death. "*Blood* is a more vivid expression for the death of Christ in its redemptive significance" (J. Behm, *"haima,"* in *TDNT* 1:172-76). Vincent Taylor writes, "To explain the allusions to 'blood' as synonymous for 'death' is mistaken. One can hardly fail to be conscious of a loss of meaning if, instead of 'being justified *by his blood*' (Rom. 5:9), we read 'being justified in Christ crucified,' or if 'in the blood of Christ' (Eph. 2:13) [is] replaced by 'through Christ crucified'" (*The Atonement in New Testament Teaching* [London: Epworth, 1940], 92) (cf. Rom. 3:25; Eph. 1:7). "Blood" is also used of human death (Luke 11:50-51; Acts 1:19; Rom. 3:15); and as a symbol of cosmic signs (Acts 2:19); and as the redemptive effect of the blood of Christ (John 6:55; Rev. 12:11). "Flesh and blood" can mean "humankind" (Matt. 16:17).

Body

(Heb. *gᵉwiyyāh, bāśār;* Gk. *sōma;* sometimes *sarx,* strictly "flesh," or even *skēnos,* "tent.") In both Testaments "body" denotes not a "part" of a human being but a human being as seen in the public, visible world. Neither Testament exhibits a mind-body dualism, as can be seen in Plato and in Descartes. Human beings *are* bodies and souls, rather than *have* bodies and souls. *Body* is that mode of self that concerns the public and visible world. In as far as *soul* is mentioned, which occurs far less frequently, this concerns the self in a more "inner" and "private" sense, except as it is seen by God. By contrast, Plato speaks of "the liberation of the soul from bondage to the body at death" (*Republic* 611E). Meanwhile W. Pannenberg speaks of the *unity* of body and soul, and of "the biblical idea of psychosomatic unity" (*ST* 2:184). E. Schweizer urges that in the LXX *sōma* and *psychē* are used in parallel, where "each term denotes the whole man" (*TDNT* 7:1047). It is even claimed, "Ancient Semitic has no special word for 'body'" (1049).

When we come to the NT and to Paul, E. Käsemann makes the best comment of all. He asserts that for Paul the Christian life is not limited to interior piety and cultic acts. "We are quite clear that 'body' for Paul means ... that piece of the world which we ourselves are, and for which we bear responsibility because it was the earliest gift of the Creator to us.... For the apostle it signifies man in his worldliness [i.e., as his being part of this world] and therefore in his ability to communicate.... In the bodily obedience of the Christian, carried out as the service of God in the world of everyday, the lordship of Christ finds *visible expression,* and only when this *visible expression* takes personal shape in us, does the whole thing become *credible as Gospel message*" ("Primitive Christian Apocalyptic," in *New Testament Questions of Today* [London: SCM, 1969], 135, italics mine). This "body" makes discipleship *visible and public,* and therefore communicable to others. In the world, for the self to be embodied is a blessing from God.

The supreme example of the importance of public visibility comes in the phrase "The Word became flesh" (John 1:14). This is not only a matter of solidarity with humanity, but also a condition for a public life of obedience and suffering. In apocalyptic it allows for suffering, struggle, and temptation. Paul declares, "Present your bodies as a living sacrifice, holy and acceptable to God" (Rom. 12:1), and "Glorify God in your body" (1 Cor. 6:20). The phrase that follows "Glorify God in your body" in the KJV/AV, "and in your spirit, which are God's," depends on a questionable and doubtful manuscript reading, which suggests a later assimilation to the Greek notion of "body," not Paul's. In Paul the body provides a vehicle of self-discipline (1 Cor. 9:27), and the body is the temple of the Holy Spirit (1 Cor. 6:19-20). The suffering of the body is not a mark of its inferiority, but a mark of apostleship (2 Cor. 4:10-11; 11:24-25; Gal. 6:17). The body also demonstrates human accountability (2 Cor. 5:10). The heart of the Lord's Supper comes in the words "This is my body" (1 Cor. 11:23-25; Mark 14:22-23).

The body allows for the *relational* aspect of human life on earth. Pannenberg calls this "the being with others as others" (*ST* 2:193), and ascribes "the awareness of I-relativity of one's own consciousness" to "body" (2:194). He comments, " 'I' always indicates the physical individuality of the speaker," but often in relation to others. One's own corporality and its history are important. Pannenberg writes, "We achieve our particularity in our encounter with others" (2:200). Nevertheless, early on, "Christian Alexandrian theology" tended to devalue the body and to focus on human reason, especially in its account of the divine image (Clement of Alexandria, *Stromata* 5.94.5; Origen, *On First Principles* 1.1.7, 24; Gregory of Nyssa, *Sermon* 5).

In the NT and especially in the second century, as Robert Jewett comments, in three-quarters of the instances in Paul, the issue about "the body" "appears in arguments or exhortations directed against the Gnostics, the enthusiasts or the libertinists" (*Paul's Anthropological Terms* [Leiden: Brill, 1970], 456). It is well known that in Gnostic circles there was often disdain of the body as a physical organ. Yet Jewett rightly stresses: "For the structure of individualistic existence, the word *sōma* has lost all meaningful connection with physical bodiliness" in much Pauline thought (210). He sees Käsemann's German monograph *Leib und Leib Christi* (1933) as decisive for NT studies. It was the Gnostics, not Paul, who believed that "all bodily relationships are irrelevant to the quest of salvation" (259).

In the Bible the resurrection of the body and the phrase "the body of Christ" both have distinctive significance. But, Paul asserts, "You do not sow the body that is to be, but a bare seed" (1 Cor. 15:37). "God gives it a body as he has chosen" (v. 38). Thus Paul does not suggest that in the postresurrection mode of existence the body is still *"physical."* As we have seen, the characteristic of "body" is not simply that it is always physical, but that it is *recognizable, visible, public,* and able to *communicate*. To be sure, the body of Jesus Christ that was resurrected during "the forty days" had "flesh and bones" (Luke 24:39) and could eat bread and fish (John 21:13-14). But this was while he remained within the conditions of this earth and its space-time before his ascension. In 1 Cor. 15:44 the body is raised "a spiritual body," which means animated by, and under the control of, the Holy Spirit (A. C. Thiselton, *Life after Death* [Grand Rapids: Eerdmans; London: SPCK, 2012], 120-26). Clearly *God* raises Christ, and will raise those in Christ with a "body" like his (Rom. 8:11). "Spiritual body" cannot mean "immaterial body," which corresponds with Greek, not Christian, usage.

The body of Christ also has a distinct secondary meaning in which it usually denotes the church. In Col. 1:24 Paul speaks of the body of Christ that is "the church." Col. 1:28, 2:19, and Eph. 1:23 are similar. However, this is not peculiar to the later epistles. In Rom. 12:4-5 Paul borrows from Livy and other Greco-Roman writers the analogy of the body and its members *(melē),* which in 1 Cor. 12:12-27 need one another. Together the members make up "one body." D. B. Martin points out that whereas Livy uses it as an elitist analogy, to argue that menial slaves are to work for the good of the whole body, Paul uses the "body" analogy to show that the humblest and least-esteemed members are honored and needed. In 1 Cor. 6:13-15 Paul makes two points: first, "the body is meant . . . for the Lord" (v. 13); second, "your bodies are members of Christ" (v. 15). In his book *The Body* (London: SCM, 1952), J. A. T. Robinson says "members" may suggest too loose a status, like "members" of a golf club or motoring organization. Paul regards Christians as "limbs" of Christ's body, who are integral to it. Robinson even claims, "The [resurrection] appearance on which Paul's whole faith and apostleship was founded was the revelation of the resurrection body of Christ, not as an individual, but as the Christian community" (58). D. E. H. Whiteley, however, questions his exegesis. Robinson, he says, "has both complicated and illuminated" the subject (*The Theology of St. Paul* [Oxford: Blackwell, 1971], 192).

The secondary use of "body" to denote the solidarity of the Christian community with one another and with Christ should not distract us from the primary emphasis upon the *public, visible, and communicative* nature of Christian identity, personhood, and discipleship. Käsemann's conclusions remain a key to the NT use of the term. Some periods of historical theology have unwittingly surrendered to the "Greek," Platonic, and Cartesian use of the term, which has distorted the gospel. Further, the early-modern association of the body with sex and food sometimes led to its being regarded as less than "spiritual." Nothing could be further from the truth. The body provides the sphere in which, in Käsemann's words, discipleship becomes visible and public, and therefore also credible. (*See also* **Ecclesiology; Gnosticism; Resurrection of the Dead.**)

Reading: E. Best, *One Body in Christ* (Cambridge: CUP, 1955); J. D. G. Dunn, *The Theology of Paul the Apostle* (Edinburgh: T. & T. Clark, 1998), 55-64; R. Jewett, *Paul's Anthropological Terms* (Leiden: Brill, 1970), 201-304, 456-58; W. Pannenberg, *Systematic Theology*, vol. 2 (Grand Rapids: Eerdmans, 1994), 182-86; E. Schweizer and F. Baumgärtel, *TDNT* 7:1024-94; D. E. H. Whiteley, *The Theology of St. Paul* (Oxford: Blackwell, 1971), 190-99.

Boethius

Boethius (c. 480-525) held office as consul in the administration of Theodoric the Great. He came from an aristocratic family, and his learning was encyclopedic. He wrote on astronomy, arithmetic, music, geography, logic, and rhetoric. He translated and commented on parts of Plato, Aristotle, and Porphyry. He also wrote on Christology and the Trinity, and deeply influenced the theology of the Middle Ages. He attempted to combine Christian thought with classical culture. He was influenced by Augustine, and attempted to employ his own logic and philosophy to clarify such terms as "person," "nature," "substance," and "eternity." Some have described him as a bridge between Chalcedon and Neoplatonism. His most famous work was *The Consolation of Philosophy*, written in prison. It remains a controversial work, since it is not explicitly Christian. Yet he portrays God as the ultimate good of all things. On his notion of eternity as simultaneity of time, see entries **Time** and **Eternity**.

Bonaventura

Bonaventura (c. 1217-1274) was a prolific writer, and practiced rigorous asceticism. He drew on Peter Lombard and the mystics for much of his theology. On the Trinity he tended to follow Augustine and Richard of St. Victor. He studied in the University of Paris, and entered the Franciscan Order in 1243. D. Knowles, the eminent medievalist, declares, "With St. Bonaventura . . . we reach one of the true summits of mediaeval theology." Sometimes he appears as the equal of Thomas Aquinas, with whom he was almost an exact contemporary. In his *Itinerary of the Mind,* "contemplative love" follows "purification," illumination, and perfection or consummate union (1.7). He introduced the notion of *vestigia,* footprints or traces of God (1.2). He declares, "By . . . praying we are led to discern the degrees of the soul's ascent to God" (1.2). Like Aquinas, he was a Scholastic, but unlike Aquinas, he resisted the influence of Aristotle. The cross of Jesus, he argued, is the supreme act of divine humiliation, and the revelation of God's love. He remained faithful to the theology of Augustine and Anselm, and denied the doctrine of the Immaculate Conception. He was declared to be "the Seraphic Doctor," perhaps because of his combination of theology and mystical experience.

Bonhoeffer, Dietrich

Dietrich Bonhoeffer (1906-1945) was the son of a professor of psychiatry in a middle-class family loosely attached to the Lutheran church, which he considered an "extension of bourgeois culture, closed to intellectual change." From the first he looked for "something different," and even as an adolescent determined to become a theologian. At eighteen, in 1923, he studied theology at Tübingen, and then continued his studies at Berlin (1924-1927). At twenty-one he completed his doctoral dissertation, which he published as *Sanctorum Communio* (1930; Eng. 1963). In this work he reacted against the individualism of Descartes and Kant, and stressed how closely "sociality" was rooted in God. The church was not simply a community of like-minded people. He also studied at Union Theological Seminary, New York (1929-1930), and after ordination published *Act and Being* in 1931, and lectured at the University of Berlin (1932-1933).

Hitler became chancellor of Germany in 1933, and Bonhoeffer became seriously involved in the struggle against Nazism. He had to leave Germany, and served as pastor at Forest Hill, London (1933-1935). But as the struggle in Germany increased, he returned as director of the "illegal" Confessing Church, and taught at its seminary in Finkenwalde. During these years he wrote *The Cost of Discipleship* (1937; London: SCM, 1959) and *Life Together* (1939; Eng. 1954). Starting in 1934 he corresponded with Karl Barth in Switzerland and Sir Edwin Hoskins in England. In *The Cost of Discipleship* he stressed the twin themes of grace and obedience, urging obedience to the call of Jesus "to leave one's nets and follow after Jesus" (39). He attacked "cheap grace," in which he saw "the preaching of forgiveness without repentance, baptism without church discipline, communion without confession . . . , grace without discipleship" (38). Costly grace is like the pearl of great price; to gain it a person must sell all that he has. Luther had taught that pure grace provided the basis for glad giving of the self in costly service. The kingdom of God demanded exclusive obedience to Christ (51). Jesus said that if any wanted to follow him, "let him deny himself and take up his cross" (71). This book became extraordinarily influential, and was related to his earlier *Sanctorum Communio* by seeing the church as "under the cross" (85), or as "the community of the Crucified" (97).

Bonhoeffer reflected on moral dilemmas in his posthumously published *Ethics* (1949; Eng. 1965). He declined offers to move to Britain for safety, as John Bailey had invited him, or to America, as Reinhold Niebuhr had invited him. In 1939 he became a member of the resistance centered in the *Abwehr*, or military intelligence, and in 1941 corresponded with Bishop Bell of Chichester. The same year he wrote *Meditations* (Eng. *Meditation on the Word* [Cambridge, Mass.: Cowley, 1986]). In this volume he wrote: "Either I determine the place in which I will find God, or I allow God to determine the place where he will be found. If it is I who say where God will be, I will always find a God who corresponds to me, is agreeable to me, fits in with my nature. But if it is God who says where he will be … that place is the cross of Christ" (44-45).

In 1943 Bonhoeffer was arrested and imprisoned in Tegel, near Berlin. In July 1944 the bomb plot to assassinate Hitler failed, and he was imprisoned at Buchenwald. In April 1945, one month before the Nazi surrender, he was hanged at Flossenbürg. But during 1943-1945 he worked on his *Letters and Papers from Prison* (1951; Eng. 1967; London: SCM, 1971). Many of these letters were smuggled to his friend Eberhard Bethge. These represented a new phase of Bonhoeffer's thinking. They lay behind much of the debate about "worldly Christianity" and "modern man," which consumed much energy during the 1960s. In these last writings he attacks much traditional preaching and apologetics, which "seems to me like an attempt to put a grown-up man back into adolescence, i.e. to make him dependent on things on which he is, in fact, no longer dependent"; for example, on guilt over sexual or other sins, or the need for additional strength (327). In his own words, "God is being increasingly pushed out of the world that has come of age" (341). This book became highly controversial. In England, J. A. T. Robinson lauded its insights into "modern man" in his book *Honest to God* (1963). Gerhard Ebeling of Switzerland believed that Bonhoeffer was highly valued, not *because of*, but *in spite of*, his *Letters and Papers from Prison*.

Reading: D. Bonhoeffer, *Ethics* (New York: Macmillan; London: SCM, 1955); D. Bonhoeffer, *The Cost of Discipleship* (London: SCM, 1959); D. Bonhoeffer, *Letters and Papers from Prison* (London: SCM, 1971); D. Bonhoeffer, *Meditation on the Word* (Cambridge, Mass.: Cowley, 1986); J. W. de Gruchy, ed., *The Cambridge Companion to Dietrich Bonhoeffer* (Cambridge: CUP, 1999).

Boniface

Boniface (c. 675-754) was born in the west of Britain, but is popularly known as "the Apostle of Germany" because of his missionary endeavors there. After an initial unsuccessful attempt, Boniface was commissioned by Gregory II of Rome to preach there in 719. His legendary courage in confronting the religion of Woden with the legend of felling the oak tree of Thor led to the conversion of many in Hesse. Eventually he established stable churches east of the Rhine. He was appointed as the first bishop and then archbishop without a specific see, and engaged in much preaching and in the establishment of monasteries.

Book of Common Prayer

The Book of Common Prayer is the official service book of the Church of England, in spite of more recent introductions of *The Alternative Service Book* (1980) and *Common Worship* (2000). In the history of the Reformation, four versions of *The Book of Common Prayer* were produced: in 1549 and 1552, under Edward VI; in 1559 under Elizabeth I; and in 1662 under Charles II. The first prayer book of 1549 was compiled largely by Thomas Cranmer to provide Morning and Evening Prayer, the communion and baptism with other rites, and the Psalter for daily use. Much of it was drawn from the Sarum Breviary (1543) and other sources. An ordinal was introduced in 1550. But under Edward VI Martin Bucer and Peter Martyr assisted in the revision of the 1549 edition, to compile a much more Protestant and Reformed prayer book. They abolished prayers for the dead, Mass vestments, the invocation of the Spirit in the Communion Canon, omitted all references to "the Altar," rather than the communion table, and introduced the Black Rubric to indicate that kneeling to receive communion did not constitute veneration of the sacrament. Mass vestments were replaced by the surplice.

On the death of Edward VI, the Catholic Queen Mary repealed the use of the *Book of Common Prayer* and restored medieval Catholic services (1553). But with the succession of the Protestant Elizabeth I (1558), the Elizabethan prayer book (1559) replaced the Mass with a prayer book similar to the 1552 version, except that the Black Rubric was omitted. Under James I the Hampton Court Conference of bishops and Puritans added the second part of the catechism. Under Charles II the Black Rubric was reintroduced, to satisfy concerns of the Puritans, and the KJV/AV for readings at communion. Since that time only the lectionary has been seriously revised. In 1927 the Church Assembly (forerunner of General Synod) attempted to introduce a revision with more Anglo-Catholic and liberal leanings, but the House of Commons rejected it. Although the archbishops presented the Queen with a copy of *Common Worship* in Synod in 2000, Elizabeth II graciously accepted it with the personal reminder that it was legally only an optional supplement or optional alternative to the 1662 *Book of Common Prayer*. Many had virtually agreed that the *Alternative Service Book* of 1980 was what some called "cheap and cheerful," without the depth and gravitas of the prayer book, and lacked its deeper theology. *Common Worship* offers a compromise, which is closer to the prayer book. Probably the majority of English churches use *Common Worship* now, but many churches retain the *Book of Common Prayer* for some or all of their services, and it remains legally the doctrine and practice of the Church of

England. Many may use a different ordinal, and the Church in Wales is not bound by the Parliamentary rejection of the proposed 1928 prayer book.

Bousset, Wilhelm

Wilhelm Bousset (1865-1920) was professor of NT theology at Giessen, and was one of the leaders of the so-called history-of-religions school. He wrote on the Jewish religion in NT times (1903) and a work entitled *Kyrios Christos* (1913; Eng. 1970).

Brueggemann, Walter

Walter Brueggemann was born in Nebraska in 1932, graduated from Eden Theological Seminary, and was awarded doctorates by Union Theological Seminary, New York, and St. Louis University. In 1986 he became professor of OT at Columbia Theological Seminary, Decatur, Georgia, where he stayed until retirement in 2003. His exegetical work can be seen in his commentaries on Genesis (1982), Exodus (1994), Deuteronomy (2002), 1 and 2 Samuel (1990), Isaiah (1998), and Jeremiah (1991). He wrote monographs on David, 1 and 2 Kings, the Prophets, hope, the land (1977), and especially OT theology (1997). His concerns extend both to exegesis and to theology, exploring theological method. He remains concerned with history, but also with Israel's confession of faith, and with canon as exemplified in B. S. Childs. He also has a concern for the social function of biblical texts, and for the church today.

Brunner, Emil

Emil Brunner (1889-1966) was a Swiss Reformed theologian. After eight or nine years (1916-1924) spent as pastor in the Reformed Church, he became professor of systematic theology and practical theology in the University of Zurich from 1924 to 1953, and finally visiting professor in Tokyo from 1953 to 1955. In the popular mind he is often associated with Karl Barth, partly because of their common attack on nineteenth- and early-twentieth-century liberalism, and partly because of their common defense of Reformed theology, the theology of crisis, and dialectical theology. But there are at least three great differences. (i) Whereas Barth addressed his theology primarily to the church, Brunner addressed his theology to the contemporary world; (ii) whereas Barth's major influence was mainly in Germany and partly in America, Brunner visited England for two years (1913-1914), learned to speak English fluently, and had an affinity with Anglo-Saxon culture; (iii) whereas Barth dismissed all natural theology on the ground that the image of God in humanity was entirely lost, Brunner believed that it was only partly lost. He said the possibility of repentance and such ordinances as marriage and the state suggested natural ordinances. Brunner studied in the United States (1919-1920) at Union Theological Seminary, and traveled in Asia in 1949.

Brunner's first major book, *The Mediator* (1927), is often regarded as a classic in Christology, although in 1961 he observed that his 1937 book *Man in Revolt* constituted, in his view, his greatest contribution to theology. Like Barth, in *The Mediator* he stressed God's initiative in revelation, but he also valued historical research ([London: Lutterworth, 1934], 21-200). Reflecting Barth, he begins: "Through God alone can God be known" (21). But he addresses this theme more widely than Barth does, and includes other religions. In Christianity, however, "revelation is a unique, absolute, decisive fact" (34). He values historical inquiry, since "The Word became flesh. . . . Historical criticism has forced us to perceive this" (156), even though "definite results" elude us (170). He urges, "The doctrine of the Two Natures itself is right," but metaphysical misunderstandings cause difficulty (343). He adds: "The God-Man as *God*-Man would be perceived by all" (343). Christ holds the key to our understanding of ourselves: "We do not perceive the mystery of our person so long as we do not perceive the mystery of the Person of Christ" (347). Yet the person of Christ and the cross can appear "foolish" (1 Cor. 1:18-25) to those who separate the world "above" from the world "below" (562). The work of Christ is "a movement from God to God," but this must pass "through this lowest point, as through our own place. . . . The Crucified is the One from above — this alone gives meaning to His Cross" (562). This movement is the dwelling of God with his people. In the light of all this, contrary to Herrmann's and Harnack's liberalism, he asserts: "Doctrine expresses what ought to be proclaimed in the Church" (597); "Only in the Mediator Jesus Christ do we know ourselves as we really are" (600). Further, Brunner concludes, "Only in the Mediator is the will of God, that is, the God known as Love" (603). He asserts: "Only in faith in Christ the Mediator is our arrogant self-will broken and God honoured" (606). This leads to the reality of justification by grace (610-13) and an ethical lifestyle (613-17).

A small volume, *Natural Theology,* records the break with Barth over natural theology in 1934 (Eng. 1946). While delivering a lecture series in Sweden in 1937, Brunner attacked both biblical literalism or ultraconservatism and subjective "enthusiasm" such as was found in mysticism or the Radical Reformers. In 1938 he published *Truth as Encounter* (Eng. 1964), in which he sought to overcome the subject-object opposition in Western thought. "Encounter" is partly indebted to Buber's *I and Thou,* and became a major theme in Brunner. In 1937 he began to produce his series on Christian doctrine; the first volume was *Man in Revolt* (London: Lutterworth, 1939). His starting point is "man's own view of his significance" (29-53), which can vary from asking no questions in naïve lack of reflection to a consciousness of the hunger for power or sex, as Freud and Nietzsche suggest. He then moves to "foundations" in the Word of God, in God as Creator, and in his gift of creating humankind in the image of God (*see* **Image of God**). God implants his Word in our hearts and as Trinity reveals "Being-for-love" as the key to human existence itself (74): "In Himself . . . He is the One who loves" (75).

Brunner leads us on to "The Contradiction: The Destruction of the Image of God" (114-67). We need to interpret the OT in the light of the NT and church doctrine (119-20). In this process he dismisses Schleiermacher as "not dealing with sin at all, but with stages of development" (124; *see* **Sin: Historical**). The origins of evil lay "solely in the will" and "personal decision" (125). Many try to escape a doctrine of radical evil by stressing "autonomous reason," but this would be an illusion. Precisely the problem is "the assertion of human independence over against God" (129). Here we see common ground with Barth, and his further attack against liberalism. Humankind wants "to measure itself against God. That is presumption, arrogance" (130). Brunner develops this theme further in examining the consequences of this in the decay of personality (228-36), the problem of freedom (256-77), and the relation between men and women (345-61). Sexuality is implanted deep in humankind, but men and women's "otherness gives even their sinfulness a different stamp" (353). The man becomes dominating and arrogant; the woman too easily adapts herself and "loses herself in nature-mysticism," losing her "universal destiny." Brunner anticipates later feminist diagnoses of sin (*see* **Sin: Historical**). The remainder of the book traces disruption in various forms.

Brunner produced three volumes in his series of dogmatic theology or doctrine. Volume 1 is *The Christian Doctrine of God*; volume 2, *The Christian Doctrine of Creation and Redemption*; and volume 3, *The Christian Doctrine of the Church, Faith, and the Consummation* (London: Lutterworth, 1949-1962). He had addressed the question of ethics in *The Divine Imperative* (1932). God is self-giving love, and we are to obey him. He also produced *The Misunderstanding of the Church*. The NT church is not an "ecclesiastical institution" but a free fellowship of faithful Christians. "Institutionalization" began in the Pastoral Epistles, followed by "early Catholicism." He has severe reservations about those churches that enjoy the favor of the state. By all accounts, he was an outstanding teacher. It is a mistake to see Brunner as merely a softer or watered-down version of Barth. They each have their distinctive insights. (*See also* **Barth, Karl; Dialectic; Liberalism; Natural Theology; Theology of Crisis**.)

Reading: Emil Brunner, *The Mediator* (London: Lutterworth, 1934); Emil Brunner, *Man in Revolt* (London: Lutterworth, 1939); Emil Brunner, *Dogmatic Theology*, vol. 1, *The Christian Doctrine of God*; vol. 2, *The Christian Doctrine of Creation and Redemption*; vol. 3, *The Christian Doctrine of the Church* (London: Lutterworth, 1949-1962); C. W. Kegley, ed., *The Theology of Emil Brunner* (New York: Routledge, 1962).

Buber, Martin

Martin Buber (1878-1965) was born in Vienna, and studied philosophy at the Universities of Vienna, Zurich, and Berlin. In his early years he was an active Zionist, but later turned to Hasidism, a mystical movement of Judaism that originated in eastern Europe in the eighteenth century. From 1938 to 1951 he taught philosophy at the Hebrew University, Jerusalem. He is best known for his seminal work *I and Thou* (New York: Scribner, 1970). He first claims that "basic words" are "not single words, but pairs," and Buber's "basic word is the word-pair I-You" (53). He adds, "There is no 'I' as such, but only the 'I' of the basic word 'I-You,' and the 'I' of the basic word 'I-It' " (54). The world of objects belongs to the world of "I-It."

I may contemplate a tree: I perceive this perception as an I-It. Buber declares, "When I confront a human being as my You . . . he is no thing among things" (59). Similarly, the human being is "I-You," is not "He" or "She." Relation, Buber insists, "is reciprocity. My You acts on me as I act on it" (67). The language of objects, he says, "catches only one corner of actual life" (69).

Buber thus seeks to expose the *relational* and *personal* character of all beings (71), and especially the uniquely person-to-person, or subject-to-subject, character of personal encounter. He writes, "The innateness of the longing for relation is apparent even in the earliest or dimmest stage" (77). One problem is that "Occidental Christendom accepted the Greek I-it world" (87). This would mean "silence toward the You" (89). But the relation with God is I-You: "In relation to God unconditional exclusiveness and unconditional inclusiveness are one" (127). Buber influenced a number of Christian theologians and philosophers, including E. Brunner, J. Baillie, K. Barth, R. Niebuhr, P. Tillich, and G. Marcel.

Bucer, Martin
Martin Bucer (Butzer) (1491-1551) was a moderate Protestant Reformer. His particular significance is his trip to England at Cranmer's invitation, where he became Regius Professor of Divinity at Cambridge and contributed to the second edition (1552) of the *Book of Common Prayer*. He worked for concord among Protestants together with Melanchthon. W. P. Stephens writes, "Bucer . . . was a biblical scholar, reformer, statesman, apostle of unity" (*The Holy Spirit in the Theology of Martin Bucer* [Cambridge: CUP, 1970], viii). As a theologian he not only addressed Reformation theology, seeking to reconcile Luther and Zwingli, but he also expounded a theology of the Holy Spirit, and used the Greek Testament of Erasmus. Like Luther, he opposed the Radical Reformers and Anabaptists.

Bulgakov, Sergei Nikolaevich
Sergei Nikolaevich Bulgakov (1871-1944) was drawn to Kant and Hegel. He became a priest in 1917, but was expelled from Russia in 1923, to spend most of his life in Paris as dean of a seminary for immigrant Russians. He became a prolific writer. He firmly rejected a dualism of matter and spirit. His work is often seen as obscure.

Bullinger, Heinrich
Heinrich Bullinger (1504-1575) succeeded Zwingli as Cathedral preacher in Zurich in 1531. In effect, he consolidated the Swiss Reformation, building on Zwingli's foundations. His writings were prolific, exceeding, it is claimed, even those of Luther and Calvin. He stressed the faithfulness of God and the need for faithfulness in human conduct. He became a key figure in the relation between Lutheran and Reformed churches. He was influenced by Melanchthon, and was well read in Augustine, other Church Fathers, and Peter Lombard. He stressed God's sovereignty, providence, grace, and the covenant. He worked on the relation between

church and state, and influenced Beza. Next to Calvin, he is regarded as probably the most influential of the second-generation Reformers.

Bultmann, Rudolf

Rudolf Bultmann (1884-1976) is widely considered the most influential NT scholar of the first half of the twentieth century, and a significant influence on Christian theology during that period. Between 1903 and 1912 he studied at Tübingen, Berlin, and Marburg. His teachers included H. Gunkel on the OT, through whom he was introduced to form criticism; A. Jülicher, Adolf von Harnack, and J. Weiss on the NT, deriving a liberal approach from Jülicher and Harnack and apocalyptic from Weiss; and W. Herrmann in systematic theology, from whom he learned the neo-Kantian distinction between fact and value. Herrmann also represented hostility to doctrine, a neo-Kantian legacy of value in contrast to fact, the very broadly Lutheran approach to justification by grace through faith, and a dualism between faith and works, and grace and law. What emerged as Bultmann's extreme historical skepticism cohered with a disdain for "bare facts" and the "intellectual work" of discovering historical authenticity. He later wrote that to believe in the cross of Christ "does not mean to concern ourselves ... with an objective event *(ein objektiv anschaubares Ereignis)* ... but rather to make the cross of Christ our own" ("New Testament and Mythology," in *Kerygma and Myth*, ed. H. W. Bartsch, vol. 1 [London: SCM, 1964], 36; Ger. *Kerygma und Mythos*, 1:46).

(i) **Contributory Factors to Bultmann's Form Criticism and Historical Skepticism.** Gunkel's work on form criticism of the OT had influenced Bultmann. He eventually came to apply this to the NT, although in Gunkel's case it was more plausible to postulate a long period of oral tradition, in which an OT form might come to be shaped by a later setting-in-life. Bultmann proposed that a given form suggested a particular setting in the life of the early Christian community *(Sitz im Leben)* over a shorter period. He drew on Weiss, Schweitzer, and Bousset for their history-of-religions-school approach. In the first few pages of his *History of the Synoptic Tradition* (Ger. 1921, 2nd ed. 1931; Eng. Oxford: Blackwell, 1972), Bultmann cites Wrede's notion of the "messianic secret," Gunkel's form criticism, and the work of K. L. Schmidt on Mark. M. Dibelius had also been working on the history of forms. These provide four chief influences for this work (1-5). He suggests many settings from early *Hellenistic* communities, not from the Palestinian church. Bultmann tells us later that he looked back on the liberalism of Harnack and on Krüger's "unchurchly theology" as fostering an atmosphere of truth and freedom, which actually "led men into doubt, to shatter all naïve credulity" (*Faith and Understanding*, vol. 1 [London: SCM, 1969], 29-30). He recalls that in 1927, "I [had] never yet felt uncomfortable with my critical radicalism. ... I calmly let the fires burn. ... 'Christ after the flesh' is no concern of ours. How things looked in the heart of Jesus I do not know, and do not want to know" (132).

Partly on the basis of Schmidt's work on Mark, Bultmann believed that the *framework* and *chronological sequence* of Mark were secondary, and imposed at a later stage of tradition. The earliest tradition consisted of small isolated units, independent of any connection in time and place. Links between these small units were artificial. As a whole, "there is no life of Jesus in the sense of an evolving biography." Bultmann used and assimilated Schweitzer's negative conclusions in his *Quest of the Historical Jesus*. In his book *Jesus* (Ger. 1926) Bultmann wrote, "No attempt is made to render Jesus as a historical phenomenon psychologically explicable.... Interest in the personality of Jesus is excluded.... We can now know almost nothing concerning the life and personality of Jesus, since the early Christian sources show no interest in either, and are moreover fragmentary" (*Jesus and the Word* [London: Collins/Fontana, 1958], 13-14). A host of later scholars has now rejected such an assessment, including, notably, G. N. Stanton, *Jesus of Nazareth in New Testament Preaching* (Cambridge: CUP, 1970), and R. J. Bauckham, *Jesus and the Eyewitnesses* (Grand Rapids: Eerdmans, 2006).

The supposed value of Bultmann's work was to suggest that every *form* of the narrative suggested a particular *setting (Sitz im Leben)* in the community. Bultmann himself ascribed the *Sitz im Leben* largely to the *needs* of the early church. For example, the tradition contains a series of apothegms, or pithy "sayings," of Jesus (e.g., "the Sabbath was made for man, not man for the Sabbath"), and these are placed in settings of the life of the church. These may be controversies in the church. A second category was dominical sayings, which may be legal pronouncements, prophetic or apocalyptic words, or church rules. Under narratives came miracle stories and other forms. The problem about all this is that, in the well-known words of T. W. Manson, "A paragraph of Mark is not a penny the better or worse as historical evidence for being labelled 'apophthegm' or 'pronouncement story' or 'paradigm'" ("The Life of Jesus: Some Tendencies in Present-Day Research," in *The Background of the New Testament and Its Eschatology*, ed. W. D. Davies and D. Daube [Cambridge: CUP, 1956], 212). Manson's view became widely held among scholars outside Germany, but Bultmann insisted that the purpose of form criticism was to recover the origin and history of particular units. Manson insisted that a second problem was one of circular argument. Material in the Gospels is used to define situations in the church, and then assumed situations are used to account for material in the Gospels. Vincent Taylor in England followed Manson's view. To him it was at best a descriptive, not a historical, project.

(ii) **Factors behind Bultmann's Existentialist Concerns.** The popularity of form criticism has largely or at least partly faded in the form in which Bultmann practiced it. Why was it so highly valued, when many saw it as speculative? The explanation lies perhaps more in Bultmann's other achievements, including his emerging *existentialist perspective,* with a disjunction (following Kant) between fact and value. In Germany it is impossible for others to understand the influence of a "school." Before 1921 Bultmann owed much both to his background of nineteenth-century neo-Kantianism and to the influence of Kierkegaard. For this reason, among others, he denigrated "facts" and valued existential situations in life. In neo-Kantianism, scientists such as H. Hertz utilized "models" rather than "facts," while Kierkegaard had emphasized subjectivity and personal involvement in his search for truth. This is partly why, perhaps surprisingly, Bultmann welcomed Barth's *Romans,* with its emphasis on *address* and personal application in the present, rather than historical and exegetical reconstruction of the past. For a very brief period both Barth and Bultmann were advocates of dialectical theology. In *Faith and Understanding,* volume 1, Bultmann asserts: "God represents the total annulment of man, his negation, *calling him in question, indeed judging him*" (46). This emphasis received total support from Bultmann's Lutheranism. The dualism between fact and value becomes correlated with the contrasts between faith and works, and grace and law. In his essay "What Does It Mean to Speak of God?" Bultmann appeals to Luther, and expounds "the concept of God as the 'Wholly Other'"; we are not to speak *about* God: "We are speaking directly *from* God" (*Faith and Understanding,* 56-57).

This existential or practical approach was confirmed when Martin Heidegger became professor at Marburg in 1923 and served until 1928. At one level it confirmed Bultmann's concern for hermeneutics and understanding. At another level it underlined the importance of *decision,* as in Bultmann's essay, "Adam, Where Art Thou?" (in *Essays* [London: SCM, 1955], 119-32). This narrative tells how God "once called the first man out of his concealment from the eye of his judge," while this call has "become the call of grace" (132). Bultmann's appropriation of Kierkegaard and Heidegger explains his comment that in a system of cognitions (*Erkenntnissen*) "God would be objectively given *(Da wäre Gott eine Gegebenheit)*... and could be achieved at will" ("What Does It Mean?" 32). Like Kierkegaard, Bultmann believes that God's Word comes as a challenge that demands a response. He insists, "Faith must not aspire to an objective basis in dogma or in history, on pain of losing its character as faith."

Bultmann drew on Heidegger for a clarification of concepts in an existential, rather than a substantival, way. This pays dividends when Bultmann considers Paul's doctrine of the human being. *Body* and *soul* are not substantival "parts" of humankind, but modes of being. Further, Heidegger's *Dasein* does not have a viewpoint *outside* history, but is *within* history and conditioned by it as historicity or historicality *(Geschichtlichkeit).* Bultmann explicitly states: "I learned from him (Heidegger) not *what* theology has to say but *how* it has to say it" ("Reply," in *The Theology of Rudolf Bultmann,* ed. C. W. Kegley [London: SCM, 1966], 276). A human being's "world" is made up of practical concerns, of what is ready-to-hand *(zuhanden),* not substances. Heidegger and Bultmann share a common rejection of "objectivism," which ultimately came from Kierkegaard. The horizon of time, which governs all understanding, is not merely chronological, but concerns *attitudes, experiences,* and personal *perceptions.* This features when Bultmann turns to hermeneutics. It also dominates his contrast between authentic and inauthentic existence. In accordance with his Lutheranism, he sees inauthentic existence as a closed system of cause and effect under the Law. By contrast, grace opens the future; the Holy Spirit is "the power of futurity."

(iii) **Bultmann's Hermeneutics.** No doubt the influence of Heidegger encouraged Bultmann's close engagement with the hermeneutical tradition of F. Schleiermacher, W. Dilthey, and Heidegger himself. Although his thought on this subject goes back to earlier years, particularly significant essays include his "Problem of Hermeneutics" (1925), in German in *Glauben und Verstehen,* volume 2, but translated into English and appearing in *Essays Philosophical and Theological* (London: SCM, 1955), 234-61; and "Is Exegesis without Presuppositions Possible?" (1957), in *Existence and Faith* (London: Collins, 1964), 342-52; as well as others. He argued in the latter that *"There cannot be any such thing as presuppositionless exegesis"* (343-44; Ger. *voraussetzungslose Exegese*). Like Schleiermacher and Heidegger, he argued that every interpreter begins with a preliminary understanding *(Vorverständnis)* of the text, that is, a content and context in life into which he can fit the text to make sense of it. This "preunderstanding" becomes corrected and revised in the light of the text, and this process can continue to move between the text and the interpreter in a form that Schleiermacher and Heidegger called the "hermeneutical circle." Thus Bultmann argued in "Hermeneutics": "An interpretation is, it follows, *constantly orientated to a particular formulation of a question.* To put it more precisely, it is *governed always by a prior understanding of the subject"* (239).

Bultmann also drew on Dilthey's maxim that it is not by introspection but through history that we gain self-understanding. Bultmann quotes Dilthey: "Exegesis is a work of personal art ... conditioned by the mental make-up of the exegete" ("Hermeneutics," 238). He concludes: "The 'most subjective' *(subjektiviste)* interpretation is ... the 'most objective' *(objectiviste),* that is, only those who are stirred by the question of their own existence *(der eigenen Existenz)* can hear the claim which the text makes" (238; Ger. 215). For example, a person understands a mathematical or musical text only if the person knows something about mathematics or music in the first place. This involves human "historicity": a person's given place in the historical situation into which the person has been born and educated.

(iv) **Myth and Demythologizing.** Everything discussed so far leads up to Bultmann's well-known essay of 1941, "Demythologizing the New Testament." Seldom has any essay caused more controversy. The key to his proposals can be summed up as the desire to "de-objectify" most of the language of the NT. To understand the NT as primarily "describing objects" is, in Bultmann's view, to misunderstand it. This is why he uses the term "myth." He writes, "The real purpose of myth is not to present an objective picture of the world as it is, but to express man's understanding of himself in the world in which he lives. Myth should be *interpreted* not cosmologically, but anthropologically, or better still, existentially" ("New Testament and Mythology," in *Kerygma and Myth,* 1:9). Mythology may *look like* objective description in narrative, but *in reality* it serves a different purpose. D. F. Strauss called myth the expression of ideas in narrative. Bultmann sees myth as expressing the "otherworldly" in terms of this world. It brings challenge, judgment, and grace.

This much is clear, and draws on his existentialism and work in hermeneutics. It also draws on his form criticism as expressing practical faith-concerns, not depicting objective events. But Bultmann now detracts from his aim by proposing three incompatible definitions of myth, which the British philosopher R. W. Hepburn noted. First, he appears to define myth as analogy, which is a straightforward account of most religious language. H. Thielicke suggests that if this is myth, it cannot be "demythologized." But Bultmann then confuses this formal definition with one of content: myth expresses an outdated first-century worldview. He calls this the notion of a "three-decker" universe, with angels above, humans in the middle, and demons in an underworld. According to such a worldview, "miracles are by no means rare. . . . Man is not in control of his own life" (1:1). He even argues, curiously, "It is impossible to use electric light and the wireless and to avail ourselves of modern medical and surgical discoveries, and at the same time to believe in the New Testament world of spirits and miracles" (1:5). It is as if thousands of Christians did not simultaneously on occasion take medication and pray for health, believing that God is sovereign but often works *through medication.* John Macquarrie called this "a pseudo-scientific view of a closed universe that was popular half a century ago" (written in 1955, more than fifty years ago!). On top of all this, "de-objectification" looms large over both definitions.

Bultmann applies his proposals to a number of specific areas of theology. The easiest to understand, and perhaps sympathize with, is probably that of eschatology. Most Christian believers would not imagine that heaven is literally "up" beyond the sky. As Ramsey pointed out, even the hymn "There Is a Friend for Little Children Above the Bright Blue Sky" is well enough "qualified" in other verses to exclude a purely *spatial* understanding. But again Bultmann seems to confuse two things. We may well interpret "clouds of heaven" as symbols or metaphors in 1 Thess. 4:17. But Bultmann appears to suggest that we cannot even expect "the return of the Son of Man" since history has long continued after the resurrection of Christ ("New Testament and Mythology," 1:11-17, and *Jesus Christ and Mythology* [London: SCM, 1970], 14). On the work of Christ, it is understandable that Bultmann has concerns about "a process wrought outside of us and our world" ("New Testament and Mythology," 1:136; *Jesus Christ,* 35), as if to imply that believers are not involved. But to extend this to question the status as "an objective event" goes much further (*see* **Anselm; Atonement; Aulén, Gustaf**). On the resurrection, Bultmann concludes, "Faith in the resurrection is really the same thing as faith in the saving efficacy of the cross. . . . The risen one encounters us in the word of proclamation and nowhere else" ("New Testament and Mythology," 1:39, 41; cf. 1:36-41). Again Macquarrie replies, "How can it make sense of being raised with Christ unless Christ actually died and was raised?" (in Kegley, *The Theology of Rudolf Bultmann,* 141). The process also applies to Christology, in which "Christ is God" is said to be false, except "as the event of God's acting" (287).

The problem, yet again, lies in Bultmann's lack of awareness of multifunctional operations of language. Much language does not have to be *either* descriptive *or* existential, *either* myth *or* kerygma. In Anglo-American philosophy of language, stretches of language that are recognized to be self-involving avoid the one-sided nature of existential language. The isolated German language tradition has proved to be a fatal flaw and handicap to Bultmann. Put in a more positive light, he often uncovers "the point" of much NT language, revealing its personal and practical challenge in the present. But while achieving this, Bultmann has also thrown away things that are irreplaceable, as I. Henderson argues. The NT is not like a code, when once decoded we discard the original, but more like a masterpiece, to which we constantly return. Admittedly he claims *not to abolish myth,* but to *interpret* it. However, most of his critics agree that the price of this is too high to pay.

(v) **Bultmann's Theology of the NT and Commentary on John.** Bultmann published his *Theology of the New Testament* in German in 1948 and 1953 in three volumes (Eng. vol. 1, 1951; vol. 2, 1964; double volume, 1970), and his *Gospel of John* in German in 1941 (Eng. 1971). Volume 1 of *Theology of the New Testament* first considers the message of Jesus and the kerygma of the earliest church only as "presuppositions" of the theology of the NT. Part 2 expounds the theology of Paul as focusing on "man prior to the revelation of faith" and "man under faith." This concerns the righteousness of God, grace, faith, and freedom. Arguably pages 270-352 represent his best and most creative work. He begins: "The message of Jesus is a presupposition for the theology of the New Testament rather than a part of that theology itself" (*Theology of the New Testament* [New York: Scribner, 1951], vol. 1, p. 1; the following page references are from vol. 1). He continues, "The dominant concept of Jesus' message is the Reign of God. . . . Reign of God is an eschatological concept" (4). Jesus proclaims that the end is here (6). Hence "Jesus' call is the call to decision" (9). Jesus also protests against Jewish legalism (11), although "God did declare his will in the Old Testament" (16). His eschatology and ethics form a unity (19). Jesus pointed to God as providential Carer and Judge (23, 25).

In the earliest community "the bearer of the message" (Jesus) became "its essential content" (33). The church perceived the Spirit at work within it (41). Bultmann allows that Jesus called disciples to follow him, and that "Jesus' call to decision implies a Christology" (43). But the rise of the Easter faith becomes "a way of understanding the cross" (45). The earliest church conceived of the death of Jesus "as an expiatory sacrifice" (46). The titles ascribed to Jesus were drawn from Jewish messianic tradition (48). The direction of the church was in the hands of the Twelve (58). They preached Christ and demanded faith (65-67). Preaching resurrection is inseparable from judgment (77). Finally, the church became conscious of itself as "the true Israel" (93), and excluded itself from non-Christian cults (99); but the interpretation of the OT therefore became a "problem" (108). The church saw itself as God's temple (115-19). In the "Hellenistic" church the title of Lord *(Kyrios)* became a widespread term for Jesus Christ, and baptism became prominent (121-33). Christians saw themselves as the property of Christ their Lord

(137). The Eucharist spoke both of sacrifice or atonement and covenant (146). The "Hellenistic" Christian community saw the Spirit as "miraculous divine power" (153), which became manifest especially in missionary activity (161).

In part 2 Bultmann appreciates Paul not as an independent freelancer, but as originating in the context of "Hellenistic Judaism" (187). His assertions about God are "simultaneously assertion(s) about man, and vice versa" (91). Hence Bultmann examines "body" *(sōma); psuchē, pneuma* and *zōē;* "mind" and "conscience" and "heart." *Psuchē* is little used by Paul; "heart" "may designate the hidden tendency of the self" (223), that is, it represents the subconscious. He then turns to the mode of existence characterized by flesh, sin, and the world. "Man has always already missed the existence that at heart he seeks" (227). "Flesh" denotes several things. It may sometimes denote "carnality" or "weakness" (234). Theologically it denotes "trust in oneself as being able to procure life by the use of the earthly and through one's own strength.... 'Flesh' is the self-reliant attitude of the man who puts his trust in his own strength ... a life of self-reliant pursuit of one's own ends" (239, 240, 241). Thus it relates to human "boasting" (242). Paul saw death as a "punishment" (even though Bultmann refuses to see it in this way). He writes, "Death grows out of fleshly life like a fruit — organically" (247). The Law plays its part in this self-defeating situation (Gal. 3:19).

The section "Man under Faith" begins with the possibility of becoming "rightwised" (270). Righteousness can be "already imputed to a man in the present" (224). God pronounces his eschatological verdict over the man of faith (276). Rom. 1:18–3:20 shows that this is "without works of the Law" (279). Rom. 5:15, 17 show that the source of this is grace and gift. This results in reconciliation, "removing the objective state of enmity" (187). Grace becomes an "event," God's eschatological deed that is part of the word of the cross. In his " 'Confession of faith' the believer turns away from himself" (319). Bultmann asserts: "The decision of faith has done away with the past" (322). He adds that the Christian "lets this care [of himself] go, yielding himself entirely to the grace of God" (331). Further, "The Spirit may be called the power of futurity" (335). It would be difficult to find a better account of law and grace from a Lutheran perspective, as well as existential contrasts.

Volume 2 of *Theology of the New Testament* does not continue in this vein, as indeed it could not, since John is not Paul. But Bultmann makes far too much of what he calls "Johannine dualism." He attributes this to the influence of Hellenism and Gnosticism. But since he wrote, the epoch-making discoveries of Qumran (the Dead Sea Scrolls) have shown that Jews of the first century held views of light and darkness, of knowledge and ignorance, and of truth and error that should be called dualistic. It is neither necessary nor plausible today to account for these as later developments influenced by Greek or Gnostic sources.

Bultmann's commentary *The Gospel of John* (Oxford: Blackwell, 1971) contains more varied and perhaps insightful material. For example, in his exposition of the vine (John 15), he sees "the life of faith as a growing, vital activity" that is "the prime concern here.... Nobody can rest content in the knowledge of having borne fruit; no-one can rely on what he has achieved.... 'Enough is enough!' ... God as the vine-dresser 'purifies' the fruit-bearing tendril, that it may bear more fruit" (533). "Faith is the unconditional decision to base oneself on the act of God, at the cost of giving up one's own ability" (535). Some may find Luther and even Heidegger here, but no one can doubt that Bultmann wrestles with the text to bring out its meaning for Christian discipleship today. He would doubtless claim that his form criticism, his hermeneutics, his demythologizing proposals, and his theology of the NT all have this positive aim. (*See also* Atonement; Biblical Criticism; Existentialism; Form Criticism; Heidegger, Martin; Kerygma; Kingdom of God; Liberalism; Myth.)

Reading: Rudolf Bultmann, *Theology of the New Testament*, vol. 1 (London: SCM, 1952); Rudolf Bultmann, "New Testament and Mythology," in *Kerygma and Myth*, ed. H. W. Bartsch, 2 vols. (London: SCM, 1953), also in *New Testament Mythology*, ed. S. M. Ogden (Philadelphia: Fortress, 1984); Rudolf Bultmann, *Essays Philosophical and Theological* (London: SCM, 1955); Rudolf Bultmann, *The Gospel of John* (Oxford: Blackwell, 1971); D. F. Ferguson, *Bultmann* (London: Chapman, 2000); A. C. Thiselton, *The Two Horizons* (Grand Rapids: Eerdmans, 1980), 205-92.

Bushnell, Horace

Horace Bushnell (1802-1876) remains a controversial figure. Probably his greatest contribution was on the nature of language and symbol, although he has also been called "the father of American religious liberalism" and the "American Schleiermacher." On the other hand, some see him as inheriting the New England Puritan tradition, with a Romanticist trend. He was born and lived in Connecticut, and at first had doubts about the Christian faith. He studied law at Yale. But in 1831 he underwent an experience of renewal, and became a Congregational pastor at Hartford. His first major publication was *Christian Nature* (1847), and his central work was probably *God in Christ* (1849). He also wrote *Vicarious Sacrifice* (1866) and *Forgiveness and Law* (1874). On the basis of the importance of symbol, he attempted to reformulate a doctrine of the Trinity, seeing God as experienced in terms of three *aspects* (verging on modalism), and taught a *moral influence* interpretation of the atonement. Because of the particular *use* he made of symbol and metaphor, the conservative Charles Hodge probably overreacted in his advocacy of the literal language of biblical and doctrinal propositions. Unwittingly Bushnell and Hodge transposed the conservative-liberal polarity into one of literal versus symbolic interpretation of the Bible in America, which still lingers popularly today. (*See also* Atonement; Modalism.)

Butler, Joseph

Joseph Butler (1692-1752) was educated at Oriel College, Oxford, and became bishop of Bristol and bishop of Durham. In 1736 he published his famous work *The Analogy of Religion,* which was a work of apologetics largely aimed at Deism.

He also attacked the work of Thomas Hobbes. He argued that Christian belief was reasonable, and corresponded with truths of nature. He respected the principle of probability, and as bishop of Bristol also criticized the "enthusiasm" and supposed "certainty" of Wesley and Whitfield as "a horrible thing." His defense of natural theology remained a widely read classic until the end of the nineteenth century.

C

Caird, George B.

George B. Caird (1917-1984) gained his D.Phil. degree from Oxford University for a thesis on the NT concept of glory. In 1970 he became principal of Mansfield College, Oxford, and subsequently was appointed as Dean Ireland's Professor of the Exegesis of Holy Scripture at Oxford. Like F. F. Bruce, he was exceptionally competent in both OT and NT studies. He wrote *The Apostolic Age* (1955), *Principalities and Powers* (1956), *The Gospel of Luke* (1963), *The Revelation of St. John the Divine* (1966), *Paul's Letters from Prison* (1976), and especially a major work, *The Language and Imagery of the Bible* (London: Duckworth, 1980). Caird distinctively argued that neither Jesus in the Gospels, nor Paul in the Epistles, nor John in Revelation believed in the immediate imminence of the End. With S. Ullmann, a professor of semantics at Oxford, he believed that NT scholars had grossly underestimated the role of metaphor. Metaphorical imagery, Caird argued, "telescoped" events within history and the ultimate triumph of Christ at the End. They took "end of the world" language too literally, as both "ends" were overlapped in meaning. To attribute "a mistake" to Jesus and Paul was naïve. Language, exegesis, and preaching remained his special interests. He was writing a work titled *New Testament Theology* when he died (1984), and L. D. Hurst completed it in 1994.

Calendar

Those not accustomed to using a liturgical calendar may be surprised at its profound theological roots. O. Cullmann rightly noted that time was more fundamental than space in Hebrew and Christian thought, and that the *linear conception of time* marked God's purposive action in history and human life, as the primary conception of time in Christian theology. Yet a *cyclical view of time* contributes to meaning in life as well. The main Christian and Jewish festivals provide a paradigm. Every year begins with Advent and looks forward to the coming (as well as to the return) of Christ; then Christmas celebrates his birth, followed by, or in the Eastern Church bracketed with, Epiphany, or his manifestation to the Gentiles. Ash Wednesday and Lent remember Christ's temptations and trials. Maundy Thursday recalls the institution of the Last Supper; Good Friday, the death of Jesus; Holy Saturday, his descent into hell; Easter Day celebrates the resurrection; Ascension Day, the ascension; Whitsun or Pentecost, the coming of the Holy

Spirit; and Trinity Sunday the culmination of Christian doctrine in the celebration of the whole Trinity. Many of the Reformation churches also retained "red letter" saints' days, that is, those who are mentioned in Scripture. Traditionally the Feast of the Annunciation became "Lady Day" on 25 March, and the Feast of Michael and All Angels became "Michaelmas," which provided in secular life key dates for the payment of rent in commerce or for term dates in academia. Biblical saints' days include those of Paul (25 January), Mark (25 April), Peter (29 June), Matthew (21 September), Luke (18 October), and many others; All Saints' Day is celebrated on 1 November.

Later some Protestant churches inserted more saints' days from the Roman Catholic calendar. But alongside the ecclesiastical calendar, the season of nature also preserved God's cyclical calendar, together with, in the church calendar, Rogation Day, for asking God's blessing on sowing the crops, and Harvest for the ingathering of the harvest. The influence of the more detailed Roman Catholic calendar has been assimilated, for better or worse, by much of the Anglican Church and other Protestant churches. The date of Christmas differs between 25 December in the Western Church and 6 January in the Eastern Orthodox Church, although, as Cullmann argues, we cannot be certain of the original historical date at all. Clement of Alexandria had suggested a day in May; 25 December did not emerge until the fourth century; in the East Christmas was associated with Epiphany, beginning perhaps in the fifth century.

The date of Easter is clearly related closely to the OT and Jewish Festival of the Passover (Exodus 12 and Deuteronomy 16). Traditionally it celebrates redemption from Egypt, although some have associated it originally with agricultural festivals. The OT and Judaism also celebrated the Feast of Weeks (Exod. 23:16), when the grain harvest had been gathered, and the Feast of Tabernacles (Exodus 25–31; 35–40; 33:7-10; also called Feast of Booths; Lev. 23:33-36, 39-43). Again, the cyclical festivals of the OT and Judaism find parallels in the Christian liturgical and seasonal calendar.

It remains theologically important, however, to place the primary emphasis on linear time, as proposed by Cullmann and others, which forms the framework for the purposive acts of God in history and of human life. But within this frame the color and variety of a liturgical and seasonal calendar lend further significance to observations of habit and regularity. Both directly impinge on human life, and function both to facilitate memories of the key events of the gospel and, secondarily, to relieve the possible monotony of a life unmarked by seasonal festivals. Protestants tend to resist overelaborate ceremonies, especially if they become assimilated into folk religion.

Calvin, John

John Calvin (1509-1564) was born at Noyon, Picardy, and went to the University of Paris in 1523. In 1528 he moved to Orleans to study law, and then to Bourges, which had humanist and Protestant tendencies. The French king, however, supported a papal bull against Lutherans, and in 1535 Calvin fled to Basel. In 1536, at the age of twenty-six, he had already completed the first edition of the *Institutes,* which by its succinct and organized exposition of Protestant doctrine made him, in effect, the theological leader of the Reformation. His two purposes were to facilitate an understanding of Scripture and to defend Reformation theology against false or hasty accusations. He partly followed the Apostles' Creed, expounding a doctrine of God in part 1, of Christ the Redeemer in part 2, of the Spirit and grace in part 3, and of the church in part 4. While he worked, he studied especially not only the Bible and the Fathers, but also Luther, Melanchthon, and Bucer. He subsequently produced larger editions of the *Institutes* in 1539, 1541, and 1559. The last was the definitive edition, although a final edition was published posthumously in 1586. In due course he also wrote numerous biblical commentaries and further theological treatises, some of which are collected by J. K. S. Reid in *Calvin: Theological Treatises,* LCC 22 (1954). His systematic theology in the *Institutes* allowed him to produce commentaries wholly of exegesis, without doctrinal digressions (*Institutes,* "Epistle to the Reader," 1:25).

(i) **Life.** Calvin was returning to Paris and Strasbourg from Italy when war forced him to pass through Geneva. G. Farel, when he heard that Calvin was temporarily in Geneva, implored him to stay there to counter failed Reformation hopes in Geneva, insisting that his pleading would represent the voice of the Holy Spirit. Calvin agreed to remain as professor and preacher. He stayed from 1536 to 1538, before moving to Strasbourg. This was Calvin's first stay in Geneva, and it was not easy. He sought to instruct and organize the church in accord with Reformed principles, and urged the Roman Catholics who opposed him to study the Church Fathers more carefully before appealing to them. In 1537 he published a catechism. But as J. Atkinson observes, "Calvin always remembered the agony and tumult of those days; how he was insulted in the streets, and fireworks were put in his door, while lewd louts sang obscene songs in his window at night" (*The Great Light* [Grand Rapids: Eerdmans, 1968], 164).

At the urging of Farel, Calvin returned to Strasbourg, where he again worked as a professor and preacher, and published the French translation of the *Institutes* and his *Treatise on the Holy Communion.* During this period he became close friends with Melanchthon and Bucer, and married in 1540. In response to Bucer and others, including the Councils of Zurich and Basel, he reluctantly returned to Geneva in 1541, where he remained until his death. Much of Geneva was still disunited and in tumult, but Calvin's cause was helped by some French Protestant refugees. Steady, patient instruction and careful organization won through. He wrote in the fifth edition of the *Institutes* that he was one of those who, like Augustine, "write as they learn, and learn as they write" (the Beveridge edition translates "by profiting, write, and by writing profit," "Epistle to the Readers," 1:26). While undertaking all this work, not least the writing of numerous commentaries and the founding of the Genevan Academy (1559), Calvin was shaping the practical governance of the Genevan church. He believed in the appointment of four orders of ministry: pastors, doctors, elders, and deacons (discussed further below). In other words, although incomparably a theologian, he was also an ecclesiastical statesman, a religious controversialist, an educationalist, and an author in several genres. He provided daily sermons for the people as well as lectures. He tried hard to teach concord and unity among the Reformation churches, and at least at a formal level achieved the *Consensus Tigurinus* (1549) with the Zwinglians, even if he was perhaps less flexible than Melanchthon. In February 1564 he appeared to anticipate his death in May, and appointed Beza as his successor in Geneva, and as editor of the final edition of his *Institutes*. He had become an international figure and founder of "Reformed theology." It is time now to turn to his systematic theology in the *Institutes*. All direct quotations of Calvin are from the Beveridge edition of the *Institutes,* in which all biblical quotations are from the KJV/AV. In this entry only we shall follow this practice.

(ii) **Doctrine of God.** The first part (or "book") of the *Institutes* bears the heading "The Knowledge of God the Creator," and is eighteen chapters long. The first chapter argues that "the knowledge of God and of ourselves" are interdependent (1.1.1). They are "bound together by a mutual tie" (1.1.3). In chapter 3 Calvin argues that knowledge of God is naturally implanted in the human mind. But two things qualify this. First, humankind has corrupted, distorted, and neglected this knowledge (chap. 4); second, God remains transcendent and unique (chaps. 10–13), and is revealed by the Holy Spirit in Scripture (chaps. 6–9). He quotes Rom. 1:22, "Thinking to be wise, they became fools" (1.4.1); "The fool hath said in his heart, There is no God" (1.4.2; Pss. 14:1; 53:1). He quotes Lactantius with approval but attacks the pagan notion that "fear made the gods." On the other hand, the works of nature point to God's being and action (Acts 17:27; 1.5.3). He sums up his view of pagan "religion": "All worship of man's device is repudiated by the Holy Spirit as degenerate" (1.5.13). As for divine transcendence, Calvin writes: "How can the human mind . . . bring down the boundless essence of God to its little measure?" (1.13.21).

Chapter 6 begins Calvin's exposition of the need for Scripture. Here he draws on his famous analogy of the need of many elderly people for spectacles. They are "scarcely able to make out two consecutive words, but, when aided by glasses, begin to read distinctly" (1.6.1). The human mind, he comments, easily falls into forgetfulness of God; hence we need Scripture. Chapter 7 shows how the Holy Spirit gives "full authority" to Scripture. Paul testifies that the church is "built upon the foundation of the apostles and prophets" (Eph. 2:20; 1.7.2). This includes "the writings of the prophets, and the preaching of the apostles" (1.7.2). Calvin appeals not only to Scripture but also to Augustine, who has been twisted by some to imply the authority of the church *in contrast to* Scripture. But he "had no intention to suspend our faith in Scripture on the nod or decision of the Church" (1.7.3). He examines Augustine in historical context. He also cites numerous biblical passages (1.7.5). In chapter 8 Calvin recognizes the dilemma that if we place too much emphasis on arguments or rhetoric for Scripture's authority, "the authority of Scripture remains in suspense" (1.8.1). God does, in his grace, reveal himself through human words, but we rely "not on 'the wisdom of men,' but on 'the power of God'" (1.8.1, citing 1 Cor. 2:5). As far as the reception of Scripture is concerned, scarcely an age has passed during which its authority was not confirmed and renewed (1.8.9). Calvin admits that in the NT, three Evangelists give a narrative in a mean and humble style, but John, "fulminating in majesty, strikes down ... the petulance of those who refuse to submit to the obedience of faith" (1.8.11). Scripture will "burn into their consciences as with a hot iron" (1.8.11). Scripture has been sealed with the blood of many witnesses, but it remains "foolish to attempt to prove to infidels that the Scripture is the Word of God" (1.8.13).

Chapter 9 becomes important again in an era that often cites "spiritual visions" as supplements to Scripture. Calvin maintains that the apostles remained faithful to salvation given in the Word of God and we need the Holy Spirit to confirm this witness. But when he declares "quench not the Spirit," Paul does not carry them aloft to empty speculation "apart from the word." Like Luther, Calvin attacks "swelling enthusiasts" (1.9.3). Chapter 10 reasserts the main theme of book 1: "God, the creator of heaven and earth, governs the world which was made by him" (1.10.1). He exercises "loving-kindness, judgment, and righteousness, in the earth" (Jer. 9:24; 1.10.2). On God's revelation and love, Calvin writes that, having tasted his fatherly love, he, the believer, is drawn to love and worship him in return (1.3.3). Chapter 11 attacks idols and images of God, including "images" of "the priests." He appeals to Gregory, Lactantius, and Eusebius (1.11.5, 6), as well as to Scripture. But Calvin adds, "I am not, however, so superstitious as to think that all visible representations of every kind are unlawful. . . . sculpture and painting are gifts of God . . . [but] if it be unlawful to make any corporeal representation of God, still more unlawful must it be to worship such a representation instead of God, or to worship God in it" (1.11.12).

Chapter 13, again, is a keynote chapter. God is a unity, but a unity in three persons: "While he proclaims his unity, he distinctly sets it before us as existing in three persons" (1.13.2). Christ the Son of God is "the express image of his person" (Heb. 1:3). Yet a subsistence *(hypostasis)* distinguishes him from the Father (1.13.2). This chapter also expounds God's mercy as his "accommodation." Just as nurses "lisp" to infants, so forms of speaking do not so much express clearly what God is like, as accommodate the knowledge of him to our slight capacity (1.13.1). Calvin rejects the argument that "person" is not a scriptural term (1.13.3). He explicitly follows Hilary and Augustine (1.13.5-6). The divinity of Christ and the Holy Spirit cannot be doubted (1.13.9-16). In particular, Calvin also follows and quotes Gregory of Nazianzus (1.13.17), and admits that he is "not sure" about drawing on analogies to try to expound the Trinity (1.13.24). He adds that the Scriptures teach that there is essentially but one God (1.13.25). He explicitly affirms Nicaea (1.13.29).

Calvin returns to the doctrine of creation in chapter 14. Whatever we may think about seven "days," the point of the language in Genesis is to stress "progressive steps" and the "order of events" (1.14.2). Angels are ministers appointed to execute the commands of God (1.14.4). Calvin, however, contrary to his frequent popular reputation, is willing to admit limits to speculative knowledge. He writes, "Whether or not each believer has a single angel assigned to him for his defence, I dare not positively affirm" (1.14.7). He does not join those who presume to dogmatize on the ranks and numbers of angels (1.14.8). We simply know that angels are "ministering spirits" (Heb. 1:14; 1.14.9). He also discourages speculation and dogmatism about "devils." He does quote biblical passages about them, but the "point" of these references is to guard us against demonic assault (1.14.13), to see that all creatures, including angels and devils, are created by God (1.14.16); that Satan is an adversary of God (1.14.17); and that God turns evil spirits "hither and thither at his pleasure" (1.14.18). We must beware of "empty speculators" (1.14.19). God created all things for the sake of man (1.14.22).

Many would argue that Calvin's next subsection is more speculative. It concerns "original righteousness," or the human condition *before* the Fall. Certainly he could argue that "before" the Fall humankind was immortal (1.15.2). Humankind was indeed "created in the image of God" (1.15.3). He discusses the debate about "image" and "likeness," and argues that when humankind became alienated from God, the image of God was not utterly effaced and destroyed; it was, however, "so corrupted, that any thing which remains is fearful deformity" (1.15.4). We need Christ to restore the perfect image of God. The image of God, before the Fall, "shone in Adam," but was afterward vitiated and almost destroyed (1.15.4). There remains, however, human intellect (1.15.8). Calvin in his next chapter affirms that humans are still cherished and protected. In his goodness God still preserves and governs the world (1.16.1). Calvin rejects the Deist notion of a deity "sitting idly in heaven" (1.16.4). That would render God governor only in name, not in reality. Particular events are "evidence of the special providence of God" (1.16.7). But Calvin rejects the Stoic notion of an endless chain of causes (1.16.8). God is utterly transcendent; "our sluggish minds rest far beneath the height of Divine Providence" (1.16.9). God works through means (1.17.1). Calvin applies this doctrine, speaking of the stupidity of those who presume to undertake anything without God (1.17.4). Even thieves and murderers, Calvin urges, are instruments of divine Providence (1.17.5). He argues that Christians will not overlook inferior causes (1.17.9). Calvin adds typically: "[The] heavenly Father ... so regulates ... by his wisdom, that nothing takes place save according to his appointment" (1.17.11).

In chapter 18 Calvin rejects the distinction between the permissive will and active will of God (1.18.1), which would be widely controversial today. He cites the example of the affliction of Job. The believer's only response should be, "The Lord gave, and the Lord has taken away; as it pleased the Lord, so it has been done." Many Christians would claim such a view is Islamic rather than Christian. But Calvin insists that this distinction is based on an "improper confusion" between *will* and *precept* (1.18.4). Would "permission" not imply some force other than God's will? This is one of the few theological controversies about which many minds have changed over the years — in both directions. (*See* **God, Trinity: Historical Development.**)

(iii) **Doctrine of Christ, or Christology.** Book 2 concerns knowledge of God the Redeemer, in Christ. 2.1.1-8 recapitulates and develops earlier work on the fall and revolt of humankind. Humans have "no confidence" by the standards of divine justice (2.1.3). On the results of the Fall, Calvin comments, "This is the hereditary corruption to which early Christian writers gave the name of Original Sin, meaning by the term the depravation of a nature formerly good and pure" (2.1.5). He rejects Pelagius's "profane fiction." Augustine demonstrated this innate corruption. Calvin cites Ps. 51:5, "I was shapen in iniquity, and in sin did my mother conceive me" (2.1.5), alongside Rom. 5:19, "By one man sin entered into the world. . . . All have sinned; even so might grace reign" (2.1.6). The whole depends on the parallel between Adam and Christ. Calvin uses extreme language: "Their whole nature is, as it were, a seed-bed of sin" (2.1.8), which is what is meant by "total depravity" (*see* **Sin: Historical**).

In 2.2 Calvin expounds the dominion of sin (2.2.1). To claim any righteousness would rob God of his honor. He comments that Augustine does not hesitate to call the human will a slave (2.2.8). Calvin tends to set the Church Fathers, to whom he appeals, against the medieval Scholastics, whose view of freedom he rejects. Chapter 3 uses, if possible, even stronger language. Calvin writes, "The will is enchained as the slave of sin, it cannot make a movement towards goodness, far less steadily pursue it." To will ill is part of corrupt nature (2.3.5). He concludes, "Not one particle remains to man as a ground of boasting. The whole is of God" (2.3.6). Chapter 4 concerns how God works in human hearts. Calvin writes that God is very often said to blind and harden the reprobate (2.4.3). Chapter 5 recapitulates and develops arguments on free will. His view here differs from that of Erasmus, and inclines toward Luther. The purpose is to show that humankind cannot will to do the good except by God's grace.

In chapter 6 Calvin expounds redemption. Christ is both Redeemer and Mediator. But here Calvin refers mainly to OT prophecies, including that of the Davidic king. He boldly asserts that by familiarizing the Jews with these prophecies, God intended to teach them to turn their eyes directly to Christ (2.6.4). Chapter 7 considers the Law and its purpose. The Law was to keep alive the hope of salvation in Christ. The Mosaic legislation pointed to Christ (2.7.1). Law also discloses guilt. "The Law is a kind of mirror. As in a mirror we discover any stains upon our face, so in the Law we behold . . . our iniquity" (2.7.7). Paul declares that the Law pronounces its sentence of guilt "that every mouth may be stopped" (Rom. 3:19; 2.7.8). Calvin understands by the word "Law" not only the Ten Commandments, but also the form of religion handed down by God through Moses (2.7.1). He adds that a sober interpretation of the Law goes beyond the words (2.8.8). Chapters 9–11 compare the OT and the NT. In summary, the function of the Law is threefold: it provides a mirror of sin and the need for God's mercy, it provides a restraint on evil, and it conveys the will of God for the life of the believers. Calvin distinguishes between *ceremonial* laws of the OT, which are no longer binding on the Christian, and the *moral* law, which expresses God's will for daily life.

Chapters 12–17 explicitly concern mediation and redemption through Jesus Christ. Chapter 12 introduces Christ as Mediator and closely follows the argument in Hebrews. Calvin declares that Christ was to be our Mediator, and was therefore "very God and very man" (2.12.1). He is true God, to represent God (as descending Mediator), and true man, to represent man (as ascending mediator). Further, as Barth also argues, it was necessary for the Son of God to become for us "Emmanuel," that is, "God with us" (2.12.1). This is almost like the Eastern notion of deification, except that a "mediator" is one who stands "in between" two parties. Thus, in his *prophetic* work Christ conveys the voice and presence of God to us; in his *priestly* work, Christ conveys the needs, prayers, and praise of his people to God. This is the key to the Son of God voluntarily assuming our nature (2.13.3). In chapter 14 Calvin follows the "two natures" Christology of the Church Fathers and the ecumenical councils. He writes that the true substance of Christ is most clearly declared in those passages that comprehend both natures at once (2.14.3).

Chapter 15 expounds Calvin's famous exposition of Christ as Prophet, Priest, and King. Pannenberg considers that the kingly office is perhaps the most important, for Jesus proclaims the kingdom of God as breaking into the new age in his own person. Even so, Calvin comments that the meaning of the kingdom of Christ cannot be fully perceived without recognizing it as spiritual (2.15.4). He also comments that the "honor" of his priesthood belonged only to Christ, because "by the sacrifice of his death, he wiped away our guilt, and made satisfaction for sin" (2.15.6). By his priestly office, he brings reconciliation with God (2.15.6).

In chapters 16 and 17 Calvin sums up his theme that everything needful is given through Christ (2.16.1). Christ has merited grace for us (2.17.1). Calvin urges that we must seek righteousness, deliverance, life, and salvation in Christ alone (2.16.1). He is explicit on penal substitution: "Christ . . . took the punishment upon himself, and bore what . . . was impending over sinners; with his own blood expiated the sins which rendered them [sinners] hateful to God" (2.16.2). He cites Rom. 3:25, "whom God hath set forth to be a propitiation through faith in his blood," and 2 Cor. 5:21, "He hath made him to be sin for us, . . . that we might be made the righteousness of God in him" (2.16.5). Christ used the language "imputed to us" (2.16.6), and suffered the curse and wrath of God (2.16.11). Chapter 17 continues the theme, stressing Christ's obedience in the incarnation. Calvin writes that Christ by his obedience purchased and merited grace for us (2.17.3). The righteousness of *Christ* has been imputed to the believer as *his* or *her* righteousness. Finally Calvin quotes Rom. 5:8, "God commendeth his love toward us, in that . . . *Christ* died for us" (2.17.6).

The third part, or book 3, concerns the Holy Spirit and the mode of obtaining the grace of Christ. Calvin declares: "the Holy Spirit is the bond by which Christ effectually binds us to himself" (3.1.1). Paul calls him "the Spirit of adoption" (3.1.3), and this is symbolized by oil, unction, and fire. Calvin regards faith as his principal work (3.1.4). In chapter 2 the Spirit and the Word of God operate together (3.2.6). Most of the chapter concerns faith and promise. The Holy Spirit works as Mediator between Christ and believers, just as Christ is Mediator between God and humankind. The Holy Spirit is both "seal" and "guarantee" for "confirming the faith of the godly," because until he illuminates these merits, they may waver among doubts (1.7.4). Faith depends on the Holy Spirit, but faith also arms and fortifies itself with the Word of God (3.2.21). Calvin adds that the Spirit gives good ground for understanding and accepting all the promises of Christ (3.2.32). Again he declares, "The illumination of the Spirit is the true source of understanding" (3.2.36; *see* **Holy Spirit: The Spirit in Historical Theology**). The Spirit makes us what we shall become. Calvin leaves no room for purgatory (3.5.10).

Like most Reformation theologians, Calvin regards the Holy Spirit's work most of all as sanctification, following regeneration (3.6.1-4). The Spirit gives us love of righteousness, and holiness because God is holy (3.6.2). Holiness is practical; it involves self-denial (3.7.4), since we belong to God (3.7.2). Self-denial reflects the cross (3.8.2). Christians should not fear death but meditate on it (3.9.5). But Calvin counsels Christians to avoid excessive austerity (3.10.3). In chapter 11 he returns to justification, which means that the Christian "by faith lays hold of the righteousness of Christ, and clothed in it appears in the sight of God not as a sinner, but as righteous" (3.11.2). Chapters 12–18 then consider objections to the doctrine and its relation to sanctification. Chapter 20 urges prayers, with the need for reverence (3.20.5), adjustment to what God wills, mediation, faith, vigor (3.20.7), and confidence (3.20.10-12).

Chapters 21–25 are of special interest today since they address issues of election, predestination, and the last resurrection. Many probably assume that election and predestination constitute the center of Calvin's theology. In fact, chapters 21–24 occupy only 56 pages out of two volumes that occupy *1,287 pages* in English. This amounts to 0.04 percent of the whole *Institutes*. In earlier editions this had been still less, and the subject is never discussed as a metaphysical problem. Like Augustine, Calvin attempts to show that *all* is from God: God's will cannot be defeated. He is aware that some "lay hold of the subject of predestination to carp, or cavil, or snarl, or scoff" (3.21.4). But he replies, "The secret things of God are not to be scrutinised," and the doctrine is clear in Paul. Calvin asserts that God adopts some to the hope of life, and judges others to eternal death (3.21.5). He collects some sixteen passages to affirm God's sovereignty, and contrary to today's trend toward egalitarianism, adds, "All are not created on equal terms" (3.21.5). This surely implies the sheer fact of the varied circumstances of birth and upbringing. The doctrine, he insists, serves to crush all pride. The grace of God is seen in the election of Abraham and Jacob (3.21.6). On Paul, he cites Rom. 9:8 on "the children of promise," and Gal. 3:16, "The promises were made to Abraham" (3.21.7). Chapter 22 wholly contains "proof from Scripture," such as Eph. 1:4: "chosen in Christ before the foundation of the world" (3.22.1), and "called ... according to his own purpose" (3.22.3). (For more on this, *see* **Election and Predestination**.) Much depends on divine omniscience, which includes knowledge of the future, the purpose of election and predestination, and the role of human freedom. Chapter 25 discusses the truth and necessity of the doctrine of final resurrection (3.25.3). As we should expect, Calvin appeals to the example of Christ's resurrection (3.25.3), to the sovereign creative power of God (3.25.4), and to the glory of the postresurrection condition (3.25.10).

Book 4 concerns "the holy catholic church." The church, the sacraments, and civil government are all indispensable means through which God keeps us in eternal life. Calvin begins with the Augustine-like statement, "To those to whom [God] is a Father, the Church must also be a mother" (4.1.1). Both Augustine and Cyprian used this analogy. In contrast to Rome at the time, Calvin declares, "Wherever we see the word of God sincerely preached and heard, wherever we see the sacraments administered according to the institution of Christ, there we cannot have any doubt that the Church of God has some existence" (4.1.9). He distinguishes between the visible and invisible church (4.1.2 and 4.1.7).

Calvin further explains that all the elect are so joined together in Christ that they are one body, sharing the same Spirit (4.1.2); hence we may speak of the "communion of the saints" (4.21.3). Again, the visible church is the "mother" of believers (4.1.4). Preaching is not in word only, but in power (1 Thess. 1:5; 4.1.6). The church belongs to God, and is holy (4.1.10). The church, however, remains sinful, fallible, and capable of splits, as 1 Corinthians vividly demonstrates (4.1.10).

In chapter 2 Calvin feels obliged to attack the "false church" of the papacy. We see there "a perverted government. . . . In place of the Lord's Supper, the foulest sacrilege has entered, the worship of God is deformed by . . . intolerable superstitions" (4.2.2). This theme continues throughout the chapter. Chapter 3 concerns the ministry. Paul names, first, apostles; second, prophets; third, evangelists; fourth, pastors; and last, teachers (4.3.4). Pastors have individually "the government of a particular church . . . [and] have the *same function as apostles*" (4.3.5, italics mine). They preside over the church as watchmen and preachers (4.3.6). The titles "bishops," "presbyters," and "pastors" function "indiscriminately" (4.3.9). The calling of the ministers is both through inward conviction and externally by the church. The appointment of pastors is not by one single person, but other pastors preside and the people consent (4.3.15). The Holy Spirit and the laying on of hands constitute ordination (4.3.14). Elsewhere Calvin lists "doctors" and "elders" as having a prominent place in doctrine and church discipline. Chapter 4 confirms this by examining the primitive church of the NT, while chapter 5 argues that the medieval Roman Church had corrupted NT practices. Chapters 6–8 attack the primacy of the Roman See.

Calvin does not regard the NT as a blueprint for ministry and the church, which was simply to be replicated (*see* **Pentecostals, Pentecostalism**). Calvin respects and values the decrees of such general councils as Nicaea, Constantinople, Ephesus, and Chalcedon because, he explains, "they contain nothing but the pure and genuine interpretation of Scripture" (4.9.8). But as the Anglican *Book of Common Prayer* asserts, "councils may err," and Calvin distrusts later councils. He declares that no power was given to the church to set up any new doctrine (4.9.13). The interpretation of Scripture, however, is another matter. He alludes to Rome again when he speaks of ceremonies, "heaped one upon another," which have become "such a multitude, that it is impossible to tolerate them in the Christian Church" (4.10.13). He firmly advocates church discipline. Since the church is the body of Christ, he argues, it must not bring disgrace upon its Head (4.12.5). He warns against rash vows (4.13).

Calvin's final section concerns the sacraments (chaps. 14–19) and civil government (chap. 20). He writes, "Baptism is the initiating sign by which we are admitted to the fellowship of the Church, that being ingrafted into Christ we may be accounted children of God" (4.15.1). "Grafted" is a helpful word, for it suggests a particular event, followed by a process of ever-closer relationship between what is grafted and what it is grafted on to. Calvin asserts that it is applicable to the children of Christians in the present day (4.16.5; *see* **Baptism; Lord's Supper**). On civil government he parts company with the Anabaptists (4.20.1). The state is by divine appointment for the well-being of God's creation. In T. H. L. Parker's words, "since the magistracy is appointed by God, the people should accept its authority as God-given and therefore to be obeyed" ("John Calvin," in *A History of Christian Doctrine,* ed. H. Cunliffe-Jones [Edinburgh: T. & T. Clark, 1978], 399). Admittedly Calvin concedes that Christ and civil government are things "very widely separated." But to regard the state as polluted or irrelevant is the way of "the Fanatics." Calvin approves of civil order that is directed to an appropriate end, namely, to prevent true religion from being with impunity openly violated (4.20.3). The alternative would be anarchy (4.20.5). Taxes, he states, are the legitimate revenues of princes (4.20.13). Here he follows Luther, as against the Radical Reformers.

We do not have space to expound Calvin's wonderful and insightful work in his commentaries, which his exegesis and attention to language and historical context make still helpful and relevant today. His *Institutes,* however, remain a masterpiece of coherent, well-argued, well-organized, systematic theology. He has produced a classic worthy of attention by all. Even if some will not follow him on predestination or on the time-bound attacks on the papacy of the period, it is difficult not to acknowledge the power and influence of this masterpiece of Protestant Christian theology. (*See also* **Bucer, Martin; Luther, Martin; Melanchthon, Philip; Reformation; Reformed Theology; Zwingli, Ulrich.**)

Reading: John Calvin, *Institutes of the Christian Religion,* trans. H. Beveridge, 2 vols. (Grand Rapids: Eerdmans, 1989); A. N. S. Lane, *"Calvin's Institutes": A Reader's Guide* (Grand Rapids: Eerdmans, 2009); A. E. McGrath, *A Life of John Calvin* (Oxford: Blackwell, 1990); Donald K. McKim, ed., *The Cambridge Companion to John*

Calvin (Cambridge: CUP, 2004); T. H. L. Parker, *Calvin: An Introduction* (London: Chapman, 1995); D. C. Steinmetz, *Calvin in Context* (Oxford: OUP, 1995).

Cambridge Platonists

The Cambridge Platonists flourished at Cambridge in the seventeenth century. Their most influential leaders were Ralph Cudworth (1617-1688), master of Christ's College and Regius Professor of Hebrew, and Benjamin Whichcote (1609-1683). In contrast to the Puritans before them and the Anglo-Catholics after them, they championed the cause of *tolerance within the church,* and held that reason should be the arbiter of revelation. God, they believed, indwelt the mind, for "the spirit is the candle of the Lord." They uncritically found affinities between Platonism and the OT. Superficially their agenda looks like that of Deism, but their piety was warmer, and their emphasis on tolerance was probably partly a reaction against the English Civil War and strident theological controversy.

Canon

"Canon," from Greek *kanōn,* "rule," "standard," "measuring rod," or "straight line," can denote two main things and have many secondary meanings. The first meaning denotes the canon of Scripture, which includes those books of the Bible that have emerged in Christian tradition. The term was used in this technical way by Origen in the early third century, and by others in the fourth century. F. F. Bruce articulates a key issue. It is sometimes argued that the church "created" the canon. But Bruce observes, "We are not dealing so much with the recognition of the biblical oracles as authoritative ... as with the formation of these writings which had *already* the stamp of authority upon them" (*The Books and the Parchments* [London: Pickering and Inglis, 1953], 95). Since the "rule of faith" also uses the same Greek word, *kanōn,* it is significant that it is used in Clement of Alexandria, *Stromata* 6.15 and 4.15, and in Hippolytus, *Heresies* 10.5 in the late second century or early third century (Lampe 701). The date of the completion of the OT canon remains controversial. Most regard it as closed by the beginning of the Christian era, but some argue for a later date. Diaspora Jews and most Church Fathers (except Jerome) included the longer canon of the LXX. Some have argued that the formal notion of an NT canon occurred only in reaction to Marcion (d. c. 160) and "fringe" books perhaps later on (e.g., Hebrews, 2 Peter, and Revelation).

A second meaning of "canon" denotes the canon of the Lord's Supper, Eucharist, or Mass. It was relatively formalized by the time of Ambrose (c. 339-397) in his work *On the Sacraments,* but this may go back to Hippolytus's *Apostolic Tradition* in the second or third century. The heart of it is the words of institution in the pre-Pauline tradition, as in 1 Cor. 11:23-26. In many traditions it also includes the Gloria, the Peace, "Lift up your hearts," the *Trisagion,* the Prayer of Consecration, the Lord's Prayer, the Agnus Dei, and the Prayer of Humble Access.

"Canons of the church" may denote rules or regulations for the lives of clergy and laity. Sometimes a system of canons becomes "canon law."

Canons is also the name given to priests or sometimes laypeople appointed by the bishop in association with the work of the cathedral and diocese. They may be residentiary or honorary canons, or canons theologian.

Canon Criticism

"Canon criticism" is often used as a general term to denote the different "canonical" approaches to the biblical writings represented primarily by Brevard S. Childs and James A. Sanders, but also by Rolf Rendtorf, Gerald T. Sheppard, and Christopher Seitz. Sanders is said to have coined the term "canon criticism" in his major work *Torah and Canon*. But the acknowledged founder and pioneer of the canonical approach is B. S. Childs, although he has reservations about the term "canon criticism." Rather than offering a genetic or purely historical approach, he explores "the sacred Scriptures of the church" as a "living and active text addressing each new generation" (quoted in A. C. Thiselton, "Canon, Community, and Theological Construction," in *Canon and Biblical Interpretation*, ed. Craig G. Bartholomew et al. [Grand Rapids: Zondervan, 2006], 5). He looks at the Bible in more extensive textual expanses, rather than in terms of very small units. But does this mean regarding the biblical writings as a uniform or monochrome landscape? Would this avoid engaging with the distinctive thrust of smaller units? On the other hand, some critics still accuse him precisely of this, in spite of disclaimers. But he is well aware of this problem, as his lifelong work on the shortcomings of the older biblical theology movement shows, and he strenuously seeks to avoid this. Sheppard was an acknowledged follower of Childs. (*See also* **Biblical Theology; Childs, Brevard.**)

Cappadocian Fathers

The name given to the three great Eastern Fathers of the late fourth century: Basil of Caesarea (c. 330-379), his younger brother Gregory of Nyssa (c. 330-395), and his friend Gregory of Nazianzus (c. 330-390). Basil wrote *On the Holy Spirit*, in which he defended the deity of the Spirit and the threefold Gloria. Gregory of Nyssa and Gregory of Nazianzus both wrote on the Holy Trinity, in which they rejected a "numerical" approach, as if "three" were a number that quantified objects. We consider each under separate entries.

Carthusian Order

The Carthusian Order was founded in 1084 by St. Bruno, for living in contemplation, silence, renunciation, prayer, and mortification. The Carthusians adopted a formal Rule c. 1125, and were approved by Pope Innocent II in 1133.

Cassian, John

John Cassian (c. 360–c. 435) is best known for his writings on monasticism, namely, his *Institutes* and *Conferences*. He studied monasticism in Egypt and founded monasteries near Marseilles. The *Institutes* sets out rules for monastic life. The *Conferences* comprises conversations with the leaders of Eastern monasticism. He also had reservations about Augustine's doctrine of grace. His main works are available in *NPNF,* ser. 2, vol. 11.

Casuistry
Casuistry aims to apply general moral principles to particular cases. Historically it is often associated with Jesuit morality, and with the Roman Catholic custom of confession and penance. It usually presupposes an objective moral order.

Catechism
Catechetical (from Gk. *katēcheō,* "to make hear, to instruct") teaching denotes any kind of Christian instruction, but especially Christian teaching of basic or elementary doctrine to new converts, to candidates for adult baptism, and to candidates for confirmation (catechumens). Catechisms were emphasized in the early church and reinstated at the Reformation. Luther, Calvin, and the major Reformers did not want believers to be passive spectators of the Mass, but well-instructed, active participants. Calvin believed that a catechism for children should be simple, in accordance with his principle of accommodation. Catechisms were not only for information, but also for spiritual formation. Both the Westminister Confession and *The Book of Common Prayer* contain catechisms, and there are several Roman Catholic catechisms.

Cathars
The name Cathars (or Cathari) is generally applied to a sect that flourished from the eleventh to the thirteenth century; S. M. Burgess calls it "the greatest single threat to the Roman Catholic Church in the High Middle Ages." The Cathars' fundamental theology was radically dualist, and they were condemned at four councils, the last being the Fourth Lateran Council of 1215. In the battle between good and evil, they condemned marriage, procreation, eating, and war. Their Christology was Docetic, and they viewed sacraments as a deception. They appear to have anticipated baptism in the Spirit as a way of escape from evil powers. They rejected belief in the resurrection of the body. The name is also secondarily applied to earlier "purist" and dualist sects in the time of Novatian and the time of Augustine.

Catherine of Siena
Catherine of Siena (c. 1347-1380) was a Dominican nun who lived much of her life in solitude and silence. At twenty-one she believed she was mystically espoused to Christ. She practiced maximum abstinence from food and sleep, and gave herself to the service of the poor and sick. In 1377 she underwent a still-deeper mystical experience, and reported a multitude of visions. Many involved metaphor. She speaks of "ladders," "castles," and "dark nights" as ways of communicating what transcends simple description. She writes of a bridge "from heaven to earth,"

which is "moistened with his [Christ's] blood ... united with the mortar of divinity ... and with the fire of love" (*Dialogue* 11). Many of her visions might have invited the corrections of Walter Hilton. But her visions were Christ-centered, and she died at thirty-three, largely through self-denial and exhaustion. She was a true mystic, and envisaged God as addressing her: "Oh best-beloved, dearest, and sweetest daughter, my spouse, rise out of yourself" (*Treatise on Prayer* 18).

Catholicity
This word derives from Greek *katholikos*, which means general or universal. In theology it is applied to the universal church in contrast to local churches or congregations. Ignatius, for example, wrote, "Whenever the bishop *(episkopos)* appears this is the congregation *(plēthos)*; where Jesus Christ is, there is the Catholic Church" (*hē katholikē ekklēsia*; *To the Smyrnaeans* 8.2). The traditional "marks of the church" are that it is "one, holy, catholic, and apostolic." A secondary meaning of "catholicity" arises in the distinction between "catholic and apostolic" and heretical sects that are not in accord with apostolic doctrine and the major Church Fathers.

The definition was challenged when the Roman Catholic criteria of catholicity was contrasted with the Reformation or Protestant criteria, which are further complicated by their relation to Eastern Orthodoxy. Before Vatican II this was defined by the Roman Catholic Church in *institutional* terms, especially in an unbroken line allegedly from Peter, and transmitted by the laying on of hands to subsequent popes or bishops. By contrast, most Protestant churches insist that the "catholic" church is truly present wherever the apostolic gospel is preached and the dominical sacraments duly administered. But within both communions a spectrum of views has emerged. Some Catholics incline toward a more Protestant as well as institutional view. Some Protestants incline toward stressing the institutional view as well as the traditional Protestant one. At the other end of this spectrum, some Protestants scathingly criticize the mechanistic or "pipeline" transmission of grace, when this is primarily institutional, while some Catholics stress the absolute necessity of an institutional continuity. But whatever the final interpretation, catholicity stresses the universality of the church, in contrast to a federation of "independent" units, and above all the continuity of the church's tradition in time and place. Even many "independent" churches would claim that wherever the apostolic gospel is preached, there is the one true universal or "catholic" church.

Cause, Causality
Traditionally cause appears as the antecedent of an effect. But can "cause" as such be observed, or do we merely observe constant conjunction, as Hume claimed? Aristotle divided causality (Gk. *aitia*) into four aspects. In producing a statue, or building a house, matter *(hylē)* would be the *material* cause; the impact of the tools *(archē tēs kinēseōs)* would be the *efficient* cause; the design or pattern used

by the sculptor or architect would be the *formal* cause; the purpose for which the statue was carved or the house built would be the *teleological* cause. This demonstrates that we must know what we mean when we speak of "cause." In popular thought this is often the efficient cause.

Hume shows the limits of strictly empirical observation. We see constant conjunction, but "laws of causality" spring from our reflection on what we see. Kant reacted by proposing that cause is an a priori category, and is virtually imposed on phenomena by the mind, as a means of making sense of things. It introduces order into what would otherwise be random succession. An *ordered* nature requires a cause-effect law or assumption. He regarded pace and time also as organizing categories. Leibniz had appealed to "the Principle of Sufficient Reason" to argue that nothing occurs without sufficient reason for it, that is, some cause. Today there is still debate about "laws of causality." Some regard such "laws" as a mechanistic system of controlling significance; others regard them as "progress reports" or generalizations about what usually occurs in an "open" universe. Critical realism is more helpful than simple or naïve realism, while Kant accords too much to the mind. (*See also* **A Priori; Critical Realism; Empiricism**.)

Celsus

Celsus was a late-second-century pagan philosopher who attacked Christian belief in the incarnation, the crucifixion, and the miracles of Christ, although he accepted the church's *Logos* doctrine and its standards of morality. Origen wrote a counterattack in *Against Celsus,* which argued that Christian belief is not irrational. (*See also* **Origen**.)

Celtic Christianity

Celtic Christianity refers to a twentieth-century "ideal" picture of a type of Christian faith and practice distinct from the more hierarchical structures of Rome or the Latin world, and supposedly more sensitive to nature and to the feminine, and less concerned with sin and Augustinian theology. But, since the 1970s and especially during and after the 1990s, this "romantic" and idealized picture of Celtic Christianity has been exposed largely as a popular myth, in conflict with genuine historical and archaeological research and evidence. Writer after writer since at least 1990 has used such phrases as "It was supposed that . . ." According to the romantic and popular view, early medieval Britain (mainly Wales, Scotland, and Cornwall) and much of Ireland reflected a non-Roman version of Christianity, which might then be traced in theory almost up to the Reformation. But the term "Celtic" cannot denote some unified tradition of this kind.

The "romanticized" version traces Celtic Christianity from a century after the withdrawal of Roman power to the Synod of Whitby (664), a council held to regularize the date of Easter, the style of tonsure for monks, and other minor customs. Bede made this council a turning point in his *History of the Church*.

But the synod discussed only its main agenda, and no alleged deep theological divergences appeared. Whitby's conclusion was not at all a decision in favor of the Roman theology against "Celtic" Ireland and parts of Scotland. Moreover, primary sources for the phenomenon of "Celtic Christianity" do not exist, and Bede is misleading. Any notion of Celtic unity or solidarity is simply wrong. Admittedly Patrick (c. 390-461) sought to evangelize Ireland when he traveled from Britain, and the Irish Columba (c. 521-597) brought the gospel to the northern Picts, as confirmed by the abbot of Iona. But K. Hughes asserts that Celtic church unity is a "product of modern imagination." At best, as T. O'Loughlin urges, in *every* region of the Latin West we find distinctive localized features. J. Bruce asserts that the "Celtic isolation theory" is challenged by history and archaeology. G. Markus declares that Celtic theology was hierarchical and *not* egalitarian, anti-Roman, pro-woman, or Pelagian ("The End of Celtic Christianity," *Epworth Review* 24 [1997]: 45-55). Ian Bradley, *Celtic Christianity* (Edinburgh: Edinburgh University Press, 1999), also sees this as an example of popular mythmaking.

Cessationalism

This is usually defined as "the position which holds that miracles or 'extraordinary' charismata were terminated at or near the end of the apostolic age" (J. Ruthven, *On the Cessation of the Charismata* [Sheffield: Sheffield Academic Press, 1993], 15). The classic exposition of the cessationist argument is B. B. Warfield, *Counterfeit Miracles* (1918). But the "cessationist polemic," as Ruthven calls it, was notable in Calvin, and anticipated in Justin, Origen, and Cyril, with a possible implied belief in 1 Cor. 13:10. Speaking in tongues was often a target of criticism even more frequently than miracles, although Enlightenment thinkers certainly stressed the latter. It was usually argued that miracles and tongues-speech might be a witness to the gospel until the final formation of the biblical canon, when, it was suggested, they then became unnecessary. False claims to charismatic "prophecy" became an easy target. Special gifts of healing also relate to the extent to which the kingdom of God is present or future. The exegesis of 1 Cor. 13:8-13 also gives fuel to both sides of the debate, depending on their exegesis. (*See also* **Holy Spirit**.)

Chalcedon, Council of

Occurring in 451, this is known as the fourth ecumenical council (after Nicaea [325], Constantinople [381], and Ephesus [431]). It was formally based on the *Tome* of Leo I of Rome, although it also embodied the conclusions of the other three ecumenical councils. It formally excluded the Christology of Eutyches, although it also took account of Nicaea's address of issues raised by Arius, Constantinople's exclusion of Apollinarianism, and Ephesus's condemnation of Nestorianism. The findings of the council were universally approved, even by Nestorius. It set the climate of christological orthodoxy until at least the beginning of the modern era, when Kant, Hegel, and others began to express fresh formulations.

Chester Beatty Papyri

A group of papyrus codices that date from the second, third, and fourth centuries, the Chester Beatty Papyri were acquired in 1931 by A. Chester Beatty, and the majority are preserved in Dublin. They are at least a century older than the earliest vellum manuscripts. They include 30 leaves of Paul's Epistles, and 30 leaves (out of 220) from the Gospels and Acts. Both are from the early third century. They therefore provide very valuable evidence for the text of the Greek Bible. Some manuscripts are at the University of Michigan.

Childs, Brevard

Brevard Childs (1923-2007) was primarily an OT scholar, but his work extended to the New Testament, theology, and the history of reception. He is especially well known for his canon criticism and for his monumental commentary *The Book of Exodus* (1974), which produced distinct layers of interpretation, including OT exegesis and its reception in Judaism. He also examined reception history in historical eras of the Christian church, and usually also in contemporary theology. He studied the OT under W. Eichrodt at Basel, and was also influenced by K. Barth. His first book, *Myth and Reality in the Old Testament* (1960), distinctively discussed "broken myth," a concept G. B. Caird later explored in the NT. He took up a teaching post at Yale, where he remained for forty-one years until his retirement in 1999, latterly as Sterling Professor of Divinity. In 1992 he published his *Biblical Theology of the Old and New Testaments*. His aim in this was to redefine biblical theology in the wake of the virtual collapse in the 1960s of the biblical theology movement. (*See also* **Biblical Theology; Canon Criticism.**)

Christology

Jesus of History

The phrase "the quest of the historical Jesus" was coined by the English publisher or translator of Albert Schweitzer's book *The Quest of the Historical Jesus* (London: Black, 1910, 1911, 1954), in German entitled more informatively *Vom Reimarus zu Wrede: eine Geschichte der Leben-Jesu-Forschung* (Tübingen: Mohr, 1906). Yet since the publication of Schweitzer's book in English, all inquiries into the Jesus of history have begun with this Quest, giving rise to the term "the New Quest" for that of Bultmann's pupils, E. Käsemann, G. Bornkamm, and E. Fuchs, and even a supposed Third Quest in the 1990s and early twenty-first century. In effect, Schweitzer's book constituted a critique of mainly nineteenth-century "lives of Jesus," beginning with H. J. Reimarus (1694-1768) in the eighteenth century. Schweitzer states, "Before Reimarus no one attempted to form a historical conception of the life of Jesus" (*Quest*, 13). We shall explore the three so-called Quests at length, but if the reader's main interest is in the *teaching* or theology of Jesus, see **Christology: Ministry of Jesus**.

(i) **The First Quest.** Schweitzer admits that not much is known about Reimarus (14). We know that he was born in Hamburg and taught Oriental languages there. In 1754 he published a book on the distinctive truths of natural religion, and a defense of Deism. But his most famous work was *Fragments by an Unknown Author,* which G. E. Lessing, a librarian, published only after Reimarus's death, in 1774-1778. Only one of Reimarus's "fragments" was on the life of Jesus; the others defended Deism, toleration, reason, and the alleged falsity of the resurrection. Schweitzer called the section on Jesus "a magnificent piece of work" (*Quest,* 15). The kingdom of heaven, Reimarus argued, was "according to Jewish ways of thought" (16), and Jesus did not supposedly break with the Law (Matt. 5:18; *Quest,* 17). However, Jesus falsely expected the kingdom of God to come in his lifetime. In Matt. 10:23 he says that it will come before the disciples "have gone through the towns of Israel," and in Matt. 23:39, "Until you say, 'Blessed is the one who comes in the name of the Lord.'" Both hopes were disappointed: "The people in Jerusalem refused to rise." This, of course, cohered with Schweitzer's own distinctive view. As a rationalist and Deist, Reimarus excluded all mysteries and miracles from the life of Jesus. Jesus did call for repentance and readiness for the kingdom of God (Mark 1:15). Reimarus saw the Last Supper as a normal Passover meal, and accepted that Jesus criticized the Pharisees for excessive legalism. When he uttered the words "My God, my God, why have you forsaken me?" (Mark 15:34), however, this expresses his sense of disillusionment (*Quest,* 19-20). For the disciples, "the hope of the Parousia was the fundamental thing" (21). The death of Jesus meant "the destruction of all the dreams for the sake of which they had followed Jesus" (20). Hence they now invented *for themselves* a "spiritual" conception of Messiahship and "the event of Easter" (24). Schweitzer approved of Reimarus's "eye for exegetical detail" (25). But he agreed that he wrote "only [as] a historian" (15), and that he "hung a mill-stone about the neck of the rising theological science of his time" (26). He expressed surprise that even J. S. Semler attacked his work as a historian.

Schweitzer then assessed "rationalist" approaches: J. J. Hess in effect paraphrased the Gospels; F. V. Reinhard removed all dogmatic data from his strictly "historical" study; and J. G. Herder in practice favored art and literature to rationalism. H. E. G. Paulus provided "fully developed rationalism" (48). On miracles, Paulus insisted, "The truly miraculous thing about Jesus is Himself" (51), and he regarded miracle as "a subsidiary question," although it did really exist as a problem. But in detail he "explained away," for example, "the Feeding of the Five Thousand" as an occasion when the rich provided for the poor (52). Raisings of the dead were supposedly cases of coma. Surprisingly Schweitzer chose Schleiermacher to represent "the last phase of rationalism." Admittedly Schleiermacher's attitude to the supernatural often came under this category. The resurrection was a case of "reanimation after apparent death" (64). The ascension "conjecturally supplemented" what was incomplete (65). The messianic temptations had "no intelligible meaning" (65).

At this point Schweitzer devoted a number of chapters to D. F. Strauss (1808-

1874). We have provided details under that entry. Schweitzer was unsympathetic with his "negative Hegelian theology" (73), and his wholesale application of "myth" to Gospel narrative. He commented on his *Life of Jesus,* "It was a dead book, in spite of the many editions which it went through" (76). Many theologians viewed it as bankrupt, and even Nietzsche found fault with it. For Strauss's contemporary readers it seemed to make an end of miracles as a matter of historical belief. He concluded: "Scarcely ever has a book let loose such a storm of controversy, and scarcely ever has a controversy been so barren" (97). W. Hoffmann cited an aphorism of Bacon: "Let the mind be expanded to the greatness of the mysteries, not the mysteries contracted to the compass of the mind." The conservative E. W. Hengstenberg saw it as bringing "the spirit of the age to a clear consciousness of itself" (106).

With Bruno Bauer (1809-1882) we encounter what Schweitzer called "the first sceptical life of Jesus" (137). Bauer thought that *theological* apologists had "reduced" the life of Jesus. It should be given a living relation to *history.* Schweitzer commented, "His purpose was really only to continue the work of Strauss" (145). The messianic temptations merely reflected the experience of the early church. The cross was not connected with the work of salvation. Jesus must perform miracles, Bauer writes, because he was the Messiah, and needed to prove this (149). In the end, "Mark has loosed us from the theological lie" (153). In his book *Criticism of the Gospel History* (1850-1851), Bauer concludes, "There never was any historical Jesus" (*Quest,* 157).

Ernest Renan (1823-1892) was born in Brittany, and originally planned to enter the Catholic priesthood. But he came to doubt the truth of Christianity in the light of German criticism. In 1862 he became a professor of Semitic languages, and later librarian of the Imperial Library. His purpose in writing a life of Jesus was "purely historical" (180). But he marked everything with "artistic imagination" (181), and his description of Jesus became wholly romanticized. Renan recounted how "The sweet theology of love won him [Jesus] all hearts. His preaching was gentle and mild, full of nature, and the fragrance of the country" (185). On the death of Jesus, Renan reflected: "Rest now, amid Thy glory, noble pioneer. Thou conqueror of death, take the sceptre of Thy kingdom." The book passed through eight editions in three months. But critics were at least as numerous as admirers. T. Colani commented, "This is not the Christ of history" (189). In Schweitzer's view, it was "untimely and an over-easy popularisation of the ideas of the critical school." The NT was foreign to Renan; he "must perfume it with sentimentality in order to feel himself at home in it" (192).

Schweitzer's criticism of W. Wrede (1859-1906) is one of the most polemical in the book. In 1901 Wrede published *The Messianic Secret in the Gospels,* which Schweitzer saw as suggesting a new era in "life of Jesus" research. Wrede focused on prohibitions on speaking in Mark about the true Messiahship of Jesus (e.g., Mark 1:23-25, 34, 43-45; 3:11-12; 5:43; 7:36; 8:26). Wrede understood these not as historical facts about the life of Jesus but as *theological constructs* imposed into a narrative by Mark. They served to reconcile a life that did not appear to be messianic with the church's post-Easter proclamation of Jesus as Messiah. This undermined liberal confidence in Mark as a primary basis for reconstructing the life of Jesus. Schweitzer commented, "In order to find in Mark the life of Jesus . . . modern theology has to read between the lines" (330). Wrede argued that as history Jesus' comments not to confess him as Messiah are incomprehensible; as theology their purpose is clear. The idea of Jesus as Messiah did not originate with Jesus, but with the Christian community (ET *Messianic Secret* [London: James Clarke and Co., 1971], esp. 72-80, 218-20, 227-28). In Mark 9:9 the Sonship of Jesus could not be known until after the resurrection.

Astonishingly, Bultmann, Dibelius, and many form critics would later consider Wrede's argument as self-evident. Schweitzer, however, asked a deluge of questions that suggested a different verdict. His chief criticism was that Wrede ignored many of the arguments of J. Weiss and others for an eschatological and apocalyptic understanding of the kingdom of God. Schweitzer also attacked Wrede's hypothesis in detail, a criticism that today may be helpfully supplemented by J. D. G. Dunn, *Jesus Remembered* (Grand Rapids: Eerdmans, 2003), 625-27.

In his last chapter Schweitzer declared, "The historical foundation of Christianity as built up by rationalistic, by liberal, and by modern theology no longer exists; but that does not mean that Christianity has lost its historical foundation" (*Quest*, 397). Modern "lives of Jesus," he complained, are *too general* in their scope. His ending was pessimistic, although from his viewpoint less so, because allegedly it sweeps away false foundations. He concluded: Jesus "comes to us as One unknown, without a name. . . . To those who obey Him, whether they be wise or simple, He will reveal Himself in the toils, the conflicts, the suffering which they shall pass through in His fellowship. . . . They shall learn in their own experience Who He is" (401).

This First Quest is generally regarded as a failure. But few seem to ask *why* it failed. Throughout the writers we have investigated, mainly through Schweitzer, it is apparent that most regard *history* as an *exclusive alternative* to *theology*. This does not imply that every critic was an unbeliever. But many of those we have considered under the First Quest were so. Time and time again the word "dogmatics" is taken to mean "excluding genuine historical inquiry." There are hints that Schweitzer recognized this, but one might not think so from the widespread reaction to Schweitzer's book. In practice, his false alternative history *or* theology dominated the First Quest from Reimarus and Schweitzer to Bultmann. Francis Watson has exposed the naïveté of the supposed alternative in his *Text, Church, and World* (Edinburgh: T. & T. Clark, 1994). Citing B. Childs, he writes: "Approaches which start from a neutral ground never can do full justice to the theological substance because there is no way to build a bridge from the neutral, descriptive content to the theological reality" (31).

Bultmann endorses the negative verdict of Schweitzer's work. Because the "lives of Jesus" have largely failed, Bultmann writes, "No attempt is here made to render Jesus as a historical phenomenon psychologically explicable, and nothing really biographical . . . is included" (*Jesus and the Word* [London: Collins/Fontana, 1958], 13). He then writes: "Interest in the personality of Jesus is excluded. . . . I do indeed think that we can now know almost nothing concerning the life and personality of Jesus, since the early Christian sources show no interest in either; and other sources about Jesus do not exist" (14). He repeats Schweitzer's verdict that over 150 years, the "lives" of Jesus are "fantastic and romantic," as *Quest of the Historical Jesus* has "brilliantly" shown (14). The words of Jesus, however, encounter "*us* with the question of how we are to interpret our own existence" (16). This reflects Schweitzer's conclusion. It would be tempting to claim that Bultmann endorses M. Kähler's verdict that the real Christ is the *preached* Christ. But Bultmann does not sit quite so loose to history. His *History of the Synoptic Tradition* (Oxford: Blackwell, 1972; Ger. 2nd ed. 1931) is largely a *historical* reconstruction of more than 400 pages, admittedly *not* of the life of Jesus, but of the editorial tradition of the early NT church and the Synoptic Evangelists. It is the history of "forms," which supposedly imply situations in the life of the church.

Hence, with this proviso, ultimately Bultmann, like Kähler, qualifies the phrase *historische Jesus* with the adjective *sogenannte* (so-called), and turns not to history as such but to the narrated story of Christ *(der geschichtliche, biblische Christus)*. As H. Anderson reminds us, the name Jesus (the historical man) Christ (the church's object of worship) is what Sir Edwyn Hoskyns and Noel Davey called "the middle of the New Testament" (*Jesus and Christian Origins* [New York: OUP, 1964], 17). Thus Bultmann is prepared to speak of the "that" *(der dass)* of the existence of Jesus, to argue that Jesus called disciples, and was crucified. Bultmann writes, "Jesus knows that he is called to sinners as the physician to the sick" (Mark 2:17; *History of the Synoptic Tradition*, 64), and that "Jesus actually lived as a Jewish rabbi" (49). His call to disciples is said to imply a "Christology." But in more important respects, Bultmann argues, "Faith must not aspire to an objective basis in dogma or in history, on pain of losing its character as faith" (*Faith and Understanding*, vol. 1 [London: SCM, 1969], 14). This aspect is drawn from the influence of neo-Kantian philosophers, and of Herrmann, Heidegger, and nineteenth-century Lutheranism (A. C. Thiselton, *The Two Horizons* [Grand Rapids: Eerdmans, 1980], 205-26). In the same volume Bultmann disparages those conservative scholars who attempt to vindicate or to defend a historical basis for faith. Referring to Krüger, he states: "I calmly let the fires burn, for I see that what is consumed is only the fanciful portraits of Life-of-Jesus theology. . . . How things looked in the heart of Jesus I do not know and I do not want to know" (*Faith and Understanding*, 1:132). All this comes to a climax in his *Theology of the New Testament* (London: SCM, 1952), volume 1, in which he writes, "The message of Jesus is a presupposition for the theology of the New Testament rather than a part of that theology itself" (3).

(ii) **Later Scholarship up to the New Quest.** Bultmann tended to dominate NT studies for much of the first half of the twentieth century. It has become almost conventional to date the emergence of the New Quest from 1954, when Bultmann's former pupil Ernst Käsemann, professor of New Testament at Göttingen, delivered the lecture "The Problem of the Historical Jesus," which was published in *Zeitschrift für Theologie und Kirche* 51 (1954). He declared, "We cannot deny the identity of the exalted Lord with the incarnate Lord without falling into Docetism and depriving ourselves of the possibility of distinguishing . . . the Easter faith of the Church from myth" (141). One of the key themes of the New Quest was to be the identity of the risen Lord with the incarnate Jesus.

However, a number of scholars, both inside and outside Germany, did not follow Bultmann in his modified disregard for history. In America F. C. Grant attacked what he called "existentialist exegesis," although H. Anderson comments that he was also "unashamedly liberal" (*Christian Origins,* 68). The same can be said of A. Barnett's "Jesus as theologian" model, and less clearly of A. Wilder's more moderate work (73-76). In British scholarship Anderson cites C. H. Dodd, T. W. Manson, and Vincent Taylor. He refers to Dodd with particular reference to *The Apostolic Preaching and Its Developments* (1936); to Taylor's *Jesus and His Sacrifice* (1937) and the *Person of Christ in New Testament Teaching* (1958); and to Manson's *Teaching of Jesus* (1931). These were all eminent scholars, and represented Congregational, Methodist, and Baptist traditions, respectively. All three undertook careful research on Jesus Christ without forcing apart the Jesus of history and the Christ of faith, and using moderate biblical criticism.

In Germany Anderson cites the work of E. Stauffer, O. Cullmann, and more recently J. Jeremias. Stauffer, *New Testament Theology* (London: SCM, 1955; 1st Ger. ed. 1941), begins by alluding to the First Quest and to Bultmann, and comments: "The New Testament has another answer: the Way of Jesus" (25). Cullmann had at first embraced Schweitzer's and Bultmann's approach, but from 1931 to 1938 located the ministry of Jesus Christ in an eschatological and promissory timeline between the "now" and the "not-yet"; after 1946, in *Christ and Time,* he understood Jesus in the context of "history of salvation" *(Heilsgeschichte).* This led to his classic *Christology of the New Testament* (London: SCM, 1959, 1963; Ger. 1957). He declared that God's "history . . . must be related to this centre in Christ, to this earthly Jesus of Nazareth, the crucified and risen. . . . All Christology is *Heilsgeschichte* and all *Heilsgeschichte* is Christology" (325-26). Jeremias at first took relatively little interest in the Jesus of history. But in 1935 he published his classic *The Eucharistic Words of Jesus* (ET London: SCM, 1966), in which he spoke of the *ipsissima vox Jesu* (201-2). From Dodd to Jeremias we should not underestimate the serious treatment of the history of Jesus by eminent scholars, in spite of the claims of Bultmann.

In 1954 E. Käsemann began what is conventionally called the New Quest, chronicled by James M. Robinson, *A New Quest of the Historical Jesus* (London: SCM, 1959). Apart from Käsemann, its leading figures are G. Bornkamm and E. Fuchs, both former pupils of Bultmann. Bornkamm lectured before the war at Königsberg, until 1936, when his post was terminated by the Nazis because of his membership in the Confessing Church. After the war, in 1946, he was appointed to Göttingen, and in 1949 to Heidelberg. He partly continued Bultmann's existentialist and kerygmatic tradition, but also positively modified it. He published his classic *Jesus of Nazareth* in 1956 (Eng. 1960), and *Tradition and Interpretation in Matthew* in 1960 (Eng. 1963). Bornkamm agreed with Käsemann on the identity of Jesus, and elucidated Jesus' distinctive message. His account *(Geschichte)* of Jesus did not focus on his personality as such, but distinguished enough of his message to suggest features of the teaching of Jesus. But like Bultmann, he doubted whether Jesus was conscious of being the Messiah. Jesus, however, is not merely "the Bearer of the Word." Jesus proclaimed the kingdom of God and obedience to God with authority. Jesus makes present the reality of God. Bornkamm used a considerable amount of Synoptic material. His criticisms of Bultmann seemed too mild to many who were outside the Bultmann school. But he marked a step ahead of Bultmann.

E. Fuchs studied in Tübingen and Marburg, and received his doctorate under Bultmann. He became a controversial figure, and the church hierarchy censured him for some of his views. But eventually he became Bultmann's successor at Marburg (1961). He contributed to the New Quest mainly through his concern with language. He argued that words and deeds of Jesus constituted a language event *(Sprachereignis)*. He wrote on hermeneutics in 1959, and also *The Question of the Historical Jesus* (Ger. 1960; part Eng. *Studies of the Historical Jesus* [London: SCM, 1964]), which selected essays from his *Gesammelte Aufsätze*. Typical of Fuchs's New Quest approach is his view that Jesus allows us "to understand his conduct as God's conduct. . . . Jesus' proclamation . . . went along with his conduct" (*Studies*, 36-38). Jesus becomes a model of faith. "God accepted the conduct of Jesus as a valid expression of his will. . . . Jesus does not give a new law, but substitutes himself for the law" ("The Parable of the Unmerciful Servant," in *Studia Evangelica* [Berlin: Berlin Academy, 1959], 491-92). Jesus "stands together with the hearer," and so becomes a model for faith "and the way of love" (*Studies*, 80-82). He declared, "To have faith in Jesus now essentially means to repeat Jesus' decision" (28). He adds: "The so-called Christ of faith is none other than the historical Jesus. . . . God . . . *wants to be encountered* by us in the historical Jesus" (30-31).

Why then should Fuchs become so controversial, especially with the church? This is largely because, despite talk about the "actions" of Jesus, everything, including the resurrection, became what most people would regard as "intralinguistic." It all takes place within language. The language event is part of the language world that in Fuchs's view gives it its reality. His work depends on Heidegger's view of language. He places hermeneutics in the dimension of language. He does include some positive insights. For example, in the parables of Jesus: "Love does not just blurt out — Instead it provides in advance the sphere in which meeting takes place" (129). But it remains true that the "common world" of communication in effect belongs to Heidegger's *"existentialia,"* which all takes place in and through language: "The language of faith brings into language the gathering of faith" (208-9). The New Quest, not surprisingly, seemed to inch the debate forward a little, but for many not far enough. In fact, the movement only lasted roughly ten years, from 1954 to 1964, even though Fuchs wrote into the late 1960s and beyond.

(iii) **The Jesus Seminar and the Scope of the Debated Third Quest.** The term "the Third Quest" began to emerge about 1980, largely in contrast to the so-called New Quest. The obvious problem is that people mean utterly different things by this term. In 1985 Robert Funk founded the Jesus Seminar in the Society of Biblical Literature. Scholars were to discuss Jesus material, which extended beyond the four canonical Gospels and included the apocryphal *Gospel of Thomas*. The material was graded as authentic, probably authentic, probably not authentic, and inauthentic. N. T. Wright underlines two problems. First, the presuppositions of the group were never made clear. Second, there is an implicit (not explicit) reversion to the nineteenth-century "history versus theology" polarity (*Jesus and the Victory of God* [London: SPCK, 1996], 31-35). The fact that Burton Mack and J. D. Crossan are leading members may suggest that the seminar stands on the radical or postmodern end of a spectrum of scholarship. Mack reflects the tradition of Wrede and Bultmann, together with an interest in the social history of early Christianity. Crossan is a distinguished Irish American NT scholar who has increasingly turned to postmodernism as well as the NT.

In his later work Crossan portrays Jesus as a follower of John the Baptist from a rural peasant background, who practiced healing and common eating, and uttered "wisdom" aphorisms. He regards many of the Gospel narratives as fiction, but sees Jesus as a "magician" and sage who utters pithy "wisdom" sayings. In *The Historical Jesus* (1991) he dates the *Gospel of Thomas* in the 50s, whereas he dates the Synoptic Gospels as probably from about 70 onward. The resurrection seems to be a "vision" experience. In 1999 he published *The Jesus Controversy*, a debate with William Craig. N. T. Wright expresses admiration for his "brilliance" and learning, but attacks the content of *The Historical Jesus* as "almost entirely wrong" (*Jesus*, 44). He argues that to treat the so-called Q sayings as a Gospel remains highly controversial (48), while to rely on several of the NT apocryphal gospels is "extremely shaky" (49). His sociological study of village life is more important, but this area is still "in comparative infancy" (53). Wright is dubious about "the heart of Jesus' activity" as what he calls "magic and meal" (57). We do not have space to consider all Wright's counterarguments (on which see his *Jesus*, 44-74, and the entry on him in this book).

It is difficult to define the scope of this Third Quest. Wright argues that Marcus J. Borg occupies "a kind of middle position, straddling the Jesus Seminar on the one hand and the Third Quest on the other" (75). His comment suggests a difference between the two movements. Most scholars in both movements attempt to examine the historical and sociological background of Jesus. But Borg is clear about his Christian commitment, and, like Wright, follows G. B. Caird in arguing that the apocalyptic language of Jesus was wrongly assumed to denote the end of the world. He argues that Jesus had ecstatic experiences, was a healer, and was a wisdom teacher and prophet. Borg portrays Jesus as thoroughly Jewish. But he expresses reservation about his dying an atoning death. It is understandable that Borg should reflect both conservative and liberal positions. On the one hand, he is an American and a fellow of the Jesus Seminar, and studied at Union Seminary, New York. On the other hand, he is a Lutheran and studied also at Mansfield College, Oxford, where Caird had been principal. His doctoral supervisor was W. D. Davies. In 1987 he wrote *Jesus: A New Vision;* in 1994 he coauthored *The Search for Jesus* with Crossan; in 1999 he coauthored *The Meaning of Jesus* with Wright; in 2001 he coauthored *The Apocalyptic Jesus;* and in 2006 he wrote *Jesus: Uncovering the Life.*

We see the extreme difficulty of defining the scope of the Third Quest. Wright sees its starting point in 1965 with G. B. Caird. It is understandable that he should include M. Hengel, G. Vermes, B. F. Meyer, A. Harvey, Borg, B. Witherington, J. P. Meier, and others (84). These scholars all explore the history of Jesus of Nazareth and his environment. They are all removed from the assumption and methods of the First and New Quests. Wright was writing in 1996. He could therefore have not been able to include at least two outstanding contributors from the twenty-first century: J. D. G. Dunn, *Jesus Remembered* (Grand Rapids: Eerdmans, 2003); and R. Bauckham, *Jesus and the Eyewitnesses* (Grand Rapids: Eerdmans, 2006), and *The Testimony of the Beloved Disciple* (Grand Rapids: Eerdmans, 2007). Dunn traces the Third Quest more specifically as arising from a more Jewish perspective on Jesus, especially in the work of Geza Vermes, *Jesus the Jew* (London: Collins, 1973), or from a reaction against "the denigration of Judaism" (88), and greater knowledge of the Dead Sea Scrolls and Second Temple Judaism (85-92).

(iv) **The Historical Jesus in Dunn, Bauckham, and Wright.** Since Dunn's *Jesus Remembered* exceeds a thousand pages, it will not be possible to summarize it all in two or three paragraphs. Dunn begins by reviewing the Quests in NT scholarship, and the question of sources. Chapter 8, "The Tradition," brings us to the heart of his work. He sets out the argument in six clear subsections. (a) He follows G. N. Stanton and others in pointing out that new converts to Christian faith would have *wanted* to know about Jesus. Many who were Christian would have witnessed about Jesus and remembered Jesus (177-80). Teachers would have transmitted the early tradition. (b) There are no grounds for assuming that early prophets and prophecy would have added questionable material, for the earliest church was well aware of the dangers of false prophecy. Dunn questions some of the arguments of Bultmann, Käsemann, and M. E. Boring (186-91). (c) Knowledge of oral tradition is important for understanding its reliability and occasional variability. B. Gerhardsson and W. Kelber, in earlier years, and especially Kenneth Bailey today are specialists on the subject of oral tradition. Bailey has studied and observed Middle Eastern village life ("Middle Eastern Oral Tradition and the Synoptic Gospels," *ExpTim* 106 [1995]: 563-67; and *Through Peasant Eyes* [Grand

Rapids: Eerdmans, 1980]). Kelber has written in *Semeia* and elsewhere. (d) The priority of Mark in the Synoptic tradition can still be vindicated, and Markan traditions should not be underrated. Nor should we doubt material common to Matthew and Luke, often called the Q source. Dunn includes detailed textual examples of veracity (217-22). (e) Teachings as well as sayings and the sheer "impact of Jesus' life" (254) would have made an indelible mark, including such phenomena as the Lord's Prayer and the words spoken at the Last Supper (226-31). (f) Oral tradition remained firm until the time arrived when the tradition began to be written down.

Dunn discusses numerous details of historical context: the mission of Jesus, including his baptism by John, his proclamation of the kingdom of God, and his call to discipleship; his identity and role; and his climax in the resurrection. He concludes by reconsidering the historical context, respecting the intention of the text, drawing on hermeneutics, and stating: "Any historical study of Jesus has to take seriously the character of the Judaism of the time and the social and political circumstances in which Jesus undertook his mission, as illuminated by archaeology" (882). He insists that *"the primary formative force in shaping the Jesus tradition was the impact made by Jesus during his mission on the first disciples"* (882). This is the impact of the pre-Easter call to faith. This set in train first an oral and then a written tradition. The tradition goes back *"to the consistent and distinctive character made by Jesus himself"* (884). The tradition includes, for example, his baptism by John, his preaching the kingdom in Galilee, his mission to bring good news to the poor and to call sinners, the realization of many prophetic hopes, the theme of Sonship and Jesus' relation to God. The resurrection and the people of God come under the theme of "eschatological reversal." Easter could not have created "such a weighty Christological affirmation" had not the pre-Easter Jesus been seen as bearing *"divine authority and power"* (892). Through this tradition the would-be disciple *"encounters Jesus"* (893).

Like Dunn, Richard Bauckham, *Jesus and the Eyewitnesses,* begins with comments on the Quest and oral tradition, but also reintroduces the Achilles' heel of much form criticism, namely, the status and value of eyewitness testimony (5-11). Papias, for example, learned from the testimony of Peter (Eusebius, *Historia ecclesiastica* 3.39.9). He collected oral traditions from those who had been eyewitnesses (19). The "living voice" carried much weight in the ancient world (22). Bauckham undertakes research on the memory of particular names of characters in the tradition, as exemplified in his table 5, "Names in the Four Gospels" (65-66). Some names are preserved in all four Gospels: Joseph of Arimathea and Mary Magdalene. Many who might not perform a prominent role feature in all the Synoptic Gospels: Simon the leper; Simon of Cyrene; Mary, mother of James and Joses. Many occur in two of the Gospels: for example, Levi and Jairus. Bauckham lists forty-eight names in all. He then compares occurrences of these names in Palestinian and Egyptian environments, with striking results (71-92). His research includes the use of nicknames and related occupations. He considers the place and role of the Twelve, concluding, "The status of the Twelve in relation to the renewed people of God explains their authoritative status in the early church.... The Twelve were disciples of Jesus the teacher, appointed in the first place to be 'with him' (Mk. 3:14)" (95). Bauckham's point is especially useful since many scholars claim that "the Twelve" merely represent a construction or fiction of Luke. He also addresses the alleged minor differences between names of the Twelve (97-113). He accepts the possibility that Thaddaeus and Judas, son of James, are one person. But he shares honest doubts that Matthew and Levi are (108-13).

Bauckham then turns to the continuity of the proclamation with Acts. In Acts, he says, "Luke depicts Peter preaching a summary of the gospel story with precisely the same parameters and with the claim to witness linked specifically to the resurrection appearances" (Acts 10:36-42; *Eyewitnesses*, 115). He then appeals to the careful preface to Luke's Gospel (Luke 1:1-4), with its reference to "events ... among us, just as they were handed on to us by those who from the beginning were eyewitnesses and servants of the word" (Gk. *paredosan hēmin hoi ap' archēs autoptai kai hupēretai tou logou*). He comments, "The *autoptai* are simply firsthand observers of the events" (117). The phrase "from the beginning" *(ap' archēs)* is common to Luke and John. Bauckham dissents from those who suggest that this belongs only to the tradition of Greek historiography. This introduces a consideration of eyewitnesses "from the beginning" in Mark, John, and Luke (124-32). He then compares this with extrabiblical literature. Again he provides useful tables of those we might consider in this context (table 11, 148-49; and table 12, 150-54). The next logical step is to reconsider the traditional testimony of Peter behind Mark's Gospel. Many will know the traditional arguments on both sides. But, as ever, Bauckham is detailed and meticulous. Mark refers to Peter more frequently than other Gospels do. Sometimes Mark's narrative moves to the singular, to give the point of view of one of the disciples. "Point of view" is one of several key devices used in analyzing narratives in literary theory. Moreover, Mark seems more reluctant than Matthew or Luke to give emphasis to "treatment of Peter's preeminent role" (171), though he does emerge as an individual. Bauckham writes, "Peter is ... the most fully characterized individual in the Gospel, apart from Jesus" (175). He concludes, "Mark's Gospel ... claims Peter as its main eyewitness source" (179). There are many more engagements with recent scholarship and with further issues than we can explore here, as was the case with Dunn. Bauckham wrote a further book on testimony in the Fourth Gospel. But we have shown enough of his work to vindicate Rowan Williams's verdict, when he presented the Michael Ramsey Prize to Bauckham, that "it has blown much previous New Testament scholarship out of the water."

N. T. Wright, like Dunn, begins his volume *Jesus and the Victory of God* by reviewing the Quests of the historical Jesus and the Jesus Seminar. He considers Schweitzer, Bultmann, the New Quest, Mack, Crossan, and Borg. On the so-called Third Quest, he comments, "Serious historical method, as opposed to the

Christology

pseudo-historical use of home-made 'criteria,' is making a come-back in the Third Quest" (87). Anticipating Dunn, Wright insists on the setting of Jesus "within the history of first-century Judaism" (91); "Jesus cannot be separated from his Jewish context" (98). On the aims of Jesus, Wright answers that the Third Quest, in its narrower sense, can simply say that it has "something to do with the kingdom; something to do with the Temple; something to do with Jesus himself; just possibly something to do with his death" (105). Wright insists that we must go much further and deeper than this. Jesus "had the public persona of a prophet," but he was much more than this, as the confession at Caesarea Philippi indicates (197). Jesus announced what Wright calls his "major kingdom-theme of the defeat of evil" (243). This proclaimed both welcome and warning: welcome to the needy, enacting the return from exile; and warning of the need for repentance. The story of the kingdom was Israel's story. Those Jesus welcomed could see themselves as "restored Israel." The notion that Jesus did not intend to found a church rests on a misunderstanding. It undervalues the corporate and communal implications of Jesus' teaching about the restoration of Israel (317). Matthew and Mark both summarize his theme as repentance and welcome (Mark 1:15; Matt. 4:17; *Jesus*, 246). The vocation of Israel has come at last (309).

Wright considers in detail the preaching and teaching of Jesus. This is "not to be squashed down into witty or proverbial aphorisms. It is not to be reduced to timeless moral or doctrinal teaching. He spoke as he acted, as a prophet through whose work YHWH was doing a new thing, indeed *the* new thing for which Israel had waited for so long" (367). In considering this "newness" in contrast to traditional Pharisaism, Wright seeks to move *beyond* two standard ways of interpreting this controversy. It is *not* a matter of outward observance versus inner attitude, nor is it E. P. Sanders's new account of the Law. He rejects, as Sanders does, the critique of "the older, caricatured position" (372), but understands Jesus as attacking the symbols that are resistant to his vision of the kingdom, and as announcing his vision of the kingdom through different symbols. Sabbath, food, and family represent some of the old symbols. "Return," restored land, and redefined family represent some of the new ones (428-38). This brings us to one of the climactic points of Wright's argument. Here he builds on the classic work of G. B. Caird. He cites some of the standard sayings about the kingdom, for example, "Some standing here ... will not taste death until they see ... the kingdom of God" (Mark 9:1; Luke 9:27; cf. Matt. 10:23; 16:28; Mark 13:30). He comments, "To read this saying as though it were a prediction of Jesus' 'return,' or *'parousia'* in some ... end-of-the-world sense, is simply to fail to think historically" (470). The effects of this comment are momentous. Caird argued that a reference to a historical event was "taken up into the myth of the end" (*The Language and Imagery of the Bible* [London: Duckworth, 1980], 265). He claimed the two questions of Mark 13 were confused by many interpreters; one was: "When will the end of the world come?" The other was: "When will the end of the Temple at Jerusalem come?" (266-68). Caird was almost alone in this view, but he argued that NT specialists do not understand adequately the scope of "myth." C. E. B. Cranfield argued that Mark 9:1 refers to the transfiguration, and Vincent Taylor referred it to Pentecost. He dismissed Caird's suggestion that it refers to the destruction of Jerusalem, but he wrote some twenty years before Caird's careful work on semantics. Wright points also to the ambiguity of the Greek *ēngiken* (471-72).

Wright's part 3 concerns Messiahship, the crucifixion, and the return of the King. The Messiahship of Jesus "redefined itself around Jesus' own kingship-agenda" (538), and it pointed to a fulfillment of Israel's destiny. The return of God to "Zion and Temple-theology . . . are the deepest keys . . . to gospel christology" (653), which are more significant than the "titles" of Jesus. Jesus went to Jerusalem to die. The present system, he taught, was corrupt: "it is ripe for judgment" (609). Jesus must have known that to proclaim this would have invited his death: "The death of the shepherd would result in YHWH [God] becoming king of all the earth" (610). Further, he says, "Jesus was raised from the dead" (659). This would be the subject of Wright's next major book, *The Resurrection of the Son of God* (London: SPCK, 2003). (*See also* **Bauckham, Richard J.; Bultmann, Rudolf; Crossan, John Dominic; Dunn, James D. G.; Strauss, David F.; Wright, N. Thomas.**)

Reading: R. J. Bauckham, *Jesus and the Eyewitnesses* (Grand Rapids: Eerdmans, 2006); J. D. G. Dunn, *Jesus Remembered* (Grand Rapids: Eerdmans, 2003); E. Fuchs, *Studies of the Historical Jesus* (London: SCM, 1964); A. Schweitzer, *The Quest of the Historical Jesus* (London: Black, 1910, 1954); G. Vermes, *Jesus the Jew* (London: Collins, 1973); N. T. Wright, *Jesus and the Victory of God* (London: SPCK, 1996).

Ministry of Jesus

The title of this section does *not* imply that the Quests have not taken theology seriously. Indeed, Dunn, Bauckham, and Wright, for example, have clear theological concerns. But the very notion of a "historical" Jesus implies not simply the need for historical research, but in many cases the need, it is claimed, for *purely* historical research, in isolation from theological research. This results in the impressive work of Jürgen Moltmann, for example, appearing to inhabit a different world from the Jesus Seminar, although he and Wolfhart Pannenberg are not only insistent on the need for historical research, but also draw on the wider and deeper picture provided by theology. Indeed, the beginning of Moltmann's *Way of Jesus Christ* (London: SCM, 1990) makes this very point. He pleads for a clear continuity "between the Christian gospel and the Jewish history of promise found in the Old Testament" (3). The *historical* origins of the messianic hope, he argues, are found in Israel. He laments the "'turn to anthropology' in modern European times," typified in the liberal "Jesusology" (38). The account of Jesus of Nazareth, and indeed Christology, "presupposes belief" (19). This does not prevent Moltmann from saying also: "Christological statements have to be verified as originating historically . . . in the Bible" (43). He continues: "Anthropological Christology is simply Jesusology and nothing else" (55).

Pannenberg makes the same point. He describes the "historical-critical procedure" as being often, even usually, guilty of "anthropocentricity" (*BQT* 1:39). The Jewish thinker Martin Buber also laments this modern "turn." It may appear that Moltmann's "Christology from below" (55), which is also strongly advocated by Pannenberg, might also run this risk. But Pannenberg advocates "the total character of the coming of Jesus and his history in order to find a basis for confession of his deity" (*ST* 2:280). Although "the foundation is the history of Jesus," he continues, "Christology must ask and show how far this history of Jesus is the basis for faith" (282). Pannenberg cannot be accused of "narrowing" Christology; indeed, he broadens its horizons. Scholars as varied as O. Cullmann, G. B. Caird and J. Jeremias, J. A. Baird, D. C. Allison, M. Bockmuehl, M. Hengel, and B. Witherington (as well as Dunn, Bauckham, and Wright) *broaden* the context of history to include a critical theology.

To this group of scholars we turn now. If we begin with the birth of Jesus, Cullmann makes an illuminating point in his essay "The Origin of Christmas" (in *The Early Church* [London: SCM, 1956], 21-36). He points out that 25 December was unknown as the date of Jesus' birth to Christians for three centuries. In the end, the West tried to persuade the Eastern churches to accept this date, but especially Syria refused, in spite of Chrysostom's attempts to advocate the idea. Cullmann writes, "Christians have never kept Christmas on a historically accurate date, whether on December 25th or January 6th. . . . Christmas did not commemorate a date at all." Historical and chronological accuracy is not always necessary in every case for healthy theological and pastoral application.

If we can follow not only a host of NT scholars but also Moltmann and Pannenberg, the narrative of Jesus of Nazareth begins long before his birth. The historical context of the ministry of Jesus stretches back several hundred years to prophetic and apocalyptic expectations about his coming. A study of hermeneutics suggests that to establish bare facts about Jesus without historical understanding would be to chase an abstraction. The two distinct themes of prophetic and apocalyptic expectation each contribute a different aspect of understanding. However, with some irony we may cite the historically concerned Albert Schweitzer in chapters 4 and 5 of *The Mysticism of Paul the Apostle* ([London: Black, 1931], 52-100). The background to "to wait for his Son from heaven" (1 Thess. 1:10), Schweitzer argues, comes from "the earlier and later Prophets, mainly the Book of Enoch, the Psalms of Solomon, and the Apocalypses of Baruch and of Ezra" (54). Admittedly Schweitzer sometimes cites sources that postdate Jesus and Paul, and admittedly he believes that Jesus expected the immediate end of the world. But those two shortcomings do not invalidate the double appeal to the prophetic and apocalyptic tradition. In short, "The pre-Exilic and Exilic prophets expect a Messiah of David's line to come as the God-anointed Ruler, endowed with wisdom and power, to rule the great Kingdom of Peace which was to form the consummation of world history" (76). On the other hand, in apocalyptic "the Law has no more validity" (188). Whereas the prophetic stream looked for a prophet or *human king* who would be preeminently *equipped by the Spirit* to bring in an era of liberty and deliverance from oppression, apocalyptic saw that human leaders constantly failed, and that "in terms of 'the above' ... *the triumph of God*" is expected; God would intervene in history to overcome the failure of man (D. S. Russell, *Method and Message of Jewish Apocalyptic* [London: SCM, 1964], 106; *see* **Apocalyptic**). At the risk of oversimplification, we might suggest that Jesus as a man equipped by the Holy Spirit fulfills the hopes of the *prophetic* stream; Jesus as representing the direct intervention of *God* and the birth of *new creation* and the new age responds to *apocalyptic* hopes. Pannenberg writes that in his acts of authority, Jesus "put himself in God's place" (*Jesus — God and Man* [London: SCM, 1968], 67).

The prophetic hope is fulfilled explicitly in the descent of the Holy Spirit at the baptism of Jesus (Matt. 3:13-17; Mark 1:9-11; Luke 3:21-22; John 1:32-34). This is clearly authentic. Jeremias points out that this account risked being offensive to the early church on two grounds: first, the apparent subordination of Jesus to John the Baptist (Matt. 3:14-15); second, it may have appeared that Jesus underwent baptism "for the forgiveness of sins." Jeremias observes, "Such a scandalizing piece of information cannot have been invented" (*New Testament Theology* [London: SCM, 1971], 45). In his baptism, as C. K. Barrett comments, Jesus "became one of the prepared people of God, able to await the coming judgement without fear" (*The Holy Spirit and the Gospel Tradition* [London: SPCK, 1958], 33). Jeremias comments, "Jesus stood among the people, who immersed themselves in the Jordan at a sign or a call from John" (51). The Spirit descends also to call Jesus to embody and to enact his message.

This event is not only well attested in multiple traditions; it is pivotal for the installation of the messianic ministry in which God the Father expressed his love for the Son, and the Spirit descended upon him to empower him for his work and lead him to his messianic temptations. The virgin birth is not placed by the Gospel writers in so prominent a position. Even Moltmann acknowledges, "The virgin birth is not one of the pillars that sustains the New Testament faith in Christ" (*Way*, 79). "The narrators' aim is not to report a gynaecological miracle" (82). The purpose of the narrative especially in Matthew is to recount "Emmanuel ... God with us," and that from beginning to end the life and ministry of Jesus were sustained and overshadowed by the Holy Spirit. It is significant that in the fourth century to call Mary "the Mother of God" was not a statement about Mary, but a statement about the true humanity of Jesus. The confession in the creeds, "Conceived by the Holy Spirit, born of the Virgin Mary," serves to underline, as Moltmann comments, "that *God alone is the Father of Jesus* Christ" (82).

In the messianic temptations or tests (Mark 1:12-13; Matt. 4:1-11; Luke 4:1-13), clearly the Holy Spirit "immediately drove him *(ekballei)* out into the wilderness" (Mark); Matthew softens this to "was led up by the Spirit"; and Luke recounts that Jesus was "full of the Holy Spirit ... and was led by the Spirit." Could Jesus have been tempted to sin? The point of the temptation was to persuade him in each example to take a convenient *shortcut* to *obeying* God's purpose, but not *in the way that God intended.* To turn stones into bread might have gathered followers more quickly than otherwise, and clearly outdo Moses' miraculous "manna" in the wilderness. To jump from the temple platform into the Valley of Hinnom would guarantee popular appeal, and force God's hand to take premature action. All three temptations aimed specifically to disrupt the intimacy of Jesus with God's Way of his being the Messiah, and to disrupt his trust in God. The proximity of the temptations to the baptism is significant. Ringing in his ears, Jesus had last heard, "This is my beloved, on you have I set my choice." This recalls Isa. 43:1 on the function of God's servant. The Son's *obedience* to God's *Way* would involve the necessity of the passion (Mark 8:31; 9:31; 10:32), and "not what I want, but what you want" (14:36). This, in turn, necessitates confrontation with evil, and response to God's timing *(kairos)*. Jesus' opening message in Mark 1:14-15 concerned the arrival of the right time in God's purpose.

To understand the unfolding of events in the four Gospels, it is crucial to appreciate narrative speed and narrative time *(see* **Narrative; Ricoeur, Paul**). The Gospels never claim to follow strictly *chronological* time or *clock* time. It is well established that Mark depicts the ministry of Jesus using *narrative* time. In the first section of Mark the work and status of Jesus are known only to himself, and the narrative tempo moves rapidly onward. Then, as W. Manson argues, "In the second section, the Christhood comes out into the open, but solely in relation to the historical events of his rejection, suffering, and death (8:31; 9:31; 10:32-3 and 45)" *(Jesus and the Christian* [London: J. Clarke, 1967], 35). Manson could have added Peter's confession in 8:29 to the publicizing of his Messiahship. As E. Best (1983) and W. A. Kort point out (Kort, *Story, Text, and Scripture* [University Park: Pennsylvania State University Press, 1988], 44), the pace of the first section of Mark "is very quick," as the use of *euthus* and a rapid succession of events indicate. The second section still uses indirect communication with parables and enigmatic sayings, but now becomes "normal" time, moving ahead at a moderate rate. The third section of Mark depicts the passion in slow motion, pausing over every detail of events. This should warn us not to expect "natural" chronology in Mark, and perhaps other Gospels.

In addition to narrative time, other Gospels deploy narrative *sequence.* The temptations, which reveal differences of sequence in Matthew and Luke, and the cleansing of the temple, which reveals differences of sequence between John and the Synoptic Gospels, use *standard devices* of narrative telling. Today we are used to flashbacks in most detective stories. But this always has a specific purpose. In a detective story there would be no suspense of plot in a simple chronological account. In Mark the three variations of speed, for example, are to cast the spotlight on the cross. It is as if to say: "This is what the whole narrative has been leading up to, as its climax and purpose."

So the baptism and temptations set the narrative going, with added scene settings in Matthew, Luke, and John. Jesus clearly begins in direct continuity with John the Baptist, and with him, calls Israel to repentance. But Jesus also proclaims the good news of the gospel, and announces that the kingdom of God "has drawn near" (Gk. *ēngiken;* Mark 1:15). Then his call to his first disciples (1:16-20) begins in Galilee. The ethos of Galilee is well described by G. Vermes (*Jesus the Jew* [Philadelphia: Fortress, 1981], 42-57), even if Bultmann dismisses Mark 1:16-20 as "legends" (*Jesus and the Word* [London: Collins/Fontana, 1958], 35). Jeremias finds "considerable intrinsic probability in Jesus' calling of disciples of John the Baptist" (*New Testament Theology,* 47-48). After this initiating call, Mark relates a ministry in Capernaum, which constitutes the beginning of accounts of healings and conflict. Mark 1:23-28 recounts the healing of the demoniac in the synagogue, resulting in the question, "What is this? A new teaching — with authority!" (v. 27). Five episodes of healing follow (1:29–2:12), culminating in the healing of the paralytic. Specialist NT scholars and Pentecostals rightly link "healings" with the announcement of the kingdom of God. The problem, however, is that the kingdom is *near*: it is *both present and future,* or both *manifest and hidden.* In as far as it is *present,* healings are a sign of this; in as far as it is still *future,* healings may be genuine but certainly not "normal," even in the ministry of Jesus.

The call of Levi (Mark 2:13-17) provokes more open conflict with "scribes and Pharisees" (2:16-17), and is followed by Jesus' teaching on newness and new creation (2:21-22). The saying about "new wine and old wineskins" is reminiscent of "wisdom aphorisms" supposedly belonging to the Q source in Matthew and Luke, and indeed we find parallels in Matt. 9:16-17 and Luke 5:36-38. Mark includes a "wisdom aphorism" in the call of Levi: "Those who are well have no need of a physician, but those who are sick" (Mark 2:17). This is followed by a pronouncement of implied authority: "I have come to call not the righteous but sinners" to repentance (2:17). The controversy with scribes and Pharisees soon broadens into a debate about the respective priority of grace and "justice," together with new creation or Sabbath observance (2:23–3:6). Jesus calls to the kingdom "the poor," which "covers the hungry, the unemployed, the sick, the discouraged, the sad and the suffering . . . oppressed and humiliated people . . . sick, crippled, homeless" (Moltmann, *Way,* 99; cf. Luke 14:21-23; Matt. 11:2-5). Mark reports the oppressive demons as saying, "Have you come to destroy us?" (Mark 1:24).

Matthew and Luke supplement Mark's tradition. Mark's episode of the call of Levi is parallel with "This fellow welcomes sinners and eats with them" (Luke 15:2). Virtually every student of the Synoptic traditions would be familiar with Matthew's softening of Mark's "He *could* not do mighty work there" (*ouk edunato ekei poiēsai oudemian dunamin;* Mark 6:5) to "He *did* not do . . ." (*ouk epoiēsen;* Matt. 13:58). Jeremias comments, "The rephrasing in Mt. 13:58 . . . guarantees the trustworthiness of the account" (*New Testament Theology,* 91). He also argues that Jesus' disputes over the Sabbath "have a firm place in the tradition" (91). In spite of Bultmann's claim that the miracle stories have a Hellenistic setting, Jeremias urges, "Even when strict critical standards have been applied to the miracle stories, a demonstrably historical nucleus remains" (92). The conflict with the Pharisees when Jesus called a tax collector is partly due to his concern for those with "despised trades," namely, those which in popular thought led to dishonesty or immorality. These included "gamblers, usurers, tax collectors... and herdsmen (these last were suspected of leading their herds into other people's land and pilfering the produce of the herd). When the gospels talk of 'sinners,' they are thinking of those occupied in despised trades as well as those whose way of life was disreputable" (110). In those terms the indignation of the Pharisees that a prophet or rabbi should choose to consort with these is understandable and "natural," for they especially prized loyalty to every iota of the Law.

This very roughly covers the first part of Mark's Gospel, where with about half a dozen exceptions in various forms the triple tradition of Matthew, Mark, and Luke, or at least Mark and Luke, recounts broad parallels (pericopes 13 to about 110 in K. Aland, *Synopsis of the Four Gospels*). Major gaps in Mark are: (i) the early synagogue sermon that expands the Jubilee: "The Spirit of the Lord is upon me, because he has anointed me to bring good news to the poor..." (Luke 4:16-30); (ii) a more detailed narrative of the call of the disciples (Luke 5:1-11); (iii) Matthew's Sermon on the Mount (Matthew 5–7); (iv) Luke's Sermon on the Plain (often paralleled with Matthew; Luke 6:20-49); (v) the naming of the Twelve (Luke 6:12-16); (vi) the fate of the disciples (Matt. 10:16-25; Luke 12:11-12), and division within households (Matt. 10:34-36; Luke 12:51-53); (vii) longer sayings about John the Baptist (Matt. 11:7-19; Luke 7:31-35); (viii) the thanksgiving to the Father (Matt. 11:25-27; Luke 10:21-22). This is not an exact comparison, but indicates the outline of the earlier part of the ministry of Jesus.

We have yet to explore what is also widely recognized as authentic, namely, Jesus' intimate relationship with his Father. One problem is that Jesus frequently stresses God as his Father in the tradition of Matthew and John, but Mark and the so-called Q source seem to show reluctance or reserve in doing so. Does this suggest that it is authentic to Jesus, even if Matthew and John call special attention to it? N. Perrin uses the now old-fashioned "criteria of dissimilarity" to suggest that Jesus uses it. However, relatively few today regard this creation as definitive rather than perhaps useful. T. W. Manson holds the opposite view: "Father" is "a common theme of Rabbinic teaching, and 'Father' is a common mode of address in prayer," but "Jesus spoke of God as Father... not presenting a new... doctrine" (*The Teaching of Jesus* [Cambridge: CUP, 1963], 92, 93). G. Vermes agrees with Manson that there is rabbinic evidence for the use of "Father," and that "for Jesus, God is *Abba*" (*Jesus the Jew*, 211). He proposes that the term "Son of God" is ascribed to Jesus more because of his activities as miracle-worker and exorcist than because of his intimacy with God. A middle course between Vermes and Jeremias is broadly adopted by J. D. G. Dunn. As we saw above, he thinks that Jeremias may be broadly right about Jesus' use of "Abba" as an intimate and affectionate term, but that Jeremias has perhaps overstated his case. Jeremias insists that the Fatherhood of God cannot be taken for granted (*New Testament Theology*, 180). At all events, it constitutes the *supreme expression of trust*. Jeremias suggests, "The riddle of evil is left in God's hands" (184). Just as what "Lord" denotes is best seen by the work of the servant *(doulos)*, so to be a "little child" who trusts sheds light on God as Father. Matt. 11:25-27 speaks of "infants" (NRSV) as those who receive God's revelation in trust. Remarkably, in retrospect, Heb. 2:13 applies "I will put my trust in him" to Jesus.

Just as it is natural for children to talk with their father, so this introduces for Jesus the subject of prayer. The earliest traditions preserve the prayer that begins "Our Father . . ." Dunn and Jeremias point out that the value of prayer to Jesus occurs in all four strata of the Synoptic Gospels: Mark (Mark 11:17, 24); Q (Matt. 7:7-11; Luke 11:9-13); Matthew (Matt. 6:5-8); and Luke (Luke 11:5-8). In addition to teaching the liturgically memorable "Lord's Prayer," the prayer in Gethsemane uses the "Abba" of address. The Pauline churches then reflect this usage in Rom. 8:15 and Gal. 4:6. The Lord's Prayer reflected "the desire of the disciples to have a prayer of their own" (Jeremias, *New Testament Theology*, 196-97). Manson argues, "The Lord's Prayer is the sum of all the teaching of Jesus on the Fatherhood of God" (*The Teaching of Jesus*, 115). Some of the sayings about the Father would be unlikely to be created. One example might be: "About that day or hour no one knows, neither the angels in heaven, nor the Son, but only the Father" (Mark 13:32, and parallel Matt. 24:36, *ei mē ho patēr*). Both Manson and Jeremias examine the Aramaic or Semitic background of these sayings. Jeremias also develops this in terms of God's providence and care, arguing that "Nothing is too small for God." Jesus always used the word "Father" in his own prayers.

Two classic sources on the teaching of Jesus should not be ignored. J. A. Baird's *Audience Criticism and the Historical Jesus* (Philadelphia: Westminster, 1969) has been unduly neglected, even though Baird in some respects anticipated much in reader-response theory and is meticulously careful in his research. He rightly declares, "The Evangelists were intensely concerned to identify the audience that surrounded Jesus at any given moment. . . . In 94% [of the Huck-Lietzmann Synopsis] the audience is clearly designated. . . . The general picture is one of an audience that is constantly shifting" (32). Apart from special nuances, there are four basic types of audiences: the Twelve, the "crowd" of disciples, the opponent crowd, and opponents of Jesus. The Twelve were always present; the larger group of disciples was often, but not always, in the background. Following Manson, Baird calls the Twelve the "D" group; the crowd of disciples, "DG"; the opponent crowd, "GO"; and the opponents, "O." Those in the "D" category, the Twelve, receive authority for missionary activity (Matt. 18:18), the explanation of parables (Mark 4:33-34), and "the secret of the kingdom of God" (Mark 4:10-12, 33). Baird then provides detailed charts to illustrate this (34-36). Members of the "DG" category are "with Jesus" and listen to his instruction, and the Seventy even share in his mission (37-43). The "GO" group varies in their response from astonishment bordering on suspicion (Mark 1:21-28) to full-scale opposition (Mark 15:8-15). Finally the "O" group is a hard-core opposition (Luke 13:17). Baird gives a detailed list under such headings in Greek (37-49). We cannot take the reader through the 200 pages of Baird's book, but the purpose of his early chapters is to correlate particular teaching with particular audiences. The origin, Baird argues, is "the single mind of the historical Jesus" (153).

The other book is Jeremias's *Parables of Jesus* (London: SCM, 1963). His reconstruction of the *teaching* of the parables is mainly *retrospective,* and therefore, as R. W. Funk rightly argues, it tends to wreck the hermeneutical dynamic of the parables by treating them as flat propositional truths (*see* **Parables of Jesus**). But this does not invalidate their function in allowing us to grasp their content, not as operational parables, but as a retrospective account of the teaching of Jesus. They no longer have the cutting edge that Funk finds in Fuchs, but as a survey of former teaching Jeremias offers an invaluable tool. Jeremias suggests nine themes, from which we make a selection from each category. The first theme is "Now Is the Day of Salvation." The parables include the new garment and new wine, traditional metaphors for the new age (117). The allusion to the strong man bound refers to the defeat of Satan (Mark 3:27; *Parables,* 122). A second theme traces God's mercy for sinners. The parables of the lost coin and lost sheep are obvious examples, but so are those of the Pharisee and the publican (Luke 18:9-14) and the prodigal son (Luke 15:11-32). Parables of eschatological reversal are relevant (142). Third come parables of assurance: the parables of the mustard seed (Mark 4:30-32) and of the leaven (Matt. 13:33) belong here. They speak of God's miraculous power (149). Jeremias sees the parable of the sower as also eschatological, with the message: "Whatever the obstacle, go on sowing."

Some parables speak of the imminence of catastrophe, and warn "it may be too late." The parable of the ten virgins, well expounded by Dan Via, provides a good example (171). Jeremias sees the theme of the challenge of the hour in the parable of the rich man and Lazarus (Luke 16:19-31), which shows that "evasion is impossible" (182). The parable of the guest without a wedding garment (Matt. 22:11-13) may be less disputable (187). He calls the seventh theme "Realized Discipleship," which is illustrated by the pearl of great price (Matt. 13:45-46), for which a person will give everything. Jeremias also places the parable of the Good Samaritan (Luke 10:25-37) here, of which we note Crossan's interpretation under the entry **Parables**. It is not a mere "example story." The eighth theme concerns the suffering and exaltation of the Son of Man, and the ninth the consummation. What is hidden will become manifest, the blind will receive their sight, and numerous "reversals" will take place (221-22).

Those who work with very strict or exacting criteria of authenticity may refer several of the above themes to the Evangelists or to the tradition. But there are good reasons for seeing the parables as distinctive to Jesus. Moreover, in the next phase of Jesus' ministry, namely, the passion, many rigorous NT scholars, including Raymond E. Brown, include a mass of detail about the passion narrative (*The Death of the Messiah,* 2 vols. [London: Chapman, 1994]). He considers events from the arrest, through the trial, to the condemnation and the cross. "It is the largest consecutive action recounted of Jesus. . . . No previous work has required research so lengthy, or bibliography so ample" (1:vii). In the end, "what the evangelists 'intended and conveyed' is the key to the meaning of the Passion Narratives," and Brown's "primary concern" (9). He may not think of the Evangelists as *direct* eyewitnesses, but ultimately there were eyewitnesses and "earwitnesses" who were in a position to know the broad lines of Jesus' passion (14; see above on Bauckham). He adds, "It is inconceivable that they [the disciples] showed no concern about what happened to Jesus after the arrest" (14). Jesus predicted his death in Mark 10:45 and John 10:15. The interdependence of the Gospels "is a very complex and disputed issue" (40), but the priority of Mark and the influence of oral tradition command a reasonable consensus, especially (as Bauckham also argues) in the light of work on orality by Gerhardsson, Kelber, and others. Orality is "very important in giving nuance to the Gospel's historicity" (51).

Brown divides the passion narrative into four dramatic acts, of which the first is the prayer of Jesus and his arrest in Gethsemane on the Mount of Olives. Jesus utters a foreboding prediction of the fate of his disciples in Mark and Matthew (Mark 14:27-28; Matt. 26:31-32), while Luke recounts that Jesus prays for Peter (Luke 22:32). The flight of the disciples "was on a par with denying Jesus" (*Death*, 122). Peter tries to protest (Mark 14:29-31). But Jesus predicts Peter's denials (Mark 14:30; *Death*, 134). Brown pays special attention to the prayer of Jesus in Gethsemane (146-234), to which Hebrews also refers (Heb. 5:7-10). The arrest now follows (act 1, scene 2) with the arrival of Judas, recounted in each Gospel. According to Baird's analysis, the opponents are surrounded by a group, including Roman and Jewish troops (*Audience Criticism*, 250). Part 2 of the arrest concerns accompanying incidents, including the response of Jesus to the sword-wielder (Matt. 26:52-54). Part 3 (Brown, *Death*, 294-304) concerns the naked flight of the young man (Mark 14:51-52), who cannot be a merely symbolic figure, but must be an anxious young man (302-4).

Act 2 of the passion narrative portrays Jesus before the Jewish authorities. This includes Jesus before the high priest and his interrogation, the mockery by the Jewish authorities, and Peter's three denials (315-660). Scene 1 is the interrogation by Jewish authorities. Brown discusses governance in Palestine. Antipas, son of Herod the Great, was tetrarch, or "king" (4 B.C.-A.D. 39). The governor of Judea had independent authority from the legate of Syria, and Tacitus alludes to the *procurator*, Pontius Pilate (336). He would have had power to execute. Rome, not the Sanhedrin, had these full powers (364-72). There may be a tendency in the Gospels to make some Jews more "guilty" for the death of Jesus than the Romans, but "guilt" is not as accurate a term as "responsible." The interrogation took place in the house of the high priest (402-4). John maintains that both Caiaphas (five times) and Annas (twice) held the office of high priest. Annas had been high priest some fifteen years before, and Josephus still calls him "high priest" at the end of Caiaphas's reign. Against Bultmann, Brown sees no problem here. Brown comments, "The question of the high priest centres on Jesus' disciples and on his teaching" (413). In his teaching, his interrogators would have found it offensive that Jesus called "God his own Father, thereby making himself equal to God"

Christology

(John 5:18; *Death,* 413). Jesus replied that he was present daily. On the precise sequence of events, Brown includes detailed chronological charts (418-19) and a huge wealth of bibliography, as he does throughout.

Part 3 of act 2 examines the Sanhedrin proceedings with reference to Jesus' response, and part 4 considers the reaction of the Jewish authorities (484-547). Mark 14:55-59 recounts false witnesses whose testimony was inconsistent. Both Mark and Matthew record the saying about destroying and raising the temple. This is repeated in Acts 6:12-14. Brown considers the host of theories about a different emphasis on the part of each Evangelist. Much would depend on how the statement was understood (449). But Brown counsels caution about making judgments of "historicity" on this basis (459). At its core, this saying has "high historical probability" (459-60).

The scene now shifts to the high priest's questions (Mark 14:60-61 and parallels). He poses "Christological questions" (462). The silence of Jesus becomes a model for Christians undergoing suffering (1 Pet. 2:21, 23). There is an endless flow of articles on this question (466). Brown comments on Mark's "Are you the Messiah?" that "we should not assume it is a Marcan creation" (467). We must take previous passages (e.g., Mark 8:29) into account. The "Son of Man" saying relates to Mark 13 and the destruction of the temple. We have noted above the comments by Caird and Wright on these passages. Matthew uses the term "Son of God," which relates to Peter's confession in Matt. 16:16. "Messiah" simply means "Anointed One" (*Christos* in Gk.; *Death,* 473). Brown declares, "There is no preserved passage where Jesus ever denies he is the Messiah" (477). On the other hand, he argues, "The key to the logic is once again that Messiah was not a universal concept" (477). On the other term he comments, "The frequency and early date of the Christian usage of 'the Son of God' for Jesus is impressive" (481), for example, in the 50s (cf. 1 Thess. 1:10; Gal. 1:16; 1 Cor. 1:9).

Scene 2 of act 2 concerns the mockery and abuse of Jesus, and Peter's denials. As in every section, once again Brown gives impressively voluminous bibliographies. He comments that the mockery of Jesus implies that he is a false prophet; he will later be mocked as a (supposedly false) king. Some of this echoes the abuse heaped on the Suffering Servant (569). He writes on Luke, "Mockery so dominates this scene for Luke that he has eliminated the physical abuse narrated in Mark that is not related to the mockery" (583). He concludes, "Such abuse is not at all implausible historically" (586). Brown concludes, "All the Gospels correlate the cockcrow with Peter's third denial" (607).

Act 3 of the passion narrative concerns the accounts of Jesus before Pilate (665-877). Once again there is a huge bibliography on the Roman trial (665-75). Brown regards the Roman trial as "neither a legal report . . . nor an eyewitness testimony"; yet "there is a historical kernel" (725). The Greek of the key question and answer is identical in the four Gospels. This is "one of the most fixed elements in the Passion Narrative" (729) for Mark. Brown comments, "The scene is a kerygmatic dramatization of formulae preserved in the tradition" (730). Mark again uses the historical present tense with a strong sense of narrative. For example, "He says... You say..." is transposed into the past tense in Matthew and Luke. Brown is scrupulous in tracing similarities and differences among the four Gospels.

Act 4 of the passion narrative, and the whole of Brown's second volume, consists of two scenes: in the first scene Jesus is crucified and dies; in the second scene he is buried. The bibliography on the crucifixion covers sixteen pages (2:884-99). We cannot explore this act in the same detail as we could acts 1-3 (although *see* **Cross**). Mark, however, includes seven events or subjects: the name of the place, the initial offering of wine, the crucifixion, the division of clothes, the timing of events, the inscription, and the two bandits (935). Matthew includes six of these seven items, and Luke and John include five. The place in Semitic is *Golgotha,* or in Greek, *kranion,* "skull." The refused drink underlines Jesus' determination in Mark to give himself fully to his passion. The crucifixion is the centerpiece of the passion narrative (945). The term "cross," Brown comments, prejudices our modern understanding. Normally, he argues, a stake or pole, rather than a cross, would bring about a slow and painful death (945). All four Gospels include the division of clothes among the soldiers (952). John quotes Ps. 22:19 (LXX) exactly. Mark 15:25 recounts the event as occurring at the third hour, although Brown doubts whether this explicit timing belongs to the earliest tradition. Mark's purpose, he argues, is to show that God took care of the events. All four Gospels narrate a written description of the charge. Here Brown comments, "I see no convincing objection to its historicity" (968). The two bandits illustrate "the indignity to which the innocent Jesus was subjected" (969). The prayer of Jesus, "Father, forgive them ... ," has an almost equal weight, he claims, of *textual* evidence for it as against it (975). On the other hand, many consider it to be secondary to Stephen's speech in Acts 7:60.

For detailed theological interpretation of key points in the ministry of Jesus, *see* **Atonement; Cross; Sacrifice; Soteriology;** among other entries. On the resurrection of Jesus as the climax of his ministry, *see* **Pannenberg, Wolfhart; Resurrection of the Dead.**

Reading: J. A. Baird, *Audience Criticism and the Historical Jesus* (Philadelphia: Westminster, 1969); R. E. Brown, *The Death of the Messiah,* 2 vols. (London: Chapman, 1994); L. W. Hurtado, *Lord Jesus Christ* (Grand Rapids: Eerdmans, 2003); J. Jeremias, *New Testament Theology* (London: SCM, 1971); Jeremias, *The Parables of Jesus* (London: SCM, 1963); W. Pannenberg, *Systematic Theology,* vol. 2 (Grand Rapids: Eerdmans, 1994), 277-396.

Christ's Resurrection and Lordship

(i) **Resurrection.** It is essential to the post-Easter church that resurrection, both the resurrection of Christ and the general resurrection of the dead, is enacted by *the sovereign and creative power of God,* not primarily by Christ. To be sure, Jesus declares in John that he has power to reclaim his life, but the resurrection of Christ is essentially God's vindication of his identity and of his death for human sin. In Paul this is clear and decisive, whether in 1 Cor. 15:1-11 or in Rom. 4:16-25, 2 Cor. 1:9, 5:1-10, and 1 Thess. 4:14-17. God raised Christ (Rom. 8:11) and will in the future raise all "in Christ," that is, those who share in his death and resurrection. It is also fundamental that resurrection is not resuscitation, or restoration to postmortal life in the same body, as was the case for Lazarus in John 11. It entails *transformation* into a new mode of existence. Any language about the resurrection of the "body" is meant to stress not its "physicality" as such, but its status as a phenomenon in the *public and intersubjective* world. When the resurrected body of Jesus appears during the forty days between the resurrection and the ascension, it appears within the space-time conditions of this world. Hence we see the "body" tailored to this-world conditions. But this does not provide a model or paradigm for the resurrection body in another context of existence (*see* **Body**).

1 Cor. 15:1-11 embodies the earliest apostolic tradition, transmitted long before it reached Paul. Paul explicitly calls it the tradition that he proclaimed and that had been proclaimed or transmitted to him (15:1-4), indicated by the NRSV translation "handed on" (Gk. *paredōka . . . parelabon*, v. 3). This tradition is not the creation of Paul. The tradition recounts the earlier appearance to Peter and to the Twelve (v. 5). Paul includes James, "all the apostles" (v. 7), and "five hundred brothers and sisters at one time, most of whom are still alive" (v. 6). Richard Hays comments that Paul did not think of the resurrection "as some sort of ineffable truth beyond history: rather it was an event . . . for which historical eyewitness testimony was readily available" (*First Corinthians* [Louisville: John Knox, 1997], 257). G. D. Fee comments that "all at once" is not an indication of sequence, but indicates "the reality and objectivity of the appearances" (*First Epistle to the Corinthians* [Grand Rapids: Eerdmans, 1987], 730). A full and comprehensive discussion is available in A. C. Thiselton, *The First Epistle to the Corinthians* (Grand Rapids: Eerdmans, 2000), 1169-1213. To summarize some key points: verse 5, "that he appeared" (NRSV, REB, NJB; Gk. *ōphthē*, passive of *horaō;* KJV/AV, "was seen"), normally means "was seen by the eyes." W. Marxsen and H. Conzelmann, however, understand this as "to see with the mind." It is almost like the dawning of the answer to an intellectual puzzle, when we often say "I see!" (Marxsen, *The Resurrection of Jesus of Nazareth* [Philadelphia: Fortress, 1970], 72, 81; Conzelmann, "On the Analysis of the Confessional Formula in 1 Cor. 15:3-5," *Interpretation* 20 [1966]: 15-25). Bultmann also insists, "It was not an objectively given historical event" *(ein historisches Ereignis)* but "faith in the saving efficacy of the cross" (in *Kerygma and Myth* [London: SPCK, 1962], 1:41; Ger. *Kerygma und Mythos*, 6 vols. [Hamburg: Reich & Heidrich, 1948], 1:47).

However, this view has hardly remained the dominant one since Pannenberg has argued to the contrary, supported by W. Künneth, Fee, Hays, N. T. Wright, and many others. Pannenberg asserts that 1 Cor. 15:5, together with the whole pre-Pauline tradition, constitutes something *"decisive for confidence in the facticity of the resurrection of Jesus,"* including *"the primitive Christian testimonies to the appearances of the risen Lord . . . along with the discovery of the empty tomb of Jesus in*

Jerusalem" (*ST* 2:352-53). Pannenberg insists on speaking of a "factual core" in the accounts of the appearances and empty tomb (2:254; for many more details, *see* **Pannenberg, Wolfhart**). A. Eriksson also argues positively for the common pre-Pauline tradition (*Traditions as Rhetorical Proof* [Stockholm: Almqvist & Wiksell, 1998]). Wright similarly argues, "Not only was Jesus' resurrection in principle a datable event. . . . It was always something that took place not immediately upon his death, but a short interval thereafter" (e.g., the traditional "three days"; *The Resurrection of the Son of God* [London: SPCK, 2003], 322). The many witnesses must be taken seriously (323-26). Importantly, Pannenberg sees this confession of belief not only as a post-Easter confession, but also as one that earlier provides proleptic or anticipatory vindication of Jesus in the Gospels. But whatever the details, Moltmann asserts: "For earliest Christianity as we know it, God's raising of Christ was the foundation for faith in Christ, and thus the foundation of the church of Christ as well. And it is in fact true that the Christian faith stands or falls with Christ's resurrection. . . . Faith in the God 'who raised Christ from the dead' and the confession that 'Jesus Christ is the Lord' are mutually interpretative" (*The Way of Jesus Christ* [London: SCM, 1990], 213).

Having established the common apostolic tradition that emerged before his time, and that he received through witnesses, Paul recounts his own witness, and then in 1 Cor. 15:12-34 the impossible consequences of denying the resurrection of Christ. Eriksson points out that the *narratio,* or key thesis (vv. 1-11), is followed by a first *refutatio* (vv. 12-19) and first *confirmatio* (vv. 20-34), characteristic of deliberation rhetoric. If Christ had not been raised, Paul argues, the consequences are dire, and virtually unthinkable: the apostolic proclamation has been in vain (v. 14); the apostles were guilty of misrepresenting God (v. 15); the present faith of many Christians is futile (v. 17a); Christians are still in bondage to sin (v. 17b); and Christians are pitiable, wretched people (v. 19). The first *confirmatio,* however, follows: in reality Christ has been raised (v. 20a); and he has become the "firstfruits" *(aparchē)* of the harvest of the dead, that is, the beginning of the harvest proper, and a pledge of more to come of the same kind (v. 23). Hence "As all die in Adam, so all will be made alive in Christ" (v. 22). Resurrection has become a corporate event, which both holds out future promise and, in the present, vindicates Christ as Lord.

(ii) **Christ as Lord, Son of God, and God.** Paul's favorite term for Jesus Christ is "Lord" (Gk. *kurios* or *kyrios*), although often he uses all three terms together. Vincent Taylor calls the conception of Christ as Lord "the dominating idea in the Pauline theology" (*The Person of Christ in New Testament Teaching* [London: Macmillan, 1963], 42). The NT traces two different routes to this confession. Paul uses both. The first is that God enthroned him as exalted Lord at the resurrection (Rom. 1:4). The second concerns the correlated status of the Christ as servant and as slave (Rom. 1:1). The slave or servant (Gk. *doulos*) no longer belongs to himself (1 Cor. 6:19). This opens up a positive dimension to this situation. Bultmann cites Rom. 14:7-8 as a wonderful declaration of freedom: "We do not live to ourselves, and we do not die to ourselves. If we live, we live to the Lord, and if we die, we die to the Lord; so then, whether we live or whether we die, we are the Lord's." Bultmann comments, "The believer . . . no longer 'belongs to himself' (1 Cor. 6:19). He no longer bears the care for himself, for his own life, but lets this care go, yielding himself entirely to the grace of God: he recognizes himself to be the property of God (or of the Lord)" (*Theology of the New Testament,* vol. 1 [London: SCM, 1952], 331).

This coheres precisely with the status of a slave in the Roman world. The slave was often regarded as a mere "thing" (later, *res*), but had a different status under some "good" masters. J. Weiss and Bultmann draw on this concept for the existential condition of submission to the Lordship of Christ. Weiss argues, "What it means in a practical religious sense will best be made clear through the correlative concept of 'servant' or 'slave' of Christ" (Rom. 1:1; 1 Cor. 7:22-23; Gal. 1:10; Phil. 1:1; Col. 4:12; *Earliest Christianity* [New York: Harper, 1959], 458). But they both follow Bousset in ascribing this to the Hellenistic community. But this has some degree of ambiguity and generalization. Weiss comments, "What appears in the Greek as ignoble or servile appears rather, in the Semitic, as a proud title. We can understand how Paul . . . designated slavery as a mark of liberty" (460). The fact of the matter is that slavery and its status vary from case to case. Dale Martin, in *Slavery as Salvation* ([New Haven: Yale University Press, 1990], ix), calls attention to the "manager slave," who is sufficiently literate to work as an administrator, secretary, or finance director, probably with many menial slaves under him. Hence Paul may speak of slavery in terms of serving a "good" lord, as well as the self-emptying of Jesus Christ (Phil. 2:7) and of the freedom of the Christian (Rom 14:7-8). To be the manager-slave of an important lord provided in many ways better security and comfort than to be an impoverished freeman.

A separate category are those born of a woman in slavery (a third of the slave population), usually in urban centers. O. Patterson, *Slavery and Social Death* (Cambridge: Harvard University Press, 1982), 105-31, suggests that 85 percent of the population of Rome were slaves of slave origin. Others sold themselves into slavery to pay off debt; others were taken in battle. Everything depended on the attitude and outlook of the lord or master. Slave owners without scruples could indulge a sense of power and control over slaves, using torture, rape, and oppression regularly. Educated slave owners such as Seneca or other "good" Stoics might accord slaves dignity and even management roles. The key point, however, is that they were always under the protection and care of their masters, and in this respect some could have advantage over a free person. There was often a potential for "upward mobility." Inscriptions on tombs show that relations within a "nuclear family" could be respected. Martin includes a range of employment of slaves, from barbers and goldsmiths to architects and business managers (*Slavery as Salvation,* 11-12). On Paul's varied uses of the metaphor of slavery, see I. A. H. Combes, *The Metaphor of Slavery* (Sheffield: Sheffield Academic Press, 1998).

While the existential significance of Lordship is given added emphasis by

Weiss, Bultmann, and others, it is grossly one-sided. The acclamation of Christ as Lord does not simply depend on *human acknowledgment;* it depends also on *God's* declaring and making him "Lord" through the resurrection (Rom. 1:4), and by vindicating the claims of the earliest Christian community. "Lordship" thus implies an ontological grounding as well as an existential experience. The gospel is the preaching of Jesus Christ as Lord (2 Cor. 4:5), and this implies the tradition of Christ Jesus as Lord (since Paul uses the language of "as you received" and "continued" in Col. 2:6). In 1 Cor. 12:3 the confession of Jesus as Lord becomes the decisive test that faith is inspired by the Holy Spirit. The connection between the Lordship of Christ and his resurrection is not limited to Rom. 1:4, but is made even more explicit in Rom. 10:9: "If you confess with your lips that Jesus is Lord and believe in your heart that God raised him from the dead, you will be saved." We have already noted Rom. 14:9 and Phil. 2:6-11. Further, to confess Christ as Lord is not restricted to the church: "God .. exalted him ... so that at the name of Jesus *every* knee should bend, in heaven and on earth and under the earth, and *every* tongue should confess that Jesus Christ is Lord, to the glory of God the Father" (2:9-11). J. D. G. Dunn also cites the very early Christian use of Ps. 110:1, in which the Lord (God) addresses "my Lord" (Christ). Dunn argues, "The text was clearly in mind in several Pauline passages" (Rom. 8:34; 1 Cor. 15:25; Col. 3:1; *The Theology of Paul the Apostle* [Grand Rapids: Eerdmans, 1998], 246). Ps. 8:6 also complements Ps. 110:1.

To all this weighty evidence Dunn adds: "The greatest significance in Paul's use of the term *kyrios* for Jesus lies in the fact that '(the) Lord' was already a customary way of speaking of God in Jewish circles" (249). Even if the Greek sometimes transliterates the Hebrew *Y-H-W-H,* a Greek-speaking synagogue would pronounce *Kyrios* in *speech* when they needed to refer to the written *Yahweh,* or God. Similarly in the Pauline Epistles there are parallels between "Lord" as referring to God and the mention of Christ (e.g., the use of Isa. 40:13 in 1 Cor. 2:16). Dunn also compares Jer. 9:24, "Let him who boasts, boast in the Lord," with 2 Cor. 10:17-18 (250). Similarly Larry W. Hurtado calls the term "Lord" a "key christological title, used about 180 times in the undisputed Pauline letters" (*Lord Jesus Christ* [Grand Rapids: Eerdmans, 2003], 108). He also cites its use for "God," in addition to any general honorific sense, almost like "sir" (109-10). He also alludes to the use of *marana tha,* "Our Lord come," in 1 Cor. 16:22, which reflects Aramaic-speaking Christian circles. He concludes that in the early years the double devotion to God and to Jesus reflects a "Trinitarian" devotional pattern (110-11). Like others, he regards W. Bousset's hypothesis of locating the origin of Christian use of this term in Greek cults as a "desperate proposal." This does not conflict with Jewish monotheism, which Paul affirms, but refigures and modifies it, because Christ "is directly and uniquely associated with God" (112). If God and Christ are *one* in will and purpose, monotheism is not fragmented when both are honored as *Kyrios.*

Various contexts now emerge in Paul in which the title "Lord" finds characteristic use. Werner Kramer emphasized that of *worship,* as Hurtado showed. A second would be action or *conduct,* where *obedience* enters the public sphere. Christians are concerned "to please the Lord" (1 Cor. 7:32) in what they *do,* in practical terms. They want to "serve the Lord" (Rom. 12:11) and to engage in "the work of the Lord" (1 Cor. 15:58). The collection for the Jerusalem church is related to the Lord's work (2 Cor. 8:5, 19). A third context is that of the return of Christ or the *Day of the Lord.* For example, the Aramaic *"Marana tha"* (1 Cor. 16:22) witnesses to this. Rom. 10:9 uses the term "Lord" as a public *confession:* "If you confess with your lips that Jesus is Lord and believe in your heart that God raised him from the dead, you will be saved." O. Cullmann, V. H. Neufeld, and Hurtado all include the Lordship of Christ among the earliest Christian confessions of faith (Cullmann, *The Earliest Christian Confessions* [London: Lutterworth, 1949], esp. 54-64; Neufeld, *Earliest Christian Confessions* [Grand Rapids: Eerdmans, 1963], esp. 42-68; Hurtado, *Lord Jesus Christ,* esp. 137-53).

Paul uses many other terms for Jesus Christ. Examples often cited include "Image of God," "Firstborn," "Beloved," "Wisdom of God," and "Last Adam." Other key names occur in other writings of the NT. The pre-Pauline tradition includes "Rabbi," "Teacher," "Master," "Prophet," "Son of David," "Son of Mary," "Son of Joseph," "Son of Man," "King of Israel," and "He Who Comes" (Taylor, *Person,* 34-35). R. Brown includes passages "where Jesus is clearly called God." These include Heb. 1:8:

> "Your throne, O God, is forever and ever,
> and the righteous scepter is the scepter of your kingdom."

These are the words of Ps. 45:6-7, spoken by God. Brown defends the traditional textual reading (*Jesus: God and Man* [London and Dublin: Chapman, 1968], 23-24). H. Montefiore calls it "an outright assertion of his divinity," and Cullmann shares this view. Psalm 45 is a gospel psalm, paralleled by Ps. 102:25-27. John 1:1 is probably the best-known verse of all: "In the beginning was the Word, and the Word was with God, and the Word was God" *(kai theos ēn ho logos).* Moffatt prefers "the Word was Divine," but Brown regards this as "too weak" (26), and it is grammatically questionable, as J. Wenham argues. Brown also translates *(ho) monogenēs Theos* in 1:18 as "God the only Son" (27), and in John 20:28 the climactic confession is that of Thomas, "My Lord and my God" *(ho Theos mou).* Brown regards these three passages as "clear," with five passages suggesting "probability" (28). Probable passages include Gal. 2:20, where a number of textual witnesses read *tou theou kai Christou* instead of "Son of God" (10). Another is Acts 20:28, of which Brown comments that "church of God" seems more original (11), and is purchased "by his blood." Other probabilities include John 1:18, Col. 2:2, 2 Thess. 1:12, Titus 2:13, and John 5:20.

G. O'Collins explores further passages to reach a similar conclusion. 2 Peter puts together "Lord and Saviour" (2 Pet. 2:20). Luke recounts the angels as declaring: "A Saviour who is Christ the Lord" (Luke 2:11). Paul states, "We await a Saviour, the Lord Jesus Christ" (Phil. 3:20; biblical quotations from O'Collins, *Christology* [Oxford: OUP, 1995], 143). It is Pannenberg, however, whose work is most widely known in this context. He writes, "The historical reality of Jesus of Nazareth can be appropriately understood only in the light of his coming from God" (*ST* 2:288). In the resurrection "God confirmed the claim that was implicit in the work of Jesus ... that the imminent rule of God ... was about to break in, and in fact was already doing so for those who trusted his message" (345). Pannenberg asserts, "The first Christians could not have successfully preached the resurrection of Jesus if his body had been intact in the tomb" (358). Hence God himself has vindicated every declaration of Jesus about his intimate relation with God as his Father. In the light of the history of the phrase, to assert that Jesus is "Son of God" may seem today to understate this relationship. But given the *derived* nature of the status of Christians as sons of God, and the uniqueness of Jesus' relation to God, we may quote Pannenberg: "The relation of Jesus to the eternal God ... finds expression in the concept of divine sonship" (367). But he goes further, declaring, "We cannot think of the Father apart from the Son. . . . The Son was linked to the Father before the beginning of the earthly existence of Jesus" (367). Thus: "The idea of a pre-existence of the Son of God, who manifested himself historically in Jesus' relation to the Father, is inescapable" (370). He further declares, "The origin of the divine sonship of Jesus can lie, then, only in the eternity of God himself" (371). Finally, Pannenberg gives expression to the impossibility of separating the person and work of Christ. He concludes, "By the incarnation of the Son sinners who are under the penalty of death are saved, reconciled, brought into the Trinitarian fellowship of God, and thus made participants in eternal life" (390). He adds, "Not least of all, then, the Father suffers with the suffering of the Son. . . . The *basileia* is actualized by the Son as he glorifies the Father (John 17:4), i.e., as he reveals his deity on earth" (391).

We have not exhausted the "titles" ascribed to Jesus Christ in the NT. He is, for example, the "Messiah," the "Last Adam," the human Jesus, and the "Wisdom of God." 1 Cor. 15:21-22 and Rom. 5:14 talk about Christ being the last Adam. "Son of Man" may imply "man" or an eschatological figure. Col. 1:15-18 also sees Jesus as the cosmic Christ, and there are echoes of Wisdom in Proverbs 8. But it appears no longer fashionable to think of the person of Christ in terms of "titles," in spite of Cullmann's magisterial book *The Christology of the New Testament* (London: SCM, 1963). (*See also* **Moltmann, Jürgen; Pannenberg, Wolfhart; Resurrection of the Dead.**)

Reading: R. E. Brown, *Jesus: God and Man* (London and Dublin: Chapman, 1968); J. D. G. Dunn, *Christology in the Making* (London: SCM, 1980, 1989); K.-J. Kuschel, *Born before All Time?* (London: SCM, 1992); J. Moltmann, *The Way of Jesus Christ* (London: SCM, 1990); W. Pannenberg, *Jesus — God and Man* (London: SCM, 1968); Pannenberg, *ST*, vol. 2 (1994), 325-96; R. D. Williams, *Resurrection* (London: DLT, 1982).

History of Thought

The major or classical heritage from the patristic era is the "two natures" Christology of the four great ecumenical councils: Nicaea (325), Constantinople (381), Ephesus (431), and Chalcedon (451). But the transition from the biblical era to the early church at the beginning of the era retains value for today.

(i) **Christian Thought before Nicaea.** The subapostolic writings between c. 90 and c. 140 have relatively little to say on Christology. Clement of Rome (c. 96) emphasizes Christ's humanity and passion. He showed lowliness of mind: "Christ is of those who are humble-minded . . . he came not with pomp or arrogance, for all his power . . . as the Holy Spirit spoke concerning him" (*1 Clem.* 16.1-2, in K. Lake, *The Apostolic Fathers*, vol. 1 [London: Heinemann, 1912], 34-35). He quotes from Isaiah's Servant Songs: "The Lord delivered him up for our sins" (Isa. 53:7). *The Epistle of Barnabas* cites the same passage: "He was wounded for our transgressions" (5.2), and also the prophecy that Jesus would be "a light to lighten the Gentiles, to be for salvation to the ends of the earth" (14.8). On the other hand, *The Epistle to Diognetus* speaks of Christ as Creator of the Universe, "who became as a King and was sent as a Saviour" (9); Christ is the only begotten Son (10) and the Word who was from the beginning (11). Ignatius (c. 110-112) asserts the reality of Christ's human life in contrast to Docetism. Jesus, he asserts, "was of the family of David, the child of Mary. He was truly born, ate and drank, and truly persecuted under Pontius Pilate, and truly was crucified and truly died . . . and was truly raised from the dead" (*To the Trallians* 9.1-2; Gk. and Eng. in Lake, vol. 1, 220-21). Ignatius speaks further of believers as "nailed to the cross of our Lord Jesus Christ . . . by the blood of Christ . . . of the family of David . . . God's Son by the will and power of God, truly born of a Virgin, baptized by John . . . truly nailed to a tree . . . under Pontius Pilate and Herod the Tetrarch . . . that he might set up an ensign . . . through his resurrection" (*To the Smyrnaeans* 1.1-2). He refers again to "his Passion and Resurrection both of flesh and spirit in union with God" (12.2). God and Christ are like two sides of the same coin (*To the Magnesians* 5.2; Gk. and Eng. in Lake, vol. 1, 252-53). On the borderline of the patristic era, Justin in the second century sees Christ as the *Logos*, who fulfills many prophecies and hopes in Israel and Greek philosophy.

Writers in the patristic era are far more involved in christological issues. (a) *Irenaeus* (c. 140–c. 200) expounds the true humanity and deity of Christ, especially against all Gnostic claims. Christ is "the only true and steadfast teacher, the Word of God." He writes, "The Lord, revealing Himself to His disciples, that He Himself is the Word, who imparts knowledge of the Father. . . . 'neither knoweth any man the Father, save the Son'" (*Against Heresies* 4.6.1; *ANF* 1:467; cf. Matt. 11:27). He opposes the teaching of Basilides that Jesus was "without body" and came "to destroy the God of the Jews" (1.24.2). Irenaeus recounts various episodes of the earthly life of Jesus (2.22.3-4): Jesus was descended from David, born of the Virgin Mary, and was Son of God through the Holy Spirit and the resurrection (3.16.2-3;

ANF 1:440-41). He quotes Paul in Gal. 4:4, "When the time had fully come, God sent forth his Son" (3.16.7). Christ is "the holy Lord, the Wonderful, the Counsellor, the Beautiful in appearance, and the Mighty God" (3.19.2; *ANF* 1:449; cf. Isa. 9:6). He is "the Son of God, our Lord, ... Word of the Father" (3.19.3; *ANF* 1:449). To conclude: Christ is "God with us," yet although he became fully human *(homo, hominem)*, he rose from the dead (3.19.3).

(b) *Tertullian* (c. 150–c. 225) insists on the unity of the Holy Trinity. He writes that the Father, the Son, and the Holy Spirit differ not in degree or in substance, but only in form; the three are of one substance, "not in power, but in aspect; yet of one substance, and of one condition, and of one power ... He is one God ... without division" (*Against Praxeas* 2; *ANF* 3:598). Jesus Christ was "sent by the Father into the Virgin, and to have been born of her — being both Man and God, the Son of Man and the Son of God.... We believe Him to have suffered, died, and been buried ... raised again ... and taken back to heaven, to be sitting at the right hand of the Father, and that He will come to judge the quick and the dead" (2; *ANF* 3:598). Elsewhere Tertullian recounts the ministry and healing miracles of Jesus Christ (*Against Marcion* 4.9-11). He shows the characteristics of the Creator God (4.15). Christ appeared to the women and to the apostles after his resurrection (Luke 24; *Against Marcion* 4.48). Christ is "the image of the invisible God" (Col. 1:15; *Against Marcion* 5.19). Tertullian also uses the analogy of two metals fused together to form a new compound (*Against Praxeas* 27), even if in the 1970s J. A. T. Robinson explicitly rejected this analogy as suggesting a hybrid figure of two natures, in his language, like a "bat-centaur" (discussed below). Clearly the road that led to Constantinople and Chalcedon is well established.

(c) *Origen of Alexandria* (c. 185-254) clearly taught that Christ is coeternal with God the Father, but is also subordinate to him. Christ is "a second God" (*Against Celsus* 5.39). Christ's generation is as eternal and everlasting as the brilliance produced from the sun (*De principiis* 1.2.4). In *De principiis* 2.6.3 Origen declares: "The Only-begotten of God, therefore, through whom ... all things were made, visible and invisible, according to the view of Scripture, both made all things, and loves what He made.... This substance of a soul, then, being intermediate between God and the flesh ... the God-man [*Deus-Homo*] is born ... that substance being the intermediary to whose nature it was not contrary to assume a body" (*ANF* 4:282). Here we see a highly developed Christology, in part based on the Bible, but also drawing elements from Greek and probably Stoic philosophy. In one respect it represents a step forward, but in another it represents a speculative digression. It is not surprising that later much of Origen's theology was condemned by many parts of the church. J. N. D. Kelly shows how his Christology was bound up with his belief in the preexistence of spiritual beings *(ta logika)* and of human souls. The preexistent soul of Jesus "was attached to the Logos" (*Early Christian Doctrines* [London: Black, 1977], 155). Hence, "With this theory of the mediating role of Christ's human soul as its basis, Origen expounds the doctrine of the incarnation *(enanthrōpēsis)*" (155). On the one hand,

Origen holds the duality of a divine and a human nature *(phusis)*. On the other hand, the incarnate Lord "is a unity — a 'composite thing' *(suntheton chrēma)*, as Origen forcefully describes Him" (156). In *Against Celsus* 1.66 Origen speaks of "the composite nature of the incarnate Jesus." This approach, coupled with his subordinationism and universalism, led to doubts about his Christology, in spite of his enormous influence especially in the East. Like Tertullian, Origen presupposes a Trinitarian and biblical framework for his Christology. Athanasius was to draw certain elements from Origen, but ultimately his philosophical culture led to a "soul communion" rather than an "enfleshment" of Jesus as both God and man. Origen also tended to ascribe the "higher" roles of Jesus, such as Word, Wisdom, and Truth, to his eternal being, and "lower" roles such as Shepherd and Priest to his incarnation. Behind this notion, the dualism of Plato might be seen. Among Origen's later critics was Methodius of Olympus, although Dionysius of Alexandria still defended much of his teaching.

(d) *Arius* (c. 250-336) receives a separate entry in this book, in which the important work of Rowan Williams on him is discussed. To sum up, Arius argued that God is the only source of all creation, and that God is one. Hence the Son must be regarded as "created," although he hesitated to say that the Son was "made." He also argued that there was a time when God was alone and not yet "Father." Hence the Son did not always exist, and was not coeternal with the Father. Arius asserted: "Before he was brought into being, he [Christ] did not exist." He had a beginning as far as his created existence is concerned. Alexander, bishop of Alexandria, summoned a synod, which excommunicated Arius and his followers. Conflict, however, became sharp and bitter. Hence the emperor Constantine tried to intervene to bring about peace. He summoned the Council of Nicaea in 325.

(ii) **From the Council of Nicaea to the Council of Constantinople.** After much debate, (a) *Eusebius of Caesarea* brought forward the traditional baptismal confessions or creed of the pre-Nicene church, in which believers declare: "We believe in one Lord, Jesus Christ, the Word of God, God from God, Light from Light, Life from Life, the Only-begotten Son, Firstborn of all creation, before the ages begotten from the Father" (cf. *NPNF,* ser. 2, 14:3). The council adopted very similar wording, including "the Son of God, the only-begotten of his Father, . . . God of God, Light of Light, very God of very God, begotten *(gennēthenta)*, not made, being of one substance *(homoousion;* Lat. *consubstantialem)* with the Father . . ." (3). The Nicene Creed, or more strictly the Nicene-Constantinopolitan Creed (381), is based, in effect, on the theology of Athanasius.

(b) *Athanasius* argued that only the Creator can redeem creation and re-create it, and that Christ is not a creature. To worship created things would be idolatry, but Christians worship Christ and pray to him. He saw the compromise term "of like being" *(homoiousios)* as being insufficiently decisive. Thus "of the same being" became the official form. In his treatise *On the Incarnation,* Athanasius begins by discussing the doctrine of creation, stressing that only through Christ can God's purpose in creating humankind be fully realized (4-19). On the cross "all creation was confessing that He [Christ] that was made manifest and suffered in the body was not man merely, but the Son of God and Saviour of all. . . . Christ is known to be God and the Son of God" (19; *NPNF,* ser. 2, 4:46). Sections 20-32 expound the victory of the cross. Athanasius writes, "By faith in Christ, death is trampled down. . . . It is none other than Christ Himself that has displayed trophies and triumphs over death" (29; *NPNF,* 4:51). Sections 33-40 offer replies to Jewish objections, and sections 41-54 represent replies to Greek objections. In his epilogue (55), Athanasius calls Christ "the true God, Word of the Father," and alludes to "martyr for the deity of Christ" (56).

There are at least two convenient English translations of *De incarnatione.* Perhaps the more readable is *St. Athanasius on the Incarnation* (London: Mowbray, 1946; New York: Macmillan, 1953), and "Athanasius," in *Christology of the Later Fathers,* ed. E. R. Hardy (Philadelphia: Westminster, 1954), 41-110. A multitude of letters and other treatises may be found in *NPNF,* ser. 2, vol. 4. Hardy called Athanasius "a central figure in the exposition and defense of orthodox theology" (43), and *On the Incarnation* "among those Christian classics which are read not only as documents in the history of Christian thought, but as treatments of the subjects in which they deal" (44). In his *Letter to Serapion* 4.14, Athanasius wrote, "Being God, he became as a human being. . . . He raised the dead, heals all by a word. These are not the acts of a human being. But as a human being he felt thirst and tiredness, he suffered pain. . . . As God, he said, 'I am in the Father and the Father in me'; as a human being he criticized, crying; 'Why do you seek to kill me when I am a man who told you the truth?'" (PG 26:656C). (*See* **Holy Spirit: The Spirit in Historical Theology.**)

(c) *Apollinarius of Laodicea* (c. 310–c. 390) was a friend of Athanasius and stressed the deity of Christ, as did the Alexandrian church as a whole. He joined with Athanasius in arguing that Christ was not a created being. But he pressed this point one-sidedly, as if to underestimate the humanness of Jesus. In particular he appears to *deny* that Jesus had a *human mind.* He seceded from the church in c. 375, and was condemned by a synod at Rome. Many of his writings have been lost, and it is difficult to give an accurate account of his teaching on the basis of firsthand sources. What remains clear, however, is that the "divinization" of Christ's flesh implies a kind of Docetism. Kelly suggests four probable objections to Apollinarianism (*Early Christian Doctrines,* 296).

(d) *The Cappadocian Fathers: Basil of Caesarea* (c. 330-379), *Gregory of Nazianzus* (c. 330-390), and *Gregory of Nyssa* (c. 330-395). Basil was some thirty years junior to Athanasius; Gregory of Nazianzus was Basil's friend, and Gregory of Nyssa was Basil's brother. These three thinkers, especially Basil, focused on the coequality and eternity of the Holy Spirit with the Father and with Christ (*see* **Holy Spirit: The Spirit in Historical Theology**). The two Gregorys were provoked by Apollinarianism to think through Christology further. Basil clearly stressed the unity and mutual association of the Father, the Son, and the Holy

Spirit (*On the Holy Spirit* 13.29). He explicitly refers to the Trinity in 1 Cor. 12:4-11. Gregory of Nazianzus considered Christology especially in the *Theological Orations* (in *NPNF*, ser. 2, 7:203-434). In *Orations* 3.29.3, he declared, "The Father is the Begetter and the Emitter. . . . The Son is the Begotten, and the Holy Ghost the Emission; for I know not how this could be expressed . . . altogether excluding visible things" (7:301). He continues, "There never was a time when He [the Father] was not. And the same thing is true of the Son and the Holy Ghost" (3.29.3). He then discusses possible objections to this, including the linguistic and conceptual status of "begot" and "begotten" that is beyond time (3.29.4-15). He concludes, "We have learnt to believe in and to teach the deity of the Son" (3.29.17; 7:307). Nevertheless, Christ "was born of a woman — but she was a Virgin. . . . In His Human Nature He had no Father, but also in His Divine Nature no Mother. Both these belong to Godhead" (3.29.19; 7:308). Gregory presses the point: "He hungered — but . . . is the Bread that giveth life. . . . He dies, but He gives life, and by His death destroys death. He is buried, but He rises again" (3.29.20). Ultimately we "will hold fast to the Trinity, and by the Trinity may we be saved" (3.29.21; 7:309).

In his years of retirement Gregory was still troubled by continuing controversy with Apollinarianism in Cappadocia. His *Letters on the Apollinarianism Controversy* are published in translation in Hardy, *Christology of the Later Fathers*, 215-29, and in *NPNF*, ser. 2, 7:437-46. It is well known that Gregory insisted on belief that "holy Mary is the Mother of God." However, this is not to venerate Mary, but to insist that Jesus Christ was "divinely and humanly formed in her" (*Epistles* 101). Gregory laments that the church is "being torn asunder and divided" by vanity and "heresy." But he cannot accept "two contrary doctrines on the same subject [as] being both true" (*Epistles* 202).

Gregory of Nyssa was elected bishop of Nyssa in 372, and exiled by Valens in 374. He wrote *On "Not Three Gods"* in 375 (*see* **Holy Spirit: The Spirit in Historical Theology**). He returned to his diocese in 378. He wrote *On the Holy Trinity* in 380 and *Against Eunomius* in 382-383. *The Great Catechism* appeared in 385. Apollinarius had found it self-contradictory to declare that Christ had free will, since the "Word of God" would allegedly be changeable. Thus he argued that the Word of God took the place of *the human mind* in Jesus. In reply, Gregory stressed the independence of the "two natures," even if their connection remains unbreakable. He spoke of "that ineffable and inexpressible conjunction" of the two natures that resulted in the incarnation (*The Great Catechism* 16; *NPNF*, ser. 2, 5:489), The God-man was "one Person" *(hen prosōpon)*, "because of their conjunction and fusion" (*dia tēn sunapheian te kai sumphuian; Against Eunomius* 3.2-4).

(e) *The Council of Constantinople* (381) is known as the second of the ecumenical councils, after Nicaea. Formally it excluded Apollinarianism, and was decisively influenced by Athanasius and the Cappadocian Fathers, just as Nicaea excluded Arianism. The "Nicene Creed" used widely today is really that of Constantinople, and this underlines the close similarity of wording between them. It confirmed the clause "of the same being" (Gk. *homoousios*). But the clause used in Western churches, "proceeds from the Father and the Son" *(filioque),* did not form part of the original creed. The Eastern Church has in general disowned it. The council was called by the emperor Theodosius, who expelled an Arian bishop. Gregory of Nazianzus, "who excelled in eloquence and piety all those of the age in which he lived," was present to guide its discussions (Socrates, *Ecclesiastical History* 5.7.2).

(iii) **Antiochene, Nestorian, and Alexandrian Christologies.** (a) *From Theodore and Nestorius to the Council of Ephesus.* The period between the Council of Constantinople (381) and the third ecumenical council of Ephesus was largely dominated by two factors: the controversy about Nestorius, who was archbishop or patriarch of Constantinople from 428 to 441, and the political and theological initiatives of Cyril, archbishop or patriarch of Alexandria (378-444). During this period so-called Antiochene Christology was represented by Theodore of Mopsuestia (350-428) and John Chrysostom (c. 347-407). If the Council of Constantinople gave a reply to Apollinarianism, the Council of Ephesus answered the teachings of Nestorius. This great debate about Christology was inaugurated by the relatively minor controversy over whether Mary should be described as *Theotokos,* God-bearer or Mother of God, or simply *Christotokos,* Mother of Christ. *This difference turns more on the nature of Christ than on the veneration of Mary.* Nestorius insisted on "Mother of Christ," but Cyril of Alexandria argued that "Mother of God" was steadily becoming embedded in orthodox liturgy. In the nineteenth century it was fashionable to regard Cyril as a devious political manipulator, and as late as 1925 Sidney Cave argued: "The traditional account of Nestorius' teaching owes as much to Cyril's malice as to Nestorius' heresy" (*The Doctrine of the Person of Christ* [London: Duckworth, 1925], 110).

Traditionally the Antiochenes have been credited with stressing the humanness of Jesus, and the Alexandrians his divinity. But this is an oversimplification, even if it represents some truth. Theodore and Chrysostom were primarily exegetes and preachers, rather than dogmatic theologians. Theodore studied at Antioch, was a close friend of Chrysostom, and his diocese was in Cilicia in Asia Minor. In addition to his biblical exegesis, he gave *Catechetical Lectures* on the Nicene Creed, and his work *On the Incarnation* attacks both Arius and Apollinarius. He defended the Council of Constantinople. But he had reservations about describing Mary as *Theotokos,* and preferred *anthropotokos.* He was not a "heretic," but followers of Nestorius appealed to part of his teaching.

(b) *John Chrysostom* was the third "Ecumenical Doctor" of the church, the first two being Basil and Gregory of Nazianzus. He was ordained at Antioch in 386, where he remained for twelve years, earning the title "Golden Mouth" *(Chrusos* or *Chrysos* and *Stoma)* because of his incisive and popular preaching. He was elected bishop of Constantinople in 397-398, but aroused the hostility of the empress Eudoxia for his forthright sermons, as well as the hostility of Theophilus, archbishop of Alexandria. H. Bettenson comments, "He was not a speculative thinker, nor a systematic theologian: he was essentially a pastor, preacher, and reformer. In his Trinitarian theology he expands the Nicene faith.... He asserts the reality of the true nature of Christ" (*The Later Christian Fathers* [Oxford: OUP, 1977], 19-20).

(c) *Nestorius* became archbishop or patriarch of Constantinople in 428, and was Antiochene in his Christology. Cyril of Alexandria condemned him in 430 at Rome, and launched twelve anathemas against him. The condemnation was confirmed at the Third Ecumenical Council of Ephesus, though Bettenson again argues, "There was more than a hint of sharp practice in Cyril's conduct at the Council" (28). His condemnation took place, for example, before the Antiochene bishops from Syria had arrived; and when they did arrive, they held a counter-synod to depose Cyril. Both Cyril and Nestorius were briefly imprisoned. The latter was removed from his office in 431, the date of the Council of Ephesus. It was argued that he had separated or confused the two natures of Christ, holding to two centers of consciousness in Jesus Christ. Nestorius explicitly denied this. Hence some of the debate focused on his denial of the *Theotokos* ascription to Mary. From the point of view of Nestorius, Alexandrian Christology verged on Doceticism.

(d) *Cyril of Alexandria* (c. 375-444) supported the Christology of Athanasius, and above all stressed the *deity* of Christ. Christ, he urged, shared the same nature as God. He attacked not only Arius, but also Apollinarius's alleged understatement of the humanness of Christ. His deity did not absorb or assimilate his humanity, but transfigured it. The "deification" of humanity became a theme of the Eastern Church. J. Stevenson and W. H. C. Frend have conveniently collected an English translation of some of the correspondence between Cyril and Nestorius (*Creeds, Councils, and Controversies* [London: SPCK, 1989], 295-321). These record Isidore of Pelusium claiming that Cyril was guilty of "private animosities" against Nestorius (319). Cyril wrote to Nestorius that, according to Paul, "all the fullness of the Godhead dwelt in Christ bodily" (303; cf. Col. 2:9). He declared: "To one person, therefore, must be attributed all the expressions used in the Gospels... for the Lord Jesus Christ" (305). He adds, "God [is] personally united to the flesh, for this reason we say of her [Mary] that she is *Theotokos*... for he [Christ] is co-eternal with the Father" (306). Finally, he concludes, "If anyone ... divides the personalities, i.e. the human and the divine, after the union... let him be anathema" (307).

(e) *The Path to Chalcedon.* Each of the latter three ecumenical councils gathered up the anathemas and endorsements of the previous council. In summary: first, Nicaea (325) addressed Arianism; second, Constantinople (381) addressed Apollinarianism and the Pneumatomachi or "Tropici" (*see* **Holy Spirit: The Spirit in Historical Theology**); third, Ephesus (431) addressed Nestorianism (whether real or supposed); and fourth, Chalcedon (451) addressed all three of these, together with Eutychianism. Allegedly the Eutychians denied the distinction and coexistence of the two natures, holding that this mingling constituted a *tertium quid*. They were sometimes called Monophysites, as if to imply that the two natures were reduced to one (Gk. *monos + phusis*).

The most active participants at the first three ecumenical councils came, apparently, largely from the Eastern Church, especially from Antioch and Alexandria. By contrast, the Council of Chalcedon is based in essence on the *Tome* of Leo of Rome, in the West. Leo the Great (Leo I) was pope, or bishop of Rome, from 440 to 451. As pope he pressed claims of jurisdiction over Africa, Spain, and Gaul. The Eutychian controversy drew him into Eastern affairs. His *Tome* (449) became widely accepted as the standard of christological orthodoxy in both the Eastern and Western provinces. Benedict XIV declared him "a doctor of the church," but his main gifts were administrative rather than theological. He was a shrewd politician on behalf of the church and his see, and he is said to have been clear and forceful.

Meanwhile, the main theologians of the West had been already affirming an orthodox Christology. Hilary of Poitiers (c. 315-368) was familiar with the work of Athanasius, and opposed Arianism. He had been called "the Athanasius of the West." Ambrose of Milan (c. 339-397) insisted on the oneness of Christ and the Holy Spirit with God. He asserted: "Let us observe the distinction between the divinity and the flesh. [But] it is the one and the same Son of God who speaks in both, for both natures are present in one and the same subject. . . . In him you may see at one time the glory of God, at another the feelings of man" (*On the Faith* 2.77). Bettenson reproduced selections from the Christology of Hilary and Ambrose in *The Later Christian Fathers* (53-55 and 178-80). Augustine of Hippo (354-430) also taught two natures, one person. The flesh of Jesus Christ was not "a false flesh and a feigned appearance of a human body" (*On the Christian Struggle* 20; see Bettenson, 218). The Council of Chalcedon read the Nicene Creed, two letters from Cyril, and Leo's *Tome*. Even Nestorius, now in exile, heartily approved of its decision. Issues in Christology seemed to have been settled for the next thirteen or fourteen hundred years. A. H. Strong, writing in America between 1886 and 1906, confidently claimed that by 451 "history had exhausted the possibilities of heresy" (*Systematic Theology* [New York: Armstrong and Son, 1889], 672). Apart from the *filioque* clause about the Spirit, Christology would remain settled until the rise of modern Christology, almost after Strong had written.

(iv) **The Middle Ages and the Reformation.** Among medieval thinkers, Thomas Aquinas stands out as thoroughly orthodox in his Christology. He expounds the incarnation of Christ in part 3 of his *Summa Theologiae*. He explicitly quotes from Chalcedon: "It is said . . . 'We confess that . . . the son of God appeared in two natures, without confusion, without change, without division, without separation — the distinction of natures having been taken away by the union'" (pt. 3, qu. 2, art. 1). He continues, "*Person* has a different meaning from 'nature.' . . . The Word has a human nature united to him. . . . The union [with divine nature] took place in the Person of the Word" (qu. 2, art. 2, reply). He adds, "In the Lord Jesus Christ we acknowledge two natures, but one hypostasis composed from both" (qu. 2, art. 4).

At the Reformation Luther and Calvin entirely endorsed the Christology that was agreed on by the Church Fathers at both Constantinople and Chalcedon. Christology was not controversial at the Reformation. Luther clearly expresses this in his critique of Nestorianism in 1539. "Christ is God and human being in one person because whatever is said about him as a human being must also be said about him as God, namely 'Christ has died,' and, as Christ is God, it follows that 'God has died' — not in isolation, but God united with humanity" (LW 36:280). John Calvin discusses "the two natures" of Christ in *Institutes* 2.14. "He who was the Son of God became the Son of man, not by confusion of substance, but by unity of person.... The two natures constitute only one Christ" (2.14.1; Beveridge, 1:415). He continues, "The true substance of Christ is most clearly declared in those passages which comprehend both natures at once" (2.14.3; 1:417). He cites such NT passages as Phil. 2:8, 10, and Heb. 2:7, as well as 1 Cor. 15:24-28. His one criticism of some ancient writers is that of "not attending to the office of Mediator" (2.14.3; 1:417).

(v) **Earlier Modern Christology.** (a) J. Macquarrie traces the rise of "modern Christology" from *I. Kant* (1724-1804). We noted the radical departures of H. S. Reimarus and G. E. Lessing in the "Jesus of History" section above. Reimarus entirely reflected the skepticism of David Hume and the rationalism of the Enlightenment. Macquarrie calls Kant's approach "rationalist Christology" (*Jesus Christ in Modern Thought* [London: SCM; Philadelphia: Trinity, 1990], 175-91). This is correct in the sense that Kant takes to task "a religion that declares war on reason" (*Religion within the Limits of Reason* [New York: Harper and Row, 1960], 9); yet most of Kant's work also concerns the *limits* of reason. He aims to found faith on *"practical* reason" and the moral imperative as absolute. Hence he transposes Christology into timeless and abstract truth. Macquarrie urges that Kant interprets Jesus as "the archetype of a life well pleasing to God, or the ideal of a perfected humanity ... [but] fundamentally Docetic" (184-85). He adds, "The historical ... did not interest him as much as did the archetype itself" (185).

(b) *F. Schleiermacher* (1768-1834) has as his central theme "feeling" *(Gefühl)* as absolute dependence on God *(Schlechthinig Abhängigheit von Gott)* (*The Christian Faith* [Edinburgh: T. & T. Clark, 1989], sect. 4, p. 12). His emphasis is not here on feeling as such, or as a psychological state, but on what this is a feeling *of.* His emphasis is upon having the highest degree of consciousness of God, or God-consciousness. "There is no general God-consciousness which has not bound up with it a relation to Christ, and no relation to the Redeemer which has no general bearing on God-consciousness" (sect. 62, p. 261). Christ represents "our finite limited nature ... from the perspective of the divine" (sect. 50). One of Schleiermacher's strengths is the integral connection between the person and word of Christ or Redeemer. He portrays Christ as the second Adam, and, like orthodox Lutherans, opposes Docetism and Ebionism. Yet while A. McGrath sees his view of the consciousness of Jesus as distinctive *in kind,* Macquarrie sees it as distinctive *only in degree* from that of other human beings. In section 94 of *The Christian Faith,* Schleiermacher declares, "The Redeemer, thus, is like all men in virtue of the identity of human nature, but distinguished from them all by the constant potency of his God-consciousness, which was a veritable existence of God in Him" (p. 385). He insists that the Redeemer "should be entirely free from all sinfulness." But this sinlessness does not separate him from humankind, for sin is only, he imagines, "a disturbance of nature" (385). He regards the classical formulations of Christology as products of controversy. McGrath perhaps describes his *intention;* Macquarrie, the actual *effect.* Macquarrie calls this "humanistic Christology" (*Jesus Christ,* 192-211). Kathryn Tanner similarly traces a "humanistic and this-worldly outlook" of Schleiermacher and others that sees the humanity of Jesus as "purportedly endangered by the emphasis on Christ's divinity in the creeds" (K. Tanner, "Jesus Christ," in *The Cambridge Companion to Christian Doctrine,* ed. Tanner and C. Gunton [Cambridge: CUP, 1997], 246).

(c) *Georg W. F. Hegel* (1770-1831) tended to bypass the classical formulations of Christology because he approached the divine-human union of incarnational theology within the terms of his own philosophical system (cf. J. Heywood Thomas, "Hegel," in *Nineteenth Century Religious Thought in the West,* ed. N. Smart and others, vol. 1 [Cambridge: CUP, 1985], 103). In its place he speculates about God's "self-differentiation" from the incarnate Jesus and from the Holy Spirit, a concept Pannenberg also develops today. The life history of Jesus remained central for Hegel, and in the crucifixion "God is dead," to become spiritually present again through the Holy Spirit. The role and person of Christ, however, are shaped by dialectical conflict between opposites, and "absorption" or "reconciliation" of those opposites. Macquarrie comments: "Absolute Being, actualized in self-sacrifice ... becomes a self ... that is transitory and passes away" (*Jesus Christ,* 219). *Christ becomes an episode in the history of God.* There can be nothing enduring about the historical, and thus Macquarrie calls it "Idealist Christology" (212-34). Yet the larger framework within which Hegel views the incarnation is suggestive. Moltmann and Pannenberg draw constructively on selected aspects of this picture to take the subject forward.

(d) The next decisive step was the emergence of *"kenotic Christology,"* first expounded by G. Thomasius (1802-1873). In England it was developed by Charles Gore (1853-1932), bishop of Oxford and editor of *Lux Mundi* (1889). His most controversial contention was that because of his self-emptying or *kenosis* in the incarnation, the earthly Jesus would not have been infallible in his knowledge or predictions. For example, Gore disputed the Davidic authorship of Psalm 110. In 1895 Gore developed this further, arguing that "real self-impoverishment" firmly restricted foreknowledge of his death. On a broader and less specific scale, liberalism promoted a growing divide between biblical Christology and early Christian doctrine. Thus, while H. B. Swete was tracing the Apostles' Creed to a very early creed in Rome (*The Apostles' Creed* [Cambridge: CUP, 1899]), A. Harnack was arguing that even the earliest Roman creed went well beyond the apostles' teaching of the NT. We traced the growing divide between the so-called Jesus of history and the Christ of faith in the section "Jesus of History" above, which began largely with Lessing.

(e) *British Christology intensified a growing attack on Chalcedonian "two natures" Christology in the late 1960s and 1970s.* Some of the essays in S. W. Sykes and J. P. Clayton, eds., *Christ, Faith, and History* (Cambridge: CUP, 1972), mounted such an attack, especially those by J. A. T. Robinson and Maurice Wiles. Robinson argued, "Jesus was not a hybrid ... a sort of bat-man or centaur, an unnatural conjunction of two strange species" ("Need Jesus Have Been Perfect?" 39-52). Other essays proposed "replies" to such skepticism, including one by Peter Baelz, later dean of Durham Cathedral. Meanwhile, Robinson developed his proposal into a full-length book, *The Human Face of God* (London: SCM, 1973). In 1968 he had predicted that Christology would be the next focus of debate and outlined his own proposal in the Cambridge Hulsean Lectures of 1970 (preface, vii). He rejected the charge that he was merely reformulating the old patristic debates, arguing that we must genuinely ask "*our* questions" today (x). His double target of attack was that of "a Christ who was God in disguise and of Jesus the perfect man. Both have removed him from 'the likes of us'" (3). He aimed to remove Christology from language and concepts that may seem remote. He admitted, however, "the danger ... that each generation simply sees its own Christ" (15); hence we must use rigorous historical criticism. We need, he urged, a change of conceptual framework. For example, the early church saw "a timeless being, in the categories of substance rather than will" (33). While this general comment has some weight, we have noted some counterevidence, especially in Gregory of Nyssa and Gregory of Nazianzus (*see* **Holy Spirit: The Spirit in Historical Theology**).

A further claim concerns the preexistence of Christ, for which Robinson draws mainly on John Knox, *The Humanity and Divinity of Christ* (Cambridge: CUP, 1958). The preordination by God of Christ's mission "became translated as the preexistence of Christ" (37). This has become almost the stock-in-trade of many, if not most, NT scholars (for example, J. D. G. Dunn), although not of most systematic theologians. Dunn collects a representative sample of Knox, Wiles, Lampe, Cupitt, Craddock, and others. Dunn has doubts about the traditional concept of the preexistence of Christ, writing, "There was ... no concept of 'the preexistence of Christ' apart from this application of Wisdom categories to Jesus.... It would be inaccurate to say that Christ was understood as a pre-existent being become incarnate" (*Christology in the Making*, 2nd ed. [Grand Rapids: Eerdmans, 1989], 210, 211). However, we may compare, for example, L. W. Hurtado in 2003. He responds to Dunn that in his view Phil. 2:6-11, 1 Cor. 8:6, 15:47, and Gal. 4:4 suggest the traditional conclusion. Moreover, "two key christological convictions" would be otherwise compromised: "(1) Jesus' origins and meaning lie in God, above and before creation and human history ... ; and (2) Jesus' agency in creation corresponds to his central role in redemption" (*Lord Jesus Christ* [Grand Rapids: Eerdmans, 2003], 126; cf. 118-26).

Yet it would be unwise to dismiss the search for a fresh *conceptualization and formulation* of the issue. One monumental study both of the exegetical and of the theological material is provided by K.-J. Kuschel, *Born before All Time?* (London: SCM, 1992). In his review in the *Journal of Religion,* Hurtado calls Kuschel's book "remarkable" and "informed, critical, and devout." Yet Kuschel wishes to take whatever is meant by "preexistence" more seriously than many, while at the same time he calls for new understandings and formulations. He even concludes, "If we take texts at their Word ... there is no sign of any unambiguous and explicit statement about pre-existence in the Christology outlined by Paul himself. ... The texts call for sobriety, caution, and restraint" (303). On the other hand, many may dissent from even Kuschel's exegesis of relevant biblical passages.

Meanwhile, Robinson easily finds examples in patristic thought of undervaluing the humanness of Jesus. Clement of Alexandria observed, "It would be ridiculous to imagine that the body of the Redeemer... had the usual needs of a man" (*Stromata* 6.9; Robinson, 39n.). Even Athanasius argued, "The Word disguised himself by appearing in a body.... He showed himself to be not Man but God the Word" (*On the Incarnation* 16.18; Robinson, 39). Cyril of Alexandria claims that his nature was "timeless and incapable of grief" (*Commentary on John* 7; Robinson, 40n.). The Alexandrians do provide an understandable target for Robinson. By contrast, Robinson claims that "the nexus of biological, historical, and social relationships" is part of Christ's humanness (41). He imagines that notions of the virgin birth will obscure this. Moreover, he urges, "The Church has appeared to present him as *sexless*" (64). Robinson attacks any way of describing the manhood of Jesus as "an unreal figure with the static perfection of flawless porcelain, rather than a man of flesh and blood" (68). Jesus was *not* "the all-rounder of whom it could be said, 'You name it: he's got it'" (70). As Barth insists, he was not "a great man" in this sense (72). Robinson urges, "Jesus was fully a man like ourselves, sharing the same unconscious drives and libido" (85). His temptations were genuine temptations. Yet Robinson affirms: "The gospels ascribe to Jesus no trace of the consciousness of sin or guilt" (97).

Too many of the Fathers, Robinson claims, held the astonishing doctrines of *anhypostasia*, "the view that Christ assumed human nature without assuming human personality" (105). This point had been made even more forcefully by John McIntyre in *The Shape of Christology* ([London: SCM, 1966], 93-98). The Alexandrians, Robinson claims, were too much influenced by Platonism. After discussing in what sense Jesus represents God, Robinson quotes C. F. D. Moule as declaring: "*Kenōsis* actually is *plerōsis;* which means that the human limitations of Jesus are seen as a positive expression of his divinity rather than a curtailment of it" (Robinson, 208). The relation between manhood and deity in Jesus is not to be stated in metaphysical terms as two levels or "storeys"; but as two *languages, two narratives, or two stories.* One is "historic-scientific." Unfortunately, following Strauss and Bultmann, he calls the more theological language "mythological," which is a term that causes massive confusion (118).

In *Christ, Faith, and History* Wiles explained the same model that Robinson proposed, stating that to confuse "the human historical story with the divine mythological story" constitutes "a category mistake" ("Does Christology Rest on a Mistake?" 11). But Peter Baelz replied by rejecting that the two "stories" are "utterly divorced from each other" with no logical relations between them ("A Deliberate Mistake?" 23; cf. 13-34). The two "stories" at least overlap. A fourth essayist in this volume is Don Cupitt, who contributed the essay "One Jesus, Many Christs." He argued that the way in which Jesus is Christ "for me" may be "very different from the way he is Christ for some other person" (143). Cupitt thus falls into the very trap to which, we noted, Kathryn Tanner gives due warning.

(vi) **More Recent Modern Christology.** Karl-Josef Kuschel points to a fresh and perhaps more creative phase in the history of Christology. Beginning with what he calls "failed conversations of yesterday" (*Born before All Time?* 35-176), Kuschel criticizes the hermeneutical assumptions of Harnack, Bultmann, and even Barth, and then takes a fresh look at biblical material (177-395). His part 3 focuses on the contemporary (or near-contemporary) Christologies of Pannenberg, Moltmann, and Jüngel among Protestant thinkers. He also discusses Rahner, Kasper, Küng, and Schillebeeckx in the Roman Catholic tradition (397-481). Metz argued that Rahner represented "a departure from the jaded and often fossilized world of the formulae of neo-scholastic thought and language," confronting it "with the questions posed by modern transcendental and existentialist philosophy" (Kuschel, *Born before All Time?* 411).

(a) *Karl Rahner* (1904-1984). He explored not only a Christology of the incarnation but also the connection between Christology and theological anthropology. Rahner generally shared the presuppositions of Chalcedon, but increasingly stressed the need to view them within the frame of a transcendental philosophy and to understand Christology in relation to humankind. Much of Rahner's Christology is presented in summary form in *Foundations of Christian Faith* (New York: Seabury Press; London: Darton, Longman, and Todd, 1978), chapter 6 (hereafter *FCF*); with further material in *Sacramentum Mundi*, vol. 3 (London: Burns and Oates, 1969), 192-209, and *Theological Investigations*, 22 vols. (New York: Seabury Press; London: Darton, Longman, and Todd, 1961-1969), and vol. 6, 153-77; and in his *Lehrsätze* on Christology, cowritten with W. Thüsing, and published in *A New Christology* (New York: Seabury Press; London: Burns and Oates, 1980). Whereas Bultmann had reduced everything to the existential dimension, Rahner considers both Jesus Christ "in himself" (the ontological) *and* "what he 'means for us'" (*FCF* 204). To put it differently, these are one "in the relatedness of the faithful to Jesus as the absolute eschatological mediator of salvation" (*Lehrsätze*, 5). No less important is Rahner's insistence that the Chalcedonian formulation can be understood *only within a transcendental frame.* The term "transcendental" relates to "conditions for the possibility of" reality or knowledge. Rahner explicitly declares that "An a priori doctrine of the God-man must be developed in a transcendental theology"; but this must be developed *not* prior to encounter with Christ, but must represent "the conditions of possibility for a reality which we have already encountered" (*FCF* 177). Only thus can we *exclude mythological misunderstanding* of orthodox *doctrine* (240). Like Robinson in his comments on Clement of Alexandria, we must not misperceive the humanity of Jesus or "merely the livery which God donned in order to appear among us" (W. Dych, *Karl Rahner* [London: Chapman, 1992], 68). Rahner declares, "An explicit transcendental Christology is necessary, a Christology which asks about the *a priori* possibilities in man which make the coming of the message of Christ possible" (*Lehrsätze*, 9). Rahner might have drawn directly from Heidegger. In Heidegger "man" denotes only *what concerns him* and what are his *interests.*

This phrase immediately points to man or human being not as a solitary being, but in his social and historical context. Hence Rahner speaks of human "active self-transcendence" and of God's creative presence as the ground of his creation (*FCF* 184). Thus a theology of Christ concerns not only an isolated human being or a "Soul," but humankind in their material environment and as part of creation. In actuality self-transcendence becomes the world's self-transcendence into the life of God. There is, according to Rahner, a self-transcendent movement of all creation to God that reaches its culmination in Christ. In expounding Rahner's Christology, Macquarrie comments, "A human being is a finite creature who is nevertheless conscious of moving towards an infinite horizon" (*Jesus Christ,* 304). Humans move from one horizon to another without even coming to a stopping place. As Macquarrie also observes, the human nature of Jesus is never "a mere instrument required for the incarnation" (307).

Christology and creation are closely related in Rahner. Jesus Christ is the climax of God's communication of himself to humankind, which began at creation. Rahner believes that even in evolutionary processes God has been progressively excommunicating himself. Jesus Christ constitutes "both the absolute promise of God to spiritual creatures as a whole" and the fulfillment of the promise in "the acceptance of self-communication" (*FCF* 195). Like Pannenberg, Rahner sees the coming of Christ as a unique moment in universal history.

All this signifies that Rahner maintains belief that "the Word became flesh," but with a much fuller and deeper meaning than the Church Fathers could ever have grasped in their day. Like Robinson, his concern is for the incarnation to make sense in today's world, but unlike him, he uses Heidegger and the transcendental philosophy of Kant. Some Protestant critics may suspect that, like so many contemporary Catholic theologians, he seems to wish to hold on to orthodox formulations while giving them a new meaning. But, first, this is bound up with the problem of hermeneutics. Second, Rahner is incredibly complex and sophisticated, and casts new light on old questions. Moreover, as Macquarrie observes, his books are huge, offering a comparison even with Barth in learning and quantity, He is careful to guard against misunderstanding. He continues to challenge theology afresh.

(b) *Edward Schillebeeckx* (1914-2009) was born in Antwerp, trained as a Jesuit, entered the Dominican Order in 1934, and was ordained priest in 1941. After a year at the Catholic University of Leuven (Louvain), he became professor of systematic theology at Nijmegen. He shared preparatory discussions for Vatican II with Rahner, Congar, and Kuhn, and was active at the council. Traditionally a Thomist, he turned in preparation for his work on Christology to the exegesis of the NT, the discovery of which he described as a "great joy." Schillebeeckx then wrote *Jesus: An Experiment in Christology* ([Dutch 1974; Eng. London: Collins, 1979], 767 pages) and *Christ: The Christian Experience in the Modern World* (Dutch 1978; Eng. London: SCM, 1980); as well as a third volume on church and ministry, *The Church: The Human Story of God* (London: SCM, 1990). Macquarrie calls these "perhaps the most detailed study of the person of Jesus Christ to have appeared in the twentieth century" (*Jesus Christ*, 308).

In his first volume, *Jesus,* Schillebeeckx seeks to probe the earliest traditions that lie behind the Gospels. He realizes that the Christ of church formulations is far removed from much contemporary thinking in the Netherlands. Like Robinson in England and Rahner in Germany, he wishes the presentation of Christology to be on the wavelength of modern readers and hearers; hence he calls it "an experiment." As a systematic theologian, he is dismayed by disagreements among NT specialists about almost every question and task. It is said that he spent three years on NT exegesis before beginning to write the first volume (Macquarrie, *Jesus Christ*, 309). He declares, "As a believer, I want to look critically into the intelligibility for man of Christological belief in Jesus, especially its origin.... I want to look for what a Christological belief in Jesus of Nazareth can intelligibly signify for people today" (*Jesus,* 33). He continues, "A historical fact is therefore our most justifiable point of departure" (44). This stands in contrast with the average church person's confession of "Christ who died for our sins," which at once enters the realm of faith. As he looks back on previous work, he observes that "Every period has its own way of representing Jesus" (64). This has always been the case, even in primitive Christianity. But he rejects the conclusions of Reimarus, Schweitzer, Bultmann, Käsemann, Fuchs, and Bornkamm (67-76). Rejecting "liberal" approaches, he turns to "a post-critical, narrative history" (77; *see* **Narrative; Ricoeur, Paul**). He takes up the discussion among NT scholars about "criteria of authenticity," and even hermeneutics. For example, "consistency" may bring in a cluster of criteria (96). Rightly, like Pannenberg and others, he values both the prophetic and the apocalyptic background and context (116-26), and that of John the Baptist (126-36). The conclusion emerges that "the context of Jesus' living and speaking is the future purposed by God" (140). His focus is proclamation of the kingdom of God.

This at once suggests two key points about Jesus. First, Schillebeeckx calls attention to *"praxis"* and to parables. Jesus' "person, his stories, and his actions" are one (158). His ministry is lived action. The beatitudes and the miracles show "Jesus' caring and abiding presence among people, experienced as salvation coming from God" (179). Special importance is given to "Jesus' eating and drinking in fellowship with his men and with 'outcasts,' tax-gatherers, and sinners" (206). Jesus is "man's liberation" (229). The key is Jesus' "caring and loving service of, and solidarity with, people" (310). One christological conclusion is that "The New Testament clearly shows that in his lifetime Jesus of Nazareth had made on many people the impression of being 'a prophet' — something by then already rare" (475). To be *the* eschatological prophet, "the prophet like Moses" (Deut. 18:15), is the oldest of all christological beliefs. Psalm 2 and Psalm 110 were certainly given a messianic interpretation retrospectively. Schillebeeckx writes, "The choice of the very first followers of Jesus . . . fell upon the Jewish model of the eschatological prophet, with which they were familiar" (473). He explores passages that portray Jesus as a new Moses, including Johannine references. He speaks of "the prophetic self-understanding of Jesus" (479), and sees this as a link to the earthly, kerygmatic Christ. This prophetic role is explained by "the identification of Jesus with Wisdom" (489).

Contrary to Pannenberg and many others now, Schillebeeckx disappointingly follows Bultmann in assessing the resurrection of Jesus as the *consequence* of faith, rather than its *cause*. He declares only, "When Christians affirm that Jesus was raised from the dead on the third day, they are affirming that God's rule has assumed the aspect of the Crucified-died-risen One, Jesus of Nazareth" (531). Hermeneutically we must explore the relation between resurrection and exaltation (533-44). Unlike Pannenberg, he dismisses the apocalyptic view of resurrection. Macquarrie cites his explicit statement: "In no way does the affirmation of belief in Jesus' being taken up into heaven depend on a possible empty tomb or on appearances" (538; cf. Macquarrie, *Jesus Christ*, 311). Hence Macquarrie concludes, "I do not find his Christological speculations persuasive," in spite of his learning (312).

Schillebeeckx's second volume, *Christ*, begins with the helpful claim that experience is always "interpreted experience" (31-36). "There is no experience without 'theorizing,' without queries, hypotheses and theories" (34); "we would never know exactly whether we were dealing with 'reality' " (35). But the supposed alternative, he urges, between the NT and "experience" is false (21-80). This leads him into an exposition of the NT theology of the experience of grace. This occupies the whole of part 2, which covers three sections and six chapters (81-628). He examines the Hebrew *chēn* and the Greek *charis;* and grace and suffering in Paul, Hebrews, and John, in which the theme becomes love. He then explores the book of Revelation. Parts 3 and 4 concern the experience of God's grace and God's glory. He also considers man's truth, well-being, and happiness. He writes, "God . . . shares his true *countenance* to Christians in the unselfish involvement of Jesus . . . in search of his wandering sheep" (639). Kuschel describes this as sketching out "a biblical theology of grace" (Kuschel, *Born before All Time?* 476).

Schillebeeckx's Christology, Kuschel further comments, has been vigorously questioned by Rome's Congregation of the Faith. Schillebeeckx defended himself in 1977, especially over the rather technical issue of why he seemed not to use "hypostatic identification," as at Chalcedon. He proposed "human mode of being" for the purpose of intelligibility in the modern world. In 1978 and 1979 further questions were presented to him, the last a few days before Küng was deprived of his right to teach as a Catholic theologian. As elsewhere in the world, his use of the term "hermeneutics" seemed also to arouse suspicion. Suspicion, however, is not surprising when we recall that his bold book *The Church* specifically attacks the Roman Catholic view of apostolic succession.

(c) *Hans Küng* was born in 1928 in Switzerland, and studied in Rome and Paris. In 1960 he was appointed professor of fundamental theology in the Catholic Faculty of the University of Tübingen. He is one of the four most influential Catholic theologians of today, along with Rahner, Congar, and Balthasar. He was heavily involved in Vatican II (1962-1965). But after his books *The Church* (Ger. and Eng. 1967) and *Infallible?* (Ger. 1970; Eng. 1971), as well as *On Being a Christian* (Ger. 1974; Eng. 1977) and *Does God Exist?* (Ger. 1978; Eng. London: Collins, 1980), his license to teach as a Catholic was withdrawn in 1979 by the Vatican, although he retained the post of ecumenical professor at Tübingen until his retirement in 1996. His main book on Christology is *The Incarnation of God* (Ger. 1970; Eng. Edinburgh: T. & T. Clark, 1987). This, he suggests, should be read in close interaction with *On Being a Christian* (London: Collins, 1977) and *Does God Exist?*

In the first chapter of *The Incarnation of God,* Küng argues that Hegel's thought is seminal for any truly creative thought up to the present. The world of Christology had been virtually static through the centuries up to Hegel. But with Hegel German idealism reached its climax, and, Küng comments, "the after-effects of Hegel are immense" (20). Further, "the greatest anti-Hegelians, Kierkegaard and Marx, draw upon him the most" (21). Although Hegel was brought up as a Protestant, he was a child of the Enlightenment, for whom Christianity was seen "in its aridity and intellectuality" (28). Enlightenment Christianity spoke of God, but not so much of Christ. Hegel perceived the limits of the Enlightenment. At first "Hegel appeals to the earthly Jesus as an ideal of virtue" (71). But he began to see that such an understanding could not account for the "eternal truths" of Christianity (95). In his period at Bern, he began to be impressed by the pantheism of Spinoza, Schelling, and Hölderlin. Then at Tübingen he was influenced, by Kant, Lessing, and Goethe, to study the debate about pantheism. An "epoch-making shift of direction" then occurred (103). This became "a monism of Spirit" (*Geist:* 106). He began to take seriously a union of God and man. In this period Hegel wrote, "The Son of God is also the Son of Man; the divine in a particular shape appears as a man. [It is] the connection of the infinite and finite . . . a 'holy mystery' " (111). The reconciliation between the finite and the infinite emerges in the concept of love; in the "true spiritual beauty [which is] more clearly seen in Jesus" (121). Küng concludes, "For Hegel, religion is the fulfilment of love" (123). Hegel now comes to relate "the Word made flesh" to an individual, namely, to Jesus (126). Faith may give us a "relationship with Jesus" (129).

On the brink of exploring a Hegelian Christology, Küng considers his turn to philosophy in his next period of thought. However, even when he focuses on God, he perceives the incarnation as "the Absolute [becoming] objective to itself in a perfect totality" (162). On Good Friday "God himself is dead." Christ's interesting history is "a movement of the absolute Spirit in the world" (206). In spite of Macquarrie's comments about Doceticism in Hegel, Küng quotes Hegel's declaration: "the truly historical existence of Jesus is at stake" (209). According to Küng, understanding the incarnation in this way is *"for the understanding of the true nature of God"* (209). Hegel's dialectic, he proposes, shows Jesus not only in history, but also in *historicity,* or *historicality.* Jesus is conditioned by his place in history. We must cling to the insight: "God in the *World,* transcendence in *immanence,* the beyond in the *here-and-now"* (237). The dialectic of love, Küng urges, is to create a space both for "God to be himself [and] also for *man* to be himself" (239).

Küng agrees that this is bound up with Hegel's "philosophy of world history" (325). But Jesus Christ is not just "a historical figure of the past" (329). His appearance as God is "unique." Christ died and was raised. Now reconciliation "becomes universal" (330). In the NT God does not appear as an apathetic God. Küng quotes Rom. 8:32: "He who does not withhold his Son . . . will he not give us all things?" At issue here is "how God appears when he identifies himself with man" (449). Christ reveals God both in his glory as God (Phil. 2:6) and in the human *kenosis* of the form of a servant (Phil. 2:7). In the light of Hegel's framework of thought, Küng suggests that "God's transcendence, immortality and unchangeability be subjected to a thoroughgoing reinterpretation" (455). There is more than an echo of Rahner on the transcendental approach here. The simple traditional formula "God became man" remains true, but remains, he argues, unintelligible, until it is placed within a different conceptual framework. This does not imply that Küng accepts *everything* in Hegel. He has doubts about his "speculative necessity against the 'contingency' of free grace" (457). He also refuses to follow Hegel on the impersonal or subpersonal nature of the Absolute. But we need to use "the insights painfully gained during this study" (457). There is "no going back behind Hegel" (465).

Nevertheless, even if Dilthey and York used or coined the term "historicity," this term remains invaluable for understanding the incarnation of God (466). Further, like Barth, whom Küng studied for his dissertation, he sees the redemptive (or for Hegel, dialectical) process as occurring *within God,* not outside him. Third, like Jüngel and Moltmann, he also sees the intense *suffering* of God himself as a central part of this occurrence in God. Some may regard the critique of Hegel and Küng by Grenz and Olson a little overhasty and perhaps misplaced. Their pinpointing of the above three insights (on historicity, on occurrence within God, and on the suffering of God) surely commands a fair degree of assent (S. J. Grenz and R. E. Olson, *Twentieth-Century Theology* [Downers Grove, Ill.: IVF, 1992], 265-67). It seems to accord with K.-J. Kuschel's conclusion in *Born before All Time?* (460-68). Admittedly, three of Küng's key themes are "transcendence, creatorship, and historicity." But he comments, "God does not remain in himself . . . but is a God who emerges from himself and empties himself, already through the coming-to-be of the world, which has its climax in God's becoming human" (460). This leads on to the relation between a dispute over Jesus as a dispute over God, and proposing the question, "How do we understand God today?" (462-64).

(d) *Eberhard Jüngel* (b. 1934) is emeritus professor of systematic theology and the philosophy of religion in the Protestant Faculty of Theology at Tübingen. He was born into a nonreligious home in the German Democratic Republic, yet came to faith, perceiving that truth could be, or was, spoken in the church. He studied theology at Berlin and Zurich. Influenced by G. Ebeling and K. Barth in Switzerland, he undertook postgraduate research under E. Fuchs. He taught at Zurich until 1969, and then became professor at Tübingen. His close relationship with Fuchs explained his lifelong interest in language event *(Sprachereignis)* and metaphor, as well as in NT studies. Yet his primary areas were systematic theology and philosophy of religion. He remained at Tübingen until his retirement in 2003. His lifelong concerns are also in the theology of Luther and Barth. Indeed, in his discussion of his Christology, Kuschel heads a section "Like Barth and Yet Not Like Barth" (*Born before All Time?* 433-35; cf. 432-40). His greatest affinity with Barth concerns Barth's period of dialectical theology or theology of crisis in the years 1919-1933. Barth even characterized this early period as "between theism and atheism." Like Pannenberg and Moltmann, Jüngel sees the coming of Christ as the emergence of a distinction within the Godhead, as had Küng with reference to Hegel.

In his major work, *God as the Mystery of the World* (Edinburgh: T. & T. Clark, 1983), Jüngel begins with the status of language about God in the modern world, a basic question in the philosophy of religion. Recalling the often complex and sometimes obscure language of Fuchs, we find Jüngel saying, "God is thinkable only as the unthinkable" (8). Yet, he argues, "One of [language's] essential functions is that of *address*" (11). Fuchs makes the same point in the New Hermeneutic. This makes a purely philosophical approach questionable, and Kuschel calls this "like Barth" (*Born before All Time?* 433-34). Jüngel argues, "The metaphysical concept of God was undermined by the *cogito* ('I think'). . . . God is thinkable as God solely on the basis of his self-sharing of his being, which has taken place" (*God as the Mystery*, 298). God is without analogy. But the death of Jesus Christ is drawn "into the event of which it speaks. . . . The event character of this event, its *dynamic* ('power') is . . . not just information about it" (287). Metaphor, parable, and the cross of Christ "are *addressing* speech" (290). Jüngel declares: "The word of the cross is the self-definition of God in human language, which implies a definition of man" (229). As a central principle of Christology he asserts: "God defines himself as love in the cross of Christ. God *is* love" (220; cf. 1 John 4:8). Very profoundly he comments: "His 'inner being' *is* itself a turning toward what is 'outside.' God communicates with himself without holding himself from others. As love, he makes it possible to share in his life." It is worth quoting his words at exceptional length. He continues, "His identification with the man Jesus is, consequently, the *revelation* of the *eternal* being of God, as a special and unique event.... *God is in and of himself,* in such a way that he is *In* man.... 'If God is for us, who can be against us?' (Rom. 8:31)" (220-21). God is identified with the crucified and raised Christ.

The death of Jesus Christ, then, is profoundly significant for the nature, or better, the history, of God. But any Hegelian talk of the death of God can be dangerous. He offers a critique of both Bonhoeffer (57-63) and Hegel (63-100), as well as of the death-of-God movement (100-111). God's being "is thinkable again" in his identification with Jesus and his resurrection (111). Yet it is possible to speak, as Pannenberg does, of "the differentiation of God from God within himself. Jesus," Jüngel urges, experienced "God-forsakenness ... on the Cross ... to become a curse *for* us" (362). There is a union of death and life. This is grounded in "the God who is love" (314-31). Jüngel states, "One can love neither God nor the other if one has not *already* been loved by God and let oneself be loved by him. 'He first loved us' (1 Jn. 4:19)" (327). "Love," like "Father," is a relational term.

Hence, as in Barth, the doctrine of God remains central, but the event of the incarnation and cross permits *"thinkability"* concerning the One who thereby addresses us. God's self-identification with Jesus becomes a key theme. Moreover, Jüngel's talk of language event and love further recalls the writings of Fuchs on hermeneutics and the parables of Jesus. The Being and action of God, and the person and work of Christ, are all inextricably entwined, and enter speech in language and love. In his short essay "My Theology," Jüngel explains: "I believe, therefore I speak. Not of me and of my faith.... I speak of the God in whom I believe and his lifelong truth ... the God who has come into the world as a human being, and who has for our salvation revealed himself as God in the person of Jesus Christ" (in *Eberhard Jüngel: Theological Essays,* ed. J. B. Webster, vol. 2 [Edinburgh: T. & T. Clark, 1995], 1-19, here 5). He adds, "Theology acquired its method by repeating in thought the movement of God's coming to the world.... God distinguishes himself from the world by sharing himself with it" (11).

(e) *Jürgen Moltmann* (b. 1926). Moltmann's theology is profoundly affected by his early life. In 1943-1944 he was conscripted into the army, and witnessed terrible destruction and the death of a friend who stood beside him in an air raid on Hamburg. He was taken prisoner of war, and spoke of "the death of all my mainstays." But from Psalm 139 he read, "If I make my bed in hell, you are there," and came to see that "God is with those who are of a broken heart.... Nothing is shut off from God" (cf. *History and the Triune God* [London: SCM, 1991], 165-82, and *A Broad Place* [Minneapolis: Augsburg Fortress, 2008]). On his return to Germany he became influenced by Luther's theology of the cross, as well as by O. Weber, H.-J. Irvand, and Gerhard von Rad. In 1964 he published *Theology of Hope,* for which he became famous, and then in 1972 *The Crucified God.* On the person and work of Christ, he asked: "What does Jesus' suffering and death mean for God himself?" (*A Broad Place,* 182).

One of Moltmann's two major books on Christology was *The Way of Jesus Christ* (Ger. 1989; Eng. London: SCM, 1990). But before that he had also published *The Trinity and the Kingdom of God* (Ger. 1980; Eng. London: SCM, 1981). In this 1981 volume he asked, first, not "What does God mean to me?" but "What do I mean for God?" (3). Second, he declared, "A God who cannot suffer cannot love either" (38). God is not the God of "theism," as Jüngel also urges. Third, the narrative of the Trinity permeates the Gospels and the life of Jesus Christ. These three principles determine his approach to Christology in *The Way of Jesus Christ*. He argues in his first chapter that the uniqueness of Jesus can be seen only in terms of the messianic expectations of the OT and Israel's history. This means that "messianology" should not be split into "Christology on the one hand and eschatology on the other" (4). Like Barth, he sees the climax of the hope in "Immanuel," God with us. The Messiah is "a historical figure of hope," but through his rule "the coming of God himself" is announced (12). God's Servant in Deutero-Isaiah is both messianic and "the corporate person of Israel itself" (20). The message of repentance does not begin with John the Baptist, but with the prophets. Meanwhile, even the Sabbath represents "an advance-pledge" of the Messiah (27).

Moltmann is not impressed by a supposedly value-neutral Christology. He urges, "Every Christology presupposes belief.... Believing and thinking inevitably belong together" (39). Jesus is Lord because God raised him from the dead. "Christopraxis" is the source of Christology. Moltmann argues that "anthropological" Christology is simply Jesusology, and nothing else (55). If "Christology from below" is merely centered in "the human being Jesus of Nazareth," this is not enough (55). This would be all part of the modern retreat into "subjectivity" and the "secularization" of society. The Enlightenment and Schleiermacher provide ready examples of this trend. Even the *later* writings of Rahner betray this trend. What is important is "Jesus' history with God," or "the Trinitarian history of the Father, the Son, and the Spirit" (71). Like J. Zizioulas, he insists that the messianic mission of Christ begins with the Holy Spirit. The Spirit descends on him at baptism and "leads him" into the messianic temptations in the descent. This still traces the development of Christology from the OT and Jewish hopes. On the virgin birth, the Evangelists were not aiming "to report a gynaecological miracle," but to point "to the divine origin of (Jesus') person" (82). The Father saw this event as proclaiming the humanity of Jesus, rather than his divinity. Inevitably "Jesus' unique baptismal experience" and his experience of God as "Abba" remain crucial for this approach. Jesus then "makes conversion possible" and calls men and women to discipleship (102-3). He initiates them into "a way of life" (116-19), which is reflected in the title of *The Way of Jesus Christ*.

This messianic "way" means that Jesus does not redeem "through powerful signs and wonders of liberation" (164). Jesus experiences "the frightening eclipse of God" in Gethsemane (Mark 14:32-42) and "God-forsakenness" at Golgotha (166-67). He faces "God's silence, the hiding of his face, the eclipse of God, the dark night of the soul, the death of God, hell" (167). This section can be supplemented from *The Crucified God*. Many will detect affinities with Luther's hidden

God here. Through all this humankind may experience "the justification of sinners," the liberation of "man and woman who are closed in upon themselves into the open love of God" (*The Way of Jesus Christ*, 185). The goal is "the wiping away of the tears from every eye" (210). Moltmann adds, "God's raising of Christ was the foundation for faith in Christ" (213). He cites the witness of the women at the empty tomb, Christ's appearances to different people, the early date and tradition of 1 Corinthians, and Paul's "sight" of Jesus (216). Moltmann concludes, "Seeing history in the perspective of the resurrection means participating through the Spirit in the *process of resurrection*" (240). It is not just assent to dogma; it is participation in this creator's act of God. Praxis must be bound up with the hope of resurrection. This opens up "a way of moving forward in the discovery of 'the always greater Christ,'" who becomes "the cosmic Christ" (275; Col. 1:15-20). Moltmann comments, "The ontological foundation of cosmic Christology is Christ's death" (282). This leads to "the renewal of creation" (291) and "The Day of the Lord" (326).

(f) *Wolfhart Pannenberg* (b. 1928). Further details of Pannenberg's life and Christology are available under the entry for Pannenberg in this volume, but some degree of repetition is unavoidable. The culmination of his work is his three-volume *Systematic Theology* (Grand Rapids: Eerdmans, 1991-1998). But earlier, his book *Jesus — God and Man* (Ger. 1964; Eng. Philadelphia: Westminster; London: SCM, 1968) burst upon the scene to suggest a widespread reappraisal of Christology. Many called it "the great new alternative to Bultmann." Whereas Bultmann and many of his pupils had insisted that belief in the resurrection of Christ grew out of post-Easter faith, Pannenberg urges that the resurrection of Jesus Christ was the *cause* of post-Easter faith. He endorses the view of P. Althaus: the resurrection kerygma "could not have been maintained in Jerusalem for a single day, for a single hour, if the emptiness of the tomb had not been established as a fact for all concerned" (100). He urges that *both* the "appearances" tradition *and* the "empty tomb" tradition remain independently valid. Too many doubts depend simply on a positivist assumption that "dead men do not rise" (109). He urges, "The tomb tradition and the appearance tradition had come into existence independently of each other" (105). He carefully replies to H. Grass, W. Marxsen, and H. Conzelmann on this subject.

Nevertheless, Pannenberg respects and values a Christology "from below" in principle, citing Luther's conviction that he saw "in Jesus the representation of all men before God" (43). Like Moltmann, he values the prophetic and apocalyptic background to OT and Jewish expectation. In particular, the apocalyptic literature suggested, "If Jesus had been raised, then the end of the World had begun" (67). He writes, "If Jesus had been raised, this for a Jew can only mean that God himself has confirmed the pre-Easter activity of Jesus" (67). The life, death, and resurrection of Jesus are firmly embedded in the history of the tradition of Israel. As he has often stated in earlier writings, "the unity of event and word" remains crucial, and the event of Jesus "had its own meaning within the sphere in the

Christology

history of traditions" (73). Resurrection is not without appropriate analogy: "The familiar experience of being awakened and rising from sleep serves as a parable for the completely unknown destiny expected for the dead" (74).

The ministry of the pre-Easter Jesus, therefore, remains important. Pannenberg declares, "God's presence in Jesus was characterized by the concept of the Spirit" (116). He rejects notions of the "divine man." He discusses Barth and Brunner on the virgin birth. But on the question of "preexistence" he affirms "Jesus' unity with God." This precedes, he suggests, "the time of Jesus' earthly life" (150). He adds, "Paul presupposes the pre-existence of the Son" (Gal. 4:4; Rom. 8:3). When thinkers such as Rahner claim that a different framework of concepts implies a different principle for today, it is impossible to undervalue Pannenberg's philosophical sophistication, just as on the resurrection it is hard to ignore his detailed concerns for history and historicity. He asserts, "The point of departure for all further considerations [is] that Jesus' person cannot be separated from God's essence, if Jesus in person is God's self-revelation" (158).

Pannenberg readily discusses Jesus as "the true man" (191-211). He is "representative of man before God" (195). Jesus is "the man well-pleasing in the eyes of God in the dedication to his office, in the obedient acceptance of his faith" (197). He accepts Calvin's belief in the importance of being, but is reserved about Christ's priesthood, even if he concedes that his prophetic office is seen in his preaching. He states, "The title of King . . . designates the position that is due to Jesus because of his resurrection" (218). When we consider the death of Jesus, in as far as people no longer have to die, "Jesus' death has vicarious significance for all humanity" (263). The pre-Pauline tradition affirms that "Christians die with Christ and are raised up with him" (264). On the issue of Christ's "decent into hell," Pannenberg discusses in an excursus (269-74) the Reformed view that this was "a part of his passion, the deepest point of his humiliation," and also the Lutheran view that it constitutes "the first act of his exaltation" (273). Pannenberg criticizes bad exegesis of 1 Pet. 4:6, and sees some truth in both views: the Reformed view stresses the suffering and humiliation of Jesus; the Lutheran view sees it as victory over Satan (*see* **Descent into Hell**). He then considers the notions of concern and satisfaction in relation to the meaning of his death.

In part 3 Pannenberg brings together the divinity of Christ and the man Jesus. He does not regard the "two natures" conceptuality of Chalcedon the best way forward; indeed, it seems to promote an "impasse." Pannenberg affirms the true divinity and true humanity of Jesus (284-85). He traces the twists and turns of the patristic era. He concludes that more "conceptual flexibility" is needed. This can largely be achieved with the notion of mutual *interpenetration* of the two natures. He writes, "The term for mutual interpenetration *(perichōrēsis)* . . . prevailed because it suggested less strongly the notion of a blending of the two natures to form a third. The Cappadocians explicitly strived to express the distinction between the two natures as well as this unity, but succeeded only in a series of figurative illustrations that later became famous." He continues, "Divinity saturates Jesus' humanity as fire makes the iron glow, and the humanity dissolves itself in the divinity, as a drop of vinegar in the infinite sea" (297). The weakness of these illustrations is that they can be interpreted differently. But, again, "the retroactive meaning of Jesus' resurrection as divine confirmation of his previous activity" seems largely to overcome the dilemma that they leave (307). Conceptual understanding from the nature of the Trinity also helps us here. The way forward is a deeper understanding of the relationship between God as Father and Jesus as his Son. Pannenberg concludes, "The execution of Jesus' dedication which (confirmed by his resurrection) mediates his unity with God and is related to the Father" surpasses the formulation of his human nature as such (339). Yet in the incarnation we see "the hiddenness of the Lordship of Christ in this World" (377). Eschatology, the Holy Trinity, and a disciplined *perichoresis* save Pannenberg from utilizing the conceptuality of Hegel or of other extrabiblical sources.

In theory we ought to explore Pannenberg's *Systematic Theology* further. But this has been done in the entry under his name, and some sympathetic critics have ventured to suggest that rather than developing these theories further, the *Systematic Theology*, of later and more recent years, is more concerned with caveats, qualifications, and accuracy. This simply shows the complexity and creativity of Pannenberg's Christology in the earlier volume. (*See also* **Aquinas, Thomas; Arius, Arianism; Athanasius; Basil of Caesarea; Chalcedon, Council of; Dualism; Gnosticism; Hegel, Georg Wilhelm Friedrich; Holy Spirit: The Spirit in Historical Theology; Jüngel, Eberhard; Küng, Hans; Liberalism; Moltmann, Jürgen; Pannenberg, Wolfhart; Rahner, Karl; Robinson, John A. T.; Schillebeeckx, Edward; Schleiermacher, Friedrich D. E.; Subordinationism; Transcendental.**)

Reading: H. Küng, *The Incarnation of God* (Edinburgh: T. & T. Clark, 1987); J. Macquarrie, *Jesus Christ in Modern Thought* (Philadelphia: Trinity; London: SCM, 1990); J. Moltmann, *The Way of Jesus Christ* (London: SCM, 1990); G. O'Collins, *Christology* (Oxford: OUP, 1995); W. Pannenberg, *Jesus — God and Man* (London: SCM, 1968); E. Schillebeeckx, *Jesus: An Experiment in Christology* (London: Collins, 1979).

Chronology

Because this is *not* a companion to *biblical studies*, it is inappropriate to discuss here the numerous problems posed by biblical chronology in specific terms. The key question for theologians in their use of the Bible concerns the genre of the text in question, and above all, hermeneutics. Is chronology the prime concern of the writer of the text? Clearly the writers or editors of 1 and 2 Kings and 1 and 2 Chronicles do not have as their primary aim the writing of a value-neutral or chronological history of Israel. They have other concerns, although they may use historical sources and traditions as best they can. In the NT, Luke writes *both* as a theologian *and* as a historian. His famous triple dating in Luke 3:1-2 seems at first sight to exemplify his purpose. He establishes a date in Roman imperial terms (the fifteenth year of the reign of the emperor Tiberius when Pontius Pilate was governor of Judea); in Jewish political terms (Herod was ruler of Galilee and his brother Philip ruler of the region of Iturea and Trachonitis); and in Jewish religious terms (during the high priesthood of Annas and Caiaphas). But is this mainly a *chronological* concern? J. A. Fitzmyer observes, "Luke relates his narrative to the history of the Roman world by several references in the Gospel and Acts. He connects the birth of Jesus with a decree of Caesar Augustus" (Luke 2:1; *The Gospel according to Luke I–IX* [New York: Doubleday, 1981], 175). On 3:1-2, Fitzmyer comments: "The sixfold synchronism serves to connect the historical perspective of Lucan theology [but] cannot be understood as an exact dating" (453). This negative comment on dating has been challenged, but Fitzmyer's main point is generally recognized by theologians. The Gospel, in Luke's view, is no private, inner thing; it is related to God's acts in world history. Therefore, the issue of chronological accuracy, whether correct or not, is subservient to Luke's overall concern *to anchor the public appearance of Jesus Christ in the public world: in public history and in a public tradition.*

Secondly, it is now beyond question that many types of narrative do not strictly adhere to chronology because, without any intention to deceive, this is not their primary concern. Detective stories, for example, are frequently forced to use flashbacks and flash-forwards to construct a meaningful *plot*. This is clearly the case in Mark, where rapid events at the beginning of his Gospel eventually become slow-motion events in the passion narrative. Mark's purpose is to show that the cross and the death and suffering of Jesus are key events to which the events of the Gospel lead. The death of Jesus was no tragic accident. Mark *structures* his *narrative time* to make this point. (*See also* **Narrative; Ricoeur, Paul.**)

Once we grasp the subservience of narrative to plot and purpose, we shall be less troubled about the sequence of the temptations of Jesus in Matthew and Luke, or the sequence of the cleansing of the temple in the Synoptic Gospels and John. This does not imply that the biblical writers sit loose to chronology. Sometimes it becomes very important, and the writer usually makes clear that he is especially concerned with chronology at this point. Even in terms of the chronology of eschatological events, Hendrickson, among many others, points out that some events in the book of Revelation are portrayed in cyclical, not linear, terms.

All this, however, paints only one side of the picture. Chronology has an important place in biblical studies. Recently Marcus Borg has published *Evolution of the Word* (New York: HarperCollins, 2012), which seeks to place NT writings in chronological sequence. We should not underrate such attempts to disentangle chronological problems as that of F. F. Bruce, *Chronological Questions in the Acts of the Apostles* (Manchester: John Rylands, 1986), or some of the essays in *Historicity and Chronology of the New Testament* (London: SPCK, 1966), particularly those by Allan Barr, H. E. W. Turner, and others. Specialist studies include C. Blomberg, *The Historical Reliability of John's Gospel* (Downers Grove, Ill.: IVP, 2001), and similar studies.

Chrysostom, John

John Chrysostom (c. 347-407), bishop of Constantinople, studied under Diodore of Tarsus, the leader of the Antiochene School. He was recognized by his contemporaries as an outstanding preacher and orator, and hence he bore the nickname *Chryso-stoma*, "Golden Mouth." His writings are available in English in *NPNF*, ser. 1, vols. 10-14. These contain *Homilies on St. Matthew* (vol. 10); *Homilies on Acts and Romans* (vol. 11); *Homilies on First and Second Corinthians* (vol. 12); homilies on epistles from Galatians to Philemon (vol. 13); and homilies on John and Hebrews (vol. 14). In 387 he delivered sermons "on the statues" after a riot at Antioch, and he also preached on Genesis, Psalms, and Isaiah. Often he divides the sections of his homilies first into careful exegesis, looking at the context, and second into "applications" that may include a "spiritual" meaning. Nevertheless, in principle he was opposed to Alexandrian allegorizing. When he was made bishop in 398, he courageously reformed corruption in the city, in the court, and among the clergy. The empress Eudoxia tried to oppose him, and he was temporarily removed from his diocese, but the court recalled him shortly afterward. In medieval times he was called "A Doctor of the Church," alongside Gregory of Rome, Ambrose, Augustine, and Jerome.

Church, Doctrine of. *See* Ecclesiology

Clapham Sect

This term described a group of wealthy Anglican evangelicals who lived near Clapham in southwest London around the end of the eighteenth and beginning of the nineteenth century. Most belonged to Clapham Parish Church, whose rector from 1792 to 1813 was John Venn. The group included William Wilberforce, who led the struggle against the slave trade. They exercised considerable influence on Parliament and public opinion, and gave the lie to the misunderstanding that evangelicals were not concerned with social reform, justice, and the state. They extended missionary work, and founded the British and Foreign Bible Society.

Clement of Alexandria

A pupil of Pantaenus, Clement of Alexandria (c. 150–c. 215) became head of the catechetical school of Alexandria in about 190. He came from a pagan background, and he later wrote *Exhortation to the Greeks (Protrepticus)* to exhort pagans to embrace the Christian faith. This work shows a close knowledge of pagan literature, including its philosophy and mythology. He continued this work in *The Instructor (Paedagogos)*, while his third major work was *The Miscellanies (Stromata)*. He also wrote *Extracts from Theodotus;* Theodotus was a Valentinian Gnostic. Clement aimed to steer a middle way between Christianity and Gnosticism. In his view, the Christian faith represented the fulfillment of the OT and Greek philosophy. He even regarded Plato as "Moses with an Attic (the Athenian dialect of Greek) accent." He presented Christianity as the faith of "the Christian Gnostic." During his lifetime Alexandria was the second city of the Roman Empire, and a strong intellectual center. If he leaned perhaps too much in the direction of Gnosticism and intellectual issues, his aim nevertheless was to communicate with his Greek readers, and to evangelize many for the Christian faith.

Clement of Rome

Clement of Rome (fl. c. 96) was almost certainly the author of *1 Clement*. Clement addressed his epistle on behalf of the church of Rome to the church in Corinth. Presbyters at Corinth had been duly appointed, but some younger members of the church sought to depose them. Clement's aim is to plead for unity and loyalty. He speaks of "unholy sedition," which is foreign to the "elect of God" (1.1). He calls for humility, as can be seen from the sufferings of Christ (2.1). Like Paul in 1 Corinthians, he rebukes "jealousy and envy" (Gk. *zēlos kai phthonos*, 3.2), and the rebellion of the young against the old. He cites the jealousy of Moses and the faithfulness of Abraham (4.12 and 10.1-7). Some teaching seems to wander from orthodoxy, such as Rahab's being saved "for her faith and hospitality" (12.1). Yet at this early date he states that Christ "bore the sins of many, and for their sins he was delivered up" (16.14), and looks to the promise of resurrection (26.1.2). He attributes the inspiration of Scripture to the Holy Spirit (13.1, "the Holy Spirit says..."; 16.2, "the Holy Spirit spoke concerning him" [Christ]). He quotes here from the Servant Songs: "The chastisement of our peace was upon him; with his bruises were we healed... the Lord delivered him up for our sins" (16.4-7). Part of the value of this letter is the early witness to vicarious atonement. The document known as *2 Clement* was not written by Clement of Rome.

Cloud of Unknowing, The

This is an anonymous book of contemplative prayer, which reflects affinities with the mystical theology of Walter Hilton. The title reflects the approach of apophatic or "negative" theology, in which God is beyond human words. It belongs to the fourteenth century.

Coakley, Sarah

Presently Norris-Hulse Professor of Divinity at the University of Cambridge (from 2007), Sarah Coakley (b. 1951) is a systematic theologian and Anglican priest. She was educated at Cambridge, took the Th.M. from Harvard (1975), and was awarded the Cambridge Ph.D. for her work on Ernst Troeltsch (1983). She has taught at the University of Lancaster (1976-1991), has been a visiting professor at Princeton, and was also a member of the Church of England Doctrine Commission. In addition to her wider work in systematic theology, she has interests and expertise in patristics, feminist theology, and science and religion. She published a revision of her thesis entitled *Christ without Absolutes* (1988); edited *Religion and the Body* (1997), *Powers and Submission* (2002), *Rethinking Gregory of Nyssa* (2003), and *Pain and Its Transformations* (2007); and wrote

Sacrifice Regained (2012). She is engaged in writing a four-volume systematic theology. The first volume, *God, Sexuality, and the Self: An Essay on the Trinity*, developed her Gifford Lectures given at Aberdeen (2012), and was published by CUP, Cambridge, in 2013.

Codex Bezae

This codex is one of the four most important Uncial manuscripts of the Gospels and Acts, conventionally named "D," the Western text, alongside Sinaiticus ("א"), Vaticanus ("B"), and Alexandrinus ("A"). It is bilingual, in Greek and Latin, and dates from the fourth to sixth century. Its most distinctive feature is that it has some extensive additions to the text, mainly in Acts, as well as some omissions, and some inaccuracies in the Greek. E. J. Epp published *The Theological Tendency of Codex Bezae Cantabrigiensis in Acts* (Cambridge: CUP, 1966), and D. C. Parker, *Codex Bezae* (Cambridge: CUP, 1992). T. Beza donated it to the University of Cambridge.

Codex Sinaiticus

Known as "א," Codex Sinaiticus was discovered by C. Tischendorf between 1844 and 1859, and was donated to the tsar of Russia in 1869. The manuscript was sold to the British Museum in 1933 for £100,000. It was found in St. Catherine's Monastery on Mount Sinai, and probably dates from the mid-fourth century. Westcott and Hort regard its joint witness with Codex Vaticanus ("B") as a basic or "neutral" witness to the biblical text.

Coleridge, Samuel Taylor

Samuel Taylor Coleridge (1772-1834) was born in Devonshire, England, and began studies at Jesus College, Cambridge, which he then abandoned. In 1795 he met William Wordsworth, with whom he collaborated in literature and poetry. In 1798 he published *Lyrical Ballads,* which included his famous poem "The Ancient Mariner." He studied Kant in Germany, and wrote several great poems. But from 1802 his powers declined, probably because he was struggling with his growing addiction to opium. Yet in 1816 he published "Christabel" and "Kubla Khan." In theology and religion he reacted against the rationalism of his early years, and came under the influence of the Pietist J. Boehme and the pantheism of Spinoza. Many date his "Christian" period from about 1810. He urged the use of imagination and creativity, and attacked rationalistic orthodoxy. As is well known, J. S. Mill described him as, with Jeremy Bentham, one of "the two great seminal minds of England of their age." Newman and Maurice were also greatly impressed by him.

In Coleridge's thought, Bernard Reardon writes, "The basis of faith, then, is not argument but experience" (*From Coleridge to Gore* [London: Longman, 1971], 65). As regularly occurs in hermeneutics, he distinguished between reason and understanding. He followed Kant in excluding religion and morality from logic alone. Like Schleiermacher, he understood God as One with whom humankind can hold communion. A Christian creed, he held, should not be as cheerless as atheism. He was also influenced in this period by Schelling and Romanticism. Sin, he believed, is the subjection of the will to an external control. He called for a "new and more perceptive approach to the Bible" (*From Coleridge to Gore*, 81), and was familiar with much current German NT scholarship. Whatever in the Bible "finds me," he wrote, demonstrates the witness of the Holy Spirit. Reardon considers him "The first of the great nineteenth century 'thinkers'" (88). Truth, he believed, concerns *life*, not simply thought.

Communion of Saints
The communion of saints is mentioned in the ninth article of the Apostles' Creed. W. Pannenberg traces the origin of the clause to Bishop Nicetas of Remesiania in Serbia, to whom it may have come from southern Gaul. Originally it appears to have had a double sense, indicating the fellowship or communion *(koinōnia)* of believers who have now died with the living, and also fellowship between living Christians. Luther thought it denoted the congregation of believers. In both meanings it indicates that believers are not solitary individuals, and it is usually associated with the mutuality, participation, and solidarity of believers at Holy Communion. Pannenberg suggests that it also indicates "the universal unity of the church across the ages, which finds manifestation in the worship of the local congregation that exists in view of its apostolic basis, having fellowship with past saints and martyrs" (*ST* 3:101). But J. Pearson insists that it is communion between living believers and the Holy Trinity and the angels. Some understand it as participation in "holy things," that is, the sacraments, since the Latin *sanctorum* can denote either masculine or neuter. Pannenberg sets out these three views in *The Apostles' Creed* (London: SCM, 1972), 149-59.

Compatibilism. *See* **Freedom**

Comte, Auguste
Auguste Comte (1798-1857) was the founder of French positivism. Comte wrote six volumes on positivist philosophy, and applied purely "positivist," materialist, or "scientific" method to the study of economics, politics, and the social sciences. Only what can be directly observed, he claimed, could be used in the study of any object. He proposed three stages in the history of human knowledge. In the first, or primitive, stage, humankind resorted to theology to explain phenomena; in the second, humankind appealed to metaphysical considerations; in the third, or positivist stage, appeal was restricted to observable objects. In effect, it is an evolutionary defense of materialism.

Concept
Many regard concepts as constituents of propositions or thoughts, much as a word is the constituent of a sentence. Hegel distinguished between "concept"

(Begriff) as the material of critical philosophy and "image" *(Vorstellung)* as the uncritical expression of religion. J. Barr has criticized the tendency in some theology to confuse concept with word. Concepts may be used to categorize phenomena, or as building blocks to produce ideas. Empiricists often regard concepts as arising from critical reflection on perceptions. Yet no definition of "concept" is entirely without criticism, especially as it operates in different contexts. These may include logic, linguistics, semantics, philosophy, and theology. Locke viewed concepts as the capacity to distinguish between ideas. Kant stressed the differences between percepts and concepts. Wittgenstein related concepts not to language but to the *use* of language. In positive terms, they make generality possible, as well as differentiation and categorization. But concepts may also have limits, as thinkers since Kant have noted.

Conditional Immortality

Conditional immortality rejects the notion that all human beings are immortal without condition. It renders immortality conditional upon a fresh act of grace from God. Unbiblical or popular forms make it conditional upon a righteous life, and often equate it with annihilationism. Irenaeus in the second century repeatedly exclaimed: "How can man be immortal, who in his mortal nature did not obey his maker?" (*Against Heresies* 4.39.2). He declared, "[Unbelievers] are deprived of his [God's] gift, which is eternal life" (3.19.1). "Life does not arise from us, or from our own nature, but is *bestowed* according to the grace of God" (2.34.3). The ancient church was divided on the subject. Irenaeus represents conditional immortality; Origen tends toward Universalism; Augustine believes in unconditional immortality, either to eternal bliss or to eternal torment (*see* **Hell**). None of the three views was sufficiently widely held to constitute "orthodoxy." Augustine's view was later held by Thomas Aquinas and Calvin, but in modern times Christians are uncertain about the issue. The Roman Catholic view of purgatory seems in general to support Augustine and Thomas. The Fifth Lateran Council of 1513 condemned conditional immortality. In 1846, however, a Congregationalist minister, Edward White, attempted to reformulate and defend the doctrine. Charles Gore was largely uncertain, but called the view "tolerable." Debate continues.

Confirmation

Some exponents of confirmation sometimes appeal to Scripture. B. Neunheuser declared, "Three New Testament texts make it certain that a laying on hands for the imparting of the Spirit existed in the earliest apostolic times. These texts are Acts 8:4-20; 19:1-7; and Heb 6:1-6" (*Baptism and Confirmation* [Freiburg: Herder; London: Burns and Oates, 1964], 42). Philip administered baptism (Acts 8:38), and the Ephesians had been baptized by John the Baptist (Acts 19). But against A. J. Mason, L. S. Thornton, G. Dix, and Neunheuser, G. W. H. Lampe, E. C. Whitaker, and J. D. G. Dunn have decisively shown that such exegesis is anachronistic and invalid. Indeed, although there is evidence that confirmation went back to earliest times among the Church Fathers, there is no clear evidence or consensus about any NT origins or its theological significance or timing.

A variety of practices of the laying on of hands and anointing occurred in subapostolic times and in the early Fathers. In Tertullian the rite appears to be part of baptism (*On Baptism* 8), but some argue that they are separate rites in Cyprian (*Epistles* 70; 74). In the West confirmation was separated from baptism. In the East it was more directly related to baptism, but could be administered by the priest, not necessarily the bishop. Its theological significance is disputed, and Dunn and many others reject the notion that the rite conveys the gift of the Holy Spirit, on analogy with ordination.

At the Reformation the 1552 *Book of Common Prayer* prescribed that the bishop should pray that the candidate may "daily increase in Thy Holy Spirit more and more." Aquinas declared that it was instituted by Christ, and was one of the seven sacraments (*Su Th* 3, qu. 72). Luther and Calvin insisted, by contrast, that the rite was not scriptural; Luther called it "monkey business" (*Affenspiel*) and mumbo jumbo (*Glaukelwerk*), although in most Lutheran and Anglican churches it is regarded as a personal and public endorsement or confirmation of baptismal vows. The admission of children to communion prior to confirmation has, however, largely reduced the significance of confirmation for many Anglicans.

Congar, Yves M. J.

Yves M. J. Congar (1904-1995) stands among the half-dozen best-known and most influential Roman Catholic theologians of the twentieth century. He greatly influenced Vatican II (1962-1965), and is especially known for his ecclesiology, theology of tradition, theology of the Holy Spirit, and ecumenism. He entered the Dominican Order in Paris in 1925; he was awarded his doctorate for work on the unity of the church according to Aquinas. He also worked on Johann A. Möhler, and was influenced by the Catholic philosopher Jacques Maritain and the Dominican theologian Réynold Garrigou-Lagrange. He was ordained priest in 1930. Like Balthasar, he became attracted to Barth's theology, especially on the sovereignty of God, divine grace, and his defense against liberalism. In 1937 he visited England, where Michael Ramsey introduced him to the Anglican tradition. He was drafted into the French army as a chaplain in 1939, and was a prisoner of war from 1940 to 1945. After attempts to escape, he was imprisoned in the notorious Colditz, where he came to know many Protestants. He had already written his first book, *Divine Christendom*, in 1937 (Eng. 1939), and in 1958 Pope Pius XII criticized his alleged "false irenicism." When he openly supported the worker-priest movement, he was explicitly forbidden to teach. This difficult period abruptly changed, however, when John XXIII was elected pope in 1958. He appointed Congar as a specialist theologian in preparation for Vatican II, where he made significant contributions on revelation, ecumenism, and mission. Congar also influenced Karol Wojtyla (the future Pope John Paul II).

Congar was an ardent advocate of the ecumenical movement, and had criticized the papacy and Roman Curia. He also criticized ultramontanism and clerical pomp and privilege, and encouraged the role of laypeople in the church, especially in his work *Lay People in the Church* (Fr. 1953; Eng. 1957). He advocated ordaining laypeople as priests where there was real need. In 1960 and in 1963 he published *La Tradition et les traditions* in two volumes, one dealing with history and the other with theology (Eng. *Tradition and Traditions* [New York: Macmillan, 1966]). Many regard this as his most important publication. The recovery of tradition is a real, living, self-communication of God. It is not a mere collection of conventions and customs. This stands as one of the distinctive contributions of Vatican II. Congar published a shorter account of the subject in English as *The Meaning of Tradition* (New York: Hawthorn Books, 1964; rev. San Francisco: Ignatius, 2011). He also published *True and False Reform in the Church* (Fr. 1963; Eng. 1964).

During this period Congar also turned to the doctrine of the Holy Spirit, and later produced *I Believe in the Holy Spirit,* 3 vols. (Fr. 1979-1980; Eng. New York: Seabury Press; London: Chapman, 1983). This combines solid theology with pastoral sensitivity, providing biblical and historical material in volume 1, and material on the relation between the Spirit and everyday life in volume 2. He avoids the dualism between the institutional and charismatic, and argues, "The Church is made by the Spirit" (2:5); and "The Spirit is the principle of love" (2:67). He is very supportive of the Renewal Movement, but recognizes that "the style of ... meetings is not acceptable to everyone" (2:156). Later he produced *The Word and the Spirit* (Fr. 1984; Eng. 1986). There followed two books on Vatican II, and *Fifty Years of Catholic Theology* (Eng. 1988).

This does not provide a complete list of Congar's books, and he published numerous articles. In 1936 he launched a series of ecclesiological inquiries under the title *Unam Sanctam,* or "one holy (church)," from the creeds, of which his work *Divided Christendom* constituted the first volume. In his book *The Mystery of the Church* (Fr. 1941; Eng. 1960) he stressed the continuity between Aquinas and the Church Fathers, and gathered material from Aquinas for a theology of mission in his own times. In *True and False Reform,* he expounded the holiness of the church on the basis of its divine call and origin, and the sinfulness on the basis of its human composition. This reform, he argued, must follow from "a return to the sources," a phrase, Aidan Nichols notes, borrowed from Charles Péguy (Nichols, *Yves Congar* [Wilton, Conn.: Morehouse-Barlow, 1989], 10). Congar sought changes that would not disrupt the church and its history.

In his *Lay People in the Church* (London: Chapman, 1959), Congar aimed to produce a theology of the laity. He wrote that although Greek *laikos* is not found in the Bible, the Greek *laos* occurs frequently, often in contrast to the Gentiles, to denote the people of God. The Greek *klēros* denotes "lot" or "heritage." But by the time of Origen and Cyprian in the third century, a fixed pattern of laity, clerics, and monks had been established (*Lay People,* 1-7). Much later in the history of the church, "the laity, concerned in temporal affairs, have no part in the sphere of sacred things" (10). From the eleventh to the sixteenth century the church was often divided into the pope, bishops, priests, and monks, and on the other side the emperor, princes, knights, peasants, men, and women (11). The Reformers rightly insisted that Christ did not have two "bodies" (12). But after the eleventh century, a "deep change" took place (14). Nevertheless, the NT insists on "the inheritance of the saints in the light" (Col. 1:12). Congar concludes, "Lay people are called to the same end as clergy or monks" (16). This does not mean exclusion from the affairs of the world. The clerical condition may become "full of danger" (17), as laity gather more tasks to themselves.

This should not mean a counterreaction that exaggerates "the communal or democratic tendency" (33). Congar rejects "anti-hierarchical spiritual sects," "individualist-representative" theories, or "strict Congregationalist premises" (45). But the laity nevertheless share in the kingly, priestly, and prophetic anointing of Jesus Christ (61, 66). John in the Apocalypse calls all Christians "kings and priests" (67; cf. Rev. 1:6; 3:21; 5:10). But the laity "exercise this kingly and priestly ministry at the 'suture' of Church and World" (Nichols, *Yves Congar,* 10). Christ's kingship is "universal," including the world (Congar, *Lay People,* 75). Thus there is still a "duality of orders" (77). Continuity exists between "human work of this world" and the kingdom of God (81). Thus there are "the acts of a holy Christian life" (127). Congar adds, "In early Christianity ... the whole Christian community, lay people included, is said to celebrate or offer the Lord's sacrifice" (203). He concludes, "The faithful are called to live 'in the world'"; but they are not to be "of the world" (380). The laity are called to be holy.

Tradition and Traditions was written as Vatican II was proceeding. Congar had by then given increasing attention to the Holy Spirit and his gifts to the church. The concept of tradition was firmly rooted in the Scriptures; it was certainly not a "rival" source, as some had claimed at the Reformation. Tradition is indeed the gospel. Congar opposed the modernist notion of an evolutionary theory of doctrine. The Church Fathers constituted a valuable but secondary "source" of tradition. Like Gadamer, Congar insists, "Tradition always implies learning from others" (*The Meaning of Tradition,* 3). "For every Catholic, Scripture ... enjoys pride of place, since its value is absolute" (4). The basis of appeal to tradition is *ressourcement* (a return to the sources) (6). It does not merely convey formal conventions. It is a living "handing on," as Gregory of Nyssa calls it (29). At the heart it is *apostolic* tradition. Admittedly, from the third to the fifth century the Church Fathers spoke of "traditions" (plural) such as Lenten fasts, baptismal rites, prayer facing east, the sign of the cross (37). But these are all "secondary" details. The apostolic tradition is not secret or merely oral. Often these traditions (plural) "have no connection with Scripture" (39). The Reformers realized this. This may look reassuring to Protestants, until Congar addresses such phenomena as the immaculate conception of the Virgin Mary and the doctrine of her bodily assumption. If these were "alien" to Scripture, Congar maintains, they would not belong to authentic tradition. But the Roman magisterium claims that these doctrines "were not alien to formal Scriptural statements" (106), even though they are not explicit in Scripture. Congar maintains that they supplement and complete tradition. He argues for a synthesis between Scripture and what comes from related sources. He concludes, "The texts of the *Magisterium* are next in importance immediately after the Holy Scriptures, at least with regard to its major pronouncements" (130).

Congar includes within tradition the transmission of a task, especially the task of mission. Tradition also reflects the life of God, so that this task shares in God's will for mission. The ultimate source or subject of tradition is God, and in Jesus Christ we see especially the mission of the Word. The Holy Spirit brings about unity and continuity in the handing on of tradition. Thus tradition makes the gospel "ever new" for each generation. Nichols writes, "The Church is the immanent subject of Tradition, just as the Spirit is the transcendent subject" (*Yves Congar*, 31). The role of the whole community of God's people shows "togetherness." In Russian Orthodox language, it shows *sobornost*. Tradition is like the flowing river of water promised in the Fourth Gospel. In practice, it also facilitates hermeneutics, or interpretation of Scripture. Its historical expressions of truth are called "monuments," such as the liturgy, the Church Fathers, and "ordinary expressions of the Christian life" (Congar, *Tradition and Traditions*, 355; *The Meaning of Tradition*, 129-56).

In *I Believe in the Holy Spirit,* Congar argues that the Holy Spirit is known by his *effects*. He also claims that the Holy Spirit empties himself of his own personality in *kenosis,* where J. Fison and others often speak of his self-effacement. Congar speaks of "the two missions" of the apostles and of the Holy Spirit (2:42). He appeals to John 13:16, 20; 17:18; 14:16, 26; 15:26. He also insists that we should not put revelation and experience against each other; they are complementary.

On the OT Congar accepts that gifts of the Spirit are temporary and for a given task, but they always bring forward God's purpose in history. This occurs through the prophets, through the messianic figure, and through cosmic wisdom. Congar addresses the gift of the Spirit to judges, warriors, prophets, and wise men in 1:5-14. These include Othniel (Judg. 3:10), Gideon (6:34), Jephthah (11:29), and Samson (13:25; 14:6, 19), among others. Congar then writes, "The Spirit has effects in man, and brings about an experience of seeing and wisdom" (*I Believe*, 1:7). The NT witness begins with the public ministry of Jesus, including his conception, birth, and baptism (1:15-19). Congar then considers Paul, Luke-Acts, and John (*I Believe*, 1:29-63). In John, Jesus gives, as well as receives, the Holy Spirit. Congar then turns to history, in which he includes the mutual love of the Father and Son in Augustine, the Middle Ages, the Reformers, George Fox, Pietism, and Edward Irving (1:85-150).

Volume 2 begins with "the 'two missions,'" the Holy Spirit as the principle of Catholicity, and the Spirit and the church's holiness (2:5-66). The church is a holy temple (Eph. 2:21) and a pure bride (2 Cor. 11:2); the Spirit sustains "the communion of Saints" (*I Believe,* 2:59-60). He writes further, "The Spirit is the principle of love and realizes our lives as children of God in the form of a Gift" (2:67). The church, he repeats, is God's temple (2:80; 1 Cor. 3:16). Sometimes his indwelling relates to mystical experience. The life of the Spirit is a filial one (*I Believe,* 2:104), and he rightly sees a frame of reference in the "already and not yet" of eschatology (2:106-8). He prompts prayer and provokes sanctification. Part 3 of this volume concerns renewal. Renewal in the Spirit, he points out, has "spread like wildfire in the traditional churches" (2:149). It is not merely compensation for a depressed and humiliating way of life; it is a worldwide movement. It represents "a rising up of vitality from the source into the present" (2:150). We need both institutional and charismatic emphases. The renewal movement can also enliven the sacraments. Congar welcomes free prayer meetings. He appeals to Cardinal Suenens. He does not disparage reason, but sees the perils of an "exclusively organized and cerebral religion" (2:154), against which Pentecostalism warns us. Congar, however, expresses one serious reservation. "I do not believe that Renewal, in the form in which it appears now, can be extended to the whole Church" (2:156). First, this is because "the style of its meeting is not acceptable to everyone" (2:156). Love will avoid imposing these manifestations on everyone. Second, we need to retain a full theology of the Trinity (2:158). Charismata must serve the whole church. Like Barth, Congar is cautious about overconcern with the phenomena, rather than with that to which they point (2:168).

The third volume of this work reflects mainly on the double procession of the Holy Spirit, and the *filioque* clause, which divides East from West. He is sympathetic with Lossky, and believes, rightly, that "Common understanding is possible." He looks to Gregory of Nyssa as one way forward. The two formulations, he asserts, are "equivalent and complementary." Congar may well have done more than almost anyone to reconcile Catholic and Protestant perspectives on major doctrines. (*See also* **Double Procession;** *Filioque;* **Liturgy; Vatican II.**)

Reading: Yves Congar, O.P., *Lay People in the Church* (London: Chapman, 1959); Yves Congar, *I Believe in the Holy Spirit,* 3 vols. (New York: Seabury Press; London: Chapman, 1983); Yves Congar, *The Meaning of Tradition* (San Francisco: Ignatius, 2011); Yves Congar, *True and False Reform* (Minnesota: Glazier, 2011); T. MacDonald, *The Ecclesiology of Yves Congar* (Lanham, Md.: University Press of America, 1984); Aidan Nichols, O.P., *Yves Congar* (Wilton, Conn.: Morehouse-Barlow, 1989).

Conscience

For the Greek word *syneidēsis* Hebrew has no special word but usually uses *lēbh,* "heart," and Latin uses *conscientia,* "knowledge with." (On the OT uses, *see* **Anthropology; Heart.**) Wolff calls "heart" the most important word in the vocabulary of OT anthropology (*Anthropology of the Old Testament* [London: SCM, 1974], 40). It occurs nearly 600 times in the OT, or 850 times if cognate forms are included. Often it denotes the core of a person's being. But often it also has moral overtones akin to conscience. Hence God tells Moses concerning Pharaoh, "I will harden his heart, so that he will not let the people go" (Exod. 4:21). The "hardening" of Pharaoh's heart occurs in Exod. 7:3, 13, 14, 22; 8:15, 19, 32; 9:12, 34-35; 10:1, 20, 27; 11:10; 14:4. In Josh. 11:20, "It was the LORD's doing to harden" the hearts of enemy kings. In these passages the equivalent English would perhaps be "without conscience" or "obstinate." The word is even more akin to conscience in 1 Sam. 24:5, "David was stricken to the heart because he had cut off a corner of Saul's cloak." BDB offers ten distinct uses of *lēbh*, of which the fifth is "conscience" (1 Sam 24:5) and the sixth is "moral character," for example, God tries the heart (Ps. 17:3; Jer. 12:3) or refines hearts (Ps 26:2; BDB 525). The later medieval debate about whether conscience stems from affection or will (as Franciscans maintained) or from reflection and reason (as Aquinas and the Dominicans argued) would be subsumed under Hebrew *lēbh*.

The NT uses *syneidēsis*, which most scholars render "conscience," although some translate it as "self-awareness," in most parts of 1 Corinthians 8–10. The term has a long history of research as R. Jewett has demonstrated in *Paul's Anthropological Terms* ([Leiden: Brill, 1970], 402-46). H. J. Holzmann (1911) argues that the term is borrowed from Hellenism, but its *use* there is broader than in the NT. The basic point is simply that in the Greek, Latin, and NT writers "conscience" denotes a knowing *(-eidēsis)* with *(syn-)*, in the sense of scrutinizing one's own attitudes and conduct. Thus, as Spicq (1938) points out, in 1 Cor. 4:4 Paul says that he knows (Gk. *sunoida*) nothing against himself. Bultmann (1948) and Dupont (1948) also note affinities at times with its wider Greek and Stoic usage. But a new stage in research began with C. A. Pierce, *Conscience in the New Testament* (London: SCM, 1955), esp. 13-20 and 111-30, and J. N. Sevenster, *Paul and Seneca* (Leiden: Brill, 1961), 84-102. Pierce strongly argues that the NT dependence on Stoicism rests on "insufficient evidence" (15). It has nothing to do with a "divine voice" (13-22). Conscience in the NT denotes "the pain consequent upon the inception of an act believed to be wrong" (22). Thus he urges that in 1 Cor. 8:7, 10, 12, the "strong" have an undersensitive conscience while the "weak" have an oversensitive one. Like "the little ones" in Matt. 18:5-6, they can be easily hurt and damaged. D. E. H. Whitely endorses this: conscience is retrospective; we know that we have done wrong (*The Theology of St. Paul* [Oxford: Blackwell, 1964, 1971], 44 and 210).

A third phase of research began in 1967 with Margaret Thrall's modification to Pierce's approach. She argues that he was largely correct, but that he had not accounted for passages in which conscience was more positive and even prospective ("The Pauline Use of *Syneidēsis*," *NTS* 14 [1967]: 118-25). R. A. Horsley (1978) and P. W. Gooch (1987) not only agree, but also consider whether "self-awareness" would promote a better translation in 1 Corinthians 8–10. The classic study now becomes that of H.-J. Eckstein, *Der Begriff Syneidēsis bei Paulus* (Tübingen: Mohr, 1983), alongside the studies of Horsley, Gooch, and Gardner (1994). Eckstein endorses Pierce's work on inflicting damaging blows on the "weak," and the relative indifference of the "strong." This self-awareness is too narrowly vested in self-interest, at the expense of the weak.

Several passages outside 1 Corinthians witness to "a good conscience" (Acts 23:1; 24:16; Rom. 9:1; 2 Cor. 1:12; 1 Tim. 1:5, 19; 3:9; 1 Pet. 3:16). Some passages are neutral (Rom. 13:5; 2 Cor. 4:2); some speak of a corrupted or distorted conscience (Titus 1:15; Heb. 10:22; cf. 1 Cor. 8:7). Certainly it is universally agreed that *conscience may be fallible,* and is *relative to* learned attitudes.

In the history of theology, Franciscans regarded conscience as an expression of feeling and will, while Aquinas and the Dominicans regarded it as a cognitive and reflective capacity. Thomas devoted a section to conscience in *Summa Theologiae* (1a, qu. 79, art. 13). He wrote, "Conscience may be resolved into *'cum alio scientia,'* i.e. knowledge applied to an individual case.... Conscience is said to witness, bind, or to incite, and also to accuse, torment, or rebuke." But Thomas also used the unexpected term *synderesis,* taken from Jerome, to denote something slightly different. Most scholars today ascribe this term in Jerome to a scribal error. The Reformers, however, tended to stress only the retrospective or consequent function of conscience in a way similar to Pierce's analysis of 1 Corinthians 8–10. On the other hand, they also spoke of a "good conscience" as virtually equivalent to assurance. Although the biblical writings do not explicitly promote this, the Radical Reformers often regarded conscience as the voice of the Spirit perhaps because of the egalitarian rejection of church tradition. The Quakers associated it with the "inner light." Samuel Clarke continued the Thomist theme of conscience as reason, and Joseph Butler saw it as a faculty of the mind, or as a natural moral sense. Outside the Christian tradition, some insist that it is simply a moral habit, or a personal conflict with social convention. But Christians rank it more highly, even though virtually all agree that it can be fallible and requires teaching and education.

Reading: P. D. Gooch, "'Conscience' in 1 Corinthians 8 and 10," *NTS* 33 (1987): 244-54; D. Langston, *Conscience and Other Virtues: From Bonaventure to MacIntyre* (University Park: Pennsylvania State University Press, 2001); C. A. Pierce, *Conscience in the New Testament* (London: SCM, 1955); A. C. Thiselton, *First Corinthians* (Grand Rapids: Eerdmans, 2000), 612-61.

Constantinople, Council of

Although known as the second "ecumenical" council, the Council of Constantinople (381) was attended for the most part by the Fathers of the Eastern Church. The emperor Theodosius I convened it to resolve the Arian controversy, as well as Apollinarianism and the debate with Pneumatomachi or "Tropici." One hundred fifty orthodox bishops and thirty-six from the Pneumatomachi took part. Gregory of Nazianzus was its leading orthodox theologian, and he heavily relied on the work of Athanasius. (*See* **Christology: History of Thought; Holy Spirit: The Spirit in Historical Theology**). The creed used in most churches is drawn from the Nicene-Constantinopolitan Council.

Contingent

Contingent propositions or objects are those that might or might not have occurred, in contrast to logically necessary propositions or beings. To claim that the world is contingent means that in principle the world might not have existed. A favorite philosophical example is the statement "It is raining," which might or might not be the case. On the other hand, "a triangle has three sides" and "water boils at 100° Centigrade" are logically necessary statements because their truth is built into their definitions, and they are true a priori. For theologians, statements about "cause" are contingent when applied to finite or created beings, but necessary when applied to God as first cause. Among philosophers the term "contingent" goes back to Aristotle, and is implied by the distinction in Aquinas between substance and accidents (*see* **Lord's Supper**). Leibniz and Lessing applied "contingent" to truths of history, in contrast to "necessary" truths of reasons (*see* **A Posteriori; Biblical Criticism; Lessing, Gotthold Ephraim**).

Cosmological Argument

The cosmological argument for the existence of God has always had widespread popular appeal. In spite of sophisticated theories from physicists, it is often popularly argued that the world cannot have come from nothingness, but must have had an ultimate cause. Such an argument was formulated by Plato and ancient Greeks, by Maimonides and Jewish thinkers, by al-Kindi and Islamic thinkers, and by Thomas Aquinas and many other Christian philosophers and theologians, including Duns Scotus. An Islamic formulation, known as the *kalām* cosmological argument, runs as follows: (i) whatever has a beginning of existence must have a cause; (ii) the universe began to exist; (iii) the universe must have been caused to exist. In most formulations the issue turns on the nature of cause, and whether an infinite regress of caused causes would be possible. In popular thought the counterreply arises: If we can call who or what caused the universe "God," who or what caused God? Almost all versions of the argument concede that in the case of the universe and of everything in the world, we know only of *caused* causes.

Most arguments therefore distinguish between a free, intelligent, and first cause and a caused cause, which is part of a causal chain of events. Aquinas made such a distinction between a caused cause and a first cause, or, in his language, between a moved mover and an unmoved mover, or Prime Mover. Avicenna drew on Aristotle for the distinction between contingent and necessary causes. Objects in the world have contingent existence; they might or might not be. But we cannot have an infinite chain of contingent objects, which might or might not be. They must derive in the end from what exists of *necessity*. Others besides Aquinas formulated this argument, but Aquinas formulated different versions in his famous "Five Ways." He declared, "There are five ways in which one can prove God" (*Su Th* 1, qu. 2, art. 3, reply). "The first and most obvious way is based on change."

The shift from causality to change or movement is the least easy to understand today, but was considered the most powerful and convincing "way" in the thirteenth century, mainly in the light of Aristotle. Hence his discussion becomes technical, referring to issues in medieval and Aristotelian philosophy. Aquinas states: "Anything in process of change is being changed by something else ... because ... things in process of change ... do not yet have that perfection towards which they move.... To cause change is to bring into being what was previously only able to be [potentiality], and this can be done by something that already is [actuality]. Thus fire, which is *actually* hot, causes wood, which is *able* to be hot, to become actually hot, and in this way causes change in the wood.... The same thing cannot be ... both actually *x* and potentially *x*" (qu. 2, art. 3, reply). Some call this the kinetological argument. Philosophically it rests on Aristotle's contrast between *the potential and actual*. Aquinas concludes: "We must stop somewhere, otherwise there will be no first cause of change.... [This] everybody understands [as] God" (qu. 2, art. 3, reply). In other words, what is complete (i.e., God) is the first cause or Prime Mover of whatever is incomplete (the everyday world). The other "ways" are less technical.

The second way is "based on the nature of causation," as popular formulations today express this (qu. 2, art. 3). We can never observe "something causing itself." It cannot "precede" itself. A string of causes cannot be infinite, but must imply a first cause. The third way depends, like the *kalām* argument, on the contrast between contingency and necessity. We find contingent beings "springing up and dying away, thus they are sometimes 'in being' and sometimes not. But *everything* cannot be like this, for a thing that *need* not be, once *was not*. But, if *everything* need not be, once upon a time there was *nothing*" (qu. 2, art. 3). We are forced to suppose that there must be a necessary Being, or God. Such a Being possesses aseity. Duns Scotus reproduced a formulation of the argument that closely reflects the third way, arguing also from efficient cause.

The fourth and fifth "ways" of Aquinas are not strictly versions of the cosmological argument. The fourth way argues from degrees of being *(ex gradibus qui in rebus)*. This again appeals directly to Aristotle. The fifth is a formulation of the teleological argument from "the guidedness of nature" *(ex gubernatione rerum)*. Everything intelligent works toward a goal or end *(ad finem)*. He writes, "An arrow, for example, requires an archer." Ultimately, "this we call 'God'" (art. 3).

Samuel Clarke (1675-1729) defended the cosmological argument in the light of Sir Isaac Newton's laws of motion. John Locke also defended the argument. But David Hume attacked and challenged it. In strictly empirical terms we cannot actually observe causation, but only "contiguity" or "constant conjunction." In strictly empirical terms we can observe only habit, convention, or regularity, which we mentally construe as "cause." Hume concedes this (*A Treatise of Human Nature* [1739; reprint, Oxford: OUP, 1978], 79-94). Immanuel Kant pressed this attack further. Space, time, and cause, he argued, are all categories imposed by the mind in order to make sense of things.

Søren Kierkegaard offers a more theological counterargument. What kind of "God," he asks, would really be *God* if his existence could be *proved*? If "God" can be inferred from a chain of causes or inferences, would not this imply that God is part of the world? But if he is not "within" the world, can we expect to infer his existence by purely rational or inferential argument? Can we dispense with the need for *revelation*? The misguided attempt to "prove" God, he declared, is "a most shameless affront" to God. This resonates with Kant's argument about the difference between "caused cause" and "uncaused cause" or "First Cause." A logical syllogism is valid only if the terms used in the major premise and minor premise and conclusion have exactly the same value or identity. If we argue from a chain of *caused causes* to the need for an *uncaused cause,* this would clearly not be the case. If the first cause is "above" the causal chain, would it not be outside it?

Of the three major arguments for the existence of God, the ontological argument is an a priori argument, while the other arguments, the cosmological (and teleological), are a posteriori arguments. The former is in effect analytical, that is, independent of our experience of the everyday world, while the latter draws inferences from our daily experience. Christian theologians tend to belong to one of three theological groups. Some urge that the arguments cannot function as *arguments,* but simply assert or imply the transcendence of God. Indeed, they may follow Barth in dismissing them *as arguments,* which would amount to "natural theology." A middle group may insist also that these are not valid as *positive arguments,* but negatively show that theistic or Christian *belief is not unreasonable.* A third group suggests that these arguments show the *probability* of the existence of God, if not more. Often these last are followers of Aquinas, or neo-Thomists, for example, Herbert McCabe (in *New Blackfriars* 61 [1980]); and Elizabeth Anscombe (in *Analysis* 34 [1974]), who exposed fallacies in Hume's conception of causality. Alvin Plantinga and W. L. Craig also defend the argument. (*See also* **Aquinas, Thomas; Contingent; Necessary.**)

Reading: W. L. Craig, *The Cosmological Argument from Plato to Leibniz* (London: Macmillan, 1980); B. Davies, *Philosophy of Religion* (Oxford: OUP, 2000), 179-244; A. Plantinga, *Warranted Christian Belief* (Oxford: OUP, 2000); W. Rowe, *The Cosmological Argument* (Princeton and London: Princeton University Press, 1975).

Counter-Reformation

The Counter-Reformation is usually dated from about 1540 to 1640. In 1540 Pope Paul III confirmed St. Ignatius Loyola's foundation of the Jesuits, who became a spearhead for Catholicism in Europe, and a missionary force in America and the East. In 1562-1563 the Council of Trent was held, which confirmed the position of the pope. Discipline and efficiency within the Curia at Rome improved. Spanish improvements to church discipline were supported by the Spanish Inquisition, where Philip II became the strongest military power of this era.

Covenant

A covenant denotes a binding agreement between two parties, often between God and humankind, but sometimes between human persons, nations, or tribes.

In the latter case "treaty" often does duty for "covenant." The covenant between God and humankind, as W. Eichrodt comments, is a declaration of the terms of the relationship, so that people know where they stand. Covenant with God in the Old Testament is made between God and Noah (Gen. 6:18; 9:9, 11-16); between God and Abraham (15:18; 17:2, 4, 7, 9, 19); between God and the patriarchs, Abraham, Isaac, and Jacob (Exod. 2:24; 6:3-4); between God and Israel through Moses (19:5; 24:8; 31:16; 34:10); and between God and his people in the "new covenant" (Jer. 31:31). The New Testament church saw itself as heir to the covenant (Acts 3:25; Heb. 8:6, 8, 10; 10:16; 13:20). A covenant was made between David and Jonathan (1 Sam. 18:3); between husband and wife (Mal. 2:14); and between tribes (Judg. 2:2; 1 Sam. 11:1).

The normal Hebrew word is *berîth,* "covenant, treaty, alliance, agreement"; its derivation is uncertain. The Greek equivalent *diathēkē* means either will or testament, or covenant. Heb. 9:15-17 may provide a play on both meanings; see also Gal. 3:15, 17. Both meanings presuppose *promise* and *commitment.* God shows his grace in being willing to bind himself, pledge himself, and make promises, by which he voluntarily chooses to limit his range of actions. God's willingness to enter into a covenant shows that he wills a relationship with his people. Since this relationship has explicit terms, this provides God's people with assurance. They may believe his promises. At times in the Old Testament, opportunities arose to renew the covenant with God.

Covenants may include signs or guarantees of the covenant promise. The phenomenon of the rainbow became such a sign for Noah; the Passover became a sign for Israel (renewed in the Passover seder); and the dominical sacraments of baptism and the Lord's Supper became signs of the covenant for Christians. A covenant may have a mediator, who, for Christians, is Jesus Christ (Heb. 8:6). In the climax of the Holy Communion service, Christians hear, "This cup is the new covenant in my blood" (1 Cor. 11:25; cf. Mark 14:24; Luke 22:20). The covenant and its relation to *testament* are discussed in Hebrews 8:6–9:22.

In the history of theology, covenant became less prominent in many Church Fathers than it was in Scripture, although Augustine contrasts the old and new covenants in *The Spirit and the Letter* 19.32–20.35. In the eleventh century the baptismal covenant was extended beyond Scripture, and applied to loyalty to the pope. At the Reformation, Luther saw God as present in the sacraments not because of the sacraments themselves, but because they were effective signs of covenant grace (Luther, *The Pagan Servitude of the Church* [1520] 2.2). Zwingli agreed that the sacraments were "signs" of the covenant, but separated the sign in effect from what it might signify (Zwingli, *On Baptism,* sect. 1). The place of covenant in Calvin is debated, but it is implied in his work on promise (*Institutes* 2.9-10) and in his sermons on Deuteronomy and on Jeremiah 31. The covenant of grace is featured in the Westminster Confession and in the writings of many Puritans. In modern theology Karl Barth revived the notion of covenant, seeing it as the basis of creation, and preferring the term "covenant history" to "salvation history" (*CD* III/1, chap. 9, sect. 41).

Reading: W. J. Dumbrell, *Covenant and Creation* (Carlisle: Paternoster, 1984); W. Eichrodt, *Theology of the Old Testament*, vol. 1 (London: SCM, 1961), esp. 36-69; E. W. Nicholson, *God and His People* (Oxford: Clarendon, 1986).

Cox, Harvey

Harvey Cox (b. 1929) is emeritus professor at Harvard Divinity School. In 1957 he was ordained as a Baptist minister, and rose to fame in 1965 with his book *The Secular City* (Penguin ed. 1968), which sold over a million copies. He wrote, "The idea of the secular city exemplifies maturation and responsibility. Secularisation denotes the removal of juvenile dependence from every level of a society; urbanization designates the fashioning of new patterns of human reciprocity" (109). The secular city, he declared, is a good symbol of the kingdom of God. This may owe something to Dietrich Bonhoeffer's *Letters and Papers from Prison*, and certainly conveys the mood of much theology in the 1960s. From 1965 until his retirement from teaching at Harvard in 2009, he wrote a number of books, including *The Feast of Fools* (1969), *The Seduction of the Spirit* (1973), *Fire from Heaven* (1994), and *The Future of Faith* (2009).

The Seduction of the Spirit (London: Wildwood House, 1974) still breathes the spirit of the times, namely, a surprising degree of cynicism and skepticism, almost reminiscent of Nietzsche. He writes, "The theologian is the 'demythologizer,' the exposer of fraudulent meanings.... He is ... jester or holy fool ... who pricks pretences and shouts out ... that the king has no clothes" (319). But in *Fire from Heaven* (Cambridge, Mass.: Da Capo Press, 1995) he acknowledges, "It is secularity, not spirituality, that may be heading for extinction" (xv). He examines the worldwide phenomenon of global Pentecostalism. He surveys the movement from Seymour and Parham to the present. He respects the Pentecostal "widespread appeal" (81), even though he is understandably critical of the past "pattern of division and proliferation" (78). He understands the appeal of what he terms "primal speech," "primal piety," and "primal hope," especially for those who are young or black. He is at times critical, but always respectful, and no longer cynical, even if he does not yet warm to the established traditions of the church. This is more a symptom of the positive values of the 1990s than of much of the 1960s and 1970s.

Cranmer, Thomas

Thomas Cranmer (1489-1556) was educated at Cambridge, ordained as a fellow of Jesus College in 1523, and became archbishop of Canterbury in 1533. He was probably Henry VIII's chief agent in overthrowing the papacy in England. In 1533 he also annulled Catherine's marriage to Henry. But Cranmer was motivated by theological conviction, on the basis of biblical and patristic texts, and not simply by service to the king. He assembled a large range of key texts on Reformation principles, and in 1528 wrote to refute Zwingli on the Lord's Supper. Under Edward VI he introduced worship in the vernacular in the two versions of the *Book of Common Prayer,* in 1549 and 1552 respectively. The 1549 version still reflected compromises, but the 1552 book has been called "the high-water mark of Protestantism" (*see Book of Common Prayer*). He consulted closely with Continental Reformers, including Martin Bucer and Peter Martyr. His aim was to transform "the Mass" into "Holy Communion," and to promote worship "understanded of the people." Mary Tudor succeeded Edward VI in 1553, and at first spared Cranmer's life. But in the end he was tried for treason and burned at the stake in Oxford in 1556.

Creation

It is unavoidable that this entry will overlap with the article on God, and even repeat some initial comments. Both entries need to stress, for example, that God chose to create the universe and other orders of created being *out of love,* and to go forth, as it were, out of himself to enter into relationships with the *other* (*see* **Other, Otherness**). The world is "other" than God; it is not an emanation; God remains transcendent as well as immanent. Creation is also an act of *creativity and love* on the part of the *whole Holy Trinity:* the Father, the Son, and the Holy Spirit. All this is expanded in the entry **God**.

Nevertheless, certain points must be added, which are less explicit in the other entry. Creation is not only an act of the past but it also signifies the *present dependence* of all created beings and things on God. It is not merely a comment about origins, but also a comment about continuous dependence. If God were to withdraw his creative life and power, all creation would disintegrate and perish. As J. Moltmann declares, the continual outflow of the divine Spirit forms (Heb. *bārā'*) humankind: "the Spirit preserves it, makes it live, and renews it" (*God in Creation* [London: SCM, 1985], 10). He is the fountain of life: "Everything that is, and lives, manifests the presence of this wellspring" (11). But God is not to be understood as if he himself were part of the world; he dwells within it, but is also beyond it.

The often-used phrase *creatio ex nihilo,* moreover, absolutely excludes dualism and stresses monotheism. God alone is Creator. Unlike the myths of pagan religions, God did not have to overcome some hostile or chaotic force to create the world. Further, "matter" and the physical are not evil, as most strands of gnosticism and many pagan religions, and some Greek philosophers, maintain. God created man in his bodily existence in his own image.

It has long been debated whether God created the world as an act in time. But, as Augustine declared, God did not create the world "in" time, but created it "with" time. Everything that God has created, including the world and the universe, participates in time. Another well-worn debate is the alleged priority of history (in Hebrew thought) over nature (in Greek thought). While there is some truth in this, as J. Barr among others has shown, this should not be exaggerated. God is Lord both of nature and of history. Third, the divine ordering of the world entails differentiation or distinction. The day is "separated" from night

(Gen. 1:14), and light from darkness (1:18). Fourth, it is clear that Genesis 1 is not intended to give a strictly chronological account of creation. The creation of "light" (1:3) and day and night (1:5) precedes the creation of the sun, moon, and stars (1:14-18). On the other hand, the general sequence is often said to match biological research, and broadly offers the sequence also suggested in the Babylonian creation myth *Enuma Elish,* and the Egyptian myth. But parallels abruptly cease when we compare their respective purposes. Pagan parallels reflect conflicts among deities, and some such preexisting material as the body of Tiamat, in contrast to the utterly monotheistic *creatio ex nihilo.* The words "without form and void" (Heb. *tōhū wābōhū*) signify only confusion, waste, and nothingness (Gen. 1:2). "Chaos" may be misleading.

Creation accounts may be found in the OT outside Gen. 1:1–2:7. Psalm 8 recalls God's founding of the earth (v. 1), the creation of the heavens (v. 3) and humankind (vv. 4-5), together with the gift of "dominion" over the animal world. This is part of bearing the image of God (vv. 6-8). The purpose of the account is mainly praise. Ps. 19:1-6 sees creation as an expression of the glory of God, and Ps. 24:1-2 recounts God's "founding" creation and his sovereignty over it. Several psalms recount the *present* significance of God's creation. In the NT creation is seen as the work of the whole Trinity. In Col. 1:16 Christ is Mediate Creator, and in 1:17 the coherent focus in whom "all things hold together" (Gk. *panta en autō sunestēken*). In 1 Cor. 8:6, "Through whom (Christ) are all things and through whom we exist," Paul regards Christ as Mediate Creator. Heb. 1:10 addresses Christ:

> "In the beginning, Lord, you founded the earth,
> and the heavens are the work of your hands."

John 1:3 declares, "All things came into being through him (Gk. *di' autou*), and without him not one thing came into being." Calvin wrote, "Without proceeding to his Providence, we cannot understand the full force of what is meant by God being the Creator" (*Institutes* 1.16.1). (*See also* **Gnosticism; God; Image of God.**)

Reading: B. W. Anderson, ed., *From Creation to New Creation* (Eugene, Ore.: Wipf and Stock, 2005); Z. Hayes, *The Gift of Being: A Theology of Creation* (Collegeville, Minn.: Liturgical Press, a Michael Glazier Book, 2001); J. Moltmann, *God in Creation* (London: SCM, 1985); H. Schwarz, *Creation* (Grand Rapids: Eerdmans, 2002).

Creationism

The term is used in two distinct ways. One meaning is the belief that God directly created each species, in contrast to using evolutionary processes. Perhaps its strongest argument is that natural selection appears to rest on random factors of chance. Its weakest is whether God's creative and providential power usually works through natural means or processes (e.g., medical healing), and especially whether the writer of the early chapters of Genesis intended to convey a scientific cosmology and literal or historical account of God's actions (*see* **Creation**). Creationism in a second sense denotes the belief that each person is created afresh in body and soul, in contrast to traducianism, which understands a person's body and soul to be transmitted from parents to children. Both views are represented in the Church Fathers and in Reformed theology, and are not formally regarded as dogmas in Catholicism. (*See also* **Traducianism**.)

Critical Realism

Critical realism is not to be equated with the "naïve" realism of the empiricists, nor does it fully accept the role of the mind in constructing and ordering reality, as in Kant and Fichte. Like realism, it asserts the existence of the external world. But in the process of knowing, critical realists, unlike realists, accept the modified role of a creative filtering by the mind. Most of all, critical realists reject positivism, as if the mind knows only brute facts. Critical realism also rejects value-free inquiry. Realism had reacted against the idealism of the nineteenth century (e.g., G. E. Moore's criticisms of F. H. Bradley). But critical realists also seek to avoid sheer representationalism. There are mind-dependent aspects of knowledge of the external world. In Christian theology one advocate often cited is Bernard Lonergan, who combines a theory of cognition, a theory of knowledge, and metaphysics. Knowledge involves experience, but also intelligence, reflection, and judgment (*Method in Theology* [New York: Herder and Herder, 1972]). Other practitioners often cited are Ben Meyer (*Critical Realism and the New Testament* [Allison Park, Pa.: Pickwick, 1989]). Many also cite the theology and historical method of N. T. Wright (*The New Testament and the People of God* [1996]). In philosophy critical realism is often associated with W. Sellars. "Reality" is wider-ranging than the mere sense-data of the empiricists. This becomes important for critical realists' approach to history.

Critical Theory

Critical theory was first developed by Max Horkheimer to denote the Frankfurt School of social theory and its revision of Marxism. The Frankfurt School was founded in 1929, and in addition to Horkheimer included Theodor Adorno, Herbert Marcuse, and, later, Jürgen Habermas. Although it retains its social dimension, the term "critical theory" can be used much more widely today. Sometimes it denotes sociology of knowledge. Characteristically it attacks positivism, empiricism, and value-free or value-neutral knowledge. It is often marked by an acceptance of historicality. The thinking of a person or of a group is radically conditioned by the historical situation and society into which it is born. Hence in theology there is considerable overlap with feminism, black theology, and hermeneutics. It attacks abstract or instrumental reason, and is especially concerned with legitimation based on convention, as are many postmodernists. Critical theory must not be confused with critical realism, which is quite different. The latter is associated with Bernard Lonergan, N. T. Wright, and others.

Cross

It is impossible to exaggerate the divide between the NT, Paul, and Luther, on one side, and popular misperceptions of the cross today, on the other. J. Moltmann, quoting H. J. Iwand, observed, "We have surrounded the cross with roses.... This is not the bleakness inherent in it placed in it by God.... Here God is non-God. Here is the triumph of death, the enemy" (*The Crucified God* [London: SCM, 1974], 36). He continues, "'The religion of the cross' is a contradiction in itself" (40); "the suffering of abandonment is overcome by the suffering of love, which is not afraid of what is sick and ugly" (46). Thus Paul writes, "The message about the cross is foolishness to those who are perishing, but to us who are being saved it is the power of God" (1 Cor. 1:18). Paul continues, "Christ crucified [is] a stumbling block [Gk. *skandalon*] to Jews and foolishness to Gentiles" (1:23). He defines the gospel as "the message about the cross." Christ redeemed us from the "curse" of the law, he declares, "by becoming a curse for us — for it is written, 'Cursed is everyone who hangs on a tree'" (Gal. 3:13; cf. Deut. 21:23).

Martin Hengel has done more than most writers to elaborate the significance of the cross and crucifixion. The cross was "particularly offensive" (*The Cross of the Son of God* [London: SCM, 1986], 94). It was "a sign of shame" (99). Crucified victims were "punished with limbs outstretched" (101), and Romans regarded it as "barbarian" (115), not fit for Roman citizens, but for slaves, terrorists, and rebels. To a Roman it was "a horrific, disgusting business" (129), not the subject of polite conversation. It was "a particularly cruel and shameful death, which as a rule was reserved for hardened criminals" (175). It satisfied "primitive lust for revenge and sadistic cruelty.... Crucifixion also represented his [Christ's] uttermost humiliation" (179).

Luther, therefore, contrasted the theology of the cross with theologies of glory. "The theologian of glory says bad is good, and good is bad; the theologian of the cross calls them by their proper name" (Heidelberg Disputation 21). The cross represents "the hinder parts of God" (20). Following Luther, D. Bonhoeffer wrote: "Either I determine the place in which I will find God or I allow God to determine the place where He will be found. If it is I who say where God will be, I will always find there a God who in some way corresponds to me, is agreeable to me.... But if it is God who says where He will be,... that place is the cross of Christ" (*Meditating on the Word* [Cambridge, Mass.: Cowley, 1986], 44-45). The cross, then, is not only the source of atonement, salvation, and redemption for all Christians; it also enacts a full-scale reversal of all values, as Paul explains in 1 Cor. 1:18–2:6 and elsewhere. (*See also* **Atonement**.)

Crossan, John Dominic

John Dominic Crossan (b. 1934) has no place, many would argue, in a *Companion to Christian Theology*. At best, they might suggest, he is a historian of Christian origins, and strictly an NT scholar, not a theologian. But his work has had considerable effect on Christian theology. An Irish American, he was ordained in the

Catholic Church in 1957, but has since resigned his orders. For twenty-five years he taught undergraduates comparative religion at DePaul University. However, in 1985 he cofounded (with Robert Funk) the SBL Jesus Seminar, and became president of SBL in 2012. His early work on the parables of Jesus was very useful, especially that on "parables of reversal," such as the Good Samaritan (*In Parables* [1973]). But in a succession of volumes, beginning with *The Dark Interval* (1975), Crossan moved increasingly toward postmodernism. In the 1990s he portrayed Jesus as a rural peasant wisdom teacher, drawing evidence mainly on sayings or aphorisms from the supposed document "Q" (where Matthew and Luke overlap). Crossan depends here on the thesis of J. Kloppenborg (*The Historical Jesus* [1991]). In *God and Empire* (2007), he portrayed Jesus as opposing Roman power and violence.

Cullmann, Oscar

Oscar Cullmann (1902-1999) was born in Strasbourg, and began his teaching career at the seminary there. He also taught in Paris, and after 1938 was professor in Basel. He was a Lutheran and widely associated with "biblical theology" rather than a purely descriptive and historical account of the biblical writings. Among his many works, probably the most influential are three: *Christ and Time* (Eng. London: SCM, 1951); *The Christology of the New Testament* (London: SCM, 1963; Ger. 1956); and *Salvation in History* (London: SCM, 1967). "Salvation history" or "redemptive history" translates the German term *Heilsgeschichte*, which denotes *not* simply history as observed by the secular historian or scientific investigation, but the *history of God's self-revelation* in Israel, Jesus, and the early church. Hence he aimed to write biblical *theology*.

In *Christ and Time* Cullmann distinguishes between the two Greek terms for time, *kairos* and *chronos*. *Kairos* denotes "the moment in time which is especially favourable for an undertaking" (39). *Chronos* normally denotes time as duration. The Bible knows nothing of "timelessness," which is a Platonic notion. Between the present and the future, as Kümmel has argued, lies a period of tension between the "now" and the "not yet." The Holy Spirit operates in the present to make human beings what they have *yet to become* in the future. He writes, "Upon the basis of the Holy Spirit . . . man *is* that which he *will become* only in the future" (75). Hence Cullmann coins a distinctive metaphor. "The decisive battle in a war may already have occurred . . . yet still the war continues" (84). He illustrates this by the well-known contrast in the Second World War between the decisive landing in France (D-Day) and the eventual victory of the Allies (V-Day). The cross and the resurrection constitute D-Day; the final consummation constitutes V-Day.

The Christology of the New Testament is not to be dismissed because it is no longer fashionable to focus on "the titles" of Jesus Christ; Cullmann does more than discuss and cite "titles." To answer the question "who is Christ?" he asks and answers "what does he *do*?" He first addresses the role of Christology for the earliest Christians. They never isolate the person of Christ "without at the same time speaking of his work" (3). Jesus is the eschatological prophet who pronounces a prophetic message, in continuity with John the Baptist, the OT, and Judaism. But Jesus is more than this; he is the *ebed Yahweh,* the Suffering Servant, who also represents Israel. Did Jesus think of suffering and death as part of his prophetic mission? Cullmann emphatically answers "yes," in spite of denials by many liberals and by Bultmann. He declares, "Three times Jesus prophesied his death following Peter's confession at Caesarea Philippi, Mk. 8:31; 9:31; 10:33-34" (63). He "came to give his life a ransom *(lutron)* for many" (65; Mark 10:45). He thus combined the Suffering Servant and "Son of Man" themes.

In further chapters Cullmann expounds the themes of "Jesus the High Priest," "Jesus the Messiah," "Jesus the Son of Man," and "Jesus the Lord." He examines the concept of high priest in Judaism and Hebrews, claiming of Hebrews, "the whole letter deals with him [Christ] in this role" (89). He fully shares the humanity of humankind, but now "always lives" to make intercession (102). John 17 also shares this theme. The notion of Jesus as Son of Man occurs not only in the Gospels but also in Phil. 2:5-11 and elsewhere in Paul. Finally Cullmann explores the terms "Lord" (and its Aramaic form *Maran* or *Marana*), "Savior," "Son of God," and "Word of God." Clearly these are in Cullmann's work not mere "titles," but ways of describing his role and activity on salvation history.

This becomes even clearer in *Salvation in History* (Ger. *Heil als Geschichte* [Salvation "as" History]). Cullmann accepts the importance of hermeneutics and the illusion of the "empty head" approach. The requirement begins with "a simple listening" (67). But he distances himself from Bultmann and an "it all depends on me" approach. Cullmann combines the "given" with the "confessional" in his *Early Christian Worship* (1953) and *Earliest Christian Confessions* (1949). Today his work is perhaps unduly neglected, partly because of the demise of the "biblical theology" movement, and partly because he is, perhaps unjustly, accused of oversimplification. He has done much to halt the divide between NT specialists and Christian theologians, and has offered a valuable contribution to both areas. (*See also* **Biblical Theology**.)

Curia
The Curia is usually defined as the papal court at Rome, which administers the government of the Roman Catholic Church, under the pope. It includes pontifical councils and tribunals. Current regulations for its function were approved by the pope in 1992. In medieval times the term could apply to any ecclesiastical court.

Cyril of Alexandria
Cyril of Alexandria (c. 375-444) was an eminent theologian in the tradition of Athanasius, but also seems to have relished controversy and was arguably ruthless in his politics. In particular, as patriarch of Alexandria, he strenuously attacked Nestorius, patriarch of Constantinople, and raised the profile of the antagonism between the two sees. Cyril became patriarch (or archbishop) in 412, and imme-

diately initiated clashes with Novatianism, the Jews, the imperial prefect, and the philosopher Hypatia, who was murdered. When Nestorius's chaplain, Anastasius, preached against applying *"Theotokos"* (Bearer of God) to the Virgin Mary, Cyril defended the use of the term in his paschal letter of 429. For neither side was the status of the Virgin Mary the main issue. Anastasius (and probably Nestorius) claimed that Mary was the mother of the *human* Jesus; Cyril insisted, however, that she was *Theotokos,* Bearer of God, and that this reflected a long-established tradition, which affirmed that Mary was mother of God incarnate.

In modern scholarship it is often doubted whether the contrast between "Antiochene" and "Nestorian" Christology was as sharp and clear-cut as Cyril portrayed it to be. But Cyril accused Nestorius of Apollinarianism, and Nestorius was condemned at the Council of Ephesus (431), over which Cyril presided, and ultimately also at Chalcedon (451). At the Council of Ephesus Cyril saw to it that Nestorius was condemned before the Antiochene bishops had arrived. But they held their own council, which pronounced Cyril deposed. In 433 Cyril had this reversed by more moderate Antiochenes. Throughout Cyril's time as patriarch we see a constant mix of theology and politics.

Cyril of Jerusalem

Cyril of Jerusalem (c. 315-387) has provided a detailed account of baptism and the Eucharist or Lord's Supper as it was in the fourth century, especially in his *Catechetical Lectures* and *Mystagogic Lectures* (c. 348), which were given for those preparing for baptism. In particular, lectures 16 and 17 expound the doctrine of the Holy Spirit. The Spirit is "a Power most mighty, a Being divine and unsearchable" (*Lectures* 16.1-2; 1 Cor. 2:10-13). Cyril also urges, "Let no one separate the Old from the New Testament" (16.4). On the basis of Rom. 8:9, he observes, to receive the Spirit is synonymous with becoming a Christian (17.5). Cyril was bishop of Jerusalem from about 349, but suffered exile because he opposed Arianism. He was recalled in 359, yet suffered two further exiles. The Arian bishop of Caesarea had claimed ecclesiastical jurisdiction over Jerusalem.

D

Dante
Dante Alighieri (1265-1321), an Italian poet, was bereaved by the death of his wife in 1290, and this led to the writing of the *Divine Comedy*. After this he turned to the study of philosophy. His major poem depicts the three realms: inferno, purgatory, and paradise. His vision travels down to hell, passes up through seven terraces of purgatory, to an earthly summit of paradise. His symbolic guide is Virgil. Bernard presents him to the Blessed Virgin Mary, who grants him a glimpse of the beatific vision.

Darby, John Nelson
John Nelson Darby (1800-1882) is the well-known originator of dispensationalist eschatology; after his death, the *Scofield Reference Bible* (1909) popularized his views. Darby was at one time an Anglican clergyman, and also a leader of the Plymouth Brethren. He interpreted a number of themes in Daniel and in Revelation as prophecies of the future, some still to be fulfilled. Dispensationalism perceives the present dispensation as beginning with the fall of Jerusalem in A.D. 70 and as culminating with the so-called rapture. Darby proposed that Christ will return twice. The first return involves the rapture of the faithful (1 Thess. 4:17); the second will occur after the great tribulation. Cyrus Scofield annotated the KJV/AV in 1909 in accordance with Darby's views. In spite of a thoroughly literalist interpretation of the language of eschatology, many in America are still influenced by Darby, and his view was partly popularized by Tim LaHaye and Jerry Jenkins's *Left Behind* series of novels, which have sold in the millions.

Darwin, Charles R.
Darwin's account of natural selection, which is a theory of evolution, constitutes what postmodernists call one of the three "grand narratives" that have dominated post-nineteenth-century thought. The others derive broadly from Freud, and perhaps less plausibly from Marx. Charles Darwin (1809-1882) attended the Universities of Edinburgh and Cambridge, and was then offered a voyage on the HMS *Beagle* (1831-1836), during which he made extensive observations of flora and fauna. On his return he reflected on his findings, and wrote *The Origins of Species* (1859), and later *The Descent of Man* (1871). The first book popularized the thesis that all creatures had evolved by natural, even random, processes. This the-

ory of natural selection was viewed by many as displacing the widespread belief that species had been designed by God, and seemed to threaten the teleological argument for the existence of God. "God," it seemed, was replaced by a purposeless mechanism. Mechanisms of change persisted that proved to be useful for the survival of species; others died out. Herbert Spencer popularized the slogan "the survival of the fittest," and even applied it to ethics. Massive controversy was provoked by Darwin's work. Even some scientific colleagues expressed reservations about supposed oversimplification. In religion he was opposed by Bishop Wilberforce, bishop of Oxford, and by W. E. Gladstone.

Darwin denied that he was an atheist, and held a religious belief that wavered between theism and Deism. He preferred to argue that these approaches could be reconciled, but that this was beyond human intellect. Many Christians regarded his work as incompatible with the account of creation in Genesis, even though Augustine and Calvin had rejected a "literal" account of the early chapters of Genesis. The later work, *The Descent of Man*, was more specific about the origins of humankind, and provoked further questions in psychology, ethics, social theory, and theology. Today most theologians seek to accommodate these theories within theology, while a minority still regard evolution only as theory. (*See also* **Evolution**.)

Day of Atonement

The Day of Atonement (Heb. *yōm kippurîm*; Gk. *hēmera exilasmou*) was and is celebrated annually on the tenth day of the seventh month (Tishri), and entails a series of rituals. Although Yom Kippur is still a regular feature of Judaism, it is prescribed in the OT only in Leviticus 16, and is presupposed in the theology of Christ's complete sacrifice in Heb. 9:1-14. Lev. 16:1-2 begins with a warning about approaching the Holy God unprepared. Aaron's two sons Nadab and Abihu "offered unholy fire before the Lord . . . and fire came out from the presence of the Lord and consumed them, and they died before the Lord" (10:1-2). The institution of the Day of Atonement begins "after the death of the two sons of Aaron, when they drew near before the Lord and died" (16:1-2). God is holy, and approach to God is not a human "right," but demands preparation and purification by expiation. Hence 16:3-10 sets out elaborate preparations for the act of atonement.

The ritual and ceremony demand the use of five animals, to be used for different purposes. Two bulls are required, and many scholars argue this represents the conflation of two older ceremonies. But Aaron must prepare a young bull for a sin offering and a ram for a burnt offering (16:3; *see* **Sacrifice**). He is to wear priestly robes of linen (16:4a) and first purify himself by washing (16:4b). Aaron's first sacrifice is that of "the bull as a sin offering for himself . . . and for his house" (16:6). Of the two goats, one is "for the Lord and the other . . . for Azazel" (16:8). The former will constitute a sin offering; the latter will become the scapegoat, which will be presented to the Lord and then sent away into the wilderness (16:9-10).

The ceremony itself involves, first, the purification of the sanctuary (16:11-19), then the purification of the people (16:20-22), and only then the sacrifices (16:23-28). The verb *kipper* (16:11, 16-18) is usually translated "expiate" or "atone" (as NRSV), but in this context also denotes "purify" or "cleanse." The acts involved are numerous and elaborate, requiring purification of the mercy seat (16:13-14). A goat is then sacrificed "for the people," but its blood is also sprinkled on the mercy seat (16:15) and the sanctuary (16:16). After this double purification and cleansing, Aaron is to present the live goat to the Lord (16:20), and "shall lay both his hands on the head of the live goat, and confess over it all the iniquities of the people ... sending it away into the wilderness.... The goat shall bear on itself all their iniquities" (16:21-22). The culmination of the proceedings is intended to cover any sin not covered by other sacrifices. When the sacrifice and cleansing are complete, Aaron is to discard his priestly linen clothes, ritually wash them again, and become reclothed in festal robes (16:23-28). Several interpretations of Azazel are possible. (See also *1 En.* 6–16.)

Hebrews 9 takes up this theme of the Day of Atonement in its insistence that the Aaronic priesthood and OT sacrifices can never fully, finally, and completely atone for human sin. Heb. 9:1-5 sets the scene for purifying the sanctuary: both the Holy Place and the Holy of Holies (9:2-4). 9:6 stresses that the priests "continually" repeat this ritual, and "cannot perfect the conscience of the worshiper" (9:9). Christ, however, made atonement once-for-all *(ephapax)* when he offered not a heifer, but himself (9:12-14). His work is complete and perfect. The allusion to the heifer comes from Num. 19:2-3. The Day of Atonement provides a prime example of *ad infinitum* regression. Acts in the series are meant to complete each previous act, but the series in principle could go on forever. Christ's offering is an unrepeatable definitive offering for all time; it is once-for-all.

The Mishnah devotes a whole tractate to the Day of Atonement *(m. Yoma)*, with additional details; it is reshaped in *Temple Scroll* 25.10–27.10. Israel still observes Yom Kippur as the holiest day of the year, retaining the theme of atonement as well as repentance. It is a twenty-five-hour period, usually involving fasting and intense prayer, with services in the synagogue. Yom Kippur has five services, and these may include public confession. (*See also* **Azazel; Scapegoat.**)

Reading: M. Douglas, *Leviticus as Literature* (Oxford: OUP, 1999); J. Milgram, *Leviticus 1–16*, AB (New York: Doubleday, 1991); G. J. Wenham, *The Book of Leviticus* (Grand Rapids: Eerdmans, 1979).

De Lubac. *See* **Lubac, Henri de**

Dead Sea Scrolls
The Dead Sea Scrolls comprise some 900 manuscripts that were discovered shortly after 1945 in eleven caves near Qumran on the northwest shore of the Dead Sea. The identification and cataloguing of manuscripts continued into the 1950s, and in many cases into the 1980s and beyond. A proportion of them are

papyrus scrolls, others are leather, and one is copper. Some are texts of the OT; others reflect the life of the Qumran community. In the early years the *Rule of the Community, War Scroll, Damascus Document,* and *Thanksgiving Hymns* appeared to shed special light on Judaism in the time of Christ and the apostolic age. The scrolls were given shorthand titles, usually with a number to indicate their cave and a letter to indicate the document. This library was probably hidden in these caves shortly before the first revolt of A.D. 66-70.

Rule of the Community (1QS) exists in a longer version, which suggests a hierarchical organization suppressed by the sons of Zadok, and in a shorter version (4Q256 and 4Q258) that reflected a more egalitarian community. For Johannine specialists it was of special value for dating the Gospel of John. Bultmann and others had argued that dualism in John suggested a very late date for the Gospel, which was probably influenced by Gnostic dualism. The sharp contrasts in John between light and darkness, truth and falsehood, good and evil, and above and below appeared to date the Gospel much later than the time of Jesus. However, 1QS (as well as the *War Scroll*) is full of such dualism, indicating that Judaism in the time of Jesus, and Jesus and John, would have been familiar with this way of thinking. The Gnostic dating of John now looks bizarre and misleading. 1QS contains the notion of the two spirits (3.13–4.26), linked respectively with truth and falsehood, and with light and darkness. A. R. C. Leaney traces numerous affinities with the Fourth Gospel (*The Rule of Qumran and the Meaning* [London: SCM, 1966], 37-56, 143-46). F. F. Bruce calls this rule "our most important source of information for the organisation of the Qumran community," and Leaney's work authoritative and reliable. Its doctrine stresses the order of the world and predestination, and compares biblical and extrabiblical texts. The Qumran community is a particular form, Leaney argues, of the Essenes in Palestine.

The *Damascus Document* (CD) urges holiness in the community, and draws on what OT scholars usually call "the Holiness Code" in Leviticus. The document, from Caves 4, 5, and 6, anticipates a tenth- and twelfth-century medieval writing of the same kind, and perhaps celebrates the giving of the law. The *War Scroll* (1QM), also known as *The War Rule* or *War of the Sons of Light against the Sons of Darkness,* was published in 1954-1955, with the definitive English text edited by Yadin in 1962, mainly from Cave 1, but also partly from Cave 4. Columns 1-9 describe a plan of war and campaigns depicting formations and weaponry; columns 10-14 are mainly liturgical pieces and speeches; and columns 15-19 portray the battle against the "Kittim" (probably Romans), conducted by the priests and chief priest or "Prince of the Congregation," who is virtually a priestly messianic leader. These last columns depict an eschatological confrontation between light and darkness, underlining the dualism of the Scrolls. The date appears to be either first century B.C. or early first century A.D. The *Thanksgiving Hymns* (1QH), or *Hodayoth,* are mainly songs of praise, but survive only in fragments. They contain elements of Aramaic and late Hebrew. Their style is like that of Psalms. The first-person "I" is sometimes identified with "the Teacher of Righteousness."

A number of the Scrolls are biblical texts. Well-known examples include Isaiah and *Pesher Habakkuk* (1QpHab). The dating is uncertain, and similarities with, and differences from, the Hebrew text suggest to some a fluidity among a number of manuscript readings.

Reading: George J. Brooke, *The Dead Sea Scrolls and the New Testament* (London: SPCK; Philadelphia: Fortress, 2005); F. M. Cross, *The Ancient Library of Qumran* (Minneapolis: Fortress, 1995); J. A. Fitzmyer, *Responses to 101 Questions about the Dead Sea Scrolls* (New York: Paulist, 1992); Y. Hirschfield, *Qumran in Context* (Peabody, Mass.: Hendrickson, 2004); Geza Vermes, *The Complete Dead Sea Scrolls in English* (London: Penguin, 1998; 5th ed. 2011).

Death and Mourning

The experience of death and mourning may at first sight seem less prominent in the biblical writings than we might imagine. The reason is that "the last things" for the NT writers denote primarily the cosmic and corporate events of the return of Christ, the resurrection of the dead, and the Last Judgment rather than the individual event of death. Nevertheless, the Bible universally teaches the mortality of all humans and the inevitability of death. There is a tendency in the modern West to push away thoughts of death. Moltmann declares, "To push away every thought of death, and to live as if we had an infinite amount of time ahead of us, makes us superficial and indifferent.... To live as if there were no death is to live an illusion" (*The Coming of God* [London: SCM, 1996], 50). Those who repress the thought of death turn life into an idol. As recently as in Victorian times, Geoffrey Rowell points out, the death rate itself made confrontation with death inevitable. "In 1840 the annual death rate per 1,000 persons in England and Wales was 22.9; by 1880 it had fallen to 20.5; and in 1900 it was still 18.2.... In 1840 there were 154 infants under a year old who died out of 1,000 live births, and this figure remained constant until 1900" (*Hell and the Victorians* [Oxford: Clarendon, 1974], 1; these figures are taken from T. Lambert, *A Brief History of Life Expectancy*). Today many in the "two-thirds world" are experiencing what America and Europe think they have left behind.

Further, in previous generations the elderly lived and died at home, often amid a circle of family and friends, rather than being shunted off to die in hospitals and care homes, out of sight and mostly out of mind. A churchyard was often located in the center of a town or village, not as it is today; cemeteries and crematoria are often established at the margins of population centers. Moltmann urges: "Dying and death are privatized.... There is an unconscious suppressive taboo on dying, death, and mourning" (*The Coming of God,* 56).

The OT saw death as a tragedy, involving even possible separation from God. The notion of a descent to Sheol (Gk. *hádēs*) occurs sixty-five times. The dead barely exist. Ryder Smith calls existence in Sheol "a bloodless, juiceless" shadow existence (*The Bible Doctrine of Salvation* [London: Epworth, 1946], 92). The one who descends to Sheol does not come back (Job 7:9; 10:21), but fades and vanishes. Ezekiel condemns Pharaoh to the Pit or Sheol (Heb. *bôr*; Ezek. 31:16).

In a very few passages there begins to be a hope that "Your dead shall live, their corpses shall rise" (Isa. 26:19). Those intertestamental writings influenced by Greek thought might hint at "immortality," but the NT is fully committed to belief in the resurrection of the dead through Christ. In 1 Cor. 15:26 Paul speaks of death as "the last enemy to be destroyed." It is both "last" and an "enemy." Victory over death, however, is assured in Christ (1 Cor. 15:54-56) through the power of the Holy Spirit (Rom. 8:11).

Meanwhile in this earthly life, a person's life can be "cut off" before a hoped-for completion. Moltmann and Niebuhr both address this problem. We must not forget the real pain of premature bereavement or disability. There is the need for grieving and mourning, even though God is in control of time, and we are bidden to maintain trust. Children often die at birth, and boys and girls can be fatally injured in road accidents. In the OT and NT, mourning customs are explicit and elaborate because we need to grieve. Moltmann observes, "The greater the love, the deeper the grief; the more unreserved the surrender, the more inconsolable the loss. Those who give themselves utterly in love with someone else die themselves in the pains of grief, and are born again" (*The Coming of God*, 119).

The Hebrew *'ābal*, "to mourn," and *'abēl*, "mourning," occur some forty-five times in the OT, and Hebrew *sāphad*, "to mourn, beat the breast, lament," some forty times. Gen. 37:34-35 recounts that Jacob "mourned for his son many days. . . . He refused to be comforted." Abraham mourned and wept for Sarah (Gen. 23:2); "David mourned for his son day after day" (2 Sam. 13:37). All Judah and Jerusalem mourned for Josiah (2 Chron. 35:21-25). In the NT Jesus saw Mary weeping for Lazarus, and "Jesus began to weep" (John 11:33-36). Paul urges Christians, "Rejoice with those who rejoice, weep with those who weep" (Rom. 12:15). No Christian should have to mourn *alone*. Mourning in biblical times was *long, serious, and public*. Moltmann warns us that to suppress mourning or cut it short may lead to depression, and worse.

The stages of grief and mourning, as these usually occur, have been set out by Elisabeth Kübler-Ross in *On Death and Dying* (New York: Simon and Schuster, 1969; London: Tavistock, 1970). The first stage is often disbelief or denial. Then very often comes anger, as the bereaved seek to blame God or another person or even themselves for the event. Third, "bargaining" sometimes follows. Fourth, few can escape a period of prolonged depression. Finally come acceptance, reconciliation, and hope. The process is not invariable in sequence, but most of these symptoms of bereavement occur. Others suggest that an initial numbness and shock are followed by a yearning for a restored life, followed by despair. Only then can there be resolution and return to an ordered life. Psychologists often claim that the death of a child can be even more painful than the death of a spouse.

Nevertheless, Paul states: "If for this life only we have hope in Christ, we are of all people most to be pitied" (1 Cor. 15:19). The resurrection life will be characterized by the ever-fresh, ever-ongoing life of the Holy Spirit. Moreover, resurrection of the "body" promises, unlike "immortality" among the Greeks, a postresurrection mode of existence in which transformed people will be recognizable, identifiable, and above all, like Christ and holy. I have explored these themes further in *Life after Death: A New Approach* (Grand Rapids: Eerdmans, 2012); British title, *The Last Things: A New Approach* (London: SPCK, 2012). I am also especially indebted to J. Moltmann, *The Coming of God* (London: SCM, 1996). (*See also* **Body; Resurrection of the Dead**.)

Death of God Theology
Death of God theology flourished in the 1960s, especially in America. Although Luther spoke of the death of Christ as the death of God, and Hegel understood the death of God to occur in the cross, death of God theology relates perhaps more directly to the atheism of Nietzsche and Feuerbach. Nevertheless, adherents would not describe themselves as atheists, but as some kind of theists who believe that a concept of the transcendent God of traditional theism has no currency in the contemporary world. One of the most prominent leaders of this school, T. J. J. Altizer (b. 1927) is superficially close to Hegel in seeing the death of God as occurring at the cross, but unlike Hegel, he denied the resurrection and ascension of Christ. Moreover, he drew on Blake and Nietzsche as well as Hegel. Christ can be known, he claimed, as a "secular" presence. Altizer's intention, however, was to deny that God was meaningful as a transcendent, remote, self-sufficient figure. He would claim that the emphasis on "secularity" stands in continuity with Bonhoeffer's later *Letters and Papers from Prison* about "nonreligious" Christianity. But Bonhoeffer's aim was to attack a concept of God simply as a fulfiller of human need and "answer" to human guilt, in the most simplistic way.

Paul van Buren (1924-1998) and William Hamilton (1924-2012) also sought to disentangle Christian identity from belief in a transcendent God. Van Buren passed through three distinct stages in his theological career. In his middle period he became vulnerable to the attacks of logical positivism and some strands of linguistic philosophy on the credibility and meaning of Christian discourse. He therefore demanded a radical reinterpretation of "God," and pursued a radical linguistic analysis in *The Secular Meaning of the Gospel.* Hamilton coauthored *A Radical Theology and the Death of God* in 1966. G. Vattimo, J. Caputo, and J. A. T. Robinson have been associated with the movement, but Robinson mainly attacked *traditional* theism. Don Cupitt, however, might have a stronger candidacy. He denies the existence of God in any "objective" sense. This school has largely lost its influence, and "radical" theologians tend now to be involved in postmodernist critiques of religion. (*See also* **Atheism**.)

Deconstruction, Deconstructionism
This movement probably dates from 1967, when J. Derrida published his three classic works, *Speech and Phenomena, Of Grammatology,* and *Writing and Dif-*

ference. Derrida was influenced by Freud, Nietzsche, Marx, and Heidegger. He insists that "deconstruction" does *not* mean demolition, or even analysis. It is not a method of interpretation, nor is it a reductive operation. It is not, he insists, a "thing" that can be defined, but it does stand in relation to a text, begins by reading a text, and involves thinking about the reading. It involves comparing the dominant interpretation with gaps, absences, or blind spots in this "usual" interpretation. Derrida rejects the simple repetition of a text as "logocentric" reading. In short, deconstruction denotes, if anything, *undermining readings.* Christopher Norris regards it as a serious philosophy, in contrast to postmodernism, which he regards as little more than a passing fashion.

Like Ricoeur, Derrida sees most language as having a double meaning. Further, the meaning is never "closed off." Derrida writes, "It is no longer a finished corpus of writing enclosed in a book" (in H. Bloom, *Deconstruction and Criticism* [London: Routledge, 1979], 84). Following Ferdinand de Saussure and subsequent thinkers in linguistics, he sees meaning as difference. In French "difference" *(différence)* is related to "deferment" *(différance)* of meaning. The postponed or deferred meaning leaves only traces or tracks. K. Vanhoozer therefore engages in full-scale polemic that such an approach "undoes" the Bible as the Word of God (*Is There a Meaning in This Text?* [Grand Rapids: Zondervan, 1998]).

Others, however, defend deconstruction. James Smith argues that it is compatible with the Reformers' emphasis on *sola Scriptura,* and Derrida drew a huge audience when he spoke at a Society of Biblical Literature gathering in America. Perhaps the truth is more complex than either extreme. Deconstruction may be appropriate for some "open" or "poetic" texts, but not for more straightforward propositions. In *Limited Inc* (1988) Derrida seems more willing to avoid generalizations about language and texts. Perhaps like Ricoeur, his greatest value is to expose the multilayered nature of language, and our overreadiness to equate a dominant interpretation or the conventional meaning with what has been called "the 'natural' meaning." S. Fish endorses this in his radical reader-response theory. (*See also* **Derrida, Jacques; Postmodernism, Postmodernity; Ricouer, Paul.**)

Deification

Also in some contexts called "divinization" or *theōsis,* deification has often been regarded as the Eastern Orthodox Church's equivalent to what the Western Church usually calls sanctification, depending on an appropriate context. As Vladimir Lossky states, in the Eastern Church the concept is usually traced to Athanasius's dictum "God made himself man that man might become God" (*On the Incarnation of the Word* 54). Lossky also cites Gregory of Nyssa's words, "that our nature might by this transfusion of the Divine become itself divine" (*The Great Catechism* 25; *NPNF,* ser. 2, 5:495); Gregory of Nazianzus, *Dogmatic Poems* 10.5-9; PG 37:465; and Irenaeus, *Against Heresies,* preface, although the wording in Irenaeus refers to Christ, not God, "who did become what we are that he might bring us to be even what he is himself" (*ANF* 1:526). Lossky declares, "The Father and Orthodox theologians here repeated them [these words] in every century with the same emphasis, wishing to sum up . . . the very essence of Christianity" ("Redemption and Deification," in *The Image and Likeness of God* [London and Oxford: Mowbray, 1974], 97). He adds, "The descent *(katabasis)* of the divine person of Christ makes human persons capable of an ascent *(anabasis)* in the Holy Spirit" (97). In Lossky's view this transforms a mere "individual" into a true "person," who is unique and irreplaceable (107). 2 Pet. 1:4 speaks of being "participants of the divine nature," and Paul speaks of sharing the unique Sonship of Christ.

This must not be confused with the Platonic notion of assimilation into God. The Western Church may have shown reserve in using the term for this reason. But with renewed interest in patristic sources, contemporary study has paid more attention to deification. Both deification and sanctification are processes of becoming Christlike by the power of the Holy Spirit. (*See also* **Athanasius; Sanctification.**)

Deism

Deism flourished in the seventeenth and eighteenth centuries. In its popular form it expresses belief in a God who created the world, but in contrast to theism, Deism also holds that God cannot and does not engage with events in the world. Any such intervention would imply that creation was inadequate or imperfect. Deists saw creation like a mechanism that God had set going, but that he then left to run as a self-regulating machine. Some trace the origins of English Deism to Lord Edward Herbert of Cherbury (1583-1643), who believed in "common notions" of reason and "natural religion" (*On Truth* [1624]). More specifically, Matthew Tindal (1657-1733) expounded a natural theology in his *Christianity as Old as Creation* (1730), as did John Toland (1670-1722) in his *Christianity Not Mysterious* (1696). T. Carlyle attacked Deism as promoting "an absentee God, sitting idle ever since the first Sabbath, at the outside of his universe and seeing it go" (1834). Meanwhile Anthony Collins, one of the later Deists, produced his *Discourse of Free Thinking* (1713), which, like exponents of the Enlightenment, denoted free thinking "independently of any given authority." This included the Bible, the church, and clergy. He spoke of appeals to these as "superstition," anticipating some claims today. (*See also* **Theism.**)

Denney, James

James Denney (1856-1917) was educated at Glasgow University and Glasgow Free Church College, and later taught theology at the latter. He moved from a more liberal to an evangelical persuasion, and his book *The Death of Christ* (1902) became a classic for his exposition of a substitutionary understanding of the atonement. On that basis it is still used today. He also wrote *The Christian Doctrine of Reconciliation* (1917), and commentaries on Romans, 2 Corinthians, and the Thessalonian correspondence.

Deontology
J. Bentham used the term in 1826 to denote ethics or moral action. Today it is often used to denote ethical motivation in contrast to ethical consequence. More widely and less accurately, it may sometimes denote *altruistic* ethical action.

Depravity
Depravity denotes humankind under the power of sin. Reformed theology often uses the term "total depravity," but today it is popularly misunderstood. The term does not suggest that all humans are totally evil, but that there is nothing in humankind that has not been marred or infected by the power of sin. Following Paul, Calvin states on the one hand, "There is none righteous" (Rom. 3:10); but on the other hand, "In every age there have been some who . . . were all their lives devoted to virtue" (*Institutes* 2.3.2-3).

Derrida, Jacques
One of the most influential and controversial of twentieth-century thinkers, Jacques Derrida (1930-2004) was born in Algeria, taught at the Sorbonne in Paris from 1960 to 1964, and also taught in the École Normale Supérieure from 1965 to 1984. He later became professor at the University of California. In 1967 his three classic books, *Speech and Phenomena, Of Grammatology,* and *Writing and Difference,* burst upon the scene. His disciple Gayatri Spivak confirms that the major influences on his thought were Nietzsche, Freud, Husserl, and Heidegger, together with Marx and Saussure. Reading and writing, he urged, is not merely to replicate, stabilize, or embody the text. This is "logocentrism." We must look beyond the words themselves, and even often undermine them, by exposing their unfinished nature. What is most lacking in Derrida is an account of extralinguistic situations, which language and words normally presuppose. He rightly draws attention to the limitations of representational language, but some language does remain conscious representation. Derrida appears to acknowledge this in some of his later work, especially in *Limited Inc* (1988). But like Roland Barthes, he perhaps speaks too easily of "the death of the author." He has had immense, but controversial, influence on biblical studies. Kevin Vanhoozer offers a critique in *Is There a Meaning in This Text?* (Grand Rapids: Zondervan, 1998).

Descartes, René
René Descartes (1596-1650) introduced a new era into philosophy. Whereas others had often appealed to authorities and tradition, Descartes argued that "those who use only their pure natural reason" can discover certainties, in contrast to "those who believe only the books of the ancients" (*Discourse on Method* [London: Penguin, 1968], 91). He was a French philosopher and mathematician who respected Jesuit teaching, and he believed that only revelation and mathematics or logic yield "certain" truths. His two main works were *Discourse on Method* (1637) and *Meditations* (1641), although he wrote other works.

In the first part of *Discourse on Method* Descartes reflects on the multitude and diversity of human opinions, which offer "little basis . . . for certainty" (33). Nothing can be built on such a "shifting foundation" (32). In part 2 Descartes builds on a foundation that is wholly his own. He seeks "clear and distinct" ideas (43). In part 4 he states his famous dictum: "I think, therefore I am" *(cogito ergo sum)*, that is, the fact that I perceive myself thinking means that I exist, which is "absolutely indubitable" (53-54). In part 5 he attacks skepticism, and in part 6 he reemphasizes his own method of approach, namely, a priori reasoning rather than a posteriori inference. Critics such as H. Thielicke call this anthropocentric, and P. Ricoeur protests against "the immediateness, the transparency, the apodicticity of the Cogito" ("Intellectual Autobiography," in *The Philosophy of Paul Ricoeur,* ed. L. E. Hahn [La Salle, Ill.: Open Court, 1995], 16). This emerges, he claims, especially in the light of hermeneutics and modern psychology. In terms of history, it excludes all capacity to "stand on the shoulders of giants."

In *Meditations* (Chicago: Open Court, 1901) Descartes argues that systems of belief need to be demolished, but only "once in a lifetime" (*Meditation* II, 31). Tradition is to be dismantled, and then there remains "nothing but what is indubitable" (31). But by human reason "'God' is a clear, distinct, indubitable idea, which God himself has placed within the mind" (II, 81). He writes, "I cannot conceive of God without evidence" (78). This is because he adheres to the ontological argument for the existence of God, which argues for God's existence by pure, abstract logic alone. Its logic has the same status as mathematical statements about the three angles of triangles (78). This logic is attacked by Kant and others (*see* **Ontological Argument**). Descartes's famous or notorious dualism arises from this. Mind is an "essence" of thought alone, which truly is an "essence," and has extension in the world. Descartes did not doubt that emotions could affect both mind and body, but a basic dualism allowed G. Ryle to speak of Descartes's "mind" as "the ghost of the machine." Descartes has drawn this contrast between the rational and the empirical too sharply to support the radical nature of his new method. G. Vico and others attempt to reinstitute the importance of *history* and *community*. William Temple, perhaps with some exaggeration, calls the lonely individuality of the Cartesian *Cogito* "the most disastrous moment in the history of Europe" (*Nature, Man, and God* [London: Macmillan, 1940], 57). Yet even Temple's criticism demonstrates unwittingly Descartes's huge and vast influence.

Descent into Hell

This article did not originate from the earliest creeds, but became a substantial component of the later Apostles' Creed. It was inserted only in the fourth century. It is possible that its popular understanding today is the opposite of the original intention behind its inclusion. Jesus died not only a physical death, but a death that entailed an awareness of being separated from God. At death he exclaimed: "My God, my God, why have you forsaken me?" (Mark 15:34), and Paul wrote, "Cursed is everyone who hangs on a tree" (Gal. 3:13). Pannenberg argues that the original intention behind this article was "to give a more detailed description of what happened to Jesus at his death . . . namely exclusion from the presence of God" (*The Apostles' Creed* [London: SCM, 1972], 90). Luther correctly sees it as part of the agony of Christ. Calvin is even clearer: Christ not only endured corporeal death, he faced "the horrors of eternal death . . . the death which is inflicted on the wicked" (*Institutes* 2.16.10; Beveridge, 1:443). He endured "the pains produced by the curse and wrath of God" (16.11; 1:443).

Nevertheless, in the history of theology a different interpretation emerged. The descent into "hell" became "a demonstration of [Christ's] triumph . . . a triumphal progress" (Pannenberg, *The Apostles' Creed*, 92). This is usually based on 1 Pet. 3:19-20, which declares that Christ "went and made a proclamation to the spirits in prison, who in former times did not obey, when God waited patiently in the days of Noah." 1 Pet. 4:6 also declares, "The gospel was proclaimed even to the dead." Further, Eph. 4:9 speaks of Christ's descent into "the lower parts of the earth," and Rev. 1:18 ascribes to Christ "the keys of Death and of Hades" (J. M. Lochman, *The Faith We Confess* [Edinburgh: T. & T. Clark, 1985], 144). Lochman interprets this to mean that the benefits of Christ's death extended beyond "a geographical parochialism" to those who "have lived since his birth . . . and who died before Christ was born" (144). There are indeed parts of Luther's works in which he sees this as part of Christ's triumphal procession, and his victory over sin and death. But Calvin remained adamant that "hell" is not a "locatable underworld . . . it means primarily separation from God, abandonment by God" (145). On the cited biblical passages, exegesis is not clear-cut, and both Pannenberg and Lochman seek to combine the Lutheran and Calvinist interpretations. The ecumenical creed and *Alternative Service Book* (1980) replace "descended into hell" with "descended to the dead," which reflects the spirit of the times, while *Common Worship* (2000) restores the 1662 *Book of Common Prayer*'s "he descended into hell," leaving open the two main options of interpretation, namely, the victory theme and separation from God at the crucifixion.

Desert Fathers
This is the general name given to those ascetics, monks, and hermits who were drawn to the desert of Egypt for devotion to God in solitude, mainly in the late third and fourth century A.D. They especially sought prayer and ordered discipline. Although some regard Paul of Thebes as the first of this group, Anthony (or Antony) of Egypt (c. 251-356) is most widely regarded as the founder and most important leader of the movement. In about 270 he is said to have heard a sermon on Matt. 19:21, on selling one's possessions to give to the poor, and on following Christ. This led to his giving away his property to feed the poor, and to devote his life to prayer and asceticism in solitude. Around 285 he retired to the desert of Egypt for this purpose. Popularly he became renowned for his holy life and ordered discipline.

Anthony's reputation attracted many to follow his example, and in c. 305 he organized his followers into a community of hermits. Except for their solitude and lack of common life, they effectively anticipated the monastic movement, which was soon to emerge in Egypt and Syria. From c. 310 he supported the Nicene party. Athanasius is said to have written a life of Anthony, although many ascribe this to an Athanasian circle. By the time of Anthony's death, Athanasius had called the desert home of his followers "a city." As the group increasingly became more "monastic," they formed a "monastery" under Pachomius, and began to hold property in common. A figure emerged to give guidance for spiritual welfare, and was usually known as *abba* (father) or sometimes *amma* (mother). This prefigured the monastic term "abbot." Basil of Caesarea was in the group at one time, and John Cassian wrote about it. Their mystical tradition came to be known as "Hesychasm" (from the Greek, stillness or silence). Macarius of Egypt and Gregory of Nyssa are associated with the movement. Prayer, austerity, poverty, meditation, silence, and giving to the poor remain the hallmarks of the movement. (*See also* **Monasticism**.)

Dialectic, Dialectical Theology

"Dialectic" is a broader term than "dialectical theology," although the two are closely related. "Dialectic" is used in contrast to flat assertion, when the truth seems too complex to be expressed by a simple single statement or even set of statements. The term originates from the Greek *dialektikē technē*, "art of conversation." It may have originated with Zeno of Elea (fifth century B.C.), but is also reflected in Socrates and in the *Dialogues* of Plato. Socrates used question and answer in his search for truth. Plato regarded dialectic as the major philosophical method of inquiry (*Republic* 534E; *Cratylus* 390C). In view of his special interest in Plato's *Dialogues*, it is not surprising that H.-G. Gadamer gives pride of place to the question in his hermeneutics. Gadamer also drew on R. G. Collingwood for this. In linguistic philosophy F. Waismann argues for the importance of the question. In literature Bakhtin highly valued the question as a way of entry into polyphonic discourse. Clearly dialectic also has a firm place in Hegel and Marx.

"Dialectical theology," in the more specific sense of the term, applies especially to the earlier theology of K. Barth, F. Gogarten, E. Brunner, E. Thurneysen, and R. Bultmann through the 1920s. None of them believed that human beings could make *direct assertions* about God. An inbuilt tension in language that purported to describe God suggested both a "yes" and a "no" of assertion and counterassertion. Barth's *Commentary on Romans* reflected a dialectic of judgment and grace. For this he was partly indebted to Kierkegaard, who had earlier embraced the use of paradox. The heyday of dialectical theology corresponds with that of the journal *Between the Times* (1920-1933). After about 1930 the movement declined.

In a broader sense this approach to theology had flourished before this time and would continue afterward. Bultmann argued that knowledge of God is impossible without self-knowledge, but John Calvin also stressed this mutuality in his *Institutes*. Luther spoke of the God who is both hidden and revealed.

Reading: H.-G. Gadamer, *Truth and Method* (London: Sheed and Ward, 1989), 362-80; J. M. Robinson, ed., *The Beginnings of Dialectical Theology* (Richmond: John Knox, 1968).

Dilthey, Wilhelm

Wilhelm Dilthey (1833-1911) studied at Heidelberg and Berlin, and became Professor at Basel and then Berlin. He was an ardent admirer of Schleiermacher, of whom he wrote a biography. In effect, he follows him in the Romanticist tradition of hermeneutics, but with greater interest in the social sciences. He believed that hermeneutics formed the basis for all inquiry in the *Geisteswissenschaften*, or humanities and social sciences. In this respect he constitutes a link between the hermeneutics of Schleiermacher and that of Heidegger and Gadamer. He sought to apply hermeneutics not only to texts, but to *human life, institutions,* and *society.* His writings ran to twenty-six volumes. He aimed to achieve for the *Geisteswissenschaften* what Hegel had achieved for philosophy.

Three themes were fundamental for Dilthey. First, he developed Hegel's emphasis on historical reason further, believing that everything in life was radically *historically conditioned,* as Heidegger was later to emphasize. He attacked both timeless rationalism and positivism as naïve. Second, with Herder and Schleiermacher he sought to replace Hegel's emphasis on Spirit or Mind *(Geist)* with an emphasis upon "life" *(Leben)*. *Lived experiences* lie behind all human society. Dilthey argued that we must take seriously the mental processes and inner lives of people. To analyze a causal nexus of nature is insufficient for the *Geisteswissenschaften.* The human being knows himself only in history. He commented concerning Descartes, Locke, Hume, and Kant: "In the veins of the knowing subject *no real blood flows*" (*Gesammelte Schriften,* vol. 5 [Leipzig: Teubner, 1927], 4). Third, Dilthey also looked for some kind of quasi system that would do justice to the *"connectedness" (Zusammenhang)* behind various experiences of life. This could objectify the subjective experiences of human life, and express much more than any introspection could discover. Predictably, this was the feature to which Gadamer was most opposed.

On this basis Dilthey extended hermeneutics to include law, social sciences, and all human institutions, in addition to language and texts. If hermeneutics can apply to language, he argued, the hermeneutical approach can apply to all human society and its concrete institutions. But the interpreter is to *"relive" (nacherleben)* the other's experience by stepping out of his or her shoes, and exercising sympathetic *Hineinversetzen,* or "transposition" (in *Dilthey: Selected Writings* [Cambridge: CUP, 1976], 226-27). This constitutes an important contribution to hermeneutics, although some existentialist writers maintain that the repetition of the experience of one person by another would in principle be impossible. On the other hand, the attempt "to stand in the shoes of the person to be understood" remains an important principle of understanding and interpretation. To quote Dilthey directly again: "Understanding *(Verstehen)* is a rediscovery of the 'I' in the 'You.' . . . We may ask how much this contributes to solving the general problem of epistemology" (208).

It was important for the development of later hermeneutical theory in Gadamer that Dilthey rejected the value of direct introspection as a means of hermeneutical self-awareness. He also stressed the importance of *social science* within the approach of hermeneutics. Although Heidegger and Gadamer reject his move toward quasi system or "connectedness," this approach finds some resonance later with Jürgen Habermas and Emilio Betti. Betti insists that his approach and that of Dilthey are more objective than Gadamer's. Rudolf makes much of Dilthey's hermeneutics. Wolfhart Pannenberg has also developed his insight that meaning becomes possible only within the totality of the whole.

Dionysius, Pseudo-

The name Pseudo-Dionysius is used to distinguish this fifth- and sixth-century monk and mystic from the Dionysius who was converted by Paul in Acts 17:34. Three others named Dionysius come from the third century. He is also known as Dionysius, or Denis, the Pseudo-Areopagite.

For him, union with God is achieved by purification, illumination, and perfection. He became an influential figure in the mystical tradition. His work *The Celestial Hierarchy* discusses orders of angels. His treatise *The Ecclesiastical Hierarchy* discusses sacraments and the orders of clergy. *The Divine Names* concerns the Being of God. His *Mystical Theology* relates to the journey and ascent of the soul, or to deification, in the mystical or Eastern sense.

In Christian theology Pseudo-Dionysius is noted especially for two things, apart from his mysticism. First, he depends heavily on Neoplatonism, especially on the Neoplatonist philosopher Proclus. Second, he is known for his distinction between apophatic and cataphatic theology. God surpasses human concepts. Dionysius may have coined the word "hierarchy." Among twentieth-century theologians, the Russian Orthodox Vladimir Lossky has a special interest in his apophatic theology. Dionysius thinks in cosmic terms of the union of all creation with God, and in the mystical sense of the word, through "deification."

Disciples of Christ

Also called the Churches of Christ, the Disciples of Christ became a separate communion in 1832. They are congregationally organized, regard Scripture alone as the basis of faith, practice believer's baptism, and celebrate the Lord's Supper every Sunday. The original movement came from America, and from both Presbyterians and Scottish Baptists. The movement is now worldwide. In Britain many joined the United Reformed Church in 1981. Their original vision was ecumenical and evangelistic.

Dispensationalism

This theological approach divides God's dealings with the world into different "dispensations," or periods characterized by different responsibilities and hermeneutical principles. Most Christians would recognize a distinction between the Mosaic period of the Law and the new covenant instituted by Christ. But dispensationalists usually work with a more complex notion of history. Strictly, dispensationalism denotes the system of interpretation contained in the notes of the *Scofield Bible,* and in L. S. Chafer's *Systematic Theology.* This proposes seven distinct economies of God, each requiring a distinct hermeneutic.

Dodd, Charles H.

Charles H. Dodd (1884-1973) was professor successively at Manchester and Cambridge. In his book *The Authority of the Bible* (London: Nisbet, 1928), he argues that we should turn from "the narrow sense of individual experience" to the long history of the communities of the Bible that have "tested their belief in God" and "delivered us from the tyranny of private impressions" (288-89). In *According to the Scriptures* (1952), Dodd defends the NT writers' appeal to the OT in a coherent way. His *Parables of the Kingdom* (1935) remained a textbook for many years. He was widely known for his *Interpretation of the Fourth Gospel* (1953) and *Historical Translation of the Fourth Gospel* (1963). Many have dissented, however, from his "realized eschatology," arguing that the kingdom of God is not wholly present, but also still future.

Dogma, Dogmatics

These terms differ from "systematic theology." In Barth and Brunner, who use the term frequently, "dogma" not only concerns God as Trinity and Christ and arises from Scripture, but is also the public confession of faith by the church, in contrast to private opinion. "Dogma" and "dogmatics" carry with them the notion of norm or rule, from the Greek *dogma,* a formal statement relating to rules, or an established tenet. Barth is forthright about this being the *church's* reflection on revelation and on Christ. By contrast, "systematic theology" is generally more "open" and not necessarily an expression of confessional or church belief, and is therefore more readily used in purely academic or university circles to denote a systematic and coherent study of doctrinal themes. The verb *dokeō* may have the sense of "recognize," as when doctrine is received or recognized by the church.

Dominicans

The Dominican Order (*Ordo Praedicatorum,* O.P.) was founded by Dominic in 1220. The order possessed only corporate property, and served to promote preaching, study, and pastoral welfare. In Britain Dominicans were often called "Black Friars" because of their black mantles. They established a system of education, often associated with universities. Albertus Magnus and Thomas Aquinas were Dominicans. Many Dominicans worked outside Europe. Two of the most controversial historical phases were their links with Crusaders and with the Inquisition. They added a second order of nuns, and later a third order, who did not make vows. Today Dominicans often identify themselves as "O.P."

Donatism

Donatism is a heresy of the ancient church that retains relevance in the post-Reformation period and today. The emperor Decius initiated a period of sharp persecution in 249, which brought about large-scale apostasy. The bishop of Carthage, Cyprian, was forced to flee, but returned in 251. As persecution slackened, many sought to be rehabilitated and restored to church services and sacraments. Jesus had pronounced the need for limitless forgiveness to Peter, but Cyprian was largely against the readmission of lapsed Christians, and wrote *On the Lapsed* in 251 (*ANF* 5:437-47). He wrote first, "Peace is restored to the Church" (*On the Lapsed* 1). But then his tone changed: "I share in the grievous burden of sorrow and mourning" (4). He then adds: "Miserable creature, you have lost your soul" (30); "Think you that the Lord will be quickly appeased?" (35). Bishops who had committed apostasy have disqualified themselves from office.

Donatism was the expression of the desire for a "pure" church. In the fourth century this controversy split the African church, and in the renewed persecutions of 303-311 the "pure" church was defended by Donatus, whose followers others called Donatists. In 314 the Council of Arles condemned Donatism. Later, the most learned and articulate spokesman *against* Donatism was Augustine. He cited the parable of the seeds sown among the wheat (Matt. 13:24-30, 36-43) as evidence for a mixed church. Prior to the Last Judgment human beings cannot judge who truly is "saved." The Catholic Church and the mainline Reformers advocate a visible church; some, perhaps like extreme Puritans, still hankered after a "pure" church. The Donatist controversy survived for three or four centuries, while the hope for a "pure" church still seduces many today. Augustine's writings against the Donatists include *On Baptism, Answer to the Letters of Petilian*, and *The Correction of the Donatists* (*NPNF*, ser. 1, 4:411-651). In *On Baptism* he selects the example of the notorious heretic Marcion, and observes, "If Marcion consecrated the sacrament of baptism with the words of the gospel 'In the name of the Father, and of the Son, and of the Holy Spirit,' the sacrament was complete" (3.15; 4:442). He argues against "rebaptism" and a false appeal to Cyprian, and discusses the nature of the church. In our own day J. C. Wand has declared: "The Church is a school for sinners, not a museum for saints."

Reading: W. H. C. Frend, *The Donatist Church* (Oxford: OUP, 1952, 1985).

Dort, Synod of

In the classic controversy between Calvinism and Arminianism, the first country to attempt to formalize an official response was the Netherlands, where an assembly of the Dutch Reformed Church was held at Dort (Dordrecht) in 1618-1619. Several representatives from Britain and Switzerland also attended. James Arminius (1559-1609) had been professor at Leiden, and argued that Reformed theology undermined human freedom. Prince Maurice of Orange supported the Calvinist tradition. They met through the fall of 1618 and the spring of 1619. In April 1619 the Synod asserted: (i) unconditional election, (ii) a limited atonement, (iii) the total depravity of humankind, (iv) irresistable grace, and (v) final perseverance of the saints. It then drew up further rules, and confirmed the authority of the Belgic Confession and the Heidelberg Catechism.

Douai

The Roman Catholic translation of the Bible into English in the sixteenth century was widely known as the "Douai" Bible. Strictly it is the Douai-Reims Bible because translation occurred in both Douai and Reims; the College at Douai moved to Reims from 1578 to 1593, at which time it returned to Douai in northeastern France. The OT appeared in 1609-1610. The translation was not from the Greek text but from the Vulgate. Douai was founded as a college in 1562 by Philip II of Spain for Roman Catholic students from Britain.

Double Procession

The double procession of the Holy Spirit denotes the doctrine of the Western Church that the Holy Spirit proceeds from God the Father and from God the Son. The major Western Church Fathers all argue for this on the basis of such biblical verses as John 14:26, "The Holy Spirit, whom the Father will send in my name"; John 16:13-15; Rom 8:9; and others. In the East, Cyril of Alexandria is often cited for the Western view. But Theodore of Mopsuestia and Theodoret reject this doctrine, and Photius (864) made it a theological and political sticking point. The earliest ecumenical creeds did not support it, although it is part of the Western Nicene Creed. In formal terms neither the Western Church nor the Eastern Orthodox will surrender their preferred phrase. But informally it is widely recognized that in favor of double procession is the Spirit's witness to Christ, and in favor of the single procession is the early date of the clause and the originating primacy of the Father. In the West J. Moltmann argues that the Eastern form does better justice to the equality of the three persons of the Trinity. Some have tried to offer such mediating formulae as "proceeds from the Father through the Son" in place of "from the Father and the Son." In general, many theologians see right on both sides, but many church politicians and traditionalists prefer to stay with these traditional formulations. At the recent consecration of Justin Welby as archbishop of Canterbury, the older Eastern form was used in the creed.

Dove

(i) The widespread popular image of the dove as a symbol of peace probably arises from the return of the dove to Noah with an olive branch in its beak (Gen. 8:11). Even the descent of the dove at the baptism of Jesus (Mark 1:10) is often understood popularly to represent the Holy Spirit as peace. (ii) But at a more serious level this probably represents the Spirit's *new creation* and his *creative* power. If the allusion in Gen. 1:2 is to the Spirit of God *(ruach)* rather than to the wind, it may suggest a bird looking over the chaos to bring forth creation and ride in place of formless chaos, as C. K. Barrett suggests. (iii) Tertullian, Ambrose, and Augustine note that the bride is called a dove in Song of Sol. 2:14, 5:2, which therefore applies to the church. (iv) Gregory of Rome and Thomas Aquinas apply this image to theological knowledge. As we argue elsewhere, symbols are important, but can be variously interpreted.

Dualism
Dualism expresses the belief that reality is sharply divided into two. It takes various forms. It may see the world as caught between the two powers of God and Satan; it may divide off God and the world; anthropological dualism offers a sharp divide and contrast between body and "soul"; it may propose a divide between the realm of light and the realm of darkness, truth and falsehood, wisdom and folly, spirit and matter, and other such contrasts. Dualism is seen in gnosticism and in many Eastern religions. Christian theology rejects the notion that anything can challenge the total sovereignty of God. God has created *all things,* including angels, good and evil powers, humankind and nature. God is omnipresent and almighty. Within Christian thought there may remain subsidiary contrasts between light and darkness, truth and falsehood, and spirit and matter; nevertheless, all come within the sovereign governance and purposes of the one God. The Christian church has acknowledged only two orders of being: the Creator (God the Father, Christ, and the Holy Spirit) and the created (all other beings).

Many also argue that some Christians unwittingly or overreadily divide the world into the two components of natural and supernatural. This distinction emerges often in discussions of miracle and healing. A number of respected theologians accept what many orthodox conservatives and Pentecostals *wish* to say by such terminology, but point out that far from honoring the active sovereignty of God, it restricts his action to the "supernatural," as if he were not also sovereign in the everyday world. Some ascribe dualism primarily to a philosophical doctrine in which the contrast between body and mind is construed or interpreted into what G. Ryle called "the ghost in the machine." Plato and Descartes advocated such dualism, which is wholly nonbiblical (*see* **Anthropology**). Others regard it as a metaphysical contrast between good and evil (*see* **Evil, Problem of**). In modern Christology some regard the "two natures" approach of Chalcedon as unnecessarily dualistic.

Dunn, James D. G.
James D. G. Dunn (b. 1939) graduated from the University of Glasgow, was awarded the Cambridge Ph.D. in 1968, and was lecturer at the University of Nottingham from 1970 to 1982. He became professor of divinity at Durham University in succession to C. K. Barrett, was awarded the Cambridge D.D. (1991), and was elected as a fellow of the British Academy. He has become one of the most prolific authors in British NT studies. Among other writings, he has published *Baptism in the Holy Spirit* (1970); *Unity and Diversity in the New Testament* (1977, 1990); *Christology in the Making* (1980, 1989); *Romans* (2 vols., 1988); *The Epistle to the*

Galatians (1993); *The Theology of Paul the Apostle* (1998); *Christ and Spirit* (1998); *Jesus Remembered* (2003); and *The Oral Gospel Tradition* (2013). He has been an advocate of "the new perspective on Paul."

Duns Scotus, John

John Duns Scotus (c. 1266-1308) was born in Duns near the Scottish border, and was a Franciscan. He studied in Oxford and taught in Paris and Cologne. He was a major influence on medieval thought, and directly influenced William of Ockham. He believed that God's Being could be shown by natural reason, but attacked Thomas Aquinas partly for his rationalism. His major work was his commentary on the *Sentences* of Peter Lombard. The complexity and sophistication of his philosophical thought earned him the title "the Subtle Doctor." He published works on causality, freedom, and finitude. God, he argued, can actualize any *logically* possible state of affairs. Free human choices do not depend on prior causes. Duns Scotus believed that theology should be practical, in that its purpose is to inspire love. He was among the first to formulate Mary's immaculate conception, for which some called him "the Marian Doctor." Both humanists and Reformers criticized much of his work (and allegedly some coined the word "dunce" as a play on his name). All the same, his influence during the medieval period rivals that of Aquinas. His thought takes the form of a complex and highly sophisticated system.

Dysteleology

Dysteleology denotes an apparent lack of purpose in nature. It is extended to denote waste or cruelty in animal life, or to anything that runs counter to the teleological argument.

E

Ebionites
The Ebionites were an early Jewish sect of Christianity that did not do justice to the deity of Christ. After A.D. 70 they appear to have lived in rural areas of Palestine, and were especially devoted to the law. Some regard Ebionitism as a form of adoptionism. The origin of the term reflects the Hebrew for "poor," to stress this low Christology.

Ecclesiology
Ecclesiology, or the doctrine of the church, arises from both OT and NT tradition. Narrative confessions of faith in the OT have a communal framework. The confession in Deut. 26:5-9 constitutes a case in point. It begins in the first-person singular, "A wandering Aramean was *my* ancestor," but continues in the first-person plural, "The LORD brought *us* out of Egypt with a mighty hand . . . and gave *us* this land." The same singular-plural logic characterizes the Passover meal. "When your children ask you, . . . 'What is the meaning of the decrees and the statutes and the ordinances that the LORD our God has commanded you?' then you shall say to your children, '*We* were Pharaoh's slaves in Egypt, but the LORD brought *us* out of Egypt'" (Deut. 6:20-24). The identity of an individual speaker becomes one with the *corporate* or *communal* identity of Israel. G. E. Wright and Gerhard von Rad depict OT creedal forms as communal recitals of narrative.

This lays the foundation for the church as the people of God. The modern notion that a "church" denotes the sacred building in which worshipers meet constitutes an unfortunate and misleading development, which is far from the biblical and patristic meaning of the term. Indeed, the corporate and communal mind-set that persisted from at least the fourth century to the eighteenth century grew out of the OT, and was interrupted only by the individualism of Descartes, the empiricists, the Enlightenment, and the Industrial Revolution. God called and elected a "people," and Christ entrusted to a "people" the vocation of being a worshiping community, with *corporate* responsibility for mission and service to the world.

One of the classic images for "church" in the NT is the body of Christ. J. A. T. Robinson memorably attacked the intrusive individualism that too often provides a false interpretation of "the church and its members" (*The Body* [London: SCM, 1952], esp. 58, 78-79). "Members" (Gk. *melē*) are not to be understood on the analogy of members who subscribe to a golf club or a motoring organization. "Members" are not a collection of individuals who happen to subscribe to, or attend, a church. Robinson suggests the term "limbs," which has an organic and ontological relation to Christ and the church. The church would be nothing without its limbs. Indeed, Robinson suggests that Paul's doctrine of the church originated in Christ's words, "Why do you persecute *me?*" on the road to Damascus (Acts 9:4-5; cf. 22:7-8; 26:14-15). In that context Christ identified himself with his church. Admittedly, as many have argued, Robinson may have unduly pressed this to apply to every context. But the fundamental point remains. The one big problem with John Bunyan's *Pilgrim's Progress* is that while it depicts brilliantly the trials and struggles of the Christian life, his "Christian" remains primarily an *individual* believer, supported by an incidental band of Christian friends. But "members" are more than "companions" on the same journey.

Lionel S. Thornton selects the Greek word *koinōnia* to depict the "common life" of the church (*The Common Life in the Body of Christ* [London: Dacre Press, 1950]). The word *koinōnia* often denotes more than "fellowship." He argues that the fellowship of the Holy Spirit in 2 Cor. 13:13 implies that Christians have a "joint-share-together" in the common possession and presence of the Holy Spirit. His other suggestion alongside "common share" is "participation." *Koinōnia* applies to the church in Acts 2:42; 1 Cor. 1:9; 10:16; 2 Cor. 6:14; 9:13; 13:13; Phil. 1:5; 2:1; 3:10; and elsewhere. The adjective *koinōnos* denotes a shareholder or stockholder, who bears common liabilities and advantages with other shareholders. In Acts the church is characterized by common teaching, breaking of bread or common meals, common prayer and *koinōnia* (2:42). In Thornton's language, we *participate in* Christ's Spirit, Christ's love, Christ's victory, and Christ's sonship. He traces the history of Israel, who went with Christ to the grave; until finally, *"When Christ rose, the Church rose from the dead"* (282).

The Fourth Gospel and Paul use various images to press home this point. John 15:1-11 speaks of the *one entity* of the vine and its branches; John 10:1-18, of the many sheep within the one flock. Paul speaks of grafting the wild olive (Rom. 11:17-24), and of the church as God's field, God's building, and God's temple (1 Cor. 3:9-17). The church is the bride of Christ (Eph. 5:25-26, 32), and this also occurs in Rev. 21:2. Often the Greek *ekklēsia* may denote a local congregation (Matt. 18:17; Acts 13:1; Rom. 16:1; 1 Cor. 1:2; 16:19; Gal. 1:2; 1 Thess. 1:1; Rev. 1:4). The status of the local church remains complex, as Pannenberg maintains (*ST* 3:109). Yet the NT witness is as one in underlining the *shared status* of all Christians as participants in the church. The NT writers would be incredulous about the notion of permanently isolated individual Christians "doing their own thing"! In harmony with other aspects of his theology, Luke, especially in Acts, stresses the visible and public role of the church (*see* **Body**).

The biblical writings stress the nature of the church *as pointing beyond itself,* both to Christ and to service and mission to the world. In Acts, Ephesians, and the Pastoral Epistles we also begin to see it as secondarily and additionally an institutional or sociological entity within the world. Both of these aspects emerge in the history of the doctrine of the church.

Pannenberg, R. Jenson, and K. Rahner all allude with approval to Vatican II's description of the church as "a sacrament as it were" (Lat. *uti sacramentum*), and as "the universal sacrament of salvation" (*Lumen Gentium* 1.1; Austin P. Flannery, ed., *Documents of Vatican II* [Grand Rapids: Eerdmans, 1975], 350). A sacrament is a "visible sign" that points to realities beyond itself. Sociologically, the church is a concrete, visible community. Theologically, it points beyond itself to Christ and to its vocation of worship, mission, and service to the world. Rahner calls it "the community of pilgrims." Because the present church on earth contains failure and sin, Pannenberg carefully distinguishes the fallible church from the kingdom of God, in which the consummation brings perfect obedience to God as King. He writes, "The Kingdom and the Church are not herewith simply identical" (*ST* 3:30). The church is "an anticipatory sign of God's coming rule" (32). R. Schnackenburg traces this concept of the church to Cyprian (*God's Rule and Kingdom* [London: Nelson, 1963], 23-34; Cyprian, *Epistle* 69.6; *On the Unity of the Church* 4). J. Moltmann, too, insists, "The Church is her true self only when she exists for humanity" (*Church in the Power of the Spirit* [London: SCM, 1977], 66). He appeals further for this to D. Bonhoeffer. Moltmann expresses this even more strongly. He writes, "It is not the church that has a mission of salvation to fulfil to the world; it is the mission of the Son and the Spirit through the Father that includes the church, creating a church as it goes on its way" (64). The church, he says, is moving toward the eschaton, but has not already arrived.

Much thought has recently been given to *models* of the church, probably each of which has advantages and difficulties. On the institutional or sociological side, it is recognized that any society or community usually begins with a vision, and gradually develops an infrastructure to support the vision. At the beginning the vision outweighs the infrastructure. At the end the danger arises that the infrastructure can become top-heavy, or even an end in itself. The aim is to achieve the appropriate support for the vision, without undermining it. On the church, Avery Dulles offers seven models that may test how well the vision is served (*Models of the Church* [Dublin: Gill and Macmillan, 1988], 35-46).

(i) The *institutional* model, Dulles argues, may facilitate an emphasis on the church's tradition and corporate identity, but negatively it may seem to support clericalism and an overconcern with jurisdiction and law. Rahner questions the "managerial" stance of some clergy (*The Shape of the Church to Come* [London: SPCK, 1974], 58). (ii) The *liturgical* model stresses prayer, worship, proclamation, and sacraments, but may encourage the notion of a self-contained, inward-looking community. (iii) The *pilgrim* model rightly stresses that the church is en route to glory, and can be fallible. It may be complementary to other models. (iv) The *sacrament* model can remind the church that it is a visible manifestation of what points beyond itself. (v) The *communal* model stresses corporate identity, friendship, and participation, but at times can lead to self-preoccupation.

(vi) The *kerygmatic* model reminds the church of its responsibility for proclamation and mission. (vii) The *servant* model underlines the need for service, and its "diaconal" work for others. These are all *complementary* models, not exclusive ones.

Much is made of "the marks of the church." These are traditionally the four "notes" (Lat. *notae*) of the church as one, holy, catholic, and apostolic, as confessed in the creeds. The unity of the church is both given and lived out (J. R. Nelson, *The Realm of Redemption* [London: Epworth, 1951], 200-210). The church as holy should not be interpreted in moralistic terms. It is primarily holy as belonging to God. Historically this notion has invited the heresy of Donatism, and has sometimes led to division and exclusivity. On the other hand, the church is more than a religious arm of social services. The church's catholicity and apostolicity concern its continuity and identity, especially in the proclamation of the apostolic gospel and loyalty to the rule of faith. However, these notions can be controversial. It is well known that concern for the church has characterized Christian theology from the earliest times. *1 Clement* (A.D. 96) shows concern for the unity of the church, and Ignatius (c. 110) shows concern for the relation between bishops and presbyters. The *Didachē* (c. 110-120) discusses such practices as baptism, prayer, and the holiness of the church, including words of the Lord's Supper or Eucharist. Justin (c. 150) also addresses the theology of the Eucharist. Clement of Alexandria (c. 190) is concerned with the teaching role of the church and catechesis. Tertullian (c. 200) stresses the corporate prayer of the church for the emperor, and its requirement for moral purity. Many find in Hippolytus (c. 215) a model of early liturgical and creedal practice. Cyprian (c. 250) appears to have coined the saying "There is no salvation outside the church," and is greatly concerned with Donatism, governance, and episcopal succession. By contrast, Origen (c. 240) sees the church as a mixture of purity and impurity, but also as the bride of Christ.

Bryan P. Stone has edited excerpts from postbiblical writers, from Augustine, Bernard, Hildegard, Aquinas, Luther, and Calvin, to Hooker, Owen, Wesley, Schleiermacher, Barth, Temple, Küng, Moltmann, and Pannenberg, in *A Reader in Ecclesiology* (Farnham, U.K., and Burlington, Vt.: Ashgate, 2011). (*See also* **Anglican Theology; Apostle, Apostolicity; Baptism; Baptist Theology; Body; Catholicity; Lord's Supper; Methodism; Ministry.**)

Reading: K. Brower, *Holiness and Ecclesiology* (Grand Rapids: Eerdmans, 2007); R. F. Collins, *The Many Faces of the Church* (New York: Crossroad, 2003); F. J. Cwiekowski, *The Beginnings of the Church* (Mahwah, N.J.: Paulist, 1988); Avery Dulles, *Models of the Church* (New York: Doubleday, 2002); J. Moltmann, *The Church in the Power of the Spirit* (Minneapolis: Fortress, 1993); J. Moltmann, *The Open Church* (London: SCM; Philadelphia: Fortress, 1978); J. R. Nelson, *The Realm of Redemption* (London: Epworth, 1951, 1963); R. Schnackenburg, *The Church in the New Testament* (Freiburg: Herder; London: Burns and Oates, 1965); B. P. Stone, ed., *A Reader in Ecclesiology* (Farnham, U.K., and Burlington, Vt.: Ashgate, 2011).

Eckhart, Meister

Meister Eckhart (c. 1260–c. 1328) has a double interest for theology. One is his mysticism; the other is his apophatic theology, for which he is indebted to Neoplatonism and Plotinus. He was influenced by Albertus Magnus and Thomas Aquinas, and his mystical writings include *The Book of Divine Consolation* (c. 1320). Nothing that we can say, he urges, comprehends God, and "all things are a mere nothing." His creative and imaginative use of German made him an influential preacher. In 1326 he was accused of heresy under Pope John XXII, but Pope John Paul II commended him.

Edwards, Jonathan

Jonathan Edwards (1703-1758) was one of the finest minds in eighteenth- and nineteenth-century America, accredited also with playing a leading part in the Great Awakening revival. Born in Connecticut, he entered Yale at thirteen, graduated in 1720, and took a master's degree at twenty. He accepted Calvin's doctrine of "the glory of the divine King," even though he had difficulties about God's unqualified sovereignty. In 1727 he was ordained and served in the Congregational Church in Massachusetts. In his book *A Faithful Narrative of the Surprising Work of God* he recounted the First Great Awakening of the 1730s and 1740s. But in 1746 he supported the authenticity of many experiences of conversions, but he also seriously questioned the genuineness of many who did not remain faithful, in his *Treatise concerning Religious Affections*. As a theologian he accepted the majesty and power of God; as a philosopher he expanded on the peril of self-deception and "imagined" work of the Holy Spirit. Thus he was both a defender and a critic of religious revivals. True renewal is a work of the Holy Spirit.

Edwards also defended the purification of the church. In his *Qualifications Requisite for Full Communion* (1749), he insisted on true signs of grace for admission to Holy Communion. In the following years his congregation deposed him for this strict policy, and Edwards moved to Stockbridge, Massachusetts. He completed *The Freedom of the Will* in 1754, defending Calvinism against Arminianism. He held a view of the universe as an interdependent, unified system of being, combining Calvinism with Sir Isaac Newton's notions of science. He planned a lesser work, but after being appointed president of the College of New Jersey (later, Princeton), he fell victim to smallpox, and died in 1758. Imagined conversion, he asserts, owes much to "imaginations and pretences" that are "stupid and perverse."

Reading: Jonathan Edwards, *Select Works of Jonathan Edwards* (London: Banner of Truth, 1959); Jonathan Edwards, *Basic Writings,* ed. Ola Winslow (New York: New American Library, 1966).

Election and Predestination

Election has its basis in the biblical words for "to choose" (Heb. *b-ch-r* and *bāchîr,* "chosen," or sometimes *y-d-ʻ,* "to choose" or "to know"; and Gk. *eklegomai* or *eklektos,* "chosen"; or also other words, *cheirotoneō,* "to choose" or "to select"; *procheirizomai,* "to choose in advance"; *haireomai,* "to choose"; *lambanō,* "to choose" or "to take"). The secular use of *b-ch-r* in the OT is varied. One may choose a wife (Gen. 6:2) or a land (Gen. 13:12), stones for a sling (1 Sam. 17:40), or soldiers (Exod. 17:9). When human beings are the subject, they may choose a way of life (Pss. 25:12; 119:30; Isa. 7:15-16). But in at least 100 of the cases, or 60 percent, God is the subject of the verb. God chooses a place of worship some 44 times, notably in Deuteronomy (12:18; 14:25; 15:20; 16:7; 17:8; 18:6). God also chooses David (Ps. 2:6) and Saul (1 Sam. 10:24) and the priesthood (Num. 17:5). But especially relevant to election is his choice of "my servant" (Isa. 41:7-8; 42:1; 43:10; 44:1-2) and "Israel" (Deut. 4:37; 7:6-7). These choices do not depend on any merit in Israel, but on divine love and divine will: "It was not because you were more numerous than any other people that the LORD ... loved you" (Deut. 7:7-8). See *TDOT* 2:3-87; H. H. Rowley, *The Biblical Doctrine of Election* (1950); and J. G. M. McConville, *Law and Theology in Deuteronomy* (Sheffield: JSOT Press, 1984), 21-38.

In the NT the theme of choice is no less prominent. The word *eklektos,* "chosen," occurs in "You are a chosen race, a royal priesthood, a holy nation, God's own people" (1 Pet. 2:9). Rom. 9:11 speaks of "God's choice" *(eklogēn).* Sometimes the writer uses *exaireomai,* as in "chosen you" (NRSV, "rescued you"), or "God chose you as the first fruits for salvation" (2 Thess. 2:13). Luke repeats the phrase, "my Son, my Chosen" (Luke 9:35; *eklegomai*). In 2 Cor. 8:19 the NRSV uses "appointed" by the churches for the Greek *cheirotoneō.* K. Barth's perspective on election is thoroughly christological and often appeals to Johannine theology. The theme occurs even when the vocabulary is merely implicit. John 6:44 reads, "No one can come to me unless drawn by the Father who sent me." John 10:29 speaks of "what my Father has given me," and 17:6 repeats "whom you gave me."

The theme of choice or election is unavoidable on the basis of the biblical writings. The idea is present even when explicit terminology is absent. One crucial passage is 1 Cor. 4:7: "What do you have that you did not receive?" This is a perfect parallel to Deut. 7:6-7. The ground of election is the love and will of God, not the merit of humankind. This is explicit in Eph. 1:4-6: "He [God] chose us in Christ before the foundation of the world to be holy and blameless before him in love ... to the praise of his glorious grace that he freely bestowed on us in the Beloved." The basis of election is the unconditional love of God, his promise, and his faithfulness to this promise. In the teaching of Jesus, the conclusion of the parable of the laborers in the vineyard is "Are you envious because I am generous?" (Matt. 20:15; *see* **Grace**).

In the history of Christian thought, Augustine famously expounds this theme on the basis of these biblical passages. In *On Rebuke and Grace* Augustine considers Rom. 8:28-30, "All things work together for good for those who love God, who are called according to his purpose. For those whom he foreknew he also predestined to be conformed to the image of his Son.... Those whom he predestined he also called." Augustine comments, "No one perishes, because all are elected. And they are elected because they were called according to the purpose . . . not of their own but God's" (*On Rebuke and Grace* 14). Augustine links election and predestination (Gk. *kata prothesin . . . proōrisen;* only in Rom. 8:29-30; 1 Cor. 2:7; Eph. 1:5, 11; Acts 4:28). Augustine's strong emphasis arises from his conviction that in matters of salvation "all is of God," which provoked Pelagius into a counterreaction (*see* **Augustine; Pelagius**). He wrote, "The Lord anticipates us that we may be healed. . . . He anticipates us that we may be called" (*On Nature and Grace* 35.31). This clearly implies prevenient grace. The Law, he held, is unable to check sin. His emphasis on election is to stress the initiative of God's sovereign grace. He gives a still fuller account in *On the Predestination of the Saints*. He quotes 1 Cor. 4:6-7: "What hast thou that thou hast not received?" (*Predestination* 10; *NPNF*, ser. 1, 5:503). He stresses, "Such an election is of grace, not at all of merits. . . . Otherwise grace is no more grace" (chap. 11).

Augustine's emphasis has been transmitted in most of the Western Church, largely through Thomas Aquinas and John Calvin. Thomas is quite clear. He writes, "It is fitting that God should predestine men. For all things are subject to his providence. . . . Now it belongs to providence to direct things toward their end" (*Su Th* 1, qu. 23, art. 1). He appeals to Augustine and to Paul (Rom. 8:30; art. 2). He insists that this doctrine should not be considered in isolation from others. He repeats, "Predestination is a part of providence" (art. 3). It also presupposes election (art. 4). He cites Eph. 1:4, "'He chose us in him before the foundation of the world.' . . . Predestination presupposes election" (art. 4). Contrary to what some hold, foreknowledge of merits is *not* the cause of election (art. 5). Thomas concludes, "Predestination most certainly and infallibly takes effect" (art. 6; *see* **Irresistible Grace**). Again he appeals for this certainty to Augustine (art. 7). Prayer is not an ultimate *cause* of salvation, but a *means* through which God's will takes certain effect (art. 8).

Calvin discusses election and predestination in the *Institutes* 3.21-24. Like Aquinas, he readily appeals to Augustine. The doctrine is "useful, necessary, and most sweet" (3.21.1). He knows that secular men "carp . . . or scoff" at the doctrine (3.21.4). But it functions "to crush all pride" (3.21.5), and to extol God. It begins with the basic fact that "All are not created in equal terms" (3.21.5). If the agenda is "fairness," why are some born into rich families and countries while others may be born poor, weak, or blind? Yet the key to the doctrine is not "fairness" but *"the grace of God"* (3.21.6). This is the basis of God's election of Israel, Abraham, David, and Christ (3.21.7). In chapter 22 he cites numerous Scriptures, beginning with the call or election of Abraham and passing to Paul's statements in Eph. 1:4-5 (3.22.1).

Two basic principles (after grace) are that "God reigns" and that no good works can be taken into account (3.22.3). Calvin then considers Paul on the election of Israel in Rom. 9:6 (3.22.4). The will and love of God are "the origin and cause of election" (3.22.4). Why should Jacob have been "chosen" rather than Esau (3.22.5)? Paul answers, "I will have mercy on whom I have mercy" (Rom.

9:15; 3.22.6). The foreknowledge of God suggests "secret predestination" (3.22.6); Christ "makes himself the author of election" (3.22.7); Calvin discusses Ambrose, Origen, and Jerome but stands alongside Augustine. Thomas seems to Calvin to be oversubtle at this point (3.22.9). Constantly he returns to contemplate "the Father's will" (3.22.10). Following Augustine (*Contra Julianum* 5.5), Calvin rejects "the distinction between will and permission" (*Institutes* 3.23.8), as if God only "permitted" the wicked to perish. Here the notion of "double predestination" seems to constitute a background, although many later thinkers reject this concept, including Karl Barth. But Calvin insists that he follows both Augustine and the testimony of Scripture (3.23.13).

While many see ambiguity in election, namely, whether it constitutes a means or an end, Calvin is clear: "Paul teaches that we have been chosen to this end: that we may lead a holy and blameless life" (3.23.12). Election is not contingent upon faith (3.24.4). The pastoral purpose of the doctrine is a "means of establishing our assurance" (3.24.6), which "takes its origin from God alone" (2.3.8).

Just as Augustine's doctrine provoked Pelagius into action, so Calvin's provoked Arminius to write. Beza sharpened Calvin's doctrine even further, and the Thirty-nine Articles of the Church of England are broadly Calvinist in tone, as Presbyterianism was in Scotland. But under the Stuarts Presbyterianism declined in England, and it is well known that Wesley, in contrast to Whitefield, took an Arminian approach. Karl Barth revived the doctrine of election, but with a different emphasis. In Barth's view election primarily applied to Christ. Indeed, in *CD* II/2, chapter 7, Barth devotes five hundred (English) pages to "The Election of God." He writes, "The election of grace is the eternal beginning of all the ways and works of God in Jesus Christ" (II/2, 94). Jesus Christ is both "electing and elected." He is God's word, God's decree, and God's beginning. This occurs prior to the creation of time and space as we know them (101). In his oneness with humankind Christ is elected, and reveals "our election as an election which is made by Him" (115). As Son of God, Christ elects. Barth's emphasis remains on the *sovereignty of God* (II/2, chap. 7, sect. 33.2), and on the *reliability of God's faithful promise* (sect. 34.3, pp. 233-59). On the problem of election, predestination, and freedom, see **Freedom**, especially on the compatibility between freedom and prediction.

Reading: Augustine, *On the Predestination of the Saints*, in *NPNF*, ser. 1, 5:493-520; G. C. Berkouwer, *Divine Election* (Grand Rapids: Eerdmans, 1960); John Calvin, *Institutes of the Christian Religion*, trans. Henry Beveridge, 2 vols. (Grand Rapids: Eerdmans, 1989), bk. 3, chaps. 21-24; J. S. Kaminsky, *Yet I Loved Jacob: Reclaiming the Biblical Concept of Election* (Nashville: Abingdon, 2007); K. Tanner, *Economy of Grace* (Minneapolis: Fortress, 2005); *TDOT* 2:73-87.

Emanation

Emanation denotes a finite being or manifestation that is believed to flow from the Godhead. In Christian theology this would not apply to the Holy Spirit, since he is God, not finite; and it would not apply to the world, since the world is not

God, but finite. The Christian doctrine of creation, by contrast, states that God created the world "out of nothing" *(ex nihilo)*. The concept of emanations of God belongs, rather, to gnosticism and pantheism. God in Christian theology is transcendent as well as immanent.

Empiricism

At its simplest, empiricism denotes the belief that all knowledge or ideas come through one or more of the five human senses. Perceptions enter the mind, which is like a blank sheet of paper *(tabula rasa)*, through sight, hearing, and the other three senses. The mind may reflect on this sense-data to form ideas or even concepts. This view stands in contrast to rationalism, in which the notion of "innate ideas" is the polar opposite to empiricism. Locke, Berkeley, and Hume represent the three major British empiricists, whereas Descartes and Leibniz are classic rationalists. These two schools of philosophy were widely approved until the transcendental and critical philosophy of Kant saw both as inadequate, and changed the terms of the debate. More broadly, empiricism denotes the belief that *experience* is the source of all knowledge, including aesthetic, moral, and religious experience as well as sensory experience. This is often a more secondary meaning.

Encounter

Encounter denotes a face-to-face meeting between two personal subjects. It is typically prominent in those writers who value personal encounter above inferential knowledge or natural theology. We may cite Pascal, Kierkegaard, Buber, Barth, and especially Brunner. Pascal spoke of encounter with Christ but rejected "theistic proofs." In Kierkegaard subjectivity, or "being sharpened into an 'I,'" was of special value. Passion and inwardness, he wrote, allow us to meet Christ as our contemporary, not as a mere figure of past history or as an item in a philosophical argument. Emil Brunner attacked "objectivism" as being like a frozen waterfall, while at the other extreme he regarded mystics and enthusiasts as imprisoned in a romantic subjectivism of the self. He entitled one of his books *The Divine-Human Encounter* (Philadelphia: Westminster, 1943); also published as *Truth as Encounter*. He saw Jesus Christ as the place of this encounter. He repeats this theme in several writings. He writes, "Faith is knowledge as encounter" (*Revelation and Reason* [London; SCM, 1946], 9). Barth also gives a place to the theme of encounter, especially in the context of "God with us" and decision "in face of the Word of God spoken to me" (*CD* I/1, sect. 5.3).

Enlightenment, The

The classic definition of the Enlightenment came from I. Kant (1724-1804) in an essay of 1784 specifically in answer to the question "What is the Enlightenment?" ("Der Frage, Was ist Aufklärung?") in the *Berlin Monthly*. He answered: "Enlightenment is man's emergence from his self-incurred immaturity," by which he meant "courage to use one's reason, intellect and wisdom without the guidance of another." Reason meant thinking for oneself, in contrast to secondhand authorities and institutions. This constituted a reaction against accepting spoon-fed or secondhand dogma. The dating of the Enlightenment may vary between Britain and Continental Europe. In England it is often traced from the seventeenth-century Deists to the eighteenth century, but in France and Germany it is usually seen as an eighteenth-century phenomenon. Some even trace its beginnings to R. Descartes (1596-1650) with his location of reason and knowledge in the consciousness of the *individual,* and to the empiricism of J. Locke, with his emphasis on the "reasonableness" of belief. Henning Graf Reventlow traces the origins of biblical criticism to Deism, including M. Tindal (1657-1733) and J. Toland (1670-1722).

In France Enlightenment thought was explicitly antiestablishment and often directed against theism or religious belief. D. Diderot (1713-1784) spearheaded a largely materialistic thirty-five volume *Encyclopaedia* (1780); Voltaire promoted both empiricism and a measure of skepticism, as well as tolerance. Holbach (1723-1789) attacked Christianity explicitly. Many, but not all, include Rousseau (1712-1778) in this movement. In Germany Christian Wolff (1679-1754) drew on the rationalism of Leibniz. S. Reimarus and G. E. Lessing (1729-1781) were notorious for their attack on the veracity of the Gospels.

Many Christians would accept the need to think for oneself without seeing this as an *alternative* to respect for authority. Indeed, in spite of the work of Fichte and Hegel, the movement was partly overtaken by Romanticism. The eighteenth century, which Newman called "the age [of reason] when love grows cold," provoked downright critical hostility from the nominally "secular" philosopher Hans-Georg Gadamer. He regarded the Enlightenment as being as much a prejudice as that from which it sought emancipation (*Truth and Method,* 2nd ed. [London: Sheed and Ward, 1989], 270-82). Gadamer writes, "The fundamental prejudice of the Enlightenment is the prejudice against prejudice itself [*Vorurteile,* 'prejudgment'], which denies tradition its power" (270). He attacks its assumptions that "methodologically disciplined use of reason can safeguard us from all error." By this he means "Descartes' idea of method" (277). He adds: "The authority of persons is ultimately based not on the ... abdication of reason but on an acknowledgment ... that the other is superior to oneself in judgement ... and trusts to the better insight of others" (279). In this light, the Enlightenment seeks freedom and autonomy, but may often be guilty of individualism and arrogance.

Reading: H.-G. Gadamer, *Truth and Method* (London: Sheed and Ward, 1989), 270-82; P. Hyland et al., eds., *The Enlightenment: A Sourcebook and Reader* (New York and London: Routledge, 2003); Henning Graf Reventlow, *The Authority of the Bible and the Rise of the Modern World* (London: SCM, 1984), esp. 289-383.

Enthusiasm

R. A. Knox, author of *Enthusiasm* (Oxford: Clarendon, 1950), concedes that the term is an "elusive thing ... commonly misapplied as a label for a tendency" (1).

But he argues that "ultrasupernaturalism" is the closest that we may come to its meaning (2). He claims that while most Christians see grace as a heightening of nature, enthusiasts are bolder: "grace has . . . replaced it" (3). Yet Knox acknowledges, "Enthusiasm did not really begin to take shape until the moment when Luther shook up the whole pattern of European theology" (4). The "Enthusiasts" or Radical Reformers then opposed Luther.

Those who champion enthusiasm tend to applaud the Montanists and the Radical Reformers. Luther called Munzer and Carlstadt "the fanatics" *(Schwärmer)*. They led the Peasants' Revolt, disapproved of ministerial robes and styles, and encouraged "prophecy." In Luther's view they disparaged temptation and struggle, and made overhasty appeal to the Holy Spirit. They tended to view sanctification as an event, rather than a process. By 1750 Wesley had become convinced that the Montanists "were real, scriptural Christians." Bishop Butler declared, "Sir, the pretending to extraordinary revelations and gifts of the Holy Ghost is a horrid thing, a very horrid thing" *(Enthusiasm,* 450). But Knox hesitates to call Wesley an enthusiast in the fullest sense, seeing Fletcher and the Quakers as more appropriate candidates. Today the term might be used of most Pentecostals and of many in the Renewal Movement, but for its pejorative application.

Ephesus, Council of
Known as the third "ecumenical" council, after Nicaea (325) and Constantinople (381), the Council of Ephesus (431) was convened by Theodosius II to address the Christology of Nestorianism. But the opponent of Nestorius, Cyril of Alexandria, manipulated the proceedings, beginning them before the Syrian bishops had arrived. Many also argue that Cyril misrepresented the view of Nestorius. (*See also* **Christology: History of Thought.**)

Epistemology
From Greek *epistēmē,* "knowledge," epistemology denotes the study of any theory of knowledge. Often this includes a study of the limits and possibility of knowledge, as in Kant, or the justification and validity of knowledge, as in Plantinga. Empirical or a posteriori knowledge is often distinguished from rational or a priori knowledge, as in Descartes or Leibniz. (*See also* **A Posteriori; A Priori.**)

Erastianism
Erastianism denotes the control of the state over the church or churches. The name is borrowed from the Swiss theologian Thomas Erastus (1524-1583). Erastus believed that civil authorities have the right to exercise jurisdiction over the church, provided that the state professes only one religion. The Westminster Confession rejected Erastianism, and the Barmen Declaration excluded it. The Oxford Movement began as a protest against the British government's attempt to appoint Irish bishops. Critics of the establishment of the Church of England as a national church often accuse Richard Hooker of Erastian leanings.

Eristics

The term "eristics" seems mainly to have been coined by E. Brunner. He defines eristic theology as "the intellectual discussion of the Christian faith in the light of [views] which are opposed to the Christian message" (*Christian Doctrine of God* [London: Lutterworth, 1949], 98). He distinguishes eristics from apologetics, which serve to defend the Christian faith. In this area he commends Pascal and Kierkegaard.

Eschatology

Eschatology is the doctrine of the "last things" (from Gk. *eschatos*, "last"). In the Bible this refers not so much to individual death and resurrection as to the three great cosmic events: the parousia (or return of Christ), the resurrection of the dead, and the Last Judgment. Over time, however, other elements were added: the death of the individual, heaven and hell, the imminence of the end, hope, the intermediate state, the nature of eternity, and the beatific vision. Most or all of these themes are addressed under separate entries devoted to the foregoing terms in this *Companion*.

Eternity

Broadly there are four distinct views of eternity. (i) Plato regarded eternity as *timelessness*. He viewed time as the contingent "moving image" of timeless eternity, beyond the world of change. Eternity thus belonged to the realm of forms or ideas, untouched by the empirical world. (ii) A popular religious notion is that of eternity as *everlasting duration*. It is like time without beginning or end. (iii) Boethius (c. 480-525) is well known for his influential view of eternity as *simultaneity*, or "the complete possession all at once of the illimitable life." Boethius, however, drew this view largely from Plotinus. (iv) Some thinkers express discontent with all three of these views, and postulate a *radically different kind of time*. In the light of theories in physics and mathematics, reality could well consist of more dimensions than we can easily conceive. It would be difficult, for example, for a species familiar with thinking only in two dimensions to conceive of a third, fourth, or fifth dimension. David Wilkinson strongly hints at this fourth notion of time, which we find plausible.

(i) Each of the four conceptions or theories has certain advantages and difficulties. The first grasps the paradox that change and succession supposedly cannot improve upon what is "perfect." In addition to this, if Augustine is correct in arguing that God created the universe not *in* time but *with* time, eternity appears to involve the dissolution of time along with space. In any case, many interpret Einstein as suggesting that space and time are closely interdependent as space-time. A rapidly faster-than-light moving body may experience time at a radically different speed from "normal" time. Among Christian philosophers, most notably Paul Helm argues for "the eternally timeless God" (*The Eternal God* [Oxford: Clarendon, 1988], 37). For him, arguments about God's foreknowledge are accommodations to the thinking of those in time. He stresses the sovereignty of God. On the other hand, Brian Leftow argues: "A timeless God has no past, and one can remember [or forget] . . . only what is past. . . . A timeless God has no future . . . or plans" ("Eternity," in *A Companion to the Philosophy of Religion*, ed. P. L. Quinn and C. Taliaferro [Oxford: Blackwell, 1999], 257). Richard Swinburne describes such a God as "a lifeless being." A fixed or timeless God, he claims, "would be a very lifeless thing, not a person who reacts to men with sympathy or anger, pardon or chastening. . . . He chooses there and then . . . in continual interaction with men"; not "from all eternity" (*The Coherence of Theism* [Oxford: Clarendon, 1977], 214). Helm offers a reply: God's foreknowledge and decree are "timeless." He can appeal to Aquinas. Nevertheless, we may ask whether Helm's assumed question of "time" or "timeless" goes deeply enough into the nature of time and eternity (*see* **Time**).

(ii) Those who advocate a notion of eternity as an everlasting duration often appeal to the OT notion of the "living God" (Heb. *chay;* Gk. *zōn*, noun, *zōē; see* **Life**). The symbolism of the tabernacle is that of the moving, ongoing God (Exodus 23–40). The famous verse Exod. 3:14 means "I am what I am" only in the Greek translation, or LXX. The Hebrew verb is in the imperfect tense, which probably denotes a *future* sense: "I will be what I will be." The equally well known verse in Hebrews, "Jesus Christ is the same yesterday and today and forever" (13:8), is also widely misunderstood. The writer is not speaking of the immutability of God, but of the permanency of Christ as High Priest in contrast to the endless succession and constant replacement of Aaronic Jewish priests. Some attribute this view to Duns Scotus, William of Ockham, or Hegel. But there are enormous difficulties to conceiving of God as permanently conditioned by time, which is his own creation and belongs to the creaturely universe, along with space. It is uncertain whether Aquinas or Hegel genuinely held this view.

(iii) The most favored view is in broad terms that of Boethius and Plotinus, of eternity as gathering up all temporal moments simultaneously. Boethius expounded this in his *Consolation of Philosophy* 5.6. He pointed out, "There is nothing placed in time that can embrace the whole extent of its life equally." If the last event of life has special privilege, what are we to say of Christian believers who degenerate, for example, to suffer dementia or Alzheimer's disease? Henry Chadwick explains this by analogy with the center of a circle of time: "All is a simultaneous present" (*Boethius* [Oxford: Clarendon, 1992], 246). In many ways this view attempts to recognize that God is "beyond" or "outside" time, but also that for God time is real, and he engages with it. Whether this leaves the problem shrouded in ambiguity remains an open question.

(iv) In our entry **Time**, we attempt to show that time *is not one thing.* We distinguish clock time as chronological time from narrative time and subjective time. In the light of his knowledge of both theology and the sciences, David Wilkinson tends to adopt Boethius's view that "God experiences all time at once" (*Christian Eschatology and the Physical Universe* [London: Continuum/T. & T. Clark, 2010],

124). But he also discusses "the four dimensions of space-time" as if this were laid out before God. However, could we suppose that "multiple dimensions" of time were all set out before God? C. S. Lewis discussed the hypothesis of "Flatlanders" who lived in two dimensions, and attempt to understand three-dimensional reality. If we imagine (or try to imagine) a five- or six-dimensional universe, this simply becomes inexplicable to three-dimensional beings. But perhaps the relation between time-as-we-know-it and eternity involves such additional dimension(s). This eternity might not involve any of the three standard theories, but only eternity as we-do-not-(yet)-know-it. If clock time can differ from narrative time, subjective time, sociological time, and post-Einsteinian time in physics or mathematics, might this not also differ from God's time? Wilkinson points out: "Such an analogy receives support from the claim that certain models for quantum gravity require ten or even 26 dimensions for the physical universe" (126). Wilkinson also cites E. M. Conradie on "depth dimension." Predictably, objections arise. Swinburne argues that we cannot have more than three dimensions. But this caveat must apply only to our present human life or to created time, not to eternity.

The subject is complex and vast, and oversimplification must be avoided at all costs. The present conditions of space-time express how God has determined to create a temporal world. Eternity, most thinkers agree, cannot easily be conceptualized for those whose life and thought are now time-bound. It is beyond present life and thought. But either the third or fourth view may have most to commend it.

Reading: H. Chadwick, *Boethius* (Oxford: Clarendon, 1992); P. Helm, *Eternal God* (Oxford: Clarendon, 1988); R. Swinburne, *The Coherence of Theism* (Oxford: Clarendon, 1977); D. Wilkinson, *Christian Eschatology and the Physical Universe* (London: Continuum/T. & T. Clark, 2010).

Ethics

This *Companion* concentrates on Christian theology rather than on ethics as such. There are other dictionaries devoted to the subject, for example, L. C. Becker and C. B. Becker, *Encyclopaedia of Ethics,* 3 vols. (New York: Routledge, 2002), or in more distinctively Christian terms, R. Hays, *The Moral Vision of the New Testament* (Edinburgh: T. & T. Clark, 1996); G. Meilaender and W. Werpehowski, eds., *The Oxford Handbook of Theological Ethics* (Oxford: OUP, 2005); and D. Atkinson and D. Field, *The New Dictionary of Christian Ethics and Pastoral Theology* (Leicester: IVP, 1995). An older work is J. Macquarrie, *Dictionary of Christian Ethics* (London: SCM, 1967). Hence this entry is relatively short and selective.

Most ethical theories fall under the heading of one of three approaches, although many believe these should decisively overlap. (i) "Virtue ethics" stresses the role of character, but can sometimes merge into situation ethics or relativism. The roots of this approach lie in the philosophy of Socrates, Plato, and Aristotle. In Plato the four cardinal "virtues" were wisdom, courage or fortitude, temperance or moderation, and justice. His typical Greek words were *aretē* (virtue), *phronēsis* (practical wisdom), and *eudaimonia* (well-being, flourishing). The four cardinal virtues are found in *The Republic*. Aristotle especially stressed the doctrine of the mean: for example, courage constitutes the mean between fear and rashness. The "virtue" approach passed to Cicero, Ambrose, and especially Thomas Aquinas, who examines the virtues in detail in *Summa Theologiae* 1a2ac, questions 18-67. This section includes love, desire, pleasure, habits, and virtues. With the Renaissance, this Aristotelian-Thomist model fell into disfavor. In early modernism, utilitarianism frequently took over. But in 1978 Philippa Foot published *Virtues and Vices,* and more decisively for theology, Alasdair MacIntyre published *After Virtue* (Notre Dame, Ind.: University of Notre Dame Press, 1984; 3rd ed. 2007). In this he criticizes the ethics of Enlightenment thinkers (including Hume, Kant, Kierkegaard, and Marx), and calls for a return to Aristotelian teleology. Their stress on moral agency reduced ethics to subjective individualism and convention. Aristotle, on the other hand, distinguishes between the "is" and the "ought," and offers the antithesis to Nietzsche, as well as rightly stressing community. *Character* is more important than action. Later MacIntyre published *Three Revival Versions of Moral Enquiry* (London: Duckworth, 1990).

(ii) Deontological ethics (from Gk. *deon,* "duty," and *dei,* "it is necessary") stresses duty and moral obligation. For Christians and theists, this may be the command of God. It addresses the *motivation* of ethics, and often appeals to the moral imperative of Kant. Kant argued that it was not the consequences of an action that made it moral, but the motives of the agent of the action. The world perceived by theoretical reason is largely constructed, or at least organized, by the mind. The path to the Absolute is conveyed by the categorical imperative. Nothing can be good without qualification, but the good will. Hence: "If, with the greatest of efforts it should yet achieve nothing ... like a jewel it would still shine by its own light." Good consequences have nothing to do with ethics. Ethics depend on duty for the sake of duty. Motives must not be mixed. This gave rise to Schiller's witty rejoinder: "Willingly serve I my friends, but I do it, alas, with affection. Hence I am cursed with the doubt, virtue I have not attained." He imagines the reply: "This is your only recourse: you must stubbornly seek to abhor them. Then you can do with disgust that which the law may enjoin." For the Christian this does seem to cast doubt on what is motivated by love, which might also consider some effect of the action.

(iii) The third approach is *consequential* ethics, which often takes the form of utilitarianism. Thomas Hobbes basically believed in psychological hedonism, but allowed for half-conscious social contract of mutual benefits. David Hume certainly stressed consequences, in contrast to intuition or reason. But he defined them in utilitarian and conventional terms: good is the action "whose consequences most men approve." It is not an absolute, but relative to people and their situations. The greatest problem for Hume, as utilitarians know, is how, even if they are right, we can ever *measure* so many variables. Hume's appeal to common sense hardly resolves the problem. Jeremy Bentham more explicitly advocates utilitarianism. He wrote, "Morality is . . . the production of the greatest quantity of happiness on the part of those whose interest is in view." His ethical criticism is whether an action "tends to augment or diminish happiness." He attempted to sketch out such "measurements" as "intensity, duration and extent." But whether these can take us forward is doubtful, even if many people, in everyday life, may tend to adopt this ethic. The three main approaches lay out the ground for Christian theology. However, we have not included in this brief survey various particular schemes such as Herbert Spencer's evolutionary ethics, which are not mainstream approaches.

The two most widespread theological reactions are to insist that *either* (1) all three approaches must be taken into account *or* (2) "general" or "secular" ethical theories are all inadequate without a firm theological basis, as Barth would argue. In fact, the fundamental areas of social ethics, medical ethics, legal ethics, business ethics, and sexual ethics cannot be fully addressed without *both* a theological basis *and* a comprehensive account of motive, consequences, and character-and-society. In theology, for example, such themes as human sin are vital, together with law, mind, heart, image of God, and creation. Reinhold Niebuhr offers one of many examples in his *Nature and Destiny of Man*. Grace and love are also important, for which see Anders Nygren, *Agape and Eros*. Aquinas may be consulted in detail, and Augustine's concept of grace and sin is transformative for his ethics. Calvin stresses that the motivation of ethics is not achievement, but gratitude for grace. Kenneth Kirk urged readers to hold together moral analysis and love and service of God. J. Fletcher popularized "situation ethics." Oliver O'Donovan and Stanley Hauerwas are discussed under separate entries. On the Catholic side, a sweeping reorientation of political philosophy is reflected in Vatican II. On the Protestant side Helmut Thielicke, professor at Heidelberg and then at Tübingen, wrote his massive *Theological Ethics*, 3 vols. (Philadelphia: Fortress, 1966-1969). The first volume is on foundations, the second on politics, and the third on the ethics of sex. The German is lengthier than the English. He sees heterosexual marriage as reflecting the order of creation. (*See also* **Deontology; Grace; Hauerwas, Stanley; Liberation Hermeneutics and Theology; Love; O'Donovan, Oliver; Political Theology; Sin.**)

Reading: G. W. Forell, *The History of Christian Ethics*, 3 vols. (Minneapolis: Augsburg, 1979); Richard Hays, *The Moral Vision of the New Testament* (Edinburgh: T. & T. Clark, 1996); G. Meilaender and W. Werpehowski, eds., *The Oxford Handbook of Theological Ethics* (Oxford: OUP, 2005); Oliver O'Donovan, *The Ways of Judgment* (Grand Rapids: Eerdmans, 2005); Wolfgang Schrage, *The Ethics of the New Testament* (Edinburgh: T. & T. Clark; Philadelphia; Fortress, 1988); Helmut Thielicke, *Theological Ethics*, 3 vols. (Philadelphia: Fortress, 1966-1969).

Eusebius of Caesarea

Eusebius of Caesarea (c. 260–c. 339) was effectively court theologian to the emperor Constantine, and has become best known today for his *Ecclesiastical His-*

tory. He may have had more in common with Arius than some appear to realize, but he played a major role in the Council of Nicaea in 325. He added a clause on the Holy Spirit, probably to exclude Sabellianism. He asserted that the Spirit is "different" (Gk. *heteron*) from the Son, but also referred to the Trinity as "one in substance." H. B. Swete regards him as a subordinationist.

Evangelical, Evangelicalism
One popular misunderstanding is to equate "evangelical" with "evangelistic." This is wrong, although among evangelical beliefs evangelism has a high priority. But other people within the church also often prioritize evangelism. Another popular misunderstanding is to identify "evangelical" with nonliturgical, unstructured, or even "happy-clappy" worship. This would exclude some evangelical Anglican, Episcopalian, and probably Methodist churches. A third misunderstanding is to assert that "evangelical" in Britain, America, Germany, and Holland defines the same thing. In Germany since 1945 all Protestant churches have been designated evangelical *(evangelisch)* in contrast to the Roman Catholic Church. Sometimes "evangelical" refers especially to Lutheran churches in Germany, while in America "evangelical" may refer to Calvinist or Reformed churches, in contrast to Lutheran ones.

Any positive definition will include at minimum two features, although it will probably entail more than two. The first is an emphasis on the primacy of Scripture. Even within this there are variants. Anglicans who follow Hooker will stress the role of Scripture, reason, and tradition, but give priority to Scripture. Reason and tradition will be involved only if and when something is deemed "not contrary" to Scripture. Some may stress Scripture alone, with no appeal to tradition and reason, but they are thrown back onto the problem of hermeneutics. The second article of faith is the all-sufficiency of the finished work of Christ, in which the interpretation of penal substitution usually plays a leading role. Again, divisions occur between a "narrower" emphasis on penal substitution alone and a "broader" or more "inclusive" emphasis that while it is an indispensable model, it complements other models or understandings. After these two, most definitions emphasize sanctification as a process rather than an event, the sinfulness of humankind, and belief in, and experience of, a "personal" Savior, Jesus Christ. This is understood as an I-Thou relationship sustained by justification by grace and regular prayer. Today not all evangelicals have a relative disregard for the sacraments, though unlike Tractarians or "High Church" Christians, they do not hold sacraments to be of "higher" status than the ministry of the Word in preaching and teaching.

On top of these characteristics, normally evangelicals believe in the return of Christ, or the parousia, and a traditional doctrine of judgment and the resurrection of the dead. But a difference may arise between a more tightly defined eschatology in America and a looser variety of interpretation in Britain and Europe. Many evangelical Americans remain heirs to the tightly bound definitions of doctrine associated with A. A. Hodge and B. B. Warfield. American evangelicals often express concern about "premillennialism," while many British and European evangelicals find this an obscure and debatable, if not incorrect, subject. It probably derives from the tendency in earlier fundamentalism (c. 1895-1925) to defend a more literalistic interpretation of the Bible, in contrast to recognizing the place of symbol, imagery, and metaphor. Today, however, evangelical theologians increasingly distance themselves from this cluster of themes. Like every other movement or theology of this kind, there is a spectrum of beliefs with different nuances. For example, the Dutch evangelicals A. Kuyper and H. Bavinck challenged the American evangelical position of Charles Hodge and others. The Scotsman James Orr held a more flexible and "progressive" view of revelation and inspiration than the American B. Warfield. Yet in general terms we have cited some seven characteristics, of which the first two are of supreme importance. There are many implications or corollaries. For example, evangelicals in general emphasize "the priesthood of all believers." Territorially the features may vary: for example, Harriet A. Harris argues that since Pentecostals are the largest Protestant group in Latin America, the normal use of the term in that particular land-area may denote Pentecostals. But this is not the normal use of the term in Europe, Britain, or America.

Reading: D. Bebbington, *Evangelicalism in Modern Britain* (London: Unwin and Unwin, 1989); D. Dayton and R. Johnson, eds., *The Variety of American Evangelicalism* (Downers Grove, Ill.: InterVarsity, 1991); H. A. Harris, *Fundamentalism and Evangelicals* (Oxford: Clarendon, 1998).

Evidentialism

An evidence-based approach in the philosophy of religion, evidentialism demands that belief be supported by the "total evidence" of other propositions on which it rests. A rudimentary version was proposed by J. Locke against sectarians or enthusiasts, but the modern example usually chosen is that of W. K. Clifford, "The Ethics of Belief," in *Lectures and Essays* (2nd ed. 1986). Clifford suggests that a shipowner was about to launch a ship filled with emigrants. He knew the boat was old and needed repairs, but he overcame his doubts and concerns, putting his trust in "providence." His belief was sincere, but he was guilty of the deaths of the passengers, because he had no *right to believe* on the basis of the *evidence* of which he was aware. Evidentialism concerns the *ethics* of belief, and is the opposite of fideism. From a theistic viewpoint, N. Wolterstorff explores "entitlement" to believe from a very different angle.

Evil, Problem of

The Bible recognizes the reality of suffering, and the problem of what many perceive as unfair situations and tragedies in life. Job cries,

> "Let the day perish in which I was born. . . .
> Why is light given to one in misery,

and life to the bitter in soul,
who long for death, but it does not come . . . ?" (Job 3:3, 20-21)

The preacher in Ecclesiastes confesses, "I hated life, because what is done under the sun was grievous to me" (Eccles. 2:17); "The race is not to the swift, nor the battle to the strong, nor bread to the wise . . . time and chance happen to them all. For no one can anticipate the time of disaster" (9:11-12). The writer of Lamentations cries,

> Is it nothing to you, all you who pass by?
> Look and see
> if there is any sorrow like my sorrow, . . .
> which the LORD inflicted
> on the day of his fierce anger. (Lam. 1:12)

This passage later applied to Jesus on the cross. The Psalms repeatedly express puzzlement and the temptation to doubt God in the face of such phenomena. Psalm 73 admits,

> My feet had almost stumbled. . . .
> For I was envious of the arrogant;
> I saw the prosperity of the wicked. (vv. 2-3)

> In vain I have kept my heart clean. . . .
> It seemed to me a wearisome task,
> until I went into the sanctuary of God. . . .
> My soul was embittered,
> when I was pricked in heart. (vv. 13, 16-17, 21)

Ps. 116 declares,

> The snares of death encompassed me;
> the pangs of Sheol laid hold on me;
> I suffered distress and anguish. (Ps. 116:3)

Christian tradition does not make light of the reality of evil and suffering. In general a Christian "reply" to the problem of evil cannot "solve" it, but it may mitigate it. The Christian philosopher Alvin Plantinga has declared that if we do not *know* the reason for evil, this does not mean that there *is no reason* for it. There are two broadly different approaches to evil, and two subdivisions within the main tradition. The main tradition seeks to defend the coherence or consistency of belief in God, who is almighty, good, and loving, with the reality of evil and suffering in the world. This is a standard move in Christian philosophy of religion. One method is often to clarify what we mean by God's "almighty-ness." Does it exclude human freedom? Does it presuppose frequent interventions in the consequences of human actions? Another move is to question whether God's goodness and love exclude human holiness, as a testing of character, or human struggle and temptation. Within this general tradition there is also a "minority report," represented allegedly by Irenaeus and Schleiermacher, but certainly by John Hick. This makes the maturing of human character and the calculated risk of human freedom more prominent.

Against this mainstream view we may characterize a different approach as "existential" rather than "logical." Terrence Tilley, for example, attacks traditional "theodicy," or attempts to justify God's acts, as a doomed and mistaken attempt to address the problem. His book *The Evils of Theodicy* (Eugene, Ore.: Wipf and Stock, 2000) argues that the traditional approach distorts the Christian tradition, and makes evil a worse problem. He refuses to accept that writers such as Augustine offer a "theodicy," and looks especially to writers such as F. Dostoevsky, Kierkegaard, Simone Weil, and Kenneth Surin for more existential or practical approaches to evil.

There is a long history of formulations of the problem of evil. It was formulated by Epicurus (341-270 B.C.) in terms of the dilemma that was taken up by David Hume (1711-1776). Hume writes, "Epicurus' old questions are not yet answered. Is he [God] willing to prevent evil, but not able? Then he is impotent. Is he able, but not willing? Then he is malevolent. Is he both able and willing? Whence, then, is evil?" (*Dialogues concerning Natural Religion* [1779; reprint, New York: Harper, 1948], pt. 10, 66). In these *Dialogues* Hume portrays "Cleanthes" as the traditional theist or Christian, who acts as a foil for Hume's own arguments, while "Philo" (who represents Hume) argues against God's almighty-ness, goodness, and omniscience. Up to the time of Hume, most Christian apologists sought to defend the *coherence* of theism. After Hume and the Enlightenment, it was widely held that the problem of evil challenged the very truth and validity of the Christian faith. Christian responses at the logical level tend now to focus on clarifying what we mean by God's sovereignty or almighty-ness, what we mean by his love or goodness, and what role "evil" might play in the world.

(i) The ascription of sovereignty, according to the theistic reply, does not entail God's performing more than one act without logical contradiction. The classic schoolboy example of such an act can be focused on the question: Can God make a stone so heavy that he cannot lift it? Or: Can God divide odd numbers in half to leave two sets of integers? God "cannot" *(logically, not empirically)* perform such an act. Some restrict divine sovereignty even further. Edgar S. Brightman (1884-1953) speaks of a "finite" God, who is severely constrained by human freedom. Even the natural world possesses a "dysteleological" surd, which God "cannot" overrule. J. S. Mill similarly sees God in terms of an analogy with an artist who is constrained by his medium (*Three Essays on Religion* [London: Longman, Green,

1875], 176-77). Mill writes: "The author of the cosmos worked under limitations ... obliged to adapt himself to conditions independent of his will" (177). More recently a similar view of God has been sensitively promoted by W. H. Vanstone, especially in his book *Love's Endeavour, Love's Expense* (London: Darton, Longman, and Todd, 1977), which stresses both suffering and creative love. The concept of divine "omnipotence" has been criticized by Peter Geach and by G. van den Brink, who argue for the use of "almighty" rather than "omnipotent" (*Almighty God* [Kampen: Pharos, 1993]). On the other hand, many philosophical theologians support a less modified notion of omnipotence. R. Swinburne does this in *The Coherence of Theism* ([Oxford: Clarendon, 1977], 149-61). To be sure, he excludes what is "logically impossible" such as making "a square circle" or "changing the past" (149-58). Moreover, there are constraints imposed by God's own nature. For example, "God cannot lie" and "God cannot sin" because he wills to be truthful and righteous as is his habit of mind or character.

The traditional view of the sovereignty of God probably comes from Augustine, perhaps mediated through Aquinas, Calvin, and Barth. Hick observes, "From his earliest to his latest writings Augustine was continually turning to the problem of evil," especially in *The City of God, Confessions,* and the *Enchiridion* (*Evil and the God of Love* [London: Macmillan, 1966], 43). In one sense evil cannot frustrate God's will, because in the metaphysical sense it is only a privation or absence of good. At its heart, Augustine uses the so-called free-will defense argument. If God were to prevent or to restrict the consequences of human beings, would not this destroy their freedom as agents or treat them as mere machines or objects? Augustine asserts the sovereignty of God partly in reaction to the Manichaeans, who believed in a dualism of good and evil, which implied to Augustine a denial of God's sole sovereignty over the world and all creatures. He describes Manichaeism, which he once held, as "that shocking and detestable profanity, that the wedge of darkness sunders ... the very nature of God" (*Against the Epistle of Manichaeus* 24.26; *NPNF,* ser. 1, 4:140).

(ii) A second issue explores what we might mean by the goodness and love of God. Biblical and committed Christian theologians generally fully assert this quality of God. Some, like Vanstone, may place it "higher" than his sovereignty, which he may choose to compromise for the sake of his love. On the other hand, some philosophers, for example, F. H. Bradley, assert that God is "absolute," or may be characterized as "Reality-as-a-Whole," and therefore cannot have "moral" character. Many ask in this case what God's "goodness" now amounts to. John Hick argues that humankind's *telos* is "a relationship to God"; he has "made us for Himself," and *holiness* is even more important than happiness (*Evil*, 16).

(iii) A third move in "replies" to the problem is to explore whether the term "evil" might be redefined as less than tragic or disastrous. Hinayana Buddhism tends to regard evil as a necessary part of life. The quasi pantheism of Spinoza tends to accept evil as part of the whole. Simone Weil argues that to make possible the beauty of a storm at sea, a corollary has to be the possibility of shipwrecks

(*Gateway to God* [New York: Crossroad, 1974; original 1939]). Hick tends to relativize evil in terms of what he calls his "soul-making" theodicy (the phrase is borrowed from Keats). His theodicy looks not to the past, such as the fall of Adam and humanity, but to the *future,* to God's *goal* for humanity. God seeks the maturity and holiness of humankind. He calls this "the Irenaean type of theodicy," which we also find in Schleiermacher (*Evil*, 207-41). He begins with the distinction between image of God *(eikōn)* and his likeness *(homoiōsis).* He finds this in Irenaeus, *Against Heresies* 5.6.1 (217). Irenaeus perceived "likeness" to God as a goal yet to be achieved, even if most scholars today accept that the two terms are synonyms in Hebrew poetic parallelism. Irenaeus therefore thought of sinful humanity as merely "immature" (218; *see* **Sin: Historical**). Humans were at first in "the state of infancy" (219). Hence struggles and setbacks have their part in providing a path to maturity.

Hick points out that Clement of Alexandria and some of the Eastern Fathers also thought of humankind as initially a child. He writes, "With Irenaeus Clement thinks of Adam as a child" (222). Schleiermacher also ascribes sin to immaturity and is closer to Irenaeus than to Augustine (225-41). Many nineteenth-century theologians follow an evolutionary account of humankind. M. M. Adams and R. M. Adams select Hick's chapter "The Starting-Point" for their anthology *The Problem of Evil* ([Oxford: OUP, 1990], 168-88). Hick writes, "Instead of regarding man as having been created by God in a finished state . . . the minority report sees man as still in process of creation" (*Evil,* 290). His approach remains "developmental and teleological" (292). Pleasure is not "the sole and supreme value" (294). Parents do not seek unalloyed pleasure at the expense of growth and maturity. The world is "the God-given environment of man's life" (295). Space, time, and the varied events of life allow and make possible "the final fulfilment of our nature in relation to God" (296). "Evil" is thus redefined in terms of one of the conditions for maturity and holiness.

Not all writers are convinced by Hick. Many regard his approach as an unacceptably "utilitarian" view of evil. We must therefore look more closely at the traditional view in Augustine and Aquinas, and responses to it.

Aquinas follows Augustine in stating: "Evil is the absence of a good" (*Su Th* 1a, qu. 49, art. 1). For example, "blindness" is the absence of sight (qu. 5, art. 48). Augustine declares, "Each single created thing is good. . . . What, after all, is anything we call evil except privation of good?" (*Enchiridion* 3). Sometimes he uses the alternative Latin terms *deprivatio, negatio,* and *defectus.* Evil is not a "thing" that God specifically created. Evil is parasitic on the good: "evil is not a positive substance" (*City of God* 11.11). Aquinas argues that the abolition of all "evil" would destroy much that is good: "A lion would cease to live, if there were no slaying of animals" (qu. 49, art. 2). This leads to "the principle of plenitude."

The principle of plenitude includes the principle of "difference" in the universe; for example, God divided the day from the night, light from darkness, earth from water (Gen. 1:4, 7). The divine artist produces a rich, complex, diverse universe (qu. 47, art. 2). "Difference" transforms chaos into an ordered universe. Some today speak of "the rich tapestry" of life. Augustine writes, "What is more beautiful than a fire? What is more useful than its heat and comfort? . . . Yet nothing can cause more distress than the burns inflicted by fire" (*City of God* 12.4). Hick admittedly attacks this view as an "aesthetic" response to evil (*Evil*, 192). However, Aquinas points out that these "differences" or "inequalities" at once give rise to the possibility of envy, covetousness, discontent, and even theft. Gottfried Leibniz argues that God had created "the best possible world," not least because it exhibited "the principle of plenitude."

Augustine argues that it is not "difference" itself that is the root of evil, but human reactions to it. Evil arises from "a wilful turning of the self in desire from the highest good. The defection of the will is evil" (*City of God* 12.7). In his *Confessions* he acknowledges that "self-will" generates evil, and evil is "borne of self-interest which generates conflict and competitiveness." Even a child has "a wish to be obeyed" (1.6.8). God's gifts are good gifts, but humankind may choose to *misuse* them. This is part of what is generally known as "the free-will defense"; evil is based on "the wrong choices of free rational beings" (Hick, *Evil*, 65). The free will is the cause of humanity's doing evil. Over the years there have been critics and advocates of the free-will defense. However, J. L. Mackie insists, "All forms of the free-will defence fail" (*The Miracle of Theism* [Oxford: Clarendon, 1982], 176). Plantinga addresses Mackie's argument head-on, that God could (supposedly) have created humans who *always freely choose* to do the right. He speaks not of "creation" but of God's "actualizing" certain conditions. God does not "create" properties, numbers, propositions, or pure sets. Necessary states of affairs are internal to logic, not created by God. Further, Plantinga expounds the concept of "possible worlds w and w^*" that draw on modal logic. He concludes, "It is not within God's power to create a world in which E's instantiation . . . is significantly free, but always does what is right" ("God, Evil, and the Metaphysics of Freedom," in *The Problem of Evil*, 104; cf. Plantinga, *God, Freedom, and Evil* [New York: Harper and Row, 1974]). Indeed, Plantinga stands the argument on its head: "God actualises a world containing as much broadly moral good as the actual world contains" ("God, Evil," 108). He even responds to the problem of "natural" evil as well as human "trans-world depravity." Plantinga writes as a skilled logician and philosopher of the Reformed faith.

It may be a relief to turn from such logically complex and sophisticated argumentation to the work of those who discard confronting the problem of evil with logical arguments in favor of a more *existential* approach. One extreme example is T. W. Tilley, *The Evils of Theodicy* (Washington, D.C.: Georgetown University Press, 1991). He begins with an exploration of speech acts in J. L. Austin and others. He then suggests religious applications. He rightly contrasts speech acts with informative or descriptive propositions. His underlying thesis is "Theodicy is a *practice* within Christian theology" (85, italics mine). But theodicy, he claims, degenerated into the reading of texts and the formulation of abstract logical arguments, which undermine the very purpose of theodicy. To understand and appropriate the book of Job require *entering into* Job's plight and sharing his commitments or, in speech-act theory, his "commissives" and "expressives" (94). Tilley suggests: "The speech act God performs seems to be . . . a judicial verdict" (102). He concludes: "The Book of Job, then, as a speech act cannot answer the reader's questions about the meaning of suffering" (105).

Tilley next considers Augustine, and argues that each of his major writings is so closely bound to a specific context that he does not formulate a general "theodicy" in the usual sense. I was at first persuaded by Tilley, but several experts on Augustine have denounced Tilley's work as a selective and unreliable account of Augustine. The reader must judge. Perhaps more plausibly he examines Boethius and George Eliot. Many others are less black-and-white in their approach than Tilley. Vincent Brümmer warns readers that to present a bereaved person or sufferer with the Augustinian-Thomas tradition *alone* would exhibit "moral insensitivity" (*Speaking of a Personal God* [Cambridge: CUP, 1992], 128-51); but it may serve its purpose in an appropriate situation. Meister Eckhart's mysticism is content to let "what-is" disclose itself. Simone Weil's courageous acceptance of suffering and "humiliation," especially during the war, provides an inspiration to anyone, and her "Love of God and Affliction," in *Waiting for God*, is a treasure. Elie Wiesel recounts experiences of the Holocaust in his autobiographical work *Night*. J. Moltmann's exposition of Auschwitz, in which *"God is there,"* is remarkable. So is his exposition of the *God who suffers* (*The Crucified God* [London: SCM, 1974] and *The Trinity and the Kingdom of God* [London: SCM, 1981], and other works). F. Nietzsche and A. Camus, as we might expect, convey an antitheistic protest. Dostoevsky offers a *conversation* in *The Brothers Karamazov*, which may be seen as a dialogue between human protest and Russian Orthodoxy. Conversation and dialogue may prove to be the only lasting "theodicy," for, as M. Bakhtin has argued, some things are simply too big to be expressed in a monologic proposition. Literature on this subject is almost infinite, representing a huge variety of approaches. However, we have attempted to identify the most prominent in the Christian tradition. (*See also* **Dualism**.)

Reading: M. M. Adams and R. M. Adams, eds., *The Problem of Evil* (Oxford: OUP, 1990); J. H. Hick, *Evil and the God of Love* (New York: Harper and Row, 1978); N. C. Pike, ed., *God and Evil* (Englewood Cliffs, N.J.: Prentice-Hall, 1964); A. Plantinga, *God, Freedom, and Evil* (New York: Harper and Row, 1974); R. Swinburne, *The Existence of God* (Oxford: Clarendon, 1979), chaps. 10–12; T. W. Tilley, *The Evils of Theodicy* (Washington, D.C.: Georgetown University Press, 1991).

Evolution

The bare facts of Darwin's discoveries and theory and Spencer's application of evolution to ethics are contained in the entry on Darwin. Here we content ourselves with making two kinds of theological comments. First, those who look for reconciliation between theories of evolution and Christian theology focus on the creative process of God through natural processes as well as "intervention." They argue that the portrait of God as Creator does not merely refer to prehistory, but refers also to a present process that is still operative. They also argue that theologians and the Genesis narrative address the question *why* creation occurred, in contrast to scientists, who may ask *how* creation occurred. The former is the "bigger" question, and addresses the issue of the purpose of life. W. R. Matthews famously argued, "Gradualness of construction is itself no proof of the absence of ... design" (quoted by F. R. Tennant, *Philosophical Theology*, vol. 2 [Cambridge: CUP, 1930], 84). Tennant himself argues, "Lucky accidents and coincidences bewilderingly accumulate" until "purpose" may seem more reasonable than "groundless contingency" (79, 92-93). More recently, John Polkinghorne provides more detailed and contemporary argument (*Science and Creation* [Boston: New Science Library, 1989], 22; *The Way the World Is* [London: SPCK, 1992]; *see* **Teleological Argument**).

On the other side of the argument, Moltmann concedes, "The theory of evolution was the perfect instrument for developing a materialist outlook.... Friedrich Engels and Karl Marx at once welcomed the appearance of Darwin's *Origin of Species* in 1859 as affirming 'the foundation in natural history for our own view'" (*God in Creation* [London: SCM, 1985], 194). It may also represent the thought of Neoplatonism and pantheism of "God" as emerging from the world, which some might see as a possible danger in the work of Teilhard de Chardin. The whole notion of "self-reproduction" and "self-ordering" seems to ascribe to the world a self-sufficiency and autonomy that would be the opposite of what a Christian doctrine of creation affirms (*see* **Creation**). The task of theology seems to be to steer between this particular Scylla and Charybdis; between Bishop Samuel Wilberforce's extreme conservatism and Richard Dawkins's atheism.

An important study in evangelical reactions to Darwin and evolutionary theory has been provided by David N. Livingstone in *Darwin's Forgotten Defenders: The Encounter between Evangelical Theology and Evolutionary Thought* (Grand Rapids: Eerdmans, 1987). This was called "the first systematic investigation of the response of evangelical intellectuals ... to Darwin's evolutionary theories." Livingstone carefully examines the exact words of Charles Hodge, James McCosh, A. A. Hodge, B. B. Warfield, A. H. Strong, and James Orr, as well as initial contributions to *The Fundamentals* (1910-1915; pp. 100-152). He traces a hardening in the 1920s of criticisms of, and attacks on, Darwin's theory. Charles Hodge had expressed reservations based on the philosophy of an ordered universe, but could also note merit in his work (100-106). McCosh broadly agreed. A. A. Hodge was even more open (112-14). He wrote, "Evolution considered as a plan of an infinitely wise Person and executed under the control of His everywhere-present energies can never be irreligious" (114). B. B. Warfield endorsed these attempts (112). He wrote, "There is no *necessary* antagonism of Christianity to evolution," provided we do not hold to too extreme a version of evolution" (118). A. H. Strong in *Christ and Creation* (1899) offered a similar view (129). In 1905 P. T. Forsyth agreed, stating, "There is nothing in evolution fatal to the great moral and spiritual teleology of Christianity" (145). Between 1910 and 1915 G. F. Wright and others wrote similarly in *The Fundamentals* (147-52).

However, with H. Beach and W. B. Greene, the attack on Darwin became increasingly polemical. In the 1920s J. Gresham Machen was forced out of Princeton, to move to Westminster Theological Seminary. An all-out attack on Darwin was launched in 1925, mainly by "Missouri-Synod Lutherans and ... premillennialist groups" (157). In the wake of the notorious trial of John T. Scopes, creationism emerged and flourished. Livingstone comments, "Within the incredibly short space of about two decades, the old cultured evangelicalism had given way to the bitter polemics of a rampant Fundamentalism" (165-66). From Warfield to Price, he notes, is a long stretch. Then in the 1960s there came a creationist renaissance. In 1963 the Creationist Research Society was formed, and in 1964 the Biblical Science Association. In Europe Martin Lloyd-Jones and Francis Schaeffer "expressed substantially creationist sentiments" (176). Bernard Ramm remained one of the few to echo nineteenth-century concerns. Livingstone, who is an evangelical, a geographer, and a historian of thought, concludes that this controversy shows the complexity of the subject (185). But, he concludes, "If only to curtail the abyss of rhetoric, creationists and evolutionists need to be made more aware of Darwin's forgotten defenders" (189). (*See also* **Creation; Creationism; Darwin, Charles R.; Science and Religion; Teleological Argument.**)

Reading: D. N. Livingstone, *Darwin's Forgotten Defenders* (Grand Rapids: Eerdmans, 1987); J. Polkinghorne, *Science and Creation* (Boston: New Science Library, 1989); F. R. Tennant, *Philosophical Theology*, 2 vols. (Cambridge: CUP, 1930).

Exegesis
Exegesis refers to the process of interpreting and expounding a text, usually a biblical text. It is distinguished from hermeneutics, which raises wider multidisciplinary issues about the nature, theory, and practice of interpretation. Usually exegesis involves (i) *textual criticism,* or establishing a valid text from among a multiplicity of ancient manuscripts; (ii) *lexical research* into the meaning of the words of the text in question; (iii) *grammar and syntax,* which are used in the construction of sentences; (iv) an examination of *historical context,* which often also demands historical reconstruction; (v) an assessment of *literary genre* and its function; (vi) the *exposition* and often also the practical *application* of the text; and (vii) the *appropriation* of the text, which some would see as part of (vi).

Traditionally, much of the time taken on exegesis in university departments of theology and religion, and especially in seminaries or schools devoted to training for ministry, rests on the belief that all these stages remain necessary for the understanding of revelation and for preaching and teaching. But today the task of detailed exegesis is sometimes crowded out because more fashionable areas put intense pressure on the syllabus. Exegesis presupposes careful translation; but some universities and seminaries devote less time to the learning of Hebrew and

Greek than they did formerly. In the history of the church, Origen is regarded as a systematic exegete as well as a theologian, and Chrysostom's commentaries are often still used. Luther was a professor of biblical studies, and Calvin is often regarded as the first "modern" exegete, especially in his numerous commentaries.

Existentialism

Among the half-dozen philosophers generally described as existentialists we can identify certain common themes, even if existentialists insist on particularity and dislike generalizations. Human beings are too finite and too relative to their situated place in history to aspire to an objective view of reality as a system. Truth, in Kierkegaard's phrase, "is subjectivity," by which he means that in which an individual self is passionately and personally involved. Hence existentialism is characterized by fragments and viewpoints, rather than by systems. Its first task is to attend to human finite existence. The decision and responsibility of the individual become paramount. This leads to an undervaluing of reason and rationality, and often to an elevation of the absurd. In general, it is pessimistic and sometimes even caustic or ironic. But here we face again the peril of generalizing. If "the individual consciousness" is primary, we cannot define it in terms of a group. Each individual exponent has personal characteristics.

The first thinker to use the term "existential" in its proper sense was Søren Kierkegaard, probably in his *Philosophical Fragments* ([Princeton: Princeton University Press, 1985], 227). Kierkegaard was a Protestant Christian, even if also a stern critic of the Danish church. Individual existentialists, however, represent all shades of belief about Christian faith. For example, G. Marcel became Roman Catholic; K. Jaspers was in a very broad sense "religious"; M. Heidegger was, in effect, agnostic; F. Nietzsche, J.-P. Sartre, and A. Camus were atheists. Each promotes a different version of existentialism, and perhaps only Kierkegaard and Sartre lay explicit claim to the term "existentialist." The common or basic traits in most of these writers can readily be seen in Kierkegaard. His life reveals at once why he threw off assent to systems and to anything secondhand or inherited. He had once admired his father, but on discovering his father's affair with his housekeeper, he became determined to discover truth for himself. Earlier he had studied theology, which, he commented, did "not interest [him] in the least." This was because, he says, Mikael, his father, believed "that Canaan itself [lay] on the other side of a theological degree" (*Johannes Climacus* [London: Black, 1958], 21). But when his world was shattered, Søren tried to live "as himself." He first went into moral decline. However, this personal decision, he saw, involved more responsibility and seriousness, even if this was costly. After writing *Either/Or* in 1843, he wrote *Fear and Trembling* in 1844, and within five years *The Concept of Dread, Repetition, Philosophical Fragments, The Stages on Life's Way, Concluding Scientific Postscript,* and *The Sickness unto Death*. In his next book, *The Point of View for My Work as an Author,* he stated that his purpose was to show what it meant *to live* as a Christian, not simply to convey thoughts *about* Christianity.

Kierkegaard's melancholic upbringing underwent further strains and crises not only because of his father's affairs, but also because of his unhappy broken engagement with Regine Olsen, and from his unhappy brush with a satirical newspaper *The Corsair,* which made him the laughingstock of Denmark, by portraying him as an eccentric, maverick oddity. All this drove him to greater existential extremes. He saw his broken engagement as a courageous act of faith, overriding convention and ethics, and comparing him, he thought, with Abraham, who was to "slay the son of promise" in a supposedly similar way. In his journals he wrote, "My doubt is terrible. . . . It is a cursed hunger, and I can swallow up every argument" (*The Journals of S. Kierkegaard* [Oxford: OUP, 1938], 89; cf. 59-63). He spoke in these journals of his "self-isolation." His later works include *Attack upon "Christendom"* (1854-1855), in which he writes: "Christianity has been *abolished by expansion* by these millions of name-Christians. . . . [God] cannot discover that he has been hoaxed, that there is not one single . . . Christian" ([London: OUP, 1946], 127). Kierkegaard's themes, then, were historical finitude, rejection of system (for which he mercilessly attacks Hegel), personal decision, dread, death, suffering, antirationalism, and above all a deeply practical, full involvement and engagement, or "subjectivity." Nevertheless, Kierkegaard's reputation did not rise to prominence until after 1919 or 1921 in Germany, in the wake of Barth's understanding of the limitations of human reason, as well as his emphasis upon the transcendence of God, personal decision, and themes in his period of dialectical theology.

Friedrich Nietzsche (1844-1900), an opposite example, was not an explicit existentialist in the strict and fullest sense. But he was sometimes regarded so after 1919-1921, because he refused to belong to any school of thought, he repudiated a body of beliefs, he opposed philosophical systems, and he was dissatisfied with traditional philosophy. As such he provides a link between Kierkegaard and Jaspers, Heidegger, and Sartre. But he may have held a more positive view of reason than Kierkegaard. In his book *Antichrist,* his caustic critique of prevailing Christian thought is reserved for an attack on theism and Christianity. Nietzsche could more accurately be regarded as a nihilist.

Karl Jaspers (1883-1969) rejected being called "an existentialist" because "existentialism" suggested a school of thinkers to him. But he accepted the term "philosophy of existence." He was an existentialist in a limited sense, because he was concerned with the human situation, personal attitudes, and "boundary situations," which involve a person reaching the end of himself or herself. In such a situation the person's dread or anxiety is said to penetrate through to truth and authenticity far more effectively than any conventional set of beliefs. Jaspers explored the distinctive natures of human consciousness *(Bewusstsein)* and human finite incompleteness. Yet he also held to a "transcendent" beyond, and to "possibility" (*Philosophy,* 3 vols. [Ger. 1932; Eng. Chicago: University of Chicago Press, 1969], 2:42).

Martin Heidegger (1889-1976) initially focused on human situatedness in time, or "historicity" *(Geschichtlichkeit)*. The human being is Being-there *(Dasein)*, not Being as such *(Sein)*, because a human is restricted and finite in his or her point of view. He began from this starting point in *Being and Time* (1927). He used E. Husserl's "horizon," within which humans view truth, and saw the world and time in subjective terms. Time may be seen in these subjective terms as "time for a short walk," rather than in terms of objective clock-time. Everything is shaped by "my world," my aims and interests, and "my horizons," including "being-towards-death." Heidegger rejected the term "existentialist" because he was seeking ultimately an ontology. But around 1934 he turned to art and poetry for the disclosure of truth, coming to abandon a search for Being. Humankind has "fallen out of Being."

Jean-Paul Sartre (1905-1980) did accept the term "existentialist." In his *Being and Nothingness* (1943), he focused on human consciousness as "for itself" *(pour soi)*, in contrast to inanimate objects. Like Heidegger, he emphasized the limits imposed by "historical situatedness," which severely reduced human freedom and choices. Like his compatriot Albert Camus, he was militantly atheistic, and stood firmly in the French philosophical tradition. Like Jaspers, Sartre rejected convention. Decisions may further limit freedom, but also they contribute to selfhood. He declared, "Life begins on the other side of despair"; and "The idea of God is contradictory." Humankind is "a useless passion." Existentialism is a matter of life, not of thought. In Christian theology R. Bultmann has made much of existential bondage to history and to law, from which only grace can liberate us to futurity. Bultmann argued that he does not depend on existentialism, but finds its concepts and language useful, especially in the case of Heidegger. He declared: "I learned from him [Heidegger] not *what* theology has to say but *how* it has to say it" ("Reply," in C. W. Kegley, *The Theology of Rudolf Bultmann* [London: SCM, 1966], 276). Humankind, living according to *inauthentic* existence under self-achievement and the law, lives in a situation of existential estrangement; *authentic* existence, however, is characterized by grace, freedom, and futurity. The most influential era of existentialism was from the early 1920s to the late 1950s. Especially since the thought of W. Pannenberg in the late 1960s and early 1970s, existentialism and Heidegger have become far less prominent, although Kierkegaard will perhaps continue to exercise some influence on theology. Pannenberg is more inclined to look to Hegel. Existentialism also marked a huge contrast between Anglo-American ordinary-language philosophy and Continental philosophical thought, especially in Germany and France. (*See also* **Heidegger, Martin; Jaspers, Karl; Kierkegaard, Søren; Marcel, Gabriel; Nietzsche, Friedrich; Sartre, Jean-Paul.**)

Reading: H. J. Blackham, *Six Existentialist Thinkers* (New York: Harper, 1959); C. Guignon and D. Pereboom, eds., *Existentialism: Basic Writings* (Indianapolis: Hackett, 1995); W. Kaufmann, ed., *Existentialism from Dostoevsky to Sartre* (New York: World Publishing, 1956); S. Kierkegaard, *The Concept of Dread* (Princeton: Princeton University Press, 1981); J.-P. Sartre, *Existentialism and Humanism* (London: Methuen, 1973).

Existentiell

Existentiell is often distinguished from "existential" and is used in Christian theology. "Existential" is the more general and academic term, denoting the analysis of human existence found in existentialist writers. *Existentiell* is concrete and more specific, usually to a particular situation. A specific person may face a decision in an *existentiell* situation. *Existentiell* relates to a particular individual here and now; "existential" relates to the situated-ness and finitude of humankind.

Expiation

In the NT, "expiation" is a frequent translation of Greek *hilastērion,* with the alternative English translation "propitiation." In turn, the Greek translates the Hebrew *k-p-r,* which normally means "to cover, to wipe off, to cleanse," or, as a noun, a means of dealing with sin. C. K. Barrett advocates the term "expiation," and C. H. Dodd compares it to a primitive disinfectant to remove the stain of sin. But in *koine* Greek the term more often means "to propitiate." The danger in the translation "propitiation" is that if we forget that *God has initiated* it, it might seem as if God's wrath has to be appeased. The danger in the translation "expiation" is that God's dealings with humankind in Christ appear to be subpersonal, impersonal, or mechanistic. Hence Leon Morris, *The Apostolic Preaching of the Cross,* 3rd ed. (1963), 155-57, argues for "propitiation," together with J. Klausner and D. Hill. The Hebrew *kappōreth* may also denote "mercy seat," which is the meaning of *hilastērion* in Heb. 9:5, and A. Nygren and T. W. Manson suggest the translation "mercy seat" or "place of meeting" (as in Exod. 25:22). On the meaning in Rom. 3:25, C. E. B. Cranfield concludes that Dodd "failed to pay adequate attention to the content of these words," and that there is no thought of caprice or vindictiveness in God's action. He argues that "*propitiatory sacrifice* is the most accurate translation" (*The Epistle to the Romans* [Edinburgh: T. & T. Clark, 1973], 1:216). (*See also* **Atonement: Biblical; Sacrifice; Wrath of God.**)

F

Faith, Faithfulness

The Hebrew word *'-m-n,* "firm, reliable, trustworthy," or even its Hiphil form, *he'emîn,* "to trust in, to believe in, to have faith in," is used in the OT more rarely than Greek *pisteuō,* "to believe," and *pistis,* "faith," are used in the NT. Certainly the familiar examples cited in the NT occur, for example, "He (Abraham) believed the LORD; and the LORD reckoned it to him as righteousness" (Gen. 15:6; BDB 53), "to trust, to believe in," with *b^e,* the regular contraction for "in God" or "in the Lord," with the Hiphil verb. Parallel examples occur in Exod. 14:31, "the people ... believed in the LORD"; Num. 14:11, "How long will they refuse to believe in me?"; and Deut. 1:32, "You have no trust in the LORD your God." In other contexts *'^emeth* denotes security, fidelity, truth, or faithfulness. The other OT passage quoted in the NT is the famous Hab. 2:4: "The righteous live by their faith," which is quoted in Rom. 1:17. But the Hebrew has "his" faith: *be'emûnātō,* while the Greek LXX translates it as "my" faith, and Paul omits the possessive pronoun. R. W. L. Moberly refers to the complex difficulties of the context in the Hebrew text, and most OT specialists render the term "faithfulness" (in *DOTT* 1:425-33).

When it is applied to God, the root *'-m-n* often means "the faithful God who maintains covenant" (Deut. 7:9). The Niphal form of the verb can shade off into the term "promise." But the Hiphil, *he'emîn,* can share the meaning "to trust" with *b-ṭ-ch,* both of which can be translated by *pistis* or *pisteuō.* A. Weiser points out that humankind may approach God with either "faith" or "fear," and W. Pannenberg insists that "faithfulness" makes sense only if it is shown through a definite *duration of time.* Weiser further concludes that uses of *'-m-n* are fluid (*TDNT* 6:182-96).

This introduces the multiform contexts and uses of *pistis,* "faith," and *pisteuō,* "to trust" or "to believe," in the NT. A classic starting point is Heb. 11:1, "Now faith is the assurance of things hoped for, the conviction of things not seen." In the context of the argument of Hebrews, this means not the apprehension of some invisible "upper" world, but "things not seen" in the sense that they have not yet occurred, and still lie in the future. The Greek word-order *estin pistis elpizomenōn hypostasis* indicates a formal definition, and *hypostasis* denotes an underlying or undergirding reality. Attridge rightly argues for "the reality of things hoped for." The word "conviction" (Gk. *elenchos*) means "proof" or "solid ground" in the legal sense. Faith is the objective anchor in the realities that God has promised, but that have not yet come into view (*see* **Promise; Time**). Nevertheless, the difference of emphasis is striking when we compare two other famous statements about faith in the NT. One comes in Rom. 1:17, "The one who is righteous will live by faith" (NRSV), or "The just shall live by faith" (KJV/AV). Faith as an appropriation of justification by grace similarly occurs in Rom. 3:22, 27, 28; 4:5, 9, 11, 13; 5:1, 2; 9:30; 10:6; Gal. 3:2, 5, 7, 8, 11, 12, 24-26. Here faith is *"internally"* related to "justified by grace" as *appropriation*. It is the possession of every genuine Christian. It brings forward the verdict that properly belongs to the last day, and in *this* respect does offer a link with Heb. 11:1 (*see* **Justification**).

All the same, a third classic context is that in which *some* have faith, while others either have none or "less" faith. Faith almost seems to become a "virtue" in 1 Cor. 13:13, "Now faith, hope, and love abide." 1 Cor. 13:2 speaks of a faith that can remove mountains, and 12:9 speaks of "faith" as a special gift given to some but not to others. Clearly it is not justifying faith, which belongs to every Christian, but a particular robust confidence in God, which will help, strengthen, and give confidence to the whole church or congregation. This may be related to a frequent use of "faith" in the Synoptic Gospels. In the triple tradition (Matt. 9:22; Mark 5:34; Luke 8:48), "Your faith has made you well." Or, when the friends brought the paralytic to Jesus, "When Jesus saw their faith, he said to the paralytic, '. . . your sins are forgiven'" (Matt. 9:2; Mark 2:5). Matthew and Luke recount, "If you have faith the size of a mustard seed . . ." (Matt. 17:20; cf. Luke 17:6). This is quite different from Paul's meaning in justification, where "faith" is not a *ground* for God to act, but an appropriation of that act. There, as Whiteley observes, "Faith is not 'another kind of work'" (*The Theology of St. Paul* [Oxford: Blackwell, 1964], 164).

Faith in the NT is what philosophers call a "polymorphous concept." Bultmann is misleading when he declares, *"Paul understands faith primarily as obedience"* (*Theology of the New Testament* [London: SCM, 1952], 1:314). Bultmann wishes to criticize the notion of faith as doctrine, belief, or intellectual assent. But *some* uses of faith do denote this, for example, "the faith" in Gal. 1:23, Eph. 4:5, Phil. 2:17, 1 Tim. 1:19, 3:9, 2 Tim. 4:7, and Titus 3:15. Neither of these two approaches represents the approximation of the eschatological verdict "justified" in the present. Yet in James we encounter yet another viewpoint. "What good is it, my brothers and sisters, if you say you have faith, but do not have works? Can faith save you? . . . Faith by itself, if it has no works, is dead" (James 2:14, 17). Paul uses *faith in contrast to* "works" (Rom. 4:2-25); James argues that faith must be *evidenced* by works (James 2:22-26). As J. Jeremias argues, this is not a clash or contradiction; James attacks a theoretical monotheism abstracted from action and commitment. For James, the very nature of faith presupposes commitment, trust, and action (see Thiselton, *The Two Horizons* [Grand Rapids: Eerdmans, 1980], 422-27).

Believing, as Thomas Aquinas hints, is a disposition rather than a conscious state of mind. Thus L. Wittgenstein asks whether it makes sense to believe "uninterruptedly." For example, do we become an unbeliever if we fall asleep? (*Zettel* [Oxford: Blackwell, 1967], sect. 85). What counts as belief is not what is going on in the head of a believer. H. H. Price, the philosopher, writes on belief: "Dispositional statements" describe what the believer "*would* be likely to say or to do or feel if such and such circumstances were to arise. For example, he would assert the proposition . . . if he heard someone else denying it, or expressing doubt of it" (*Belief* [London: Allen and Unwin; New York: Humanities Press, 1969], 20). Belief has a performative character (30; *see* **Speech Act Theory**). Thus the "circumstances" in which faith or belief becomes operative and has cash-currency arise and vary from situation to situation in the NT. Sometimes it is indeed an expression of assent to doctrine; at other times it is trust; at still other times it may be optimistic confidence. In a more illuminating statement than the former one, Bultmann urges that what belief or faith amounts to depends on to whom it is directed. We simply add: "and in what circumstances."

Aquinas comes near to the dispositional view of faith when he rightly calls faith a habit. He quotes the NT: "He who comes to God must believe that he is" (Heb. 11:6; *Su Th* 2.2, qu. 1, art. 7). Faith is a "cognitive habit" (qu. 1, art. 1), which seeks the truth of God. Aquinas saw no tension between faith and reason (art. 2), any more than Augustine did, even if faith is directed to the unseen (Heb. 11:1; art. 4). Unlike "science," it is not directed toward what is self-evident (art. 5), but to "the articles of faith," which have been handed down from the apostles (art. 7), and "the universal Church cannot err" (art. 9). Luther emphasized several aspects of faith when he declared, "Faith is a living, daring confidence in God's grace, so sure and certain that a man would stake his life on it a thousand times. This confidence in God's grace . . . makes men glad and bold and happy" (cited in E. G. Rupp and B. Drewery, *Martin Luther* [London: Arnold, 1970], 95). Yet in early modern thought a number of thinkers began to separate faith and reason. J. Locke, for example, was suspicious of faith as enthusiastic passion, and argued for rational grounds of true belief. Too many modern debates may fall short of the subtlety of the biblical material by regarding faith as "one thing" rather than recognizing, with H. H. Price, its dispositional and thus variable character. (*See also* **Fideism; Sanctification**.)

Reading: Avery Dulles, *The Assurance of Things Hoped For* (Oxford: OUP, 1997); D. B. Garlington, *Faith, Obedience, and Perseverance* (Tübingen: Mohr, 1994); Henrik Ljungman, *Pistis: A Study of Its Presuppositions and Meaning in Pauline Use* (Lund: Gleerup, 1964); H. H. Price, *Belief* (London: Allen and Unwin; New York: Humanities Press, 1969); Victor Rhee, *Faith in Hebrews* (New York: Peter Lang, 2001); A. C. Thiselton, *The Two Horizons* (Grand Rapids: Eerdmans, 1980), 415-27.

Father, God As

It is tempting to view this "God as Father" only in terms relating to human anthropomorphisms, that is, to fathers of human children. Hence many hasten to say (rightly) that God is beyond gender, and especially in view of tragic experiences of abuse at home, or of an authoritarian father. Many cite passages in which feminine characteristics are ascribed to God, for example, the analogy of Isa. 49:15,

> Can a woman forget her nursing child . . . ?
> Yet I will not forget you.

Even more explicitly, Isa. 66:13 declares,

> As a mother comforts her child,
> so I will comfort you.

Subsequently to the NT, Julian of Norwich writes, "Jesus Christ . . . is our real mother. . . . God is really our Mother, as he is our Father. . . . I am the strength and goodness of Fatherhood; I am the wisdom of Motherhood" (*Revelations of Divine Love* 59). She adds that there are "three ways of looking at God's motherhood"; the first by being made; the second by grace; the third by a constant flowing out of grace (59). "Motherhood is so sweet . . . that it cannot properly be used of any but him" (60). In modern times the feminist Sallie McFague speaks of "the world as the body of our Mother-God" ("The Ethics of God as Mother," in *The Body of God* [Minneapolis: Fortress, 1993], 255).

Nevertheless, W. Pannenberg insists that more than God's relation to humankind is at issue. He is the God of Jesus, who taught us to pray "Abba" and "Our Father." More than this: "The idea of God as Father is by no means an arbitrary one. . . . Adoption gave the idea of God as Father a consistency which made it much more than a metaphor" (*ST* 1:261). An anthropological and sociological view of the issue is "time-bound" (1:262). Pannenberg declares, "On the lips of Jesus 'Father' became a proper name for God. It thus ceased to be simply one designation among others" (1:262). God as Father, he urges, is not a time-bound concept. "Father" is a term best understood not in relation to humankind, but in relation to the Trinity. As creator, sustainer, and provider, God's identity is uniquely that of the Father of Jesus and of those "in Christ." This does not exclude the use of feminine comparisons and imagery. (*See also* **God, Trinity; Symbol**.)

Feminist Theology

Feminist theology arguably began in embryonic form in the nineteenth century with Elizabeth Cady Stanton (1815-1902) and the publication of *The Woman's Bible* (1895 and 1898). A decisive landmark after World War II, however, was Simone de Beauvoir's book *The Second Sex* (1949; Eng. 1953), which raised questions about the relation between symbolic and conceptual perceptions of women and conventional roles for women in society. Perhaps a key theme finds expression in her words: "Humanity is male, and man defines woman not in herself but as relative to him. . . . He is the subject. . . . She is the Other" (*The Second Sex*, in E. Marks and I. de Coutivron, eds., *New French Feminisms: An Anthology* [Brighton: Harvester Press, 1981], 44). Some might trace feminism to the history of the early church, and even to aspects of the NT. More recent research has revealed that Junia was a woman apostle, that Mary Magdalene was a key witness to the resurrection of Christ, and that Priscilla and Phoebe held key leadership roles. But these are simply accepted exceptions to frequent conventions, and can hardly be attributed to "proto-feminism." Understandably, as Elisabeth Schüssler Fiorenza and others have shown, women did occupy positions of leadership in the early and medieval church. But the uncovering of these phenomena is part of a more recent feminist endeavor to "retrieve" a largely "lost" or ignored past.

Serious feminism began to emerge in the late 1960s and early 1970s. Kate Millett's *Sexual Politics* (1969) unmasked a network of social power-structures in which roles and employment promotions were determined more by sexual identity than by merit. Millett particularly attacked what she viewed as patriarchal power-structures within the family. The link with theology is the effect of an unmasking process in liberation. Germaine Greer published *The Female Eunuch* (1970) to reinforce the argument that social roles were imposed on women by the constraints of education, the family, work, and capitalist market-forces. The effect of this was "to reduce" (her term was "to castrate") women as persons. In practice feminist *theology* and hermeneutics emerged mainly in the 1970s with such studies as Phyllis Trible, "Depatriarchalizing in Biblical Tradition" (1973) and her *God and the Rhetoric of Sexuality* (1978); Letty Russell, *The Liberating Word* (1976); Rosemary Ruether and Eleanor McLaughlin, eds., *Women of Spirit: Female Leadership in the Jewish and Christian Traditions* (1979); and Mary Daly, *Beyond God the Father* (1973). These contributed to the "first wave" of the seventies, and were shortly followed by another, in the 1980s and 1990s, which we shall shortly consider.

In *God and the Rhetoric of Sexuality* (Philadelphia: Fortress, 1978), Trible begins with "the hermeneutics within scripture" (1). The hermeneutics of tradition, she argues, must be supplemented by a hermeneutics of inquiry, which may question the tradition. Women's "lost" place, she argues, must be "retrieved." One of her most influential conclusions is that it is not only "man" who is created in the image of God, but man-and-woman. God, she insists, is neither male nor female, and humankind bears God's image as both male and female. Strangely, it is often forgotten that earlier Karl Barth also insisted on this. Phyllis Bird also regarded the image of God as referring to both sexes in this creative function. Rosemary Ruether and E. McLaughlin also aimed at "a hermeneutic of retrieval" in the edited volume *Women of Spirit* (New York: Simon and Schuster, 1979). This aimed at recapturing leadership among women from the first to the third century. In this volume Schüssler Fiorenza claimed that "only a fraction of such traditions about significant women" has passed through the filter of "patriarchal" transmitter of tradition (57).

Daly and Ruether effectively founded the women's caucus in the American Academy of Religion in 1971. From the caucus Letty Russell published her moderate book *The Liberating Word* (Philadelphia: Westminster, 1976). In this she argued that God transcends gender, and warned against stereotyping. Ruether, however, proposed that "women's experience" should promote the basis for an ideological critique in hermeneutics. She declared, "Women's experience explodes as a critical force, exposing classical theology, including its foundational tradition in scripture as shaped by male experience rather than the human experience" (in *Liberating Word*, 112-13). Daly offered a more "radical" feminism, which would eventually become post-Christian feminism.

The high point of feminist theology emerged in the 1980s and 1990s, with a flood of literature. The most influential was probably Elisabeth Schüssler Fiorenza, *In Memory of Her: A Feminist Theological Reconstruction of Christian Origins* (New York: Crossroad; London: SCM, 1983). She urges "women's self-affirmation, power and liberation from all patriarchal alienation, marginalization, and oppression" (126). Her "ecclesia of women" or "women-church" has, she claims, "authority 'to choose and reject' biblical texts" (132). She presses the point: the Bible is "authorised by men, written in androcentric language, [and is] reflective of male experience" (130). It would be unjust to her intentions to tone down her polemical language. From a hermeneutical viewpoint, it is a self-fulfilling hermeneutic, like the most subjective elements and selections of texts in liberation theology. But among the polemics there is some solid historical research. She points out that Mary Magdalene is the first witness to the resurrection of Christ. In the Johannine tradition, she argues, Mary becomes "the *apostola apostolorum,* the apostle of the apostles" (332). Yet even some of this argument may be questioned. She is right to stress the faithfulness of the women, and failures of Peter and the men, but neglects the transforming effect of the resurrection to reverse failure and to bring hope out of despair. It is not surprising that she appeals to liberation theology. "Liberation theology has challenged the so-called objectivity and value-neutrality of academic theology" (6). The problem with her exegesis is that often gender may be merely one among *many* explanations for a text or historical situation, but by her own admission she selects the hypothesis that best serves her case.

To Schüssler Fiorenza goes the accolade of becoming a kind of paradigm or marker for literally scores of feminist studies over the next twenty or more years. Two immediate publications were those of Ruether, *Sexism and God-Talk* (1983), and Trible, *Texts of Terror* (Philadelphia: Fortress, 1984). Trible "recounts tales of terror *in memoriam* to offer sympathetic readings of abused women" (3). She expounds Hagar's being trapped in a circle of bondage (Gen. 16:1-16), though God protects her offspring. She then considers the rape of Tamar, whose dignity stands in contrast to Ammon's brutal violence, alongside the death of Jephthah's daughter (Judg. 11:29-40). In the "patriarchal hermeneutics" of tradition, she concludes, "we are all diminished" (27-29 and 102-8). A flood of literature then follows, with works from Schüssler Fiorenza (1984), Adela Yarbro Collins (1985), Letty Russell (1985), Elaine Showalter (1986), Mary Ann Tolbert (1989), Rebecca

Chopp (1989), Julia Kristeva (1989), Ursula King (1990), Daphne Hampson (1990), Alice Laffey (1990), and others. Ann Loades offers a helpful collection of representative extracts and essays in *Feminist Theology: A Reader* (London: SPCK, 1990). Like liberation theology, the collection challenges examples of stereotypification, injustice, and predetermined role models, as well as those of manipulation, power, and control. But it cannot escape notice that in the twenty-first century the same themes tend to be repeated, even if some believe that these themes still need to be voiced. More recently Susan F. Parsons has written on ethics in *Feminism and Christian Ethics* (Cambridge: CUP, 1996). Like liberation theology, the movement was certainly needed in former times; but whether it has become imprisoned in the same repeated themes, the reader must judge. Elizabeth Achtemeier, Susan Heine, and especially Janet Radcliffe Richards, *The Sceptical Feminist* (London: Penguin, 1983), have voiced serious reservations and criticisms, which also deserve to be heard. (*See also* **Liberation Hermeneutics and Theology**.)

Reading: Ann Loades, *Feminist Theology: A Reader* (London: SPCK, 1990); Janet Radcliffe Richards, *The Sceptical Feminist* (London: Penguin, 1983); Elisabeth Schüssler Fiorenza, *In Memory of Her* (New York: Crossroad; London, SCM, 1983); A. C. Thiselton, *New Horizons in Hermeneutics* (Grand Rapids: Zondervan, 1992, 2012), 430-62; Phyllis Trible, *God and the Rhetoric of Sexuality* (Philadelphia Fortress, 1978).

Fergusson, David
David Fergusson (b. 1956) is professor of divinity in the University of Edinburgh, and a minister of the Church of Scotland. From 1983 he was involved in parish ministry, and was appointed lecturer at Edinburgh in 1986. He became professor of systematic theology at Aberdeen in 1990, and returned to Edinburgh in 2000. He is a fellow of the British Academy, and is a worldwide speaker. He gave the Cunningham Lectures at Edinburgh in 1996, the Bampton Lectures at Oxford in 2001, the Gifford Lectures at Glasgow in 2008, and the Warfield Lectures at Princeton. He has lectured in Korea, Hong Kong, Japan, and Australia. He has a special interest in Reformed theology, and also in science and religion. But he has written on most aspects of systematic theology and theological ethics.

Fergusson has written *Bultmann* (Collegeville, Minn.: Liturgical Press, 1992; London: Continuum, 2000); *The Cosmos and the Creator: Introduction to the Theology of Creation* (London: SPCK, 1998); *Community, Liberalism, and Christian Ethics* (Cambridge: CUP, 1998); *Church, State, and Civil Society* (Cambridge: CUP, 2004); *Scottish Philosophical Theology, 1700-2000* (Ann Arbor: University of Michigan Academic, 2007); *Faith and Its Critics* (Oxford and New York: OUP, 2009); and is coeditor of *The Cambridge Dictionary of Theology* (Cambridge: CUP, 2011). His books, range of interests, and participation in theological events have made him an influential force in British and international systematic theology. He has now been elected a Fellow of the British Academy.

Feuerbach, Ludwig A.

Ludwig A. Feuerbach (1804-1872) is most famous or notorious for his radical critique of religion. He was one of the younger "left-wing" Hegelians. His central thesis was that "God" is only a human projection. The religious believer, he urged, projects and objectifies his own human being into a celestial figure, and religious belief becomes an illusion. Humankind thus creates "God" in its own image (*The Essence of Christianity* [1841]). In his *Principles of the Philosophy of the Future* (1843), he develops and broadens this thesis, and criticizes Hegel's view of "spirit" *(Geist)*. His materialism provides a seminal link with Karl Marx. He also influenced Nietzsche and Wagner. His aphorism "What distinguishes the Christian from other honourable people? At most a pious face, and parted hair" reminds us of the style of Nietzsche. Another well-known reductionist aphorism is: "Man is what he eats." He also declared, "God was my first thought; reason, my second; humankind my third and last thought." His life story is not irrelevant. He began by studying theology at Heidelberg and Berlin, passed through personal encounter with Hegel, and the study of philosophy at Berlin, and reached his climax in radical materialism.

Fichte, Johann G.

The early years of Johann G. Fichte (1762-1814) were dominated by an admiration for Kant, especially his *Critique of Practical Reason*. With support from both Kant and Goethe, Fichte became professor of philosophy at the University of Jena at the age of thirty-two in 1794; Schiller was professor of history there. Fichte strongly stressed moral absolutism. But moral consciousness, sympathy for republicanism and the French Revolution, and his idea of God as a principle rather than a person alienated him from many at the time. In Fichte God is a presupposition: the ground of all that exists. In 1799 he was forced to vacate his chair at Jena. By 1810, however, he was appointed dean of the Faculty of Philosophy in the newly founded University of Berlin. Like Kant, he sought to provide a transcendental philosophy, especially of experience. The finite continually strives toward an ideal. But whereas Kant ascribed only "categories" of thought, such as *cause* and *time,* to the creation of the mind, Fichte went much further, ascribing the notion of *necessity* and supposed *objectivity* to the mind. While subjective idealism may be applied to Schelling only with qualifications, Fichte comes more clearly under this heading.

Reading: G. Zöller, *Fichte's Transcendental Philosophy* (Cambridge: CUP, 1998).

Fideism

Fideism (from Lat. *fides,* "faith") covers a spectrum of meanings. At one end of the spectrum it asserts the primacy of faith over reason. At the other end it regards Christian faith as blind trust or belief, which cannot be rationally demonstrated as true. In this latter sense, Christian faith is *contrary* to reason, or irrational, while the other meaning regards Christian faith as *beyond* reason, but capable of demonstration that the belief is not irrational. B. Pascal and S. Kierkegaard were among the most uncompromising fideists. Augustine and Aquinas perceived reason as confirmatory, even if it could not match the scope of revelation. Barth may stand between Kierkegaard and Augustine. Today W. Pannenberg insists on the role of argument in the public arena as part of the credibility of faith, and Roman Catholics formally reject fideism.

Filioque

Filioque (Lat. "and the Son") refers to the double procession of the Holy Spirit from the Father and the Son. This clause was added by the Western Church to the Nicene-Constantinopolitan Creed; it was not an original part of that creed. Photius denounced the clause in the Eastern Church, but it has been defended in the West. The Western addition reflects the theme that the Spirit testifies to Christ and that Christ breathed on the disciples to communicate the Holy Spirit (John 20:22). But J. Moltmann and others argue that the original form does better justice to the coequal status of the persons of the Holy Trinity. At his inauguration in 2013, the archbishop of Canterbury, Justin Welby, led the confession of the creed in the earlier (Eastern) form, and Balthasar, among others, has also used the Eastern form. Both forms serve to make a valid point. (*See also* **Double Procession**.)

Forgive, Forgiveness

In the OT three Heb. words are used to denote "forgive" or "pardon," namely, *kipper* (often meaning "to cover" or "to atone"); *nāśā'* ("to forgive" or "to carry away"); and *shākach* (to let go, to forget). In the NT the normal word is *aphiēmi* (to forgive, to send away), but *apoluō* (to loose away) and *charizomai* (to be gracious) are also used. BDB lists numerous passages for the Piel of *kipper* (two and a half columns, 497-98). *Shākach* can mean to forget and to leave (BDB 1013), as in Jer. 31:34, "I will forgive their iniquity, and remember their sin no more." *Nāśā'* is used more rarely, but characteristically of Moses' pleas for the forgiveness of Israel (Exod. 10:17; 32:32). The surprise (for many) about the NT uses is that, according to Moulton and Geden, *Concordance to the Greek Testament,* the verb *aphiēmi* occurs more than 100 times in the Synoptic Gospels, 14 times in John, and only 5 times in Paul, with 8 in the General Epistles. Mark alone has about 25 occurrences of the word.

This may explain why many claim that "forgiveness" in the teaching of Jesus is equivalent to justification or reconciliation in Paul. Vincent Taylor observes, "For modern theology forgiveness is the equivalent of reconciliation" (*Forgiveness and Reconciliation* [London: Macmillan, 1948], 195). Both arise from personal issues about fellowship with God. Yet Taylor also writes, "Justification . . . is widely, but not accurately, held to be the Pauline equivalent for forgiveness" (xiii). A moment's reflection will confirm that a Christian believer is never "*not* reconciled" with God. That mutual fellowship is always active. But all Christians come at least at the beginning and end of the day to pray, "Forgive us our trespasses," and express repentance for sins. On the other side, justification and reconciliation are *independent of renewed pardon,* which every Christian needs. Christians, although renewed, still sin, just as they still die, as O. Cullmann has reminded us. Taylor writes, "The divided character of man's heart must be recognized frankly and unreservedly" (xviii). Yet Taylor cites W. H. Moberly, R. S. Franks, and R. N. Flew as defining forgiveness as "restoration of relationship," as if it were reconciliation.

Clearly forgiveness is part of the earliest preaching by the apostles (Acts 2:38; 10:43). Eph. 1:7 combines "redemption through his blood" with the forgiveness of sins. In Col. 1:14, the two, again, seem synonymous: "in whom we have our redemption, the forgiveness of sins." But in these passages it is sin that is forgiven; they do not speak of remitting penalties. Justification and redemption, however, do speak of the removal of obstacles, penalties, or bondage. Forgiveness springs from grace, generosity, or compassion. James Atkinson insists that repentance is not a *condition* of forgiveness, but a *consequence* or *concomitant* of it. It is as if to say: no one would ask for forgiveness unless they repent of what they admit before God, and hold nothing against others. In the episode of the paralytic (Mark 2:1-12) Jesus simply states: "Your sins are forgiven" (v. 9). The context is the authority of Jesus to forgive sins, rather than the attitude of the paralytic. The logic of "as we forgive those who trespass against us" is that if we seek the presence and approval of God, it is assumed that we shall want to be like him, and share his attitude of generosity to others. Whether a person has a forgiving spirit is a good test of the person's genuineness in asking for God's forgiveness. The withholding of forgiveness for blaspheming against the Holy Spirit (Mark 3:29) relates to a mind so twisted that it calls good "bad" and bad "good," and has lost the moral awareness to ask for forgiveness. For anyone that this verse troubles, the very experience of concern shows that he or she still has that needed moral awareness (*see* **Holy Spirit: The Spirit in the New Testament**). Those who in heart are merciful will be shown forgiveness (Matt. 5:7), not those who perform some such act as "penance." (*See also* **Grace; Justification; Reconciliation; Redeem, Redemption.**)

Reading: Glen Pettigrove, *Forgiveness and Love* (Oxford: OUP, 2012); Lewis B. Smedes, *Forgive and Forget* (New York: HarperCollins, 1996); Vincent Taylor, *Forgiveness and Reconciliation* (London: Macmillan, 1948); William Telfer, *The Forgiveness of Sins* (London: SCM, 1959; Philadelphia: Muhlenberg, 1960).

Form Criticism

The key to understanding form criticism is to see the relation between a given biblical "form" and its setting in life *(Sitz im Leben).* It fundamentally concerns a period of oral tradition before this tradition finally found written form. In OT studies H. Gunkel and S. Mowinckel applied it to the Psalms, where a longer oral period was involved than in NT cases. On the basis of Gunkel's OT work, R. Bultmann, K. L. Schmidt, and M. Dibelius sought to apply it to "forms" in the NT. Such forms as sermons, aphorisms, sayings, pronouncements, and narratives were believed to have been shaped by the needs of the Christian community. British scholars (such as Vincent Taylor and T. W. Manson) took issue with German form critics about how secure inferences from forms could be to hypothetical settings in life. This partly arose because German has two terms for "form." *Form* is individual and neutral in context; *Gattung* concerns a general class or genre, which has a relation to context. Manson wrote: "A paragraph of Mark is not a penny the better or worse as historical evidence for being labelled 'apothegm' or 'pronouncement story' or 'paradigm'" ("Present Day Research in the Life of Jesus," in *The Background to the New Testament and Its Eschatology,* ed. W. D. Davies and D. Daube [Cambridge: CUP, 1956], 212). But for Bultmann and Dibelius, the whole point of the exercise was to determine the historical origins of the form. Most "forms," on this view, not only postdated Jesus; they also reflected an oral tradition that had been shaped by the needs of the Aramaic-speaking or Hellenistic community.

The *Sitz im Leben* was rarely, if ever, the setting in the life of Jesus, but was the *Sitz im Leben* of the early church. Bultmann was also largely influenced (i) by W. Wrede on the "messianic secret," (ii) by Schmidt's theory that Mark presents fragments of the Jesus tradition rather than a continuous narrative history, (iii) by A. Schweitzer's negative conclusions in *The Quest of the Historical Jesus,* and (iv) by Gunkel's inferences from a much longer oral tradition in the OT. Today the work of G. N. Stanton on NT preaching (1970) and of Richard Bauckham on oral tradition and eyewitnesses (2006) invites a far more cautious and careful approach to form criticism than used to be the vogue. (*See also* **Bultmann, Rudolf**.)

Forsyth, Peter T.

Peter T. Forsyth (1848-1921) was born and educated in Aberdeen, studied also in Göttingen under Albrecht Ritschl, and spent twenty-five years in the congregational ministry in England. He then became principal of Hackney College, London, in 1901. Initially he followed Ritschl's liberalism, but soon became a firm evangelical. He published *The Work of Christ* (1910), which focused on victory, new birth, and reconciliation. He urged that the atonement involved judgment, and stressed the holiness of God. This followed his *Person and Place of Jesus Christ* (1909). He declared, "Christ's sacrifice began before he came into the world, and his Cross was that of a lamb slain before the world's foundation." He also declared, "We do not stand on the fact of our experience but on the fact *which* we experience." During 1909 he also published *The Cruciality of the Cross;* and in 1916, *The Justification of God.* Some have called him Barthian before Barth.

Fox, George

George Fox (1624-1691) is generally recognized as the founder of the Quakers. Fox expressed dissatisfaction with those Christians who looked to "theology" rather than to "experiences," and attacked the importance given to doctrines and formal liturgy. He criticized the Anglican clergy, who had been educated at Oxford or Cambridge, and sought the "inner light" of the Holy Spirit. Fox's *Journal* was published in 1694; it is a narrative classic, in effect his autobiography. He was born in Mansfield in Nottinghamshire. In early years he was a traveling shoemaker. In 1646 he abandoned church attendance, relying only on the "inner light," and in 1647 he received a "revelation" in which he learned that all earthly power was corrupt. His attack on the established church brought periods of imprisonment. By 1655 Quakerism had spread from Yorkshire to London and Bristol. Before the Restoration in 1660 Fox fled to the American colonies. He was finally imprisoned at Worcester. His *Journal* records typical early Quaker experiences: "The Lord's power began to shake them. . . . The house seemed to be shaken" (chap. 2); "I was wrapped up as in a rapture in the Lord's power" (*Journal*, 2007 ed., 14). He called parish churches "steeple houses" and rejected many "worldly" customs, including raising one's hat or swearing an oath in a law court. There are numerous resonances with the Radical Reformers, with the Holiness Movement, and with some Pentecostals. In America William Penn (1644-1718) became influential as a statesman in the Quaker tradition. Quaker universalism led many later into latitudinarianism. (*See also* **Quakers, or Society of Friends.**)

Franciscans

Francis of Assisi founded the Order of Friars Minor in 1209. Its Rule originally insisted on complete poverty for the whole order, encouraged labor to pay for living costs, and forbade the ownership of property. Francis is said to have read portions about self-denial from the Sermon on the Mount to his followers when he founded the order. Bonaventura in the thirteenth century and Pope John XXII in the fourteenth century debated the practicalities of the Rule, and permitted corporate ownership of property. A series of further reforms took place between the fifteenth and eighteenth centuries. The order encouraged preaching and mission. In addition to Bonaventura, Duns Scotus and William of Ockham were Franciscans. The order added a second order of contemplative nuns. In due time the Franciscans developed a third order, which did not require religious vows.

Francis de Sales

One of the leaders of the Counter-Reformation, Francis de Sales (1567-1622) was born at the castle of Sales in Savoy and educated in Paris. He was ordained priest in 1593, and became bishop of Geneva in 1602. He wrote *Introduction to the Devout Life* (1609) and *Treatise on the Love of God* (1616).

Frankfurt School

The Frankfurt School was set up in 1931 under the direction of M. Horkheimer in association with T. Adorno and H. Marcuse. Its more formal name was the Institute for Social Research, and it explored problems in sociology, philosophy, and psychoanalysis. It stressed the limits of "pure" reason, following Kant, and the problem of alienation, following Hegel and Marx. Its emphasis on social deception paved the way for later postmodernism, especially for M. Foucault. In effect, adherents explore what would later become sociology of knowledge. Moltmann saw value in the "negative dialectic" and "critical theory" of Adorno and Horkheimer (*The Crucified God* [London: SCM, 1974], 5, 283-54).

Freedom, Free Will

The concept cannot be defined in the abstract apart from its relation to a given context of thought. On one side it is deeply related to philosophy and to the philosophy of religion; on the other side it is deeply related to the theology of Paul, of Augustine, of Luther and Calvin, and of the Reformed. In popular thought in much philosophy, freedom and free will denote the capacity to choose from two or more alternative actions. Many see this as the precondition for moral responsibility. Many theologians, however, especially those in the Pauline, Augustinian, and Reformed tradition, note that freedom for God does not denote a free choice of any action, but freedom to express one's character without any external constraint. Few, if any, would argue that God is "free" to tell lies or to go back on his promises, because he has committed himself to be true and to honor his promises. Yet this voluntary acceptance of limited options of action would not normally be regarded as a lack of human freedom. Already, therefore, we may distinguish between a purely anthropocentric notion of freedom as the ability to choose to do any action, and a definition derived from the freedom of God as freedom to express the character of the self, without external constraint.

Even in secular philosophy, however, some have challenged the notion of autonomous freedom. Some cite scientific laws or historicality to claim that certain factors determine a limited range of actions. Yet those who are known in philosophy as "compatibilists" argue that free will can be compatible with determinism. If an action can be predicted, for example, this need not imply that the agents of the action are not free. One well-known example from philosophy envisages a man and woman who live or work close by each other, who enjoy the same hobbies, aim at the same ideals, and have had a similar education. When they declare their intention to get married, everyone in the area exclaims, "I knew it! I predicted that they would get married!" But this does not mean that this act was not *free*. Prediction and freedom are certainly compatible. Others, however, adopt an "incompatible" view, whether for philosophical or theological reasons. Some would argue that everything is determined, whether by God, by laws of nature, by historicity, or by some other means, including biology and physiology. Various forms of postmodernism regard humankind as helpless victims of forces beyond their control.

A. H. Strong, a Baptist Reformed theologian who lived near the end of the nineteenth century, defined "freedom" in four ways, which predispose the choice of an Augustinian definition: (i) physical freedom, or lack of external constraint; (ii) formal freedom, which is morally not determined; (iii) moral freedom or self-determinateness; and (iv) "real" freedom, namely, "ability to conform to the divine standard" (*Systematic Theology* [London: Pickering and Inglis, 1907], 361). This fourth definition seems to be what Paul has in mind when he declares, "For freedom Christ has set us free. Stand firm, therefore, and do not submit again to a yoke of slavery" (Gal. 5:1). This lies behind Paul's argument in Rom. 6:15-19. You are a slave, he declares, "of the one whom you obey." But God has delivered us from such slavery. Under grace, Christians often believe that they obey God "necessarily, yet freely." This notion of freedom fits those definitions of the consequences of sin that render human nature corrupt and powerless (*see* **Depravity; Sin: Historical;** and related information under entries for Augustine, Barth, Calvin, Luther, and Pannenberg).

Nevertheless, even in the NT "freedom" (Gk. *eleutheria, eleutheros*) is used in more than one way. When in the Fourth Gospel Jesus declares, "The truth shall make you free" (John 8:32) and "If the Son makes you free, you will be free indeed" (8:36), the contrast with "slavery" there seems to reflect Paul's usual meaning. Rom. 7:3 asserts freedom from the law. But 1 Cor. 7:21-22 and Col. 3:11 both speak of people who are slaves or free according to Roman law, that is, free from external constraint. Danker distinguishes *eleutheros* as "socially and politically" free, from *eleutheros* as referring to "freedom from control or obligation" (BDAG 316-17).

More than one tradition is reflected in Christian theology. Augustine, for his part, argued that originally Adam possessed both the ability not to sin *(posse non peccare)* and the ability to sin *(posse peccare)*. But after the Fall, Adam lost this equipoise, or ability not to sin. Only by grace could his original freedom be restored. He wrote to the Pelagians: "By the sin of the first man, free will perished from the human race. Through sin, freedom indeed perished" (*Against Two Letters of the Pelagians* 1.5; *NPNF*, ser. 1, 5:378). He adds, "That freedom was in Paradise, to have a full righteousness with immortality." Hence now humankind needs grace. Augustine quotes John 8:36: "If the Son shall make you free, you will be free indeed." He acknowledges that "proud" people oppose him, and demolish free will by exaggerating it (chap. 8). Luther follows Augustine. In his 1525 reply to Erasmus, entitled *On the Bondage of the Will*, he writes, "Free-will without God's grace is not free at all, but is the permanent prisoner and bondslave of evil, since it cannot turn to good. . . . What is *ineffective* power is (in plain language) *no* power" ([London: James Clarke, 1957], 104). Calvin expounds how humankind is "deprived of freedom of will" and enslaved, in the *Institutes* 2.2. The first man, he asserts, was brought under "the dominion of sin" (2.2.1; Beveridge, 1:222). He complains, "The thing meant by free will, though constantly occurring, . . . few have defined" (2.2.4; 1:226). He cites Origen, Chrysostom, Bernard, and Peter Lombard. But "free-will does not enable any man to perform good works" (2.2.6; 1:228). In a different tradition Chrysostom writes, "God, having placed good and evil in our power, has given us full freedom of choice." Although Thomas Aquinas and the Dominicans tended to follow Augustine's tradition, the Franciscans did not, nor did Duns Scotus; nor the Jesuits. N. P. Williams argues that the Council of Trent (1546) repeated the second Council of Orange, which was "a compromise" between the Dominicans and the Jesuits (*The Ideas of the Fall and of Original Sin* [London and New York: Longmans, Green, 1929], 420-21). Most Christians today will acknowledge their need of grace, but will probably presuppose a degree of freedom (however it is defined) as a precondition of moral accountability and guilt. Complete lack of freedom, many claim, would undermine the daily phenomenon of confession of sin. (*See also* **Grace; Sin: Historical.**)

Reading: W. J. van Asselt, *Reformed Thought on Freedom* (Grand Rapids: Baker, 2010); C. A. Campbell, *In Defence of Free Will and Other Essays* (London: Allen and Unwin, 1967); T. O'Connor, *Persons and Causes* (New York: OUP, 2000); R. Swinburne, *The Coherence of Theism* (1977; reprint, Oxford: Clarendon, 1989).

Frei, Hans W.

The family of Hans W. Frei (1922-1988) emigrated to the USA from Germany in 1938, when Hitler was chancellor, not least because his family was Jewish. He graduated in theology from Yale in 1945, and served first as a Baptist preacher, then as an ordained minister of the Episcopal Church. He was greatly influenced by Karl Barth's writings, which he studied for his Ph.D. He spent most of his life teaching at Yale, and his large influence is perhaps disproportionate to his relatively few writings. William K. Wimsatt, a leader of the New Criticism School, was a colleague at Yale, and Frei's most important book was *The Eclipse of Biblical Narrative* (New Haven: Yale University Press, 1974). In this work he argued that a fateful change befell the reading of the Bible in the eighteenth and nineteenth centuries. A division occurred between precritical reading of narrative as report and a critical reconstruction of narratives. The artificial choice between them led to an eclipse of narrative in a postcritical sense. Narrative could be recovered in various ways. A narrative world was that into which a reader could enter. Moreover, a more theological reading of narrative that also drew on literary criticism could more truly engage with the *meaning* of narrative.

A year later Frei published *The Identity of Jesus Christ: The Hermeneutical Basis of Dogmatic Theology* (Philadelphia: Fortress, 1975). Both books place hermeneutics on the theological agenda. Whereas his earlier book spoke of "history-like" narrative, the second book claimed that "fictional description . . . merges with factual claims," and that the identity of Jesus Christ is bound up with his presence. After Frei's death in 1988, G. Hunsinger and W. C. Placher edited the book *Types of Christian Theology* (New Haven: Yale University Press, 1992) from the manuscript and notes. Many describe him as an exponent of "postliberal theology," with G. Lindbeck. One recent study is Michael Higton, *Providence and History: Hans W. Frei's Public Theology* (Edinburgh: T. & T. Clark, 2004). (*See also* **Hermeneutics; Narrative.**)

Freud, Sigmund

Sigmund Freud (1856-1939) was born in Freiburg, and grew up devoid of any belief in God. His father was an orthodox Jew. He went to university to train as a medical doctor, and in Vienna came strongly under the influence of Brücke, whom he regarded as a "second father." He graduated in 1881 but was not drawn to a doctor's practice, preferring to continue laboratory work and scientific research. Starting in 1882 he worked in Vienna General Hospital in neuropathology with the psychiatrist Meynert, and in 1885 he worked as *Privatdozent* (honorary lecturer) at the University of Vienna. In 1886 he entered private practice as a specialist in nervous disorders. Throughout his early career he regarded mental states and processes as "interplay of forces which assist or inhibit one another." "Psychic energy" was the influx and discharge of mental tension. Hans Küng comments, "The human *psyche* [was] understood as a kind of machine, as a 'mental appliance'" (*Does God Exist?* [London: Collins, 1978], 268). From 1889 Freud began to treat hysteria and its symptoms, which he regarded as products of emotional shock or trauma, which the patient had "repressed." This path of research or speculation reached its climax in *The Interpretation of Dreams* (1899), which followed his *Studies in Hysteria* (1895, published cojointly with J. Breuer).

Freud broke new ground by proposing that it was possible to gain access to the unconscious. Many others had thought of the unconscious merely as a hidden area. Freud regarded it as a source of primary psychic processes. Patients, confronted with what was a cause of guilt or with what was superficially undesirable, "repressed" these wishes or desires into the unconscious, to hide or disguise them. The task of therapy was to discover and expose them as the repressions that they were. It was to lay bare the unconscious, in which had been hidden untreated traumatic experiences. Freud argued that therapy must examine "the dream work" and its "mechanisms." These bring about "transposition" and "distortion" *(Entstellung)* of the "dream-thoughts." Dreams constitute models of disguised, substitutive, and fictive expressions of human wishing or desire.

The dream-as-dreamed ("dream-thought") is not the dream-as-recounted or dream-as-remembered ("dream-account" or "dream-content"), but lies beneath it. It "scrambles" and condenses it. Hence it has to be "interpreted" by the psychoanalyst. This is what was decisive for Ricoeur in seeing fully the importance of hermeneutics. To interpret is to diagnose "a double meaning," as Marx and Nietzsche also argued. The deeper "text" below the dream-account seeks to hide the id from the ego by repression and disguise. Küng and Ricoeur, however, note that most of Freud's terms and metaphors draw either from physiology or economics. "Cathexis," for example, as the retention of mental energy, is indeed derived from economics.

Freud then elaborated this in terms of a sexual metaphor or image. He often used the Oedipus myth, whereby desire for the mother ends in the death of the father. In fact, Küng points out, this notion is a reflection of Freud's own early childhood, in which an early childhood passion for his mother coexisted with jealousy of his father, just as King Oedipus, without knowing it, killed his father and married his mother. These speculative conclusions emerge in Freud's *Three*

Essays on the Theory of Sexuality (1905). He took this further in *The Ego and the Id* (1923) and *Future of an Illusion* (1927; reprint, Seattle: Pacific Publishing Studio, 2010). The superego acts as a moral judge or censor; the id is the source of the primitive drives that drive the psyche and libido. The ego is the rational and conscious self. Acute conflict within the self causes neurosis, when therapy is needed. Without treatment this conflict is usually *repressed*, with negative results. The therapist will try to gain access to the unconscious through exploring dreams, "free association," and unconscious "giveaways," or "Freudian slips."

All this sets the stage for Freud's critique of religion. Basically religious people, he argued, project inner conflicts outward and upward, away from the self. This reflects Feuerbach's notion of projection. The "patient" projects the conflict upward to a god figure who both judges guilt and gives grace and comfort.

The figure of the father similarly provides both judgment, and love and protection. The face that gazes into the cradle is magnified into infinity. "Religion" is associated with this "infantile" stage. Earlier, in *Totem and Taboo* (1912-1913), Freud also explored how the "totem" animal protected the tribe or group yet prohibited certain "taboos." This allegedly provided a parallel with the Oedipus myth. Religion springs from "a longing for a father" as a "defence against childhood helplessness" (*Future of an Illusion,* 20).

Freud's influence cannot be overstated, even if many now dissociate themselves from a number of his specific claims. There are some positive features. Bonhoeffer in his *Letters and Papers from Prison* warned his fellow Christians not to invite others to regress into an infantile concern about guilt and dependence. Ricoeur owed much to Freud's method of interpretation for his discovery of the prime importance of hermeneutics and double meaning. But both Küng and Ricoeur attacked his materialist worldview and other aspects. Might it be argued that much of Freud's hostility to religion sprang from his own poor relation to his father? Do some of his observations about animals and young children spring from a certain type of evolutionary theory, now largely discarded? Does he place too much weight on terms drawn from the machine and economic forces? Can we "explain" the human mind by regarding it as a mechanism of forces? He describes religion as "the obsessional neurosis of humankind." But does this account for *all* religion, and has Freud examined alternative accounts of the human mind? A. Adler and C. G. Jung offer different accounts of "drives" and of the truth of religion. Küng comments, "Freud took over from Feuerbach ... the essential arguments for his personal atheism" (*Freud and the Problem of God* [New Haven: Yale University Press, 1990], 75). (*See also* **Atheism; Feuerbach, Ludwig A.; Jung, Carl G.**)

Reading: Sigmund Freud, *The Future of an Illusion* (Seattle: Pacific Publishing Studio, 2010); Hans Küng, *Does God Exist?* (London: Collins, 1978); Hans Küng, *Freud and the Problem of God* (New Haven: Yale University Press, 1990), Michael Palmer, *Freud and Jung on Religion* (London and New York: Routledge, 1997); Paul Ricoeur, *Freud and Philosophy* (New Haven: Yale University Press, 1970).

Fundamentalism

Fundamentalism takes its name from a twelve-volume paperback series entitled *The Fundamentals,* published between 1910 and 1915. The aim of the writers was to reaffirm the traditional Christian doctrines about Christ and the Bible. Initially the editors of the volumes were A. C. Dixon, Louis Meyer, and R. A. Torrey. Two wealthy Californians supported the endeavor, and about three million copies were distributed, to every pastor, evangelist, missionary, theological student, and Sunday school superintendent. Initially, according to D. N. Livingstone, the volumes were not radically different from the thought of Hodge, Warfield, and the older Princeton tradition, but as the movement subsequently developed, especially in the 1920s, it became more shrill and no longer represented the Princeton tradition. In particular, it was hostile to Darwin and to evolutionary theories. Whereas G. F. Wright and J. Orr looked for some kind of reconciliation with an evolutionary theory, H. Beach, W. B. Greene, and others were "pugnaciously anti-Darwin" (Livingstone, *Darwin's Forgotten Defenders* [Grand Rapids: Eerdmans, 1987], 153). As the influence of "fundamentalism" grew and hardened, even J. Gresham Machen was expelled from Princeton Theological Seminary, and moved to form Westminster Theological Seminary in 1929. In response, David Clark wrote, "Scriptures do not say *how* God created man, whether instantaneously by fiat, or by a process of slow development." *The Fundamentals* addressed the infallibility of the Bible, the doctrine of the Trinity, the virgin birth and deity of Christ, the substitutionary account of the atonement, and the bodily resurrection, ascension, and return of Christ. But in the 1920s, increasing emphasis seems to have been placed on biblical criticism, the Genesis narratives, and this "stricter" interpretation and specific theories of evolution. Most evangelicals today would not wish to be called "fundamentalists." Hence, although James Barr wrote a polemical book, *Fundamentalism,* in criticism of this movement, it is not clear who still wished to own the title.

G

Gadamer, Hans-Georg
Hans-Georg Gadamer (1900-2002) was born in Marburg, and educated in the University of Breslau, where he worked on literature, languages, and philosophy. Between 1922 and 1923 four events were decisive for the development of his thought. First, in 1922 he expressed his insight about the difference between "problems," which are fixed abstractions, and concrete contextual "questions," which form the basis of hermeneutics. This became a key to his great book on hermeneutics, *Truth and Method* (2nd Eng. ed. [London: Sheed and Ward, 1989; first Ger. ed. 1960]). Gadamer wrote, "Problems are not real questions that arise of themselves, and hence acquire the pattern of their answer from the genesis of their meaning, but are alternatives that can only be accepted in themselves"; "problems" exist only as fixed points "like stars in the sky" (377). Second, in 1923, Gadamer came to Freiburg and met Martin Heidegger. After initial disappointment, he became a close follower and friend of Heidegger, who assisted him financially during the economic crisis of that year, and shared much of his thought. Third, with Heidegger, he began to study Friedrich Schleiermacher and Wilhelm Dilthey on "the art of understanding," and developed and modified their approach. Fourth, with Heidegger he also studied Aristotle, and this led to his growing respect for the "wisdom" of the ancient Greeks. During the 1920s Gadamer became increasingly interested in Kierkegaard and in art.

In his magisterial work *Truth and Method*, Gadamer first attacked the rationalism of Descartes and the Enlightenment, in conscious contrast to the more historical and communal tradition of Giambattista Vico (1668-1744). Rationalism, he argued, might be adequate for the natural sciences alone, but a historical and hermeneutical method is more appropriate for the *Geisteswissenschaften*, or the humanities. This approach more adequately addresses culture and education, and above all keeps "oneself open to what is other" (17). Typically, Gadamer wrote, *"All encounter with the language of art is an encounter with an unfinished event, and is itself part of this event"* (99). Events are "unfinished," because history flows forward and onward.

Gadamer illustrates this point with reference to games, festivals, and concerts, each of which *cannot be precisely replicated* without undermining its very identity. He writes, "Play fulfils its purpose only if the player loses himself in the play" (102). "It is the game that is played — it is irrelevant whether or not there is a subject who plays it" (103). Most emphatically of all he writes, *"The primacy of play over the consciousness of the player is fundamentally acknowledged"* (104). Like Wittgenstein, he is suspicious of the importance of purely "mental states." He writes, "Play draws him (a child) into its domain" (109). In other words, just as a player in a game is totally absorbed in the rules and aims of the game, so a *participant* always has a different viewpoint and horizon from that of the so-called neutral spectator or observer. During the argument in the first part of *Truth and Method,* he acknowledges the turning point in Schleiermacher's hermeneutics.

In the second main part of *Truth and Method,* he examines more deeply the questions of truth, understanding, and historical reason. He commends Dilthey for wrestling with the questions left by Hegel, especially the question of how history transforms persons. Nevertheless, although he values Dilthey's notion of "life-world," he regards his conclusions as still too "scientific." Gadamer endorses Heidegger's notion of temporality *(Zeitlichkeit)*. He now introduces his well-known concept of prejudices or prejudgments *(Vorurteile)*. He concludes, "The pre-judgments of the individual, far more than his judgements, constitute the historical reality of his being" (276-77).

Gadamer also explores the rehabilitation of authority and tradition. Authority, he argues, "rests on an acknowledgement and hence on an act of reason itself which, aware of its own limitations, trusts in the better insight of others" (279). This leads to his well-known exposition of effective history, or the history of effects *(Wirkungsgeschichte)*. In this process we can see reality only from a particular vantage point. Gadamer calls this, following Heidegger, "a horizon." He writes, this is "something into which we move and that moves with us. Horizons change for a person who is moving. Thus the horizon of the past . . . is always in motion" (304). This leads us beyond Romanticist hermeneutics, and understands "application" as integral to the process of understanding. In particular Gadamer argues that we must be open to the "other." He writes: "Openness to the other, then, involves recognising that I must accept some things that are against me, even though no one else forces me to do so" (361). Finally, in part 2 he turns to Collingwood's logic of question and answer, and its contrast with abstract problems. He insists on *"The priority of the question* in all knowledge and discourse" (363). He adds, "Reflection on the hermeneutical experience transforms questions back to questions that arise, and derive their sense from their motivation" (377). Like Heidegger, he regards statements as derivative from questions.

In part 3 of *Truth and Method,* Gadamer turns to what he calls ontological hermeneutics and the nature of language. Language is the "medium of understanding" in which fresh insights arise, which could not hitherto have been predicted (384-85). No one can know in advance what will "emerge" from a conversation. This applies especially to situations in which the conversation partner is "other." The aim of the conversation partners is to bring their respective horizons as closely and creatively together as possible, although "total" assimilation between them would be impossible. Elsewhere Gadamer speaks of "The convergence of my concept of game with the concept of language games in the later Wittgenstein" ("My Philosophical Journey," in *The Philosophy of Hans-Georg Gadamer,* ed. Lewis E. Hahn [Chicago: Open Court, 1997], 42). He aims to build carefully on a theory of language, considering such linguists as Ernst Cassirer, Wilhelm von Humboldt, and others. But his tradition of the theory of language is largely Germanic and one-sided, and there is little engagement with Anglo-American and French thinkers. It is generally acknowledged that the third part of *Truth and Method* does not contribute to hermeneutics as decisively as do the first and second parts.

To sum up, Gadamer constitutes a *second major turning point* in the theory of hermeneutics, after Schleiermacher had constituted the first turning point. A second major contribution of Gadamer consists of his consistent *opposition to the Enlightenment,* and his exposure of its nonhistorical rationalism. He has shown that it is individualistic rather than communal, and relies on instrumental reason rather than tradition and history. He also exchanges the Enlightenment model of scrutinizing the text *as a mere object* for *listening to the text,* as if it were also a subject. His third major contribution is to show the importance of effective history, or the history of effects, and the importance of "prejudgments" rather than more superficial reflection.

Gadamer's work on games is imaginative and full of insights, and helps us to understand narrative worlds, and the suprarational revelation of truth in art and other modes of truth. The reader and interpreter are hermeneutical *participants, rather than value-neutral spectators.* On the negative side, as Wolfhart Pannenberg insists, he tends to undervalue the significance of statements. Although what he claims about questions and about hermeneutics remains of the utmost importance, concepts of truth that can be expressed in statements also remain no less important. It was left to Paul Ricoeur to demonstrate that in hermeneutics we need exegesis and explanation, as well as creative understanding. His overall contribution to hermeneutics remains of the most profound importance.

Reading: Hans-Georg Gadamer, *Philosophical Hermeneutics* (Berkeley: University of California Press, 1976); Hans-Georg Gadamer, *Truth and Method,* 2nd Eng. ed. (London: Sheed and Ward, 1989); Lewis E. Hahn, ed., *The Philosophy of Hans-Georg Gadamer* (Chicago: Open Court, 1997); Anthony C. Thiselton, *New Horizons in Hermeneutics* (London: HarperCollins, 1992; Grand Rapids: Zondervan, 1992, 2012) (Anthony C. Thiselton, "Hans-Georg Gadamer," in *Hermeneutics: An Introduction* [Grand Rapids: Eerdmans, 2009], 206-27, overlaps a little in parts); Georgia Warnke, *Gadamer: Hermeneutics, Tradition, and Reason* (Cambridge: Polity Press, 1987); Joel C. Weinsheimer, *Gadamer's Hermeneutics: A Reading of Truth and Method* (New Haven: Yale University Press, 1985).

Gilson, Étienne

Étienne Gilson (1884-1978) was a French Catholic Thomist philosopher. He was influenced by Bergson and Lévy-Bruhl. He founded the Pontifical Institute of Mediaeval Studies in Toronto, and became a major figure in neo-Thomism. He worked initially on the Scholastic background to Descartes. His works included studies of Duns Scotus, Augustine, Bernard, Aquinas, Bonaventura, Dante, and Abelard. He urged the importance of studying medieval philosophy.

Glory

When applied to God, "glory" denotes the splendor and majesty of God. Stephen "gazed into heaven and saw the glory of God" (Acts 7:55). The writer to the Hebrews calls Christ "the reflection of God's glory and the exact imprint of God's very being" (Gk. *apaugasma tēs doxēs, kai charaktēr tēs hypostaseōs autou;* Heb. 1:3). Paul speaks of God shining in our hearts "to give the light of the knowledge of the glory of God in the face of Jesus Christ" (2 Cor. 4:6). In terms of word history and semantics, the Hebrew word for glory, *kābôdh,* conveys that which is weighty or heavy. We may compare the Latin *gravis* and the Anglicized Latin *gravitas*. A person who has gravitas is immediately impressive and worthy of respect and attention. Hence glory becomes what makes someone impressive. This is also applicable to ancient Greek usage, where in Homer Achilles glories in his strength and Odysseus glories in his cunning. Paul is emphatic about this: "Let him who glories (Gk. *ho kauchōmenos*) glory (NRSV 'boast'; Gk. *kauchasthō*) in the Lord" (1 Cor. 1:31). To glorify God denotes acknowledging his splendor, especially in Christ, and his worthiness to be adored. In John the Holy Spirit or Paraclete will glorify Christ (Gk. *doxasei;* John 16:14). Basil of Caesarea insists that the Father, the Son, and the Holy Spirit should be coequally worshiped in the threefold Gloria of the church: "Glory be to the Father, and to the Son, and to the Holy Spirit."

When we observe more detailed aspects of the term, three or four points emerge. First, "glory" signifies not only God's presence, but also the *manifestation* of his presence. Jude declares that God will "make you stand without blemish in the presence of his glory with rejoicing" (v. 24). Heaven is permeated with "the glory of God and a radiance like a very rare jewel" (Rev. 21:11). The glory of God is light: "The city has no need of sun or moon" (Rev. 21:23). The OT speaks of "the glory of the Lord" thirty-six times: "They shall see the glory of the LORD" (Isa. 35:2). God's glory is manifest when it "fills," "rises," or "comes." Ezekiel has many passages of this kind: "This was the appearance of the likeness of the glory of the LORD" (Ezek. 1:28). "The glory of the LORD rose up . . . and the court was full of the brightness of the glory of the LORD" (Ezek. 10:4). Isa. 40:5 declares,

> "The glory of the LORD shall be revealed,
>   and all people shall see it together."

Often symbols of glory are used, as in "The glory of the LORD appeared in the cloud" (Exod. 16:10). Glory may become a manifestation of the living God. When people speak of someone who has died as having "gone to glory," their main point is "gone to be with God," even if glory also means more.

In classical Greek the meaning of glory *(doxa, doxazō)* often denoted *reputa-*

tion. This aspect has not faded away from the use of the term in the NT and LXX. God's people rejoice in the "name" or "reputation" that God has established. It is easy to see how glory can involve God's honor, splendor, or reputation. The Seer writes: "The living creatures give glory and honor and thanks to the one who is seated on the throne ... singing, 'You are worthy, our Lord and God, / to receive glory and honor and power'" (Rev. 4:9-11). This becomes even more striking when such glory is seen "in the face of Jesus Christ" (2 Cor. 4:6). For what makes God so impressive and worthy of worship is not only the history of redeeming acts, but also his gracious love in Jesus Christ. Christ is indeed "the visible manifestation" of God. Barth declares, "God's glory is God Himself.... At its core it is freedom to love.... God is the One who seeks and finds fellowship.... It is a matter of God's *love*" (*CD* II/1, 641, 643). To see God's glory is "to recognize the beauty of God in Jesus Christ" (664). When he speaks of Jesus' time "to be glorified" (John 12:23), John refers to the cross. When he faces this ignominious death, Jesus prays, "Father, glorify your name" (12:28).

God's glory, Luther shows, is not the triumphalist glory of sheer power, but involves humility and the cross. Indeed, when the term is applied to humans, "a theologian of glory" shows arrogance and self-sufficiency, whereas "a theologian of the cross" sees reality as it is. One writer speaks of "the Christlikeness of God." Barth and Hans Urs von Balthasar see the beauty of God in these terms.

Jürgen Moltmann also argues that to "glorify" God "means to love God for his own sake, and to enjoy God as he is in himself" (*The Coming of God* [London: SCM, 1996]). Moltmann draws this idea from Augustine. Unbelievers, Augustine declared, "make use" of God to enjoy the *world;* Christians "make use" of the world to enjoy God (*On Christian Doctrine* 1.12). The praise of God is not "useful," but for sheer joy. An example of this is to be "face-to-face" with God at the last day. In Hebrew the same word, *pānim,* denotes both "face" and "presence." As David Ford comments, "face" conjures up a world of meaning; it is fundamental to social relationships: "His face was like the sun shining with full force" (Rev. 1:16). Ford comments, "seeing [God's] face in worship is here the picture of unsurpassable joy and perfection" (*Self and Salvation* [Cambridge: CUP, 1999], 175). Light and shining become metaphors of glory. The priestly blessing in Num. 6:25 asks that God may "shine upon you." The King of glory is the Lord of hosts (Ps. 24:10). Yet when Jesus stoops to participate in a peasant wedding and turns water into wine, this "revealed his glory" (John 2:11). The cross glorifies the Son "so that the Son may glorify you [the Father]" (17:1). He prays to be glorified "with the glory that I had in your presence before the world existed" (17:5). Hence the threefold Gloria of the church concludes with "As it was in the beginning, is now, and shall be forever." In Protestantism "glorification" is mainly associated with the glory of the resurrection (1 Cor. 15:43). But in Eastern Orthodoxy the term denotes an elevation to "sainthood."

Reading: G. B. Caird, "The Glory of God in the Fourth Gospel," *NTS* 15 (1969): 265-77; L. D. Hurst and N. T. Wright, eds., *The Glory of Christ in the New Testament* (Oxford: OUP, 1987); C. G. Newman, *Paul's Glory Christology* (Leiden: Brill, 1992).

Glossolalia

In 1 Cor. 14:2-39 glossolalia (Gk. *glōssa*, "tongue"; *laleō*, "to speak") functions primarily in contrast to prophecy (Gk. *prophēteia*), where tongues mean unintelligible speech and prophecy denotes articulate, clear speech. 1 Cor. 12:10, 28-30 and 13:1, 8 are similar, although 12:10 and 14:10 state that there are various *kinds* of tongues. The meaning in Acts 2:3, 4, 11; 10:46; 19:6 may perhaps be akin to tongues in Paul, but many scholars debate this identification. Most Pentecostals regard "other tongues" in Acts 2:4 as known foreign languages, but this is also debated both outside and within Pentecostalism. In James 1:26, 3:5-8, and 1 Pet. 3:10 as well as in Revelation, Greek *glōssa*, "tongue," seems to have its regular, nontechnical meaning, as language.

In my commentary on the Greek text of 1 Corinthians, I identify at least five serious views among writers of what "speaking in tongues" means in chapters 12–14 (*The First Epistle to the Corinthians* [Grand Rapids: Eerdmans, 2000], 970-89, 1098-1130). (i) Ellis and Dautzenberg argue that tongues may denote *angelic speech,* and Witherington and Barrett express sympathy for this view. This may relate to angelic speech in apocalyptic or at Qumran, especially in the *Testament of Job, Testament of Judah,* and *1 Enoch* 40. Allo and Grudem are among critics of this view.

(ii) The traditional view is that tongues denote *the miraculous power to speak other languages.* Advocates appeal to the Fathers, medieval writers, and the major Reformers; Origen, Chrysostom, Theodore, and Cyril offer examples. Aquinas, Estius, and Calvin span the medieval period to the sixteenth century. In modern scholarship J. G. Davies, R. Gundry, and C. Forbes constitute examples. But in the history of Pentecostalism assumptions about foreign languages were sometimes proved false; several linguists query whether "tongues" retain a genuine "linguistic" or communicative structure; and Paul appears to conceive of them as unintelligible, unless they are interpreted. T. C. Edwards argues, "The Corinthians did not use their gift of tongues to evangelize the heathen world," and many Pentecostals agree. It remains open to question whether Luke recounts a different "kind" of tongues. L. T. Johnson argues that the miracle in Acts is not one of speech, but one of hearing.

(iii) F. Bleek and C. F. G. Heinrici proposed that tongues denote an *archaic, liturgical, or rhythmic use of language,* with novel or unfamiliar idioms. Heinrici appeals to historic uses of *glōssa* in Greek literature and poetry. Today, however, this view does not have many advocates.

(iv) J. Behm, H. Kleinknecht, S. D. Currie, and in a modified form M. E. Boring and L. T. Johnson advocate the meaning *ecstatic speech.* In 1 Cor. 12:3, W. Schmithals, J. Weiss, H. Lietzmann, and M. Thrall see the problem as "uncontrolled ecstasy." E. B. Allo and C. K. Barrett express qualified agreement. Tertullian also speaks of "ecstatic" language. This view is vigorously opposed by R. H. Gundry, M. Turner, and C. Forbes. J. D. G. Dunn speaks of "mindless" utterance (14:15, 19) but warns us against rigid classification on Paul or Corinth.

(v) To the present writer, Gerd Theissen's work on *"the language of the unconscious"* or subconscious is attractive (see G. Theissen, *Psychological Aspects of Pauline Theology* [Edinburgh: T. & T. Clark, 1987], 59-114, 292-341). If tongues reflect hidden yearnings and longings, or hidden bursts of praise and thanksgiving, it is not surprising that these should be unclear, and that "interpretation" may well benefit the congregation. This would also fit the Pentecostal F. D. Macchia's equation with "sighs too deep for words" in Rom. 8:26. Paul's phrase "sighs too deep for words" points to the hidden depths of the human heart (cf. 1 Cor. 4:3-5). Here the Holy Spirit is at work. In my commentary I cite this as a sixth view, but it is also part of the fifth. Full documentation of sources can be found there. In my second excursus on tongues (1098-1130), I also refer to K. Stendahl's classic essay ("Glossolalia: The New Testament Evidence," in *Paul among Jews and Gentiles* [London: SCM, 1977], 109-24; see E. Käsemann, "The Cry for Liberty in the Church's Worship," in *Perspectives on Paul* [London: SCM, 1971], 122-37). I also argue that "the interpretation of tongues" may be by the speaker-in-tongues, not a second person (there is no Gk. *tis*, "someone," in 1 Cor. 14:13). (*See also* **Pentecostals.**)

Reading: K. Stendahl, *Paul among Jews and Gentiles* (London: SCM, 1971), 122-37; Gerd Theissen, *Psychological Aspects of Pauline Theology* (Edinburgh: T. & T. Clark, 1987); A. C. Thiselton, *The First Epistle to the Corinthians* (Grand Rapids: Eerdmans, 2000); A. C. Thiselton, *The Holy Spirit* (Grand Rapids: Eerdmans, 2013), 54-57, 114-20, 329-38.

Gnosticism

Gnosticism (from the Gk. *gnōsis*, "knowledge") denotes a loosely related network of sects, ranging from the second to the fifth century, which stressed secret revelation and a heightened dualism. In spite of some claims that Gnosticism influenced the NT, especially Paul and John, it is more likely that elements or themes of earlier "proto-gnosticism" can be detected in the theology of some of their *opponents*, especially in the Corinthian church, among others. In particular, these saw themselves as "spiritual" (Gk. *pneumatikos*) in contrast to others who were supposedly sensual or materialistic (*sarkikos* or "hylic"), or even merely "religious" *(psychikos)*. By contrast, Paul uses the term *pneumatikos* to mean "of the Holy Spirit," and *psychikos* and *sarkikos* to mean, respectively, "unspiritual" and "centered on the self." But whereas these are fixed categorizations in Gnosticism, in Paul they denote a chosen openness to the Holy Spirit, or a chosen state of self-reliance and self-sufficiency. Irenaeus faithfully defends Christianity against Gnosticism when he insists that the transmission of a tradition of revealed truth must be *public* and open to evaluation and rational discussion, in contrast to any "secret" or "private" transmission of tradition. The NT, also followed by Irenaeus, Tertullian, and other Church Fathers, stresses the identity of the God of the OT and the God of the NT, and the positive goodness of creation and of the body; in other words, it rejects Gnostic dualism. Gnostics impose a negative dualism on both God and creation, including matter. Hans Jonas declares, "The cardinal feature of gnostic thought is the radical dualism that governs the relation of God to the world.... The deity is absolutely transmundane, its nature alien to that of the universe, which is neither created nor governs, and to which it is the complete antithesis" (*The Gnostic Religion* [Boston: Beacon Press, 1958, 1963], 42).

Hence many Gnostic systems propose a chain of beings, often called "powers" or Archons (Gk. *archontes*), which stretch "down" to earth and to darkness at one end of the chain or spectrum, and approach God or "light" at the other end. A normal minimum would be seven, arranged like concentric spheres around the earth, and representing planets. But there was a tendency to multiply these intermediaries, for which Basilides proposed 365 "heavens." Their primary function is to *separate humankind and earth from God,* both by space and by demonic forces. But "knowledge" *(gnosis)* of certain secret formulae or "names" would allow Gnostics to ascend through the heavens. Sometimes the "powers" are called by names relating to the God of the OT, such as Adōnai, Sabāōth, Elōhim, and El Shaddai. It would be naïve to imagine planetary guardians demanding passwords as such; the whole process is wrapped up in myth, symbol, and existential involvement.

The origins of Gnosticism have long been the subject of controversy. The earlier Church Fathers tended to regard Gnosticism as a Christian heresy and a gross distortion of Christian ideas. But specialists today look to Hellenic, Babylonian, Egyptian, and Iranian sources, sometimes combined with Jewish elements especially in the diaspora, and in the Wisdom traditions of Judaism. This change of viewpoint was accelerated by discoveries from 1945 onward of a library of Gnostic texts and sources at Nag Hammadi in Upper Egypt. The texts were a Coptic translation from Greek, and included the Valentinian *Gospel of Truth* and hitherto unknown writings. The *Gospel of Thomas* contains a Gnostic collection of the sayings and parables of Jesus, and the *Apocryphon* (secret book) *of John* and the *Gospel of the Egyptians* come from Gnostic sects influenced by Christians. The *Apocryphon of James* allegedly recounts postresurrection appearances of Jesus, and the *Treatise on the Resurrection,* otherwise known as *The Letter to Rheginos,* argues for a purely immaterial, nonbodily resurrection. The *Gospel of Philip* combines teaching from more than one sect.

The *Gospel of Truth* was known to Irenaeus as "comparatively recent," and "agreeing in nothing with the Gospels of the Apostles.... For God made all things"; it probably comes from Valentinus (*Against Heresies* 3.11.9; *ANF* 1:429). It includes typical Valentinian themes: aeons, fullness *(plērōma),* and first-person utterances, and tells how the elect are brought back "into the Father, the Mother, Jesus of the infinite gentleness" (*Gospel of Truth* 24.8). According to the Gnostic "redeemer myth," Gnostics are led from ignorance to knowledge *(gnōsis).* By contrast Paul tells the Corinthians that *gnōsis* (the noun) inflates pride (1 Cor. 8:1), whereas the verb *(ginōskō)* depicts the process of learning, or of gaining knowledge. In the *Gospel of Thomas,* B. Gärtner argues, "The dialogue form is put to constant use ... and may be said to be a characteristic means of expression"

(*The Theology of the Gospel of Thomas* [London: Collins, 1961], 23). He adds, "The question-and-answer form occupied a key position in Gnostic literature" (24). The story part of the parables of Jesus is often replicated: "The Kingdom of the Father is like a merchant who . . . when he had found a pearl . . . sold his goods . . . and bought this single pearl" (*Logion* 76). But the application is different, referring to treasure in heaven (Luke 12:33-34). Some parables are more faithful to the NT, for example, sowing weeds among the wheat (*Logion* 57).

This brings us to a key point argued in detail by Samuel Laeuchli in *The Language of Faith* (London: Epworth, 1962). He argues consistently that language "such as 'gnosis,' 'cosmos,' 'aeon,' 'plērōma' can be found in various books in the New Testament. The terminology of the *Gospel of Thomas* does not differ radically from the terminology of the Synoptic Gospels" (15). But this of itself is "misleading." The terminology changes its meaning within "the new frame into which it is inserted" (19). It is not biblical words that matter, but the *use* to which these words are put. Laeuchli provides ninety pages of examples of NT uses of language; seventy pages of language *uses* in the Church Fathers; and seventy more of differences of theology. He concludes, " 'Canonical language' is only possible in a chain of biblical terminology, never in a catchword or in a set phrase, but in the relation of biblical concepts to each other" (91). More recently James Dunn has argued the same conclusion with detailed comparison of the texts of the Synoptic Gospels and the *Gospel of Thomas* ("The Earliest Interpreters of the Jesus Tradition," in *Horizons in Hermeneutics* [Grand Rapids: Eerdmans, 2013], 119-47). (*See also* **Dualism**.)

Reading: W. Barnstone and M. Meyer, eds., *The Gnostic Bible* (Boston: Shambhala, 2003); Werner Foerster, *Gnosis: A Selection of Gnostic Texts,* 2 vols. (Oxford: Clarendon, 1972); Bertil Gärtner, *The Theology of the Gospel of Thomas* (London: Collins, 1961); Hans Jonas, *The Gnostic Religion* (Boston: Beacon Press, 1963); Samuel Laeuchli, *The Language of Faith* (London: Epworth; Nashville: Abingdon, 1962): R. McL. Wilson, *The Gnostic Problem* (London: Mowbray, 1958).

God, Trinity

God Creates, Speaks, or Reveals; Acts in Transcendence and Immanence

(i) **God Creates, Speaks, Reveals, or Addresses, Is Faithful and "Thinkable."** The first two revelations of God in the canonical Bible tell us that God created the world, and that God spoke with humankind. First, God created the world *because he loves us*. The act of God's creating the world represents a going out of himself to engage with creation and with humankind. He chose not to be self-sufficient or isolated. He did not create the world out of any *need*, of self-expression or of communication; an "Other" already existed in himself as Trinity. From a "formless void" or chaos he chose to bring forth *order* (Gen. 1:2), and made categorizations or *distinctions* between light and darkness, day and night, evening and morning (Gen. 1:3-5). Although the NRSV translates *ruach* as "wind" in 1:2, many argue that this verse refers to the *creativity of the Spirit of God;* in C. K. Barrett's language, the Spirit hovered over the water like a bird. Clearly this is not a chronological or purely descriptive account of creation, for "lights in the dome of the sky" (1:14-16) appear *after* the separation of light from darkness (1:4).

After creation had been prepared by the creation of seasons, seas, and natural creatures, including birds, reptiles, fish, and mammals (1:20-25; *see* **Creation**), God created humankind (1:26-28) in his own image, to represent him (*see* **Image of God**). The reason for this emerges in other parts of Scripture: God created humankind *out of love.* Since "The eternal Spirit is the divine wellspring of life — the source of life created" (Moltmann's language), there is a sense in which God gives *himself* in creation. This does *not* mean that the world is an emanation of God; he remains "wholly other" than the world. Yet he goes forth, as it were, out of himself, to give the precious gift of life, entirely because he loves us and all creation. We shall later see that "creation is a Trinitarian process: the Father creates through the Son in the Holy Spirit" (Moltmann, *God in Creation* [London: SCM, 1985], 9).

Second, *God speaks to humankind* (Gen. 2:16-17; 3:9, 11, 13, 16-19). God seeks to enter into a *relationship* that is *person to person.* The mode of speech is second-person address. As Martin Buber rightly comments, "For the 'I,' the primary word *I-Thou* is a different 'I' from that of the primary word *I-It*" (*I and Thou* [1923; Eng. New York: Scribner, 1958], 3). The Other (God) addresses us as subject to subject, in reciprocity and mutuality, treating people as ends, not as means. Address again reflects love and election, as Buber expresses it, although also command. John D. Zizioulas also stresses this capacity for relationship. He writes, "God is a relational being; without the concept of communion it would not be possible to speak of the being of God.... 'God' has no ontological content, no true being, apart from communion" (*Being as Communion* [New York: St. Vladimir's Seminary Press, 1997], 17). Bultmann has a long section on existential responsibility in his essay "Adam, Where Art Thou?" (see Gen. 3:9). Since conversation and address are initiated by God, this is the language of revelation, not human discovery.

Revelation, then, third, provides the basis of our knowledge of God. The OT regularly speaks of *knowing God* (*da'ath 'elōhim;* Hos. 4:1; 5:4; 6:6; Isa. 1:3; Jer. 2:8; 4:22; 31:34). T. C. Vriezen comments: "*This knowledge of God is essentially a communion with God*" (*An Outline of Old Testament Theology* [Oxford: Blackwell, 1962], 128). It is knowledge of the heart, not only of the intellect. The OT speaks of "walking humbly" with God (Mic. 6:8). To know God is different from having a conception or concept of God. This reaches a climax in the NT. E. Jüngel argues that Christ, as the true image of God, and his representation, make God "thinkable" and "conceivable" (*God as the Mystery of the World* [Edinburgh: T. & T. Clark, 1983], 111, 220-21, 229). He declares: "God defined himself as love on the cross. God *is* love" (220; 1 John 4:8). Jüngel sees this as integrally connected with the "essential function" of "'*address.*'... It is the address character of language which first makes it humane.... The word of address reflects not only the consciousness of the person addressed but his whole being" (11).

Address comes to Noah (Gen. 7:1; 8:15), to Abraham (12:1; 15:1, 7; 17:1-2, 9, 15; 18:22-32; 22:1-2), and to Jacob (28:13-15). But the paradigm case is the address to Moses in Exod. 3:4-6 and 3:14. God addresses him personally as "Moses" (v. 4), tells him that he stands on holy ground (v. 5), and identifies himself as the God of Abraham, Isaac, and Jacob (v. 6). He then commissions him to deliver Israel from Pharaoh (3:7-10). After Moses offers excuses, including a further need for God's identity, "God said to Moses, 'I AM WHO I AM.... I AM has sent me to you'" (3:14). The NRSV translation is misleading, and reproduces the LXX Greek: "Egō eimi ho ōn," where both verbs are the continuous present tense. The Hebrew imperfect of the verb indicates a *future,* as B. S. Childs and others argue. Childs writes, "God said to Moses, 'I will be who I will be.'" He continues, "The word-play on the name of God *(ehyeh-yahweh)* confirms the connection between name and significance" (*Exodus* [London: SCM, 1974], 76). The LXX translation is a "senseless tautology... a self-contained incomprehensible being.... God announces that his intentions will be revealed in his future acts, which he now refuses to explain" (76). Yahweh (or God) is "the God of the Fathers" (76), and will prove his *faithfulness* and his continuity of identity by his future acts.

In modern thought, W. Pannenberg shows how this revelation embodies the faithfulness and constancy of God through his acts in history. He declares, "True being is thought of not as timeless but instead as historical, and it proves the stability through a history whose future is always open. For the constancy of the biblical God is not available in advance [as the timeless view], but from time to time is disclosed in retrospect in a new way at every historical stage.... Faith ... is grounded in the experience of the faithfulness and constancy of God that has already been proven by his historical guidance" (*BQT* 2:9-10). Pannenberg also looks to a single history that is also experienced in the NT. "It is of great theological significance that the confession of Israel and that of the community of the new covenant consistently hold fast to the one history of God which binds them together. The connection between the Old and New Testaments is made understandable only by the consciousness of the one history which binds together the eschatological community of Jesus Christ and ancient Israel by means of... promise and fulfilment" (*BQT* 1:25).

(ii) **God as Transcendent, Immanent, and Holy Love.** Given what we have already said about God, in given respects God remains elusive. Job cried, "Oh, that I knew where I might find him!" God is constantly beyond some fixed location or easy comparison with humans. He is not to be located in space, or categorized in terms of what he has created. When God declares,

> My thoughts are not your thoughts,
> nor are your ways my ways. (Isa. 55:8),

admittedly he says that his grace and mercy are beyond human imagining, but the key thought is that God surpasses any comparison or analogy. K. Barth expounded this in the first half of the twentieth century. Barth's theme on the doctrine of God, we note in the entry on Barth, is "God is known through God, and through God alone" (*CD* II/1, 179). Apart from his grace and decree, God remains hidden, as Luther also declared. For God is beyond comparison with earthly experiences and people. God himself asks,

> To whom then will you compare me,
> or who is my equal? (Isa. 40:25)

Yet God can be known; we have just asserted that God is known in communion with God. As I. Ramsey convincingly argues, we may use *models* of God provided that we *qualify* these models in adequate ways. Hence, he argues, we may speak of God as *cause*, but only if we qualify this as *first* cause. We may speak of God as *wise*, but only if we qualify this as *infinitely* wise (*Religious Language* [London: SCM, 1957], 49-89, esp. 61-71).

This aspect of the reality of God is usually known as God's transcendence. Although God engages with the world, God is also *beyond* and *above* the world, to use these two words in analogical sense. Paul Tillich, who leans heavily on the depth psychology of Jung, uses symbol rather than analogy to represent the transcendent. He is too easily brought within the human conceptual sphere and hence into our world. Tillich is therefore forced to speak of the "'God' beyond God." For in his view, to use superlatives is to diminish him merely to the highest example of a class within the world. We must strive to express God's "otherness" or "beyondness." God is uniquely God. Kierkegaard, Otto, Barth, Tillich, and Niebuhr all seek ways of preserving the divine transcendence, as E. Farley argues (*The Transcendence of God* [London: Epworth, 1962], 13-102, 194-222). Pannenberg follows Barth in asserting: "Knowledge of God that is made possible by God and therefore by revelation, is one of the basic conditions of the concept of theology as such. Otherwise the possibility of the knowledge of God is logically inconceivable; it would contradict the very idea of God" (*ST* 1:2). Pannenberg sees the testing of truth not primarily in terms of comparison with the world, but "truth as coherence, as the mutual agreement of all that is true . . . and presentation of its coherence as . . . the interrelation of the parts, and the relation to other knowledge" (21-22). In this, he argues, God's Word and Spirit belong together. By contrast, "Individual experience can never mediate absolute, unconditional certainty" (47). Hence talk of God becomes doxology; "speakers rise above the limits of their own finitude to the thought of the infinite God" (55). *It is not that experience interprets God; "the concept of God serves to interpret experience"* (66, italics mine).

Kierkegaard argued, "To prove the existence of one who is present is the most shameless affront . . . it is an attempt to make him ridiculous. . . . One proves

God's existence by worship ... not by proofs" (*Concluding Unscientific Postscript* [Princeton: Princeton University Press, 1941], 485). Even to talk about God in the third person risks reducing him. The first step is to "fear God" (484). Commenting on human finitude, Kierkegaard declared: "I am only a poor existing human being, not competent to contemplate the eternal either eternally or divinely" (190). He cited the experience of Abraham, especially in Genesis 22. But earlier in Gen. 18:27 Abraham says, "Let me take it upon myself to speak to the LORD, I who am but dust and ashes."

The NT is just as emphatic. Paul exclaims, "O the depth of the riches and wisdom and knowledge of God! How unsearchable are his judgments and how inscrutable his ways! 'For who has known the mind of the Lord? / Or who has been his counselor?'" (Rom. 11:33-34). The writer to the Hebrews knows that humans have no natural right to approach God, but can only respond to his call to enter his presence through a duly appointed mediator (Heb. 9:11-28). He adds, "Our God is a consuming fire" (12:29). Very many passages in Hebrews allude to the OT. Might this verse allude to Lam. 3:22, "It is of the LORD's mercies that we are not consumed" (KJV)? To return to the OT, the visions of God in Isaiah and Ezekiel also stress his transcendence. Isaiah's vision in Isa. 6:1-13 sees God as "high and lofty" and enthroned, with seraphs in attendance, who cried, "Holy, holy, holy is the LORD of hosts." Isaiah responded, "I am lost, for I am a man of unclean lips ... yet my eyes have seen the King, the LORD of hosts" (6:3-5). Ezekiel saw "a great cloud ... and fire flashing forth" with "something like four living creatures" and wheels within wheels (Ezek. 1:4, 5, 16), all of which contributed to "visions of God" (1:1). Ezekiel continues: "Then the spirit lifted me up, and as the glory of the LORD rose ... I heard behind me the sound of loud rumbling ... the wings of the living creatures ... I sat ... stunned" (3:12-15). This is probably behind Rev. 1:10-17 and 4:5-11: "Coming from the throne are flashes of lightning ... and peals of thunder ... four living creatures" who sang,

> "Holy, holy, holy,
> the Lord God the Almighty....
> You are worthy ...
>   to receive glory and honor and power,
> for you created all things."

Yet these visions of God's transcendence are forced to use metaphors, symbols, and analogies of clouds, thunder, fire, flames, and thrones. So once again we should perhaps note Tillich's words: "The being of God cannot be understood as ... a being alongside others or above others.... Even if he is called the 'highest being' in the sense of the 'most perfect' and the 'most powerful' being ... when applied to God, superlatives become diminutives. They place him on the level of other beings while elevating him above all of them" (*Systematic Theology*, vol. 1 [London: Nisbet, 1953], 261). Hence language in these biblical passages is stretched and strained. Yet with this proven, nothing can better convey the transcendence of God.

It is important to examine God's transcendence first. Then we may assert that this transcendence stands in dialectical tension with his immanence. Once we have grasped that God is *beyond* the world, we may also assert that he chooses to work and to act *within* the world. Sometimes these two dimensions are equated respectively as holiness and love, but these cannot be separated. In practical action they are holy love. Today we should hesitate to use E. Brunner's language of "transcendence of essence," for the biblical writers are primarily concerned with God's practical actions, not with Aristotelian "essences." But we agree with Brunner that "His 'Godhood' is absolutely and irrevocably different from all other forms of being." He further comments, "God and the world must be kept absolutely distinct from one another" (*The Christian Doctrine of God: Dogmatics*, vol. 1 [London: Lutterworth, 1949], 175). Yet Brunner continues, "With the assertion that God is Wholly Other, the problem is stated of the relation of likeness or unlikeness between God and the world" (175). After all, God created the world to engage with it in love, and created humankind in his own image.

Immanence, therefore, denotes God's communion with the world; it does *not* identify the world with God, which would be more akin to pantheism than to theism. Immanence may denote seeing the world as an expression of God's love, and his presence within it to sustain it day by day. God's activity is continuous within the world, which is wholly dependent on his daily love, care, energy, and presence. Extreme mysticism may press the concept too far if it suggests an absolute fusion between God and the worshiper, which is not totally complete until the resurrection and the last day. Certainly the immanence of God is Trinitarian. The Holy Spirit indwells believers and gives daily life to the world. The incarnation of Jesus Christ expresses divine immanence, provided that we do not regard Christ as simply the greatest of Spirit-inspired men. Incarnation and immanence are best regarded as overlapping but distinct concepts. The classic biblical statement of divine immanence comes in Acts 17:28: "In him (God) we live and move and have our being." Although Luke attributes this to Paul, many consider it uncharacteristic of Pauline thought, and some follow Schweitzer in viewing it as not Pauline. But most of our knowledge of Paul comes from his epistles to *Christians*. Here he is expressing common ground at Athens with many Greek philosophers, especially Stoics. This is typical of their philosophy that God animates the universe.

The Bible contains many suggestions of divine immanence. Jesus declares in Matt. 10:29-31: "Are not two sparrows sold for a penny? Yet not one of them will fall to the ground apart from your Father. And even the hairs of your head are all counted. So do not be afraid; you are of more value than many sparrows" (paralleled in Luke 12:6-7). In response to the rejoinder, "How could the God who sustains galaxies have such detailed knowledge of birds and people?" the reply has been offered: "The greater the mind, the greater its knowledge of detail." In any case, the primary concern in Matthew and Luke is for providential care, rather than intellectual knowledge as such. This is paralleled in the OT:

> "The LORD,
> a God merciful and gracious,
> slow to anger,
> and abounding in steadfast love and faithfulness,
> keeping steadfast love for the thousandth generation." (Exod. 34:6-7)

"Merciful" *(rachûm)* is also used in Isa. 49:15-16 of God's being like a mother who shows "compassion" to her child:

> Even these [mothers] may forget,
>   yet I will not forget you.
> See, I have inscribed you on the palms of my hands.

Hosea even uses the analogy of taking Israel as a wife (Hos. 2:19). Hosea also writes,

> When Israel was a child, I loved him. . . .
> It was I who taught Ephraim to walk,
>   I took them up in my arms. . . .
> I led them with cords of human kindness,
>   with bands of love. (11:1-4)

In spite of the insistence in Hebrews on access to the holy God through Christ as Mediator, the writer concludes, "Let us therefore approach the throne of grace with boldness" (Heb. 4:16). Transcendence and immanence go together as dialectic that characterizes God.

One way of holding these together is to assert that God is holy love. Vriezen argues, "The idea of holiness is the one most typical for the Old Testament faith" (*An Outline,* 149). *Qādōsh* (Heb. for "holy"), he adds, is "the wholly Other One, as appears in Hos. 11:9: I am God, and no mortal, the Holy One in your midst." Holy, he urges, "explains why His actions are wonderful, unlike anything man could ever expect." We have already noted the vision of the holy God in Isaiah 6. The seraphim who utter "Holy, holy, holy," the *trisagion,* cover their faces so that they cannot behold him, and cover their "feet" so that he cannot behold them as they move around his throne. As we observed concerning Hebrews, "Holiness first of all involves *unapproachableness*" (149). Thus many scholars trace the term to the verb "to separate." Yet just as God's transcendence is inseparable from his immanence, so "Holy, holy, holy is the LORD of hosts" is inseparable from "the whole earth is full of his glory" (Isa. 6:3; *see* **Glory**). The

Holy of Holies in the temple was the innermost or hindmost place, which not even the priests could enter, but only the high priest. It was entered through an outer court (the "court of the Gentiles"), the court of the women, the court of the Jewish men, and the Holy Place, or court of the priests, at least in Herod's first-century temple. Yet, to cite Vriezen again, "The holiness of God is... also the continuous background to the message of love.... The two are in complete agreement" (151).

Rudolf Otto, as we note in the entry under his name, sees holiness as the divine numinous, which he calls *mysterium tremendum,* and which is different from notions of mere moral holiness. E. Brunner underlines and supports Otto's emphasis (*The Christian Doctrine of God,* 157-58). Brunner argues, "Holiness is the nature of God, that which distinguishes Him from everything else" (158). He contrasts this holiness with the *ba'alim* or nature gods of Canaan: "holiness belongs to God alone.... God will not tolerate the recognition of any other" (159, 160). Brunner entirely agrees with Vriezen: "But this movement of exclusion, of keeping human beings at a distance, is inseparable from a second opposite movement.... God wills that 'the whole earth shall be filled with his glory.'... He, the God of revelation, wills to be known and recognized.... All revelation is self-communication... attraction to Himself, 'drawing near.'... It is the dialectic of Holiness and Love" (163). He declares, "The Holiness of God is the basis of the self-communication which is fulfilled in love (Isa. 41:14; 43:3; 47:4)" (164). For the holiness that separates also sets God's people apart to be God's own people, distinct from others. In one sense, all peoples belong to God, for he has created them; but in a special sense, he sets his special love on those who, in a narrower sense, are his people who consciously belong to him. They become "his hallowed property" (165). He seeks his people as holy love. In Jesus Christ alone, he says, "God makes Himself known as He really is" (168).

Many scholars associate transcendence and holiness with divine wrath. But if they are correct (e.g., Vriezen, *An Outline,* 154-59), how can this be compatible with, let alone close to, divine love? The answer is that wrath is not the opposite of love, but the opposite of indifference. Parents may be wrathful at a child bent on self-destruction, but their reaction may be a manifestation of love for the child, and a desire for the child's welfare. But although God may show wrath, this is neither an emotion nor a *permanent* expression of character. The statement "God is love" has no parallel assertion about wrath. In the LXX the Hebrew *kā'as,* which may denote displeasure or grief, usually means "wrath" (*TDNT* 5:411). We tend to think of wrath in anthropomorphic terms. The old liberal notion that Jesus is a loving figure in the NT while God is wrathful in the OT, is a travesty of Christology and the Trinity. When he received criticism for healing on the Sabbath, Jesus "looked around at them with anger" (Mark 3:5; Stählin, in *TDNT* 5:419). Stählin insists, "Wrath is right for God, but not for man.... God's love includes wrath... love and anger are mutually exclusive in man" (419). In Rom. 1:18, "The wrath of God is revealed from heaven against all ungodliness" clearly concerns self-distortion and self-destruction, and is parallel to the revelation of righteousness and love.

Love in the OT cannot be separated from grace and election. Deut. 7:7-8 reads: "It was not because you were more numerous than any other people that the LORD set his heart on you and chose you.... It was because the LORD loved you." G. Quell writes, "With the same tenderness and depth Hosea introduces the thought of God's love in other motifs which cause us to think of fatherly love.... Ephraim has learned to put his arm in His (Hos. 11:3), and thus to be drawn by cords of love.... When He acts in love, God demonstrates... His proper character as the holy God" (*TDNT* 1:31-32). This is often a suffering love, as in Jer. 12:7-12. Nevertheless, "Because He loved Israel... He bound Himself *(ch-sh-q)* to it" (33). The command of Jesus to love one's enemies (Matt. 5:43-44; Luke 6:32-33) simply reflects the love of God to us when we were his enemies: "If while we were enemies *(echthroi)*, we were reconciled to God through the death of his Son, much more surely... will we be saved by his life" (Rom. 5:10). Paul exclaims: "Who will separate us from the love of Christ?... [Nothing] will be able to separate us from the love of God in Christ Jesus our Lord" (Rom. 8:35-39). E. Stauffer concludes, "Paul clearly sees... the new situation created by the loving work of God" ("*Agapē; agapaō*," in *TDNT* 1:49). The love of God, he urges, is one with the love of Christ, for the work of Christ was initiated by God. As Paul, followed by D. Baillie, argues, "In Christ God was reconciling the world to himself" (2 Cor. 5:19).

Karl Barth, like Brunner, holds these two aspects together. God is "the One who loves" (*CD* II/1, 272). This love is lavished by a free and sovereign choice: the Lord loved you because he loved you (Deut. 7:7-8). God's loving is his being and essence: "His love is His own" (297). His love is "free from all origination, conditioning, or determination from without" (307). In sections 29 and 30 Barth explains that "the perfections of God" include his grace, love, and holiness. God declares: "I... will show mercy on whom I will show mercy" (Exod. 33:19; *CD* II/1, 353). He speaks of "the unity of His judgment with His grace. God is holy because His grace judges and His judgment is gracious" (363). Hence in *CD* II/2 election is not some "horrible decree," but "the sum of the gospel" (II/2, 3). It denotes God "encountering man in His free love, God becomes the companion of man" (11).

Transcendence, immanence, and holy love may come together in the same psalm. Ps. 18:7-11 reads:

> The earth reeled and rocked;
> > the foundations also of the mountains trembled
> > and quaked, because he was angry....
> He rode on a cherub, and flew....
> He made darkness his covering.

But 18:16-17 adds:

> He reached down from on high, he took me;
>   he drew me out of mighty waters.
> He delivered me.

The psalmist declares in verses 28-30,

> The LORD, my God, lights up my darkness....
> This God — his way is perfect; ...
>   he is a shield for all who take refuge in him.

In Job 11:7-8 Zophar asks Job:

> "Can you find out the deep things of God?
>   Can you find out the limit of the Almighty?
> It is higher than heaven — what can you do?"

In 10:12 Job declares,

> "You have granted me life and steadfast love,
>   and your care has preserved my spirit."

In Matt. 6:9 Jesus teaches that God is "in heaven," but he is "our Father" also. In modern theology G. Newlands speaks not only of God as "creator and sustainer of his creation, acting in providence," but also of God "identified with his creatures through the presence of Jesus, suffering, sharing in life and death" (*Theology of the Love of God* [London: Collins, 1980], 18, 19). He draws attention to D. Bailey's *God Was in Christ* (1948) to point out that we see the love of *God* in the life, suffering, and death of *Jesus Christ* (27-30). In several hymns writers speak of holiness or wrath meeting with love in the work of Christ. Newlands also brings together transcendence, immanence, and holiness in a more recent book, *God in Christian Perspective* (Edinburgh: T. & T. Clark, 1994), 65-74.

O. R. Jones, *The Concept of Holiness* (London: Allen and Unwin, 1961), sees holiness as a *disposition to respond* to situations, rather than only as a general static quality. Holiness and love both have a "power" to shape. In the case of love (and perhaps holiness) this is conveyed by the Holy Spirit: "the love of God is shed abroad in our hearts by the Holy Ghost" (Rom. 5:5 KJV; 80-88). Love and holiness belong to a continuity of character and action, involving the holistic vision of holy love (188-98): "The Lord disciplines those whom he loves" (Heb. 12:6). Jones writes: "The love which is holy power is love eternal, and this implies that it reaches out to all mankind" (83). Holy love is both self-giving and transforming. (*See also* Creation; Glory; Image of God; Immanence; Other, Otherness; Otto, Rudolf; Transcendence.)

Reading: E. Brunner, *The Christian Doctrine of God* (London: Lutterworth, 1949);

O. R. Jones, *The Concept of Holiness* (London: Allen and Unwin, 1961); E. Jüngel, *God as the Mystery of the World* (Edinburgh: T. & T. Clark, 1983); W. Pannenberg, *Systematic Theology*, vol. 1 (Grand Rapids: Eerdmans, 1991); K. Ward, *The Concept of God* (London: Collins, 1977).

Almighty, Omniscient, Omnipresent

(i) **Almighty.** Traditionally, in older works, God's omnipotence, omnipresence, and omniscience are often called "his metaphysical attributes." But this term raises at least two questions or difficulties. First, the word "attributes" suggests a relation to the vocabulary of Greek philosophy rather than the Bible; second, G. van den Brink has argued convincingly that "almighty" (Gk. *pankratōr, pantokratōr*, 2 Cor. 6:18; Rev. 1:8; 4:8; 11:17; 15:3; 16:7, 14; 19:6, 15; 21:22) has numerous advantages over "omnipotent" (Lat. *omnipotens;* van den Brink, *Almighty God* [Kampen: Kok Pharos, 1993], 46-60 and throughout). He especially distinguishes between the less helpful *power-over* (which may simply denote brute force) and *power-for* (which implies *enabling* and *empowerment*). They admittedly overlap, for almightiness or omnipotence denotes exclusion of any limitation at all, except any that God may choose voluntarily and freely to place upon himself. For example, if he has freely willed always to be true, or to speak truth, he "cannot" tell a lie (logical "cannot"; not empirical "cannot"). If he has promised salvation on given conditions, he "cannot" revoke his promise. Anyone who makes a promise is no longer totally "free" to perform an alternative action. Augustine declared that it is impossible for the eternal God to die, or to make what is done undone, or to make what is false true. But these notions of what is possible are not prior to God. They are not "external" forces controlling him, but originate from what God freely wills to do and to be. The word "impossible" is virtually shorthand for "without gross incoherence," or "without *subsequent* logical contradiction."

Without such qualifications, the so-called omnipotence of God may sound like that of a tyrannical monarch. C. Hartshorne called the notion of "brute power" perhaps "the most shockingly bad of all the theological analogies," as van den Brink reminds us (3). On the other hand, W. Pannenberg declares, "The word 'God' is used meaningfully only if one means by it the power that determines everything that exists" (*BQT* 1:1). Van den Brink, however, rejects the idea that such omnipotence is a logically "necessary" truth; "almightiness is not a matter of course, but a matter of faith" (5). Peter Geach is largely in agreement with van den Brink. He suggests that almightiness denotes power over all things, whereas omnipotence indicates God's ability to do everything (46). To call God "omnipotent" is simply to pay him "metaphysical compliments." In the LXX *pantokratōr* is used some 170 times of God, often translating the Hebrew "Lord God of hosts" *(ts^ebā'ōth)*. The biblical term seems to denote a *capacity for,* not *the exercise of,* power, which may militate against Geach's suggestion. It may denote *power-for.* In fact, van den Brink distinguishes *three* concepts of God's power: power as universal dominion and authority over everything, which is often the meaning of "Almighty"; power as seen in the creation and preservation of the universe, that is, an actualized power; "Power as the capacity to realize all possible states of affairs, ... not actual but virtual" (49), namely, *power-for*. Against these three categories, van den Brink observes, there is often a blurring of original distinctions. This is confirmed by Danker. He gives the meaning of *pantokratōr* as "the Almighty, All-Powerful, omnipotent," as used only of God, and cites the LXX, Origen, *1 Clement,* and numerous NT passages and modern articles (BDAG 755).

H. Hommel and van den Brink trace the Greek word through the writings of the Church Fathers and ancient Greek. It regularly denotes the sustaining function of divine Providence, or the preservation of what God created. Gregory of Nyssa equally ascribes this quality to the Son. "God as holding and supporting the universe" is prevalent in both the Stoic and Christian tradition, and in Col. 1:17 it is Christ who holds all things together (Gk. *ta panta en autō sunestēken*). The Apostles' Creed then places together "God the Father Almighty," although *patēr* and *pantokratōr* have rarely been cojoined before. This suggests that their juxtaposition in many creedal texts "must have been intentional" (56). Acts 17:28, "In him we live and move and have our being," is again relevant. This is confirmed by G. W. H. Lampe's entry *pantokratōr* in his *Patristic Greek Lexicon* (Oxford: Clarendon, 1961, 1995), 1005: he gives the meaning "all-sovereign, controlling all things," citing Justin, Irenaeus, Origen, and others, and applying it not only to God, but also to the Logos and the Holy Spirit.

When we turn to the use of *omnipotens* in the Latin Fathers, and especially Augustine, however, we find a shift from *sovereignty and power* (the first two categories) to *the capacity to realize all possible states of affairs,* the third category. For God's creative and sustaining power Augustine tends to use *omnipotens,* "holding all together," or "sustaining" all. Van den Brink argues, "*Omnipotens* came to be interpreted more literally as being able to do all things *(qui omnia potest)*" (61). The Greek equivalent is not *pantokratōr,* but *pantodunamos.* But this brings us out of biblical thought into philosophy, where "we can imagine all sorts of hypothetical actions." In the OT, for example, the first category of *power over* is linked with the power of the Lord of hosts in military exploits that deliver Israel from oppression. But in the Latin West, by the Middle Ages the notion of omnipotence became highly complex, especially after William of Ockham (83-87). The Reformers had to dismiss much of this as "scholastic sophistry." Calvin asserted the primacy of the divine will, but could not entirely shake off this medieval complexity (87-92).

E. Jacob begins his work on God in the OT by asserting, "What gives the Old Testament its force and unity is the affirmation of the sovereignty of God: God is the basis of all things" (*Theology of the Old Testament* [London: Hodder and Stoughton, 1958, 1964], 37). He is "the living God" and "the King." Jacob adds, "The idea of power, involving also that of pre-eminence, most adequately conveys the reality designated by *El* (Ps. 36:7; Ps. 80:11[10]; Isa. 14:13)." The personal name for God, Yahweh, indicates *both power and presence.* The title *Yahweh tsᵉbā'ōth,*

Lord of Hosts, occurs 279 times in the OT, especially 60 times in Isaiah, 77 in Jeremiah, and 44 in Zechariah 1–8. These are either earthly armies of Israel; armies of the stars; or celestial armies of spirits and angels. The term, he argues, "refers to the totality of forces over which Yahweh asserts his rule" (55). It underlines his sovereignty, as does *'Ādōn*, "Lord"; *Melek*, "King"; and *'Ab*, "Father" (Isa. 52:7; 63:16; Pss. 29:10; 84:3; Jer. 31:9).

In the teaching of Jesus, the kingdom of God, or God's sovereign reign, was central to his proclamation (Mark 1:14-15; parallel Matt. 4:17). Scholars are virtually unanimous in asserting that "kingdom" denotes God's kingly rule or reign, in contrast to the older, mistaken views of Ritschl and Harnack. This phrase also occurs in Paul (Rom. 14:17; 1 Cor. 4:20; 6:9; Gal. 5:21), although he usually uses the term "Lord" *(Kurios)*, which Vincent Taylor calls his favorite term. Paul and John probably avoid the term, lest it should be mistaken for a political attempt to rival the Romans. But neither shows any reluctance to speak of God as sovereign or almighty (*see* **Kingdom of God**).

(ii) **Omniscience.** The omniscience of God is beyond analogy in human experience. As Paul readily admits, "We know only in part" (1 Cor. 13:9). Humankind is always limited in knowledge by a point of view, or situatedness in time, place, and history. As Kierkegaard insisted, "I am only a poor existing human being, and cannot contemplate the eternal," or see things "theocentrically" (*Concluding Unscientific Postscript*, 190). Superficially it appears straightforward to assert that God knows everything. He is the source and ground of all knowledge. But the matter becomes complex as soon as we ask, "Does divine omniscience extend to *the future?*" The exception is those who also believe that everything is predetermined (*see* **Election and Predestination**). If all is determined, everything can be known, for the future is seen as *fixed*. Some even argue for determinism on the ground that God can know everything *only* if everything *is determined*.

Most thinkers, however, reject such rigid determinism. One solution is to assert that God knows everything in the past or present, but that *the future has not yet entered reality* and *does not therefore exist*. Hence it is irrelevant whether God knows it, or even logically impossible for him to know it. Yet if so, how can God fulfill *promises to determine* destinies or outcomes? A further paradox emerges if we believe that God can "forget" a person's sinful past (Jer. 31:34), for he will no longer know all that has happened. Richard Swinburne asks how a proposition can be "true" if truth and falsity depend in part "on things yet to happen" (*The Coherence of Theism* [Oxford: Clarendon, 1977], 173). He cites the parallel of *omnipotence*. Aquinas explains omnipotence "not as the ability to do anything but (roughly) as the ability to do anything *logically possible*" (175). Hence omniscience, by parity of reasoning, would be defined "not as knowledge of everything true, but (very roughly) as knowledge of *everything true which is logically possible to know.*" God may know everything "except those future states and their consequences which are *not* physically *necessitated* by anything in the past" (175, italics mine). Omniscience in an absolute unconditioned sense, Swinburne urges, "is not compatible with God's freedom" (176). Certainly *God will know what may result from his own choices,* and "he continually limits himself... by not curtailing his or men's future freedom" (176). It does not alter this situation to claim that God is timeless, outside time, or can view past and future actions simultaneously (*see* **Eternity; Time**). The logical problems about omniscience are in the end parallel to those about omnipotence.

Typically in the OT God may have certain plans that he may then change, if humankind or Israel intercedes on behalf of those involved. Abraham's intercession for Sodom in Genesis 18 provides one example. Moses' intercession for Israel in Exodus 32 provides another. Swinburne comments, "God may change his plans because men change their behaviour" (177). The book of Jonah provides an example of this, when Jonah preaches judgment on Nineveh, but their repentance averts this, to the regret of Jonah! *Promises God makes* are often conditional, but why should they be conditional if everything is predetermined? Swinburne quotes Jeremiah: "It *may* be they will hear, and turn every man from his evil way" (Jer. 26:3). Moses implies that even the Book of Life is not predetermined: Exod. 32:32 reads: "But now, if you will only forgive their sin — but if not, blot me out of the book that you have written." The Spirit tells John the seer, "If you [the church of Sardis] conquer... I will not blot your name out of the book of life" (Rev. 3:5).

None of this denies that God has plans and purposes, or that his purposes will be fulfilled. Indeed, one argument that softens that of Swinburne is to suggest that humans can act *freely,* while their actions may also remain *predictable.* The classic philosophical example is that of John and Mary falling in love with no constraints, while their parents say to each other, "I knew that it would happen." But is such prediction always certain? Or might "freedom" be conditional by such circumstances as propinquity and lack of a wider competition? Many regard this as a view to be taken into account and respected, but not as finally convincing. In biblical thought the omniscience of God is a *practical* concept, often relating to individual or corporate responsibility, not a metaphysical or hypothetical one. Often the symbolism of "seven spirits" (Rev. 4:5), or creatures around God's throne "full of eyes in front and behind" (4:6), indicates God's sovereignty over the churches and indeed his sovereignty over world history. The visions of the book of Revelation regularly convey this message, and the consummation of God's purposes in history by the establishment of the New Jerusalem (Rev. 21:1-27).

(iii) **Omnipresence.** In addition to being almighty and omniscient, God is omnipresent. This is set out in a classic text from the Psalms:

> Where can I go from your spirit?
>   Or where can I flee from your presence?
> If I ascend to heaven, you are there;
>   if I make my bed in Sheol, you are there.
> If I take the wings of the morning
>   and settle at the farthest limits of the sea,

> even there your hand shall lead me,
>> and your right hand shall hold me fast. (Ps. 139:7-10)

J. Moltmann recounts how this passage made a profound and life-changing impression on him when he was a prisoner of war in Britain. As a prisoner he experienced "the death of my mainstays ... the experience of misery." But when, almost at random, he opened his "little black book" to Psalm 139, and read "If I make my bed in hell, you are there," he came to see that "God is with those who are of broken heart," and that "nothing is shut off from God" ("My Theological Career," in *History and the Triune God* [London: SCM, 1991], 165-82; *A Broad Place* [London: SCM, 2007], 30-31). This omnipresence is often associated with God's immanence, for example, in Jer. 23:24: "Who can hide in secret places so that I cannot see them? says the LORD. Do I not fill the heaven and earth? says the LORD." Unlike the Ba'alim of Canaan, God is in no way a "local" God. Yet again, however, this is not pantheism: the world is *not* an emanation of God.

Indeed, God is neither within nor outside space: God is the *condition and ground* of space; he created the world, along with time. God is thus not limited by any spatial constraint. But this does not exclude the notion of holy places, where God manifests his presence in a particular way. Jerusalem was "his holy city," as Deuteronomy stresses. Jesus and the NT have no more abolished "holy places" than "holy times." Moses was told to remove his shoes at the burning bush, "for the place on which you are standing is holy ground" (Exod. 3:5). Heb. 9:12 speaks of "the Holy Place" in the temple, though admittedly this points back to the OT, and such references in the NT are rare, more usually describing God or God's people. Further, God's presence often denotes his Holy Spirit or his activity. To say that God "is present in every point in space" means in biblical thought that he is active everywhere. Above all, he transcends the spatial order as its Creator and Ground. Paul explicitly rejects the notion in Stoicism of a divine world-soul; we receive the Spirit who comes forth from God (*to ek tou Theou pneuma;* 1 Cor. 2:12).

To conclude: philosophers often say that omnipotence, omniscience, and omnipresence arise from God's being infinite or perhaps even absolute and eternal. "Infinite" denotes what is *unlimited,* in contrast to creaturely and finite. But the NT does not use the terms "infinite" and "absolute"; only "eternal" (*see* **Eternity; Time**). This language reminds us of Hegel. The terms examined in this entry all relate to practical theology and situations and to worship, not to hypothetical or abstract metaphysics. Older books on philosophy of religion may use these terms, but they entered Christian theology often under the influence of Greek philosophy, and today are largely overlooked. They detract from the fact that God is known in situations of history and life, not rational speculation. "Eternal" may be a practical term, in the sense of not being subject to decay. But "absolute" tends to lead us away from the God who became incarnate in Christ.

(iv) **God as Suprapersonal, as Ultimate Source and End and Father of Jesus**

Christ. Everything said in the Bible and in mainstream Christian tradition presupposes that God *is not less than personal*. We have seen that in the Bible God is "the *God who speaks*"; but it would be self-contradictory to claim that an impersonal "it" could speak in the way that is meant here. God *purposes* and *promises;* but only a *person* can purpose and promise. Biblical writers speak of the *mind* and *will* of God; but only a person has a mind and will. Yet some philosophers and theologians are terrified of *anthropomorphism; God is not "personal" in exactly the same way human beings are personal.* Certainly most of the characteristics of a person overlap: God is self-consciously aware of his own purposes and thoughts. Since at least around 1900 philosophical theologians have used the term "suprapersonal" to indicate that God is more than personal, but not less than personal (G. Galloway, *The Philosophy of Religion* [Edinburgh: T. & T. Clark, 1914], 495). Furthermore, God created humankind in his own image to represent all that is characteristic of God, including his willingness and delight to relate to others on a "person-to-person" basis. Finally, Jesus Christ is described in Heb. 1:3 as "the reflection of God's glory and the exact imprint of God's very being" (Gk. *apaugasma tēs doxēs kai charaktēr tēs hypostaseōs autou*), which H. Montefiore takes to mean "all that makes God 'God.'" This includes his personhood. As we noted, E. Jüngel declares that Christ makes God "thinkable" and "speakable" (*God as the Mystery of the World* [Edinburgh: T. & T. Clark, 1983], 111, 226-50, 287-90). In our entry on the Holy Spirit, we speak of the Holy Spirit in similar terms, using the word "suprapersonal."

Paul also speaks of Christ as the image of the (otherwise) invisible God *(eikōn tou Theou tou aoratou)* in Col. 1:15. God created all things *en autō,* "in him" or "by him" (1:16). In Christ "all the fullness of God was pleased to dwell" (1:19), and in him "all things hold together" (1:17; *ta panta en autō sunestēken*). In Rom. 11:36 Paul declares (very untypically, according to Schweitzer), "From him and through him and to him are all things." C. E. B. Cranfield observes, "[This] is far from the pantheism of the Stoic use.... He [Paul] is affirming that God is the Creator, the Sustainer and Ruler, and the Goal of all things" (*Romans,* vol. 2 [Edinburgh: T. & T. Clark, 1979], 591). It is clear that the *ultimate source* and goal is God, not Christ. In 1 Cor. 15:24 Christ "hands over the kingdom to God the Father, after he has destroyed every ruler and every authority and power." Then Paul adds in v. 28, "When all things are subjected to him, then the Son himself will also be subjected *(autos ho huios hupotagēsetai)* to the one who put all things in subjection under him, so that God may be all in all" *(ho Theos [ta] panta en pasin).* (There are textual variants between B, D*, 33, and A, D², which represents this text, but the sense is similar.) J. Moffatt insists that what many have called subordinationism is due to Corinth making more of their "cult Lord" Jesus than the shadowy, more remote figure of God. But while there may be truth in this, God and Christ remain one in sovereignty, will, and purpose, even if Paul describes *ultimacy* to God the Father as the origin and goal of all things. Among the Fathers, Origen and Chrysostom stress this ultimacy.

The notion of God the Father as ultimate source is reaffirmed in the same epistle, in 1 Cor. 11:12: "All things come from God" *(ta de panta ek tou Theou)*. The use of *ek* (from) is important and significant. F. Danker has seven columns on this preposition. He first suggests the meaning "from, out of," in the sense of origin or separation. His second meaning is "marker denoting the direction from which something comes," and the third is "denoting origin, cause" (BDAG 295-96). Of itself, this may not seem very startling, but it becomes so when we realize that all creation is "from" *(ek)* God the Father, and "by means of," or "through" *(dia)*, the Son as *mediate* cause, not *ultimate* cause. In 1 Cor. 8:6 the quasi-creedal formula runs "one God, the Father, *from (ek)* whom all things . . . and one Lord, Jesus Christ, *through (dia)* whom are all things and *through (dia)* whom we exist" (Gk. *di' hou panta*). H. Conzelmann and R. Kerst wrongly attribute this phrasing to Stoic pantheism, although Kerst acknowledges that it performs a different function. L. Hurtado rightly sees this as springing from refigured Jewish monotheism, with Jesus as unique agent. O. Cullmann and N. Richardson stress the important difference between the two prepositions: *ek* or *ex* with the genitive is different from *dia* or *di'* with the accusative (Richardson, *Paul's Language about God* [Sheffield: Sheffield Academic Press, 1994], 296-304). They signify respectively "their origin" and "through." *Eis* with the accusative signifies "goal." As J. D. G. Dunn and R. Horsley suggest, the theme of wisdom at Corinth may also lie behind the phraseology. Tertullian compares 1 Cor. 1:30, "It is because of him *(ex autou)* that you are in Christ Jesus" (NIV), and K. Barth speaks of God as "originating cause," who "holds us from the abyss of non-Being" (*CD* I/1, 441-42). E. Jüngel comments, "*God . . . goes out of himself,* and only for that reason there is a *difference* between Being and nothingness" (*God as the Mystery*, 224).

In the light of all this, it is all the more important that God reveals himself as *the Father of Jesus Christ*. God has already declared his identity as "the God of Abraham, the God of Isaac, and the God of Jacob" (Exod. 3:15; cf. 6:2). The personal name Yahweh was so sacred that in later times *'Ădōnāi*, "Lord," was read in its place. *'Ēl*, "God," is used in the patriarchal period, while *'Ĕlōhîm* is certainly *not* a plural of quantity, but probably a plural of intensity. "Yahweh" is characteristic of the Deuteronomic literature. As we note in the entry on the image of God, the prohibition on setting up idolatrous images arose partly because God had intended that his people should represent him as his image, and this became possible only with the coming of Christ. The OT especially stresses that God is the *living God* (1 Sam. 17:26). The classic confession of the uniqueness of God, as we have noted, comes in the Shema of Deut. 6:4-7: "Hear, O Israel: The LORD is our God, the LORD alone. You shall love the LORD your God with all your heart, and with all your soul, and with all your might. Keep these words. . . . Recite them to your children." The struggle of the prophets from Elijah onward against the Canaanite deities was not only or primarily to defend the oneness of God, but to defend also his uniqueness as the God of Abraham, Isaac, Jacob, and Israel. It is reductionist when some philosophers call this only a defense of "monotheism."

In the teaching of Jesus, sometimes Jesus speaks of God as his Father, and more especially he addresses God as Father. There are 5 explicit references to God as Father in Mark (8:38; 11:25, 26; 13:32; 14:36). Mark 8:38 alludes to God as Father: "when he [the Son of Man] comes in the glory of his Father." 11:25 declares, "Forgive . . . so that your Father in heaven may also forgive you"; verse 26 has a parallel, but with weak textual support. 13:32 has, "About that day or hour no one knows, neither the angels in heaven, nor the Son, but only the Father." In the important passage Mark 14:36, Jesus says, "Abba, Father, for you all things are possible; remove this cup from me." H. F. D. Sparks and T. W. Manson reject 11:26 on textual grounds, and query 11:25 as reflecting Matthew's style "Father in heaven." Matthew and Luke have more passages: Matt. 6:32 (Luke 12:30); Matt. 5:48 (Luke 6:36); Matt. 11:25-27 (Luke 10:21-22); Matt. 7:11 (Luke 11:13); and Matt. 6:9 (Luke 11:2). There are 5 further references in Luke (Luke 2:49; 22:29; 23:34, 46; and 24:49). Matthew reflects Markan and Lukan passages and has 8 references in material peculiar to Matthew. John has some 120 references to God as Father. But many of these references are messianic or distinctive to Jesus. Against Harnack, Sparks declares, "There is no ground whatever for asserting that Jesus taught a Doctrine of 'the Fatherhood of God and the Brotherhood of Man'; Jesus did not teach 'Universal Fatherhood.' For Jesus . . . men were not 'sons of God' by nature, although they were capable of becoming so by Grace" ("The Doctrine of the Divine Fatherhood in the Gospels," in *Studies in the Gospels,* ed. D. E. Nineham [Oxford: Blackwell, 1967], 260; cf. 241-62). Some will accept the nature-grace distinction but still hold a broader concept of Fatherhood.

J. Jeremias is more positive and less cautious about the number of authentic references to God as Father in the Gospels. All five strata (Matthew, Mark, Luke, Q, and John) witness to this fact (*New Testament Theology,* vol. 1 [London: SCM, 1971], 62). As far as address to God as "Abba" is concerned, he insists that the OT does not contain this, even if later Judaism does (63-66). He claims that "Abba" is a children's word, and the *ipsissima vox Jesu* (67). N. T. Wright and others argue that some of Jeremias's work may be exaggerated, but that he is basically right. Christians are then invited to utter the words of Jesus to his Father in Rom. 8:15-17: "You have received a spirit of adoption. When we cry, 'Abba! Father!' it is that very Spirit bearing witness with our spirit that we are children of God, and if children, then heirs, heirs of God and joint heirs with Christ." These verses support Sparks's contention that Jesus and Paul did not teach "universal Fatherhood," but in the case of Christ, taught a unique Sonship, and in the case of Christians, a *derived* sonship from that of Christ. In the sense of *creation, generation,* and Fatherly *care,* Jesus does teach Fatherhood in the wider sense, for all creation depends on God for life and preservation. *But in the sense of adoption* (pneuma huiothesias) *and intimacy, this is exclusively derived from Christ, and from sharing his Sonship* (see **Adoption, Adoptionism, Adoptianism**).

This double meaning of Fatherhood is not as confusing as some may imagine. The chief expression of Fatherhood is not only care and preservation, but also love. Yet in the case of love, the Father's love for Christ belongs to a unique category, distinct from God's love for creation, the world, and all people. "Our Father" may be distinctive to Jesus' disciples, but his love extends to the evil as well as the good. As Pannenberg reiterates, quoting Moltmann, "Theology has to develop the thought that the creation of the world is an expression of the love of God" (*ST* 2:21). But this is always "mediated through the Son." Pannenberg continues, "Jesus . . . lets God be God as Father over against himself . . . subjecting himself to the one true God" (2:22). Pannenberg claims on this basis: "The idea of God as Father is by no means an arbitrary one, for which others might be substituted. . . . The description of God as Father has its basis in an act of election" (*ST* 1:261). Fatherhood is more than a metaphor (cf. Eph. 3:15). He adds, "On the lips of Jesus 'Father' became a proper name for God. It thus ceased to be simply one designation among others" (1:262): "The words 'God' and 'Father' are not just time-bound concepts from which we can detach the content of the message" (1:263). It is as irrevocable as Jesus' Sonship. This does not deny the place of motherly similes and metaphors:

> As a mother comforts her child,
>   so will I comfort you. (Isa. 66:13)

(*See also* **Emanation; Eternity; Holy Spirit; Image of God; Immanence; Kingdom of God; Time.**)

Reading: V. Brümmer, *The Model of Love* (Cambridge: CUP, 1993); J. D. G. Dunn, *The Theology of Paul the Apostle* (Grand Rapids: Eerdmans, 1998), 27-50; J. Macquarrie, *Principles of Christian Theology* (London: SCM, 1966), 94-110, 174-93; G. Newlands, *God in Christian Perspective* (Edinburgh: T. & T. Clark, 1994); W. Pannenberg, *Systematic Theology*, vol. 1 (Grand Rapids: Eerdmans, 1991), esp. 337-448; R. Swinburne *The Coherence of Theism* (Oxford: Clarendon, 1977).

Historical Development

(i) **The Patristic Era.** *1 Clement* (A.D. 96) underlines God's omniscience: "All things are seen and heard by God" (*1 Clem.* 28). Clement of Rome similarly stresses God's omnipresence: "Whither can any of us flee from his right hand?" (28), and quotes Ps. 139:7-10, "Whither shall I go . . . from your presence?": God is gracious and merciful, but also holy (29). He resists the proud but gives grace to the humble (he cites James 4:6 and 1 Pet. 5:5). God is also Creator (33), who rejoices in his works. God's omniscience also emerges in Polycarp (c. 69–c. 155), who speaks of "the all-seeing God" (*Epistle of Polycarp* 7). The *Letter to Diognetus* may be dated as early as 125, and speaks of God as "the Master and Maker of the Universe, who made all things and determined the proper place of each . . . slow to anger and true . . . he alone is good" (8.7). The letter exclaims: "O the overflowing kindness and love of God toward man! . . . O sweetest exchange! O unfathomable work of God! . . . One justifies the many that are sinners. . . . Look on him as Nurse, Father, Teacher, Counselor, Healer, Mind, Light, Honor, Glory, Might, Life" (9.5-6). "God rules in heaven," the writer adds, and we may begin to talk of the mysteries of God, and admire those who refuse to deny him (10.7). Athenagoras in his *Plea Regarding Christians* (c. 176) describes the contrasting view of God in Greek philosophers and poets, which amounts to words without deeds (5). The God of the Christians, however, can be "recognized from his works" (5). At least Sophocles and Plato agree with Christians that God is one, eternal, the Creator, and uncreated (6): "From the beginning there was one God who made this universe" (8). God is "the first and the last" (9); "we acknowledge one God, who is uncreated, eternal, invisible, impassible, incomprehensible, illimitable" (10). It is not "stupid" to say that he has a Son or sends the Holy Spirit (10). Athenagoras is interested in philosophical categories, but is not in debt to them. He marks the beginnings of Trinitarian theology.

Irenaeus of Lyons (c. 130–c. 200) defended the apostolic faith against Gnosticism. On the doctrine of God, this often meant distinguishing apostolic faith from belief in emanations, or *Plērōma*. He cites one pair of silent Gnostic emanations; another pair consisting of the Father and the Other; another pair, of Logos and Zoe; and another pair, of Anthropos and Ecclesia (*Against Heresies* 1.11.1). Against Valentinus and Marcion, he argues that there is one God, "the Creator, who made the heaven and the earth . . . and there is nothing either above him or after him, influenced by no one except his own free will. . . . [He is] the only God, the only Lord, the only Creator, the only Father" (2.1.1). The Gnostics' belief in the *Plērōma* is self-contradictory (2.1.3). In particular, he attacks Marcion's notion of two gods (2.1.4). God created the world. It was not created by angels nor by any other being (2.2.1-5). Irenaeus uses the phrase, later occurring in the creeds, "one God, the maker of heaven and earth" (2.9.1). Humankind is not omniscient, but God alone is omniscient: God is "all reason, all active spirit, all light . . . comprehending all things" (2.28.4, 5). God's Holy Spirit inspired both the OT and the NT (3.6.1 and 4.32.1-2). God is eternal; one and the same God spoke through the OT and the NT (3.8.1 and 9.1-3). In Christ God engages with the world: he is "God with us" (3.19.3). Finally, Irenaeus concludes, "Communion with God is life and light" (4.27.2). This coheres with everything in our previous sections, but also shows Irenaeus's special concern with the corrosive attacks of Gnosticism. Tertullian (c. 150–c. 225) similarly attacks Marcion. God is Creator of all things, "visible and invisible . . . animate and inanimate, vocal and mute, movable and stationary" (*Against Marcion* 1.6). He is one God, Creator and Judge (4.17); "He has no room for any diversity in his gods" (1.6). God is good, and not irrational, as Marcion seems to suggest (1.23). "God is eternal and rational" and "perfect" (1.24).

Clement of Alexandria is eager to find common ground with some philosophers. He argues, "God is invisible and beyond expression by words" (*Stromata* 5.12). In this context he cites Plato, to the effect that "it is difficult to discover the Father and Maker of this universe, and . . . to declare him," and likewise cites the

OT where Moses "entered into thick darkness, where God was." He agrees with philosophers that knowledge of God is a gift of God (5.13). God is universal. He quotes Paul: "Is He God of the Jews only, and not also of the Greeks?" (5.14). Where Tertullian seeks to preserve the church from heresy, Clement goes as far as he can to win over the Greek world, and find common ground with it. The Greeks, he argues, have some knowledge of God (6.5). But "God is not a subject for demonstration"; he is "the Alpha and the Omega," whom humans can truly know only through Christ (4.25).

Origen (c. 185-254), who was Clement's successor, gives a systematic treatment of doctrine in *De principiis,* expounding a doctrine of God in 1.1. God is light (1 John 1:5); Spirit (John 4:24); "incomprehensible and incapable of being measured" (*De principiis* 1.1.1-5). God is "unspeakably and incalculably superior" to any earthly object (1.1.5). Divine Providence has "the plan of this whole world" (1.1.6). God is "the mind and source from which all intellectual nature or mind takes its beginning" (1.1.6). Clearly "the nature of God surpasses the nature of bodies.... God is invisible" (1.1.8): "No one has ever seen God" (John 1:18). Moreover, "what belongs to the nature of deity is common to the Father and the Son" (1.1.8). God may be " 'seen' by those who are pure in heart" (Matt. 5:8; 1.1.9).

God rightly bears the titles "omnipotent" and "almighty," as well as "Father" (1.3.10). He has "power over all things," and is eternal (1.3.10-11). Origen quotes 1 Corinthians to the effect that even Christ is subject to God (2.3.6), and God is both the God of the OT and "the Father of our Lord Jesus Christ" (2.4.1). He is revealed in Christ, who "is the image of the invisible God" (Col. 1:15; 2.4.3). Origen adds: "In the consummation or end God is 'all in all' " (3.6.1; cf. 1 Cor. 15:28). "All in all" means "in each individual person" (3.6.3). He explains to Celsus that such models as "hands of God" and "breath of God" are merely approximate metaphors (*Against Celsus* 4.35-38). Scripture teaches us that God is "a great Lord above all gods" (cf. Ps. 97:9; *Against Celsus* 8.3). It is often argued that in his desire to extol and honor God, Origen was guilty of "subordinationism." G. L. Prestige, for example, claimed that in Origen the Logos is both uncreated and derivative from the Father (*God in Patristic Thought* [London: SPCK, 1952], 138). But sixty years later this is still open to debate. He does say that God is served through Word and Wisdom (*Against Celsus* 8.6), but Paul says as much, as well as offering at times a "high" Christology.

Hippolytus (c. 170–c. 236) declares that God is One, and "Creator and Lord of all ... alone in himself," and that he willed to bring people and things into existence (*Refutation of All Heresies* 28). But he also says that Christ was "co-existent with his Father before all time, and before the foundation of the world" (*Fragments,* pt. 1; *ANF* 5:167). There appears to be no systematic exposition of the doctrine of God in Hippolytus, and it is hazardous to draw too precise an inference from his text. Novatian, however, produced a treatise on the Trinity (c. 250). God, he declares, "included all things ... (his) perfect greatness and power, pervading all things and moving all things, and giving life to all things" (*On the Trinity* 2). It seems that God is both transcendent and immanent. God "contains all things," but there is "nothing beyond himself" (2). He is eternal, without beginning, and "always unbounded, because nothing is greater than he; he is eternal, because nothing is more ancient than he" (2). God has "all might . . . all power . . . all riches . . . all wisdom . . . all goodness" (2). Novatian quotes Isa. 40:22,

> He . . . sits above the circle of the earth,
> and its inhabitants are like grasshoppers (3),

and Isa. 45:22, "I am God, and there is no other." God is "perfect, both Parent and Judge" (*On the Trinity* 4). Novatian quotes, "I am God, I change not" (cf. Mal. 3:6), which in context denotes his stability and faithfulness, although Novatian hints at "immutability" (4). He rejects any anthropomorphic interpretation of God's wrath (5). A full doctrine of God is expounded, with reference to Scripture, in *On the Trinity* 1-9. Cyprian (d. 258) offers less explicit material on the doctrine of God.

By 325 the ante-Nicene Fathers had firmly established the confession of God in the Nicene Creed. The Creed of Jerusalem (348) followed Nicaea, and was based on the *Catechetical Lectures* of Cyril of Jerusalem. These began: "We believe in one God, Father Almighty, Maker of Heaven and earth, of all things visible and invisible." The Creed of Constantinople (381) virtually followed the same words: "We believe in one God, the Father almighty, maker of heaven and earth *(hena Theon Patera, pantokratora)*, of all things visible and invisible" (W. H. C. Frend, ed., *Creeds, Councils, and Controversies* [London: SPCK, 1989], 21, 114). The Councils of Ephesus (449) and Chalcedon (451) followed the same wording (345-65). The controversies that occurred between the death of Origen and the Council of Constantinople concerned Christology rather than the doctrine of God as such. Dionysius of Alexandria followed Origen's Trinitarian theology. He condemned Sabellianism, or modalism, which tended to fuse together the persons of the Trinity as three aspects or modes of the one Godhead, although it was alleged that he veered toward subordinationism or potential Arianism. Bishops at Antioch also condemned Paul of Samosata in 268 for teaching a Christology that verged on adoptionism.

Arius (c. 250-336), born in Libya, became bishop of Alexandria but was then excommunicated and, under the leadership of Athanasius, was condemned in 325. Arius taught subordinationism, and that Jesus Christ, as God the Son, was "younger" than God the Father. Rowan Williams notes the popular image of the heresy of Arianism from Newman and Harnack onward. Prestige regarded it as crypto-pagan; Newman regarded Arius as "other" than Christian; Harnack saw Arius as influenced by Aristotle's rationalism. H. M. Gwatkin saw Arianism as having an affinity with Deism, and also deficient in understanding metaphor, and misunderstanding God's relation to creatures and the world (Williams, *Arius* [Grand Rapids: Eerdmans, 1987, 2001], 2-25). But Williams argues that these critics too readily understood the church of the early fourth century as doctrinally well defined, with sharp boundaries, and Arianism as an equally bounded subsect. The Arian struggle, Williams argues, emerges from the tension between the "academic" explorers and a supposedly "Catholic" system (84-88). The precedent for Arius was Origen and his supposed "school." In practice *Arius held a high theology of God:* God alone has aseity, is immaterial and unbegotten *(agennētos),* without plurality or emanation; he is free, rational, and purposive. He initiated creative processes by bringing the Son into being, so there is a sense in which he is "prior" to the Son. But the Son is not just "one among others" (98). Thus there was a time when God was not a "Father," for the Son is not eternal (100). Nevertheless, Williams concludes, we must not trace a direct line from Origen to Arius (147). The point is that the debate was far more complex and blurred than many have assumed. Eusebius of Caesarea showed sympathy with Arius and his aims. He actually denies that the Father and the Son coexist eternally (167-74). Indeed, Williams concludes, "Arius was a committed theological conservative" (175). Arius's ultimate aim was that "no aspect of the created order" should "enter into the definition of God" (231). Hence, although popularly Arius is understood in the context of Christology, his prime concern was to preserve the transcendence and uniqueness of God.

Arius's formulations and explorations, however, provoked Athanasius to stress the difference in kind between the *created order* and what was *not created.* The Son and the Holy Spirit alone belonged to the *uncreated order of Being:* the Son was "begotten, not made," and the Holy Spirit "proceeds" or comes forth from God. Indeed, whereas the Creed of Jerusalem (348) simply refers to the Son of God as the "only-begotten Son of God, who was begotten from the Father as true God before all ages," the Creed of Constantinople (381) has "the only begotten Son of God, begotten from the Father before all ages, light from light, true God from true God, begotten not made *(gennēthenta ou poiēthenta),* of one substance with the Father *(homoousion tō Patri,* of one *being* with the Father)" (*Creeds, Councils,* 114). It was Athanasius together with Hilary, Ambrose, Basil, Gregory, and others who explicitly formulated a doctrine of God as Trinity, in reaction partly against Arius, and partly against those who explicitly denied the divinity of the Holy Spirit (*see* **Holy Spirit: The Spirit in Historical Theology**).

Among the Eastern Fathers, Eusebius (260-337) seeks to exclude modalism or Sabellianism from orthodox catholic faith. God as Father, Son, and Holy Spirit does not merely express himself as three "modes" of being or aspects. Cyril of Jerusalem (c. 315-387) has a biblical, pastoral, and practical approach. He writes, "Let us return to the Scriptures" (*Catechetical Lectures* 16.11). He sees the Father, the Son, and the Holy Spirit as being *one in will* and Being, but as having *distinct and separate* roles in *relation to the church and the world.* He quotes Paul in 1 Cor. 12:4-6: "There are varieties of gifts, but the same Spirit; and there are varieties of services, but the same Lord; and there are varieties of activities, but it is *the same God* who activates all of them in everyone."

In response to challenges to the personhood of the Holy Spirit, Athanasius argues that "the whole Triad is God" (*Epistle to Serapion* 1.17). Neither Jesus Christ nor the Holy Spirit is a *ktisma*, a created being or creature. Like Cyril, he quotes 1 Cor. 12:4-6, and engages in careful exegesis. Athanasius contributed decisively to the theology of God. First, he stressed that the Son was true God, but within a monotheistic framework; that is, he articulated more clearly than before that God is God as Holy Trinity. Second, he elaborated the notion that God created the universe "from nothing" *(ex nihilo)*, and insisted on the ontological distinction between the uncreated and created order of Being. Third, he asserted clearly the goodness of matter as God's creation, in an era when monasticism was beginning to invite retreat from the world. He prepared the way for the adoption of the *homoousios* (of the same being) clause in the Council of Constantinople, which was sometimes termed Christ's "consubstantiality" with the Father, especially after 360 (for more detail, *see* **Holy Spirit: The Spirit in Historical Theology**).

The three Cappadocian Fathers, Basil of Caesarea (c. 330-379), his friend Gregory of Nazianzus (c. 330-390), and his younger brother Gregory of Nyssa (c. 330-395), carried the debate further. Basil succeeded Eusebius as bishop of Caesarea, and struggled against Eunomius, who now led the Arians, and against the Pneumatomachi, who denied the divinity of the Holy Spirit. He wrote *Against Eunomius* (three books) and the treatise *On the Holy Spirit*. He sought to persuade the "semi-Arians" that their proposed creedal clause "of like being" *(homoiousios)* amounted to the *homoousios* phrasing of the Council of Constantinople. He argued that God created the heavens and the earth (*Hexaemeron* 1.1-9). It is clear that for Basil God is not "solitary" but Trinitarian. His first argument in *On the Holy Spirit* is against those who deny that Christ is "with" the Father (6.13). Basil insists that worship and glory should be ascribed to God as Father, Son, and Holy Spirit, and ranked together as one in dignity and glory. In *On the Holy Spirit* 6-8 he argues for the coequality of the three persons of the Trinity. "Our Lord ... cojoins the Spirit with the Father and Himself" in baptism (10.24). In the latter part of the treatise he stresses their coequality, deity, and coglorification (17–22). The three persons are "inseparable" in their relations to humankind (16.37-38).

Gregory of Nazianzus similarly stresses the unity of the persons as one Godhead. "To us there is one God, for the Godhead is One ... though we believe in three Persons" (*On the Holy Spirit* 14); we are not "tritheists" (17). To speak of "three" has nothing to do with *quantity* (18), as in "three Peters or three Johns" (19). Gregory of Nyssa is even more detailed and emphatic on this point. He expounds it further in his work *On "Not Three Gods."* In linguistic terms "three" has a *quantitative* function *only* if it is applied to created objects that can be counted or enumerated. It is logical nonsense to apply the term in the same way to God. It implies only distinction, quality, or function in an analogical way. He concludes, "The *activity* of the Father, the Son and the Spirit is *one*" (Gregory, *On the Trinity* 6). To speak of "one" in activity is not philosophical or metaphysical. The Son and the Spirit are "joined to the Father by His uncreatedness" (Gregory,

Against Eunomius 1.22). Gregory of Nyssa profoundly influenced the Council of Constantinople in 381.

Meanwhile in the Western Church, Hilary of Poitiers (c. 315-368) drew partly on Tertullian and Origen, but, like Athanasius, insisted, against Arius, that the Father and the Son were both "of the same being" *(homoousion),* although he allowed also "of like being" *(homoiousion).* In 362 he wrote *On the Trinity* (twelve books). In Latin terminology, he argues that God the Father and God the Son are "one" *(unus):* "no difference is revealed to sever them; their unity [does] not . . . contradict their distinct existence (*On the Trinity* 7.2). We confess "One God *from* whom are all things" (ultimate sense) and "one Christ our Lord, *through* whom are all things" (mediate source); "One Source of all, One Agent" (4.6). To be more specific, God, or the persons of the Trinity, is "one in nature, honour, power" (8.19). Hilary appeals to John 15:26 and other verses (8.2). Some have called him the "Athanasius of the West."

Ambrose of Milan (c. 339-397) also emphasizes the oneness of God as Trinity. The OT and NT witness to the same God. He declares, "The Father, Son, and Holy Spirit are of one nature *(naturae)* and one knowledge" (*On the Spirit* 2.11). Moreover, their unity is "eternal" (*sempiternae;* 2.12). In 1 Cor. 12:4-7 the Trinity is "not separated" (2.12). The Holy Spirit "is of one will and operation with God the Father" (2.12). Again in book 3 Ambrose speaks of the "inseparability" of the divine nature (3.6, 7).

Augustine (354-430) produced a vast literature of theological works. On the Trinity he tends to speak of God as a "mind," or a thinking, willing, purposive self. He accepts that "the Holy Spirit is not inferior to the Father and Son"; the Trinity is "consubstantial and co-eternal" (*On Faith and the Creed* 9.16). But "The Trinity is One God . . . as it is written, 'Hear, O Israel, the Lord your God is one God' (Dt. 6:4)" (9.16). Again, like Hilary, he ascribes Rom. 11:36 to the Trinity: "Of him and in him and through him are all things" (9.16). Unlike some of his predecessors, Augustine believes that the word "person" does not advance our understanding of the Trinity, especially since it too easily suggests tritheism. Augustine writes, "Human language labours altogether with great poverty of speech. The answer . . . three 'persons' is given *not* that it might be [completely] spoken, but that it might not be left unspoken" (*On the Trinity* 5.9). "The Trinity is called one God, great, good, eternal, omnipotent" (5.11). But the operative term is not "in the way of substance" (5.11.12; similarly 7.5.10). Humankind somehow still bears the image of God (7.6.12). Hence, "man might be the image of the Trinity: not equal to the Trinity . . . but approaching it" (7.6.12). Thus "love and mind are not two spirits but one spirit; nor yet two essences, but one" (9.2.2). The loving mind also presupposes self-knowledge (9.3.3). Hence the three are one: the mind, the knowledge of it, and love. The Trinity is the God who loves, and his self-conscious knowledge of this. But it would be absurd to suggest that this represents three beings or substances. He declares, "There remains a trinity: mind, love and knowledge . . . mutually all in all" (9.5.8), Augustine then reaches his classic formulation.

He declares, "These three, memory, understanding, and will, are not three lives, but one life, not three minds, but one mind . . . one substance" (10.11.18).

Whether this simplifies or obscures the matter has been debated over the centuries. As in some other areas, there are insights in Augustine, but Athanasius, Hilary, and the Cappadocian Fathers offer complementary insights. We find perhaps the closest link between Augustine and the Cappadocian Fathers in the Cappadocian emphasis on *perichoresis,* or *mutual interpenetration* between the persons of the Trinity as one God, which Moltmann has recently stressed. We have to wait until the late twentieth and the twenty-first century, however, for a return to a "narrative" approach to the Trinity, which some find more helpful.

(ii) **The Medieval Period.** It is false to see the medieval period as uncreative or sterile. But specifically on the doctrine of God, controversies and developments concern ways of approach to God and the grace of God, rather than the nature of God or his Being and character. While monasticism and mysticism often stress God's love and holiness, there is often also a tendency to see an "upward" ladder of human purification and progression, rather than the Reformers' stress on a "downward" movement from God to humankind in grace, though some might dispute this contrast. W. T. Davison, an older modern writer, maintains that the doctrine of God and the Trinity remained "stationary" and "unchanged" from Augustine until Kant and the Enlightenment. There are some exceptions, however. Pseudo-Dionysius (probably sixth century) stressed the unknowability and inconceivability of God the Father in his theology of negation, which influenced the mystics and others in the Middle Ages. A system of "heavenly hierarchy" seems to place the Father as the highest transcendent being, allowing communication with the world through Christ and the Spirit. This, if it is his teaching, would stand in tension with the teaching of Jesus about intimacy with the Father.

Erigena, John Scotus (or Eriugena John Scottus, c. 810–c. 877), meaning probably John the Irishman, was both a commentator on John and biblical exegete, and a philosophical theologian. He was concerned about God's relation with the world, grace, and freedom. His concept of God drew not only upon Augustine, but also on Pseudo-Dionysius and Gregory of Nyssa. Creation is seen as a process of "going out from God" and returning to him. Erigena emphasizes the activity of God in nature so strongly that he has been accused of pantheism, but it may be more accurate to suggest that he attempts to expound the immanence of God. In effect, he anticipated Christian Neoplatonism. He was primarily a philosopher rather than a theologian, but to him the fields were part of the same quest to arrive at a rational understanding of God and the world. Many would claim that despite intentions, he leaves little room for divine transcendence, although he does argue that God is a mystery above nature. He comes near to seeing the world as an emanation of God. Nature is the "totality" *(universitas)* of reality, or its unifying principle, though he also denies that creatures are part of God. God is the unchanging "first cause" of the universe. God is also the goal of the creative process.

Anselm of Canterbury (1033-1109) was strongly dependent on Augustine, but is especially known today for his work on atonement in *Cur Deus Homo (Why God Became Man)* and for his formulations of the ontological argument for the existence of God. He claimed that the existence of God is truly a priori. In about 1078 he formulated two versions of this in his *Proslogion* 2-4. In *Proslogion* 2 this takes the form of a confession or prayer: "We believe that you are that than which nothing greater *(nihil maius)* can be conceived" (*see* **Ontological Argument**). To claim that this is not reality would be a self-contradiction, which leads to debate with the monk Gaunilo. Barth insists that this is a Christian confession rather than an argument. As such, it constituted a key to his *Church Dogmatics*. But Descartes clearly formulated it as an argument, thereby inviting devastating criticisms from Kant, Russell, and others. Today the Christian philosopher Alvin Plantinga has defended Anselm by means of modal logic and his concept of "maximal greatness," which applies uniquely to God. Hence Anselm's concept of God influences philosophical discussion today. *Cur Deus Homo* is no less epoch-making on the atonement. It shows that the atonement not only integrates and unifies the person and work of Christ, but also stems from the nature of God as holy love. Humankind, Anselm argues, has offended God, and since God is infinite, owes him infinite debt or satisfaction. Only Jesus as God-man can achieve this. As God, he pays an infinite satisfaction; as man, he stands in solidarity with humankind to offer the satisfaction or to pay the debt that is due. Anselm writes, "No one but God can make this satisfaction.... But no one ought to make it except man; otherwise man does not make satisfaction" (*Why God Became Man*, chap. 6, in *A Scholastic Miscellany*, ed. E. R. Fairweather [Philadelphia: Westminster, 1956], 151). Both *Proslogion* 2-4 and *Why God Became Man* show how great God's Being and mercy are (chap. 20). Abelard and others since have offered criticisms of Anselm's theology, but it nevertheless portrayed new insights into the Being and character of God.

Thomas Aquinas (1225-1274) is usually regarded as the greatest of the medieval theologians, and his work effectively defined the theology of the Roman Catholic Church at the Council of Trent and prior to Vatican II. His twin inspirations are Aristotle and Augustine. His major work is the *Summa Theologiae*. In part 1 after question 1, on the nature of theology and knowledge, Aquinas has the following ten *quaestiones:* question 2 on the existence of God; 3 on his "simpleness"; 4 on his perfection; 5 and 6 on the term "good" and the goodness of God; 7 on his limitlessness; 8 on his omnipresence; 9 on his "unchangeableness"; 10 on his eternity; and 11 on his "Oneness." These cover 170 pages in the Blackfriars edition. We consider the existence of God under the entry on the cosmological argument. God's "simpleness" also partly relates to questions of substance and accidents (*see* **Aristotle; Lord's Supper**). On perfection, Aquinas quotes Matt. 5:48, "Be perfect as your heavenly Father is perfect *(perfectus est)*." Next, he declares, "Augustine tells us that the three divine persons are the supreme good, seen by the supremely clean of heart." He continues, "God alone is good by nature." Thomas turns next to "God's limitlessness." He writes, "The fact that God's existence itself subsists *(subsistens)* without being acquired by anything, and as such is limitless *(infinitum)*, distinguishes it from everything else" (qu. 7, art. 1). On God's omnipresence, in Jer. 23:24 God proclaims that he fills heaven and earth. Aquinas concludes, "Being everywhere outright belongs to God alone. By being everywhere outright *(ubique primo)*, I mean being everywhere in one's completeness *(totum est ubique)*." The "immutability" of God is part of traditional Thomist and Catholic theology: God is unchangeable *(immutabile)*. Aquinas quotes Mal. 3:6: "I am God, I change not." This certainly excludes growth and decay, and in as far as it concerns his faithfulness, this correctly reflects the biblical witness. But the traditional doctrine of divine "immutability" raises difficult questions today, and bears no relation to "unchanging" in Hebrews, which concerns the abolition of a changing succession of priests. On God's eternity, Aquinas cites the Athanasian Creed: "The Father is eternal, the Son is eternal, the Holy Spirit is eternal" (qu. 10, art. 2). He states, "Eternity and God are the same thing. Calling him eternal does not imply his being measured by something external" (art. 2); "Eternity, in the true and proper sense, belongs to God alone" (art. 3). Question 11 discusses God as one. Here Aquinas quotes Deut. 6:4: "Hear, O Israel, the Lord our God is one God" (qu. 11, art. 3). He also quotes Bernard approvingly, that God as divine Trinity is supremely one *(unitas;* art. 4). Creation (qu. 44-49) comes in volume 8 of the Blackfriars edition. The "operations" of God are categorized in accordance with Augustine, by "Intellect, Will and Power" (providence, predestination, and power; qu. 14-26). Aquinas declares, "The will of God is the cause of things" (qu. 19, art. 4). On the problem of evil, he comments, "God neither wills evil to be done nor wills it not to be done, but wills to permit evil to be done" (qu. 19, art. 9, reply to obj. 3). The omnipotence of God is effective, but he cannot make possible what is impossible, and cannot make the past not have happened (qu. 25, art. 3 and 4). The term "Father" also names God in a personal relationship (qu. 33, art. 2). He appeals here to Jerome and to Basil.

Among medieval mystics, Meister Eckhart (c. 1260–c. 1328) provides one example. He taught that all things flow out from God, and flow back to him. His theology is basically apophatic, or at best paradoxical. Hence he approaches near to a pantheist view of God, although he would probably have denied this. At least he stresses divine immanence. This exposes a major problem with mysticism. This partly applies to Hildegard of Bingen (1098-1179), Bonaventura (c. 1217-1274), Catherine of Siena (c. 1347-1380), and perhaps even Julian of Norwich (1342-1416). Walter Hilton (c. 1343-1396), however, retained important critical faculties more clearly than most of that era.

(iii) **The Major Reformers.** The first major exponent of explicit Reformation principles was Martin Luther (1483-1546), even if men such as John Wycliffe had earlier anticipated aspects. Luther's most distinctive theme in his doctrine of God is God as hidden and revealed *(deus absconditus et revelatus)*. God is both hidden and revealed in the incarnation and the cross. Everything must be seen through the lens of the cross. Luther wrote: "As long as man does not know Christ he does not know God as hidden in sufferings.... God is not to be found except in sufferings and in the cross.... The theologian of glory says bad is good.... The theologian of the cross calls them by their proper name" (*Heidelberg Disputation* 21, in J. Atkinson, ed., *Luther: Early Theological Works* [London: SCM, 1962], 291). He also says, "He is worth calling a theologian who understands the visible and hinder parts of God to mean the passion and the cross" (290). God is transcendent, yet comes to us in the cross. This has more content than merely describing God as transcendent and immanent.

As well as transcendent and immanent, revealed and hidden, God is *sovereign,* but exercises his sovereignty over humankind in two distinct ways. At the devotional or spiritual level, God exercises it through Scripture, preachers, and the sacraments. But, secondly, he exercises it through princes, officers of the state, and fathers of families. This is how evil is restrained. B. Drewery argues that authority, vocation *(Beruf),* station, and office *(Amt)* constitute characteristic emphases in Luther. He bitterly opposed the Peasants' Revolt, which was incited by the Radical Reformers, Carlstadt, Münster, and others. Mob tyranny, Luther urges, is excluded by Rom. 13:1: "Let everyone be subject to the higher powers." On the Trinity, J. Pelikan observes, "There is in Luther's writings very little speculation about the inner life of the Trinity.... He had surprisingly little to say even about Christ as the Second Person of the Trinity" (*Luther the Expositor* [St. Louis: Concordia, 1959], 52-53). He discusses the Trinity, it appears, only in his commentary on John 1:1-14, in which Jesus is the Word of God.

John Calvin (1509-1564) devotes the first book of the four books of the *Institutes* to knowledge of God and the doctrine of God. The first nine chapters underline the mutuality of knowledge of God and knowledge of ourselves, and point to the authority of Scripture and the testimony of the Holy Spirit. Chapters 10–18 most explicitly expound the doctrine of God. He is "the Creator of heaven and earth." Calvin selects three "attributes" for exposition, namely, "loving-kindness, judgment, and righteousness" (Jer. 9:24; *Institutes* 1.10.2; Beveridge, 1:88). God excludes false deities and idols. Calvin recognized, however, that we must allow for Scripture's "accommodation" when it speaks "in popular terms," through anthropomorphism and analogy (1.11.1; 1:91). Lactantius, Eusebius, and Augustine warn us against worshiping "pictures used in churches ... painted on walls," as if these were God himself (1.11.6; 1:95). But Calvin does not dismiss *all* "visible representations of every kind"; only their *misuse* (1.11.12; 1:100). He passes on to "the unity of the Divine Essence in three Persons," as taught in Scripture (1.13; 1:108). Certainly divinity fully belongs to the Son and the Holy Spirit (1.13.7). Calvin cites Heb. 1:2 and many other Scripture passages. The energy of "the Word" was active at creation (1.13.8). Like Gregory, he urges, "the New Testament teems with innumerable passages" (1.13.11; 1:119). Calvin cites those passages that feature in the teaching of the Church Fathers, and demonstrates the relevance of the Holy Trinity to the Christian life. He concludes, "The Scriptures teach that there is essentially but one God, and therefore that the essence both of the Son and

Spirit is unbegotten." Nevertheless, he argues, "the Father is first . . . and fountain of all the Godhead" (1.13.25; 1:134).

When he considers the creation of the world, Calvin does this in such a way as "to ponder on the paternal goodness of God" (1.14.2; 1:142). He accepts the notion of strife against Satan, with the proviso that "Satan cannot possibly do anything against the will and consent of God" (1.14.17; 1:153). Perhaps surprisingly, Calvin states that Jesus himself demonstrated that "he created all things for the sake of man" (1.14.22; 1:157; repeated in 1.16.6). He discusses the image of God, and addresses misguided objections to a doctrine of Providence by Sophists and others (1.16.1-3). Calvin rejects the notion of "the Deity, sitting idly in heaven," but believes that God "overrules all events" (1.16.4; 1:175). Calvin insists that "Fortune and Chance are heathen terms" (1.16.8; 1:179). Things are "ordered by the counsel . . . of God" but may appear to be fortuitous because God's counsel is hidden (1.16.9; 1:180). In the next chapter he repeats: "all things come to pass by the dispensation of God . . . nothing happens fortuitously" (1.17.6; 1:188). This encourages us to pray, "paying due regard to inferior causes." Adverse happenings will raise our thoughts and prayer to God (1.17.9-10). He concludes, God does not cease to be trustworthy (4.15.17). God extends his mercy even to the unworthy (3.3.25).

(iv) **The Modern Period.** During the years following the Reformation the warmth and practical concern of Luther and Calvin tended to harden into post-Reformation debates, with few exceptions. But the dominance of Christian orthodoxy received head-on challenge from two sources. Deist writers held strongly to the notion of an absentee God, who had set the world going but left it to run like a well-oiled machine without interference or interaction. The attempt to "repair" defects in the world, most Deists argued, implied serious imperfections in creation. They also denied the possibility of revelation rather than discovery or human reasoning. This struck at the heart of an orthodox doctrine of God. The other source was the Enlightenment of the seventeenth and eighteenth centuries. This also tended to undermine any appeal to authoritative texts and writers, whether the Bible or those of the patristic church, in the name of individual freedom. This trend was also aggravated by Kant, who tended to view "God" only as a presupposition of freedom and morality. He attacked "churchly" prayer in any form other than that of meditation, self-adjustment, or contemplation. These two sources take us far from the God of the Bible, and of patristic and Reformation roots.

The Enlightenment includes a large range of mainly eighteenth-century thinkers. But the works of I. Kant (1724-1804) have particular importance for the doctrine of God. At first his concept of religion as the interpretation of our moral duties as divine commandments suggests a closer relation to orthodoxy than that of Deism. But in his thought God comes to be seen as the abstract presupposition of the absolute nature of moral law. Indeed, God becomes the philosophical presupposition on which freedom, immortality, and morality can be built. E. L. Fackenheim urges that "God is an alien and indeed insufferable intruder into

Kant's moral thought" (in N. Smart and others, eds., *Nineteenth Century Religious Thought*, vol. 1 [Cambridge: CUP, 1985], 21). The same applies to his arguments for immortality: "God" lies beyond the realm of sense experience. Moreover, the notion of "First Cause" in the cosmological argument, and of "Necessary Being" in the ontological argument, becomes logically contradictory. The notion of "cause" is supposedly a product of the human mind: it provides conditions necessary for regulative reason to understand the ordering of the world. Kant's concern for transcendental thinking in his *Critique of Pure Reason* (1781) moved the argument into the realm of conditions for the possibility of knowledge and truth, that is, presuppositions of meaningful discourse. This becomes still more acute for a doctrine of God in his *Religion within the Bounds of Reason Only* (1793). In "churchly faith" *(Kirchenglaube)* prayer was thought to lead to a changed situation. But in "purely rational faith" *(reiner Vernunftglaube)*, as we have noted, prayer is seen as "conversing... with oneself," not as "superstitious illusion" (*Religion within the Bounds of Reason* [New York: Harper, 1960], 185). Thus on these two grounds, among others, the traditional orthodox view of a God who loves the world and engages with it becomes untenable.

At first sight the incarnation and Trinity appear to be central to G. W. F. Hegel (1770-1831). He opposed Kant's notion that reason served mainly to provide a regulative principle of ordering reality by the human mind, and his notion of God as a presupposition of morality. He attacked Schleiermacher and Schelling for giving privilege to human consciousness as unduly subjective. He viewed the incarnation and cross as virtually a negation or "death" of God, which God would then "sublate" or "raise" *(erheben)*, and assimilate *(aufheben)* in the event of the resurrection. He saw three eras of biblical history: the OT, the incarnation and the cross, and the resurrection and exaltation. The three represent respectively the eras of God the Father, God the Son, and God the Holy Spirit. Hegel criticized Roman Catholicism for stopping short at the cross by promoting the crucifix of a dead Christ rather than the liberating era of the Spirit. Such a sketch may suggest a more traditional doctrine of God than Kant's. But while philosophy used concepts, he urged, religion used only "representations" *(Vorstellungen)* or imagery of a less critical and more metaphorical kind.

Is Hegel's historical dialectic dictated by his logic and philosophy, or by a Christian doctrine and religion? Does the incarnation of God merely serve conceptual differentiation on the part of "infinite spirit"? He argues the "thesis" that Jewish religion and creation became "negated" in the antithesis that the incarnation of Jesus and the cross brought finitude and the "death" of God. Then Pentecost released the synthesis of the new age of the Spirit. But this looks more like a restoration of the Absolute than the new age of Peter's sermon. It all fits perhaps too neatly into Hegel's system. But the price for it is an *emergent God,* who vindicates Hegel's logical and historical system. It is not at all clear that Hegel's "God" is less "instrumental" than that of Kant. Hegel was first of all a philosopher and, second, a theologian. Kierkegaard denounced the whole system as mere theory and abstraction. In his *Lectures on the Philosophy of Religion* (1832), Hegel wrote, "In *thinking*, I lift myself into the absolute.... I am infinite consciousness while I remain at the same time finite self-consciousness... it is in myself and for myself that this conflict and this reconciliation take place" (*Lectures* [London: Kegan Paul, 1895], 1:63-64). Everything serves Hegel's theoretical concept of history-as-a-whole, which somehow embraces God.

F. D. E. Schleiermacher (1768-1834) at first sight appears far more "churchly" than the Deists, Kant, or Hegel. He regularly preached at Trinity Church, Berlin, while he was professor of theology, and saw theology, against Hegel, as serving the church. His roots were partly in Moravian Pietism, although he was also influenced by Kant and Romanticism. On the other hand, he reduced religion to "the feeling of absolute dependence on God" (*das Gefühl schlechthinner Abhängigkeit; The Christian Faith* [1821-1822; Eng. Edinburgh: T. & T. Clark, 1989], sect. 62, p. 261). He tended to disparage Christian doctrine, commenting, "Ideas, principles, are all foreign to religion" (*On Religion: Speeches to Its Cultured Despisers* [1799; Eng. London: Kegan Paul, Trübner, 1893], 46). He spoke of the "miserable love of system" (55). He was deeply concerned to promote a living relationship with God in Christ. But some might claim that he does not provide a clear doctrine of God in *The Christian Faith*, but devotes much energy and thought to God's relation to the world in the light of the current advances of natural science. In view of these advances, he asked, how can we speak of God as "causing" events in the world? He rejected Deism and pantheism, but found the infinite and the eternal "in all that lives and moves, in all growth and change, in all doing and suffering. If it is to have life and to know life in immediate feeling... in itself it is an affection, a revelation of the Infinite in the finite, God being seen in it and it in God" (*On Religion*, 36).

No doubt much in Schleiermacher reflects orthodox Christian tradition. *Perfect* consciousness of God, as he says, can be seen only in Jesus of Nazareth. He expounds the notion of the one God as eternal, omnipresent, omnipotent, and omniscient (*The Christian Faith*, 203-32). But in the end it is the *corporate God-consciousness* of this experience in the church that is decisive. Many in the patristic and Reformation tradition would see this as reductive, as if to make humankind or even faith and experience the measure of God. Further, some regard his doctrine of the Holy Trinity as the climax to which *The Christian Faith* leads. But on examination this amounts to about a dozen pages in a volume of 751 pages. Moreover, he calls this doctrine "ecclesiastically framed," for it is "not an immediate utterance concerning the Christian self-consciousness" (738). He repeats: "The assumption of an eternal distinction in the Supreme Being is not an utterance concerning religious consciousness" (739). This shows the limits set by Schleiermacher to any doctrine of God as Holy Trinity. Critics would call this "subjectivism."

A. Ritschl (1822-1889) was probably the most influential thinker of the nineteenth century, apart from Hegel and Schleiermacher. His theology has been attacked from and perhaps misrepresented by two opposite sides. He called Schleiermacher "my predecessor." Orthodox theologians, including Barth and Brunner, have attacked him for paying too much deference to "religion" as a universal phenomenon. On the other side he has been attacked for building on biblical and christological roots and, like Schleiermacher, for seeing a personal relationship with Christ as determinative for theology. Ritschl himself must accept some responsibility for this. On one side he argued that Christian doctrine "is to be obtained from the Bible alone." Yet on the other side he mediated Schleiermacher's thought to Wilhelm Herrmann and Adolf von Harnack. Like his predecessor, he built his doctrine of God on what *human faith believes* in trusting response to revelation (*The Christian Doctrine of Justification and Reconciliation* [Edinburgh: T. & T. Clark, 1902], 105).

The core of Ritschl's doctrine of God is that God is love and God is personal. In terms of philosophy, some argue that the double notion that God is both "absolute" and a "person" is contradictory. Before he became a professor of theology at Göttingen in 1870, he had been teaching NT exegesis and theology. He never abandoned his NT foundation, stressing the key theme of the kingdom of God and the "for us" of Christ's atonement. It is above all Christ who provides our revelation of God. In the sense of seeking "core" characteristics of God, he stressed the orthodox themes of love, personhood, Christ, and the kingdom of God. But to Barth and Brunner, he reduced "God" to the compass of human experience and faith. He argued that this aspect reflects Luther, and hence his work also provided a fresh impetus to research on Luther. In the twentieth century this aspect can be seen in Bultmann (*see* **Ritschl, Albrecht**).

Wilhelm Herrmann (1846-1922) and Adolf von Harnack (1851-1930) maintained aspects of Ritschl's outlook. Herrmann looked to the immediate awareness of human faith and obedience for his understanding of God, who could be conceived only in a trustful relationship. But he very strongly repudiated *doctrine,* seeing faith as virtually grounded on itself. Harnack drew on the teaching of Jesus for the central core teaching of the Fatherhood of God, the infinite value of the "soul," and the brotherhood of humankind. Doctrine, he argued, is largely contaminated by Greek philosophy, although the epistles of the NT do set forth Jesus Christ as the way to God. Meanwhile in America, Horace Bushnell (1802-1876), who was sometimes called "the American Schleiermacher," continued the liberal critique of orthodox doctrine. C. Hodge regarded him as a "dangerous" innovator. He was concerned to reach those who had become removed from the tradition. In 1849 he wrote *God in Christ,* which was especially a treatise on language. Language conveys truth about God, he argued, through *symbols, images, analogies, and paradoxes.* Like Herrmann and Harnack, he minimized the role of doctrine. Probably it was in reaction to Bushnell that many conservatives in America came to stress the "literal" meaning of the Bible and doctrinal propositions. He has been compared also with the English theologian F. D. Maurice (1805-1872). But although he began as a Unitarian, Maurice had a higher regard for traditional formularies, especially in *The Kingdom of Christ* (1838; reprint, Cambridge: Lutterworth, 2002). He believed in the organic connection between the Bible, tradition, and reason.

The reaction to liberal dominance, at least in Britain, came with the Cambridge "triumvirate," B. F. Westcott (1825-1901), J. B. Lightfoot (1828-1889), and F. J. A. Hort (1828-1892), and shortly thereafter with the Scottish theologian P. T. Forsyth (1848-1921). In his early life Forsyth was a liberal in the tradition of Hegel and Ritschl, but became effectively a "Barth before Barth" in many respects, especially in his Christology and his view of the atonement. This is seen especially in his *Person and Place of Jesus Christ* (1909) and *The Work of Christ* (1910). He rigorously opposed the liberalism of R. J. Campbell and advocated a return to Paul, Athanasius, and the Reformers. On the doctrine of God, he stressed divine grace, both in judgment and in mercy, viewing the love of God in Herrmann and Harnack as a sentimental accommodation to human love. Anticipating Barth, he saw revelation as God's deed, not simply his word: "Revelation is redemption." He also saw God's grace as God's holy love, and as God's giving himself. With Barth we see the exposition of a detailed doctrine of God, which again accords with Scripture and tradition. For the specifics of this doctrine, see the entries on Barth and Brunner.

Karl Barth devotes *CD* II/1 and II/2 to the doctrine of God. He declares, "God is known by God and by God alone" (II/1, 179). God is always active, not a static Being. Barth rejects natural theology, finding God in Christ alone. God loves humankind in freedom: "God loves because he loves" (II/1, 279; Deut. 7:7-8). His love is motivated by nothing outside the will of God. Barth stresses God's grace, mercy, and judgment. He argues for God's omnipresence, omnipotence, eternity, and righteousness (sects. 28-31, e.g., p. 639). In *CD* II/2 a central place is taken by God's gracious election and covenant. God elects Jesus Christ and the individual: "He may let go of God, but God does not let go of him" (II/2, 317). The command of God gives rise to what most call "ethics." (*See* **Barth, Karl.**)

Emil Brunner's *Christian Doctrine of God* constitutes volume 1 of his *Dogmatics* (Ger. 1946; Eng. London: Lutterworth, 1949). He begins with revelation: God is "not merely the One who *speaks;* He is also the One who *acts*" (23). God is "not an 'object' which man can manipulate . . . He is a Mystery dwelling in . . . 'inaccessible light'" (117). God is a person, not an "It" (121). He reveals himself as "Lord" (137). He writes: "God is Subject, addressing us" (139). He is holy and "Wholly Other" (157-58). The declaration "God is love" points to the heart of the gospel (183-99). He is also Holy Trinity (222-34). God is omnipresent, omniscient, and Almighty (241-65).

Further developments of the doctrine can be seen by consulting entries for Tillich, Rahner, Küng, Moltmann, and Pannenberg. In Tillich God is beyond conceptual thought and can be understood only through symbol. God is the Ground of Being and the Ultimate. But God is also whatever concerns us ultimately. Tillich writes, "Whatever concerns a man ultimately becomes God for him" (*Systematic Theology*, vol. 1 [London: Nisbet, 1953], 42). God is "beyond God." Hence, Tillich writes, if we imagine that we have hurled him out of our consciousness, "ultimately we know that it is not he whom we reject and forget, but rather some distorted picture of him" (*The Shaking of the Foundations* [1949; reprint, London: Penguin, 1962], 49). Like Tillich, Karl Rahner argues that God is "present as the abiding mystery.... The incomprehensibility of God persists also in the immediate face-to-face vision of God... in the eternal consummation" (*TI* 16:238 and 18:91-92). God transcends normal knowledge, but knowledge may imply a transcendental awareness of a horizon beyond creation. This is a love in which God gives himself, "an unfolding of his inmost self for the other in love" (*TI* 1:123). Like Barth, Rahner urges that God loves in freedom.

Hans Küng is very careful about calling God "personal," as if to imply that God were a superhuman person. He writes: "God is not a person as man is a person" (*Does God Exist?* [London: Collins, 1980], 632). Nevertheless, "A God who founds personality cannot himself be non-personal.... God transcends the concept of the personal.... God is not an 'It'" (633). The Bible portrays a God who is benevolent and absolutely reliable: "God is one who faces me, which I can address" (634). He is the one, living God, the God who acts in history. The miracle stories are "pointers to his action in the world" (651).

J. Moltmann asks not "What does God mean to me?" but "What do I mean for God?" (*The Trinity and the Kingdom of God* [London: SCM, 1981], 3). Moltmann and John Zizioulas tend to speak of God in the context of God as Trinity, so we consider their work under this entry. After an exhaustive study of God in apologetics and philosophy of religion, W. Pannenberg broadly reaches similar conclusions. He agrees first with Rahner that the word "'God' has increasingly lost this [foundational] function, at any rate in the public mind" (*ST* 1:63). Attempts to arrive at "God" on the basis of a guilty conscience, "disclosure situations," or even the cosmological argument do not quite bring us to the "wholly Other" as the key to an awareness of the totality of the world and life (66-73). Barth had claimed that natural awareness of God plays into the hands of Feuerbach, who dissolved faith into an anthropological basis. But, Pannenberg insists, the substitution of confession in place of argument is no improvement on an appeal to some religious a priori (105; cf. 115-27). As Augustine stresses, knowledge of God is inseparable from worship of him (121). God is revealed in Jesus Christ's proclamation of him, in which God reveals himself as Father (125) and as the God of Abraham, Isaac, and Jacob (260). "Father" becomes the proper name for God. But "Father" is necessarily a *relational* term (266-72). He urges that, as Athanasius argued, "the Father would not be the Father without the Son" (273). Hence we encounter the NT narrative of "the Son in self-distinction from the Father on one side and the Spirit on the other"; this is "the starting point for an establishment of the trinitarian distinctions" (273). Once this has been accepted, the other biblical characterizations of God find their proper context. Pannenberg's approach is creative and positive.

Reading: K. Barth, *Church Dogmatics* II/1 (Edinburgh: T. & T. Clark, 1957); John Calvin, *Institutes of the Christian Religion* (London: James Clarke, 1957), 1.10-18; Hans Küng, *Does God Exist?* (London: Collins, 1980); W. Pannenberg, *Systematic Theology*, vol. 1 (Edinburgh: T. & T. Clark; Grand Rapids: Eerdmans, 1991); F. M. Young, *From Nicaea to Chalcedon* (London: SCM, 1983), F. M. Young, *The Meaning of the Creeds* (London: SCM, 1991, 2002); and books cited above.

The Holy Trinity

Further to the discussion above, we distinguish three possible approaches to the Trinity. The first concerns biblical and patristic evidence, which has partly been covered in the subentry above and in the historical subsection of the Holy Spirit entry. The second concerns a narrative approach, and is extremely helpful, while the third explores classical models of the Trinity, often from the early church, to be assessed in the light of the first two approaches.

(i) **Biblical and Patristic Data.** No one can doubt the NT absorption of Jewish monotheism. Recently L. W. Hurtado has demonstrated that Christian devotion to Christ as God embraced a modified or refigured Jewish monotheism, and did not detract from it (*Lord Jesus Christ* [Grand Rapids: Eerdmans, 2003]). Christ devotion, he writes, amounts to "a 'mutation' or new variant form of exclusivist monotheism in which a second figure (Jesus) was programmatically included with God in the devotional pattern of Christian groups" (64) He refers to "this binitarian pattern" (64). In his even more recent thought Hurtado is less wedded to the term "binitarian." But, he argues, we should not expect the Holy Spirit to be the object of early Christian devotion or worship because of what J. E. Fison, Y. Congar, and many others call the "reticence" or "self-effacing" character of the Holy Spirit. In the Church Fathers, especially in Gregory of Nyssa, it emerges that God is "one" primarily in a qualitative sense, *not* in a quantitative or *numerical* sense (*see* **Holy Spirit: The Spirit in Historical Theology**). The Spirit in John 15:26 "proceeds" from God the Father, as the Spirit does in Paul (1 Cor. 2:12, *to pneuma to ek tou Theou;* "the Spirit comes forth or proceeds from God").

If the Holy Spirit is understood as the presence of *God himself,* the Spirit cannot be considered a mere force or an "It." This emerges in the synonymous parallelism of the Psalms ("Where can I go from your Spirit? / Or where can I flee from your presence?" [Ps. 139:7]), in the parallel between "finger of God" (Luke 11:20) and "Spirit of God" (Matt. 12:28), and elsewhere. The very adjective "holy" indicates "derived from God" (*see* **Holy**). Hence the detailed work of Athanasius and Hilary to show that the Spirit is *not* a created being is vindicated by their NT exegesis. Bultmann's conclusion that the Holy Spirit is not fully personal is based on a misunderstanding of language. He is correct to contrast what he calls the *"dynamistic"* language of pouring, filling, giving, and supplying with the *"animistic"* language of searching, witnessing, guiding, speaking, and revealing (*Theology of the New Testament,* vol. 1 [London: SCM, 1952], 155-56). But the two categories of language function as what Ian Ramsey calls "models and qualifiers."

The dynamistic language qualifies the animistic to show that the Spirit is not a person in the *same sense as* a *human* person; the Spirit is *suprapersonal.*

We turn to the NT exegesis of Origen, Athanasius, and Basil, which is well documented and explained by M. Haykin, *The Spirit of God: The Exegesis of 1 and 2 Corinthians in the Pneumatomachian Controversy of the Fourth Century* (Leiden: Brill, 1994). Origen argues that the persons of the Trinity are not merely "cor-related" in 1 Cor. 12:4-7, but that the NT speaks of their "oneness in will" (Haykin, 10-18; Origen, *De principiis* 1.3.1-8). Athanasius and Basil divide entities between "created" or creatures *(ktisis* or *ktisma)* and uncreated. Clearly in the NT the Holy Spirit is the latter. The Spirit anointed Christ for his work, and is "indivisible from the Son" (Athanasius, *Letters* 3.5). Athanasius appeals to 1 Cor. 2:7-13. Basil, anticipating G. Fee (*God's Empowering Presence* [Peabody, Mass.: Hendrickson, 1994]), describes the Spirit as God's presence, and the Giver of Life. Gregory of Nazianzus cites "a swarm of texts" from the Bible, while Gregory of Nyssa rightly insists that the "three" of the persons of the Trinity does not denote a numeral suggesting quantity. Ambrose and Hilary in the West appeal to the same Scripture passages with the same effect.

(ii) **The Narrative Approach.** The breakthrough in Moltmann, Pannenberg, and Eugene F. Rogers is to approach the Trinity in terms of the *NT narrative*. Moltmann declares, "The New Testament talks about God by proclaiming in narrative the relationship of the Father, the Son, and the Spirit" (*The Trinity and the Kingdom of God* [London: SCM, 1981], 64). This recounts the Father "sending" the Son, the Son obeying the Father, and the Spirit raising the Son (88; cf. John 3:16; Rom. 8:11). Pannenberg sees the Holy Spirit at work "at every critical point in his life" (*ST* 1:7-10, 36-37). The Spirit "instituted Jesus into his Sonship" (266). In the story of the baptism of Jesus, "the Spirit was imparted to him" (266; cf. Mark 1:10). Pannenberg continues: "The fellowship of Jesus as Son with God as Father can obviously be stated only if there is reference to a third as well, the Holy Spirit" (267); "Semantically Father is a relational term" (273). J. Zizioulas makes similar claims. God exists only as "being in relation (i.e. being a person)" (*Being as Communion* [Crestwood, N.Y.: St. Vladimir's Seminary Press, 1985], 88).

This seems the simplest and most effective way today of introducing the debated complexities of the Holy Trinity. As soon as we use well-worn analogies, such as a shamrock, we fall into the trap against which Gregory of Nyssa warned his readers, of treating "one" and "three" as numerals of quantity. Rogers has therefore expanded the "narrative" approach of Moltmann and Pannenberg (*After the Spirit* [London: SCM, 2006]). He declares, "The baptism of Jesus is primarily to be understood as an intra-Trinitarian event. . . . It is an event in which the Spirit bears witness to the love between the Father and the Son" (136). He compares other events in the narrative of Jesus, for example, the conception, transfiguration, and resurrection.

(iii) **Models of the Trinity.** A historian of doctrine may readily turn to the variety of models of the Trinity and their relations, which have been used since the early period of the church. (a) Harnack introduced the term "modalism" to characterize the thought of writers who so emphasized the unity of God that they underestimated the distinctive roles of Father, Son, and Spirit in relation to the world. He used this term of Praxeas, and Noetus in the second century, and Sabellius in the third. This is also referred to as Monarchianism, and springs from a fear of falling into tritheism. Tritheism suggests the notion of three equal, independent, autonomous beings, each of which is divine. To avoid such a picture, Barth prefers to speak of God's modes of being, rather than "three persons."

(b) Some have accused the model of the *social Trinity* of also verging on tritheism. Moltmann in effect holds this model, stressing that each person of the Trinity is fully subject, related as *one will* through *perichoresis,* or interpenetration, a favorite word of the Cappadocian Fathers. C. Plantinga argues: "A person who has extrapolated theologically from Hebrews, Paul, and John would naturally develop a social theory of the Trinity" (R. J. Feenstra and C. Plantinga, eds., *Trinity, Incarnation, and Atonement* [Notre Dame, Ind.: University of Notre Dame Press, 1989], 27). He draws on Gregory of Nyssa's *On "Not Three Gods"* but expounds a "strong" social theory. Thinkers in the Eastern Church have always had reservations about a supposedly one-sided Western emphasis on the unity and oneness of God as Trinity. Hence today the Greek Orthodox Zizioulas stresses their relationality. The Eastern Church often stresses the Trinity as a "community" of persons who manifest an indissoluble unity as one. Like Pannenberg, they argue that the persons *are* only what they are in *relation* to each other. Thus in John 10:38 the Father is "in" the Son, and the Son is "in" the Father. Today many feminists and liberation theologians find the concept of social Trinity helpful because it implies a coequality of a community rather than the "monarchical" Father of "patriarchalism." In reply, critics of social Trinity suggest that this concept merely reflects the egalitarianism of today's Western society, and gives force to Feuerbach's notion that our idea of "God" is merely a projection of our human wishes and concerns. On the other hand, the concept of the social Trinity has many different kinds of advocates. The Baptist Stanley Grenz, for example, is a strong advocate (*The Social God and the Relational Self* [Louisville: Westminster John Knox, 2001]).

(c) The model of the economic Trinity refers to the acts of the triune God in a sequence of events including creation, salvation, the cross and resurrection, and the formation of the church. Here the Trinity operates in history, in roles or functions performed by each person of the Trinity. The Church Fathers, however, insisted that *all* persons of the Trinity are coactive in creation, redemption, resurrection, and creation of the church. Yet some biblical passages might imply a subordinationism before or after certain times. Hence Augustine rejected an economic hierarchy within the Godhead. Karl Rahner called the economic Trinity the "immanent" Trinity. As a *comprehensive* account, it cannot perhaps stand. But as one model among others, it is suggestive. "Economic" refers to the arrangement of *activities;* hence such a statement as "God sent his Son" (cf. John 6:44; 3:16) implies some difference of function.

(d) "Immanent Trinity" usually refers not to God's operations in history (economic Trinity) but to *internal relations* between the persons of the Trinity in eternity. Many thinkers would regard this as beyond the scope of revelation and human knowledge, even if some, but not all, regard it as a useful distinction from the economic Trinity. K. Vanhoozer argues that the economic Trinity "communicates" the immanent Trinity. But as soon as he speaks of "intra-Trinitarian communicative action," the logic of Rahner's pronouncement that the economic Trinity is the same as the immanent Trinity seems perhaps less surprising. Yet, surely rightly, Pannenberg and many others associate revelation with the *acts* of God in world history and the future.

(e) Monarchical Trinity. Arius, among others, wanted to preserve the monotheistic and monarchical status of God as Father. Some today suggest a political path to connecting monotheism with the notion of one political ruler. This may have been the case in Eusebius, who sympathized with a single imperial court and government. In the end, however, the Church Fathers rejected and condemned this approach as implying an inadequate view of Christ and the Trinity.

(f) The double procession of the Holy Spirit and the *filioque* clause. The two accounts that the Holy Spirit proceeds "from the Father" and that the Holy Spirit "proceeds from the Father *and the Son*" have divided the Eastern and Western Churches. The *filioque* clause did not appear in the Greek text of the original Nicene Creed. Hilary of Poitiers described the Spirit as "from the Father through the Son" (*On the Trinity* 12.56), but in the 380s Ambrose insisted that the Spirit proceeds "from the Father and the Son" (*On the Holy Spirit* 1.11.20). The Eastern Fathers generally omitted "and the Son," although Cyril of Alexandria finds numerous sources for it. The NT can support both notions. It was not until Photius I of Constantinople called a Council of Constantinople (c. 860) in which he charged the Western Church with heresy, that a wall was finally erected between East and West. In practice, many today recognize that both forms of these words can be defended as safeguarding different truths. Moltmann belongs to those Western theologians who advocate either a compromise or accepting the Eastern form of words as guarding the coequality of the Holy Trinity. He is not alone in this.

In practice, debates about these six models probably constitute the least effective way today of introducing a doctrine of the Trinity. They do not generally describe exclusive alternatives. They serve as signposts, pointers, and markers for preserving the biblical and patristic balance between untenable extremes. The narrative approach of Moltmann, Pannenberg, and Rogers offers perhaps the most biblical and easiest way into the subject, signposted also by patristic exegesis of biblical passages.

Reading: P. S. Fiddes, *Participating in God: A Pastoral Doctrine of the Trinity* (Louisville: Westminster John Knox, 2000); S. J. Grenz, *The Social God and the Relational Self* (Louisville: Westminster John Knox, 2001); C. E. Gunton, *The Promise of Trinitarian Theology* (Edinburgh: T. & T. Clark, 1991); W. Kasper, *The God of Jesus Christ* (New York: Crossroad, 1991); J. Moltmann, *The Trinity and the Kingdom of God*

(London: SCM, 1981); W. Pannenberg, *Systematic Theology*, vol. 1 (Grand Rapids: Eerdmans, 1991); Eugene F. Rogers, *After the Spirit* (London: SCM, 2006).

Grace

The OT uses both *chēn,* noun, and *chānan,* verb and adjective, for showing grace or favor, and in many contexts *chesed,* especially for references to God's covenant mercies. The NT uses Greek *charis,* but also other terms. The subject is too large to be represented by one specific word entirely. Exod. 34:6-7 sums up much of the theme of the Pentateuch on grace:

> The LORD passed before him [Moses], and proclaimed,
> "The LORD, the LORD,
> a God merciful and gracious,
> slow to anger,
> and abounding in steadfast love and faithfulness,
> keeping steadfast love for the thousandth generation,
> forgiving iniquity and transgression."

This is further amplified by Exod. 33:19, "I will be gracious to whom I will be gracious, and will show mercy on whom I will show mercy." The latter passage indicates that grace is freely shown, without any external influence or desert. H. Conzelmann suggests that the verb *chānan* was historically connected with the meaning "to stoop," expressing the aspect of favor being bestowed by a superior onto an inferior. Nineteenth-century writers had often spoken of condescension, but the term has now gathered negative associations. The causative verb "to grant favor" is usually conveyed by *nathan chēn.* In the OT Prophets, Isa. 55:7-9 expresses the unique generosity of grace:

> God . . . will abundantly pardon.
> For my thoughts are not your thoughts,
>   nor are your ways my ways, says the LORD.
> For as the heavens are higher than the earth,
>   so are my ways higher than your ways
>   and my thoughts than your thoughts.

This passage serves to indicate that while human compassion may be measured and have limits, God's generosity reaches beyond human imagination.

Originally *chēn* may have denoted beauty or attractiveness, and it still occasionally carries this meaning. But it soon meant "God's favor" or "grace" (BDB 336), or acceptance with God. D. N. Freedman and J. R. Lundbom find sixty-seven occurrences of *chēn* in the OT, generally meaning "grace" or "favor" (*TDOT* 5:24). They agree that *chesed* is often used as "a covenant term most often meaning *covenant love*" (25), suggesting kindness or loving-kindness when used of God, or "condescending to the needs of his creatures" and "loving kindness in redemption" (BDB 339). Indeed, *chesed* and *chēn* experience "a remarkable merging" (Conzelmann, *TDOT* 9:381). Normally *chesed* expresses "Yahweh's covenant grace to his people . . . Dt. 7:9" (9:383): God is "the faithful God who maintains covenant loyalty with those who love him . . . to a thousand generations." This follows the memorable and paradigmatic example of sheer grace two verses earlier: "It was not because you were more numerous than any other people that the LORD set his heart on you and chose you — for you were the fewest of all peoples. It was because the LORD loved you" (Deut. 7:7-8). The origin of sheer, unmerited, unmotivated grace is the love of God, with no other condition or cause. This theme may occur independently of terms for "grace":

> I am He
> who blots out your transgressions for my own sake. (Isa. 43:25)

Chesed, further, occurs much more frequently in the Psalms than *chēn*, namely, about 127 times. The psalmist cries,

> Help me, O LORD my God!
> Save me according to your steadfast love *(chesed)*. (Ps. 109:26)

> According to your steadfast love, remember me. (Ps. 25:7)

It becomes virtually a liturgical form:

> O give thanks to the LORD, . . .
> for his steadfast love endures forever.
> (Ps. 136:1; cf. vv. 2, 3, to the end of the psalm in v. 26)

In the NT the supreme manifestation of grace comes in the person and work of Jesus Christ, although the meanings in the OT also remain formative for the NT uses. The covenant of grace is traced to Abraham. In the Gospels *charis* occurs in Luke and John, but not in Matthew or Mark. In Luke 1:30 Mary hears from the angel, "You have found favor with God." This reflects the greeting, "Greetings, favored one!" The text does not suggest that Mary is "full of grace." This interpretation is partly due to the Vulgate's loose translation of virtually all the Greek and Hebrew terms by the broader Latin term *gratia*, which has broader connotations. Curiously, the Greek *kecharitōmenē* becomes *gratiae plena*, "full of grace," in the Vulgate. Some argue that the perfect tense implies an abiding state. But this would not convey an innate *human* quality, but the abiding experience of *God's* unmerited favor. Luke 2:40 applies the normal usage to Jesus: "The favor of God was upon him." Even 2:52: "Jesus increased . . . in divine and human favor," does not obscure the OT usage. Luke 4:22 reverts to the older OT meaning: "All... were amazed at the gracious words that came from his mouth." In Luke 6:32, 33, and 34, *poia humin charis estin* makes *charis* equivalent to "love" and has no particular theological meaning. In John Jesus Christ as the enfleshed Word of God is "full of grace and truth" (*plērēs charitos kai alētheias*, 1:14), and "from his fullness we have all received, grace upon grace" (*charin anti charitas*, 1:16). G. R. Beasley-Murray comments that verse 16 relates directly to verse 14, while he translates "grace after grace" as "inexhaustible grace" (*John* [Nashville: Nelson, 1999], 15). E. Jauncey comments, "One measure of grace was to have gained a larger measure in exchange for it" (*Doctrine of Grace* [London: SPCK, 1925], 40). John 1:17 reiterates that "grace and truth came through Jesus Christ," which is the core message of John and the NT.

However, simply consulting a Hebrew and Greek concordance will not tell us all the truth about "grace." In the Synoptic Gospels many parables of Jesus take us further. One of the most striking concerns the laborers in the vineyard (Matt. 20:1-16). The laborers agree with the employer for a full day's wage. Some work for the day and receive what they have agreed to. But other laborers work for shorter periods, down to the cooler "eleventh hour" only. The employer gives them the same wage. On grounds of "natural fairness," those who worked the full day are indignant: "They thought they would receive more" (v. 10). The employer replied to those grumbling: "Are you envious because I am generous?" (v. 15). *Grace* causes consternation when it appears in conflict with supposed justice. Two more of the best-known parables are parables of grace. The parable of the Pharisee and the tax collector tells of grace, which sidesteps the Pharisee's acts of supposed meritorious devotion by God's acceptance of the tax collector, who makes no pretensions of desert. The parable of the prodigal son and elder brother (Luke 15:11-32) clearly offers no reason for the prodigal son to "deserve" restoration; he has spent his inheritance, and shows not even repentance, but sheer remorse. The elder son then tries to claim what he imagines he "deserves." But the Father welcomes the lost, without conditions about conduct (v. 32).

The grace of God, or God's underserved generosity, is especially prominent in the epistles of Paul. This is so not least because of Paul's personal circumstances, as witnessed by 1 Cor. 15:8-10: "Last of all, as to one untimely born, he appeared also to me. For I am the least of the apostles, unfit to be called an apostle, because I persecuted the church of God. But by the grace of God I am what I am, and his grace toward me has not been in vain." Paul explains that God chose to give life and new creation to those reckoned as dead; he was like a miscarried, abortive fetus *(ektrōma)*. J. Munck understands this as "a prematurely born dead foetus," so used in the LXX. He has also been hostile to Christ and his people. Grace *(charis)* springs from the free, sovereign love of God alone and is unmerited. God has made Paul what he is, and grace has also been operative through his subsequent ministry. This crucial passage has a close parallel in the autobiographical verses of Galatians 1 and 2, for example: "I was violently persecuting the church of God, and was trying to destroy it.... But... God, who had set me apart before I was born [hence, Paul implies, any 'merit' is impossible] and called me through his grace, was pleased to reveal his Son to me" (Gal. 1:13, 15-16).

In his earliest letter, 1 Thessalonians, the bare term *charis* is limited to the greeting and blessing (1:1 and 5:28). But Paul declares that God has chosen the Thessalonians (1:4) and that the Holy Spirit made the word of the gospel effective (1:5; 2:13). In 2 Thessalonians, Paul states that "God . . . loved us and through grace gave us eternal comfort" (2:16). Similarly in Galatians, the readers have been called "in the grace of Christ" (Gal. 1:6), yet are now turning to a "different gospel." With their initial reception of the preaching of the gospel to the Gentiles, Paul compares their subsequent attitudes. He asks: "Did you receive the Spirit by doing the works of the law or by believing what you heard? Are you so foolish? Having started with the Spirit, are you now ending with the flesh?" (Gal. 3:2-3). He then compares the paradigm or key model of Abraham, who accepted God's promise unconditionally, not relying upon "achievements" with the Galatian Christians (3:6-14): Christ redeemed us from the curse of the law (3:13; cf. 3:21-29).

1 Corinthians has no less material on the grace of God than Romans, which so many regard as the classic source on grace. In 1 Cor. 4:7 Paul asks, "What do you have that you did not receive? And if you received it, why do you boast as if it were not a gift?" He thanks God "because of the grace of God *(charis)* that has been given to you in Christ Jesus" (1:4). In 3:10 *charis* is used differently to indicate the gift of ability to perform a particular task (e.g., that of a skilled master builder). We have looked already at 1 Cor. 15:8-10, "By the grace of God I am what I am." Elsewhere, perhaps three times, the Greek word *charis* denotes "thanks" or "gift" (e.g., 16:3). In 12:1–14:40 Paul deliberately changes the Corinthians' preferred term *pneumatika*, "gifts of the Spirit," to *charismata*, "free gifts of grace from the Spirit" (e.g., 12:4, 9, 28, 31). In 2 Corinthians "grace" is used in its comprehensive sense in 4:15, "so that grace, as it extends to more and more people, may increase thanksgiving." In the Greek, *charis* is used alongside *pleonazō* and *perisseuō*, which may remind us of *Grace Abounding* by John Bunyan. A classic passage comes in 8:1-9, where Paul speaks of the grace *(charis)* of God (v. 1), which prompts the generosity of the churches (v. 2). *Charis* is then used in verses 4, 6, and 7 to indicate the reflection of God's grace in the generous giving of the Corinthian church. Then in verse 16 it passes to the meaning of "thanks." Finally in 12:9 Paul reflects on his "thorn in the flesh" (v. 7) in the light of God's assurance: "My grace *(charis)* is sufficient for you, for power is made perfect in weakness."

On Romans, Conzelmann comments, "Grace is not just the basis of justification (Rom. 3:24-25; 5:20-21). It is also manifested therein" (*TDNT* 9:395). In 3:22-28 the contrast between grace and "works of law" emerges. Justification comes "by his grace as a gift" (v. 24). "Boasting in achievements" (KJV) is excluded (v. 27). This contrast is sharpened further in 4:13-25: "The promise . . . rest[s] on grace" (v. 16). Abraham, as the paradigm of promise and grace, became the "father" of Christian believers: "His faith 'was reckoned to him as righteousness'" (v. 22). The AV/KJV renders 3:24, "freely by his grace," which reflects the Greek *dōrean tē autou chariti*. The NRSV has "justified by his grace as a gift." "Boasting" is not appropriate before God (4:2). Rom. 5:2 speaks of "grace in which we stand," and E. Jauncey argues that this verse suggests "a state of grace" (*Doctrine of Grace*, 58). However, C. E. B. Cranfield describes *tēn charin tautēn en hē estēkamen* as "this state of being the object of favour" (*Romans* [Edinburgh: T. & T. Clark, 1975], 1:259). In spite of universal sin and death in 5:12-21, Paul declares in verse 17 that "those who receive the abundance of grace *(hoi tēn perisseian tēs charitos)* and the free gift *(dōreas)* of righteousness exercise dominion in life through the one man, Jesus Christ." Cranfield speaks of "the effectiveness and unspeakable generosity of the divine grace" (288). The context is the dissimilarity of Christ and Adam. Similarly, 6:23 contrasts the "wages" of sin (i.e., for work done) with the "free gift" of God *(opsōnia . . . charisma)*. The principle of grace has made believers "free from the law of sin and of death" (8:2). Grace is seen in the sending of the Son (8:3). Bultmann and many others define "flesh" in this context as self-sufficiency, while life in the Spirit depends on God (8:5-17). The remainder of chapter 8 amplifies this with reference both to creation and the future (8:18-25), and to Christians (8:26-39). The love of God has the last word (8:38-39). Chapters 9–11 show God's grace and election in history. This can be seen for example in God's sovereignty (the potter and the clay, 9:20-24) and the doctrine of the remnant (9:27-33). Paul concludes: "How inscrutable are his ways!" (11:33), and

"Who has given a gift to him,
    to receive a gift in return?" (11:35)

References to *charis* also occur in 12:3, 6, and 15:15.

Ephesians is often regarded as "post-Pauline," but also as a summary of Paul's theology written either by a disciple of Paul or by Paul. It contains the classic passage: "By grace you have been saved through faith, and this is not your own doing; it is the gift of God — not the result of works, so that no one may boast" (Eph. 2:8-9). In 3:2 Paul speaks of "the commission of God's grace," while in 3:7 he became "a servant according to the gift of God's grace." He adds in 3:8: "This grace was given to me to bring to the Gentiles the news of the boundless riches of Christ." The Greek is regularly *dōrea*. Phil. 1:6 ascribes the beginning of work in Christians to God (*see* **Prevenient Grace**) and its final completion (*see* **Irresistible Grace**). In 1:7 grace is seen as a gift to the whole community: "all of you share in God's grace with me." This epistle also provides a classic reference to grace that also evokes simultaneous human response: "Work out your own salvation with fear and trembling; for it is God who is at work in you, enabling you both to will and to work for his good pleasure" (2:12-13). In terms of "works" of "achievement," Paul has "come to regard [these] as loss because of Christ" (3:7-8), "not having a righteousness of my own that comes from the law, but . . . the righteousness from

God" (3:9). Paul confirms this with "not that I have already obtained this" (3:12). In 4:13 Paul declares, "I can do all things through him [Christ] who strengthens me." This is reflected in 2 Tim. 2:1, "Be strong in the grace that is in Christ Jesus." In Titus 2:11 "the grace of God has appeared, bringing salvation to all." But in the Pastoral Epistles the term *charis* may also mean "thanks" (1 Tim. 1:12).

Hebrews uses *charis* sometimes with *eleos,* "mercy": "Let us therefore approach the throne of grace with boldness, so that we may receive mercy and find grace to help in time of need" (Heb. 4:16). In 2:9 the ministry of Jesus Christ, even his suffering and death, is "by the grace of God." The warning against "falling away" implies that the grace of God is not to be trifled with (6:4-6), and God's promise is "unchangeable" (6:17). In James, God is the Giver of "every perfect gift" and "every generous act of giving" (James 1:17; Gk. *dosis* and *dōrēma*). Yet James also stresses that a formal belief without appropriate behavioral response would be hollow (2:23-26). He expects evidence of grace and faith. Humility is a fact of grace (4:6); in the first part of the verse God increases grace *(meizona de didōsin charin).* In 1 Peter, the greeting form in 1:2 is more than conventional: "May grace and peace be yours in abundance" (Gk. *charis humin kai eirēnē plēthuntheiē*). In 1:3-5 the writer attributes the readers' progress to their being "protected by the power of God" (v. 5), suggesting the grace of preservation. In 2:20 *charis para theō* indicates God's favor or pleasure. In 5:5 God's gift of grace *(charis)* comes to the humble, and in 5:12 God is called the God of all grace. NT writers are constant about the primary meaning of *charis,* even though the concept is far wider than the actual term *(see* **Love**).

In the history of Christian thought the concept of grace has broadened beyond the biblical usage, and, unlike the NT, grace and human effort take on a more problematic relation in many writers. Clement of Rome (c. 96) writes of the "grace of repentance" *(metanoias charin),* which has come through the blood of Christ *(1 Clem.* 7.3). Grace is also conveyed through "the ministers of the grace of God" (8.1), and their gospel message is gracious (8.2). Yet on the other side Clement links "faith and hospitality" in both Abraham and Rahab (10.7; 12.1), and "hospitality and piety" in Lot (11.1). Such linkage seems surprising, as Clement otherwise has a biblical notion of grace. He writes, "We who have been called in Jesus Christ are not made righteous by ourselves or by our wisdom ... or piety ... or deeds" (32.4; *ou di' heautōn dikaioumetha* ...); and God is "our merciful Father" (29.1), who has chosen us. "Who shall say to him, 'What hast thou done, or who shall remit the might of his strength?' When he wills, and as he wills, he will do all things" (27.5). Some have suggested that limitations of intellectual capacity, rather than sitting loose to the NT, cause this apparent inconsistency.

The *Didachē* (c. 108-120) uses "grace" in the context of the Eucharist: "Let grace come *(elthetō charis)* and let this world pass away" (10.6). Conzelmann regards this as synonymous with Christ's own presence. The prophets are "ministers of the grace *(tēs charitas)* of God" (8.1). Ignatius (c. 112) speaks of prophets of God who were persecuted, but who, "being inspired by his grace *(hupo tēs charitos autou*)," convinced those led astray by "strong doctrines," which seem to have included Judaism (*To the Magnesians* 8.2). In *To the Romans* he prays for grace to complete his journey (1.1). In his epistle to Polycarp, Ignatius exhorts Polycarp to press forward "in the grace wherewith you are endued" (1.2, *en chariti hē endedusai,* "in which you are clothed"). Polycarp, bishop of Smyrna, was martyred circa 155. In his epistle to the Philippians he quotes Paul, "By grace you are saved, not by works, but by the will of God" (1.3). It is probable that he had been a disciple of John. The early-second-century *Epistle of Barnabas,* which often seems very variable, sees the gift of the Spirit as "innate grace" *(emphuton tēs dōreas pneumatikēs charin eilēphate)* (1.2). Grace in the apostolic fathers remains objective and unmerited, as in the NT, and brings salvation. Yet other statements suggest that some have begun to wander from the NT concept.

In the Church Fathers numerous scattered references to grace occur, but the three major systematic expositions of grace in the history of the church occur in Augustine, Thomas Aquinas, and John Calvin. Much of Augustine's exposition constitutes a "reply" to Pelagius. In his *Retractions* Augustine tells us that he wrote *On Nature and Grace* (c. 416) specifically in response to Pelagius's work on the nature of man, which Augustine believed opposed the grace of God whereby the unrighteous are justified (*NPNF,* ser. 1, 5:116). He acknowledged Pelagius's piety, but saw him as a man with "zeal, but not according to knowledge" (*On Nature and Grace* 1.1). Pelagius speaks as if "the righteousness of God ... lies ... in the commandment of the law," whereas it lies "in the aid afforded by the grace of Christ" (1; *NPNF,* 5:121). He quotes Paul's words "All have sinned ..." (Rom. 3:23). If Pelagius is right, Augustine urges, "Christ died in vain." Human nature was created sound, but humankind fell (*On Nature and Grace* 3). "This grace of Christ, however, without which neither infants nor adults can be saved, is not rendered for any merits, but is given *gratis,* on account of which it is called *grace*" (*gratia*) (4; *NPNF,* 5:122). Pelagius is ardent in his zeal and intellect, but this "render[s] the cross of Christ of none effect" (7).

Pelagianism had its origins at a slightly earlier date, probably around 409. Celestius was condemned for denying the transmission of Adam's sin to humanity in a council at Carthage in 411. Pelagius was accused of heresy in 415. After the correspondence with Augustine, he seems to have disappeared from the scene. Pelagius's own "pious and righteous" life as a monk signified his lack of experience of serious personal sin, such as marked Augustine's former life. Hence Pelagius saw goodness as largely springing from natural capacities; he had an inadequate view of the scope of redemption. He wrote commentaries on the Pauline Epistles before 410, when he and Celestius left Rome for Carthage in response to the attack of the Goths. In 412 Augustine wrote *On the Spirit and the Letter.* He argued that in everyone except Jesus Christ, sin has occurred (1; *NPNF,* ser. 1, 5:83-84). Sin cannot be resisted "without God's help," by the "mere power of the human will" (4). Indeed, "by the law of faith we say to God, 'Give me what you command'" (22; *NPNF,* 5:92). "Out of the kindness of God, the law is fulfilled....

The law was given in order that grace might be sought; grace was given in order that the law might be fulfilled" (34; 5:97). In his later work *On Nature and Grace*, he asks Pelagius, "Why do you affirm that man without the help of God's grace is able to avoid sin? . . . Nothing but God's grace alone delivers them, through our Lord Jesus Christ" (62; 5:142). He quotes Hilary in support (72). Later, in *On the Proceedings of Pelagius* (c. 417), Augustine appeals to Rom. 7:13-16, 23-25: "What I would, that I do not" (Rom. 7:15), and compares nature and grace (21-22; *NPNF*, 5:192-93). He repeats his arguments yet again in *On the Grace of Christ* and *On Original Sin* (c. 418). Grace is more than illumination of the mind, and cannot be merited (*On the Proceedings of Pelagius* 24). Grace works in our heart by God's wonderful power (25). Augustine's anti-Pelagian polemic continues in *On the Soul and Its Origin* (c. 419), *On Grace and Free Will* (c. 427), and in his work on predestination (c. 428-429).

Thomas Aquinas also addresses the Pauline notion of unmerited divine grace, which he calls *"actual grace."* He expounds the doctrine of grace in *Summa Theologiae* 1.2, questions 109-144. In question 112, "The Cause of Grace," he argues in article 1 that God alone can be the cause of grace. In article 2, reply 2, he writes that grace is "a help from God, who moves the soul to good. . . . No preparation is required on man's part . . . even the good movement of free will . . . God . . . moves the free will." God may prepare humans "with an infusion of grace . . . which sometimes precedes sanctifying grace, and yet is from God's motion" (art. 2, reply to obj. 1). "Man's preparation for grace is from God" (art. 3, reply). He cites Jer. 18:6: "As clay is in the hands of the potter, so are you in my hand" (art. 3, reply). In article 5, reply, Thomas quotes 2 Cor. 12:9, "My grace is sufficient for you." In question 113, "The Effects of Grace," Thomas insists that grace leads to regeneration and justification (art. 3, reply). He concludes, "The entire justification of the ungodly consists as to its origin in the infusion of grace" (art. 7, reply).

In a distinctive feature, Aquinas adds that the life of grace becomes the "habit" of being in a state of grace. He argues that "virtues and gifts are not in themselves contrasting terms"; they constitute "good habits," of which grace is the cause (qu. 68, art. 1). "Habitual grace is infused into the soul" (qu. 110, art. 2, reply). This is the aspect that the Council of Trent tended to give most attention. Habitual grace, it was argued, was conveyed especially in the sacraments. Some have argued that this obscured Aquinas's own contrast between faith and works. Some question the term "infusion," except in the broad sense of "implanting" or "pouring in."

John Calvin (1509-1564) saw the need for grace as a logical corollary of the depravity of human nature. Early Christian writers called "Original Sin . . . the depravation of a nature formerly good and pure" (*Institutes* 2.1.5; Beveridge, 1:214). But "the Lord in bringing assistance supplies us with what is lacking" (2.3.6; 1:255). God promises to give us a new heart, and his Spirit (Ezek. 36:26-27). He works in us (Phil. 2:13): "Everything good in the will is entirely the result of grace" (2.3.6; 1:256): "we are his workmanship" (Eph. 2:10). "We merit nothing, because we are created in Christ Jesus unto good works, which God hath prepared. . . .

The whole is of God" (2.3.6; 1:256). Citing Augustine, Calvin concludes that "the cause of election" is not in man (2.3.8). Many Protestants followed the traditions of Augustine and Calvin, notably George Herbert in his poem "Grace"; John Bunyan in his *Grace Abounding* (1666); Jeremy Taylor in his concept of grace in relation to duty; and William Cowper and John Newton in their hymns and poems, such as the well-known "Amazing Grace." Karl Barth has much on grace, although it is dispersed among such related subjects as election and redemption. For example, he writes, "Our own election by the grace of God directed towards us is revealed in the election of Jesus Christ" (*CD* II/2, 107). (*See also* **Holy Spirit; Irresistible Grace; Love; Prevenient Grace; Sanctification.**)

Reading: J. M. Boice and P. G. Ryken, *The Doctrines of Grace* (Wheaton, Ill.: Crossway, 2009); E. Jauncey, *The Doctrine of Grace* (London: SPCK, 1925); S. A. Long, *Natura Pura* (New York: Fordham University Press, 2010); T. F. Torrance, *The Doctrine of Grace in the Apostolic Fathers* (Edinburgh: Oliver and Boyd, 1948); M. Volf, *Free of Charge: Giving and Forgiving in a Culture Stripped of Grace* (Grand Rapids: Zondervan, 2005); P. S. Watson, *The Concept of Grace* (London: Epworth, 1959).

Gregory of Nazianzus

Gregory of Nazianzus (c. 330-390) was a contemporary and friend of Basil of Caesarea, and was one of the three great Cappadocian Fathers. He was an eloquent preacher, a firm advocate of Nicene orthodoxy, and a prominent contributor to the Council of Constantinople. His writings include the *Five Theological Orations* (from 389), which contain a theology of the Holy Spirit, and the *Philocalia*, which contain selections (in collaboration with Basil) from the writings of Origen. He cited a "swarm" of biblical texts that supported the deity of the Holy Spirit. The Spirit is not simply a force or an "it." Like Gregory of Nyssa, he insisted that the word "three," when applied to the Holy Trinity, had nothing to do with numerals. He rightly stressed the activity of the Spirit, in contrast to his being or "essence." The Holy Spirit, he argued, is not a created being, like the angels, but "proceeds" from God. Like Basil, he urged that the persons of the Trinity should be given equal honor. On the other hand, "There is one God, for the Godhead is One" (*On the Holy Spirit* 14). (*See also* **Basil of Caesarea; Cappadocian Fathers; Gregory of Nyssa.**)

Gregory of Nyssa

Gregory of Nyssa (c. 330-395) was the younger brother of Basil of Caesarea, and one of the three great Cappadocian Fathers. He passionately defended the Nicene concept of the Holy Trinity. Before he became bishop of Nyssa, he was a solitary ascetic who had also spent time as a rhetorician. He became bishop at Basil's urging, but was temporarily exiled under the Arian emperor Valens. The "Nicene" emperor Theodosius restored him in 380, and commissioned him to propagate Nicene orthodoxy. His original and creative works included *On "Not Three Gods," On the Trinity, On the Holy Spirit,* and *Against Eunomius*. He insisted that "three," when applied to the Trinity, was *not a numerical term*. He also argued that every act of creation and redemption is performed *cojointly* by the Father, the Son, and the Holy Spirit. In Christology he famously used the term *Theotokos* to urge that Jesus was truly human, not to suggest a special status for the Virgin Mary. (*See also* Basil of Caesarea; Cappadocian Fathers; Gregory of Nazianzus.)

Gregory of Rome

Gregory of Rome (c. 540-604) was an able administrator and pastor as bishop of Rome. He was not a creative theologian, although he was called "the last doctor" of the Western Church, after Ambrose, Jerome, and Augustine. He was faithful to Scripture and to the Church Fathers. He also founded monasteries, administered finances, and above all was deeply concerned with the standards of pastoral care among clergy. His *Moralia* on Job was written in a monastic collation, in which the abbot preached and monks asked questions. Gregory acknowledged that biblical interpretation was at best a communal or corporate activity. In the *Preface to the Moralia* he expounded a threefold or fourfold meaning of Scripture. He also wrote his *Book of Pastoral Rule*, or *On Pastoral Care*, and *Forty Gospel Homilies*. The Holy Spirit, he urged, turned the fisherman Peter into a preacher, and transformed a persecutor, Paul, into a teacher of the Gentiles (*Forty Gospel Homilies,* homily 30). He constituted a bridge between the tradition of Augustine and the Middle Ages.

Grotius, Hugo

Hugo Grotius (1583-1645) defended the theology of J. Arminius, and attacked a full-scale Calvinist theology. He also followed a political career, becoming advocate-fiscal of Holland from 1607 to 1613. This led, however, to his arrest and imprisonment in 1618-1619. He escaped in 1621 and fled to France, where he remained until his death. On the atonement he proposed a "governmental theory," which attacked the theory of F. Socinus. God is Ruler, not simply Judge, in demonstrating and enacting the justice of the cross (Rom. 3:25-26). He also proposed a philosophy of law, advocated "natural law," and argued for a just war theory (1625). Many regard him as a later humanist, and see some affinities with P. Melanchthon. His *Annotations of the New Testament* (from 1641) attempted a genuinely contextual exegesis. He wrote *On the Truth of the Christian Religion* as a handbook for missionaries. He contributed to thought as a jurist, historian, classicist, poet, and theologian.

Gunton, Colin

Colin Gunton (1941-2003) was a British systematic theologian. He was professor of Christian doctrine at King's College, London, from 1984, and actively involved in the United Reformed Church. He contributed especially to the doctrine of God, the Holy Trinity, and the work of Christ. In this last field he creatively explored metaphor, not least in defense of traditional church doctrine. He received honorary doctorates from Aberdeen, London, and Oxford.

H

Habermas, Jürgen

Jürgen Habermas (b. 1929) is a German sociologist and philosopher whose significance for theology is largely in connection with his hermeneutics and critical theory. In 1964 he became professor of philosophy and sociology at Frankfurt. His major works include *Theory and Practice* (Eng. 1973); *Knowledge and Human Interests* (Eng. 1971); *The Theory of Communicative Action* (2 vols., Eng. 1987); *The Philosophical Discourse of Modernity* (1985); and *The Inclusion of the Others* (1996). In hermeneutics he takes special account of the "interests" of interpreters, and the ways in which the interpreters' social world conditions them. Habermas criticizes positivist theories of knowledge, and produces a sociocritical hermeneutics, which has affinities with the hermeneutics of Karl-Otto Apel. He has reservations about postmodernism. Gadamer attacks his use of reason, while he, in turn, attacks Gadamer's lack of emphasis of social concern and social conditioning. He has close affinities with critical theory, and with the sociological-Marxist views of the Frankfurt School. *The Theory of Communicative Action* explores the relations between social practice, intersubjectivity, language, and "lifeworld" and system. He also has an interest in speech act theory. He criticizes the splitting apart of life-world and system.

Harnack, Adolf von

Adolf von Harnack (1851-1930) was primarily a church historian, but also a systematic theologian, closely associated with the school of Ritschl and with the flourishing of classical liberalism from 1900 to 1925. He believed that the teaching of Jesus could be reduced to three fundamental truths: the Fatherhood of God, the brotherhood of man, and the infinite value of the human soul. He shared Ritschl's view that Christian doctrine owed much to Greek philosophy and metaphysics, in contrast to the "simple" teaching of Jesus. He published the book *What Is Christianity?* (Ger. *Das Wesen des Christentums*) in 1900 (Eng. London: Benn, 1958), which sold an enormous number of copies and had huge influence at the time. In this he wrote of "the idea of God as Father and the infinite value of the human soul" (54-55) as "restful" and "religion itself" (55). He appealed to the teaching of Jesus in the Lord's Prayer. The brotherhood of humankind arises "from the commandment to love" (59-61). On doctrine, he published his *History of Dogma* in 1886-1889 (3 Ger. vols.; 7 Eng. vols.).

Hauerwas, Stanley

A well-known American theologian and ethicist who currently teaches at Duke University, Stanley Hauerwas (b. 1940) grew up as a Methodist and went to Southwestern University. He graduated as B.D., M.A., M.Phil., and Ph.D. at Yale, and has honorary D.D. degrees from Edinburgh and elsewhere. In 1970-1983 he taught at Notre Dame, and then became professor of theological ethics at Duke Divinity School. *Time* magazine called him "America's best theologian." He is the first American in forty years to have delivered the Gifford Lectures at the University of St. Andrews (2001). He writes and lectures on a multitude of theological and ethical subjects, most often in political theology. He is a robust and witty, if sometimes provocative, speaker, often leaving his audience helpless with laughter. He advocates virtue ethics, postliberalism, and pacifism. In addition to his early debt to Methodism, he has firm Anabaptist and Mennonite roots, but is also partly indebted to Anglican and Catholic theology.

Hauerwas has published an enormous quantity and range of books, about forty in number. His work on postliberal and narrative theology is often associated with Frei, Lindbeck, and Childs, but he has also received some criticism from Wolterstorff. John Berkman and Michael Cartwright have recently produced *The Hauerwas Reader* (Durham, N.C.: Duke University Press, 2001). Berkman calls him "North America's most important ethicist" (*Reader*, 3). His book *Resident Aliens* (1989) may be short, but its argument expresses most of his leading themes. He rejects the "Constantine" era between Constantine and the Enlightenment, characterized by so-called state religion, and the interdependence of church and state. Yoder and the Mennonite movement adopt a similar stance.

Hauerwas allies himself with the Anabaptists and Radical Reformers. He focuses on Luke 16:13, "[No one] can serve two masters." His aim is for the church to regain its biblical vitality. In his book *Community of Character* (Notre Dame, Ind.: University of Notre Dame Press, 1991), he applies the narrative theology of the formation of the Christian church to the fields of social and political theology. He attacks uses of the Bible that make it match "preformed" themes of ethics. John Thomson, *The Ecclesiology of Stanley Hauerwas* (Aldershot, U.K., and Burlington, Vt.: Ashgate, 2003), expounds Hauerwas's relation to liberation theology, especially with reference to *The Peaceable Kingdom* (1983), and as a critique of the Enlightenment and liberalism. Typical quotations from Hauerwas's writings are as follows: "A social order bent on producing wealth as an end in itself cannot avoid the creation of a people whose souls are superficial"; and "The basis for the ethics of the Sermon on the Mount is not what works, but rather who God is."

Healing

Three fundamental principles should be borne in mind as we approach the biblical material. First, the Hebrew *rāpā'* and its synonyms may mean "heal," "restore," or "repair" (BDB 950-51). But it does not *uniformly* denote *physical* healing of the human body. Elijah "repaired" broken-down altars (1 Kings 18:30), but more significantly the word sometimes denotes a more *holistic* healing, which *includes healing of sin,* for example,

> Return, O faithless children,
>   I will heal your faithlessness. (Jer. 3:22)

Isa. 35:5,

> The eyes of the blind shall be opened,
>   and the ears of the deaf unstopped,

comes in the context of restoring the fortunes of Israel, when "the desert shall rejoice and blossom ... the glory of Lebanon shall be given to it ... they shall see the glory of the LORD ... be strong" (35:1, 2, 4). The NT takes up this holistic theme, applying it especially to the hope of the Messiah. This applies especially to *sōzō* in the NT.

Second, the Gospels regard healing (Gk. *iaō* or *therapeuō*) as bound up with the arrival of the kingdom of God. Healings are a sign that the kingdom *has come* in Jesus Christ. But the kingdom is *not wholly present.* Virtually all NT specialists agree that the kingdom is *both present and future* in the teaching of Jesus (*see* **Kingdom of God**), although C. H. Dodd argued, "The kingdom of God has come to you" (Matt. 12:28; Luke 11:20; Gk. *ephthasen*). But when he summarized his message, Jesus declared, "The kingdom of God has *come near*" (Mark 1:15; Gk. *ēngiken*). Dodd tried to argue that this represents the Aramaic for "has come," but this suggestion has not been widely accepted, especially if it excludes a future dimension. Even "has come" in Mark 9:1 refers to an event yet to come. Jeremias coined the term "in process of realisation"; and Cullmann famously applied the analogy of D-Day as the decisive battle (won in the coming of Jesus) and V-Day as the final victory (achieved at the end; *see* **Cullmann, Oscar; Time**). Jeremias spoke both of parables concerning "*imminent catastrophe" and* of those that look forward to the future. *Hence healings do occur,* because in one sense the kingdom has come in Jesus; *but healings are neither universal nor automatic,* because there is a sense in which the kingdom of God has not yet arrived, or reached its climax. Often whether God chooses to heal depends on the *timing* of God's purposes.

Third, in the ancient world sickness was so widely regarded as a sign of God's disfavor (or a deity's disfavor) that "healing" *became an essential part* of assurance of restoration to God's favor, in a way that is not the case in most societies today. To declare to a sufferer in the first century that God has accepted and restored the person but still abandoned him or her (it would seem) to sickness, would appear to undermine the message of a restored relationship with God. A huge amount of research and literature has examined sickness and medicine in the ancient world. In the ancient period, not only is illness or disability perceived as a sign of punishment. Divine healing and healing through "medical" or natural means were *not perceived in the dualistic terms* in which they are too often perceived today. No one in the ancient world asked, "Was healing from God or the doctor?" They asked, "Will God choose to heal now, whether with or without a doctor or pharmaceutical medicine?"

Now that we have established a contextual frame of reference, we may return to more specific biblical material. The Hebrew *rāpā'* does have several synonyms. The Hebrew *g-h-h* is rarely used, but occurs in parallel with *r-p-'*. Hebrew *chābash* may denote "to bind up a wound," but may also mean "to wrap around"; and *chobēsh* may denote a surgeon or a saddle. In Ezek. 30:21 NRSV translates the verb as "bound up for healing," and Hos. 6:1, "he will bind us up," stands in parallel with "he will heal us." But the most usual word is *rāpā'*, especially for "restored to life," as in Ps. 30:3; or simply "be healed," as in Isa. 6:10. In the NT *iaomai* may be used in the literal sense as a medical term, or also in a metaphorical or theological sense. *Iasis,* "healing," and *iatros,* "physician," are used both physically and more holistically or broadly. Greek *therapeuō* is also used. The *kind* of healing depends on the source of the dysfunction. But this is not always clear or easy to determine. "Leprosy," for example, in biblical language may not necessarily or always denote Hansen's disease, but any of a number of skin conditions. Leviticus 13–14 seems to imply that leprosy befalls someone as a sign of divine curse, and results in exclusion from the everyday life of the community. In terms of modern medicine, however, skin diseases are often not contagious, and in the ancient world were often regarded as a source of ritual impurity. Hence, after the cure of a leper, Jesus counsels, "Go, . . . show yourself to the priest" (Luke 5:14).

Exorcisms were regarded as challenges to satanic power. One classic example is the healing of the Gerasene (or Gadarene) demoniac (Luke 8:26-39). The demoniac lives "in the tombs" (v. 27), that is, apart from the community. His speech oscillates between the singular (v. 28) and the plural (vv. 30-32). Only by the transference of demonic forces into the swine and their destruction in the sea (vv. 32-34) could the restored man be convinced that his condition would not recur. This is a classic case of the *arrival* of the *kingdom of God*. In the so-called Q passage of Luke 11:20 and Matt. 12:28, Luke (probably the earlier version here) writes, "If it is by the finger of God that I cast out demons, then the kingdom of God has come to you." Matthew repeats the sentence but replaces "finger of God" with "Spirit of God." There follows the analogy of the attacking and overcoming of the "strong man" by a stronger one (Luke 11:21-22; Matt. 12:29). Matthew repeats the account of the "Gadarene" demoniac (this time, two demoniacs) in 8:28-34. The chapter includes the healing of the leper (8:2-4), the centurion's servant (8:5-13), and Peter's mother-in-law (8:14-15), including "many who were possessed with demons" (8:16), concluding with the quotation "He took our infirmities and bore our diseases" (8:17, quoting Isa. 53:4). But BDB suggests that Isa. 53:4-5 involves "forgiveness and Yahweh's blessing" (951). John Nolland comments that this is linked with "a generalised statement about healings and exorcisms," but in the context of deliverance to "the people who sat in darkness," it is also linked to a "release from suffering" (*The Gospel of Matthew* [Grand Rapids: Eerdmans, 2005], 361). The LXX, however, has *tas hamartias hēmōn pherei kai peri hēmōn odunatai*. This couples "sins" with "pain, misery, mental pains, torment," or "spiritual pain" (BDAG 692). The Pentecostal scholar David Petts concluded that Isa. 53:4-5 entailed *more than* physical healing, if it was "physical" at all, after his Ph.D. on this one passage.

Luke offers a summarizing verse in 5:17: "The power of the Lord was with him to heal." This precedes the healing of the paralytic (Luke 5:18-26), which couples healing with Jesus' pronouncement of forgiveness of sins. Mark also recounts early on in the ministry of Jesus: "He commands even the unclean spirits, and they obey him" (Mark 1:27). At evening "they brought to him all who were sick and possessed with demons . . . and he cured many" (Mark 1:32, 34). Mark 1:40-45 recounts the healing of the leper. A. Oepke comments, "Many of the accounts authenticate themselves by their vividness and simplicity" (*"Iaomai,"* in *TDNT* 3:206). He adds, "Nature miracles are found in the oldest strata of the tradition" (3:207). The key factor, however, as Joel Green argues, is that "Episodes of healing point beyond themselves to the genuine identity and glory of Jesus" (*NIDB* 2:759).

No doubt these healings were connected with Jesus' messianic office as *prophet*. Elijah had been instrumental in restoring a widow's son to life (1 Kings 17:8-24), and Elisha had been involved in the healing of Naaman the Syrian (2 Kings 5:1-15). Although Jesus according to the Fourth Gospel worked "signs" rather than performed "miracles," episodes of healing occur, as in the case of the paralyzed man by the pool of Bethzatha (or Bethesda; John 5:2-9). After the feeding of the five thousand (John 6:1-14), the people inferred from the miracle: "This is indeed the prophet who is to come into the world," that is, the expected eschatological prophet.

It is often said that there is a *universal* command to heal the sick. This is implied in the Church of England report *A Time to Heal* (London: Church Publishing, 2000). But of the eleven members of the Review Group, none seem to have been mainline NT specialists, although they did consult widely, and only 10 out of 412 pages are devoted to "the Scripture and Tradition." The direct command by Jesus "to cure diseases . . . to proclaim the kingdom of God and to heal" comes in Luke 9:1-2, which concerns the mission of the Twelve. Healing seems to have a relatively minor place in the mission of the Seventy (Luke 10:9; cf. 10:1-12). On their return the Seventy did report, "The demons submit to us," but Jesus replied, "Do not rejoice at this . . . but rejoice that your names are written in heaven" (10:17-20). There is no doubt that apostolic healings continue in Acts. The main thrust of the early chapters, however, concerns the apostles' teaching, fellowship, breaking of bread, and prayer (Acts 2:42), and the outreach and expansion of the church. Nevertheless, we have to decide what is included in "wonders and signs" (2:43). Peter and John healed a lame man (3:2-10). Aeneas, who was paralyzed and bedridden, was healed (9:32-35), and Tabitha was resuscitated (9:36-42).

Acts 19:12 tells the surprising tale of the healing effect of "handkerchiefs or aprons that had touched his [Paul's] skin." But clearly James, Stephen, and, later, Paul were not delivered from death, illness, or martyrdom. In 2 Cor. 12:7-10 Paul suffered from "a thorn . . . in the flesh, a messenger of Satan to torment me." Paul prayed three times for its removal, but God chose *not* to remove it, with the words "My grace is sufficient for you" (12:9). Paul then expressed himself "content with weaknesses" (12:10).

A classic passage on "gifts of healing" comes in 1 Cor. 12:9, where Paul speaks of *kinds of healing*. He uses the plural *charismata iamatōn*, which is best explained as a *generic* plural. The greatest difficulty attaching to this verse is the temptation to distinguish natural and "supernatural" healing. As W. Hollenweger laments, this contrast would impose on Paul a *modern* Cartesian dualism, which he simply would not have recognized. This particular dualism followed especially in the wake of Deism. We should exclude *neither* of these alleged components. Paul believed in the "Almighty-ness" or omnipotence of God to heal, whether by natural or medical means or by means that transcend obvious known cause-and-effect. After the close of the NT, the early apologist Justin refers to people who "perform exorcisms in the name of Jesus Christ . . . who have healed and do heal those who could not be cured . . . by others or by incantations and drugs" (*Second Apology* 6). *Kinds* of healing do not appear in the gifts enumerated in Rom. 12:3-8 and Eph. 4:11, although the term occurs again in 1 Cor. 12:28, 30. The specific verb *iaomai* occurs nineteen times in the Gospels (twelve in Luke), four times in Acts, once each in Hebrews, James, and 1 Peter, but never in Paul. *Therapeuō* occurs forty times in the Gospels, but again, never in Paul. Following Justin, Tertullian and Cyril connect the gift of healing with Jesus Christ's anointing by the Holy Spirit, especially the sevenfold gifts of Isa. 11:1-3. (*See* **Holy Spirit**.)

In the modern era the gift of healing has again become controversial. Today Francis McNutt, for example, claims, "It is always God's normal will to heal" (*Healing* [Notre Dame, Ind.: Ave Maria; New York: Bantam Books, 1972] and *The Power to Heal* [Notre Dame, Ind.: Ave Maria, 1972]). But by contrast, Peter Mullen gives eleven reasons why God does *not always* heal (in D. Martin and P. Mullen, eds., *Strange Gifts?* [Oxford: Blackwell, 1984]). However, some agreements have been reached. K. McDonnell, editor of *Presence, Power, Praise*, 3 vols. (Collegeville, Minn.: Liturgical Press, 1980), includes in the book the Anglican joint-report "Gospel and Spirit: A Joint Statement." On "healing," this report asserts: "All true wholeness, health, and healing, come from God. We do not therefore regard 'divine healing' as being always miraculous. We also look forward to the resurrection knowing that only then shall we be finally and fully free from sickness, weakness, pain and mortality (cf. 1 Cor. 15:44)." The report continues, "At the same time we welcome the recovery by the Church of a concern for healing . . . but also wish to express caution against giving wrong impressions" (305). This "caution" may relate to guilt, if expectations are not fulfilled; or to demands for faith if these are understood individualistically; or to a naïve equation between sickness and sin. The Pentecostal Donald Gee declares that "healing" does not preclude "medical healing" (*Spiritual Gifts* [Springfield, Mo.: Gospel, 1963]). The Pietist J. A. Bengel also asserted that "healing" does not preclude "natural remedies" (*Gnomon*, 652). Concerning God's will, we conclude that the key question is not *whether* God heals, but *how* and *when*, and in *what circumstances*.

Reading: Church Report, *A Time to Heal* (London: Church House Publishing, 2000); C. S. Keener, *Miracles*, 2 vols. (Grand Rapids: Baker Academic, 2011); K. McDonnell, ed., *Presence, Power, and Praise*, 3 vols. (Collegeville, Minn.: Liturgical Press, 1980); A. C. Thiselton, *First Epistle to the Corinthians* (Grand Rapids: Eerdmans, 2000), 935-89; A. C. Thiselton, *The Holy Spirit* (Grand Rapids: Eerdmans, 2013); M. Turner, *The Holy Spirit and Spiritual Gifts Then and Now* (Carlisle: Paternoster, 1996).

Heart

Biblical witnesses use the Hebrew *lebh* and Greek *kardia* to denote depth of feeling, firmness of will, subconscious depths, or the center or core of the whole human personality. John Calvin uses "heart" especially in the last sense; hence he urges that it represents the human organ where the Holy Spirit is characteristically at work (Rom. 5:5: "God's love has been poured into our hearts through the Holy Spirit that has been given to us"). But Calvin anticipates such modern scholars as Rudolf Bultmann and Gerd Theissen by underlining the hidden depths of which a person may not even be aware: "The human heart has so many recesses for vanity, so many lurking places for falsehood, is so shrouded by fraud and hypocrisy, that it often deceives itself" (*Institutes* 3.2.10; Beveridge, 1:478).

In the OT, Judaism, and the NT alike, "heart" may sometimes call attention to the human capacity to experience strong *feeling* or *emotion*. Prov. 14:30 commends "a tranquil heart" (NRSV, "mind"), whereas passion "makes the bones rot." The heart can "envy sinners" (Prov. 23:17); but it can also "exult" or "feel glad" (1 Sam. 2:1; Ps. 4:7); can "tremble" with anxiety or fear (1 Sam. 4:13); or can be "sad" (1 Sam. 1:8) or courageous; cf. H. W. Wolff, *Anthropology of the Old Testament* (London: SCM, 1974), 44-45. God created humans with a heart so that they could have feelings. When Ezekiel conveys God's promise of "a heart of flesh" (Ezek. 36:26), he means tenderness and sensitivity. But in addition to the emotional states of joy, sorrow, anxiety, fear, and courage, the term "heart" can refer to *the will*. Deut. 2:30 refers to the "defiant" (NRSV) or "obstinate heart"; Deut. 15:7 and Ps. 95:8 speak of hardening one's heart. Yet many passages refer to intellectual assessment and decision. Deut. 7:7 refers to reflection; Exod. 7:23 to attention; Deut. 4:9 to memory; 1 Kings 3:9 to understanding; and Exod. 28:3 to technical skill. H. Wheeler Robinson refers to five categories, which include the physical activity, the inner life, emotions, intellectual activity, and volition or purpose (*The Christian Doctrine of Man* [Edinburgh: T. & T. Clark, 1911], 22-26; confirmed by Wolff, 40-44).

Nevertheless, the use of "heart" to convey "the core of one's being" can be found in such passages as Deut. 6:5, "You shall love the LORD your God with all your heart"; 1 Sam. 16:7, "They look on the outward appearance, but the LORD looks on the heart"; Gen. 20:5, "the integrity of my heart"; and Deut. 30:2, "with all your heart." The NT takes up their meaning: "Blessed are the pure in heart" (Matt. 5:8); "I am gentle and humble in heart" (Matt. 11:29); "This people honors me with their lips, / but their hearts are far from me" (Mark 7:6); "Where your treasure is, there your heart will also be" (Luke 12:34); "Do not let your hearts be troubled" (John 14:1); "Your heart is not right before God" (Acts 8:21); "God's love has been poured into our hearts" (Rom. 5:5); "God, who searches the heart" (Rom. 8:27); and, "If you ... believe in your heart" (Rom. 10:9). Many of these dimensions of meaning in the OT can be rendered by different Greek words, especially in the LXX: *nous*, "mind"; *splanchna*, "affections, compassion"; *thelēma*, "will"; *boulai*, "strivings"; or even with the sense of "conscience."

Nevertheless, together "the core of one's being," the most significant theological aspect, is roughly equivalent to the use of the word "subconscious" or "unconscious." R. Bultmann, following Calvin, argues that heart or will "need not penetrate into the field of consciousness at all, but may designate the hidden tendency of the self" (*Theology of the New Testament*, vol. 1 [London: SCM, 1952], 223). As in 1 Sam. 16:7, it stands in contrast to outward appearance. No one has done more to shed light on this than Gerd Theissen (*Psychological Aspects of Pauline Theology* [Edinburgh: T. & T. Clark, 1987]). In Rom. 2:12-16 the secrets of the heart are revealed to God; in 1 Cor. 14:20-25 Paul speaks of preaching or disclosing the secrets of the heart. Theissen writes, "Paul is familiar with the idea of unconscious influences within human beings" (57). He especially examines 1 Cor. 4:1-5, Rom. 2:16, and 1 Cor. 14:20-25 (59-80). In 1 Cor. 4:1-5 Paul is unaware of accusations of conscience against himself, "but I am not thereby acquitted." The eschatological light will reveal the true state of affairs. Rom. 2:16 speaks of "the secret thoughts of all." In 1 Cor. 14:20-25 prophecy (or preaching) can expose what is hidden from a person and from others. The key phrase is "the secrets of the heart" (*krupta tēs kardias*, 78). Hans Küng admits that in Sigmund Freud preconscious drives are viewed entirely as mechanistic forces of nature in a positivist world. But he and Paul Ricoeur give Freud credit for showing how unconscious forces need to be reckoned with as disturbing and powerful factors behind human action. In modern preaching many of these complexities need to be explained prior to using the term "heart" as it is understood in popular currency.

Reading: R. Jewett, *Paul's Anthropological Terms* (Leiden: Brill, 1971), 305-35; G. Theissen, *Psychological Aspects of Pauline Theology* (Edinburgh: T. & T. Clark, 1987); H. W. Wolff, *Anthropology of the Old Testament* (London: SCM, 1974) 40-44.

Heaven

Heaven (Heb. *shāmayîm*; Gk. *ouranos*) has two distinct but related meanings in the OT. It may mean "the sky" in certain contexts. But it also denotes the dwelling place of God and the angels. Sometimes the two meanings overlap, as when

Elijah ascended "upwards" to the sky, but also into the more immediate presence of God (2 Kings 2:1). Both the plural and the phrase "heaven of heavens" denote not numerical multiplicity, but qualitative or intensive description. Normally in the OT the dead depart from life to enter Sheol. Ryder Smith has described this as a "bloodless and juiceless" kind of existence, in no way like the NT concept of heaven. Heaven emphatically remains God's creation. This applies not only to the sky, firmament, or "dome" (NRSV; Heb. *rāqîaʿ*) in Gen. 1:6-7, but also to the "heaven of heavens" (NRSV) in Neh. 9:6. But heaven should not be thought of as God's "location." At the dedication of the temple, Solomon exclaims, "Will God indeed dwell on the earth? Even heaven and the highest heaven cannot contain you, much less this house that I have built!" (1 Kings 8:27). Psalms brackets the creation of heaven with the creation of the heavenly host:

> By the word of the LORD the heavens were made,
> and all their host by the breath of his mouth. (Ps. 33:6)

God is exalted "above" the heavens (Ps. 57:11).

In the NT at the ascension Jesus Christ was "lifted up, and a cloud took him out of their sight . . . they were gazing upward toward heaven" (Acts 1:9-10). More explicitly in Luke 24:51, Jesus "was carried up into heaven." With regard to the destiny of Christians, Paul asserts that if our earthly "tent" is destroyed, "we have a building from God, a house not made with hands, eternal in the heavens" (2 Cor. 5:1). Yet Jesus may also speak of heaven symbolically, as in "treasure in heaven" (Luke 12:33; cf. Matt. 6:20). Jesus teaches his disciples to pray, "Our Father in heaven" (Matt. 6:9). Matthew regularly uses the term "kingdom of heaven" as a reverential replacement for kingdom of God in Mark and Luke. In Mark 1:11 the voice "from heaven" at the baptism of Jesus probably combines the two ideas of "above" and the realm of God. The most explicit book on this subject is the Revelation of John. The NRSV translates, "There in heaven a door stood open! And the first voice . . . said, 'Come up here.' . . . I was in the Spirit, and there in heaven stood a throne, with one seated on the throne" (Rev. 4:1-2). Some commentaries crudely call this a trapdoor in the sky. But the whole thrust of Revelation is to see the earthly struggles and sufferings of the church from the viewpoint and perspective of heaven. Heaven reveals the ceaseless worship of God (Rev. 4:8-11). Those who come through earthly trials will acknowledge the following in heaven:

> "Just and true are your ways,
> King of the nations!" (15:3)

To open the "scroll" is to see the plan and purposes of God for the world and church (5:1-8; 6:1-17; 7:1-8). The innumerable company of saints praise God for his ways, and "have come out of the great ordeal; they have washed their robes and made them white in the blood of the Lamb" (7:14).

The seer who wrote this book knew full well that he frequently used symbolic language. For language about superearthly or heavenly realities, how could he do anything else? As G. Beasley-Murray comments, did he imagine that the heavenly horsemen (6:2-8) returned their horses to be replenished in heavenly stables? The absolute center of the stage is God: God's sovereignty over history; God's purpose for the church and the world; and God and the once-crucified Christ, sending out the power of the Holy Spirit. Hence the old aphorism is fully justified: "It is not in heaven that we find God, but in God that we find heaven." The description of the New Jerusalem draws on symbols from Ezekiel and elsewhere in the OT. Symbols portray what Robert Gundry calls "the sheer happiness" of the city. God "will wipe every tear from their eyes"; "crying and pain will be no more" (21:4). Those who "conquer" (21:7) are those who have been faithful, as Beale asserts. The city is no literal city, for it measures 12,000 stades, or 1,500 miles, in each direction, including vertically. God's glory is symbolized as a rare jewel.

The experience of heaven, however, will be grounded in the presence and power of God as Trinity. The heavenly hosts and the church are portrayed as worshiping the "Lamb standing as if it had been slaughtered" (5:6), or "the Lamb that was slaughtered" (5:12); and the martyrs "have washed their robes... in the blood of the Lamb" (7:14). Calvary and the cross may be in the past, but their memory and significance abide through eternity. Further, resurrection will have taken place in the power of the Holy Spirit (Rom. 8:11), and the redeemed in heaven will enjoy a mode of existence that is sustained by the Holy Spirit (1 Cor. 15:44). Hence, like the Spirit himself, it will be ongoing, ever-fresh, and in no way stagnant. (*See also* **Glory; Metaphor; Resurrection of the Dead; Symbol.**)

Reading: Paula Gooder, *Heaven* (London: SPCK, 2011); A. C. Thiselton, *Life after Death* (Grand Rapids: Eerdmans, 2012), 185-215; also called *The Last Things* (London: SPCK, 2012).

Hegel, Georg Wilhelm Friedrich

Georg Wilhelm Friedrich Hegel (1770-1831) was probably the most creative mind among all philosophers of the nineteenth century. He believed that only the whole is real, and that the real is the rational. He first introduced the concept of "historical" reason, which was epoch-making for theologians. He first lectured at the University of Jena, where Fichte was professor, and shared Fichte's rejection of the subjectivism of Romanticism. He collaborated closely with Friedrich Schelling, seeking an increasingly objective idealism. He parted from Schelling when Napoleon sacked Jena. In 1807 he published his *Phenomenology of Mind (Phänomenologie des Geistes)*. In 1818 he succeeded Fichte as professor of philosophy at the newly founded University of Berlin, where he worked with Schleiermacher as his great rival until his death. His politics were shaped by a philosophy of freedom. In 1821 he published his *Philosophy of the Right* (also translated *Philosophy of Law*), anticipating Marx by postulating successive eras of history representing Oriental despotism, Greek oligarchy, post-Reformation capitalism, and post-Revolution egalitarianism. From 1818 to 1831 he exercised massive political influence in Berlin.

Hegel worked for a sophisticated and complex recovery of rationality through a "historical" and dialectical redefinition of reason. In contrast to the ultimacy of the categorical moral imperative in Kant, the absolute moral principle in Fichte, and consciousness in the later Schelling, Hegel argued that only the rational is real and ultimate, provided that this reason could *look back* from the standpoint of the completed process. This particular theme has been expounded in theology by W. Pannenberg. Reality merely *appears* not to be rational because we normally tend to view it as disparate pieces. A rational, critical concept *(Begriff)* is discovered and used by differentiation. This is in marked contrast to the later Schelling, of whom Hegel remarked that in Schelling's night "all cows are black," and hence cannot be differentiated. Difference is part of negation, which is inevitable in conflict. The conflict, however, may belong to a specific time; resolution may follow, and create a synthesis from the dialectic. The synthesis "sublates" or subsumes the disparate parts into a new whole, and thus the whole historical process moves forward and advances. Wherever Schelling had sought for the "whole" as a unity, Hegel believed that it could not be reached except by an earlier stage of differentiation, or conceptual distinctive.

This historical principle undoubtedly has value, and offers a useful explanatory hypothesis of much in history and human life. Perhaps most of all, "historical reason," as he termed his distinctive method, leads on to an appreciation of historicality, or conditioning by the place of the self in history. It leaves the problem, however, of whether *all* conflicting situations or ideas can operate in this way. Hegel recognized this by distinguishing between the negation of cancellation, the absolute "not" of contradiction, and the negation of dialectic, which can lead to the higher stage. In his *Encyclopaedia of Philosophical Sciences* (1817) he distinguished between the science of logic and the philosophy of Spirit. He also attempted to formulate his doctrine of the Holy Trinity in these terms. The triune God is absolute or "complete." But God as Absolute Being is somehow "negated" when Jesus Christ takes flesh and dies. The "pieces" or "fragments" in midprocess do not make rational sense; for the "immortal" dies. "Religion" cannot conceptualize this, but works with "representations" *(Vorstellungen)* rather than concepts. Indeed, in Hegel's view Roman Catholicism is self-contradictory because it stops with a crucifix. But the work of Christ leads on to the era of the Holy Spirit, which "sublates" this work into a "higher" whole. The finished process is therefore coherent and wholly rational.

Hegel was not the first to see the work of Christ as "the death of Death," and his scheme has some appeal. But whether his doctrine of the Trinity can be arrived at independently of his philosophy of history may be doubted. Many theologians have argued this. But his perspective has revolutionary consequences. His influence can be seen on Heidegger, Kierkegaard, Gadamer, Moltmann, Pannenberg, and many others. He was primarily a philosopher, but his work on historical reason introduced a new era in theology, at least as decisively as did his rival Schleiermacher. (*See also* **Historicality; Pannenberg, Wolfhart; Reason.**)

Reading: P. C. Hodgson, *Hegel and Christian Theology* (Oxford: OUP, 2008); P. C. Hodgson, *Shapes of Freedom* (Oxford: OUP, 2012); P. C. Hodgson, ed., *G. W. F. Hegel: Theologian of the Spirit* (Minneapolis: Fortress, 1997); H. Küng, *The Incarnation of God* (Edinburgh: T. & T. Clark, 1987); T. P. Pinkard, *Hegel's Dialectic* (Philadelphia: Temple University Press, 1985); R. D. Williams, *Wrestling with Angels* (London: SCM, 2007).

Heidegger, Martin

Martin Heidegger (1889-1976) dominated German philosophy almost completely from about 1923 to the late 1960s, when Pannenberg and others began to break the mold of his thought. He did not make a comparable impact on the English-speaking world, where his philosophy remains, at best, highly controversial. He was professor of philosophy at Freiburg and Marburg, and wrote his most famous work *Being and Time* in 1927 (Eng. Oxford: Blackwell, 1962). From 1923 he shared seminars with Bultmann, Gadamer, and Jonas, all of whom he profoundly influenced. He is also one of the half-dozen major thinkers who contributed fundamentally to hermeneutics.

Although he disowned the specific term "existentialist," Heidegger is widely regarded as the founder of existentialist hermeneutics. He prefers to speak of *Dasein,* "being there," or of human beings as "thrown" into a concrete existential situation. This becomes his starting point in exploring human existence. In other words, humankind is radically conditioned by its *"world"* within human *history.* Heidegger called the view that a person is radically conditioned by his place in history *Geschichtlichkeit,* which is translated "historicity," or sometimes "historicality." *Time,* Heidegger argued, is the horizon that makes it possible to understand the meaning of Being. *"Time needs to be explicated primordially as the horizon for the understanding of Being, and in terms of temporality (Zeitlichkeit) as the Being of Dasein, which understands Being"* (*Being and Time,* 39). We often quote Heidegger's own phrases, often with the German, because his use of technical (some would say "idiosyncratic") terminology is notorious.

Humankind, Heidegger argues, is not only "thrown" into a given situation, but also sees people and objects around it in existential or practical terms. Thus, unlike most English philosophers, he defines a hammer, for example, not as a piece of wood and metal, but as something with which to drive in nails. A hammer does not consist of its "properties," which are "present at hand" *(vorhanden),* but, for Heidegger, in terms of possibilities for human action. Rather than being present to hand, phenomena are "ready to hand" *(zuhanden).* All conceptualizing takes place in terms of the world within which we view it. Heidegger and Bultmann view this as a new *conceptuality (Begrifflichkeit).* Thus in his hermeneutics Bultmann regards human beings as modes of being, not as a collection of properties. This is totally different from the world of Descartes or Locke.

This leads on to Heidegger's discussion of *understanding, interpretation,* and *language.* These do not constitute an independent subject, but flow from his understanding of "world" and *Dasein.* He suggests that our moods or states of mind *(Befindlichkeit)* convey a disclosure of what characterizes our existence. This is no mere subjective emotion. On this basis, understanding *(Verstehen)* is existential, and prior to rational cognition. Hermeneutics arises because Heidegger insists that the notion of projection *(Entwurf)* plays a vital part in the process. He argues, "Understanding projects Dasein's being upon its 'for the sake of which'" (185). The laws of logic alone cannot be adequate for hermeneutical inquiry. What we see is not simply an array of isolated objects. To *understand* them we need to regard them as integral with our particular surroundings and "world." In other words, they are grounded "in something we grasp in advance — in a 'fore-conception'" (*Vorgriff*; 191). Heidegger explains: "An interpretation is never a presuppositionless apprehending of something presented to us" (191-92). It belongs to the same category as preunderstanding or prior understanding *(Vorverständnis)* in Schleiermacher and Dilthey. Heidegger concludes, "Meaning is the 'upon-which' of a projection in terms of which something becomes intelligible as something" (193). Like Schleiermacher, he insists on "the hermeneutical circle."

Anticipating Gadamer, Heidegger considers the significance of assertions *(die Aussage).* He does not see these as the locus of truth. They point out rather than represent. In the English-speaking world Gilbert Ryle and others have especially criticized this approach. Assertions, Heidegger claims, are a *derivative* mode of interpretation. But the best way to understand this is perhaps to note that in hermeneutics there is a *historical* and *situational* dimension to interpretation. This is not always the case with abstract assertions.

The second half of *Being and Time* may not take us much further in the understanding of hermeneutics. It becomes more specifically philosophical and specialist in its use of terms. It concerns the "falling" of *Dasein,* Being as "care," and "anxiety." Heidegger considers that "idle talk" yields the possibility of understanding things *without previously appropriating them* as one's own (211). Idle talk inhibits any fresh angle of vision, because the anonymous crowd or the "they" have taken the place of a personal "me" and "mine." Heidegger also considers the role of death. He declares, "*Dasein* reaches its wholeness in death.... In *Dasein* there is undeniably a constant 'lack of totality,' which finds an end with death" (281 and 286). This expresses Heidegger's view that history always remains open. Finally, Heidegger introduces the notions of "call" and "conscience." This begins to anticipate his later thought, which many describe as a kind of mysticism, in which Being calls *(ruft) Dasein,* even against its wishes.

The later thought of Heidegger is different from the thought of *Being and Time.* Most describe it as a "turn" *(Kehre)* in his thought, although some regard it as a "reversal" of it. During this period Heidegger gives increasing emphasis to the role of poetry in revealing truth. Some, but not all, regard it as obscure and esoteric. The major work from this period is his book *On the Way to Language*

(1959), although the first systematic outline of Heidegger's later thought emerged in his book *An Introduction to Metaphysics*. This was first published in 1953, but represents lecture material produced in 1935. The beginning of his later thought is usually placed in about 1935.

Heidegger's conviction is that language and humankind have "fallen out of Being *(Sein)*." This fallenness from being, he believes, is bound up with the disintegration and fragmentation of life, which in turn reflect a tradition of technology and "leveling down." This is the time of "the darkening of the world, the flight of the gods, and the destruction of the earth." Men have been transformed into a mass, hating everything that is free and creative. Heidegger bemoans "the standardisation of man, the pre-eminence of the mediocre," and the rise of technology. In *Gelassenheit,* he draws a contrast between calculative thinking and meditative thinking (Eng. *Discourse on Thinking* [New York: Harper and Row, 1966], 46 and 53).

Calculative thinking belongs only to the natural sciences; meditative thinking brings us into relation with life and reality. The basic source of this, he urges, has been the dualism of Plato and Descartes, which reduced everything to the status of technological, calculative tools. Time, he writes, "has ceased to be anything other than velocity, instantaneousness, and simultaneity, and time as history has vanished from the lives of all peoples" (*Introduction to Metaphysics* [New Haven: Yale University Press, 1959], 38). Language now merely serves *information.* It can no longer produce anything genuinely creative. A chasm has been created between being and mere concepts. The theologian Gerhard Ebeling repeats much of this negative verdict in *Introduction to a Theological Theory of Language* (1973).

If there is any solution, according to Heidegger this will come from waiting for a language event *(Sprachereignis),* or a new coming to speech. This new coming to speech, he urges, must collect together fragmented reality and provide a "gathering call" (*On the Way to Language,* 108). In theology, Fuchs and Ebeling make much of this in their "New Hermeneutic." Meanwhile, Heidegger advocates renunciation and waiting. Language, he insists, is "the House of Being." Humankind must wait in patience for the revelation of Being, "if necessary for a whole lifetime." Hans Jonas has criticized this attitude of passivity. Humankind, he argues, shapes reality by specific actions. Heidegger prefers to rely on meditative thinking and poetry, especially that of Hölderlin.

Reading: Martin Heidegger, *Being and Time* (Oxford: Blackwell, 1962); Martin Heidegger, *On the Way to Language* (New York: Harper and Row, 1971); Anthony C. Thiselton, *The Two Horizons* (Grand Rapids: Eerdmans, 1980), 143-204 and 327-42.

Heilsgeschichte

Heilsgeschichte is the German term usually translated "salvation history." It featured in the earlier work of J. C. K. von Hoffmann (1810-1877), but became especially prominent in O. Cullmann's *Christ and Time* (London: SCM, 1951). Cullmann traced a "redemptive line" (107) that provided a theological history of the acts of God, and demonstrated God's Lordship over the whole of time and history as a linear process. The coming of Christ constituted its climax. This brought the era of the Gentile mission, and will culminate in the arrival of the End. This is not to be confused with the empirical history of the historian. Cullmann expanded this approach in *Salvation in History* (Eng. 1967; Ger. *Heils als Geschichte* [1965]). Since around 1970, however, the term is also contrasted with "universal history," or the "universal correlative connections of human history . . . not in a ghetto of redemptive history" (Pannenberg, *BQT* 41). Pannenberg seeks a broader understanding of history-as-a-whole, of which God is also Lord.

Hell

Since the earliest days of the church, Christian thinkers have promoted three different views of this subject. It would be a mistake to view "everlasting punishment" as the "orthodox" view, since it has been one of three possible views, each prominent among the Church Fathers, and each arguable in principle from Scripture. Origen tended to hold a universalist view, but his view was condemned at the Council of Constantinople in 553. Irenaeus so strongly believed in the resurrection of the whole person, that he tended to hold what today is called conditional immortality, which in practical terms means extinction for unbelievers. Augustine declared that unbelievers would be "punished, together with the devil and all his angels. . . . This damnation is certain and eternal" (*Enchiridion* 23.92). Many have equated Augustine's view with "orthodoxy," perhaps because of its dominance in the medieval West.

(i) Irenaeus wrote, "How can man be immortal, who in his mortal nature did not obey his Maker?" (*Against Heresies* 4.39.2). Unbelievers are "deprived of God's gift, which is eternal life" (3.19.1). "God alone is without beginning and without end" (2.34.2). He concludes, "Life does not arise from us . . . but is bestowed according to the grace of God" (2.34.3). It is possible that he inherited this view from Polycarp. This approach has the advantage of avoiding an eternal dualism. If God alone is sovereign, will some eternally resist his will? A second advantage is the gift of the resurrection mode of existence by grace, not by natural right. Is not the rejection of the presence and love of God the rejection of life? Yet the NT speaks of the "hell of fire" *(geenna tou pyros)* in Matthew 5, and "gehenna" in Matt. 10:28 and Mark 9:45, 47; but it is ambiguous about the duration of this condition.

(ii) Gregory of Nyssa believed that *all* humanity was destined to enjoy immortality. With Origen, he believed in "the restoration of all things" (Acts 3:21 KJV). Today he would be a "universalist," though he rejected some of Origen's eccentricities. Life, he urged, can destroy death: "That which was dead can be restored to life" (*Catechism* 24). Resurrection, he declared, is "the restoration of the fallen . . . bringing back to Paradise him who was cast out from it" (*The Making of Man* 17.2). He cites Ps. 145:9, "The LORD is good to all." This harmonizes with biblical passages that speak of God's will that all will be saved. J. Moltmann among today's theologians regards the exclusion of some from final salvation as "a defect for the love of God, especially since his ultimate purpose is that 'God may be all in all'" (1 Cor. 15:28); that "all things will be united in Christ" (cf. Eph. 1:10); and that "all things will be reconciled to him" (cf. Col. 1:20; *In the End — in the Beginning* [London: SCM, 2004], 148; *Sun of Righteousness, Arise!* [London: SCM, 2010], 130).

(iii) Augustine of Hippo did believe in "unending physical torment" for the wicked, although it is difficult to see what "physical" may mean here. He wrote, "The soul . . . is tormented. In that final and everlasting punishment . . . the soul is said to die, because it does not live in connection with God. . . . This feeling is . . . painfully final" (*City of God* 13.2). In the *Enchiridion* he asserted, "Pain perpetually afflicts, but never destroys; corruption goes on endlessly. This state is called in Scripture 'the second death' (Rev. 2:11; 20:6, 14; *Enoch* 23:92)." In the Middle Ages this view was dominant. The Fourth Lateran Council (1215) spoke of "perpetual punishment," and this view was promoted by both Anselm and Thomas Aquinas. At the Reformation Calvin argued for the Augustinian-Thomist view, quoting the Gospel language about "wailing and gnashing of teeth" and "cast him into the exterior darkness" (cf. Matt. 13:42; 8:12; 22:13; Mark 9:43). Probably the harshest writer was Thomas Vincent, who wrote of the "fire and brimstone" that burn the wicked in hell "continually" (*Fire and Brimstone in Hell,* chap. 5).

What are we to make of these diverse views? David Powys was commissioned by the Evangelical Alliance to examine these views in *Hell: A Hard Look at a Hard Question* (Milton Keynes, U.K., and Waynesboro, Ga.: Paternoster, 1997). At minimum he set out the three traditions, to show that the Augustine-Thomas-Calvin one was not the only possible view. Even the report of the Evangelical Alliance in Britain reflected more than one approach. In theological scholarship the rise of liberalism shunted the issue off the scene. Although F. D. Maurice was supposedly a universalist, he simply held out the *hope* of universal salvation. This is perhaps Balthasar's and N. T. Wright's view. They reject the *two* very different views of "dogmatic universalism" and everlasting torment. Wright warns us not to be seduced by exotic medieval imagery, and notes that even several Catholic theologians, including Rahner and Ratzinger (Pope Benedict XVI), have modified the traditional doctrine (*Surprised by Hope* [London: SPCK, 2007], 177-98). Perhaps most powerful of all is Balthasar's position. He insists that there is a huge difference between *knowing* whether salvation will be universal and *hoping* that it might be. The question for him is not which view is right, or whether we should affirm or deny universal salvation. We must allow two or three traditions, and two or three series of biblical texts, to stand side by side, and perhaps express our *hope on* this basis (*Dare We Hope "That All Men Be Saved"? With a Short Discourse on Hell* [San Francisco: Ignatius, 1988]).

Reading: Hans Urs von Balthasar, *Dare We Hope "That All Men Be Saved"?* (San Francisco: Ignatius, 1988); J. Moltmann, *Sun of Righteousness, Arise!* (London: SCM, 2010); D. Powys, *Hell: A Hard Look at a Hard Question* (Milton Keynes, U.K., and Waynesboro, Ga.: Paternoster, 1997); A. C. Thiselton, *Life after Death* (Grand Rapids:

Eerdmans, 2012; also entitled *The Last Things* [London: SPCK, 2012], 145-59); N. T. Wright, *Surprised by Hope* (London: SPCK, 2007).

Hengel, Martin
The early years of Martin Hengel (1926-2009) were interrupted by war service, but in 1947 he entered Tübingen to study theology, and in 1949 moved to Heidelberg. In 1951 he became a Lutheran parish minister. However, in 1954 his father insisted that he join the family business, which led to what he later referred to as "ten wasted years." For a while he served as assistant to Otto Michel, and after another interval succeeded Michel in 1972 as professor of New Testament and early Judaism at Tübingen. He held this post until 1992. Most of his work is both constructive and conservative. Whereas many had looked to "Hellenistic Judaism" as a clearly defined entity, Hengel demonstrated that there was much overlapping and blurring between the Aramaic-speaking Judaism of Palestine and the Greek-speaking Judaism of parts of the Holy Land and the Diaspora. He argued that the origin of Mark as "interpreter of Peter" was entirely credible. His book on the cross became a classic. His most influential books include *Judaism and Hellenism* (1969; Eng., 2 vols., 1974 and 1981); *The Son of God* (1975; Eng. 1976); *Jews, Greeks, and Barbarians* (1976; Eng. 1980); *Acts and the History of Earliest Christianity* (1979; Eng. 1980); *Paul between Damascus and Antioch* (Eng. 1997); and *The Cross and the Son of God* (Eng. 1986). He was president of Studiorum Novi Testamenti Societas, and received honorary doctorates from St. Andrews, Durham, and Cambridge, as well as from Uppsala, Strasburg, and Dublin.

Henry, Carl F. H.
Carl F. H. Henry (1913-2003) was an American conservative evangelical thinker who served as the first editor in chief of *Christianity Today*. Many saw him as an informed voice for evangelicals in their challenge to liberalism. He entered Wheaton College in 1935, and obtained a D.Theol. degree from Northern Baptist Theological Seminary, and a Ph.D. from Boston University (1949). In 1947 he published *The Uneasy Conscience of Modern Fundamentalism,* and became one of the four cofounders of Fuller Theological Seminary. In 1978 he signed the Chicago Statement on Biblical Inerrancy. His major work was *God, Revelation, and Authority,* 6 vols. (Waco: Word, 1976-1983). He opposed the narrowest kind of fundamentalism but rallied evangelical forces against liberalism in theology. Henry, however, tended to stress the "propositional" character of the Bible and theology regardless of biblical genre, including poetry and imagery.

Herbert, George
George Herbert (1593-1633), poet and theologian, was a fellow of Trinity College, Cambridge, and public orator of the University. He was ordained a priest in 1630, and W. Laud persuaded him to accept the post of rector, at a parish near Salisbury. His most famous work is *A Priest to the Temple,* or *The Country Par-*

son (1652). His devotion to prayer, pastoral care, and duty cannot be overstated. Today some of his hymns are still sung. These include "Teach Me, My God and King" and "Let All the World in Every Corner Sing."

Hermeneutical Circle

The term is used to emphasize that understanding (Ger. *Verstehen, Verständnis*) is normally a process, even if within that process it may involve a sudden dawning. The process begins not with a blank mind (as B. Lonergan has rightly urged) but with what is called "preunderstanding" (from Ger. *Vorverständnis, vorverstehen*), although idiomatic English would render it "preliminary understanding." To borrow Bultmann's example, to understand a mathematical or musical text requires at least a rudimentary understanding of mathematics or music. In its basic form the concept can be found in the hermeneutics of F. Ast, but was worked out in detail by F. Schleiermacher. In a long process a "difficult" book or concept can become increasingly understood more adequately when the reader or interpreter seeks to understand it more than once, allowing it "to speak back" to improve the initial engagement each time the process is repeated; hence the term "circle." G. Osborne and others suggest the term "spiral" for this. The hermeneutical circle also applied to the relation between understanding "parts" of the text (e.g., pieces of vocabulary, grammar, or historical context) and its sense as a whole. Schleiermacher stressed this dual and reciprocal emphasis in the parts and the whole. After Schleiermacher the term became stock-in-trade for hermeneutics in Dilthey, Heidegger, Bultmann, Gadamer, Ricoeur, and virtually all serious writers on hermeneutics. Heidegger stresses that if we see the circle as a vicious one, we have misunderstood it even before seeking to use it.

Hermeneutics

Hermeneutics explores how we read, understand, and interpret texts, especially biblical texts, or those written in a different time, culture, or context from our own. It includes understanding, reading, and application. Hence it involves not only biblical studies and exegetical practice, but also philosophical questions about understanding; linguistic questions about meaning; questions in literary theory about reading, narrative, and genre; and sociological and historical questions about the situatedness of the self, including sometimes class, gender, and belief. It includes both theory and practice. In recent years it has become ever more crucial in theology, where so much is determined by how we read the Bible and even documents of history. Differences of interpretation appear to be more deeply questions of hermeneutics. It is also increasingly recognized that, as E. Betti suggested, hermeneutics can promote patience, tolerance, and respect for the other, as well as the understanding of a text and of other interpreters. On this ground Betti argued that hermeneutics should become an obligatory subject in universities.

In a more simplistic sense, hermeneutics in theory and practice occurred among the Greek Stoics and the Jewish rabbis of the ancient world. In the fifth and fourth centuries B.C., many Greeks viewed Homer and Hesiod as sacred texts, but recognized the anthropomorphic difficulty of stories of pagan deities and their love affairs. Hence Theagenes of Rhegium and Hecataeus found that they could defend the text as sacred if they allegorized stories of the deities as forces of nature. Hephaestus was said to represent fire; Poseidon represented water; Hera represented air; and so on. Metrodorus of Lampsacus used allegory to denote parts of the body. Zeno, founder of the Stoic school, read Hesiod in this way, and most Stoics adopted this method. Not all Greeks, however, did this. Plato expressed serious reservations about it. By the first century it had become a matter of serious debate. Philo and many in Greek-speaking Judaism followed the Stoic method. But the Jewish rabbis tended to follow stricter rules. Rabbi Hillel formulated seven "rules" *(middōth)* of interpretation. These arose partly from questions about specific situations in life, for example, the respective priority of the Passover or the Sabbath. The first five "rules" remain largely matters of deductive logic, for example, that the greater includes the less. The sixth, however, concerns support from other passages in Scripture, and in effect the seventh recognizes the importance of context. Rabbi Ishmael Ben Elisha, Hillel's pupil, expanded these seven into thirteen, and "rules" became more numerous. Rabbi Akiba interpreted the Song of Songs allegorically. Some Jewish apocalyptic literature applied references to "oppressors" directly to the Romans (cf. *Psalms of Solomon,* c. 50-40 B.C.).

The place of allegorical interpretation in the NT is still debated. Most believe that Paul used allegory in Galatians, but Otto Michel and others prefer to speak of typology, which involves historical parallels, rather than a simple parallel between ideas (*see* **Typology**). J. W. Aageson speaks of "correspondence." (*See* **Allegory, Allegorical Interpretation**; on Judaism and the NT, see A. C. Thiselton, *Hermeneutics* [Grand Rapids: Eerdmans, 2009], 60-94.) From the second century onward, however, allegory became more widely used, especially among the Alexandrian Church Fathers, Clement of Alexandria, Origen, and their successors. It was less widespread among the fathers of the Antioch School, including John Chrysostom, but it is simplistic to categorize the differences between Alexandrian and Antiochene exegesis entirely in this way. Augustine and Gregory of Rome formed a bridge to the medieval period, but the next hermeneutical debate in effect emerged at the Reformation.

In his early thought, Luther used allegorical interpretation. But he came to see that it allowed the teaching of the church to dominate and to shape the message of Scriptures. In his well-known "Tower Experience" (*see* **Luther, Martin**), he came to understand Rom. 1:16-17 and "the righteousness of God" in a new way, which differed from normal church teaching. Whereas Erasmus had argued that the Bible was too complex to allow readily for action, Luther insisted that it was always clear enough to determine practical action at the next stage. He wrote many commentaries, however, which suggests that the Bible needs careful interpretation in the light of the meaning of words and sentences and their historical context. His commentaries and lectures included Psalms, Romans, Galatians, and many other books. Luther's commentary on Galatians often applies the text to the pope and to contemporary situations. His respect for the power of Scripture was immense. He said of one of his conflicts with Roman opposition: "I did nothing.... The Word did it all." Interpretation overlaps with translation, and one of Luther's many legacies was the German Bible, in the language of the people. William Tyndale applied many of Luther's insights to the English church. He saw the Bible as conveying God's promise, and as performing various *actions* of commission, forgiveness, liberation, and so on. Nowadays these are called speech acts. Most important of all, he produced the English translation that largely lies behind the KJV/AV (*see* **Tyndale, William**).

John Calvin was in many ways more meticulous than Luther. He wrote commentaries on virtually all the books of the OT and NT, including Romans, in which he acknowledged the exegesis of Melanchthon and Bucer. He saw the chief virtue of the commentator as "lucid brevity," which expounds the mind of the biblical writer in its proper context. As such, he has rightly been called "the father of modern commentators." He compared the Bible with the use of glasses with which to see more clearly, and strongly argued against the use of allegory. An overuse of allegory, he urged, was folly, and belittled God's acts in history. Apart from the relatively major hermeneutical insights from Chladenius on "point of view," and from Bengel on solid exegetical practice, the next major advance in hermeneutics came with Ast and Schleiermacher. The work of the English Deists had a negative effect on the status and authority of the Bible, and J. S. Semler, in effect, was the founder of biblical criticism (*see* **Biblical Criticism**).

F. D. E. Schleiermacher provided the first great turning point that introduced hermeneutics as a modern discipline. Before his work, hermeneutics was often described as "the science of interpretation." He defined it not as "rules" but as "the art of understanding" (*Hermeneutics* [Missoula, Mont.: Scholars Press, 1977], 113 and 35-79). As well as being influenced by Pietism, the Enlightenment, and Kant, Schleiermacher also fell under the influence of Romanticism. He stressed the "divinatory" pole *(divinatorisch)* of understanding a text, which he described as "the feminine" or suprarational. This dimension of understanding could perceive a whole, sometimes intuitively. He did not, however, dismiss the rational: the comparative reflection and divinatory perception were entirely complementary, even if the "feminine" was perhaps more important. He illustrated this in his book *The Celebration of Christmas,* in which after Christmas Communion the men discussed conceptual difficulties of the incarnation while the women sang hymns to Jesus. Their understanding seemed more complete to him.

From Kant Schleiermacher grasped the importance of transcendental questions. In parallel with Kant, he asked, how is interpretation or understanding *possible?* Too often, he observed, interpretation or hermeneutics had become a merely retrospective exercise in which, where there is disagreement, each side appeals to hermeneutics to justify an *already arrived at* interpretation. This turns it into an instrumental or service discipline. We should ask about the *possibility* of understanding a text with an open mind. But this does *not* mean with an *empty* mind. We all approach texts with a reservoir of *preliminary* understanding *(Vorverständnis)*. We come with assumptions about the meaning of words, the force of grammar, the purpose of the author, and so on. We should *not* suppress or dismiss these. We should allow them, however, to become corrected and reshaped in the light of the text itself. This could mean traveling between the preliminary understanding and the more mature one several times. Schleiermacher called this the hermeneutical circle. F. Ast had already formulated a version of this. But Schleiermacher's version was so definitive that it became central for Dilthey, Heidegger, Bultmann, Gadamer, Ricoeur, and for modern hermeneutics. All these explain that this is more than a circle; G. Osborne calls it a hermeneutical spiral. The hermeneutical circle also means that understanding the *parts* can lead to understanding the *whole* (by the comparative method); and the *whole* (by divinatory method) can shed light on the *parts*. The two are interdependent and mutually corrective.

Schleiermacher established hermeneutics as an independent discipline in its own right. It enables one "to step out of one's own frame of view" (*Hermeneutics*, 42). We must understand "how a way of speaking originated" (47); "the content of the text and its range of effects" (151); and in the NT, how to do justice "to the rootedness of the text" in history, and "the author's way of thinking" (207). In this sense, interpretation can be "the reverse of composition" (69). We need to ask what set this stretch of language or speech going. Schleiermacher valued his regular preaching at Trinity Church, Berlin, no less than his professorship in the University of Berlin. The purpose of hermeneutics was to set the text alight, and to communicate it to the congregation with fire, freshness, imagination, understanding, and accuracy. He explains further: "The divinatory method seeks to gain an immediate comprehension of the author. . . . The comparative method proceeds by subsuming the author under a general type" (150). He adds: "If we follow only the divinatory method, we become 'nebulists'; if we follow only the comparative, we risk pedantry" (205). Hermeneutics may share in the provisional and fallible nature of all human knowledge. But Schleiermacher shows how it is also capable of growth, expansion, and multidisciplinary inquiry. Human work and thought, he stresses, do not exclude the work of the Holy Spirit.

Wilhelm Dilthey became in effect Schleiermacher's successor. He was professor at Basel and Berlin. He aimed to make hermeneutics the foundation of the "human sciences" *(Geisteswissenschaften)*, that is, the humanities, arts, letters, and social sciences. His complete writings take up twenty-six volumes in German. He greatly admired Schleiermacher but sought to add two further components to his work. First, following Hegel, he believed in the "historicity" *(Geschichtlichkeit)* of all human life and thought in time and place. The interpreter, the author, and the text are radically conditioned by how they are situated in history. Second, he aimed to extend hermeneutics from texts to human life *(Leben)*, to society and to institutions. His central theme was *lived experience (Erlebnis)*. He rejected positivism.

When he compared the work of Locke, Berkeley, Hume, and even Kant, he argued that "in the veins of the knowing subject, *no real blood flows*" (*Gesammelte Schriften,* vol. 5 [Leipzig: Teubner, 1924]). He also postulated a "connectedness" *(Zusammenhang)* behind social diversity and individual experience that bound together disparate individuals. This found expression in such shared phenomena as symbols. Subjective experience learns more from history and life than from introspection. The ultimate aim in hermeneutics is "to relive" *(nacherleben)* the other's life experience *(Leben, Erlebnis)* by stepping out of his shoes and exercising "sympathy" *(Hineinversetzen)* or "transposition" (*Selected Writings* [Cambridge: CUP, 1976], 226-27). This brings us back to the core of Schleiermacher's concerns, but with the addition of "historicality" and social life and institutions.

It is not surprising that Heidegger, Bultmann, and Gadamer draw on Dilthey. What *is* surprising is the relatively minimal concern for hermeneutics and Dilthey in sociology. To be sure, he features in Z. Bauman, *Hermeneutics and Social Science* (London: Hutchinson, 1978), and to some extent in P. Berger, J. Schutz, and P. Winch. He has made a small impact on sociology of knowledge. But some also lament the use of clinical and therapeutic models in pastoral psychology, when Dilthey's hermeneutics may have taken them much further. While Dilthey was writing, Bishop George Ridding of Southwell, England, was compiling a pastoral litany of prayer that suggested we should empathize with others but not measure their feelings entirely by our own.

Martin Heidegger is dominated by the concept of historicity. Hence he cannot begin his work *Being and Time* by speaking of "man" or "human beings" in the abstract, but by speaking of *Dasein,* "being-there." *Dasein* does not have a viewpoint outside history. He declares, "The phenomenology of *Dasein* is a hermeneutic" (*Being and Time* [London: SCM, 1962]). "An interpretation *(Auslegung)* is never a presuppositionless apprehending of something presented to us" (*eines Vorgegebenen,* 191-92). The "world" of *Dasein* is determined, shaped, and bounded by the horizons of practical concerns of the "I." Heidegger states, "The essence of *Dasein* lies in its existence *(Existenz)*" (67). "Things" may be merely present-at-hand *(vorhanden),* which is a *derived or secondary* mode of conceptualizing. On the other hand, *Dasein* apprehends what is "ready-to-hand" *(zuhanden),* that is, what plays a practical part in the world of the self, or in "my" world. We understand things *as* that which has a practical significance in our world. Thus Heidegger appropriates preliminary understanding *(Vorverständnis)* and the hermeneutical circle as Schleiermacher and especially Dilthey formulated it. He writes: "*If we see this circle as a vicious one and look out for ways of avoiding it . . . the act of understanding has been misunderstood from the ground up. . . .* The 'circle' in understanding belongs to the structure of meaning" (194-95). This principle renders understanding a *process* conditioned by historicality.

What we seek to understand is necessarily also conditioned by its place in time and history, that is, by its historicality. Heidegger had originally hoped to arrive at some kind of anchorage in Being. But in his later work he sees human beings as "fallen out of Being" *(Introduction to Metaphysics* [New Haven: Yale University Press, 1959], 36-37; *Sein)*. He traces this to the negative effects of dualism from Plato onward. We cannot fully understand our lost relation to Being, but we can understand existentially what is related to our interests as historically finite and situated beings. Heidegger gives no more than proleptic hints of "the call of Being" in such later works as *On the Way to Language* (Ger. 1960; Eng. 1971) and *Discourse on Thinking* (Ger. 1959; Eng. 1966). E. Fuchs and G. Ebeling offer their theological hermeneutics of "language event" *(Sprachereignis)* with affinities to this thought. Meanwhile in *Being and Time*, Heidegger explores time and temporality. *Temporality (Zeitlichkeit)* is the transcendental *possibility* of time. Temporality is experienced in understanding in a subjective and practical way, or in Heidegger's language, "in an *existentiell* way" (357). This is bound up with the phenomena of "projection towards the future" and "authentic" existence. *Dasein* remains in each case my own *(die Jemeinigkeit)*. If language concerns only the theoretical and "objective," it becomes mere "idle talk" (213). Clearly, in Heidegger, *Dasein*'s understanding relates to authentic existence in history and in time.

Rudolf Bultmann utilizes the hermeneutics of Dilthey and Heidegger for his own purposes in theology. Following these authors, as well as Schleiermacher, he observes that preliminary understanding *(Vorverständnis)* is "not a prejudice, but a way of raising questions" (*Existence and Faith* [London: Collins, 1964], 346). The interpreter must not suppress his questions. In his essay "The Problem of Hermeneutics," he explicitly appeals to Dilthey's work more than a dozen times (*Essays Philosophical and Theological* [London: SCM, 1955], 234-61). For example, one cannot understand a text about mathematics, music, or love unless one knows at least *something* about mathematics, music, or love (*Faith and Understanding*, vol. 1 [London: SCM, 1969], 53). Bultmann asserts: "The 'most subjective' interpretation *(subjektiviste)* is . . . the 'most objective' *(objektiviste)*, that is, only those who are stirred by the questions of their own existence can hear the claim which the text makes" (*Essays*, 256). Here we can see clear echoes of both Dilthey and Heidegger. He concludes, "There cannot be any such thing as presuppositionless exegesis" (*Existence and Faith*, 344). Bultmann is explicit about this: "Heidegger's analysis of existence has become for me faithful for hermeneutics" (in C. W. Kegley, *The Theology of Rudolf Bultmann* [London: SCM, 1966], 275). J. Macquarrie argues that this dependency extends not to content, but to "ways of raising questions" and to seeking a better scheme of concepts. (For detailed proposals of Bultmann to demythologize the NT, *see* **Bultmann, Rudolf; Myth**.)

Hans-Georg Gadamer constitutes a second major turning point for hermeneutics, after Schleiermacher's. Both, in effect, provided a new agenda for a new concept of hermeneutics, in relation to their times. At Marburg University Gadamer read philosophy under the neo-Kantians P. Natorp and N. Hartmann, and then turned to art, history, and Plato. In 1923 he moved to Freiburg and met Heidegger. Their common interest in art, history, philosophy, and (later) hermeneutics established a ready bond. Historical situatedness and finitude, or "historicality," remained a central theme for both. Gadamer especially reacted against Enlightenment knowledge in the sciences and all fixed abstractions. He contrasted "problems" and "questions." J. Grondin comments: "Problems are not real questions from the genesis of their meaning" (*Hans-Georg Gadamer* [New York: Yale University Press, 2003], 84). "Problems" are *fixed* points "like stars in the sky" (Gadamer, *Truth and Method* [London: Sheed and Ward, 1989], 377). From 1923 to 1927 Heidegger collaborated with Natorp and Bultmann at Marburg, and with Gadamer, Arendt, and Jonas as younger scholars. Heidegger and Gadamer studied Dilthey and Schleiermacher in "the art of understanding," and especially Dilthey's preference for historicality over introspection as a source of knowledge. Increasingly Gadamer was convinced by Heidegger's rejection of objectification and generality. In the 1930s he worked on Plato, the poets, and Kierkegaard, and in 1936 he lectured on art and history. He later lectured on Hegel and Plato.

Part 1 of Gadamer's magisterial work on hermeneutics, *Truth and Method*, expounds the limits of "technical reason" and of the Enlightenment for all but the sciences. In place of the individualist appeal to inner consciousness by R. Descartes, he appeals to the communal and historical tradition found in G. Vico, and the *sensus communis* of ancient Rome. He argues that hermeneutics began "from the experience of art and historical tradition" (xxiii). He traces this method of history, tradition, and historicality through Droysen, Dilthey, and others, urging the importance of formation *(Bildung)* over technical knowledge or mere information. *Bildung* teaches one to be "open to the other" (17). The whole of part 1 constitutes a blistering attack on Enlightenment rationalism, much of which is repeated in part 2. By contrast, Gadamer writes: *"All encounter with the language of art is an encounter with an unfinished event and is itself part of this event"* (99).

Part 2 explicates this further, under the theme of "the ontology of the work of art." He offers the paradigmatic illustration of play: "Play fulfils its purpose only if the player loses himself in the play" (102); "It is the game that is played — it is irrelevant whether or not there is a subject who plays it" (103). He stresses: *"The primacy of the play over the consciousness of the player* is fundamentally acknowledged" (104). Players lose themselves in the aims of the game; the rules of the game determine how the players act and rank their priorities. They are determined by the "world" of the game: "Play draws him into its domain" (109). "Objectivity," if we can use this term, is found in the game, not in the consciousness of the player, as Descartes had imagined. Similarly, a festival, like a game, *exists* in its celebration. The center of gravity of the game or festival is also *present* in experience. Gadamer criticizes Schleiermacher for giving too much privilege to the origination of the text. Gadamer writes: "Historical interpretation in Schleiermacher's sense is too subjectivist. Question and answer receive minimal attention" (185). According to Gadamer, Schleiermacher is too influenced by the Romanticism of his time.

The central place given to "historicality" in Dilthey and in Gadamer owes much to Hegel and his work on historical reason. In part 2 Gadamer expresses his disillusion with Husserl's phenomenology, except for his coining of the useful term "horizon." Although human beings begin from a given situation and viewpoint, this given horizon may expand and change, and provide a fresh viewpoint. The term "lifeworld" is also useful in this respect. Gadamer agrees with Heidegger: "A person who 'understands' a text . . . has not only projected himself . . . toward a meaning. . . . [It] constitutes a new state of intellectual freedom" (260). He examines "prejudice" or prejudgment *(Vorurteile):* "The fundamental prejudice of the Enlightenment is the prejudice against prejudice (pre-judgement) itself; which denies tradition its power" (270). Our prejudices "constitute our being" (*Philosophical Hermeneutics* [Berkeley: University of California Press, 1976], 9), or "the historical reality of our being" (*Truth and Method,* 277). Hence he explores "the rehabilitation of authority and tradition" (277-85). Authority, he argues, "rests on . . . an act of reason itself, which, aware of its own limitations, trusts in the better insight of others" (279).

This leads Gadamer to consider *effective history,* or *the history of effects (Wirkungsgeschichte).* This entails asking appropriate questions. Toward the end of this second part he argues, "Understanding always involves . . . *applying* the text to be understood to the interpreter's present situation" (308). This applicatory dimension is not some "third thing" after explanation and understanding, but is integral to understanding. Legal hermeneutics offers a parallel. In legal hermeneutics, we "understand" when we see how a law embodied in a text is applied: application "is the central problem of hermeneutics" (315). This is one reason why hermeneutics transcends "science" and "rules." We build up an *expectation,* which may be reversed, fulfilled, or suppressed. This approach will later lead to reception theory, and be developed further by H. R. Jauss. Meanwhile Gadamer urges "*the priority of the question* in all knowledge and discourse" (363). He illustrates this point from Socrates, and from H. G. Collingwood. "Problems" become part of rhetoric; "questions" remain part of philosophy. Hermeneutics leads back to understanding the questions that arise (377).

In the third part of *Truth and Method* Gadamer turns to language, which he sees as "the medium" of understanding (384). Admittedly he speaks of the linguistics of E. Cassirer, but there is no engagement with contemporary "names" in linguistics from Ferdinand de Saussure onward, especially in the Anglo-American tradition. Gadamer has much outdated discussion of language as "names." The two serious advances are his approval of John's "the Word became flesh" (419, 429) and his agreement with Plato that language is far more than a second-class imitation of inner thought. He rightly implies that language and speech facilitate formation of character, and form concepts: "Concept-formation . . . occurs in language" (428). Language, he urges, is creative, not merely instrumental. Not surprisingly, the profound influences on hermeneutics have come mainly from parts 1 and 2; much less has come from part 3. The lasting legacy is "how questions arise"; the priority of the game over consciousness, the rehabilitation of tradition and the concept of historicality and the history of effects. This last theme has encouraged further work on reception theory. Finally, to risk a generalization, in biblical hermeneutics Gadamer's work leads to a reappraisal of the Enlightenment and an emphasis on *listening to texts* as the active "subject" to which the reader assumes the role of a more passive "object," although Gadamer aims to transcend the subject-object division. Gadamer writes, "Hermeneutics is above all a practice. . . . In it what one has to exercise above all is the ear" ("My Philosophical Journey," in *The Philosophy of Hans-Georg Gadamer,* ed. E. Hahn [Chicago and La Salle, Ill.: Open Court, 1997], 17).

Paul Ricoeur was a French Protestant, although primarily a philosopher. He was influenced by G. Marcel and M. Merleau-Ponty, but as a prisoner of war in Germany he studied Jaspers, Husserl, and Heidegger. Briefly after the war, J. Derrida became his assistant. In 1960 he published *Fallible Man,* on the problem of the will, finitude, and guilt, and also *The Symbolism of Evil.* The human will, subjectivity, and symbol remained lifelong concerns. The turning point to hermeneutics appears in his book *Freud and Philosophy* (Fr. 1965; Eng. New Haven: Yale University Press, 1970). From Freud he learned the special importance of interpretation. In one of the most important statements ever made on hermeneutics, he declared. "Hermeneutics seems to me to be animated by this double motivation: willingness to suspect, willingness to listen; vow of rigour, vow of obedience. In our time we have not finished doing away with *idols,* and have largely begun to listen to *symbols*" (*Freud and Philosophy,* 27). When patients recounted their dreams to him, Freud distinguished between the dream as dreamed (dream thoughts) and the dream as recounted. "Overdetermination" means both suspicion and care in interpreting *dreams as actually dreamed.* Reports could not be accepted at face value. The psychiatrist had to use interpretation based on hermeneutics.

Ricoeur does not accept the *materialist* aspects of Freud's language. Like H. Küng, however, he sees Freud as helpful on specific issues, including those of disguise and interpretation of layered texts. The self, Freud argues, seeks defensively to hide from itself forces and wishes of which it might feel ashamed, and often represses these into the unconscious. Conversely, thoughts or wishes arise from the unconscious that may invite disguise. Hence interpretation of desires and dreams must be undertaken with care. Often a concealed text lies beneath the reported text. Ricoeur is well aware of the narcissism of the self. His next book, *The Conflict of Interpretations* (Fr. 1969; Eng. 1974), examines a variety of topics. These include Descartes on consciousness, double-meaning expressions, structuralism, Freud, and faith. He examines the work of R. Barthes and A. J. Greimas. In 1975 Ricoeur called attention to the multilayered functions of language in *The Rule of Metaphor.* What symbols are to words, metaphors seem to be for sentences. This book is almost an encyclopedia of metaphor, exploring models, figures, and the theory of Max Black, as well as R. Jakobson and J. Ladrière.

From 1983 to 1985 Ricoeur wrote his magisterial *Time and Narrative* (3 vols. [Chicago and London: University of Chicago Press, 1984, 1985, 1988]). In volume 1 he compares Aristotle and Augustine on time. Augustine sees time as extension or "discordance"; Aristotle explores the logic of "plot," which brings coherence or "concordance." Ricoeur comments, "Through the experience of human time (memory, attention and hope) we came to understand the world . . . and our own present" (16). Aristotle's *Poetics* shows how this is brought together as "plot" *(mythos)* through the concordance or "organisation" of events (33). The third part of volume 1 explores "emplotment" through "temporality" *(Zeitlichkeit)* as a condition of understanding that gives to events their unity. Hermeneutics "makes present" this plot, and provides narrative understanding. This leads to a discussion of narrative and history.

Volume 2 considers change or "configuration" in fictional narrative, examining *mimēsis* in Plato, Aristotle, and Auerbach. Here he discusses Gérard Genette's view of order, duration, and frequency in narrative time. This sheds a flood of light on the arrangement and sequence of the four canonical Gospels. Flashbacks and *prolepses,* or flash-forwards, may be used, just as they are constantly in detective stories. Ricoeur examines Virginia Woolf, Thomas Mann, and Marcel Proust. Volume 3 addresses the relation between narrative time and chronological time. If the Gospels, for example, use narrative rather than chronological time, this casts "chronological" problems in a different light (my example). Ricoeur examines Heidegger's *Dasein* and historicality. Anticipation and expectation are more authentic than bare futurity, especially in terms of subjectivity. Like Dilthey, Ricoeur has a special interest in *lived* time. His notion of "world" comes close to Gadamer's. He explores tradition further.

Ricoeur's last genuinely magisterial work is *Oneself as Another* (Chicago: University of Chicago Press, 1992). Here he returns to his earlier concerns about the self, will, and identity. Descartes merely suggests *"what"* I am. Even P. F. Strawson does not, he claims, entirely escape this problem. J. L. Austin, F. Recanati, and J. R. Searle advance to a "speaking subject," but not far enough beyond this. E. Anscombe and Davidson go further, but still not far enough. H. L. A. Hart's "ascribing" provides only a partial solution. When he finally sets out positive criteria for personal identity and narrative identity, Ricoeur introduces *ethical* factors. He writes: "Keeping one's word in a promise is a basic sign of . . . continuity and stability . . . keeping one's word in faithfulness to the word that has been given" (123). Ricoeur has addressed one of the most long-standing problems of philosophy, that of the self and its continuity and identity. Locke and Hume had addressed this without success. Ricoeur argues that the good life is "with and for others in just institutions" (180). Where philosophers will speak of justice, Christians will speak of love (219). We come near to Gadamer's emphasis when Ricoeur similarly speaks of the place of practical wisdom. He concludes,

"Otherness is not added to selfhood . . . but belongs to the ontological constitution of selfhood" (317).

Finally, we must go behind this work to note that in hermeneutics Ricoeur values *both "explanation" (Erklärung) and "understanding" (Verstehen)*. This is quite different from Gadamer, who stakes everything on *understanding alone*. Gadamer is hostile to anything that smacks of "science" or rationalism. Ricoeur recognizes, as Schleiermacher did, that comparative explanation *(Erklärung)* performs necessary linguistic tasks, even if "explanation" may prevent distortion or illusion; "understanding" grasps the deeper meaning and appropriation of the text.

Schleiermacher, Dilthey, Heidegger, Bultmann, Gadamer, and Ricoeur remain the key thinkers behind contemporary hermeneutics. Nevertheless, other contributors deserve note. E. Betti offers a more carefully critical and controlled alternative to Gadamer. Many regard Gadamer as too relative and "open," offering no genuine *criticism* for understanding. So, too, does J. Habermas. J. L. Austin, J. R. Searle, and F. Recanati offer the additional hermeneutical tool of speech act theory, while D. D. Evans also produces many insights in his *Logic of Self-Involvement* (London: SCM, 1963). Fresh progress has also been made in reception theory, which owes its impetus to Gadamer and to H. R. Jauss. Furthermore, great strides have been made in literary theory, including G. Genette's theory of narrative, R. Alter on OT narratives, and many others. B. Lonergan has produced relevant material in the theory of knowledge, and Habermas and Z. Bauman on the interface between hermeneutics and social theory or sociology. Hermeneutics has become a demanding multidisciplinary subject area, which is now of growing importance for theology, for biblical studies, and for the church. (*See also* Allegory, Allegorical Interpretation; Biblical Criticism; Bultmann, Rudolf; Dilthey, Wilhelm; Exegesis; Gadamer, Hans-Georg; Heidegger, Martin; Hermeneutical Circle; Historicality; Historicism; Narrative; Reception Theory and Reception History; Ricouer, Paul; Schleiermacher, Friedrich D. E.; Speech Act Theory; Typology.)

Reading: H.-G. Gadamer, *Truth and Method* (London: Sheed and Ward, 1989); A. S. Jenson, *Theological Hermeneutics* (London: SCM, 2007); S. L. Mackenzie, ed., *The Oxford Encyclopedia of Biblical Interpretation* (Oxford: OUP, 2013); S. E. Porter and J. C. Robinson, *Hermeneutics* (Grand Rapids: Eerdmans, 2011); P. Ricoeur, *Freud and Philosophy* (New Haven: Yale University Press, 1970); P. Ricoeur, *Time and Narrative* (Chicago: University of Chicago Press, 1984-1988); A. C. Thiselton, *Hermeneutics* (Grand Rapids: Eerdmans, 2009); A. C. Thiselton, *New Horizons in Hermeneutics* (Grand Rapids: Zondervan, 1992, 2012).

Herrmann, Wilhelm

Wilhelm Herrmann (1846-1922) firmly allied himself with A. Ritschl, especially while teaching at Marburg. He was concerned for the possibility of faith in the modern scientific world, but argued more radically than Ritschl for the exclusion of metaphysics from theology. He believed that doctrine cannot bring religious certainty about God. The certainty of faith comes from a different source than either doctrine or historical evidence. Rather, the path of trust and truthfulness brings immediate communion with God. He argued that "a communion of the soul with the living God [comes] through the mediation of Christ" (*The Communion of the Christian with God* [London, 1906], 9). His emphasis on immediacy and consciousness derives ultimately from Schleiermacher, and his notion of faith as its own ground leads to Bultmann. He claims, as did Bultmann, to stand in the tradition of Luther. But such a notion of faith is contested head-on by W. Pannenberg.

Hilary of Poitiers

Hilary of Poitiers (c. 315-368) was profoundly influenced by Athanasius and the Eastern Church, although he also drew on the thought of Tertullian and Origen. He has been described as "the first exegete in the West, before Ambrose and Augustine." He was elected bishop of Poitiers c. 350. In 362 he produced his major work, *On the Trinity*, in twelve books, previously entitled *On the Faith*. He argued that the Father and the Son are one *(unus)*: "Their unity [does] not ... contradict their distinct existence" (*On the Trinity* 7.2). The Holy Spirit "is joined with Father and Son" (2.9). This suggests the validity of the term *homoousion*. He declared, "The Father and the Son are one in nature, honour, and power" (8.18). The Holy Spirit "proceeds from the Father" (8.20). Virtually every declaration is supported by a number of biblical passages. For example, in 1 Cor. 12:4-11, all three persons of the Trinity are involved in gifts and salvation. Hilary stressed that the descent of the Holy Spirit and the Sonship of Jesus are involved in his baptism. Not for nothing has he been called "the Athanasius of the West."

Hildegard of Bingen

Hildegard of Bingen (1098-1179) was an outstanding twelfth-century mystic. She is noted for her visions, writings, preaching, and musical compositions. She became abbess of her convent in 1136. From 1141 she wrote *Scivias,* or *Know the Ways of the Lord*. Bernard of Clairvaux advised and encouraged her. At sixty she embarked on several preaching tours, at Bamberg, Trier, and Cologne, seeking to reform lax clergy. She also sought to correct the Cathars. Her visions involved many "pictures": light as representing Christ; fire and flashes as representing the Holy Spirit (*Scivias* 2.2). She urged that the Holy Spirit drives out sin and creates faith in baptism (1.6; 3.9).

Hilton, Walter

Walter Hilton (c. 1343-1396), mystical theologian, wrote especially on contemplation. He wrote *The Scale of Perfection*, which was hugely influential in the fifteenth century. Hilton declares, "Contemplative life consists in perfect love and charity ... and knowledge of God" (*Scale*, chap. 3). "Knowing God" includes "study in holy Scripture" (chap. 4) and prayer and hymns (chap. 7), "with burning love" (chap. 9). However, Hilton is emphatic in warning about the limits of mysticism. "Visions" too readily encourage "imaginary" notions and deception by a wicked angel (chap. 10). The devil can too easily create "counterfeit visions and imaginings" (chap. 11). The first section is written to an ex-anchoress (*see* **Anchorites**) to correct her "perverted" visionary experiences and "inordinate loves and fears of earthly things" (chap. 1). Hilton is a jewel: he advocates moderate mysticism, but shrewdly urges correction and care in interpreting visions and "pictures."

Hippolytus

Hippolytus (c. 170–c. 236) was a presbyter of Rome, and is regarded by many as the most significant third-century theologian of Rome. He attacked the teaching of Sabellius and modalism, and sought to prevent Callistus of Rome from undertaking his own election as bishop in his place. His main work is *The Refutation of All Heresies*. His authorship of the *Apostolic Tradition* is probable, even if sometimes debated. He regarded Montanism as a heresy. Most of the *Apostolic Tradition* has been lost, but fragments are preserved, and deemed important for early Roman liturgy. This laid down criteria for the appointment of bishops (*Apostolic Tradition* 2) and for elders or presbyters (7) and for deacons (8). He used the threefold Gloria (3.6; 4.11; 6.4). He was passionate but inflexible. He was exiled to Sardinia in 235, and martyred in 236.

Historicality

"Historicality" translates the German *Geschichtlichkeit*, sometimes termed "historicity," but the term has more than one meaning. Historicality denotes being radically conditioned by one's place in history. Although Hegel introduced the notion of historical reason for the first time, it was probably Dilthey and Heidegger who gave the term its most characteristic use. Heidegger argued that a human being was "thrown," as it were, into his or her historical situation. As such, a human being was being-there *(Dasein)*. The person's viewpoint or horizons depended on the place in history in which the person found himself or herself. Purely objective or value-neutral knowledge is impossible. The concept was then expounded by Bultmann and Gadamer, for whom it became crucial. Every exploration into hermeneutics must take this view seriously. The radical historical finitude of human beings eventually led on to postmodern views, in which humankind is a victim of its social and historical environment. A belief that human beings are conditioned by their place in history, however, need not lead to such radical and arguably extreme conclusions. At one level the concept appeals to common sense as useful and true, with less pessimistic consequences than relativists and postmodernists claim or imply.

Historical Theology

Historical theology stands in contrast to church history, although the two substantially overlap. It traces, expounds, and assesses themes and ideas from biblical sources and foundations, through patristic, medieval, Reformation, and modern thought, up to the present. It thus constitutes the building blocks and groundwork of systematic theology. It is a cardinal principle of hermeneutics that we seek to understand theology through historical events and contexts (expounded especially in A. C. Thiselton, *The Hermeneutics of Doctrine* [Grand Rapids: Eerdmans, 2007]). Theology is never purely abstract. It answers questions that arise from a series of specific contexts and events. Unlike church history, however, historical theology does not focus primarily on the events themselves, but on their influence in the formation of theology and doctrine. Christian theology also claims a continuity of faith. This begins with the "rule of faith" as seen in the Scriptures and the earliest Church Fathers. Historical theology then traces continuities and discontinuities in the formulations of doctrine at given times. Historical theology also allows the latest generation to understand why previous generations expounded or rejected earlier formulations within the context of their own times. The two disciplines of biblical and historical theology are vital for a mature systematic theology, although the biblical material remains primary and normative, while the historical material provides a substantial indication of continuity and guidance for thought. Luther and Calvin respected the tradition of the Church Fathers more than is often realized. (*See also* **Tradition**.)

Historicism

Historicism is usually defined as the view that any event, person, culture, or situation is capable of explanation and understanding solely in terms of historical cause and effect. In this sense it verges on positivism, objectivism, and belief in value-neutral inquiry. In theory Leopold von Ranke aimed to reconstruct what "actually happened," but in practice brought his own assumptions to the subject. It is essentially a nineteenth-century phenomenon, although still practiced in many circles today. Thinkers in hermeneutics and "theological interpretation" tend to reject this approach as inadequate.

History of Religions School

The history of religions school *(Religionsgeschichtliche Schule)* names an influential group of scholars who argued that the comparative study of religions would be useful and illuminating for the interpretation of Christian origins. It typically flourished between 1880 and 1920. H. Gunkel (1862-1932), one of its leading exponents, applied this method to the OT, and E. Troeltsch (1865-1923) regarded himself as the leading systematic theologian of this school. He emphasized its special place within the expertise of the faculty at Göttingen. W. Bousset, J. Weiss, and R. Reitzenstein were prominent leaders in this school. It arose partly through dissatisfaction with Ritschl's "dogmatic" theology, which arguably underrated the importance of history. One of the major works from this school was Bousset's *Kyrios Christos* (1913); Bultmann wrote a foreword to the English edition (1970). This claimed that the "Lord" of a cultus had affinities with a deity that was worshiped in a Greek "local" cult. However, G. Wagner, among others, has questioned the dating of alleged Hellenistic and Oriental sources, arguing that later parallels do not imply dependency, at least in the case of Paul and Paul's view of baptism.

Hodge, Charles

Charles Hodge (1797-1871) studied under Ernst Hengstenberg, among others, and taught at Princeton for most of his life. He published solid commentaries on Romans (1835), Ephesians (1856), 1 Corinthians (1857), and 2 Corinthians (1859), and wrote the very influential three-volume *Systematic Theology,* published in 1871-1873. He suspected that original and creative thinking would lead scholars away from Reformed orthodoxy. Hence he stated proudly of Princeton: "A new idea never originated in this Seminary" (P. C. Gutjahs, *Charles Hodge* [Oxford: OUP, 2011], 368). He championed Calvinist and Reformed theology, in contrast to the more liberal theology of H. Bushnell at Yale.

In his *Systematic Theology* Hodge devoted forty pages to "the Protestant rule of faith" (1:151-90). Together with B. Warfield, he argued that the Scriptures were both infallible and inerrant, and advocated belief in their plenary inspiration. This inspiration is "supernatural" (154-55). Plenary inspiration includes "all parts of Scripture" (168), and "extends to words" (164-65; i.e., is verbal inspiration). On the other hand, Hodge hints at more flexibility than Warfield might seem to concede. Hodge acknowledges, "As to all matters of science, philosophy, and history, [the sacred writers] stood on the same level with their contemporaries" (1:165). It is difficult to overemphasize the influence of Hodge and Warfield among American evangelicals, and at one time also fundamentalism. (*See also* **Evolution; Warfield, Benjamin B.**)

Hollenweger, Walter J.

Walter J. Hollenweger (b. 1927) is a Swiss theologian widely known for his work on Pentecostalism. He was Professor of Mission at the University of Birmingham, U.K., from 1971 to 1989. He has written *The Pentecostals* (1972) and *Pentecostalism: Origins and Developments Worldwide* (1997). The VU University Amsterdam has established a Hollenweger Centre for Pentecostal and Charismatic Studies.

Holy, Holiness

"Holy, holiness" is in Hebrew *qādōsh, qādesh,* in Greek *hagios, hagiazō.* The Hebrew *q-d-sh* stands in contrast to *chōl,* "common" or "profane" (1 Sam. 21:5-6; Ezek. 22:26; 42:20; 44:23), just as *hagios* stands in contrast to *koinos.* Thus both terms denote "withheld from ordinary use." In the OT the most extensive uses relate to cultic texts. But more broadly the term also denotes what in any way pertains to God or his worship. Thus the Sabbath is called a "holy day" (Isa. 58:13). God is "majestic in holiness" (Exod. 15:11), and God's Spirit is called "his Holy Spirit" (Isa. 63:10-11). Lev. 20:3 refers to God's "holy name." T. G. Vriezen insists that "the Holy God" is *"The Wholly Other One"* (*Old Testament Theology* [Oxford: Blackwell, 1962], 149). In Hos. 11:9 the prophet says,

> I am God and no mortal,
> the Holy One is in your midst.

"Holy," Vriezen argues, shows that God is different from human beings in nature. Thus Isaiah speaks repeatedly of God's holiness in the context of his miracles and wonderful acts. One classic reference is the vision of Isaiah in Isa. 6:1-7. The angels covered their faces, and cried, "Holy, holy, holy is the LORD of hosts" (v. 3). In this context holiness denotes "unapproachableness." Holiness is associated with glory *(kābōd)*. In a cultic setting the "Holy of Holies" is "the hindmost part of the Temple, shut off from all human coming and going" (151). E. Jacob concurs with Vriezen in elucidating the themes conveyed by this term (*Theology of the Old Testament* [London: Hodder and Stoughton, 1958], 86-93). BDB underlines the same themes: separateness, apartness, sacredness, to be hallowed (871-74).

F. Danker considers several words in the NT that are cognate with *hagios*. *Hagiazō* denotes "to set aside, to sanctify, to reverence" (BDAG 10). *Hagiasmos* denotes "holiness, consecration, sanctification" (10). *Hagios* means "being dedicated or consecrated to the service of God"; or, in the case of things, "sanctuary, holy place," or "that which is holy" (10-11). It may then in the plural become a term for *Christian believers, as those set apart for God* (11). One classic verse is 1 Pet. 1:15-16: "As he who called you is holy, be holy yourselves in all your conduct; for it is written, 'You shall be holy, for I am holy'" (see O. Procksch, *TDNT* 1:101; cf. 88-115). Jesus is addressed as "the Holy One of God" (Mark 1:24). Peter exclaims, "You are the Holy One of God" (John 6:69). In Rev. 3:7, Christ is "the holy one, the true one." In 1 Cor. 3:12-17 Christians are "God's temple," "for God's temple is holy, and you are the temple" (cf. A. L. A. Hogeterp, *Paul and God's Temple* [Leuven: Peeters, 2006]).

Among modern works on holiness, one of the most distinctive is O. R. Jones, *The Concept of Holiness* (London: Allen and Unwin; New York: Macmillan, 1961). Jones faithfully reflects the biblical witness but brings to bear on it a conceptual, logical, and philosophical analysis akin to what Wittgenstein might have done had he addressed the subject. Holiness, he begins, is not simply a "quality," like "loudness" or "sweetness" (19). It is discerned intellectually and in effect should be regarded as a *disposition*. He uses the analogy of an electrical charge, and writes of a worshiper's response to holiness: "What he has is not so much a constant fearful emotion as a constant disposition to behave in a certain way in relation to electrically charged objects," for example, when something goes wrong or there is a short circuit (41). The believer has "a disposition to behave in a certain way with respect to certain situations" (44). This can explain why "holiness" has its operative currency in such a wide variety of situations. Sometimes, but not always, it entails "undaunted perseverance and unflinching decision" (69). At other times the term overlaps with "completeness" or "wholeness," and yet again with "Christlikeness" (89). We become "one with him (Christ) in his submission and self-revelation" (99). "Separateness" is not a permanent quality; but in worship and other situations it may merit appropriate behavior. In a dispositional sense it may relate to the numerous, as when Paul exclaimed, "Depart from me for I am a sinful man" (131). But this does not invite relativism. Jesus concludes that God is the paradigm case of holiness (158; cf. 195).

This dispositional account also helps to explain how the original notion of "majesty" holiness, when it is connected with God's glory, shades into "moral" or "ethical" holiness, which demands growth in sanctification and righteous conduct. Both aspects belong in principle to the church as holy, in the sense of aspirations to sanctification and holiness, which have sometimes been misunderstood. At one end of the spectrum the Donatists and some Puritans aimed at a "pure" church, often by excluding Christians who had lapsed or fallen in some way below expected standards. Luther lamented that enthusiasts or Radical Reformers had blunted his message of justification by grace. At the other end of the spectrum are "radicals" who believe that "anything goes" in the life of the church. Paul struggled with libertines and legalists equally in Galatia. Yet a third group believe that holiness, or sanctification, comes instantaneously as an event, rather than as a long process of being conformed increasingly to Christ. (*See also* **Ecclesiology; Sanctification; Temptation.**)

Reading: O. R. Jones, *The Concept of Holiness* (London: Allen and Unwin; New York: Macmillan, 1961); Thomas Merton, *Life and Holiness* (New York: Doubleday, 1964); David Peterson, *Possessed by God* (Leicester: IVP, 2001); John Webster, *Holiness* (London: SCM; Grand Rapids: Eerdmans, 2003).

Holy Spirit

The Spirit of God in the Old Testament and in Judaism

(i) **In the OT the Hebrew word for "spirit" is *ruach*.** It occurs about 400 times in the OT, and may denote "Spirit of God," "human spirit," "wind," or "breath." The LXX usually translates the Hebrew by Greek *pneuma*. At the beginning of Genesis the NRSV translates "a wind from God swept over the face of the waters"; but other versions more plausibly translate "the spirit of God moved..." (AV/KJV; RSV, "was moving"; Gen. 1:2). According to the more traditional translation, the Spirit of God brings order out of chaos. The Hebrew *tohu wa-bohu* denotes an unproductive waste, to which the Spirit brings life and order. W. Pannenberg stresses the creative power of the Spirit; C. K. Barrett and others suggest the creative hovering of a bird over the water (Heb. *mᵉrachepheth*, "brooding" or "hovering": Barrett, *Holy Spirit and the Gospel Tradition* [London: SPCK, 1958], 18-19). This would offer a parallel with Ps. 104:30: "When you send forth your Spirit, they are created." "Life" appears in J. Moltmann's title *The Spirit of Life* (London: SCM, 1992). This theme reappears in Ezek. 37:1-14, where the Spirit brings life to a dead and dried-up community, as if it were "dry bones." The specific term "Holy Spirit" occurs only three times in the OT: Ps. 51:11, Isa. 63:10, and the parallel in 63:11. These verses are: "Do not take your Holy Spirit from me" (Heb. *rûach qôdhshekā*), and "They grieved his Holy Spirit." "Holy" signifies "derived from the holy God."

Second, the Spirit offers empowerment to the individual, but also in the context of the community of God's people. The gift of the Spirit may be a temporary gift to match a particular task, in contrast to the permanency of the gift in the NT. A classic example arises from the empowerment of the judges. The Spirit is given to Othniel (Judg. 3:7-11), to Ehud (3:12-30), to Deborah and Barak (4:1-24), to Gideon (6:11–8:35), to Abimelech (9:1-57), to Jephthah (11:1–12:7), and to Samson (13:1–16:31). All receive the Spirit to deliver Israel from oppression. Hence they are called "saviors." But they cannot deliver Israel in their own strength. Each has a perceived weakness: Ehud is left-handed; Deborah is a woman; Gideon has to reduce the size of his army; Abimelech is overambitious; Jephthah makes a rash vow; and Samson abuses his gift. But they all accomplish this task because God gives them his Spirit. These exploits benefit the whole people of Israel; the gift is not primarily for individual advantage. This will also be true of the gift in the NT.

The Spirit can *give strength*, as in a warrior. But the Spirit also gives *wisdom*, a craftsman's skill, revelation, insight, and prophecy. For example, Bezalel receives the gift of craftsmanship in Exod. 31:3-5. The Spirit inspires Micaiah to prophecy (1 Kings 22:13-28). The Spirit brings peace and justice (Isa. 32:15), and well-being or salvation (Isa. 11:6-10). The Spirit gives what is required for leadership and administration (Num. 11:16-25, the seventy elders). Indeed, although the Spirit gives power, Zechariah insists that this is not brute force: "Not by might, nor by power, but by my spirit, says the LORD of hosts" (Zech. 4:6). In Isaiah the Spirit *anoints the messianic figure,* just as the Spirit anoints judges or kings. The classic passage comes in Isa 11:1-2:

> A shoot shall come out from the stump of Jesse,
>   and a branch shall grow out of his roots.
> The Spirit of the LORD shall rest on him,
>   the Spirit (or spirit) of wisdom and understanding,
>   the Spirit of counsel and might.

Such a figure will be king on David's throne, and in the NT this is applied to Christ. He will bring restoration to the remnant of Israel (v. 11). Isa. 28:6 and 32:15 speak of the Spirit (spirit?) of justice (Heb. *rûach mishpāt*).

Two further themes concern *prophecy* and new life. Micaiah (1 Kings 22:13-28) constitutes one of many examples of prophecy. An early example comes in Numbers 22–24. Balaam appears as a non-Israelite prophet who defies King Balak of Moab by blessing Israel. Num. 24:2-4 declares: "The Spirit of God came upon him, and he uttered his oracle, . . . the oracle of one who hears the words of God." Prophecy provides the backcloth for the confrontation between Elijah and Ahab. Deut. 18:9-22 raises the problem of false prophecy. Claims to prophecy must be tested. Hence the canonical prophets Amos, Hosea, Isaiah, and Jeremiah are reticent about claims to possess the Spirit. But such are nevertheless regularly made. Micah exclaims:

> As for me, I am filled with power,
> > with the Spirit of the LORD, . . .
> to declare to Jacob his transgressions. (Mic. 3:8)

Jeremiah attacks false prophecy: "I did not send the prophets" (Jer. 23:21; cf. 23:25, 32; 14:14). Elisha derives his share of the Spirit from Elijah (2 Kings 2:15; cf. 2:9-14). Isa. 61:1, by contrast, asserts:

> The Spirit of the Lord GOD is upon me,
> > because the LORD has anointed me;
> he has sent me to bring good news to the oppressed.

In the NT, Jesus probably used a composite quotation from Isa. 40:3-5 and 61:1-2. *New life,* as we noted, comes into prominence in Ezekiel, especially Ezek. 37:1-14. In 37:14 God declares, "I will put my Spirit within you (Israel), and you shall live." The "dry bones" exemplify a long-dead, lifeless body. Earlier in Ezekiel, the Spirit transports both the prophet (3:12, 14; 8:3; 11:1) and the majestic throne of the awesome God (1:19-21). Unlike Jeremiah, Ezekiel has no hesitation in claiming to be filled with the Spirit for prophetic utterances (2:2-3; 11:24-25). Yet he is also aware of the deep-seated problem of false prophecy (14:9).

A final positive theme is that of the Spirit as the *presence of God*. Eight or nine prayers in the Old Testament imply this, but at least these are explicit. In synonymous parallelism the psalmist prays,

> Do not cast me from your presence,
> > and do not take your Holy Spirit from me. (Ps. 51:11)

The psalmist similarly uses synonymous parallelism in Ps. 139:7:

> Where can I go from your Spirit?
> > Or where can I flee from your presence?

Job declares:

> "The Spirit of God has made me,
> > and the breath of the Almighty gives me life." (Job 33:4)

Further references are clear, but are more open to debate. Ps. 33:6 asserts:

> By the word of the LORD the heaven was made,
> and all their host by the breath *(ruach)* of his mouth.

Isa. 31:3 reads:

> The Egyptians are human, and not God;
> their horses are flesh, and not spirit.

Haggai declares, "I am with you.... My Spirit abides among you" (Hag. 2:4-5). Psalm 104:29-30 has

> When you hide your face *(pānîm,* "presence"), they are dismayed; ...
> When you send forth your Spirit, they are created.

We may compare, perhaps not as directly, Isa. 59:21 to the same effect. Gordon Fee calls the Spirit "the personal presence of God himself," and cites Old Testament roots for this, as well as the NT.

In spite of these seven or more characteristic uses in the OT, some OT passages use *ruach* to denote the *human spirit*. In Gen. 45:27, "When he saw the wagons that Joseph had sent to carry him, the spirit of their father Jacob revived." Similarly, "When he drank, (Samson's) spirit returned, and he revived" (Judg. 15:19). In Josh. 5:1, "There was no longer any spirit in them," where "spirit" is parallel to "heart." Num. 16:22 speaks of "the spirits of all flesh"; and in Ps. 77:6 is "I ... search my spirit," which is parallel to "I commune with my heart." There is no doubt that we find an anthropological use of "spirit" as a rough equivalent to "heart." But this is not sharply dualistic, as in the modern Western sense. Characteristically, the Spirit stands in contrast, not with the material, but with all that is weak and human. The Spirit is above all *transcendent*. Even when the Spirit is immanent, the Spirit is "the Beyond, who is within."

(ii) **The Spirit of God in Judaism.** The mistaken notion that the Spirit is silent between the Testaments is based on one solitary text, Tosefta *Sotah* 13:2-4. It apparently declares that "the Holy Spirit ceased" when Haggai, Zechariah, and Malachi, the last of the prophets, died, to be replaced by the *Bath Qōl* (literally, daughter of the voice). But this text is disputed, and even if it is genuine it belongs to the third or fourth century A.D. Where Judaism speaks of the Spirit, its major themes concern prophetic inspiration *(Jub.* 31.12), holiness and purification, and the obedience of the community (1QS 3.7-8).

It is no longer considered accurate to contrast "Palestinian" and "Hellenistic" Judaism clearly. Martin Hengel has demonstrated an extensive overlap. However, a more authentic contrast would be between "Greek-speaking Judaism" and "Aramaic-speaking Judaism." Greek-speaking literature tends to lay more stress on an immanent and rational Spirit of God. Philo and Josephus typify this trend, together with Wisdom of Solomon (all first century B.C. and A.D.). But on the other side, Ben Sirach defends the distinctiveness of Judaism *against* a Hellenistic culture. God sends to his people a "spirit of understanding" (Sir. 39:6). As in Ezra, the scribe is trained to transmit a pure tradition. Philo seeks to commend Judaism to a Greco-Roman audience. The Spirit is God, and agent in creation; and God seeks a "holy spirit" to dwell within humankind (Philo, *Allegorical Interpretation* 1.31-42). The Spirit is diffused everywhere (*On Giants* 32).

Of the twenty occurrences of *pneuma* in the LXX during this period, only two or three denote *the Spirit of God*. Often the word refers to a human disposition. The Spirit of God, however, "holds all things together" (Wis. 1:7), as Christ does in Col. 1:17. "Spirit" is virtually on loan to humankind, until it returns to God when death intervenes (Wis. 15:16). Wisdom also suggests that the holy spirit is a gift from God, as is the Holy Spirit in 1 Cor. 2:10-15. Wisdom remains a major figure (Wis. 7:7-30), all-powerful, steadfast, and overseeing all (7:22-23). Similarly "Spirit" can be an "emanation of the glory of the Almighty," "a spotless mirror of the working of God" (7:25-26).

Wisdom literature constitutes one bridge between the OT and the NT; apocalyptic literature provides another. Some uses of "spirit" merely denote the human spirit, or a human disposition (*1 En.* 13.6). At other times "spirit" may denote an evil spirit, or even an angelic spirit (*1 En.* 15.10; 39.8, 9-13; 60.6, 8, 25). *Testaments of the Twelve Patriarchs* (probably c. 109-106 B.C.) covers a similar range, as a Pharisaic book written first in Hebrew. Apocalyptic also uses the concept of *Bath Qōl* (*Apoc. Baruch* 8.1; 13.1; *1 En.* 65.4). In *Psalms of Solomon* (c. 50-40 B.C.) an apocalyptic "Son of David" is anointed by the Spirit to purge Jerusalem "from all Latin men," perhaps alluding to Pompey's visit to the temple. The *Apocalypse of Baruch* (probably first century A.D.) speaks of both messianic expectations and the creative or sustaining power of the Spirit.

Rabbinic literature stresses the relation between the Spirit and obedience. But obedience can make a person "worthy that the Holy Spirit should rest upon him" (*Mekilta Exodus* 15:1; cf. *Numbers Rabbah* 15:20), whereas Paul sees the Spirit as the *cause* of obedience (Gal. 3:1-5). Yet the rabbis were at one with Christians in seeing the Holy Spirit as "the Spirit (spirit?) of prophecy" (*Jub.* 25.14; 31.12), who inspired the prophets of the Scriptures. The Targums see the spirit as a source of revelation. In rabbinic thought, according especially to Erik Sjöberg, the Spirit becomes fully personal, in speaking, crying, admonishing, sorrowing, weeping, and rejoicing. He claims: "The Spirit proceeds from God himself." Finally, in the Dead Sea Scrolls of Qumran, God's Spirit is a "holy Spirit," whom God gives to the Messiah (1QS 4.20-21). In the *Thanksgiving Hymns* the Spirit is also holy (1QH 7.6; 9.32; 12.1). The Spirit will cleanse the community (1QS 3.6-8; 1QH 16.12). 1QS 4.26 has the well-known contrast between "the spirit of truth" and "the spirit of error." In 1QH 7.6-7, the Holy Spirit upholds the believer. Therefore there are differences of emphasis in Aramaic-speaking Judaism, Greek-speaking Judaism, the Wisdom literature, rabbinic Judaism, apocalyptic Judaism, and the Dead Sea Scrolls, Philo, and Josephus. (*See also* **Judaism.**)

Reading: (i) OT: W. Eichrodt, *Theology of the Old Testament,* vol. 2 (London: SCM, 1967), 46-69; E. Jacob, *Theology of the Old Testament* (London: Hodder and Stoughton, 1958), 121-27; G. T. Montague, *The Holy Spirit* (Eugene, Ore.: Wipf and Stock, 1976); A. C. Thiselton, *The Holy Spirit* (Grand Rapids: Eerdmans, 2013), 3-22. (ii) Judaism: H. Kleinknecht, F. Baumgärtel, and E. Sjöberg, *"Pneuma,"* in *TDNT* 6:332-96; J. R. Levison, *The Spirit in First-Century Judaism* (Leiden: Brill, 2002); Max Turner, *Power from on High* (Sheffield: Sheffield Academic Press, 1996), 82-139; M. Welker, *God the Spirit* (Minneapolis: Fortress, 1994), 50-182.

The Spirit in the New Testament

(i) **Holy Spirit in the Synoptic Gospels.** All three Synoptic Gospels stress the baptism and messianic temptations of Jesus. Mark 1:10 recounts: "As he [Jesus] was coming up out of the water, he saw . . . the Spirit descending like a dove *(hōs peristeran)* on him" (cf. Matt. 3:16-17; Luke 3:21-22). Luke adds "in bodily form" *(sōmatikō eidei).* The Father, the Son, and the Holy Spirit are all involved in this act. The Father declares his love and approval; the Son undergoes baptism "as one of the prepared people of God" (C. K. Barrett); the Holy Spirit descends visibly upon Jesus, and anoints and empowers him for his messianic temptations or trials. The Spirit actually instigates the wilderness experience of Jesus: "The Spirit . . . drove him out" *(ekballei,* Mark 1:12); or in Matthew, "Jesus was led up by the Spirit . . . to be tempted by the devil" (Matt. 4:1). Luke recounts that Jesus was "full of the Holy Spirit" *(plērēs)* when he "was led by the Spirit in the wilderness" (Luke 4:1).

All three Synoptics then record works of Jesus in the power of the Spirit that imply that the kingdom of God has arrived in the person of Jesus. Matt. 12:28 and the Lukan parallel read: "If it is by the Spirit of God that I cast out demons, then the kingdom of God has come to you" (Luke has "by the finger of God"). Matthew and Luke also see the Spirit at work in the conception and birth of Jesus Christ (Matt. 1:18-20; Luke 1:35). The temptations in the wilderness are distinctively *messianic* trials or tests *(peirazomenos).* Jesus is not tempted to do evil or wickedness, but to take shortcuts to do God's will, but not in God's way. Jesus is not to be recognized as messianic King by spectacular miracles of feeding (Matt. 4:3-4), nor by a miracle of spectacular preservation (Matt. 4:6-7), nor by the methods of the world and the devil (Matt. 4:8-10), including popular appeal. God's will is the way of humility and the cross, in the power of the Holy Spirit.

Luke stresses healings, exorcisms, and miracles more than Matthew and Mark do, but all three portray the intimacy of Jesus with his Father in the power of the Spirit. In Luke 4:18-19 Jesus declares: "The Spirit of the Lord is upon me, because he has anointed me to bring good news to the poor . . . release to the captives . . . sight to the blind . . . the year of the Lord's favor" (partly from Isa. 42:1; mainly from Isa. 61:1). G. W. H. Lampe urges that prayer, the Word of God, and the Holy

Spirit come together here ("The Holy Spirit in St. Luke," in *Studies in the Gospels*, ed. D. E. Nineham [Oxford: Blackwell, 1967], 159; cf. 159-200). We find a different emphasis respectively in C. K. Barrett and J. D. G. Dunn. Barrett insists: "Lack of glory and a cup of suffering were his Messianic creation, and part of his poverty was the absence of all the signs of the Spirit of God" (*The Holy Spirit and the Gospel Tradition* [London: SPCK, 1958], 158). J. E. Fison also refers to this *kenosis* of the Spirit in the incarnation. On the other hand, Dunn stresses the miracles of Jesus, his words of power, and intimacy with God, all in the strength of the Spirit: Jesus, he argues, was "a charismatic figure"; "an ecstatic"; with "supernatural power" (*Jesus and the Spirit* [London: SCM, 1975], 68-92). Max Turner and the Pentecostal writers R. Menzies and R. Stronstad stress the Lukan emphasis on the empowerment of Jesus (Turner, *Power from on High* [Sheffield: Sheffield Academic Press, 1996], 188-212; Stronstad, *The Charismatic Theology of St. Luke* [Peabody, Mass.: Hendrickson, 1984]).

All writers agree, however, that the temptations of Jesus were not limited to the three "messianic" temptations that followed his baptism. Luke records that the devil departed "until an opportune time" (Luke 4.13; *achri kairou*). Hebrews stresses that Jesus endured temptations throughout his earthly life (Heb. 4:15). They also stress the relation of Jesus to his Father as exemplified in his address of *"Abba,"* "dear Father" (Mark 14:36), which is consciously replicated in Christians in Rom. 8:15 and Gal. 4:6 under the inspiration of the Holy Spirit. All three Synoptic Gospels also record the saying of Jesus about blasphemy against the Holy Spirit (Mark 3:28-30; Matt. 12:31-32; Luke 12:10). This concerns anyone who willfully distorts good and evil. How can such a one retain any capacity to repent, if he or she calls good "evil" and evil "good"?

In the Gospels Jesus also promises that the Holy Spirit will guide Christians in moments of crisis (Mark 13:11; Matt. 10:20; Luke 12:12). When disciples are brought to trial, they are not to fear, "for it is not you who speak, but the Holy Spirit" (Mark 13:11). This is an encouragement, but R. T. France comments, this does not encourage "lazy preaching," following a similar comment from Aquinas. Luke distinctively sees the future gift of the Holy Spirit in the context of prayer: God gives the Spirit "to those who ask" (Luke 11:13; Matt. 7:11 has "good things" in place of "the Spirit"). These promises reach a climax for both Matthew and Luke in the postresurrection Great Commission of Matt. 28:19 (with baptism in the threefold name, although many question its authenticity to Jesus). Luke speaks of "power from on high" (Luke 24:49), and offers no reasons for doubt.

In what they stress, rather than deny, Barrett and Dunn make valuable points. As Barrett argues, the Synoptic Gospels are restrained in their language about the Spirit, because the resurrection and Christ's victory have not yet occurred. Yet as Dunn stresses, the kingdom of God is already bursting through, and the dawn is beginning to rise. Fison rightly speaks of the Holy Spirit's "self-effacement," as he leads Jesus to humiliation and the cross. But as Dunn and Turner imply, there are also conspicuous moments of the Holy Spirit's visible activity, especially in the fulfillment of the prophecy. Jürgen Moltmann and Eugene Rogers, however, stress that "the narrative of Jesus" gives us the most helpful way of approaching a New Testament notion of the Holy Trinity. For all persons of the Trinity are involved in every critical event of the life of Jesus: his conception and birth; his baptism and temptations; his incarnate life of prayer and action; his transfiguration; and his cross and resurrection (Moltmann, *The Trinity and the Kingdom of God* [London: SCM, 1981], 64 and elsewhere; E. F. Rogers, *After the Spirit* [London: SCM, 2006], 75-175).

(ii) **The Holy Spirit in Acts.** The general impression of the Spirit in Acts is of his enabling the church to fulfill the will and purposes of God (Beverly Roberts Gaventa, *The Acts of the Apostles* [Nashville: Abingdon, 2003], 25-60). This takes the specific form of missionary expansion. Ronald Williams subtitles his 1953 commentary on Acts *Nothing Can Stop the Gospel*. W. G. Kümmel traces five clear sections in Acts that correspond with progressive stages of outreach: Jerusalem (Acts 1:15–8:7); Samaria (8:4–11:18); Antioch and the Antiochene mission (11:19–15:35); lands around the Aegean Sea (15:36–19:20); and "from Jerusalem to Rome" (19:21–28:31). Persecutions and setbacks serve only to promote the expansion (8:1, 4). It is not strictly accurate to speak only of "Luke's interest in history"; it is more accurate to speak of "Luke's interest in God's acts and purposes in history."

Peter appeals to the inspiration of the Spirit in the Psalms (Acts 1:16-21; 4:25-26), and the Day of Pentecost (2:1) is perceived as the fulfillment of the prophecy of Joel 2:28,

> I will pour out my spirit on all flesh;
> your sons and your daughters shall prophesy. . . .

Arie Zwiep rightly calls it a "barrier-breaking event" (*Christ, the Spirit, and the Community of God* [Tübingen: Mohr, 2010], 116). Acts 2:2 speaks of "a sound (*ēchos*) like the rush of a violent wind," and in the LXX of Exod. 19:16, 1 Sam. 4:5, and Ps. 45:3, *ēchos* indicates a theophany. "Tongues of fire" (Acts 2:3) may be an image of judgment and cleansing (Isa. 5:24; Luke 3:16). Many argue that this fulfills the promise of a baptism in the Holy Spirit and fire (Luke 3:16). However, while many Pentecostals think in terms of an individual experience of "baptism in the Spirit," Zwiep, F. D. Bruner, and other NT scholars assert a "communal" or corporate baptism in the Spirit.

The significance of the "other tongues" (*heterais glōssais;* Acts 2:4) is disputed. Many early Pentecostals saw this as an evangelistic tool. But today some Pentecostals (e.g., Jane Evert Powers, in *JPT* 17 [2000]: 40; cf. 39-55) argue that there is "no biblical evidence" for seeing tongues as a missionary gift; the early apostles "preach in the vernacular, not tongues." Further, she and others claim that Jewish visitors to Jerusalem would normally speak Greek, the required language of commerce, except in remote areas. John Chrysostom, J. E. Hull in modern times, and many others, however, do relate "tongues" to foreign languages. Kirsopp Lake argues that this is "clear," and constitutes a reversal of Babel. Yet others see this as a miracle of hearing, not of speaking. Don Carson argues that this is *"xenoglossia,"* foreign languages never learned by the speaker (*Showing the Spirit* [Grand Rapids, Baker, 1987], 138). C. S. C. Williams and the NEB opt for "ecstatic utterance," which is rejected by Robert Gundry and others. H. B. Swete returns to the view that the crowd would have understood at least Greek or a dialect of Aramaic. The theological explanation that Luke conveys, however, remains a unique removal of barriers. K. Stendahl describes tongues as "a high voltage experience" that removes inhibitions, but cannot normally be sustained over many years (*Paul among Jews and Gentiles* [London: SCM, 1977; Philadelphia: Fortress, 1976], 109-24; cf. G. Theissen, *Psychological Aspects of Pauline Theology* [Edinburgh: T. & T. Clark, 1987], 59-80, 96-114). In classic Pentecostalism, by contrast, the tongues-speaking is seen as initial evidence of baptism in the Spirit (Gary McGee, ed., *Initial Evidence* [Eugene, Ore.: Wipf and Stock, 1991], 41-95, 219-34). Today, however, not all Pentecostals agree. The Pentecostal Frank Macchia compares it (at least in Paul) with "sighs too deep for words" (Rom. 8:26), but the relation between tongues in Luke and tongues in Paul is also unclear. Macchia also compares this phenomenon with the Babel event, as J. G. Davies did. Max Turner stresses the theme of "power for witness" (Acts 1:8; 2:22, 37-38).

Is Pentecost "repeatable"? Most biblical scholars reject the view that Luke offers a model of events to be replicated. Such a view reflects a "restorationist" hermeneutic. Narrative takes place for several purposes. Perhaps only most Pentecostals and some in the Renewal Movement see it in a restorationist way. However, at least three events in Acts appear to replicate the phenomenon of Pentecost. These concern the Samaritans (Acts 8:14-24), Cornelius (10:17-48), and the Ephesians (19:1-7). Some add Paul receiving the Spirit to this list. The usual scholarly explanation of these events is that, like Pentecost, they signal "barrier-breaking" events. The Samaritans represent, in a sense, a halfway house to Gentiles (John 4:9; Acts 1:8). To win and convert Samaritans was to cross a barrier, or to form a bridge to a new area. Hence Luke sees the need for visible evidence of some kind (8:15). A more "Catholic" interpretation sees the laying on of hands by Peter and John as of great significance for apostleship. Even Dunn calls it "the riddle of Samaria" (*Baptism in the Holy Spirit* [London: SCM, 1970], 55-72). Geoffrey Lampe believes that this episode has unique status as "a turning-point in the missionary enterprise" (*The Seal of the Spirit* [New York and London: Longmans, 1951], 70-72). In the end, Dunn also adopts this conclusion. Both argue that it is utterly anachronistic to see this as "confirmation." Luke wanted to avoid a fragmented church; hence Peter and John are involved.

The Cornelius episode in Acts 10:44 (cf. 11:15, 17) invites a similar explanation. Cornelius was a Gentile, even a "God-fearer" (i.e., a Gentile who worshiped with Jews). The Holy Spirit "fell upon all who heard the word," and the Jewish believers "were astounded that the gift of the Holy Spirit had been poured out even on the Gentiles, for they heard them speaking in tongues and extolling God" (10:44-46). It is plain and visible that the Holy Spirit has unfolded the next step in God's plan, passing over the barrier between Jew and Gentile. There is, incidentally, no reference to laying on of hands. There is mention, however, that this event took place while Peter was preaching the Word. Spirit and Word belong together. Many Pentecostals appeal to Paul's receiving the Holy Spirit in Acts 9:13-17. But the Pentecostal Robert Menzies and the Renewal Movement's exponent Max Turner see this as a moment of empowerment and commission, as in the OT. There is much debate about the status of the Ephesians in 19:1-7. The Ephesians had heard only of John's baptism and had not received the Spirit. Paul laid his hands on them, and they received the Spirit and spoke in tongues (19:6). Many see this supposed anomaly as a "catching-up exercise," in which the Ephesians demonstrate oneness with the rest of the church. This notion may have some relevance today.

(iii) **The Holy Spirit in Paul.** We begin with eight basic themes in Paul, which are not generally controversial. (a) The work of the Holy Spirit is centered on Christ. No one can say "Jesus is Lord" except by the Holy Spirit (1 Cor. 12:3). The Spirit is "the Spirit of his Son," who gives us the same attitude to God as *Abba* as Jesus had (Rom. 8:15-16; Gal. 4:6). (b) Every Christian receives the Holy Spirit (Rom. 8:9). J. D. G. Dunn comments that this verse excludes the notion of a Christian not possessing the Spirit; he does not simply come to Christians after some crisis experience. (c) Like the OT, the NT and Paul see the Holy Spirit as given to chosen individuals for a special task; but *also* as poured out on the whole community of God's people. Gifts are given "to each one individually" (1 Cor. 12:11). The OT scheme is surpassed but not eliminated. Gifts are "for the common good" (1 Cor. 12:7). (d) The Holy Spirit is the agent of the resurrection. This applies to the resurrection of Christ and to the resurrection of the dead (Rom. 8:11). This is a cosmic act of new creation. (e) The Holy Spirit brings home the preaching of the gospel (1 Thess. 1:5; 4:1-10; 1 Cor. 2:4-5). (f) The Holy Spirit is "holy" because he makes actual the presence and power of God himself. Gordon Fee stresses this. The Holy Spirit "proceeds from God" (Gk. *to pneuma to tou ek Theou,* 1 Cor. 2:12). J. E. Fison urges, "*Qōdesh* [holy] ... is something ... reserved for Yahweh" (*The Blessing of the Holy Spirit* [London and New York: Longman, Green, 1950], 43). (g) The Holy Spirit is the "firstfruits" (Gk. *arrabōn*) of the future that God has promised; he is the first installment of more to come, and also a guarantee of such a future (2 Cor. 5:5; Rom. 8:21). (h) The Holy Spirit is also prophetic and revelatory. He inspires not only the preaching of the gospel, but also Scripture and prophecy (1 Cor. 2:6-16), although we have yet to comment on the range of the word "prophecy."

Paul makes it clear that when he speaks of the Holy Spirit he is not speaking of human spirit or of the Stoic world-soul. A few texts remain ambiguous. Rom. 12:11, *tō pneumati zeontes,* may perhaps refer to the human spirit (as in "be ardent in spirit," NRSV), or to the Holy Spirit ("be aglow with the Spirit," RSV).

Rom. 1:4 and 2 Cor. 4:13 share this ambiguity. But normally the different senses of *pneuma* are clear. The danger in English is to let the adjective "spiritual" *(pneumatikos)* slide into "pertaining to the human spirit," when Paul uses it mainly to mean "of the Holy Spirit" (cf. 1 Cor. 3:1). Fison also warns us about the "self-effacing" character of the Holy Spirit. The Spirit usually points away from himself to Christ, as he does in John (*Blessing*, 11, 22, 27, 72, 107, and throughout). A further issue that arises is the meaning of "the Lord is the Spirit" in 2 Cor. 3:17. It is true that the Spirit is related closely to Christ. But Paul has been discussing Exod. 34:34, and implicitly comparing Christ and Moses. The majority of scholars understand the "is" to be an exegetical "is," as George Hendry and Vincent Taylor call it. Taylor renders it: "Now *Kurios* in the passage I have first quoted denotes the Spirit, and where the Spirit of the Lord is, there is liberty" (*The Person of Christ in New Testament Teaching* [London: Macmillan, 1958], 54). Dunn and Moltmann concur (Moltmann, *The Spirit of Life* [London: SCM, 1992], 101-2; Dunn, *Theology of Paul the Apostle* [Edinburgh: T. & T. Clark, 1998], 421-22). Parallels between Christ and the Holy Spirit clearly occur in 1 Cor. 12:4-7; 12:10; 2 Cor. 6:6; 13:13; Rom. 6:3-11; 8:1, 14-17. In the list of "gifts of the Holy Spirit" in 1 Cor. 12:4-11, we may note that call and endowment always go together in Paul. If we are called to perform a task, the Holy Spirit will enable us to do it.

In the remainder of this section we take up more controversial issues. They are controversial because they become a matter of hermeneutics, not simply of exegesis and lexicography. We begin with the more straightforward gifts of the Spirit. (a) The phrase "utterance of wisdom" (NRSV; Gk. *logos sophias*) requires two broad comments. First, *logos,* "utterance," does not simply mean "a word." It means any intelligible communicative act or unit, often a sentence or statement (BDAG 599-601). The translation "word" might imply a more staccato, even spontaneous, communication than Paul implies. Second, "wisdom" has already been defined for those at Corinth. It is used sixteen times in 1 Corinthians, compared with eleven in all the other Pauline epistles. In 1 Cor. 1:18–4:21 it plainly concerns the wisdom of *the cross,* God's wisdom, the gospel. Hence it is almost certainly a communication relating to the gospel; it is not a private revelation about a number of people in the congregation and their physical or mental state. Normally wisdom comes from experience and training, as exemplified in the Wisdom literature of the Bible, in Jesus, and in James. In James 3:13-18 it concerns teaching, humility, justice, discipline, and integrity.

(b) The phrase "utterance of knowledge" (NRSV; Gk. *logos gnōseōs*) commands no clear consensus about its difference from "communication of wisdom." *Gnōsis* recurs in 1 Cor. 8:1, 2, 3, 7, 10, and 11, if we include the verbal form. It also occurs in Rom. 11:33; 15:14; 1 Cor. 1:5; 13:2, 8; and six times in 2 Corinthians. In spite of the negative comparison with love in 1 Cor. 8:1, this chapter uses the term to denote a creedal confession of belief in God. The probability exists that *logos gnōseōs* could be the recital of a common creed, or of shared doctrine. P. Carrington and V. Neufeld have shown the importance of creeds and confessions in the NT. If the congregation contains new Christians, this may well mean instruction in the basic truths of the gospel.

(c) The third gift of faith in 1 Cor. 12:8-9 cannot be justifying faith, as all agree, for not every Christian necessarily receives this gift. Since the gifts are all "for the common good," it may well constitute a gift of glad, bold, even daring confidence in the future, especially for the congregation. The congregation would be encouraged and energized by such an expression of confidence in God. As many have rightly said, *faith* is never "one thing" in Paul, but achieves its definition by how, when, and for what purpose it is exercised and directed. The remaining gifts of the Spirit in 12:8-10 and 28-30 require more careful hermeneutical consideration.

(d) "Gifts of healing" (NRSV; Gk. *charismata iamatōn*) is in the plural in the Greek. This is probably a *generic* plural, meaning "kinds of healings" (like the English "cheeses" or "fruits"). It should therefore not be restricted to "supernatural" healing. An interesting list of Christian advocates could be cited: the Pentecostal Donald Gee; the Pietist J. A. Bengel; and commentators on the Greek text, T. C. Edwards, W. Hollenweger, F. Godet, and A. Robertson and A. Plummer. Furthermore, Hollenweger and others warn against imposing onto Paul an alien *dualism* of "natural" and "supernatural," which would be entirely foreign to his thought. Whichever *kind* of healing is in question, it is from *God*. In any case, the gifts are "as the Spirit of God wills." Healing may be given because the kingdom of God has come; or healing may be withheld, because the kingdom of God is still in process of coming, and the future final victory is yet to come.

(e) "The working of miracles" (NRSV, NJB, AV/KJV: Gk. *energēmata dunameōn*) is an overtranslation of the Greek. The Greek is literally "workings of power," which may best be translated "effective deeds of power." Karl Barth, for one, argues that "power" *(dunamis)* in 1 Corinthians denotes what is *effective* against any obstacle (*The Resurrection of the Dead* [London: Hodder and Stoughton, 1935], 18). The same Greek word as "effective deeds" in 12:6 is translated here "varieties of activities" *(diaireseis energēmatōn)*. John Calvin doubts whether verse 10 refers to miracles, but that power *(virtutem)* denotes "effective working" against demons or hypocrites (*The First Epistle to the Corinthians* [Edinburgh: Oliver and Boyd, 1960], 262). H. Thielicke concurs (*The Evangelical Faith,* vol. 3 [Grand Rapids: Eerdmans, 1982], 79). Hollenweger warns us against imposing a "God of the gaps" dualism or Deism onto Paul. Danker includes "capability" among the meanings of these words (BDAG 262-63). This is *not to reject* the inclusion of "miracle" among the possible meanings of this gift; it is to point out that it conveys other, more important qualities *as well,* which may be at least as primary. At all events, "supernatural" is not an entirely appropriate meaning to impose onto Paul. (*See* **Miracles**.)

(f) Prophecy, the sixth of the gifts, raises parallel hermeneutical issues, as well as those of exegesis. The Pentecostal writers R. Menzies and R. Stronheim, and the Renewal writer Max Turner, make much of the spirit of prophecy, especially in Luke-Acts. This cannot be denied. But how broad and many-faceted is *proph-*

ecy? We know that this may sometimes, but not always, denote *prediction*. Might it also denote *applied practical preaching,* as U. Müller, D. Hill, and T. Gillespie argue today, and as Thomas Aquinas, Calvin, and many others argued over the years? K. O. Sandnes stresses that Paul regarded himself as a prophet (*Paul — One of the Prophets?* [Tübingen: Mohr, 1991]). Yet as G. Bornkamm, W. Pannenberg, and others point out, Paul did not use "revelation speech," such as "Thus says the Lord," but did not spare himself the trouble and toil of persuasive, discursive argument (Bornkamm, "Faith and Reason in Paul," in *Early Christian Experience* [London: SCM, 1969], 29-46; Pannenberg, *BQT* 2:34-35). The acknowledged purpose of prophecy, to build up, encourage, and comfort, would not conflict with the aims of applied preaching (A. C. Thiselton, *First Epistle to the Corinthians* [Grand Rapids, Eerdmans, 2000], 956-70, 1087-94).

Nevertheless, others propose different views. Earle Ellis proposes "pneumatic exegesis." Dunn, Turner, and C. Forbes support the quasi-popular view of largely "spontaneous" utterance. Dunn insists, "It does not denote a previously prepared sermon. . . . It is a spontaneous utterance" (*Jesus and the Spirit* [London: SCM, 1975], 228; cf. 205-300). C. M. Robeck believes that prophecy is addressed only to believers. Nevertheless, D. Hill, U. Müller, and T. Gillespie insist that God acts *through* thought and reflection, not *instead of* it. The debate is parallel to that about dualism and miracles. We do *not altogether exclude* the more popular understanding of prophecy. But Gillespie insists, convincingly, on "the dialectical movement of judgement and grace that structures Paul's presentation of the gospel" (*The First Theologians* [Grand Rapids: Eerdmans, 1994], 136). It is "the activity of speaking or proclaiming" (132). Prophets are "mediators of divine promise" (134). "The proclamation of the prophet is *pastoral preaching* which, by its very nature, offers guidance and instruction to the community" (141). The teacher may be less immediately practical and pastoral, and more long-term; prophecy may include teaching doctrine. In postbiblical interpretation, this view of prophecy follows Augustine, Thomas Aquinas, Calvin, Estius, John Wesley, and James Denney.

(g) "Discernment of spirits" probably relates to the testing of prophecy. Self-styled prophets arise from self-deception, subjective understanding, or unreflective ecstasy, especially if this gift is "spontaneous." A trail of such damage can be traced from the OT, through the *Didachē,* probably through Montanism, the Radical Reformers, and Irvingites, to the present day. The need for a testing of prophecy occurs in 1 John 4:6, *Didachē* 11.7-8, and probably 1 Cor. 14:33-36. Testing prophets is enjoined in 1 Thess. 5:20-21. G. Dautzenberg argues for "interpretation of prophecy" here, but "discernment" is the more usual meaning of the Greek *diakrisis* or *diakrinō*. W. Grudem dissents from Dautzenberg.

(h) The eighth gift is speaking in tongues. But Paul uses the phrase *genē glōssōn* to indicate that there are different *kinds* of tongues (1 Cor. 12:10). Above all, "those who speak in a tongue do not speak to other people but to God" (14:2). Paul does commend the use of tongues in private devotion (14:15). But he also refers to the possibility that people use tongues-speech "to build up themselves" (14:4). P. Vielhauer argues that this refers to an ungodly self-affirmation or self-indulgence (*Oikodomē: Das Bild vom Bau in der christlichen Literatur* [Karlsruhe: Harrassowitz, 1940], 91-98). W. Schrage also links this with 10:24, "Do not seek your own advantage." Gordon Fee, however, dissents from this conclusion, but sees 14:4 as endorsing private prayer and praise (*God's Empowering Presence* [Carlisle: Paternoster; Peabody, Mass.: Hendrickson, 1996], 219). We saw in our examination of Acts 2 that some view tongues-speech as *xenoglossia,* or speaking unlearned foreign languages. But Paul regards tongues as unintelligible, and not a communicative action. It is difficult to harmonize this with Turner's view: "In Paul's view *glōssai* are most probably languages of some kind, not merely ecstatic shouts" (in M. J. Cartledge, ed., *Speaking in Tongues* [Milton Keynes: Paternoster, 2006], 12).

Many regard tongues-speech in Acts as a reversal of the confusion of tongues at Babel. But whether this is Paul's view is uncertain. In my commentary on the Greek text I have listed more than half a dozen views of what constitutes "tongues" in Paul (*First Epistle to the Corinthians,* 970-88). As we noted, the Pentecostal F. D. Macchia compares "sighs too deep for words" in Rom. 8:26. K. Stendahl and G. Theissen understand tongues as the welling up of unconscious longings and desires without the inhibitory censor, to express, for example, praise from the heart to God. This is akin to E. Käsemann's "Cry for Liberty." Stendahl sees the value of tongues, but warns us, "Few human beings can live healthily with high-voltage religious experience over a long period of time" ("Glossolalia," in *Paul among Jews and Gentiles,* 11; cf. 109-24). Theissen examines the subconscious and unconscious in Paul in a full-scale study, concluding that tongues are "the language of the unconscious" (*Psychological Aspects,* 79; cf. 59-114, 276-341).

(i) The interpretation of tongues (1 Cor. 12:10; Gk. *hermēneia glōssōn*) is amplified in 14:13: "One who speaks in a tongue should pray for the power to interpret" (Gk. *hina diermēneuē*). On the basis of Theissen's approach, the tongues-speaker needs to become conscious of what was buried in the depths of his unconscious mind. In contrast to many older English versions, the intrusion of "someone" *(tis)* is simply not in the Greek; 14:13 refers to the one who speaks in tongues. I have argued since 1979 that "interpretation" is not the best translation of *hermēneia* or the cognate verb *diermēneuō.* This Greek word *in this context* means to *"put into articulate speech."* I have shown that this is a frequent meaning in the Greek of Paul's lifetime, as evidenced by this meaning in Philo and Josephus ("The Interpretation of Tongues? A New Suggestion in the Light of Greek Usage in Philo and Josephus," *JTS* 30 [1979]: 15-36). It is fair to state, however, that this view remains controversial in many quarters.

(j) The list of "gifts of the Holy Spirit" ends in 12:10, but Paul adds others in verses 28-30. The first part of verse 28 recapitulates earlier discussions. But "forms of assistance" (NRSV, v. 28b; Gk. *antilēmpseis*) takes us beyond those we have discussed. The AV/KJV "helps" and RSV "helpers" are fairly colorless terms. The

Greek *antilambanō* normally means not only to help, but also to commit oneself to share a task. The most natural equivalent is "administration" or "administration assistant." We know that secretaries and administrators were a familiar feature of life in the first century, as they have become in many churches today. Of course, we could not have a "spontaneous administration" without self-contradiction.

(k) "Forms of leadership" (NRSV, v. 28b; Gk. *kubernēseis*) again seems a colorless translation, even if it opts for safety, and is not wrong. Moulton and Milligan translate the usual meaning in papyri as "steersman" or "pilot" (MM 363). The Greek word may well mean "strategic thinkers" or "church strategists" who point the way ahead through hazards.

(l) We cannot discuss apostles, prophets, and teachers without rehearsing long-past discussions, and engaging with the vast literature on apostleship. Chrysostom, Schrage, and Crafton see apostleship as a sign of humility, which points away from the human agent to Christ and his cross (J. A. Crafton, *The Agency of the Apostle* [Sheffield: Sheffield Academic Press, 1991], 33-103).

We may add an appendix to Paul that is unfashionable and unconvincing to most NT specialists. L. W. Hurtado has advanced the case for the deity of Jesus Christ in the NT by showing that the earliest Christians of the first century worshiped and venerated Christ as God, as determined on the basis of their devotional practices (*Lord Jesus Christ* [Grand Rapids: Eerdmans, 2003]). He acknowledges Paul's Jewishness and his monotheism (Rom. 9:1-5; Gal. 2:15; 1 Thess. 1:9; 1 Cor. 8:1-6). He then discusses the practical meaning of "Jesus is Lord," examining hortatory passages, eschatological passages, and worship passages (117-53). He concludes that Paul reflects "binitarian worship" (134-43), and cites such phenomena as his "grace benedictions" (Rom. 16:20; 1 Cor. 16:23; 2 Cor. 13:13). He comments that there is "explicit indication of direct, personal prayer to Jesus in 2 Corinthians 12:8-9" and elsewhere (140). But can we go further than "binitarianism"?

Hurtado argues that Paul's Jewish roots and monotheism provide the foundation for Jesus worship. This applies equally to recognition of the Holy Spirit as belonging to the same order of existence as God, not that of contingent beings. The Holy Spirit, after all, comes forth from God and conveys God's presence and power to the Christian community. He is not a subpersonal force. Bultmann's appeal to the "dynamistic" imagery of "pouring out" or "filling" *does not imply that the Spirit is subpersonal.* As I. T. Ramsey has argued, for every model or analogy we need "qualifiers." To qualify the personal models of "coming to our help," "interceding," or "crying," we need other symbols also. These qualifiers show that the Holy Spirit is not "personal" in the same way that a human is personal. Rather, the Holy Spirit is *"superpersonal"* or suprapersonal, in the sense that God is *more but not less* than personal. It is a mistake to think that Trinitarian theology emerged only in the fourth or fifth century. Hilary and Ambrose in the West and Athanasius and Basil in the East simply developed what they found in the Pauline text (Michael A. G. Haykin, *The Spirit of God: The Exegesis of 1 & 2 Corinthians in . . . the Fourth Century* [Leiden and New York: Brill, 1994]).

(iv) **The Holy Spirit in John and the Rest of the New Testament.** In John the importance of the Holy Spirit for the earthly life of Jesus is contested. A. Heron, Dunn, and the majority of scholars stress its importance. The Holy Spirit "remains" on Jesus (John 1:32), and he gives the Spirit "without measure" (3:34); Jesus "baptizes with the Holy Spirit" (1:33). Yet E. Schweizer argues, "Jesus is not represented as a pneumatic. His inspired speech and his miracles are nowhere attributed to the Spirit. The path taken by Luke does not satisfy John" ("Pneuma," in *TDNT* 6:438-39; cf. 438-44). Fison similarly comments on John 14:10, "He will not speak on his own (Gk. Aph' heautou) . . . He will glorify me." He writes, "The Spirit . . . effaces himself, and advertises Jesus" (*Blessing*, 137). The Holy Spirit also resists control and manipulation (3:8).

The Holy Spirit is admittedly more prominent in the Paraclete passages of John 14–16 than in 1–12. This is partly because the whole Gospel focuses on Christology, culminating with the confession of Thomas, "My Lord and my God!" (20:28). In the prologue it is Jesus Christ as God's "Word" who makes God communicable and "thinkable" (Jüngel). Christ is the source of life and light (1:4), and relates perhaps to preexistent Wisdom (Prov. 8:23-24). But the Holy Spirit brings truth from above (Gk. *anōthen;* John 3:5-7), and God is Spirit (4:24). The Spirit descends upon Jesus at his baptism (1:32-34). On the other hand, Fison asserts: "There is no sign whatever that Jesus spoke with tongues" (*Blessing*, 100). G. R. Beasley-Murray argues that Jesus spoke God's words "since the Father has given him the Spirit 'without measure'" (*John* [Nashville: Nelson, 1999], 53). Some argue on the basis of the Targum of Isa. 44:3 that the Spirit relates to the water of life in John 4:14 and 7:37-38. Other OT passages have also been cited.

The four Paraclete sayings (John 14:15-17; 14:26; 15:26-27; and 16:5-15) become very significant. Hans Windisch argues that these belong together and could readily be extracted from John, leaving a smooth text. But Barnabas Lindars doubts whether this is true of chapters 15 and 16, even if it might be applicable to 14:15-17. The verb *parakaleō* means "to call alongside [to help]," and Danker sees *Paraklētos* in the first instance as "One who appears on another's behalf" (BDAG 766). But he also notes that J. Behm translated the term as advocate or defending counsel in a legal context (rejected by K. Grayston), while C. K. Barrett allows the meaning "prosecuting counsel," alongside others. The Holy Spirit convicts of sin. Both "Comforter" and "Exhorter" are equally possible. As Heron observes, this range of vocabulary can be applied to Jesus also (*The Holy Spirit* [Philadelphia: Westminster, 1983], 52). In 14:18 Jesus declares, "I will not leave you orphaned; I am coming to you." The phrase "another Paraclete" *(allon paraklēton)* demonstrates their unity of operation. John is also interested in Christian experience. The experience of Christ and the experience of the Holy Spirit are one, as many of the Church Fathers will insist. In terms of early doctrine, John 15:26-27 confirms that the Spirit comes, or proceeds, from the Father *(to pneuma . . . ho para tou Patros ekporeuetai).* In terms of activity, the Spirit's further ministry is "to convict" (Gk. *elenchei*) the world of sin, righteousness, and judgment: the sin of the world, the righteousness of Christ, and the judgment of God. Finally, the Christ-centered nature of the Spirit's work is corroborated with the insufflation. Christ breathed on them and said, "Receive the Holy Spirit" (20:22).

There are overlapping themes in the rest of the NT. 1 John relates the Spirit to truth and revelation (1 John 5:6). The epistle also raises the problem of false prophecy (4:1), and the rejection of the ways of the world (4:1-6). 1 John also takes up the theme of witness (5:6). H. B. Swete observes, "The Spirit of Christ is known by the witness which he bears to Christ" (*The Holy Spirit in the New Testament* [New York and London: Macmillan, 1909], 269).

1 Peter explicitly takes up the theme of sanctification (1 Pet. 1:2), and then that of prophetic inspiration (1:11). As in Paul, Peter's readers were brought "good news by the Holy Spirit sent from heaven" (1:12). The allusion to "the spirits in prison" (3:19) reflects unusually a different use of "spirit," not the Holy Spirit. 4:6 may refer to living in the Spirit, but this is not clear. 2 Peter has parallels with Jude and may come from a different hand, but it again stresses that prophecy comes not from human will, but as prophets were "moved by the Holy Spirit," they "spoke from God" (2 Pet. 1:21). The probable allusion is to Scripture. Like 1 John 2, Peter warns us against false prophecy (2 Pet. 2:1-22). Jude refers to the Spirit only in verses 19-20: "worldly people, devoid of the Spirit, . . . are causing divisions."

The Epistle of James has few references to the Spirit, but what there is has importance. Swete paraphrases the difficult Greek in James 4:5 as "The Spirit of Christ in us longs after us, but jealously, with a love which resents any counteracting force such as friendship of the world" (*The Holy Spirit in the New Testament* [London: Macmillan, 1909], 257). The adverbial phrase *pros phthonon* denotes "with yearning jealousy." Hence this again clearly ascribes full personhood to the Holy Spirit. It is parallel with Eph. 4:30, "Do not grieve the Holy Spirit of God." Peter Davids argues that the Wisdom theme in James is "a wisdom pneumatology" (*The Epistle of James* [Grand Rapids: Eerdmans, 1982], 56). But such a conclusion seems speculative.

The Holy Spirit does not feature prominently in Hebrews. Some uses of "spirit" are anthropological (Heb. 4:12; 12:23), or refer to angelic beings (1:7, 14). There are, however, four clear references to the Holy Spirit. Heb. 2:4 refers to "gifts of the Holy Spirit, distributed according to his will." This is parallel with 1 Cor. 12:4-11. This passage urges the seriousness of the Christian calling, as against merely drifting. Heb. 6:4 makes a similar point. Those who have "shared in the Holy Spirit" must not lapse and fall away. The Christian life is ongoing. In F. F. Bruce's words, "continuance is the test of reality" (*The Epistle to the Hebrews*, rev. ed. [Grand Rapids: Eerdmans, 1990], 144). Heb. 3:7 refers to the Spirit's inspiration of Ps. 95, while Heb. 10:29 also warns against apostasy. A fifth reference, 9:14, is ambiguous, but may refer to empowerment by the Spirit.

In Revelation, the "seven spirits" (1:4; 3:1; 4:5; 5:6) may denote the Holy Spirit in his completeness, since "seven" in Revelation is seldom numerical but usually symbolic. The seer sees his visions "in the Spirit" (1:10; 4:2; 17:3; 21:10). The visions come from beyond himself, from God. Rev. 11:11, "the Spirit of life," reflects Ezekiel 37 and its parable of resurrection. Rev. 14:13 refers to the Spirit of prophecy. Both reflect NT themes. Finally, "The Spirit and the bride say, 'Come'" in Rev. 22:17. This suggests the yearning in the church at the prompting of the Holy Spirit. The Holy Spirit has given to the seer an ever-fresh vision of the sovereignty and purposes of God.

Reading: J. D. G. Dunn, *Jesus and the Spirit* (London: SCM, 1975); Gordon Fee, *God's Empowering Presence* (Carlisle: Paternoster; Peabody, Mass.: Hendrickson, 1996); L. W. Hurtado, *Lord Jesus Christ* (Grand Rapids: Eerdmans, 2003); J. Moltmann, *The Trinity and the Kingdom of God* (London: SCM, 1981); H. B. Swete, *The Holy Spirit in the New Testament* (New York and London: Macmillan, 1909); A. C. Thiselton, *The First Epistle to the Corinthians* (Grand Rapids: Eerdmans, 2000), 956-70, 1087-94.

The Spirit in Historical Theology

(i) **The Church before Nicaea.** (a) The Apostolic Fathers and apologists have relatively few references to the Holy Spirit, and half of the earliest references allude to the Spirit's inspiration of the OT. *1 Clement* (c. 96) exhorts readers to do what is written, and cites the Spirit's origin of Scripture (1.1). Ignatius (c. 110) asserts that the Holy Spirit speaks through bishops, presbyters, and deacons (*To the Philippians* 7.1). The *Didachē* warns us about false prophecy (11.3-12; 13.1, 3). More significantly in *1 Clement,* the Holy Spirit brings repentance (8.1), strength (18.1), illumination (21.2), desire for life (22.1-2), and especially the unity of the church (46.5-6). In a famous analogy, Ignatius speaks of God's carrying us up "using the rope of the Holy Spirit" (*To the Ephesians* 9.1), and attributes the conception and birth of Jesus to the Holy Spirit (18.2). References also occur in Polycarp, *Barnabas* (13.5), and the *Shepherd of Hermas* (2.1.1; *Similitude* 9.1-2).

(b) Among the apologists, Justin Martyr (c. 100–c. 165) sees the Holy Spirit as resting in Jesus (*Dialogue with Trypho* 87), descending on him like a dove at his baptism, and empowering him (88). Gifts are given through the Spirit (*First Apology* 6), and the Spirit is associated with reasonableness, not with ecstasy (13). Athenagoras (c. 180) formulates an embryonic doctrine of the Trinity: the Father, the Son, and the Spirit are one "by the unity and power of the Holy Spirit" (*Embassy* 10.3). God is not "separate" from Christ or the Spirit, any more than the rays of the sun are separate from the sun (10.3). Theophilus (second century) saw the Spirit in Gen. 1:2 as creative, acting cojointly with the Son as Logos, and as the Spirit of Wisdom (*To Autolycus* 1.7). The Holy Spirit embraces, and is embraced by, the hand of God (*hypo cheiros Theou,* 1.5). He uses the words *trias* (triad) and "Trinity" (2.13).

(c) In the second century, Irenaeus (c. 130–c. 200) employs the memorable metaphor of Christ and the Spirit as "the two hands of God": distinct but inseparable (*Against Heresies* 1.4; 4.20.3). The Spirit shares in creation (1.4), anoints

Christ (3.17-18), and plays a part in the virgin birth, the incarnation, Christ's baptism, and the resurrection of Christ (3.18.3; 3.9.3). The Holy Spirit indwells the believer, and brings about the resurrection of the dead (5.8.1-4; cf. Rom. 8:9, 15). In both Testaments the Spirit is the Spirit of prophecy and of revelation (3.4.1; 4.33.1). Clement of Alexandria (c. 150–c. 215) examines 1 Cor. 3:1-3, and urges the need to advance from "fleshly to spiritual" (*The Instructor* 1.6). This stands in contrast to the fixed categories of Gnosticism. In *Miscellanies* he expounds the gifts of the Spirit in 1 Cor. 12:7-11 (*Stromata* 4.21). He alludes to the Trinity, calling the Son "second" and the Spirit "third." Tertullian (c. 150–c. 225) also urges the creativity of the Spirit in Gen. 1:2 (*On Baptism* 4), and the role of the Spirit in the conception of Christ (*Prescription against All Heresies* 13). As we should expect in his Montanist phase, he sees the work of the Spirit as the "New Prophecy," and the Spirit's union with the Father as rays to the sun (*Against Praxeas* 8 and 13). Indeed, the Spirit "proceeds . . . from the Father" (*Against Praxeas* 4). By about the end of the second century, then (c. 210-220), most of the basic themes of the NT on the Spirit had been noted and had received comment.

(d) In the third century, Origen (c. 185-254) gives a succinct, systematic exposition of the doctrine of the Holy Spirit in *First Principles* 1.3. Against Gnosticism, he stresses the unity of the two Testaments (1.3.2). Like his predecessors, he urges a close relationship between the Holy Spirit and Christ, as in 1 Cor. 12:3. The Holy Spirit is not a "creature" or creative being (*First Principles* 1.3.3), but, rather, he gives life (2.7.2). He works in cooperation with the whole Trinity (1.3.5). The Spirit also gives increasing sanctification (1.3.8). Hippolytus of Rome (c. 170–c. 236) calls the Spirit a guardian of church order (*Refutation of All Heresies*, preface, 5). He attacks Montanism and their "wretched women" (10.21). He insists on the role of bishops, and anticipates Basil on the threefold Gloria. He is most concerned about order, although many describe as "charismatic" his exposition of the gifts of the Spirit. Yet he stresses confirmation and the Lord's Supper. His near-contemporary Novatian stresses the role of the Spirit in the virginal conception of Jesus Christ, and the "outpouring" of the Holy Spirit in Acts 2:17, alongside the "Spirit of truth" in John 14:17. He expounds the gifts of the Spirit in 1 Cor. 12:7-11 (*On the Trinity* 29). He uses much Pauline material, including Rom. 8:9, the Spirit as a pledge of the inheritance, and sanctification. The Spirit comes forth from God (1 Cor. 2:12). Cyprian (d. 258) writes during the time of the Decian persecution, and with the Donatists argues against the readmission to the church of lapsed Christians. The unity of the church is held together by its bishops, according to Cyprian. Moreover, martyrs are "full of the Holy Spirit" (*On the Lord's Prayer* 69.14). In spite of this, Burgess sees Cyprian as strongly "charismatic." Much depends on how we define "prophecy." In spite of their importance for church order and liturgy, none of these thinkers can perhaps approach Tertullian and Origen in coherent and creative work on the Holy Spirit.

(ii) **The Post-Nicaean Church.** (a) The key thinkers of the Western Fathers were Hilary of Poitiers (c. 315-368) and Ambrose of Milan (c. 339-397). Some have called Hilary "the Athanasius of the West." His exegetical work is impressive. His main work, *On the Trinity* (c. 362), extends to twelve books. He insists that the Father, Son, and Spirit are one *(unus);* the Spirit "is joined with the Father and Son" (*On the Trinity* 7.2). The Spirit is one in honor and power with God. He proceeds from the Father (John 15:26; *On the Trinity* 8.19-20). The Spirit is deity, not a "creature," or a creative being. Yet he has distinctive roles also, for example, in the giving of "the gifts of the Spirit," according to God's will (1 Cor. 12:4-11). His formula is *ex Patre per Filium.*

Ambrose of Milan also drew on the theology of the Eastern Church. He gave examples of "spiritual interpretation," for example, of the Gideon narrative (*On the Holy Spirit* 1.1-8), and urged that the Holy Spirit is not a mere "creature." He anointed Jesus for his messianic task (1.3.32), and bestowed diversities of gifts. He is Giver of life, and is worthy of worship. He inspires the Christian to pray. He is "of one will and operation with God the Father" (2.12.142-143). He sanctifies Christians in holiness, making them a holy temple, which he indwells (1 Cor. 3:16; 6:19; *On the Holy Spirit* 3.11.81; 3.16.109).

Augustine of Hippo (354-430) approaches the Trinity from a number of contexts (against the Pelagians, the Donatists, and the Manichees), stresses the unity of God as Trinity, and elaborates an analogy with the human condition, expounding it as "Memory, understanding, and will, not three lives, but one life ... one essence" (*On the Trinity* 1.3). The union of God is "consubstantial and co-eternal," especially in love (*caritas;* 6.5.7). "The Holy Spirit ... is of both [the Father and the Son] ... a mutual love, wherewith the Father and the Son reciprocally love one another" (15.17.27). This may suggest a lessening of the Holy Spirit as a "person," but Augustine also attacks the Arian view that the Holy Spirit "was not God, but a creature" (*Sermon* 21.5). He glorifies Christ, and does not speak "of himself" (John 16:13-14; Gk. *aph' heautou*; *On the Gospel of John* 99.2). "The Spirit may be given by the laying on of hands" (*On Baptism* 3.16). Both the gifts of the Spirit and church order are important (*Reply to Faustus* 21.8). The Spirit is active at creation in the breathing of God (Gen. 2:7). Again, Augustine expresses the characteristic creedal form of the Western Church: he is "the Spirit of the Father and the Son" (*City of God* 13.24).

(b) The Eastern Fathers. (1) Eusebius of Caesarea (c. 260–c. 340) and Cyril of Jerusalem (c. 315-387). Eusebius's statement about the Holy Spirit serves mainly to exclude Sabellianism, the doctrine that the Father, the Son, and the Holy Spirit constitute modes or aspects of God. Cyril of Jerusalem has a more pastoral and practical approach in his *Catechetical Lectures* 16 and 17. The Spirit is "a Power most mighty, a Being Divine and unsearchable" (16.3; 1 Cor. 2:10-13). But Cyril avoids speculative theology, urging: "Let us return to the Scriptures" (16.11). He adds: "He will not declare his substance with exactness" (16.5). The Holy Spirit helps us to pray (Rom. 8:26), and gives a variety of gifts for service (*Catechetical Lectures* 16.11, 12, 17-20, 22; and 1 Cor. 12:8-11). He rejects Montanism and "enthusiasm." H. B. Swete remarked that of the *work* of the Spirit, no writer of the fourth century has spoken more fully or convincingly. He is sober, pastoral, and practical.

(2) Athanasius (c. 296-373) insists that the Holy Spirit is not a created being (Gk. *ktisma*), nowadays an "it." He distinguishes between different meanings or uses of "spirit" *(pneuma)*. The Son and the Spirit cannot be separated. Indeed, "the whole Triad is one God" (*Letters to Serapion* 1.17). When the Holy Spirit is given to us, "God is in us" (1.19). The transcendent Spirit "comes forth from God" (1.22; 1 Cor. 2:12). He anointed Christ for his messianic work and dwells in Christians as God's temple (1 Cor. 3:16-17). The Spirit is "the image of his Son" (Rom. 8:29; *Letters to Serapion* 1.24). He cites 1 Cor. 12:4-6: "diversities of gifts, but the same Spirit . . . the same Lord . . . the same God" (1.30). This reflects the creeds, councils, and Scripture (2.2-6). Citing "the grace" in 2 Cor. 13:13, he insists that the Spirit is "indivisible" from the Father and the Son (3.5). Finally, he is the Spirit of sanctification (1.22-23). He also uses the term *homoousion* of the Spirit, sometimes translated "coessential," but meaning "of the same being" (1.27).

(3) Basil of Caesarea (c. 330-379) reflects the strong influence of Athanasius, but together with him represents a peak in the theology of the Spirit in the Eastern Church. The Holy Spirit is of the same order of Being *(homoousios)* as the Father. His work approximates to the formulation of the Nicene Creed, of the Second Ecumenical Council called by Theodosius. The Holy Spirit is "the Lord, and Giver of Life, who proceeds from the Father, who with the Father is worshipped and glorified, who spoke by the prophets." The Pneumatomachian controversy (i.e., debate with those who denied the deity and coequality of the Spirit) provoked Basil to develop his doctrine, both in *Against Eunomius* (364) and in *On the Holy Spirit*. Basil insisted on the importance of the threefold Gloria to the Father, the Son, and the Holy Spirit (*On the Holy Spirit* 1.3; *NPNF*, ser. 2, 8:3; cf. *On the Holy Spirit* 1-8). Our Lord "co-joined the Spirit with the Father and Himself in baptism" (10.24). He refers to the anointing of Jesus by the Holy Spirit (12.28), and explicitly to Paul's associating together the Father, the Son, and the Holy Spirit (15.34-35). On the work of the Spirit, he writes: "The Spirit gives us the earnest of life . . . having our fruit in holiness . . . the Spirit pours in quickening power, renewing our souls from the deadness of sin" (15.37; *NPNF*, 8:23). In *On the Holy Spirit* 17-22, Basil underlines further the deity and coequality of the Spirit with the Father and the Son (19.49). He "makes intercession for us" (19.50; cf. Rom. 8:26-27). He fully expounds "gifts" in 1 Cor. 12:4-11, urging the unity of the Spirit (16.61; *NPNF*, 8:38).

(4) Gregory of Nazianzus (c. 330-390), Basil's close friend and fellow "Cappadocian Father," also stressed the unity of the Trinity. "Three" persons has nothing to do with numerals. Like many modern theologians, Gregory urged a unity of *activity,* or "identity of activity" with God. In 380 he delivered his *Theological Orations,* which H. B. Swete calls the "greatest of all sermons on the Holy Spirit." These repeat themes from Basil: the Spirit is not a creature *(ktisis),* and "proceeds from God" (*On the Holy Spirit* 8). The Spirit prays in us and deserves "co-equal

honour" with the Father (12; *NPNF,* ser. 2, 7:321). Again "three" (of the Trinity) does not denote numerals (19 and 29; *NPNF* 7:327). We cannot deny "personality" to the Spirit (32).

(5) Gregory of Nyssa (c. 330-395), Basil's brother, like Gregory of Nazianzus, insists that "three" in this Trinitarian context has a context beyond any analogy with numerals. He concludes: "Every operation [of God] has its origin from the Father, and proceeds through the Son, and is perfected in the Holy Spirit" (*On "Not Three Gods," NPNF,* ser. 2, 5:334). This activity is one (*On the Trinity* 6). Again, many themes are common to all three Cappadocian Fathers, although Gregory of Nyssa especially examines linguistic questions, and those about analogy. He was a major figure at the Council of Constantinople (381).

(iii) **The Medieval Church.** (a) The First Half of the Middle Ages. Gregory of Rome (c. 540-604), Philoxenus of Syria (c. 440-523), Bede (c. 673-735), Alcuin (c. 740-804), Photius (c. 810-895), Anselm (c. 1033-1109), Rupert of Deutz (c. 1075-1129), and most writers up to the twelfth century tended to be dominated by the agenda of the Fathers. Gregory stresses some pastoral concerns about the Holy Spirit, including his gift of wisdom and tongues; the best example of the Spirit's gifts, however, can be seen in Christ (*Moralia* 14). He asserts that the Spirit "proceeds from the Father and the Son" (*Homily on the Gospels* 26; cf. *Moralia* 5.65; 27.34). He stresses the life of holiness that the Spirit gives (*Homily* 30). Bede is largely a transmitter of Augustine. Alcuin stresses the Spirit's coequality with the Father and the Son (*Commentary on John* 15.26), and follows the Western Church's "proceeds from the Father and the Son." He also speaks of receiving the Spirit from the bishop through the laying on of hands (*Letters* 80). Photius of Constantinople summarizes the work of the Church Fathers, but in *Mystagogy of the Holy Spirit* defends the Eastern Church's view of the simple procession of the Spirit from the Father. Anselm's *Monologion* reflects Augustine's *On the Trinity.* The Spirit is coeternal with the Word. He declares, "The Spirit possesses in every respect the attributes [or character] of the Father and the Son.... The whole Father *(totus Pater)* is present in the Son and the common Spirit" (*Proslogion* 58, 59). Like Augustine, Anselm sees the Trinity as memory, understanding *(intelligentia),* and love *(amor).* Rupert of Deutz presupposes the agency of the Father, but also stresses especially the renewal of the Spirit (*On the Holy Trinity* 21.126). This involves the Spirit's gifts, but as a "cooperative" work of the Trinity. The subject seems less prominent in Abelard, who has other concerns.

(b) The Second Half of the Middle Ages. In general there is a change of emphasis from the twelfth to the fifteenth century. (1) Bernard of Clairvaux (1090-1153) stresses the *work* of the Holy Spirit more than his person. He especially focuses on love *(caritas),* distinguishing between types or "degrees" of love ("The Four Degrees of Love," in *On the Love of God* 8-10). Humans begin by loving God with some self-interest for their own sake. Then, in the second degree, a person "loves purely and without self-interest." In the third degree, he loves God "for himself," while the fourth degree is an indescribable perfection. But all this is made possible by the Holy Spirit. Similarly in his *Sermons on the Song of Songs* the fellowship between Christ and his church is also made possible by the Holy Spirit: "It is by giving the Spirit [that] he reveals that he shows us himself" (*Sermon* 8.5). He writes of attending "gift-laden visits of the Holy Spirit" (*Sermon* 17). The Holy Spirit, he urges, both "leads us to salvation" and "outwardly endows us with serviceable gifts" (*Sermon* 18.1). The origin of the gifts is sheer grace.

(2) Hildegard of Bingen (1098-1179) is an outstanding example of twelfth-century mysticism, notable for her visions, pictures, music, and preaching. In 1141 she began writing her *Scivias*, which is short for "Know the Way of the Lord." She also opposed the dualism of the Cathars. In advance of Pentecostalism the Cathars claimed to have received the "baptism in the Holy Spirit." Many will regard the extensive use of "pictures" as controversial, for as Wittgenstein has observed in our day, a picture can be "variously interpreted." In her visions she saw fire, light, and flashes of light as the Holy Spirit (*Scivias* 2.2). She uses analogies of flame, stone, and red burning fire. But she also formulates conceptual theology: "The three persons [of the Trinity] are inseparable" (2.2). She draws material from biblical and patristic traditions. In her time many regarded her as a prophet.

(3) Richard of St. Victor (c. 1123-1173) acknowledges the sovereignty of the Holy Spirit: "The Spirit flows where he wills" (*The Mystical Ark* 3.17). The Spirit in a sovereign way distributes the gifts of 1 Cor. 12:4-11 (*The Mystical Ark* 3.24). His view of the Holy Trinity is partly Augustinian, but he seeks to be more "personal" than Augustine. Richard stresses the "spontaneous" nature of several of the Spirit's gifts. The Trinity consists of "a co-eternity of persons" (*On the Trinity* 3.6).

(4) Bonaventura (c. 1217-1274) stresses both the theme of mystical contemplation and the upward ladder, or ascending journey, of which many in Reformed theology disapprove as undermining grace. In this ascent the seventh stage is mystical, becoming "ecstatic love." God leaves his "footprints" *(vestigia)* for believers to follow (*Itinerary of the Mind* 1.2). Untroubled contemplation is "a garden of delights" (1.7). Jesus is the Way, the Door, the Ladder (7.1). But the desire for such vision comes only to one "inflamed by the fire of the Holy Spirit" (7.4). Eternal light brings "certitude" (*Disputed Questions* 3.11). True knowledge of God is mediated by the Holy Spirit, and his "sevenfold grace" (*Tree of Life* 49). The Spirit's action is "the love with which the Father loves the Son" (*Commentary on the Sentences of Peter Lombard* 11.1).

(5) Thomas Aquinas (1125-1274) devotes part 1 of the *Summa Theologiae* to God, the source of all, especially as Trinity (qu. 27-43, Blackfriars ed. vols. 6-7). In question 36, article 2, reply, Thomas asserts: "The Holy Spirit is from the Father and the Son, not created, not begotten, but proceeding." Question 37 expounds the Holy Spirit as love, following Augustine. In question 38 he discusses God's "giving" of the Holy Spirit: "Gift is properly an unreturnable giving, a gratuitous donation . . . the Holy Spirit proceeds as love" (art. 2, reply). In part 1.2, question 28, Thomas relates the work of the Holy Spirit to habits of action, or to virtues. In part 1, question 70, he considers "the fruit of the Spirit" (Gal. 5:22-23). He dis-

cusses the nature and gift of prophecy in Paul (2.2, qu. 171-173). The goal, however, is to be conformed to Christ (qu. 68, art. 1, reply). Among the fruit of the Spirit, "we reckon 'charity' *(caritas)* ... the highest ... since He Himself is love" (qu. 70, art. 3). Commenting on 1 Thess. 5:19-20, Aquinas sees prophecy as including especially preaching (qu. 173, art. 3, reply to obj. 4). The earlier part, however, remains a reflection of Augustine, where the Spirit is the bond of love between the Father and the Son.

(6) Catherine of Siena (c. 1347-1380) lived as a mystic for some years, but in 1377 she underwent a still deeper mystical experience, leading to her *Dialogue*. Like Hildegard, she portrayed her life with God largely through pictures and visual imagery. She explicitly spoke of "metaphors ... ladders, castles and dark nights," describing what is indescribable in terms of concepts. She sees "a bridge as the way to heaven.... The soul ... is overflowing with love ...; when my Son was lifted up on the wood of the most holy cross" (*Dialogue* 8-11). The disciples "received the plenitude of the Holy Spirit" (20). She reflects in her thoughts the Lord saying: "I love you of *grace*, not because I *owe* you My love" (42). Nevertheless, unlike the Reformers, she exclaims, "The whole of your faith is founded on obedience" (*A Treatise on Obedience* 2). On the Trinity and the Holy Spirit, she follows Augustine and Aquinas (*Dialogue* 78). Her constant use of pictures and images may be a cause of concern today if Wittgenstein is right about them being "variously interpreted," but the patristic tradition gives her a sense of direction, perhaps more than the "Third Wave" renewal of today.

(7) Julian of Norwich (1342-1416) also spent much of her life in contemplation as a mystic. She recounts her sixteen revelations of Christ in *Revelations of Divine Love*, or *Showings* (shorter text, 1393; longer text, after 1393). Her two most widely known revelations are: "I shall make all things well" (*Revelations of Divine Love* 15) and "Our Saviour is our true mother" (57). She speaks of "our Mother, Christ" (58). The imagery surrounding God as Father and Christ as Mother becomes complex, especially in relation to the Holy Spirit, who gives "love and goodness" (58). But she also stresses the Trinity (4), although most of all sharing in the sufferings and the blood of Christ (7). More controversially, she assured Margery Kempe (c. 1373-c. 1440), her fellow mystic of neighboring King's Lynn, also Norfolk, that her excessive outbursts of emotions and tears were a sign of the Holy Spirit.

(8) Walter Hilton (c. 1343-1396) urged moderation in the explanation or description of mystical visions. He advocated the contemplative life (*The Scale of Perfection* 1-9), but recognized that this could too easily pass into "imagining" (10-11). He urged the possibility of self-deception. To desire Christ, he stated, is more important than "songs and sounds to the ear, all tastes and smellings" (pt. 3, chap. 3). A person cannot "suddenly" reach a high point in grace. In harmony with Hilton, the anonymous *Cloud of Unknowing* (c. 1390) warns mystics about pride and arrogance in receiving "revelations." It has affirmation with Pseudo-Dionysius, but urges meekness.

(9) Teresa of Ávila (1515-1582) and John of the Cross (1542-1591) take us beyond

the Middle Ages, and belong to the sixteenth-century Spanish mystics. In her work *Interior Castle,* Teresa undergoes "assaults of the devils" (1.13) and experiences "several kinds of raptures" (4.2). "Ecstasy" (4.18) seems to receive more emphasis than the Holy Spirit, although the persons of the Trinity reveal themselves as "distinct," yet "of one substance," in *The Seventh Mansion* (1.9).

(iv) **The Reformers.** (a) Martin Luther (1483-1546) and the "enthusiasts" or "fanatics" *(Schwärmer).* In 1513 Luther came across the word "righteousness" in Ps. 31:1. He confessed that until then he had "hated" the term "righteousness." But in the light of Rom. 1:16-17, he wrote, "I began to understand . . . that a just man lives by the gift of God. . . . I felt myself born afresh and to have entered . . . into paradise itself" (cited in G. E. Rupp and B. Drewery, eds., *Martin Luther* [London: Arnold, 1970], 6). He nailed his Ninety-five Theses on the door of Wittenberg's castle church in 1517. In 1521 the Roman Church excommunicated him. R. Prenter comments: "The concept of the Holy Spirit completely dominates Luther's theology. In every decisive matter . . . we are forced to take into consideration his concept of the Holy Spirit" (*Spiritus Creator* [Philadelphia: Muhlenberg, 1953], 147). In addition to the tradition inherited from Augustine and Richard of St. Victor, he stressed the Spirit's work of sanctification. Luther declared, "The Holy Spirit enlightened me with his gifts . . . gave me the saving knowledge of Jesus" (*Small Catechism* [1529]). He added: "By faith he works a renewal of my life." Kärkkäinen writes: "Luther took the designation *Holy Spirit* to mean the sanctifying work" (*The Large Catechism;* V.-M. Kärkkäinen, *The Holy Spirit and Salvation* [Louisville: Westminster John Knox, 2010], 154-55).

However, Luther appealed to the Holy Spirit to grant "that we may be protected against the enthusiasts, i.e. spirits who boast that they have received the Spirit without . . . the Word" (*The Smalcald Articles,* pt. 3, art. 8, sect. 19). On the subject of the Holy Spirit, Luther was compelled to attack the enthusiasts more than the Roman Church. He declared, "It is the devil himself . . . the Spirit without the Word" (prop. 8). Where Christ is not preached, "there is no Holy Spirit" (*The Large Catechism,* Creed, art. 3). Unlike the enthusiasts, Luther stressed *Anfechtung,* or trials and struggles, as part of sanctification. The *Schwärmer* (as Luther called them) were Radical Reformers who preached against monastic vows, the Mass, clerical robes, images, the baptism of infants, and all titles of dignitaries. They contrasted and privileged "the leading of the Spirit" with and over theological learning. Andreas Carlstadt and Thomas Müntzer were their leaders. Worst of all, in Luther's view, they encouraged and led the Peasants' Revolt. In 1523-1524 Carlstadt urged people to empty themselves to listen to the Spirit. Luther condemned these "new prophets" as "satanic." In 1525 the princes of Saxony defeated Müntzer's rebellion, when he lost 8,000 men. Prenter sees the two different conceptions of Christianity in Luther and the enthusiasts. They made the Holy Spirit the reward of the perfect. To Luther this undermined justification by grace. While P. Melanchthon, Luther's collaborator, was less harsh on the Radical Reformers, Luther saw them as enemies of the gospel, and betrayers of grace.

(b) Ulrich Zwingli (1484-1531) at first gave more credit to the enthusiasts, but in the end he found himself forced to agree with Luther. He wrote: "Whether the Spirit of God is with you is demonstrated above all by whether the Word is your guide" (*The Defense of the Reformed Faith* [Allison Park, Pa.: Pickwick, 1984], 46). Heinrich Bullinger (1504-1575), Zwingli's successor, also stressed the relation of the Spirit to the Word. Martin Bucer (1491-1551) followed Luther in stressing the work of the Spirit as sanctification and new truth. He also urged that the Spirit does not lead to self-glorification, as did the enthusiasts. The Holy Spirit produces deep love for God, and enables the interpretation of the Bible. The gift of teaching, he claimed, is not in the least to be less valued than prophecy.

(c) John Calvin (1509-1564) draws on both Scripture and several of the Church Fathers (especially Augustine and Gregory of Nazianzus) to stress the coeternity of the Father, the Son, and the Holy Spirit. He expounds this doctrine in *Institutes* 1.13, and also in 3.1. 1.13 expounds the person of the Holy Spirit; 3.1 turns to his work and empowerment. He stresses the argument of Rom. 8:9, "Anyone who does not have the Spirit of Christ does not belong to him" (3.1.2). "He that raised up Christ from the dead shall also quicken your mortal bodies by his Spirit" (3.1.2; cf. Rom. 8:11). He expounds the biblical metaphors of water, fire, oil of anointing, and earnest of our inheritance (3.1.3). Calvin concludes: "Our justification is his work; from him is power, sanctification, truth, grace, and every good thought ... from the Spirit alone" (1.13.14). Calvin's work on the person and work of the Holy Spirit eminently reflects Paul and other biblical writings.

(v) **From the Post-Reformation Era to 1800.** (a) The Post-Reformation Era. John Owen (1616-1683) is probably the leading writer on this subject in the post-Reformation era. He became vice-chancellor of Oxford University and was a leader of the Puritans, and onetime chaplain to Oliver Cromwell. His book *The Holy Spirit* (1674) is a major source (Grand Rapids: Kregel, 1954). Chapter 1 begins with names and titles of the Spirit, his personality and gifts. Chapter 2 concerns the new creation; 3, regeneration; and 4, sanctification. Owen examines the *charismata* of the Holy Spirit in 1 Cor. 12:8-10, including prophecy. We can pretend, he argues, to "supernatural agitations from God," when these are really inspired "by the devil" (*The Holy Spirit* 25). He admits that the meanings of *ruach* and *pneuma* are "very various." But many refer to the Holy Spirit "who proceeds from God" (*to Pneuma to ek tou Theou*, 1 Cor. 2:12) "as a distinct Person." For he is "the Spirit of God" (*The Holy Spirit* 37-39). The Spirit is "a distinct, living, powerful, intelligible, divine person" (41). The Spirit works both through nature and through grace, for example, in "garnishing the heavens" (Ps. 19:1) or the galaxy or Milky Way (122). Sanctification comes from the Spirit "by degrees." His is a *progressive* work (461). Owen warns us against undue introspection. Owen's contribution is robust, biblical, and full of commonsense realism.

(b) The Pietists. The first of the Pietists was Philipp Jakob Spener (1635-1705). He sought to "improve" Lutheran orthodoxy. For example, he encouraged "spiritual gifts," including speech, from the congregation and argued that a simple-minded minister was better than a worldly person "with double doctorate degrees." But he remained loyal to Luther. The Word and the Spirit belong together and must "penetrate the heart" (*Pia Desideria,* in *Pietists,* ed. P. Erb [London: SPCK, 1983], 48). He rejected the extremes of the Radical Reformers or "enthusiasts." He wrote, "Scripture is a light for our enlightenment, but it is a word of the Spirit" (*The Necessary Reading and Useful Reading of the Holy Scripture* [1694], in *Pietists,* 72). However, Spener's disciple, A. H. Francke (1663-1727), encouraged ecstatic experiences, visions, and "prophecy," and nursed apocalyptic expectations. In Germany Pietism spread from Leipzig to the followers of Nicholas von Zinzendorf (1700-1760). Zinzendorf founded the Moravians, who to some extent influenced Wesley, and in part eventually Johann A. Bengel (1687-1752) and Friedrich Oetinger (1702-1782).

(c) George Fox (1624-1691) became the founder of the Quakers, or Society of Friends. They clearly emphasized the "experience" of the Holy Spirit (like later Pentecostals) and earned their popular name because of their trembling or shaking at the Spirit's presence. They also stressed, however, silence to hear the Spirit, and the "inner light" of the Holy Spirit. Fox's *Journal* (1694) was an autobiography mixing spiritual experience with natural events. In 1647 he received the "revelation" that all earthly power was corrupt. He suffered intermittent imprisonment for his opposition to the established church and the establishment in general. In 1648-1649, "The Lord's power began to shake them . . . as in the days of the apostles" (*Journal of George Fox* [New York: Cosimo Books, 2007], 13). He called the parish churches of the Church of England "steeple houses" (14). By contrast, "the Friends" sought "fellowship . . . in the Holy Spirit" (14), and had "Meeting Houses." In 1650-1651 he was imprisoned for "diverse blasphemous opinions" (31), but believed that the Holy Spirit of God commanded them. What most galled the established church was his preaching of *sinless perfection:* "They could not bear to hear victory over sin and the devil. . . . They could not believe that any could be free from sin this side of the grave" (32). Fox, in the name of the "inner light" of the Holy Spirit, opposed the use of doctrine, reason, and education, in contrast to "experience."

(d) John Wesley (1703-1791) is considered elsewhere. But in an age of formal rationalization, it is understandable that he should emphasize experience. His decisive experience came in 1738, after ordination and missionary work in Georgia, America, when he read Luther's preface to the book of Romans. He afterward wrote, "I felt I did trust in Christ, Christ alone, for salvation; and an assurance was given to me that he had taken away my sin" (*Journal* [London: Isbister, 1902], 43). After a brief consultation with the Moravians in Germany, he followed Whitefield to Bristol, then preached as an itinerant in London, Newcastle, and elsewhere. We find less explicit material on the Holy Spirit in his *Journal* than we might expect. Clearly, he believed in "healing" (145) and lay preaching. In America he ordained Francis Asbury (1745-1816). Whether he actually advocated sinless perfection has long been debated. Unlike Fox, he stressed the Bible, reason, tradition, and the sacraments, *as well as* "experience." He certainly believed that the Holy Spirit was given to every Christian believer for salvation and sanctification. He even preached: "How many have mistaken the voice of their own imagination for the witness of the Spirit of God" (Sermon 10, "The Witness of the Spirit," ed. D. Leonard, in *Christian Classics Ethereal Library*, online). Wesley's sermons reveal a Trinitarian orthodoxy.

(e) Jonathan Edwards (1703-1758) is associated with the Great Awakening in America of the 1730s and 1740s. He led a huge revival in his Congregationalist church of Northampton, Massachusetts. In 1737 he published *A Faithful Narrative of the Surprising Works of God;* and in 1746, his *Treatise concerning Religious Affections* (*The Works of Jonathan Edwards*, vol. 2 [New Haven: Yale University Press, 2009]). As a philosopher and also a Calvinist, he expounded the peril of self-deception, and the need for discernment. Like Paul, he used "spiritual" for what is of the Holy Spirit, not for mere "religious feelings." He wrote, "Holiness is the nature of the Spirit of God" (*Religious Affections* 1.2). He added, "There is a *pretended* great humiliation ... emptied of self ... [but] confident, noisy, assuming humility" (sect. 6). Real, authentic Christians are "Christ-like" (sect. 8). "The Spirit is the water of life." He hesitated to call the Spirit "supernatural," preferring the terms "from beyond," "surprising," and "from outside man."

(vi) **The Nineteenth Century.** Apart from George Fox and the Quakers, there was general unanimity about the person and work of the Holy Spirit, admittedly with variations, until the modern era from about 1820 onward. The nineteenth century witnessed at least three or, more probably, four traditions: with the rise of liberalism, F. D. E. Schleiermacher and G. W. F. Hegel developed their own streams of thought; Reformed orthodoxy expressed itself through such scholars as Charles Hodge in America, George Smeaton in Scotland, and Abraham Kuyper in Holland; anticipations of aspects of the later Pentecostal approach found advocates in Edward Irving, Albert Simpson, and Benjamin Irwin; and in the Roman Catholic Church, John Henry Newman reacted against the dry rationalism of much in the eighteenth and nineteenth centuries, and sought creatively to recapture the reality of the unseen world.

(a) Friedrich Schleiermacher (1768-1834) began his early life under the influence of Pietism and the Moravians, wrote of Christ as "my Savior," and always regarded preaching as "my proper office." But when he entered the University of Halle, he found the intellectual climate one where he could breathe freely. He was profoundly influenced by Kant's philosophy and the Enlightenment. He also fell under the influence of Romanticism. In 1799, as a young man, he wrote *On Religion: Speeches to Its Cultured Despisers* (London: Kegan Paul, Trench, 1893). Piety, he wrote, is "a revelation of the infinite in the finite" (36). In 1809-1810 he wrote his *Aphorisms on Hermeneutics*. For most of his life he was professor of theology at Berlin, and preached regularly at Trinity Church. He called this "the sweetest desire of my life." On the subject of the Holy Spirit he combined traditional Pietist aspects with immanentism or panentheism. On the first aspect, he wrote in his major theological work *The Christian Faith* (2nd ed. 1830): "*Every regenerate person partakes of the Holy Spirit, so that there is no living fellowship with Christ without an indwelling of the Spirit,* and vice versa" (*The Christian Faith* [Edinburgh: T. & T. Clark, 1989], 574). But on the second aspect, the Holy Spirit is manifested as the religious consciousness of the church. This is focused as "a feeling of utter dependence on God" (*Gefühl schlechthinger Abhängigheit;* 12-31). This experience is not mere "feeling," but a feeling *of* the reality that the Spirit gives.

G. W. F. Hegel (1770-1831) was professor of philosophy at Berlin from 1818, while Schleiermacher was professor of theology there. The Spirit plays a key role in his thought, but this is partly speculative and the fruit of his philosophical idealism. The Spirit became part of Hegel's philosophical system. In his *Phenomenology of Spirit (Phänomenologie des Geistes)* (1807), Hegel saw thought as a ladder that culminated in critical philosophy. God as Trinity spiritualizes himself (or itself) in the world-historical process. All knowledge is also bound to history, or historical finitude, or how a person is situated within history. This "historical situatedness" was called by M. Heidegger and H.-G. Gadamer *Geschichtlichkeit,* "historicality" or "historicity." Race, class, and upbringing largely determine what a person *counts as* "knowledge." Into this philosophical scheme Hegel fits his philosophy of the Spirit. God the Father is "Absolute Spirit." The incarnation, in which Jesus Christ takes flesh, constitutes the antithesis of this, or its negation. God *differentiates* himself from the experience of the Son. (This principle has value, and in a different context finds its way into the contemporary theology of J. Moltmann and W. Pannenberg.) God's identity is both himself as Eternal Spirit and the "other" as the incarnate and crucified Christ. In a mediating *synthesis* the Holy Spirit raises Jesus from the dead, once again to reign as Spirit. Hegel criticizes the Roman Catholic Church for absolutizing the crucified Christ as a static crucifix, and thereby failing to be a religion of the Spirit. How far his theology of the Spirit is determined by his philosophy, or philosophy of history by his view of the Spirit and Christ, is debatable. In the end he tends to identify the work of the Spirit with the merely ethical (*Sittlichkeit; Phenomenology of Mind* [New York: Harper and Row, 1967], 460). His system is very different from Schleiermacher's more Christ-related and church-related thought.

(b) Charles Hodge (1797-1871), G. Smeaton, and A. Kuyper were motivated by a need to defend orthodoxy, especially Reformed orthodoxy. Hodge championed Calvinism at Princeton, in contrast to Horace Bushnell's liberalism at Yale. He argued for the personality of the Holy Spirit as "sanctifier, teacher, comforter, and guide" (*Systematic Theology,* 3 vols. [Grand Rapids: Eerdmans, 1946], 1:525). "The Holy Spirit is the executive of the Godhead"; "the source of intellectual life"; and "involved in the experience of all Christians" (1:529, 530, and 532). Hodge was unimpressed by Hegel (2:781). He concluded, "Predominantly sanctification is referred to the Holy Spirit" (3:214).

George Smeaton (1814-1889) was professor at Aberdeen and then at Edinburgh in the Free Church of Scotland. He had a firm doctrine of the Trinity, discussed the procession and personality of the Spirit, and argued for his empowerment of Christ: "Jesus received the Unction of the Spirit" (*The Holy Spirit* [London: Banner of Truth, 1958], 118). He was happy to speak of "supernatural" gifts in the NT in the first century, but insisted: "These ... gifts ... were no longer needed when the canon of Scripture was closed" (140). This is the so-called cessationist view, usually associated with Benjamin Warfield. Smeaton saw such "miracles" as all of a kind with Roman Catholic accounts of miracles, especially in the Middle Ages (140-59). The Holy Spirit, however, initiates "prevenient grace" (211), and love becomes the Spirit's principle of unity. The goal is the formation of "the character of Christ" (223). Smeaton attacked the "crude utterances, ecstasies, and prophecies" of Montanism (265; cf. 256-368). He also attacked the Pelagianism and the "synergism" of Melanchthon. "Irvingism" offered an "ostentatious parade of supernatural gifts" (355).

Abraham Kuyper (1837-1920) was a Dutch Calvinist, who with others founded the Free University of Amsterdam in 1880. The Holy Spirit is transcendent, above nature, but God is also immanent within nature. In *The Work of the Holy Spirit* (New York: Funk and Wagnalls, 1900; Dutch 1888), he declared: "Man is fallen.... The Holy Spirit must purify and sanctify him.... The work of the Spirit is continuous and perpetual" (11). He argued, "Power to bring forth proceeds from the Father; the power to arrange, from the Son; the power to perfect, from the Holy Spirit" (19). But their work is inseparable. The Spirit inspires natural talents (39). Like Smeaton, he urged: "The Irvingites completely lack the marks of the apostolate" (139). *"Ordinary"* ministerial gifts are no less of the Spirit (199). Sanctification, love, and prayer characterize the work of the Spirit; they are more reliable than bursts of "fire" (433). Sanctification is "a gradual process" (477). His is a "never-finished work" (532).

(c) Edward Irving (1792-1834) was Scottish, but reacted against the doctrine of the Church of Scotland. He championed an outbreak of speaking in tongues in 1828 and another in 1830. He was excommunicated by his church in London, and together with Henry Drummond he formed the Catholic Apostolic Church. By 1835 the new church had "apostles," "prophets," and "angels," that is, in effect, bishops, of whom Irving became one. In 1827, he preached on baptism in the Spirit. Most seriously of all, against the emphatic position taken by Hodge, Smeaton, and Kuyper, he insisted that sanctification took place as an *event*, not as a *process*. (C. G. Strachan, *The Pentecostal Theology of Edward Irving* [London: DLT, 1973; Peabody, Mass.: Hendrickson, 1988]). In the light of this, B. Warfield and others attacked his doctrine. Meanwhile Irving established prayer groups to pray for a new outpouring of the Spirit. In 1833 the London Presbytery charged Irving with heresy. F. D. Bruner traces a line from Montanism through the Radical Reformers to Irving and Pentecostalism.

Benjamin H. Irwin (b. 1854) received around 1891 a "sanctification experience" through the Holiness Movement in Iowa. In 1895 he received what he called "a baptism in fire," and began teaching the need for "a third blessing." He founded

"Fire-Baptized Holiness Associations." But in 1900 he confessed to "open and gross sin," and fell from leadership to obscurity. Albert Benjamin Simpson (1843-1919) resigned from the Presbyterian Church in Canada to establish an independent church, urging "the fourfold gospel" of Christ as Savior, Sanctifier, Healer, and Coming King, which became an identity-marker of many Pentecostals and the "Foursquare Gospel" movement. On the basis of Joel 2:23, he looked for "the latter rain" of a new Pentecost. This approach found sympathy with Charles Finney, some Wesleyan Methodists, and, later, classical Pentecostalism.

(d) The fourth of the four streams of the nineteenth century may be represented by John Henry Newman (1801-1890), probably the most creative Roman Catholic thinker of that century. He had been ordained into the Church of England, but became strongly associated with the leadership of the Tractarians, or Oxford Anglo-Catholic Movement. In 1833 he produced *Tracts for the Times* in collaboration with John Keble and E. B. Pusey. They all rejected liberalism and any compromise with the state. Newman insisted, "Dogma has been the fundamental principle of my religion" (*Apologia Pro Vita Sua* [Oxford: Clarendon, 1967], 127). In 1843 he preached on "the parting of friends" and converted to the Roman Catholic Church. Newman emphasized the Holy Spirit's indwelling. He distanced himself from both the dry rationalism of liberalism and the concern for the extraordinary among enthusiasts. He criticized "religious ecstasy ... impassioned thoughts, a soft and languid tone of feeling" (*Parochial and Plain Sermons* [London and New York: Longmans, Green, 1891], 2:267). The Holy Spirit works in and through human actions. Newman did not disparage reasoning as such, but it needs the light of the Spirit. He cannot be identified entirely with any of the other three traditions, although in general he valued orthodoxy over liberalism or enthusiasm. On the Trinity and the Spirit Newman sought to follow Athanasius and Ambrose, and other Fathers.

(vii) **The Twentieth Century and Beyond.** (a) Earlier Years of the Twentieth Century. In mainline Christian theology the two most notable achievements in the earlier years of the century were the publication of two thorough volumes by H. B. Swete — *The Holy Spirit in the New Testament* (London: Macmillan, 1909) and *The Holy Spirit in the Ancient Church* (London: Macmillan, 1912) — and work on the Holy Spirit by the theologian Karl Barth *(The Holy Spirit and the Christian Life,* lectures of 1929, subsequently published, as well as the later monumental *Church Dogmatics).* The most startling development, however, came with the emergence and rise of Pentecostals. This has now become a huge worldwide phenomenon, and we discuss it in a separate entry.

(1) H. B. Swete (1835-1917) was Regius Professor of Divinity at Cambridge, and wrote over 400 pages on the Spirit in the New Testament and over 400 pages on the Spirit in the ancient church. His work is mainly descriptive and exegetical, and represents a scholarly classic in each area. The books contain relatively little innovative material, but constitute a reliable survey, within the limits of its time. Swete stresses *progressive* holiness, especially in Paul; it is not an "event," or

"perfectionism" (*Holy Spirit in the New Testament*, 172). Prophecy can be fallible, and needs to be tested (189). Love, he argues, is more significant than tongues or "power"; the Holy Spirit nurtures likeness to Christ. The Spirit is also agent of Christ's resurrection, and initiates prayer in the Christian. He directs the new life (202-10). Part 3 of his book offers a summary of NT doctrine (283-360). His later book, *The Holy Spirit in the Ancient Church*, constitutes a reliable survey from a historian of doctrine. His dialogue between Athanasius and the Tropici is especially detailed. Part 3 then gives a more theological assessment of the relation of the Holy Spirit to God, the deity of the Spirit, inspiration, the Paraclete, and sanctification (359-409).

(2) Karl Barth (1886-1968) had already described the Holy Spirit as "the operation of God in faith, the creative and redemptive power of the Kingdom of Heaven . . . the eternal 'Yes'" in his *Epistle to the Romans* (Oxford: OUP, 1933, 1968), 157. In 1929 he gave oral lectures that were subsequently published under the title *The Holy Spirit and the Christian Life* (Louisville: Westminster John Knox, 1993). He described the Spirit as Creator, whose activity must be firmly distinguished from the human spirit's attempts at "religion." Following Augustine, Barth saw the Holy Spirit as God's love, inconceivable and undeserved. Through the Spirit we are "equipped by God for God." He gave a view of sanctification as progressive, not instantaneous: "No one other than the Holy Spirit will give real faith" (35). In his still earlier book *The Resurrection of the Dead* (London: Hodder and Stoughton, 1933), Barth declared concerning "spiritual gifts" in 1 Corinthians 12–14, "What we are really concerned with is not *phenomena* in themselves, but with their *whence?* and *whither?* To what do they point?" (80).

Barth began publishing his magisterial *Church Dogmatics* in 1932. Here he insists, "The Holy Spirit . . . cannot be separated from the Word" (*CD* I/1, 150). The Word of God spoken through the Spirit is a speech act (162). The Holy Spirit is of "both the Father and the Son" (453). In *CD* I/2, he underlines the point that the Spirit is the subjective reality of revelation (I/2, 203). Christ is revealed in the Bible by the work of the Holy Spirit (513). The Holy Spirit opens our blind eyes, and "in the Holy Spirit . . . we are free for God" (243). The Holy Spirit also works moment by moment in relation to time. Volume II concerns God, and Barth reiterates that redemption comes from the Father, the Son, and the Holy Spirit (II/1, 3). Further, "It is God the Holy Spirit who makes the existence of the creature as such possible" (III/1, 56). In volume IV he speaks of the Holy Spirit as "the awakening power in which Jesus Christ . . . renews His body . . . [the] Church" (IV/1, 643). Justification and sanctification are "two different aspects of . . . salvation" (IV/2, 503). To sum up, the Holy Spirit, in Barth's view, constitutes a major personal agent of God, or God himself, in all thirteen volumes of *Church Dogmatics*.

(b) Middle Years of the Twentieth Century. (1) During these years J. E. Fison, later bishop of Salisbury, wrote *The Blessing of the Holy Spirit* (New York and London: Longman, Green, 1950). Like Paul Tillich, he warned against confusing penultimates, or vehicles of the Spirit, with the Holy Spirit himself. His most distinctive theme is "the incurable self-effacement of the Holy Spirit Himself, and His determination . . . only to point to . . . Jesus Christ" (22). He is more than cautious about ecstatic states, and even "seeking the Holy Spirit" (213). (2) L. S. Thornton wrote on a broader subject in *The Common Life in the Body of Christ* (London: Dacre, 1950), but stressed participation in the Spirit. The "grace" in 2 Cor. 13:13 refers to *sharing in* the Holy Spirit, not having him as a companion (67, 71, 66-95). (3) N. Q. Hamilton, *The Holy Spirit and Eschatology in Paul* (Edinburgh: Oliver and Boyd, 1957) took up Oscar Cullmann's thesis of the eschatological framework of the Spirit in the NT, in his classic study *Christ and Time* (London: SCM, 1951). The decisive battle over sin has been won, but final victory lives in the future, Cullmann argued (73-93). (4) Lindsey Dewar published *The Holy Spirit and Modern Thought* (London: Mowbray, 1959). The first eighty or so pages concern biblical teachings. In general this replicates Swete, although he urges that the Spirit is "fully personal, as 'he' and not an 'it'" (71). Part 2 provides a very brief and sketchy historical outline. Part 3 discusses some recent speculative psychology.

(5) The very long article on *pneuma* by Eduard Schweizer (1915-2006) in Kittel's *TDNT* (6:332-455) is far more significant. On the Synoptic Gospels, Schweizer agrees with C. K. Barrett: "It is no doubt a historical fact that Jesus Himself seldom referred to the Spirit" (403). Luke-Acts does contain some thirty-seven references, but in Luke's Gospel Jesus is "not a pneumatic, but Lord of the *pneuma*" (407-9). He stresses that Luke shares with Judaism "the view that the Spirit is essentially the Spirit of prophecy" (409). He inspires the *utterances* of Jesus. (Stronstad, Menzies, and Turner will take up these claims later.) As a Hellenist, Schweizer argues, Luke stresses physical and visible phenomena. In Paul the Spirit is closely associated with Christ, and is the first installment *(arrabōn* and *aparchē)* of more to come in the future. In John, "there is no thought of the sporadic coming of the Spirit, the extraordinary nature of His manifestations . . . or miraculous acts" (438).

(6) John V. Taylor (1914-2001), who became bishop of Winchester, wrote a practical and influential study, *The Go-Between God* (London: SCM, 1972). In it he emphasized mission, and made the practical comment that for most Christians the Holy Spirit excluded any attitude of "It all depends on one" (3). The Spirit is transcendent, yet also operates in the ordinary, everyday things of life. He is not just an upsurge of the unconscious, and does not necessarily prompt "a fever of activity" (55). The *charismata* are not "the essence of a Spirit-filled life" (202).

(7) Geoffrey W. Lampe (1912-1980) wrote an article on the Spirit in Luke in 1962; *The Seal of the Spirit* in 1976; and *God as Spirit* in 1977. In "The Holy Spirit in the Writings of St. Luke" (in *Studies in the Gospels,* ed. D. E. Nineham [Oxford: Blackwell, 1967], 159-200), Lampe sees the Spirit as the connecting thread between Luke and Acts (159). *The Seal of the Spirit* expressly addresses "the relationship between Baptism and Confirmation." In Lampe's view, "High Church Anglicans" represented by A. J. Mason and Gregory Dix had unduly el-

evated confirmation, making baptism "no more than a prelude to confirmation" (x). Lampe discusses "sealing" in 2 Cor. 1:21-22, Eph. 1:13, and 4:30. The term means "to set a mark of ownership upon" (5). He regards supposed references to confirmation in Acts as anachronistic, and also reviews the second century and patristic literature. On Luke-Acts he stresses the outreach to the Gentiles, and the concern for prophecy. In *God as Spirit* he argues that in Jesus we encounter *God's indwelling presence*. Like many Pentecostals, he sees the Holy Spirit as pouring down "rain on a thirsty land, showers on the dry ground" (*God as Spirit* [Oxford: OUP, 1977], 63; cf. Isa. 44:3-5).

(8) James D. G. Dunn (b. 1939), Lightfoot Professor Emeritus of Divinity at Durham, wrote *Baptism in the Holy Spirit* in 1970 and *Jesus and the Spirit* in 1975 (both London: SCM). Since then he has published a huge quantity of books on the NT, especially on Christology and on Paul. Many regard his 1970 work as a "landmark" for Pentecostalism, as the first book by a "mainline" scholar to take seriously the claims of Pentecostals. He recognizes that "The Pentecostal doctrine is built chiefly on Acts" (5). Dunn criticizes, however, the "two-stage" scheme of salvation advocated by most Pentecostals. He argues that "Spirit-and-fire baptism is not offered as an alternative to John's water baptism" (11). The Spirit's descending on Jesus at his baptism is a "unique anointing" (26). Pentecost "inaugurates the age of the Church" (49). "The riddle of Samaria" (Acts 8:5-8) and the conversion of Cornelius (Acts 11:15-17) are *barrier-breaking events,* in which the context of hostility between Jews and Samaritans, and the huge step of the admission of Gentiles fully into the church, require Luke to offer a *visible* sign. In different ways these events are "beginnings" (52; cf. 59). Dunn concludes, "The possession of the Spirit was *the* hallmark of the Christian" (66). When he discusses Paul, he concludes, "Rom. 8:9 rules out the possibility both of a *non*-Christian possessing the Spirit, and a Christian *not* possessing the Spirit: only the reception and consequent possession of the Spirit makes a man a Christian" (95). Throughout this work Dunn challenges both the Pentecostal notion of a "second blessing" and the "Catholic" tying of the Spirit either to baptism or to confirmation. For example, 1 Cor. 6:11, "You were washed," is not necessarily a "baptismal aorist"; this is merely an assumption. Dunn sees the "separation of Spirit-baptism from the event of conversion-initiation" as "contrary to New Testament teaching" (226). Dunn's work is widely respected, although some Pentecostals claim (predictably) that it gives higher priority to Paul than to Luke.

In *Jesus and the Spirit* (1975), Dunn suggests that there is more about the Spirit in the life of Jesus than C. K. Barrett, H. B. Swete, and J. E. Fison allow. Indeed, he claims: "Jesus is . . . a charismatic figure" (68). He was a miracle-worker, exercising *dunameis,* or acts of power, and "had the reputation of a prophet" (82). Yet he admits: "there is no evidence of ecstatic behaviour" (85). The action of the Holy Spirit is implicit, he argues, in such experiences as Jesus' relation to God as *Abba,* his prayer life, and so on. All this led Christians to place their hope not in themselves, but in the exalted Jesus. When he moves to Paul, Dunn recognizes that "*For Paul, the religious experience of the believer is characterized* by *paradox and conflict*. . . . It is a religion of *Anfechtung* . . . (Rom. 8:22-23; 2 Cor. 5:4) . . . a life-long tension" (338). This results from the eschatological situation of the "now" and "not yet."

(c) *Later Twentieth Century to 2012.* (1) Four major theologians stand out from most other writers during this period: Yves Congar, Jürgen Moltmann, John Zizioulas, and Wolfhart Pannenberg. Congar (1904-1995) wrote *I Believe in the Holy Spirit,* 3 vols. (New York: Seabury Press, 1983), in addition to other works. It had appeared in German in 1979-1980. In the first volume he examines biblical and historical material. The Spirit is known by his effects, and Congar, like Fison, insists that the Spirit empties himself of his personality. We should not pit "revelation" and "experience" against each other. Like Augustine, Congar sees the Spirit as the bond of union between the Father and the Son. He enters history as "messianic gift and . . . eschatological gift" (1:15-16). The church is "the sphere of the Spirit." Patristic tradition avoids setting up a contrast between the "institutional" and the "charismatic." In volume 2 he sees two parallel "sendings" by the Father of Christ and the Spirit. On the question of postbiblical prophecy, he asks: "Does the Spirit still speak through the prophets? Who would dare to say that he does not?" (2:30). The Holy Spirit, he argues, preserves the church's apostolicity, which means "conformity with the origins of Christianity" (2:39). The Spirit gives "dynamic catholicity" (2:50). In our personal lives "the Spirit is the principle of love" (2:67), but "every action performed by God is common to all three persons of the Trinity. . . . Even the incarnation is common to all three persons" (2:85). As a Roman Catholic theologian, he is more than sympathetic to the Renewal Movement, but also insists, "I do not believe that the Renewal, in the form in which it appears now, can be extended to the whole of the Church," because "the style of meetings is not acceptable to everyone" (2:156-57). He traces the phrase "baptism in the Spirit" to the Holiness Movement. It is better to avoid this term (2:198). In the third volume he turns to Eastern Orthodoxy. Both East and West are complementary. The Father is the ultimate source of the Spirit; the Son is the mediate source.

Moltmann (b. 1926) wrote *The Spirit of Life* in German in 1991 (Eng. London: SCM, 1992). It draws partly on his earlier work *The Trinity and the Kingdom of God* (London: SCM, 1981), although he was already widely known for his *Theology of Hope* and many other volumes. In the earlier book he avoided abstractions about the Holy Spirit. He wrote: "The New Testament talks about God by proclaiming in narrative the relationships of the Father, the Son, and the Spirit" (*Trinity,* 64). All three persons of the Trinity play a part in the conception, truth, baptism, testing, life, passion, and resurrection of Jesus Christ (88). From 1970 to the 1980s, he wrote in *The Spirit of Life,* we have moved from "forgetfulness of the Spirit" to "obsession" with the Spirit (1). Like Congar, he does not see "experience" and "revelation" as alternatives (3). Like Schleiermacher, he accepts that the experience of God may encounter "the infinite in the finite, the eternal in the temporal"

(35). Nevertheless, the Spirit is "the creative power of God" (42). We see this in the OT. When they speak of the Holy Spirit, OT writers always mean "God himself." He is both "God himself" and yet "distinct from God." The Holy Spirit also inspires the relation of Jesus to God as *Abba;* Jesus is "filled with the Holy Spirit" (60). The Spirit also nurtured eschatological longing for the new creation (71-77).

Part 2 of *The Spirit of Life* examines liberation for life, rebirth, sanctification, and charismatic power. The Holy Spirit invites trust, as against self-sufficiency, bringing "hitherto unexplored creative power of God," which is "life-giving through love" (115). He declares, "To go forward in God's ways means continually beginning afresh" (155). He also discusses views of the Spirit in Zinzendorf and Wesley. *Charismata* may include "special gifts," but *also* those of ordered church ministry (182-83). Tongues-speech is a possible gift, and even "the weak and handicapped members" of the church can constitute a needed *charisma* for the church (193). Christocentric and theocentric mysticism must be distinguished from counterfeit mysticism. Part 3 of the book concerns the fellowship of the Spirit and his personhood. The fellowship of the Spirit takes place "between the generations" (237). We discover God's love in the love between human beings (248). "Love makes life worth living" (259). As a person, the Spirit is "the Lord and Giver of life" (270). His personhood is such that "his subjectivity is constituted by his [Trinitarian] inter-subjectivity" (289). Like Basil, Moltmann affirms the threefold Gloria of the Trinity (304).

Zizioulas (b. 1931) represents the Greek Orthodox Church. His most influential book to date is *Being as Communion* (New York: St. Vladimir's Seminary Press, 1997). He declares: "There is, so to say, *no Christ until the Spirit is at work*" (127). For Christ's identity as church depends on his incarnation and messianic vocation, both established by the Spirit. He also argues, "God is a relational being: without the concept of communion it would not be possible to speak of the being of God" (17). Both God and the Spirit are seen in terms of their relationships, not simply as abstract or static Being or "substance." He claims that Vatican II failed to see that "Christology is essentially conditioned by Pneumatology" (110-11). Further, the Holy Spirit "ensures the importance of the local church in ecclesiology" (132). Like his earlier Russian Orthodox colleague Vladimir Lossky (1903-1958), he argues for a hermeneutical understanding and re-presentation of the work of the Eastern Church Fathers. Truly personal being, Lossky had argued, is not merely a matter of "nature." It involves no defensive isolating wall of self-protection, but becoming more like God, or deification, which is a work of the Holy Spirit.

Pannenberg (1928-2014) wrote numerous epoch-making works before his climactic *Systematic Theology*, 3 vols. (Grand Rapids: Eerdmans, 1991-1998). In his earlier works he attacked "an anthropocentric world-view" and the notion of reducing God's acts to the "ghetto of redemption history," that is, in practice only to Israel and the church (*BQT* 1:39-41). Thus Pannenberg sees the event of creation as a Trinitarian event, involving Father, Son, and Holy Spirit: "The

Spirit is at work already in creation" (*ST* 3:1). Nor must we restrict his work to "supernatural" gifts; he is "the Creator of all life" (2). The Father and the Son work together in sending the Spirit (5). In granting salvation, the Spirit is "a lasting possession of believers," enabling them to participate in the life of God (12). In Paul and in John "The Spirit and the Son mutually indwell one another as Trinitarian persons" (17). The Holy Spirit may help us break free of dead tradition, but also acts "as a brake in unregulated enthusiasm" (20). There can be no "pure" church; for the church is not the same as the kingdom of God, which remains the future goal (32-37).

(2) Other Writers between c. 1980 and c. 2012. Gerd Theissen (b. 1943) published an important book called *Psychological Aspects of Pauline Theology* (Eng. 1987). We take this up in the entry on the Renewal Movement, not because he is Pentecostal or an advocate of "renewal," but because his work is very important for the discussion of tongues and the subconscious. In 1991 the Church of England Doctrine Commission produced *We Believe in the Holy Spirit* (London: Church House Publishing). This affirmed the personhood of the Holy Spirit, his witness to Christ, his "self-effacing" character, and his nurturing in prayer so that Christians "are graciously caught up in a divine conversation" between the Spirit and God (108). The report urged: "Openness to change, vitality, warmth and surprise all need to be balanced by continuity, regularity, stability, and nationality" (55). "Continuous euphoria" cannot be a model for all Christians. Yet the Spirit is the one Beyond, and yet Within (171). F. W. Horn wrote in the 1990s on the deposit of the Spirit *(Das Angeld des Geistes)*, stressing eschatology and those passages in which Paul speaks of the Spirit as *pledge, earnest,* or *down payment,* and suggesting three phases of development in Paul. In his *Prophecy and Inspired Speech* (1995), C. Forbes attacked any undue emphasis on parallels between inspired speech in early Christianity and in Greek religions.

Michael Welker wrote *God the Spirit* (Minneapolis: Fortress, 1994), and edited *The Work of the Spirit* (Grand Rapids: Eerdmans, 2006). He engages with A. N. Whitehead and process thought, and more surprisingly with pluralism and postmodernism, which he sees as largely positive for a doctrine of the Spirit. There are "powerful and invigorating forms of pluralism," as well as debilitating forms (*God the Spirit*, 23). He sees "totalization" as hostile to the work of the Spirit (475; cf. 37). He offers "creative readings" of biblical passages, especially from Judges (52-91). The Spirit's descent "from heaven" denotes "a domain of reality that is relatively inaccessible to us" (137-39). We must recognize "the specific selflessness of the Spirit of God" (295). In his 2006 book he speaks again of "the multi-contextual and polyphonic presence of the Spirit" (*Work of the Spirit,* 231).

Harvey Cox, Amos Yong, Jim Purves, Frank Macchia, and V.-M. Kärkkäinen have made noteworthy and often creative contributions to Pentecostal theology. Other writers who also come under this heading are Gordon Fee (discussed in the entry on Pentecostalism), who writes mainly on Paul, and R. Stronstad, R. Menzies, and M. Turner (discussed in the entry on the Renewal Movement), who write mainly on Luke-Acts. Eugene F. Rogers published *After the Spirit* (Grand Rapids: Eerdmans, 2005; London: SCM, 2006), which sheds much light on the Trinity and Holy Spirit in the NT. He repeats Moltmann's claim that the NT offers a Trinitarian approach *in narrative form*. The annunciation, baptism, transfiguration, resurrection, and ascension of Jesus Christ, he argues, all demonstrate "intra-Trinitarian relations" in this narrative form. "The baptism of Jesus is primarily to be understood as an intratrinitarian event.... The Spirit bears witness to the love between the Father and the Son.... 'This is my Son, my beloved'" (136-37). Rom. 8:11 also demonstrates the same common working in the resurrection of Christ.

F. Philip wrote *The Origins of Pauline Pneumatology* in 2005. His thesis comes close to that of Horn, stressing especially the eschatological background to Paul. N. Q. Hamilton had trodden the same general path earlier, but Philip places more emphasis on the gift of the Spirit to the Gentiles. A. W. Zwiep (b. 1964) published *Christ, the Spirit, and the Community of God* (Tübingen: Mohr, 2010). He emphasizes both the "now" and the "not yet" context of eschatology (116), but most of all the *communal* or *corporate* context of baptism. He cannot see on what basis the Pentecostal writer Robert Menzies can speak of "every individual believer" (111), on "baptism in the Spirit." It is the *community* who receives such barrier-breaking events. This study of Acts and related issues brings the debate forward. (*See also* **Montanism; Pentecostals, Pentecostalism; Pietism; Renewal Movement; Sanctification; Sinless Perfection.**)

Reading: S. M. Burgess, *The Holy Spirit: Ancient Christian Traditions* (Peabody, Mass.: Hendrickson, 1984); Y. Congar, *I Believe in the Holy Spirit*, 3 vols. (New York: Seabury Press, 1983); M. A. G. Haykin, *The Spirit of God* (Leiden: Brill, 1994); V.-M. Kärkkäinen, *Holy Spirit and Salvation* (Louisville: Westminster John Knox, 2010); J. Moltmann, *The Spirit of Life* (London: SCM, 1992); H. B. Swete, *The Holy Spirit in the Ancient Church* (London: Macmillan, 1912).

Homiletics

Homiletics is the study and practice of preaching. It includes the history, theology, composition, and reception of preaching, as well as rhetorical or technical guidelines. The NT contains examples of preaching by Jesus (Luke 4:16-21), Peter (Acts 2:14-36), and Paul (Acts 20:18-35; 1 Thess. 2:1-16). The latter contains a sample of Paul's missionary preaching, describing his behavior, mode of delivery, and motives. Paul concludes: "You accepted it not as a human word but as what it really is, God's word" (2:13). Augustine offers a comprehensive study in his *On Christian Doctrine* 4. He begins by claiming that skill in rhetoric is not part of his aim (4.1.1, 2), but then concedes that rhetoric is useful in enforcing truth (4.2-4). He praises wisdom above rhetoric (4.5-7). He acknowledges that biblical exegesis is the real beginning of the exercise (4.9), although Cicero's rhetoric may offer suggestions on how to delight and move the hearers (4.12). The hearer must be moved as well as instructed (4.13-14). Prayer should precede preaching (4.15).

The Christian teacher must use different styles on different occasions (4.19-21). He draws examples from Ambrose and Cyprian (4.21.46-50). The "orator" should aim at perspicuity, beauty, and persuasiveness (4.26), although truth is more important than expression (4.28), and prayer is vital (4.30).

In the medieval period Alan of Lille published his book *The Art of Preaching* (c. 1200), and by the thirteenth century homiletics had become a recognized academic discipline. The Dominicans and Franciscans were Orders of Preachers. Preaching was important to the Reformers, not least to educate a Christian mind. Calvin wrote of those whose pride and arrogance led them to read only "in private, and thus to despise public meetings and deem preaching superfluous" (*Institutes* 4.1.5). These are especially the "enthusiasts" or fanatics. In Calvinist churches, ministers are often known as "preachers." In early modernity F. Schleiermacher considered theology in the university as consisting primarily of training for the ministry, as law was for lawyers and medicine for doctors. In contrast to Fichte, he wrote *A Brief Outline of the Study of Theology* (Eng. Eugene, Ore.: Wipf and Stock, 2007). Even "the dogmatic procedure has reference entirely to preaching" (*The Christian Faith* [New York: Harper, 1963], 1:88). Preaching, he urged, is like "striking up the music" to kindle a spark of faith. In his view, NT studies and hermeneutics served this purpose. Before Schleiermacher, J. Wesley made much of preaching. But by the end of the nineteenth century preaching as an art and practice occupied a smaller and smaller place in university courses, and was often subsumed within "practical" or "pastoral" theology. But handbooks on homiletics still flourished. Austin Phelps, *The Theory of Preaching: Lectures on Homiletics* (London: Dickinson, 1882), contains forty lectures on the sermon, including lectures on sources and texts, introductions, propositions, divisions, conclusions, and so forth. Phelps was professor of sacred rhetoric at Andover Theological Seminary.

Preaching began to experience new life in the mid–twentieth century with the theology of K. Barth and the rise of a literary criticism, which reinstated more action to the hearer or reader. Interest and concern about communication have often been reserved for seminaries and divinity schools rather than university departments of religion or theology. But many writers either in seminaries or (within Britain) in Scottish universities wrote on preaching in the twentieth century. P. T. Forsyth wrote *Positive Preaching and the Modern Mind* (London: Independent Press, 1907); James Black wrote *The Mystery of Preaching* (London: James Clarke, 1924; rev. ed., London: Marshall, 1977); and R. E. O. White published *A Guide to Preaching* (London: Pickering and Inglis, 1973). Vatican II (1962-1965) strongly urged the importance of biblical preaching, not only in the context of the sacraments.

Homiletics includes not only history, but also guidelines for practice. In 1982 J. Stott published *I Believe in Preaching* (London: Hodder and Stoughton), in which he discussed the glory of preaching; objections to preaching; preaching as bridge building; the call to study; preparing sermons; and sincerity, courage, and humility. In 2012 P. E. Brown recalled the homiletics class of E. F. Kevan, former principal of the London School of Theology. The class included a mass of detailed guidelines, such as: "An effective sermon must be focused around one formative idea"; "The Introduction must never overtop the sermon; this is like a large porch on a small house"; "Never be afraid to be too simple"; "Stop when you come to the end"; "Beware of unbearably long stories"; "Gesture is the result of acting how you think; not thinking how you will act"; "Forget homiletics when you are preaching, but not when you are preparing" (*Ernest Kevan* [Edinburgh: Banner of Truth Trust, 2012], 163-65). (*See also* **Dominicans; Franciscans; Kerygma**.)

Reading: James Black, *The Mystery of Preaching* (London: Marshall, 1977); P. T. Forsyth, *Positive Preaching and the Modern Mind* (London: Independent Press, 1907); A. Phelps, *The Theory of Preaching* (London: Dickinson, 1882); R. E. O. White, *A Guide to Preaching* (London: Pickering and Inglis, 1973).

Hooker, Richard

Richard Hooker (1554-1600) was the primary theologian to mark out the contours of Church of England (Anglican) theology during the reign of Elizabeth I. Characteristically he appealed to Scripture, tradition, and reason. He sought to defend the Elizabethan settlement especially against independent or Calvinist Puritans. His major work is his *Treatise of the Laws of Ecclesiastical Polity* (books 1-4, 1593; book 5, 1594; and books 6-8, after his death). He attacks what today is often called a restorationist view of the Bible, namely, that Scripture constitutes an unalterable blueprint for everything in life. While some Puritans insisted that Christians should do only what the Bible directs, Hooker argues that they should do what reason and the church suggest, provided it is *not contrary* to Scripture. Hooker's moderate and balanced approach led to his earning the title "the judicious Hooker." It is symptomatic of Hooker's respect in both evangelical and Anglo-Catholic traditions that John Keble edited an 1836 edition of the treatise. The first book discusses various kinds of "laws": the law of God, reason, and Scripture: "by reason man attains to the knowledge of things that are and are not sensible [i.e. sense-data]" (1.7.1; 1:219). He declares, "Laws... human... are available by consent" (1.10.8; 1:246). Book 2 also considers Scripture. "To hold that only... the Scripture must be the rule to direct in *all* things" is an overstatement (2.1.2; 1:287). "For Scripture is not the only law whereby God has opened his will touching all things" (2.2.2; 1:291). Alongside Scripture we must also respect the Church Fathers (2.5.1-3; 1:313-18). He concludes: "The determination of bare and naked Scripture has caused here much pains" (2.7.1; 1:318). In effect, Hooker is widely regarded as the founder of Anglican theology, although many would stress this alongside the major Reformers.

Reading: Richard Hooker, *The Works of Mr. Richard Hooker*, 7th ed., 3 vols. (Oxford: Clarendon, 1888); T. Kirby, *A Companion to Richard Hooker* (Leiden: Brill, 2008).

Hope

The Hebrew uses four words for hope: *beṭach, chāsāh, yāchal,* and *qāwāh;* the Greek uses mainly *elpizō* in the sense of confidently looking forward to some future good. The words may denote the process, disposition, or act of hoping, or sometimes also the object of hope. In Hebrew, *beṭach* primarily denotes "confidence," but the AV/KJV translates Ps. 16:9 "my flesh also shall rest in hope"; cf. also Job 6:20. *Yāchal* means to wait with hope in Ps. 31:24, translated "you who wait for the LORD" in NRSV, but "ye that hope in the LORD" in AV/KJV. Ps. 33:18 speaks of "those who hope in his steadfast love"; 71:14 declares, "I will hope continually"; 119:114 reads "I hope in your word." Luke-Acts uses *elpizō* in a normal, nontheological way: for example, Luke 23:8, where Herod was hoping to see Jesus perform a sign; Acts 24:26, where Felix "hoped that money would be given him by Paul." But it may also be used theologically, especially in Paul, of "hope in Christ" (1 Cor. 15:19); "we hope for what we do not see" (Rom. 8:25). In Heb. 11:1, "Faith is the assurance of things hoped for." "Faith, hope, and love abide" (1 Cor. 13:13), which may suggest the dynamic, ongoing nature of life after death.

In the context of prophecy and apocalyptic, it has often been noted that hope arises from the contradiction between the present and what has been promised for the future. In the OT many covenant promises have not yet been fulfilled. The basis of hope in this case is the faithfulness of God. The Psalms and Job especially witness to that kind of hope. The exile triggered hope of a return (Jer. 32:9-15). In the NT the greatest ground of hope is the resurrection of Christ (*see* **Christology**). Hope also becomes an expression of eschatology in the process of realization. The Christian life is characterized by "now" and "not yet." Hence Peter admonishes, "Always be ready to make your defense . . . for the hope that is in you" (1 Pet. 3:15). Suffering also provokes hope (Rom. 5:3-5). Bereavement and death should not lead to grieving or despairing, "as others do who have no hope" (1 Thess. 4:13).

The multiform contexts in Scripture give rise to broad definitions in the history of theology. For example, N. T. Wright, *Surprised by Hope* (2002), includes paradise, resurrection, the parousia (or return of Christ), the Last Judgment, and in effect all that comes under the heading of eschatology. J. E. Fison, *The Christian Hope* (1934), is about the Day of the Lord, the parousia, and eschatology. John Macquarrie, *Christian Hope* (1978), follows a similar path. Brian Daley, *The Hope of the Early Church* (1991), concerns patristic eschatology in general. Richard Bauckham and Trevor Hart's book *Hope against Hope* (1999) carries the subtitle *Christian Eschatology in Contemporary Theology.* Its "images of hope" include the resurrection, the Antichrist, the millennium, the City of God, Sabbath rest and marriage feast, and the vision of God. See the separate entries in this book for more on these eschatological themes.

Horizon

"Horizon" is not simply a code word used by those who practice hermeneutics. It does not have precisely the same meaning as "presupposition" or even "point of view." The key point about "horizon" is that it moves as we move, and can expand its scope. Whereas "presupposition" suggests a fixed, defensive standpoint, "horizon" permits negotiation, whether with a text or with a person. More important, it also allows self-correction, as reading and listening to a text reshape our horizon. It also allows expansion of vision, as it allows us to see more of God and human life. All the major exponents of hermeneutics use and defend the term, including Heidegger, Gadamer, and Ricoeur. The term must be retained as being of distinctive value. (*See also* **Hermeneutics; Preunderstanding.**)

Hume, David

David Hume (1711-1776) is the most radical of the British empiricists, developing further the work of John Locke and George Berkeley, but differing in his conclusions. He was born and educated in Edinburgh, and served as a librarian and administrator. His cardinal principle was that we cannot go beyond experience. He published his classic *Treatise of Human Nature* when he was about twenty-eight. In 1748 he published *An Enquiry concerning Human Understanding;* his *Natural History of Religion* was published in 1757; and his *Dialogues concerning Natural Religion* (1778) was published after his death. Curiously, although he is most widely known for his skepticism and his philosophy, he also published a six-volume history of England.

The *Enquiry concerning Human Understanding* was published in a third edition (1975) edited by Peter Nidditch. Sense-data, Hume argued, enter the mind as "impressions" of sensation, or as "more lively perceptions" (sect. 2, para. 12). The less lively are "thoughts" or "ideas." He concluded, "Nothing can ever be present to the mind but an image or perception" (sect. 12, pt. 1, para. 118). This has a direct implication about the nature of the self. Hume wrote, "The mind has never anything present to it but the perceptions" (para. 119). The mind is little more than a bundle of perceptions. There are difficulties with this approach. C. A. Campbell argues, for example, that if the self is only a vehicle of transient perceptions, to hear a clock striking nine o'clock would be perceived as it striking one o'clock nine times *(On Selfhood and Godhood)*.

Hume is otherwise entirely consistent, however. Cause or causality cannot strictly be observed empirically, as Kant confirmed. Hence Hume admitted that the limits of experience mean that we perceive only constant conjunction (sect. 4, pt. 1, paras. 23-26). He admits that in daily life we can make only *assumptions* about causality and probably time. His skepticism remains genuine. He admits that "God" remains for him an enigma. Yet he is keen to silence "bigotry and superstition" (sect. 10, pt. 1, paras. 86-101). In *The Natural History of Religion* he argues that monotheism encourages intolerance. *Dialogues* was completed in 1761, even if it waited seventeen years for publication. Of the three figures involved in dialogue, "Cleanthes" represents theists; "Demea" is a rationalist; and "Philo" almost entirely represents Hume. Cleanthes appeals to the teleological argument (pts. 2 and 3); while Philo argues that too much depends upon the use of anthropomorphism (pt. 4). When Demea appeals for rational foundations (pt. 6), Philo rejects this on the basis of lack of adequate data (pt. 7). Parts 10 and 11 give us Hume's well-known discussion of the problem of evil. Philo maintains that there is lack of evidence from "experience" to prove it (anticipating some of Paley's arguments), while dysteleology and other counterarguments seem more convincing. He claims that Epicurus's old question remains unanswered (pt. 10, para. 66). Hume is not polemical for the sake of being polemical; he is simply unwilling to go beyond experience.

In his essay on miracles Hume remains skeptical about genuine evidence. This includes historical evidence about the resurrection of Jesus Christ. These are all the more difficult, he concludes, since they do not appeal to regularities of nature but to unique events. On the other hand, if we cannot observe causality, what kinds of laws (regularities) could we expect to see "broken"? Many see in Hume the spirit of an age that has largely transposed "scientific method" into a "scientific worldview," and luxuriates in an "evidence-based culture," whatever the question. Kant claimed that Hume's skepticism awoke him from his "dogmatic slumber." While many Christians in Continental Europe see practical atheism bound up with Feuerbach, Nietzsche, Marx, and Freud, many Anglo-Americans have to contend with a skepticism or agnosticism still largely in the tradition of Hume, even if advanced by later arguments. (*See also* **Cause, Causality; Empiricism; Evil, Problem of; Science and Religion; Skepticism.**)

Huss, John

John Huss (c. 1372-1415), like Wycliffe, was an early advocate of Reform before the Reformation. He was Czech, and entered Prague University c. 1390. In 1400 he was ordained, and in 1401 he became dean of the faculty of philosophy. He translated one of Wycliffe's works into Czech, and preached on the morals of clergy, as well as more generally. In 1409 a royal decree gave him control over the university. He was excommunicated by Pope John XXIII, but Bohemia became a center for Huss's and Wycliffe's doctrines. In spite of this, Huss was martyred in 1415. After his death he was celebrated as a national hero. Huss had contrasted the biblical account of the apostolic community with the power-hungry church of the papacy. He was also opposed to indulgences, and consistently drew his arguments and theology from Scripture.

Husserl, Edmund

Next to Heidegger, Edmund Husserl (1859-1938) influenced Continental philosophy perhaps more than any other person. In 1900-1901 he published *Logical Investigations,* and in 1913 *Ideas,* which was the first systematic exposition of phenomenology. Probably the greatest influence on him was F. Brentano. His legacy to German theology has three aspects: (1) his work on perception; (2) his influence on Heidegger; and (3) his concept of *horizon.* He argues that we do not simply perceive "facts" in a so-called objective sense; we perceive a lifeworld. A horizon constitutes the point of view from which we perceive, but this is not fixed; it can move and expand as we move. In hermeneutics this idea became influential not only in Heidegger, Bultmann, and Gadamer, but also through Wolfgang Iser, especially on reader-response theory. *Horizon* has been taken up by many theologians, including Pannenberg. (*See also* **Horizon; Phenomenology.**)

Hypostasis

A Greek word, the meaning of which depends largely on its context, although in the later Fathers it became almost equivalent to "being." In Heb. 11:1 faith as the *hupostasis* of things hoped for *(elpizomenōn)* may mean "realization" (BDAG 1040), but it may also mean "foundation" or "basis" (*Grimm-Th* 643). For its use in patristic thought, Lampe devotes fifteen columns to its meaning (Lampe 1454-61). It may denote "origination" (Hippolytus; Gregory of Nyssa); in Heb. 11:1, Irenaeus and Chrysostom insist that it may denote "ground of confidence"; in the Cappadocian Fathers and others it may also denote "having substantive existence"; in Heb. 1:3 it is "variously interpreted" (1457). Many of the Church Fathers use *hypostasis* as the equivalent of *ousia*, "substance" or "being" (1458). Lampe cites references in Origen, Cyril of Jerusalem, and many others, to this effect. In Christology it was used prior to Chalcedon to denote "state of being" (Origen, Gregory of Nyssa, and others; 1458-59). After Chalcedon it could even sometimes approximate to the modern notion of person (1461). In the fifth century and earlier, it comes to be contrasted with *ousia*, "being," to mean individual reality, especially in a Trinitarian context. The formula "three *hypostaseis* in one *ousia*" came to be widely accepted. Thus it becomes crucial to identify not only the context of discussion, but also its date. Since the rise in modern times of linguistic philosophy, Gilbert Ryle and others have warned against "hypostatizing an abstraction," that is, rendering a concept as a thing or a reality.

I

Iconoclasm, Icons
Icons (from Gk. *eikōn,* "image") are flat pictures, usually created by special paint or crafted in mosaic, which are venerated especially by the Russian and Greek Orthodox Churches. Icons often commemorate a biblical character or event. "Iconoclastic" (from Gk. *eikonoklastēs,* "image-breaker") alludes mainly to the iconoclastic controversy of the eighth and ninth centuries, when Emperor Leo III (717-741) regarded an excessive use of icons as a constraint on the conversion of Jews and Muslims. In 726 he ordered their destruction. Disturbances broke out, with persecution. Persecution was relaxed under Leo IV, and this policy was reversed in 787. But iconoclasm continued in a more subdued form until 842.

Idealism
Idealism traditionally denotes the school of philosophy that regards ideas or the mind, rather than material objects alone, as constitutive of reality. Some credit G. Leibniz (1646-1716) with coining the term, but it could be applied to many before him, of whom Plato offers one example. In spite of the emphasis on sense-data by empiricists such as Locke, Berkeley, and Hume, since they regard perceptions as combining to constitute ideas, empiricism is not incompatible with idealism. But in Kant idealism became dominant. The mind, he argued, actively shapes and forms reality. It brings order and intelligibility to what would otherwise remain chaotic and meaningless sense-data.

After Kant, German idealism was represented especially by Fichte, Hegel, and Schelling. Fichte attempted to go further than Kant in postulating an even more extensive role played by the mind. Hegel is sometimes described as an "objective idealist" in distinction from the "subjective idealism" of Schelling or even perhaps Kant. The Absolute Idea in Hegel is called God. His fundamental theme is *Geist,* "mind" or "spirit." As is well known, Feuerbach and Marx reversed Hegel's perspective by replacing idea or spirit by matter and means of production. In England, F. H. Bradley maintained Hegel's tradition, while in America Josiah Royce has sometimes been called the "American Hegel." Nevertheless, we should show caution about overeasy generalizations and simplistic classifications.

Ignatius of Antioch

The seven letters of Ignatius of Antioch (c. 35–c. 108) partly concern his last journey from Antioch, where he was bishop, to Rome, where he expected martyrdom. While he was in Smyrna, he wrote letters to the Ephesians, the Magnesians, the Trallians, and the Romans. When he reached Troas, he wrote to the Philadelphians, to the Smyrnaeans, and to Polycarp, bishop of Smyrna. Eusebius dates his martyrdom in the tenth year of Trajan, in 108. In the nineteenth century W. Cureton published a Syriac collection that contained only three letters; he claimed this "short recession" was the only authentic version. J. B. Lightfoot and others argued convincingly for seven letters, and a longer version was thought to date from the fourth century.

The letter to the Romans witnesses to Ignatius's passionate devotion and longing for martyrdom. He writes, "Grant me nothing more than that I be poured out (Gk. *spondisthēnai*, 'poured out as a libation') to God" (*To the Romans* 2.2). "Suffer me to be eaten by the beasts.... I am God's wheat, and I am ground by the teeth of the wild beasts that I may be found pure bread of Christ" (4.1). "I long for the beasts that are prepared for me.... Let there come on me fire and the cross, and struggles with wild beasts, cutting and tearing asunder... and cruel tortures.... May I but attain to Jesus Christ" (5.2-3). He wants his journey to be "to the glory of God" (10.2).

In other letters Ignatius warns his readers against Docetism, insists on the deity and humanity of Christ, urges unity under the bishop, and warns against Judaizing. For example, Jesus was born "of the family of David and Mary... he both ate and drank... was truly crucified... truly raised from the dead" (*To the Trallians* 9.1-2). Ignatius is also seen as giving special prominence to obedience to the bishop (2.1-2): "You should do nothing without the bishop." Again: "He who does anything apart from the bishop, the presbytery and the deacons is not pure in his conscience" (7.2). He says the same in *To the Philadelphians* 7.1-2. He is almost as enthusiastic for monarchical episcopacy as he is for martyrdom. Whether he represents a view of episcopacy held by most contemporaries is debated.

Image of God

An "image" in the ancient world often served to *represent* God. In pagan religions the image of the deity, usually erected within a temple devoted to that deity, often represented the distinctive qualities of that deity. In Hebrew religion images of God were forbidden (Exod. 20:4-6), mainly because Israel, as the people of God, had been given the vocation of being God's image, that is, of representing him to the world (D. J. A. Clines and Jürgen Moltmann). To construct an image from wood or stone would become an excuse for delegating this task and vocation to someone or something else. There was also the secondary danger that people would confuse the image with God, and render it worship as an "idol" (same word, e.g., Exod. 20:5). Thereby it would rob God of his uniqueness and transcendence, by identifying him with something he created as a mere "it."

Until about 1960 it had been customary to list the qualities or attributes that mark the image of God. Traditionally since Augustine and Aquinas, these have been rationality, dominion or sovereignty, freedom, and more recently relationality, or the capacity to relate to others (Barth, Migliore). Rationality is stressed by Augustine and especially Aquinas as marking out a human being or humanity in contrast to animals. Dominion gains plausibility not only from the explicit words "and let them have dominion over the fish of the sea ... over the birds ... over the cattle" (Gen. 1:26), but also from Ps. 8:6-8:

> You have given them dominion over the works of your hands; ...
> all sheep and oxen, ...
> the birds of the air, and the fish of the sea.

Relationality may be most important of all, because in creation God chose to go forth out of himself to engage with creation, which he loved. The statement "God is love" (1 John 4:16; cf. 4:7-21) suggests that self-giving in relation to others is the most fundamental aspect of God's being. Those who represent God must show these qualities, especially the last.

The Russian Orthodox writer Vladimir Lossky, as well as others, however, argues that we must understand "image of God" as a whole, and not as a string of diverse qualities. Lossky declares, "Creation in the image and likeness of God implies the idea of participation in the divine Being, of communion with God. That is to say, it presupposes grace" (*The Mystical Theology of the Eastern Church* [Cambridge: Clarke, 1991], 118). Lossky certainly appeals to the image of God to distinguish humanity from the rest of creation. As a mere "individual," a human is still part of "nature"; but as a "person," a human participates in God: "individual and person mean opposite things" (121). This draws on what the Fathers called "deification," or becoming like God. "Man is a creature called to *attain* union with God" (117). Hence the Greek Orthodox writer John Zizioulas insists, "God is a relational Being. ... God has ... no true being, apart from communion" (*Being as Communion* [New York: St. Vladimir's Seminary Press, 1997], 18). Many have recently appealed to intra-Trinitarian relationality (Stanley Grenz).

These arguments confirm that to be made in, or called to, the image of God is to represent God. Clines and others argue that the Hebrew in Gen. 1:26, traditionally translated as "*in* our image" (*bᵉtsalmēnû*), should in fact be translated as "*as* our image," or "in the capacity of our image," on the ground that b^e is "the *beth* of essence," signifying "as our representative" (Clines, "The Image of God in Man," *Tyndale Bulletin* 19 [1968]: 75). This is further confirmed by the fact that the Hebrew for "likeness" (*dᵉmūth*) is a synonym for "image" *(tselem)*. Irenaeus's attempt to make a theological distinction between them runs against the logic of synonymous parallelism in Hebrew.

Before we turn to "image of God" in Christ, we note that "dominion" does not denote *exploitation* or *mastery*, as if this were the dominion of brute force.

Certainly God is King, as the message of Jesus proclaims. But this is above all a stewardship of care and concern: the exercise of sovereignty for the benefit of those over whom God and humans are sovereign. Moltmann, Niebuhr, and many others have rightly stressed this. Further, rationality or reasonableness includes many dimensions of wisdom. Even so, Paul and the biblical writers do not underrate "reason." Only self-sufficient reason is criticized. As Wolfhart Pannenberg urges, Paul could have spared himself much trouble if he had believed in simple declaration or assertion, rather than argument. Also, freedom in this context does not denote freedom to act out of character (e.g., God cannot lie; the "logical" "cannot"). It denotes freedom to express that which accords with character.

The majority of references to "image of God" in the biblical writings probably refer to Jesus Christ. If he is God's representative, this is what we should expect. The significant Greek terms are *eikōn*, "image," and *homoiōsis*, "likeness." *Morphē*, "form," and *charactēr*, "exact imprint," are also relevant. Paul speaks of Christ as the image of God in 2 Cor. 4:4: "the glory of God in the face of Jesus Christ, who is the image of God"; in Col. 1:15, Christ is "the image of the invisible God." But the Epistle to the Hebrews perhaps has even more significant passages. Christ is "the exact imprint *(charactēr)* of God's very being" (Heb. 1:3). *Charactēr* may denote engraving or exact representation. In Heb. 2:5-6 humankind has lost its God-given capacity to represent and to show forth God, including its dominion over the nonhuman world. But Jesus Christ alone now embodies the true image of God. In the words of the Fourth Gospel, "Whoever has seen me has seen the Father" (John 14:9; cf. 12:45).

Christ gathers up in his own person the entire manifestation of the invisible God. Eberhard Jüngel drives home this point. He writes: "God defined himself as love on the cross of Christ.... Paul unmistakably identifies the being of God concretely with love ... in the death of Jesus" (*God as the Mystery of the World* [Edinburgh: T. & T. Clark, 1983], 220-21). This echoes Phil. 2:6-11 on Christ "in the form of God." God becomes intelligible and visible in Jesus Christ. Thereby, Jüngel argues, God becomes "thinkable," "conceivable," and "speakable." Christ as "the image of God" and as "the Word of God" belong together.

Reading: D. J. A. Clines, "The Image of God in Man," *Tyndale Bulletin* 19 (1968): 53-103; E. Jüngel, *God as the Mystery of the World* (Edinburgh: T. & T. Clark, 1983); V. Lossky, *The Image and Likeness of God* (London: Mowbray, 1974); V. Lossky, *The Mystical Theology of the Eastern Church* (Cambridge: Clarke, 1991); D. L. Migliore, *Faith Seeking Understanding* (Grand Rapids: Eerdmans, 1991), 120-29; J. Moltmann, *God in Creation* (London: SCM, 1985).

Immaculate Conception

The Immaculate Conception of the Virgin Mary was a dogma first decreed for the Roman Catholic Church in a papal bull by Pope Pius IX in 1854. It claimed that "from the first moment of her conception the Blessed Virgin Mary was ...

in view of the merits of Jesus Christ . . . kept free from all stain of original sin." Sometimes it is claimed that Gen. 3:15 and Luke 1:28 support this. But Gen. 3:15 is hardly relevant to this issue, and Luke 1:28 describes Mary not as "full of grace," as in the Vulgate, but as "favored one" (NRSV). This does not specify what the grace of God will bring, other than the birth of Jesus Christ. Traditions in some of the Church Fathers about Mary as a "new Eve" hardly provide a firm basis for the Roman interpretation. We note elsewhere that the term *Theotokos* related to Christology rather than directly to Mary. Neither Eastern Orthodox nor Protestant theologians generally endorse this doctrine explicitly. Bernard and Thomas Aquinas also did not seem to endorse this idea explicitly.

Immanence

Traditionally in Christian theology the immanence of God denotes God's being or acting *within* humankind or *within* the world, in contrast to God's transcendence, which denotes his being *beyond* or *above* humankind or the world. But this contrast alone is too simple. For in Christian theology God is both transcendent and immanent; the terms are complementary, not alternatives. Indeed, pantheism, not theism, regards God as entirely immanent in the world, without qualification. It is more accurate to regard God's immanence as his animating and sustaining the world and humankind by his near presence, and God's transcendence as denoting his otherness, holiness, and difference from the world and humankind. As immanent, God energizes the wills of human beings by his Holy Spirit; as transcendent he is never to be equated with the world, the "All," or his creatures, and his Spirit is holy. Pantheism and Deism are exaggerations of only one side of this dialectic. Popular thought sometimes accuses liberalism of urging God's immanence, and Karl Barth and others as urging his transcendence. But this would be a simplistic caricature, although one can see why such a caricature is sometimes drawn and that it is not entirely invalid. (*See also* **Transcendence**.)

Imminence of the End

This term is most likely to be used in connection with belief in the imminent return of Christ, or the imminent parousia of Christ. Most NT specialists, but not all, ascribe this belief to Jesus, Paul, and the earliest Christians. They often cite some well-worn NT texts. The most frequent in the Gospels is Mark 9:1: Jesus "said to them, 'Truly I tell you, there are some standing here who will not taste death until they see that the kingdom of God has come with power.'" This is supplemented by Matt. 10:23, "You will not have gone through all the towns of Israel before the Son of Man comes." G. B. Caird and others trace to J. Weiss and A. Schweitzer the "imminence" interpretation, that is, "the belief that the end was imminent" (*The Language and Imagery of the Bible* [London: Duckworth, 1980], 250). Caird argues, however, that there is considerable counterevidence against this view. According to Mark 13, Caird argues, "the Son of Man is to come only after a long series of warnings — wars, famines, earthquakes, persecution, the ravaging of Judaea ... the falling of the stars from heaven" (251-52). He declares, "The great day cannot happen for a long time yet" (252). Further, the kingdom of God has a double timing; it is both present and yet to come. Jeremias spoke of "inaugurated eschatology." C. E. B. Cranfield calls the saying in Mark 9:1 "one of the most puzzling in the Gospels," and gives seven plausible interpretations of it, including the fall of Jerusalem, Pentecost, and the transfiguration (*The Gospel according to St. Mark* [Cambridge: CUP, 1963], 285-89).

In the Epistles the key verse often cited is 1 Thess. 4:16-17, where Paul asserts that Christ "will descend from heaven" (v. 16); then "we who are alive, who are left, will be caught up in the clouds ... to meet the Lord" (v. 17). The operative word is "we." Similarly in Heb. 10:37, the writer declares,

> "In a very little while,
> the one who is coming will come and will not delay";

and James 5:8, "The coming of the Lord is near." Ernest Best, a moderate scholar, declares, "This imminence is clear." The majority of commentators share this view. But John Chrysostom argued that "we" did not signify Paul himself, but the faithful at Christ's coming, which might be "ten thousand years away" (Homily 7 on 1 Thessalonians, in *NPNF*, ser. 1, 13:353). Theodore of Mopsuestia, Rabanus Maurus, Thomas Aquinas, John Calvin, J. Bengel, and others follow this view.

It would not be correct to assume that this is simply harmonization to defend a less embarrassing view of the later church, which is also precritical. If we appeal to the generally accepted view in linguistics that "meaning is choice," we must ask what the alternative "they who remain" or "those who remain" might imply. First, it would exclude the *possibility* of an early return, and would imply a lack of seriousness on Paul's part of facing such a possibility. Second, as P. F. Strawson points out, there is all the difference between *presupposition* and explicit *statement*. He argues that their logic is different. Paul does indeed wish to show *solidarity* with his fellow believers, but he does not make an explicit statement of the timing, which "no man can know." As far as charges of a "precritical" attitude are concerned, Arthur L. Moore argues eloquently for the "conservative" view in his *Commentary on 1 and 2 Thessalonians* (London: Nelson, 1969) and in his book *The Parousia in the New Testament* ([Leiden: Brill, 1966], 108-10); N. T. Wright has even stronger reservations about the "mainstream" view (*Surprised by Hope* [London: SPCK, 2002], 140-46).

"The imminence of the end" may well have become a widely used phrase, but we should perhaps regard it as a hypothesis rather than a fact. A number of scholars have argued that it is a fatally flawed hypothesis, even if it must be taken seriously because of the number of supporters it claims.

Reading: G. B. Caird, *The Language and Imagery of the Bible* (London: Duckworth, 1980); A. L. Moore, *The Parousia in the New Testament* (Leiden: Brill, 1966); N. T. Wright, *Surprised by Hope* (London: SPCK, 2002).

Impassibility of God

The doctrine that God is incapable of suffering has been, in effect, the orthodox tradition of the church from the patristic era, through the medieval and Reformation periods, to the late nineteenth century. This doctrine has been challenged by many theologians in the twentieth century and today, of whom Jürgen Moltmann is probably the most well-known. In one form "passibility" means the capacity to be acted upon from without. In another form the term denotes the capacity to experience such changing emotions as pain. Whether love can be construed as an emotion in this sense is debated. Many argue that because in human beings love can be commanded, love cannot be an emotion. In the history of Christian theology the impassibility of God has been urged especially under the influence of Greek philosophy, and on the ground of the supposed "immutability" of God. He is depicted often as absolute and unconditioned. On the other side, appeal is frequently made to the biblical witness. "God was in Christ" (2 Cor. 5:19 KJV) appears to imply that God shared with Jesus the pain of the cross. In Judg. 10:16 God "could no longer bear to see Israel suffer," and raised up Jephthah to be a judge and leader against the Ammonites. In Gen. 6:6-7, "The LORD was sorry that he had made humankind on the earth, and it grieved him to his heart. . . . 'I am sorry that I have made them.'" In Judg. 2:18 "the LORD would be moved to pity by their groaning because of those who . . . oppressed them."

On the other hand, with one possible exception, the patristic church unanimously affirmed the impassibility of God. They argued that God could not experience *changing* joys and sorrows, pleasures and pains, or certainly any frustration of will. God is "without passions." Aristotle, the Stoics, and even Epicureans believed in the passionless God, remote from the world. Very early on the Fathers endorsed this. Ignatius is admittedly ambiguous: God, "who cannot suffer *(apathē)*, for our sakes accepts suffering" refers only to the incarnation (*To Polycarp* 3.2). Justin explains that Christians once worshiped Bacchus and Apollo, but have turned from such gods "to the unbegotten and impassible God" (*First Apology* 25). Clement of Alexandria writes: "God is impassible, free from anger, destitute of desire . . . one in the immutable state" (*Stromata* 4.23). Tertullian explicitly declares, "The Father was not associated with the Son in suffering with the Son" (*Against Praxeas* 29). He adds: "The Father is incapable of suffering in company with another" (29). Origen argues that to speak of the wrath of God does not "indicate any passion on His part" (*Against Celsus* 4.72); "Wrath is no passion on the part of God" (72). After Nicaea, both Eastern and Western Fathers maintained this tradition. Gregory of Nyssa asserts that "the Divine nature is incapable of suffering and mortality" (*Against Eunomius* 6.1). In the West Augustine states: "in God there can be no suffering" (*On Patience* 1).

In the Middle Ages Anselm affirmed: "Without doubt the divine nature is impassible" (*Why God Became Man* 1.8). Thomas Aquinas asserted that God cannot "repent, nor be angry or sorrowful, since all these denote passion and defect" (*Summa contra Gentiles* 2.25), and that God cannot have "potentiality" or change

(*Su Th* 1, qu. 9, art. 1). During the era of the Reformation, the Thirty-nine Articles of the Church of England (1549, 1552, and 1662) declared, "There is but one living and true God, everlasting, without body, parts or passions" (art. 1). The Westminster Confession (1647) stated: "There is but one living and true God, infinite in being and perfection, a most pure Spirit, invisible, without body, parts, or passions" (chap. 2.1). This view generally prevailed at least until its affirmation by M. Randles, *Impassibility* (1900). He urged that this doctrine viewed God as a source of "unsullied happiness," in place of a God to be pitied.

Nevertheless, by the 1920s many began to challenge this doctrine, perhaps partly because of the suffering brought about by the First World War (1914-1918). J. K. Mozley wrote, "There is a sense in which God may be said to bear our sorrows" (*The Impassibility of God* [1926]). By 1980 J. Moltmann wrote, "A God who cannot suffer cannot love either; a God who cannot love is a dead God" (*The Trinity and the Kingdom of God* [London: SCM, 1981], 38). In the cross "'God' is forsaken by 'God.' . . . The Father loses His Fatherhood" (80); God shares fully in the pain of the cross.

Moltmann had argued earlier, "God renounces his honour in the beginning at creation. . . . He descends into the thorn bush. . . . He meets men in those who are in straits. . . . These *accommodations* of God . . . contain anticipations of his future" (*The Crucified God* [London: SCM, 1974], 273). "God has taken upon himself death on the cross . . . and real life" (277). He wrote, "Like the cross of Christ, even Auschwitz . . . is taken up into the grief of the Father, the surrender of the Son, and the power of the Spirit"; "God himself hung on the gallows" (278). Many other theologians took this path. W. H. Vanstone wrote *Love's Endeavour, Love's Experience* in 1979. An early hint of such a radical change came in 1959 when D. D. Williams called this "a structural shift in the Christian mind." Paul Fiddes wrote *The Creative Suffering of God* (Oxford: OUP, 1988), in which he traced the roots of the newer approach to Moltmann, Whitehead, Hegel, and Barth. He declared, "The belief that God is a suffering God has become compelling for recent theology" (16). This is perhaps because more reflection has been given to the love of God and to God's role or even share in the cross, as well as to the problem of human suffering.

Reading: Thomas Aquinas, *Summa Theologiae* 1, qu. 9, esp. art. 1; P. Fiddes, *The Creative Suffering of God* (Oxford: OUP, 1988); J. Moltmann, *The Crucified God* (London: SCM, 1974); J. Moltmann, *The Trinity and the Kingdom of God* (London: SCM, 1981).

Incarnation. *See* **Christology**

Incarnational Theology
Incarnational theology has been defined in many ways. At its simplest it suggests that the incarnate ministry of Jesus Christ is as essential to redemption as are his death and resurrection. A concern about the cross should not obscure the essen-

tial redemptive significance of the incarnation, in which Jesus became "one with humankind." At the opposite extreme, it has come to stress the embodiment and visibility of God's actions in such a way as to emphasize not only the incarnation, but also the sacramental principle in the broadest sense. Between these two ends of the spectrum, Charles Gore edited *Lux Mundi* in 1889 under the subtitle *Studies in the Religion of the Incarnation*. This also stressed the relation of faith to the intellectual and moral problems of the times. Thus in the broadest sense, once again, incarnational theology came to stress the role of culture and civilization in the world. The social concern of F. D. Maurice and Charles Kingsley sprang in part from the concerns of Jesus for the poor, seen in the incarnation. At best, however, it is a protest against reducing Christianity to a set of abstract ideas that fail to interact with everyday life. It opposed Docetism. (*See also* **Christology**.)

Incommensurability

"Incommensurability" properly functions as a term in the philosophy of science, but is now frequently, almost fashionably, used in theology with both its correct and its incorrect meaning. Thomas Kuhn applied the term to two conceptual systems that do not actually contradict each other, but find no common arbiter to decide between their competing claims (T. S. Kuhn, *The Structure of Scientific Revolutions* [1962; 2nd ed. 1970]). He proposed that usually "normal" science works within a given conceptual scheme or paradigm. But "revolutions" in science take place when a new paradigm is adopted, which cannot be measured (i.e., it is incommensurable) in terms of the old one. The customary example often cited is the overtaking of Isaac Newton's system of physics, with its "normal" gravitational laws, by Albert Einstein's "new" paradigm of quantum physics. Einstein does not "contradict" Newton, but opens the possibility of addressing problems that were insoluble within the "old" paradigm. Hans Küng and many others urge the need for new paradigms in theology. However, Lyotard and some postmodernists urge that no arbitration is possible for numerous, far-reaching problems, and perhaps overstate the role of incommensurability. Some, including Saul Kripke, have criticized Kuhn's notion, and have even spoken of interparadigmatic standards.

Indirect Communication

Indirect communication offers a very important means of communication by avoiding the use of direct or transparent propositions. It may be used for more than one reason. (i) In the thought of S. Kierkegaard, it facilitates *decision* between different possibilities. (ii) In the thought of M. Bakhtin, it would allow for a polyphonic communication of truth that was too complex to be communicated by a single proposition. (iii) To E. Fuchs it represents the way of love, by avoiding confrontation, and by allowing the hearer to find a place of meeting within the world of narrative or speech event. (iv) Aside from its more technical meaning in Kierkegaard, Jesus taught in parables as a model of indirect communication. In the OT, had Nathan confronted King David with an overt accusation of adultery and murder, his language might not have succeeded. But by inviting David into the narrative world of hospitality, David saw the point, for the parable "wounded from behind."

Inspiration

The one explicit allusion to the inspiration of Scripture in the biblical writings appears to come in 2 Tim. 3:16, where the writer asserts that Scripture (presumably the OT) is inspired or "God-breathed" (Gk. *pāsa graphē theopneustos kai ōphelimos pros didaskalian*). Danker translates it as "inspired by God"; W. D. Mounce renders it "God-breathed" (*Pastoral Epistles* [Nashville: Nelson, 2000], 565-67). After the NT period, Clement of Rome asserts that the Holy Spirit habitually inspires the Scripture (*1 Clem.* 13.1-2). The subapostolic *Epistle of Barnabas* declares that the Spirit was active in inspiring the OT (9.7); and Athenagoras (second-century apologist) compares the Spirit inspiring Scripture to a flute player playing his flute. Theophilus (late-second-century apologist) also affirms this (*Ad Autolycum* 2.9-22). Clement of Alexandria declares that "the Spirit by the mouth of Isaiah is an unimpeachable witness" to what Jesus teaches (*The Instructor* 1.5.15; *ANF* 2:213; cf. *Stromata* 6.14). Irenaeus affirms "the rule of faith," which incorporates Scripture. A critical point was reached when Marcion (c. 150) attempted to ascribe the OT and NT to different deities, in reaction to which the church insisted that "one" Holy Spirit inspired both Testaments. Origen states, "The sacred books are not compositions of men.... They were composed by the inspiration of the Spirit" (*De principiis* 4.1.9).

John Webster may be correct in claiming, "The Patristic era contains little formal treatment of the nature of biblical authority" (in *DTIB* 724), but this is relative to post-Reformation Protestant orthodoxy, and hardly applies to inspiration. It is true, however, that, as H. B. Swete suggests, the second century may have shown more concern than the fourth, but Swete cites Cyril of Jerusalem and Gregory of Nazianzus as major exceptions (*The Holy Spirit in the Ancient Church* [London: Macmillan, 1912], 200-201; Cyril, *Catechism* 4.2, 16; 16.1, 2; 17.3; and Gregory, *Theological Orations* 5.1, 18, 24).

The term "inspiration" came into prominence in the sixteenth century. Luther identified the inspiration of the Holy Spirit with witness to Christ. In terms of detail, he admitted that there were errors in the prophets; he evaluated Kings as more reliable than Chronicles; he argued that James "mangles Scripture"; and he rejected the book of Revelation as virtually valueless. John Calvin was less radical. But, in the words of Paul Achtemeier, Calvin argued that the Holy Spirit "does not delegate it [inspiration] to the *words* of Scripture, but rather *uses* those words to convince people of the *content* of the message to which Scripture bears witness" (*The Inspiration of Scripture* [Philadelphia: Westminster, 1980], 140). We find the same view in J. K. S. Reid, *The Authority of Scripture: The Reformation and Post-Reformation Understanding* (London: Methuen, 1957), 48-49 and

156-76. In the post-Reformation period, however, this view tended to revert to the *words* of Scripture rather than its *writers* and *purpose*. Eventually the high point of this trend was reached in B. B. Warfield, A. A. Hodge, and probably Carl Henry. These three writers, contrary to Luther and probably Calvin, argued for the "inerrancy" of Scripture. Among evangelicals this stands in sharp contrast with the view of James Orr, who distinguished between a "maximum" level of biblical inspiration and inspiration that operated on a "lower plane" with "feebler energy" (*Revelation and Inspiration* [New York: Scribner; London: Duckworth, 1910], 177-78).

Karl Barth, Emil Brunner, and Bernard Ramm argue that questions about revelation are prior to questions about inspiration. Revelation constitutes a major biblical theme from the revelation to Abraham and certainly to Moses at the burning bush (Exodus 3). Only in the light of God's self-revelation can we then discuss theories of biblical inspiration by the Holy Spirit. Even in his definitive study *Catholic Theories of Biblical Inspiration Since 1810* (Cambridge: CUP, 1969), J. T. Burtchaell states, "The real issue here is what confounds scholars in so many areas: the manner in which human events are jointly caused by both God and man" (279). This issue can be addressed only by considering at greater length the questions of the authority of the Bible and of the nature of revelation. (*See also* **Authority of the Bible; Revelation.**)

Reading: Paul Achtemeier, *The Inspiration of Scripture* (Philadelphia: Westminster, 1980); G. C. Berkouwer, *Holy Scripture* (Grand Rapids: Eerdmans, 1975); J. T. Burtchaell, *Catholic Theories of Biblical Inspiration Since 1810* (Cambridge: CUP, 1969); James Orr, *Revelation and Inspiration* (New York: Scribner, 1910); J. K. S. Reid, *The Authority of Scripture: The Reformation and Post-Reformation Understanding* (London: Methuen, 1957).

Intention
A whole generation of biblical scholars were mistakenly put off seeking for "the intention of the author" in biblical exegesis. In English literature R. Wellek and A. Warren formulated what they called "the intentional fallacy" (in W. K. Wimsatt, *The Verbal Icon* [1954; New York: Noonday Press, 1966]). They argued that "Intention as an account of meaning is quite mistaken." As exponents of the New Criticism of the 1950s and 1960s, they argued that the text is "autonomous," and detached from the author. The author, they claimed, concerned merely the text's origin. The supposed fallacy was also called "the genetic fallacy." What biblical scholars failed to realize, however, was that these writers were primarily referring to *poetic* or *literary* texts. Poetic speech about a "red rose" often does not require reference to the author. There are biblical genres of which the same could be said.

It was also argued that "the mental state" of an author was inaccessible and unreliable. This objection runs counter to Schleiermacher's hermeneutics. It also fails to take into account the view of Wittgenstein and others that intention does not *primarily* denote a mental state. If a person acts "intentionally," the act is willed and deliberate. Intention denotes an act of will, as its adverbial use implies. Wittgenstein, Searle, and many in linguistics understand intention as *directed toward a goal*. It may be more fruitful to ask how an author *wills* a text to be *directed,* and this does not exclude intention. Work on speech acts makes this clear. Detailed accounts of these arguments can be found in A. C. Thiselton, *New Horizons in Hermeneutics* (London: HarperCollins, 1992; Grand Rapids: Zondervan, 2012), with numerous references in the index, for example, 598-600.

Intermediate State
The intermediate state generally denotes the supposed condition after death in which Christians await the general resurrection of the dead. This belief invites doubts from many, who cite biblical passages in which the dead appear to enter Christ's presence immediately. For example, Paul declares: "I am hard pressed between the two: my desire is to depart (Gk. purposive infinitive, *eis to analysai*) and be with Christ, for that is far better" (Phil. 1:23). Greek *analyō*, "to depart," is a euphemism for death. Similarly, he states, "We would rather be away from the body and at home with the Lord" (2 Cor. 5:6 ESV). Jesus declared to the dying thief, "Today you will be with me in Paradise" (Luke 23:43). Why, then, does belief in an intermediate state persist? Elsewhere we have expressed doubts about the existence of purgatory. The substantial difficulty is the unfolding of eschatological events before the resurrection. In O. Cullmann's words, "The transformation of the body does not take place until the End, when the whole creation will be made new by the Holy Spirit, when there will be no death or corruption" (*Immortality of the Soul or Resurrection of the Dead?* [London: Epworth, 1958], 37). Thus Paul writes, "The Lord ... will descend from heaven, and the dead in Christ will rise first. Then we who are alive, who are left" (1 Thess. 4:16-17; *see* **Imminence of the End**).

Martin Luther proposes that the dead will sleep in an unconscious, dreamless way, "removed from space and time" (*Commentary on 1 Corinthians 7 and 15* [St. Louis: Concordia, 1973], 110; WA 36:947). J. Moltmann argues that the intermediate state is "not empty, like a waiting room. It is filled with the Lordship of Christ over the dead and the living, and by the experience of the Spirit" (*The Coming of God* [London: SCM, 1996], 104). Christians are "hidden with Christ" (Col. 3:3). They cannot be separated from the love of God (Rom. 8:38-39). The Roman Catholic theologian Karl Rahner argues for a qualified universalism and points to the grace of God, but he allows for a period of postmortal growth and insists that purgatory remains official Catholic doctrine (*TI* 19:181-93).

There is a way to maintain the truth of each set of biblical passages, by the tools of conceptual analysis, as suggested in a different context by linguistic philosopher Gilbert Ryle (1900-1976). He addresses "conflicts between theories" in *Dilemmas* ([Cambridge: CUP, 1966], 1 and throughout). He takes up and discusses the ancient paradox of "Achilles and the tortoise," clearly demonstrating that the paradox arises from confusing an "observer" logic with "a participant" logic. In this confusion "Achilles never catches the Tortoise" (36-37). If we adhere to observer language, no problem arises. If we confound it with participant language, confusions abound. We suggest an even more homely analogy. When a child falls asleep on Christmas Eve night, we can use "participant" language to say, "The sooner you fall asleep, the sooner Christmas morning will be here." But for the rest of the household we may need to use "observer" language. We may say: "You only have three hours to finish the tree and wrap up all the presents." Both are true. In "participant" language, the next thing that dying Christians know is meeting Christ. In "observer" language, the great events of Christian eschatology unfold. There is no contradiction.

In one sense it is misleading to speak of an intermediate state. But in a different sense, it is essential. In *pastoral* comments to the dying, it tends to mislead. In *theological* contexts, in terms of God's purposes for the whole world, it may become necessary. The issue simply cannot be addressed in the abstract. (*See also* **Imminence of the End; Parousia; Purgatory; Resurrection of the Dead.**)

Intersubjectivity

Intersubjectivity relates to communication between, and attitudes toward, fellow humans, especially in their plurality or community, rather than simply as one-to-one. Under the entry on subjectivity, we note that another person is not to be depersonalized into a "thing" or a passive *object*. Kierkegaard stressed the active and transforming nature of subjectivity. In this sense, *inter*subjectivity recognizes mutual transformation in the *interaction between* people. In Buber's thought it is crucial to regard each person as the other, or as a "You" or "Thou," not an "It." Merleau-Ponty sought a theory of intersubjectivity. Both the self and the other communicate and interact as active and responsive subjects. (*See also* **Subjectivity.**)

Irenaeus

Irenaeus (c. 130–c. 200) became bishop of Lyons in 180. Some regard him as the first theologian of the church. One of his distinctive qualities lies in his having roots in both the Eastern and the Western Church; he also had a possible oral link with the apostles through Polycarp. He urged observance of "the rule of faith," or biblical and apostolic tradition, especially in contrast to Gnostic systems. He rejected the Gnostic notion of "secret" revelation or tradition, and argued for faithfulness to the public transmission of knowledge from the apostles. Thus, against Gnostics, Irenaeus declared, "God is Creator of the world" (*Against Heresies* 1.9.1). He rejected the notion of divine emanations (1.12.7). In a famous passage he described God the Son and the Holy Spirit as the two "hands of God," and saw Christ and the Spirit as the same order or being as God. They are "anterior to all creation" (4.20.3). The Holy Spirit anointed Jesus Christ for his incarnate ministry (3.17-18). Another distinctive feature is Irenaeus's notion of "recapitulation" on the basis of Eph. 1:10. "These things therefore he (Christ) recapitulated in himself, by uniting man to the Spirit, and causing the Spirit to dwell in man" (5.20.2; cf. 5.21.1-2). He used Eph. 1:10 four or more times. The Latin term is *recapitulatio*, "recapitulation, repetition, summing up"; the Greek term is *anakephalaiōsis*, also in the verbal form, "to sum up, to recapitulate, to complete." In addition to his five books *Against Heresies*, he wrote a shorter work, *The Demonstration of the Apostolic Preaching*, and some works that have become lost.

Reading: J. Lawson, *The Biblical Theology of St. Irenaeus* (Eugene, Ore.: Wipf and Stock, 2006); J. R. Payton, *Irenaeus on the Christian Faith: A Condensation* . . . (Cambridge: James Clarke, 2012).

Irresistible Grace

This is the doctrine that the grace of God cannot be finally resisted or ultimately be rejected by human beings. Although it may not be prominent in Augustine, it remains a corollary of his theology of election and predestination. It is held in Calvin and in Reformed theology, as defined by the Synod of Dort, as well as among the Jansenists. This doctrine does not necessarily oppose free will. Jürgen Moltmann regards the victory of grace as inevitable only at the last day. (*See also* Grace.)

Irving, Edward

Edward Irving (1792-1834) is associated with the origins of the Catholic Apostolic Church, together with Henry Drummond. Irving was born in southwest Scotland and educated in the University of Edinburgh. In 1819 he ministered in Glasgow, and in 1822 moved to London. But he reacted strongly *against* the theology of the Church of Scotland. In 1828 there were outbreaks of speaking in tongues in Scotland, and in 1831 another outbreak followed in his London church, with his support and approval. His presbytery ejected him, and with Drummond he formed the Catholic Apostolic Church. This revivalist group expected the imminent return of Christ, and by 1835 they had appointed twelve "apostles," as well as evangelists, prophets, and teachers. "Apostles" were, in effect, "bishops" of the new church. He also undermined notions of the sinlessness of Christ, on the ground that Christ shared *fallen* human nature. In many respects his theology of the Holy Spirit anticipated many aspects of Pentecostal theology and of the Renewal Movement. In 1833 he was charged with heresy. Many compare him with the *Schwärmer* or Radical Reformers, who aroused Luther's hostility, and with the Holiness Movement in America. His followers were often called "Irvingites."

Irwin, Benjamin H.

Benjamin H. Irwin (1854-?) underwent a "sanctification experience" through the Iowa Holiness Association. In 1895 he received a "baptism of fire," and founded the Fire-Baptized Holiness Association. But in 1900 he confessed to "open and gross sin" and entered obscurity.

Iser, Wolfgang

Wolfgang Iser (1926-2007) was a foremost theorist of reader-response criticism. He drew on the philosophical background of Roman Ingarden, who in turn was a disciple of E. Husserl. His philosophical interest was largely in perception. Following Ingarden, Iser argued that there is a measure of *incompleteness* in what we perceive. For example, when we "perceive" a table or a chair, what we perceive may be three, rather than four, of the legs; yet we "fill in" the rest of what we cannot actually see. Ingarden produced the model of "filling in the gaps" of our perceptions. Iser applied this to the act of reading. Reading with intelligence involves "completing" the passage's meaning, or making explicit what we presupposed or construed. He argued, "Effects and responses are properties neither of the text nor of the reader; the text represents a *potential* effect that is realized in the reading process" (Iser, *The Act of Reading* [Baltimore and London: Johns Hopkins University Press, 1978], ix, italics mine). Actualization in reading involves "filling in the blanks." Further, actualization requires "interaction" between the text and the reader (21).

The upshot of this approach is to see that the reader must be *active* in the process of reading, and must *contribute* something. The "ideal" reader will have a competence that allows a close matching of the code of the text with the reader's assumptions. In biblical reading this leads to reader-response in engaging fully with the text. S. Wittig, J. Bassler, J. Resseguie, and R. Fowler have explored this with profit for biblical studies. Admittedly some confidence may be lost in seeing that biblical reading is never entirely objective. This point is pressed by S. Fish, and to a more moderate extent by U. Eco, D. Holland, and others. But the insight of interaction between the text and readers is inescapable, and constitutes one of the central issues in hermeneutics. It discourages the illusion of a "take it or leave it" attitude to the Bible, making it a demanding experience. Yet Fish is wrong to insist that there are no "givens" in the Bible at all. Creeds and traditions would function only in certain communities if this were so. To Iser we owe a sober, realistic, and balanced exposition of reader-response theory, as well as a pioneering one, in spite of Fish's blistering criticisms that he should go further.

J

Jansenism
Named after Cornelius Jansen (1585-1638), Jansenism is a strict and extreme version of the Augustinian doctrine of grace, which flourished within Roman Catholicism mainly in the seventeenth and eighteenth centuries. It was condemned as a heresy by Pope Innocent X in 1653. In his work on Augustine, Jansen had asserted that it was impossible to obey God's commandments without God's special grace; and that grace was irresistible (*see* **Irresistible Grace**). The Jansenists specifically opposed Jesuit theology and practice. They urged that assertions of human freedom compromised divine grace and God's deterministic sovereignty.

Jaspers, Karl Theodor
Karl Theodor Jaspers (1883-1969) became a doctor of medicine at Heidelberg in 1909, practiced psychiatry, and became professor of philosophy at Heidelberg in 1921. He regarded his three-volume *Philosophy* (1932) as his major work. He did not accept the term "existentialist," but he nevertheless focused on the human situation and the nature of human consciousness, leading others to use this term of him. He believed that human finitude pointed to a transcendent "Beyond." But truth, for Jasper, was not a fixed or abstract property, but that for which "*we* search" (*Philosophy* [Chicago: University of Chicago Press, 1969], 1:37). Life involves struggle, suffering, and guilt (2:178). A human being can "find his real self" especially in "boundary situations" (1:48). If the transcendent confronts a person in a boundary situation, for example, when he comes to the end of his tether, he may discover what is true "for him." Jaspers sought to hold together a positive view of "religion" or "God" with a pluriform, perhaps relativist and subjective, view of truth. He defended human freedom and the ability of people to pass beyond convention. He was influenced by Kierkegaard and Nietzsche.

Jerome
Jerome (c. 345-420) first studied at Rome, and traveled in Gaul, before he entered the ascetic life and became a biblical exegete. In 374, at about thirty, he traveled to Palestine via Antioch, and then settled in the Syrian desert, where he learned Hebrew. By 385 he had returned to Rome as secretary to the pope, or to Bishop Damasus. Shortly afterward he moved to Bethlehem, where he devoted himself

to study, accompanied and supported by a wealthy Roman widow, Paula, and her daughter. Her wealth established a monastery.

Jerome was outstanding as a biblical exegete and translator, especially in an age when few of the Church Fathers were familiar with Hebrew. His most widely known work remains the translation of the Bible into Latin, known as *versio vulgate*, or the Vulgate, which was accepted as authoritative by the Roman Catholic Church. He also translated Origen into Latin. Anticipating the Reformers, he advocated acceptance of the Hebrew canon rather than that of the LXX. He was also a controversialist and a polemicist, and attacked Arianism, Pelagianism, and Origenism. He advocated extreme asceticism.

Jesuits

The Society of Jesus (the Jesuits) was founded by Ignatius Loyola (1491-1556) with nine companions, among whom was Francis Xavier. Pope Paul III approved the society in 1540. Ignatius, who came from Loyola, south of the Pyrenees, wanted to rekindle fervor and practice in the church. The society aimed at "the propagation of the faith" through the "Spiritual Exercises" of Ignatius. From the beginning, Jesuits vowed to travel and be mobile. They formed three "colleges" in Rome: for themselves, for English Catholics, and for German Catholics. In effect they became itinerant missionaries for Rome. Francis Xavier established the order in India and Japan, and other orders were founded in Brazil, Africa, and China. By 1600 the order numbered 8,500 members. In 1580 Edward Campion came to England, and a province was formed in 1623.

In South America they attempted to protect the indigenous population against slave traders. In the seventeenth century, however, they met with opposition from Rome and Pope Paul V over the issue of grace and free will. But they reestablished themselves, and Pope Pius VII formally restored them in 1814. Today estimates of their numbers vary from more than 25,000 to about 40,000. They oversee Vatican Radio, and publish the *Heythrop Journal* and *Theological Studies*. Their educational work is highly valued, especially in founding and maintaining schools and universities. Among serious theologians, Teilhard de Chardin, Bernard Lonergan, and Karl Rahner are global figures. In 2013 the cardinals elected the first Jesuit pope, Francis of Argentina, known for his humility and simplicity.

Joachim of Fiore

Joachim of Fiore (c. 1135-1202) is known especially for his work on apocalypticism and millennialism. His three major works include *An Exposition of the Apocalypse, Ten-Stringed Psaltery,* and *Book of Concordance of the Old and New Testaments*. He stressed the involvement of the Holy Trinity in world history. His view of history was not totally unlike that espoused by later dispensationalism. He divided history into "ages," calculated by generations, and saw the millennium as the age of the Holy Spirit, which would come after the Antichrist, or between Antichrists. The first age, he stated, was that of God the Father, when humankind lived under the law; the second was that of God the Son, when humankind lived under grace. He also developed a complex scheme of hermeneutics, which drew on typology. He was a monk of the Benedictine Order, and he founded a new house at Fiore.

John of Damascus
John of Damascus (c. 655–c. 750) was known as a strong defender of images in the iconoclastic controversy. Little is known of the events of his life, except that he came from a wealthy family, served for a time in a Muslim administration, and then became a monk. His work *The Fountain of Knowledge* became influential as an exposition of Orthodox theology. In the Orthodox Church he is often considered "the last great theologian of the patristic era."

John of the Cross
John of the Cross (1542-1591) was a Spanish mystic who was a friend and colleague of Teresa of Ávila. He took charge of Teresa's Carmelite Order, and is author of *The Dark Night of the Soul*. The "dark night," he suggests, is an experience that occurs "when God wants to purify [believers], and move them on to greater heights. . . . The soul is nurtured and caressed by the Spirit" (*Dark Night* 1.1, 2). Like Hilton, he corrects some arbitrary interpretations of mystical visions, and seeks reformation within the Roman Catholic tradition.

Jowett, Benjamin
Benjamin Jowett (1817-1893), master of Balliol College, Oxford, represented both the Anglo-Catholic and Broad Church, or liberal, traditions. In the controversial collection *Essays and Reviews* (1860), he famously declared that the Bible should be interpreted "like any other book." In 1859 he published a commentary on Thessalonians, and held a subjective view of the atonement. He wrote on Plato and Aristotle. Many suspected that he fell short of Christian orthodoxy.

Judaism in the Time of Jesus
The term "Jew" (Gk. *Ioudaios*) was originally used by foreigners to denote those living in Judea. But by the era of the Maccabees (second century B.C.), the term was used by Jews themselves as a self-designation, which also entailed a distinctive religious identity. In the same period "Judaism" (Gk. *Ioudaismos*) also emerged (2 Macc. 2:21; 8:1; 14:38). Within Judaism, however, further distinctions need to be made.

(i) **Aramaic-speaking or "Palestinian" Judaism and Greek-speaking, "Hellenistic," or Diaspora Jews.** It used to be conventional to distinguish between "Palestinian" and "Hellenistic" Judaism. But this may now be regarded as simplistic for two reasons. First, not all of "Palestine" was Aramaic-speaking. Matthew speaks of "Galilee of the Gentiles" (Gk. *tōn ethnōn*; 4:15). Second, Martin Hengel and others have shown decisively that these constituted not two self-contained groups, but groups between which there were blurred edges, interaction, interchange, and two-way influences. Today it is customary to use the terms "Aramaic-speaking" Jews (mainly from Judea as *part* of "Palestine") and "Greek-speaking" Jews (mainly but not exclusively from the Diaspora). All Jews looked on Jerusalem and the Holy Land as their home, but by the first century the majority of Jews lived further afield, mainly in several "Jewish" centers in the Roman Empire. The three strongest centers in the Roman Empire were as follows:

(a) Jews had lived in *Mesopotamia* since the Assyrian-Babylonian deportations in the seventh and sixth centuries B.C. Under the Persian Empire some returned, but many remained. (b) Jews settled in *Egypt* from the sixth century onward. The Elephantine papyri (from the island of Elephantine in the Nile) recount the fortunes of one such community c. 590 B.C. More Jews followed in the wake of the conquests of Alexander the Great, and later the assimilation of Egypt as a province of the Roman Empire. Philo of Alexandria estimated about a million Jews in Egypt in A.D. 38. Even if this is exaggerated, one out of five wards of the city of Alexandria was entirely Jewish, and Alexandria came to be the second-largest city of the empire. (c) Jews had migrated to *Rome* since the second century, especially after Pompey's conquest of Judea in 63 B.C. Roman Jews were usually Greek-speaking and bore Greek names. Jewish influence was strong. Many Jews eventually returned to Rome after Tiberius's expulsion of Jews. These three were the main centers, but not the only ones.

Acts 6:1 recounts the complaint from "the Hellenists" (NRSV) against "the Hebrews" (NRSV) because their widows were neglected in the daily distribution of food. The NRSV gives a literalist rendering of the Greek *goggusmos tōn Hellēnistōn pros tous Hebraious*. But Danker gives the first meaning of *Hellēnistēs* as "one who uses the Greek language," or a Greek-speaking Israelite, in contrast to one speaking a non-Semitic language (Acts 6:1; BDAG 319). He translates *Hebraios* either as "Hebrew" or "Jew," or as "Hebrew–Aramaic-speaking Israelite, in contrast to a Greek-speaking Israelite," in Acts 6:1 (BDAG 270). It is significant that the appointed arbitrators of the dispute all had Greek names, and were presumably Greek-speaking Jews. In Acts 2:8-11 the main centers of Judaism are mentioned, together with other Diaspora centers. Artaxerxes III of Persia had resettled some of the Mesopotamian Jews in Hyrcania by the Caspian Sea. Pontus was in northern Asia Minor; and virtually all Asia Minor was covered, together with parts of North Africa. The audience at Pentecost is a credible picture of Diaspora Jews visiting their "home," Jerusalem, for the festival.

(ii) **Literature Associated with the Two Respective Settings.** A vast amount of Jewish literature emerged in the period between the two Testaments. On the "Hebrew" or Aramaic-speaking side, clearly the Hebrew Masoretic Text of the OT was the most fundamental influence, just as the LXX became the Bible of the Diaspora Jews. Also on the "Hebrew-speaking" side, we may mention the *Psalms of Solomon,* which is a vivid account of Pompey's invasion of Jerusalem (c. 63 B.C.). This prophesies the coming of a messianic figure, the Son of David, who will "purify Israel of Latin men" by conquest. This probably emerged from the Essenes or *chasidīm* in Judea, and is probably to be dated in the first century B.C., or shortly thereafter. Another example is the Wisdom of Ben Sirach, known also as Ecclesiasticus. Although it was translated into Greek, it was originally composed in Hebrew, and mirrors the style of Proverbs. Further, 1 Maccabees recounts the opposition of Judas and his brothers, Jonathan and Simon, to the oppression of Antiochus Epiphanes and the Seleucids, and is usually dated c. 104 B.C. With the discovery of Qumran in 1948 and following, such books as the *Damascus Document, Rule of the Community*, and *Temple Scroll* should be added.

The literature of "Hellenistic" or Greek-speaking Diaspora Judaism is in many cases even easier to define. The Wisdom of Solomon came probably from Alexandria in the first century B.C. or shortly afterward, and shared many themes with Philo. 2 Maccabees is more difficult to date and locate, and although it overlays with 1 Maccabees, has a suggestion of the intercession of saints (15:12-14). 3 Maccabees and 4 Maccabees are clearly from the Diaspora. 2 Maccabees was written in Greek, possibly originated in Alexandria, and was probably written before A.D. 70. 4 Maccabees is virtually a misnomer, and was also called "On the Power of Absolute Reason." It is a Hellenistic philosophical discourse, and praises virtue (1:1, 7, 15, 30; 2:24; 6:7). The two key sources from Greek-speaking Judaism are Philo and Josephus (*see* **Philo of Alexandria**). Flavius Josephus (c. A.D. 37-110) took a leading part in the Jewish War against Rome in 66-70, although he claims he was a reluctant recruit. He somehow escaped when the Romans were on the brink of victory, and devoted his life thereafter as an advocate of Judaism to the Romans. He apparently was befriended by Vespasian. His two major works were *The Jewish War* and the *Antiquities of the Jews*. The latter partly paraphrases the earlier narrative of the OT, with allegorical interpretation, especially where any OT text might offend the Romans. Yet both Philo and Josephus were loyal to their Jewish faith. Much of the Greek-speaking Jewish literature took the form of apologetic to Gentiles or accounts of loyalty in the face of Jewish persecution.

(iii) **The Temple, Synagogues, and the Home.** Next to the vital role of the Hebrew Bible, arranged as the Law, the Prophets, and the Writings, the home and the temple stood at the heart of Judaism. (a) In the home, circumcision and the Passover meal marked out the Jews as God's covenant people. At the Passover meal the father presided and the oldest son added the meaning of the rite. It bound the family together and reminded it of its roots in the past.

(b) The temple was the linchpin of Judaism in the time of Jesus. Solomon had built the first temple, but it was destroyed by Babylonian armies in 587 B.C. It was refounded seventy years later under Zerubbabel, but in a much more modest form. This second temple also suffered defilement, under Antiochus Epiphanes in 167-164 B.C., when the Seleucids oppressed the Jews, but the Maccabees led a Jewish revolt. Herod I (37-4 B.C.) curried favor as a Roman collaborator, and from 37 to 27 followed the Oriental custom of devoting himself to domestic affairs and, where necessary, trying potential rivals or rebels, and executing them. The second phase of his reign from 27 to 13 B.C. was one of cultural expansion, including the erection of magnificent public buildings, partly designed to impress the Romans. The renamed "Caesarea," for example, was virtually re-created as a Hellenistic city, with a palace, a theater, an amphitheater, and a stadium. Work on the "third" temple began in 20 B.C.; it took nine years to rebuild and extend. The disciples of Jesus commented on its "wonderful stones" (Mark 13:1; cf. Luke 21:5). The temple area became one of the largest such areas in the ancient world, and the temple itself extended to at least twice the area of the former temple. Apart from the golden eagle of the sun god, Herod made every effort to respect the religious sensibilities of the Jews, and his building was indeed impressive.

The temple was designed around five "courts," each symbolizing exclusion because of divine holiness and invitation to entry because of divine grace. The outermost court was called the Court of the Gentiles, and was a terrace surrounding the temple, with beautiful colonnades. On the east was "the portico of Solomon," where Jesus and later the apostles often spent time (John 10:23; Acts 3:11). Within this "court," that is, nearer to the temple itself, was the Court of the Women, which Gentiles were forbidden to enter on pain of death. The main gate from the Court of the Gentiles to the Court of the Women, with steps from the east, was called the Beautiful Gate (Acts 3:10), with inscriptions in Greek and Latin warning Gentiles not to enter. West of the Court of the Women was the men's court, on a higher level, which only Jewish men could enter. There stood the altar of burnt offerings. An inner court beyond this was the Court of the Priests (cf. Acts 4:15), where they slaughtered the sacrifices twice a day, and carried out a rinsing. The sacrifices were enacted probably at dawn at the ninth hour (three o'clock). Finally, the most sacred "court" of all was that of the high priest, called the Holy of Holies. The high priest made a solemn sacrifice once a year on the Day of Atonement, to make a sacrifice of atonement for the whole people of Israel.

(c) The origins of the synagogue are uncertain. Synagogues may have emerged during the period of exile. They had become a fixed feature of Jewish life before the time of Jesus both in the Diaspora and the Holy Land, and even in Jerusalem. Worship took place especially on Sabbaths, and at the great festivals. There was always a place for the reading of the Law, and there is evidence of a yearly cycle of readings (*see* **Lectionary**), or in some cases three-yearly. In Palestine the reading of the Hebrew text was accompanied by an oral reading (called a Targum). On the Sabbath a reading from the Law was followed by one from the Prophets — in Luke 4:16-19 Jesus read from Isaiah. Acts 13:15 alludes to Paul and Barnabas giving "a word of exhortation," often the synagogue reading. Apart from this very basic pattern, there could be variations in form, which would include praise, prayer, reading, exhortation, and blessing. A minimum of ten Jewish men would constitute a congregation. Acts recounts some eight or more synagogues in Diaspora cities.

(iv) **Priests, Scribes, Pharisees, Sadducees, Essenes, and Other Groups.** Sadducees and Pharisees both revered the Law, but differed politically. Luke describes them as "parties" (Gk. *hairesis*) of Judaism (Acts 5:17; 15:5; 26:5). The Mishnah calls them different schools of biblical interpretation (*m. Yadayim* 4:6). They were politically conservative and emphasized responsibility for one's actions. Traditionally they supported aristocrats, and resolutely opposed popular movements. Many, but not all, were priests. The Pharisees traced their name to the Hebrew *pārash* and Aramaic *pᵉrash*, "to separate," because of their concern for religious purity. But they were also an expansionist, popular party, made up of laypeople (Matt. 15:2; Josephus, *Antiquities* 18.12-15). They analyzed the laws of the Bible in meticulous detail, and supplemented them, legislating for every conceivable situation. They developed a tradition of observances *(halākā)* and a tradition of narration *(haggadāh)*. This led to the Mishnah and later the Gemara. Although the Sadducees became the larger party in government, the Pharisees were also fully involved. Their strict observance included washing of hands (Matt. 15:2) and the wearing of phylacteries and tassels (Matt. 23:5). Unlike the Sadducees, they believed in the resurrection (Acts 23:8; Josephus, *Antiquities* 18.14; see **Resurrection of the Dead**). They would have resented Jesus' critique of Pharisaic traditions.

The scribes (Heb. *sōphēr*; Gk. *grammateus*) had originally been secretaries to Oriental governors or kings in the Persian Empire, and were certainly part of the Jewish Council. The Jewish scribe came to serve as a government official, as well teacher and judge, and had close knowledge of the Mosaic Law. Scribes organized synagogues (1 Macc. 2:42). They often drew a circle of disciples around them, just as Paul sat at the feet of Gamaliel (Acts 22:3). Recognized scholars were given the courtesy title "Rabbi." The Jewish priests were not officially a ruling body. But they alone could enter the Court of the Priests (see above). Priests and Levites were appointed by their descent. They performed the daily sacrifices in the temple, and were organized through divisions, so that they might be "on duty" about twice each year. Further offerings were required at the great festivals: the Day of Atonement, the Feast of Booths, the Dedication of the Temple, the Feast of Weeks, and the Passover. Some were reserved for the office of high priest.

The first documentary evidence for the term "Essene" comes from about 144 B.C. Essenes believed in God's plan for salvation history, and developed a *community* life. In 1948-1949 a settlement of Essenes was discovered at Qumran. They rejected the worship of the temple, and looked on themselves as led by true Zadokite priests. Philo speaks of *essaioi*, and Josephus, of *essēnoi*. They may perhaps best be understood as a monastic order.

Much changed, as we should expect, after the destruction of the temple by the Romans in A.D. 70. Judaism became an honorable, living tradition, which included such later thinkers as Maimonides. We have restricted our entry, however, to that period that directly relates to the time of Jesus.

Reading: M. C. Boys, ed., *Seeing Judaism Anew* (New York and London: Sheed and Ward, 2005); F. F. Bruce, *New Testament History* (London: Nelson, 1969); F. V. Filson, *A New Testament History* (London: SCM, 1965); C. Hezner, ed., *Oxford Hand-*

book of Jewish Daily Life in Roman Palestine (Oxford: OUP, 2010); Jacob Neusner, *First Century Judaism in Crisis* (Philadelphia: Westminster John Knox, 2006); Bo Reicke, *The New Testament Era* (London: Black, 1964); John Riches, *The World of Jesus* (Cambridge: CUP, 1990).

Julian of Norwich

Julian of Norwich (1342-1416) was a Benedictine nun who lived as an anchoress, a solitary who had withdrawn from the world. Her life is a classic example of mysticism. Her major work is *Revelations of Divine Showings* (London: Penguin, 1998), and exists in a longer and a shorter version. The main focus of the visions concerns the sufferings of Christ. She comments, "God was showing . . . the bodily sight of plentiful bleeding from Christ's head. . . . Great drops fell down under the crown of thorns" (*Revelations* 7; Eng. 50-51). One of her most famous sayings comes in *Revelations* 15 (Eng. 23): "I will make all things well . . . I can make all things well." Another is: "Our Saviour is our true mother in whom we are eternally born" (*Revelations* 57). Most of her revelations, or showings, focus on God's love or on Christ's sufferings. However, it is characteristic of mysticism that a dialogue takes place between God and the self as "I" and "You." This can lead in many cases to visual representations, which may need to be checked against the language of revelation. Julian showed more careful and critical self-discipline (as advocated by Walter Hilton) than her associate, Margery Kempe of King's Lynn (c. 1373-1458).

Jung, Carl Gustav

Together with Sigmund Freud and Alfred Adler, Carl Gustav Jung (1875-1961) is thought of as one of the three great founders of psychoanalytical theory. He argued for the importance of the "collective" unconscious, especially as the source of collective symbols and archetypes. He believed that these archetypes were prior to the formulation of concepts and ideas. Symbols may combine "double meanings," a phrase that P. Ricoeur frequently uses. Indeed, Ricoeur owes much to both Jung and Freud, although he also criticizes what he perceives as their errors. Ricoeur also employs interactive metaphor as a creative device. Jung holds that often the "shadow side" of a person may suggest something that has been suppressed or neglected. P. Tillich owes even more to Jung than Ricoeur does, especially in his use of symbol and his concern for wholeness in contrast to fragmentation. He regards fragmentation as "demonic." Unlike Freud, Jung believes that religion can be a positive force. It may often be useful, although this is no guarantee of its truth. Tillich and Jung both seek to ground religion in the pre-cognitive and in the "depths" of the self.

Jüngel, Eberhard

Eberhard Jüngel was born in 1934 in a part of Germany that, after World War II, became the German Democratic Republic, which was dominated by Stalin. He reacted against this materialistic background, and his intention to study theology was met by astonishment on the part of his parents. In the University of Berlin, however, he studied under Ernst Fuchs, and also worked under K. Barth and Gerhard Ebeling in Switzerland. He presented his *Habilitation* in Berlin in 1962. From 1966 to 1969 he taught at Zurich, and in 1969 was appointed professor of systematic theology in the Protestant faculty of the University of Tübingen, where he remained until his retirement in 2003. Jüngel was heavily influenced by Fuchs on language event and hermeneutics; by Ebeling on the importance of Luther; and by Barth on justification, the Trinity, and the work of Christ. His own approach, however, is not primarily as an imitator; he is innovative and suggestive, and publishes seminal ideas, mainly on these areas.

Jüngel's early book *God's Being as Becoming* (1975; Eng. 2001) studied aspects of Barth's theology of the Holy Trinity. His magnum opus was *God as the Mystery of the World* (Ger. 1977; Eng. Edinburgh: T. & T. Clark, 1983). Here he first stresses the function of language as address, and argues that this affects the hearer's "whole being" (11). There are echoes of Fuchs here. We do not simply talk *about* God: *we listen* to his call. But there is confusion and uncertainty in the whole world-order about thought and language concerning God. Many talk of the death of God in various ways, and ask, "Where are you?" Jüngel discusses Bonhoeffer on God's letting "himself be pushed out of the world" (61), as well as Hegel on the frailty and weakness of humankind (93). He distinguishes between the christological origin of this concept of the death of God and "atheism, which defines the modern period" (97). But thinking of God is *possible*. Jüngel writes, "God's being is *thinkable again*" (iii). Indeed, "God is dead" has become a code word for "the end of metaphysics" (203). "The word of the cross," he urges, opposes this (204). "God defined himself as love on the cross of Jesus: God *is* love (1 Jn. 4:8)" (220). Through the cross, Jüngel declares, God discloses uniquely the depths of his deity. God, he says, "happens as love" in the death of Jesus (221). Thereby, in the cross, he argues, "The problem of the speakability of God" is addressed (229). This is a particular "speech event," as Fuchs would also say. Jüngel concludes, "The word of the cross is the self-definition of God in human language" (229). The world now appears in a completely new light (285). He adds, "The event character of this event, its *dunamis*, 'power'... is not just information" (287): "God is thinkable as one who speaks" (289).

Jüngel, it is clear, has a fine rhetorical turn of phrase, and it is not surprising that he has a widely appreciated preaching ministry. Unlike Fuchs, his speech event is not simply intralinguistic, but embodied. Toward the end of his book he discusses metaphor, as he does in *Theological Essays,* vol. 1 (Edinburgh: T. & T. Clark, 1989), 16-72. He asserts: "A theological theory of language has to accord to metaphorical speech" (23). He declares, "Metaphors are the articulation of discoveries" (51). Again, in this essay, he stresses "the address-character of language" (57); "the language of faith is metaphorical through and through" (58). He holds an interactive theory of metaphor. In volume 2, Jüngel offers "My Theology — a Short Summary" (Edinburgh: T. & T. Clark, 1995). Here he expresses concern about speaking of "my" theology. Theology, he declares, is listening to God, and "God distinguishes himself from the world by sharing himself with it" (11). Revelation is essentially from God, as Barth would argue.

There are many other aspects of Jüngel's work. He gives a dynamic account of justification elsewhere, and has many insights on Luther. But we have tried to indicate the heart of Jüngel's thought.

Reading: "Eberhard Jüngel," in *The Modern Theologians,* ed. D. F. Ford (Oxford: Blackwell, 2005), 250-55; Eberhard Jüngel, *God as the Mystery of the World* (Edinburgh: T. & T. Clark, 1983); Eberhard Jüngel, *Theological Essays* (Edinburgh: T. & T. Clark, vol. 1, 1989; vol. 2, 1995); J. B. Webster, introduction to *Theological Essays,* by Eberhard Jüngel, 1:1-15.

Justification

The term broadly denotes "being in a right relationship with God." It is no less a personal term than Paul's distinctive use of "reconciliation," which generally denotes a restored relationship between two people (e.g., in marriage) or between institutions or groups (e.g., peace between nations). It is a mistake to think of it as *exclusively* a legal term, in contrast to forgiveness. The contrast with forgiveness arises because whereas *forgiveness has to be renewed,* justification signifies a *once-for-all state.* If God is the subject of the verb, "to justify" (Heb. *ts-d-q;* Gk. *dikaioō*) denotes mainly "to put things right."

It is true that in the NT the fullest expression of justification by grace through faith occurs in Paul, especially in Galatians and Romans, and that God's "gift" of righteousness remains central to Martin Luther and the Reformation in the first place through Luther's new reading of Rom. 1:16-17. But it also occurs in other Pauline epistles and especially in the teaching of Jesus. Jesus' famous parable of the prodigal son (Luke 15:11-32) runs closely parallel with reconciliation and justification in Paul. More startlingly, the parable of the laborers in the vineyard, or the good employer and grumbling workers (Matt. 20:1-15), compares the unlooked-for generosity and grace of God with the standards of "fairness" or justice expected by the laborer. Grace eclipses justice. (This is parallel with Paul on law and grace.) Those who had worked an eleven-hour day received the day's wage that they had agreed on. Those who worked for only one hour received the very same wage, to the consternation of the others. The employer responded: "I am doing you no wrong; did you not agree with me for the usual daily wage?" (v. 13). He then asked the pivotal question: "Or are you envious because I am generous?" (v. 15). Humanity's cry of "it's not fair!" runs up against the offense and primacy of grace over that of law. The parable of the Pharisee and the tax collector (Luke 18:9-14) provokes the same attitudes and contrast. It is addressed to those "who trusted in themselves that they were righteous" (18:9). The Pharisee was obviously pleased with his achievements (vv. 11-12). The tax collector pleaded with God to be "merciful to me, a sinner" (v. 13). The tax collector "went down to his home justified rather than the other" (v. 14).

In Paul we find the two major themes that characterize the teaching of Jesus in the Gospels. First, justification depends on the sheer sovereign grace of God, as exemplified in the parable of the laborers in the vineyard (Matt. 20:1-15; *see* Grace). Second, it involves a declaration or verdict from God; it is not primarily a form of human behavior. Otherwise grace would not be grace (Gal. 2:21; Rom. 11:6). However, when we come to a more detailed interpretation of Paul, there are differences among modern scholars and in the history of Christian thought.

(i) The traditional approach of Luther and Calvin is carried into modern thought by J. Weiss, R. Bultmann, and C. K. Barrett. Weiss sees justification in Paul as "the 'non-imputation of sins' . . . peace with God" (Rom. 5:1-2; *Earliest Christianity* [New York: Harper, 1959], 2:498). It alludes by analogy to "heavenly book keeping," or "reckoning" by God: "It does not say what a man is in himself, but it states that he is considered, in the eyes of God . . . right with God" (499). Weiss continues: "God 'declares the ungodly just' . . ." In Rom. 3:24, "We are justified freely *(dōrean)*" (499). Herein, as Luther saw, "the righteousness of God is revealed" (Rom. 1:17; 3:21, 25-26); hence any self-glorifying is excluded: "man is always only the receiving agent" (*Earliest Christianity,* 501). It brings "a new relationship to the Lord Jesus" (503). Bultmann distinguishes between righteousness in a forensic sense and the word in an ethical sense (*Theology of the New Testament,* vol. 2 [London: SCM, 1952], 271). In Paul, "forensic righteousness . . . is already imputed to a man in the present" (274). He concludes: "The paradoxicality . . . is this: God already pronounces his eschatological verdict . . . in the present" (276). This is not "ethical perfection." Righteousness "has its origin in God's grace" (284). As a Lutheran, Bultmann expounds this in accordance with Lutheran tradition. Barrett similarly comments that Rom. 1:17 refers to God's righteousness, not to a human virtue, in the sense of vindication. In 3:21 it denotes "setting things and persons right" (*Epistle to the Romans* [London: Black, 1962], 73).

(ii) A minor modification to the traditional Lutheran interpretation of Paul can be found in C. Müller, K. Kartelge, and P. Stuhlmacher. Following Bultmann's emphasis on eschatology, they stress the apocalyptic context of this divine declaration or verdict. But the most decisive rejection of an alternative approach comes from E. Käsemann. He utterly repudiates the view taken by A. Schweitzer and especially K. Stendahl (see below), according to whom, in Käsemann's judgment, "the Church takes precedence over the Scriptures" (*Perspectives on Paul* [London: SCM, 1969], 62). Stendahl, he suggests, sees justification *only* as "an early Christian defence against Judaism" (63). Käsemann rejects a narrowing down of justification to legalistic issues, rather than placing it in the wider context of salvation history (60-78). His one agreement with Stendahl is "in protesting against the individualist curtailment of the Christian message" (74).

(iii) J. Ziesler's approach attempts to reconcile the largely earlier Roman Catholic "behavioral" view of righteousness with the traditional Protestant "declarative" view. If we restrict our attention to the verb *dikaioō,* "to rightwise," the Lutheran declarative view is right. The noun *dikaiosunē*, "righteousness," however, may often refer to the behavioral aspect. Ziesler writes, "If God looks on believers only as they are found in Christ, he may properly declare them righteous, for in him ... they are righteous.... There is nothing fictional here" (*The Meaning of Righteousness in Paul* [Cambridge: CUP, 1972], 212). But the noun and adjective often describe "behavior within relationships." The status precedes the state: Christians must become what they are. Some find the verb/noun approach not entirely convincing.

(iv) As for the traditional Roman Catholic interpretation, *The Catholic Encyclopaedia* still maintains that its view corresponds with that of the Council of Trent (1547; for which, *see* **Trent, Council of**). It explains: "Justification denotes that change or transformation in the soul by which man is transferred from the state of original sin ... to that of grace and Divine Sonship" (Trent, chap. iv). Nevertheless, this is not quite the same as Luther's maxim "at the same time sinners and righteous" *(simul peccator et iustus)*. Indeed, a traditional Catholic Pauline scholar observes of the Protestant view: "How can the false be true or how can God declare true what he knows to be false?" (F. Prat, *The Theology of St. Paul*, 2 vols. [London: Burns and Oates, 1945], 2:247).

(v) In modern theology the debate took a new turn with Stendahl, E. P. Sanders, and the so-called "New Perspective on Paul." An earlier attack on the Reformation interpretation of Paul had been made by A. Schweitzer, who attacked "being right with God" as a purely *individualistic* affair, whereas Paul's perspective was communal. Its logical context was different from the Pauline theme of death and resurrection with Christ, and was addressed to the "subsidiary" problem of addressing Judaizing Christians in Romans and Galatians. Stendahl agreed in 1977 that the central theme, even in Romans and Galatians, was not justification by grace, but the *equal* status of Jewish and Gentile Christians before God (*Paul among Jews and Gentiles* [London: SCM, 1977]).

Sanders pressed Stendahl's critique further. The Jewish background, he urged, concerns not "works," but remaining in the covenant by faithfulness to God's gracious provisions, which included the law. He termed this *covenanted nomism* (*Paul and Palestinian Judaism* [London: SCM, 1977], 511-15; cf. 75 and 426-28). The issue behind the relevant passages in Galatians and Romans concerns faithfulness to what God requires of his people in and under grace. Justification denotes not judgment on human "works," but "being saved by God's gracious election" (517). Righteousness in *Judaism* "implies the maintenance of status among the group of the elect; in *Paul* it is a *transfer term*" (544). For Christians, the term "justification" may be "a term indicating getting in" (544). The concept in Sanders is therefore more communal and broader than is the traditional view. Sanders softened the contrast between law and grace, so that they are no longer antithetical. Obedience does not "earn" grace, but "maintains one's position in the covenant" (420).

J. D. G. Dunn has firmly defended the positive insight of Sanders's detailed work on Judaism. Jewish scholars have been puzzled that too often Christian reconstructions of Judaism appear to be caricatures of a Judaism for which there is little or no evidence (*The Theology of Paul* [Edinburgh: T. & T. Clark, 1998], 339). He has sought to defend and to develop Sanders's approach. However, there has been resistance to Sanders, notably in Seyoon Kim, *Paul and the New Perspective* (Grand Rapids: Eerdmans, 2002). Kim argues that Paul related his doctrines of justification more directly to the OT and to the teaching of Jesus, and also to his Gentile mission. He engages most directly and critically with Dunn (1-34), especially in his interpretation of Paul's Damascus Road experience. He concludes his first chapter: "Sanders's definition of Judaism as covenantal nomism is in need of correction.... We cannot simply elevate it to the status of a dogma" (83). In the rest of his book he reconsiders justification by grace in 1 Thessalonians, Galatians, 2 Corinthians, and Romans, as well as Paul's use of Isaiah 42. The key issue in Galatians is " 'freedom' from the law of sin and death" (164).

(vi) In *The Two Horizons* (Grand Rapids: Eerdmans, 1980), 415-31, I attempt to illustrate how L. Wittgenstein and D. D. Evans might help to clarify what Prat called a "contradiction" in the traditional Reformation interpretation of Paul. Bultmann, Käsemann, and Stuhlmacher had begun to explore justification in the contrasting contexts of history and eschatology. The use of *dikaioō*, "to put right," is not a *factual assertion* about history in the present, but a *future verdict* or *evaluation*. Hence it becomes relevant to explore Wittgenstein's logical analysis of "seeing ... as ... ," or seeing *x* as *y* (*Philosophical Investigations* [Oxford: Blackwell, 1967], sect. 74 and II. xi, 193-214; and *Zettel* [Oxford: Blackwell, 1967], sects. 195-235). To interpret how we see something *as* something, Wittgenstein observes, "depends on the system to which the sign belongs" (*Zettel*, sect. 228). If there is more than one *evaluation*, these *do not "contradict" each other*, if their context or system is different. Wittgenstein gives an example that was suggested by Jastrow, in which the same drawing may be seen at one time as a duck, at another as a rabbit, or as both simultaneously. My thesis was that to see those "in Christ" as *righteous* functions *within the system of eschatology;* Luther's insistence that they are "at the same time sinners" functions as a verdict *within the system of history, or present human life*. There is no "contradiction" here, or even what Käsemann calls a "tension." This approach finds strong support from Evans's work on *"onlooks."* Evans writes, "Looking on *x* as *y* involves placing *x* within a structure ... or scheme" (*The Logic of Self-Involvement* [London: SCM, 1963], 124-41).

Is this true of Paul? Many years ago Weiss declared that "justification is an occurrence which will take place only in the day of the divine judgement" (Rom. 2:12-13, 16; Gal. 5:5; *Earliest Christianity*, 502). Bultmann urges both present and future poles: "Righteousness ... is already imputed to a man in the present" (*Theology of the New Testament*, 274). This "does not rob it of its forensic-eschatological meaning" (276). Bultmann has no need to call this present-future contrast a "paradox." To quote Weiss again, it is "the significant 'pre-dating' of what is really an eschatological act of salvation" (*Earliest Christianity*, 502). Gal.

5:5 is especially clear: "We eagerly wait for the hope of righteousness," alongside Rom. 5:1: "we are justified by faith." As Wittgenstein argues, there is no "contradiction" between two different evaluations of the word "exact": exactness in measuring miles between the earth and sun does not contradict exactness in carpentry or microbiology. Kartelge and Stuhlmacher view justification in the context of an apocalyptic verdict. But no one doubts the sinfulness of humankind purely in terms of past causal processes in history and life.

(vii) N. T. Wright finds himself in a mediating position between the Reformation tradition (as exemplified in Calvin, not Luther) and Sanders and Dunn. He agrees with Sanders and Dunn about *the communal and covenantal framework,* and about the need to study *Jewish* thought and religion, not to rely on a caricature of it. But he argues: "Torah . . . functioned . . . within not only a covenantal framework but also within a broadly *eschatological* one. The 'age to come' would see Israel vindicated at last" (*Justification* [London: SPCK, 2009], 57, italics mine). Righteousness, he concludes, "denotes the status that someone has when the court has found in their favour" (69). In that context it does *not* denote "moral character." But "to be in the right" is *to be vindicated,* and Romans 3 sees the whole human race as in the dark, guilty before God (70). Nevertheless, he also follows Augustine in seeing self-involving consequences, namely, "*transforming the character of the person,* albeit in small, preliminary ways" (70). On the other hand, the foundational starting point for Paul is the covenant (111-14). For Wright, the Reformation tradition is too narrow, and needs to be broadened.

The differences between these seven interpretations suggest that we need to be accurate in determining what the precise issue is between Paul and the Galatians or Romans, and not to set up "Judaism" as an unreal antithesis to Paul. As Sanders and Dunn stress, the issue does include the equal footing of Jews and Gentiles, and a *communal* perspective. Many of a more traditional frame of mind accept this, and Wright does not exclude a legal and declarative framework when it is not regarded as all there is to say. The "New Perspective" makes sense of Romans 9–11, and does not treat it as a mere appendix to 1–8 (as it seems to be in A. Nygren's otherwise excellent commentary). Yet Käsemann holds together salvation history with a basically Reformation interpretation, within an apocalyptic framework. He insists that it would be reductive to make the church, rather than Christ, the focus of Romans and Galatians (*Perspectives on Paul,* 60-78). It would be unwise to dismiss any of these seven interpretations of Paul too hurriedly.

(viii) The postbiblical or historical period sheds further light upon justification. (a) From earliest times something akin to the Reformation approach can be found. In *1 Clement* (c. 96) it is put this way: "We . . . are not justified by ourselves, nor by our own wisdom . . . or godliness, or works . . . but by that faith through which, from the beginning, Almighty God has justified all men" (32). Augustine, especially in his anti-Pelagian writings, makes this case; he firmly declares that "nobody is justified by [works]" (*On the Spirit and the Letter* 21). This is the context of his "Give what You command, and command what You will"

(22). It is faith, not law, which provides the approval verdict of justification (51). Justification springs from pure grace (56). Justification is never procured by one's own resources, but by grace alone (*On the Grace of Christ* 9.8). Augustine may be among the most prominent of the Fathers to reflect on grace, but the Eastern Fathers also have many references to this. For example, John Chrysostom writes on Rom. 3:25-28: Paul " 'declares' righteous those filled with the putrefying sores of sin. . . . 'Boasting' is excluded; 'by faith a man is justified' " (*Homilies on Romans* 7). Augustine cites 1 Cor. 4:7, "What do you have that you did not receive?"

(b) In the Middle Ages a number of writers show that this early tradition remains alive. Peter Abelard insists that Rom. 3:24-25 conveys the idea of "being justified freely." He explains that this is "not by any previous merits of their own, but by the grace of . . . God, who first loved us" (*On Romans* 3.19-26).

(c) Luther made justification by grace through faith alone the keystone of his theology. God "imputes" or "reckons" the righteousness of Christ to sinful believers. The believer is *simul iustus et peccator,* at once justified and a sinner. In his famous "Tower experience" he recounts how even as a monk he used to hate the phrase "righteousness of God" because it threatened and intimidated him. But when he reflected on the context of "He who through faith is righteous shall live" (Rom. 1:17), he began to understand that "the righteous lives by a gift of God, namely by faith. . . . Here I felt that I was altogether born again and had entered paradise itself. . . . A totally other face of the entire Scriptures showed itself to me. . . . Later I read Augustine's *The Spirit and the Letter,* where . . . I found that he, too, interpreted God's righteousness in a similar way" (*LW* 34:336-37). When the Christian belongs to Christ, there is a "happy exchange" *(froelich wechtzel)*: Christ bears our sin; we are declared righteous. Justification comes "by faith alone" *(sola fide).*

John Calvin shares many of Luther's themes: the declaration or forensic aspect; union with Christ; justification without merits; certainty of salvation. But in *Institutes* 3.11-16 he associates it more closely with sanctification and eschatology. He writes, "A man is said to be justified in the sight of God when in the judgment of God he is deemed righteous, and is accepted on account of his righteousness" (*Institutes* 3.11.2; Beveridge, 2:37-38). He agrees with Luther that it "is the principal ground on which religion must be supported" (3.11.1; 2:37). He writes, "*To justify* . . . is nothing else than to acquit from the charge of guilt " (3.11.3; 2:39). We "place our righteousness in the obedience of Christ" (3.11.23; 2:59). The believer is "clothed in it [righteousness of Christ] . . . in the sight of God" (3.11.2; 2:38). But in 3.11.6 Calvin adds further comments on Christ union, and in 3.11.11 on the rejection of a "frigid" or isolated doctrine.

(d) The Council of Trent (1545-1563) saw justification as imputed righteousness, but also stressed the transformation of the Christian into a righteous person. Indeed, as A. E. McGrath notes, Trent saw justification as a process continuing as sanctification does. Canon 9 of Trent states, "If anyone says that the sinner is justified by faith alone, meaning that nothing else is required to co-operate in order to obtain the grace of justification . . . let him be anathema." Trent doubted Luther and Calvin on the certainty of salvation, as assured by faith alone. Defenders of Trent would argue that this expounds the doctrine of justification in its proper wider context; critics of Trent would claim that the differences between justification and sanctification are blurred and confused.

(e) In modern theology we have already noted the debates about Pauline theology by Bultmann, Käsemann, Stendahl, Sanders, Dunn, Seyoon Kim, Wright, and others. Paul Tillich defined justification as "an act of God by which he accepts as not estranged those who are indeed estranged. . . . There is nothing in man which enables God to accept him. But man must accept just this. He must accept that he is accepted; he must accept acceptance" (*Systematic Theology*, vol. 2 [London: Nisbet, 1957], 205, 206). Hans Küng, as a Roman Catholic thinker, investigated Barth's view of justification. He concludes that it springs from "the supremacy of God's grace" (*Justification* [London: Burns and Oates, 1964], 187). The grace of God is his "generous kindness . . . something entirely personal" (189). The believer is "in Christ," or united with Christ, hence receives the righteousness of Christ. Küng appears willing to accept "by faith alone," as it is in Luther and Barth, provided that "man has to respond to the justifying activity of God." Yet *sola fide* makes good sense when it affirms "the total incapacity of man for any kind of self-justification. . . . The sinner can give nothing which he does not receive by God's grace. He stands there with his hands entirely empty" (238). (*See also* **Forgive, Forgiveness; Grace; Reconciliation; Sanctification.**)

Reading: John Calvin, *Institutes* 3.11-16 (Beveridge, 2:36-102); J. D. G. Dunn, *The Theology of Paul the Apostle* (Edinburgh: T. & T. Clark, 1998), 334-89; Seyoon Kim, *Paul and the New Perspective* (Grand Rapids: Eerdmans, 2002); H. Küng, *Justification* (London: Burns and Oates, 1964); A. E. McGrath, *Iustitia Dei: A History of the Christian Doctrine of Justification*, 2 vols. (Cambridge: CUP, 1986); N. T. Wright, *Justification* (London: SPCK, 2009).

K

Kairos

Kairos is the Greek word for a point in time, in contrast to the Greek *chronos,* which usually denotes time as duration. *Kairos,* however, also denotes time of a specific and limited duration. Characteristically it may denote "an acceptable time" (2 Cor. 6:2), or may be translated as "the right time" or "the proper time" (Matt. 24:45) or "a defined period" (BDAG 497-98). In secular use it denotes a time favorable for action or understanding, and often in the NT "a point of time that has a special place in the execution of God's plan of salvation" (O. Cullmann, *Christ and Time* [London: SCM, 1951], 39). J. Marsh calls it "a time of opportunity." Hence, in spite of J. Barr's warnings of the need for more lexical precision, P. Tillich and others use the term theologically. Some point to Isa. 55:6, "Seek the LORD while he may be found"; and Psalm 95, "O that today you would listen to his voice," quoted in Heb. 3:7-8 as "Today, if you hear his voice, do not harden your hearts." In 1985 a group of South African theologians published *The Kairos Document* to facilitate the opportunity to end apartheid. It was signed by 151 church leaders to mark their belief that God had provided this "right time" for action.

Kant, Immanuel

Immanuel Kant (1724-1804) superseded the rationalism of Leibniz and the empiricism of Locke and Hume by formulating a new critical transcendental philosophy. His *Critique of Pure Reason* (1781) constituted a landmark in the history of philosophy. He also stressed human autonomy, and defined the Enlightenment as secondhand dependence on earlier authorities, finally breaking ties with medieval thought. Transcendental philosophy no longer asks, "How do we know?" or "What do we know?" but "What are the preconditions for the possibility of knowledge?" Kant was born in Königsberg in Prussia, and taught at Königsberg University.

Kant agreed with Hume that some truths seem neither to be a priori analytical propositions nor a posteriori empirical or synthetic propositions. Cause, for example, is not the result of a priori propositions, since its denial would not be self-contradictory. Yet "cause" is not the conclusion of a posteriori arguments, for it cannot strictly be observed. The notion of *cause,* he concluded, arises from "regulative reason," that is, what the mind construes from phenomena to make sense of the world. Kant showed the limits and scope of reason not least by formulating his antinomies. For example, "the edge of space" and "the beginning of time" are concepts we may want to apply, but cannot do so without conceptual confusion. How can time have a beginning? If we try to fence off "space," we cannot help imagining space on the other side of our "fence." We insist on ordering the world by spatiotemporal categories. C. E. M. Joad once compared Kant's view of the activity of the mind with seeing the world through blue spectacles. We should then have no way of telling whether it was "really" blue. Hence the overt agenda of the *Critique of Pure Reason* was to demonstrate the limits of reason.

Kant next produced *Groundwork of the Metaphysics of Morals* (1785), and his two remaining major works, *Critique of Practical Reason* (1788) and *Critique of Judgment* (1790). In the first of these he postulates the absolute of the categorical imperative of morality that constitutes the presupposition of God, freedom, and immortality. In *Critique of Practical Reason* he develops the notion of a self-contained world, and practical reason could reveal that "rational faith" has an absolute claim on us. "Rational faith" differs from "churchly faith." For example, in intercessory prayer churchly faith expects prayer to influence the world; in natural religion prayer facilitates mental adjustment to the world, as Kant explains in his further book, *Religion within the Limits of Reason Alone* (1793). Kant's third great work was *The Critique of Judgment* (1790). This "third" critique extended Kant's philosophy to aesthetics, and to the methods of science.

The conclusion of Kant's three critiques is that evidence of human freedom cannot come simply from empirical observation. The spatiotemporal realm does not exhaust reality. To try to define ultimate reality in terms of the laws appropriate to the empirical realm results in self-contradiction. This must be a *transcendental* deduction. Antinomy results when two a priori arguments conflict. In theology K. Rahner, H. Küng, and B. Lonergan, among others, have utilized his transcendental approach in their own ways. Kant's philosophy is broadly characterized as transcendental idealism. Freedom, morality, and God are postulated, but not by natural law or pure reason. Kant was followed by more radical idealists: namely, Fichte and Schelling.

Kelsey, David H.

David H. Kelsey (b. 1932) is often grouped with Hans Frei and George Lindbeck as major theologians of the "Yale School," and sometimes of postliberalism. He is Luther A. Weigle Professor Emeritus of Yale Divinity School. Yale awarded him the B.D. (1958) and Ph.D. (1964). He has taught at Yale since 1965. His most influential contributions are on the use of the Bible and on narrative. He published *The Uses of Scripture in Recent Theology* (London: SCM; Philadelphia: Fortress, 1975). The Bible, he argued, functions within the church primarily to shape people's identities. In his words, biblical texts serve *"to shape persons' identities so decisively as to transform them"* (91). G. Lindbeck and Frances Young had made exactly this point. Kelsey argues that Scripture, especially in its narrative mode, establishes the identity of Jesus Christ and forms both the communal identity of the church and the individual identities of Christians. Hence he attributes the authority of the Bible to God through the Holy Spirit (316).

In his further work Kelsey has stressed the primordial nature of narrative as an expression of human personhood (Kelsey, "Biblical Narrative and Theological Anthropology," in *Scriptural Authority and Narrative Interpretation*, ed. G. Green [Philadelphia: Fortress, 1987], 121-43). Kelsey urges this point together with S. Crites and S. Hauerwas. Later, Paul Ricoeur would develop this further still and in greater detail. Kelsey also published *Imagining Redemption* (Louisville: Westminster John Knox, 2005), and especially *Eccentric Existence: A Theological Anthropology*, 2 vols. (Louisville: Westminster John Knox, 2009). This is a full-scale theological anthropology. Kelsey argues that humankind is related to God: first, to God as Creator; second, to God as End; and third, to God as Reconciler. While some reviews commend this work highly, others have been mixed, especially because of his supposedly tedious style.

Kenotic Theology

Kenotic theology derives from Christ's "emptying himself" (Gk. *heauton ekenōsen*) in Phil. 2:7. The verse states that although he was in the form of God, he did not seek his divine quality or self-interest, but took

> the form of a slave,
> being born in human likeness. . . .
> He humbled himself. (vv. 7-8)

The "self-emptying" of Jesus led to his anguish, suffering, constraints, God-forsakenness, and death on the cross. Jesus did not rely on himself, but looked to God in trust, and to the anointing and power of the Holy Spirit. Y. Congar and J. Moltmann stress the *kenosis* of the Holy Spirit (Moltmann, *The Way of Jesus Christ* [London: SCM, 1990], 91). J. E. Fison speaks regularly of the "self-effacement" of the Holy Spirit (*The Blessing of the Holy Spirit* [London and New York: Longman, Green, 1950], 21, 22, 27, 72, 93, 107, etc.).

The nineteenth and early twentieth centuries saw a flourishing of "kenotic theology." A. B. Bruce wrote *The Humiliation of Christ* (1876), and Charles Gore's Bampton Lectures, *The Incarnation of the Son of God* (1891), provided a popular exposition of kenotic theology. In Germany Gottfried Thomasius (1802-1873) was the best-known exponent of the approach. Kierkegaard also stressed this theme. It became a way of accepting the deity of Christ while avoiding the so-called dualism of Chalcedon. At one level it may suggest an inadequate Christology. But at a more important level it urged that it is the key essence of love to *accept limitations and constraints*. Karl Barth stressed the humility of God in this sense. Recently John Polkinghorne has edited a remarkable book, *The Work of Love: Creation as Kenosis* (London: SPCK; Grand Rapids: Eerdmans, 2001), in which many of the contributors argue that "Suffering is a key to transformative love" (31), or that regeneration in natural science leads to new birth but "is always in travail" (58; cf. Rom. 8:22). W. H. Vanstone also firmly emphasizes this. The principle is arguably valid in soteriology. But in the nineteenth century it was sometimes used to argue for the historical relativity and ignorance of Jesus, for example, by Gore. The concept of *kenosis* is crucial for theology. It need not become embroiled in controversies in Christology.

Kerygma

Kerygma is the Greek word for "preaching," and denotes the earliest Christian proclamation of the gospel. Classic references appear in the NT even before Paul; he "received" it as a given apostolic tradition and passed it on to others. The classic NT passage comes in 1 Cor. 15:3-5: "I handed on (Gk. *paredōka*) to you as of first importance what I in turn had received (Gk. *parelabon*): that Christ died for our sins in accordance with the scriptures, and that he was buried, and that he was raised on the third day in accordance with the scriptures, and that he appeared to Cephas, then to the twelve." This was the conventional form for declaring the absolute fundamentals of Christian faith (Thiselton, *The First Epistle to the Corinthians* [Grand Rapids: Eerdmans, 2000], 1186). Paul tells the Corinthians that he did not originate the gospel, but "received" it as common apostolic doctrine, agreed on before he entered the scene. He also recounts this kerygma in his explanation about the Lord's Supper: "I received from the Lord what I also handed on to you" (1 Cor. 11:23).

This is not confined to 1 Corinthians. Most scholars agree that Paul's exposition of the theology of baptism also appeals to pre-Pauline teaching, often signaled by "Do you not know that . . . ?" (Rom. 6:3-4). Many argue that 1 Peter contains several traces of early kerygma, for example, 1 Pet. 3:18-19, "Christ . . . suffered for sins, the just for the unjust" (KJV). B. Gerhardsson argued that oral and written summaries were often confirmed by the community (*Tradition and Transmission in Early Christianity* [1964; Grand Rapids: Eerdmans, 1998], 44). Each time they refer to the sufferings and resurrection of Christ as "for our sake" or "for us." This use of the term probably goes back to C. H. Dodd, who distinguished kerygma as "preaching" or "proclamation" from *didachē*, or "teaching" (*The Apostolic Preaching and Its Developments* [London: Hodder and Stoughton, 1944], 17). It has more recently been expounded by R. Mounce in *The Essential Nature of New Testament Preaching* (Eugene, Ore.: Wipf and Stock, 2005). The term is frequently used by Barth, Bultmann, and others. The adjective "kerygmatic" is used to denote "relating to gospel proclamation."

Kierkegaard, Søren

Søren Kierkegaard (1813-1855) was born in Copenhagen, and his childhood and youth were dominated by an attempt to please his father, Mikael. Mikael was a stern disciplinarian and believed "that Canaan itself lay on the other side of a theological degree" (*Johannes Climacus* [London: Black, 1958], 21). Søren later in his *Journals* wrote of "the dread with which my father filled my soul" (*The Journals of Søren Kierkegaard* [Oxford: OUP, 1938], 841). But in 1835, at the age of twenty-two, he discovered that his father had had an adulterous affair with his housekeeper. His "righteous" idol crashed to the ground. From that moment onward, therefore, Kierkegaard determined to discover all truth and values *for himself*, relying on no secondhand authorities or systems. At first he experienced wretchedness, desolation, guilt, and solitude. But he began to discover what it meant to live *as himself*, not according to roles imposed on him by others. His search for truth eventually carried him to seek truth "before God." This threefold emphasis on the rejection of all authorities; personal decision and commitment; and acute individualism made him, in effect, the father of existentialism.

Christian truth, Kierkegaard urges, emerges from passionate individual *commitment*, not with assenting to inherited doctrines or attending church. He cites Paul: "Only one receives the prize" (1 Cor. 9:24). He writes: "Christianity has been abolished by expansion — by these millions of name-Christians" (*Attack on "Christendom"* [Princeton: Princeton University Press, 1944, 1968; London: OUP, 1946], 121). Elsewhere he writes: "The whole of my work as an author is related . . . to the problem of 'becoming a Christian,'" as against the illusion that "all are Christians" who live in "Christian" Denmark (*The Point of View for the Work of an Author* [London: OUP, 1939], 5). Truth, he argues, is not just a matter of assenting to right doctrines or belief; truth should be *lived out*. In this work he also stresses indirect communication, in which he questions, presents paradoxes, and expounds opposing arguments. In a startling phrase, he declares, "Truth becomes untruth in this or that person's mouth" (*Concluding Unscientific Postscript* [Princeton: Princeton University Press, 1974], 181). Or, quoting again his well-known memoirs: "Truth is subjectivity" (169-224). Since truth involves life, in the case of Jesus the incarnation, suffering, and the cross remain important. In terms of his existentialist philosophy, he stressed human finitude and creatureliness, and opposed the grandiose system-building of Hegel. He compared the armchair ease of the builder of abstract systems in philosophy with his own vocation of suffering. Two crises in his life contributed to his suffering: his broken engagement to Regine Olsen, and his ill-judged challenge to the newspaper *The Corsair*, which satirized him until he became the laughingstock of Denmark.

Kierkegaard's individualism seeks to find theological foundations. He writes: "The most ruinous evasion of all is to be hidden in the crowd in an attempt to escape God's supervision . . . to get away from hearing God's voice as an individual" (*Purity of Heart Is to Will One Thing* [London: Fontana, 1961], 163). This, he suggests, is what Adam did when he tried to hide from God among the trees (Gen. 3:8-10). R. Bultmann later expounded this theme in his existential theology. Kierkegaard saw himself as perplexed and venturesome. Abraham, in his prayer or in his imagination and faith, believed he was called to sacrifice his only son, Isaac, just as Kierkegaard was supposedly "called" to "sacrifice" Regine Olsen. Faith could boldly venture to perform even a conventionally unethical act. In *Fear and Trembling* he addresses the problem of whether there could be "a theological suspension of the ethical." In Abraham's willingness to sacrifice Isaac, his only son, "the individual becomes higher than the universal." Kierkegaard comments, "This is the paradox which does not permit of mediation" (*Fear and Trembling* [London: Penguin, 1985], 83-89). Like subsequent existentialists, Kierkegaard elevates personal decision over accepted norms, or mere conventions.

The reference to subjectivity calls to mind that an encounter with truth involves "an inner transformation ... an infinite passionate interest" (*Concluding Unscientific Postscript*, 51). It denotes "being sharpened into an 'I,' rather than being dulled into a third person ... staking his life on it" (*Journals*, 533). He adds, "*The objective accent falls on What is said, the subjective accent on How it is said....* This inward 'how' is the passion of the infinite, and the pursuit of the infinite is truth" (*Concluding Unscientific Postscript*, 181). Decision and commitment translate us, Kierkegaard believed, into a genuine human person. In the twentieth century Bultmann agreed that the truth of the gospel is bound up with human response to God's addressing humankind as a "Thou," and how humankind responds.

Existentialism inherits Kierkegaard's individualism, his stress on subjectivity, and his claims for the primacy of personal decision. It also inherits his emphasis on human finitude. He ridicules Hegel's lofty concept of history-as-a-whole, or the manifestation of the Absolute. He ironically calls the project "the System," and argues that this system can never be finished. The philosopher talks of perfection, but has a patch on his elbow, and needs his paycheck. Kierkegaard states with deep irony that, like everyone else, he is "ready to worship the system; but it is never finished" (*Concluding Unscientific Postscript*, 97-98). He explains ironically: "For I am only a poor existing human being," and cannot "contemplate the eternal" or view reality "theocentrically" (190).

In the twentieth century many existentialist philosophers (Nietzsche, Heidegger, Marcel, Sartre, Camus, and others) borrowed and developed particular themes from Kierkegaard, and theologians such as R. Bultmann and F. Gogarten were heavily influenced by him. However, this did not last beyond the middle years of the century. More recently Wolfhart Pannenberg and Jürgen Moltmann have developed insights perhaps more akin in origin to Hegel in the service of Christian theology. But Kierkegaard remains one of the half-dozen most influential thinkers of the nineteenth century. He recognized that his work consisted of scattered insights, rather than a system of thought. Perhaps his greatest legacy is the close relation between faith and life. (*See also* **Existentialism; Subjectivity**.)

Reading: J. Gariff, *Søren Kierkegaard: A Biography* (Princeton: Princeton University Press, 2005); S. Kierkegaard, *The Point of View for My Work as an Author* (London: OUP, 1939); S. Kierkegaard, *Concluding Unscientific Postscript* (Princeton: Princeton University Press, 1974); S. Kierkegaard, *Philosophical Fragments* (Princeton: Princeton University Press, 1985); A. McKinnon, "Søren Kierkegaard," in *Nineteenth Century Religious Thought in the West*, ed. N. Smart et al. (Cambridge: CUP, 1985), 1:181-214.

Kingdom of God

"Kingdom of God" occurs regularly in Mark and Luke; Matthew normally uses the reverential circumlocution "kingdom of heaven." The Hebrew term *malkhuth* is derived from *melekh*, "king"; similarly the Greek term *basileia* is related to *basileus*, "king." It is universally agreed that the term denotes the *royal reign of God as King*, not primarily a "kingdom" in the sense of an arena or sphere. It may sometimes mean this in particular cases. It is also universally agreed that it is synonymous with Matthew's term "kingdom of heaven." It is generally agreed that this phrase occurs in authentic and historical sayings and the message of Jesus, for example, "Jesus came to Galilee, proclaiming the good news of God, and saying, 'The time is fulfilled, and the kingdom of God has come near'" (Mark 1:14-15, *ēngiken hē basileia tou Theou*; cf. Matt. 4:17, *ēngiken hē basileia tōn ouranōn*). Both Jesus and John the Baptist associated the kingdom of God with the gospel as good news (*euangelion*, Mark 1:14; or "forgiveness of sins," Luke 3:3) and also with repentance (*metanoeite*, Mark 1:15; Matt. 3:2; cf. Luke 3:3). This is because on the one hand God's own rule would bring deliverance from oppression, but on the other hand it would demand righteousness. In contemporary theology W. Pannenberg and others distinguish the kingdom of God from the church, because the church remains sinful and fallible, in spite of its redemption, whereas the future kingdom of God demands absolute obedience and righteousness. Hence in the preaching of Jesus, especially before his death and resurrection, the kingdom is *in process of arrival*. Many describe this as eschatology *in process of* realization.

In modern theology several phases or stages of research can be distinguished. The first phase is that of Schleiermacher, Ritschl, and Harnack, roughly from 1820 to 1920. Schleiermacher identified the kingdom of God with "corporate God-consciousness" (*The Christian Faith* [Edinburgh: T. & T. Clark, 1989], sect. 164; Eng., 723), where "consciousness" is the object of focus more than "divine governance." Ritschl stressed the importance of the concept as "divine end," and his emphasis mainly concerned ethics. In Harnack the message of the kingdom concerns only divine Fatherhood, human brotherhood, and the infinite value of the "soul." The second phase is the pseudo-eschatological phase of Dalman, Weiss, and Schweitzer. Gustav Dalman's work on Aramaic deserves respect as revealing the meaning of "kingdom" as divine reign, not a territory. He also stressed righteousness and obedience in rabbinic theology. Johannes Weiss argued that the kingdom of God was God's work, in contrast to both Satan's rule and human striving (*Earliest Christianity* [New York: Harper, 1959], 34). Schweitzer, however, pressed this eschatological emphasis in an eccentric way, with the result that, as Moltmann argues, his "eschatology" could not be appropriated by readers today. He especially urged the imminence of expectation of the End, providing the basis for Bultmann's later claim that Jesus was mistaken about it. The third phase, following the work of C. H. Dodd and J. Jeremias, was to retain Dalman's emphasis on the reign of God but to see this both fulfilled in the coming of Christ, and yet also with greater fulfillment ahead. Dodd perhaps overemphasized its presence in his "realized eschatology"; J. Jeremias saw the kingdom as "in process of realization"; R. H. Fuller used the term "proleptic eschatology."

To return to the NT evidence, such facts as demons yielding to exorcisms seem to be a sign of the present or proleptic arrival of the kingdom of God. Thus Jesus declares, "If it is by the Spirit of God that I cast out demons, then the kingdom of God has come to you" (Gk. *ephthasen,* Matt. 12:28; cf. Luke 10:17-18). On the other hand, such passages as the Beatitudes (Matt. 5:3-12; Luke 6:20-26) speak of future promises, as does Matt. 10:26, which says the hidden shall be revealed, and Matt. 18:4, which says the lowly shall be exalted. Indeed, the Greek verb *ēngiken* is usually translated "has drawn near," from the verb *engizō.* The well-known petition in the Lord's Prayer reads "Your kingdom come" (Gk. *elthetō hē basileia sou;* Luke 11:2 has identical Greek). The result of this present-future double emphasis would be simply bland if these were played off against each other. As Oscar Cullmann asserts, the decisive victory has been won in Christ; to this extent the kingdom of God is here. But the war, to use Cullmann's metaphor, is not over; much yet remains before we experience the ultimate triumph of God's kingdom. Some aspects are already visible; others remain hidden before the End. This has many practical effects in life. For example, those who deny the possibility of healing in unexpected ways, deny that the kingdom of God has come in any sense. Those who expect *every* believer to be always healed, deny that the kingdom of God is also future, and awaits consummation.

The OT often ascribes kingly rule to God and acclaims him as king (Pss. 47:2; 103:19; 145:13). The term "kingdom of God" is used in Wis. 10:10. There are clearly two streams of hope in the OT, which converge in the humanity and deity of the person of Christ. One stream of hope is usually called the *prophetic.* Israel repeatedly hopes for a king who will be anointed by the Spirit to expel wickedness and injustice, and to bring in a reign of peace and prosperity. This hope began with the kingship of David and his line. But such a king never materialized; all the kings had flaws. Hence they hoped for a preeminent king in the last times. Zech. 9:9, for example, promises,

> Your king comes to you;
> > triumphant and victorious is he,
> humble and riding on a donkey.

The second stream is well described as *apocalyptic.* Since all earthly agents continually fail to bring in the kingdom, God himself will intervene in the last days. The apocalyptic passages of Isaiah express this hope, for example, Isa. 25:8,

> Then the Lord GOD will wipe away the tears from all faces,
> > and the disgrace of his people he will take away from all the earth,
> > for the LORD has spoken. (also Isa. 40:10)

A. Schweitzer traces this dual background (*Mysticism of Paul the Apostle* [London: Black, 1931], 76-90). Although he draws his own different conclusions, these two streams of hope merge in Jesus Christ: he is a man, anointed for his work, anointed by the Holy Spirit as Son of David. But he is also the One through whom God acts, acting in God's stead. The phrase "your God reigns" comes from Isa. 52:7, but is mediated through the messianic figure probably in Isa. 40:9-10.

Norman Perrin gave a useful account of the present/future debate among NT scholars (*The Kingdom of God in the Teaching of Jesus* [London: SCM, 1963]), looking at Dodd, T. W. Manson, and Bultmann. He then argued for the "tensive" and symbolic nature of the kingdom of God in *Jesus and the Language of the Kingdom* (London: SCM, 1976). This time he turned to the hermeneutics of E. Fuchs, E. Jüngel, A. Wilder, R. W. Funk, and J. D. Crossan. The parables of the kingdom "proclaim the coming dramatic reversal, in a clash of worlds" (195): "God is to be experienced precisely in the shattering of that everyday world" (199). But this new vision is largely conveyed through metaphor. He wrote, "The further problem of hermeneutics . . . is the problem of the similes and metaphors," which leave the interpreter to sort out much of the meaning-currency of the kingdom of God (203). Perrin himself concluded, "Kingdom of God is a symbol evoking a myth," though this last term has many definitions (203). Two points cannot be denied. First, as Bruce Chilton comments, "A clear prosaic description of the kingdom" is not to be easily found. Second, one reason for this is the transcendence of God, which makes prosaic description difficult, if not impossible.

The phrase also occurs in Paul (Rom. 14:17; 1 Cor. 4:20; 6:9; 15:50; Gal. 5:21; Col. 1:13; 1 Thess. 2:12) and in John (John 3:3, 5; 18:36). However, both Paul and John choose to avoid the term, largely because of its political overtones. Paul often prefers to speak of "being in Christ" or "calling Christ 'Lord' "; and John prefers to speak of "eternal life." But the kingdom of God remains central in the proclamation of Jesus, and ensures that his basic message is centered on God, rather than primarily on himself.

In the early Fathers sometimes the kingdom of God was linked with millennial eschatology, and in the later Fathers after Constantine it was sometimes linked with the Roman Empire, as in Eusebius. But Augustine expounded the notion of two different orders in his work *City of God*. If he seemed to identify the kingdom of God with the church, he nevertheless denied that the kingdom was (yet) visible on earth. In the Middle Ages, Joachim of Fiore reintroduced a link with millennial hopes. During the Reformation Luther developed the theme of two kingdoms, in which the kingdom of God and the kingdom of the world are at war with each other. In the kingdom of God Christ is King and Lord. Christians, he believed, belong to both kingdoms, but the two kingdoms cannot be intermixed. This has far-reaching consequences. God rules the world in two ways, through earthly agents and structures, and through his spiritual kingdom. Hence Luther regarded highly those whom he saw as godly princes, instituted by God for human welfare. He thus resisted the Peasants' Revolt, set in motion by his former followers, the

Radical Reformers, such as Müntzer. Law and gospel ruled in parallel. The two kingdoms reflect two different kinds of righteousness. This leads to a concept of the visible church, which is interrelated with state institutions. Secular authorities are to be respected (cf. Romans 13), but they must not coerce spiritual beliefs. Zwingli also connected the kingdom with the ordering of secular states, and Calvin believed that in one sense God rules over creation, though in another sense creation still awaits the consummation of God's power and sovereignty.

The Pietists tended to look for the transformation of the world into the kingdom of God, while Hegel saw the kingdom in terms of the philosophy of history. Schleiermacher, Ritschl, and Harnack, during the nineteenth century, saw the kingdom, as we have seen, differently from Weiss and Schweitzer. The kingdom of God held a prominent place in Karl Barth's Barmen Declaration (1934), in which Christ is proclaimed as sole Lord, in contrast to allegiance to earthly rulers. The World Council of Churches in 1983 distinguished between the church and the kingdom: the church is a witness to the kingdom. J. Moltmann and W. Pannenberg also press this distinction, and have developed this theme of God's sovereignty.

Reading: G. R. Beasley-Murray, *Jesus and the Kingdom of God* (Grand Rapids: Eerdmans, 1986); B. Chilton, *Pure Kingdom: Jesus' Vision of God* (Grand Rapids: Eerdmans, 1996); J. Moltmann, *The Trinity and the Kingdom of God* (London: SCM, 1980); W. Pannenberg, *Theology and the Kingdom of God* (Philadelphia: Fortress, 1969); N. Perrin, *Jesus and the Language of the Kingdom* (London: SCM, 1976).

Kingsley, Charles

Charles Kingsley (1819-1875) was educated at King's College, London, and Magdalene College, Cambridge, and was ordained in the Church of England in 1842. He was strongly influenced by F. D. Maurice, and became a leader of the Christian Socialist Movement. He was a theological writer and novelist, and is mostly known today for his children's story *The Water Babies*.

Küng, Hans

Hans Küng was born in 1928 at Sursee in the Swiss Catholic Canton of Lucerne, in a devout Catholic home. In 1948 he went to Rome to commence studies for the priesthood at the Gregorian University. He was ordained in 1954. During the 1950s Pope Pius XII aimed to suppress modernism in the church, and in the early 1960s he silenced Teilhard de Chardin and Henri de Lubac. After initially supporting the regime, Küng became increasingly uncomfortable with the treatment of the French theologians. He studied at the Sorbonne and elsewhere, and began his doctoral thesis "Justification: The Doctrine of Karl Barth and a Catholic Reflection," a revised version of which was published (New York: Nelson, 1964). He came under the influence of several more "open" or moderate Catholic scholars, including most notably Yves Congar and Hans Urs von Balthasar. Barth encouraged him to attend his seminars in Basel. The upshot was Küng's conclusion, "On the whole there is fundamental agreement between the theology of Barth and that of the Catholic Church" (*Justification*, 282).

In 1960, shortly before Vatican II, Küng was called to the Chair of Fundamental Theology in the Catholic faculty of the University of Tübingen, which was astonishing for a man of thirty-two. That year he also published his second book, *The Council, Reform, Reunion* (London and New York: Sheed and Ward, 1960); and then *The Structures of the Church* (New York: Nelson, 1962). In 1962 Pope John XXIII invited him to be a special theological adviser for Vatican II, together with Congar, Karl Rahner, and Joseph Ratzinger. In his book *The Living Church* (London and New York: Sheed and Ward, 1963), Küng set out hopes for Vatican II, quoting Pope John: "There will be one fold and one shepherd," and the need to provide "an outstanding example of truth, unity, and love" (23-24). Küng commented, "The reunion of separated Christians is bound up with renewal within the Catholic Church" (24). He repeated that the pathway to these goals is "through a renewal of the Catholic Church" (31). He recognized, however, that "the Council's rules of procedure were initially very imperfect" (133). On certain specific points, he saw the need to reform the Mass according to the pattern Christ instituted in "the Last Supper with the Apostles" (153). This involves intelligible and clearly spoken words, in which the Liturgy of the Word should involve "communal prayer and singing, together with an intelligible reading and exposition of the biblical texts" (154). Latin is not really a bond of unity, and to many is "not intelligible" (162).

A turning point came with Küng's book *Infallible? An Unresolved Enquiry* (1970; Eng. London: SCM, 1994; Seabury Press, 1980). Küng begins by pointing out that the infallibility of the Papal Teaching Office is problematic not only to Protestants, but also within the Catholic Church (29-52). He writes concerning the encyclical on the subject: "The Pope, on his own showing, evidently did not closely consider the original gospel message" (40). The "Curial group" did not base their case on more than "the consensus of Pope and bishops" (47). A bishop's first task, however, is "the proclamation of the gospel" (57). Vatican I asserted papal infallibility solely on three grounds: Petrine origination, perpetual continuity, and Roman origins and tradition (77). Yet are these firm foundations? Küng raises some "critical questions" (88-102). He concludes, "The case for the dogma of infallibility based on Scripture and tradition is plainly as meagre as it is brittle" (99). Yet he argues, "Our criticism of the unhappy relations between leadership and teaching in the Church has been so outspoken only in order to clear the way for positive co-operation" (195). The book concludes with a postscript written in 1979.

In December 1979 the Vatican declared Küng no longer to be a bona fide Catholic teacher and theologian. Rome's Sacred Congregation for the Doctrine of the Faith deprived him of his Catholic chair, but not of his membership in the church. The result was startling. There were demonstrations at Tübingen and in various parts of the world. His books sold more copies, and the University of Tübingen created a special ecumenical chair for him, so that he could remain a Tübingen professor. Even Karl Rahner, however, called Küng a liberal Protestant, and even Balthasar criticized him. But Küng criticized infallibility not only because he found the defense of it unconvincing, but more especially because only God, not his church, could be infallible.

Meanwhile in 1970 Küng published one of his most learned works, *The Incarnation of God* (Ger. 1970; Eng. Edinburgh: T. & T. Clark, 1987). It is subtitled *An Introduction to Hegel's Theological Thought as Prolegomena to a Future Christology*. He suggests that this should be read in conjunction with the more popular books *On Being a Christian* (London and New York: Collins, 1977) and *Does God Exist?* (London and New York: Collins, 1980). Küng rightly argues that Hegel's thought remains seminal for creative thought today. Moltmann and Pannenberg make or imply similar claims. Up to the time of Hegel, Christology had tended to be static, but Hegel perceived the limits of the Enlightenment. At first, Hegel may have appealed "to the earthly Jesus as an ideal of virtue" (71). But he also saw that this limited approach could not do justice to the "eternal truth" of Christianity. Küng notes "a momentous change in the concept of God ... which comes to fruition in Hegel's Frankfurt period" (94). Hegel rejected an absolute opposition between God and humankind, and an unqualified divine transcendence. During his period in Bern, Hegel began to be impressed by Spinoza's pantheism, and that of Schelling and Hölderlin. What was yet to come, however, was "a principle of unity, namely a monism of Spirit ... recognition of the antithetical nature of life, that is, of the dialectical structure of reality in general" (106). Hegel wrote, "The divine in a particular shape appears as man, the connection of the infinite and finite ... a holy mystery" (111; *see* **Christology: History of Thought**). This is the Word made flesh (126).

The sequence of Küng's thought so far is clear. Chapter 1 of *The Incarnation of God* showed the inadequacy of the "Enlightenment" Christ; chapter 2 focused on Jesus and the "Lives"; and chapter 3 concentrated on the "God-man" with life "reconciled in love" (117-22), and true to the NT (131-42). In chapter 4 Küng turns to philosophy more explicitly, first examining the development of Hegel's idealism. Christ is "the *one* divine-human reconciler through the Spirit into all" (157). A concrete history is needed before a universal and systematic way of thinking can be possible. Hegel's doctrine of salvation was "above all in the Bible" (161). He then considers the "infinite pain" and "absolute suffering" of Good Friday (162). This becomes "the death of God" (162-74); Christ's history becomes "a movement of the absolute Spirit in the world" (206). In the death of Jesus we understand *"the true nature of God"* (209). God has created a space for "God to be himself," and man to be himself (239). Here are echoes of Barth.

In Christ's being raised (*aufgehoben*), reconciliation becomes universal. God reveals himself both in his glory as God (Phil. 2:6) and in human *kenosis* (Phil. 2:7). Again there are echoes of Barth. Christ has become "sublated in the system" (279). Hegel addresses both intra-Trinitarian relations and reconciliation (277-

78). The NT sees this as "simply God's act and gift of grace" (287). This leads on to chapter 7, "Jesus Christ in History." Küng declares, "Hegel rediscovered his youth in his old age ... by re-discovering history" (316). Throughout this book Küng brilliantly expounds each stage of Hegel's thought against the background of his life. He finally concludes, "God's transcendence ... and unchangeability require a thoroughgoing *reinterpretation*" (455, italics mine). This is part of his eighth chapter, "Prolegomena to a Future Christology." With echoes of Barth, Küng regards "the humiliation of God" as announced in the OT, which also points to "a vicarious mediator" (451). He arrives at "an undreamt of *vitality* in the Being of God" (453). Küng rejects "a Christology from below" as suggesting a positivist understanding of history and neglecting the course of the atonement as essentially the act of *God* (691). Yet, he urges, the kerygma can be known only in history. Küng concludes that to regard Christ as both God and man requires a new conceptual frame, if it is to be meaningful. Catholic theology is too concerned with simply repeating the familiar phrases within an old, well-worn, conceptual frame. He concludes, "We should consider afresh the problem of change and becoming in God" (537).

It is worth noting the careful and positive verdict on Küng's Christology by Karl-Josef Kuschel. Kuschel is professor at Tübingen. Küng gives a warm commendation to his book *Born before All Time? The Dispute over Christ's Origin* (London: SCM, 1992), in its foreword. Kuschel provides a useful evaluation of *The Incarnation of God* and *On Being a Christian* (460-82). He argues that these two books form a turning point in Küng's thought. His overview of Christology in *The Incarnation of God* largely follows Hegel's "Christology from above," while this is balanced in *On Being a Christian* by a greater attention to the earthly Jesus and to history. The first book successfully shows that "Jesus does not fit into any historical, political, or religious order" (461). It stresses his "otherness." Moreover, Küng rejects a "timeless," static God. In the second book we see more of Jesus as "a God for the godless" in a historical dialectic of revelation (464). Küng asserts, "The one who was crucified and raised up has from God's standpoint such a unique, fundamental, decisive importance, must he not always have been in God's thoughts? ... Was he not as Son and Word with God from eternity?" (465). This advances beyond many NT scholars in affirming Christ's preexistence, while practicing careful exegesis. He is at one here with W. Kasper. Küng resists the dissolution of the ontological and metaphysical into the merely psychological and subjective (466). Küng will expound this further in *Does God Exist?* (1978). Functional and ontological statements are not exclusive alternatives, as Bultmann failed to see.

This brings us to *Does God Exist? An Answer for Today* (Ger. 1978; Eng. New York: Doubleday; London: Collins, 1980). Many regard this as Küng's magnum opus. It is over 800 pages in length. He begins by examining Descartes, with his emphasis on mathematics, rationalism, and certainty, and his departure from reliance on tradition. Descartes opened further debate on faith, reason, and certainty, as he searched for a firm ground for belief. He acknowledged that everything could be "deception" (12); but God's goodness suggests otherwise; for the end, "Throughout all doubt, the Archimedean point had been found: the fact of one's own existence . . . is the basis of all certainty" (13). Thus Descartes arrives at his *cogito;* the self is a *res cogitans* (14). The path to belief in the existence of God is that of the ontological argument, found also in Anselm. God's "perfection," however, includes the fact that he cannot be a deceiving spirit. Deception is a sign of imperfection. Küng stresses that Descartes was a Christian, even if not a very zealous one. He was not simply a natural scientist (17), but he aimed at clarity in theology (22).

Nevertheless, Küng sees a dualist tendency in Descartes, which affected the relation between mind and body (27), and subject and object (28). The latter is too static in Descartes. On the other hand, Küng does advocate "critical rationalism" (31), which indirectly stems from Descartes. The foundations of the philosophy of mathematics remain open today. On the other hand, "It became increasingly impossible to appeal in matters of faith solely to the authority of the Bible, the Fathers of the Church [and] Councils, or Popes" (35). Hence Küng turns to examine the debate in reason and faith in B. Pascal and other thinkers. Pascal stressed the capacity of the human heart, but also the role of intuition and certainty in mathematics. He did not want to return to the time before Descartes, but choice and wager cannot be sidestepped either (61). In pursuing his problem of "cultural rationalism," Küng compares the work on philosophy of science of Karl Popper and Thomas S. Kuhn. Popper's appeal to reason is utterly different from that of A. J. Ayer and logical positivism. His appeal to "falsification" is not quite the same, however, since "theories are not simply derived inductively from experience" (103). Popper's "critical method" is largely that of "trial and error." He is a fallibilist. Kuhn, an American historian of science, undertook the first comprehensive study of how scientific revolutions were structured (*The Structure of Scientific Revolutions* [Chicago: University of Chicago Press, 1962; rev. 1970]). In view of Küng's regular appeal to "new paradigms," Kuhn is clearly important to him. Küng distinguished between "normal science," which is based on past achievements as its foundation, and "a new paradigm," which bursts upon the scene when increasing anomalies are discovered in the "normal" system (107-11). The new paradigm can handle "new, unexpected phenomena" that cannot easily be fitted into the old paradigm (107). Küng observes, "Neither the verification nor the falsification procedure can explain the really far-reaching upheavals in science" (108). The progress is not cumulative, as in "normal" science, but revolutionary. Küng applies this by comparing "the hyper-Cartesian rationality of an abstract positivistic logic" with the logic of new discovery (109). One example might be J. Habermas's "social-critical de-ideologizing" (110).

Küng now seeks to explore revolutions in theology, which involve the replacement of one paradigm by another. Too often, he claims, the church has stressed continuity. But in historical terms it is possible to argue that new paradigms were offered, first, by Clement and Origen; then by Augustine; then perhaps by Aquinas, with his use of Aristotle; then especially by Luther; and finally by historical biblical criticism (111). All this calls for a rationality that takes account of "changes in the world-picture" (115). We need "new critical-dialogic collaboration between theology and natural science and technology . . . a radical course-correction" (115). In the history of philosophy Hegel provides one such example, with his emphasis on history. Küng concludes this section by arguing that "critical rationalism" offers a more adequate approach than either the narrower rationalism of Descartes or the uncritical fideism of Pascal. Hegel and Kuhn have their place in distinguishing between narrow rationalism and critical rationalism.

Küng then examines Hegel on God and the world, focusing especially on *Phenomenology of Spirit*, "Hegel's most brilliant and most obscure book: a pioneer work" (144). Since we have looked at Hegel's thought in *The Incarnation of God*, we shall consider this only briefly. This finds "dialectic in God himself," in which we see "development" even in God (147). Here is the beginning of process thought. But Hegel does provide a philosophy of world history, which Pannenberg will later explore. Separation is "sublated" (157). Küng declares, "His teaching on the Trinity is not an unrealistic conceptual arithmetic, but a Trinitarian 'economy' related to the world, salvation history" (159). Moreover, God is not a despotic God in all this. Later, in his words, Küng summarizes this point: "God does not operate on the world *from above or from outside* as unmoved mover, but from within as the *dynamic, most real reality* in the process of the evolution of the world, which he makes possible, directs and completes . . . he is not threatened by man's freedom . . . he (man) is not crushed by God's freedom" (649, italics mine).

Küng then writes on the challenge of atheism. He considers Feuerbach's claim that "God" is a projection, Marx's claim that "God" is the production of vested interests, and Freud's claim that "God" is an infantile illusion (191-341). First, he looks at the background of the "young" Hegelians and Bruno Bauer. Feuerbach literally moved from theologian to atheist; hence his aphorism: "God was my first thought; reason, my second; man, my third and last thought" (cited on 192). Feuerbach studied to become a Protestant pastor; then he saw the value of reason under Hegel; finally he saw man as the center of his atheism. He was helped on his way by Strauss and his rejection of orthodox Christology (197-98). Finally, he believed, "God appears as a pure projection of human understanding" (Feuerbach, *The Essence of Christianity* [New York: Harper, 1957], xxxiv). The consciousness of the infinite is nothing other than the consciousness of the infinity of consciousness. The divine is also the human projection unto the hereafter. The notion that God is love is a "projection of the human heart" (*Does God Exist?* 201). Feuerbach calls atheism "the secret of religion." Küng asks, however, not only whether wish guarantees reality, but also whether wish can guarantee *nonreality*. This, he urges, is "the crude scientific materialism of the 1850s and 1860s" (211). Further, against Feuerbach's accusations, Küng insists, "Theology does not attempt to dissolve anthropology into theology, but asserts the objective priority of theology over anthropology, not to weaken the reality of being human but to add to it" (215).

The next section on Karl Marx is no less astute. Küng rightly calls his thought "sociopolitical atheism." The year 1841 constituted a watershed. Marx was greatly indebted to Feuerbach, but regarded his sociopolitical thought as grossly inadequate. He saw religion as "the opium of the people" (228-31). When appropriate social developments occur, he believed, religion would become superfluous (239). Küng not only follows Marx's thought and life step by step, but discovers contradictions within his sociopolitical program. In the end his critique of religion can be seen as no more than a hypothesis, not a proof (244-45). It is simply not true that where good social conditions occur, religion is dying out. His thesis defies verification.

Perhaps the subtlest atheism is that of Freud. Küng traces how the natural scientist emerged as an atheist. Freud grew up devoid of any belief in God, and despising his father, who was an orthodox Jew. He had negative experiences of religion. Freud believed that all mental processes arose from "the interplay of forces which assist or inhibit one another" (*Psycho-Analysis,* in Freud, *The Complete Works,* standard ed., 24 vols. [London: Hogarth, 1956-1974], 20:265; *Does God Exist?* 268). So much, perhaps everything, depends on quasi-physical or physiological "forces," understood in mechanistic terms. He entered private practice in 1886, and in 1889 began to treat hysteria by such methods as hypnosis and electrotherapy. The key, Freud believed, lay in what was "repressed." This view emerged in his work *The Interpretation of Dreams* (1900). Dreams were often the disguised emergence of repressed wishes. Freud regarded his greatest achievement as "laying bare unconscious, untreated, traumatic experience and affects" (*Does God Exist?* 272). As early as 1895 Freud had asserted, "Dreams are wish fulfilments." Many or most repressed wishes were sexual, and in 1905 Freud published *Three Essays on the Theory of Sexuality.* This set the stage for his account of the origins of religion, which related to "infantile wishes" rooted in "the father-complex" (*see* **Freud, Sigmund**). Küng's critique of Freud can also be found in our entry on Freud, and in *Does God Exist?* pp. 228-323.

After considering the atheism of Feuerbach, Marx, and Freud, Küng turns to the nihilism of Friedrich Nietzsche. He begins with Nietzsche's statement, "God is dead. God remains dead. And we have killed him" (from *The Gay Science* [1882], cited in *Does God Exist?* 352). Nietzsche "diagnosed the destruction of values," and in this sense was not an absolute nihilist (393). Küng considers the widespread negative verdict on Nietzsche "not much more than hot air" (399); he allows for a diversity of interpretations. In fact, Nietzsche did not seek to justify his claim. Indeed, he claims the work *The Antichrist* (vol. 16 of *Complete Works,* 18 vols. [London: Allen and Unwin, 1909-1913]) is a "provocation for Christians which can be salutary" (*Does God Exist?* 408). Küng cites Nietzsche's critique of the church, of priests, and of concepts of God as partially deserving of critique. On the church, Nietzsche declares, "A theologian, a priest, or a pope . . . lies with every word that he utters" (*The Antichrist,* 177; aphorism 38). On priests, Nietzsche declares, "God forgives a person who repents" really means, "He who submits himself to a priest" (161; aphorism 26). On concepts of God, he regards "God" as excluding the "strong, brave, and heroic" and welcoming "the sick, weak, decadent, a poor man's God" (*Does God Exist?* 408). Christianity, Küng suggests, has sometimes "actually been presented as it was seen by Nietzsche" (409). It was consciously to avoid such a crude caricature that Moltmann portrays the Holy Spirit so positively as the Spirit of life, joy, and release.

Küng now addresses what he calls "Yes to Reality," "Yes to God," and "Yes to the Christian God," which includes the God of the Bible and the Holy Trinity (425-702). These all entail trust in what sustains the self. He declares, "Fundamental trust manifests its essential reasonableness in its realization." He continues, "Such a positive fundamental attitude is rationally justifiable" (447). Küng repeats this theme in various ways. Trust in reason is not credulity. This kind of trust is not infantile or childish; it is "the cornerstone of the psychologically healthy personality" (459). Trust is also the basis of ethics, for in his section entitled "Yes to God," Küng takes account of the multidimensional nature of humankind. He turns to Being in Heidegger, and to silence before God, in the way in which the later Heidegger saw Being as beyond words, other than poetry. Wittgenstein, too, saw the "inexpressible" as often of great importance for life. He quotes Wittgenstein as saying, "To believe in God means to see that life has a meaning" (506; Wittgenstein, *Notebooks, 1914-16* [Oxford: Blackwell, 1961], 74). He considers Barth's attack on "natural theology" (515). Part of Barth's protest, however, was directed against Vatican I, with its dualist "cleavage" between "natural" and "supernatural." Küng agrees with Barth about the necessity of revelation. But de Lubac, Balthasar, and others have queried such a stark cleavage between natural and supernatural. These are "abstract, quasi-Aristotelian, ambiguous ... categories" (522). Even Barth is not so negative about natural theology, Küng claims, in *CD* IV, *The Doctrine of Reconciliation,* written some forty years after his initial attack. The "creaturely world" has its own lights and truths. He concludes, once again, that we need "not a blind, but a justifiable belief ... a belief related to reality" (528).

Küng now considers the traditional arguments for the existence of God. His evaluations of the four traditional arguments match traditional assessments (531). But these are not "proofs." He writes, *"Belief in God cannot be proved to a person if the existential constituents are neglected.... There is no purely rational demonstration of God's existence that could carry universal conviction"* (533). Clearly "critical rationalism" does *not* simply mean "rationalism." In the end, Küng concludes, "Both denial and affirmation of God are possible" (568, 569). But faith or trust may assume God: "Belief in God," he says, is "ultimately justified fundamental trust" (571); it is "rationally justified" (573). Belief, he urges, is a gift. Küng is attempting to stand on a knife edge. He does not, in the end, embrace natural theology. He writes, "We did not assume an autonomous reason capable of demonstrating a foundation of faith, but having nothing to do with faith" (577). Yet he insists that it is rationally justified to believe in God in faith.

Küng's last chapter is entitled "Yes to the Christian God." The God of the Bible takes account of Jewish monotheism and liberates the oppressed people in the exodus. The God of the philosophers, he argues, is nameless (604-7). The Bible helps us to see God as a person, "who faces us as benevolent and absolutely reliable: not an object, not an empty ... silent infinite" (634). He takes up Heidegger's question, "Why is there something and not nothing?" The Genesis accounts "do not provide scientific information," but they do imply God's "gracious turning to the world and man" (639). The God of Jesus Christ is no tyrant, but is good and loving (671). He declares, "From eternity, there is no other God than the one who manifested himself in Jesus" (683).

In this book Küng's "critical rationalism" does appear to tread a careful path through the traditional faith-versus-reason debate, avoiding both rationalism and fideism. It also provides superb exposition and criticism of Feuerbach, Marx, and Freud, while seeing Nietzsche's work as not wholly negative. It seeks to do justice to the transcendence and even hiddenness of God, and to continue to reformulate Christology, while placing faith and trust in a positive and prominent light. It is not certain that criticisms which accuse him of making too much of God as a mystery can be defended. He also shows that the "why" of creation is even more important than the "that" of creation, which physicists and astrophysicists address.

In 1982 Küng published *Eternal Life?* (Eng. London: Collins, 1984; London: SCM, 1991); in 1992 *Credo: The Apostles' Creed Explained for Today* (London: SCM, 1993); and in 1994 *Christianity: Its Essence and History* (London: SCM, 1995). *Eternal Life?* discusses death as entry into light, and dying with dignity; considers whether the hereafter is "wishful thinking"; and provides models of eternity, the resurrection, and the end of the world. This book does not leave behind the questions and answers of *Does God Exist?* For example, in "Eternal Life: Wish or Reality?" (30-34), Küng returns to Feuerbach and to his theory of projection. But he also considers fresh ground: Sartre and the supposed absurdity of death, Jaspers and "borderline situations," consensus and difference today, and the final state. Although he returns to "trust," trust becomes especially relevant to belief or hope in the resurrection. Küng rightly takes account of "the horizon of apocalyptic ideas" (91), but also faces difficulties about belief in the resurrection of Jesus Christ. He examines the role of early testimonies, the Easter message, and the resurrection of the body (99-112). He addresses issues concerning hell and heaven (129-45). He comments, "The fear of hell ... has done immense harm over the course of centuries" (131). Further, "Religious fanaticism still leads Christians to condemn others to hell" (132). The "particle of truth" in the idea, he concludes, is "purification, cleansing, liberation, enlightenment" (137). But he admits that purgatory finds no place in the OT or NT. Küng's last three chapters discuss the consequences of his earlier work on eschatology. This includes "Dying with Dignity," in which he takes account of medical ethics, the importance of grieving, and assisted dying (165-75). There is a difference between active euthanasia and passive assisted dying. He concludes, "The patient is not obliged in every situation to submit to any possible form of therapy or operation in order to prolong his life" (167).

Küng's book *Credo* is fully engaged with the meaning of the creed *for today*. On the incarnation he approves much of the work of his colleague K.-J. Kuschel, and concludes, "In this original sense Jesus of Nazareth is the Word become flesh, God's Logos in person, God's wisdom in human form" (61). He considers creation in relation to biology, cosmology, and evolution, arguing that God's creation is not restricted to *past* acts only, but includes present processes. On the other hand, "We should avoid mixing up scientific knowledge and religious confessions: we will not follow Teilhard de Chardin... [on] a particular Omega point" (25). On the death of Christ, Küng quotes 1 Cor. 1:18-31, which he calls "a paradox, but not a contradiction" (87). He resists the Patripassian view that God the Father died, and also protests against "a sadistic, cruel picture of God, according to which a bloodthirsty God calls for the sacrifice of his Son" (87). But he accepts that it is "an unprecedented abandonment of the one sent by God" (87-88). On the resurrection Küng is less clear than usual: "It is not a historical event, an event which can be envisaged... but it is nevertheless a real event in the divine sphere" (111). This appears perhaps to represent a point midway between Pannenberg and Conzelmann and Marxsen. He is on safer ground when he asserts, "Death and resurrection do not abolish the identity of the person, but preserve it in an unimaginable, changed form, in a completely different dimension" (111). Meanwhile, his book *Christianity* not only addresses issues of our own times, but offers a martially historical survey of the church, in which are embedded six "paradigm changes" between the first century and the present day.

Two books show Küng's vision for the future of theology and his hopes concerning paradigm change. They are H. Küng and D. Tracy, eds., *Paradigm Change in Theology* (Edinburgh: T. & T. Clark, 1989), and H. Küng, *New Horizons for Faith and Thought* (London: SCM, 1993). Throughout his writings Küng's strength is his philosophical and apologetic concern to explain the Christian faith to people of today. His work on Christology draws creatively on Hegel. His early works *The Living Church* and *Infallible?* point the way to a post–Vatican II church, which is largely reformed along biblical lines. If there is any reservation, many would argue that he is too ready to adapt Christian theology to appeal to "modern man," like many Protestant liberals. But he is far too learned and the author of too many books and articles to be categorized in any simplistic way. He is often creative, and his works will always repay study. His greatest contributions make an impact on many areas, but these include especially the concept of God, Christology, and apologetics. His thought is consistent, and part of a whole. (*See also* **Christology; Feuerbach, Ludwig A.; God, Trinity; Hegel, Georg Wilhelm Friedrich; Marx, Karl; Nietzsche, Friedrich; Resurrection of the Dead; Vatican II.**)

Reading: John Kiwiet, *Hans Küng* (London: Harper-Collins, 1985); Hans Küng, *Does God Exist?* (London and New York: Collins, 1980); Hans Küng, *The Incarnation of the Son of God* (Edinburgh: T. & T. Clark, 1987); Hans Küng, *Infallible?* (London:

SCM, 1994); Hans Küng, *Christianity* (London: SCM, 1995); Hans Küng, *Justification* (Louisville: Westminster John Knox, 2004); H. Häring and K.-J. Kuschel, eds., *Hans Küng: His Work and His Way* (London: Collins; New York: Doubleday, 1980).

Kuyper, Abraham

Abraham Kuyper (1837-1920) was ordained into the Dutch Reformed Church, was educated at Leyden, and in 1880 took a prominent part in the founding of the Free University of Amsterdam. He became increasingly concerned about theological liberalism, and in 1892 his Christian Reformed Church merged with the Reformed Churches of the Netherlands. He also involved himself in national politics, and became prime minister of the Netherlands from 1901 to 1905. In 1888 he published *The Work of the Holy Spirit,* of some 550 pages (New York and London: Funk and Wagnalls, 1906). This includes major Calvinist themes: "the redeemed and the lost"; "sovereign grace alone"; "the vindication of the Counsel of God"; and contemplation of an "architect forming his plans" (11-17). The Holy Spirit "effects only that which is invisible and inseparable" from the work of the Father and the Son (25). Much of his book builds on the work of Hodge and Smeaton, except that, unlike Hodge, he describes as "foolish" the view that the church never received the gifts described in 1 Cor. 12:8-10 for eighteen centuries (186). Kuyper is realistic about sanctification: this takes time, struggle, and perseverance. It remains "a gradual process" (479). In 1898 he delivered the Stone Lectures at Princeton Seminary. He remains a central figure of neo-Calvinism.

Reading: J. D. Bratt, *Dutch Calvinism in Modern America: A History of a Conservative Subculture* (Grand Rapids: Eerdmans, 1984); J. D. Bratt, *Abraham Kuyper: A Centennial Reader* (Grand Rapids: Eerdmans, 1998); Abraham Kuyper, *The Work of the Holy Spirit* (New York and London: Funk and Wagnalls, 1906).

L

Lactantius
Lactantius (c. 250–c. 325) is generally thought to have been a convert to Christianity. The emperor Constantine appointed him to be tutor to his son. His main work is *The Divine Institutes,* which he began to write in 305-311, using the language and style of Cicero, but constituting a Christian apologetics in content and aim. He subtitled it *An Introduction to True Religion.* Book 1 concerns the worship of false gods, in contrast to God as a spiritual being; book 2 concerns the origin of error; book 3 is on the false wisdom of philosophers; and book 4 concerns true wisdom and religion. Books 5-7 concern justice, true worship, and a happy life. Lactantius concludes with a section on eschatology. He also wrote on the anger of God, the creation of humankind, and death of persecutors.

Lampe, Geoffrey W. H.
Geoffrey W. H. Lampe (1912-1980) was a British theologian, who was Ely Professor of Divinity at Cambridge (1960-1970), and then Regius Professor (1970-1979). He was an Anglican priest and a member of General Synod. He won the Military Cross for rescuing troops under fire. He edited the massive volume *A Patristic Greek Lexicon* (Oxford: Clarendon, 1961), with 1,569 quarto pages; edited *The Cambridge History of the Bible,* volume 2 (1975); and published *The Seal of the Spirit* (1951) and *God as Spirit* (1977), as well as other works. We discuss the two volumes on the Holy Spirit under **Holy Spirit: The Spirit in Historical Theology.**

Language, Religious
Most aspects of this subject have been covered in detail by a succession of separate articles. Hence this general survey merely outlines a number of concerns that are expounded more fully in these separate articles. One of the oldest and most traditional defenses of the validity and currency of religious language depends on the virtually universal use of analogy. Aquinas and many other thinkers have expounded this approach. Analogy is also supplemented by metaphor and symbol, which are defended and expounded by writers as different from each other as Tillich and Ricoeur. Personal language in religion is often expounded in work on the nature of narrative by Frei, Hauerwas, Ricoeur, and others. Ian Ramsey has offered a unique contribution in his work on models and qualifiers.

Many advances in linguistic philosophy and in the philosophy of language have enriched this area. The work of L. Wittgenstein has been seminal and creative in this area, although he does not write as a Christian theologian, and has been followed to some extent by J. L. Austin, G. Ryle, and P. F. Strawson. In speech act theory immense progress has been made by Austin, Searle, Recanati, and many Christian theologians.

From time to time materialists have attacked the validity of religious language, among them A. J. Ayer and logical positivists. They have misconceived arguments that religious language is merely emotive, or constitutes recommendations to adopt certain forms of behavior. Such a view occurs in R. B. Braithwaite, *An Empiricist's View of the Nature of Religious Belief* (1955). F. Nietzsche argued that such language as "the salvation of the soul" meant only "the world revolves around me," with no further referent (*The Antichrist,* vol. 16 of *Complete Works* [London: Allen and Unwin, 1909-1913], aphorism 43). Wittgenstein clearly recognized that the logical grammar of religious language is distinctive, for example, "You can't hear God speaking to someone else (That is a grammatical remark)" (*Zettel* [Oxford: Blackwell, 1967], sect. 717). Such language is a distinctive "language game"; but this does not mean that it is isolated from ordinary language. Between language games there are "overlappings and criss-crossings." Defenses against negative criticisms and positive defenses of religious language are expounded in more detail in the separate articles elsewhere in this book. (*See also* **Analogy; Aquinas, Thomas; Austin, John L.; God, Trinity; Jüngel, Eberhard; Logical Positivism; Metaphor; Myth; Narrative; Ramsey, Ian; Speech Act Theory; Strawson, Peter F.; Symbol; Wittgenstein, Ludwig.**)

Last Judgment

We are accustomed to conceive of the Last Judgment as concerned with accountability. Often popular imagination assimilates it into notions of the judge's sentence in a law court. The Last Judgment includes this aspect, but only as one among others. Paul writes, "All of us must appear before the judgment seat of Christ, so that each may receive recompense for what has been done in the body, whether good or evil" (2 Cor. 5:10). Why, then, is the future judgment so frequently contemplated with joy? In Ps. 96:10-13 the writer looks forward to God's judging "with equity," and comments,

> Then shall all the trees of the forest sing for joy
>   before the Lord: for he is coming,
>   he is coming to judge the earth.

We read of similar joy in Ps. 67:4:

> Let the nations be glad and sing for joy,
>   for you [God] judge the peoples with equity.

This joy arises largely because the primary emphasis of God's judgment concerns vindication and "putting things right," where there has been oppression or injustice. Many millions in the world have been tempted to think they have been treated unfairly, and that power-hungry oppressors have "got away with it." In Ps. 98:2, 4, 9 God

> has revealed his vindication in the sight of nations. . . .
> Make a joyful noise to the LORD. . . .
> He is coming to judge the earth.

Second, illusion and deceit of all kinds will be abolished. Self-proclaimed achievers and so-called celebrities will be seen in their true colors; so will sincere, hardworking, but unrecognized laborers. Third, God will be revealed as universal sovereign, King of creation, who comes genuinely to put right wrongs. Trust in God's providence in this age will come fully into sight, into full public view. The persecuted church will come to acknowledge: "Just and true are your ways" (Rev. 15:3).

The whole world will witness this. The Last Judgment will reveal God's definitive evaluation of all human claims and endeavors. But Stephen Travis observes, "The emphasis on restorative justice is not on 'paying back' the offender, but on positively 'putting right' what has gone wrong between the offender and the victim" (*Christ and the Judgement of God* [Milton Keynes: Paternoster; Colorado Springs: Hendrickson, 2008], 8). The Hebrew for judgment *(mishpāt)* is expressed in the Greek *krima* or *krisis* both in the LXX and the NT. These terms relate to God's manifestation of "righteousness," rather than primarily "equality," as in Aristotle and Aquinas. But this reminds us that "putting things to rights," in turn, relates to justification. The believing Christian has had things "put to rights" by grace through faith in Jesus Christ. This still requires the event of the Last Judgment. For what is appropriated in faith must be vindicated and proven to be the case publicly in the sight of all. This especially applies to a right relationship with God, but, as J. P. Miranda and others have argued, it also relates to a broader social relation with others. The so-called parables of reversal in the teaching of Jesus confirm this. Jeremias comments, "Conditions are reversed; what is hidden becomes manifest (Mt. 10:26 and parallels); the poor become rich (Lk. 6:20); the last are first (Mk. 10:44); the small become great (Mt. 18:4); the hungry are filled (Lk. 6:21); the weary find rest (Mt. 11:28)" (*The Parables of Jesus* [London: SCM, 1963], 221-22).

Once again (as in other entries) this concerns speech act theory. For in uttering what J. L. Austin calls a "verdictive," God will perform a speech act. God's verdict is not first an evaluation or opinion to be listened to; it is a pronouncement that *makes* the situation what God definitively *declares* it to be. If a duly appointed judge *says*, "I acquit," the accused goes *free*. If a duly appointed umpire *says* "Out," the player or the ball *is* out. It is in this sense definitive and irreversible.

The Last Judgment may have a special relevance to ministry. In 1 Cor. 4:3-5 Paul states that he does not judge how well or badly he has performed: "I do not even judge myself" (4:3). For only he who is the Lord truly knows. But at the Last Judgment "the Day will disclose it" (3:13; cf. 3:10-15). Yet the same may be said of any Christian, whatever the Christian's vocation. There is no conflict between justification by grace and judgment of "works." Travis comments, "There is no suggestion here of reward or punishment in accordance with the quality of good or evil deeds done" (94). K. L. Yinger broadly agrees. "Questions as to the quantity of transgressions or righteous deeds are pointless. There is . . . no tension or paradox between salvation by grace and judgement according to deeds" (*Paul, Judaism, and Judgement according to Deeds* [Cambridge: CUP, 1999], 287). Both aspects turn on a relationship with God. The Last Judgment will reveal things as what they are or were. The notion of "public" revelation should not cause needless anxiety or worry. We shall be seen as we are "in Christ"; in the Reformed language, "clothed in the righteousness of Christ." Anthropomorphic analogies such as that of the law court or the headmaster may even mislead us. On the other hand, it does entail accountability. God's judgment must be understood within the whole frame of reference of the vindication of the oppressed and the gospel of Jesus Christ.

Reading: C. D. Marshall, *Beyond Retribution* (Grand Rapids: Eerdmans, 2001); O. O'Donovan, *The Ways of Judgment* (Grand Rapids: Eerdmans, 2005); S. H. Travis, *Christ and the Judgement of God* (Milton Keynes: Paternoster; Colorado Springs: Hendrickson, 2008); K. L. Yingen, *Paul, Judaism, and Judgement according to Deeds* (Cambridge: CUP, 1999).

Latimer, Hugh

Hugh Latimer (c. 1485-1555), one of the first generation of the Reformers, became bishop of Worcester. He was born in Leicestershire, and educated in the University of Cambridge. In about 1524 he underwent a dramatic conversion to Reformation doctrine. He defended himself before Wolsey, and in 1530 preached before Henry VIII, which won his favor. When Henry broke with the pope in 1534, he became a royal chaplain, and in 1535, bishop of Worcester. His sermons denounced both papacy and social injustice, attacking purgatory, images, and the monasteries. In 1539, however, he opposed Henry's Act of the Six Articles, which retained transubstantiation, celibacy, monastic vows, and private masses. He was forbidden to preach, and in 1546 confined to the Tower of London. On the succession of Edward VI he was released, and in 1548 preached his famous sermon of the plough, commending the reading of Scripture by all. His preaching was learned, witty, and popular. But upon Mary's succession as Queen in 1553, he was imprisoned, and in 1555 martyred at Oxford together with Cranmer and Ridley.

Latitudinarians

This name was applied in the seventeenth century to a group of Anglicans who nominally conformed to the doctrines of the Church of England but attached little importance to dogmatic theology or to ecclesiastical organization. They tended to sympathize with Arminian theology and the Cambridge Platonists. They were forerunners of the Broad Church, or more extreme liberals in later centuries.

Laud, William
William Laud (1573-1645) was fellow of St. John's College, Oxford, and became archbishop of Canterbury. He was influential under Charles I. In advance of Anglo-Catholicism, he represented a "High Church" view within the Church of England, attempting to make the Lord's Supper, rather than the sermon, the center of church worship. As dean of Gloucester, he moved the communion table to the east end of the church, prompting hostility from the Puritans. In 1640 he proclaimed "the divine right of kings," and at the instigation of the Long Parliament was imprisoned in the Tower, and executed on Tower Hill in 1645.

Law
The law (Heb. *tōrāh;* Gk. *nomos*) at first seems to receive different evaluations in the biblical writings, but on reflection these are seen to be different meanings or functions of the term (cf. esp. J. D. G. Dunn, *The Theology of Paul the Apostle* [Edinburgh: T. & T. Clark; Grand Rapids: Eerdmans, 1998], 719-22; D. E. H. Whiteley, *The Theology of St. Paul* [Oxford: Blackwell, 1971], 79-86; and Peter Ens, "Law of God," in *NIDOTTE* 4:893-900). Such differences are confirmed by Luther, Melanchthon, and Calvin, who speak of two, three, or even four "uses" of the law. *Torah* occurs about 220 times in the OT, and in all the major writings of the OT. It denotes God's standard of conduct for his people. The LXX translates it by *nomos*. The plural *tōrōth* may denote regulations, especially in ceremonial law to direct sacrifices and offerings (Lev. 6:25; 7:7); Sabbaths, temple worship, and feasts (Ezek. 43:11-12; Neh. 8:13); and the Passover and consecration of the firstborn (Exodus 12; 2 Chron. 30:16; Neh. 10:36). But the law also directs social and judicial matters (Isa. 51:4). A dozen passages in Deuteronomy concern upright or moral behavior. It may speak of "the book of this law" (28:61; cf. 29:21), and other books speak of godly living. A father may teach the law (Prov. 3:1), or "teachers" may undertake this work (Neh. 9:34). The law is the psalmist's delight (Pss. 1:2; 119:70, 77, 92), and a source of wonder and grace (Ps. 119:18, 29).

The NT seems to present an ambiguity at first glance. But this multiple evaluation is due to multiple meanings and functions. (1) Paul can use *nomos* to refer to the revealed will of God, or to "The Torah as God's supreme self-revelation" (Whiteley, *Paul*, 79; cf. Dunn, *Theology of Paul*, 722). Paul inherits this use directly from the OT and Judaism (Gal. 3:19-20; Rom. 7:12-13). God's commandment is "holy, just and good." (2) But the law also brings consciousness of sin (Rom. 5:13; 7:7). Dunn states that it can be "the cat's-paw of sin" (*Theology of Paul*, 721). It brings sin to consciousness (Rom. 6:14-15; 7:14-17; Dunn, 155-59). (3) It stands therefore in contrast to the gospel, which brings life through the Holy Spirit (2 Cor. 3:1-18; Rom. 5:12-21; Dunn, 143-55). (4) For those "in Christ" and under the power of the gospel, the law may facilitate the learning of what is pleasing to God. This fourth function has been controversial.

These differences of meaning and function can be found throughout the NT, as when Jesus both attacks bondage to the law and also says that he has not come to destroy it (Matt. 5:17). Of the Gospel writers, Matthew is the most overt in promoting the positive role of the law, even if he also recounts the "woes" to false leaders, whether leaders of the Jews or of the church (Matt. 23:1-36). Gerhard Ebeling attributes to Melanchthon the classic three "uses" of the law ("On the Doctrine of the *Triplex Usus Legis*," in *Word and Faith* [London: SCM, 1963], 62-78). This is mainly on the basis of Gal. 3:23-29. But, as is well known, Luther primarily focused on the contrast between law and gospel, and the Augsburg Confession (1531) stated, "All Scripture ought to be distributed into these two principal topics, the Law and the Promises." In Reformed theology Louis Berkhof called the law and the gospel "the two parts of the means of grace." Thus Calvin stressed three uses of the law: (1) it warns, informs, convicts, and lastly condemns (*Institutes* 2.7.6); (2) people may be careless, unless they are mindful of the threats of the law (2.7.10); and (3) it admonishes believers and urges them on in well-doing (2.7.8-12). It is this third point that sometimes remains controversial for many. But those in the Reformed tradition insist that God uses both the Holy Spirit and the law in the process of sanctification. This principle is well argued in E. F. Kevan, *The Grace of Law: A Study in Puritan Theology* (Grand Rapids: Baker, 1966).

Lectionary

In the nontechnical sense, a lectionary is an ordered system of biblical readings, set for each day and for special festivals in the Christian year. It avoids allowing the readings to be determined by the personal whim of the preacher or pastor, and guarantees a reasonable coverage of balanced readings from the OT and the NT. Lectionary readings go back to the Jewish synagogue, at least for festivals and Sabbaths. The addition of apostolic writings to the OT is witnessed as early as c. 150 in Justin (*First Apology* 67). In the West Alcuin standardized readings for the Mass. Cranmer ensured that both the OT and the NT were read at daily offices, and where possible lections reflected the theme and mood of the season of the Christian year.

Leibniz, Gottfried Wilhelm

Gottfried Wilhelm Leibniz (1646-1716) was born in Leipzig, and educated at Leipzig, Jena, and Altdorf. His main contributions were to mathematics, logic, and philosophy, but he also contributed to law, historical inquiry, natural science, and politics. He served as a librarian and diplomat in the court of Hanover. Popularly he is probably best known in theology for his optimistic response to the problem of evil, claiming that God had created "the best possible world." In philosophy he was a rationalist. He produced a complex ontology, partly on the basis of his dissatisfaction with Descartes. He postulated "units of one" or "monads," which were the smallest indivisible things. But these were not spatial; they were units of force. Monads do not interact: "monads have no windows" (*Monadology,* sect. 7). They may, however, mirror reality, as a microcosm of the universe. Leibniz's central concern was logic. He realized that there must also be room for freedom and possibility, and attempted to address "the labyrinth of freedom."

Leibniz accepted the ontological and cosmological arguments for the existence of God. He declared, "God is without limits, without negation ... without contradiction" (*Monadology,* sect. 45). The ground of contingent objects or events must lie outside themselves, and point to a necessary being, who is God. By free choice, God chose to create "the best possible world" (*Theodicy,* 1710). Evil is necessary for the world to be the best possible world. Leibniz appealed to "the principle of sufficient reason" for God's creation of such a world. His emphasis on "possibility" may have been a stepping-stone toward modern modal logic. He and Sir Isaac Newton independently discovered infinitesimal calculus, each blaming the other for plagiarizing his work. (*See also* **Evil, Problem of; Rationalism.**)

Lessing, Gotthold Ephraim

Gotthold Ephraim Lessing (1729-1781) is most famous, or notorious, for his aphorism "Accidental truths of history can never become the proof of necessary truths of reason" (*Theological Writings* [London: Black, 1956], 53). Lessing was not primarily a theologian, but first made his name as a drama and art critic and as a playwright. However, he had an interest in theology, and in 1774-1778 he edited the notorious *Wolfenbüttel Fragments of H. S. Reimarus,* which attacked historic Christianity. A. Schweitzer drew attention to Reimarus in his classic book *The Quest of the Historical Jesus: From Reimarus to Wrede,* the subtitle of which was the main title in German (1906). In fact, Leibniz had begun the faith and history debate c. 1686 by contending that rational truths were necessary truths and historical reconstructions were contingent, or not more than probabilities. Lessing contended that there was "a broad ugly ditch" between the certainties that reason could establish and the probabilities gleaned from history. This devaluation of historical accounts was a dominant influence in theology from Lessing to Bultmann, becoming reversed only in the late 1960s, mainly with Pannenberg. Cf. D. Pailin, "Lessing's Ditch Revisited," in *Theology and Change: Essays in Memory of Alan Richardson,* ed. R. H. Preston (London: SCM, 1975), 78-103.

Lexicography

Lexicography includes the practice of compiling or using dictionary meanings. The larger the lexicon or dictionary, the more it will take account of specific contexts in texts, or even of unusual examples. The standard resource for NT studies is F. W. Danker's third edition of W. Bauer-Arndt-Gingrich, *A Greek-English Lexicon of the New Testament and Other Early Christian Literature* (Chicago: University of Chicago Press, 2001). An older lexicon is J. H. Thayer, *A Greek-English Lexicon of the New Testament* (Edinburgh: T. & T. Clark, 1901), based on the work of C. G. Wilke (1851) and C. L. W. Grimm (1879). On the patristic period, the standard work currently remains that of G. W. H. Lampe, ed., *A Patristic Greek Lexicon* (Oxford: OUP, 1961). For classical Greek, perhaps the classic edition is the lexicon by Liddell, Scott, and Jones.

Liberalism

Liberalism has its origins in the thought of the Enlightenment. In essence, Kant defined the Enlightenment as freedom from all authorities except one's own thought, or freedom to think for oneself without subservience to authorities. Prior to Kant, most of the Deists promoted this project. A. Toland, *Christianity Not Mysterious,* suggested that human reason alone could fathom Christianity without either the Bible or tradition. A. Collins wrote his *Discourse of Free Thinking* (1713) at a time when political liberalism and theological liberalism seemed to be virtually the same (*see* **Natural Theology**).

The theological liberalism of Germany contained a varied spectrum of more radical and more moderate views. G. E. Lessing argued that history and tradition could provide no absolutes, as against reason. He declared that a broad, ugly ditch lay between the contingent truths of history and the "necessary" truths of reason and logic. Schleiermacher, however, who is sometimes called a "liberal evangelical," rejected some, but not all, traditional and Pietist formulations. He argued in his *Speeches* that in religion, one should attend to the views of "experts," as in other subjects. In most semipopular theological thought liberalism is associated characteristically with Ritschl and Harnack, to whom many would add Herrmann and Troeltsch. Harnack sought the "essence" of the teaching of Jesus in the Fatherhood of God, the brotherhood of humankind, and the infinite value of a human soul.

Liberalism in Britain and America was perhaps narrower and more specific. It related especially to the authority, role, and status of the Bible. In England liberalism was also attacked by the Anglo-Catholic Movement, while liberals attacked Anglo-Catholic concerns for early tradition. At certain points, however, the two movements overlapped, and still today many use the term "liberal Catholic" of themselves. In England J. H. Newman firmly rejected liberalism in favor of respect for doctrine and tradition. Thomas Arnold, Benjamin Jowett, and Frederick Temple promoted liberal education and theology, the latter two contributing to the controversial volume *Essays and Reviews* (1860). Jowett wrote in this volume that the Bible should be interpreted "like any other book," while Temple argued that reason had no imposed limits, and that no special knowledge comes from God's direct communications. Liberalism became later exemplified in the Modern Churchman's Union (1872-1961). Hastings Rachdall was also an acknowledged representative. In America liberalism began later under the guise of "progressive" orthodoxy. It spread initially through Union Theological Seminary, New York, and A. C. McGiffert; through Horace Bushnell, president of Yale; and through Shailer Mathews, dean of Chicago Divinity School. Christian theology lost much of its distinctive character when it attempted to enter into mutual dialogue with sociology and ethics. Thus Walter Rauschenbusch published *A Theology for the Social Gospel* in 1919, in which he argued that Jesus was concerned primarily with reform of the social order and political action. Mathews similarly saw the kingdom of God as "a conventional symbol of the supreme good to be enjoyed by humanity."

Voices were raised in criticism of liberalism in America, Britain, and Germany. In America Charles Hodge, president of Princeton, insisted that the Bible was a "storehouse of facts." In reaction against Bushnell and others, he discouraged "new ideas." In Britain the reaction came from Newman, Pusey, and Keble, but soon evangelical opposition also became strong and articulate, especially on the Bible. Even those who were moderate biblical critics, such as B. F. Westcott and J. B. Lightfoot, opposed the liberal tendency. A similar reaction took place in Germany, where Hengstenberg and others rejected the tide of liberalism. Many view the heyday of liberalism as 1900-1925, although the emergence of fundamentalism in America saw reaction and counterreaction, sometimes reaching heights of passion on both sides. Polemics still continue today, although perhaps in new and more considered forms. It is inaccurate to describe radicals or *all* nonevangelicals as "liberals" today. A relatively small tradition of liberals exists within the Roman Catholic Church, perhaps following A. Loisy and others. In America another sign of the demise of liberalism is the so-called postliberal approach of Hans Frei, George Lindbeck, and others. (*See also* **Enlightenment, The; Rationalism;** *and names of individual theologians.*)

Reading: K. Cauthen, *The Impact of American Religious Liberalism* (New York: Harper and Row, 1962); B. Reardon, *Liberal Protestantism* (Stanford: Stanford University Press, 1968).

Liberation Hermeneutics and Theology

Liberation hermeneutics denotes the interpretation of the Bible in liberation theologies. These theologies emerged especially in Latin America toward the end of the 1960s and throughout the 1970s, and have had influence from the 1980s to today. The themes have also emerged in Africa, India, and other parts of the world, but today the emphasis often moves to postcolonial hermeneutics. In a weak sense origins may be traced to the sixteenth century, as chronicled by Enrique Dussel, ed., *The Church in Latin America, 1492-1992* (London: Burns and Oates; New York: Orbis, 1992), esp. 1-184, particularly 43-48. Dussel selects Bartolomé de Las Casas (1474-1566) as the seminal theologian of the sixteenth century. But in a stricter sense, liberation hermeneutics stems from the Peruvian Gustavo Gutiérrez, when he devised an agenda for the Conference of Latin American Bishops at Medellín, Colombia, in 1968. His ideas were developed in his seminal book *The Theology of Liberation* (Lima, Peru, 1971; Salamanca, Spain, 1972; and Maryknoll,

N.Y.: Orbis, 1973). Gutiérrez argued that biblical texts needed reinterpretation because the framework of most Western (usually American, British, and German) interpretation was thought-centered, academic, and bourgeois-capitalist.

Philip Berryman traced the roots of liberation hermeneutics and liberation theology to Central America, notably Guatemala, El Salvador, Honduras, Nicaragua, and Costa Rica (*The Religious Roots of Rebellion* [London: SCM, 1984], esp. 13-38). The forces of the Spanish Crown, he claims, constituted "an act of conquest and domination" in 1542 and thereafter (35). Only missionaries denounced the cruelties. This ushered in a "colonial" period, which contributed to rebellion in the 1960s and early 1970s. Some loosening of the grip occurred earlier when in 1838 Central America divided into five republics. But more liberal types of economic "development" did not bring material improvement for the poor. In El Salvador, Guatemala, and elsewhere, the military were upgraded, largely to protect the landowning elite. By the 1950s a policy of "development" had collapsed. Moreover, the church appeared to support the landowning elite, and to reinforce traditional values. All this must be seen against the background of calls for revolution in Latin American liberation theology. Moreover, amidst the downward economic spiral only Marxist Cuba appeared to provide greater prosperity for the poor.

By contrast, Catholic Action had emerged in the 1930s and later in the 1950s and 1960s to lend support to the poor. In 1955 a first conference of Latin American bishops was held, and the "New Catholic Left" emerged. While some hoped still for "economic development," an increasing number saw revolution as the only option for progress. The inspiration for revolution came not only from Cuba's revolution in 1959, but from the "Paris Manuscripts" of the earliest writings of Karl Marx. His early work before 1843 was in general not specifically antitheist, but largely based on the goals of the French Revolution to promote liberty, equality, and fraternity. Marx believed that capitalism contained the seeds of its own destruction. Only later did he develop a materialist view of history, which left no room for Christian faith. In 1844 he met F. Engels, and together they wrote *The German Ideology* (1845-1846), which embodied Feuerbach's atheism. In 1848 they wrote the *Communist Manifesto,* and in London Marx wrote *Das Kapital.* These *later* writings inspired Vladimir Lenin and Joseph Stalin. "Marxism" in Latin America was that of the Paris Manuscripts, not that of Lenin and Stalin.

A further crucial factor in the emergence of liberation theology and liberation hermeneutics was the freedom of conscience given to Catholic individuals by Vatican II. It is not too strong to say that Vatican II changed the face of the Catholic Church. The Council encouraged concerns for justice and the plight of the poor and oppressed. Indirectly, its stress on the laity encouraged the base communities, which would shortly emerge. It promoted changes in social structures (*see* **Vatican II**). In 1964 Dom Helder Camera became archbishop of Recife, in northeastern Brazil, and described the oppression of the poor as "a second violence." In Brazil Paulo Freire also began his mission of "consciousness raising" *(concientización)*. To make the poor and oppressed aware of their condition appeared to have its basis in God's command to Moses to make the Hebrews aware that "the LORD . . . had seen their misery" (Exod. 4:31). Hence Freire established a program of literacy classes.

All these factors became explicit in the work of Gutiérrez. His key theme was solidarity with the poor. We may further distinguish five major themes, as follows. First, he saw theology as *critical reflection on praxis* (*Theology of Liberation*, 6-15). The term "praxis" is often misunderstood in Western churches to mean simply "practice." But it has a technical history in Aristotle, Hegel, Feuerbach, and Marx. It does involve change in behavior, but also change in its theoretical basis. Second, Gutiérrez is concerned with the *total social condition* of poverty and oppression in not only Latin America, but also in Africa and Asia, and what used to be called "the third world" but is now often referred to as "the two-thirds world." He questions whether "development" could be the main solution to this, rather than "a total social process" (23-24). The poor must become masters of their own identity, as Marx insisted (29). A social revolution is needed (32). He appeals to "freedom" in Gal. 5:1.

Third, Gutiérrez appeals to *theology and "a new Christendom"* (54-57, 63-67). This rejects disengagement from "the world," for Christ is the universal Lord of all reality, not only of the church. He includes Paulo Friere's "pedagogy of the oppressed" (89, 91). Theology must be committed to "revolutionary political groups" (102). Fourth, attention must be given to hermeneutics and eschatology. The symbolism and typology of Israel's deliverance from Egypt must be applied to Latin America. "Egypt" stands for "the land of oppression and slavery" (Exod. 20:2; Deut. 5:6). Gutiérrez declares, "The God of the Exodus is the God of history and politics" (157). Hence he is the God of eschatological promises of new creation. Fifth, *to honor God is to do justice to the neighbor.* He cites numerous biblical passages, including Prov. 14:20, Deut. 24:14-15, Luke 1:47-49, and 1 John 4:7-8. He declares, "To evangelise . . . is to incarnate the Gospel in time" (271). He adds: "The class struggle is part of our economic . . . and religious reality" (273).

To gain a fuller picture of developments after Gutiérrez we must consider several other theologians, of whom within the "first generation" José Porfirio Miranda and Juan Luis Segundo assume special importance. Miranda (1924-2001) wrote some eleven books, of which the best known is the classic *Marx and the Bible* (Maryknoll, N.Y.: Orbis, 1974; London: SCM, 1977). He wrote from Mexico, and his primary purpose was not to find parallels between Marx and the Bible, but, as his subtitle indicates, to show that both the Bible and Marx provide "A Critique of the Philosophy of Oppression," which overlaps at various points. He aims at building "a classless society" (xiii), and turns therefore to philosophies of power. The biblical writings, he urges, demand justice. From the start he challenges the system of "wages." He is skeptical about most "academic" scholarship, which, he alleges, burden us with interpretations that have no relevance. Inevitably he appeals to Amos (Amos 5:21-25) and Exodus (Exod. 6:2-8). One creative section interprets justification by grace as a *corporate and communal* "putting right with God" the global situation of the oppressed (169-99). "Unrighteousness" *(adikia)* in Rom. 1:15–3:20 includes *structural* injustice in the world. Recent scholarship in Europe tends also to suggest this more corporate and communal emphasis.

Segundo (1925-1996), of Uruguay, was a Jesuit, who wrote especially on hermeneutics. He studied in Argentina and Louvain, Belgium, where he met Gutiérrez. He later lectured in Brazil, Canada, and America. His major work was *The Liberation of Theology* (Dublin: Gill and Macmillan, 1977), written after the Medellín conference. It makes considerable use of the "hermeneutical circle" (7-39). His distinctive approach is that preunderstanding must be shaped by practical sociology and active compassion for the oppressed. He attacks "academic" theology for ignoring this. The hermeneutical circle "proves that a theology is alive" (23). He rejects the notion of a theology without commitment; it needs "a commitment to liberation" (83).

Besides these three liberation theologians, if we had unlimited space, we should discuss J. Severino Croatto (1930-2004) of Argentina, who also shows a major concern for hermeneutics. He published *Exodus: A Hermeneutics of Freedom* (Span. 1978; Eng. Maryknoll, N.Y.: Orbis, 1981), in which he considers Paul Ricoeur and H.-G. Gadamer. He followed this with *Biblical Hermeneutics* (Maryknoll, N.Y.: Orbis, 1987). Hugo Assmann (1933-2008) also belongs to this first generation. He published *A Practical Theology of Liberation* (London: Search Press, 1975). We should probably also include in this first generation of thinkers Leonardo Boff (b. 1938) of Brazil, who published *Jesus Christ Liberator* (Port. 1972; Eng. 1978); and Jon Sobrino (b. 1938), another Jesuit, who wrote *Christology at the Crossroads* (Maryknoll, N.Y.: Orbis; London: SCM, 1978). Clodovis Boff (b. 1944) is the younger brother of Leonardo, and began writing in the 1980s, and is therefore on the borderline of the "first generation" of liberation theologians.

In 1984 Segundo distinguished between two theologies of liberation. First, the theologians mentioned above used training in biblical studies and hermeneutics to formulate a hermeneutics of suspicion and to use neo-Marxist tools. Second, many focused on "doing" rather than "thinking," and worked among the poor "on site." The best-known examples are the base communities. Ernesto Cardenal, in *The Gospel of Solentiname,* and to some extent the work of Julio de Santa Ana and of Carlos Mesters, a Dutchman working in Brazil, chronicle and describe this grassroots work.

Without doubt liberation hermeneutics and liberation theology articulated the cry of the oppressed and poor in Latin America, and spread to cries for liberation and justice in Africa and even among some African Americans. Nevertheless, critics of the movement argue that the biblical texts are endlessly repetitive and highly selective. Some in the Roman Catholic Church ask whether "democratization" is the right model for the church. Especially in Roman Catholicism two opposite evaluations seem to be emerging. Vatican II gave much momentum and encouragement to the movement. After Vatican II, Cardinal Joseph Ratzinger (later Pope Benedict) and a number of more conservative Catholics expressed concern that the movement might be going too far. Pope Francis seems to be showing more sympathy with it. Whether the initial call of this movement is still urgent or whether it has already decisively made the point remains controversial, and varies considerably in different parts of Latin America, and in different parts of the world. Certainly different leaders in Rome adopt different attitudes to it. (*See also* **Base Communities; Postcolonial Theology.**)

Reading: L. Boff and C. Boff, *Introducing Liberation Theology* (London: Burns and Oates, 1987); C. Cadorette et al., eds., *Liberation Theology: An Introductory Reader* (Maryknoll, N.Y.: Orbis, 1992); Gustavo Gutiérrez, *The Theology of Liberation* (Maryknoll, N.Y.: Orbis, 1973); J. A. Kirk, *Liberation Theology* (London: Marshall, Morgan and Scott, 1979); José Porfirio Miranda, *Marx and the Bible* (Maryknoll, N.Y.: Orbis, 1974); Juan Luis Segundo, *The Liberation of Theology* (Dublin: Gill and Macmillan, 1977).

Life, Eternal Life

(i) **Life in the Old Testament.** The Hebrew *chayyîm* and *chayyah* initially denoted "span of life" or "allotted life" (Gen. 23:1, of Sarah; 25:7, of Abraham). In the verbal form, the Qal usually means "to be alive"; in the Piel it may denote preservation of life ("to keep alive") or restoration of life ("to restore to life," Ezek. 13:18; 2 Kings 8:1, of Elisha). The adjective, in such phrases as "living water," denotes *running water,* which *moves* and flows, in contrast to the stagnant water of a cistern (Jer. 2:13, "They have forsaken me, / the fountain of living water, / and dug out cisterns for themselves, / cracked cisterns"; Heb. *mayim chayyîm*). *Living water* is pure, ever-fresh, and in motion. The two articles in *TDOT* and *TDNT* provide a picture of life in the OT put together by G. von Rad, H. Ringgren, and R. Bultmann. Often *nephesh,* usually translated "soul" in the AV/KJV and the RV, means "life" rather than "soul," like the Greek *psuchē*. Its semantic contrast is not with "body" but with "death." As von Rad indicates, the acquisition of vitality is ascribed to a creative act by God (*TDNT* 2:844). To live is not to die (Gen. 42:2, of Jacob).

In Deut. 30:15 and 19, Moses announces to Israel, "I have set before you . . . life and death, blessings and curses. Choose life so that you and your descendants may live." He adds that life entails loving God and obeying his commandments (v. 20). Ps. 80:18-19 repeats the theme:

> Give us life, and we will call on your name.
> Restore us; . . .
> let your face shine.

Prov. 4:4 reads, "Keep my commandments, and live." In Prov. 8:35, Wisdom declares:

> "Whoever finds me finds life
> and obtains favor from the LORD."

Those who miss Wisdom "love death" (v. 36). To the Pentateuch, Psalms, and Proverbs, we may add the prophets: Amos 5:6 declares, "Seek the LORD and live." G. von Rad comments, "The curse is not death, but the making of life bitter" (*TDNT* 2:844). Similarly, H. Ringgren observes: "'Life' has nuances besides purely physical life.... 'Living water'... is fresh running water or spring water ... (Lev. 14:5f., 50-52; 15:13; Nu. 19:17).... The concept is also used figuratively" (Jer. 2:13; 17:13; *TDOT* 4:333). Zech. 14:8 speaks of living water that will flow from Jerusalem in the end-time. Malachi states that the divine covenant is one of "life and well-being" (2:5). Life means blessing.

Often in the OT the restoration of life is not primarily physical, but relates to states of well-being or rescue from despair. The psalmist cries:

> You ... will receive me again;
> from the depths of the earth
> you will bring me up again. (71:20)

Hezekiah thanks God for restoration to life and health (Isa. 38:16). "Sickness and distress impair the forces of life, and represent, as it were, a potential death; deliverance is therefore appropriately termed 'life'" (Ringgren, *TDOT* 4:334). Genesis refers to a "tree of life" (2:9 and 3:22, 24). This theme is not developed, but it implies the capacity to live forever, which is otherwise denied to humankind. Any prospect of future life depends on God. In the OT there are hints of this (Dan. 12:2), since God can give life or terminate it (2 Kings 5:7), in contrast to the NT, which develops a full-scale, explicit doctrine of resurrection in Christ (1 Corinthians 15). Exod. 32:32 also speaks of a book of life. In God are "life" and "length of days" (Deut. 30:20).

The phrase the "living God" becomes important. The people of God were proud to be called "sons of the living God" (Hos. 1:10 RSV). God is called the living God not only in contrast to lifeless idols, but also as creative Giver of, and Restorer to, life, and as one who is ever active. He is *ʾelōhîm chayyîm* in Josh. 3:18, 1 Sam. 17:26, Deut. 5:26, Jer. 10:10, 23:36; and in Aramaic in Dan. 6:20, 26. Ps. 42:2 speaks of thirsting for the living God *(ʾēl chai)*. The living God intervenes actively in the world and history. Humankind, unlike God, does not possess life as an *inherent* or *independent* possession. Without God, human beings face being cut off from "the land of the living." Ringgren is explicit. He says the attainment or loss of life "depends solely on the Word of God, so that there is constant need of the blessing in life" (*TDNT* 2:845). Jesus is quoting from Deut. 8:3 when he declares that life does not depend on bread alone but on the Word of God. Sheol portrays a cheerless, colorless, bloodless, shadowy existence, where one cannot even praise God (Isa. 38:18). God is the God of life, which humans cannot control.

(ii) **Life in the New Testament.** The NT follows the LXX in using *zōē* and *zēn* to represent the Hebrew *chayyîm* and *chayyāh* (roughly 150 times). It also uses other Greek terms for "life," namely, *bios* and *psuchē*. *Bios* usually means "everyday life," the condition of being alive, or "means of subsistence" (Mark 12:44, what the widow who donated a mite had to live on; Danker, BDAG 176-77). *Psuchē* usually refers to an individual's life, occasionally to "soul," and in Paul in the form of an adjective, *psuchikos,* to denote what is *not of the Holy Spirit. Zōē* may sometimes also overlap with this ("during your life," Phil. 1:20; cf. Luke 16:25; "life or death," 1 Cor. 3:22). More characteristically, however, *zōē* refers either to *quality* of life or to *eternal* life *(zōē aiōnios);* 1 John 5:20, "He [Christ] is the true God and eternal life"; John 5:26, "Just as the Father has life in himself, so he has granted the Son also to have life in himself"; John 12:50, "His commandment is eternal life"; 1 John 5:11-12, "God gave us eternal life, and this life is in his Son. Whoever has the Son has life; whoever does not have the Son of God does not have life"; John 6:35, "Jesus said to them, 'I am the bread of life,'" also 6:48; John 6:54, "Those who eat my flesh and drink my blood have eternal life" (Danker, BDAG 430-31).

The climax of the NT teaching on life comes in John. The prologue introduces the theme in 1:3-4, where the NRSV follows the Greek manuscript reading by translating "What has come into being in him was life" *(en autō zōē ēn).* R. Schnackenburg comments, "Light and life . . . form a closely aligned pair, life being the more basic" *(The Gospel according to St. John,* vol. 1 [New York: Herder and Herder, 1968], 241). In the body of the Gospel, Jesus declares: "I came that they may have life *(zōēn),* and have it abundantly" (10:10). He declares to Martha, "I am the resurrection and the life" (11:25). He says concerning his "sheep," "I give them eternal life, and they will never perish" (10:28). It is generally agreed that to enter the kingdom of God in the Synoptic Gospels "is the same as to 'have eternal life'" in John (E. K. Lee, *The Religious Thought of St. John* [London: SPCK, 1950], 198; see **Kingdom of God**). To appropriate his sovereign rule in one's life is the same as appropriating his gift of life. But life more decisively becomes a present possession in John, although "eternal" points to the gift of resurrection at the endtime. Like the OT, John can speak of living water (John 4:14), which denotes both running water and ever-fresh, ever-new water in limitless supply. Living bread in 6:25-59 stands in contrast to "the food that perishes" (v. 27, i.e., ordinary food), and especially in contrast to the "bread from heaven," namely, the manna God gave to Israel through Moses in the wilderness (vv. 32 and 58; cf. Exod. 16:4-20). Jesus contrasts the living bread of his flesh both with everyday food and with the manna that became putrefied normally after one day (Exod. 16:20).

Eternal life in the Fourth Gospel is bound up with "believing" in Jesus. Jesus declares, "Whoever believes has eternal life" (John 6:47). *Believing* in John usually approximates to Luther's sense of *appropriating.* To *appropriate,* or to *believe* in, his flesh and blood denotes *assimilation or identification.* The analogy with eucharistic experience is so close that most scholars see John 6:53-58 as a eucharistic allusion. However, G. R. Beasley-Murray is hesitant to see the eucharistic experience as the *primary* thrust in these verses, stressing the anti-Docetic theme ("eating," i.e., appropriating, the real, genuine bodiliness of the earthly life of Jesus; *John* [Nashville: Nelson, 1999], 96). This is also a key theme in 1 John (4:2). R. E. Brown points out that "flesh and blood" means "the whole man" in the OT and Hebrew idiom (*The Gospel according to John*, AB 1 [New York: Doubleday, 1966], 282). Brown also argues that Eucharist themes come to the fore in John 6:35-50 and 51-58 (284). The phrases "Bread of Life" and "living bread" are interchangeable, just as "living water" is equivalent to "water of life." John 17:3 states: "This is eternal life, that they may know you." Many regard the episode of the raising of Lazarus (11:1-44) as the climax of the Book of Signs (John 1–12) and perhaps the whole of the Gospel of John. The event is not strictly resurrection, for Lazarus presumably died again, and did not have a transformed body. But it is a parable of resurrection, and evokes the saying "I am the resurrection and the life" (11:25). F. V. Filson even argues that Lazarus was the author of the Fourth Gospel.

In the Synoptic Gospels, "life" often refers to the life of Jesus, as in "The Son of Man came . . . to give his life a ransom for many" (Mark 10:45). Yet "life" plays a part in the warnings of Jesus against materialism and greed: "One's life does not consist in the abundance of possessions" (Luke 12:15). Similarly, with more relations to Christ and the cross, "Those who find their life will lose it, and those who lose their life for my sake will find it" (Matt. 10:39). In the parable of the prodigal son, the younger son is "dead" when he is alienated and estranged, but "alive" when he returns (Luke 15:24). Eternal life does occur, for example, when Jesus is asked, "What must I do to inherit eternal life?" (Mark 10:17).

In Paul, the theological role of life can most easily be seen when we examine its semantic opposition with death. In Rom. 5:12 Paul states: "Death came through sin, and so death spread to all because all have sinned." He adds, "Death exercised dominion from Adam to Moses" (v. 14). "It was sin, working death in me" (7:13). He concludes, "Who will rescue me from this body of death?" (7:24). "Body of death" stands in contrast to "the Spirit of life in Christ Jesus [that] has set you free from . . . death" (8:2). Paul (or, according to some, a later summarizer of Paul) exclaims: "You were dead through the trespasses and sins" (Eph. 2:1), "but God . . . even when we were dead . . . made us alive together with Christ . . . and raised us up with him" (2:4-6). In Rom. 5:21 Paul parallels life and death: "Just as sin exercised dominion in death, so grace might also exercise dominion through justification leading to eternal life through Jesus Christ our Lord." Death, as Calvin comments, represents a condition in which human beings can do nothing to help themselves; hence only grace can reverse this situation of helplessness and hopelessness by giving life.

Although even the body may be dead, the Spirit of life can operate without the resources of humankind to raise it from the dead, first as the same Spirit that raised Christ from the dead (Rom. 8:10-11). Paul expresses this more generally: "If you sow to the Spirit, you will reap eternal life from the Spirit" (Gal. 6:8). Like writers in the OT, Paul speaks of "the word of life" (Phil. 2:16). Paul's logic sees *eternal life,* in the fullest sense, as dependent on resurrection that is derived from the resurrection of Christ. Yet in his fullest exposition of resurrection (1 Corinthians 15), he seems not to speak explicitly of *life,* except in 15:22, "In Christ shall all be made alive *(zōopoiēthēsontai)"* (RSV). Otherwise the Greek phrase seems to occur in Paul only in Rom. 5:21; Gal. 6:8; and perhaps 1 Tim. 1:16.

As we noted, the explicit phrase "eternal life" appears in the Synoptic Gospels occasionally with full force, but usually almost incidentally (Mark 9:43-45 and parallel; Matt. 25:46). In John, however, it is intimately related with "believing" *(pisteuō)* (John 3:15-16; 5:24; 6:47, 68; 10:28; 12:50). Sometimes this link is with "knowing" (17:3). In the rest of the NT, the OT phrase "the living God" is taken up four times in Hebrews (Heb. 3:12; 9:14; 10:31; 12:22). The book of Revelation speaks of "living creatures" (Rev. 4:6-9; Gk. *zōon*), and "living waters." It also uses the phrases "book of life" (3:5), "crown of life" (2:10), river of life (22:1), and water of life (22:17). (*See* **Eternity; Resurrection of the Dead; Time.**)

(iii) **Postbiblical Debates and Questions.** Christian theologians have seen life as a precious gift of God to be nurtured and lived in thankfulness. To be careless of life is to be indifferent to a gift of God. Secular philosophers vary radically in their estimate of life's value. A. Schopenhauer, in his *The World as Will* (1818 and 1844), saw humans as shaped by a will to life, which they had not chosen. Life turns against itself. He wrote: "We have not to rejoice, but rather to mourn at the existence of the world . . . non-existence would be preferable to its existence." Human life might just as well never have been. Schopenhauer influenced the atheism of F. Nietzsche. Thus W. Pannenberg sees humanity *without God* as "misery" (*see* **Sin: Historical**). C. Darrow sees life as an "awful joke." On the other hand, many Christian theologians see life not only as a gift from God to enjoy, but they often see a variety of grounds for its sacredness. Appeal is often made to "You shall not murder" (Exod. 20:13) in the Decalogue. Many argue that only God can give or terminate life as his gift. Many (for example, V. Lossky) argue from the uniqueness of the image of God. Some Christians and many secular thinkers argue on the basis of "a right to life," although the scope of "rights" is debatable. All theists argue for human worth and human value to God.

Reading: R. Bultmann and G. von Rad, *"Zaō, Zōē,"* in *TDNT* 2:833-75; G. M. Burge, in *NIDB* 3:655-61; C. H. Dodd, *The Interpretation of the Fourth Gospel* (Cambridge: CUP, 1933), 144-51, 333-45; H. Ringgren, *"Chāyāh, Chai,"* in *TDOT* 4:324-44.

Lightfoot, Joseph Barber

Joseph Barber Lightfoot (1828-1889) was one of "the Cambridge Triumvirate," as it was called, with Westcott and Hort. He was Lady Margaret's Professor of Divinity at Cambridge, and one of the leading revisers of the Revised Version from 1870 to 1880. He was appointed bishop of Durham in 1879. He was a first-class NT scholar, writing commentaries on Galatians, Philippians, and Colossians, with a well-known essay entitled "The Christian Ministry" in his commentary on Philippians. He also worked in patristics, publishing *The Apostolic Fathers* and volumes on Clement of Rome and Ignatius. He defended orthodox theology and, like Westcott and Hort, integrated Christian theology with his NT research and moderate biblical criticism.

Lindbeck, George

George Lindbeck (b. 1923) is an American theologian who is well known as the founder of "postliberal" theology and is involved in ecumenism. He was born in China and educated in Korea before entering Yale University for postgraduate work (B.D., 1946; Ph.D., 1955). He also studied medieval thought with Étienne Gilson in Toronto, and submitted his Ph.D. on Duns Scotus. He was an observer at Vatican II, and wrote *The Future of Roman Catholic Theology* (1970), *Infallibility* (1972), and *The Church in a Post-Liberal Age* (2003), but his reputation largely depends on *The Nature of Doctrine: Religion and Theology in a Post-Liberal Age* (London: SPCK, 1984).

Lindbeck begins this book with a discussion of ecumenism and "growing dissatisfaction with the usual ways of thinking about those norms of communal belief and action which are generally spoken of as the doctrine or dogmas of churches" (7). He adds, "All the standard theological approaches are unhelpful" (7), which is a huge claim for a book of 138 pages. He calls for a "postliberal" approach, which involves a new conceptualization and new language. Perhaps because of his ecumenical concern, his argument "is designed to be doctrinally and religiously neutral" (10). There is indeed some precedent in linguistic philosophy for dissolving confusions by paying closer attention to language; we need think only of the later Wittgenstein and of Gilbert Ryle in the context of other problems. Lindbeck is right to focus on sentences that are "theory laden" (11), and also on historical context (12).

In his first main chapter Lindbeck distinguishes between theologians who base their theology largely on the use of "informative propositions"; those who stress experience by "experiential-expressive" religious utterances; and those who seek to combine these approaches (16). "Propositionalists" view doctrine as true or false; experientialists may retain often the same meaning; but the third approach is "weak in criteria" (17). His aim is commendable: to avoid "insoluble collision" while offering criteria of truth. Whether there is overgeneralization in chapter 2 about "a common core experience" (31), others must judge. His "cultural-linguistic alternative" (32) tries to build on Wittgenstein's "language games," which stress the relation between language uses and forms of life. This looks at first promising, although it might have been developed further. Where he is right is his diagnosis of "anomalies" that arise in applying old conceptual schemes to new contexts (39). In Luther, for example, the "Tower experience" makes possible a variety of fresh symbolisms (39).

In chapter 3 Lindbeck examines "unsurpassable truth," which can be criticized if seen in rationalist terms (51). The concept depends on dialogue. But "classical cognitivists" are not convincing in claims about "a general revelation" (57). Lindbeck turns to Wittgenstein's analogy of a child learning a language. In spite of critiques of "Hellenization," this at least provided a stretching of language. A "cultural linguistic," he argues, is compatible with "unsurpassability" (69). In chapter 4 he examines "theories of doctrine" as the critical text for the theological and ecumenical usefulness of cultural-linguistic approaches to religion (73). Lindbeck considers "creedless" Christianity artificial, and notes that controversy becomes a driving force for explicit doctrine, as we see in Luther's life. Faithfulness to doctrine does not mean simply repetition, but following these directives. Classical doctrines of the Trinity and Christology seem "unconditionally permanent" (87 and 92). In chapter 5, however, their "irreversibility" depends on the "irreversibility of the conditioning circumstances." Lindbeck adds, "That is, on Greek philosophy" (92). Some may doubt such an unqualified statement. Moreover, the claim that things may be "true in other religions" may suggest an overflexible view of truth. Some may think that Lindbeck may be overreliant on Kuhn's notion of "paradigm" (95) as determinative of research, questions, and language.

In the final chapter Lindbeck is undoubtedly correct in observing, "Systematic or dogmatic theology has generally been thought of . . . as especially concerned with faithfulness, practical theology with applicability, and foundational or apologetic theology with intelligibility, but each of these concerns is present in every theological discipline" (112). Postliberalism, he argues, overcomes polarization between tradition and innovation. He seeks to give attention to "the interpretative framework within which believers seek their lives and understand reality" (117). He also warns us against inserting *extra*biblical material into a biblical world. He takes up with fellow Yale theologian Hans Frei about the Bible's "history-like" nature (122).

Much of Lindbeck's material is creative, innovative, and useful. What is surprising is why so many, notably in America, seem to accord a book of 140 pages the status of an almost guru-like volume, as if it changed everything in theology. Most of the proposals are useful rather than epoch-making. Perhaps it seemed more revolutionary in 1984. Most theologians admire the work. But its hugely ambitious claims for novelty should perhaps be treated with caution. However, it rightly separates postliberalism from liberalism; majors in methodology, and problems of concepts and language; and contributes to ecumenism.

Reading: P. De Hart, *The Trial of the Witnesses: The Rise and Decline of Postliberal Theology* (Oxford: Blackwell, 2006); George Lindbeck, *The Nature of Doctrine* (London: SPCK, 1984); George Lindbeck, *The Church in a Postliberal Age* (Grand Rapids: Eerdmans, 2003); A. Vidu, *Postliberal Theological Method: A Critical Study* (Milton Keynes, U.K., and Colorado Springs: Paternoster, 2007).

Liturgy, Liturgical Movement

"Liturgy" derives from Greek *laos*, "people," and *ergon*, "work," which combine to form *leitourgia*, "public service," or service in general. In Luke 1:23 it is used of Zechariah's service as a priest; in Heb. 8:6 of the ministry or high-priestly office of Jesus; and in Heb. 9:21 of the vessels used in worship. Thus "public worship" or "public service" constitutes the earliest Christian meaning. It soon came to denote either public worship or the Lord's Supper. From the *Didachē* onward it began to denote a relatively focused form, or a form with fixed elements. In about 150 Justin tells us that the Lord's Supper, or Eucharist, was celebrated every Sunday, with a reading from Scripture, a sermon by the president, and intercessions with a kiss of peace, after which the bread and wine were brought to the president. The president prayed a prayer of thanksgiving over them, and after the administration of the bread and the wine a collection for the needy was taken (Justin, *First Apology* 65; *ANF* 1:185). Hippolytus (c. 210) wrote the *Apostolic Tradition*, which set out the text of a eucharistic prayer similar to Justin, and also the consecration or ordination of bishops. But the original text has been lost, and there is now only a fifth-century Latin version. Fourth-century liturgies come from Egypt, Antioch, and Syria.

The Liturgical Movement is a modern phenomenon. In the nineteenth century the Roman Catholic Church in France sought to recover an authentic Gregorian liturgy. But the Liturgical Movement as such began in the twentieth century. It sought to rediscover and renew liturgy as a pastoral aid. Jean Daniélou and Louis Bouyer are often regarded as contributors. The Roman Catholic Church and Anglo-Catholics stressed the centrality of the Eucharist. The climax in the Church of England was the now largely outmoded *Alternative Service Book* (1980). This stressed intelligibility, participation, and simplicity. But by the time of *Common Worship* (2000), this 1980 revision was recognized as too reductive in both language and theology, veering at times toward what some called "the cheap and cheerful." However, the Liturgical Movement deeply influenced Vatican II for good, which stressed greater participation of the laity and vernacular language. (*See also* **Lord's Supper.**)

Locke, John

John Locke (1632-1704) was one of the three classic British empiricists, along with Berkeley and Hume. He was born in Somerset and educated at Christ Church, Oxford. Philosophically he was initially influenced by Descartes. His major work was *An Essay concerning Human Understanding* (1690). However, he also wrote on political philosophy in *The Letter on Toleration* (1689) and *Two Treatises on Government* (also 1689), in which he defended strongly free inquiry. Parts 1, 2, and 3 of *An Essay concerning Human Understanding* constitute basic texts on empiricism, and have traditionally been most valued. But D. J. O'Connor and N. Wolterstorff have more recently called attention to part 4 on reasonableness and "entitled" belief (Wolterstorff, *John Locke and the Ethics of Belief* [Cambridge: CUP, 1996]). Locke also wrote notes on several epistles of Saint Paul.

Like Socrates and Plato, Locke begins his *Essay* by distinguishing human opinion from human knowledge, and by exploring grounds and degrees of belief (1.1.1). We need to know the powers and limits of our minds. He attacks the rationalist and Platonist notion of "innate ideas," which Descartes advocated. He writes, "Consent proves nothing innate" (2.3). Book 2, "Of Ideas," argues, "All Ideas come from Sensation or Reflection" (2.1.2). We "experience" ideas as they enter our minds through one or more of the five senses. Reflection may combine "simple" ideas into complex ones. This led to his famous distinction between "primary qualities," such as solidity and extension, and "secondary qualities," such as colors, sounds, and tastes. These secondary qualities may be perceived differently by different people, as the sense-data streams into the mind, which is otherwise like a "blank sheet" *(tabula rasa)*. Toward the end of book 2 he considers personal identity. In his famous analogy or parable of the soul of a prince and the body of a cobbler, he compares the introspective identity of the prince with the public perception of the cobbler (*see* **Ricoeur, Paul**, for a critique). This draws on Descartes's dualism, which cannot give an adequate account of ideas, as Ricoeur later showed.

In part 3.1-11 a modified dualism characterizes Locke's philosophy of language. "Words" constitute "sensible marks of ideas" (3.2.1). He gives an "ideational" account of language. "Ideas" are merely a middle term in what is basically a theory of reference. Part 4 is different in tone. It concerns reasonable belief. Wolterstorff urges, "Locke was the first to develop with profundity . . . that we are all responsible for our believing" (*John Locke*, xiv). Reason gives a discovery of certainty; faith depends on the credit of the proposer, as representing God (4.18.2). Locke attacks "enthusiasm," because mere intensity of conviction is no guarantee of truth. He concludes, "Reason must be our last judge and guide in everything" (4.19.14).

Locke pleaded for religious freedom for all except Roman Catholics and atheists. He supported the national church and the Whig Revolution of 1688. He wrote *The Reasonableness of Christianity* in 1695, and *Discourse on Miracles*. Locke's "classical liberalism," as it sometimes is called, influenced the Declaration of Independence in the USA (1776) and Thomas Jefferson, and less directly Voltaire and Rousseau.

Logical Positivism
Logical positivism is associated with the philosophy of A. J. Ayer (1910-1989), and especially his book *Language, Truth, and Logic* (London: Gollance, 1936; 2nd ed. 1946), which he originally published at the age of twenty-six. He later became Wykeham Professor of Logic in the University of Oxford (1959-1978). But critics such as H. J. Paton called it "positivism in linguistic dress." Ayer's positivism had a background in the so-called Vienna Circle of Rudolf Carnap, Moritz Schlick, and others. Some also trace it to Wittgenstein's earlier logical atomism, but this is to misunderstand Wittgenstein's earlier work, which was primarily concerned with *logical* relations. After 1933 the center of the positivist movement changed from Austria and Germany to the United States and England. In the USA it was combined with a pragmatic approach, especially in the philosophy of C. Morris and W. V. Quine.

The distinctive focus of the first edition of *Language, Truth, and Logic* was the criterion of verification. Ayer maintained that only two categories of propositions were meaningful: either they were logically analytical statements, or tautologies (such as "bodies are extended," or "a triangle has three sides"); or they are capable of being verified by sense observation, that is, they could be seen, heard, touched, or verified by other senses. Metaphysics, ethics, and religion and theology failed such a criterion of meaning, and were therefore said to be "non-sense." But critics asked: What is the logical status of the principle of verification? It is neither tautologous nor verifiable. Hence H. J. Paton and J. L. Evans compared it to "a weighing machine trying to weigh itself" (Paton, *The Modern Predicament* [London: Allen and Unwin, 1955], 40).

In his second edition Ayer modified his claims to what could be "verified in principle," such as, at the time, "There are mountains on the moon." This could be verified by observation in principle if rockets could travel far enough. The other modification was to extend or to modify verification *to falsification*. How could the denial of a proposition be verified? This gave rise to the famous parable of the invisible gardener. What practical difference would it make if someone claimed that a plot of land was regularly tended by a gardener who was invisible, intangible, silent, odorless, and so on? The argument was often applied to the existence of God, although critics claimed that we draw influences from divine activity. Yet the main criticism remains. Ayer had purported to be formulating a theory of language and meaning. Yet it proved to constitute simply old-fashioned positivism or materialism, clothed in the disguise of a linguistic theory. Relatively few philosophers would question the status of language about anything except the material world, including ethics, art, poetry, and so much more. After the 1960s the theory was generally regarded as old-fashioned, in the light of more sophisticated theories of language. In Christian theism much clarification was achieved by such writers as Ian Ramsey, Basil Mitchell, Eric Mascall, F. Ferré, and many others.

Lombard, Peter

Peter Lombard (c. 1100-1160) was especially well known for his *Sentences* (1148-1151) and for his exegetical work. He was born in Lombardy and studied in Rheims and Paris. In 1159 he became bishop of Paris. The *Sentences* was a collection of sources that addressed especially creation, the Trinity, redemption, sin, grace, and other doctrines. Bernard of Clairvaux regarded him highly, and his *Sentences* was very influential in the Middle Ages. He was a sober and careful exegete, who consciously prevented his doctrine from overinfluencing his exegesis. Lombard cited various Fathers, especially the two great Western Fathers, Ambrose and Augustine. He wrote his commentaries in the light of other commentaries before him. Like Abelard, he stressed the love of God in his exposition of the atonement. His method of producing commentaries on biblical passages was largely overtaken by Calvin.

Lonergan, Bernard

Bernard Lonergan (1904-1984) was born in Quebec, was ordained a priest in 1936, and studied in Montreal. His four years of study in Rome, however, proved more formative for him, as he developed an interest in the theory of cognition, metaphysics, and history. During the early part of his career he was virtually unknown to the general public. But in 1957 he published the first of his two greatest works, *Insight* (1957; New York: Harper and Row, 1978). This confronted a range of problems in the theory of knowledge and understanding. He rejected straightforward representational realism as unduly simplistic. But he also argued that a "residue" of reality lies beyond the empirical realm. Reality is not constructed entirely by the mind, but the mind nevertheless acts as "sensing, perceiving, imagining, inquiring, understanding, formulating, reflecting, and affirming" (*Insight*, 319). Many thinkers call this mediating position critical realism. In Lonergan's view, "reasonableness and groundedness" are essential to knowing; "reasonableness discovers groundedness in its reflective grasp of the unconditioned" (323). This calls for "balanced judgement." "Fact" thus combines the concreteness of experience with "accurate intelligence and the absoluteness of rational judgement" (331). He contrasts this with Kant's view, and concludes, "Concepts and theories ... have to be checked against the data" (340). Lonergan cannot be accused of relativism.

Lonergan's second major work, *Method in Theology* (London: DLT, 1971), has been described as the fruit of a lifetime of study and reflection on human cognitive processes. He sought a transcultural framework and transcendental method for his approach. The tasks are successive, but each "sublates" the previous task or level. The human mind, he argued, operates at four levels: observation, intellectual reflection, judgment of fact, and decision or judgment of value (15, 120-21). Similarly, in exegesis there are three operations: "(1) understanding the text; (2) judging how correct one's understanding of the text might be; (3) stating what one judges to be correct" (155). This is "embedded in the problem of hermeneutics" (155). Initial understanding may be inadequate, but a "self-correcting process of learning may change one's outlook" (161). This is very near to the process of the hermeneutical circle. Throughout the process this requires self-transcendence: it is not simply an empirical operation. Research, he claimed, made textual data available; this must be followed by interpretation. Finally, history discerns a wider social context. We may then arrive at "foundations" for the construction of systematic theology and doctrines. Lonergan gives much space to the concept and study of history (175-234). This leads on to the concept of "horizon," which denotes a perspectival viewpoint that can expand and be corrected. He wrote, "Differences in horizon may be complementary, or genetic, or dialectical. Workmen, foremen, supervisors ..., managers, doctors, lawyers, professors, have different interests. They live in a sense in different worlds. Each is quite familiar with his own world. But each also knows about the others.... Many horizons in some measure include one another.... What in one is found intelligible, in another is unintelligible" (236). This begins to look like Wittgenstein's language games. But hermeneutics explores the art of bringing them into communicative interaction.

The first three chapters of this book seek to apply the foregoing to doctrines and systematic theology, as well as to discovery. Clearly Lonergan's work is extraordinarily complex, and this brief survey cannot do justice to it. Just as Thomas Aquinas drew upon Aristotle to meet many of the issues of his day, so Lonergan sought to use multiple resources, including the theory of mind, cognitive studies, and hermeneutics, to address the difficulties that confront modern humankind. Today there are Web sites, newsletters, and conferences dedicated to his thought. He is sometimes associated with K. Rahner as a "transcendental Thomist." He has also produced many other works. (*See also* **Critical Realism**.)

Reading: F. E. Crowe, *Lonergan* (London: Geoffrey Chapman, 1992); Bernard Lonergan, *Method in Theology* (London: DLT, 1972); Bernard Lonergan, *Insight* (New York: Harper and Row, 1978); P. McShane, ed., *Foundations of Theology* (Notre Dame, Ind.: University of Notre Dame Press, 1972); J. Stebbins, *The Divine Initiative* (Toronto: University of Toronto Press, 1996).

Lord's Supper
(i) **In the Bible.** Lord's Supper, Eucharist, and Holy Communion, the three names for this sacrament, are all used in the NT. Paul speaks of the Lord's Supper in 1 Cor. 11:20 (Gk. *Kuriakon deipnon*); the word "communion" or "fellowship" *(koinōnia)* occurs in 1 Cor. 10:16; Eucharist reflects the Greek word for "thanksgiving" *(eucharistēsas),* which features in 1 Cor. 11:24 and in the Synoptic Gospels. It is an unfortunate accident that these tend to be associated with particular church traditions: respectively, evangelical or Reformed; Anglican; and "High Church" or Catholic. The word "mass" is postbiblical, drawn from the Latin at the end of the Roman Catholic liturgy in the dismissal, literally *missa. Deipnon* is not necessarily related to timing; it may denote the main meal of the day.

The Lord's Supper has the function of anchoring the Christian faith and life-experience in *the death and resurrection of Christ,* much as baptism also does. In the Lord's Supper or Holy Communion the whole congregation proclaims the death and resurrection of Christ (1 Cor. 11:26), both corporately and individually. It is also a bond of union (1 Cor. 10:16-17), in which Christians pledge themselves to one another as "one body" and to God in Christ. The breaking of the bread and pouring out of the wine are a "memory" (*anamnēsis,* which is more than intellectual) of the cross; the receiving of the bread and wine is an appropriation of God's pledge of grace "for me." The sign, symbol, or sacrament constitutes a promised, visible, tangible, and audible proclamation of Christian dependence in Christ's cross and resurrection to receive life and nurture or "preserving" or "feeding." It is a participatory act in the dramatic events of the passion, cross, and resurrection. It is public, not private, as a public witness and proclamation of God's grace and personal reception of it.

Some scholars, especially Hans Lietzmann, misleadingly draw a sharp line between two forms or types of the Lord's Supper in the early church. In 1926 Lietzmann proposed that the liturgy of Hippolytus at Rome derived from "the Pauline type" (*Mass and Lord's Supper* [London: Brill, 1979], esp. 172-86). This stood in contrast to the "Jerusalem type," which allegedly reflected the more joyous mood of fellowship meals, and was a development of the Jewish fellowship meal or *Chaburah*. E. Lohmeyer and the Anglo-Catholic writers Gregory Dix and A. B. J. Higgins developed and modified Lietzmann's theory as a contrast between a "Galilean" type and a "Pauline" type (Higgins, *The Lord's Supper in the New Testament* [London: SCM, 1952], 13-63). This view had considerable influence in the middle years of the twentieth century. But it then received devastating criticisms from J. Jeremias (*The Eucharistic Words of Jesus* [London: SCM, 1966]), O. Hofius, C. F. D. Moule, and I. H. Marshall. Jeremias concludes, "Unfortunately ... we have ... a conjecture for which there is absolutely no evidence" (30; cf. 16-36). Moule and others embrace Jeremias's view that "every meal had religious solemnity, because of the grace that was always said." Marshall entirely endorses the criticisms of Lietzmann and Lohmeyer (*Last Supper and Lord's Supper* [Grand Rapids: Eerdmans, 1980], 108-23).

Jeremias, F. J. Leenhardt, and others strongly support the context of the *Passover* (Exod. 12:1-51), as Mark 14:14, Matt. 26:12-18, and Luke 22:7-13, 15 indicate, for the Last Supper. In the *seder*, or Jewish liturgy, of the Passover, those who participate in the Passover meal in effect "relive" the dramatic narrative of the Passover. The Mishnah declares: "In every generation a man must regard himself as if he came forth himself out of Egypt" (*m. Pesahim* 10:5; Eng. conveniently in H. Danby, ed., *The Mishnah* [Oxford: OUP, 1933], 150-51). The *seder* begins with a blessing on God, or directed to God, which is equivalent to a "grace" at table. A later blessing is also a blessing on God, which some English versions mistranslate as "blessed it" (the bread) when this is foreign to the text. To regard this as "consecrating the bread" is an anachronism reflecting later church practice. The haggadah (Jewish narrative) declares, "This is the bread of affliction that forefathers ate in the land of Egypt." Leenhardt notes the surprise of the disciples when Jesus replaced this with "This is my body" (Leenhardt, "The Relationship Established by Christ," in *Essays on the Lord's Supper*, ed. O. Cullmann and F. J. Leenhardt [London: Lutterworth, 1958], 39-43). The Jewish haggadah repeats this principle: "It is a man's duty to regard himself as if *he* had gone forth from Egypt.... Because of what the Lord did to *me* (singular) when I came forth from Egypt ... Not our fathers only ... but us also ... 'And he brought *us* out'" (C. Roth, ed., *The Haggadah* [in Hebrew and English] [London: Soncino Press, 1934], 36). The Lord's Supper, like the Passover, involves both "us" and "me": it is both corporate and individual, and deeply self-involving or participatory.

Hence *"remembrance"* (Gk. *anamnēsis*) is more than simply an intellectual calling to mind in Luke 22:19 and 1 Cor. 11:24. The Greek reflects the Hebrew *zēker* and *zākar*. Virtually all scholars agree on this point. But *to what extent* it is more than subjective is highly debatable. Some argue that it means "to make present."

But this, if taken too far, would undermine the *once-for-all* nature of the cross, represented by the Greek *ephapax* (Heb. 7:27; 9:28). The most serious *mistake* is to regard this as an actual *repetition*. Many trace this mistake in part to the exaggerated claims by the "myth and ritual" school of A. Bentzen, S. H. Hooke, and probably S. Mowinckel, who applied "cultic reenactment" to the Lord's Supper. A number of writers seek a middle way between the two extremes, arguing that the death of Jesus Christ becomes "contemporary" or "self-involving," not by bringing it into the present, but by enabling the communicant to participate dramatically in the past event. The black spiritual "Were You There When They Crucified My Lord?" seems to sum up their position very well. The ARCIC (Anglican–Roman Catholic International Commission) seems to express this in its Windsor Agreed Statement of 1971. It declares: "Christ's redeeming death and resurrection took place once and for all in history ... the one, perfect, and sufficient sacrifice for the sins of the world" (II, 5). The statement continues: "There can be no repetition of, or addition to, what was thus accomplished once for all by Christ." It also uses the language of "effective signs." This closely matched Anglican doctrine and liturgy. On the other hand, Vatican II reaffirms transubstantiation, and does not seem to endorse the Agreed Statement.

We must recall that the Passover operates in a *covenant* context. Moreover, Luke recounts the words of Jesus at the Last Supper: "This cup ... is the new covenant in my blood" (Luke 22:20). Similarly Paul's older tradition repeats: "This cup is the new covenant in my blood." In the Lord's Supper God confirms his covenant promise and pledge. The theme of the *bond of unity* is also reinforced by Paul's reaction to the divisions or splits *(schismata)* at Corinth (1 Cor. 11:28-34). This has become vivid through the discovery of large villas near the suburbs of Corinth at Anaploga, where Roman dining customs applied. Early arrivals and the friends of the host or household would have dined on couches in the privileged reception room (the *triclinium*) with first-class food and wine, while slaves and late-comers ate and drank in the hall (the *atrium*) on second-class food and wine. This is why Paul claims that a formal dinner undermines the purpose of the Lord's Supper, by contradicting the unity of the church. He urges participants to eat and drink at home (11:33-34). More than one major Roman author (including Tacitus) witness to the divisive effects of these Roman dining customs.

(ii) **In the History of the Church.** First, we consider the patristic church. One of the earliest accounts of the Eucharist in postbiblical times comes in the *Didachē* (probably late first century). It reads, "Hold Eucharist thus: first, concerning the cup, 'We give thanks to thee our Father, for the Holy Vine of David ... made known to us through Jesus ...' And concerning the broken Bread, 'We give thanks for the life and knowledge ... through Jesus. ... As the broken bread was scattered upon the mountains, but was brought together and became one, so let the Church be gathered together from the ends of the earth into thy kingdom, for Thine is the glory" (9.1-4). In his *First Apology* (c. 150), Justin recounts a regular administration that includes "hearty prayers in common" and the kiss of peace; "there is then brought to the President of the Brethren *(tō proestōti tōn adelphōn)* bread and a cup of wine mixed with water, and taking them [the President] gives praise and glory to the Father . . . through the name of the Son and of the Holy Spirit. . . . All the people express their assent by saying Amen." The deacon then distributes the bread and wine "to each of those present to partake" (*First Apology* 65; *ANF* 1:185). Only those who are believers and have been baptized are "allowed to partake" (66), and the Words of Institution are repeated or recited, as in the NT. Many argue that Hippolytus of Rome (c. 170–c. 236) offers a valuable source. He may well have composed *The Apostolic Tradition* (c. 215), although much of the manuscript is lost. He includes two Eucharists in 21.27-33, which in broad terms appear to follow Justin. The Words of Institution are called the *anaphora*. Later developments emerge in the *Apostolic Constitutions* (c. 350-380), probably reflecting the Syrian Church. This offers detailed descriptions of liturgy, including the place of women; the kiss of peace; biblical readings of the OT, the Epistles, and the Gospels; an exhortation from the bishop or one of the presbyters; praying looking toward the east; and the deacon "ministering the Lord's body with fear." The liturgy includes an *epiklēsis*, or invocation of the Spirit on the elements. The administration of the elements appears twice: "Let every rank partake of the Lord's body and precious blood . . . and approach with reverence and holy fear" (*Apostolic Constitutions*, sect. 7; *ANF* 7:421). After the Council of Nicaea the Eucharist is further expanded. The liturgy of Basil is used by the Coptic Church today.

Second, we consider the four major views of the medieval and Reformation church. These emerged between the thirteenth and sixteenth centuries. (a) Thomas Aquinas (1225-1274) formulated a doctrine of transubstantiation, drawing especially on Aristotle's distinction between substance and accidents. An object might be said to have a substance or essence, which consists of its underlying identity *(substantia)*, in which contingent, visible, and tangible qualities *(accidentia)* inhere. Aquinas states: "The complete substance *(tota substantia)* of the bread is converted into the complete substance of Christ's body" (*Su Th* 3a, qu. 75, art. 4, reply; Eng. Blackfriars ed., 58:73). But the visible and tangible perception does not appear in this way. "Accidents" are the everyday qualities that we may perceive by sight, sound, taste, or any of the five senses. Thus, Aquinas asserts, "it is through the accidents that we judge the substance" (qu. 75, art. 5, 2). "The accidents of the bread . . . are the object of our self-knowledge" *(subjecta sensibus;* art. 5, 3). The bread retains accidents but loses its substance when it has been consecrated; the *body of Christ retains its substance* but appears under the *accidents* of *bread and wine*. Hence: "Our Catholic Faith makes it absolutely necessary to profess that the whole Christ is in this sacrament" (qu. 76, art. 1, reply; Eng. 58:95). The Council of Trent (1551) endorsed this doctrine of transubstantiation as Catholic doctrine. Vatican II (1962-1965) appears also to embrace it. It reads: "Even in the reserved sacrament he [Christ] is to be adored because he is substantially present through the conversion of bread and wine, which as the Council of Trent tells us, is most aptly called transubstantiation" (*Sacred Liturgy:* "Sacred Instructions on the Worship of the Eucharistic Mystery," May 1967, Eng. in A. P. Flannery, ed., *Documents of Vatican II* [Grand Rapids, Eerdmans, 1975], 104).

(b) Martin Luther (1483-1546) advocated a view that must be distinguished on one side from that of Aquinas, and on the other from that of John Calvin and Ulrich Zwingli. Like Aquinas, and unlike Zwingli, he insists that in the Lord's Supper the bread and wine become "the real flesh and blood of Christ," but like Zwingli and Calvin, he argues that they remain "real bread and real wine" (*On the Babylonian Captivity of the Church* [1520], in *Luther's Primary Works,* ed. H. Wace and C. Buchheim [London: Murray, 1883], 147-48). Luther believed that he did not in principle dissent from Rome and from Aquinas about the real presence of Christ in the Eucharist, but he violently disagreed with their descriptions of the process, which depended on the pagan philosopher Aristotle, rather than Scripture alone. Luther's criticisms of Zwingli, his fellow Reformer, were much sharper. He declared, "It is . . . the devil who now assails us through the fanatics. . . . They would like to make mere bread and wine a symbol and memorial supper. . . . They will not accept that the Lord's body and blood are present, even though the plain, clear words stand right there: 'eat, this is my body.' . . . They say 'the word *is* must mean the same as *represents*,' as Zwingli writes. . . . There is no proof of representation . . . in the passage that they quote" (*LW* 37:18-19).

(c) John Calvin (1509-1564) insisted on the parity of word and sacrament as a means of grace. However, he comments, "In regard to our sacraments, they present Christ the more clearly to us . . . the Supper of the Eucharist [testifies] that we are redeemed" (*Institutes* 4.14.22; Beveridge, 2:507). Christ "gives himself" both in the sacrament and in the word of the gospel (4.17.5). He avoids any crude, localized idea of the presence of Christ, as if this were tied to the elements of bread and wine, but refuses to exclude the notion that *Christ* himself is present, in contrast to the mediation of the Word by the Holy Spirit (4.17.7). He unreservedly *attacks transubstantiation.* Such a view, he claims, renders the bread "but a mask" on the basis of a "fictitious" change in the elements (4.17.13-14). This view implies that Christ is "transmitted by the bodily mouth into the belly. . . . The cause of this brutish imagination was, that consecration had the same effect with them as magical incantation" (4.17.15; Beveridge, 2:567). Whereas Luther regarded transubstantiation as too specific and philosophical, Calvin regarded it as downright false, offensive, and the work of the devil. In the *Genevan Confession* (1536) Calvin expounds the Lord's Supper as "spiritual communion," in contrast to "the mass of the Pope . . . a reprobate and diabolical ordinance . . . condemned by God" (in J. K. S. Reid, ed., *Calvin: Theological Treatises* [London: SCM, 1954], 30). In the *German Catechism* Calvin is more positive: the Lord's Supper brings "promises which he . . . gives us and at the same time implements" (in Reid, 137).

(d) Zwingli explicitly distinguishes "three groups" in their approach to the Lord's Supper. These are Catholics, Lutherans, and Calvinists (*On the Lord's Sup-*

per, in *Zwingli and Bullinger,* ed. G. W. Bromiley [Philadelphia: Fortress; London: SCM, 1953], 188; cf. 185-238). He rejects all these as "falsehoods," because in his view they go beyond Scripture. This is the charge that especially provoked Luther. Zwingli compares "This is my body" with "I am the vine" (John 15:1). "Is" and "am," he asserts, are used in a figurative, symbolic, or metaphorical way (*On the Lord's Supper,* 191-93). His strongest point, perhaps, is that the sacrament of the Lord's Supper constitutes a *sign;* but a sign does not convey the *reality* to which it points. His article 3 examines metaphorical or symbolic language further, including "Behold, the Lamb of God" (John 1:29), while article 4 addresses possible counterarguments to his view.

Anglican doctrine has long embraced a spectrum of views with traditions that go back respectively to Luther, Calvin, and Zwingli. This is striking if we compare the first *Book of Common Prayer* of 1549 with the more "Protestant" or "Low Church" revisions of 1552, and then the "compromise" or synthesis of 1662. Peter Martyr and Martin Bucer influenced the 1552 version, while Thomas Cranmer influenced both the 1549 and 1552 versions. The 1552 edition removed mass vestments; prayers for the dead; kissing the Gospels; the use of "Hail Mary!"; ablutions before administration; and references to the merits of saints (*The First and Second Prayer Books of Edward VI* [New York: Dutton; London: Dent, 1910). The 1549 edition came largely from Sarum Rite. This version, however, removed the *epiklēsis* and introduced the Black Rubric. The Black Rubric explained that the posture of kneeling was not to be understood as worshiping the sacrament, but was done "to acknowledge gratefully the benefits of Christ."

The difficulty of assessing Anglican or Church of England doctrine is that in many quarters it is still in process of development, although many would question this by appealing to the Prayer of Consecration in the 1662 prayer book and to the Thirty-nine Articles. Under Elizabeth I and her 1559 prayer book (the third), Richard Hooker affirmed "the real presence of Christ," but qualified this, asserting that this presence was "not therefore to be sought in the sacrament, but in the worthy receiving of the sacrament" (*The Works of Mr. Richard Hooker,* 3 vols. [Oxford: Clarendon, 1888], 2:353). Until the mid–nineteenth century the Church of England position approximated to that of Calvin, but with the Tractarian Movement (or Anglo-Catholic tradition) a spectrum has emerged between Luther's view and that of Calvin or even Zwingli, perhaps by way of reaction against Tractarian theology. Today's *Common Worship* largely mirrors the 1662 prayer book in doctrine, and the 1662 prayer book retains its authority, supplemented by some modern, largely optional variants. Most denominational traditions in the Western Church can trace their roots to one of the three Protestant figures, or even a combination of them. As noted above, the Windsor Agreed Statement of 1971 by ARCIC suggests a growing together of Catholic and Protestant traditions, especially in the light of biblical research on the Passover and *anamnēsis.* However, Vatican II remains at present opposed to advance. (*See also Anamnēsis;* Sacraments.)

Reading: O. Cullmann and F. J. Leenhardt, eds., *Essays on the Lord's Supper* (London: Lutterworth, 1958); K. W. Irwin, *Models of the Eucharist* (New York: Paulist, 2005); J. Jeremias, *The Eucharistic Words of Jesus* (London: SCM, 1966); I. H. Marshall, *Last Supper and Lord's Supper* (Grand Rapids: Eerdmans, 1980); B. F. Meyer, ed., *One Loaf, One Cup* (Mason, Ga.: Mercer University Press, 1988); sources in Luther, Calvin, and Zwingli, often found in LCC.

Lossky, Vladimir

Among the most influential and important Russian Orthodox theologians of the twentieth century, Vladimir Lossky (1903-1958) studied at the University of St. Petersburg. After he was expelled by the Soviet government in 1922, he worked first in Prague and then in France, in the Sorbonne; he remained in France until his death. He opposed the doctrine of Bulgakov, and was especially well known for his work on deification, the image of God, and the mysticism of Meister Eckhart. He cofounded the Brotherhood of St. Photius in Paris. At least three of his works are in English translation: *The Mystical Theology of the Eastern Church* (New York: St. Vladimir's Seminary Press, 1976; Cambridge: James Clarke, 1991); *Orthodox Theology* (New York: Crestwood, 1959; New York: St. Vladimir's Seminary Press, 1997); and *The Image and Likeness of God* (London and Oxford: Mowbray, 1974).

On the image of God, Lossky argues, "Individual and person mean opposite things" (*Mystical Theology*, 121). "Individual" belongs to the empirical realm of biology, or the chain of cause and effect, unlike "person." As individual the self is cut off from the other. The individual is the self-contained narcissistic ego of Descartes. But when by grace the image of God is restored, the self may relate to the other. Then the "person" can mirror the nature of God as self-giving, loving, and engaged with others. On deification, Lossky regularly quotes Athanasius, Irenaeus, and Gregory of Nazianzus: "God made himself man, that man might become God" (*Image and Likeness*, 97). "Creation in the ... likeness of God," Lossky argues, "implies the idea of participation in the divine being, of communion with God" (*Mystical Theology*, 118). The transition to bearing the image of God fully as a person is due entirely to grace, not to some inherent natural quality in humankind.

The Western Church may have underestimated Lossky for a number of years. His influence appears to be growing once again. (*See also* **Deification; Image of God**.)

Love

Heb. *'āhēb,* verb, and *'ahăbāh,* noun; Gk. *agapaō,* verb, *agapē,* noun, but not only these words. See BDB 12-13; *TDNT* 1:31-55 (E. Stauffer); and BDAG 5-7. In the OT *'āhēb* is the main word for "to love," translated by *agapaō* in the LXX, and only seldom by *phileō.* G. Quell calls it "basically a spontaneous feeling which impels to self-giving" (*TDNT* 1:22). It is used of people loving God with all one's heart and soul and strength (Deut. 6:5; 13:4). It may be used of humans' love toward humans in Jeremiah, Hosea, and Ezekiel. In Hos. 3:1 it is a euphemism for the sexual act. The verb is used thirty-two times of God's love (*NIDOTTE* 1:278), of which twelve occur in Deuteronomy and five in Hosea. In Hos. 3:1 the command "Go love a woman who has a lover and is an adulteress" is explained by "just as the LORD loves the people of Israel." In Deut. 7:7-11 the context is the utter lack of attraction, merit, or desert on Israel's part that led to God's love for Israel in sovereign elective grace, and his utter faithfulness to Israel. There love is an important basis for the covenant. Hosea's use of love to express his understanding of God "reflects the original meaning of *'ahăbāh* as love between husband and wife" (*TDNT* 1:113). God's love for Israel is sovereign, unconditioned, and elective. Quell declares, "To love God is to have pleasure in Him" (*TDNT* 1:28). We consider the related Hebrew words *chēn*, "grace," and *chesed*, "loving-kindness," under separate entries, especially the entry on grace.

In the NT Jesus urges, You shall love the Lord your God and love your neighbor as yourself (Mark 12:28-34; Matt. 22:37-39). An emotion cannot be commanded, as Wittgenstein argues, hence love in the NT is not an emotion, but an act of will or a disposition. Both love for God and love for the neighbor are quoted from the OT, and from rabbinic thought. Stauffer rightly stresses that love "is a matter of will and action" (*TDNT* 1:44-45). He adds, "The love of prestige is incompatible with the love of God" (45). The second danger is love of possessions and riches (Matt. 6:19-21). Such love ministers to a false sense of control and self-security, whereas love for God is the fruit of trust and dependence. Persecution may also be a cause of distraction (Matt. 10:16-23). In Matt. 7:12 Jesus formulates "the golden rule": "Do to others as you would have them do to you" (cf. Luke 6:31). Philo formulates this in negative terms. However, Jesus goes even further by insisting, "Love your enemies" (Matt. 5:44). He adds, "If you love those who love you, what reward do you have? Do not even the tax collectors do the same?" (5:46). God gives his grace to the evil and the good (5:45). The motivation for love is clearly seen in the extent to which a person is conscious of being the recipient of grace. After the parable of the two debtors, Jesus asks Simon the Pharisee, "Which of them will love him more?" (Luke 7:42), to which Simon replies, "The one for whom he canceled the greater debt" (v. 43). Jesus comments, "Her sins ... have been forgiven; hence she has shown great love. But the one to whom little is forgiven, loves little" (v. 47). Hence his followers are to "be merciful, just as your Father is merciful" (Luke 6:36). God also expresses his special love for Jesus as "my Son, the Beloved" (Mark 1:11; cf. 12:6; John 3:16).

Paul the apostle lays out a whole range of forces that humankind fears, and concludes that nothing, "in all creation, will be able to separate us from the love of God in Christ Jesus our Lord" (Rom. 8:39). However, his most detailed explanation of the qualities of love comes in the classic passage 1 Cor. 13:1-13. C. Spicq lists over a hundred "activities" or "effects" that may be inferred from Paul's reflections on *agapē* (*Agapē in the New Testament*, 3 vols. [London and St. Louis: Herder, 1963], 2:139-81). The noun is relatively rare in Greek outside the NT, although the verb is more frequent in the Bible, and very frequent in the LXX (cf. LSJ; H-R; and BDAG), and in specialist studies including Wischmeyer, Stauffer, Spicq, Moffatt, and Nygren. Nygren and Moffatt agree that Paul wishes to disengage his own theology of love from Greek and pagan ideas, which are primarily emotional or sexual. They argue: "Agape comes to us as a quite new creation of Christianity ... without it nothing that is Christian would be Christian" (Nygren, *Agape and Eros* [London: SPCK, 1957], 48; cf. Moffatt, *Love in the New Testament* [London, 1929; New York: Richard Smith, 1930], 5). Moffatt and Nygren may well exaggerate the distinctiveness of *the word,* as against the NT *uses* of the word. Nevertheless, it remains true, as Nygren indicates, that Paul's *use* of the term *agapē* is "unmotivated"; "indifferent to [prior] value" of that which is loved; "creative of value" (by virtue of God's love set upon it); and relational to the one who loves (*Agape and Eros,* 75-81). The word does not *always* imply these connotations, although his comments remain true for *most* of its uses. Above all, *agapān* enters Paul's mind as the usual LXX translation of the Hebrew *'āhēb.* M. M. Mitchell argues that while Paul distances himself from the Greek word *erōs* on many occasions, the word *philia* may denote the mutual respect for which Paul pleads after division in the church in 1 Cor. 13:1-13 (*Paul and the Rhetoric of Reconciliation* [Tübingen: Mohr, 1992], 165-71). But it signifies a deeper meaning in Paul than specific rhetorical contexts may suggest.

Agapē in 1 Corinthians 13 denotes above all a *stance* or *attitude* that shows itself in acts of will as regard, respect, and concern for the welfare of the other. Since the paradigm of this attitude is seen in Christ, it is not a devotional or pietistic jump to regard it as profoundly christological. Moltmann and Jüngel rightly relate it to the self-giving grace of the cruciform God. Paul has argued that tongues, by contrast, may indirectly minister to the self (14:4; 13:1), whereas "love does not seek its own personal good" (13:5, translation mine). Tongues without love would be "sounding brass" (AV/KJV) or "a noisy gong" (NRSV) (W. W. Klein, "Noisy Gong or Acoustic Vase?" *NTS* 32 [1986]: 286-89; W. Harris, "'Sounding Brass' and Hellenistic Technology," *BAR* 8 [1982]: 38-41). Love is not a mere resonating jar, which transmits mere noise (cf. Thiselton, *First Epistle to the Corinthians: Greek Text* [Grand Rapids: Eerdmans, 2000], 1032-39). Even if a Christian has the gift of prophecy, and "all knowledge," and the gift of faith, but, after all, lacks love, the Christian is "nothing" (13:2). Nygren contrasts the "Gnostic-mystical 'vision of God'" with the Pauline way of love (*Agape and Eros,* 134). The catalogue of parallels and comparisons genuinely reflects the contrasting condition of the Corinthian church. Moffatt rightly argues, "This 'hymn of love' has been written out of a close and trying experience" (*Love,* 182). Even better, C. T. Craig argues, "On closer examination it is seen that almost every word in the chapter has been chosen with this particular situation at Corinth in mind.... The mood is instructive fully as much as lyrical" ("1 Corinthians," in *IB* 10:165). Paul could well have fashioned the polished, rhetorical nature of the composition, with its special vocabulary, phrases, and rhythm, while reflecting in Corinth. The church's prizing of *gnosis* (1 Cor. 8:1), tongues, and "gifts" of the Spirit, and the power-hungry jealousies, perfectly fits the chapter. Even if Paul is borrowing some poetic source, it is still what he chooses to include.

In the second stanza (13:4-7) the practical and dynamic character of love is evident. It waits patiently, judging the right time for action. It shows kindness *(chrēsteuetai)* or generosity, does not burn with envy (cf. 1 Cor. 3:1-3), and does not begrudge honor shown to another. In Moffatt's words, "it makes no parade," or better, in Barrett's, "does not brag" (*The First Epistle to the Corinthians* [1968 and 1971], 303). It is not "inflated" with its own importance. "Inflated" suggests exactly the point, when Paul uses *phusioutai* elsewhere (4:6, 18, 19; 5:2; 8:1). It is not attention-seeking. The Greek *ouk aschēmonei* means "does not behave with ill-mannered impropriety." Spicq comments, "*Agapē* is not ill-mannered" (*Agapē in the New Testament*, 2:153), as when speakers interrupt in worship or continue to speak endlessly. Love is courteous. REB renders *ou zētei ta heautēs* as "is never selfish." Spicq suggests "disinterested." Love does not "exasperate" people or irritate them, or turn to "pique." It is the opposite of aggressive triumphalism. It does not "reckon up" a score of wrongs, but joyfully celebrates the truth. The only way of translating the bland "bears all things, believes all things, hopes all things, endures all things" (NRSV; which sounds soft and overly credulous) is to use negatives: "never tires of support, never loses faith, never exhausts hope, never gives up" (A. C. Thiselton, *The First Epistle to the Corinthians* [Grand Rapids: Eerdmans, 2000], 1057-60). The third stanza (13:8-13) tells of the permanence of love. Much will be redundant in heaven, but never love.

Elsewhere in Paul this picture is confirmed. Love holds us captive (2 Cor. 5:14); love is poured into our hearts by the Holy Spirit (Rom. 5:5). In the work of salvation, love is God's goal. Christians are called to share this. In Galatians love forms part of the fruit of the Spirit (5:22), and Paul urges, "Through love become slaves to one another" (5:13). Stauffer declares that "John and Paul are one" (*TDNT* 1:52). Jesus is the Mediator of the love of God. The Son loves "those whom the Father has given him." 1 John also reflects this: "Little children, let us love, not in word or speech, but in truth and action" (3:18). 1 John repeats, "Beloved, let us love one another, because love is from God" (4:7). In 4:19, John declares, "We love because he first loved us." In the postapostolic period *1 Clement* continues the tradition: "Let him who has love in Christ perform the commandments of Christ. Who is able to explain the bond of the love of God? . . . Love unites us to God" (*1 Clem.* 49.1-4). Clement of Alexandria quotes from Jesus, "Love your enemies" (Matt. 5:44-45), that "you may be the children of your Father in heaven" (*Stromata* 4.14.1).

Augustine writes frequently of love, arguing that in Latin *amor, dilectio,* and *caritas* are similar (*City of God* 14.7; *NPNF*, ser. 1, 2:266). "Well-directed love" should be the aim of all Christians (14.7). He declares, "Charity *(caritas)* is that affection of the mind which aims at the enjoyment of God for His own sake, and the enjoyment of one's neighbour." He adds, "By lust *(cupidas)* I mean that affection . . . which aims at enjoying one's self" (*On Christian Doctrine* 10.15; 2:561). Elsewhere he writes, "Your will is that we should love not only you but also our neighbour" (*Confessions* 37.61). Thomas Aquinas writes, "Charity *(caritas)* extends even to our enemies, whom we love out of charity in relation to God, to whom *caritas* is chiefly directed" (*Su Th* 2.2, qu. 23, art. 1, reply to obj.). Thomas repeats, "To love belongs to charity *(caritas). Caritas* is a virtue. . . . Friends are more to be commended for loving than for being loved" (qu. 27, art. 1). God, Thomas adds, can be loved, "not for anything else, but for himself" (art. 3). He reminds us, "Bernard says . . . that 'God is the cause of our loving God'" (art. 6). John Calvin writes about love when he discusses the Ten Commandments, especially the tenth. He concludes, "The whole human race, without exception, are to be embraced with one feeling of charity. . . . All are to be viewed not in themselves, but in God. . . . [But] if we would hold the true course in love, our first step must be to turn our eyes . . . to God" (*Institutes* 2.8.55; Beveridge, 1:359). In modern theology, among many studies Anders Nygren's remains a classic. He writes, "*Agapē is spontaneous and 'unmotivated.'* This is the most striking feature of God's love as Jesus represents it." He continues, "God's love is 'groundless.' . . . The only ground for it is to be found in God himself. . . . It does not look for anything in man that could be adduced as motivation for it" (*Agape and Eros*, 75-76). He further writes, "[A person's] value is precisely the fact that God loves him" (78). (*See also* **Grace**.)

Reading: K. Barth, "The Holy Spirit and Christian Love," in *CD* IV/2, sect. 68, pp. 727-840; R. Canning, *The Unity of Love of God and Neighbour in St. Augustine* (Louvain: Augustinian Historical Institute, 1993); J. Moffatt, *Love in the New Testament* (London and New York: Richard Smith, 1930); A. Nygren, *Agape and Eros* (London: SPCK, 1957); G. Outka, *Agapē: An Ethical Analysis* (New Haven: Yale University Press, 1972); C. Spicq, *Agapē in the New Testament,* 3 vols. (London: Herder, 1963).

Lubac, Henri de

Henri de Lubac (1896-1991) was a French Jesuit theologian. He studied in England and France, and was made cardinal in 1983. His pupils included J. Daniélou and Hans Urs von Balthasar. He wrote on ecclesiology, grace and the supernatural, Augustine, Joachim of Fiore, and Teilhard de Chardin. However, he is equally well known in Britain and America for his *Medieval Exegesis,* 3 vols. (Grand Rapids: Eerdmans, 1998-2009). He and Daniélou were founding editors of Sources chrétiennes, which epitomizes his concern to go back to sources. De Lubac has special significance for his influence on Balthasar, especially in Balthasar's reading of the Church Fathers. His books *Catholicism, Corpus Mysticum,* and *Surnaturel* (Fr. 1946), as well as many others, make him one of the leading Catholic theologians of the twentieth century. His claim that we have a "natural desire for the supernatural" implies self-transcendence, or the need to look beyond ourselves. (*See also* **Balthasar, Hans Urs von**.)

Luther, Martin
Martin Luther (1483-1546) was effectively the founder of the Reformation, especially in Germany. He was born in Eisleben, Saxony, was educated at Magdeburg and Eisenach, and entered Erfurt University in 1501. In 1505 he entered the Augustinian monastery at Erfurt, and was ordained a priest in 1507. He lived as a devout monk, receiving the tonsure and cowl, begging for bread in the streets as an act of humility. He had professed vows of poverty, chastity, and obedience. After ordination he began a life of study and teaching, and in 1508 was called to the University of Wittenberg. There he taught both Aristotle and the Bible. During all this time, however, he wrestled with intense doubts about his relationship with God, regarding himself as imprisoned in wretchedness and misery. In 1509 he returned to teach at Erfurt.

At Erfurt there was a desire to reform the Augustinian monasteries, and to bring lax communities up to the standard of stricter houses. The Order assigned Luther to the company of a senior monk, to take their appeal to Rome. When he arrived in Rome, contrary to high expectations, Luther underwent deep disillusionment. He was troubled by the ignorance of many priests, and their wish to pass through masses hastily. He crawled on his knees, like many others, up the twenty-eight steps of the Scala Sancta, kissing each step, and reciting a Pater Noster, in the hope of being freed from purgatory. He was shocked by the disproportionately lavish expenditure of the papal Curia, and the conduct of the populace. The two returned to Germany four months later, in 1511. Luther became convinced that somehow the Roman Church had missed its way.

On his return John Staupitz transferred Luther to Wittenberg. Staupitz was his vicar-general, and a professor of theology at Wittenberg, and he convinced Luther that his vocation was to be a doctor and preacher. The years 1512-1519 were to prove a very difficult time of heart-searching and transition for Luther. He went through agonies of despair, doubts, and misgivings. His monastic "works" seemed to deepen his despair. Even the confessional did not seem to absolve him. J. Atkinson writes, "He felt an overpowering fear of God, a trembling awareness of Him as the destructive power over against a sinner" (*The Great Light* [Grand Rapids: Eerdmans, 1968], 16). Atkinson adds, "He had scaled the heights by the ladder of mysticism, but, when he reached the summit, he found there was nothing there" (17). There were, however, some positive elements. Staupitz had tried to turn Luther's mind away from the system of penance to the biblical notion of repentance, that is, in a new direction. But although he tried to trust in the merits of Christ, Luther also relied on the merits of the Virgin Mary and the saints, over which he was to have misgivings.

Luther took a step forward in 1513. His lectures included teaching on the Psalms. The phrase "In your righteousness deliver me" (Ps. 31:1) began to disturb him and provoke thought. How can there be "deliverance" in God's righteousness? Then he began to compare Rom. 1:17, "The righteousness of God [is] revealed through faith to faith: as it is written, 'The just shall live by faith'" (AV/

KJV), or in the NRSV, "The one who is righteous will live by faith." To understand Luther's change in 1513, we must assess the context of his thought. There are both negative and positive factors. On the negative side, there were three: first, Luther had been disillusioned by his visit to Rome, and not least by the mechanical attitude to indulgences, which could allegedly shortcut future periods in purgatory, either through gifts of money or by undertaking prescribed "works." Second, before he even entered his monastic order, he had been terrified by a violent storm in which his friend was struck dead by lightning. He regarded this as a sign of God's wrath. Third, he later recounts, "I was a monk for twenty years. I tortured myself with prayers, fasting, vigils, and freezing.... It caused me pain.... What else did I seek by doing this but God?... I did this all for the sake of God"; but all this gave him no peace or assurance (WA 24:23-24). Before 1513-1514 Luther regarded Christ as "a severe and terrible judge."

On the positive side, however, there were four noteworthy factors: first, Luther's vicar-general, Staupitz, had been a wise guide and counselor, directing him to trust in the shed blood of Jesus Christ, even if alongside the merits of Mary and the saints. Second, Luther studied deeply William of Ockham (c. 1285-1349), who regarded Scripture as supreme, even infallible. He wrote that a person could not be required to believe "what is not contained in the Scriptures" (*Dialogus* 1.2.1). He believed that unaided human reason could not arrive at certain knowledge of God. Third, Luther looked to Augustine as patron of his order, and gradually came to appreciate his emphasis on grace, divine sovereignty, and even predestination and election. He highly valued Augustine's exposition of the Psalms, and his *City of God*. Fourth, he also drew on the thought of Peter Lombard (c. 1100-1160) and his *Sentences,* which he had studied for his doctorate and on which he now lectured. Staupitz generously vacated his chair at Wittenberg so that Luther could succeed him as professor of biblical exegesis in 1512. Luther became "Doctor of Sacred Scripture" in the same year. He never abandoned patristic tradition, using, among other sources, Chrysostom's homilies on Hebrews for his commentary on Hebrews, and Jerome's biblical work for his commentaries on Galatians and Titus.

With this contextual background, we may reenter Luther's struggle and pondering on Psalms 31 and 70 during 1513-1515. On Ps. 31:1, Luther stressed "Your" (or "Thy") righteousness, not "mine." "My righteousness," he added, "is nothing." His initial wrestling in 1513 did not constitute an immediate breakthrough, but was the beginning of one. A. Skevington Wood associates this time with the "Tower" experience of perhaps a year later. Luther recalls that on his first engagement with Rom. 1:17, "I hated Paul with all my heart," but later, "by the mercy of God, meditating day and night, I gave heed to the context of the words.... I began to understand that the righteousness of God is that by which the righteous lives by a gift of God, namely by faith.... I felt that I was altogether born again and had entered paradise itself through open gates. There a totally other face of the entire Scripture showed itself to me" (*LW* 34:336-37, cited by Wood, *Captive to the Word* [Exeter: Paternoster, 1969], 52; cf. Atkinson, *The Great Light*, 20). From this moment onward Luther also saw that the church is *always* in need of *constant* reformation: "The *ecclesia reformata* is always the *ecclesia reformanda*" (*The Great Light,* 21). Thus the years 1513-1517 were deeply formative for Luther. He was given a light teaching load of two lectures a week (though also three seminars). His deep reflection during those four years prepared him to speak on indulgences in 1517. His contrast between God's free grace and human ecclesial "works" sharpened. He could no longer tolerate the sale of indulgences for money or prescribed "works" to escape purgatory or "buy" the grace of God. Atkinson comments, "Luther's break-through was not the burst of a single intense experience but rather the growth of years that one day proved overwhelming" (23). During this crucial period Luther lectured on Genesis (1513), Psalms (1513-1515), Romans (1515-1516), Galatians (1516-1517), Hebrews (1517-1518), and Psalms again (1518-1521).

In his lectures on Romans Luther stressed that God does not want to save us "by our own personal and private righteousness and wisdom." He wants to save us "by a righteousness and wisdom apart from, or other than, this," namely, the righteousness of Christ. Faith is not assent. Faith is by appropriation (WA 56:370). In Christ's new law, he urged, "all things are free.... Love is all that is necessary" (cited in *The Great Light,* 32). Luther declared, "A man ... is always a sinner, always penitent, always justified" (WA 36:422). In his commentary on Galatians (1516-1517) he drew further contrasts between the law and the gospel. In April 1517 he warned of a "purity" that suggests that we should not be classed or associated with sinners, for, he wrote, "Christ only dwells among sinners.... If by our own efforts we are to attain peace of conscience, why then did Christ die?" (cited by E. G. Rupp and B. Drewery, eds., *Martin Luther* [London: Arnold, 1970], 8).

For Luther things came to a head on the subject of indulgences in 1517. He nailed up in public his famous Ninety-five Theses against indulgences and the pope's "plentitude of power" on 31 October, the vigil of All Saints' Day, 1517. (In many churches 31 October is observed as Reformation Day.) Rupp and Drewery trace the history of papal indulgences, with full texts. They explain, "An Indulgence is a remission of temporal punishment due for sin, and has its origin in the medieval developments concerning the sacrament of penance" (11). These were normally paid for by money, or "bought," either by the pope, the church, an approved patron, or the penitent. In 1300 Pope Boniface VIII issued a Jubilee Indulgence, and to assist a financially embarrassed papacy, indulgences became increasingly frequent. In 1343 Pope Clement VI attempted to justify them by claiming "a treasury for the Church militant." Pope Sixtus extended the indulgence to souls in purgatory in 1476. Finally, Rupp and Drewery declare, the Jubilee Indulgence of Pope Julius II in 1507 and Leo X in 1513 "sparked off the Reformation" (11). Luther had already protested about indulgences in 1515 and in a sermon in Wittenberg in 1516. This latest affront to the sufficiency of Christ's work was to go toward paying off the huge debts of Archbishop Albert of Mainz, who was also archbishop of Magdeburg. Some 26,000 ducats were due to the papacy. Albert ordered the Dominican John Tetzel to sell the indulgences.

Pope Leo had declared to Albert that this indulgence granted, first, "the plenary remission of all sins" (*Martin Luther*, 15). The "penitent" is to make oral confession, say five Pater Nosters and five Ave Marias, and pay honor to the wounds of Christ. Then money must be placed in Tetzel's box. The "second indulgence" relates to the confession to a priest, who can "apply plenary indulgence for all sins" (16). The fourth indulgence is for "all sins for the souls that exist in Purgatory" (17). Luther wrote to Albert on 31 October 1517 about "false promises of Indulgences which do not promote the salvation or sanctification of their souls" (18). In the Ninety-five Theses, Luther showed that "penitence" was an attitude or disposition that followed repentance, and that "The Pope has neither the will nor the power to remit any penalties . . . beyond canon law" (19). He can "only declare and confirm that it (sin) has been remitted by God." The theses are conveniently available in *Martin Luther*, 19-25, and elsewhere. Luther had opposed what Bonhoeffer would later call "cheap grace."

The years 1517-1518 saw three very different types of writing from Luther. In his *Disputation against Scholastic Theology* (1517), Luther posited that Scholasticism had both strengths and weaknesses, but it asked questions that no one in real life asked, and, especially in its Aristotelian form, did not serve theology well. His *Lectures on the Epistle to the Hebrews* (1517-1518) constitutes a commentary, still largely in medieval form, with glosses, *scholia*, and notes. The Heidelberg Disputation (1518) makes clear the heart of Luther's Reformation theology. All are collected in J. Atkinson, ed., *Luther: Early Theological Works*, LCC 16 (London: SCM; Philadelphia: Westminster, 1962), together with Luther's *Answer to Latomus* (1521).

Among the Schoolmen who most influenced Luther, we have noted, was William of Ockham. Ockham attacked abstractions. Ahead of Kant, he denied the existence of "causality" as a phenomenon outside the human mind. It was Aquinas who introduced Aristotle into Scholasticism. Luther therefore did not dismiss the entire tradition of Scholasticism, only its overfussy hairsplitting and constant appeal to authorities, as if to escape active thinking. He began his treatise with Augustine, whom he defends. He welcomes his thought on grace, predestination, and total depravity (286). But, he insists, "The whole Aristotelian ethic is grace's worst enemy" (269). Aristotle, he claims, is like darkness to light for theology. Contrary to some Scholastics, Luther sees grace as "a living, moving, and active spirit" (270), whereas "the law is a tyrant over the will and makes sin to abound" (271). He concludes, "to love God is to hate oneself and to know nothing apart from God" (273). We are to want "what God wants" (273). The treatise then is less a "dispute against Scholasticism" than a criticism of Aristotle's influence on it.

Luther's lectures on Hebrews may reflect a medieval form and style, but in content they proclaim the sacrifice of Christ and the power of God's Word. On "the word of God is living" (Heb. 4:12), Luther alludes to Nicholas of Lyra, and concludes, "It makes alive those who believe it" (94). He then refers to Chrysostom, who speaks of the Word as "more cruel than any sword" (95). On the ministry of the High Priest, who is Christ in 4:14, this makes "our faith certain" (99). Similarly in 4:16, "Let us draw near with confidence," Luther paraphrases, "Let us not be hindered by scruples of conscience or fear of sins" (101). On 11:1, "Faith gives substance to our hopes," Luther renders "faith" as *proof, conviction,* or a "kind of certainty" (202). Again, for support he cites Chrysostom, who understands faith here as *reality.*

Luther's Heidelberg Disputation (1518) constitutes his reply to the indulgences controversy, and to Tetzel's countercharges. In the event, it was more warmly received than Luther had expected or feared. He expounded "the righteousness of God" in Rom. 3:21, appealing to Augustine on the weakness of the law (281), and condemned the works of humankind as "loathsome" (282). Even the works of the righteous would be mortal sins if performed without fear of God (284). He then contended that free will after the Fall "exists only in name" (287), but this should not lead to despair (289). If a person despairs of himself, he becomes fit to receive the grace of God (290). A famous thesis is reached in section 21: "The theologian of glory says bad is good and good is bad. The theologian of the cross calls them by their proper name"; God is "hidden in sufferings" (291). Luther adds, "The righteousness which comes from faith in Christ is sufficient for him. Christ is his wisdom, his righteousness and all, as it says in 1 Cor. 1:30" (sect. 25, p. 294).

In spite of the warm reception of Luther's work by such men as Martin Bucer, Tetzel continued to oppose Luther, and the Dominicans awarded a doctor's degree to Tetzel and pressed charges against Luther at Rome. In due course these charges were sent to the learned Cardinal Cajetan in Augsburg. Luther was to appear before Cajetan in Rome. But Luther requested to be tried in Germany, and argued that his theology was acceptable as "catholic" theology. These were troubled times, not least involving the succession of Charles V as emperor; Elector Frederick the Wise's defense of Luther; and Rome's declaration that Luther was a heretic. The upshot was that Luther was to appear before Cajetan at Augsburg in October 1518. The "trial" at Augsburg was in some respects more intimidating than the earlier one at Heidelberg, or the one at Worms in 1521. Cajetan was a powerful and learned opponent, who published biblical commentaries, and theological works on Aquinas. Staupitz begged Luther to escape. But Luther replied, "Christ rules in Augsburg even in the midst of his enemies." The "trials" that Luther had faced or would face included (i) Heidelberg (April 1518); (ii) Augsburg (October 1518); (iii) Leipzig (July 1519); (iv) the Bull of Pope Leo X (June 1520); and (v) Worms (April 1521). Luther's opponents or "judges" were, respectively: (i) the Augustinian Order and Dominicans; (ii) Cardinal Cajetan; (iii) John Eck; (iv) the papacy; and (v) the emperor Charles V.

At Augsburg Cajetan announced that the pope required that Luther repent of errors and recant, that he not teach them again, and that he cease to disturb the peace of the church. Luther respected Cajetan's learning and sincerity, but he told Cajetan that such a request could have been considered at home, and asked what these errors were (Atkinson, *Martin Luther and the Birth of Protestantism* [London: Penguin, 1968], 170). Cajetan instanced Thesis 58, on the treasury of merits, and Thesis 7, where Luther stated that faith justifies, not the sacraments. Luther replied that these were scriptural doctrines, which took precedence over papal decrees. Later in the "trial" he added, "The Pope does not have this treasure in a purse or treasure chest"; Christians look for grace and gift (171). On justification through faith Luther stated eleven arguments, and appealed to Rom. 1:17 and John 3:18. He argued that he "cherished and followed the Church in all things" except when the Roman Church erects a "Babylon" as if Scripture did not exist. Cajetan promised to send Luther's reply to Rome, but Luther seemed to stand alone in a dangerous and vulnerable position. In the dead of night a well-wisher seized him and smuggled him out of the city. Once he was home Luther wrote, "I await my excommunication from Rome any day now. . . . I shall be ready." Meanwhile political machinations continued between the pope and Elector Frederick, which involved offering Frederick bribes and rewards, and Luther's situation was unresolved.

The Leipzig Disputation with John Eck took place in July 1519. Eck chose to make a strong attack on the Wittenberg school of theology, especially on Andreas Carlstadt, who was technically Luther's senior. Carlstadt would later lapse into radical enthusiasm and egalitarianism or socialism, but at this point held to a biblical theology. But he did not entirely embrace Luther's approach, and Luther insisted on accompanying him, in spite of opposition. Eck and Carlstadt debated for a week, and Carlstadt utterly failed. Luther then entered the fray. Eck accused Luther of following Huss, but Luther appealed once again to Scripture and protested his loyalty to the church. Eck supposed that he had won the debate, and left in triumph. But not everyone recognized the debate in this way. Eck had also attacked Melanchthon, who wrote a convincing reply, and Luther wrote an account of the debate for the German people. Atkinson argues, "At Leipzig the ship of the Reformation was launched on the high seas, and Luther found himself at the helm" (*Birth*, 181). The humanist scholars resented Eck's attack on Melanchthon, and the University of Wittenberg gathered strength, while the Universities of Paris and Erfurt withdrew support from Eck. Luther continued to write and to preach. He recalled, "I simply taught, preached, and wrote God's Word; observe I did nothing . . . I left it to the Word" (cited by Atkinson, *The Great Light*, 55).

In June 1520 a papal bull was issued by Leo X. It is set out in Rupp and Drewery, *Martin Luther*, 36-40. As we noted, this came as no surprise. In May 1520 Luther had published *The Papacy at Rome,* in which he argued that God's church was not to be identified with the institution in Rome. Luther began to suggest that "Antichrist" ruled in Rome. The same year he produced the *Open Letter to the Christian Nobility of the German Nation Respecting the Reformation of the Christian*

Estate. He wrote, "We must renounce all confidence in our natural strength and take the matter in hand with humble trust in God" (*Martin Luther,* 42). Luther continued, "ALL Christians are truly of the spiritual estate . . . as St. Peter says, 'You are a royal priesthood, a holy nation' (1 Pet. 2:9)" (43). Luther attacked the "indelibility" of priesthood. Biblical interpretation, he urged, did not belong to the pope alone (text in *Martin Luther,* 42-47). Within weeks Luther also published *The Prelude on the Babylonian Captivity of the Church*. In this Luther denied "that there are seven sacraments." He also proved from the first three Gospels that the cup should not be withheld from the laity, for Jesus said, "Drink you *all* of this" (text in *Martin Luther,* 47-50; comment in Atkinson, *The Great Light,* 59-62, and *Birth,* 187-93). Luther attacked the notion of good works and sacraments as *opus operatum*, "surrounded with vestments and incense, gestures and ceremonies" (*Birth,* 191). Luther translated the papal bull into German for the people to understand, and put the bull in the fire at Wittenberg.

The last remaining "trial" was the Diet of Worms in April 1521. The emperor Charles V was present; forty-one propositions by Luther had been condemned in the June papal bull. Luther's excommunication was ratified in January 1521. His friends tried to dissuade Luther from going. At Worms Luther was simply commanded to recant, or retract his words. Luther uttered the famous reply, "Unless I am convinced by the testimony of the Scriptures or by clear reason . . . I cannot and will not recant anything. . . . May God help me. Amen" (cited by Wood, *Captive to the Word,* 72; Atkinson, *The Great Light,* 67; and *LW* 32:110-11). The equally famous dictum "Here I stand, I can do no other" was added to the manuscript after the earliest printed version. R. Bainton argues that the words "may nevertheless be genuine" (*Here I Stand* [London: Lion, 1978], 185), but Skevington Wood and others doubt their originality. This forms the climax of Luther's patient and courageous work to lay the foundations of the Reformation. However, while his "trials" were dramatic, what was even more important was the steady development of Protestant theology, largely through Luther's struggle, from 1517 to 1521.

The real thrust of the Reformation lay in Luther's writings and his work as a teacher. In the formative years the former included the Heidelberg Disputation, *The Open Letter to the German Nobility, On the Babylonian Captivity of the Church,* and *Concerning Christian Liberty*. In the same period he produced a commentary on Hebrews, and revised commentaries on the Psalms, Galatians, and Titus (all 1518-1521). There now followed lectures or commentaries on Romans (1522), Deuteronomy (1523-1525), the Minor Prophets (1524-1526), Ecclesiastes (1526), 1 John, Titus, and Philemon (1527), 1 Timothy (1528), Isaiah (1527-1530), Song of Solomon (1530-1531), a revision of Galatians (1531), a revision of Psalms (1532-1535), and a revision of Genesis (1535-1545). This biblical work anchored his Reformation theology in biblical writings. In all this Luther was aided by humanist method and by humanist lexicography.

Slowly Luther's method of exegesis developed, from a medieval-like form in Hebrews to a greater suspicion of allegorical interpretation in the later commentaries. Luther declared, "I am the first to place primary emphasis on the importance of laying hold upon the meaning of the book, what it wants to say, the essential viewpoint of the author." In his *Preface to Romans* (1522) he wrote, "To begin with we must have knowledge of its language and know what Paul means by the words 'law, sin, grace, faith....'" He added, "Faith is a living, daring confidence in God's grace, so sure and certain that a man would stake his life on it a thousand times."

After the Diet of Worms, life was still unsafe for Luther, and Elector Frederick persuaded him to take temporary shelter in the Wartburg. Regin Prenter, the Lutheran specialist on the Holy Spirit, observes that after his return from the Wartburg Luther had to fight on two fronts: "He had to take up the struggle with the Roman Church. He had also to take up the struggle with the new enthusiastic movement" (*Spiritus Creator: Luther's Concept of the Holy Spirit* [Philadelphia: Muhlenberg, 1953], 205). These "fanatics" *(Schwärmer)* included Nicolaus Storch, Thomas Müntzer, and Andreas Carlstadt. Atkinson comments, "It is not always understood that Luther's worst enemy was not Catholicism, but rather that wild left-wing radicalism identified with fanaticism and 'socialism'" (*Birth,* 221). Luther saw himself as standing in the tradition of Augustine, Bernard, and Richard of St. Victor, emphasizing the Spirit's work of sanctification. Above all, the Holy Spirit promotes the doctrine of Christ. The Spirit gives life and sanctification. Luther claimed that the enthusiasts boast that they have the Spirit "without and before the Word" (*Smalcald Articles,* pt. 3, art. 6). These "Radical Reformers" saw sanctification as an event, whereas Luther saw it as a process that involved *Anfechtung,* or inner conflict and struggle. There is no precise English equivalent. They are trials sent by God to test and strengthen believers.

While Luther was at the Wartburg, Carlstadt came to Wittenberg and preached against monastic vows, celibacy, and the Mass, and wore lay clothes rather than robes. He denounced the baptism of infants, images, and pictures; ridiculed theological learning; and wanted to abolish titles and dignitaries. He appealed to the Holy Spirit as the grounds for this. In 1521-1522 Luther returned from the Wartburg to unmask all this. Müntzer made a similar appeal to the special revelation of the Holy Spirit. In 1520 Müntzer moved to Zwickau as a self-proclaimed prophet, which gave rise to Luther's description of "the Zwickau prophets." In Prague they produced the "Prague Manifesto," which expounded this enthusiast doctrine of the Holy Spirit, imminent apocalypticism, and believer's baptism. In 1524 Luther reformulated his views against those of Carlstadt and Müntzer in *Against the Celestial Prophets* (January 1525). He noted the irony that "the left-wing radicals" hit him harder than his enemies, although they were originally "our own people." By 1524 Carlstadt was teaching people to cultivate a passive emptiness "to listen to the Spirit." He was now advocating polygamy, rejecting the real presence, and destroying images and crucifixes, allegedly at the instruction of the Spirit. Luther now viewed these prophets as satanic. Müntzer, on the basis of "revelation" from the Spirit, encouraged the peasants and mob to revolt, burning convents and cities, and redistributing land in the name of the Holy Spirit. Luther called Müntzer "the Arch-devil."

In June 1525 the Saxon princes attacked the Peasants' Revolt and defeated Müntzer. Luther entreated the princes to be merciful, but repudiated the radicals' false doctrine of the Spirit. For him, the Spirit and the Word spoke together. An "inward word" did not have priority over Scripture. Prenter calls the doctrine of the prophets "a peculiar type of piety different in principle" from Luther's view of Christianity. They turned the gospel "upside down" (*Spiritus Creator,* 248). Even worse, Luther regarded their emphasis on human acts and attitudes as undermining his doctrine of justification by grace through faith. Admittedly Melanchthon argued less harshly, but Zwingli was just as strongly opposed to them as Luther.

During his period in the Wartburg Luther had time to begin his most important work of all, namely, the translation of the Bible into German. He probably contemplated this task as early as 1520, but it was after Worms that he began systematically and in earnest, probably in 1522 or shortly thereafter. His translation was to be for Germany what both Tyndale and (later) the AV/KJV were together for England. Luther translated the NT from the Greek text of Erasmus. Skevington Wood calls this "a work of genius" (*Captive to the Word,* 101), and quotes Koolman as saying, "Rarely, if ever, has a book that exerted such influence been written so rapidly." It was completed in less than three months. Within two months five thousand copies were sold, and in twelve years a quarter of a million (102). Luther left the Wartburg for Wittenberg and immediately began the OT translation. He translated from the Hebrew, and could draw on the advice of Aurogallus, the newly appointed professor of Hebrew, as well as that of Melanchthon. This more complex task took twelve years. The translation appeared in stages between 1522 and 1534. The work of the translation, Luther declared, required not only knowledge of the ancient text, but also present experience of the subject matter, or at the very least deep rapport with it and imagination. His German language, Wood concludes, is clear and vigorous.

We have seen Luther as a controversialist, a reformer, a theologian, a teacher, a preacher, and a translator. He was also a pastor and spiritual counselor, as may be seen above all from numerous letters, some of which are collected in English in Theodore G. Tappert, ed., *Luther: Letters of Spiritual Counsel,* LCC 18 (London: SCM; Philadelphia: Westminster, 1955). Tappert comments, "In Luther's eyes . . . spiritual counsel is always concerned above all else with faith — nurturing, strengthening, establishing, practising faith" (15). He does not aim at getting people to *do* things, such as fasting, good works, a pilgrimage, or becoming a monk. Ministry includes counseling troubled hearts, and those who are ill or sick. Thus he counsels Elector Frederick when he is ill (1519; *Letters,* 26-28), George Spalatin (1527; 29), his father (1530; 29-32), and others. He counsels the anxious and despondent (82-108), including his wife, Catherine or Katie (1546; 105-8). He counsels the bereaved (53-81); the perplexed and doubting (109-38), including again George Spalatin and Elector Frederick; and the persecuted and imprisoned (190-227).

In addition to his many roles, however, he continued working as a theologian and Reformer. His controversy with Erasmus produced Luther's reply in *The Bondage of the Will* (1525). All had gone well before about 1522. Atkinson paints a largely sympathetic picture of Erasmus, arguing that Protestants owe him a special debt. Erasmus had produced the Greek Testament from which Luther and Tyndale worked, and had firmly advanced classical and patristic studies. Negatively, he criticized the ignorance of many monks, and disapproved of the event at Worms and of much of Rome's activity against Luther. He was essentially a good-humored man of peace. Although he was born and lived in Rotterdam, he traveled widely in Europe, and twice visited England. He made friends with Thomas More, Cardinal Wolsey, and even Henry VIII. For a time he held the Lady Margaret chair at Cambridge. Until about 1522 in general he approved of Luther's work, except for what he saw as provocative or polemic. Erasmus was a loyal but critical Catholic. In 1521 Henry VIII wrote a defense of the seven sacraments, and encouraged Charles V to use force to exterminate Luther. Luther replied with scorn and, in even Atkinson's words, "abused the King's person mercilessly" (*Birth*, 227). In 1525 Luther apologized, but it was too late. Among other former friends, Luther entirely lost the sympathy of Erasmus. By 1524 he had completely withdrawn from the Reformer, and in September 1524 attacked Luther's doctrine of total depravity in his work *The Freedom of the Will*.

In June 1525 Luther married his wife Katie, and in December published his reply to Erasmus: *On the Bondage of the Will*, one of his most famous theological works. It is available in English (London: Clarke, 1957). Its English editors call it "the greatest piece of theological writing that ever came from Luther's pen" (*Bondage*, 40), which was also apparently Luther's own assessment. Luther held that Augustine's and Paul's doctrine of bondage was "the corner stone of the gospel" (43). Not all will agree with these comments by ardent supporters of Luther. Many Anglicans still tend to follow Erasmus more closely. But Luther was not merely arguing about human choice. The basic issue was that of the inability of a human to save himself or herself. For Luther, God's grace is all, and the work of Christ is all. He saw the defense of free will by Erasmus as being about human capacities, perhaps unintentionally undermining the all-sufficiency of the grace of God. "Free will" in Erasmus suggests "an inherent power in man to act apart from God" (*Bondage*, 52). Luther also appeals to God's hidden purposes (55). The editors maintain, "Martin Luther and John Calvin . . . Ulrich Zwingli, Martin Bucer . . . stood on precisely the same ground here" (58).

Luther first reviews Erasmus's work. Much depends on "the perspicuity *(claritas)* of Scripture" (73). By this term Luther was attacking the skepticism that could follow study with practical action. Had he meant that *nothing* could be obscure, he would hardly have produced so many commentaries. But "God foreknows and wills all things" (83). Luther continues, "'Free-will' without God's grace is not free at all, but is the permanent prisoner and bond-slave of evil" (104). He adds, "Scripture is called a *way* and a *path,* doubtless by reason of its entire certainty" (126). If Scripture is equivocal, why should God give it (128)? He states, "I hold that the Scriptures are perfectly clear" (135), that is, for the next practical step of action. Again, he reviews the arguments of Erasmus, especially of texts (190-272). Luther's counterreply concerns universal sin and guilt, for which he appeals to Rom. 1:18-32 (273-78). He then examines Rom. 3:9-18 and 19-23, where Paul asserts, "All have sinned" (3:23) and "There is no one who is righteous" (3:10; 278-84). He then passes on to the role of the law, which provokes sin (287-88). Finally he expounds the doctrine of salvation by faith in Christ (288-92), and the irrelevance of "works" (295-97). In Rom. 8:5 and elsewhere he also appeals to the work of the Holy Spirit (299-301). Last of all, Luther speaks of "the comfort of knowing that salvation does not depend on 'free-will'" (313).

We must finally glance briefly at his work in liturgy and the reorganization of parishes. For details on this, see the second part of the entry on the Lord's Supper above. In liturgy he strove to make the "Mass" or Lord's Supper more true to its biblical roots and the Church Fathers. In 1527 he insisted that Christ's words "This is my body," against the claims of both Zwingli and the "fanatics," or enthusiasts, mean what they say, and suggested what is often called the real presence of Christ. He also attacked Zwingli for a merely symbolic understanding of the Lord's Supper. He renewed his attack in 1529, but also sought a "friendly conference" with Zwingli, Melanchthon, and Bullinger at Marburg in the same year (Rupp and Drewery, *Martin Luther,* 135-36). In July 1529 he produced his *Short Catechism,* addressed "to all faithful, pious pastors and preachers." It included creation, redemption, and sanctification. We have not had space to speak of Luther as a hymn writer. The hymn "A Safe Stronghold Our God Is Still" probably came from this period. Then in 1530, with Melanchthon, he produced the Augsburg Confession. This included the doctrines of God, original sin, Christ, justification, the ministry, the church, and other articles. Atkinson writes, "The Confession at Augsburg was the first evangelical confession and is the most famous ... written and modified by Melanchthon" (*Birth,* 287). Part 1 contained twenty-one positive articles, while part 2 lists seven articles of perceived abuses by Rome. These included the withdrawal of the cup from the laity, the celibacy of the clergy, the sacrifice of the Mass, compulsory confession, fasts and feasts, monastic vows, and the secular power of bishops.

In his remaining years Luther was anxious about the disunity of the Reformation churches, as well as the spiritual condition of the city of Wittenberg, which had been his spiritual home. By 1545 he was suffering from failing sight, general weakness, and creeping old age. In January 1546 he preached his last sermon, although he began one in February but was forced to abandon it. Finally, he died with his friends beside him, commending himself to God and thanking God for Jesus Christ. They heard him murmur "God so loved the world ..." (John 3:16; *Birth,* 331).

Many dispute Luther's legacy. Some argue that his greatest influence is exercised through the catechisms (David Yeago); others through his translation of the Bible (Skevington Wood); some through his *Bondage of the Will* and other theological writings (probably Packer and Johnston). Whatever may be the critiques of his doctrine of justification by grace through faith, Luther always saw this in relation to the church and to other aspects of salvation, not the solitary faith of the private experience. His work as an exegete and biblical scholar should not be underrated, as Atkinson insists. His writings are so extensive that controversial "Luther quotations" can easily be extracted from any of them. His work was not systematic in the way that Calvin's was. As one of his interpreters observes, Luther never did anything by halves. He was both an acute intellect and a man with a huge heart. Often he was compelled to fight on two or three fronts. Some may try to fault him for his contrast between law and gospel. But Luther was always addressing specific situations. None can overlook his unique founding place in beginning the Reformation, and his influence on the history of Europe. Interpretations of Luther abound, including the "New Finnish Interpretation." (*See also* **Enthusiasm; Faith, Faithfulness; Grace; Justification; Melanchthon, Philip.**)

Reading: James Atkinson, *The Great Light* (Grand Rapids: Eerdmans, 1968); James Atkinson, *Martin Luther and the Birth of Protestantism* (London: Penguin, 1968); Carl E. Braaten and R. W. Jenson, eds., *Union with Christ: The New Finnish Interpretation of Luther* (Grand Rapids: Eerdmans, 1998); Bernhard Lohse, *Martin Luther's Theology* (Minneapolis: Fortress, 1999); Martin Luther, *On the Bondage of the Will* (London: James Clarke, 1957); E. G. Rupp and Benjamin Drewery, eds., *Martin Luther: Documents* (London: Arnold, 1970).

M

Manichaeans. *See* Augustine

Marcel, Gabriel
Gabriel Marcel (1889-1973) was born in Paris, and raised by an agnostic family. He regarded his childhood as a "desert," with a "dehumanizing" demand for academic excellence. The intellectual, at best, he believed, formed only one dimension of life. He became a convert to Roman Catholicism in 1929. In his philosophy, sometimes called "the human face of existentialism," he urged "availability" to "the other." In his major work *Being and Having* (1935), he saw other human beings as persons or subjects, rather than case studies, numbers or statistics, or mere objects. He associated objects with "having"; but "being" was characterized by presence, dignity, and sacredness. He wrote *Creative Fidelity* (1940) and *The Mystery of Being* (1950).

Marcion
Marcion (d. c. 160) made his way to Rome c. 140, and in 144 organized his followers into a community separate from the church. Irenaeus, Clement, Tertullian, Hippolytus, and Origen regarded his system of thought as heretical. Marcion claimed that while the NT taught a gospel of love, the OT was to be rejected as teaching only law. Indeed, the "God" of the OT was a Demiurge, who had nothing in common with God, the Father of Jesus Christ. Marcion claimed that only Paul genuinely understood this, with his antithesis between law and grace. He rejected the theology of the Evangelists in the four Gospels, or at least Matthew, Mark, and John. On Christology he was Docetic, and triggered reflection on the biblical canon. Justin, his contemporary, witnesses to the number of Marcionite "churches" scattered throughout the Roman Empire. His influence lasted until at least c. 200, although some Marcionite sects survive today. Marcionism became part of the growing influence of Gnosticism.

Marx, Karl
Karl Marx (1818-1883) stands with Feuerbach, Nietzsche, and Freud as one of the four great advocates of atheism. They all regard "God" as a human projection of thought. In his earliest works, known as the Paris Manuscripts, Marx was primarily concerned with sociology and freedom from oppression. Hence liberation

theology appeals to these earliest writings. But especially after his meeting with Friedrich Engels (1820-1895), Marx became increasingly hostile to religion. In the short *Communist Manifesto* (1847), written jointly with Engels, he began to argue that projected beliefs about God were used by a ruling class to keep the proletariat submissive. Religion is seen as "the opium of the people." His well-known slogan was "Workers of all countries unite" (*Communist Manifesto* [London: Penguin, 1967], 121).

In terms of his worldview, Marx believed that the material and conditions of production constituted a more basic force for change and ongoing history than "ideas." Idealism tended to trade in myths. In 1845 Marx wrote in his *Eleven Theses on Feuerbach:* "Philosophers have only *interpreted* the world in various ways; the point is to *change* it" (*Early Writings* [London: Pelican, 1975], 423). In *The German Ideology* (1845-1846) Marx criticizes even Feuerbach on this ground. Marx's classic work is *Capital* (*Das Kapital,* 3 vols. [1867, 1885, 1895]). Here we see his view of world history as the exploitation of the working class until "the expropriators are expropriated." The transition to state socialism must come through revolution. Then the final era of communism may dawn, as the Marxist eschaton. He chided the "young Hegelians" for failing to see the radical implications of Hegel's view of history. Economic forces, he claimed, were more fundamental than "consciousness" or "ideas," which Hegel had failed to see. Class struggle is worked out in dialectical materialism (Engel's term). In practice, for Marx, this means the transition from oligarchy to the feudal system; from the feudal system to commercial and industrial capitalism; and from hitherto oppressed labor through revolution to the victory of the proletariat over the bourgeoisie. As for religion, Marx wrote, "Man makes religion; religion does not make man" (*Early Writings,* 244). He added, "The abolition of religion as the *illusory* happiness of the people is the demand for their real happiness" (244). No doubt it was in relation to this approach and kindred approaches that Bonhoeffer and others stressed the *costly* aspect of Christianity; this is not to be understood primarily as a source of "happiness." Nor is it always "submissive," as Nietzsche and Marx claimed. N. Lash, H. Gollwitzer, and others have developed various criticisms of Marx. But his early Paris Manuscripts do not explicitly oppose religion. (*See also* **Liberation Hermeneutics and Theology.**)

Materialism

Materialism denotes the view that only material entities or objects exist. It is then an ontology, or theory of reality, which stands in contrast to idealism, theism, and dualism. It is virtually akin to positivism, which confuses the methods of natural science with a "scientific" worldview, and behaviorism, which is a psychological version of materialism, usually associated with J. B. Watson and B. F. Skinner. In ancient Greek philosophy, Democritus held that the whole world was composed of material, solid atoms. Epicurus held roughly similar views, but might more accurately be called an evidentialist. The ancients raised the question: Is consciousness simply the physical in greater complexity?

In modern thought it is simplistic to describe Thomas Hobbes as a materialist. Materialism first emerged again in its strong form with J. O. de La Mettrie, D. Diderot, and Henri d'Holbach. La Mettrie's title *Man the Machine* (1747) reveals the mechanistic laws of his materialism. Holbach regarded the whole world as a machine. Some theories of evolution seemed to undermine the teleological argument, but in modern times F. R. Tennant and J. Polkinghorne, and others, have regarded moderate evolutionary theories as compatible with theism. Another argument for materialism has been "epiphenomenalism," as if to imply that the human mind could emerge from material processes. But Arthur O. Lovejoy formulated the following paradox: If the "reason" by which someone reaches a materialistic view is simply a matter of physical processes, on what can we base its validity as genuine reasoning? (*See also* **Atheism; Positivism; Science and Religion; Skepticism.**)

Maurice, F. D.

F. D. Maurice (1805-1872) has attracted admiration, controversy, and hostility. It is probably an exaggeration to call him "the greatest thinker of the English Church in the nineteenth century," as some do, although B. M. G. Reardon calls him "arguably the most original theological thinker that the nineteenth century produced [in Britain]" (*From Coleridge to Gore* [London: Longman, 1971], 162). He is "impossible to classify" (164). He began life as a Unitarian, and was later attracted to evangelicals in the Church of England. He was ordained an Anglican in 1834. His initial study was in law and English literature. Eventually he became professor of divinity at King's College, London, and was an effective preacher as chaplain of Guy's Hospital. However, he was eventually dismissed from his chair at King's College because of his controversial views, especially on Universalism. His major published work was *The Kingdom of Christ* (1838, rev. 1842; 2 vols. [London: James Clarke, 1959]). In the first part he addressed the Quakers in the form of a dialogue, first to describe the Quaker system (45-51), and then to consider objections to it (52-73), and to advocate loyalty to church "principles, ordinances and constitution." The volume was dedicated to S. T. Coleridge, whom Maurice admired as opening a new direction of inquiry. He then considered the theology of Luther, of Calvin, of Zwingli, and of Unitarianism, noting sympathetically the strengths of each, but also exposing negative criticisms. His special themes were the nearness of God and God's rule over the whole of humanity, not simply a part of it. For example, in his consideration of baptism (261-93), he describes this as a "sign of a spiritual and universal kingdom" (265).

Maurice published much else. In his *Life* he states, "I could address all kinds of people as members of Christ." Baptism, he argues, tells people that they are children of God; they are to live as such. Critics, for example, R. Candlish, responded that the gospel was not to inform people of what they are, but to change them. Maurice was well known in previous years for his "Christian socialism." He formed the Christian Socialists with Charles Kingsley. But Maurice insisted that his work was primarily theological rather than political. Throughout his life he was a controversial figure. O. Chadwick described his *Theological Essays* (1853) as "a stream of rhetorical questions littered . . . with parentheses, dashes, inversions, notes of exclamation. The reader is battered and fatigued by the demand to feel indignation on subjects where he did not know himself to feel anything; unable to grasp the author's meaning while seeing that this meaning is life or death to the author" (*The Victorian Church,* vol. 1 [London: SCM, 1966], 545). Although he was dismissed from his chair for "Universalism," Maurice's language merely offered *the hope* of universal salvation, not "dogmatic Universalism."

Maximus the Confessor

Maximus the Confessor (c. 580-662) was a Greek and Byzantine theologian and monk (later abbot) of the monastery of Chrysopolis. He was not a systematic theologian, but his work covered a range of topics from biblical exegesis to doctrinal, ascetic, and liturgical subjects. His work reflects both the political and ecclesiastical situations of the times. His *Mystagogia* provides an exposition of biblical passages; his *Quaestiones ad Thalassium* addresses questions raised by a fellow monk. He especially studied Gregory of Nazianzus. Nevertheless, he was caught up in the political violence of the times, and suffered torture grievously in Constantinople, from which he died. He maintained a two-nature Christology against the Monothelites.

Mediator, Mediation

A mediator (Heb. *mēlīts;* Gk. *mesitēs*) denotes one who stands between two parties, a go-between, one who represents one party to the other. Priests are classic "ascending" mediators, representing the prayers and plight of the people to God. Prophets are classic "descending" mediators, representing the works and commands of God to the people. In the OT many agents perform the task of mediation, notably Moses, the prophets, the king, priests, the servant of the Lord, angels, and the Wisdom of God. In the NT Jesus Christ is "mediator of a better covenant" (Heb. 8:6), and "the mediator of the new covenant" (9:15; 12:24). In Romans Christ intercedes for us at the right hand of God (Rom. 8:34). Two presuppositions determine the role of one who "stands between" two parties: (i) in the case of God and humankind, sin has brought alienation and fallenness; (ii) the task of the mediator is reconciliation between the two parties. Paul asserts, "In Christ God was reconciling the world to himself, not counting their trespasses against them, and entrusting the message of reconciliation to us" (2 Cor. 5:19).

In the OT the supreme example of a mediator is Moses. As ascending and priestly mediator he pleads for the people of Israel to God; as descending and prophetic mediator he conveys the commands of God to the people. A climax is reached in Exod. 32:32: "If you will only forgive their sin — but if not, blot me out of the book that you have written." Moses pleads on behalf of Israel, but if he is unsuccessful in this ministry, he is willing for God to blot him personally out of his book. C. Ryder Smith comments that Moses was one with the people, and with God. He was like a man torn in two (*The Bible Doctrine of Salvation* [London: Epworth, 1946, 1955], 27-28). Elijah often ranks second to Moses. He, too, proclaims God's words as prophet, but also pleads on the people's behalf in intercessory, priestly ministry (1 Kings 18:24, 37; 19:15-16). In addition to prophets and priests, the king was a mediating figure. He represented God to the people, and the people to God. Hence King David is to be "a man after his own heart" (1 Samuel 13:14), and had power to enforce God's will on earth. On God's behalf he is to protect, shepherd, and care for the people. Ps. 2:2 calls him the Lord's "anointed," and in the NT Peter and the Epistle to the Hebrews take up Ps. 110:1 and 4 as applicable to the Messiah (Acts 2:32, 34-35). The four Servant Songs of Isa. 42:1-4, 49:1-6, 50:4-11, and 52:13 allude to the Servant of the Lord both as a corporate and as an individual figure, who stands as mediator before God. In the later OT writings it is arguable that angels and Wisdom sometimes assume this function.

In the NT the term "mediator" occurs six times: Gal 3:19 and 20, 1 Tim. 2:5, Heb. 8:6, 9:15, and 12:24. Jesus is the mediator of the new covenant (Heb. 8:6), and also becomes a "testament" (Gk. *diathēkē* means both covenant and testament). 1 Tim. 2:5 insists that Jesus Christ is the "one mediator between God and humankind." This explains a controversy between Luther and Calvin on one side, and the Roman Catholic Church on the other. In Calvin Jesus is Mediator as prophet, priest, and king. He writes, "He who was to be our Mediator should be very God and very man" (*Institutes* 2.12.1; Beveridge, 1:400). His "three offices" are those of prophet, priest, and king (2.15.2-6). The Roman Catholic Church did not have any doubt about Christ's role as Mediator; it affirmed it; but was Christ uniquely sole Mediator? The Council of Trent declared, "We were saved through the merits of the Mediator, our Lord Jesus Christ" (session 5, canon 31). But over the years many secondary mediators were added: earthly priests, angels, and especially the Virgin Mary in heaven. Pope Pius XII declared Mary *Mediatrix*, in the twentieth century. The Reformers recognized a plurality of mediators in the OT era, but insisted on the unique status of Christ as sole mediator in the NT and thereafter. Luther insisted that God alone, not earthly priests, could enact forgiveness of sins. Much may depend on definition, for clearly ministers plead in prayer on behalf of people, and declare God's commandments to them. This lies behind many Protestant objections to applying the term "priest" to ministers. Evangelical Anglicans often quote John Milton's earlier aphorism, "New Presbyter is but old Priest writ large."

Emil Brunner's book *The Mediator* (London: Lutterworth, 1934) appeared in English after the German, *Der Mittler,* had appeared in 1927. He said the book had "grown out of that conflict with modern theology," which he believed had become unhealthy (16). Mediation, he insisted, presupposed both the deity of the Mediator (201-85) and his humanity (316-54). He makes a similar point to that in Hebrews. He attacks the tendency in "modern" theology to soften the contrast between God and humankind, both in the Western and Eastern Churches (399-415). The work of the Mediator must not be relegated to a "subordinate position" (407). He concludes, "The being of the Mediator is the gift and the act of God" (409). This Mediator entails not only his death, but his entire "humiliation," in which he became one with humankind. This movement of Christ's work is "from God to God" (562). The cross is meaningful only if Christ is also "the One from above." Even though it was written in 1927, Brunner's book is still needed as a reminder of a key theme in biblical writings and the Reformation.

Reading: E. Brunner, *The Mediator* (London: Lutterworth, 1934); C. Eastwood, *The Priesthood of All Believers* (London: Epworth, 1960); R. P. Martin, *Reconciliation* (London: Marshall, 1981); T. McGovern, *Priestly Identity* (Dublin: Four Courts Press, 2002); R. C. Moberly, *Ministerial Priesthood* (London: SPCK, 1969); Vincent Taylor, *Forgiveness and Reconciliation* (New York and London, 1948).

Melanchthon, Philip

Philip Melanchthon (1497-1560) graduated at Heidelberg (1511) and Tübingen (1514). In 1518 he became the professor of Greek at the new University of Wittenberg, where he remained for most of his academic career. He soon fell under the influence of Luther. In addition to works on biblical exegesis and theology, he worked on several confessional documents, especially the Augsburg Confession (1530). Although this confession was Lutheran, the language was moderate in order not to offend Catholics. He was more indebted than Luther to humanism and rhetoric. Like Luther, he distinguished between law and gospel. Against Carlstadt and other Radical Reformers, but with Luther, he distinguished civil righteousness, which was still valid for the Christian, from the saving righteousness that comes from God. He lectured in Greek and Latin literature as well as on theology. He indirectly influenced Martin Bucer and John Calvin.

Melanchthon's use of rhetoric and dialectic contributed to his *Loci communes.* He also produced commentaries on Romans, Colossians, and Proverbs. He advocated justification by faith, but in a form intended to meet Roman Catholic criticisms of the Lutheran doctrine. Matthias Flacius accused him of synergism, and this led to debates among the Lutheran churches. During 1521-1527 he corrected Luther's translation of the Bible. Alone among the Reformers, he stopped short of outright condemnation of the papacy. He even sought to unite the churches, and certainly to bridge differences within the Lutheran church. (*See also* **Luther, Martin.**)

Mennonites

These believers derive their name from Menno Simons (1496-1561), who left the Roman Catholic Church in 1536 to join the Anabaptists. He insisted on believer's baptism and congregational church government, and urged nonresistance or pacifism, and withdrawal from magistracy. These congregations became numerous in the Netherlands in the seventeenth and eighteenth centuries. In the twentieth century there were about 226,000 Mennonites in America, about 18,000 in Germany, and the same in the Netherlands. Each congregation remains independent. Mennonites are widely known for their pacifism and social work.

Metaphor
In any significant or creative sense, metaphor does not denote merely an illustrative or decorative function of language. It is not mere literary flourish, or a rhetorical substitution of what could otherwise be expressed in sober prose. George Lakoff and Mark Johnson often receive credit for perceiving the more creative capacities of metaphor in *Metaphors We Live By* (Chicago: University of Chicago Press, 1980). But this had already become a matter of wide agreement by the mid–twentieth century. Admittedly Aristotle regarded it as a compressed simile (*Rhetoric* 4.1-3), which offered a comparison. But several essays appeared in Max Black, ed., *The Importance of Language* (Englewood Cliffs, N.J.: Prentice-Hall, 1963), that explored its creativity. In that volume Owen Barfield compared metaphors with applications to new situations in law in his essay "Poetic Diction and Legal Fiction," and C. S. Lewis, in "Bluspels and Flalansferes," described ornamental metaphors as "pupil" metaphors and creative, conceptual metaphors as "master" metaphors. Black traced the interactive function of metaphor in *Models and Metaphors* (Ithaca, N.Y.: Cornell University Press, 1962). P. Wheelwright spoke of "double-language" function in *Metaphor and Reality* (Bloomington: Indiana University Press, 1962). This brings us close to Paul Ricoeur's view of symbol as "double meaning" that can "give rise to thought" (*The Rule of Metaphor* [Toronto: University of Toronto Press, 1977], 6). Only very recently David Parris explored this approach in "Metaphors, Cognitive Theory, and Jesus' Shortest Parable," in *Horizons in Hermeneutics,* ed. S. E. Porter and M. R. Malcolm (Grand Rapids: Eerdmans, 2013), 148-74.

Ricoeur points to the tension that exists between the convention of so-called literal meaning and the second or target meaning of the metaphor, when the metaphor is placed in a different context. As Ian Paul has commented, Ricoeur moved metaphor "from the perceptual to the cognitive" ("Metaphor," in *DTIB* 507). Mary Hesse explored this in *Models and Analogies in Science* (London: Sheed and Ward, 1963), and Janet Martin Soskice in *Metaphor and Religious Language* (Oxford: Clarendon, 1985). Metaphors not only extend the boundaries or horizons of what we already know, they also provide solidly based *cognitive* grounds for doing so, and therefore make truth claims. To cite Ian Paul again, "Metaphors make real and substantial claims about reality that cannot be expressed in alternative propositional forms" (508). This provides a way in which reality can *expand*. This is a key part of W. Pannenberg's agenda. Theology can provide a more comprehensive horizon than any other individual subject-discipline. We are familiar with such simple biblical metaphors as "I am the light of the world." But what began as live metaphors can soon become dead ones. Originally, as Ian Paul argues, "inflation" was applied only to the expansion of a balloon, or, we might add, metaphorically, to the pride of the human ego in the apostle Paul's use of *phusioō* in 1 Cor. 8:1. But in the twentieth and twenty-first centuries, this overfamiliar metaphor has become so much a part of our vocabulary in economics that its original metaphorical status has been forgotten; it has become a "dead" metaphor, and now tells us nothing new. Daily life is riddled with dead metaphors. A person who "fishes" for compliments is not going fishing; a person who has a "broken heart" has not let his or her heart fall into bits; a "bubbly" personality does not produce bubbles or boil over; an "inflammatory" news article does not actually cause a fire. These expressions originally created an impact that dull propositions could not. But over time and regular use they have lost much of their creative power.

There is also a darker side to metaphor. Some are so suspicious of language that they are already hostile to metaphor. Friedrich Nietzsche, for example, wrote: "What is truth? A mobile army of metaphors, metonyms and anthropomorphisms" (*On Truth and the Lies* [1873]). Wittgenstein laments that in his earlier period, "A picture held us captive" (*Philosophical Investigations* [Oxford: Blackwell, 1958], sects. 109 and 115). Jacques Derrida makes a similar claim in his essay "White Mythology." We have been led astray, he argues, by "so-called philosophical metaphors" (*Margins of Philosophy* [London: Harvester, 1982], 213). The Barthian Christian theologian Eberhard Jüngel, however, does not dismiss Nietzsche too hastily. Nietzsche, he claims, wishes both to discredit truth and to honor metaphor (*Theological Essays*, 2 vols. [Edinburgh: T. & T. Clark, 1989], 1:28). He concedes that Nietzsche stresses "deception, flattering, lying, deluding, talking behind the back, putting up a false front, living in borrowed splendour, wearing a mask, hiding behind convention" (29). But all this has to do with preserving the self, and seeks to represent the "actuality" of a fallen world. By contrast, "metaphors are the articulation of discoveries" beyond actuality (51). Nietzsche's language about "a moveable host, or army, of metaphors" can be "turned in another direction, and . . . taken positively" (53). He sees falsity in metaphor's depiction of *actuality*, but leaves room for the depiction of *possibility*. Jüngel writes, "The language of faith is metaphorical through and through" (58). Metaphor brings together not only two semantic domains, but "two horizons" (60).

Metaphor, he argues, draws on the language and vocabulary of this earthly world, and with "a hermeneutical tension" also finds anchorage in the "strange world" of the Bible, as Barth calls it, and most of all of Christ and God. God is transcendent and different from the world. Yet we also need everyday worldly language and vocabulary because there is no other. Thus, Jüngel argues, "The cross of Jesus Christ is the ground and measure of the formation of metaphors which are appropriate to God" (65). He repeats, "If the cross, as the world's turning-point, is the foundation and measure of metaphorical language about God, then such language itself has the function of bringing about a turning around, a change of direction. God cannot be spoken of as if everything remained as it was," that is, by descriptive propositions about the world or human existence (65). Jüngel completes his study of metaphor by reinforcing our earlier points, but for a theological purpose. He comments, "The horizon of this world is *expanded*" (71, italics mine). We can see its actuality and possibilities from a new perspective. He concludes, "The hermeneutical end-point of theological metaphors is thus *invocation of the Holy Spirit*.... Working out a theological theory of metaphor is an urgent desideratum for both Dogmatics and practical theology" (71). Paul Avis also argues for the theological importance of metaphor in *God and the Creative Imagination* (New York: Routledge, 1999).

If metaphor is so vital for theological hermeneutics, we must attempt to round off this consideration of metaphor with a few further comments on its practical application in biblical hermeneutics.

First, it is obvious that metaphor, by opening new horizons, must constitute an antidote to narcissism, to self-centeredness or limited focus on the preexisting concerns of the self. Yet this exposes a difficulty. If the whole point of metaphor is to employ familiar language from the everyday world at the level of the "vehicle," or everyday comparison, may there not emerge the danger of *reducing* the content, the possible, the unexpressed, or the as-yet-unknown to the familiar? This, again, is the problem of dead metaphor and overfamiliarization. The author of the book of Revelation uses the metaphor of four horsemen, or a seven-branched candlestick, from Ezekiel and Zechariah. But these have become so familiar that their metaphorical or symbolic status sometimes becomes forgotten. G. Beasley-Murray is forced to ask literalists, for example, do the four horsemen stable their horses in heavenly stables? How can "streets of gold," if taken literally, be part of a city that is several miles in length and width, and several miles high, like a cube? Perhaps we should spend less time expounding the immediate historical context of the first readers, and more time expounding the history of the metaphorical aspects of the image. This will lift the eyes of hearers beyond themselves and even beyond the text, to that to which the text points (*see* **Symbol**).

Second, imagery and metaphor seem often to denote picture. But pictures have various functions. Sometimes a picture can be mental. Wittgenstein explains, "A picture held us captive. And we could not get outside it" (*Philosophical Investigations,* sect. 115). This would be the very opposite to opening new horizons. In the middle of section 23 he imagines a picture representing a boxer in a particular stance. This may be used, he explains, "to tell someone how he should stand ... ; how he should not hold himself; or how a particular man did stand in such-and-such a place; and so on" (11). In his *Zettel* (Oxford: Blackwell, 1967) he adds, "A picture, whatever it may be, can be variously interpreted.... When one has the picture in view by itself, it is suddenly dead" (sect. 236). The difference between simply *seeing* a picture and determining how it is *used or applied* lies at the heart of visionary pictures such as those that sometimes occur in mysticism or Pentecostal or charismatic renewal circles. "Pictures" seen by Hildegard of Bingen in her *Scivias,* or those of Catherine of Siena in her *Dialogues* 67 and 141, or by Julian of Norwich in her *Revelations of Divine Love* or *Showings,* may be impressive. But because of their loyalty to the Christian tradition and the cross, they operate within reasonable bounds, at least most of the time. Teresa of Ávila seems more speculative, however, in her *Interior Castle*. As Wittgenstein reminds us, a picture can be *variously interpreted*. This point can be clarified further by considering symbol and Ian Ramsey's models and qualifiers.

A third problem arises from the vagueness and overlap in popular use between the terms "metaphor," "symbol," "analogy," and "myth." Symbol has a sound exposition in Ricoeur, but also contains some suspect aspects about the collective unconscious in Paul Tillich and Carl Jung. R. Bultmann could have avoided some mistakes if he had used the term "myth" consistently, and also spoken not of myth but of metaphor and self-involvement. G. B. Caird suggests that serious misunderstandings about Mark 13 might have been avoided if readers and scholars had perceived the metaphorical status of the end-of-the-world language used by Jesus. This chapter, Caird argues, shows "a curious interplay between the metaphorical and the literal" (*The Language and Imagery of the Bible* [London: Duckworth, 1980], 246). He explains, "Mark 13 begins with Jesus predicting the destruction of the Temple" (266). This will happen within a lifetime. If we conflate with this a very different question, "When is the world coming to an end?" this confusion gives "serious justification for supposing Mark to be a fool." But those passages in Mark 13 that concern the coming or return of the Son of Man answer a different question, and do not imply that this will happen within a generation: "the day and hour are known only to God" (cf. 13:30, 32). It is vital, Caird concludes, to understand what language is used metaphorically, and what conventionally or literally, when we are expressing passages about eschatology (243-71). (*See also* **Analogy; Myth; Ramsey, Ian; Ricoeur, Paul.**)

Reading: Paul D. L. Avis, *God and the Creative Imagination* (London and New York: Routledge, 1999); M. Black, *Models and Metaphors* (Ithaca, N.Y.: Cornell University Press, 1962); E. Jüngel, *Theological Essays*, vol. 1 (Edinburgh: T. & T. Clark, 1989); G. Lakoff and M. Johnson, *Metaphors We Live By* (Chicago: University of Chicago Press, 1980); P. Ricoeur, *The Rule of Metaphor* (New York: Routledge, 1978); J. Martin Soskice, *Metaphor and Religious Language* (Oxford: Clarendon, 1985).

Metaphysics

Metaphysics is closely related to ontology, or to the exploration of the nature of reality. In its broader sense it inquires into the nature of all that is. In a narrower sense it sometimes stands in contrast to our everyday experience of the world. Aristotle's *Metaphysics* included "large" philosophical questions such as potentiality, actuality, causation, and substance. But the term "metaphysics" arose from an accident in the classifying of Aristotle's works. Andronicus of Rhodes placed the work "after" (Gk. *meta*) the treatise entitled *Physics*, hence *meta physics*.

Methodist, Methodism

Methodism was associated in its origins with John Wesley (1703-1791) and his brother Charles. The name "Methodist" derives from their student days at Oxford, when the two brothers, with George Whitefield and their friends, were nicknamed "the Holy Club" and "Methodists," because of their strict rules in pursuit of holiness. They sought to return to the devotional practices of earliest Christianity. The entry in this book under Wesley records John's journey to Georgia, USA, his link with the Moravians, and his conversion experience in 1738, together with his recollections of it in his *Journals*. He and Whitefield sought to preach the gospel to Bristol, and his famous dictum, "All the world is my parish," seems to have emerged in 1739. When he preached at Moorfields, London, some ten thousand were affected, and what Wesley called "the true, old Christianity" began also to be called "Methodism." John Wesley was an ordained Anglican, and he never wished to leave the Church of England and to found a new denomination. Charles felt even more strongly about remaining in the Church of England, and never left it. The trouble and potential breaking point arose because of Wesley's "lay preachers." He sought to commission them as "true ministers," and explicitly asked the bishop of London to ordain them. But the Anglican authorities recognized only those who were episcopally ordained. This has long been a source of contention between most Methodists and most Anglicans. It was not Wesley, but Wesley's preachers, who in effect founded a new denomination.

In America, the rift became confirmed when Wesley ordained Francis Asbury and Thomas Coke. In practice they performed the role of bishops, though at first they were called general superintendents. In England, Wesley and his group established "preaching houses," later called chapels, with centers especially in London, Bristol, and Newcastle, with local preachers who exercised a Sunday ministry. At first the chapels were called "societies," operating under the "Rules of the United Societies." A system of "circuits" was set up. In 1744 Wesley convened his preachers together to form the first Methodist conference, still today the supreme authority in English Methodism. But by 1784 a strain arose between John and Charles (see below). Charles wrote that, even with all her blemishes, Anglicanism was nearer the scriptural plans than any other in Europe, and he disapproved of the drift away from the Church of England. In practice the link with the Church of England was sustained until John's death in 1791. But by 1789 the membership of Wesley's chapels and societies had risen above 56,000. In 1784 a Deed of Declaration regularized the "Methodist" constitution. A hundred preachers were given authority to oversee administration and the ministry, and to fill new vacancies. This "Legal Hundred" admitted laypeople to their numbers in 1788. There was prolonged discussion about the administration of Holy Communion, and in 1795 preachers were allowed to conduct these services, if approval was granted by trustees, stewards, and "class leaders." The separation became complete in 1836. In 1838 there was a membership of about 339,000.

The church now had a polity that mixed central oversight with the quasi autonomy of local congregations. It was less "congregational" than the Baptist model, but also less centralized than the Church of England, with its bishops. Presbyterianism sought the same kind of middle way. However, in the first half of the nineteenth century Jabez Bunting was a strong and quasi-autocratic leader who caused some controversy. In 1842 Didsbury College was opened for the training of ministers; Headingly, Hansworth, followed in 1843; and Wesley House, Cambridge, in 1925. Meanwhile in America, Wesley had appointed Thomas Rankin as superintendent in 1773, and there were already Methodists in Maryland (under Robert Strawbridge) and New York (led by Philip Embury and Thomas Webb). The main centers of Methodism were Delaware, Maryland, and Virginia, and Virginian preachers began to withdraw from the Anglican Church in 1779. Francis Asbury convened a Methodist conference in Baltimore, together with Thomas Coke, and they designated their superintendents as "bishops." In effect the Methodist Episcopal Church was thus founded in 1784. Their liturgy was a revised or modified version of the Anglican *Book of Common Prayer,* and their doctrinal basis was a shortened form of the Thirty-nine Articles. In 1792 a General Conference was constituted as the lawmaking body of the American Methodist Episcopal Church.

In both America and England divisions *within* Methodism also occurred. In 1811 the Primitive Methodist Church was formed in England by Hugh Bourne and William Clowes. This stemmed largely from a revival. By 1850 it had become a denomination; by 1860 it had 675 ministers and 11,000 lay preachers. In 1857 the Wesleyan Methodists joined with "Wesleyan Reformers" to form the United Methodist Free Church. It took until 1932 for the Primitive Methodists and the United Free Methodists to come together as the Methodist Church, with 800,000 members. In America a division occurred in 1830. The Methodist Protestant Church formed to curb the power of the Methodist bishops, and disowned the name "Episcopal." There was further tension between the southern Methodists and others over the problem of slavery. In 1843 the Wesleyan Methodist Church was formed. In 1845 the Methodist Episcopal Church South was formed. But in 1870 steps were taken toward reunion, and by 1876 the rift was healed. Further union with the Methodist Protestant Church took place in 1939. The Canadian Methodist Church was slower to form, with several branches in 1834, and a United Methodist Church in 1874. In 1925 it combined with the Congregationalist Church.

Methodists in Scotland remained few in number. Methodists globally, however, were noted for their social work, schools, and missions. In America Methodists sponsored Boston University School of Theology (1841), Garrett Theological Seminary (1853-1855), and Duke Theological Seminary (1867). The southern Methodists founded Vanderbilt University in Nashville (1872). Hospitals were founded in Brooklyn (1881), and at Emory University in Atlanta (1905). The Methodist Missionary Society was founded in 1819. (*See also Book of Common Prayer;* Holy, Holiness; Sanctification; Sinless Perfection; Wesley, John.)

Reading: T. Campbell, *Methodist Doctrine* (Nashville: Abingdon, 1999); J. Craske and J. Marsh, eds., *Methodism and the Future* (London: Continuum, 1999); N. B. Harmon, ed., *Encyclopaedia of World Methodism,* 2 vols. (Nashville: Abingdon, 1974);

G. S. Wakefield, *Methodist Spirituality* (London: Epworth, 1999); Kenneth Wilson, *Methodist Theology* (London: Continuum/T. & T. Clark, 2011).

Millennium
Belief in a millennium, or thousand-year period in which the saints will rule while the devil is bound, appears to depend for biblical evidence virtually wholly on Rev. 20:1-10, while the Synoptic Gospels, John, Paul, and Hebrews either ignore it or seem to reject it. Some appeal to a forced exegesis of 1 Cor. 15:22-28 and 1 Thess. 4:15-17. Among those who believe in the promise of a millennium, premillennialists believe that the millennium will *follow* the parousia, or return of Christ (i.e., the return *pre*dates the millennium); postmillennialists believe it will occur *before* the return of Christ (i.e., the return *post*dates it). Both sorts of millennialists tend to believe in plenary inspiration of the Bible, so that the dependence of the belief on only ten verses in the book of Revelation does not trouble them. Nevertheless, the key issue remains one of hermeneutics: How should we interpret the book of Revelation, and these verses in particular?

In chapter 20 an angel descends and seizes "the dragon, that ancient serpent, who is the Devil and Satan," to bind him for a thousand years (Rev. 20:2). He throws him into the abyss, locks and seals it, and prevents his deceiving the nations "until the thousand years were ended" (20:3). Then the martyrs who were beheaded for their testimony to Christ are raised to life, and they reign "with Christ a thousand years" (20:4). This is called "the first resurrection" (20:5), in which to share is counted blessed (20:6). When the thousand years are ended, "Satan will be released from his prison and will come out to deceive the nations" (20:7). Finally, Gog and Magog march to attack the Holy City (20:8), and the devil is "thrown into the lake of fire" forever (20:10).

A premillennialist interpretation is defended by J. F. Walvoord (*The Revelation of Jesus Christ* [Chicago: Moody, 1966], 291 and elsewhere, and *Armageddon: Oil and the Middle East* [Grand Rapids: Zondervan, 1990], esp. 218). This interpretation also emerged from J. N. Darby (1800-1882) and the Scofield Reference Bible (1909), together with the "dispensationalist" approach. This view also indirectly influences conservative American politics, especially in relation to Israel and Zionism. In popular thought it is associated with Hal Lindsey. Others who interpreted the millennium in a literalistic way were William Miller (1782-1849) and the "Millerites," who were forerunners of Seventh-Day Adventists. This belief is also known as *chiliasm*. Those who favor this view may appeal to Justin, Irenaeus, Tertullian, Lactantius, and possibly Hippolytus (cf. Justin, *Dialogue with Trypho* 77-79; *ANF* 1:237-38). On the other side stand Origen, Tyconius, Augustine, and later, Luther and Calvin.

G. B. Caird argues that belief in the millennium is "demonstrably false" (*The Revelation of St. John the Divine* [London: Black, 1966], 250). In conservative circles the decisive breakthrough was achieved by William Hendriksen in his commentary *More Than Conquerors: An Interpretation of the Book of Revelation*

(1940; Grand Rapids: Baker; London: Tyndale, 1962], 182). He demonstrated that Revelation is not intended as a sequential chronological history of world history or posthistory. He showed, for example, that Rev. 12:5-11 is closely parallel with 20:1-3; while 11:2-6 and 12:14-17 are closely parallel with 20:2; 11:7 is parallel with 20:7-10; and 14:14-16 is parallel with 20:11-15 (185-88). The events, he concludes, are symbolic. He writes, "The theory of the premillennialists is at variance with the facts here" (185). Hendriksen argues that the binding of Satan begins with the first coming of Jesus Christ, even if Satan still exercises limited power. In the Gospels Christ is "the stronger man" who "binds" the strong man who had held the household in bondage (Mark 3:27). Robert Mounce repeats the view of Caird and Hendriksen, commenting, "There is no specific indication that their [the saints'] reign with Christ takes place on earth, or that it necessarily follows the second advent" (*The Book of Revelation* [Grand Rapids: Eerdmans, 1977], 351). He believes that the strictly controlled and limited activity of Satan exactly fits the present age, in which he is not "completely inactive" (352). The context concerns the steadfastness of the martyrs (359), not *all* the saints. To turn parallel events into a time chart is to ignore the symbolism of the book of Revelation. In Caird's words, such a view is "to unweave the rainbow." He adds, "John uses his allusions not as a code, . . . but for their evocative and emotive power" (25).

Once we insist on a literalist rather than a symbolic view of Revelation, we open the door to a torrent of confusion. In interpreting numerals, for example, what are we to make of seven stars and seven lampstands (Rev. 1:20); of seven spirits (1:4; 4:5; 5:6); of the Lamb with seven horns and seven eyes (5:6); of the beast with seven heads, or seven plagues, or seven mountains (12:3; 15:1; 17:9)? Revelation uses "seven" sixty times; its ancestry includes Leviticus (eighty times) and Genesis (sixty-seven times). It usually signifies wholeness or completeness, although it may occasionally function as a numeral. John Calvin recognizes Revelation as prophecy, as well as perhaps apocalyptic, but he comments that prophecy relates to reconciliation with God, not to speculation about the future (*Institutes* 4.3.4 and 1.9.3). A "millennial" interpretation deserves respect, but it flies in the face of exegetical and hermeneutical evidence. (*See also* **Darby, John Nelson; Dispensationalism; Parousia; Scofield Reference Bible.**)

Reading: G. K. Beale, *The Book of Revelation: Greek Text* (Grand Rapids: Eerdmans, 1999); G. B. Caird, *The Revelation of John the Divine* (London: Black, 1966); R. G. Clouse, ed., *The Meaning of the Millennium: Four Views* (Downers Grove, Ill.: InterVarsity, 1977); W. Hendriksen, *More Than Conquerors* (Grand Rapids: Baker, 1962); R. Mounce, *The Book of Revelation* (Grand Rapids: Eerdmans, 1977).

Ministry

Ministry, whether ordained or lay, is designed to serve the church. It can be argued that ministry and ministers do not form the basis of the church. On the other hand, the ministry is an essential feature of the church, not an option. Paul establishes three principles in 1 Corinthians. First, he warns his readers both against too high a view of ministry and against too low a view of ministry. In 1 Cor. 3:5 he asks, "What (Gk. neuter *ti*) then is Apollos? What (Gk. *ti*) is Paul? Servants through whom you came to believe." They perform contingent or specific tasks, which are denoted by Greek aorists, in contrast to a *continuous tense* for the activity of God: "God went on giving the increase" (3:6, translation mine). Paul explicitly concludes, "So neither the one who plants nor the one who waters is anything, but only God who gives the growth" (3:7). On the other hand, their tasks are "as the Lord assigned to each" (3:5). Those Corinthians who choose only their favorites as ministers, or use self-selection, are "cheating themselves" (Gk. *mēdeis heaton exapatatō*) out of God-given ministerial resources (3:18). For boasting about human leaders leads to excluding others, and Paul declares, "All things are yours, whether Paul or Apollos or Cephas" (3:21-22), which clearly looks back to "I belong to Paul," "I belong to Apollos," and "I belong to Cephas" in 1:12.

Second, church and ministry operate together as a guarantee of continuity and apostolicity. Some Roman Catholics and a few Anglo-Catholics may still regard continuity and apostolicity as somehow transmitted by the laying on of hands in an unbroken institutional quasi-physical line. In terms of assurance and public visibility, this perhaps still has some value. But most Christians, including many Catholics today, regard it as equally important that, in Luther's language, the pure gospel is preached, and see this as a sign of authenticity and continuity. In this respect both the church and ministry together carry forward genuine apostolicity. Lesslie Newbigin traced the three lines of Catholic, Protestant, and Pentecostal as offering different accounts of continuity (*The Household of God* [London: SCM, 1953]). But there is no reason why these three traditions should not be complementary. Traditionally the bishop has been the guardian of doctrine and continuity, in cooperation with fellow bishops and others. Paul's view of apostolicity is set out in the entry on **Apostle, Apostolicity**.

Third, Paul does not operate as a freelance minister. A. T. Hanson recommended that rather than impose a doctrine of ministry onto the NT, we look and see how ministry was actually carried out (*The Pioneer Ministry* [London: SCM, 1961], 46). Paul worked *collaboratively* with a host of colleagues, including Barnabas, Silvanus, Apollos, Timothy, Titus, Epaphras, Mark, Luke, Priscilla, Aquila, and many others (Rom. 16:3, 9, 21; 2 Cor. 8:23; Phil. 2:25; 4:3; Col. 4:11; 1 Thess. 3:2; Philem. 24; and elsewhere). Although some NT passages speak of a local church, Paul seems concerned to promote a translocal orderliness and identity. At a bare minimum, the churches are mutually supportive, as may be seen from Paul's concern for the collection for the church in Jerusalem (1 Cor. 16:1-4; 2 Cor. 9:1-15).

In the Pastoral Epistles Paul (or his disciple) is concerned for the order and infrastructure of the church, with respect to the appointment of ministers. W. D. Mounce sets out admirably both the question of doubts about the identity of the author, and characteristics expected of bishops (or overseers), elders (or presbyters or priests), and deacons, in his *Pastoral Epistles,* Word Biblical Commentary, vol. 46 (Nashville: Nelson, 2000), introduction, 149-92, and 406-19. The bishop or overseer (Gk. *episkopos*) in 1 Tim 3:1-7 is to be "above reproach" (Gk. *anepilēmptos*); "a one-woman man"; "clear-minded" (Gk. *nēphalion*); "self-controlled" (Gk. *sōphrōn*); "dignified" (i.e., with gravitas; Gk. *kosmios*); "hospitable" (Gk. *philoxenos*); "skilled in teaching" (Gk. *didaktikos*); "not a drunkard, not violent," "gracious" (Gk. *epieikēs*); "not quarrelsome, not a lover of money, managing his household well"; "not a recent convert" (Gk. *mē neophutos;* Mounce's translations, 156-57). The elder is to share many of these qualities: "above reproach"; "disciplined" (Gk. *enkratēs*); and "not arrogant" (Gk. *mē authadēs*). Many of these characteristics, although fewer in number, are expected of the deacon. It clearly is not a formal list, for Paul was not married. But Mounce rightly observes, "It was important to confirm management abilities, as seen in their families" (159). In 1 Cor. 4:1 Paul had spoken of ministers as stewards, or better, managers (Gk. *oikonomos*), and in 1 Cor. 3:10 as a wise "building-manager" (Gk. *sophos architektōn*). In 1 Cor. 12:28 he had listed "first apostles, second prophets, third teachers." Many later commentators, including Thomas Aquinas, regarded prophets as teachers or elders. A similar list of characteristics for ministers appears in Titus 2:1-10 (*The Pastoral Epistles,* 408-16).

The Pastorals appear to speak of bishops (Gk. *episkopos*), although Mounce cites a number of scholars who insist on a different translation. But there are no adequate grounds for Harnack's claim that this organizational structure is foreign to the nature of the gospel (*see* **Ecclesiology**). Certainly by the time of Ignatius (c. 112) bishops were a distinct order from presbyters. On the other hand, many today (English Methodists and Scottish Presbyterians) argue that presbyters may exercise an episcopal ministry. Recently John Collins has argued that *deacons* are deputies for the elders or presbyters, and do not exercise simply a "social" or administrative ministry. Some argue that "bishops" and "elders" are used interchangeably in *1 Clement,* Polycarp, and Clement of Alexandria. But no doubt the pattern of ministry developed in accordance with the needs of the church. By the time of Theodore of Mopsuestia (350-428), bishops had authority to ordain and had authority over a whole province, not a single church. (*See also* **Apostle, Apostolicity; Baptist Theology; Bishop; Presbyterian, Presbyterianism.**)

Reading: Paul Avis, *A Ministry Shaped by Mission* (New York and London: T. & T. Clark, 2005); S. Croft, *Ministry in Three Dimensions* (London: DLT, 1999); A. T. Hanson, *The Pioneer Ministry* (London: SCM, 1961); John Macquarrie, *Theology, Church, and Ministry* (London: SCM, 1986); W. D. Mounce, *Pastoral Epistles* (Nashville: Nelson, 2000).

Miracles

(Heb. *'ōth* and *mōpēth;* Gk. *dynamis* and *sēmeion;* and many more terms.) If we try to define "miracle," we immediately run into problems. Most agree that a miracle is a publicly observable event, or empirically verifiable event, but not all agree on its cause or purpose. Traditionally, Christian theologians have claimed that such an event was caused by an unusual intervention of God, which, in the words of Thomas Aquinas, is not "against" nature but "beyond" nature. Miracles are also not ends in themselves, but serve some higher, or ethical, purpose. In recent years theologians have tried to avoid the words "supernatural act." This is not because they limit God's omnipotence, but because, as W. Hollenweger has argued about "gifts of the Spirit," this language seems to promote a dualism between two kinds of acts of God in the world. As Craig Keener argues, "Philosophers debate the meaning of 'miracle'" (*Miracles*, 2 vols. [Grand Rapids: Baker Academic, 2011], 1:109). He describes the traditional definition of "an extraordinary event with an unusual supernatural cause" as "problematic," because "all that is natural has an ultimate supernatural cause" (110). Moreover, the term "extraordinary" depends on subjective judgment. What we call *unusual* is also a matter of degree. At the opposite end of the spectrum, Keener rejects David Hume's definition as that which "breaks" laws of nature as "circular" (112). Clearly, any definition would be difficult for atheists such as Feuerbach, pantheists such as Spinoza, and Deists such as Toland. If "God" is identical with the natural order, or else totally outside it, "miracles are self-contradictory" (114).

In the OT *'ōth* occurs some seventy-eight times, for which the LXX translation is *sēmeion*, normally "sign." But on twelve occasions it is coupled with wonders, often as "signs and wonders." Deut. 13:1-2 (NRSV, "omens and portents") alludes to false prophets and hence can be ignored. "A sign and a portent" (NRSV) also occurs in Deut. 28:46, as a warning against disobedience, curse, and destruction. "The signs, and those great wonders" (Deut 29:3) are warnings directed at Pharaoh. Notably "signs and wonders" were usually not to confirm faith. Sometimes, however, "signs and wonders" may be to provide encouragement (Exod. 4:30; 7:3; Deut. 4:34). The word *'ōth*, on its own, often denotes a visible sign of the presence, power, and will of God. In 2 Kings 20:8-9, when Hezekiah asks Isaiah, "What shall be the sign that the LORD will heal me?" Isaiah replies, "This is the sign . . . : shall [the shadow] retreat ten intervals?" The KJV/AV translates *mōpēth* twice as "miracle," eight times as "sign," and twenty-three times as "wonder." K. H. Rengstorff sees it as expressing God's power, but in Isa. 38:7-8 it is not only as a sign of assurance to Hezekiah, but also as an equivalent to Greek *teras*, "portent" or "wonder" (*TDNT* 8:118). Signs and portents can be used for such purposes as healing (2 Kings 5:10, Naaman the Syrian). They can be used to meet a need: Exod. 15:25, 16:4-15, 17:5.

In the NT Jesus regularly performs "mighty works" or "deeds of power" (Gk. *dynamis* in Matt. 7:22, "Many deeds of power in your name," although these may not be authentic miracles; Matt. 13:54, "Where did this man get . . . these deeds of power?"; Mark 5:30 and parallels, "Power had gone forth" [to the woman with a hemorrhage]; and Mark 6:2). In general *sēmeion* occurs no less often than *dynamis*. In Matt. 12:38 the scribes and Pharisees "wish to see a sign *(sēmeion)* from you," but Jesus will give them no sign but the sign of Jonah (v. 39). There are a couple of dozen occurrences of *sēmeion* in the Synoptic Gospels (although not all with the same meaning), and eighteen occurrences in John. John links "sign" with what we usually call "miracle," for example, at the wedding at Cana (John 2:11-23). *Sēmeion* occurs in the discourse with Nicodemus (3:2); the recovery of the centurion's dead son (4:54); the crowd's appetite for "signs" (6:2); the feeding of the multitude (6:14, together with the warning about signs, 6:26, 30); the Feast of Booths (7:31; cf. 9:16; 10:41; 11:47); and the raising of Lazarus (12:18, 37; cf. 20:30). The notion of "signs" to confirm faith or to exhibit Jesus' power seems more often to come from the Jews than from Jesus.

Alan Richardson sums up the problem admirably. He writes, "We need feel no surprise at the paradox that, while Jesus refused to give a sign to those who demanded one, he nevertheless regarded his miracles as signs which would be understood by those who had responded to the proclamation of ... the reign of God" (*Introduction to the Theology of the New Testament* [London: SCM, 1958], 96). His miracles were signs to those who recognized him. Earlier Richardson commented, "the first-century question was not whether Jesus could perform miracles, but by what authority he performed them (Mark 11:28)" (95). To those who recognized them, they were confirmation that the kingdom of God had come near (Luke 4:16-30). The exorcisms constitute such signs (Matt. 12:28; Luke 11:20). Jesus is in process of putting an end to the reign of Satan. The greatest and most decisive act of God is the resurrection, which opens the new age. On miracles as such, Jesus observes, "Neither will they be convinced even if someone rises from the dead" (Luke 16:31). The miracles are part of the preaching of the gospel.

Jesus delegates his power to the apostles (Mark 6:7; Matt. 10:1, 8; Luke 9:1; 10:19; John 14:12; Acts 1:8). The miracles point not to the power of the church, but to God's presence and power within it. The Epistles speak of special gifts of powerful deeds or miracles, given to some, but not to all (1 Cor. 12:28-30; Rom. 12:4-8; Eph. 4:11-12). But *dynamis* now more characteristically refers to Christ and the power of the gospel (1 Cor. 1:18; Col. 1:11).

Even in ancient times some had misconceptions about miracles. Hence Augustine has to insist that miracles are not "contrary to nature," but "contrary to *what is known of* nature" (*City of God* 21.8; *NPNF*, ser. 1, 2:459). Thomas Aquinas asserts, "Some miracles are not true, but imaginary deeds, because they delude man ... while others are true deeds, yet have not the character of true miracles, because they are done by the power of natural cause" (*Su Th* 2.2, qu. 178, art. 2, reply). True miracles are worked by God "for man's benefit." He quotes Augustine as arguing against a greater number of miracles lest "the weak be deceived" (art. 2, reply to obj. 4). Calvin is writing of the deity of Christ when he exclaims, "How clearly and transparently does this appear in his miracles" (*Institutes* 1.13.13; Beveridge, 1:121). Such belief reflects Christian orthodoxy. But the rise of the natural sciences in the seventeenth and eighteenth centuries brought new problems. As Craig Keener comments, "The most influential voice contributing to the long-standing modern prejudice against miracles was undoubtedly the eighteenth-century philosopher David Hume" (*Miracles*, 1:118). However, he quotes Colin

Brown's verdict that Hume's contemporaries were far less impressed by Hume's philosophy and arguments than subsequent generations. Hume astonishingly defines a miracle as "a violation of the laws of nature," since "immutable experience establishes these laws" ("Of Miracles," in *Enquiries concerning Human Understanding*, 3rd ed. [Oxford: Clarendon, 1975], sect. 10, pt. 1, para. 90). "Uniform experience," Hume writes (for example, that dead men do not come to life), amounts to a *proof*, as if "the laws" were regulatory, not descriptive, in a closed or self-contained universe.

Yet Alastair McKinnon and many others argue, "The idea of suspension of natural law is self-contradictory.... If we substitute the expression 'the actual course of events,' *miracle* would be defined as 'an event involving the suspension of the actual course of events'" ("Miracle," *American Philosophical Quarterly* 4 [1967]: 309). R. Swinburne quotes McKinnon in *The Concept of Miracles* (London: Macmillan, 1970), 20. The deathblow to Hume's argument is the advent in more recent thought of the "open dynamic" universe of today. Swinburne considers "laws" in the context of quantum theory. In the light of Einstein's equations of general relativity and Kepler's theory of planetary motion, Swinburne comments: "One must distinguish between a formula being a law *and* a formula being (unreservedly) true, or being a law which holds without exception" (*The Concept of Miracles*, 28). John Polkinghorne offers a parallel comment. "Science simply tells us that these events are against normal expectation.... The theological question is: does it make sense to suppose that God has acted in a new way? ... God can do unexpected things.... The laws of nature do not change ... yet the consequences of these laws can change ... when one moves into a new regime" (*Quarks, Chaos, and Christianity* [London: SPCK/Triangle, 1994], 82). Miracles, he argues, may be credible acts of the faithful God if experience expands with new possibilities in a new regime (88). The resurrection exemplifies this.

Hume's notion of laws and causality has been questioned from many angles. W. Pannenberg, while considering the contrast between explanation and understanding, cites E. Scheibe, who argues that we seek a cause "when something surprising or unexpected occurs, something which 'is not among the implications of the assumptions from which I started.' ... Hume's interpretation of causality [is] an expression of habit.... Surprise is the impulse of a search for causes" (Pannenberg, *Theology and the Philosophy of Science* [Philadelphia: Westminster, 1976], 151). From a completely different angle, A. Boyce Gibson attacks positivism as if "experience" contradicts the notion of any "new" event (*Theism and Empiricism* [London: SCM, 1970], 149). The whole notion in science of an *open universe*, and in theology of God's *ongoing, creative power* as not limited to a *past event* of creation in Genesis 1, has changed everything. These two factors set the whole debate about miracles in a new key. It is not that theology holds to an outdated notion of the universe, but that Hume and his positivist colleagues do. Keener concludes, "A human approach is not neutral.... Most important, it is no longer possible to tout 'uniform human experience' as a basis for denying miracles, as in the traditional modern argument" (*Miracles*, 2:763, 764). (*See also* **Aquinas, Thomas; Augustine; Creation; God, Trinity; Holy Spirit; Hume, David; Materialism; Positivism; Science and Religion; Teleological Argument.**)

Reading: Colin Brown, *Miracles and the Critical Mind* (Grand Rapids: Eerdmans, 1984); David Hume, *Enquiries concerning Human Understanding*, 3rd ed. (Oxford: Clarendon, 1975); Craig S. Keener, *Miracles*, 2 vols. (Grand Rapids: Baker Academic, 2011); John Polkinghorne, *Quarks, Chaos, and Christianity* (London: SPCK/Triangle, 1994); Richard Swinburne, *The Concept of Miracle* (London: Macmillan, 1970); Graham Twelftree, *Jesus the Miracle Worker* (Downers Grove, Ill., and Leicester: IVP, 1999).

Modalism

Modalism is an unorthodox formulation of the doctrine of the Trinity, which denies a *permanent* distinction between the persons of the Holy Trinity. Sabellius (early third century) and Praxeas (c. 200) were modalists; Monarchianism and adoptionism are modalist systems of belief. (*See also* **Adoption, Adoptionism, Adoptianism.**)

Moltmann, Jürgen

Jürgen Moltmann (b. 1926) has provided at least three autobiographical accounts of his life and career. This alone should alert us that his life and faith bear decisively on his theology. In 1943 he was conscripted into the German auxiliary army in Hamburg and witnessed both immense destruction and the death of a friend standing by his side. In 1944 he was sent to the front, and witnessed the terrible bloodshed at Arnhem. He was captured and became a prisoner of war, and was eventually placed near Nottingham. He spoke of "the death of all my mainstays ... the experience of misery ... and daily humiliation." A well-meaning army chaplain gave him "this little black book," the Bible, with which Moltmann was largely unfamiliar. When he had nothing better to do, Moltmann opened it to Psalm 139, to read "If I make my bed in hell, you are there." As he pondered, he came to see that "God is with those who are of a broken heart," and that "nothing is shut off from God." He later wrote that far from searching for God, "God found me." God was on the prisoners' side of the barbed wire.

Moltmann returned to Germany determined to study theology, and to understand "the power of hope to which I owed my life" ("My Theological Career," in Moltmann, *History of the Triune God* [London: SCM, 1991], 166). He became influenced by Otto Weber, by Martin Luther's theology of the cross, and by eschatology and promise in van Ruler, Irwand, and Gerhard von Rad. For a time he worked as a rural pastor and became passionately interested in Ernst Bloch's philosophical work *The Principle of Hope*. Although he volunteered to work in East Germany, with its many deprivations, the authorities rejected his services. He began his work on what became his best-known classic, *Theology of Hope* (Ger. 1964; Eng. 1967; [London: SCM, 1987]). In the early 1960s he saw signs of hope in Vatican II (1962-1965); the Medellín Conference of Latin American Bishops (1963); the Czechoslovakian Alexander Dubček's "socialism with a human face" as an alternative to Stalinism; and above all in Christian eschatology and the God of promise. The living God changes the present. He wrote, "Faith, whenever it develops into hope, causes not rest but unrest" (*Theology of Hope*, 21). "Presumption is that premature self-willed anticipation of what we hope for from God; despair is the premature . . . anticipation of non-fulfilment" (23). Both presumption and despair destroy hope. Eschatology promotes change, as well as inviting hope. The work of J. Weiss and A. Schweitzer on eschatology had failed to go to the heart of the matter. For Christians much of the future may remain hidden; but the hidden God is not an absent God. Here Moltmann draws on Zimmerli on hope and on Gadamer for the history of effects. Horizons of promise are not static, but are capable of enlargement. Death brings not sheer nothingness, but a "not yet." The resurrection of Christ is the annihilation of nothingness (190).

Moltmann's next great classic work was *The Crucified God* (Ger. 1972; Eng. London: SCM, 1974). Many hopeful beginnings of the early 1960s had collapsed or petered out. The Warsaw Pact armies invaded Czechoslovakia; Martin Luther King was assassinated; there came the "crass absurdity" of the Vietnam War, student unrest and its consequences, and the hardening of Catholic conservatism. This seemed to invite Moltmann to look further into the experience of "Godforsakenness." But he wrote of "a surprising turning point" "or a reversal." Most ask what the cross means for the church. Moltmann asked, "What does Jesus' suffering and death mean for God himself?" (*A Broad Place* [London: SCM, 2007], 182). The language that God "sent" his Son must not be taken to imply that God was not present in the death of Jesus, and in the cross. God himself is deeply involved in the suffering of the cross. Moltmann rejected the notion of the "God of theism" who is too often seen as "eternally in love with himself . . . without any concern for others." Such a God would be an idol and a monster. "If we ask what the cross means for God himself, we discover the Trinitarian mystery of God" (194). If it was painful for Jesus to become separated from God, would it have been any less painful for God? It is the mystery of God's "giving himself" for the world.

Looking back from a later vantage point (2007), Moltmann acknowledges how far-reaching this book was for his subsequent work. He writes, "A true theology of the cross must be a Trinitarian theology" (*A Broad Place*, 195). So much turns on this. We must discard romantic notions of the cross: "we have surrounded the scandal of the cross with roses" (*The Crucified God*, 36). The cross does not allow contentment with present conditions: "those who followed this call abandoned everything, others . . . remained what they were" (*The Crucified God*, 54). "The theology of the cross leads to criticism of the self-glorification of dehumanized man and to his liberation" (70). "Even Auschwitz is taken up into the grief of the Father, the surrender of the Son, and the power of the Spirit" (278). The problem of human suffering can be addressed only in the light of the cross. "Unless it apprehends the pain of the negative, Christian hope cannot be realistic and liberating" (5). The cross stands in tension with "building self-identity," with "struggling to maintain itself and reaching out for security" (19). Those who ignore the cross "build a defensive wall round their own little group" (20). Each one of these themes reappears in Moltmann's later work: on God, the Trinity, the Spirit, the church, and the End. Behind much of this thinking lies a rediscovery of Luther's theology of the cross; his contrast between *theologia gloriae* and *theologia crucis*.

It is not surprising that this gave rise to *The Church in the Power of the Spirit* (1975). Moltmann pursues his discussion of the sense in which God experiences suffering. God goes out of himself and engages with his creation. Unlike Deists, Moltmann does not envisage God idly watching it. The church participates in the Trinitarian history of God. The fallibility and vulnerability of the church are acknowledged. Clearly ecclesiology depends entirely on Christology and eschatology. The Holy Spirit is constantly moving toward the goal of history. Hence the Spirit empowers the church for mission. The church does not exist in or for itself. The saying "Whoever loses his life . . ." applies as much to the church as to the individual disciple. Moltmann followed this work in 1977 with *The Open Church* (Eng. 1978) on messianic lifestyle, friendship, and the church of the people.

Moltmann's next major work on the doctrine of God was *The Trinity and the Kingdom of God* (London: SCM, 1981). In parallel with his question about the cross, Moltmann asks not "What does God mean to me?" but "What do I mean for God?" (3). Today, he urges, we suffer from a culture of narcissism or self-centeredness. We must look beyond the self, as indeed God does, which we see in "a social doctrine of the Trinity" (19). Moltmann emphatically rejects the "apathy" of God, or "his essential incapacity for suffering" (23). The whole of chapter 2 attacks this traditional doctrine. On the contrary, he declares, "A God who cannot suffer cannot love either. A God who cannot love is a dead God" (38). He is not the living God of the Bible, but the self-contained God of "theism." Cannot God feel as a husband or a mother? He rejects Spinoza's and Maimonides' claim that God is free from passion. This does not compromise God's sovereignty, for God chose to suffer voluntarily with his creation.

All this, Moltmann argues, becomes intelligible in the light of God as Trinity. "The Father sends the Son through the Spirit; the Son comes from the Father in the power of the Spirit; the Spirit brings people into the fellowship of the Son with the Father" (75). In Jesus' experience on the cross of being forsaken by God, "the innermost life of the Trinity is at stake" (81). "The Father withdraws. God is silent" (77). The meaning of God as Trinity is not seen in abstract models such as the shamrock or the notion of "three in one," but in the narrative of the Gospels, when every act of Jesus involves also the Father and the Spirit. This runs from the conception and baptism to the cross and resurrection. Moltmann is unhappy with speaking of "three modes of being" (142), even if Barth comes too near to this. But equally he rejects tritheism. He discusses the details of patristic and modern formulations in his chapter 5 (129-90). He prefers the Cappadocian notion of *perichoresis,* or interpenetration (199), as "social" without rejecting monotheism.

In his next major work, *God in Creation: An Ecological Doctrine of Creation* (London: SCM, 1985), Moltmann begins with a perichoretic model of coanimating, coworking, and cosuffering. He declares, "Creation is a Trinitarian process: the Father creates through the Son in the Holy Spirit. All divine activity is pneumatic in its efficacy" (9). The essential being of creation in the Spirit "is therefore co-activity" (11). Moltmann does firmly emphasize "the *difference* between God and the world" (13). Believers who worship "forces of fertility" become idolatrous. Nevertheless, it is more accurate to speak of "indwelling, sympathizing, and participating" than of "making" and "preserving," which lose the mutuality of the preferred terms. Moltmann cites for comparison the rabbinic doctrine of the Shekinah, and again discusses "mutual interpenetration" (16-17).

After outlining the ecological crisis caused by the misuse and misunderstanding of human "domination" of nature (Gen. 1:26-28), Moltmann discusses the alienation of nature and its promised liberation. Descartes's emphasis on mastery is far from the Bible's concern for care and stewardship (26-27, 33, 46-47, 250-52). God created the whole world, human and nonhuman creatures, "out of love" (75). Humankind is called to share in God's creative love. In creating, God commends himself (86). "God makes room for his creation by withdrawing his presence" (87). Moltmann pays special attention to history and to the multiple interrelations of time and space (104-57). "There is not just a single past, present, and future" (128).

A renewed and transformed creation must be part of the new creation of heaven, whereas "if heaven is reduced to God himself, it ceases to be a part of creation" (181). The evolution of life raises questions not just about "evolution," but about "a whole series of different evolutionary processes" (197). The image of God in humanity and in Christ means that "human beings represent God on earth; as his similitude, they reflect him" (219), and therefore "the fellowship of God within the Trinity" (220). But likeness to God "comes about in the fellowship of believers with Christ: since he is the messianic *imago Dei*" (226). Like Oetinger, Käsemann, and others, Moltmann stresses the importance of "embodiment" (244-75). He attacks Descartes for his "mechanistic" view of the body. In contrast to the dualism of Plato and Descartes, he expounds a perichoretic relation of body and soul.

Moltmann produced *The Way of Jesus Christ: Christology in Messianic Dimensions* in 1989 (London: SCM). The "Way" indicates the process of traveling, since Christians still belong to the "not yet" of eschatology. Their journey is one of drama and going on. Yet it is also the way of Christ, in the sense of becoming more like Christ. Moltmann writes, "An *account* of Christ presupposes a living *faith* in him" (39). There is no separation between the Jesus of history and the Christ of faith. Jesus is Lord because God raised him from the dead; we cannot reduce Christology to the earthly life of Jesus. Christology entails "Christ praxis" (41-43). Jesus also remains relevant to eucharistic *anamnēsis*. As we might expect, Moltmann relates Christology to the kingdom, or rule, of God, and to new creation. The miracles of healing do not primarily raise issues about "religion and science," but about the in-breaking of eschatological hope, given the delay of the parousia (104-12, esp. 109). They also witness to God's acceptance of the poor and outcasts (112-16). All this introduces "the messianic way of life" (116-50), including nonviolence and love. History needs to be viewed in the light of the resurrection of Jesus Christ (227-36). In hermeneutical and historical terms, like Pannenberg and Jauss, Moltmann speaks of "the horizon of expectation" (228, 236-40).

Christ was anointed by the Holy Spirit. In the cross we see the death of God's child, and his suffering God-forsakenness (167). Jesus died for others and "for me" (Gal. 2:20). But God was in Christ (2 Cor. 5:19) and shows "com-passion" (178-81). The "sinless" Son of God "cannot have died his own death" (169). Now Christ lives in the Spirit (263-64).

The Spirit of Life: A Universal Affirmation followed in 1991 (London: SCM). Humankind is expected to be "open to the Spirit" (27). The Spirit is "the wellspring of life," who is in all things (35). Moltmann stresses the personhood of the Spirit, although this becomes comprehensible in the light of his close relationship with the Father and the Son (11). Moltmann writes, "Personhood is always being-in-relationship.... The Spirit has a wholly unique personhood" (11, 12). He is no less a "person" than Jesus Christ is. Moltmann looks to H. Mühlen in Catholic theology and to Martin Buber in Judaism to place "personhood" on a new footing. What can be more personal than the Spirit's acting in intersubjectivity?

In considering "experience of the Spirit," Moltmann tries to hold together immanence and transcendence, although some would dispute his total success. He writes, "to experience God in all things presupposes that there is a transcendence which is immanent in all things and which can be inductively discovered. It is the infinite in the finite, the eternal in the temporal, and the enduring in the transitory" (35). Again, the Spirit is "the well of life." Yet he insists that we need "a revision of anthropocentric pneumatology" (37). We must avoid "a cleavage in reality," in favor of a more holistic view. It is more helpful to consider the Spirit, like the Shekinah, as God himself, "yet distinct from God" (48). Hegel speaks of "God's self-distinction." This may lead to a coworking and cosuffering of wills. Once again, as in his book on God and the Trinity, Moltmann looks to the Cappadocian Fathers for *perichoresis,* and the Spirit's anointing and empowerment of Jesus. In stressing the equal mutuality of the Trinity, he proposes removing the controversial *filioque* clause from the creeds of the Western Church, expressing a preference for the Eastern tradition (71-73).

Part 2 of the book concerns "life in the Spirit." The new life of the Holy Spirit goes beyond mere "morality," but involves "love of life" (86). He rightly rejects a gnostic frame in favor of an apocalyptic one. He attacks Nietzsche's caricature of the Christian. The Spirit brings liberation from the compulsive power of sin (101). There is also critical dialogue with Sartre and Bloch about true freedom, and some appreciation of liberation theology. A human person does not find liberation in "the autonomous right of disposal over oneself and one's property" but in "the hitherto unexplored creative power of God," which is "life-giving through love" (115). In place of striving for "domination" we should seek "sociality" (118).

In the rest of part 2, Moltmann considers justification, rebirth, sanctification, and charismatic gifts and powers. While Moltmann endorses many aspects of the traditional Protestant view of justification, like José Porfirio Miranda, he broadens it to include the social dimensions of righteousness or justice. God creates justice for victims (129-43). Attempts at self-justification bring self-destruction: "Atonement is ... possible only for God" (134). "Rebirth," Moltmann insists, means more than being "born again." It belongs to an apocalyptic, cosmic context (145). It involves renewal through the Holy Spirit. Rebirth is to a living hope, to a future that comes to meet us. Moltmann quotes Luther: "To go forward on God's ways means continually beginning afresh" (155). Sanctification includes personal holiness, as Wesley stresses, but also "defending God's creation against human aggression" (172). On *charismata* he stresses the relation between call and endowment, or task and gift (180-86). He urges that any gift for a task "becomes a *charisma*. ... *Every* life in faith is charismatic" (182).

Moltmann has reservations about distinguishing between "supernatural" and "natural" *charismata* (183). God acts in one world by various means. The gifts of the Spirit promote "unity only in diversity, not unity in uniformity" (184). "There are varieties of gifts, but the same Spirit" (1 Cor. 12:4). Regarding speaking in tongues, Pentecostal and charismatic congregations are growing everywhere. Any powerful experience of emotion can give rise to what cannot be expressed in comprehensible language: intense pain can cause unrestrained weeping; extreme joy may produce jumping or dancing. Prophecies and testimonies may spring up spontaneously (185). Mainline churches display a wealth of ideas in sermons, but are "poverty stricken" in their forms of expression. Healing can be found today but not always independently of modern medicine. Prophetic speech is a special charisma. Moltmann also speaks of "the *charisma* of the handicapped life," which should be honored as giving a congregation a sign of vulnerability among Christians (192-93).

A final part 3 concerns the fellowship of the Spirit and his personhood. Fellowship denotes sharing (as L. S. Thornton stresses). The Spirit makes possible the creation of community. Fellowship also means "opening ourselves for one another, giving one another a share in ourselves" (217). We can "discover God's love *in* the love between human beings, and the love between human beings *in* God's love" (248). The Spirit may free us from "ego-mania" (251). Metaphors such as the Spirit as energy or fire do not detract from his personhood. He is more than "the third person" of the Trinity, but exhibits *perichoresis* with the Father and the Son (304). Moltmann again argues that "the Filioque addition ... contributes nothing new to the statement about the procession of the Spirit from the Father. It is superfluous" (306).

Apart from Moltmann's *Experiences in Theology: Ways and Forms of Christian Theology* (2000), the final classic and major work was *The Coming of God:*

Christian Eschatology (1995; Eng. London: SCM, 1996). He begins with a critical survey of eschatology from Albert Schweitzer and Oscar Cullmann to Karl Barth and Rudolf Bultmann, and of the rebirth of messianic theology in Judaism in Bloch, Franz Rosenzweig, Gershom Scholem, and others. The phrase "who is to come" can be found in Rev. 1:4 (*The Coming of God,* 23). God "goes ahead of his people" and will transform creation. The new "does not *emerge* from the old" (27). The new "does not annihilate the old, but gathers it up and creates it anew" (29). In this sense, *novum,* the genuinely new, differs from *futurum,* which mainly develops out of the past. Even Scholem can speak of "a forward-looking hope," directed to a state of things that have never been.

In his chapter "Eternal Life" Moltmann considers personal eschatology. To push away the thought of death "makes us superficial and indifferent.... To live as if there were no death is an illusion" (50). We must face up to "the deadliness of death" (55). Our consumer society seduces us to believe that only work, enjoyment, and the present moment matter (56). He declares, "The inability to mourn becomes an inability to love" (57). The Psalms encourage personal trust in God at the moment of death (80). Moltmann rejects the doctrine of purgatory, also explaining why the Reformers, and Calvin in particular, regarded it as "a pernicious invention of Satan" (100). The resurrection at the last day will be reminiscent of Luther's notion that God will awaken the whole person, calling, "Dr. Martin, get up!" (101). Concepts of "intermediate time" are "not empty, like a waiting room." They are "filled by the lordship of Christ" (104). Nothing can separate us from God's love (Rom. 8:38-39). After considering premature deaths, Moltmann turns once more to mourning: "The greater the love, the deeper the grief" (119). Weeping is better than frozen calm. Mourning should be taken seriously, although it need not involve melancholia or be endless (119-28).

Moltmann retains the main New Testament perspective when he next considers last things in the context of apocalyptic in part 3. The suffering of the oppressed is a major theme of apocalyptic, as are resurrection, judgment, the parousia, and history, as well as perhaps a notion of "ages," sometimes with millenarian aspects. He discusses theories about a "rapture" and millenarian Christianity. Part 4 is more distinctive about a new heaven and a new earth. Human life involves "participation in nature" (260). "The annihilation of the world is comprised in its transformation" (271). "Completion in God must by no means be thought of as non-corporeal.... It is a heavenly transfigured bodily life" (277). Earth is not dead matter, and not expendable material. The temporal world ends in God's eternity. Earth time involves entropy, but "the hell 'day of God' will dawn" (293). We await the vision of the heavenly Jerusalem (308-19). Finally, part 5 considers "glory." "To 'glorify' God means to love God for his own sake and to enjoy God as he is himself" (323). Again Moltmann observes, "God then goes out of himself and expresses himself in this 'other' of his own self" (327). Hence God's glory comes solely from himself, but remains love and self-giving, not self-congratulation. "The glory of God is the feast of eternal joy" (336; cf. Matt. 25:21).

Moltmann's last major work is *Experiences in Theology* (London: SCM, 2000). Theology is shared by all believers, not just theologians. It is important to all theology that God's word comes as promise, to make the future present. "A promise is a speech-act, which is authenticated by the person who promises" (94). This involves exploring "the logic of promise" (87-113). Moltmann also explores the "Trinitarian hermeneutics of Holy Scripture" (134-50) and theological epistemology (151-79). He still maintains his central interest in liberation theology: in black theology, Latin American liberation theology, and feminist theology. He ends with the "broad place" of the Trinity. This explains the title of his largest autobiography, *A Broad Place* (2007). We do not propose to list or to catalogue the many smaller books that have come from Moltmann's pen. These are numerous, not least after *The Coming of God* from 2000 onward.

It will immediately be seen how Moltmann's experiences, from his coming to faith onward, have influenced his theology indelibly. That God is with those of a broken heart has never been forgotten. Nor has the initial concern with hope and promise, and his resolve that his theology should address contemporary situations. He sees the cross as the work of the whole Trinity, reminding us of Donald Baillie's book *God Was in Christ,* but going so much further. Yet from this point onward Moltmann did not flinch from expressing his belief that "A God who cannot suffer cannot love either." This finds full expression in *The Trinity and the Kingdom of God.* For some, in spite of replies to the contrary, this seems to fall into the patristic "heresy" of Patripassianism, and to rob God of his sovereignty and status as the Absolute. But Moltmann would regard questions about "the Absolute" as belonging to Greek metaphysics, not to the Bible. God loves his creation with passion, and shares in the suffering of Christ and of the world.

Richard Bauckham, his main English expositor, argues that by now Moltmann's theology is becoming more "pneumatic." This is expressed partly through his emphasis on *perichoresis,* partly in the Trinity, coequally in *The Trinity and the Kingdom of God,* and partly in his subsequent works, especially *The Spirit of Life.* Some may suggest that his doctrine of the Trinity gives too much to a "social" doctrine of the Trinity. Barth and Rahner tend to stress the oneness of God. But for Moltmann God's going forth from himself in "relationality," or in relation with Christ, the Spirit, and creation, gives the fundamental pattern of "the image of God," and thereby of human life. Some may also claim that his doctrine of creation veers too much toward immanentism. But Moltmann does try to preserve transcendence also. He is certainly incisive in his attacks on the "mastery" and abuse of nature. Here he is not the first, for Reinhold Niebuhr and others have made this point.

It is also to the credit of Moltmann that he approaches the Holy Trinity in terms of *the narrative of Jesus* in the New Testament and especially the Gospels. This doctrine has nothing to do with numerical models, as the Church Fathers pointed out. All persons of the Trinity are active in the conception, baptism, life, death, and resurrection of Christ, and in the creation of the world. He also approaches Christology without the dualism between Jesus and "the Christ of faith," which has bedeviled so much theology since Lessing.

Moltmann's *Spirit of Life* remains practical and inspiring. He rightly emphasizes the personhood of the Spirit, stresses love of life, and stresses liberation. He has a sympathetic but critical view of "Pentecostal" gifts of the Spirit (although some might claim that an explicit use of Gerd Theissen on tongues might have been helpful). He refuses a two-story division between natural and supernatural. He argues that mainline churches may well be enriched by the "charismatic" movement. He reopens a key ecumenical debate by his proposal to drop the Western *filioque* clause in the creed. Moltmann's emphasis on liberation from narcissism is valuable. *The Coming of God* constitutes yet another classic. Many will find inspiration in his comments on the new creation, on death and mourning, on resurrection, and on the new heavens and new earth, which is transformed rather than annihilated. One or two points on time may be controversial. However, most readers will treasure his work on glory. It is not surprising that many younger clergy who may after ordination read relatively little theology say that they find Moltmann "inspirational." Together with Pannenberg, Moltmann stands among the four or five most influential and respected contemporary theologians in the whole world.

Reading: Primary texts of Jürgen Moltmann: *The Crucified God* (London: SCM, 1974); *The Church in the Power of the Spirit* (London: SCM, 1975); *The Trinity and the Kingdom of God* (London: SCM, 1981); *God in Creation* (London: SCM, 1985); *Theology of Hope* (London: SCM, 1987); *The Way of Jesus Christ* (London: SCM, 1989); *The Spirit of Life* (London: SCM, 1991); *The Coming of God* (London: SCM, 1996); *Experiences in Theology* (London: SCM, 2000); *A Broad Place* (London: SCM, 2007). Studies: Richard Bauckham, ed., *God Will Be All in All* (Edinburgh: T. & T. Clark, 1999).

Monasticism

Monks and nuns believe they have received a call from God to serve him through worship, prayer, asceticism, and often also community life. Historically they were called either to the life of a hermit in solitary contemplation or to a common life within a monastic community. They enjoy seclusion from the world, and normally renounce property, marriage, and autonomy. The primary focus is praise and prayer, but many orders also encourage labor, usually in the fields or in teaching. In the Eastern Church they looked to John Cassian, among others, and in the Western Church often to Benedict's Rule. (*See also* **Dominicans; Franciscans**.)

Montanism

Montanism was regarded by most of the Church Fathers as a heretical sect. It sprung up in the second century and emphasized prophecy, speaking in tongues, the gift of the Holy Spirit, and the imminent end of the world. The founder of the movement, Montanus, was a self-proclaimed prophet from Phrygia, who prophesied the imminent end of the world. Montanists claimed the title "the new prophecy," and were accused of encouraging ecstatic phenomena. They looked for an outpouring of the Holy Spirit, and practiced an ascetic discipline. Eusebius dates the prophecy of Montanus to 172 (*Church History* 16), but Epiphanius argues for 156-157 (*Refutation of All Heresies* 48.1). Two women disciples, Prisca and Maximilla, joined him, and the movement spread from Phrygia to North Africa. They regarded themselves as Spirit-filled, and the mainline church people as "psychicals" or "ordinary" people. Tertullian, however, was attracted to many of their tenets, including their asceticism and the immediacy of the Spirit.

Evaluations of Montanism vary dramatically. Tertullian regarded Montanists as issuing an authentic call to a lax and formal church. In more recent times, John Wesley saw them as issuing an authentic call to holiness. Some feminists regard them as promoting the positive role of women. But their claims were usually exclusive. Eusebius calls them "elated, and not a little puffed up . . . seducing spirits . . . estranged from the true faith." He comments, "The arrogant spirit taught them to revile the entire universal Church. . . . [They have] the spirit of false prophecy" (*Church History* 5.16). By this emphasis on immediate inspiration, H. M. Gwatkin argues, "They threw preaching into the background for a thousand years." There are echoes of this teaching in the Radical Reformers, whom Luther called "fanatics" *(Schwärmer)* or enthusiasts. Some, but not all, aspects can be found in Pentecostalism. To call Montanism strictly a "heresy" may be questioned, but its exclusiveness and apocalypticism perhaps represented its worst features. Many acknowledge its high ethical standards. The perennial question raised by Montanism is that of true and false prophecy, and claims to "possess" the Holy Spirit.

Moral Argument

The moral argument for the existence of God did not emerge with full seriousness until the time of Kant (1724-1804). Kant limited the scope of theoretical reason, and rendered the ontological, cosmological, and teleological arguments incapable of reaching beyond the world to a transcendent God. Hence Kant sought to find a new basis for an Absolute in practical reason (*Critique of Practical Reason*, bk. 2, chap. 2, sect. 5). Even then, however, this moral argument does not actually "prove" God, but proposes that the existence or reality of God is a *postulate* of practical reason. God, freedom, and immortality, Kant argued, are *presupposed* by the categorical imperative of moral experience. Kant presupposed a correlation in reality between the good will or virtue and human happiness. "God" will ensure the validity of such a correlation. The "highest good" *(summum bonum) presupposes* God and human freedom. This "God," however, is hardly the *personal* God of the Bible or theism. Many of Kant's comments in *Religion within the Limits of Reason* imply this. The "highest good" is necessary. But this may seem contradictory when Kant dismissed the ontological argument for relying only on *logical* necessity. Most thinkers see little force in this argument, outside Kant's assumptions, although some regard it as an intuitively valid argument, not a rational one. The "ethics" of Hobbes, Hume, Bentham, and Nietzsche suggest a different starting point.

In the nineteenth and early twentieth centuries the most convincing advocate of the moral argument was perhaps Hastings Rashdall. He was a liberal Oxford theologian who became influential in ethics. He wrote *The Theory of Good and Evil* (Oxford: Clarendon, 1907), and addressed the moral argument for the existence of God in book 3, chapter 1. He argued that the human self is no mere "thing," but an active agent with an inbuilt sense of right and wrong, as well as of pleasure and pain. Morality, he urged, is not a purely human creation. The sense of moral obligation comes from "beyond." Most people believe in their hearts that cruelty and similar acts or attitudes are wrong, and hence there is a ground or absolute outside us that implants this moral sense within us. Rashdall urged, "Moral law has a real existence," and "there is such a thing as absolute morality" (chap. 1, sect. 4). For those who believe in, or accept, an objective moral law, this theory is convincing; for those who regard right and wrong as mere expediency or convention, this argument may cut little ice. Increasingly in modern times the debate boils down to whether we believe in a naturalistic explanation of moral norms and values. A more recent statement and argument comes from H. P. Owen, *Moral Argument for Christian Theism* (London: Allen and Unwin, 1965). He argues that it is impossible to derive a moral "ought" from a merely naturalistic "is." A good conscience is far more than a gratified wish. Against A. J. Ayer and others, Owen argues that moral obligation cannot be reduced to mere corporate or individual approval. We cannot merely rest content with "disapproving" of the Nazi Holocaust; we must assert that it is wrong or evil. Owen also points out that such reductionism often depends on reducing morality to *acts* rather than *dispositions* or *character*. Owen argues that this sense of the moral points beyond itself to God (54-60). (*See also* **Ethics; God, Trinity; Kant, Immanuel; O'Donovan, Oliver; Sin; Transcendence.**)

Moravians

The Moravians originated with the Pietist vision of Count Nikolaus Ludwig von Zinzendorf (1700-1760), whose chief concern was evangelism. In 1722 he inherited an estate, on which he founded a colony of largely Bohemian Brethren, called Herrnhut. This grew into a strong Pietist force, linked with the Lutheran church. Its primary aim was the evangelization of those hitherto unreached by the gospel, and the Moravian community sent missionaries to the West Indies, Greenland, South Africa, and Labrador. Their zeal and concerns influenced John Wesley, and they established a "society" in London. They emphasized fellowship and service as well as evangelism. Moravians accepted the ecumenical creeds, the doctrinal statements of Lutheranism and Anglicanism, and the threefold ministry of bishops, priests, and deacons, as surviving groups still do today.

Mysticism

Mysticism has been defined in a variety of ways, and in both positive and negative terms. Often it denotes a state of consciousness in which the contemplative worshiper seeks the presence of God. A sense of the immediacy of God's presence overwhelms the worshiper. Many medieval monks and nuns sought to cultivate union with God in Christ in a mystical experience. At the negative end of the spectrum of attitudes, Martin Luther and many Reformed theologians, first, criticized mysticism as too often thinking or speaking of "ladders" or stages *upward to* God, in contrast to divine grace, which descends *from* God to humankind. Second, they suspected the higher regard for feelings, over against reason and will. Third, Luther also suspected that mysticism might imply aspects of a Platonic view of God. At worst, some Christians regard it as too close to pantheism.

Exponents of mysticism may sometimes point to biblical notions of union with Christ. Some could point, for example, to Paul's theme of being "in Christ," or John's passage about the branches being part of the vine. Paul mentions having been "caught up to the third heaven" (2 Cor. 12:2), but is also reluctant to speak about it or emphasize it. In Gal. 2:20 he declares, "It is no longer I who live, but it is Christ who lives in me." (But many would argue that this refers not to "experience," but to justified "status" in Christ.) Within the Eastern Church mysticism is closely connected with deification, and in the Orthodox Church, V. Lossky declares, "In a certain sense all theology is mystical, inasmuch as it shows forth the divine mystery: the data of revelation" (*The Mystical Theology of the Eastern Church* [Cambridge: James Clarke, 1957, 1991], 7). On the other hand, even Lossky admits that mysticism is "frequently opposed to theology as a realm inaccessible to understanding, as an unutterable mystery, a hidden depth" (7). H. Bergson also distinguishes the "static religion" of the churches from the "dynamic religion" of mystics. Pseudo-Dionysius (Dionysius the Areopagite) argued in *The Mystical Theology* that "Timothy" should ascend above sense perceptions and concepts, to union with God, who is beyond concepts. He profoundly influenced medieval Christian thought, and wrote of the "truly mystic darkness of unknowing" (*Mystical Theology* 1.3). Johannes Scotus of Erigena followed Dionysius and the Neoplatonic tradition, and translated Dionysius. He was condemned in 1210 for pantheism.

Bernard of Clairvaux might in some respects be called a mystic. His work *On the Love of God* speaks of "the four degrees of love," and he views the Song of Solomon as an allegory of God's love for the church. He wrote, "Delight yourself in Christ" (*Sermons on Song of Songs* 20.4). But this is "wholesome" mysticism, tempered by careful theology. Hildegard of Bingen more readily speaks of "visions" and "pictures," which include flame, stone, and burning fire (*Scivias* 2.2). The problem here is that, as Wittgenstein urged, "Pictures can be variously interpreted." Richard of St. Victor wrote *The Mystical Ark*, but was more skilled in biblical exegesis. Walter Hilton was a mystic, but also formulated some commonsense safeguards against uncontrolled and excessive mysticism. His *Scale of*

Perfection concerned "the contemplative life," which for him included study in the Scriptures. He warned that mystics may be deceived by wicked angels appearing as "angels of light" (*Scale of Perfection* 10 and 16). *The Cloud of Unknowing* (c. 1390) takes its title from Dionysius, pointing to negative or apophatic theology.

The climax of Western mysticism is perhaps found in the Spanish mystics Teresa of Ávila and John of the Cross. Like many mystics, Teresa speaks often of a journey of the soul, and symbols and pictures. In one respect she and Luther find a little common ground. In *Interior Castle* she encounters "assaults of the devils" (1.13). But later come "raptures" (402) and "ecstasy" (1.18). This aspect would merit Luther's fears about ascent to God. The problem also remains of ambiguous interpretations of pictures.

In one sense both the mystics and Luther are right. Too much hinges on "experience" rather than on "faith." Much mysticism can be open to severe deception, and even to pantheistic notions of God. However, mysticism that is controlled and disciplined by Scripture, theology, and the tradition of the church can invite living and precious experiences of God in Christ, which should not necessarily be regarded as inauthentic. But, like prophecy, such experiences need to be tested. This may become difficult if the mystic claims to have passed beyond conceptualization through thought and language. After all, Christ comes to us as God's Word. (*See also* **Apophatic Theology; Deification; Dionysius, Pseudo-; Word of God.**)

Reading: U. T. Holmes III: *A History of Christian Spirituality* (New York: Seabury Press, 1980); F. Von Hügel, *The Mystical Element of Religion* (London: James Clarke, 1953); V. Lossky, *The Mystical Theology of the Eastern Church* (London: SPCK, 1957); M. A. McIntosh, *Mystical Theology* (Oxford: Blackwell, 1998).

Myth

Any definition of myth will be highly controversial, beyond three basic characteristics. Evaluations of myth often depend on beginning with a particular definition. Myths have the status of *believed* truth within a given community. The popular notion of myth as false stories about Greek and Roman deities arose because the modern West does not share the presuppositions of Greece or Rome about polytheism. *Within* the communities in which they are believed, however, they often have the status of legitimating formulae. D. F. Strauss defined myth as ideas expressed in the form of narrative. As such, this would not suggest that the narrative transmits a *literal* account, or any truth value outside the community of belief. It has also been a convention to distinguish between *myth* and *legend*. Legends may be about human heroes or leaders; whereas myths are supposedly about deities. But some, for example, M. Dibelius, do not retain this distinction clearly. The three core principles generally agreed about myth are that it is *communal,* it assumes *narrative* form, and it is *believed to be true* within the community in question.

Beyond this we encounter immediate controversy. O. Eissfeldt argues, "A real myth presupposes at least two gods" (*The Old Testament: An Introduction* [Oxford: Blackwell, 1965], 35). But E. Brunner (*The Mediator* [London: Lutterworth, 1934], 386; cf. 377-96) regards it as compatible with monotheism, even showing Christ as "personal," although he admits that it is "childlike" (396). It does not help us that Greek *mythos* may mean thought, account, story, speech, or conversation (BDAG 660). If used in contrast to *logos,* it does indeed denote a fictional or contrived story. In his *Myths, Dreams, and Mysteries* (Eng. 1960), M. Eliade has shown how very complex the term has become. At one end of the spectrum Ernst Cassirer regards myth as a prephilosophical tool of language, and G. Hartlich and W. Sachs tend to associate it with a primitive worldview. At the other end of the spectrum, C. Jung, K. Jaspers, and P. Tillich tend to associate it with symbolic language that draws on the collective unconscious. It is used in R. Bultmann and others to denote language about Christ or Christology that lies beyond empirical facts about the earthly Jesus. Thus in 1981 I hazarded the conclusion: "The term 'myth' in fact raises more problems than it solves" ("Knowledge, Myth, and Corporate Memory," in *Believing in the Church,* by Doctrine Commission of the Church of England [London: SPCK, 1981], 68; cf. 45-78). It is not necessarily a "prescientific" mode of discourse, but is often used in that way.

Thus in earlier biblical scholarship Genesis 1–11 is regularly compared with the creation myths of the ancient Near East. These include the Babylonian creation myth, *Enuma Elish,* discovered in the nineteenth century and published in 1875 (cf. A. Heidel, *The Babylonian Genesis* [1942], and J. B. Pritchard, ed., *Ancient Near-Eastern Texts* [1950], 60-72), which recounts Marduk as utilizing the body of Tiamat for creation. The Babylonian myth *Epic of Atrahasis* is also compared (*Anet* 104-106), which includes creation and a cosmic flood. But a host of criticisms of any notion of *dependence* on the part of Genesis had been offered by W. G. Lambert, A. R. Millard, D. F. Payne, and others. Perhaps most constructively of all, B. S. Childs on the OT and G. B. Caird on the NT claim that even if the biblical writers used language that was mythological *in origin* (e.g., in Genesis 1–11, Job, and Revelation), it no longer *functioned as myth.* They have both suggested the term "broken myth" for this (Childs, *Myth and Reality in the Old Testament* [London: SCM, 1960, 1962]; Caird, *The Language and Imagery of the Bible* [London: Duckworth, 1980]). Genesis gives no hint of primal conflict or dualism (*see* **Creation**). Genesis 1–11 is no more dependent on "myths" of Paradise and the Fall, or of the flood, even if there are parallels with *The Epic of Gilgamesh* in Genesis 6–8. The story of a divine decree, the building of a boat, the salvation of a family, and a concluding sacrifice could be predicted in such parallels. A. R. Millard also considers the parallels in the *Atrahasis* story from Babylonia. The chief problem, as Caird argues, is the need to distinguish between myth and metaphor. "Leviathan" may represent "broken myth" in Job 41:1, Pss. 74:14, 104:26, Isa. 27:1; "the dragon" may perhaps represent it in Ps. 74:13, Isa. 27:1, and 51:9. Sources from Ugarit also suggest parallel imagery, but emphatically not dependence.

The so-called Myth and Ritual School of S. Mowinckel, S. H. Hooke, and

A. Bentzen is also best regarded as a phenomenon of the 1920s and 1930s. Hooke claimed in *Myth and Ritual* (1933): "The mythology of Israel was largely drawn from Canaanite... Mesopotamian, and Egyptian sources, although it was modified" (173). Bentzen insisted that myths were "re-lived" in the Christian Eucharist (*King and Messiah* [Eng. 1955], 77-79). But W. F. Albright, A. H. Frankfort, P. J. Minear, G. E. Wright, and others have shown the unsatisfactory character of this approach. Wright concluded, "The God of Israel has no mythology" (*God Who Acts* [London: SCM, 1952], 26). The fallacies include that of "the three-decker universe." Albright insisted that "up" was often construed symbolically for transcendence, just as no modern people would think of the sun rising from the depths, but happily speak of "sunrise" without implying rejection of a scientific view of earth (*New Horizons in Biblical Research* [1966], 17-35).

In 1941 Rudolf Bultmann introduced the term "myth" radically into NT studies in his classic essay "New Testament and Mythology," in *Kerygma and Myth*, ed. H. W. Bartsch, vol. 1 (London: SCM, 1953); also in *New Testament Mythology*, ed. S. M. Ogden (Philadelphia: Fortress, 1984). Bultmann's intention and motive were no doubt to enable the NT interpreter to understand "the point" of much NT language. He viewed the NT as embodying a kerygma, which transformed human existential self-understanding, and which was often reversed and revalued through the cross. His application of *Sachkritik*, or reappraisal of the NT subject matter, was to expose and rescue the NT kerygma, or preaching, from the mythological framework that threatened to disguise it. He wanted to replace "bare facts" *about* Jesus by an existential challenge addressed *from* God, not a discourse *about* God.

Nevertheless, Bultmann's intention is frustrated by a number of misapprehensions or confusions. First, he offers three definitions of "myth," which together are self-contradictory. These are set out in detail in A. C. Thiselton, *The Two Horizons* (Grand Rapids: Eerdmans, 1980), 205-92, esp. 252-92. First, Bultmann defines "myth" as "the use of imagery *(die Vorstellungsweise)* to express the other worldly *(das Unweltliche)* in terms of this world, and the divine in terms of human life" ("New Testament and Mythology," in *Kerygma and Myth*, 1:10). For example, he cites transcendence as being described as "up." H. Thielicke and J. Schiewind replied at once that in that case we cannot dispense with myth; it is like analogy or symbol. Later G. Miegge made the same point (*Kerygma and Myth*, 1:141; Miegge, *Gospel and Myth* [1956], 98-99). Second, Bultmann switches his definition of "myth" to its association with a given worldview *(Weltbild)*. In effect, it is the notorious "three-decker" universe, with "heaven above, and the world underneath.... The underworld is hell," the abode of "Satan and his demons" (*Kerygma and Myth*, 1:1). Humankind is not in control of its life, but is controlled by God, angels, or demons. Two British scholars argued that the first and second definitions contradict each other; they were the Scottish theologian Ian Henderson and the English Nottingham philosopher Ronald Hepburn. One definition concerns the *form* of myth; the other, its *content*. Even the American

Schubert Ogden, in many respects a supporter of Bultmann, argues that "the resulting complex of ideas... takes the form of a double history" (*Christ without Myth* [London: Collins, 1962], 30). This is a very different assessment of myth from that of Eliade, Jaspers, or Jung.

Bultmann's third definition of myth brings us even nearer to the heart of the matter. He writes, "The real purpose of myth is not to present an objective picture of the world as it is *(ein objektives Weltbild)*, but to express man's understanding of himself in the world. . . . Myth should be interpreted . . . anthropologically, or better still, existentially" (*Kerygma and Myth*, 1:10). He is partly indebted to Hans Jonas for this understanding, and partly to M. Heidegger. It is in one respect correct. The NT does not provide descriptive information as its primary objective. It challenges humankind with the gospel and seeks to transform the reader. However, as G. N. Stanton, Richard Bauckham, and others have argued, this does not imply that there is no residue of fact. Bultmann's interpretation of myth, as Henderson has argued, is too readily *without remainder*. For Bultmann "de-objectification" became virtually an obsession. This is partly because of the influence of existentialism, Kierkegaard, and Heidegger's philosophy, and partly because of the influence of form criticism. In Bultmann's view the purpose of most pericopes in the Gospels was not to give information, but to provide testimony and preaching of an existential nature. While German scholarship was largely convinced by this, we include in our entry on form criticism some sharp criticisms from commentators ranging from T. W. Manson to G. N. Stanton and R. J. Bauckham. It is unthinkable that the earliest Christians never wanted to know "about" Jesus; only to hear his call to a new life. Kierkegaard provides another influence, but Kierkegaard saw his emphasis on subjectivity as no more than "a little piece of cinnamon" to correct a prevailing theology. Specific examples of Bultmann's interpretation of "myth" can be found in the Bultmann entry and in *The Two Horizons*.

The "Bultmann School" of Bultmann and Gogarten soon split apart into "left-wing" Bultmannians, who thought he had not gone far enough, and "right-wing" critics, who had reservations about his whole program. The "left-wing" critics, Herbert Braun, Karl Jaspers, and Schubert Ogden, suggested that even language about "God" could be demythologized as merely useful symbols. Bultmann's "reply" to Jaspers was simply to relapse into Lutheranism, repeating Peter's words, "Lord, to whom can we go? You have the words of eternal life." With such critics as Barth, Thielicke, and Gollwitzer, he stood his ground, in spite of their criticism that he had dissolved Christology into soteriology. But his confusions about the definition of "myth" seem never to have been fully answered, even if it remains true that he struggled, albeit with unhelpful categories, to retrieve the true "point" of many NT passages. The crowning difficulty for him has been the gradual fading of Heidegger's monopoly on philosophy and language, and the new start of such theologians as W. Pannenberg with a wholly different approach. (*See also* **Bultmann, Rudolf; Existentialism; Form Criticism.**)

Reading: H.-W. Bartsch, ed., *Kerygma and Myth,* vol. 1 (London: SCM, 1953); G. B. Caird, *The Language and Imagery of the Bible* (London: Duckworth, 1980), 144-271; D. F. Ferguson, *Bultmann* (London: Chapman, 2006); J. W. Rogerson, *Myth in Old Testament Interpretation* (New York: ZAW, 1974); A. C. Thiselton, *The Two Horizons* (Grand Rapids: Eerdmans, 1980), 205-92.

N

Narcissism
The term simply denotes self-love or self-centeredness, as in the Greek myth of Narcissus. The term is used by Ricoeur, Moltmann, and many other theologians, as well by S. Freud.

Narrative
Narrative has become an urgent subject in exegesis and especially in hermeneutics. Pentecostals have now become a huge global force, and the majority of Pentecostals (although not Pentecostals alone) regard biblical narratives, especially in Acts, as accounts of events to be *replicated today,* as if the purpose of all narrative was to provide a blueprint for current imitation. Many regard narrative as detailed chronological report. Some narratives (e.g., the passion narratives) may constitute such accounts, but far from all. Many therefore become unduly anxious about what they perceive as chronological discrepancies in parallel accounts. Most readers, or at least many, are unaware of such standard devices in narrative as "plot" (stressed by Ricoeur); "point of view" (stressed by Alter); narrative speed (stressed by Genette and Ricoeur); and reader-response (stressed by Iser), among others. These devices are not designed to manipulate or to deceive the reader, but to make clearer the plot and purpose of the narrative. Gérard Genette, Seymour Chatman, Emile Beneviste, and Paul Ricoeur all distinguish between a chain of events in a bare report and a plot or structural narrative as it has been *organized* by a narrator.

In *Great Expectations,* for example, Charles Dickens withholds from the reader the identity of Pip's benefactor until toward the end, because this shapes the story and the plot. Most detective stories withhold the identity of the criminal until near the end, because sharing the clues and puzzles with the investigator gives spice and point to the plot. In the realm of fact, where history is close to narrative, devices such as narrative speed, and often narrative sequence, are still vital to a plot. Most scholars agree, for example, that the Gospel of Mark begins rapidly, with one event following on top of another, often introduced by the Greek word *euthus,* "immediately, at once" (Mark 1:10, 12, 18, 20, 21, 23, 28, 29, 30, 42, 43; 2:8, 12; 3:6; 4:5, 15, 16, 17, 29; at least thirty-two times before Peter's confession of Jesus as the Messiah in 8:29). It then occurs only six times before the beginning of the passion narrative. The usual interpretation is that Mark hurries the narrative of events along until we reach Peter's confession; then events proceed at a medium pace until the passion. Then Mark depicts the passion virtually in slow motion, taking over 100 verses to describe the final week; or over 150 if we include chapter 13 and events until the first resurrection appearance. Is this to deceive or manipulate the reader? Not at all; it is to highlight *the work of Christ on the cross* as the major point, goal, and climax of the narrative, to which other events point. Peter's confession about *the person of Christ* serves the subsidiary purpose of the plot. The reader's attention is directed toward these two key events in a *structural, organized narrative.* One scholar who advocates this approach is Wesley A. Kort (*Story, Text, and Scripture* [University Park: Pennsylvania State University Press, 1988]).

In 1969 Tzvetan Todorov drew attention to work on narrative as a serious subject of research by proposing the term "narratology" for the network of approaches associated with G. Genette, S. Chatman, R. Barthes, and others. Chatman used the word "story" for events that occurred in *"natural"* sequence, and "discourse" for a story-as-told in the telling, or for a *structured plot* (*Story and Discourse* [Ithaca, N.Y.: Cornell University Press, 1978], 19-42). Genette developed this further, distinguishing between order, duration, and frequency, in which he included flashbacks and other tools (*Narrative Discourse* [Ithaca, N.Y.: Cornell University Press, 1980], chaps. 4-6; and *Narrative Discourse Revisited* [Ithaca, N.Y.: Cornell University Press, 1988]). Although they often spoke primarily of fictional works, as Ricoeur argues, historical events can also be shaped to present a "point of view" or organized plot. Thus people tend to *prejudge* the purpose of Matthew and Luke when readers worry about the sequence of the temptations of Christ, or the Synoptic Gospels and John when they worry that the cleansing of the temple seems to occur at a different point in the ministry of Jesus.

Often "point of view" can assist the integrity and harmony of narratives. Robert Alter achieves this in *The Art of Biblical Narrative* (New York: Basic Books, 1981), 147-53, when he compares the narratives of David's rise to kingship in 1 Sam. 16:4-13 and 1 Sam. 16:14–2 Sam. 5:5. These two accounts are often considered inconsistent doublets. In the first, Samuel comes to Jesse and anoints his youngest son, David (1 Sam. 16:13); the whole process seems rapid and straightforward. In the second account, especially in chapter 17, David battles with Goliath, and gradually wins his way to power, mainly by popular acclaim. These narratives, Alter insists, are not at variance. One records David's anointing by *divine decree* as the narrator's point of view. The other records "the *brawling chaos*" of human situations, *through* which God actualizes his purposes. Stephen Crites likewise speaks of "the inner bond" between tellers and hearers, while Ronald Thiemann argues that the responsible reader must "enter the world of the text" ("Radiance and Obscurity in Biblical Narrative," in *Scriptural Authority and Narrative Interpretation,* ed. G. Green [Philadelphia: Fortress, 1987], 35-36).

We explore now reader-response theory and drawing the reader into a narrative world before returning briefly to narrative reading as replication. Reader-response theory has become enormously complex, but at its heart stands the aim of enabling the reader to take a more *active* and *involved* part in reading. Coupled with this, the technique of *defamiliarization,* borrowed from Russian formalism, helps the reader to perceive the familiar as something fresh. This addresses one of the most notorious problems faced by preachers and ministers. How can congregations be stirred or provoked into active thought or positive transformation when they are already totally familiar with the narrative or the text being read to them? Defamiliarization is designed to place the overfamiliar in an unfamiliar setting, and to rob it of what many may perceive as its apparently trite, dull, familiar, or obvious nature.

Viktor Shkovsky was one of the pioneers of defamiliarization. He argued that poetic, aphoristic, and parabolic imagery appears to make strange what would otherwise seem to be overfamiliar, habitual, or routine. Jesus, as we know, taught frequently in parables to convey a new perspective, and more recently he has also been shown to offer wisdom pronouncements in the form of crisp, terse aphorisms, especially in the so-called Q material, where Matthew and Luke overlap. For example, "The Son of Man has nowhere to lay his head" (Luke 9:58; Matt. 8:20); or "Blessed are you who are poor, for yours is the kingdom of God" (Luke 6:20; cf. Matt. 5:3); or "Hallowed be your name" (Luke 11:2; Matt. 6:9; A. C. Thiselton "Wisdom in the New Testament," *Theology* 115 [2011]: 163-72). In my recent Festschrift *Horizons in Hermeneutics* (Grand Rapids: Eerdmans, 2103), John Goldingay comments, "In the Old Testament, poetry is the dominant form of speech in the Wisdom writings, the Psalms, and the Prophets" (15). He continues, "Poetry makes more use of imagery such as simile, metaphor, and symbol, which enable it to say things that cannot be said by means of straightforward statements" (16). "Each of these images constitutes a compressed story, as is characteristic of images" (20). Broadly it is "saying the unsayable" (23-29). He concludes, "The genius of prose is a capacity to make things clear. The genius of poetry is a capacity to obscure them.... Enigmatic poetic utterances have the potential to make people think.... Poetry attacks the mind not frontally (like prose) but indirectly and subversively" (29). In a second essay in the same volume, David Parris points out: "A metaphor is the result of a 'blend' that draws from both source and target" (150). Thereby it takes us forward beyond preexisting thought, conventions, and expectations. Many biblical texts thus convey "inter-textual information" (193). A third contributor, John Thomson, argues that a proper use of hermeneutics can transcend "past perspectives," especially by "polyphonic" reading, and "as hermeneutics of altereity" (273), both of which I shall consider later.

The pioneer of constructive reader-response theory is Wolfgang Iser. From E. Husserl and Roman Ingarden he drew the idea that most texts are characterized by incompleteness; they contain gaps, which the reader is invited to fill in. He calls this "filling out a schema." A good example in everyday life is seeing a table. Usually we cannot see all four legs; one is covered by the tabletop. But we "presuppose and construe" the fourth leg from our regular experience of life. Hence, Iser declares, "The text represents a potential effect that is realized in the reading process" (*The Act of Reading* [Baltimore: Johns Hopkins University Press, 1978, 1980], ix). A number of biblical scholars have followed Iser. Susan Wittig follows him on the parables. Robert Fowler follows him on the important question of the relation between the feeding miracles in Mark 6:30-44 and Mark 8:1-10 (*Loaves and Fishes* [Chico, Calif.: Scholars Press, 1981], esp. 134-35). Mark 6 tells of five thousand men, being fed from five loaves and two fish; Mark 8 tells of four thousand, being fed from seven loaves and a few fish. The puzzle comes in Mark 8:4. If we allow chronological or narrative sequence, the disciples have just witnessed the feeding of the *five* thousand two chapters earlier. Yet they say in verse 4, "How can one feed these people with bread here in the desert?" According to Fowler, this is not the result of clumsy editing. Mark's strategy is to provoke the reader to think "Poor simpletons! Don't they realize that Jesus can feed them?" Or, in more sophisticated terms, the reader begins to understand that the Christology of the disciples is far from adequate. It is twenty-five verses later that Jesus finally elicits the beginning of a fuller christological confession from Peter (v. 29).

The remaining point is that narrative creates "worlds," or "narrative worlds," *into which readers may be drawn.* When a person is drawn into a narrative world, he or she may suspend many everyday beliefs. Millions are drawn in every evening to the narrative world of soaps on TV, in which normal judgment or prejudices become weakened. Many narrative theorists make this point, including V. Propp, A. Greimas, Ricoeur, Genette, and Chatman. But the most forceful philosophical approach comes from M. Heidegger and H.-G. Gadamer. Gadamer compares the narrative world to the world of the game. In the game world what counts are the rules, strategy, and aims of *the game,* which are quite different from those of everyday life. For example, the narrative parable of the laborers in the vineyard and the employer (Matt. 20:1-16) sets up a "world" in which the laborers do not receive what they expect. Within that world, two possible responses emerge. One response is: "That's not fair; we have worked longer and harder than the recent day-laborers." The second response is: "That's generous! Everyone is given a full day's wage, though some worked for less time." As Ernst Fuchs observes, to see reality from within this world is far more transformative than a "pallid" discourse on the doctrine of grace. The crowd is not merely *informed* that God's grace eclipses his justice; they *feel it in their bones.* The strategy of the narrative world catches the hearer off-guard, and can reverse natural resistance and natural expectations. This is the way of love, Fuchs comments, like all the ministry of Jesus. As George Stroup comments, if reading entails entering a world, it is a creative *act,* not just a replication of thoughts.

This, finally, brings us back to the issue of reading the narrative in Acts as a model to replicate today. The purposes of the Acts narrative may be manifold: to draw readers into a narrative world, to defamiliarize readers from conventional expectations, to provoke them into thinking for themselves, to see the events structured as Luke intends, to show them how the church left behind a primitive structure once suited to being the church as an emergent sect of Judaism, etc. We must be careful about what we assume. Acts is a *narrative,* not a modern newspaper report. Two of many diverse approaches to Acts seem attractive. One was formulated by R. R. Williams, former bishop of Durham, in a commentary to which he gave the subtitle *Nothing Can Stop the Gospel* (*The Acts of the Apostles,* 3rd ed. [London: SCM (Torch), 1959]). Every setback and persecution turned out to lead to the spread of the gospel. Thus in Acts 8:4 persecution scattered the believers, but they "went from place to place, proclaiming the word." The second approach is that of Beverly Roberts Gaventa, *The Acts of the Apostles* (Nashville: Abingdon, 2003), in which she regards Acts as setting out the purposes of *God* for the church. It would not be incompatible with this to understand the first few chapters as depicting what the earliest church *once* was, and out of which it has since grown as a body with elders, councils, infrastructure, and all that the later chapters depict. God reveals the church as it was stage by stage in salvation history. The narratives of the earliest chapters would then not be models still to replicate today. But whatever our conclusions on this particular matter, narrative invites careful reflection on what its purpose may be, out of up to a dozen serious possibilities. (*See also* **Iser, Wolfgang; Ricoeur, Paul.**)

Reading: Robert Alter, *The Art of Biblical Narrative* (New York: Basic Books, 1981); Beverly Roberts Gaventa, *The Acts of the Apostles* (Nashville: Abingdon, 2003); Gérard Genette, *Narrative Discourse* (Ithaca, N.Y.: Cornell University Press, 1980); D. M. Gunn and D. N. Fewell, *Narrative in the Hebrew Bible* (New York and Oxford: OUP, 1993); Wesley A. Kort, *Story, Text, and Scripture* (University Park: Pennsylvania State University Press, 1988); Paul Ricoeur, *Time and Narrative,* 3 vols. (Chicago: University of Chicago Press, 1984-1988).

Natural Law

Natural law theories postulate (i) the objective reality of an intelligible world order, as against its being a construct of human reason alone; and (ii) that this world order is a source of moral direction, moral consciousness, and ethical criteria. The origins of the idea go back to Greek and Roman philosophy, especially to the Stoics, and it was formulated as a theological principle by Thomas Aquinas. In *Summa Theologiae* 1-2, question 91, article 2, Aquinas appeals to Rom. 2:14, and comments, "Although they [Gentiles] have no written law, yet they have the natural law, whereby each one knows, and is conscious of, what is good and what is evil." It implies a rejection of utilitarianism, even if some argue that it elevates universal human reason unduly.

Natural Theology

Natural theology denotes knowledge of God that can be obtained by human reason alone, without the aid of revelation. Thomas Aquinas formulated an explicit distinction between natural and revealed theology. He argued that reason can assure us that God is, and that through analogy humankind could infer certain truths about God; however, only revelation can provide the truth that belongs to revealed theology, such as that of the incarnation, the atonement, and the doctrine of the Holy Trinity. In this sense most Roman Catholics defend the use, within limits, of natural theology. Karl Barth opposed natural theology, and engaged in a famous correspondence with Emil Brunner, in which he entitled one of his replies, *No!* (1934). Brunner defended natural theology in a weakened sense, by appealing to the divine ordinances of marriage and the state, the possibility of repentance, and Paul's allusion to knowledge of God in Rom. 1:19-20. William Paley's use of the teleological argument for the existence of God provides an example of rational argument from analogy. Others argue that evidence from the natural world is ambiguous, and requires revelation and faith. (*See also* **Barth, Karl; Brunner, Emil; Revelation.**)

Necessary

In philosophical theology "necessary" denotes *logically* necessary, in contrast to *contingently* necessary, which might or might not be the case. For example, "All bachelors are unmarried" is a standard example of a logically necessary proposition, because it is true by definition. "All triangles have three sides" would be another. It is significant for theology that "God cannot tell a lie" is a *logically* necessary proposition, because it is entailed by his nature as the truthful God. It is not a contingent proposition, which might suggest that some external force could constrain God against his will.

Negative Theology

Negative theology, or a theology of negation, is identical with apophatic theology. Since God is transcendent, many have argued that analogies and anthropomorphisms are misleading and inappropriate. Paul Tillich argued that often superlatives can become reductive diminutives. Hence some argue that we can say only what God is *not,* or remain silent. But since Jesus Christ is the Word of God, others argue, as Jüngel does, that Christ makes God "conceivable" and "speakable." (*See also* **Apophatic Theology; Dionysius, Pseudo-; God, Trinity; Jüngel, Eberhard.**)

Neoplatonism

Neoplatonism was in effect founded by Plotinus (c. 205-270), and was also represented by Porphyry (c. 232-303). Both of these are considered under separate entries. Neoplatonism flourished from the third to the sixth century, and built on many centuries of Greek philosophy. Platonism had become familiar to the Church Fathers largely through Philo, Clement of Alexandria, and Origen. But the main focus of Neoplatonism was the One, the unknowable source, from which the world and everything emanate. Emanation (Gk. *proödos*) flows outward from the One, and encounters an ascending movement of return *(epistrophē)*. This may involve contemplation and purification, which explains why Luther regarded Neoplatonism as a negative influence on mysticism. Knowledge exists as varied degrees of "contemplation," and this implies levels of knowledge. (*See also* **Plato; Plotinus; Porphyry.**)

Neo-Thomism

Neo-Thomism denotes a movement in philosophical theology, largely of the late nineteenth and twentieth centuries, whose goal was the revival of the study of Thomas Aquinas. It began with an encyclical of Pope Leo XIII in 1879. It probably reached its peak in the 1950s with Jacques Maritain, Étienne Gilson, at one stage Karl Rahner, and Bernard Lonergan. Neo-Thomism also includes some Anglicans, such as Eric Mascall.

New Hermeneutic

The New Hermeneutic is most closely associated with the work of E. Fuchs and G. Ebeling, and flourished from the mid-1950s to the 1970s. Fuchs asked how the language of the Bible could "strike home" (Ger. *treffen*) to the modern hearer. The clue to an answer came in a twofold form: the creation of a *"language world"* through a *"language event" (Sprachereignis)*. Both Fuchs and Ebeling stressed that the word should *create* faith, rather than presuppose faith. Fuchs insisted, "The text is itself meant to live" (*Studies of the Historical Jesus* [London: SCM, 1964], 193). This is achieved, Ebeling claims, not by "cheap borrowing of transient modern jargon," but by a new "coming to speech" (Ebeling, *The Nature of Faith* [London: Fontana, 1961], 16). They borrowed this latter phrase *(das Zur-Sprache-kommen)* from Heidegger. Clearly, like Schleiermacher and Heidegger, they saw hermeneutics as meaning *understanding*. Understanding is achieved when there comes to be a rapport, "mutual understanding" or agreement *(Einverständnis)*, between the text and the interpreter. It is like the language of the home, or among intimate friends. Fuchs finds this exemplified in the language of many of the parables of Jesus. In the parable of the employer and laborers in the vineyard, for example (Matt. 20:1-16), Jesus sets up a "world" that we enter as participants and can understand. We *feel* consternation and shock, or gladness and relief, that the day laborers who worked only an hour still receive a living wage for the day. We hardly need to think about it: either we are shocked at supposed injustice, or we rejoice because generosity or grace eclipses justice. Fuchs comments, "Is not this the way of true love?" Love does not simply "blurt out" or deliver a lecture on grace. The word of grace interprets the hearer.

All this can be helpful. But Fuchs was a former pupil of Bultmann, and learned his language theory from Heidegger. Hence, in the end, everything always becomes *intralinguistic,* even the event of the resurrection of Jesus Christ. Fuchs was a highly controversial figure in Germany, who was sometimes at odds with the Lutheran church. (*See also* **Christology: Jesus of History; Hermeneutics.**)

Newman, John Henry

John Henry Newman (1801-1890) was probably the most creative Roman Catholic thinker of the nineteenth century, certainly in England. His early influences were evangelical. But at Oxford University he became strongly influenced by J. Keble and E. B. Pusey. They were pioneers of the "High Church" party in Anglicanism, and believed that the church was divinely ordered, and far from being part of the state. All three believed in the importance of doctrine, and opposed liberalism and rationalism. Newman was ordained to the Church of England ministry in 1824, and remained in that ministry for nineteen years. But from 1833 onward he shared the leadership of the High Church "Tractarian" Movement with Keble and Pusey. This "Oxford Movement" took a firm stand against liberalism, regarding "certitude" as a habit of mind. Newman also believed that evangelicals were plagued by subjectivism, and by "hypochondriac" religion. The formal cause for founding the Oxford Movement was governmental interference with an appointment to a diocese in Ireland. But the main thrust was a call for a more wholehearted devotion in accordance with "Catholic" creeds and doctrine. Newman, together with Keble and Pusey, began to publish "Tracts for the Times"; hence the popular name for their movement. Newman came to believe that mainline Roman Catholic doctrine was coherent with that of the *Book of Common Prayer*, and expressed this view in his famous Tract 90, in 1841. The years 1841-1843 became a period of deep controversy.

Newman had long retained his belief that while rationalism detracted from the church's truth, Roman Catholicism added to it. But in 1843 he resigned from his parish, preaching "The Parting of Friends." In 1845, at the age of forty-four, he was received into the Roman Catholic Church. The same year he published *The Development of Doctrine*, which B. Reardon calls "one of the most significant books of the century" (*From Coleridge to Gore* [Harlow: Longman, 1971], 146). He argued that the bubbling spring of the NT becomes a full-flowing river in the modern Catholic Church. He suggested "seven tests" of doctrinal continuity, but many consider these inadequate and ineffective. His general perspective on organic growth, however, is still influential today. Owen Chadwick cites the analogy of the caterpillar becoming a butterfly (*Newman* [Oxford: OUP, 1983], 47). But the work left unresolved the problem of how we detect invalid or false developments. W. Gladstone argued: "He places Christianity on the edge of a precipice." In 1847 Newman was ordained a Roman Catholic priest, to the regret of Keble and Pusey, who was now professor of Hebrew at Oxford. Newman had always stressed the need for "the training of the mind." In 1852 he published his second major volume, *The Idea of a University*. Its immediate purpose was to found a new Roman Catholic University of Dublin, using Oxford education as a model. This encouraged not simply the transmission of information, but more especially independence of judgment and wisdom. Newman argued that while *information* could be conveyed by post, *judgment and wisdom* are learned through personal contact. Wisdom is not knowledge. Students are to learn "freedom from littleness and prejudice" (*Idea of a University* [Dublin: Ashfield, 2009], 123-24). Religion must be included in such education, as well as the sciences.

The period from 1864 to 1890 was one of the defense and exposition of the Catholic faith. In 1864 Newman published his famous *Apologia Pro Vita Sua* (London: Penguin, 1994). Charles Kingsley had charged him with lack of integrity. Newman replied by means of a powerful theological autobiography. He looked back on the stand against liberalism taken with Pusey and Keble (125), and their common defense against "German" theology (143). He regarded Kingsley's complaint as "miserably insufficient" (28). Since becoming a Catholic, he concluded, "I have been in perfect peace and contentment" (275). In 1865 he wrote the *Dream of Gerontius,* a dramatic poem on purgatory and the afterlife. In 1870 he wrote *The Grammar of Assent,* which included the moral dimension of certainty. "Pure" intellect is insufficient; "the human mind is made for truth" (*Assent,* 145). It needs the "illative" sense. Finally, he was appointed cardinal in the Roman Catholic Church.

Reading: O. Chadwick, *Newman* (Oxford: OUP, 1983); I. Kerr, *The Achievement of John Henry Newman* (London: Collins, 1990); John Henry Newman, *The Development of Doctrine* (Harmondsworth: Penguin, 1974); John Henry Newman, *The Grammar of Assent* (Oxford: Clarendon, 1985); John Henry Newman, *Apologia Pro Vita Sua* (London: Penguin, 1994); John Henry Newman, *The Idea of a University* (Dublin: Ashfield, 2009); B. M. G. Reardon, *From Coleridge to Gore* (Harlow: Longman, 1971).

Nicaea, Creed and Council of

The Council of Nicaea (325), known as the first ecumenical council, was convened by the emperor Constantine to address the Arian controversy. Eusebius of Caesarea, in effect court theologian, probably presided, unless this was Eustathius. What we familiarly call the "Nicene Creed" is really the Nicene-Constantinopolitan Creed of 381. Athanasius was present as a deacon. (*See also* **Arius, Arianism; Christology: History of Thought.**)

Nicholas of Lyra

Nicholas of Lyra (1270-1349) was born in Normandy, entered the Franciscan Order, and became a lecturer in the University of Paris between 1300 and 1310. He made a special study of Hebrew and of Jewish commentaries on the Hebrew Bible. He was essentially a research scholar, focusing on the literal meaning of the Bible, and writing *postillae,* that is, analyses on each verse or passage. Nicholas became a household name for sober biblical exegesis.

Niebuhr, H. Richard

H. Richard Niebuhr (1894-1962) was born in Missouri, and graduated from Elmhurst College (1912) and Eden Theological Seminary (1923). He was ordained in the Evangelical and Reformed Church in 1916, and took his Ph.D. at Yale Divinity School in 1924. He became president of Elmhurst College (1924-1927), and professor of theology and Christian ethics at Yale from 1931 until his death in 1962. His first major book was *The Social Sources of Denominationalism* (1929), in which he exposed the social sciences as a cause of fragmentation into Christian denominations. He attacked especially economic class and nationalism, as his elder brother Reinhold also had done.

Far more important was Richard Niebuhr's book *The Kingdom of God in America* (1937; reprint, New York: Harper and Row, 1988). In this he argued that liberalism and the Social Gospel had domesticated the sovereignty of God. One of his more lasting aphorisms was that, in response to liberalism, "Too often we want a God without wrath [who] brought men without sin into a kingdom without judgment through the ministrations of a Christ without a cross" (193). His next book was *The Meaning of Revelation* (1941; reprint, Louisville: Westminster John Knox, 2006). In his preface he acknowledged his indebtedness both to Ernst Troeltsch and to Karl Barth. He accepted the thrust of much of Troeltsch's concern about historical relativism and universalism, but he also argued, "Revelation cannot mean history, if it also means God" (40). From Barth he also stresses the theocentric and christocentric nature of revelation. Jesus did not simply proclaim love; above all, Jesus proclaimed God.

Niebuhr's two most important and influential books, however, have been *Christ and Culture* (1951; reprint, San Francisco: Harper, 2001) and *The Responsible Self* (published posthumously in 1962, but edited and reprinted, New York: HarperCollins, 1999). In *Christ and Culture* he set out five possible relations between Christ and culture: (i) Christ against culture; advocates of this position included Tertullian, Tolstoy, and the Mennonites, who pitted a rising church against a dying secularism. He criticized these, because while they stressed God as Redeemer, they tended to understate the role of God as Creator (76-82). (ii) The Christ of culture stresses the Spirit's work in nature. Some would suggest the influence of Paul Tillich in this direction, but it may overlap at either end of the spectrum with adjacent formulations of the relationship between Christ and culture. (iii) Christ above nature similarly covers the spectrum ranging from a dualist type of approach in which Christ becomes divided off from the world in order to be "above" the world to a more careful emphasis on divine transcendence. Yet such dualism may characterize the fourth category more clearly. (iv) Christ and culture in paradox offers a category in which faith struggles against unbelief and secularism. Finally, (v) Christ transforming culture provides a pattern of divine grace and human response, which matches the present period of an eschatology in process of realization. God's grace brings about a "now"; but the ambiguity of human response, as Tillich also urges, expresses the "not yet" of eschatology.

Prior to his next key book, Niebuhr wrote *The Church and Its Ministry* (1956) and *Radical Monotheism and Western Culture* (1960). But without doubt the climax of these works came in 1962 with his book *The Responsible Self*. In contrast to regarding humans as makers or citizens, Niebuhr stated that being human implies responsibility on the part of "man-the-answer, man engaged in dialogue, man in response to action upon him" (56). His book seeks to formulate an ethics of responsibility in response to grace. Before he died, he had outlined this material in his Robertson Lectures at the University of Glasgow, and also in his Earle Lectures. J. M. Gustafson has provided a preface and introduction, and the influence of this book in America has been immense. Yet one possible qualification may be offered: Paul Ricoeur published *Oneself as Another* (Fr. 1990; Eng. 1992), which progressively builds toward an even deeper understanding of accountability and moral responsibility. Many would argue that the Ricoeur work is even more profound than Niebuhr's in its philosophical underpinning. Both authors, however, deserve recognition and note for their important ethical approach. (*See also* Ethics; Hermeneutics; Ricoeur, Paul; Political Theology.)

Niebuhr, Reinhold

Reinhold Niebuhr (1892-1971) was the son of a Lutheran pastor who emigrated from Germany to the USA. He was educated at Elmhurst College, Eden Theological Seminary, and Yale Divinity School. From 1915 to 1928 he served as pastor in Detroit, Michigan, working largely among Ford factory workers. In his early years he became deeply concerned over exploitation, and was initially influenced by Rauschenbusch's "Social Gospel," socialist politics, and liberal theology. But he became steadily influenced by Barth and by Brunner, with their Reformed theology of sin and grace. He reached national prominence, and became a teacher, and subsequently a professor at Union Theological Seminary, New York. In the realm of public affairs Richard Harries, former bishop of Oxford, described him as "the most influential theologian of our century." In 1943 he received an honorary D.D. from Oxford University.

In one of his first books, *Leaves from the Notebook of a Tamed Cynic* (1929), he looked back to earlier preaching on the basis of liberal theology, with the comment: "Now that I have preached about a dozen sermons, I find that I am repeating myself. A different text simply means a different pretext for saying the same thing" (4). As he increasingly explored the seriousness of sin, he also wrote, "The culture of every society seeks to obscure the brutalities on which it rests" (80).

Niebuhr's first main book was *Moral Man and Immoral Society* (1932; London: SCM, 1963). He argued two themes, among others. First, "In every human group there is . . . more unrestrained egoism than the individuals who compose the group reveal in their personal relationships" (xi-xii). The second is: "Conflict is inevitable, and in this conflict, power must be challenged by power" (xv). He argues, "All social cooperation on a larger scale . . . required a measure of coercion" (3). Diagnosing the self-deception of groups, he observes, "Napoleon . . . could bathe Europe in blood for the sake of gratifying his lust for power, as long as he could pose as the tool of French patriotism. . . . The will-to-live becomes the will-to-power" (17-18). Liberal rationalists look simply to human intelligence and social science for progress, but this is superficial. Niebuhr spoke of "the insinuation of the interests of the self into even the most ideal enterprises" (45).

If we give ourselves to some good cause or community, the will to power remains. This applies to work supposedly for the family: "The family may still remain a means of self-aggrandisement" (47). A person may kick another down the ladder of promotion "for the sake of the family." "The same may be said of class groups" (75). Further, "the selfishness of nations is proverbial"; they always act from self-interest (84). Nations are held together "much more by force and emotion than by mind" (88). Nationalism pretends to altruism, but this is a disguise; it is "self-deception and hypocrisy" (95). Landholders, according to Niebuhr, provide further examples, together with the class of "professional people, clerks, small retailers, and bureaucrats" (115). In Marxism "the relation of social classes . . . is conceived wholly in terms of the conflict of power with power" (146). But this suffers from "moral cynicism" (161). In spite of Niebuhr's reservations, the *New York Times* greeted this book with the headline "Doctrine of Christ and Marxism Linked."

Five years later came *Beyond Tragedy* (1937). Christianity, Niebuhr argues, transcends tragedy; it offers victory over tragedy. In Dionysian or Freudian tragedy, passion and interests lie below the level of consciousness. Niebuhr writes: "The unconscious sin, of which all men are guilty . . . reaches down into the furthest depths. . . . There is no solution on the purely moral level" (165-67). But his Gifford Lectures, published as *The Nature and Destiny of Man*, 2 vols. (London: Nisbet, 1941-1943), are probably his most influential writings. To understand man, Niebuhr argues, faith grasps "that he is seen from beyond himself; that he is known and loved of God, and must find himself in terms of obedience to the divine will" (1:16). He continues: "The paradox of man as a creature and man as a child of God is a necessary presupposition of a concept of individuality" (24). Naturalism, idealism, and romanticism all lead to loss of the self: "It is the essence of man to love himself" (113). Rousseau, Nietzsche, and Freud all come under attack, in contrast to the Christian view of man as revealed in the Bible, where he is God's creature.

Niebuhr then includes a chapter on "man as a sinner." He dismisses Ritschl as inadequate (*see* **Sin**). Sin is not simply unethical, but includes "man's rebellion against God, his effort to usurp the place of God" in its religious dimensions; in its moral dimension "sin is injustice" (101). Here will to power leads to pride: "Pride is more basic than sensuality" (198). As he has argued in *Moral Man*, "The group is more arrogant, hypocritical, . . . and more ruthless in the pursuit of its ends than the individual" (221-22). There is a certain inevitability about "man's coercive and inordinate love of self," which Pelagianism ignores (268). "The self lacks the faith and trust to subject itself to God" (267). Yet humankind is responsible for this condition.

Volume 2 opens with the expectation of the Messiah, and the disclosure and the fulfillment of the meaning of life. Christ "disclosed the sovereignty of God over history," and is "the perfect norm of human nature . . . the 'second Adam' as well as the 'Son of God' " (2:71). He gives meaning to the paradox "Whosoever loses his life shall find it." In his cross we see the love *(agapē)* of God "in terms of the divine involvement in history" (74). The purpose of Christ's life is to confirm the love of God: "Sacrificial love *(agapē)* completes the incompleteness of mutual love" (86). He adds, "The cross represents a transcendent perfection which clarifies obscurities of history" (90). Niebuhr then turns to the Pauline theme of grace, in which Paul is "crucified with Christ" (112). Christ breaks and shatters the self's preoccupation with itself. Paul's "yet not I" shows the priority of grace (118).

Finally, Niebuhr explores debates about human destiny, the kingdom of God, and the struggle for justice; the parousia, the Last Judgment, and the resurrection; and the end and the meaning of history. He writes: "The final consummation of history lies beyond the conditions of the temporal process" (301). The ambiguities of history, he believes, "do not obviate the necessity and possibility of a *final* judgment" (302). "The resurrection transcends the limits of the conceivable.... Only God can solve this problem" (305). This is precisely the logic of Paul in 1 Corinthians 15. Anticipating Pannenberg, he sees the meaning of history as disclosed only after its completion, when the love of God reigns over all.

Niebuhr never lost touch with ordinary people. He must be credited with the much-used prayer: "Give us grace to accept with serenity the things that cannot be changed, courage to change the things that can, and the wisdom to know the difference." On an even more everyday note, he declared: "Democracy is finding proximate solutions to insoluble problems."

Reading: L. Gilkey, *On Niebuhr* (Chicago: University of Chicago Press, 2001); M. Lovatt, *Confronting the Will-to-Power* (Carlisle: Paternoster, 2001); Reinhold Niebuhr, *Moral Man and Immoral Society* (1932; London: SCM, 1963); Reinhold Niebuhr, *The Nature and Destiny of Man,* 2 vols. (London: Nisbet, 1941-1943).

Nietzsche, Friedrich Wilhelm

Friedrich Wilhelm Nietzsche (1844-1900) at first shared with Schopenhauer and with the pre-Socratic philosophers some kind of affirmation of life. In his early work he explored "driving force" and raw energy of the kind we find in Euripides' tragedy *The Bacchae.* Nietzsche saw himself as "Dionysian," or life-affirming and unrestrained, in contrast to the "Apollonian" principle of restraint, harmony, and moderation. In his student days in Leipzig he enjoyed a friendship with Richard Wagner, at first admiring his use of German mythology. But by 1879 he had broken with Wagner, whom he saw as insufficiently radical. In *The Gay Science* (1882) and in *Thus Spoke Zarathustra* (1883-1885), he looked toward nihilism, which would follow the announcement "God is dead." In 1886 he wrote *Beyond Good and Evil,* and in 1888 both *The Twilight of the Idols* (published in 1889) and *The Antichrist* (published in 1895). Religion, he argued, consisted of "fictions" and "lies." He stressed human will over rational system, and rejected theism.

"Master" morality became for Nietzsche sheer self-assertion. As early as his *Notebooks* of 1873 he had written: "What is truth? A mobile army of metaphors, metonyms and anthropomorphisms" (in W. Kaufman, ed., *The Portable Nietzsche* [New York: Viking Press, 1968], 46). He declared, *"Truth is that kind of error* without which a certain species of being cannot live" (*Works*, 18 vols. [London: Allen and Unwin, 1909-1913], vol. 15; *The Will to Power*, vol. 2 of *Works*, aphorism 481). In the same aphorism he wrote, "All that exists consists of *interpretations*." Truths, he said, are "illusions which we have forgotten are illusions" (*Notebooks*, 46). Theology, he believed, is simply a manipulative tool to help the weak and insecure to cope with life. He offered three reasons for its persuasiveness. First, in *The Twilight of the Idols*, he declared, "We shall never be rid of God so long as we still believe in grammar" (*Works*, vol. 12, *Twilight*, 22, aphorism 5). He utterly distrusted language. Second, religion, he urged, is concerned with power. In *The Antichrist* he maintained that "the salvation of the soul" means only that "the world revolves around me" (*Works*, vol. 16, *The Antichrist*, 186, aphorism 43). He added: "A theologian, a priest, or a pope ... lies with every word that he utters" (*The Antichrist*, 177, aphorism 38). The words "God forgives a person who repents" really mean, he declared, "him who submits himself to a priest" (*The Antichrist*, 161, aphorism 26). Third, as we have noted, he insisted: "All that exists consists of interpretations." There are no "givens" in life. He cited Paul's view of Christ as based on a dishonest manipulation of texts.

No doubt Nietzsche had perceived some half-truths in distorted "religion." Religion can admittedly be used as a tool for gaining power and prestige. But this is not the religion of Jesus. It *can* be manipulative, especially over the vulnerable, and even encourage misplaced guilt. This was a target for D. Bonhoeffer in his later *Letters and Papers from Prison*. It can detract from fulfillment and affirmation. This is also Moltmann's point in his book *The Spirit of Life*, which he subtitled *A Universal Affirmation*. But if we place self-assertive human will in the place of reason, and regard truth simply as "interpretation" or viewpoint, what tools are left for the assessment of truth? This is not only naked nihilism and atheism, but a deliberate and specific attack on Christianity. Again, we need not reject a controlled suspicion of language, as Wittgenstein and others show us. But this is different from an unrestrained critique. Many themes in Nietzsche have been taken up and amplified by such thinkers as M. Foucault and J. Derrida. It is not surprising that in 1889 Nietzsche's mental health collapsed. He never recovered his mind before his death eleven years later.

Reading: R. J. Hollingdale, *Nietzsche* (Cambridge: CUP, 1999); F. Nietzsche, *The Antichrist* (London: Penguin Books, 1969); R. Schacht, *Nietzsche* (London: Routledge and Kegan Paul, 1983).

Nominalism

Nominalism attacks the nature of abstract entities or universals, which it denies. It thus opposes Platonic ideas or forms, insisting that only specific "particulars" exist. Abelard and William of Ockham were particularists. Ockham argued, with "Ockham's razor," that we can explain all phenomena without appealing to universals. Nominalists argue that language about universal concepts are no more than *linguistic constructions* or "names" (Lat. *nomen*, plural *nomina*).

Novatian of Rome

Novatian of Rome (c. 200-258) was a presbyter at Rome who lapsed during the Decian persecutions but was restored. He wrote *On the Trinity,* which developed Tertullian's theology. He held a two-natures Christology, and produced material on the Holy Spirit, including an emphasis on new birth, eschatological pledge, sanctification, and holiness (*On the Trinity* 29). Some regard him as a bridge between Tertullian and Augustine. H. B. Swete declares of part of this work, "No passage in the ante-Nicene literature is more rich in the New Testament doctrine of the work of the Spirit" (*The Holy Spirit in the Ancient Church* [London: Macmillan, 1912], 108-9).

Nygren, Anders T. S.

Anders T. S. Nygren (1890-1978) was a Swedish Lutheran theologian who became professor of systematic theology at Lund University starting in 1924, and served as bishop of Lund from 1948 until his retirement in 1958. He is best known for his work *Agape and Eros* (Swed. 1930-1936; Eng. 1957). He was ordained in 1912, and served as pastor until 1924. His range of theological concerns was broad. In 1920 he visited Ernst Troeltsch and Rudolf Otto in Germany, where he was exploring the "religious a priori" and its presuppositions, and preparing *The Scientific Foundations of Dogmatics* (1922). In his early academic career he focused on more philosophical questions of objectivity, method, and criticism; in the 1930s he focused on the contrast between Greek concepts of *erōs* and biblical concepts of *agapē*. In the 1940s he worked on NT interpretation (especially in his *Romans;* Swed. 1944; Eng. 1949). In the 1950s he was openly concerned with ecumenical affairs. We concentrate on his *Agape and Eros* and *Romans.*

From his earlier interest in the scientific study of theology, Nygren remained concerned with "motif research," which takes its place early on in *Agape and Eros* ([London: SPCK, 1957], 30-44). Motif research is concerned "less with historical connections" than with "characteristic content and typical manifestations" (35). It comes dangerously near, some would say, to seeking the essence of phenomena. *Agapē* is "the fundamental motif of Christianity" (46). He writes, "Between Vulgar Eros and Christian Agape there is no relation at all" (51). It has been disastrous for *agapē* that it should meet with "another conception exhibiting enough similarities ... to be ... confused with it" (53). *Erōs* comes from the Greeks and Plato; Jesus seeks to bring "a near fellowship with God ... the new wine" (68; cf. Matt. 9:17). "*Agapē is spontaneous and 'unmotivated.'* This is the most striking feature of God's love as Jesus represents it" (75). He explains: "God does not love that which is already in itself worthy of love, but on the contrary that which has no worth acquires worth just by becoming the object of God's love.... *Agapē is a value-creating principle*" (78). *Agapē* is therefore creative. Nygren illustrates this from the parables, especially from the parable of the laborers in the vineyard (86-91; Matt. 20:1-16). Christians are commanded to show their love, which is not a love based on a rational calculation or reward (97-102).

Nygren then considers the love of the cross, and Paul's new evaluation of it. *Agapē* puts an end to the righteousness of the law (111-23; Phil. 3:4-7; 2 Cor. 13:11). Nygren also contrasts the way of love with the way of *gnosis* (1 Cor. 8:1-3). Love builds up, and seeks not "its own" (1 Cor. 13:5). He concludes, *"Gnōsis ... is only another name for the Eros motif"* (142). "God is Agapē" (147; 1 John 4:8, 16). In the next section Nygren traces the *erōs* motif "back to its source in ancient Mystery-piety," noting the connection between love in Plato and Orphism (163). He then follows developments in Aristotle and in Neoplatonism and Plotinus (182-99). The rest of his book is devoted to expounding the contrast between *agapē* and *erōs*, beginning with the Hellenization of love in the NT, and various reversions in the history of Christian thought. For example, Pseudo-Dionysius says, "it is from the Deity Himself that Eros takes its place" (578). He proposes, "the Chain of love that joins heaven and earth, that leads the divine Eros-forces down the lower world, and . . . the lower world up towards the Divine again" (583). The emphasis now lies on "attainment," which is foreign to *agapē*. Similarly he argues, "The religious temper of the Middle Ages can be summarily categorised by the phrase 'the upward tendency.' . . . The religious life as a ceaseless ascent" (615). Martin Luther sees what is wrong with all this: "God has not willed us to raise a ladder in order to come up to Him, He Himself has prepared the ladder, and come down to us" (707). He states: "Agapē comes to us as a quite new creation of Christianity" (48).

In general terms such a reexamination of *agapē* has been timely, not only in Nygren's work on Jesus and Paul, but also in the contrast between the latest patristic and medieval tradition and the Reformers. The one criticism Nygren invites concerns his claims for the *word agapē*, and distinctive *uses* of the word in the NT and in Luther. J. Barr has shown that there is often a mismatch between words and concepts. Nygren is right, however, to disengage uses of *agapē* from sensual, erotic, emotional, or even ecstatic uses of "love." The love of God is indeed unmotivated, spontaneous, and creative of value (Deut. 7:7; 1 Cor. 13:1-13), in contrast to the largely different origins and history of *erōs*. Love is not an emotion, for one cannot easily "command" an emotion.

Nygren's *Commentary on Romans* (London: SCM, 1952) shows his gifts as an expositor. As a Lutheran, however, he devotes nearly 350 pages to Romans 1–8 and a mere hundred to Romans 9–16. Many today argue that chapters 9–11 constitute the climax of the epistle. He also tends to belabor "the two aeons" of Adam and Christ (26-37 and 206-29). On the other hand, it is a masterly exposition within a Lutheran perspective. He writes: "The resurrection . . . refers to an all-inclusive event which is thought of as placed at the end of time" (49). The righteousness of God is Paul's "central idea," which "did not originate in us . . . [it is] not our own righteousness but a 'righteousness from God' " (74). Paul's use of Hab. 2:4 becomes decisive in Rom. 1:17. Luther's autobiographical reflections are quoted (90-91). In 5:12-21 "Adam did not signify for Paul something independent of Christ . . . only as the antitype to Christ" (211). When he came to earth, "Christ burst all patterns" (219). "The law can demand the good, but it cannot bring it about" (225); hence it becomes "a power of destruction, along with Wrath, Sin and Death" (227). Rom. 7:14-25 does not describe "the divided state . . . of men" (291), but man as belonging "both to the new and the old aeons" (296). In 8:18-30 the whole creation and the Christian look forward to the consummation of God's eternal purpose (335-46). Nygren may use less space on chapters 9–16, but he sees the heart of the matter to be "God's sovereignty in mercy and in wrath" (364-74; Rom. 9:14-29). He ends with Paul's exhortation to live as the new creation that we have become. Thus Paul declares: "You are light. . . . Walk as children of light Eph. 5:8: walk in love (Rom. 12:9-21)"; "It is a life in harmony with the new era" (431; Rom. 13:8-10).

Reading: T. Hall, *Anders Nygren* (Waco, Tex.: Word, 1978); A. Nygren, *Commentary on Romans* (London: SCM, 1952); A. Nygren, *Agape and Eros* (London: SPCK, 1957).

O

Occasionalism
This philosophical theory denies that finite things have efficient causality. Generally, therefore, it ascribes all causes to God, and eliminates human agency. A particular version of occasionalism denies or questions a causal relation between mind and body. Nicolas Malebranche (1638-1715) sought to continue both versions. As a Catholic priest, he asserted, first, the unlimited sovereignty of God. Second, he thought that occasionalism could respond to central problems of a mind-body dualism. However, this approach is out of favor in modern thought. In the light of such biblical passages as

> The LORD has established his throne in the heavens,
>   and his kingdom rules over all (Ps. 103:19),

it is not surprising that some see God's causal sovereignty in the smallest details of everyday life, and appeal to occasionalism. But even the NT declares that the kingdom of God is in process of realization, and Jesus also teaches the prayer "Your Kingdom come." Moreover, if all free will is defined only as freedom to express human character, further questions arise about the scope of human responsibility.

Ochs, Peter
Peter Ochs (b. 1950) has become well known and influential especially for two of his many achievements. First, in 1995 he coined the term "scriptural reasoning" to denote an activity that brought together Jews, Christians, and Muslims around the biblical text. Second, he published *Peirce, Pragmatism, and the Logic of Scripture* (Cambridge: CUP, 1998), which provided a new view of Charles Peirce and his distinctive species of pragmatism. Ochs was awarded his M.A. from the Jewish Seminary, and his Ph.D. from Yale. He was formerly senior lecturer in philosophy at the Hebrew University of Jerusalem, and is currently Edgar Bronfman Professor of Modern Judaic Studies at the University of Virginia.

Few have achieved more to facilitate constructive dialogue between Jews, Christians, and Muslims. It is part of the scriptural reasoning project that Jews, Christians, and Muslims participate together around a biblical text in mutual respect and hospitality. Ochs cofounded this group in collaboration with D. F. Ford and D. Hardy of Cambridge. He also founded and chaired the Textual Reading Group, mainly for Jewish philosophers studying the Talmud together. His book on C. S. Peirce attempts a new approach in which Peirce's so-called pragmatism is regarded as equivalent to what Ochs has called scriptural reasoning. He has also written *Reviewing the Covenant: Eugene B. Borowitz and the Postmodern Renewal of Jewish Theology* (Albany: SUNY Press, 2000), and *Reasoning after Revelation: Dialogues in Postmodern Jewish Philosophy* (with R. Gibbs and S. Kepnes [Boulder, Colo.: Westview Press, 1998]). He has also co-edited *Textual Reasoning* (Grand Rapids: Eerdmans; London: SCM, 2002), and *Crisis, Call, and Leadership in the Abrahamic Traditions* (New York: Macmillan, 2009). He is currently editing a volume entitled *A Tent of Meeting,* on Jewish-Christian-Muslim study. All this indicates only a small part of his many influential interests and writings.

O'Donovan, Oliver

Oliver O'Donovan (b. 1945) is probably Britain's most distinguished specialist in Christian ethics and political theology. He is currently professor of Christian ethics and practical theology in the University of Edinburgh (from 2006). Earlier he had taught at Wycliffe Hall, Oxford; Wycliffe College, University of Toronto; and as Regius Professor of Moral and Pastoral Theology, University of Oxford (1982-2006). His doctoral thesis was on Augustine, and he is a fellow of the British Academy. He has lectured in Princeton, Rome, Australia, Canada, and elsewhere. He was ordained in the Church of England.

One of O'Donovan's key books remains *Resurrection and the Moral Order: An Outline for Evangelical Ethics* (Grand Rapids: Eerdmans, 1986). A sense of moral order is not imposed by the human mind: "The order of things that God has made is *there*. It is objective, and mankind has a place within it" (17). Christian freedom entails a "pattern of free response to objective reality" (25). The doctrine of creation is not merely about origins and causes, but about "the order and coherence *in* which it [creation] is composed" (31). Divine providence does not act arbitrarily. O'Donovan's ethics are grounded in God and theology. Redemption involves ethical transformation. Like Barth, for O'Donovan ethics derives from Jesus Christ, and like Brunner, he insists on the objective moral order within creation. With respect to the incarnation, this constitutes a "worldly moral authority" in which "Christ's particularity belongs to his divine nature. . . . As the one whom God sent, he is irreplaceable. . . . He is the pattern to which we may conform ourselves" (143). The resurrection of Christ is the decisive argument for this.

O'Donovan explicitly calls his next great book *The Desire of the Nations: Rediscovering the Roots of Political Theology* (Cambridge: CUP, 1996). He urges, "Theology must be political if it is to be evangelical," or grounded in the gospel (3). The public tradition of Israel provides a promise "for the full socialization of God's believing people. . . . Social forms and structures must be referred to a normative critical standard: do they fulfil [the] will of God?" (25). O'Donovan has published numerous other books, including *The Ways of Judgment* (Grand

Rapids: Eerdmans, 2005), but also books on Augustine (1979), on the Thirty-nine Articles (1986), and on common objects of love (2002). His contribution to Christian theology is unique.

Ontological Argument

The ontological argument for the existence of God constitutes one of the four traditional arguments for belief in God, the other three being the cosmological argument (from cause), the teleological argument (from purpose or design), and the moral argument. More strictly, the ontological argument is (especially in modern thought) an attempt to demonstrate the impossibility of the nonexistence of God. It constitutes an a priori argument. Its originator was Anselm, who presented it in the form of a statement of faith, or prayer. But René Descartes reformulated it as a philosophical argument. Immanuel Kant and Bertrand Russell proposed devastating criticisms of it, and in the second half of the twentieth century it once again became the subject of lively debate in the light of logical reformulations by J. N. Findlay, A. G. A. Rainer, G. Hartshorne, N. Malcolm, and A. Plantinga, who represented both sides of the debate.

Anselm formulated his first version of the argument in his *Proslogion* 2-4 (c. 1078, Eng. "Proslogion," in *St. Anselm: Basic Writings* [Chicago: Open Court, 1962], and "Anselm's Prologium," in *Mediaeval Sourcebook* [Fordham University Centre for Mediaeval Studies, 2006], online). Karl Barth insists that Anselm put this forward as a confession, not as an intellectual argument (Barth, *Anselm* [1931]). *Proslogion* 2 begins as a prayer of confession: "O Lord, you give understanding to faith.... We believe that *you are that than which nothing greater (nihil maius) can be conceived.*" But to be "greater" in reality is to be "greater" than a mere concept or something in a human mind. Anselm imagines "the fool" in Psalm 14 protesting "there is no God," when this concerns only his *perception* of God, not what is reality. If he is indeed as we have confessed him to be, God exists in reality. Indeed, to claim, like the fool, that such a God does not exist in *reality* constitutes a *self-contradiction,* since in that case God would not then be "greater than" anything that we can conceive. Thus he asserts: "You so truly *are* that you cannot be thought not to be; and rightly so." To exist in actuality *(in re),* Anselm claims, is "greater" than to exist exclusively in the mind *(in intellectu).* Some will regard this as confusing *logical* and *ontological* necessity.

Anselm's contemporary, the monk Gaunilo, countered this argument by suggesting that it could equally well be used to deduce the existence of a perfect island: "an island none greater than which could be imagined." But Anselm responded that this kind of perfection is not the kind of perfection that we attribute to God. Perfect trees, rivers, springs, and mountains all remain contingent things. Later, in the twentieth century, Alvin Plantinga, the Christian philosopher, would clarify and sharpen Anselm's response by using the term "maximal greatness," which applies uniquely to God.

Immanuel Kant, followed later by Bertrand Russell, argued convincingly that

Anselm's fallacy was to regard or categorize *existence* as a *property*. We should not say, for example, that an orange is round, sticky beneath its skin, and an existing object, as if this added to its description. Russell insisted that existence is a presupposition or, better, *instantiation* of descriptive properties. *Being* is not a property or predicate. Russell expressed instantiation in the logical form "for all x, x is y," that is, $(Ex)(xy)$. To oversimplify, *existence* is not a quality or attribute, in the same sense as other qualities or attributes.

René Descartes reformulated Anselm's argument in his *Meditations* 5 (1641). This is part of his quest for certainty as a mathematician and rationalist. He argued that the idea of God as "a supremely perfect being" was no less *certain* than "any figure or number. . . . Eternal existence pertains to his nature." *Existence* cannot be separated from *essence* in *God,* any more than the three angles of a triangle can be other than two right angles. The problem with Descartes's version of the argument is that it exposes it as a purely analytical statement. Truths of logic are often simply true-by-definition, without any practical cash-value in the world. They belong to the familiar class in logic: "all bachelors are unmarried," "$2 + 2 = 4$," or "water boils at 100° C" when this is how "100° C" is defined in the first place. Again, Kant's counterargument that existence is not a predicate still applies. He claimed that a hundred dollars *that exist* are not "greater" than the concept of a hundred dollars *in the mind,* because "greater" is not an appropriate way of describing such a contrast.

The argument was revived in the twentieth century by the attempt of J. N. Findlay to use it as a *disproof* of God's existence. If God's nonexistence is unthinkable, God belongs to the category of *logical necessary* beings. But what is *logically necessary* cannot be said to exist *contingently,* that is, in everyday life. Hence it is self-contradictory to claim that God "exists" in the sense of making any practical difference to human life. "God" would remain in the abstract world of the philosopher or formal logician. A. G. A. Rainer, however, replied that *logical* necessity is not the kind of necessity that believers invoke when they claim that God "must" exist. Charles Hartshorne takes the debate further by applying modal logic to the argument. He argues that to deny a self-evident or "necessary" proposition would be self-contradictory. Indeed, "God does not exist" cannot be a "necessary" proposition. He rejects such a denial of the ontological argument. Norman Malcolm distinguished in 1960 between two versions of Anselm's argument respectively in *Proslogion* 2 and 3. Against 2, he supported the argument of Kant and Russell, that existence is not a predicate. But he believed that this criticism did not apply simply to *Proslogion* 3. This argued for the perfection of "necessary" existence, which constituted an acceptable argument.

Alvin Plantinga distinguished between "excellence" and "greatness." "Excellence" can apply to a being only in a particular world. But, drawing on modal logic, he argued that a being's "greatness" depends on its properties in *all* "possible" worlds. The greatest "possible" being must have maximal excellence in *every* "possible" world. Modal logic explores logical "possibility" as well as logical necessity. Plantinga argues that if a Being with maximal greatness exists in *every* possible world, that Being exists in this world. The ontological argument has now become a sophisticated debate in logic, as well as a theist confession of faith.

For Christian theology the argument operates on two distinct levels. At one level it becomes a sophisticated debate, usually in philosophy of religion or logic, exploring such thinkers as Findlay, Malcolm, and Plantinga. At another level, it takes up the issue raised by Barth, which concerns faith, confession, and the transcendence and uniqueness of God. Thereby, it also concerns theological method. Barth saw Anselm's confession as a key to the whole of his *Church Dogmatics*. It is usual for a first degree in theology to include both levels of argument, even if at a modest level. (*See also* **A Priori**.)

Reading: K. Barth, *Anselm, Fides Quaerens Intellectum* (London: SCM, 1960); J. Hick, ed., *Classical and Contemporary Readings in the Philosophy of Religion* (Englewood Cliffs, N.J.: Prentice-Hall, 1964), 28-67; A. Plantinga, *The Ontological Argument* (New York: Doubleday, 1965).

Ontology

Ontology denotes the study of being or what-is, although the modern equivalent in ordinary speech would be the study of reality (from the Gk. *ta onta,* the neuter plural participle of *ōn,* "being"). Plato contrasted appearance and reality, which in his philosophy corresponded with, respectively, the contingent, or everyday, world and the eternal realm of ideas or reality. The term extensively overlaps with metaphysics. Heidegger contrasted Being *(Sein)* with being-there, or being-in-the-world *(Dasein).* He lamented that humankind had "fallen out of Being." Duns Scotus saw the task of intellectual inquiry as to explore Being, but Martin Heidegger eventually reluctantly concluded that, especially after Plato's dualism, this task had become impossible. Heidegger's earlier question, "Why is there something rather than nothing?" becomes in theology the study of creation by the will of God. In theology, or more strictly the philosophy of religion, the adjective "ontological" is usually associated with the ontological argument for the existence of God.

Open Theism

To those who advocate it, "open theism" means simply that God is open to the world in two respects, both of which resist the Thomist notion that God is changeless. (i) While nothing can force him to take action, God may choose to limit his absolute sovereignty voluntarily in such a way as to respond to human actions. In biblical terms God chooses to avert judgment when a people repents (Jon. 3:10). The verse "Jesus is the same yesterday and today and forever" (Heb. 13:8) is widely misunderstood. It means that he is always our great High Priest, unlike successors in the Aaronic priesthood in Judaism. (ii) More controversial is the second aspect of God's being open to the future. If the future does not yet exist, this may suggest that there is not some "closed" preordained succession of events, even if the ultimate goal of such events is determined. For many, therefore, it allows a doctrine of so-called free will. At opposite ends of the spectrum today, W. Hasker and D. Bassinger, and Clark Pinnock in North America, advocate a full open theism, while Paul Helm in England resists it to the point of defining eternity as timeless. In the sense of the first aspect, J. Moltmann and J. Polkinghorne tend toward this view, but classical Thomism would see this as compromising God's sovereignty and perfection.

Opus Operatum

Opus operatum denotes "work done," and expresses the belief that a sacrament can confer grace objectively, independently of any attitude of faith or other subjective condition on the part of the believer. An alternative phrase is *ex opere operato*, which means "on the basis of work done." The term was used from the thirteenth century, and the idea was vigorously opposed by the Reformers.

Origen

Origen (c. 185–c. 254) was born in Egypt, probably in Alexandria, into a Christian family. He received a Christian education, and in early years hoped for martyrdom during a period in which the church underwent persecution (c. 202). He led a rigorously ascetic life. In his midthirties, perhaps in 218, he was ordained a priest, and determined to devote his life to writing, in response to the call of God. A wealthy friend, Ambrosius, paid for him to have the benefit of stenographers and copyists. Epiphanius claims he penned as many as six thousand writings, only a small proportion of which has survived. His work represented four kinds of Christian scholarship: (i) on textual criticism and translation; (ii) on biblical exegesis or the writing of commentaries; (iii) on work on Christian doctrine and theology; and (iv) on practical work on prayer and on the ethics and discipline of the Christian life. He was recognized as head of the catechetical school in Alexandria by Demetrius, when Clement fled the city. Eusebius recounts his ascetic life of fasting, vigils, and even self-mutilation. He was well informed in Plato's philosophy, and visited Rome and Palestine. The main period of his writing in Alexandria was c. 218 to 230, although he continued to write at Caesarea from 231 to 250. In the Decian persecution, he was imprisoned and tortured, and died shortly afterward.

(i) Regarding textual criticism and translation, Origen spent many years on *The Hexapla,* a work of six volumes, which provided the Hebrew text of the OT; a Greek translation of the Hebrew; and the LXX and translations of its versions: Aquila, Symmachus, and Theodotion. (ii) Origen's exegetical works and homilies include notes on Exodus, Leviticus, and Numbers, and commentaries on some thirty books of the Bible. His commentaries on Matthew and John have survived, with a few sections of other works. (iii) His work on doctrine or theology finds expression especially in his treatise *On First Principles (De principiis* or *Peri Archōn),* and also in his apologia *Against Celsus (Contra Celsum).* (iv) Origen produced *On Prayer* and *Exhortation to Martyrdom,* which are available in at least two English translations: Rowan A. Greer, ed., *An Exhortation to Martyrdom, Prayer, and Selected Works* (London: SPCK; New York: Paulist, 1979), and J. J. O'Meara, ed., *Origen: Prayer and Exhortation to Martyrdom* (New York: Paulist, 1954).

On First Principles and *Against Celsus* are available in English in *ANF* 4:239-384 and 395-669. *De principiis* 1 begins with the doctrine of God, then expands Christology, and third, expounds the doctrine of the Holy Spirit. Origen declares that God is light (1.1.1; 1 John 1:5); that he is a consuming fire (1.1.2); that he is a sanctifying power (1.1.3) and Spirit (1.1.4; John 4:24). He is "incapable of being measured" (*inestimabilem;* 1.1.5). To Christ Origen ascribed having deity (1.2.1), being fully personal (1.2.2), and being the eternal Word (1.2.3). In Christ all things exist (1.2.4; Col. 1:15). The Holy Spirit inspired the Scriptures (1.3.1), descended onto Christ, and anointed him for service, and enables us to call him Lord (1.3.2). The Holy Spirit was not created or made (1.3.3), and brings forth "the fruit of the Spirit" (1.3.4; Gal. 5:22). He was the means or medium of revelation (1.3.4). Origen considers the incarnation in 1.6. Christ, Origen urges, is the "only begotten of God ... the God-man" (1.6.3). In 1.7 he further considers the Paraclete in John. In book 4 Origen considers biblical interpretation. Typically he introduces "spiritual meaning" (4.1.9), and interpretation "in a threefold manner ... the common and historical sense ... something more ... the very soul of Scripture ... body, soul and spirit" (4.1.11). Gwatkin has called Origen "beyond comparison the greatest scholar and the greatest teacher of his time."

Original Righteousness

Original righteousness denotes the theory that God imparted perfect righteousness to humankind before the Fall. It was officially a Roman Catholic doctrine, but first found expression in Ambrose and Augustine (evidence in N. P. Williams, *Ideas of the Fall* [London and New York: Longmans, 1929], 300-301). Ambrose and Augustine, Williams comments, wished to "maximize" the effects of the Fall. Today, however, most theologians hesitate to enter speculation about humankind before the "Fall."

Other, Otherness

Other and otherness cannot be taken for granted, but the words imply more than their everyday use might suggest. By contrast, Iris Murdoch has described the thought of Descartes and his philosophical tradition as narcissistic, or wholly centered on the self. But beyond the consciousness of the self stands the Other, whether in the form of a Thou or You (in M. Buber's sense of I-Thou), or a community of listeners or readers, or especially God. Concern for the other lifts us out of self-preoccupation or self-absorption, and makes possible a relation of *address* and love, as Jüngel stresses. To approach this from a different angle, God chose to create the world as a choice to relate to what is "other" than God. Barth maintains that he also decreed the creation of two genders in order that each may relate to the other in marriage.

Admittedly in this context the notion of "otherness" can be abused as if it were to be secondary to the self. In the immediate postwar phase of feminism, for example, Simone de Beauvoir in her book *The Second Sex* lamented that man defined woman not as she is in herself but as relative to him: "He is the subject.... She is the other." But this is not the otherness that Barth or Buber has in mind. In an "I-Thou relation," *both* partners are subjects; neither is object. This would reduce the "I-Thou" relation to what Buber calls an "I-It" relation. In biblical exegesis and hermeneutics God speaks through the text as subject. The Bible, too, is "other." Hermeneutics is undermined if the Bible is simply "studied" or scrutinized as a passive object, rather than the text being thought of as a medium of communication with the Other, who is Subject. Here "listening" to the other becomes no less important than responding with thoughts of our own.

This aspect of otherness is stressed by Hans-Georg Gadamer. In his intellectual autobiography Gadamer writes, "Hermeneutics is above all a practice, the art of understanding.... In it what one has to exercise above all is the ear, the sensitivity for perceiving prior determinations, anticipation, and imprints," that is, those of the other ("Reflection on My Philosophical Journey," in *The Philosophy of Hans-Georg Gadamer,* ed. L. E. Hahn [La Salle, Ill.: Open Court, 1997], 17). This happens, he explains, in a conversation. If all the emphasis is placed on a "closed" message from the author or speaker, how is there a conversation? The interpretation of the text is "not only something meant; it is also something shared, something held in common" (53). David Ford follows Emmanuel Levinas in warning us not to assimilate the other to the self, and to that end Levinas and Ford explore the otherness of the "face" of the other, which we cannot assimilate into our own. A face is unique, conjuring up unique past events and a narrative history. Ford writes, "Each face is uniquely individual yet it is also a primary locus for relating to others and the world: the face as relating, welcoming, incorporating others, is fundamental to social life" (*Self and Salvation* [Cambridge: CUP, 1999], 19). So much of the other is epitomized in the face. Ford speaks of "the inexhaustibility of the face of the beloved . . . and its capacities for differentiation, many-levelled communication, ambiguity," and so forth (21).

In biblical hermeneutics, as Gadamer implies, this relates to preaching, where at a bare minimum eye contact, and not simply reciting a prepared script, provides at least the beginnings of a conversation, rather than a discourse. One can pick up gestures and experiences of understanding, puzzlement, boredom, or interest at the very least (*see* **Bakhtin, Mikhail; Polyphonic Discourse**). In a smaller Bible study group the possibilities of genuine conversation are far greater. Ormond Rush, following H. R. Jauss on reception theory, speaks of "a hermeneutics of *alterity*" (in *The Reception of Doctrine* [Rome: Pontifical Gregorian University, 1997], 109-16). Engagement with the other may change a horizon of expectation. Where Gadamer speaks of a fusion of horizons, Jauss places more emphasis on differentiation of horizons and even "provocation," although both aspects feature in both writers. George Ridding, first bishop of Southwell, warns us against measuring the feelings and attitudes of the others by our own. In *Horizons in Hermeneutics* (ed. S. E. Porter and M. R. Malcolm [Grand Rapids: Eerdmans, 2013]), Tom Greggs calls this a hermeneutics of *love* (201-16). It relates hermeneutics to the community.

For Barth and Jüngel this otherness applies most of all to God. Here the task of "listening" and being open to the other is essential for hearing the Word of God, and what Barth calls "the strange new world within the Bible." Barth says of this world: "There is only — 'the other,' new and greater world" (*The Word of God and the Word of Man* [London: Hodder and Stoughton, n.d.], 42).

Reading: M. Buber, *I and Thou* (Edinburgh: T. & T. Clark, 1942); Paul Ricoeur, *Oneself as Another* (Chicago: University of Chicago Press, 1992); Ormond Rush, "A Hermeneutics of *Alterity*," in *The Reception of Doctrine* (Rome: Pontifical Gregorian University, 1997), 109-16.

Otto, Rudolf

Rudolf Otto (1869-1937) is most widely known for his classic work *The Idea of the Holy* (Oxford: OUP, 1923; Ger. *Das Heilige*, 1917). In contrast to a merely rational or ethical approach to religion, Otto stressed the feeling of awe and wonder that he termed *"the numinous."* A creaturely and finite human person experiences such reverential awe in the presence of the transcendent God. At the beginning of his book Otto contrasts the rational and the nonrational (1-4), and then proceeds to examine the numinous (5-11). He further describes this "creature-feeling" as *mysterium tremendum* (12-30), which contains "the element of awefulness" (13-19); "the element of overpoweringness ('majestas')" (20-23); and "the element of 'energy' or urgency" (23-24). Together these amount to "the wholly other" (24-30). This gives rise partly to "horror and dread" (31), but at the same time to "something more . . . the *fascinans*" (35).

Otto sees practical consequences arising from this work of religious phenomenology. He comments, "Rationalism lacked understanding of what 'sin' is. Mere *morality* is not the soil from which grows . . . the need of 'redemption'" (55). He traces examples of the numinous in the OT, the NT, and Luther, as well as in other religions (74-115). Job provides a clear example (83). So does Heb. 10:31: "It is a fearful thing to fall into the hands of the living God," or Heb. 12:29, "Our God is a consuming fire." The "holy" is an a priori category (116-46). Otto draws a working distinction between a derived "moral-holiness" and the deep "majesty-holiness of God." For the latter he favors Schleiermacher's term "divination" (147-78), but with careful qualifications. God appears as "suprapersonal" in the numinous (201-8). Otto's book remains a classic, especially in the philosophy of religion.

Reading: R. Otto, *The Idea of the Holy* (Oxford: OUP, 1923); H. J. Paton, *The Modern Predicament* (New York: Macmillan; London: Allen and Unwin, 1955), 129-45.

Oxford Movement. *See* Anglo-Catholic; Tractarianism

P

Panentheism
Panentheism is deliberately contrasted with pantheism. Panentheism is the belief that God penetrates the whole universe, but is not coextensive with it. Pantheism identifies God with the All.

Pannenberg, Wolfhart
Wolfhart Pannenberg (1928-2014) stands among the most impressive, learned, and outstanding two or three contemporary Protestant theologians in the world. Single-handedly he moved theology from the existentialism of Bultmann and his school to explore new avenues, which placed a firmer emphasis on ontology, Christology, and the resurrection of Christ. He investigated a dialogue with atheism, addressed fundamental questions in theology, and suggested new methods of exploring philosophy, the sciences, and hermeneutics. He appealed to some of Hegel's ideas, rather than those of Heidegger. The culmination of his work is a three-volume *Systematic Theology*, which shows immense learning in biblical, historical, and contemporary theology, together with philosophy, and betrays a huge depth, meticulous detail, and innovative creativity.

Pannenberg was born in Stettin, Germany, and was baptized as an infant in the Lutheran church. He had little involvement with the church in early years, but at around sixteen underwent an intense Christian experience, which he later called his "light experience." He began reading philosophical and theological thinkers, and after a few years experienced an "intellectual" conversion, involving among other things belief in the resurrection of Christ. This became his call to the work of a theologian. E. Schlink influenced his thought, especially on theology as doxology, or truth disclosed in and through worship. In 1950 he studied under K. Barth at Basel, and became intensely concerned with revelation, history, and apocalyptic. In philosophy, rather than engaging closely with Heidegger, like so many others, he became fascinated by Hegel and his notion of an unfolding history, together with history as God's self-revelation. Pannenberg also shared Hegel's view of futurity, freedom, and a new era. This, in turn, harmonized with his view of Jewish and biblical apocalyptic. In Basel he also studied philosophy under Jaspers.

In the years during and after his doctorate and "Habilitation" thesis at Heidelberg, Pannenberg became a leading influence among a group of younger scholars who came to be known as "the Pannenberg Circle." These included Klaus Koch, an OT scholar who wrote *The Rediscovery of Apocalyptic;* a second OT scholar, R. Rendtorff, who wrote on tradition; U. Wilkens, who wrote on the NT; D. Rössler, who shared an interest in NT apocalyptic; J. Moltmann, who wrote on systematic theology; and T. Rendtorff, who wrote on society. Additionally at Göttingen, the philosopher N. Hartmann and K. Löwith had concerns about the meaning of history; while at Heidelberg, Gerhard von Rad influenced Pannenberg on history and tradition, and Hans von Campenhausen on a philosophy of world history, especially in the light of Augustine's *City of God,* which sought to take account of the fall of Rome. Hence the stage was set for Pannenberg's thought on a Christian understanding of the history of tradition and world history. Like O. Cullmann, Campenhausen was also concerned with continuity and context in history. Yet another influential voice was that of Zimmerli on the theology of hope, later to be developed by Moltmann. J. M. Robinson traces the influence of Zimmerli and Rendtorff in his essay "Revelation as Word and History" (in *New Frontiers in Theology,* vol. 3, *Theology as History* [New York: Harper and Row, 1967], 42-65). He also considers the influence of Wilckens (75-89) and of Moltmann (89-98).

During his time at Wuppertal in collaboration with Koch, Rössler, Wilckens, and others, Pannenberg gave a lecture in 1959 entitled "Redemptive Event and History," which was first translated in C. Westermann, ed., *Essays in Old Testament Hermeneutics* (1963), and then reprinted in Pannenberg's *Basic Questions in Theology,* vol. 1 (London: SCM, 1970), 15-80. He begins by declaring: "History is the most comprehensive horizon of Christian theology. All theological questions and answers are meaningful only within the framework of the history which God has with humanity and through humanity with his whole creation — the history moving toward a future still hidden from the world, but already revealed in Jesus Christ" (25). This is "the presupposition of Christian theology" that must be defended today, on one side "against Bultmann and Gogarten's existential theology, which dissolves history"; on the other side against Martin Kähler, whose position is "suprahistorical" (15). He, like Cullmann, remains in the ghetto of redemptive history *(Heilsgeschichte)* as over against ordinary world history *(Historie).*

This statement is programmatic, for it will govern much of what he says about Christology. We can understand the identity and work of Jesus Christ only in the light of God's prophetic and apocalyptic promise about history and the world. Thus, Pannenberg continues, "Israel not only discovered history as a particular sphere of reality; it finally drew the whole of creation into history. History is reality in its totality" (21). But historical consciousness is "eschatologically orientated"; the end of history is "the goal of fulfilment" (23). Hence "Christological statements about Jesus" are understood within this framework (28). This "anticipated . . . the end of history in the midst of history" (36). Pannenberg adds a section in which he states, "Historical-critical procedure," as in Bultmann and others, makes them guilty of "anthropocentricity" (39). Again he alludes to the "ghetto of redemptive history" (41), and to the domination of historical-critical inquiry by an overemphasized and simplistic use of analogy (45). It passes over the uniqueness of contingent events in history.

In 1961 Pannenberg followed this by his celebrated work *Revelation as History*. In this he proposes a different model of communication from the *"language event" (Sprachereignis)* of Ernst Fuchs and Gerhard Ebeling. They both end by suggesting that truth and reality are virtually intralinguistic, and disparage straightforward assertions. In the transmission of traditions too much is bound up with contingent and specific situations. They ignore, moreover, the *apocalyptic* dimensions of the primary context for interpreting the history of Jesus. He supports Moltmann's rejection of an existential approach, even if Moltmann suggests that Pannenberg at times owes too much to a "Greek" approach. Pannenberg replies that a biblical model also shows concern for rationality and universality. Moltmann, in turn, is troubled that Pannenberg seems unduly concerned with "facts," not kerygma, but both agree that the *future horizon of promise and hope* provides a key interpretative role in theology.

Although Pannenberg's *Basic Questions in Theology* appeared later in English (3 vols., 1970, 1971, and 1973), several of its essays go back to 1961-1964. In "The Crisis of the Scripture Principle" (vol. 1, 1962), Pannenberg argues that "this universality of theology is unavoidably bound up with the fact that it speaks of God . . . God as the Creator of all things" (1). To speak of all reality is part of the intellectual obligation involved in speaking of God. We must recall that "in a changed situation the traditional phrases, even when recited literally, do not mean what they did at the time of their original formulations" (9). He cites Gadamer on "how to span the distance between the texts and the present" (9). Hence the "crisis" is a double one: to speak of God, and to take seriously the problems of hermeneutics. In 1961 he first published "Kerygma and History" (81-95). This elaborates G. von Rad's concept of history, tradition, and address in his *Old Testament Theology*. History deals with "once-occurring" matters, and the biblical writings deal with acts of God, not "general religious truths" (83). The witnesses speak of God's past, present, and future acts, which offer interpretation of the work of Jesus (85). One of several problems with the Bultmann school is its overready acceptance of "the neo-Kantian distinction between being and value" (86). The OT tradition of a "Yahweh-effected history" is one of von Rad's achievements (88). His is an OT theology of history in which historical events are "binding upon each generation" (90).

In 1962 Pannenberg wrote "What Is a Dogmatic Statement?" (182-211). Here he argues again: "The hermeneutical question has become the actual focal point of theological dialogue dealing with . . . the authority of Scripture" (188). After discussing Luther's principles of translation, again he insists that the history of Jesus must be "understood in its original historical content" (196). He questions H. Diem's argument that these contexts should be seen as only "points of view" in the interest of the unity of the Bible. In 1963, in "Hermeneutic and Universal

History," Pannenberg expounds Gadamer's concept of "fusion of horizons" *(Horizontverschmelzung)* between the interpreter and the text (117). He also refers to Gadamer's concept of "openness" (121), his model of question and answer, and his background in Hegel (134). But in Christian theology the future is realized only in a "provisional" and anticipatory way (135).

Five of the essays in volume 2 also originated between 1959 and 1962. In the essay on a philosophical concept of God, Pannenberg finds an overlap between Greek and Christian concepts of God as origin of the world or reality (122-26), and as a unity or "one" (126-28). Yet he concedes that the Greek view also endangers the uniqueness and otherness of God in the biblical tradition (158-73). In "What Is Truth?" (1-27) Pannenberg draws a line between Greek and biblical conceptions of truth. The Hebrew word *'emeth* means "reliability" and "dependability," which is not "timeless" but occurs in events "again and again" (3). This aspect is lacking in Greek thought. He declares, "The truth of God must prove itself anew in the future" (8). Descartes and even Kant followed the "Western" approach. On the other hand, Hegel considered what was visible as the end of history. He adds: "The proleptic character of the destiny of Jesus is the basis for the openness of the future for us" (25); "the unity of all reality is conceivable only as history.... Truth is possible only if it includes the contingency of events and the openness of the future ... [and] the proleptic revelation of God in Jesus Christ" (27).

In "Types of Atheism" two main types of atheism are those of Feuerbach and Nietzsche. In "Insight and Faith" Pannenberg utterly annihilates the concept of faith held by Bultmann. He writes, "Paul speaks of ... the grounding of faith upon knowledge (Rom. 8:8-9; 2 Cor. 4:13).... An otherwise unconvincing message cannot attain the power to convince simply by appealing to the Holy Spirit.... Argumentation and the operation of the Spirit are not in competition with each other. In trusting the Spirit, Paul in no way spared himself thinking and arguing" (32, 34, 35). Volume 3 mainly comes from the 1970s. The essay on eschatology and meaning is especially important.

Many of these themes are gathered up and applied to Christology in *Jesus — God and Man* (Ger. 1964; Eng. Philadelphia: Westminster; London: SCM, 1968). Pannenberg begins by distinguishing between "Christology from above" and "Christology from below." He cites Karl Barth as propagating a Christology from above. More urgently he distances himself from Martin Kähler. He sympathized with Kähler's desire to avoid a historical quest that makes of Jesus "a mere man" (22). But he queries his aphorism "The real Christ is the preached Christ." The all-important step, Pannenberg urges, is to understand Jesus in his proper historical context, in the light of divinely inspired tradition-history in Israel and promise. Pannenberg writes, "Only on the basis of what happened in the past, not because of present experience, do we know that Jesus lives as the exalted Lord" (28). He admits that "Christology 'from above' was far more common in the ancient Church, beginning with Ignatius of Antioch," but this would be less appropriate today (33), even though E. Brunner shares this approach with Barth.

Pannenberg does not overlook or reduce the human nature of Jesus: "Luther saw in Jesus the representative of all men before God" (43). However, in his ministry "Jesus' unity with God is substantiated in most cases by the claim to authority in his proclamation and work" (53). Even E. Fuchs and G. Bornkamm concentrated on "the *conduct* of Jesus as the real context of his preaching" (57). He enacted "saving deeds"; for example, his casting out demons meant that the kingdom of God had come (Luke 11:20). However, this in itself does not adequately validate and indicate the identity and status of Jesus. Paul tells us that Jesus Christ is "the firstborn from the dead" (Col. 1:18), "the first fruits of those who have died" (1 Cor. 15:20), and "the firstborn among many brothers" (Rom. 8:29; *JGM* 67). The end-time and the new creation have begun in Jesus. Pannenberg writes: "If Jesus had been raised, this for a Jew can only mean that God himself has confirmed the pre-Easter activity of Jesus." In his acts of authority, Jesus "put himself in God's place" (67). The resurrection of Jesus demonstrates that he is the eschatological Son of Man. Pannenberg states, "If Jesus, having been raised from the dead, is ascended to God, and if thereby the end of the world has begun, then God is ultimately in Jesus" (69). The resurrection of Jesus means the beginning of the "End."

In the resurrection appearances "the unity of event and word" is important in establishing faith. This event has its meaning only within the sphere of the history of traditions (73). The resurrection is not unintelligible: "The familiar experience of being awakened and rising from sleep serves as a parable for the completely unknown destiny expected for the dead" (74). Admittedly this uses parable and metaphor, but it gains our understanding. Resurrection will involve transformation of the body and self, not simply resuscitation. There is a "qualitative difference between the resurrection life as imperishable and the present life as perishable" (81). This forms a traditional Jewish expectation of the end of history, rooted in apocalyptic. It is a presupposition of the resurrection of Jesus (1 Cor. 15:16). Pannenberg concludes: "The basis of the knowledge of Jesus' significance remains bound to the original apocalyptic horizon of Jesus' history, which at the same time has also been modified by this history. If this horizon is eliminated, the basis of faith is lost, then Christology becomes mythology" (83). He notes the appearances of the raised Jesus to Peter, to the Twelve, to five hundred Christian brothers, and to Paul (89). A second strand of the tradition of Easter events reports the empty tomb. Pannenberg takes this tradition seriously as an independent "historical fact" (100). He agrees with the verdict of P. Althaus: "The resurrection Kerygma 'could not have been maintained in Jerusalem for a single day, for a single hour, if the emptiness of the tomb had not been established as a fact for all concerned'" (100). Pannenberg repeats his conclusion that the "appearances" tradition and "empty tomb" tradition are valid independently of each other. This is convincing, he urges, if we do not begin with the positivist assumption that "dead men do not rise" (109).

The doctrine of the Holy Spirit represents an early understanding of "God's presence in Jesus" (116). The account of his baptism is relevant here. God's presence in Jesus is also implied in the patristic doctrine of the incarnation. Further, as Mediator, Jesus represents both God and humankind (123-24). In Jesus we find the epiphany of God. Further, the terms "Son of God" and "Lord" *(Kurios)* underline this point. Against some NT specialists, Pannenberg insists, "Paul presupposed the pre-existence of the Son (Gal. 4:4; Rom. 8:3)" (151). The Christ hymn in Phil. 2:6-11 confirms this. Finally, Pannenberg sees traces of the Trinity in the NT. He writes, "A distinction in the essence of God himself is the beginning point for the doctrine of the Trinity systematically as well as historically" (169). The Holy Spirit was a reality for the earliest Christians; hence "Trinity" is more *accurate* than "Duality." Contemporary theology lacks here the depth of the biblical concept of the Spirit (171). Jesus was raised through the Spirit (Rom. 1:4; 8:2, 11; cf. 1 Pet. 3:18). God is "not only Father and Son, but Spirit as well" (175).

This concludes part 1 of *Jesus — God and Man*. Part 2 expounds "Jesus the man before God." That Jesus was genuinely and really human seems self-evident today. Only from the perspective of Christ's divinity does it seem problematic in theology. Nevertheless, what it means to be truly human is revealed through Jesus (193). Jesus is "representative of men before God" (195-208). He fulfills the human destiny to become one with God, for in the resurrection God legitimated his life and office. His acceptance of his death was part of his dedication to God and his obedience to the will of the Father. He was "well pleasing in the eyes of God" (197). He was open to God, and took "the risk of trust" (203). Pannenberg also considers the three offices of prophet, priest, and king, which ultimately go back to A. Osiander (1530). But he doubts whether they can each be derived from the term "Anointed One" *(Christos)*. A "prophet" does not *need* to be anointed. Admittedly Zech. 4:12 does speak of the two messianic figures, Joshua as anointed priest, and Zerubbabel as anointed king, and Qumran broadens the concept. However, "Christ" primarily represents kingship, "at best, priesthood as well" (215). In Reformation dogmatics the "prophetic" office is seen as Jesus' ministry of *teaching*. But if "kingship" is the prominent "office," this is most of all because of the *resurrection* and the eschatological situation. This carries with it "the nearness of God's Kingdom" and the "nearness of God himself expressed in addressing God as 'Father'" (229). This carries such consequences as obedience and love, not least in the life of Jesus himself. The notion of "imminent expectation" cannot literally be replicated, although the expectation of the resurrection of the dead stands "in continuity with it" (242).

On the cross Jesus died a vicarious death. The context of tradition makes Jesus' language about suffering and the resurrection "unambiguous": "it could only be understood as dying for us, for our sins" (247). This is expressed in Mark 10:45: "The Son of Man came . . . to give his life a ransom for many." Paul also understood it in this way, but also as the end of the Law (2 Cor. 5:21; Gal. 3:13). The substitutionary nature of Jesus' suffering and death is seen first from the Lord's Supper tradition, and second, from his sayings about his coming to serve. Again, it is the resurrection that reveals that Jesus died as a righteous person (259). To go further, "substitution" has a universal horizon; it can be understood outside the traditions of Israel. His "descent into hell" partly expresses the uniqueness of his death as "one who had been expelled" (270). It meant "exclusion from God's nearness," when all his life Jesus had lived in fellowship with God. Admittedly the "pictorial" nature and "imagery" of hell are inadequate, but the notion of exclusion from God's nearness remains. Reformed dogmaticians "understood Christ's descent into hell as part of his passion." It was first, however, debated among Lutherans, but then came to be regarded as "the first act of his exaltation" (273). It became associated with Christ's preaching of judgment proclaimed by the victor, according to 1 Pet. 4:6. But this is "bad exegesis." There is truth both in the Lutheran notion of "victory" and in the Reformed notion of the passion. Pannenberg then expounds and evaluates the atonement theories of ransom and satisfaction (274-80).

In part 3 Pannenberg expounds the crowning theme of Jesus' unity with God. This unity or union, however, runs up against difficulties if we construe it with Chalcedon as a unification of two "substances." Pannenberg affirms the "true divinity and true humanity of Jesus" (284-85) as "indispensable." But the Chalcedonian definition invites problems, not least the application of "nature" or "substance" to God and man in a univocal way. Schleiermacher noted this. Ritschl and Harnack attempted to address it. While he accepted it, Barth expressed reservations about it, while Brunner, perhaps surprisingly, also rejected it. The difficulty was exacerbated by the effort to find a way through several unfortunate polarizations: between Alexandrian and Antiochene Christology; between Nestorian and Monophysite Christology; and between kenotic and Logos Christologies. Each "mediation," however, resulted in compromise. Athanasius in effect founded Alexandrian or Egyptian Christology, partly influenced by Stoicism, which led to an incarnational view that stressed Christ's divinity, and the role of the Logos in Christ. In Antiochene theology, Jesus in his humanity became too independent of God. "Two natures" restricted the conceptual flexibility on both sides. An advance came in 638 when it was argued for "one will," not two. The term for this was "Monothelitism," in contrast to the "two wills" of Dyothelitism. These tensions were largely solved with the notion of the *"mutual interpenetration"* of the two natures (although *perichoresis* had already featured in the Cappadocian Fathers).

At the Reformation Luther taught the interpenetration of the two natures, using the analogy of the glowing iron in which two elements could be fused. Zwingli saw this more as a figure of speech. Calvin focused this idea of interpenetration especially in the role of the Mediator. The notion of Christ's self-emptying or *kenosis* in Phil. 2:7 was often debated in the patristic era, but humiliation as a human person and exaltation as divine must apply to a *genuinely human nature* (309). Even the kenotic Christology of the nineteenth century was unable to overcome the difficulty. Karl Rahner stressed the self-giving of Jesus, which offers an advance. But the issue remains "the synthesis of two natures" (322). Pannenberg himself explores the "personal community" or communion of Jesus with the Father (324-34). This focuses on Jesus' Sonship, in which Jesus knew of the meaning of existence as a human living in self-sacrifice to the Father (339). As a human, Jesus had freedom of choice (349), even though he was without sin. This book remains a classic of Christian theology.

While he was still professor in the University of Mainz, Pannenberg published "The Revelation of God in Jesus of Nazareth" (in J. M. Robinson and J. B. Cobb, eds., *New Frontiers in Theology: Theology as History* [New York: Harper and Row, 1967], 101-33). Here he emphasizes once again that Jesus "stood in a tradition that expected the coming of... God" (102), and that Jesus gave reasons for trust in his person rather than simply demanding it. He urged that "the Jewish tradition had been transformed from within" (108). Yet the situation for the Gentiles could be analogous. His key statement is that "Only in the light of the End" does revelation become fully understandable (113); further, "the general resurrection of the dead at the End had already occurred in Jesus' case" in a proleptic sense (114). The second important assertion concerns "an intertwining both of prophetic *words* and of *events*" (120, italics mine). Further, in harmony with apocalyptic, "the eschatological event... binds history into a whole" (122). Again Pannenberg asserts, "Knowledge is not a stage beyond faith, but leads into faith" (129), and adds: "Faith or trust presupposes a knowledge of the trustworthiness of the partner... faith must not be equated with a merely subjective conviction that would allegedly compensate for uncertainty" (130-31). All this constitutes an utterly convincing critique of the Bultmann school, and coheres with *Jesus — God and Man*. These volumes admirably introduce his climactic *Systematic Theology*.

Meanwhile we must take note of Pannenberg's important work *Theology and the Philosophy of Science* (Philadelphia: Fortress, 1976; Ger. 1973). Although this includes philosophy of science in the Anglo-American sense, it also includes what in German would be the *Geisteswissenschaften,* or a coherent and systematic critical study of the humanities, letters, arts, and social sciences. A theme of the volume is coherence and self-criticism. For example, biblical exegesis and church history are part of theology. Theology relates not only to God, but also to "temporal phenomena" (10). As early as the second century, apologists attempted to establish the general truth of the Christian message by generally accepted rational criteria. If theology were to disappear from universities, the results would be "a severe attack" for the Christian understanding of truth (13). It must remain open to evaluation by inquiry into historical fact. H. Diem and K. Barth miss something crucial in making theology a discipline for the church only. "The unity of truth" becomes vital (19).

Hence part 1 considers theology between the unity and multiplicity of sciences. It must respect "a public standard" (27). Predictably Pannenberg rejects positivism and logical positivism. He alludes to A. Flew's well-known "invisible gardener" parable (i.e., a gardener who was supposedly invisible, inaudible, intangible, and odorless), which allegedly supported positivism. He explores K. Popper's claim that we learn by trial and error (35-43). Theology can welcome "critical rationalism." This does not mean "a rational excuse for irrational commitment" (45). He rejects "a hermeneutical immunisation technique" that can supposedly save theology from current criticism. Popper is willing to accept a necessary element of conjecture in the sciences, and an "anticipatory understanding of truth." Ultimate truth depends on some understanding of "the totality of reality" (70). This is more than the abstract closed system of positivism. In a second chapter Pannenberg traces the emancipation of the human sciences from the natural sciences. The former recognize the unity of *human life*. Here Pannenberg follows Dilthey, including his view that "the uncompleted whole of life" is still not enough for genuine understanding. Life becomes intelligible "only if the whole can be presupposed at least implicitly" (79). On sociology, he seeks to advance beyond Weber, Mead, and Parsons, noting the critique of J. Habermas (88-96). But even Habermas's work on knowledge and interests cannot be complete without a broader theological understanding. Pannenberg also notes the part played by "purpose" in Troeltsch, but "Troeltsch does not fit the eschatology of the kingdom of God"; the kingdom is "not an extension of human purposes" (110). Nevertheless, Troeltsch was right to question the relation of the individual to the whole of reality. This brings us back to the fundamental distinction between "exploration" (often *Erklärung*) and understanding *(Verstehen)*, which was important to Dilthey, Gadamer, Apel, and others. This distinction impinges on "systems-theory" (143). Apel shows that history is concerned with understanding; too often it relates only to explanation.

In chapter 3 Pannenberg considers hermeneutics. Understanding entails the relation of parts to the whole, within a structure of life. As our entry under Schleiermacher indicates, the modern history of hermeneutics begins with Schleiermacher and proceeds to creative understanding in Dilthey (160-63). But Gadamer criticizes Dilthey's pseudo-objectifying, and stresses tradition and community. Nevertheless, as Betti points out, Gadamer goes too far in eliminating "objectivity." What is often called "hermeneutical theology" tends to focus on E. Fuchs and G. Ebeling, but they suffer badly "from the devaluation of the linguistic function of the *statement*" (177). They are too much influenced by Heidegger. Pannenberg comments, "The interpretation assists understanding by putting this horizon [of the interpreter] into an explicit statement" (184). He concludes the discussion by evaluating Apel, Habermas, Gadamer, Dilthey, and Wittgenstein, and concludes, "The domain into which the uttered word enters is inter-subjective" (211). In the later Wittgenstein, "language game," as Nygren argues, is often the equivalent of "context of meaning," which is reminiscent of J. Trier on field theory.

Part 2 now addresses "theology as a science." Theology is a practical science, relevant to professional training, as Schleiermacher argued. In chapter 5 Pannenberg insists, "God is the true object of theology" (298). He continues, "God is the all-determining reality" (302), and adds, "The reality is God is always present only in subjective anticipations of the totality of reality" (310). Theological propositions have a cognitive character that invites and allows the test of coherence. This is true not only in the assertions of believers. He concludes, "The presence of the all-determining reality in a historical phenomenon can be investigated only through an analysis of the totality of meaning implicit in the phenomenon" (338).

In chapter 6 Pannenberg reiterates: "Truth must be systematic in order to correspond to the unity of truth" (347). A theology of religions would include philosophy of religion. In biblical studies, careful exegesis is needed to avoid "unhistorical and forced interpretations" (379). Biblical theology is also necessary. Church history, systematic theology, and practical theology complete the picture of necessary tools. Practical theology includes "the social and therefore church-forming nature of Christian practice" (438). All this leads up to Pannenberg's great crowning work, *Systematic Theology*, 3 vols. (Eng. Grand Rapids: Eerdmans, 1991, 1994, 1998; Ger. 1988, 1991, 1993).

Volume 1 of *Systematic Theology* addresses the truth of Christian doctrine, the concept and truth of God, revelation, the Trinitarian God, and his unity and attributes. Pannenberg's passion for truth emerges at once. He writes: "Only conviction of the divine *truth* of the Christian religion can establish and justify the continued existence of Christian churches and therefore the training of their leaders" (7). He appeals to patristic and Reformation theology for this. There must, however, be a consensus that is free from coercion, although we must avoid "a consensus theory of truth in general" (12). This can degenerate into mere subjective conviction. Luther added to the consensus "the normative function of the Word of God" (14). The qualification to this is that we need *hermeneutics and exegesis* to search the subject matter of Scripture (15). Melanchthon used the term "dogmatic" for the doctrinal content of Scripture, although Aquinas had favored the term "doctrine." But after the eighteenth century, "systematic theology" became the preferred term. Whichever term we use, the truth of this discipline must be coherent and rational. It involves "a very specific understanding of truth, namely, *truth as coherence*" (21). Although he often doubts the value of "subjective certainty" alone, he nevertheless respects Calvin's further notion of the testimony of the Holy Spirit: "Word and Spirit belong together" (33). He pauses to engage in dialogue with Schleiermacher, Herrmann, and Barth on the relation between faith and truth. He writes yet again: "Individual experience can never mediate absolute, unconditioned certainty" (47). As we also observed earlier, truth embraces the reality of the world "from its creation to its eschatological consummation" (49). Yet a third theme from earlier work is that "our talk about God becomes doxology, in which the speakers rise above the limits of their own finitude to the thought of the infinite God" (55).

Chapter 2 focuses more sharply on the concept of God. Pannenberg admits: "'God' has increasingly lost [its] function... in the public mind" (63). Statements about God no longer seem to count as "factual statements" (63). However, if "God" were to lose its meaning, "faith in Jesus of Nazareth loses its foundation"

(64). The word "God" constitutes "a key word for awareness of the totality of the world and of human life" (71). The traditional arguments for the existence of God tend to function not as "proofs," but as ways of clarifying our concept of God (83-102). Yet Pannenberg would not go as far as Barth in seeing them *simply* as Christian confessions of faith. He concludes: "What Paul calls the knowledge of God from creation through his works (Rom. 1:20) may be only a vague sense of infinitude.... The knowledge of Rom. 1:20 is not innate ... but acquired" (117).

In chapter 3 Pannenberg considers God and "religion." He agrees with Barth concerning the primacy of revelation. But he comments, "Direct assertion is not enough; the mediation of reasoning is needed" (127). He criticizes Troeltsch's view of the psychological value of religion, although he sympathizes with his search for universal validity. In the end this may help us to discover a deeper understanding of *finite* reality. But "defining the nature of religion does not answer the question of its truth" (151). It is useful to understand that human behavior is not simply centered on the self, but expresses openness to the world as "eccentricity, or self-transcendence" (155). Chapter 4 resumes the discussion of revelation. Like Barth, Pannenberg insists: "A true knowledge ... corresponds to the divine reality only if it originates in the deity itself" (189). He repeats: "The loftiness of the divine reality makes it inaccessible to us unless it makes itself known" (189). In ancient Israel reception of the word was described as "seizure by the Spirit or by the hand of God" (201). Revelation is a key feature of apocalyptic, which appears in Matt. 10:26 and Luke 12:2: "Nothing is covered that will not be revealed" (209). 1 Cor. 2:7-9 is also used of the apocalyptic mystery. Pannenberg refers back to his earlier discussion *Revelation as History*.

In chapter 5 Pannenberg considers "the Trinitarian God." It is significant that (together with Moltmann and Rogers) *he grounds an approach to the Holy Trinity in the life and narrative of Jesus*. Jesus' coming meant that the reign of God was near (259). The teaching of Jesus points to "God's fatherly goodness" (259). Jesus invoked God as *Abba* (260). His reality as "Father" is not arbitrary, but has its basis in election and adoption. Pannenberg writes, "On the lips of Jesus 'Father' became a proper name for God" (262). It is *not* simply a time-bound concept. Similarly, or in parallel, Jesus is declared to be "Son" at his resurrection (Rom. 1:3-4; 264). Pannenberg does not see this contradicting his preexistence (on which even Dunn has doubts). In Paul, he urges, "The title *Kyrios* implies the full deity of the Son" (266). This statement must be understood in the light of all Pannenberg's previous work, not least *Jesus — God and Man*. Like Moltmann and, later, Rogers, he notes that "In the story of his baptism the Spirit was imparted to him on this occasion (Mk. 1:10)" (266). He adds, "The fellowship of Jesus as Son with God as Father can obviously be stated only if there is reference to a third as well, the Holy Spirit. The Spirit of God is the mode of God's presence in Jesus" (267). He appeals to Rom. 8:9-16, 1 Cor. 12:4-6, and 2 Cor. 13:13, among other passages. Pannenberg then discusses "three hypostases in all divine activity." Athanasius and the Cappadocian Fathers have expounded this. In the light of biblical and patristic evidence, "semantically Father is a relational term" (273; *see also* God, Trinity: Historical Development; Holy Spirit: The Spirit in Historical Theology). In the eighteenth century the doctrine of the Trinity suffered decay because of a disconnection between Trinitarian statements and divine unity. But after Hegel and Dorner the doctrine revived. The "self-distinction" between the Father, the Son, and the Spirit is "reciprocal" (308-19), and the NT leaves us with "three centers of action." But there is also "a unity of consciousness with the unity of divine life" (319). Pannenberg concludes: "The Father acts in the world only through the Son and the Spirit" (328).

In the last chapter of volume 1 Pannenberg considers the unity and majesty of God, and his "attributes." For example, his omnipresence is evident from Ps. 139:2, 13-15. Isaiah speaks of God's divine plan in history, which "will be open to all eyes only when God contemplates his work" (Isa. 5:12, 19; 387). The judgment of the world will disclose the true character and nature of people and things. Further, "Paul puts the resurrection of the dead alongside creation out of nothing" (417). To summarize again: "The Father is the Father only in relation to the Son.... The Son is the Son only in obedience to the sending of the Father.... The Spirit exists hypostatically as Spirit only as he glorifies the Father in the Son and the Son as sent by the Father" (428).

Volume 2 of *Systematic Theology* considers creation, the dignity and misery of humanity, Christology and the deity of Christ, and the reconciliation of the world. Creation is a "free act of God," which may be celebrated by his people as "recital" along with God's other acts (8). The beginning of covenant history goes back to creation, and constitutes part of the basis for worship. Pannenberg writes that creatures are all that they are because of God's almighty creative action. He declares, "The patience and humble love with which God seeks his creatures ... do not proceed from weakness" (16). He approves Moltmann's comment: "The creation of the world is an expression of the love of God" (21). He adds, "The goodness of the Father as Creator ... is not different, however, from the love with which the Father from all eternity loves the Son," and this is "always mediated through the Son" (21). Thus the eternal Son is "the ontic basis of the human existence of Jesus in his relation to God as Father" (23). Pannenberg takes up Hegel's philosophy of religion as a starting point, but certainly does not stop there. In the end Hegel's "principle of otherness" is not compatible with the Christian doctrine of creation. Pannenberg states, "The life of creatures as participation in God ... transcends their own finitude ... [through] the Spirit" (33). Further, he writes, "Preservation goes with creation ... it is a living occurrence ... a constantly new creative fashioning" (34). God is constantly bringing forth new things.

God's act of creation extends not only to humanity but also to creatures. The world must be understood "as the creation of the biblical God" (59). What is striking about this is God's love of "a plurality of what is finite ... a plurality of creatures" (61). The world also exhibits order and unity, and the regularity of events of nature. This reveals not only God's faithfulness "as Creator and Sustainer," but also "the development of the ever new and more complex forms in the world of creatures" (72). In all this "the Spirit of God is the life-giving principle" (cf. Ps. 104:30), and even resurrection is "a work of the divine Spirit" (*ST* 77; Rom. 8:11; 1 Cor. 15:44-45). Pannenberg discusses some current theories in modern physics and biology, including concepts of space. He also considers the sequence of forms, but notes concerning the language of the early chapters of Genesis the creation of "light prior to the stars" on one hand, and "vegetation as a presupposition of animal life" on the other (118). The formation of the sequence is "astonishing."

Chapter 8 carries the title "The Dignity and Misery of Humanity" because on the one hand human destiny is fellowship with God, but on the other hand "Misery ... is the lot of those who are deprived of the fellowship with God that is the destiny of human life" (178). Pannenberg explains: "To speak of human misery is better than using the classical theological doctrine of sin to describe our situation of lostness.... The term 'misery' sums up our detachment from God" (179). He adds, "The term 'alienation' has a similar breadth" (179).

Part of Pannenberg's doctrine of humanity or theological anthropology can be found also in his *Anthropology in Theological Perspective* (New York: T. & T. Clark/Continuum, 1985). In *Systematic Theology* he asserts: "The early fathers defended our psychosomatic unity as a basic principle of Christian anthropology" (2:182). He adds: "Hence a resurrection of the body is necessary, for the soul alone is not the whole person" (183). The biblical material also differentiates between spirit and reason (190). One of the significant features about "body" (as Käsemann and Robinson have noted) is its capacity to relate to others. "Soul" might suggest some inner world, but "body" means that "my consciousness is there for others as well as myself" (194). Human beings are capable of standing "outside ourselves," that is, of "the 'ecstasy' of consciousness" (197). Intersubjectivity is a presupposition of some kind of grasp of "the whole." Pannenberg writes: "We achieve our particularity in our encounter with others" (200). Self-identity emerges in interaction with others, not in isolated introspection.

Pannenberg turns to human destiny and to the image of God. Divine image and likeness are "a standard for our ordination to rule over the creation" (205). But this does not simply entail the use of reason alone. The key to this subject lies in seeing Jesus Christ as the image of God (2 Cor. 4:4; Col. 1:15; Heb. 1:3) and in transforming believers into this image (Rom. 8:29; 1 Cor. 15:49; 2 Cor. 3:18). In the course of discussing the wider subject, Pannenberg comments on "original righteousness": "Little is left of the traditional dogma of a perfect first estate" (*ST* 214). On Gen. 1:26 he asserts, "The text speaks of humans' representing God" (216). More important than "a perfect first estate" is our human destiny to be made like God at the End: "to move on constantly to new experiences" (229).

The doctrine of misery or alienation is refreshingly robust. Pannenberg writes: "The decay of the doctrine of original sin led to the anchoring of the concept of sin in *acts* of sin, and finally the concept was reduced to the *individual act*" (234, italics mine). He makes no bones about *sin as a state or condition, not simply an act.* In our culture the concept is marginalized. But this does not mean people today "are no longer aware of the reality of evil" (236). We cannot, however, master its destructive *effects.* Pannenberg therefore scrutinizes the biblical vocabulary for sin. This includes not just "mistakes" or careless omission, but "the wickedness of the heart" (239). The Hebrew *'awōn* (which portrays effects of sin) becomes especially important. Moreover, he adds, "The classical significance of Augustine" elaborates "the Pauline links between sin and desire more deeply than Christian theology had hitherto managed to do" (241). Where Augustine meets with criticism, "This should not blind us to this extraordinary achievement" (241). Many modern treatments "overhastily" dismiss Augustine's teaching (*see* **Sin: Historical**). He saw sin as "an autonomy of the will that puts the self in the center and uses everything else as a means to the self as an end" (243). When he discusses the universality of sin, Pannenberg observes, "At work here is the implicit form of absolute self-willing that alienates us from God by putting the self in the place that is God's alone" (261).

Chapter 9 concerns Christology, but we have already explored much of this in our discussion of *Jesus — God and Man.* Similarly chapter 10 concerns the deity of Christ. "Messiah," Pannenberg argues, "implies the thought of divine Sonship" (*ST* 277). Only God could "send" his Son into the world (Gal. 4:4; Rom. 8:3). After considering historical church confessions, he insists that the foundation of Christology must be the history of Jesus, and God's legitimization of his pre-Easter work in the resurrection. This tends to repeat, but to formulate differently, his "Christology from below" in *Jesus — God and Man.* He comments, "We cannot regard a Christology from below as ruling out completely the classical Christology of the incarnation" (288). Christ's humanity is unique: he is the "New Man," the Author of a new humanity. Jesus is "the new eschatological Adam" (315). Chapter 10 states reasons for maintaining the unity of Jesus with God. Again, it is the resurrection of Jesus that constitutes God's vindication and justification of Jesus Christ. As in his earlier work, he repeats, "The first Christians could not have successfully preached the resurrection of Jesus if his body had been intact in the tomb" (358). Against Bultmann and even Barth, he writes: "The event took place in this world, namely, in the tomb of Jesus in Jerusalem before the visit of the women" (360). He also asserts, "In truth he suffered in our place as sinners" (374).

The last chapter of the second volume concerns salvation and reconciliation. Paul certainly understood the death of Jesus in terms of its bringing reconciliation (Rom. 5:10). Again, the biblical teaching is extended through Irenaeus, Peter Lombard, Calvin, Schleiermacher, and others. Pannenberg also examines Christ's "death as expiation for human sins." Expiation removes "the offense, the guilt, and the consequences of sin (Rom. 3:25)." He refers to its background on the Day of Atonement in Leviticus 16. He repeats, in effect, that "The crucifixion of Jesus [has] atoning force only in the light of his resurrection by God" (412). He approves of Barth's connection between resurrection and reconciliation. Pannenberg uses simple and basic language here: in Gal. 3:13 Jesus Christ bore the curse of the Law "for us"; representation may include doing "something for others." We see "a co-human solidarity" (419). Expiation, therefore, is "vicarious penal suffering" (421). If a later age finds these traditional ideas hard to understand, this is "not a sufficient reason for replacing them" (422). He rightly describes the work of Christ as "the vicarious suffering of the wrath of God at sin" (427). He declares, "God's act in reconciling the world certainly took place in Christ's passion" (437).

This brings us to volume 3, which concerns the outpouring of the Holy Spirit, the kingdom of God and its consummation, the church and ministry, election and history, and the consummation of creation. Pannenberg begins by reinforcing the point that the Holy Spirit is active, together with the Father and Son, in *every* act of creation, redemption, and bringing in the End. His work is ever-creative and ever-transforming. In the NT Jesus is seen "as a recipient of the Spirit and his work" (5). The Spirit brings life and movement, and is God's eschatological gift (12). He notes, "The Spirit and the Son mutually indwell one another as Trinitarian persons" (17). Further, "the only criticism of authentic spirituality is the relation to confession of Christ" (18).

The church is not equivalent to the kingdom of God: "Not only Protestant but also Roman Catholic theology achieved a new sense of the difference between church and kingdom" (35). Like Moltmann, Pannenberg rightly urges, "The church's nature is to be that of a pilgrimage towards a future that is still ahead" (36). On the other hand, the kingdom of God represents *obedience* and God's *total rule*. Pannenberg accepts Rahner's notion of the church as a sacrament that points beyond itself, "as a sign and tool of the coming kingdom of God," not as an end in itself (45). He also notes, "Describing the church as the congregation of believers has been basic and typical for the Reformation concept of the church" (99). But this must include "proclamation of the pure preaching of the gospel.... The universal unity of the church across the ages finds manifestation in the worship of the local congregation that exists in virtue of its apostolic basis" (101). Admittedly "local church" sometimes means congregation, sometimes diocese, sometimes province. But the key lies in "common confession of faith" (111).

Pannenberg concludes this section with a consideration of the Holy Spirit's work in individual Christians, especially in faith, hope, and love, and in Christ's presence in the sacraments. He writes: "Faith here is not just acquiring information or assenting to doctrine" (138). Faith is trust in response to promise, but as in his earlier work, Pannenberg does not see it as a *replacement* of knowledge and argument. Faith and trust in God's promises are "never apart from hope.... A sense of the incompleteness of life as it now is [is] related to ... confidence" (173). He cites Gen. 15:6, Rom. 4:3, and Rom. 4:19-21, and declares, "Faith lifts us above our entanglement in the vicious circle of sin and death by uniting us to Jesus and giving us a share in his Spirit" (177). Hope and love "belong together." However, he warns us, "Equating love of God and love of neighbor can easily lead to a moralistic interpretation of Christianity" (189). There follow illuminating discussions of adoption and justification.

Baptism takes place in time, but has a lasting effect. Death and resurrection with Christ are "grounded in baptism" and have been understood as "sharing in the destiny of Jesus in his dying and rising again" (241). Baptism does not simply mean the washing away of sins. Its form is that of "an enacted sign" (242, 243), and this coheres with "the once-for-all-ness of baptism" (243). It is unrepeatable. In the earliest church "conversion took place once for all in baptism" (246). He cites the classic passage, Rom. 6:3-14. Pannenberg discusses the relation between baptism and penitence, and Luther's rejection of their supposed equivalence. He admits that in the earliest church and in missionary situations faith came first and then baptism, as in Acts 8:37. But Cyprian and Origen witness to the practice of infant baptism. To defend it or to attack it, however, is not "just a question apart," but bound up with "the nature of baptism" (260). If baptism is primarily a confession of faith, the question has already been settled. But if baptism relates to "*something that* even those already converted . . . *cannot do for themselves* . . . namely, the definitive linking . . . to the destiny of Jesus, then the matter is obviously much *more complex*. . . . *Baptism can no longer be viewed primarily as a human act*" (260, italics mine). Pannenberg compares Luther, Aquinas, and others on this issue. He also considers "confirmation of baptism by the bishop," which seems often to assume a higher profile in Lutheran churches than in some Anglican ones.

The institution of the Lord's Supper by Jesus is "basic to the celebration" of it (1 Cor. 11:24-25; *ST* 283). Pannenberg discusses relevant biblical passages, together with the Fathers, Luther, Zwingli, Aquinas, Roman Catholic theology (including Rahner), and others. He concludes, "To belong to Jesus Christ means to participate in his giving of himself to God and his kingdom . . . in fellowship with all who are related in this way to the same Lord" (326). He also addresses numerous practical issues, including admission to Holy Communion. He declares, "Discipleship as a prerequisite of participation at this Supper means first the relation between admission to it and baptism" (330). Today there is a laxity of discipline, but this is hardly an advance. The Lord's Supper is also united with the proclamation of the gospel. Finally Pannenberg comments, "The significatory nature of the sacramental presence of Christ and God's kingdom in baptism and the Supper is an expression of the 'not yet' of our Christian life in tension as we move on to the eschatological consummation of salvation" (353).

This appropriately brings us to the final two chapters: to chapter 14 on election and history, and to chapter 15 on the consummation of creation. Much of Pannenberg's argument is considered under our entry on election. In summary, he regards the legacy of Origen and Augustine as too abstract and individualistic to do justice to biblical content and concerns. It is abstract because (i) "it makes the divine decision timeless, in abstraction from the concrete historicity of the divine acts of election as the Bible bears witness to them"; (ii) "it detaches individuals as the objects of election from all relations to society"; and (iii) "it restricts the purpose of election to participation in future salvation in disjunction from any historical function of the elect" (442). Israel's election is always a historical act. In the NT such a view depends on "detaching... Rom. 8:29-30 and 9:13, 16, from the context of salvation history in which Paul sets them" (444; *see* **Election and Predestination; Time**). Luther and Calvin wrestled with this, but also tended to presuppose an "eternal" will of God. Election in the Bible is less abstract, and refers mainly to the *election of a people for service;* "the election of the people was the chief issue in Israel's election traditions" (455).

The consummation of creation and God's kingdom "transcends all our concepts," as the reality of God also does (527). Yet the future is *"the final horizon of the definitive meaning and therefore of the nature of all things and all events"* (531, italics mine). We can use "extrapolation from the knowledge of possible wholeness (salvation)" (544). The future differs from all human incompleteness and failure. We think of an ending that has not been reached in human experience. Pannenberg writes, "The future consummation is the entry of eternity into time" (603). We look forward to the return of Christ with glory. The Holy Spirit will raise us (Rom. 8:11). He adds, "The light of divine glory is identical with the fire of judgment," which may purify (625). Pannenberg declares, "The coming again of Christ will be the completion of the work of the Spirit that began in the incarnation and with the resurrection of Jesus" (627); "we shall be changed into the image, not just a copy, of the risen Lord" (628). He concludes, "Only the eschatological consummation in which God will wipe away all tears (Isa. 25:8; Rev. 21:4) can remove all doubts concerning the revelation of the love of God... at work... at each stage in the history of creation" (645).

We have not included every detailed discussion in Pannenberg's *Systematic Theology*. One omission concerns the detailed discussions of historical theologians from the Fathers up to today on virtually every issue. More might have been said also on the ministry of the church and on election. Nevertheless, the three volumes leave us with the impression of huge learning, a practical concern, originality, and a survey of theology and Christian tradition that is doxological. Technical and learned it often is, but it is also devotionally inspiring. There is much about Christ's resurrection, the resurrection of the dead, and the creative work of the Holy Spirit and Holy Trinity. That ever-fresh life-giving movement might have been said to characterize even the final state of the redeemed, for whom "rest" is also coupled with yet "new things."

Reading: S. Grenz, *Reason for Hope: The Systematic Theology of W. Pannenberg* (New York: OUP, 1990); Wolfhart Pannenberg, *Jesus — God and Man* (Philadelphia: Westminster; London: SCM, 1968); Wolfhart Pannenberg, *Basic Questions in Theology*, 3 vols. (London: SCM, 1970-1973); Wolfhart Pannenberg, *Theology and the Philosophy of Science* (Philadelphia: Westminster, 1976); Wolfhart Pannenberg, *Systematic Theology*, 3 vols. (Grand Rapids: Eerdmans, 1992-1998); E. F. Tupper, *The Theology of Wolfhart Pannenberg* (London: SCM, 1974; Philadelphia: Westminster, 1973).

Pantheism

Pantheism is the opposite of Deism. Broadly, it denotes the belief that God is everything (Gk. *pan*). It usually identifies God with the world, or identifies the world with an emanation or outflow of God. Christianity is emphatic that God is not to be identified with the world, which is God's creation. While Judaism, Christianity, and Islam are theistic, many Eastern religions, including often Hinduism and Buddhism, are pantheist. It is the religious equivalent of monism in philosophy. G. H. MacGregor argues that pantheism is self-contradictory. If God is all, for example, why can't I give up smoking? But pantheism does not usually identify God with each individual entity in the world, but only with the "whole" or the All in the fullest sense. Historically B. Spinoza was a philosophical advocate of pantheism, partly in reaction against widespread Deism toward the end of the eighteenth century. Spinoza realized, however, that to suggest that all finite things were drawn into a single god or "substance" failed adequately to explain diversity within the universe. Some argue that Hegel was pantheistic, and he also stressed the historically finite. The idea that God is all-inclusive and barely personal (except in the sense of suprapersonal) remains alien to Christianity. One of the various dangers of Christian mysticism is that on occasion it may veer toward pantheism, certainly if it is not Christ-centered. Two other standard criticisms MacGregor seeks to highlight are an inadequate explanation of the problem of evil and inadequate concepts of free will within the single system. Emotionally the vision of the universe as a single, all-pervading system may appear to be attractive. But its problems are numerous, and it is incompatible with Christianity. Some find that negative theology provides the only rational answer. Plotinus argued that the One is beyond all thought and being; we can describe only emanations. Spinoza argued: "all things must have followed of necessity from a given nature of God" (*Ethics* 1, proposition 33). (*See also* Deism; Panentheism.)

Parables of Jesus

The parables of Jesus constitute an entry in a book on Christian theology not only because they represent a teaching method often used by Jesus, but also because a variety of methods have been used in their interpretation in hermeneutics. They stand in contrast to direct discourse. Hence, as C. H. Dodd commented, they provoke the mind of the hearer into active thought, because there is sufficient doubt about their precise application to tease the mind into thinking. In R. W. Funk's words: "The parable is not closed, so to speak, until the listener is drawn into it as a participant" (*Language, Hermeneutic, and Word of God* [New York: Harper and Row, 1966], 133). Nevertheless, some parables do not fit this pattern. Some have self-evident meanings, built from human life. A. Wilder and J. Jeremias stress this variety of their types. Jeremias points out that the Hebrew term *māshāl* may cover "parables, similitudes, allegory, fable, proverb ... riddle, symbol ... jest" (*The Parables of Jesus* [London: SCM, 1963], 20). Most NT scholars draw a line between the function of a parable and that of an allegory. C. L. Blomberg, however, insists that many parables contain allegorical elements and some are indeed allegories. On the other hand, certain principles of interpretation distinguish the two forms in general.

E. Linneman calls attention to the key points. First, a parable functions to assert and convince outsiders. An allegory is addressed to "insiders" who know the "code" in terms of how to apply or interpret it. She writes: "Allegories... serve to transmit encoded information, which is only intelligible to the initiated" (*The Parables of Jesus* [London: SPCK, 1966], 7). Second, parables convey a coherent story from everyday life. Allegories offer a string of encoded applications that may not cohere together as an intelligible story. Examples of both features abound in the OT and the NT. Nathan tells David a coherent story about a selfish rich man who would not take from his abundant flock of sheep to feed a visitor, but stole his neighbor's precious lamb. He then pronounced, "You are the man" (2 Sam. 12:1-15). Nathan would not have been wise to accuse a king of adultery directly to his face. But the injustice of the story overwhelms King David; the parable, so to speak, "wounds from behind." Hence this operates as *parable*. However, in Ezek. 17:1-10 we read of a "mighty eagle," who represents Nebuchadnezzar, which comes to "Lebanon," which represents Jerusalem. His seizure of the "topmost branch of a cedar" is not part of a coherent story, but represents the fate of Jehoiachin. This is *allegory*, addressed to the initiated. It has no "narrative world," and it presents a string of representations (*see* **Allegory, Allegorical Interpretation**).

In English literature *The Pilgrim's Progress* by John Bunyan draws on a host of allegories. John Bunyan's interpreter speaks of a room, but this represents the Holy Spirit cleansing a heart. By contrast, in the parable of the lost coin (Luke 15:8-9) a real woman sweeps a genuine room to find a coin. The parable of the prodigal son (Luke 15:11-32) remains a coherent story or a parable, until the "father" is read as "God," at which point it becomes an allegory. The parable of the laborers in the vineyard and the employer remains a parable (Matt. 20:1-16). Each worker receives an agreed-upon day's wage. But when the employer generously gives the same wage to those who had worked only one hour, the other workers are shocked and envious. Grace has eclipsed justice. There is little or no need to allegorize the parable. A few parables are mixed; one Evangelist tells the story as a parable, and another as an allegory. In Luke 14:16-24 Luke tells a coherent story of a great supper to which the host sends out invitations that are refused. So the owner of the house instructs his servant "to bring in the poor, the crippled, the blind, and the lame" (v. 21). The purpose of the parable is to address outsiders, either Pharisaic critics or the outcasts. However, in Matt. 22:1-10 Matthew begins with the parable: the same invitations are sent, and the same refusals received, but the host is now "a king" who gave a wedding banquet. Here the reaction to the refusals becomes disproportionate to a coherent story. "He sent his troops... and burned their city" (v. 7). Now this becomes an allegory of the fall of Jerusalem.

Jeremias considers that a trend toward allegorizing the parables betrays the influence of the NT church, not Jesus. It is part of the trend of change of audience, embellishment, the hortatory use of parables, conflations and changes of setting (*Parables of Jesus*, 27-114). Many NT scholars accept this. But it is doubtful whether such generalizations always stand up. It is plausible for any traveling evangelist or teacher to use the same imagery for different purposes on different occasions. For example, Luke's telling of the parable of the lost sheep (Luke 15:4-7) may well be addressed to grumbling scribes (v. 2). But Matthew tells the same story (Matt. 18:12-14) after a different introduction to the setting: "Take care that you do not despise one of these little ones" (v. 10). It clearly matched Matthew's concern for the church and its pastors (Matt. 18:6-9, 15-20). It is not impossible that Matthew took up a different situation in the life of Jesus. However, that is usually regarded, with Jeremias, as editorial, and there is a limit to how many times this kind of explanation can be used convincingly.

More important are the varied resources for interpretation that hermeneutics has provided. G. V. Jones, D. O. Via, J. D. Crossan, and others have expounded on existential interpretation. The parable of the prodigal son (Luke 15:11-32), Jones argues, traces the younger son's "flight into estrangement and return through longing" (*The Art and Truth of the Parables* [London: SPCK, 1964], 175). He adds, "He finds life empty and meaningless without personal relationships, and he seems desperate ... nobody wants him" (185). Even after his return the elder son treats him not as a *person*, but as a *type*. The new self living in destitution is "different from the confident, defiant self, at the moment of departure. . . . He is a stranger, unwanted and anonymous, experiencing the utter nausea of dereliction" (175). In other words, Jesus anticipates the later, modern, existential themes of depersonalization, estrangement, and the effect of personal decision upon the self. The father in the story restores his personhood, of which his gifts of the robe and ring become indicators.

Via and many others also call attention to "plot" within the parables, as Ricoeur does more widely in narratives as such. The "tragic" parables represent a story with a downward movement to disaster, while "comic" plots achieve the reverse, upward dynamic. "Comic" parables include the ones about the dishonest manager (Luke 16:1-9) and the prodigal son. "Tragic" parables include the parables of the talents (Matt. 25:14-30) and of the ten maidens (Matt. 25:1-13). The one-talent man perceives himself as a victim: "I knew that you were a harsh man." He refuses to take the risk of venture, or to reach a life-changing decision. The consequence of his action is that his rejection in taking *responsibility* leads to loss of *opportunity:* he is not given rule over cities, like the others who acted with courage and determination (*The Parables* [Philadelphia: Fortress, 1967], 120). Similarly the foolish maidens "presumptuously believed that their well-being was guaranteed ... that someone else will pay the bill" (126). These, too, constitute anticipations of existential themes concerning human existence, together with a clear narrative plot.

In his early work, J. D. Crossan expounds "parables of reversal" in his book *In Parables* (New York: Harper and Row, 1973), 53-78. In the parable of the Good

Samaritan (Luke 10:25-37), the hearers confront the impossible, in which "their world is turned upside down" (65). They had expected the Samaritans to be "bad" and the priest "good," but they have to rethink their values from the ground up. This is *not* a mere example story, for the priest, certainly not the Samaritan, would play the hero if it were. It is a challenge to assumptions and to conventional values. Other parables of "reversal" are the rich man and Lazarus (Luke 16:19-31) and the Pharisee and the tax collector (Luke 18:10-14). In his later work Crossan turned to postmodernism. He wrote books on parables published in 1975, 1976, 1979, and 1980. In *The Dark Interval* (1975) he argues that while myth creates "world," parable subverts it. In *Raid on the Articulate* (1976) he draws on Shklovsky's device of *defamiliarization,* in which the familiar is made strange. In *Cliffs of Fall* (1980) he focuses on paradox and polyvalence. The parables, he argues, mean what a reader makes of them.

E. Fuchs uses the method of his "New Hermeneutic." The word of Jesus "singles out the individual and grasps him deep down" (*Studies of the Historical Jesus* [London: SCM, 1964], 35). When the audience hears the narrative of the parable of the laborers in the vineyard (Matt. 20:1-16), it is shocked and stunned. The audience does not engage in long reflection. Hardly realizing it, the audience is "drawn over to God's side and learn[s] to see everything with God's eyes" (155). Love does not deliver a lecture on grace. Fuchs writes, "Is not this the way of true love? Love does not just burst out. Instead, it provides in advance the sphere in which a meeting takes place" (129). Fuchs is perhaps at his best in parables and biblical poetry. On more propositional texts his "intralinguistic interpretation," even on the resurrection, leaves much to be desired.

Fuchs may provide a starting point for understanding the nature of narrative and "narrative world." Heidegger, in a different context, uses "world" in the way suggested by a narrative world, but H.-G. Gadamer and P. Ricoeur open up the notion further. We may be "drawn in" when we read a narrative as *participants, not as mere spectators.* We become more than spectators; we are involved (*see* **Self-Involvement**). Gadamer gives the example of "world" of play, when the game determines the action for the players; it is different for the spectator (*Truth and Method* [London: Sheed and Ward, 1989], 101-21). Similarly Ricoeur expounds "world" in the context of narratives (*Time and Narrative*, vol. 2 [Chicago: University of Chicago Press, 1985], 67-69, and vol. 3 [1988], 157-92). We could continue almost endlessly to distinguish various approaches. Mary A. Tolbert, for example, uses a *semiotic* approach to provide a "Freudian" interpretation of the parable of the prodigal son.

The more we consider "polyvalent" and postmodern approaches (once fashionable during the 1970s and 1980s in the journal *Semeia*), the more we may prefer to return to the more "historical" approaches of Dodd, Jeremias, and Linneman, even if supplemented and corrected by the insights of Funk and others. The problem with these "historical" approaches is that they tend too readily to provide only retrospective, cognitive, and propositional readings of what was originally often indirect communication, as Funk points out. Probably the key hermeneutical principle is *not to generalize* about *all* parables, as if a parable were one kind of thing, but to apply each parable in the way that particular parable genuinely invites. The "historical" approach may often remain a starting point, but after that each method has its place. (*See also* **Allegory, Allegorical Interpretation; Hermeneutics; Narrative.**)

Reading: C. L. Blomberg, *Interpreting the Parables* (Leicester: Apollos, 1990); M. Boucher, *The Mysterious Parable* (Washington, D.C.: American Catholic Biblical Association, 1977); J. D. Crossan, *In Parables* (New York: Harper and Row, 1973); J. Jeremias, *The Parables of Jesus* (London: SCM, 1963); K. Snodgrass, *Stories with Intent* (Grand Rapids: Eerdmans, 2008); R. H. Stein, *An Introduction to the Parables of Jesus* (Philadelphia: Westminster, 1981).

Paradox

From Greek *para,* "contrary to," and *doxa,* classical Greek, "opinion," "paradox" may denote "that which is against common opinion." But more often it represents two well-argued propositions that *appear to contradict* each other. Whereas a self-contradiction would be irrational, many wish to retain a paradox, and to defend its rationality. S. Kierkegaard argues that, although God is beyond contradiction, when humankind seeks to describe God's acts, paradoxes occur, which must be retained. Jesus Christ, he claims, represents the central paradox or the eternal in time, who has become man as well as God. Paradoxes, Kierkegaard maintains, have the power to evoke faith. M. Bakhtin argues that monologic discourse is sometimes inadequate to express complex truth, and that therefore polyphonic discourse, or discourse with more than one voice, is essential. In their earlier thought Barth and Brunner argued for the use of dialectic in theology. Modern linguistic philosophy has often considered different kinds of paradoxes, and sought to offer logical solutions to them. Sometimes this leads to the exposure of one of the paradoxical propositions as resting on false premises. G. Ryle gave a series of answers to classic paradoxes from Zeno onward, showing that they often depended on clumsy formulations or misunderstandings. (*See also* **Dialectic, Dialectical Theology; Polyphonic Discourse.**)

Parousia

The parousia, or return of Christ, together with the resurrection of the dead and the Last Judgment, constitutes one of the three great themes of Christian eschatology. As we shall see, in spite of this, some underrate what this term denotes, noting that it may be derived from apocalyptic, and may in translation denote both "coming" and "presence." It has even been understood by some as a "coming" and "presence" at the Lord's Supper, or Eucharist. But the teaching of Jesus, especially in his parables, points to an end-time and future climax when all God's purposes will be finally fulfilled. At that end-time the hidden will become manifest (Matt. 10:26), the poor will become rich (Luke 6:20), the blind will receive their sight (Matt. 11:5), and so on. J. Jeremias provides many examples of the resolution of an ambiguous present into a clear and decisive future: wheat is sown among the weeds but cannot yet be separated, or both are damaged (Matt. 13:24-30); and a seine net catches good and bad fish, which cannot be sorted until the End (*The Parables of Jesus* [London: SCM, 1963], 221-22, 224-27). The name "parables of reversal" is often given to those that depict a radically new situation at the End. (On the joy of the oppressed at the coming vindication, *see* **Last Judgment**).

The ministry, cross, and resurrection of Jesus will bring a final overthrow of all evil forces that has certainly not fully taken place yet. In the Gospels three apocalyptic passages can be found in Mark 13, Matthew 24, and Luke 21. These apocalyptic discourses, however, become open to misinterpretation because they combine allusions to the parousia, or final coming, of Christ with allusions to the destruction of Jerusalem or some other historical event (*see* **Imminence of the End**). The discourse in Mark begins with the question of the overawed disciples visiting the capital city, "Look, Teacher, what large stones and what large buildings!" To which Jesus said, "Not one stone will be left here upon another; all will be thrown down" (Mark 13:1-2; and parallel Matt. 24:1-2; cf. Luke 21:5-6). Jesus begins to unfold an imminent future, "but the end is still to come" (Mark 13:7). G. B. Caird, N. T. Wright, G. Beasley-Murray, and R. T. France offer several possible schemes of how these chapters address two questions or two issues, which are often interwoven (Caird, *The Language and Imagery of the Bible* [London: Duckworth, 1980], 265-68; France, *The Gospel of Mark: A Commentary on the Greek Text* [Grand Rapids: Eerdmans, 2002], 497-546; and Beasley-Murray, *Jesus and the Last Days* [Peabody, Mass.: Hendrickson, 1995]). Clearly, for example, "the desolating sacrilege set up where it ought not to be (let the reader understand), then those in Judea must flee" (Mark 13:14), refers to the desecration of the temple. But the cosmic events, "The sun will be darkened, / and the moon will not give its light.... Then they will see the Son of Man coming in clouds with great power and glory" (13:24-26), refer primarily to the end of the world and the parousia, even if it may still apply, as Caird argues, to the "end of the world" for the Jews.

On the actual "dating" of the parousia Jesus is clear: "About that day or hour no one knows, neither the angels in heaven, nor the Son, but only the Father" (13:32). The task of Christian disciples is "Keep alert; for you do not know when the time will come" (13:33). It is incredible that down through the centuries self-proclaimed prophets should claim to know what God hid from Jesus. As far as the slightly different version in Luke is concerned, Joel Green also finds multiple issues and multiple fulfillments (*The Gospel of Luke* [Grand Rapids: Eerdmans, 1997], 739-40). Luke Johnson also sees both "the fall of a city" and a glimpse of "the last days of the Son of Man" in these verses (*The Gospel of Luke* [Collegeville, Minn.: Glazier/Liturgical Press, 1991], 324). S. G. Wilson also finds both an "imminent" strand and a "delay" strand in Luke's language about the parousia (*The*

Gentiles and the Gentile Mission in Luke-Acts [Cambridge: CUP, 1973], 67-85; cf. J. T. Caroll and Alexandria Brown, *The Return of Jesus* [Peabody, Mass.: Hendrickson, 2000], 26-45). Acts continues the theme of ignorance of the date or time: "It is not for you to know the times or periods that the Father has set" (Acts 1:7).

Outside the teaching of Jesus, the earliest reference to the parousia comes in 1 Thess. 4:16-17, where Paul uses traditional apocalyptic imagery. He declares, "The Lord himself, with a cry of command, with the archangel's call and with the sound of God's trumpet, will descend from heaven, and the dead in Christ will rise first. Then we who are alive, who are left, will be caught up in the clouds with them to meet the Lord in the air; and so we will be with the Lord forever." Christ is described as "the man of heaven" in 1 Cor. 15:49, and the passage shows that the parousia is bound up with the resurrection of Christ and the resurrection of the dead. Clearly much of the language is deliberately symbolic. The sound of the trumpet is an alert for a sleeping army, and, once again, it is used later in 1 Cor. 15:52. Similarly, "caught up in the clouds" is a symbol for the gathering together of believers, which takes place beyond the confines of earth. Numerous OT passages prepare us for the symbolic status of this language. But this does not rob it of content. It suggests that we take care not to define these superearthly events too precisely, because this is not a descriptive map of celestial geography.

This gives no cause for an effectively dismissive reference to these verses, as if they could be taken seriously only by biblical or apocalyptic literalists. Caird describes the passage as "a curious interplay between the metaphorical and the literal" (*Language and Imagery*, 248). Even the resurrection is "bodily" rather than "physical" (*see* **Resurrection of the Dead**). Even the parousia is a metaphorical application of a tradition, for the eventful arrival in pomp and glory of the emperor, king, or visiting dignitary. Paul uses it of the return of Christ in 1 Cor. 15:23 and 2 Thess. 2:8. In 2 Cor. 7:6 the parousia of Titus denotes his presence or arrival. In view of its parallel with *epiphaneia* (2 Thess. 2:8; 1 Tim. 6:14), it may be rendered "public appearance" or "manifestation of what was hidden." Parallels with *apokalypsis* suggest "disclosure" or "revelation" (Gal. 1:12; 2:2; 2 Cor. 12:7).

Those scholars who insist that this language is *wholly* symbolic *without remainder* of any kind tend to dismiss it as merely a conventional survival of Jewish apocalyptic. This is often based on a mistaken notion of an increasingly realized or present eschatology in Paul. R. H. Charles, for example, proposed four distinct stages of developmental thought in Paul, moving away from the future to the present. But such a view cannot be sustained. John Lowe demonstrated as long ago as 1941 that Paul included futurist and apocalyptic elements in his theology throughout his life ("An Examination of Attempts to Detect Developments in St. Paul's Theology," *JTS* 42 [1941]: 129-42). The majority of Pauline specialists recognize the dual "now" and "not yet" in epistles of various dates. Phil. 3:12, 14, and 21, for example, still retain the hope of a future goal and transformation in the future resurrection. E. Käsemann rightly stresses Paul's crucial debt to apocalyptic as a major theological principle. J. C. Beker, J. L. Martyn, and A. R. Brown make a similar point.

We discuss the phrase "We who are alive and remain" in our entry on the imminence of the end. There are several good exegetical reasons for resisting a simplistic view of this verse, not least P. F. Strawson's distinction between presuppositions and statements, and the careful exegesis of A. L. Moore and others (Moore, *1 and 2 Thessalonians* [London: Nelson, 1969], 69-71, and *The Parousia in the New Testament* [Leiden: Brill, 1966], esp. 108-10).

Hebrews is the only NT writing that explicitly speaks of the "second coming of Christ." Christ, having been offered once (Gk. *hapax*, "once-for-all") to bear the sins of many, "will appear a second time . . . to save those who are eagerly waiting for him" (Heb. 9:28). "The Day" is approaching (10:25). The parousia plays an important role, for "completion" constitutes a major theme. Believers seek a "homeland" (11:14). In Rev. 21:1-2 the home is New Jerusalem. Even in the Fourth Gospel, the future resurrection and the End are taught, as well as resurrection with Christ in the present (John 5:28-29; 6:37, 40, 44, 54). Rev. 22:12 declares, "See, I am coming soon; my reward is with me," that is, the "reward" of Christ's presence.

After the close of the NT canon, the *Didachē* still expresses longing for Christ's return (*Didachē* 10.5-6; 16.1). Clement of Rome warns readers against skepticism concerning the coming of Christ (*1 Clem.* 23.5; cf. 2 Pet. 3:4-5). Justin Martyr speaks of "two advents of Christ" (*First Apology* 52), as does Irenaeus (*Against Heresies* 4.32.1). Tertullian quotes 1 Thess. 4:13-18 almost verbatim (*On the Resurrection of the Flesh* 4; ANF 3:562; *Against Marcion* 5.15 and 20; ANF 3:462 and 473; and *On Prayer* 29; ANF 3:691). Origen also quotes Paul on the parousia (*Against Celsus* 2.65 and 5.17; ANF 4:458 and 550). Lactantius alludes to 1 Thess. 4:14-16 in *The Divine Institutes* 2.13 (ANF 7:61). After Nicaea the allusions in the Fathers became too numerous to quote. In later years, death overtook Aquinas before he could elaborate on the parousia, but he spoke of the future hope in God (*Su Th* 2.2, qu. 17, arts. 1 and 2). The Reformers reaffirmed the creeds: "He shall come again with glory to judge both the living and the dead."

Since the Reformation modern theology has embraced many twists and turns concerning belief in the parousia. Process theology and the work of Teilhard de Chardin affirm futurity, even if their view of the parousia is not conventional. However, in recent years a powerful advocate of a traditional view of the parousia has been J. Moltmann, especially in *The Coming of God* (London: SCM, 1996) and related works. (*See also* **Imminence of the End; Last Judgment; Resurrection of the Dead.**)

Reading: G. R. Beasley-Murray, *Jesus and the Last Days* (Peabody, Mass.: Hendrickson, 1995); J. T. Caroll and A. R. Brown, *The Return of Jesus* (Peabody, Mass.: Hendrickson, 2000); E. Daley, *The Hope of the Early Church* (Cambridge: CUP, 1991); J. Moltmann, *The Coming of God* (London: SCM, 1996); A. L. Moore, *The Parousia in the New Testament* (Leiden: Brill, 1966); N. T. Wright, *Surprised by Hope* (London: SPCK, 2007).

Pascal, Blaise

Blaise Pascal's experience of conversion was the foundation of his spirituality. Pascal (1623-1662) had already established a serious reputation as a scientist and mathematician when he discovered a direct and personal experience of Christ in 1654, subsequent to an earlier experience of 1646. He planned to write an *Apology for the Christian Religion,* which remained unfinished, but was part-published posthumously in his *Pensées* (1670). In his religious thought, he never questioned his scientific method. He argued, "Religion is not contrary to reason," although reason is worthy of reverence and respect. He argued not against metaphysical claims, but against obstacles to faith within the self, especially what he called careless skepticism. He is often mistakenly called a fideist, because of his language about "reasons of the heart." But he retained a positive evaluation of reason and did not defend irrational faith. He argued that Christian faith gives the best explanation of the human condition, which is both "wretched" and proud, but also capable of knowing and meeting Jesus Christ.

Pastoral Theology

Pastoral theology is sometimes called *practical theology,* although the latter is usually more narrowly geared to training for the ministry. Scotland still has ministerial training in universities, but this usually takes place in theological seminaries in America and theological colleges or "courses" in England. Schleiermacher defended ministerial training within the university, in parallel with law and medicine. It primarily includes pastoral care and flourishing, but to this end it may also include education, preaching, mission, and even liturgy, doctrine, and social work. Such writers as Richard Baxter, *The Reformed Pastor* (1656), and George Herbert, *A Priest to the Temple* or *The Country Parson* (1652), have contributed classics on the subject.

Very frequently pastoral theology relates to individual or particular situations. Don Browning, for example, argues that it is "mediated to individuals and groups in all their situational, existential, and developmental particularity" (*Practical Theology* [San Francisco: Harper and Row, 1983], 187). Paul Ballard declares, "Pastoral theology is reflection on the pastoral situation. The pastoral situation is by definition particular in time and space" ("Pastoral Theology or Theology of Reconciliation," *Theology* 91 [1988]: 375). Thus pastoral theology resists the merely general or quantifiable. Edward Farley regards it as "wisdom-based action" (in Browning, *Practical Theology,* 23).

In America, Anton Boisen developed the Clinical Pastoral Association in the 1930s, and greatly influenced pastoral theology not least through the Chicago Theological Seminary. S. Hiltner effectively succeeded him, working in pastoral care and psychotherapy, partly through his pastoral counseling. In England, Frank Lake also combined clinical practice and pastoral counseling, including fashionable talk about the "reconciliation of memories" and aspects of Jüng. However, many now regard this "clinical" approach as overdone and perhaps passé. Charles Gerkin in *The Living Human Document: Re-envisioning Pastoral Counselling in a Hermeneutical Mode* (Nashville: Abingdon, 1983), and to a lesser extent David Capps, *Pastoral Care and Hermeneutics* (Philadelphia: Fortress, 1984), attack the outworn "therapeutic model" in pastoral theology, calling for a deeper application of a "hermeneutical model" for understanding interpersonal action. Capps is more theological in his emphasis. Very recently, in 2013, Glynn Harrison, emeritus professor of psychiatry at Bristol, warned readers against the current trend of "self-esteem" as bordering on undue "liking of the self," after the self-esteem movement took off in the 1960s. He concludes, "The primacy of self-admiration became the default cultural mode," but repeatedly results in "negative findings" ("The Ego-Trip Generation," *Commentary* [Summer 2013]: 17).

The Bible offers many examples of addressing pastoral problems. Job confronts the problem of suffering; Ecclesiastes confronts a sense of chance and meaninglessness; Hosea speaks of God's passionate love; Mark addresses the cost of discipleship; Paul takes on the opposite problem of legalism and license in Galatians; 1 Corinthians stresses the need for "building up" and unity, and for generous, patient love. 1 Corinthians and the Pastoral Epistles abound in instructions and guidance about ministry. Some of this may call into question Hiltner's case-study approach, although in another sense it underlines the importance of context and situation. There is always scope for serious and respected pastors to take younger "beginning" pastors around their parish with them, much as hospital consultants may add practical training to their teaching of their successors. A useful current survey is M. Percy, *The Ecclesial Canopy* (Aldershot: Ashgate, 2012).

Patriarchate
In the history of the church the term "patriarch" emerged as a title for the bishops (in practice, primates or archbishops) of the five major sees of Rome, Alexandria, Antioch, Constantinople, and Jerusalem. Rome, Alexandria, and Antioch were recognized as patriarchates at the Council of Nicaea (325), and Jerusalem and Constantinople at Chalcedon (451). More recently the title has been extended in the Eastern Orthodox Church.

Patripassianism
Patripassianism flourished in the early third century, especially in the cases of Praxeas and Noetus. They so strongly emphasized the deity of Christ that they asserted that God was born, suffered, and died. It is also known as modalism or Monarchianism, in which Sabellius was involved.

Patristic/Patristics
Patristics is the theological study that relates to the Fathers (Lat. *patres*) of the church. The patristic period ranges from at least Irenaeus (c. 130–c. 200) until Augustine (354-430), Gregory of Rome (c. 540-604), or John of Damascus (c. 675-749). Chronologically the period is divided into the Ante-Nicene and Post-Nicene

Fathers, and geographically into the Eastern and Western Fathers. Some include the Apostolic Fathers from Clement to Barnabas or the apologists, while at the later end the Eastern Church sometimes includes Photius (c. 810-895). Gregory in some respects better represents the beginning of the medieval church. From 1951 patristic conferences were called, originally by F. L. Cross.

Pelagius

Pelagius (c. 355-420) was an Irish ascetic layman and monk who attempted to promote stricter moral rigor in the church. He believed that Augustine's dictum "Command what you will and grant what you command" (*Confessions* 10.29) undermined necessary moral struggle. He wrote a *Commentary on Romans* between 406 and 410. Shortly afterward he was supported by Caelestius in his promotion of human freedom and moral choice. Sin, he argued, required an act of will; humankind is not so corrupted by an inherited nature as to render a moral act of will powerless. He appeared in Rome shortly after 400. Against Augustine, he asserted that human nature is absolutely unimpaired by sin, and is in a position of equilibrium. He rejected the notion of "sins of weakness." Augustine's teaching was not a reaction to Pelagius, for he had written *Ad Simplicianum* by 397, before Pelagius publicized his ideas. Pelagius claimed that Adam was created mortal, whether he sinned or not, and he rejected Traducianism. He saw redemption as the *completion* of human nature. He rejected the derivation of human sin from Adam, as arguably Origen did. Augustine conceded that he was "a holy man, who has made no small progress in the Christian life" (*On the Merits and Remission of Sins* 3.1; *NPNP*, ser. 1, 5:69). Nevertheless, Augustine wrote at least thirteen treatises that are collected under the title "Anti-Pelagian" writings (*NPNF*, ser. 1, vol. 5).

Pentecostals, Pentecostalism

(*See also* **Renewal Movement**.) Most Pentecostals trace their historical roots to Charles F. Parham (1873-1929) and William J. Seymour (1870-1922). Prior to them, one could find more indirect roots in Edward Irving (1792-1834), who stressed the gifts of the Spirit in 1 Cor. 12:8-10; in Benjamin H. Irwin; in John Fletcher, successor to Wesley; and in the Holiness Movement. A. B. Simpson (1843-1919) also emphasized the "fourfold gospel" of Christ as Savior, Sanctifier, Healer, and Coming King, and looked for the "latter rain" of a new Pentecost with reference to Joel 2:28. Nevertheless, Pentecostals generally trace a more direct link with Charles Parham in about 1901 and with William Seymour's revival in 1905-1906. Others point to outbursts of speaking in tongues in India, and even to vague affinities with Montanism, Tertullian, and the early Syrian church.

Parham has become partly eclipsed by Seymour because at times he showed a racist tone. Parham founded a Bible school in Kansas at Topeka, and began to teach a "full" gospel of justification, sanctification, Spirit baptism, divine healing, and the imminence of the end-time, or return of Christ, in a premillennial mode.

Donald Dayton argues, "These . . . themes are well-nigh universal within the [Pentecostal] movement" (*Theological Roots of Pentecostalism* [Grand Rapids: Baker Academic, 1987], 22). Like Simpson, Parham looked for "the latter rain" of a new Pentecost, and in 1901 this outlook spread to his community. It was believed that healing and miracles would follow "dryness," and in that year speaking in tongues became "an inseparable part of the Baptism of the Holy Spirit" (*A Voice Crying in the Wilderness* [Baxter Springs, Kans.: Apostolic Faith Bible College, 1902], 35). Parham called this "the Apostolic Faith Movement," arguing that it reflected the age of the apostles. Several thousand were converted to the movement, among whom was Seymour, and it reached its peak in 1906. However, this soon split apart in what can only be regarded as a power struggle.

Meanwhile Seymour pastored an Apostolic Faith mission at Azusa Street, Los Angeles. The three years 1906-1909 became the time of revival. As an Afro-American he preached in the "call and response" mode familiar to black churches. Surprisingly, when he visited the scene in 1906, Parham was unimpressed with "animalisms . . . shaking, jibbering, chattering . . . meaningless sounds" (C. M. Robeck, "Seymour," in *International Dictionary of Pentecostal and Charismatic Movements,* ed. S. M. Burgess [Grand Rapids: Zondervan, 2003], 1055-56). Speaking in tongues remained the main criterion for baptism in the Spirit, although Seymour himself gave greater priority to the fruit of love. He also called for unity, even though Parham set up a rival community nearby. From 1907 to 1919 he traveled to a number of other states. Eventually his congregation dwindled, and Robeck comments that he was forsaken "by the people he had been called to serve" (1057).

A. Anderson and W. Hollenweger call attention to the rise of "speaking in tongues" in independent churches in Africa, India, and "non-white indigenous churches" (*Pentecostals after a Century* [Sheffield: Sheffield Academic Press, 1999], 34). This involved the Pyongyang Revival of 1907 in Korea, and the community at Mukti, India. Some cite the Welsh Revival of 1904. To those outside the movement, however, the most puzzling phenomenon is the ready divisions and splits that seem to have more to do with desire for power and with personal relationships and personalities than with doctrine, when we might have imagined that the Spirit would bring unity.

We cannot trace every figure of this movement in detail. Alfred Garr (1874-1944), a graduate of Asbury College, saw speaking in tongues as the "initial" experience of the Spirit. In Calcutta, however, he discovered that "tongues" had nothing to do with Bengali or Tibetan languages, as he had supposed. He also ventured a "prophecy" that failed. Frank Ewart (1876-1947) received "baptism in the Spirit" in 1908, but became assistant to W. H. Durham, who stressed more strongly "the finished work of Christ." Eudorus Bell (1866-1923) chaired the founding of the Assemblies of God in 1913, after receiving "baptism in the Spirit" in 1908. Yet Bell became associated with the "Oneness" Movement, and became rebaptized. Mention must be made of Aimee Semple McPherson (1890-1944) and her Four Square Gospel Movement. She was ordained in the Assemblies of God, and became a "faith" missionary in China. On the death of her husband she returned to Los Angeles, and in 1923 founded the Lighthouse for Intentional Foursquare Evangelism Bible College. The four elements of this were: Christ as Savior, Christ as baptizer in the Spirit, Christ as healer, and Christ as coming king. She had an enormous impact on millions of people. Yet, like Parham and many other leaders, her ministry ended in ambiguous and controversial circumstances after 1926. She suffered a breakdown in 1930. In 1933 I. Q. Spencer founded the Elim Fellowship of Churches. Hence, broadly within the Pentecostal tradition we have (i) Assemblies of God, (ii) the Foursquare Gospel Movement, and (iii) the Elim churches. In Britain the history and ethos of these movements may differ in details from their American counterparts.

The main themes of Pentecostalism include: first, a "restorationist" understanding of the NT as offering a blueprint of the apostolic age for today. Second, premillennialism and the rapture, following H. Drummond, E. Irving, and J. N. Darby, are believed by most streams. Today this kind of eschatology is associated with John F. Walvoord of Dallas Theological Seminary, and at a more popular level with Hal Lindsey. Third, baptism in the Holy Spirit remains *the* hallmark. F. D. Macchia calls Spirit baptism "an organizing principle of a Pentecostal theology" and "a central theological concern" (*Baptized in the Spirit* [Grand Rapids: Zondervan, 2006], 17 and 21). A number of "mainstream" church theologians would affirm the validity of the *experience* to which this term refers, but also strongly dispute whether Paul or other NT writers *understood the term* in the sense accepted among Pentecostals. They often prefer some such term as the Spirit's "filling" or "equipping." More seriously, Luther, Hodge, Kuyper, and many others would see *sanctification as a process, not as an event.* Their understanding of such passages as 1 Cor. 12:13 remains initiatory and corporate, as A. Zwiep strongly argues. The fourth theme is speaking with tongues. Whether this is "xenolalia," or speaking in known foreign languages, or praise from the heart to God is debated. Most Pentecostals see this as "initial evidence" of baptism in the Spirit. But some, for example, Veli-Matti Kärkkäinen, dissent from this evaluation of tongues. The fifth theme is the link between divine healing and the coming of the kingdom of God. Perhaps surprisingly many mainline NT scholars would agree with this link, but would also argue that since the kingdom of God is both "now" and "not yet," we cannot *always* expect divine healing, to the extent to which it is too often "expected" in Pentecostal and charismatic circles.

Other phenomena, such as postbiblical "prophecy," are not distinctive or peculiar to Pentecostals. This was found among the Montanists, many medieval mystics, and others. The interpretation of "gifts of the Spirit," for example, in 1 Cor. 12:8-10, is shared with many in the Renewal Movement. One problem of tracing a "general" history of the movement is that such sources as *The International Dictionary of Pentecostal and Charismatic Movements* include some fourteen subgroups under "Pentecostals," such as Pentecostal Church of God, Pentecostal Assemblies of Canada, and so forth. Each has its particular emphasis. Further,

Pentecostalism is now a global phenomenon, and the history of its manifestation in Africa, the Middle East, Brazil, Indonesia, the Philippines, Japan, and Korea may have taken different paths. Harvey Cox states that both the Pentecostal Movement and especially women within it "have become the principal carrier of the fastest growing religious movement in the world" (*Fire from Heaven* [Cambridge, Mass.: Da Capo, 1995], 137). He sees a clue to this widespread appeal in their "primal speech" (tongues), "primary piety" (vision, healing, dance), and "primal hope" (the imminence of the End; 82). Preaching often uses narrative, illustration, and testimony, which tend to have priority over technical exegesis, logic, and theory. But the Bible still remains a primary authority, even if seen through the "lens" of experience. Indeed, in recent years attention has been given to hermeneutics.

In recent years more attention also has been given to NT scholarship, especially in Luke and Acts. The Assemblies of God introduced a five-year B.Th. degree in 1947, and by 1957 the Central Bible Institute had introduced a graduate school of religions, with an M.A. in religion. In 1963 the healing evangelist Oral Roberts opened a university in Tulsa, Oklahoma, but others still made accusations of "arid intellectualism"! The largely black Church of God in Christ introduced a more ecumenical degree course in 1970. In 1973 the Melodyland School of Theology was established, although it had collapsed by the 1980s. The Assemblies of God Theological Seminary was established in 1984 and nowadays offers M.Div. and D.Min. degrees. In the early 1980s the institution now known as Regent University, Virginia Beach, Virginia, fulfilled Pat Robertson's vision of a graduate charismatic university. California Theological Seminary was founded in 1984, and Vanguard University and King's College are ongoing. But perhaps more significant is the opening to Pentecostal staff and students of the long-established evangelical seminaries Gordon-Conwell, South Hamilton, Massachusetts, and Fuller Theological Seminary, Pasadena, California. Meanwhile a number of Pentecostal seminaries flourished outside America. In Singapore, the Asia Theological Centre may be mentioned, together with seminaries at Seoul and Taejeon, Korea, and Mattersly Hall in England, as well as many others.

In Pentecostal theological research, a number of new journals since around 1990 are important. Brill of Leiden first published the *Journal of Pentecostal Theology* in 1993, with over twenty volumes up to the current year. Its list of contributors includes established theologians who are not strictly Pentecostals, such as Jürgen Moltmann, as well as those who are, such as Amos Yong. In 1979 the journal *Pneuma* was founded by the Society for Pentecostal Studies, edited by Amos Yong and Dale Coulter, which includes charismatic exponents as well as Pentecostals. There are now almost forty Supplements to the Journal of Pentecostal Theology, now published by Deo, including a work by Simon Chan, *Pentecostal Ecclesiology*, several works on eschatology, and some on Luke-Acts.

The most outstanding Pentecostal biblical scholar is probably Gordon Fee (b. 1934), who taught at Gordon-Conwell Seminary and Regent College, Vancouver.

His major books include a commentary on 1 Corinthians (1987) and *God's Empowering Presence* (Peabody, Mass.: Hendrickson, 1994), which examines Paul's view of the Holy Spirit. He is firmly Pentecostal but does not accept the Pentecostal view of baptism in the Spirit. He sees the Holy Spirit as "the personal presence of God himself" (5-6). Paul understands the Spirit as God's "person, presence, and power" (8). Fee recognizes the christocentric character of 1 Corinthians (85-86). He also acknowledges that "word of wisdom" (1 Cor. 12:8) refers to the message of the crucified Christ as God's true wisdom, and "word of knowledge" as relating to interpreting Scripture or Pauline tradition rightly (166-68). It is surprising that he considers that "gifts of healing" require little comment, since W. Hollenweger and others have accused Pentecostals of holding an oversharp dualism between "supernatural" and "natural." The Greek plural probably denotes "different *kinds* of healing" (*see* **Renewal Movement**). In contrast, Fee recognizes that "tongues" *are* of different kinds, though he views "prophecy" as a spontaneous utterance. He rightly sees 2 Cor. 3:8, 17 in terms of Paul's allusion to Exodus. He accepts that reception of the gospel is a matter of faith in Gal. 3:1-3 (381). In Rom. 8:26-27 he agrees with Macchia that "inexpressible sighs" made to God may include tongues. He finds that some views more in accordance with the NT sometimes provide "an uphill battle" with his fellow Pentecostals.

Among younger Pentecostal scholars, Roger Stronstad wrote *The Charismatic Theology of St. Luke* (Peabody, Mass.: Hendrickson, 1984) and *The Priesthood of All Believers: A Study in Luke's Charismatic Theology*, JPT Supplement, no. 16 (Sheffield: Sheffield Academic Press, 1999); while Robert Menzies wrote *Empowered for Witness: The Spirit in Luke-Acts* (Sheffield: JSOT Press, 1994) and *The Development of Early Pneumatology* (Sheffield: JSOT Press, 1992). Stronstad argues that too many read Luke through Pauline eyes, including even J. D. G. Dunn (*Priesthood*, 10). By contrast, to him Luke's view of the Spirit has as much to do with vocation as with salvation. The Spirit anoints Jesus, for example. Speaking in tongues seems almost to be more "of God" than ordination or the sacraments (30-34). He tends to trust the narrative of Luke-Acts as a *paradigm* or blueprint for much later situations. Yet his books also attempt to draw on Lukan scholarship, as Menzies does, who may perhaps be less extreme.

The entry of Pentecostals into serious scholarship since at least 1990 offers one strong advantage. A second is their self-evaluation and self-criticism, which seem largely to have escaped the Renewal Movement, or at least much of it. This can be seen on Pentecostal Web sites and in journals. They raise queries about social action, pacifism, baptism in the Spirit, and several controversial areas. Yet more exegetical work needs to be done on the "gifts of the Spirit" in 1 Cor. 12:7-10 and 28-30, in conjunction with other passages. A. Zwiep has demonstrated the corporate dimension of "baptism in the Spirit" in 1 Cor. 12:13 and elsewhere (*Church, the Spirit, and the Community of God* [Tübingen: Mohr, 2010], 100-137). More work also needs to be done on Pentecostal hermeneutics, which usually regards a Pentecostal preunderstanding as a fixed presupposition or "lens" of the reader, rather than a moving horizon that the text can correct and expand. Pentecostal hermeneutics also needs to appreciate the diversity of narrative, which is only in some cases a "paradigm" for today. Above all, the notion derived from the Holiness Movement of sanctification as *an event, not a process*, needs to be reexamined in the light of biblical texts, and the scope of "prophecy" and "tongues" also greatly scrutinized with an open mind. Finally the inseparability of the work of the Father, the Son, and the Holy Spirit, much stressed by the Church Fathers, needs more attention, together with the *partial* coming of the kingdom of God in Jesus Christ in relation to healing. Nevertheless, a genuine hunger for the living God in times of dryness, routine, or formalism remains permanently valid and healthy for the church. We assess more related issues under "spiritual gifts" and other questions in the entry under the Renewal Movement. (*See also* **Baptism in the Holy Spirit; Montanism; Renewal Movement; Sanctification.**)

Reading: A. H. Anderson and W. J. Hollenweger, *Pentecostals after a Century* (Sheffield: Sheffield Academic Press, 1999); M. J. Cartledge, *Testimony to the Spirit* (Farnham, U.K., and Burlington, Vt.: Ashgate, 2010); Harvey Cox, *Fire from Heaven* (Cambridge, Mass.: Da Capo, 1995); M.-V. Kärkkäinen, *Pneumatology* (Grand Rapids: Baker Academic, 2002); M.-V. Kärkkäinen, *Holy Spirit and Salvation* (Louisville: John Knox, 2010); F. D. Macchia, *Baptized in the Spirit* (Grand Rapids: Zondervan, 2006); G. B. McGee, ed., *Initial Evidence* (Eugene, Ore.: Wipf and Stock, 1991, 2007).

Perichoresis

Perichoresis is used in the context of the Holy Trinity to denote an *interpenetration* of the persons of the Father, the Son, and the Holy Spirit. Each person remains distinct from the others, but participates fully in their Being and action as one. Athanasius appeals to "I am in the Father and the Father is in me" (John 14:11; cf. 17:21), for what one translator calls *coinherence*. John of Damascus, *De Fide orthodoxa liber quattuor* 1.14 (PL 94:860B), uses *perichoresis* of the Trinity, and J. Moltmann follows his example.

Perseverance

The perseverance of the saints explicitly teaches that God's grace so effectively works in the hearts of believers that God will bring this process to full completion, and that no genuine believer can be "lost" at the End. Believers cannot fall away *finally* from the state of grace. The doctrine is more explicitly called "the final perseverance of the saints." It was first explicitly expounded by Augustine as an implication of election, predestination, and grace, although not prominently. Luther is a little ambiguous, since perseverance still depends on faith, although this is still God-given. Calvin is clear and emphatic in affirming this doctrine. He states, "As to perseverance, it would undoubtedly have been regarded as the gratuitous gift of God, had not the very pernicious error prevailed, that it is bestowed in proportion to human merit" (*Institutes* 2.3.11; Beveridge, 1:261). He cites Augustine in support of this doctrine. It has since become part of Reformed theology, as expounded by H. Bavinck, *Reformed Dogmatics;* G. C. Berkhouwer, *Studies in Dogmatics;* L. Berkhof, *Systematic Theology;* and Charles Hodge, *Systematic Theology*, vol. 2 (Grand Rapids: Eerdmans, 1946), 333-35. The doctrine has been considered most recently by Judith M. Gundry-Wolf, *Paul and Perseverance: Staying In and Falling Away* (Tübingen: Mohr, 1990). This provides a careful exegetical consideration of Pauline material.

The doctrine was stated most explicitly at the Synod of Dort. It declared: "God, who is rich in mercy, according to his unchangeable purpose of election, does not wholly withdraw the Holy Spirit from his own people, even in their grievous falls; nor suffers them to proceed so far as to lose the grace of adoption and forfeit the state of justification" (5, art. 6). Arminius held to a softer approach, and his followers rejected the doctrine. It seemed to them to encourage complacency, and to compromise freedom. Calvin, however, feared that human "cooperating" with God would compromise grace, and assurance, and would hint at the role of human merit. Certainly we cannot judge this doctrine from empirical observation. There are too many unknown factors, and this is not a legitimate human task. Many Christians quote such verses as "No one will snatch them out of my hand" (John 10:28) and nothing "will be able to separate us from the love of God in Christ Jesus our Lord" (Rom. 8:39).

Phenomenology

Phenomenology is not a unified doctrine, but a movement in philosophy. It is most closely associated with E. Husserl (1859-1938), but Heidegger, Sartre, and Merleau-Ponty all interpreted phenomenology differently. It has two basic features: it studies human consciousness, often with an emphasis on directedness or intentionality; and it claims to remain purely descriptive, suspending or "bracketing" any value judgment on the part of the observer or philosopher. It claims to undermine materialism, positivism, and skepticism. Its philosophical analysis of the experiencing subject is complex, but the phenomenology of religion, especially in Karl Jaspers, seeks to remain neutral and purely descriptive. Some of its critics may doubt whether this is actually possible, especially in critical theory, sociology of knowledge, and hermeneutics.

Philo of Alexandria

Philo of Alexandria (c. 20 B.C.–A.D. 50) was broadly contemporary with Paul, and is said by Henry Chadwick and others to be hugely important for understanding Paul and the NT, and for understanding Greek-speaking Judaism (*St. Paul and Philo of Alexandria* [Manchester: Manchester University Press, 1966]). Philo (also called Philo Judaeus) was an exegete and a writer who was fundamentally loyal to Judaism, and wrote to commend Judaism to the Greco-Roman world. In A.D. 39 or 40 he was chosen to lead a Jewish delegation to the Roman emperor, Gaius Caligula, and hence had reasonable means or influence. He was fully familiar with Greek philosophy, especially Plato and the Stoics. He showed courage in explaining why Jews could not accept statues of Caligula in their synagogues. He is known mainly for his allegorical exegesis of the OT, and for his view of the Logos as a creative agent of God. He interpreted the narratives of the Pentateuch allegorically, viewing the Mosaic laws as the product of right reason and virtue. Abraham is seen as migrating from bondage to virtue, and as a prototype to the true sage. Sarah represents Wisdom or Virtue. Moses is also a savior who liberates humankind from bondage to matter. Philo left a prodigious corpus of literature. Whereas he used to be regarded as a lone, perhaps eccentric, speculative thinker, nowadays he is more readily understood as representing a wider tradition in Alexandria and in Greek-speaking Diaspora Judaism. He could never have agreed with John that the Logos became flesh (John 1:14), although there are various terminological parallels with Paul.

Photius of Constantinople
Photius of Constantinople (c. 810–c. 895) was the most prolific writer of the ninth-century Byzantine renaissance. He had originally planned to enter a monastery, but decided to seek the career of a scholar and statesman. In 838 he became imperial ambassador to Baghdad, and was endlessly embroiled in political upheavals. In the field of scholarship he wrote the *Bibliotheca,* a massive reference work of some 280 volumes of the Church Fathers, collected in analyses and extracts. His *Amphilochia* considers numerous exegetical and doctrinal issues. His politics, however, brought him into conflicts over the appointment of patriarchs and the iconoclastic controversy, and with the bishop or pope of Rome. He regarded Rome's missionaries in Bulgaria as an intrusion into the jurisdiction of the patriarch in the East, and his *Treatise on the Holy Spirit* provided numerous reasons for rejecting the Western *filioque* clause in the creed, that is, the double procession of the Spirit from the Father and the Son. Photius was seen by many as an outsider imposed on the church by the emperor, and he became heavily involved with political extremists. Through his influence, it became virtually impossible to dialogue and to solve the controversy about the double procession between East and West. Today there is greater sympathy for what each side hopes to protect, at least among theologians. Some have suggested: "From the Father through the Son."

Pietism
Pietism constitutes an influential post-Reformation movement, which chronologically ranged from P. J. Spener (1635-1705) to F. C. Oetinger (1702-1782) and Nikolaus Count von Zinzendorf (1700-1760). Generally it characterizes a reaction of many eighteenth-century religious practitioners to secular rationalism, on one side, and arid Protestant orthodoxy on the other, which in many cases followed the Reformation. Pietism is not limited to Lutheranism, nor is it necessarily antagonistic to moderate biblical criticism. Pietists were primarily concerned about personal renewal, in contrast to systems of doctrine or theology.

They emphasized the work of the Holy Spirit in personal renewal. Regeneration, new birth, or "being born again" was their keynote. They stressed justification, conversion, sanctification, and vocation. Spener is often recognized as the first of the seventeenth-century Pietists. Those who suggest a later date tend to refer to his ardent follower A. H. Francke (1663-1727), who defended his work. Francke was not a theologian, but stressed new birth *(Wiedergeburt)*.

Under Francke's leadership Halle became a center for the movement. The Pietists stressed not only education, but also social concern and foreign mission. Yet, like most movements within the church, Pietism included a spectrum of positions. For example, Gottfried Arnold promoted mysticism, separatist tendencies, and support for Boehme and quietism. Many refer to him as a radical Pietist. By contrast, the philosopher Oetinger, and especially the expositor J. A. Bengel (1687-1752), were competent scholars and exegetes in the Lutheran tradition. In many respects Zinzendorf was more moderate than the radical Pietists, but placed great emphasis on missionary concern. Zinzendorf also emphasized the human heart, and shared many concerns with John Wesley. The movement gave rise to some terminological confusion. It remains active today largely under the term "Moravian," which stresses social concern and mission.

Pilgrimage

Pilgrimage has two distinct meanings in Christian theology. Perhaps the more popular use of the term concerns pilgrimages to holy places as specific acts of devotion, or sometimes in the Roman Catholic Church as acts of penance. Well-known examples would include pilgrimages to Lourdes or one of the Marian shrines, or to the Holy Land. The Catholic and Orthodox Churches often encourage these, but Reformation churches often have suspicions about "works" of devotion. The more theological meaning of "pilgrimage" is that for every Christian the *whole* of the Christian life is a pilgrimage. In Heb. 11:13 Christians are "strangers and pilgrims on the earth" (Gk. *xenoi kai parepidēmoi*). Danker translates *parepidēmos* as "staying for a while in a strange or foreign place" or "residing temporarily," as also in 1 Pet. 1:1 (BDAG 775). Paul declares, "Our citizenship is in heaven" (Phil. 3:20). But, more than this, Hebrews depicts the whole Christian life as an ongoing, forward-looking pilgrimage. Robert Jewett entitles his commentary on Hebrews *Letter to Pilgrims* (New York: Pilgrim Press, 1981), and E. Käsemann calls his commentary *The Wandering People of God* (Minneapolis: Augsburg, 1984). W. Manson called this epistle the call to take "an irreversible step" into the horizon of eschatology. C. K. Barrett speaks of "the central place of eschatology in Hebrews," which longs for future rest and completion, but meanwhile must suffer hardships ("The Eschatology of the Epistle to the Hebrews," in *The Background to the New Testament and Its Eschatology*, ed. W. D. Davies and D. Daube [Cambridge: CUP, 1956], 363-93). The onward call is part of the "now" and "not yet" of eschatology; Christians are like Abraham, who "set out, not knowing where he was going" (Heb. 11:8), but sought a city to come. The whole of Hebrews 11 maintains this theme. J. Moltmann applies it in general to the Exodus theme of the journey to the Promised Land.

Within this theological home, pilgrimages in the more popular sense can have a place. They are not necessarily "works," but symbols or sacraments (in the broad sense) of the Christian tradition. They follow spiritually the journeys of Abraham (Gen. 12:1) and Jesus (Matt. 8:20), and recognize that Christians are only temporary residents on the earth, whose goal lies ahead. For the sake of the goal, they will accept struggles, difficulties, and hardships. Barrett likened Hebrews to John Bunyan's *Pilgrim's Progress*.

Reading: C. Bartholomew and Fred Hughes, eds., *Explorations in a Christian Theology of Pilgrimage* (Aldershot, U.K., and Burlington, Vt.: Ashgate, 2004).

Plantinga, Alvin

Alvin Plantinga (b. 1932) is emeritus professor of philosophy at the University of Notre Dame, and for many years taught at Calvin College, Grand Rapids. He is widely known in many parts of the world for his work in philosophy of religion, epistemology, Christian apologetics, and metaphysics. *Time* magazine called him "America's leading orthodox Protestant philosopher of God." Although his research and writing include the most technical and rigorous work on modal logic, his Web site includes extraordinarily clear and basic answers to questions that ordinary people ask about belief in God.

Plantinga studied at the University of Michigan under William Alston, the philosopher of language, and then took his Ph.D. from Yale in 1958. He began teaching at Yale, moved to Calvin College in 1963, became a professor of philosophy at Notre Dame in 1982, and formally retired in 2010, when he returned to Calvin. He holds honorary doctorates from Glasgow, Calvin, North Park, the Free University of Amsterdam, and elsewhere. One of his most widely known formulations is a defense of the ontological argument through the method of modal logic. He argues that while Kant and Russell may effectively counter Anselm's first formulation of it, in which Russell substitutes "instantiation" for predication, this still leaves the second formulation intact. Plantinga extends the modal logic of Hartshorne and Malcolm to argue that "maximal greatest" can be instantiated in all "possible worlds." Logical necessity as such does not exhaust the multiform sense in which we may ascribe necessary being to God (Plantinga, *The Nature of Necessity* [Oxford: Clarendon, 1974], and *The Ontological Argument* [New York: Doubleday, 1965]). In *God and Other Minds* (Ithaca, N.Y.: Cornell University Press, 1967, 1991), Plantinga considers the three main arguments of the existence of God. He argues that we should be less hasty to dismiss the teleological argument, because we can make a commonsense affirmation of it, in the same way we accept a commonsense view of the existence of other minds. There is an analogy, he concludes, between the two issues. "Belief in other minds and belief in God are in the same epistemological boat; hence if either is rational, so is the other" (cf. 245-72).

In his book *God, Freedom, and Evil* (Grand Rapids: Eerdmans, 1974), Plantinga is no less robust of a theist in his reply to the problem of evil. On his Web site he declares that even if we do not *know* why God permits evil, this does not mean that God *has* no reason. Why should he choose to tell us everything? In his main work he sets out the "Free Will Defense Argument," and considers the four key presuppositions that Epicurus, Hume, and J. L. Mackie have considered to be logically contradictory: God is omnipotent and *could* prevent evil; God is omniscient, and therefore *aware* of evil; God is good, and would therefore *will* to prevent evil; but there is evil in the world. Plantinga argues that there could be evil in the world if moral goodness requires free moral creatures (i.e., those which are not forced only to do good, as if they were robots). God cannot *cause* or *determine* humans to do only what is right, if they are to be *free moral beings*. A wholly good world peopled by free moral beings is not *logically* possible. Even if such a world is "possible," it cannot *logically* be actualized. Plantinga also takes into account what he calls "transworld depravity." Robert Adams and William Alston are sympathetic with this argument, although J. L. Mackie predictably objects that it presupposes a given view of freedom, which philosophers usually call "incompatibilist."

In his epistemology Plantinga developed his notion of "basicality," the legitimacy of holding theistic beliefs *without* these beliefs being dependent on *other* nontheistic beliefs. This approach is entitled "reformed epistemology." He argues both against evidentialism and classical "foundationalism." The beginning of this approach had appeared in *God and Other Minds* and (with Wolterstorff) *Faith and Rationality* (Notre Dame: University of Notre Dame Press, 1984) and is further developed in three books on warrant and belief, namely, *Warrant: The Current Debate; Warrant and Proper Function;* and *Warranted Christian Belief* (all New York: OUP, 1993, 1994, and 1999). The books argue that theistic belief is not irrational, unqualified, or unwarranted. In the first part of *Warranted Christian Belief* Plantinga argues that "natural" knowledge of God is impossible. In the second part he attacks Kant's dualism of the two "worlds." He then looks at justified or reasonable belief, as Wolterstorff argues in his book on Locke. He next considers "warrant" in the light of Aquinas, Calvin, and Paul in Rom. 1:18-20. He attacks Freud and Marx as reductionist and insufficiently comprehensive. Finally he considers the issue in the light of human sin.

Plantinga has continued to write. He's written, for example, *Knowledge of God* (with M. Tooley, 2008) and *Science and Religion* (with Daniel Dennett, 2010). He is without doubt one of the most fertile, creative, and learned philosophers of the Christian faith today.

Plato

Plato (428-348 B.C.), probably the most influential philosopher of the Greco-Roman world, has hugely influenced Christian thought, even more perhaps than Aristotle. He was born in Athens into a distinguished, aristocratic family, and came strongly under the influence of Socrates (c. 470-399), especially in his earlier thought. The medium of his early writings is usually that of dialogue, which often involves sophisticated argument and a fine literary style. His *Protagoras* and *Symposium* constitute two outstanding examples.

Some of Plato's earliest dialogues constitute defenses of Socrates, of which *The Apology of Socrates* represents a classic example. This work seeks to reproduce speeches that Socrates gave at his trial, but it is difficult to know how much is due to Plato's editing and elaboration. Another work, which many date early (although some place it in the middle period), *Gorgias,* presents a dialogue about the choice between a philosophical and a political life. The dialogue partners include rhetoricians, sophists, and exponents of religion. Other early works focus on ethical problems, as in *Charmides,* which urges moderation. From Socrates Plato reproduces the basic philosophical distinction between mere *opinion* (Gk. *doxa*) and genuine *knowledge (epistēmē).* Opinion might change; but genuine knowledge remains constant.

Plato's *Symposium, Meno, Phaedo,* and the *Republic* belong to his middle period. Metaphysics, psychology, and epistemology become more prominent. Most references to Socrates now become expositions of Plato's own views. The dialogue form fades, and is more of a contrived way to express these views. The dominating themes that have sometimes influenced Christian thought are his dualism (both of mind and body, and of the noumenal and phenomenal worlds) and his theory of forms. These embrace both the middle and the later periods. The middle period presents constructive philosophical doctrines, rather than argumentative discourse. The theory of forms seems to be first formulated in the *Symposium,* and more fully expounded in *Phaedo* and the *Republic.* As centuries later, in the later work of Wittgenstein, much time is devoted to exploring definitions of words, which Wittgenstein called their "logical grammar." We might try to define "a straight line." This might be as straight as a draftsman can make it. But usually even the best attempt will deviate at least a little from "pure" straightness. We have in our minds an a priori concept, not derived from the everyday world, the idea of absolute straightness. This constitutes the standard to which everything attempts to aim. This cannot exist in the "phenomenal" world of contingent objects. Absolute straightness exists only as a "form" or an "idea" (Gk. *eidos*) in the realm above the phenomenal. This realm was known by Plato as the "noumenal," perhaps originally from the Greek *nous,* "mind." The same principle applies to trying to draw a perfect circle: this can be "perfect" only as a form or an idea. But we derive our daily verdict about a "good" or "bad" circle only from the form or idea. This principle can be applied even to abstract nouns. Is a person, for example, "fearless"? Fearlessness in the absolute sense cannot be achieved in this world, where fearlessness, according to Plato, is the absolute form of fearlessness. It is similar, he argues, in the case of goodness, beauty, or virtue. On this basis some speak of the "ontology of concepts." It may be asked: Do these absolutes actually exist, or are they merely mental constructs? On the basis of a commonsense approach to reality, it looks as if ordinary language demands that an absolute exists. But if we move down the road from Locke to Berkeley to Kant, it need not surprise us if these are simply instrumental constructs created by the human mind to cope with, or make sense of, reality. Plato, many argue, does not seem to give a definitive reply to this question, although he often speaks as if forms inhabit a suprasensory realm of reality.

Plato raised another question throughout this period; it concerns the immortality of the soul. The soul seemed to Plato to be eternal and changeless, because it belonged to the suprasensory realm. In the phenomenal world all is change and decay or simply copies of the absolute forms. He believed that the body (Gk. *sōma*) is contingent and mortal. It might, or might not, have existed. Indeed, the whole phenomenal world is inhabited by "copies" of ideal forms. In *Republic* 7, Plato portrays people who are condemned to live in a cave, with fire illuminating them from behind. He comments, "they see nothing of themselves, but their shadows. . . . The only real things for them would be the shadows." Nevertheless, a "higher world" exists, as it were, outside the cave. In the cave people see only changing, imperfect, time-conditioned appearances. The *Republic* also presents a political argument on the basis of forms. Plato imagines a good society ruled by a philosopher-statesman, who provides a blueprint for goodness and happiness. His mind has been prepared for abstract thought by philosophical training. Mathematics also has its place in the realm of forms. The phenomenal world can only approximate to the true and unblemished principles of mathematics.

In Plato's late period, *The Laws* and *Parmenides* raise particular problems. *Parmenides* offers a series of criticisms of the theory of forms. For example, since large objects may exist, does this imply the existence of a form of "largeness"? But if this were the case, could there be a limitless number of forms, which represent different types of largeness? In *Timaeus* Plato discusses the perfect order of forms, and compares it with the phenomenal world, which is obviously disordered. Does the world of forms contain such diverse ideas as the soul, triangles, objects, people, and space? But in this work Plato also speaks of a creator god. Other later works include *The Sophist* and *Theaetus*, which, in turn, attack Protagoras's relativist theory of truth. *The Sophist* confronts the problem of how "what is not" cannot be an object of thought or language.

In Christian thought the influence of Plato varied considerably, depending on the Christian thinker in question. Clearly he influenced the Jewish philosopher Philo of Alexandria, who was a near contemporary of Paul's letter-writing period. The early apologists used Platonic concepts to present a rational case for Christianity. Justin Martyr spoke of his pilgrimage from Stoicism to Aristotle and the Pythagoreans until he met a Platonist, whose "perception of immaterial things . . . furnished my mind with wings" (*Dialogue with Trypho* 2). Clement of Alexandria declared, "What is Plato but Moses speaking Attic Greek" (*Stromata* 1.22). Origen provides another example, and Augustine of Hippo praised Plato's account of nonmaterial reality, and considered that he offered a limited natural theology

(*City of God* 8.4-12). On the other hand, other Christian thinkers, for example, Tertullian, declared their hostility to philosophy, whether Plato's or not. In the first two centuries "Middle Platonism" and Plotinus urged a sharp dualism between the changing material world and the world of eternal forms. Neoplatonism is associated with Plotinus's successor, Porphyry (c. 232-303). Christian Platonism was espoused in the fifteenth century by J. Colet, and later by the Cambridge Platonists. W. R. Inge (1860-1954) was a follower of their work.

Reading: P. Friedländer, *Plato* (London and New York: Routledge, 1969); L. P. Gerson, *God and Greek Philosophy* (London and New York: Routledge, 1990); G. Grube, *Plato's Thought* (London: Athlone, 1980); R. Kraut, ed., *The Cambridge Companion to Plato* (Cambridge: CUP, 1992); Plato, *Complete Works* (Indianapolis: Hackett, 1997).

Plotinus

Plotinus (c. 205-270) was the founder of Neoplatonism. He was a disciple of Ammonius Saccas, traveled to Persia to explore Eastern thought, and returned to Rome in 244 to found his own school of philosophy. He is also regarded as a mystic with tendencies toward pantheism. He rejected both Gnostic dualism and Christian notions of revelation. God, as the first principle, or the One (Gk. *hen*), lies beyond thought and speech. However, below the One in Plotinus's hierarchy comes the divine mind (Gk. *nous*), which enters the world of ideas, or Plato's "forms." Finally, the third order of reality below this is "the soul" (Gk. *psuchē*), which interacts with the material world. Like his pupil and biographer Porphyry, he advocates intellectual contemplation. This may purify the soul, remove attachment to the world of sense, and perhaps attain union with God. In contrast to the Christian doctrine of grace, human beings may achieve this by reason. Neoplatonism became the dominant philosophical movement of the Greco-Roman world in late antiquity. His writings are the so-called *Enneads,* which share much of Plato's philosophy. The material world of the senses constitutes imperfect copies of supersensible ideas or forms. Plotinus's dualism extends not only to the world of forms and the material world, but also to the dualism of mind and body.

Pluralism

It is sometimes implied that religious pluralism is a new phenomenon of the late twentieth and twenty-first centuries. But Christians faced "pluralism" from the very first, until at least the sixth century. Even then, Christianity tended to hold sway as an "official" religion only in the lands of the former Roman Empire since Constantine (313), and eastern Europe and America, until the twentieth century. In lands beyond Europe, Christianity regularly constituted a minority religion, or at least one of several religions. The NT Christians and the Church Fathers expected to face the problem of pluralism, and the church grew in numbers, faith, and influence, no less. Some would argue that it grew with more zealous faith. Missionary activity and Christian witness were obvious imperatives. Thinkers such as Clement of Alexandria and Origen saw alien cultural themes as phenomena from which they could learn, and even Tertullian, who radically opposed Greek thought, nevertheless assimilated aspects of Stoicism, for better or worse. Attitudes to Jewish faith were often ambiguous, valuing insights that ultimately rested on the OT or Hebrew Bible, while attacking some features of later Judaism.

In the modern era, however, the scope and significance of pluralism have dramatically changed. We must formally distinguish extrareligious pluralism, which in effect denotes interreligious dialogue, and intrareligious pluralism. This denotes relations between traditions within one given religion. The philosophical pluralism of postmodernism adds to the complexity of the subject, while ethically the problem of the limits of tolerance has again raised its head, after the issue was first raised by the Deists and others. As far as postmodernism is concerned, F. Lyotard has grossly overpressed Kahn's notion of incommensurability to argue that different viewpoints simply cannot be reconciled, because there can be no rational arbitration between them. In *The Differend* (Manchester: Manchester University Press, 1990) he argues that one view will impose "rules of discourse" on the other, and that we can only settle for a plurality that he calls "paganism," in contrast to the monotheism of the three Abrahamic religions.

In extrareligious pluralism some draw a careful distinction between the three "Abrahamic" faiths of Judaism, Christianity, and Islam, and on the other side Hinduism, Buddhism, and other "Eastern" religions. Some emphasize overlappings in the Christian use of the Hebrew Bible, or Islam's reverence for Jesus as a prophet, and seek common ground in shared ethics. In interreligious dialogue, Küng and Rahner, on the Catholic side, and Hick on the Protestant side have made overtures to other religions, which some would call generous, and others compromising. Both Küng and Hick argue that there can be no peace between rival Absolutes. Küng argues that there can be no common language as long as each religion claims "unique superiority over all the others." Hick hopes for dialogue to lead to "mutual acceptance of world religions as having an equally valid relation to ultimate reality" (lecture delivered to the Institute for Islamic Culture and Thought, Tehran, February 2005). Rahner endorses the assertion by Vatican II that "Those who through no fault of their own do not know the Gospel of Christ . . . may achieve eternal salvation." Rahner declares that everyone depends on Christ, but that a "person lives in the grace of God and attains salvation outside explicitly constituted Christianity." This can be achieved through what he calls "Anonymous Christianity."

Many insist, on the contrary, "There is salvation in no one else, for there is no other name under heaven . . . by which we must be saved" (Acts 4:12), in explicit and concise terms. Such advocates are often called "exclusivist." Küng and Hick would be called "inclusivist." The Church of England Doctrine Commission has called for a "third model," which would transcend both of these, or even "an open and generous exclusivism," or "a Christian exclusivism," or "Trinitarian pluralism" (*The Mystery of Salvation* [London: Church House Publishing, 1995], 171). These comments suggest the ongoing nature of the problem of pluralism, and the difficulty of reaching an acceptable resolution. Most Christian thinkers are also unhappy with the divisions of intrareligious pluralism within the Christian churches. (*See also* **Clement of Alexandria; Küng, Hans; Rahner, Karl.**)

Pneumatomachi

The Pneumatomachi (from Gk. *pneuma,* "spirit," and *machē,* "battle, strife, dispute") held that the Holy Spirit is only a creature (Gk. *ktisma*), created or made by God, and differing from the angels not in kind but in degree. They flourished in the fourth century, and were opposed especially by Athanasius and Basil. Athanasius also called them "Tropici," probably because he accused them of distorting Scripture. (*See also* **Holy Spirit: The Spirit in Historical Theology.**)

Political Theology

Political theology has sometimes been regarded as emerging in the late twentieth and early twenty-first centuries. But its origins lie partly in biblical writings about such concerns, for example, as those expressed by Amos about social justice, by Jesus in the Sermon on the Mount, and by Paul in Rom. 13:1-7. Then in the patristic era, Tertullian stood at one end of the spectrum and Eusebius stood at the other. The latter was virtually court theologian to Constantine in the fourth century. Eusebius retained the favor of Constantine even when he opposed Athanasius. By contrast Tertullian had said, "We have no pressing inducement to take part in your public meetings, nor is there anything more entirely foreign to us than the affairs of state" (*Apology* 38; *ANF* 3:45). In the Middle Ages Thomas Aquinas declared, "The natural order . . . demands that the power to declare and counsel should be in the hands of those who hold the supreme authority" (*Su Th* 2.2, qu. 40, art. 1). Again, "Those who wage war justly aim at peace" (qu. 40, art. 1, reply to obj. 3). Justice, to Aquinas, is a virtue, including "legal justice" (qu. 58, arts. 1 and 2). At the Reformation, the magisterial Reformers, Luther and Calvin, believed that "godly princes" and duly appointed magistrates were to be supported by the church, and could be invoked to sustain order and justice. By contrast the Radical Reformers, or Anabaptists, rejected the notion of dignitaries and a state-controlled civil order.

In the nineteenth century political theology emerged in specific forms. F. D. Maurice, Charles Kingsley, and J. M. F. Ludlam formed the Christian Socialists, and in 1854 started a "Working Men's College" in London. In the same tradition, R. H. Tawney, a close associate of William Temple, was involved with the Worker's Education Association. In 1926 he published his influential *Religion and the Rise of Capitalism,* and in 1920, *The Acquisitive Society.* Carl Schmitt joined the Nazi Party in 1933, and defended "dictatorship" first in Germany, and then in Franco's Spain. In 1922 he wrote *Political Theology* (Eng. 1985). Meanwhile H. Richard Niebuhr, brother of Reinhold, would write *Christ and Culture* (1951). He set out the options "Christ against Culture," "Christ of Culture," and "Christ Transforming Culture." Later his work would be criticized by Hauerwas and Yoder, and also by J.-B. Metz, a Catholic theologian and former student of Rahner, who advocated the cause of liberation theology. He identified himself with the oppressed in *The Emergent Church* and *A Passion for God* (1998). Another theologian identified with liberation theology was Dorothee Sölle, author of *Christ the Representative* (1967) and *Political Theology* (Philadelphia: Fortress, 1974).

Liberation theology should itself be regarded as a political theology, and we have described it and assessed it in a separate entry. Jürgen Moltmann has often been called a political theologian, especially in relation to *Theology of Hope* (1964) and *The Experiment Hope* (1974). But Moltmann later expressed concern that his theology embodied much more than political and social concerns, and expressed hesitation about a simple identification. More obvious and less controversial candidates would be Leonardo Boff, Míguez Bonino, and A. Friero, who famously promoted and developed literacy and reading among poor and oppressed people in Latin America. In Britain a more moderate theologian would be Duncan Forrester, former director of the Centre for Public Theology in the University of Edinburgh, who published *Theology and Politics* in 1988.

In a recent book, *Beyond Suspicion* (Milton Keynes: Paternoster, 2009), Paul Doerksen considers two crucially important political theologians, Oliver O'Donovan and John H. Yoder. They have brought to the subject an entirely new approach, although from very different angles. In O'Donovan's *Desire of Nations: Rediscovering the Roots of Political Theology* (Cambridge: CUP, 1999), biblical interpretation is combined with a historical discussion of the Western political situation and theological tradition. The book involves theological construction, and, as Doerksen argues, an alternative to traditional political theology. O'Donovan regards the influence of Latin American liberation theology as inadequate for a political theology, and believes that the major theological tradition of the West offers more and better resources than liberation theology. He argues that "reflection on praxis" does not necessarily entail "obedience to God's word" (13-14). Political theology as a *theoretical* discipline must precede political ethics (15). We need to refine political concepts. We need to give "detailed attention to the structures of authority" (18). Democracy is vulnerable to mass communication. We do not need "political theology," but philosophically motivated critics of modernity. O'Donovan's "central thesis" is that "theology, by developing its account of the reign of God, may recover the ground traditionally held by the notion of authority" (19). The focus should be on divine action. This is why, he explains, he wrote *Resurrection and Moral Order*. This is a *revealed* history. Gutiérrez was right to stress much of the Exodus event and salvation.

On the NT O'Donovan makes much of Paul's concern for Israel in Romans 2–4 and 9–11 (25). Wycliffe in "the high period of political theology" went back to the grace of God in such passages. Israel's history is the history of redemption, and a hermeneutical principle for political theology. The kingship of God is seen on a national and international level (cf. Psalm 99), as well as in the cosmic order. In Hebrew thought, salvation, judgment, possession, and praise are grouped around the kingship-of-God theme (36). Judgment is a theme of legal and cosmic stability. In the biblical tradition, "[If] *any regime should actually come to hold authority, and should continue to hold it, [it] is a work of divine providence in history, not a mere accomplishment of the human task of political service*" (46). Mediation is necessary, because authority is holy. The authority of Moses provides one of many examples. In the NT the Mediator is Jesus Christ, the "desire of nations." The church's mission then anticipates the obedience of political authorities. This is how Augustine and Barth approach the problem. O'Donovan attacks the notion of Western modernity that "*we* set up political authority." Like Augustine, he defends "Christendom" as a sign of God's blessing.

Critics of O'Donovan are likely to complain of an antibiblical tendency in this, and also of a reliance on power. I recall an Anglo-American seminar in 2001 when O'Donovan gently rebuked an American colleague with the comment, "We are not citizens, but subjects, responsible to the Queen." A second comment concerned human construction, especially in postmodernism, including the ever-extending notion of "human rights." O'Donovan asked, to what do we have rights? The third striking feature of the seminar was O'Donovan's constant return to biblical history and biblical narrative. The convener of the seminar, Craig Bartholomew, said his political theology was "like a dose of cold water on a hot day" (*A Royal Priesthood? The Use of the Bible Ethically and Politically: A Dialogue with Oliver O'Donovan* [Grand Rapids: Zondervan, 2002], 19).

John H. Yoder is a Mennonite, whereas O'Donovan is Anglican. Yoder completed his Th.D. at the University of Basel on Anabaptism in Switzerland. He is American, and taught first at Goshen Biblical Seminary and then at the University of Notre Dame. He mainly worked in Christian ethics, and is well known as a pacifist. He labels any mutual dependence on church and state as "Constantine-ism." He is mostly known for his book *The Politics of Jesus* (Grand Rapids: Eerdmans, 1972). Jesus, he argues, was "the spokesman of a counterculture" (11). We should return to the words of Jesus today. Several scholars or theologians have tried to sidestep his ethics by calling them "interim ethics," or the teaching of a merely rural figure, or by insisting that Jesus dealt with "spiritual, not social, matters" (16-17). Paul, Yoder argues, also tried to "correct" Jesus by his attitude to the Roman government and "Stoic conceptions of ethics" (21). By contrast, Yoder focuses on Luke. In Luke 4:14-30, Jesus applied to himself "release to the captives . . . the year of the Lord's favor" (vv. 18-19), and the Year of Jubilee, when debts were canceled (36). This was confirmed in Luke 6:12-29, where the call of the disciples leads on to the Sermon on the Plain: "Blessed are you who are poor" (v. 20), and "Love your enemies, do good to those who hate you" (v. 27; *Politics,* 40-41). Yoder writes: "Jesus is here calling into being a community of voluntary commitments, willing for the sake of its calling to take upon itself the hostility of the given society" (45). Such a lifestyle culminates in the cross. Jesus rejected violence especially in his temptations (56-59). The key to all this is the perfection of the kingdom of God.

The Jubilee Year, Yoder continues, means "the re-distribution of capital" (74).

In the exodus Israel does not fight, but God fights on Israel's behalf. The conquest raised more difficult problems for him, though he claims that fighting was by "the angel of the Lord" (84). He quotes Zech. 4:6, "Not by might, nor by power, but by my Spirit, says Jahweh of Hosts" (87). He declares, "The believer's cross must be like his Lord's, the price of his social nonconformity" (97). He appeals to "incarnational theology" (101) and self-denial (125). Discipleship entails "the abandonment of earthly security" (130). Whereas Reinhold Niebuhr discusses the proper use of power, Yoder rejects "power" altogether (138-62). The ethic of Jesus creates "a whole new value" (189). Finally he relates all this to justification by grace through faith (215-32), in which we approach God through "Jesus as sacrifice" (252). The "victory" of the Lamb is "accepting powerlessness" (244), especially in martyrdom.

Much of the argument is impressive, but much can also be found in the Anabaptists and Radical Reformers. Yoder's achievement is to place on the agenda the debate that Luther and Calvin had with the Radical Reformers, as seen in the light of more careful exegesis. But the alternative remains that of Oliver O'Donovan, who is at least as thorough in his biblical exegesis and uses a rather more sophisticated and less selective view of the Bible. Both Yoder and O'Donovan, however, as Doerksen suggests, present new alternatives to traditional political theology. (*See also* **Ethics; Hauerwas, Stanley; Liberation Hermeneutics and Theology; O'Donovan, Oliver.**)

Reading: Craig Bartholomew et al., eds., *A Royal Priesthood* (Grand Rapids: Zondervan, 2002); Luke Bretherton, *Christianity and Contemporary Politics* (Malden, Mass., and Oxford: Wiley-Blackwell, 2013); Duncan B. Forrester, *Theology and Politics* (New York and Oxford: Blackwell, 1988); H. Richard Niebuhr, *Christ and Culture* (New York and San Francisco: HarperCollins, 1951, 2001); Oliver O'Donovan, *The Desire of Nations* (Cambridge: CUP, 1999); John H. Yoder, *The Politics of Jesus* (Grand Rapids: Eerdmans, 1972).

Polyphonic Discourse
For the basic principles of polyphonic discourse, see the Mikhail Bakhtin entry. Under that entry we noted his claims (i) for seeking a multiplicity of voices; (ii) for seeking an ongoing dialogue; and (iii) that the whole was "owned" by a community, not a lone author. We briefly develop this further. Bakhtin nowhere explicitly defines polyphonic discourse. But he clearly argues for its ability to address issues too complex for monologic discourse, noting that A. Einstein's paradigm outstrips that of Newton not because Newton was wrong, but because Einstein could address issues that seemed to be stark contradictions in Newton's paradigm. While some kind of unity is necessary to make sense of life, Bakhtin prefers the term "concordance" to "unity," which would imply a finished system. Nevertheless, he writes, "The polyphonic approach has nothing in common with relativism" (*Problems of Dostoevsky's Poetics* [Minneapolis: University of Minnesota Press, 1984], 6). In literary terms he dismisses the "thought" in favor of

what literary theorists call "point of view" (93). But here a possible tension arises. Bakhtin insists that all "voices" should be given *equal weight;* he advocates "a plurality of independent and unmerged voices" (6). Yet on the other hand he accepts that "point of view" can be clearly identified and expressed.

This means that while the polyphony remains open, a point of view can also be identified. Bakhtin's examples come from F. Dostoevsky. The great examples of plural voices are found especially in *The Brothers Karamazov,* and we can hear them in *The Idiot* and *Crime and Punishment.* But in the first example Zozima probably expresses Dostoevsky's point of view; while in *The Idiot* it is Myshkin; and in *Crime and Punishment* it is Sonia.

In biblical studies and theology the value of this approach can be seen in a respect for a diverse audience, which represents many different situations. Its open-ended style invites or provokes thought. It also explains why Christians operate with a canon of Scripture as a *concordance,* not a flat unity, of diverse voices. But this is a drawback if we propose a "nonfinalizable" message. Perhaps we may say that this model applies to *much* biblical literature, such as parables and Wisdom literature, but *not to all literature.* In theology, in contrast to biblical studies, the Catholic theologian Hans Urs von Balthasar explores polyphonic discourse especially in his *Truth Is Symphonic: Aspects of Pluralism* (San Francisco: Ignatius, 1987), 7-15 and 37-64. In Reformed Protestant theology Vern S. Poythress explores this in *Symphonic Theology: The Validity of Multiple Perspectives in Theology* (Phillipsburg, N.J.: Presbyterian and Reformed, 1987), esp. 69-91. An orchestra must be "pluralist" in terms of notes and instruments, but in such a way that the total effect is an enriched harmony. Balthasar regards truth in Christ as "in-finite," which is not to be contained in a single set of statements. It is not surprising that many find distinctive theologies within the biblical canon or theological tradition. Polyphonic discourse would be one answer to H. Räisënen's critique of theological differences within the canon.

Porphyry

Porphyry (c. 232-303) was a Neoplatonist philosopher, and native of Tyre, who traveled in Syria, Palestine, and Alexandria in early life. It is uncertain whether he ever espoused the Christian faith, but he was certainly anti-Christian in later life. He studied philosophy in Athens, where Plotinus convinced him to adopt Neoplatonism (c. 262). He produced a treatise *Against the Christians,* which survives only in fragments. He attacked both the OT and the Gospels, arguing that there were inconsistencies in the Gospels. Methodius, Eusebius, and Apollinarius sought to reply to him. He composed philosophical works on a variety of subjects, urging withdrawal of the soul from the world of sense.

Positivism

"Positivism" first emerged as a descriptive term to denote the work of the French social theorists who restricted their studies to economics, politics, and social life, but excluded metaphysical belief. Auguste Comte (1798-1857) popularized the term "positivism." In effect, positivism limited "reality" to what could be observed or assessed by evidential or empirical criteria. It is virtually synonymous with materialism. Logical positivism, associated with Carnap and Ayer, attempted to disguise positivism as a theory of logic and language. (*See also* **Empiricism; Evidentialism; Metaphysics.**)

Postcolonial Theology

Postcolonial theology is regarded by many as complementing liberation theology and developing it a stage further. Both movements are concerned to extricate Christian theology from an imperialist conceptual framework and substructure. Nevertheless, R. S. Sugirtharajah, a major exponent of postcolonial theology, argues that these are different movements. Postcolonial theology, he argues, is less closely related to neo-Marxism and a particular form of oppression. However, on the other side, Gerald West rejects such a distinction (West, "What Difference Does Postcolonial Biblical Criticism Make?" in *Postcolonial Interventions,* ed. Tat-Siong Benny Liew [Sheffield: Phoenix Press, 2009], 256-73). Both movements, in fact, seek a grassroots theology nurtured by indigenous peoples, and both movements encourage "voices from the margins," as reflected by the title of R. S. Sugirtharajah, ed., *Voices from the Margins: Interpreting the Bible in the Third World* (London: SPCK; New York: Orbis, 1991, 1995). In liberation theology not only G. Gutiérrez, but more especially Itumeleng Mosala and Vincent Wimbush have written from a postcolonial perspective.

The turning point in secular thought was probably Edward Said's book *Orientalism,* which unmasked "Eurocentric" assumptions, which were then ascribed to Oriental life. In the wake of this the aim of postcolonial theology is to enable former colonial groups to speak for themselves. The aim is admirable, but many argue that the method often involves the blurring of traditional distinctions between truth and falsehood, the relativization of monotheistic belief, and the abolition of messianic categories such as "king" and "rule," and such titles as "slave of Christ." The latter was a cause for thankful glorying, for Paul. Theology is seen rightly to engage with ethics and politics. But it may give a disproportionate place to "housing, health-care, social security, education, or homeland" (Sugirtharajah, *Postcolonial Reconfigurations* [St. Louis: Chalice, 2003]). These concerns may become so dominant as to become at times like "the tail wagging the dog." The concerns of postcolonial theology address necessary problems, but, like many young movements, it uses contemporary methods in ways many regard as extreme. (*See also* **Liberation Hermeneutics and Theology; Political Theology.**)

Postliberalism

Postliberalism has been defined in at least two ways. From the 1940s until the early 1970s, the term generally denoted those orthodox theologians who opposed liberalism, especially in the form associated with Harnack and related thinkers.

Sometimes it was used to suggest a broad sympathy or affinity with such thinkers as Karl Barth and Emil Brunner. In 1984, however, the second, and nowadays virtually universal, meaning was coined by George Lindbeck in his classic work *The Nature of Doctrine: Religion and Theology in a Postliberal Age* (London: SPCK). He entitled his final chapter "Towards a Postliberal Theology" (112-38). Here he argued that postliberal theology could avoid "polarisation between tradition and innovation" (113), and could employ C. Geertz's "thick description," or close study, of a coherent linguistic intertextual world (114-15), in which "A scriptural world is thus able to absorb all the universe" by its interpretive framework (117); it also holds that the cross is no mere metaphor for human suffering, but is a messianic and cruciform event in history (118). As Calvin and Hans Frei had also argued, Scripture would function "as the lens through which theologies viewed the world" (119). (For a critical assessment, see A. Vidu, *Post-Liberal Theological Method* [Milton Keynes, UK: Paternoster; Eugene, Ore.: Wipf and Stock, 2010.)

Several broadly like-minded thinkers shared Lindbeck's general approach, notably Frei and David Kelsey, and later, many argue, also S. Hauerwas, R. Thiemann, W. Placher, and Kathryn Tanner. Brevard Childs is also often seen as part of this "Yale School," but Childs has expressed reservations about lumping together these Yale theologians as a particular "school." This extension of the term "postliberal" has occasionally been described as a third meaning of the term. All these thinkers are sometimes criticized for overestimating the importance of the church at the expense of wider concepts of truth, but Tanner has also firmly related theology to the issues raised by secular culture, including social and economic questions. (*See also* **Frei, Hans W.; Kelsey, David H.; Lindbeck, George; Tanner, Kathryn.**)

Postmodernism, Postmodernity

D. Harvey defines postmodernism as a reaction against "positivist, technocratic, and rationalist universal modernism" (*The Condition of Postmodernity* [Oxford: Blackwell, 1989], 9). Many Christians therefore welcome this phenomenon as a dethronement of Enlightenment rationalism and positivism, which has blighted theology since the eighteenth century. They will also welcome the postmodern move against "the standardization of knowledge," which too often gives privilege to natural science as the paradigm for all kinds of knowledge; or reduces wisdom to information. Exponents of postmodernism distrust the surface grammar of language, as sometimes failing to represent the underlying purpose of a stretch of discourse. Roland Barthes has been a master of unveiling such disguises in language, and Michel Foucault has also shown where apparently innocent language-uses disguise bids for power or control. As T. Docherty argues, postmodernism denotes a *mood* rather than a *period*. D. Lyon and G. Ward use the term "postmodernism" to denote a philosophical and intellectual framework in contrast to "postmodernity," which denotes more social or sociological phenomena. Helpful and accurate as this might be in theory, in practice most writers blur this distinction without difference. As a huge generalization, Harvey and Hassan associate modernism with coherence, hierarchy, purpose, and reason, and postmodernism with fragmentation, anarchy, indeterminacy, rhetoric, and irony.

M. Welker is one of several Christian theologians who welcome aspects of this mood or movement as liberating. He claims that it takes seriously pluralism and "differentiated realities and forms of consciousness created by modern society," in contrast to supposed "keys" to experience. "A theology of the Holy Spirit can be developed better against this background than in the artificial light of an apparently unbroken reality and rationality continuum" (*God the Spirit* [Minneapolis: Fortress, 1994], 37 and 39-40). The Holy Spirit, he argues, relativizes the fixed forms of European thought, metaphysics, "universal history," and "totality of meaning" (41-42). The Holy Spirit, however, brought order out of chaos at creation, and Pannenberg shows how revelation relates to "totality of meaning."

For many Christian theologians there is a dark side of postmodernism. To be sure, Jean-François Lyotard, one of its leading exponents, has defined postmodernism as "incredulity towards metanarratives," that is, toward a "universalizing" narrative such as Marx and Freud and Darwin have offered as an explanation for so much in human history and life (*The Postmodern Condition* [Manchester: Manchester University Press, 1984], xxiv). In his later work Lyotard welcomes the term "pagan" as signifying a plurality of religions and deities, and in *The Differend* (Manchester: Manchester University Press, 1990) he argues that genuine debate is no more than a device to browbeat a weaker party to conform to the rules, language, and views of the stronger party. This trend began when Lyotard borrowed Kuhn's notion of "incommensurability" from the philosophy of science. This term denotes two self-consistent viewpoints that cannot be submitted to impartial arbitration or reconciled. In *Just Giving* (Eng. 1985) and *The Differend*, he despairs of any attempt at rational arbitration between two such contrasting views, and reduces the rational, in effect, to the rhetorical task of persuasion. He concludes that the stronger party will win over the weaker by imposing "rules of discourse," or a pseudologic, which favors the case of the stronger. This belief or device excludes rationality from theology and interpretation, including causing the collapse of biblical and general hermeneutics.

Some aspects of Lyotard's thought do remain positive for humanities and theology. For example, he and J. Baudrillard reject the notion of language and knowledge as a *commodity*. Lyotard suspects "computerization" of conveying the pretense of objective, value-free knowledge. However, he warns us: "Knowledge in the form of an informational commodity indispensable to productive power is already ... the major stake in the world-wide competition for power" (*The Postmodern Condition*, 5). Baudrillard similarly sees this process as dissolving a hold on reality and sustaining an initial reality. He questions the impartial power of the media in *The Mirror of Production* (Eng. 1983). The media usually construct a "virtual reality."

Much of Foucault's work paved the way for this. His basic thesis was that "knowledge" is power. For example, concepts of "madness" constitute valuable social constructs. In the ancient world, "madness" was construed either as animal-like and subhuman behavior, or as inspired by the gods. Nineteenth-century liberal reformers saw it as a mental *illness*. Asylums were allegedly places of safety, but in reality they served to protect bourgeois society and families from engaging with this phenomenon. Foucault regularly questions the genuine innocence or objectivity of social institutions, such as prisons, hospitals, and the police. Such "regimes" arbitrarily impose their authority in the interest of dominant classes. He speaks of psychiatrists and doctors as "the smile in the white coat" (*Madness and Civilization* [New York: Pantheon, 1965], and *The Birth of the Clinic* [Eng. 1973]). He concludes: there is no knowledge of truth outside networks of power relations. In *Discipline and Punish* (New York: Pantheon, 1977), he explores how "surveillance" and "regimes" produce "docile bodies." Examples include "disciplinary battalions, prisons, hospitals, almshouses" (300).

Most of these French postmodernists are atheists. They rightly expose the power obsessions of some religious leaders. But any notion of the divine institution of such things as marriage, kings, or law courts would fall outside this view of the world. Ethics also seems to fall largely outside the notice of *American* postmodernists such as Richard Rorty or Stanley Fish, in spite of their protests to the contrary. After some initial work in linguistic philosophy, Rorty argued that knowledge cannot "mirror" nature or reality (*Philosophy and the Mirror of Nature* [Princeton: Princeton University Press, 1979]). Mere convention is construed, he argues, as the rational. He attacks "the myth of the given." He develops this in *Contingency, Irony, and Solidarity* (Cambridge: CUP, 1989). "For liberal ironists there is no answer to the question 'Why not be cruel?' — no backup for the belief that cruelty is horrible" (xv). Rationality is simply "what society lets us say" (*Philosophy*, 171). Can he find *no* criteria for belief and action? It lies in what the *community* sees as *beneficial to it*. The community allegedly finds truth in "what benefits the community," never in "getting it right." Rorty makes extensive use of the American pragmatists W. James and J. Dewey. He agrees with James that "the true is the name of whatever proves itself to be good in way of belief" (*Truth and Progress* [Cambridge: CUP, 1998], 21). Since he explicitly rejects any evaluating criteria from "outside" the community, this has negative consequences for seeking to apply the truth-criterion of the cross, except as seen already through the lenses of a given community. The notions of reformation and correction seem to find no permissible place.

The work of Fish runs largely parallel with Rorty in the field of literary theory. Meanings, for Fish, do not lie "innocently in the world; rather they are constituted by an interpretive act" (*Is There a Text in This Class?* [Cambridge: Harvard University Press, 1980], 13). We should not ask about meaning, but about what a text *does*: "The reader's response is not *to* the meaning; it *is* the meaning" (3). This is ultimately the same kind of pragmatism as we find in Rorty. Fish builds his argument, first, by setting up "formalism" as the only alternative to his approach;

and second, by offering (as Rorty does) a radically pluralist interpretation of Wittgenstein, which most specialists on Wittgenstein would reject. Wittgenstein regularly qualifies much of his language by such disclosures as "largely," "usually," or "often," and speaks of "overlapping," "criss-crossing," and *transcontextual bridges* that would invalidate the use Fish and Rorty make of him. Moreover, Wittgenstein, of all people, rejects the stark choice between the sharply bounded purity of formalist concepts and the grossly unstable blurred boundaries of contextual pragmatism.

American and European postmodernism are two different kinds of animals, although in some respects they overlap. In summary, in France the semantics and semiotics of Roland Barthes set the ball rolling legitimately, by claiming that linguistic codes could convey subtexts of social force and significance, which may not be immediately apparent. Furniture arrangement or clothes, for example, may not always be chosen for comfort and utility, but to convey aspirations of social class. From these beginnings Jacques Derrida developed his theory of the deconstruction of language. Foucault explored power, and Lyotard attacked "grand narration" in ways that combine some positive insights for theology with some disastrous implications and claims, which have seduced some easily led Christians. The testimony mode, for example, may seem to free us from rational criticism, but are we to surrender all appeal to common sense, reasonableness, argument, and rationality, in exchange for autobiography? The appeal of W. Pannenberg and others to attempt to see Christian truth as part of a larger whole is lost in a proliferation of little stories or "small things." Kevin Vanhoozer has explored the devastating effect of Derrida's deconstruction and postmodernism in his exposé *Is There a Meaning in This Text?* (Grand Rapids: Zondervan, 1998, 2009). With this European version, it would be naïve to be an unreserved admirer or an unreserved critic from the viewpoint of Christian theology. Theologians need to call attention to some insights, but also to resist and to attack many more seductions. In addition to other factors, the primary advocates of this European or largely French movement are often extremely far to the left in politics.

American postmodernism is even more insidious. It appears on the surface to be anchored in the philosophy of language, especially the later Wittgenstein, and in literary theory. But on closer examination it is a dubious interpretation of both. Further, nothing can rescue it from a largely disguised pragmatism and distaste for nonpragmatic questions of truth. "Good" is internally relative to the community in question. Many American theologians have observed that on the surface Rorty and Fish appear to promote a pluralistic tolerance, but that this disguises a self-generated and sinister authoritarianism. If we cannot appeal to any recognized criticism, authoritarianism becomes inevitable. American postmodernism becomes as destructive for questions of truth, negotiation, and rational argument as Lyotard's *Differend*. In the end, Vanhoozer rightly observes that both types of postmodernism promote the notion of "the social construction of biblical meaning" (*Is There a Meaning?* 171). He claims this also for Derrida and deconstruction.

"Deconstruction lifts up every voice so that no one voice . . . the author's . . . dominates" (88). He concludes: "Derrida's deconstruction of the author is a more or less direct consequence of Nietzsche's announcement of the death of God" (48). (*See also* **Deconstruction, Deconstructionism; Derrida, Jacques.**)

Reading: M. Foucault, *Discipline and Punish* (New York: Pantheon, 1977); D. Harvey, *The Condition of Postmodernity* (Oxford: Blackwell, 1989); J.-F. Lyotard, *The Differend* (Manchester: Manchester University Press, 1995); R. Rorty, *Truth and Progress* (Cambridge: CUP, 1998); A. C. Thiselton, *Interpreting God and the Postmodern Self* (Edinburgh: T. & T. Clark, 1995); A. C. Thiselton, *Hermeneutics* (Grand Rapids: Eerdmans, 2009), 327-48; K. J. Vanhoozer, *Is There a Meaning in This Text?* (Grand Rapids: Zondervan, 2009).

Pragmatism

Pragmatism denotes the belief that the truth or validity of a truth claim may be assessed in terms of its usefulness or success. The first question is to whom the truth claim proves to be successful or useful. One ready answer, offered by the philosopher R. Rorty and others, is that of the local community. But two difficulties then arise. First, communities are numerous and varied; which community do we have in mind? Second, as history proceeds down the centuries, what appears to be "true" to communities in one generation may appear "false" in another.

Pragmatism is often associated with the American philosophical tradition. William James and John Dewey were classic exponents of the pragmatic tradition. Many trace the roots of this approach to Charles S. Peirce (1839-1914), who probably introduced the term "pragmatism" (technically, "pragmaticism"). P. Ochs, however, has recently defended Peirce's distinctive approach, suggesting that some of his insights are equivalent to the logic of Scripture (*Peirce, Pragmatism, and the Logic of Scripture* [Cambridge: CUP, 1998]). Peirce defined pragmatism as conceiving of meaning in terms of "practical consequences" (Peirce, "What Pragmatism Is," *Monist* 15 [1905]: 161-81, and *Collected Papers,* 6 vols. [Cambridge: Harvard University Press, 1931-1935], vol. 5). For Peirce, pragmatism is primarily a philosophy of action and consequences.

Through James, pragmatism became known to a wider public especially in his essay "The Will to Believe" (1897). James goes further than Peirce in claiming that pragmatism "makes" truth, rather than discovers it. He argued, "The true is the name of whatever proves itself to be good in the way of belief" (*Pragmatism and the Meaning of Truth* [Cambridge: Harvard University Press, 1975], 42). Dewey went at least as far in terms of action, progressivism, and instrumentalism. R. Rorty combines postmodernism and pragmatism. He claims to follow James and Dewey, and paraphrases Dewey in defining truth in terms of "intersubjective agreement" (*Truth and Progress* [Cambridge: CUP, 1998], 6-7). Truth is "what works" (305). Rorty agrees with W. Sellers in attacking what they call "the myth of the given." He also prefers the term "local" or "locality" to "relativity."

Most traditional orthodox theologians insist that this approach would replace truth with consumerism and relativism, and that it may also undervalue history, rational argument, and coherence as tests of truth. Indeed, the philosophers C. Norris and C. West, among others, regard Rorty's philosophy as a potentially authoritarian approach masquerading as liberal pluralism. This would be partly akin to Lyotard's *The Differend*. R. S. Corrington laments that pragmatism too easily dominates American hermeneutics (*The Community of Interpreters* [Macon, Ga.: Mercer University Press, 1987]). The theologian R. Bauckham even warns us that this approach attempts "the Americanisation of the world" (*The Bible and Mission* [Carlisle: Paternoster, 2003], 89). (*See also* **Ochs, Peter; Postmodernism, Postmodernity; Reason.**)

Prayer

Prayer may include many modes of humankind's communicative relation to God. It instantiates what Buber called an "I-Thou" relationship with God. It may assume such forms as adoration, confession, thanksgiving, petition, lament, and intercession. At its highest the apostle Paul sees it as a "divine dialogue," which is prompted by the Holy Spirit, and addressed to God the Father, through the mediation of Jesus Christ (Rom. 8:15, 27). Prayer is so essential to communion with God, and so complex in its various forms, that two distinct types of theological literature have emerged over the centuries to consider it in detail. One type emerges from Scripture and the history of the church, and stresses the nature of prayer in Christian experience. The other usually addresses the specific mode of petitionary or intercessory prayer in the context of the philosophy of religion, and God's relation to the world. As many popularly express this: Does petitionary prayer make any actual difference to the life of others, or to events in the world? If we pray for healing or for nations and governments, for example, does this have any effect on the lives of those for whom we pray?

The biblical material presents prayer as a simple act, often as a son or daughter to the heavenly Father. But "prayer" is offered in many modes and guises. No single Greek or Hebrew word covers all biblical prayers.

(i) *The New Testament.* We list ten Greek terms or modes of prayer, which may not be comprehensive. (a) The Greek *euchomai* is the general word for "to pray," and is used in 2 Cor. 13:7, "we pray to God that you . . . ," and James 5:15, "The prayer of faith will save the sick." But *euchomai* is only one of a dozen Greek words denoting some kind of prayer. (b) In BDAG 213, Danker suggests that Greek *deēsis* (from *deō*) means "to make an urgent request to meet a need," as in Phil. 1:19: "through your prayers and the help of the Spirit"; or in 1 Pet. 3:12, "his [the Lord's] ears are open to their prayer"; Rom. 10:1, "My heart's desire and prayer to God for them is that they may be saved"; and Luke 5:33, "John's disciples . . . fast and pray." (c) The Greek *entunchanō* (BDAG 341) denotes "appeal," or "to make earnest request." It occurs in the LXX, in the classic references to the Holy Spirit in Rom. 8:27, and in Rom. 8:34. Further, the NT refers to "Christ Jesus . . . who intercedes for us"; and in Heb. 7:25, "He [Christ] always lives to make intercession for them." Danker also considers Greek *aiteō* and *aitēma* (BDAG 30) in Phil. 4:6, "Let your requests be made known to God"; and James 4:3, "You ask wrongly." (d) A fourth word, the Greek *parakaleō*, "to call for help," seems to be used more often for human-to-human relationship (Eph. 4:1, "I beg you").

Not all prayer, however, is petitionary or supplicatory. (e) Greek *proskuneō* denotes, in Danker's words (BDAG 882-83), "Complete submission or dependence on God, or on a figure of authority." The NRSV usually translates it "worship," as in: "Jesus said . . . 'Worship the Lord your God, / and serve only him'" (Matt. 4:10; parallel Luke 4:8); "Jesus said . . . 'You will worship the Father neither on this mountain nor in Jerusalem'" (John 4:21); "Let all God's angels worship him" (Heb. 1:6). Rev. 19:4 has special significance: "The twenty-four elders and the four living creatures fell down and worshiped God." (f) In BDAG 587, *latreuō* can range from "serve" in general to "serve God acceptably with reverence and awe," as in Heb. 12:28, "We offer to God an acceptable worship with reverence and awe." The noun *latreia* also means "worship of God" (Rom. 9:4). Greek *sebomai* (BDAG 918) may also mean "worship" (Matt. 15:9; parallel Mark 7:7). (g) Thus "adoration" and "worship" can be covered by three Greek words: *proskuneō, latreuō,* and *sebomai,* and cognate terms. Phil. 2:10 also uses *kamptō*, "to bend the knee."

(h) The Greek *eucharisteō*, as is well known, means "to express appreciation for blessings," or "to render thanks" (BDAG 415-16). A classic example includes "Thanks be to God" (Rom. 7:25); or, "I thank God that . . ." (1 Cor. 14:18); Rom. 1:8, "I thank my God through Jesus Christ"; Phil. 1:3, "I thank my God every time I remember you." Sometimes the Greek *charis* is used, as in 1 Cor. 15:57, "Thanks be to God, who gives us the victory." (i) In addition to "thanksgiving," words for "confess," "confession," or "admit" also occur in the NT. 1 John 1:9, "If we confess our sins . . . ," uses Greek *homologeō*. The same Greek word occurs in Matt. 3:6, "They were baptized by him . . . confessing their sins." Nevertheless, *homologeō* also denotes "confessing the faith." But even these terms do not cover the whole range of modes of prayer. (j) The Greek *eulogeō* denotes "to bless," which is another mode of prayer (*see* **Blessing and Cursing**). Often God is the subject who blesses, but especially in the case of the corporate *eulogētos,* humans bless God; Zechariah, inspired by the Holy Spirit, said, in Luke 1:68, "Blessed be the Lord God of Israel"; Paul in Rom. 1:25, "The Creator, who is blessed forever"; and Eph. 1:3, "Blessed be the God and Father of our Lord Jesus Christ" (BDAG 408). Greek *eulogeō* can also mean "praise," "extol," or "call down God's glorious power" (408). There is a multiplicity of variations. Mary exclaims in the Magnificat: "*Megalunei he puschē mou ton Kurion,* My soul magnifies the Lord" (Luke 1:46). Sometimes in the Psalms *complaint* is a form of prayer.

All these terms in Greek may be classified in the traditional and popular Christian aphorism: *Adoration, Confession, Thanksgiving,* and *Supplication* denote four *acts* of prayer (*see* **Speech Act Theory**). They are more than merely "saying prayers," as if these were simply descriptive propositions without active force. Admittedly these four represent generalities. Jesus in Gethsemane made an *act* of *acceptance:* "Nevertheless, not what I will but what you will." The four headings do not include *contemplation,* except perhaps in Rev. 19:4. But these are the basic building blocks of biblical prayer. Many are included in A. R. George, *Communion with God in the New Testament* (London: Epworth, 1953).

(ii) **The Old Testament.** The OT provides a similar range of varieties of prayer to the NT. No single Hebrew word covers all the actions or modes of prayer. (a) An important word is Hebrew *pālal,* which in the Qal form might mean "to intervene" as well as "to pray," but in the Hithpael usually means "to pray, to intercede" (BDB 813). BDB cites Deut. 9:20: Moses interceded on behalf of Aaron; 1 Sam. 2:25: "Someone can intercede for the sinner with the LORD"; and Jer. 29:7: "Pray to the LORD on its behalf" (i.e., for the welfare of the city). (b) The verb and noun *t^{e}pilâ* occur at least seventy-four times in the OT in the sense of "prayer." In Gen. 20:7 Abraham prayed for Abimelech; Moses prayed in Num. 11:2; Hannah prayed in 1 Sam. 1:12; Solomon prayed in 1 Kings 8:28; and so on. But numerous other terms refer to prayer. (c) *Chānan* can mean "to entreat grace"; *ts^{e}lā'* can mean "to pray" or "to bend low"; *shā'al* can mean "pray for peace"; and so on. (d) Hebrew *hālal* means "to praise" (Judg. 16:24; 1 Chron. 16:36; 23:5; 2 Chron. 5:13; 8:14; 20:19; Ezra 3:10-11; Neh. 5:13; Ps. 22:22, 23, 26; etc.) (e) Hebrew *yādāh* regularly also means "to praise," as well as "to confess" (Gen. 29:35; 2 Chron. 7:3, 6; Pss. 7:17; 9:1). (f) Hebrew *shābach* may mean "to praise" or "to glorify" (Pss. 63:3; 117:1; 145:4; 147:12). (g) Hebrew *zāmar* is a similar word, meaning "praise," or "sing praises" (Pss. 7:17; 9:2; 18:49). (h) We have not even considered Hebrew *bārak,* "to bless" (Deut. 8:10, "You shall . . . bless the LORD"), where usually God is the subject, but often also the object of blessing. (i) A "vow" may constitute a prayer. Sometimes prayer may be implicit, without a special word for it.

(iii) **Historical and Philosophical Material.** The other distinct line of inquiry, in addition to the biblical material, is the controversy in the philosophy of religion. This issue was especially sparked by Kant, *Religion within the Limits of Reason Alone* (Eng. Indianapolis: Hackett, 2009). He distinguishes between the prayer of rational faith *(reiner Vernunftglaube),* and religion and prayer as practiced by the church *(Kirchenglaube).* "Rational" prayer establishes moral goodness within the one who prays; "church" faith believes that prayer causes changes in others or in the world. It achieves a change in the world, something external to the pray-er. The borderline between philosophical and biblical reflection is not clear-cut. Most Christians do not believe that even in Scripture God *invariably* grants requests. God cannot be the object of personal manipulation to personal wishes, or the subject of experiment. This is one reason why Jesus says that what we ask *in Christ's name* will be granted; what expresses God's will in Christ does not mean anything and everything. Yet philosophical problems are pressing: If God already wills "the best" for his people and creation, how could intercessory prayer or supplication "improve" on "the best"?

There is also a half-truth in Kant's emphasis on "therapeutic meditation," as Vincent Brummer calls it *(What Are We Doing When We Pray?* [London: SCM,

1984], 16-28). T. R. Miles states that "Thy will be done" means "I hereby acknowledge the need to do according to thy will" (*Religion and the Scientific Outlook* [London, 1959], 186). Thomas Aquinas asserts, "We must pray, not in order to inform God of our needs and desires, but in order to remind ourselves that in these matters we need divine assistance" (*Su Th* 2.2, qu. 83, art. 2). Prayer is not "to change his mind," but to create confidence in us (qu. 83, art. 9).

Yet the key point is that "the best possible" is not "the best," unless it is also *"the best when we pray."* The highest good is cooperation and union between humankind and God; Edgar Brightman states this formally: *"The best possible when men pray would be better than the best possible when they do not pray"* (*A Philosophy of Religion* [London: Skeffington, n.d.], 236). Providence seeks a co*sharing* between God and his children. "The best possible" is not an abstract, fixed amount, taken out of context in life.

No doubt this requires repetition or rehearsal of what we wrote under the entry **God, Trinity: Almighty, Omniscient, Omnipresent.** God cannot (the logical "cannot") change the past, or perform logically impossible acts. Nor can we invoke the argument that God knows the future, as if the future already "existed" as a thing, and everything was absolutely determined with no role for human freedom. Brummer amplifies this issue in *What Are We Doing When We Pray?* (41-48). As Peter Geach, Eleanore Stump, and Brummer all urge, prayer is *not* aimed at stimulating a grudging God to do better. God as primary cause may work through secondary agencies, and often prayer asks that secondary agencies may be attuned to God's purposes or to God's wisdom. Traditional prayer for medical doctors and healing is often so directed. Moreover, prayer in the Bible presupposes that God works through "natural" causes. Prayer does not rest on a so-called scientific *worldview* of a mechanistic universe, even if it acknowledges the place of mechanistic *method* in the sciences (*see* **Healing; Science and Religion**).

Eleanore Stump answers the question raised by Helen Oppenheimer. It is hard to believe in God, Oppenheimer complains, if he withholds his favor simply because no one is praying for the person concerned. Stump replies that God may well grant that person healing or blessing; we do not know for sure. Our task is simply to coshare with God the needs of which we are aware. Appeal is further made by some to the healing ministry of Jesus. But this brings us back to biblical theology. If the kingdom of God is wholly present in Jesus, healings may be promised. But for Christians, and even for Jesus himself, the kingdom of God is *both* present *and* future. Hence healings may *often* occur; but only when the kingdom has become fully present can we say that they are promised *inevitably* and *invariably*. We cannot conclude this subject neatly, for its ramifications and issues are virtually infinite. But the key to controversies lie in our *coworking with God*. (*See also* **Evil, Problem of; God, Trinity: Almighty, Omniscient, Omnipresent; Pentecostals, Pentecostalism.**)

Reading: P. R. Baelz, *Does God Answer Prayer?* (London, 1982); V. Brummer, *What Are We Doing When We Pray?* (London: SCM, 1984); C. S. Lewis, *Letters to*

Malcolm (New York: Harcourt, Brace, 1964); A. R. Peacock, *Creation and the World of Science* (Oxford: Clarendon, 1979); E. Stump, "Prayer," in E. Stump and M. J. Murphy, *Philosophy of Religion: The Big Questions* (Malden, Mass., and Oxford: Blackwell), 353-66; K. Ward, *Divine Action* (London: Collins, 1990).

Predestination. *See* **Election and Predestination**

Presbyterian, Presbyterianism

Presbyterianism has two related meanings: (i) in theory it relates to the heritage of Reformed theology, as seen in Calvin and in the Westminster Confession; (ii) it also reflects a church polity of government through presbyters, both clerical and lay. In practice, with both a general assembly and coequal presbyters, it claims to avoid both extremes of a centralized college of bishops and a democratic localized congregationalism, not totally unlike Methodism. If the first of these two meanings is "theoretical," this is because, while most Presbyterians affirm Reformed theology officially, some, especially in Scotland, now sit relatively loosely to their doctrinal origins, as some Methodists do to their Wesleyan origins.

Presbyterians firmly regard the NT terms for bishops and presbyters as interchangeable in origin, siding in the historical controversy with J. B. Lightfoot rather than with A. Harnack. They would regard Ignatius as representing or anticipating a distinct later development, insisting that some presbyters can perform episcopal functions. Insofar as Presbyterianism officially, at least, follows Calvin, it affirms the sovereignty of God. Presbyterians have often followed Calvin rather than the Anabaptists in their attitude to the state. They tend to hold a Calvinist, or sometimes Zwinglian, theology of the Lord's Supper. Although Calvin accepted a Reformation view of bishops, Presbyterians tend to follow John Knox of Scotland in mainly, but not always, rejecting formal episcopacy. Calvin's view of the church is expounded in book 4 of the *Institutes*. In 4.1.1 Calvin writes, "[God] has appointed pastors and teachers ... (Eph. 4:11); he has invested them with authority" (Beveridge, 2:280). He rebukes those who "despise public meetings, and deem preaching superfluous" (4.1.5; 2:285). He affirms Augustine's concept of the "visible" church, with its fallibility and failings (4.1.7-8), and commends the use of discipline (4.1.15; 1 Cor. 5:1-13). He insists, "Pastors ... have the same function as apostles" (4.3.5; 2:319). Pastors are like the watchmen in Ezek. 3:18 (4.1.6). Office bearers are supported by God (4.3.4). Indeed, "bishop," "presbyter," "pastor," and "minister" become interchangeable terms. Elders assist in the government of the churches. If discipline is required, a "consistory" of elders is the appropriate authority.

In Scotland John Knox (c. 1513-1572) was effectively the leader of the Reformation, and assisted in the preparation of Edward VI's 1552 *Book of Common Prayer*, especially, it is said, in its "Black Rubric" about the purpose of kneeling at Holy Communion. He met Calvin in 1554, but returned to Scotland in 1555. He preached the duty of fighting against "Mary, Queen of Scots," and introduced *The*

Book of Common Order as the Scottish service book. In 1581 the General Assembly of the Church of Scotland approved the second *Book of Discipline,* and the presbytery became established. By 1583 a small group of Presbyterians existed also in England. In 1647 the Westminster Confession was adopted as the official confession of all English-speaking Presbyterians. For some years fortunes waxed and waned until Presbyterianism became the Established Church in Scotland under William III in 1690, with Kirk sessions, presbyteries, and synods. There were, however, subsequent splits within the church, and only in 1900 did the United Presbyterian Church and the "United Free" Presbyterian Church unite. In Ireland, colonists from Scotland settled in Ulster, and over the years Presbyterianism became a strong presence alongside the Church of Ireland.

In America, Presbyterians arrived in considerable numbers, especially from Scotland from about 1700. Many settled in New Jersey and Pennsylvania. Under the leadership of Jonathan Dickenson, the Westminster Confession was adopted in 1729. The first General Assembly was held in 1789 at Philadelphia. Today among Protestant churches in America, the largest denominational group remains the Baptists, the second largest the Methodists, with Lutherans and Presbyterians probably respectively third and fourth, omitting the cults or sects. Presbyterian churches were formed in Canada, Australia, New Zealand, and South Africa, as well as in the Netherlands and other parts of Europe. In keeping with Calvin's theology, education has always remained a priority. In Scotland, the Universities of Edinburgh, Glasgow, St. Andrews, and Aberdeen also prepare candidates for the ministry.

Preunderstanding

Preunderstanding is a woodenly literal English equivalent to the German *Vorverständnis* (noun) and *vorverstehen* (verb). Idiomatic English would render the word "preliminary understanding." The word arises because the tradition in hermeneutics from Schleiermacher, Dilthey, and Heidegger to Bultmann, Gadamer, and Ricoeur rejects the notion of beginning the process of understanding with a blank mind, or as B. Lonergan calls it, an empty head. To begin with a blank mind would not, they urge, provide a guarantee of objectivity, but quite the reverse. A blank mind could not even understand the words and letters of a text. We begin to understand a phenomenon or a book by building on what we already understand of the subject in question. As the process proceeds, the book or the text "speaks back" to correct, revise, and refine our first, initial, preliminary understanding. This is basic to all hermeneutics. (*See also* **Hermeneutical Circle; Hermeneutics.**)

Prevenient Grace

Augustine is said to have coined the term, and it has since entered our theological vocabulary. Augustine declares: "God anticipates us . . . that we may be healed . . . anticipates us that we may be called . . . that we may lead godly lives" (*Nature and*

Grace 35). Similarly, Thomas Aquinas distinguished "prevenient and subsequent" grace in terms of their effects. Grace "comes before" human response. The memorable phrase in the *Book of Common Prayer* retains the Latinism: "Prevent us, O Lord, in all our doings, and further us with Thy continual help; that in all our doings, begun, continued, and ended in Thee, we may glorify Thy holy Name" (*Prayers after Communion*). (*See also* **Grace**.)

Process Thought

Process thought is primarily a philosophy associated with Alfred N. Whitehead (1861-1947) and Charles Hartshorne (1897-2000). Nevertheless, it has had considerable influence on process theology, especially through D. D. Williams, John Cobb, Schubert Ogden, and Norman Pittenger. In 1964 Pittenger gave a lecture entitled "A Contemporary Trend in North American Theology" (*ExpTim* 76 [1965], and *God in Process* [London: SCM, 1967], esp. 96-109). This movement stresses that God and reality are in *process* of *becoming* rather than merely in a *state* of *being*. A God only of "being" would amount to a static abstraction, like the timeless absolute of Plato. At best, this recovers the biblical notion of the *living* God, who is dynamic and purposive. The movement also focuses on history and community. Cobb argues, "Each new experience would inherit from past experiences of all" in a "total openness of each to all others" ("What Is the Future?" in *Hope and the Future of Man*, ed. E. H. Cousins [London: Gunstone Press, 1973], 13-14). Process thought rejects the notion of a static, unchanging God. Cobb produced several publications on this: *A Christian Natural Theology* (1965), *The Structure of Christian Existence* (1967), and *Christ in a Pluralistic Age* (1975). The movement readily accepts that God creates through evolution, and sees the problem of evil as part of that process. It also encourages an incarnational theology in the broadest sense. Whitehead, *Process and Reality* (1927), is perhaps the nearest to a classic text in process thought.

Today there would probably be widespread agreement with its emphasis on the creative and dynamic, as against the static and abstract. But some of its departures from traditional theology, such as its account of sin, evil, and ethics, may perhaps be questioned. The history of philosophy reflects a similar emphasis in broad terms from that of Heraclitus and Hegel as well as Bergson's notion of *élan vital*, and theories of open systems. The movement, however, also seeks to reconcile contradictions.

Promise

"Promise" occurs fifty or sixty times in the NT with the Greek word *epangelia*. The Hebrew uses more general words for "to say" or "word," *dābār* or *'āmar*. "Promise" is especially prominent in Rom. 4:13-20 (Paul on God's promise to Abraham); Rom. 9:4-9 (God's promise to Israel); Gal. 3:14-29 (God's promise to Abraham); and Heb. 6:12-17 and 11:9-39 (waiting for God's promise in faith). The Hebrew *dābār* occurs especially in Deuteronomy (God's promise to his people of the land) and 1 Kings (promises to Solomon). Characteristically God makes promises in the context of the covenant. Patience, trust, and appropriation are the requirements for God's people. Sometimes God confirms or backs up promises with an oath (Gen. 22:16; Exod. 13:5, 11; 33:1), which caused problems for Philo (who asked, is an oath from God redundant?); and in the NT in Heb. 7:20-21,

> "The Lord has sworn,
> and will not change his mind."

An oath occurs with God's promise in Heb. 6:13, 16, and 4:3. Every valid promise entails a *commitment* or *pledge*. If a human being promises to give a child a treat, the adult cannot use the promised time or money for some other purpose. At least, this is so if the promise is to remain valid. It is God's sovereign choice and will to bind himself in a promise to perform certain actions, and sometimes to offer a visible confirmation. He "cannot" (the logical "cannot") take an alternative action. If God has promised to be faithful and truthful, he "cannot" tell a falsehood.

Hence in Genesis the promise to Abraham stands firm, in spite of setbacks. God has promised a child to Abraham and Sarah. Thus, in Kierkegaard's language, Abraham "cannot" slay the son of promise (Genesis 22). Israel's bondage in Egypt must issue in deliverance (Exod. 6:6). Setbacks characterize the settlement in Canaan (Judges and 1 Samuel), but David eventually brings success (2 Samuel 5), followed by the establishment of the kingdom under Solomon. Again, covenant is the context of effective promise. In the NT the various writers see God's promises fulfilled in Christ. Paul writes, "For in him (Christ) every one of God's promises is a 'Yes'" (2 Cor. 1:20). Those who believe in Christ are "descendants of Abraham" (Gal. 3:7). Promise is the theme in Rom. 9:4 and in long stretches of Hebrews. Heb. 9:15-18 shows in the clearest terms that the basis of promise is covenant (Gk. *diathēkē*), which can also mean "testament."

In the history of theology promise becomes especially decisive for Luther, Tyndale, Barth, Rahner, Moltmann, and Pannenberg, among many others. Moltmann insists that, like much eschatology, "A word of promise . . . has not yet found a reality congruous with it. . . . It stands in contradiction to the reality open to experience now" (*Theology of Hope* [London: SCM, 1967], 103). Various "fulfilments," he continues, are expositions or "confirmations and experience of the promise" (105). Even knowledge of Christ may be "anticipatory, provisional and fragmentary," until "what he will be" comes into sight (203). Despair, Moltmann urges, is the arbitrary sin of anticipating a nonfulfillment of promise; presumption is "a premature, self-willed anticipation of the fulfilment of what we hope for" (23). Pannenberg declares, "Perhaps the most important service Luther rendered as a biblical exegete was to rediscover in the biblical texts the temporal structure of faith and therefore its nature as trust (corresponding to God's Word of promise)" (*ST* 3:138). Later he comments, "The promises put the human present, with all the pain of its incompleteness and failure, in the light of God. . . . The concept of promise links our present to God's future" (545). God's faithfulness to his promise becomes manifest over a duration of time.

In modern discussions of promise, however, the focus also turns to speech act theory. J. L. Austin's work shows that promise may be conveyed in various ways. Formally, "I promise to be there" may have the same function as "I'll be there." The word "promise" is not always *explicit*. The central issue, however, is that promise *does* something. This is the definition of speech act: it *does* something in saying something. For example, "I promise to give you . . ." entails a change in the possession of property. But the promise must be sincere and involve a personal *commitment*. Austin compares a boy whose ball broke a neighbor's window promising something with the child's mother saying, "He promises, don't you, Willie?" This is *not* a promise or a speech act at all (Austin, *How to Do Things with Words* [Cambridge: Harvard University Press, 1962], 63, 69). A person who makes a promise must take responsibility for his or her own words. Against the background of the biblical data, Christian theology, and especially speech act theory, we may sum up five components of the speech act of promise, as follows.

(i) Promise presupposes *institutional* facts. The biblical writings from Genesis to Hebrews make it clear that the terms of the *covenant* constitute those institutional facts. The promising nature of the Lord's Supper and baptism as covenanted effective signs has been emphasized by Calvin and others.

(ii) Promises entail *commitments*. Austin calls them "commissives," and Searle follows this. As Pannenberg stresses, they entail faithfulness to fulfill the promise over a certain duration of time. They relate to *character and ethics*. Psalms and Proverbs condemn rash or unmeant promises (Pss. 120:2-3; 141:3; Prov. 6:12, 19). God in his sovereignty chooses to constrain his own freedom, in order to perform his promises.

(iii) A promise *need not be explicit*. Such statements as "I'll be there" constitute promise. Some of the promises of God are buried in informal language. God's intention to act may constitute a promise.

(iv) Speech acts range in strength and intensity, as G. J. Warnock has shown. Promise is a *paradigm case* of a strong speech act. To make a promise is clearly an act of commitment.

(v) The effects of promise *change reality and the world*. They may appoint agents to a task, bequeath property to a recipient, or cause people to inherit vast resources. F. Recanati, J. R. Searle, and others expand on this. (*See also* **Speech Act Theory** for a more detailed exposition of these aspects.)

Reading: J. L. Austin, *How to Do Things with Words* (Cambridge: Harvard University Press, 1962); R. S. Briggs, *Words in Action* (Edinburgh and New York; T. & T. Clarke, 2001); J. Moltmann, *Theology of Hope* (London: SCM, 1967), 95-229; W. Pannenberg, *Systematic Theology,* vol. 3 (Grand Rapids: Eerdmans, 1998), 136-82; A. C. Thiselton, *Thiselton on Hermeneutics* (Grand Rapids: Eerdmans; Aldershot: Ashgate, 2006), 99-130; W. Zimmerli, "Promise and Fulfilment," in *Essays in Old Testament Hermeneutics* (Richmond: John Knox, 1971), 89-122.

Providence

Surprisingly, the main Greek word for "providence," *pronoia*, is not applied to God in the NT, although it occurs many times in Greek writers, including Herodotus, Plato, Plutarch, and many others (BDAG 872-23). Acts 24:2 uses the word, but with reference to Felix, the Roman governor. Nevertheless, the Bible is full of observations and events that presuppose providence. H. P. Owen argues that providence rests on a combination of four themes: (i) God foresees events; (ii) God controls events; (iii) God cares for his creatures; and (iv) God works out a purpose for them ("Providence and Science," in *Providence*, ed. M. Wiles [London: SPCK, 1969], 77). The Greek *pronoia* does occur in the LXX: "It is your providence *(pronoia)*, O Father, that steers its course" (of a vessel at sea; Wis. 14:3; cf. 4 Macc. 9:24; 13:19; 17:22). By his providence God sustains the world he has created.

God's providence in biblical thought includes even the birds: "Are not two sparrows sold for a penny? Yet not one of them will fall to the ground apart from your Father" (Matt. 10:29). The parallel in Luke 12:6 has "five sparrows sold for two pennies," of which "not one of them is forgotten in God's sight," that is, without God's knowledge and care. In both parallels the next verse adds: "Even the hairs of your head are all counted. Do not be afraid; you are of more value than many sparrows" (Matt. 10:30; Luke 12:7). The Psalms include everyone as recipients of providence:

> The Lord is good to all,
>   and his compassion is over all that he has made. (Ps. 145:9)

Both trust and prayer normally *presuppose* God's providential action. The exception would be only within a Kantian or Deist worldview. No one can trust an impotent or unloving God.

All this in no way undermines the reality of evil or freedom. One classic reference is Joseph's testimony: "Even though you intended to do harm to me, God intended it for good, in order to preserve a numerous people" (Gen. 50:20). Joseph's imprisonment and suffering were part of God's overarching purpose and plan. In the Acts of the Apostles, the church underwent setbacks, persecution, and suffering, but "those who were scattered went from place to place, proclaiming the word" (8:4). As Ronald Williams and Beverly Roberts Gaventa argue, the *purposes of God* were constantly fulfilled in Acts, in spite of, or because of, apparent setbacks.

The climactic example in the NT is the suffering and crucifixion of Jesus Christ, upon which hinged the fulfillment of God's plan of salvation. God's general providence to all is also seen in "the fixed order" of light by day and the moon by night (Jer. 31:35-36). Job 38–39 tells of God's command of the sea, storms, the life of humankind, and wild animals. Jesus declares, "If God so clothes the grass of the field . . . will he not much more clothe you — you of little faith?" (Matt. 6:30). Hence believers are not to spend time worrying about food and clothes (6:31-33).

The notion of God's "control" in no way undermines human freedom, but undergirds God's effective ability to bring all his purposes to fruition (*see* **God, Trinity: God Creates, Speaks, or Reveals; God, Trinity: Historical Development**). Israel's slavery in Egypt might look like a disaster, but it constituted the presupposition of the exodus, which lay at the roots of Israelite and Christian faith. Israel sinned in the wilderness, but God nevertheless brought them through to the Promised Land, even if this now involved more hardships than would otherwise have been their lot. Egypt, Philistia, Assyria, Babylon, Persia, and Rome became successive instruments of God for his overall control of history and his purposes for his people. Jesus was born "when the fullness of time had come" (Gal. 4:4). In Rom. 8:18-39 Paul acknowledges the reality of suffering and decay of the world, but explains that nothing "will be able to separate us from the love of God" (v. 39) and the fulfillment of his purpose. Eph. 1:10 also speaks of God's "plan" for the restoration of all things in Christ. Owen's themes of forward-seeing, controlling, caring, and purposive acts are clearly confirmed in Scripture.

Examples of these themes in the Church Fathers are numerous. Augustine's *City of God* explains how God's Lordship over history is such that the disasters and turmoil that befell the earthly city could not thwart God's purposes for the heavenly city. Thomas Aquinas discusses the governance of the world in *Summa Theologiae* 1, questions 103-5. God cares, he says, even for oxen (1 Cor. 9:9; qu. 103, art. 5). He cites for support Gregory of Nyssa and Augustine (art. 6). In question 105, article 5, he appeals to God's fixed ordering of all things, and to God as "first Agent." John Calvin discusses providence in *Institutes* 1.16-18. By "providence," he argues, we do not mean a deity "sitting idly in heaven," but one who "overrules all events" and "holds the helm" (1.16.4; Beveridge, 1:175). In Gen. 22:8 Abraham said, "God himself will provide." Calvin adds, "Particular events are evidences of the special providence of God" (1.16.7; 1:178). He quotes Ps. 104:3-4: "He maketh the clouds his chariot, and walketh upon the wings of the wind." He concludes, "The general providence of God . . . extends over the creatures . . . they are adapted to a certain and special purpose" (1.16.7; 1:175). Calvin also holds two themes together: "A Christian will not overlook inferior causes" (1.17.9; 1:191) and "the will of God is said to be the cause of all things" (1.18.2; 1:201). From the eighteenth century we may cite William Paley and his formulation of the teleological argument, and today in the light of "science" the counterarguments to alleged "difficulties" by Owen, Polkinghorne, Swinburne, and many others. (*See also* **Christology: Ministry of Jesus; Evil, Problem of; Freedom; Grace; Love; Science and Religion.**)

Reading: C. G. Berkouwer, *The Providence of God* (Grand Rapids: Eerdmans, 1952); John Polkinghorne, *Science and Providence* (London: SPCK, 1989); Maurice Wiles, *Providence* (London: SPCK, 1969); Charles M. Wood, *The Question of Providence* (Louisville: John Knox, 2008).

Purgatory

Pope Benedict XII declared in the fourteenth century: "There is a Purgatory, that is a state of punishment and purification, in which the souls which are still hardened by venial sins and the temporal punishment for sins, are purified" (*Benedictus Deus* [1336]). This distinguishes between purgatory as punishment and purgatory as purification, and combines them. Earlier, Thomas Aquinas had emphasized the first: "The punishment of purgatory is intended to supplement the satisfaction which was not fully completed in the body" (*Su Th* 2.2, qu. 71, art. 6). Protestants vehemently oppose the notion that "satisfaction . . . was not fully completed," arguing for the "all-sufficiency" of Christ. In the words of the *Book of Common Prayer* in the Holy Communion Canon, "Jesus Christ . . . made there (by his one oblation of himself once offered) a full, perfect, and sufficient sacrifice, oblation and satisfaction for the sins of the whole world." Geoffrey Rowell, however, in the Anglo-Catholic tradition, attempts to distinguish the views of the Tractarians or Oxford Movement of the nineteenth century from the classic Roman Catholic view. The "High Church" view, he argues, sees purgatory entirely as a gradual postmortem process of purification, but not as punishment.

Jürgen Moltmann represents the Protestant view with robust clarity. He urges, "The idea of purgatory seems to be incompatible with the experience of the unconditional love with which God in Christ finds us, accepts us, reconciles us, and glorifies us" (*The Coming of God* [London: SCM, 1996], 98). Paul Tillich speaks of "accepting being accepted." But Moltmann excludes the notion of a "hell" on the same basis. If Rowell is right, there are two separate issues to be addressed: whether postmortem punishment for Christians retains any validity; and whether a Christian who still harbors sin or sins at death still has to undergo a gradual process of purification. Rowell finds it incredible that a sinful Christian can suddenly be transformed in death and resurrection to a sinless or purified being. Moltmann argues that neither Scripture nor tradition supports the doctrine, but that it arose, as Luther showed, from a medieval misunderstanding of "penance" as self-inflicted punishment rather than "turning" or repentance. To be fair, most Roman Catholics would not assume that we can "add" to the suffering of Christ in a literal sense. Even Paul daringly exclaims: "In my flesh I am completing what is lacking in Christ's afflictions for the sake of . . . the church" (Col. 1:24). D. E. H. Whiteley accepts the "once-for-all" character of Christ's death, but compares the "additional" light of the moon "not as an independent source" but as reflecting the light of the sun (*Theology of St. Paul* [Oxford: Blackwell, 1964, 1970], 149). Nevertheless, this doctrine encourages a belief that Jesus' work is somehow in need of supplementation. Aquinas declared, "Purgatory is intended to supplement the satisfaction which was not yet completed" (*Su Th* 2.2, qu. 71, art. 6).

More serious for Protestants is Rowell's point about purification. He finds it unbelievable that this could occur instantaneously in the lives of all Christians. Both Roman Catholic and Protestant biblical scholars generally agree that Paul's analogy of fire in 1 Cor. 3:11-15 has nothing to do with purgatory. The "loss" here concerns ministerial faithfulness and trust, and the peril of superficial human evaluations. To be saved "as through fire" denotes a narrow escape like "a brand snatched from the fire" (Amos 4:11). First, not all the Tractarians accepted even the "milder" view of purgatory. E. B. Pusey rejected this view. Rowell cannot accept the notion of holiness "ready-made," which is doubtless true of conditions in this life. This is in spite of views of holiness among many Pentecostals and members of the Holiness Movement as an "event," not a process. Contrary to this, Paul, Luther, and the major Reformers saw struggle and temptation as part of this process in the present life.

Nevertheless, "holiness" (Heb. *qādosh*) derives its nature from closeness to God, and this will occur at the *resurrection*. There is some truth in the words of the hymn: "When I see Thee as Thou art, I'll praise Thee as I ought." While we are on the earth, temptations abound, both to forget God and to be obsessed with the self. But as O. R. Jones has extensively argued, holiness is a *disposition,* which becomes operative and manifest in appropriate conditions *(The Concept of Holiness).* Being with God in the postresurrection state, however, provides precisely these conditions. Moreover, the resurrection life becomes possible only through the Holy Spirit. When he calls this the "spiritual" mode of existence (1 Cor. 15:44; cf. Rom. 8:11), Paul declares that we shall be wholly under the influence of the Holy Spirit, who above all purifies and provides holiness. There is no need for a doctrine of purgatory, either as punishment or as purification. Understandably, the Reformers resisted such an idea.

Reading: J. Le Goff, *The Birth of Purgatory* (Chicago: University of Chicago Press, 1986); O. R. Jones, *The Concept of Holiness* (London: Allen and Unwin, 1969), 39-50; G. Rowell, *Hell and the Victorians* (Oxford: Clarendon, 1974); A. C. Thiselton, *Life after Death* (Grand Rapids: Eerdmans, 2012), 70-71 and 129-36.

Puritanism

Puritanism emerged during the reign of Elizabeth I (1558-1603), as a protest against the Elizabethan Settlement of 1559, and against the inclusion of what Puritans regarded as Romish theology and practices in the Protestant church of the time. Most Puritans disowned the title as pejorative, although some accepted it. Most Puritans rejected episcopal authority, ceremonial liturgies, and sacerdotal vestments for priests, regarding them as popish, idolatrous, and superstitious. The second *Book of Common Prayer* (1552) of Edward VI had removed vestments, invocation of saints, and the sign of the cross from the first prayer book of 1549. The Elizabethan prayer book returned some of these customs, seeking to steer a middle path. Most Puritans aligned themselves with Reformed theology on the Continent, especially with Calvinism. The movement did not have clear boundaries, especially in the Stuart era under James I (1603-1625), Charles I (1625-1649), Oliver Cromwell (1649-1660), and Charles II. For example, Richard Baxter was rooted in the Puritan tradition but was committed to church unity, and was ordained in 1638 in the Church of England; he served as chaplain in the

Parliamentary army, and declined a bishopric in 1662, although he served as a royal chaplain. At the opposite end of the spectrum, Thomas Cartwright sought a Presbyterian ecclesiology. In 1604 James I met with both bishops and Puritan leaders at Hampton Court, but contrary to their hopes the Puritans failed to win concessions from the king, in spite of his Scottish upbringing. Again, however, more moderate Puritans gained positions of influence, including Richard Sibbes, who became preacher at Gray's Inn and master of St. Catharine's Hall, Cambridge, and John Preston, who became chaplain to the then Prince Charles and master of Emmanuel College. Some Puritans remain widely read today, especially for their depth of devotion. John Bunyan is the classic example.

Q

Quakers, or Society of Friends
George Fox (1624-1691) founded the society. Quakers follow a "way," rather than subscribe to orthodox doctrine. Their community aims at friendship rather than shared doctrine. Indeed, they shun what they regard as "outward" forms of religion or formal worship, including creeds, sacraments, and liturgies. If they have any doctrine, it would simply be the "inner light," allegedly based on John 1:9 (although some argue this verse uses *phōtizō* in the sense of "shed light upon," for both judgment and grace). In the eighteenth and nineteenth centuries Elizabeth Fry led concerns for prison reform, and Joseph Lancaster for education. The original name used by others for them was "Quakers," which originates from their being said to "tremble" at the Word of God. Originally, too, they were a Christ-centered movement, but nowadays assemblies range from Christ-centeredness to very broad pacifist groups. But all retain the basic characteristics of unprogrammed worship based on the practice of silence. All can speak, including women, if they wish to pass on what their "inner light" of the Holy Spirit has revealed. They suffered persecution in the early days, but nowadays are largely recognized for their philanthropy. (*See also* **Fox, George**.)

Queer Theology
Queer theology is very recent, and in process of development. Its content, in practice, concerns human sexuality, especially among marginalized groups. It considers "heteronormativity" among gays, lesbians, and transgendered people. Like many postmodernists, especially Foucault, it rejects "givens" in theology and ethics, which it tends to regard as conventions of society, history, class, race, and gender. It often claims some affinity with *radical* hermeneutics and with radical feminism. G. Loughlin, *Queer Theology: Rethinking the Western Body* (Oxford: Blackwell, 2007), marks perhaps the beginning of a literature on the subject.

R

Radical Orthodoxy
Radical Orthodoxy constitutes a new movement in theology, dating from the late 1990s and flourishing today. Its first three main exponents were John Milbank, Catherine Pickstock, and Graham Ward, in 1999, all from Cambridge. They co-edited *Radical Orthodoxy: A New Theology* (London and New York: Routledge, 1999), to define the movement. First, Radical Orthodoxy attacks "secularism" as "defining and constructing the world," calling today's secularism a "self-conscious superficiality" (1). Second, it claims "orthodoxy" in the "straightforward sense of commitment to creedal Christianity" (2). In practice, for its exponents, although it "transcends confessional boundaries," it tends to derive its theology mainly from "Thomist currents in the wake of Gilson and Maritain," that is, the neo-Thomist tradition. Third, the adjective "radical" is intended to denote "a return to patristic and mediaeval roots, and especially to the Augustinian vision of all knowledge as divine illumination," and in particular drawing on this "to criticise modern society," aligning the movement with "the great Christian critics of the Enlightenment" (2-3). It criticizes "any alternative configuration ... independent of God" (3). It insists that every discipline must be framed by a theological perspective. If they do not participate in God, systems of thought are grounded in nothing, whether knowledge, language, the body, aesthetic experience, or politics. These systems have become deluded about their stability. Thus, as a major principle, "It recognizes that materialism and spiritualism are false alternatives," as are reason and revelation. It claims to be "incarnational theology" and participatory philosophy (4). This, as well as its neo-Thomism, may explain its sacramental perspective.

Milbank's essays explore the theme of the infinite in the finite, as well as rejecting any dualism of reason and revelation. He approaches Hamann and Jacobi in "a genuinely anti-liberal" way (23). He tends to attack a variety of positions. Barth's Christocentricity, he urges, reduces theology to "a focus on an enormous black hole" (22). He is also unhappy with Luther, in spite of the Lutheran frame of Hamann and Jacobi (24-25). But he praises Hamann for having "a non-abstractive validity in this necessary use of signs to decipher the analogically continuous aspects of reality" (27). He dismisses neoorthodox critiques of Hamann. Milbank concludes, "Because they point theology to a radical orthodoxy, they also show how theology can convert nihilism" (32). The question of language is clearly important for Radical Orthodoxy. Thus Conor Cunningham in this volume criticizes a quasi-Kantian dualism in the earlier work of Wittgenstein (75-77), and his tendency to reduce or to criticize "essences" behind phenomena, mainly in his later work (85). He concludes, "Only for theology, not philosophy, is grammar the last word" (86). The visible and bodily are also important, as Ward insists, which again harmonizes with the incarnational and sacramental theme of Radical Orthodoxy.

Much in Radical Orthodoxy will win support and perhaps admiration, including the attack on autonomous secularism and the defense of creedal Christianity. One problem for those Protestants who may resist Anglo-Catholic tendencies may be suggested by Ward's citation of Gregory of Nyssa: "He who sees the Church looks directly at Christ" (177). In one sense this is true; but in another sense Protestant and Reformation critics have long opposed the slogan "The church as the body of Christ," interpreted sometimes to mean that "to be joined to the church is necessarily to be joined to Christ." But this is a relatively minor point in contrast to the larger issues of Radical Orthodoxy. If "radical" denotes *not* what Don Cupitt argues for, but the roots of tradition in patristic sources, this is all to the good. Whether all Christian thinkers will wish to elevate Aquinas above Luther, Barth, and others, some may doubt. But, again, this may not rank as the key point of the movement. Some regard Radical Orthodoxy as stemming the tide of Anglo-Catholicism.

Rahner, Karl

Karl Rahner (1904-1984) stands with Balthasar, Küng, and Congar as one of the four most influential Roman Catholic theologians of the twentieth century, perhaps also ahead of de Lubac, Schillebeeckx, and Lonergan in influence.

(i) **Life and Beginnings.** Rahner was born in Freiburg of a devout Catholic family, and became a Jesuit in 1922. He was grounded in patristic thought and neo-Thomism, and developed a strong interest in Kant. He was ordained priest in 1932, in Munich. He then returned to his home city of Freiburg, where Martin Heidegger was professor of philosophy. Rahner was expected to undertake a doctorate in philosophy, for which he chose to study Kant and Maréchal. He studied under the professor of Catholic philosophy, who was then Martin Honecker, but also attended Heidegger's seminar on the pre-Socratic philosophers, as well as Plato, Aristotle, and Kant. Honecker did not warm to Rahner's approach in his dissertation, and his philosophical doctorate was abandoned unfinished. William Dych recalls asking Rahner whether this disappointed him, to which he replied, "I was not disappointed at all." He commented that this philosophical work would have interrupted his theological studies, and declared, "I was relieved to be delivered from this work" (Dych, *Karl Rahner* [London: Chapman, 1992], 7). Rahner left Freiburg for Innsbruck to undertake doctoral work in theology, especially in typology in the Church Fathers with special reference to John 19:34, and graduated in 1936. In 1937 he was appointed honorary lecturer *(Privatdozent)* in the University of Innsbruck. His teaching at Innsbruck lasted for some twenty or so years, and covered such topics as creation, sin, grace, justification, faith, hope, love, and the sacraments. Much of the material was collected and subsequently published as *Theological Investigations* (Ger. *Schriften zur Theologie;* Eng., 23 vols. [London: Darton, Longman and Todd; New York: Seabury Press, 1961-1992]); hereafter *TI*.

In 1938 the Nazis marched into Austria and annexed it. They abolished the faculty of theology at Innsbruck. The Jesuits withdrew from the university and set up their teaching in their own college. In 1939 the Jesuits were expelled, and Rahner was invited to Vienna, where he spent most of the war years. He had become convinced that Scholastic theology was of little help in training pastors, and revised his method and content of teaching. But in 1943 the archbishop of Freiburg sent a letter to all the Catholic bishops of Germany and Austria, warning them "of dangerous innovations in Catholic doctrine and liturgy" (Dych, *Karl Rahner*, 9). However, the archbishop of Vienna did not share these misgivings, and sent back a longer "reply," in fact drafted by Rahner. This anticipated much of the agenda of Vatican II some twenty years later. During the last year of the war Rahner served as parish priest in a small Bavarian village. He well confirmed his reputation as a priest, preacher, and pastor. In 1948 he returned to the reconstituted faculty of theology at Innsbruck, and began an era of prolific writing. Three volumes of *Theological Investigations* appeared, in 1954, 1955, and 1956, respectively. Yet Karen Kilby comments: "In the 1950s he was on the margins, his orthodoxy questioned, his work censored; in the 1960s suddenly, he was at the centre of things, a theological expert at the Second Vatican Council, and . . . one of the shaping influences upon it" (Kilby, *Karl Rahner* [London: Collins/Fount, 1997]). By 1962 objections to Rahner's theology had been voiced by Roman authorities, especially on the Eucharist and Mariology.

The turning point came when, in November 1962, Pope John XXIII appointed Rahner a *peritus* (expert adviser) to Vatican II. He was subsequently chosen as one of seven theologians to develop *Lumen Gentium,* the explication of the doctrine of the church. During the Council Rahner accepted a chair in the University of Munich. From 1967 to 1968 he edited, with Adolf Durlap and others, the well-known six-volume *Sacramentum Mundi: An Encyclopaedia of Theology* (Eng. London: Burns and Oates; New York: Sheed and Ward, 1968-1970). In 1965 he edited, with Edward Schillebeeckx, the first number of *Concilium.* Meanwhile, at Vatican II he and Joseph Ratzinger worked together on an alternative text to the document on Scripture and tradition. Dych comments, "By the time the Council ended in December 1965 Rahner had exercised enormous influence on the final shape of many of the conciliar documents" (13). This included Scripture and tradition, papal primacy, revelation, the episcopate, and the sacraments. One of the courses he delivered in his new chair at the University of Munich was "Foundations of Christian Faith." This in effect became published in 1976 by Herder in Freiburg, and in English as *Foundations of Christian Faith* (New York: Seabury Press; London: Darton, Longman and Todd, 1978); hereafter *FCF.* This is one of the best books for conveying a general impression of Rahner's theology. Then in 1967 he was called to be professor of dogmatic theology in the University of Münster, where he taught until his retirement in 1971, at the age of sixty-seven. He continued, however, to write and to undertake lecturing in Germany and overseas, including in London and Budapest.

This biography, however, does not indicate many of the most important things about Rahner. In a remarkable book, *Understanding Karl Rahner* (London: SCM, 1986), Herbert Vorgrimler, like Dych a close friend of Rahner, pinpoints two barriers to "understanding" Rahner: incomprehensible language and a lack of genuine understanding of Rahner as a human person, not just as a theologian or thinker. Hence he sees Rahner's life as "the story of a life with God . . . ; it was a search for God, a struggle with God, a taking refuge in God, a constant unmasking of idols" (2). He points to his "inexorable concern for honesty," for example, about prayer and God's apparent silence, when "we called, but no answer came" (5). Rahner, like many other theologians, sought to reach middle-class citizens who were lukewarm and halfhearted, to unsettle them. But he had "a heart devoted to humanity" and "often spoke of . . . his own love" (7-8). Love, he urged, is a power that changes people. The other side of this was his genuine anger about those who "held office" in the church but were insensitive and unctuous toward the troubled or oppressed (10). He wanted solemn liturgies to be "free from disturbances and distractions" (17). He was deeply concerned about pastoral care and the need for meditation. He regularly immersed himself in the Bible, often with the help of exegetical commentaries (21). Like Calvin, he asked, "How can the Christian speak appropriately of God unless at the same time he speaks of man?" (22). On Rahner's "difficult" language, Vorgrimler admits the complexities of his earlier writings but insists that they became simpler with the passing years. After such an introduction, he attempts to expound the events of Rahner's life and thought, pausing only to consider "difficulties." It is time now, however, to look more closely at the content and details of Rahner's theology.

(ii) **Grace and Knowledge.** Rahner is clear about the limitations of human knowledge; not for nothing had he studied Kant. *Gnosis* claims to know what is hidden from the other. But God is inscrutable. Rahner cited Rom. 11:33, "O the depth of the riches and wisdom and knowledge of God! How unsearchable are his judgments and how inscrutable his ways!" He also cited Isa. 55:8,

> My thoughts are not your thoughts,
> nor are your ways my ways.

Revelation is not primarily the disclosure of knowledge, as if to make us all gnostics, but opens the possibility of knowing a *person*. Rahner declared, "What is most specially Christian in Christianity [is] Jesus Christ" (*FCF* 176). Only because the self-communication of God "reaches the goal and climax in Jesus Christ, we can speak of 'anonymous Christians'" (176). This well-known but controversial phrase depends on Rahner's view that, contrary to the Thomist and conventional view of grace, the reception of grace does not automatically entail the conscious "knowledge" of it. In other respects grace in Rahner is christocentric. Encountering Jesus as a *person* is different from reflecting about Christology. Indeed, it begins with the faith of Jesus himself (against Bultmann). We look to Jesus as "the pioneer and perfecter of our faith" (Heb. 12:2). His faith is seen in his utter surrender to the incomprehensibility of God in the cross. Christian faith and hope, therefore, are also "a letting go of the self" and "beyond all human control" (*TI* 10:250). Faith, hope, and love reach "outwards from the self" (250). In contrast to the freedom of grace, knowledge seeks to master and to control. It involves "self-presence," "self-possession," and objectification (*FCF* 16, 17). Love of God and love of our neighbor become unified in Scripture (Dych, *Karl Rahner*, 26). Many Protestants would endorse Rahner's statement that Christian hope is trusting in God's promise, not in our own power, as indeed would Moltmann.

In his exposition of grace and of theology Rahner calls for "the courage to think" (*TI* 9:63). But faith and theology must come before philosophy. Like Pannenberg and Wolterstorff, however, he insists that faith must be reasonable, or else it becomes merely a blind leap (Dych, *Karl Rahner*, 32). In his reformation of the doctrine of grace, Rahner, in effect, follows the path opened up by de Lubac, that grace is not restricted to the "supernatural." If God had created and ordered human nature, would it not be "natural," or part of "being human," to have the capacity to receive grace? The debate turned on the relation between grace and nature, and Rahner attacked what he called the "extrinsic" view. "Extrinsicism," he wrote, is found in "the average text-book's teaching on the relationship between grace and nature" (*TI* 1:298; cited by Dych, *Karl Rahner*, 33). God's history of grace is intimately interconnected with the history of the world. Yet Rahner insists equally that grace is always free and gratuitous. Indeed, he claims that "pure nature" is an abstraction, since God's creation and providence sustain and order all nature. This offers some background to his notion of "anonymous" Christians. Yet the missing factor underlined by Augustine, Calvin, and Barth is the nature of the Fall, and its radical consequences (*see* **Sin: Historical**). Dych comments, "The claim that a universal history of grace entails a universal history of revelation is based on Rahner's understanding of the nature of human knowledge" (40-41). He draws from Heidegger the possibility of what "becomes manifest," or what can be "shown," through what Rahner calls the "luminous realm."

(iii) **Jesus of Nazareth and Christianity.** Rahner argues that Christian faith concerns events in history, not necessary or eternal ideas. Faith and reason are not schizophrenic. Nor is Docetism adequate, for "the Word became flesh." Rahner believed that "mighty deeds, signs and wonders" were part of the historical life of Jesus of Nazareth. "Jesus saw himself not merely as one among many prophets . . . but as the *eschatological* prophet" (*FCF* 245-46). He added, "Jesus lived in and was part of the religious milieu of his people and the historical situation in which he found himself" (247). But he was a radical reformer who "faced his death resolutely and accepted it at least as the inevitable consequence of fidelity to his mission and as imposed on him by God" (248). He was conscious of "a radical and unique closeness to God" (249), and proclaimed the imminence of God's kingdom. He proclaimed the kingdom, not himself, but "There was a place in his theology for his death and resurrection" (253). Kilby writes, "Rahner affirms, with the Christian tradition, the full divinity as well as the full humanity of Jesus Christ" (*Karl Rahner*, 16). Nevertheless, in comparison with the Anglican J. A. T. Robinson, Rahner believed that most Christians are "closet docetists" (18). To be truly "human" is already to be in a relationship with God.

To be truly human, Rahner believed, is to have transcendent experience. To be human is to transcend all things, "to 'go beyond' all things towards God" (19). In this sense it becomes more credible to regard Jesus as a paradigm of humanness. Rahner explicitly used the term "transcendental." He wrote, "Today an a priori doctrine of the God-Man must be developed in a transcendental theology" (*FCF* 177). These are "the conditions of possibility" for the concept of Jesus as fully human. This is part of what he called "an ascending Christology," which complements the notion of God entering history, and which he called "a descending Christology" (177).

As we note in our entry on Christology, Rahner stresses the need to view the presupposition of Chalcedon within the frame of a transcendental philosophy, which he gained especially from Kant. Rahner overtakes Bultmann's existential view of Christ by returning through this method (correctly) to an ontological perspective. He considers both the existential (what Christ means to us) and the ontological (what Christ is in himself) (*FCF* 204). This approach also places humankind in a social and historical context, not simply as solitary individuals. A human being is conscious of moving toward an infinite horizon, which fulfills the promise of God in Christ. Concerning humanity, Rahner uses the phrase found in Tillich, "ek-static," and the phrase found in Pannenberg, "ec-centric," that is, moving *beyond* the self, and *not centered* in the self. Thus "God brings about man's self-transcendence into God through his absolute self-communication to all men ... signified by hypostatic union" (*FCF* 201). Rahner wrote, "Human beings must go out and away from themselves, they must realise themselves in something other than they have done and suffered" (*TI* 3:324). This entirely reflects complex issues about the identity of Jesus Christ.

Rahner applies Christology in several practical ways. One concerns a theology of Christian vocation. If Christ, Christian believers, and human beings in general have their reason for being "outside themselves" as a vocation to serve God and to serve others, all live as Christ did. He states, "A person is always a Christian in order to become one ... in faith, hope, and love" (*FCF* 306). Salvation is not reified and static, but "occurs in the subject's knowing and loving self-surrender into the mystery of God" (309). Rahner also declares, "In Jesus God has turned to us in such a unique and unsurpassable way that in him [Christ] he has given himself absolutely" (289). One commentator observes, "Jesus is what humanity is, only more so" (Philip Endean, "Rahner, Christology, and Grace," *Heythrop*

Journal 32 [1996]: 288; cf. 284-97). Many of Rahner's christological themes are repeated in K. Rahner and W. Thüsing, *A New Christology* (London: Burns and Oates, 1980). Rahner states, for example, "We shall find that proximity of God in no other place but in Jesus of Nazareth" (17). Once again, the significance of the incarnation, the cross, and the resurrection of Christ concerns not just expiation, or a means of dealing with human sin, but God's involvement with the world. Karen Kilby sums up the point admirably. She writes that for Rahner, "Had Adam not fallen ... Christ would still have come into the world. ... Christ is not just the remedy for our sins. ... The driving motor [is] ... God's involvement with the world, not simply human sin" (*Karl Rahner,* 29).

(iv) **Concept of the Church: "Anonymous Christianity" Again?** Many Protestants will find their reactions torn in different directions on Rahner's doctrine of the church. They may well warm to the fact that Rahner's theology as a whole, like Barth's, was written in the service of the church. They may also welcome his traditional Augustinian distinction between the visible and invisible church, which loosens the absolute nature of the institutional church, which some, rightly or wrongly, perceive as a "Catholic" problem. They may also welcome the fact that Rahner's work on the church springs from a deeply pastoral concern. But on the other hand, they may experience deep anxiety and concern about one thing above others, namely, his quasi-liberal, but also pastoral, concern about twentieth-century humanity. Rahner's view of the church today in a pluralistic world leads on again to his distinctive view of "anonymous Christianity," even more clearly perhaps than his view of nature and grace. This is a point at which his pastoral concern partly overlaps, or *seems* to overlap, with many Protestant liberals in the mid–twentieth century, who also expressed concern about the dominance of scientific culture and secular thought. We might cite J. A. T. Robinson, Maurice Wiles, Denis Nineham, and others who constantly expressed their concern for "modern man," almost as if the gospel needed to be adjusted to become believable once again. They and Rahner are equally concerned about "belief" during the thirteen hundred years between around 400 and 1700 when Western culture *was* Christianity, and the later twentieth century when explicit Christian faith meant going against the stream.

In fact, Rahner is *not* suggesting a liberal agenda *in the sense of trimming or changing the gospel.* Nevertheless, he *does* agree with the diagnosis of liberals that "grace" used to come to us differently in "a homogeneous Christian society which itself provides for all strictly Christian patterns of behaviour." In this respect this "marks out a place for the decision of Christian faith, and in a certain sense facilitates it" (Rahner, *The Shape of the Church to Come* [Ger. 1972; Eng. London: SPCK, 1974], 23). This raises, Rahner believes, an acute problem for today, namely, "whether the relation between *the* faith and *the* unbelief ... ultimately decides a person's final salvation" (29). This will clarify his contrast between explicit faith and explicit unbelief in an era he calls "very much altered in our time and in our future." He argues that any notion of the church as a "little flock" does not define a "ghetto or sect" or even numbers, but a mentality or mind-set (29). People simply see lifestyles among "office holders and other Christians," which make Christianity look "historically obsolete" (31).

Few can quarrel with this diagnosis of a real problem, where many people do not fully engage with a living, committed Christian community. But Rahner's solution is radical. Hitherto, he argues, people have regarded the "true" invisible church as a kind of subset within the institutional, visible church. Rahner reverses this. Kilby explains this in simple terms (*Karl Rahner*, 31-35): "The invisible is *broader* than the visible. The invisible Church is not the hidden kernel existing within the visible, but an extension of the Church beyond the boundaries of those who explicitly confess Christianity" (31). This theme depends on Rahner's view of humankind as "a being orientated towards God" (*FCF* 322), and "the whole of human existence in its relationship to the all-encompassing God, by whom all things are born and towards whom all things are directed" (323).

Rahner recognizes that other traditions outside the Catholic Church raise "the most difficult questions ... [about] *which* church we mean" (324). Jesus Christ's founding of the church is "God's historically irreversible and historically tangible offer of himself" (329). Rahner examines the doctrine of the church in the NT, from an exegesis of the sayings about Peter in Matthew to the church in the Pauline Epistles and the Gospels. We cannot have "Christianity" without the church (342-46). But does not the church require faith? Rahner declares, "The doctrine of *sola fide* ... is nothing else but the other and subjective side of the *sola gratia* doctrine" (360). Interestingly, he views questions about the inspiration and authority of the Bible as properly within the context of the church (369-78). He quotes Vatican II as declaring that the inspired writers of Scripture write "what must be considered to be asserted by the Holy Spirit" (375). Although he rejects "verbal inspiration" as such, he accepts the notion of "inerrancy" in a broader sense (375).

On the office of the pope, Rahner asserts, "The power of primacy and the power of leadership in the church ... do not really contradict the essence of Christianity" (387). On Marian dogma, he declares that Mary "has an explicit historical role in the history of salvation" (387). She is not simply "an individual episode in a biography of Jesus" (387). He argues that Luther did not deny her status, but he acknowledges that the cult of the later Middle Ages threatened the *sola gratia* principle. For a Protestant reader, however, Rahner's treatment of the Marian dogmas remains a genuine puzzle. He claims: "The Assumption of the Blessed Virgin, body and soul, into heaven says nothing else about Mary but what we also profess about ourselves in an article of faith in the Apostles' Creed" (388). But is God's eschatological timing different for Mary alone? Was this dogma no more than a profession of the resurrection of all the dead? His treatment of the Immaculate Conception concludes that "there really is no special difficulty" because it all comes down to what God "willed from the beginning" (388). Since many Protestants treat even the virgin birth in this way, the "explanation" is understandable, but this does not make it convincing for many Protestant readers. Credit may be given for these attempts to "soften" traditional division. Rahner undoubtedly seeks to build ecumenical bridges. But whether some will suspect this simply of being a fudge, others must judge.

We have wandered from our question about the scope of the invisible church. Rahner ends his chapter on the church in *Foundations of Christian Faith* by considering again that "we live in a secular world" where there is "pluralism" (400). The church "transcends this pluralistic life with the competing groups.... the most real thing about the church itself is precisely its liberation of man of the human existence into the absolute realm of the majesty of God himself" (410). God's grace is given in Christ "even when in his historical conditioning [a] person interprets his existence without fault in a different way or in a non-Christian way, perhaps even in an atheistic way" (401). Even in such a way "he is accepting the God who gives himself in all of his incomprehensibility in ... the depth of his existence" (401). Rahner intends to argue that this notion of the invisible church arises, first, from the doctrine of grace, second, from Christology, and third, from a philosophy of consciousness and historicality as well as deep pastoral concern. It will not convince everyone, but it does address a persistent problem: "God our Savior ... desires everyone to be saved and to come to the knowledge of the truth" (1 Tim. 2:3-4). But is this as yet evident?

(v) **A Postscript on Rahner's View of the Sacraments.** When we begin to speak about "depth," "acceptance," "the unconscious," and a "secular world," it seems difficult not to be reminded of Paul Tillich. Be that as it may, Rahner's link between sacraments and symbols really does suggest Tillich's approach. Like Tillich, Rahner distinguishes between sign and symbol. Tillich argued that a symbol "participates in" that to which it points (*see* **Tillich, Paul**). One positive gain certainly arises from this: Rahner claims that the church itself is a sacrament: the visible form of invisible grace, as Pannenberg also suggests (*FCF* 411). For him, this is a part of God's self-giving in history. He has no problem with baptism and the Eucharist (or the Lord's Supper) among the sacraments. This point is almost universally agreed. But what of the other five usually listed in Catholicism? Marriage, Rahner writes, "opens out into the mystery of God" (420). Penance and the anointing of the sick are both sacraments (421), not least because "the word of forgiveness continues to live and be efficacious" (422), and these are "decisive citations of a person's life" (423). The Reformers would have agreed with Rahner's first definition of a sacrament: "A sacrament is a tangible word ... from God" (427). Like the Church of England, he sees a sacrament as an "efficacious word of God" (427). But Rahner also seems to accept that sacraments are "what is called Opus Operatum," even if they are also part of a dialogue with God (427). Rahner's "theology of symbol" occurs in *Theological Investigations* 4:221-52. There he argues that in a symbol "the symbolised becomes present." Dych comments, "The symbol is actually the medium which enables the symbolised to become present and in this sense is a cause of their presence. Rahner calls this 'symbolic causality'" (*Karl Rahner,* 119). Sacramental actions are "unfailing signs of God's grace" (119). In this sense the humanity of Christ is a symbol of God (*TI* 4:237).

Such are the outlines of Rahner's theology. Much is bold, insightful, and imaginative. Kant's transcendental philosophy is often in view, but so is a serious account of biblical passages and exegesis. It is easy to understand his influence on Vatican II. Yet there are also elements, as we should expect, that would not convince many orthodox Protestants. Nevertheless, Rahner, with Küng, Congar, and Balthasar, has ended a more sterile period of Catholic theology. His theology embraces a vast range of topics. He is deeply pastoral. His work on "anonymous" Christianity will raise questions for many, but appears bold and imaginative in the view of others. Rahner's contribution to Catholic theology is thoughtful and creative.

Reading: William V. Dych, *Karl Rahner* (London: Chapman, 1992); Geoffrey B. Kelly, *Karl Rahner* (Edinburgh: T. & T. Clark, 1992); Karen Kilby, *Karl Rahner* (London: Collins/Fount, 1997); Karl Rahner, *Theological Investigations,* 23 vols. (New York: Seabury Press; London: Darton, Longman and Todd, 1961-1992); Karl Rahner, *The Shape of the Church to Come* (London: SPCK, 1974); Karl Rahner, *Foundations of Christian Faith* (New York: Seabury Press; London: Darton, Longman and Todd, 1978); H. Vorgrimler, *Understanding Karl Rahner* (London: SCM, 1986).

Ramsey, Ian T.

Ian T. Ramsey (1915-1972) was a brilliant professor of Christian religion at Oxford (1951-1966) and an excellent pastoral bishop of Durham from 1966 until his death in 1972. He gained first-class degrees in mathematics (1936) and theology (1939) at Cambridge, and was later canon theologian of Leicester Cathedral. He worked hard on the frontier between philosophy and Christian theology, and devised a very constructive approach to religious language on the basis of exploring models and qualifiers. He took an active part in the House of Lords.

Ramsey faced criticism for his view of the language of religion from logical positivism and even from J. A. T. Robinson, and produced *Religious Language: An Empirical Placing of Theological Phrases* (London: SCM, 1957). He argued that "disclosures of God" entailed modified uses of ordinary language (19-48). Like Ricoeur's work on metaphor, he proposed that "disclosure situations" occur when two universes of discourse are placed together. Such a situation may provide a breakthrough of understanding, as when we say, "The ice breaks" or "The penny drops" (23). In his brilliant chapter "Models and Qualifiers" (49-89), Ramsey argued that a model such as cause may be applied to God only if it is adequately qualified by such terms as "first" in "first cause," "infinite" in "infinitely wise," or "eternal" in "eternal purpose." His lectures at Newcastle University were published as *Christian Discourse* (New York and London: OUP, 1965). In these lectures he examined the language of the Bible (1-27) and devoted a whole lecture to Robinson's *Honest to God* (61-90). Again he explored biblical models and careful qualifiers. Among several accounts of his life and thought are Jerry H. Gill,

Ian Ramsey (London: Allen and Unwin, 1976), and David Edwards, *Ian Ramsey* (Oxford: OUP, 1973).

Rapture
The rapture is based on a questionable exegesis of 1 Thess. 4:17, which reads, "We ... who are left, will be caught up (Gk. *harpagēsometha*) in the clouds together with them to meet the Lord in the air." Paul's main point is to console the bereaved that those who have already died will not lose out on the final coming of Christ, for all believers will be gathered together in joy at the parousia. Most of the Church Fathers see no contradiction with 1 Corinthians 15. Clement of Alexandria, Tertullian, and others comment that "taken up in the clouds" refers to all believers (Clement, *Stromata* 6.13). A history of interpretation and reception can be found in A. C. Thiselton, *1 and 2 Thessalonians* (Oxford: Wiley-Blackwell, 2011), 115-45. J. N. Darby first called attention to this technical view of the "rapture," which involved *two* events of the parousia, within the framework of dispensationalism. It was as if, in B. McGinn's words, "Prophecy took a holiday for almost two-thousand years (the Dispensation of the Gentiles) between the fall of the Second Temple in Jerusalem in 70 C.E. and the restoration of the Jewish state in 1948" (*The Antichrist* [San Francisco: Harper, 1994], 253). Faithful believers, according to Darby, would then escape a seven-year period of tribulation. Cyrus Scofield took up Darby's views in the Scofield Bible. In twentieth-century America the view was popularized through Hal Lindsey in *The Late Great Planet Earth* (1970), and fervent "prophecies" about the foundation of the Jewish state in 1948. Various political scenarios have been written, most recently associated with the Left Behind series of books by Tim LaHaye and Jerry Jenkins. These are accounts of the rapture based on poor exegesis, which have sold millions of copies. The danger of such accounts involves political attitudes toward Israel. (*See also* **Darby, John Nelson; Dispensationalism; Scofield Reference Bible.**)

Rationalism
Rationalism denotes the belief that reason is the arbiter of competing claims to truth. It stands in contrast to empiricism, which stresses the role of experience and often sense-data; to critical philosophy, which derives from Kant; and to historicality, which derives broadly from Hegel and Heidegger. In the history of philosophy the two chief exponents are Descartes and Leibniz, although many also include Spinoza, even if his themes are more complex. They stress a priori reasoning of the mind, in contrast to the a posteriori method of the empiricists.

Thoroughgoing rationalism is different from arguments from reasonableness, which the empiricist John Locke stressed. It is noteworthy that Descartes and Leibniz were also mathematicians, and that advocates of the ontological argument argue a priori, while the cosmological argument and to a large extent the teleological argument are a posteriori arguments from experience. Hegel, however, emphasized the place of historical reason, and Heidegger and Gadamer demonstrated the role of historicality. Rationalism is related in theology to natural theology and to Deism. Enlightenment rationalism flourished in the eighteenth century, which Newman called the Age of Reason, when love grew cold. Rationalism also tends to share the individualism of Descartes, which was forcefully criticized by W. Temple and others. In *Nature, Man, and God,* Temple actually called the individualism of Descartes "the most disastrous moment in the history of Europe." He was thinking of its social as well as philosophical implications. Gadamer also attacks the devaluing of authority, community, and tradition.

Realism
Realism (from Lat. *res,* "a thing") insists on the reality of the external world, in contrast to idealism, which stresses the activity of the mind in ordering it. Realism asserts that reality is not constructed by the mind. In medieval philosophy it also stands in contrast to nominalism, by understanding universals to constitute more than concepts or names. Few philosophers, however, hold to realism without qualification. They wish to accord some interpretative role to the mind. Hence critical realism is advocated by Bernard Lonergan and many others.

Reason
Reason has invited a range of conflicting evaluations in Christian theology, which are relative to the context of argument. Some of these are not usually in flat contradiction. In rationalism, reason is often opposed to revelation, and usually indicates an attitude of self-sufficiency and rejection of the need of the Bible or even revealed grace. However, John Locke rightly insists that mere intensity of feelings or convictions provides no guarantee of truth. Locke and N. Wolterstorff both speak of *entitled belief,* which includes reasonableness (*see* **Evidentialism**). W. Pannenberg rightly insists on the role of reasonable argument for the credibility of Christian truth claims. Credibility, he urges, does not mean credulity. He writes, "An otherwise unconvincing message cannot attain the power to convince simply by appealing to the Holy Spirit" (*BQT* 2:34). He adds, "In trusting the Spirit, Paul in no way spared himself thinking and arguing" (35; cf. 28-64). Even those who, like Barth, reject natural theology do not dismiss the use of reason to assess claims within the framework of a revealed theology. Reason retained an important role for Thomas Aquinas, alongside the claims of revelation (*Su Th* 1a, qu. 12, arts. 1-13; *Summa contra Gentiles* 1.2.11).

Reason receives a much more positive profile in Paul in the NT than many assume or expect. He writes to the Thessalonians that they should have a right mind (1 Thess. 5:12, 14; 2 Thess. 3:15), and that the Christians of Galatia should not be seduced or bewitched by failing to reflect or to use reason (Gal. 3:1-2). Paul prays that the Philippians will use their minds and think (Phil. 4:7). He prays for "the renewing of your minds" (Rom 12:2; cf. Eph. 4:23). Several excellent NT studies make this clear. We cite S. K. Stowers, "Paul on the Use and Abuse of Reason," in *Greeks, Romans, Christians,* ed. D. L. Balch et al. (Minneapolis:

Fortress, 1990), 253-86; R. Jewett, *Paul's Anthropological Terms* (Leiden: Brill, 1971), 358-90; and G. Bornkamm, "Faith and Reason in Paul," in *Early Christian Experience* (London: SCM, 1969), 29-46. This does not mean that Paul stresses reason *alone;* he urges the use of the heart and will, and all God-given faculties, including the wisdom of the Holy Spirit.

Recapitulation
Recapitulation (Lat. *recapitulatio;* Gk. *anakephalaiōsis*), as found in Eph. 1:10, is translated by the NRSV as God's plan "to gather up all things in him" (Christ). In Rom. 13:9 it is translated "summed up" to convey that the Ten Commandments are summed up in love. F. Danker translates the Greek as "to recapitulate" or "to sum up." The theological use of the term is normally associated with Irenaeus. In *Against Heresies* 4.6.2, he writes, "The only-begotten Son came to us from the one God... who administers all things, summing up His own handiwork in Himself" (*ANF* 1:468). In Irenaeus this tends to mean restoring human defects by reliving them without sin, as Christ did in the incarnation. What was lost from the image of God, Irenaeus argues, is restored in Christ, by passing through every stage of human life from birth to death and redeeming it. This theme has been influential in later theology also.

Reception Theory and Reception History
Reception theory and reception history are based on the belief that scholarly inquiry into the past meaning of a text must also include the effects generated by the texts. Reception history is the study of how successive generations and eras have interpreted and received texts that have been transmitted to them from the past. In general terms, these movements reject the notion of a "closed" past, since the past, and a past text, may have continuing and even changing effects. Reception history, according to Hans Robert Jauss, performs "a socially formative function." Hence theologians and biblical interpreters share the concern of this movement for how Scripture may shape, form, or be formative for successive generations of readers and communities.

Hans Robert Jauss (1921-1997) was in effect the founder of a method and approach he called *Rezeptionsästhetik,* or the aesthetics of reception. Reception theory had occupied a place in Marxism, where Marxists recognized the role of texts in social formation. Reception history involves the construction of horizons of *expectation* in different historical eras and generations, which is a central concern of Jauss. In earlier life Jauss specialized in medieval romance literature. But at Heidelberg he was influenced by his doctoral supervisor Hans-Georg Gadamer, and less directly by Martin Heidegger, with whom he shared an interest in hermeneutics, history, and art. A decisive step came with the founding of the University of Constance with its vision for interdisciplinary research. Jauss presented his inaugural lecture in 1967 as a virtual manifesto of *Rezeptionsästhetik.* Following Gadamer, he stressed the "still unfinished meaning" of works and texts in literature. He focused especially on the *historical influence* of a work. Where Gadamer spoke of the history of *effects* or effective history *(Wirkungsgeschichte)*, Ulrich Luz and others saw this term as denoting history of *influences* in Jauss. These influences are two-way. The text or work may influence readers, but readers may equally influence texts.

In addition to drawing on aspects of Marxism, Jauss also draws on literary formalism, especially on "defamiliarization," or ways of looking at the overfamiliar in new ways. Many biblical scholars have identified this disruptive device in the parables of Jesus, especially in "parables of reversal" such as the laborers in the vineyard and the Pharisee and the publican. Paul de Man compares reception theory in Germany with reader-response theory in America, but these movements have increasingly grown apart. Yet there are similarities. Jauss shares Wolfgang Iser's notion of readers "completing" a meaning for themselves. The main difference is the search in reception theory for a stable core or continuity in the meaning-effects of a text in history, although it also notes discontinuities or reversals of meaning. Jauss writes: "The work enters into the changing horizons-of-experience of a *continuity* . . . from recognized aesthetic norms to a new production that surpasses them." A work "satisfies, surpasses, disappoints or refutes the expectation of its first audience" (*Toward an Aesthetic of Reception* [Minneapolis: University of Minnesota Press, 1982], 19, 25). "Horizons of expectation" play a major part in Jauss.

There are parallels between reception theory in literary theory and current issues in biblical studies. For example, Jauss attacks a positivist or supposedly value-neutral approach to texts. He stresses the role of expectation on the part of readers when they read texts. He acknowledges that texts can contribute to a reader's formation, which includes "horizonal change." This is bound up, in turn, with how many or most readers may question the text. With R. G. Collingwood and H.-G. Gadamer, Jauss stresses the importance of what questions are brought to the text. With Ernst Fuchs and Gerhard Ebeling, he stresses the "event" character of interpretation. Finally, the exploration is not complete for the reader until there is "appropriation" or "application" of the potential of the text. The interpreter "must bring his own experience into play." Jauss argues that perception, preunderstanding, interpretation, and application are "a triadic unity." The reader must ask both "What did the text say?" and "What does it say to me?" (*Aesthetic of Reception*, 140). Every interpretation is historically conditioned. Both diachronic method (the history of meanings) and synchronic method (what it means at a given time, often the present) are involved. Most texts are formative because they expose the reader to "the other" in biblical studies, often God. A work may "provoke" new or changed horizons.

Reading: R. Evans, *Reception History, Tradition, and Biblical Interpretation* (London and New York: Bloomsbury, 2014); Robert C. Holub, *Reception Theory* (London and New York: Methuen, 1984); H. R. Jauss, *Toward an Aesthetic of Reception* (Minneapolis: University of Minnesota Press, 1982); Ulrich Luz, *Studies in Matthew* (Grand Rapids: Eerdmans, 2005), 254-79; David P. Parris, *Reception Theory and Biblical*

Hermeneutics (Eugene, Ore.: Pickwick, 2009); A. C. Thiselton, "Reception Theory, Jauss and the Formative Power of Scripture," *SJT* 65 (2012): 289-308.

Reconciliation, Reconcile

Apart from two or three uses of *katallassō* and *katallagē* in the LXX (e.g., 2 Macc. 1:5), this term demonstrates Paul's ability to coin terms that were familiar and easy to understand to Greek and Gentile ears. In the NT the term appears only in Paul, who describes the gospel as the word of reconciliation (Rom. 11:15; 2 Cor. 5:19; Gk. *katallagē*). Christians are those who "received reconciliation" (Rom. 5:11). The noun appears in Philo and elsewhere. The verb, to "reconcile" *(katallassō)*, occurs in 2 Cor. 5:18: "God was in Christ, reconciling the world to himself" (NLT), where God is the subject of the verb; and elsewhere in Paul as a plea or command to be "reconciled to God" (Rom. 5:10; 2 Cor. 5:20), or in 1 Cor. 7:11 to be reconciled to one's husband. Danker defines the Greek word as denoting "the exchange of hostility for a friendly relationship" (BDAG 521). Herodotus, Aristotle, Plato, Philo, and Josephus anticipate this meaning.

In Romans Paul expounds the condition of estrangement or alienation from God, which marks humankind without Christ. In Rom. 5:10 Paul argues, "If while we were enemies *(echthroi)*, we were reconciled to God through the death of his Son, much more surely, having been reconciled, will we be saved by his life." He continues: "The mind that is set on the flesh is hostile to God" (Rom. 8:7). Ephesians contains much about peace, reconciliation, and division. We read: "You who once were far off have been brought near by the blood of Christ. For he is our peace" (*hē eirēne hēmōn*; 2:13-14). For previously we were "aliens" and "strangers" (*apēllotriōmenoi . . . kai xenoi*; 2:12). The Greek stem *allos* signifies an *"other"* or *changed* relationship both with God and between Jewish Christians and Gentile Christians. Because the term is one of relationship, it is deeply personal, or person to person. At least as important is Col. 1:20-21: "Through him [Christ] God was pleased to reconcile to himself all things . . . by making peace through the blood of his cross. And you who were once estranged and hostile . . . he has now reconciled." Paul's emphatic statement that apart from Christ's work we should be "enemies" or "hostile" to God is not readily acceptable to modern humanity. But Paul stresses it as strongly in Romans, which all accept as Pauline, as in three later epistles that some doubt are Pauline. J. Denney, a conservative writer at the beginning of the twentieth century, declares, "Reconciliation in the sense of the New Testament is a work which is finished. . . . It is a work outside of us, in which God so deals in Christ with the sin of the world that it shall no longer be a barrier between himself and man" (*The Death of Christ* [London: Hodder and Stoughton, 1902], 145). Not all, however, agree with Denney's "objective" emphasis. R. Bultmann and M. Wiles prefer to place the emphasis of the word on human attitude and action. But Paul seems to see the process as initiated and sustained by God, even if humans are also required to respond.

Today "reconciliation" is one of the most understandable and communicable words for salvation in the NT. When there is strife between nations or groups, everyone understands the resolution of hostility in reconciliation. Children whose parents consider divorce long for their reconciliation. Industrial employment conflict needs to end in reconciliation. Estranged human relationships can often be repaired only by reconciliation. Those who are familiar with South Africa or Northern Ireland know about reconciliation, and many in Israel and Palestine long for it. In modern Christian theology Barth devotes the whole of *Church Dogmatics* IV to it (four volumes in English), expounding "God with us" and "the covenant as the presupposition of reconciliation" (*CD* IV/1, sect. 57, 1 and 2). "God with us" stands "at the heart of the Christian message," he urges (IV/1, p. 6). "'Reconciliation' is the restitution, the resumption of a fellowship which once existed but was then threatened with dissolution" (22). In his chapter on the obedience of Christ, Barth borrows the imagery of the far country. Christ has traveled to the far country to fetch us home, just like the returning prodigal son (157-210). The misery of humankind can thus be turned to justification, love, joy, and reconciliation (*CD* IV/2, 378-840; *see* **Barth, Karl**). In modern Christian theology, Karl Rahner also discusses reconciliation within the Christian church (*TI* 11:125-49). W. Pannenberg considers reconciliation in its many forms, culminating in the perfect reconciliation between God and humankind at the eschatological consummation (*ST* 3:641-42). (*See also* **Christology: Ministry of Jesus.**).

Reading: J. Denney, *The Christian Doctrine of Reconciliation* (1917; reprint, Carlisle: Paternoster, 1998); J. D. G. Dunn, *The Theology of Paul the Apostle* (Edinburgh: T. & T. Clark, 1998), 228-30; Vincent Taylor, *Forgiveness and Reconciliation* (London: Macmillan, 1948), 70-108; D. Wenham, *Paul* (Grand Rapids: Eerdmans, 1995), 59-64.

Redeem, Redemption

The two main Hebrew words for "redeem" are *gā'al* and *pādāh*, matched by the Greek *agorazō*. Both the Hebrew and Greek mean *to redeem from* bondage or a state of jeopardy, *by* a costly act of redemption, *to* a new ownership, new security, or state of freedom. However, all agree that payment *to* a particular person is often part of the imagery, except in specified cases. The classic paradigm or example in the OT is the exodus (Exod. 6:6; 15:13; Pss. 74:2; 77:15). Israel was delivered *from* bondage to the Egyptians, *by* a saving divine act, *to* safety and security in the Promised Land. Most liberation theologians treat this as a paradigm of God's will and action. Severino Croatto, for example, writes on Exodus. The sprinkling of blood on the lintel or door of houses recognizes the part of the costly act. This is then celebrated in the Passover, which every Jew must regard as if he or she were "there."

The other OT word (noun from *go'ēl*, "redeemer") is associated with the special privilege or duty of near-kinsmen. The *Go'ēl-haddām* (redeemer of blood) is permitted to "redeem" a near relative who has accidentally committed a sin against a fellow Israelite, such as allowing a bull in a field to gore the fellow Israelite to death (Lev. 25:25-28; 27:20; Ruth 4:4, 6). Both words (*pādāh* and *gā'al*), however, are used of the redemptive acts of God (Exod. 6:6; Isa. 43:1; 44:22, 23; Hos. 13:14). Job proclaims, "I know that my *Go'ēl* lives" (Job 19:25), where this means primarily "vindicator," with nuances of "near-kinsman."

The NT regularly uses *agorazō*, which is the usual word for buying merchandise from stores or from the market. Paul declares that Christ has *redeemed* Christians from the curse of the law (*exagorazō;* Gal. 3:13; 4:5); and that they are "bought with a price" (1 Cor. 6:20). A. Deissmann popularized the view that Christians were redeemed into a state of freedom, an analogy with inscriptions at Delphi, which depicted a deity "buying" freedom on the slave's behalf. But D. B. Martin has shown decisively that in the NT, especially in Paul, Christians are redeemed not to freedom, but from belonging to evil forces and sin to belonging to Christ as their new Lord. This is redemption from evil owners to a new, good owner, who cares for those who now "belong" to him. The word *agorazō* also occurs in Rev. 5:9, although the NRSV translates this as "By your blood you *ransomed* for God saints from every tribe and language." But in Rev. 14:3-4 the translation returns to "redeemed": "the one hundred forty-four thousand who have been redeemed from the earth" and "have been redeemed from humankind."

"Ransom" is a closely connected word with a similar meaning. In Isa. 51:11 it translates *gā'al;* in Isa. 35:10 and Hos. 13:14 it translates *pādāh*. But in Mark 10:45 and Matt. 20:18 the Greek *lutron* is used, where Jesus gives his life as "a ransom for many." The use of the noun connected with *luō* here stresses the aspect of release or freedom. Although Dale Martin is correct in his account of Paul's logic (redemption to a new Lord), 1 Peter also follows the *lutron* root in Mark. Peter declares, "You were ransomed (Gk. *elutrōthēte*) from . . . futile ways . . . with the precious blood of Christ, like that of a lamb without . . . blemish" (1 Pet. 1:18-19). As a whole, the NT suggests that only God, or God in Christ, can redeem, and that this redemption is brought about through the cross.

The Greek word *apolutrōsis,* which is often translated "redemption," occurs in Rom. 3:24, "the redemption that is in Christ," where it is related to justification and sacrifice of atonement (NRSV), as well as to expiation, propitiation, and place of meeting. The diverse translations of propitiation *(hilastērion)* are hotly debated. "Redemption" also occurs in Rom. 8:23; 1 Cor. 1:30; Luke 21:28; Eph. 1:7, 14; 4:30; and elsewhere.

In the history of Christian theology Clement of Rome speaks of "redemption *(lutrōsis)* through the blood of the Lord" (*1 Clem.* 1.12; A.D. 96), and Irenaeus refers to a false understanding of redemption by the Gnostics. Clement of Alexandria, John Chrysostom, and others use *agorazō* of redemption. Gregory of Nyssa speaks of Christian redemption from wickedness, and of Christ as a ransom. But he notoriously speaks of Christ as God "invested with the flesh," so that "the Enemy . . . saw opportunity" to seize him as a ransom, as a fish might seize bait (*The Great Catechism* 93; also in *NPNF,* ser. 2, 5:493). Gregory's notion of paying a ransom *to* the devil, however, is virtually universally rejected. This language became perhaps less prominent until in modern theology Gustaf Aulén, claiming to follow the Church Fathers and Luther, made "redemption" his major theme in explaining the work of Christ in his well-known book *Christus Victor* (1933). Many writers, however, see it as complementary to the approaches of Anselm and Calvin, rather than as an alternative to them.

Reading: Bruce Demarest, *The Cross and Salvation* (Wheaton, Ill.: Crossway, 2006); Trevor Hart, "Redemption and Fall," in *The Cambridge Companion to Christian Doctrine,* ed. Colin Gunton (Cambridge: CUP, 1997), 189-206.

Reformation

The term "Reformation" is used in a number of ways, as A. E. McGrath points out (*Reformation Thought* [Oxford: Blackwell, 1988, 1993], 5). (i) B. Bolton, in *The Medieval Reformation* (1983), cites the reforming work of the Cistercians, the Waldensians, and even the Cathars in the twelfth century, to reshape aspects of the church. But this does not usually come within the term "Reformation." (ii) John Wycliffe (c. 1330-1384) anticipated a later emphasis on the Bible and dissatisfaction with the papacy in England, and John Huss (c. 1372-1415) anticipated it in Bohemia (today's Czech Republic). But again, they were not altogether permanent and systematic reforms. (iii) Martin Luther (1483-1546) is undoubtedly the founder of "The Reformation," although some historians argue that the effects revolutionized in the first place primarily the German state and church, and that the English-speaking churches owe as much to the "Reformed theology" of Switzerland and John Calvin (1509-1564). However, Calvin was a second-generation Reformer, who built on and systematized the theology of Luther, Ulrich Zwingli (1484-1531), Philip Melanchthon (1497-1560), and Martin Bucer (1491-1551). (iv) Because of its permanent influence outside Germany and the seminal importance of Calvin's systematic theology, many argue that Reformed theology marks the true point of departure, which is Calvinist rather than Lutheran in content. Reformed theology spread from Switzerland to Holland and Germany, was continued by Theodore Beza, was transmitted to England partly by Bucer, and was later represented by William Perkins and John Owen. The term "Calvinist" dates from the 1560s. (v) The Radical Reformers, Andreas Carlstadt, Thomas Müntzer, and others, represent the third strand of the Protestant Reformation. In addition to their claims to "prophecy" and to a charismatic view of the Holy Spirit, they held to a Baptist theology of baptism, and were also known as Anabaptists (from the Greek for "baptize again"). They disagreed with the notion of church dignitaries and clergy robes, were radically egalitarian, and initiated the Peasants' Revolt at the alleged prompting of the Holy Spirit. (vi) On top of the three main Protestant sources of the Reformation, Roman Catholics often regard the Council of Trent (1545) and the Counter-Reformation as a Catholic reformation of the church, especially in Spain and Italy.

Much of the definition of the Reformation and its causes may depend on whether the writer is thought of as a historian or a theologian. In historical or political terms, the "magisterial reformation" denotes the close relation of secular authorities or "magistrates" with the Reformation, as envisaged by Luther, Calvin, and Bucer, but not by the Radical Reformers. The term "Protestant" derives from a reaction to the second Diet of Speyer (1529), when a number of princes and cities "protested" against the diet's attempts to end toleration of Lutheranism in Germany. But from a theological viewpoint it is the earlier theology of Luther that began the Reformation. Even within this theological vision, however, there were several progressive steps that, in different senses, were seen as initiating the Reformation. Traditionally "Reformation Sunday" is celebrated on 31 October to commemorate Luther's nailing up of the Ninety-five Theses in 1517. Yet this marked only the beginning of Luther's attack on papal indulgences. The Leipzig Disputation of 1519 was also decisive. In strictly accurate terms the Reformation can be dated only after Luther's condemnation at the Diet of Worms (1521), and his return to Wittenberg in 1522.

Meanwhile, from 1520 to 1560 the Reformation was proceeding apace in Switzerland. Bullinger succeeded Zwingli, and in the 1550s Calvin and Geneva emerged as the leading voices of Reformed theology. It would be simplistic to generalize about differences between Lutheran and Calvinist theology, but it is difficult *not* to gain the impression that justification by grace through faith constitutes a pivotal center for Luther, while the sovereignty of God forms a key center in the theology of Calvin (*see* **Calvin, John; Luther, Martin**). One problem is that Luther constantly reacted to events, while Calvin was usually able to reflect more systematically. But even then, Luther's lectures on books of the Bible and his German translation of the Bible nourished his underlying thought.

In England William Tyndale (c. 1494-1536) owed much to Luther's thought. His project of translating the Bible into English was conceived in 1522, and he completed the NT before he died. Henry VIII had opposed both Lutheranism and Tyndale's translation of the Bible into English. H. Daniel-Rops shows how complex the political context was that surrounded Henry's attempts to divorce Catherine of Aragon, which began in 1527 (*The Protestant Reformation* [New York: Dutton; London: Dent, 1961], 460-78). It was not technically a "divorce," but an annulment of papal permission to marry Catherine, supposedly on the basis of Leviticus 18 and 20, about taking a brother's wife in marriage. Cardinal Wolsey and Cardinal Campeggio were at first commissioned to assess the situation, but the matter dragged on. Eventually, however, Thomas Cranmer and Thomas Cromwell announced the end of the marriage in January 1533, and in July of that year the pope excommunicated Henry. During 1534 a whole series of measures were passed, in which the Act of Supremacy commanded that the king be recognized as "the one supreme head on earth of the Church of England" (467). Money previously sent to Rome was paid to Henry, and bishops were to be appointed by the king (as they still are, after nominations by the Crown Nomination Commission and approval by the prime minister). In 1536 an act of Parliament dissolved at least the smaller monasteries, and by 1540 all monasteries were shut down. Theological ordinances then followed, including the abolition of the cult of the saints and pilgrimages, and commission of the translation of the Bible into English. This was ostensibly undertaken by Miles Coverdale, but he was a former colleague of Tyndale, and he made considerable use of Tyndale's English. (*See* **Tyndale, William.**) Apart from the interlude of Queen Mary Tudor (1553-1558), the Reformation had permanently become established in England, first under the young Edward VI (1537-1553), son of Jane Seymour, and then under the settlement of Elizabeth I (1558-1603).

Under Edward VI the strongest theological influences were Cranmer and Martin Bucer, and also perhaps Peter Martyr. The replacement of the Mass by a Lutheran-Calvinist Lord's Supper followed (*see* **Book of Common Prayer; Lord's Supper**). The 1544 prayer book went much of the way toward the 1552 prayer book, but not all the way, and was generally Lutheran; the 1552 book was "the high-water mark" of Protestantism and was fundamentally Calvinist. Daniel-Rops observes, "At this stage the English Reformation swung towards Calvinism" (495). *(See also entries of historical figures mentioned above.)*

Reading: H. Daniel-Rops, *The Protestant Reformation* (New York: Dutton; London: Dent, 1961); A. G. Dickens, *The English Reformation* (London: Collins, 1967); H. J. Hillerbrand, ed., *The Oxford Encyclopaedia of the Reformation,* 4 vols. (New York: OUP, 1996); A. E. McGrath, *Reformation Thought* (Oxford: Blackwell, 1993); B. M. G. Reardon, *Religious Thought in the Reformation* (London: Longman, 1995); and bibliographies under Luther and Calvin.

Reformed Theology

To call Calvinism "Reformed theology" may be very broadly, but not strictly, accurate. Whereas the Lutheran churches look to Luther as their primary source of inspiration, the Reformed church looks to Calvin, partly in combination with Martin Bucer, Luther, Ulrich Zwingli, Heinrich Bullinger, and Peter Martyr. The Westminster Confession of Faith (1646) represents a consensus from among these theologians, many of whom, like Calvin, were "second generation" to Luther and Zwingli. In 1647 the Presbyterian Church adopted the Westminster Confession as its basis of faith. It had inherited, however, the fruit of several earlier confessions, including that of the Synod of Dort (1618-1619), which was largely Calvinist and Reformed in contrast to the teaching of Arminius. It had asserted election, a limited atonement, total depravity, irresistible grace, and final perseverance. The Westminster Confession was a minor modification of the Church of England's Thirty-nine Articles, which reflected an earlier quasi-Calvinist formulation, rather than a Lutheran one. Cranmer and Ridley followed the "Reformed" or Calvinist view. The *Consensus Tigurinus* (1549) had arisen from dialogue between Calvin and Bullinger, and marks a harmony between French and Swiss exponents of Reformed theology. This was followed by the Geneva Consensus in 1552 on predestination. In the seventeenth century, English Puritanism was considered the expression of Reformed orthodoxy, and the English, Dutch, and Swiss shared generally in the formulation of Reformed theology, with particular reference to the Westminster Confession. Critics view this as a hardening into "Reformed Scholastic Orthodoxy," and increasingly the term "Reformed" came to replace the term "Calvinist." But much depends on how we define Scholasticism. The term perhaps better fits Francis Turretin (1623-1687) than, for example, John Owen (1616-1683). Two celebrated examples of Reformed theology are Herman Bavinck, *Reformed Dogmatics,* 4 vols. (Grand Rapids: Eerdmans, 2008), and G. C. Berkouwer, *Studies in Dogmatics,* 14 vols. (Grand Rapids: Eerdmans, 1952-1975).

Religion
"Religion" ought, in theory, to be a fuller, richer term than "theology." The danger with "theology" is that for many it may seem too cerebral and "intellectualist," although properly understood, theology can be doxological and pastoral. Religion, on the other hand, clearly involves the practice of faith, worship, ethics, and communion with God (as James 1:26-27 implies). Yet for the Christian theologian too many definitions of religion seem to water down the concept to "a sense of the holy" or to mere sociological practice. H. Küng seems to approve of Schleiermacher's definition of religion as "a sense of the infinite." Schleiermacher wrote, "To seek and to find the infinite and eternal in all that lives and moves, in all growth and change, in all action and passion . . . in immediate feeling — that is the essence of religion." He adds, "True religion is sense and taste for the Infinite" (*On Religion* [London: Kegan Paul, Trench, Trübner, 1893], 39). This certainly does not exclude divine grace and revelation, but to many theologians, including Barth, it seems to hint of human religious aspiration rather than a personal relationship with God, founded on grace.

Biblical allusions to "religion" are partly positive but also partly confirm this negative caution. Three Greek words denote "religion." *Deisidaimonia* primarily denotes "religiosity" or "religious scruple" (BDAG 216), mainly in Josephus and Plutarch, and occurs in Acts 25:19 to refer to Jewish religious disputes. A more frequent word is *eusebeia,* often rendered "piety" or "devoutness"; it indicates "awesome respect accorded to God" (BDAG 412-13). In Acts 3:12, Peter uses it with a disclaimer: the healing was *not* due to the apostles' *eusebeia.* A positive use comes in prayers for (often pagan) kings, that their subjects may lead lives of "godliness *(eusebeia)* and dignity" (1 Tim. 2:2). The word is similarly translated "godliness" (NRSV) in 1 Tim. 4:7-8. In 1 Tim. 6:5 "godliness" is not a means of gain, but in 6:11 it is positively commended: "Pursue . . . godliness." It is entirely positive in 2 Pet. 1:3: God gives "everything needed for life and godliness." The third Greek word for religion is *thrēskeia,* which is found in the famous passage in James 1:26-27: "religious" people are empty if they cannot control their tongues (v. 26); "religion" that is genuine involves caring for orphans and widows and being "unstained by the world" (v. 27). The word *thrēskeia* denotes "devotion to transcendent beings," but also "cultic rites" as well as worship (BDAG 459). In Col. 2:18 the word is used negatively for "worship of angels," involving self-abasement.

The word *eusebeia* occurs fifty-six times in the LXX, nearly forty of which occur in 4 Maccabees (H-R 1:580). The word *thrēskeia* occurs only six times (655). In Wis. 10:12 wisdom teaches the righteous to "learn that godliness *(eusebeia)* is more powerful than anything else." In Sir. 49:3, Josiah "made godliness prevail." In Hebrew the word most often used to translate the LXX is *yir'â*, the nominalized infinite or feminine noun form of *y-r-'*, which denotes "fear" or "worship," or sometimes "fear of God." In Isa. 11:2 the servant figure is given the Spirit of the Lord, from whom the final gift is "the fear of the LORD."

The biblical writings, therefore, show some reserve about the term "religion." In the sense of "godliness" or "fear of the Lord," however, it is entirely positive. But religion can also be religiosity. The problem for the theologian is akin to the problem of "spirituality." In popular uses today it seldom means "godliness," and is usually used to denote a belief in some kind of "infinite" or "ultimate" outside Christian orthodoxy. Yet religion, though it may sometimes be man-made or idolatrous, is not necessarily to be evaluated negatively. This depends on context. It may indicate a *reaching beyond the self,* which is as yet nameless. Where religion is genuine, it is associated by James and others with care for the widows and orphans (the vulnerable and underprivileged), and with not being submerged in things of the world. Although Schleiermacher used what many might regard as a "weak" concept of religion, he also used it brilliantly to reach the educated or intellectuals of the day. Tillich has drawn positively on Otto's *Idea of the Holy,* even if many regard this as starting at too low a level. It is possible and desirable to take on board Barth's reservations about the term, and yet also to accept more positive evaluations in biblical passages. On one side early Christians were called "irreligious"; on the other side Aquinas defined religion in terms of what we owe to God. It is certainly broader than the term "theology," involving devotion and practice. Recently a "theology of religions" has added to the repertoire of exploration. The term may provide fruitful ground for dialogue with other religions outside the Christian faith.

Reading: Karl Barth, *Church Dogmatics* (Edinburgh: T. & T. Clark, 1956), I/2, sect. 17, "The Revelation of God as the Abolition of Religion," 280-361; D. Bonhoeffer, *Letters and Papers from Prison* (London: SCM, 1953, 1971); R. Otto, *The Idea of the Holy* (Oxford: OUP, 1953); F. D. Schleiermacher, *On Religion: Speeches to Its Cultured Despisers* (London: Kegan Paul, Trench, Trübner, 1893).

Renewal Movement

This entry inevitably overlaps with the entry for Pentecostalism, since several themes, although not all, are shared in common. Both movements originate from a reaction against mere religious routine or rationalism, liberalism, or pure formalism within the church, and evince a hunger to appropriate new and living experiences of God as Holy Spirit. The Roman Catholic theologian Yves Congar is more than sympathetic with this aim and ideal, but he also recognizes that the Renewal Movement incorporates features that mean it *cannot be for everyone* or the whole church (*I Believe in the Holy Spirit* [New York: Seabury Press, 1983],

2:156). While exponents of Renewal share many features of Pentecostalism, the major difference between the two is that the Renewal Movement seeks to remain within the "mainline" church or churches, and long-established traditions or denominations. At the time of this writing, Renewal Movement groups exist within all the main Protestant denominations and in the Roman Catholic Church. They should be given credit for *not* going their own way to form another denomination within the church, but for seeking to invigorate and to renew the wider community and tradition to which they belong.

It is well documented that in 1959 Dennis Bennett, then rector of St. Mark's, Van Nuys, California, received what he called "baptism in the Spirit" with several others, and by 1960, seventy members of St. Mark's had undergone a similar experience. Concerns, even hostility, were expressed at St. Mark's, and Bennett moved to St Luke's, Seattle, which became a center for the movement. The birth date of the Renewal Movement is generally accepted to be 1960. Bennett visited seminaries in various parts of the world during the early 1960s, finding a kindred spirit in the Pentecostal leader David du Plessis. In England a leading role in the Renewal Movement was played by Michael Harper, a Church of England curate (assistant pastor) who founded the Fountain Trust. From 1963 John Collins, vicar of St. Mark's Gillingham, Kent, promoted the movement, together with David Watson at York. The 1960s were heady years for an unrestrained Renewal Movement, and uncomfortable years for many outside the movement. Harper and John Stott, then rector of All Souls in central London, took very different, even opposing, views. Even well into the 1970s there seemed to be no mutual understanding. In 1970 the Renewal Movement entered the Roman Catholic Church, and some "High Church" Anglicans such as John Gunstone became heavily involved in it.

In Germany the first Renewal Movement meetings began about 1963, and the same year du Plessis led Renewal meetings in Utrecht, Holland. After 1972 the Renewal Movement in Belgium received support from Cardinal Léon-Joseph Suenens. By 1975 or 1976 Renewal meetings were held in Warsaw, Poland, with the encouragement of the archbishop of Krakow. Scandinavia, France, Italy, and Spain all saw Catholic Renewal in the early 1970s. Argentina had experienced this phenomenon in 1967 among Open Brethren, and Brazil had encountered Renewal even earlier among Methodists, Presbyterians, and Congregationalists. The Renewal Movement hit India in the early 1970s. It is difficult to trace origins in Africa, where many already held a "dualist" view of the influence of demons. The devotion and sincerity of the movement cannot be doubted, but in this first flash of enthusiasm there were also mutual hostility and serious casualties among many ordinary Christians, including those who felt "second class." In later years the movement would mellow and expand its horizons.

In America the development of the Renewal Movement within the Roman Catholic Church received publicity largely through events at Duquesne University, Pittsburgh, and at the University of Notre Dame in 1967. This followed on from Vatican II in 1962-1965, and Pope John's prayer for a new Pentecost. Leaders in the Catholic Renewal Movement included Stephen Clark and Ralph Martin. Clark published *Baptized in the Spirit* (1969) and *Spiritual Gifts* (1970). Martin moved to Brussels to work with Cardinal Suenens. "Healing" was prominently on his agenda. Among American Lutherans Larry Christenson organized Charismatic Renewal services, and Dennis Bennett remained a prominent leader in the Episcopal Church. In these earlier days there was strong opposition, for example, from the Southern Baptist Convention. In England many Protestants believed, rightly or wrongly, that while they supported Renewal, there was in the movement much confused exegesis. In particular there emerged a divorce about "healing" and conscious debate about the present or future timing of the kingdom of God, as well as too much emphasis on "tongues." These became, or were perceived as, identity marks of an elite "inner circle," together with lightweight hymn singing, very often based on simplistic interpretations of individual experience rather than the shared public theology of the church. Above all, "prophecies" concerning specific situations appeared to be given overready acceptance and privilege over exegetical reflection. Many communities became open to manipulation and control. In this they shared the character of very early Pentecostalism.

There were a number of valiant attempts to build bridges across the divide. In 1978 the Church of England General Synod expressed the wish to support Renewal in many parishes, but also identified points of tension within Anglicanism. By 1980 many in charismatic parishes had become "second-generation" exponents of Renewal, and the angularity and defensiveness of the 1960s and 1970s had become less pronounced. Much of the controversy centered on a "one-stage" versus a "two-stage" experience of salvation and sanctification. Yet, as Congar notes, a different *style* of worship still led to misunderstanding and estrangement. This probably reflected the deeper roots of division between such figures as Hodge, Warfield, and Kuyper on one side, and Irwin, Simpson, and Irving on the other. This could be caricatured as a rootedness in formal historical tradition and doctrine on one side and an obsessive concern for the present, a lack of structure, and a quest for "new things," however chaotic or discontinuous, on the other.

Just as the differences were becoming less acute, in 1983-1987 Peter Wagner began to use the term "third wave" (or "neo-charismatic"); this wave arrived in 1982-1990 as the so-called Toronto blessing. It began to cause consternation by emphasizing divine healing, "slaying" or "being slain in the Spirit," casting out demons, "holy laughter," and baptism in the Spirit. Its greatest difference from Pentecostalism was its acceptance of the possibility of *multiple* "fillings" of the Holy Spirit, and its exhibition of the excesses of a young new movement. Many reacted unfavorably to new terms introduced in England by David Watson such as "power evangelism" and "power healings." Mark Cartledge has provided an excellent account of "third wave" worship, and this particular way of interpreting "gifts of the Spirit" in 1 Cor. 12:8-10. Once again, Hollenweger's warning to Pentecostals of a sharp dualism between "natural" and "supernatural" applies emphatically to this "third wave" phenomenon.

Like most such movements, this phase passed its peak within a short time, probably by the mid-1990s. The most notable feature was that while Pentecostals were beginning to produce such scholars as Gordon Fee, Robert Stronstad, and Robert Menzies, and also to engage in serious self-questioning and self-criticism, the Renewal Movement seemed to have produced few self-critics, with the outstanding exception of Tom Smail. In scholarly research Max Turner in England is a responsible and scholarly advocate, while some emerged in North America, although more were explicitly Pentecostal. Perhaps both factors are due to Pentecostalism's going back to at least 1900, while the Renewal Movement began only in 1960. Cartledge well argues that the Renewal Movement maintains a strong emphasis on the transcendence of God and the otherness of the new creation, as well as the limits of rationalism. But he warns readers against triumphalism, and against seeking "relevance" in contrast to being anchored in the cross (*Charismatic Glossolalia* [Aldershot and Burlington, Vt.: Ashgate, 2002], 200). M. Bonnington comments that in this "third wave," "worship is often identified as ... physically and emotionally expressive of its own style of music" (*Patterns in Charismatic Spirituality* [Cambridge: Grove, 2002], 16). Cartledge and Bonnington have in mind especially John Wimber's "Vineyard" or "New Wine" gatherings.

Don Carson attempts a "bridge" or middle way in his *Showing the Spirit* (Grand Rapids: Baker, 1987), 183-88, in the wake of grievous hostility from both sides. Tom Smail has done much as a former director of the Fountain Trust to moderate the Renewal Movement in *The Forgotten Father* (1980), *The Giving Gift* (1994), *Once and for All* (1998), and *Like Father, Like Son* (2006). With Andrew Walker and Nigel Wright, he published *The Love of Power or the Power of Love* (Minneapolis: Bethany House, 1994), which is a remarkable critique of the Renewal Movement "from inside." He writes, "We are indeed rejuvenated and empowered at Pentecost, but we are judged, corrected, and matured at the cross" (19). He even recalls reacting ambiguously to Dennis Bennett in 1965, as many did, including the present writer. Nigel Wright also discusses "falling, trances, weeping, unrestrained laughter ... in a sometimes frightening manner" (38). All three authors are concerned about pragmatism, overconcern about demons, and heightened dualism, as well as a simplistic "restorationist" use of the Bible, and a "by-pass of rational faculties" (95-103). They note the promise that the Renewal Movement may indeed serve to renew the church, but with the provisos about doctrine, tone, style, and subculture, which have been expressed. (*See also* **Holy Spirit; Pentecostals, Pentecostalism.**)

Reading: M. Bonnington, *Patterns in Charismatic Spirituality* (Cambridge: Grove, 2002); M. Cartledge, *Charismatic Glossolalia* (Aldershot and Burlington, Vt.: Ashgate, 2002); Y. Congar, *I Believe in the Holy Spirit*, vol. 2 (New York: Seabury Press, 1983); F. D. Hocker, "Charismatic Movement," in *NIDPCM* (Grand Rapids: Zondervan, 2003), 477-519; Tom Smail, A. Walker, and N. Wright, *The Love of Power or the Power of Love* (Minneapolis: Bethany House, 1994).

Repentance, Repent

(Heb. *nācham, nocham,* and *shūb;* Gk. *metanoeō*). Repentance differs from remorse or regret. It is therefore a serious mistake to draw inferences from the Greek components *meta* and *noeō* or *nous* to suggest the meaning "after mind," which may simply denote regret. Its meaning is dictated by the Hebrew *shūb*, "to turn," in the dual sense of turning from and turning to. Regret might be encouraged by *metamelomai,* but not by *metanoeō*. *Nācham*, however, is used in the OT mainly of God and in the sense of "sorrow, regret, or change of purpose" (Gen. 6:6-7; Exod. 32:14; Judg. 2:18; 21:15; 1 Sam. 15:11, 35; Jer. 18:8, 10; Jon. 3:9-10). *Shūb,* on the other hand, means to repent, to turn, to return, or to restore. It occurs over a thousand times, especially in Jeremiah. To turn back physically is extended to attitudes, mind-sets, or dispositions. Humans can turn from God in rebellion or apostasy (Jer. 2:19; 3:22; 5:6; 8:5; 14:7; Hos. 11:7; Isa. 57:17). "Turn from your evil ways" occurs in 2 Kings 17:13. Repentance is a turnabout, or "about turn" in military terms.

In the NT it is integral to the message of Jesus Christ: "Jesus came to Galilee, proclaiming ... 'The Kingdom of God has come near; repent, and believe in the good news'" (Mark 1:15). (Parallel: "Jesus began to proclaim, 'Repent, for the kingdom of heaven has come near'" [Matt. 4:17]). This message also reflected that of John the Baptist (Matt. 3:2). The earliest church underlined the seriousness of repentance by making it integral with baptism: "Peter said to them, 'Repent, and be baptized ... in the name of Jesus Christ so that your sins may be forgiven" (Acts 2:38); "Repent therefore, and turn to God so that your sins may be wiped out" (Acts 3:19). Repentance may also be demanded of Christians who lapse or fail (Rev. 2:5, 16, 22; 3:3). Paul writes, "God's kindness is meant to lead you to repentance" (Rom. 2:4). He reflects, "Godly grief produces a repentance that leads to salvation" (2 Cor. 7:10).

In the postbiblical church repentance continued to be integral with baptism, as exemplified in vows of renunciation and allegiance, and in many liturgies: "Do you repent of your sins?" The other significant development was the Reformers' separation of repentance from penance *(poenitentia),* which was regarded as one of the seven sacraments in the Roman Catholic Church. Luther insisted that *poenitentia* (which was often viewed as a "work") should not be confused with *metanoia*.

Reading: M. J. Boda and G. T. Smith, eds., *Repentance in Christian Theology* (Collegeville, Minn.: Liturgical Press, 2006).

Restorationism

The word "restorationism" is used in a variety of senses, especially among Pentecostals. At its most basic it describes a hermeneutic of the NT that aims *to replicate the exact forms* of ministry, the church, and experience of the Holy Spirit that characterized the church of the NT. This especially applies to the narrative of Acts, and to the expectation of Christ's imminent return. It often also applies to miraculous healings and speaking in tongues. Yet if we accept what Beverly Roberts Gaventa, Ronald Williams, and other specialists on Acts suggest, the growth and development of the church in Acts constituted part of God's plan and purpose.

Resurrection of the Dead

The most extensive biblical treatment of the resurrection is 1 Cor. 15:1-58, although Paul also refers to the general resurrection in Rom. 4:16-25, 8:11, 2 Cor. 1:9, 5:1-10, and 1 Thess. 4:14-17. (On the resurrection of Christ, *see* **Christology**.) The emphasis in all these passages is the *free gift of God's sovereign, creative grace*, in contrast to any latent capacity for resurrection that humankind might possess. Dead people simply cannot and do not raise themselves. The Pauline view rejects Plato and many Eastern religions. Indeed, Paul goes so far as to assert that God raised Christ, and will raise all who are "in Christ," not least through the mediate cause of the Holy Spirit. "If the Spirit of him who raised Jesus from the dead dwells in you, he who raised Christ from the dead will give life to your mortal bodies also through his Spirit that dwells in you" (Rom. 8:11).

If the resurrection manner, or mode, of life is through the Holy Spirit, we should not expect it to be static. The resurrection mode of existence will be as fresh, ongoing, and renewed moment-by-moment as life led and animated by the Holy Spirit is now. He is creative and ongoing; no one will be bored, or find life dull, when the person is raised by the Holy Spirit. Equally, the raised "body" will be energized by the living, ongoing God. It will not be like the "frozen" shot of the end of a movie or film. Under our entry for "Body" we note that "body" only denotes the *physical* within the conditions of the world. The primary focus of *body* is its *public, observable, communicative,* and *recognizable identity*. As raised people, our identity will be preserved, and we shall be recognizable as individuals, even as God sees us, namely, as cleansed, guiltless, and reconciled by the work of Christ. Here is a second difference from many other religions and philosophies. We do not lose our identity by becoming assimilated into some "all," or even into God. God will continue to value us as individuals, just as he demonstrated by creating and preserving us. On the other hand, we become in Christ part of the innumerable multitude of God's raised people in Christ. As one, we are able to offer and to communicate our praise through what Paul calls "a spiritual body," that is, a way of existence characterized by the Holy Spirit and public identity (1 Cor. 15:44).

In 1 Corinthians 15, the three principles concerning resurrection are (i) contrast, (ii) continuity, and (iii) transformation. We shall return to 15:1-34 shortly, which bases the resurrection on the resurrection of Christ. Meanwhile (i) Paul asserts that "what you sow" is *not* "the body that is to be" (15:37). There is *contrast*. Sickness and suffering, for example, are left behind. So are weakness, constraints, and disabilities: all that hampers or constrains life. Paul adds, "God gives [the seed you sow] a body as he has chosen" (v. 38). One writer (Kennedy) calls the unexpected tense "an aorist of sovereignty." (ii) But there is recognizable *continuity* between the "old" body and the new. Paul's analogies from nature illustrate this point. Each kind of seed is different (v. 38b). If you sow one species of flower, another does not come up in its place. Each person carries with him or her a unique store of memories, experiences, obligations, and grounds for thanks or praise that are not interchangeable with another's. (iii) There will be *transformation.* Paul explains: "What is sown is perishable, what is raised is imperishable. It is sown in dishonor, it is raised in glory. It is sown in weakness, it is raised in power. It is sown an ordinary body (NRSV 'physical body'; Gk. *sōma psychikon*)" (15:42-44). Paul adds that the first body was characterized by "Adam," but the second will be characterized by "the man of heaven," that is, Christ (v. 49).

Paul amplifies this with a vision of the End. He explains, "We will all be changed, in a moment, in the twinkling [i.e., blink] of an eye, at the last trumpet. For the trumpet will sound, and the dead will be raised imperishable, and we will be changed" (15:51-52). He is using the image of a sleeping army. Suddenly the trumpet sounds (a standard signal in the ancient world), and the whole army springs awake, ready for action. Death has been swallowed up in victory. He adds another image or thought: "'Where, O death, is your sting?' The sting of death is sin" (vv. 55-56). But if Christ has dealt with the problem of sin, the sting of death has been removed, and transformation into a new form of existence has only to pass through a *stingless* death.

This takes us back to the first part of the resurrection chapter, 1 Cor. 15:1-34. Paul first states that the witness to the genuineness of Christ's resurrection is not just his, but rests on an earlier apostolic witness. He "received" what he now "proclaims." The Greek terms *paredōka* and *parelabon* are technical terms for receiving and transmitting an earlier creed or tradition, and Christ's death, burial, and resurrection are among the "first," that is, most important, things. A line of witnesses ends with Paul. Although Marxsen and Conzelmann understand "was seen" metaphorically (as in "Oh, I see!"), Künneth and Pannenberg insist on the normal meaning (*see* **Christology**). Paul then considers the impossible consequences of denying the resurrection, namely, "your faith has been in vain" (v. 14). But in fact, Christ's resurrection was the pledge or first fruits (Gk. *aparchē,* v. 20), which is a technical term meaning "more of the same kind to come." The nature of Christ's risen body is in principle like that of other believers who have been raised. The First Epistle of John agrees with Paul. John writes, "When he [Christ] is revealed, we will be like him, for we will see him as he is" (1 John 3:2). Elsewhere Paul speaks of the raised "body" under the image of a "house not made with hands" (2 Cor. 5:1), for which Christians long. In 1 Thessalonians Paul declares that God will bring "with him [Christ] those who have died" (1 Thess. 4:14), and "we will be with the Lord forever" (4:17).

The key principles remain. First, the resurrection of the dead comes about by God's creative, transforming power through Christ and the Spirit. It is a work in which God as Trinity is involved. Second, it is not mere resuscitation, as it was for Lazarus (John 11:17-44). It is no mere parable, as in Ezek. 37:1-14, or mere resuscitation to earlthy life, as in John 11. It is a transformed life, characterized by the ongoing life of the Holy Spirit. The old has been left behind, but ahead will be unimaginable wonders and glory, in progressive, ever-new experience. Third, transformation constitutes the bridge between continuity and contrast.

Reading: J. Moltmann, *Theology of Hope* (London: SCM, 1967), 190-229; W. Pannenberg, *Systematic Theology*, vol. 3 (Grand Rapids: Eerdmans; Edinburgh: T. & T. Clark, 1998), 555-80; A. C. Thiselton, *First Epistle to the Corinthians* (Grand Rapids: Eerdmans, 2000), 1169-1306; A. C. Thiselton, *Life after Death* (Grand Rapids: Eerdmans, 2011); also entitled *The Last Things* (London: SPCK, 2012), 111-28; R. D. Williams, *Resurrection* (London: DLY, 1982); N. T. Wright, *The Resurrection of the Son of God* (London: SPCK, 2003), 207-374 and 401-79.

Revelation

It is not surprising that virtually every major religion finds a necessary place for revelation. In traditional Jewish-Christian-Islamic theism, if God is transcendent and "other," it is not to be taken for granted that God is accessible to unaided human reason. God is not necessarily an object to be "discovered." Further, if God is omnipotent or almighty, it may be the case that God wills where and when God may be known.

(i) **Revelation in Different Traditions.** Within each of these three traditions, the relative emphasis placed upon the respective roles of revelation and reason has varied. In Islamic philosophy, al-Kindi and the predecessors of al-Farabi (c. 870-950) viewed the Qur'an as paramount in authority and in its capacity as revelation, but al-Farabi argued that at the very least knowledge of human nature came through reason *('aql)*.

Traditional Judaism looks back to the two major sources of revelation identified in the Hebrew Scriptures: the *Gilluy Sh^{e}kinah,* or manifestation of the glory of God by some wondrous revelatory act; and revelation through the gift of the Law, the Prophets, and the Writings. The Law expresses revelation of the divine will through instruction and commandment; the prophetic utterances summon and promise; the Wisdom literature and other writings explore, lament, praise, or perform varied speech acts. As Judaism developed in history, Moses Maimonides (1135-1204) affirmed the revelation of the sacred texts, but also the accommodation of Scripture and tradition to the varied backgrounds of their recipients.

In the Christian tradition Thomas Aquinas (1225-1274) argued that it is in principle possible to perceive that God exists through the right use of human reason, but to apprehend the nature or character of God presupposes and requires divine grace and the gift of revelation.

Many Protestant theologians accord less scope to natural theology, and insist that not least because of human fallenness, divine revelation is needed even to be aware that God exists. Karl Barth lays stress on the revelatory Word of God as God's gift in a threefold form: the Word (proper) is the revelation of God through the person and work of Jesus Christ; the Word written is the word of sacred

Scripture; the Word proclaimed is the eventful communication of that word in preaching and other ways, as the Spirit of God actualizes it communicatively.

In Hindu philosophy and religion wide differences of "viewpoint" find their common roots in the Vedas (c. 1500-800 B.C.), which have the status of sacred scripture *(sruti)*. The 108 Sanskrit texts of the Upanishads (c. 800-500 B.C.) count also as Vedic scripture, even though their context has become more philosophical.

That these scriptures are regarded as revelation is confirmed by the fact that the Bhagavad Gita ("Song of God") is considered sacred tradition, a little "below" Vedic scripture, but together with Vedanta is clearly also regarded as *revelation.*

(ii) **Modes of Revelation.** Arguably, if revelation is regarded as the self-disclosure of God to humankind, this self-disclosure proceeds from a free act of the divine will. It remains as free an act, and as much a free act of loving as God's free self-expression in his act of creation.

In Hebrew, Christian, and Islamic traditions, it is God who invites humankind to approach God's holy presence, not to force one's way into this presence as a "right." Hence the divine communicative act is one of sovereign grace and initiative. This is simply an aspect of the "coherence" of a theism that conceives of God as holy as well as gracious.

Thinkers have emphasized four possible modes of revelation. Such writers as Oscar Cullmann and Wolfhart Pannenberg have emphasized the unfolding of divine self-disclosure in *history*. Cullmann places the weight on "sacred history" *(Heilsgeschichte);* Pannenberg, on a more "public" or universal history in the world. Others, notably Karl Barth, stress the *mystery of divine self-disclosure of address* "where and when God wills," although usually through the medium of Christ, Scripture, and proclamation.

Yet others urge the importance of viewing the communicative act, or speech act, of revelation as a process that necessarily entails human response, and remains otherwise merely formal; or in effect, empty. Hence Rudolf Bultmann calls attention to the *existential dimension of revelation.*

Such an approach, with more equal balance on ontology, was anticipated by John Calvin, when he urged in his *Institutes* that God's revelation of God carries with it as a necessary corollary a simultaneous revelation of the nature of humankind. Thus to disclose that God is Creator is thereby to disclose the creaturely, finite, dependent status of humankind as stewards of the world. To reveal Christ as Lord is to reveal the status of Christ's people as belonging to Christ in trust and obedience.

A fourth emphasis arises from *the transmission of revelation* that has been received. Catholic tradition in particular calls attention to the role of ecclesial structures and a delegated role in regulating the tradition as part of the wholeness of the process. Other Christian traditions also see the creeds and sacraments as ways of preserving corporate memory and continuity.

Within these aspects writers as diverse as Richard Swinburne and, among conservative American writers, Carl Henry conduct discussions about revelation as "propositional" (Swinburne, *Revelation* [Oxford: Clarendon, 1991]). Clearly Scripture in the Judeo-Christian tradition performs many more functions than descriptions and performs numerous speech acts. Address *to* God in poetic psalms, and working out the meaning of parables, belongs to revelation. Yet behind the debate lies the valid recognition that revelation embodies cognitive truth, ontology, and reference to states of affairs. (*See also* **Aquinas, Thomas; Barth, Karl; Grace; Natural Theology; Pannenberg, Wolfhart; Reason.**)

Reading: W. J. Abraham, *Crossing the Threshold of Divine Revelation* (Grand Rapids: Eerdmans, 2007); Karl Barth, *Church Dogmatics* I/2 (Edinburgh: T. & T. Clark, 1950), chapter 2, "The Revelation of God"; A. Dulles, *Models of Divine Revelation* (Nashville: Doubleday, 1983); H. D. McDonald, *Theories of Revelation* (London: Allen and Unwin, 1963); H. Thielicke, *The Evangelical Faith*, vol. 2 (Grand Rapids: Eerdmans, 1977).

Richard of St. Victor

Richard of St. Victor (d. 1173) has special significance both as an exegete and theologian, and as a contemplative. His work on the Trinity is generally regarded as his most creative and profound production. In it he argues that God is necessarily a community of persons, for a solitary existence would be incompatible with love. His exegesis follows the threefold pattern of historical (or literal), allegorical, and tropological. On the literal meaning he followed his predecessor Hugh of St. Victor. The allegorical level of meaning leads on to theology, and the tropological level to the spiritual or contemplative. He wrote contemplative reflections on the two cherubim of the ark. The cherubim represent what is beyond reason. His view of the Holy Trinity has influenced "social Trinity" approaches today.

Ricoeur, Paul

Paul Ricoeur (1913-2005) was born at Valence in France of a committed Protestant family. He studied philosophy in 1934 at the Sorbonne, Paris, where he came under the influence of G. Marcel. Marcel valued the uniqueness of the human self. In 1939, with the outbreak of war, he served in the French army, but was taken prisoner by the Germans in 1940. During these years as a prisoner of war, he studied German philosophy, especially that of Jaspers, Husserl, and Heidegger. This enhanced his interest in existence, possibility, and the self. After the war he taught in the only Protestant university in France, the University of Strasbourg (1948-1954), from which he received his doctorate in 1950. In 1956 he became professor of philosophy at the Sorbonne. His earliest books were on human will, guilt, finitude, and freedom, and also symbol. In English these are translated as *Freedom and Nature* (Evanston, Ill.: Northwestern University Press, 1966); *Fallible Man* (New York: Fordham University Press, 1985); and *The Symbolism of Evil* (Boston: Beacon Press, 1969). Ricoeur would later produce magisterial volumes, and he is without doubt one of the most seminal thinkers of the late twentieth century, not only for philosophy but also for hermeneutics and theology.

Symbol and metaphor remained lifelong concerns. But his examination of Freud became a watershed for his hermeneutics, especially with the publication of *Freud and Philosophy* (Eng. New Haven: Yale University Press, 1970; Fr. *De l'interprétation: Essai sur Freud* [1965]). Although as a Christian he rejects Freud's materialistic and mechanistic worldview, he sees Freud's work on the interpretation of dreams and understanding of the human mind as a classic in hermeneutics. When a patient described his or her dreams, Freud did not see this description as an account or a text to be taken at face value. The dream as actually dreamed (the dream thoughts) is not exactly the patient's report. Another text *lies beneath* the recounted text. Displacement, condensation, and "scrambling" may result in overdetermination (93). Infantile scenes, for example, may be reported as recent experiences. Dreams often present disguised and hidden forms of what may be sources of guilt or shame. In one of his most important and seminal observations, Ricoeur declares, "*Hermeneutics seems to me to be animated by this double motivation: willingness to suspect, willingness to listen; vow of rigor, vow of obedience.* In our time we have not finished doing away with *idols* and we have barely begun to listen to symbols" (*Freud and Philosophy,* 27, first italics mine). Ricoeur had suspicions about the dream-text as recounted, and sought to recover the text that is hidden beneath the reported text.

In this volume (as well as several others) Ricoeur compares the rigorous or "suspicious" characters of "exploration" *(Erklärung)* and the "listening" axis of "understanding" *(Verstehen)*. Like Habermas and Apel, but contrary to Gadamer, he sees *both* axes as essential to hermeneutics. Only through the proper use of explanation can we reach "post critical naïveté." Four years after *Freud and Philosophy,* in 1969, Ricoeur produced a large volume of essays under the title *The Conflict of Interpretations* (Evanston, Ill.: Northwestern University Press, 1974). This considers Descartes and consciousness, structuralism, double meaning, Freud, symbols, religions, and faith. Here Ricoeur rightly considers not only the legacy of German philosophy, but also the later Wittgenstein, J. L. Austin, P. F. Strawson, and speech act theory. Earlier he had collaborated with Derrida, and to remain credible on the French intellectual scene it was necessary to engage with structuralism. He concedes that it may shed light on language as a system of possibilities *(la langue),* even if it too readily excludes the speaking subject or human agent in a speech act *(la parole)*. Gérard Genette will become important for his work on narrative.

In 1973 Ricoeur delivered in Fort Worth, Texas, lectures published as *Interpretation Theory* (Fort Worth: Texas Christian University Press, 1976). This expounded language as discourse, speaking and writing, metaphor, symbol, and explanation and understanding. In 1975 Ricoeur published *The Rule of Metaphor,* which again calls attention to the multilayered and "double-meaning" nature of language and texts. What symbol is to word, he argued, metaphor is to sentence. Here he drew on Benveniste and on Max Black's theory of metaphor as interactive. When two distinct semantic domains are placed together, metaphor may produce creatively a new thing that goes beyond both original semantic domains (*see* **Metaphor**).

This "middle period" prepares for the later period of Ricoeur's two magisterial works: *Time and Narrative,* 3 vols. (Chicago: University of Chicago Press, 1984, 1985, 1988; Fr. 1983-1985), and *Oneself as Another* (Chicago: University of Chicago Press, 1992; Fr. 1990). Ricoeur begins volume 1 of *Time and Narrative* by comparing Augustine and Aristotle. Book 11 of Augustine's *Confessions* introduces the pole of "discordance," that is, stretched-out time as duration, in which the past invites recollection or memory, the present invites attention, and the future invites expectation and hope. Augustine writes: "The mind performs these functions ... those of expectation ... attention and memory" (quoted directly by Ricoeur in vol. 1, 19, and discussed on 21). We understand the past and future through our own present. Only God can really hold past, present, and future together in what Boethius called simultaneity. In Aristotle we see the "converse" of this, in that "emplotment" *(mythos)* provides a unity to what would otherwise be mere chronological succession and extension. Ricoeur comments, "*Emplotment* gives shape and organization to what otherwise would be bare extension" (33). This makes understanding *(Verstehen)* possible. Aristotle has unified disparate events by a temporal logic. These two perspectives are now brought together in "refiguration," when the narrative and plot are reconceived. Temporality *(Zeitlichkeit)* remains crucial, but the plot can now be "made present" in hermeneutics. The readers have arrived at "narrative understanding." Vanhoozer suggests that the French title *Temps et Récit* would better be rendered *Time and Telling.* It is the *telling (récit)* that well exposes this organizing principle. It is not simply *histoire* or *fabula,* as Genette and the Russian formalists call it, but *telling, recital, or discourse.* Thus, Ricoeur insists, we must retain the "indirect connection ... between history and our narrative experience" (175).

Volume 2 provides a close-up of narrative with particular reference to fiction. Ricoeur illustrates his themes from Flaubert and Jane Austen, including such standard narrative devices as "point of view" (93-95), "narrative voice" (95-96), and the "polyphonic novel," as in Bakhtin (96-99). The refiguring of time (101-52) draws on Genette's notion of narrative discourse, including speed, flashbacks, flash-forwards, compression, and narrative sequence (81-88). Mark's Gospel, some have argued, makes the cross central by its deployment of narrative time: a fast speed marks the beginning eight chapters; then a steady pace from Peter's confession; and finally slow motion for the passion narratives. A sequential comparison of the four Gospels in terms of chronological "clock time" completely misunderstands the sequence and plot of each Gospel. Heidegger's view of "subjective" time also stands prominently in the background of Ricoeur's "refiguration."

Volume 3 reinforces the aesthetics of temporality and the poetics of narrative. In this volume Ricoeur draws more explicitly on Husserl and Heidegger. He examines Husserl on "internal time-consciousness" (23-44). He then draws on

Heidegger's concept of "making possible" (70). He explicitly draws on Heidegger's notion of *Dasein* (being there) as "superseding" the Augustine-Aristotle polarity (62) through its concept of time and care, and exteriorization of the subjective experience of past, present, and future. He writes, "Anticipation *(Vorlaufen)* makes Dasein *authentically* futural" (69). In the second main section of this volume, Ricoeur returns to the distinction between lived time, universal time, and time in history, which is so crucial for narrative. History reveals a creative capacity for "the refiguration of time" (104). Physical time, calendar time, and narrative time are distinct. As Gadamer urges also, "Historians' interpretations are guided by the theme chosen to guide their inquiries" (117). Hence a supposedly "factual" report in chronological sequence may turn out to be nearer to a "narrative" than we may imagine. Ricoeur refers to Hans Robert Jauss and to W. Iser and comments, "It is on the level of a public's horizon of expectations that a work exercises what Jauss terms the 'creative function of the work of art'" (173). So all the previous work on time and narrative (or telling) becomes intertwined again with consciousness and the human, and the horizon of time is explicitly connected with expectation and historicality. He comments, "Reading becomes *a provocation to be and act differently....Narrative identity* is not equivalent to true self-constancy, except through the decisive moment, which makes ethical responsibility the highest factor in self-constancy" (249, italics mine). The strategy of persuasion undertaken by the narrator is aimed at imposing on the reader a vision of the world that is never ethically neutral. It induces a new evaluation of the world and of the reader.

These last sentences form a bridge to Ricoeur's other magisterial work, *Oneself as Another*. *Time and Narrative* has not simply talked about plot, coherence and tension, different notions of time, and the refiguring of mere strings of "facts" into a single, purposive narrative. This alone would be enough to revolutionize our understanding of the functions of biblical narrative. Ricoeur goes further. He shows that the refigured narrative changes lives, and gives readers a new vision of the world, which includes the ethical. This brings him to the problem discussed at length in *Oneself as Another*. In the last analysis, can the continuity and stability of the self rest on anything other than our relationship to the other, ethical decision, and accountability?

It is not surprising that it takes Ricoeur 350 pages of tough and complex prose to grapple with the problem of self and self-identity that has plagued philosophers from Descartes, Locke, and Hume, through Strawson, Recanati, and other modern philosophers, to today. Ricoeur first provides his convincing critique not only of Descartes, but also of Nietzsche's attack on Descartes. In Nietzsche the search for coherence and order becomes "an illusion that conceals the play of focus under the artifice of order" (15). Next, Strawson attempts a semantic and logical analysis of "person" by means of an overlapping of M predicates and P predicates; but even this in the end also "eclipses the self" (32), failing to give enough place to its capacity for intersubjectivity. Searle's and Recanati's notion of the speech act does advance us further, with its stress on the speaking subject (against Derrida). But even so, it needs to take further "the transcendental condition of communication" (47), and a broader philosophy of language. A human being is a "Who?" not a "What?"; hence Wittgenstein and Anscombe address the logical grammar of intention, but do not quite capture what Ricoeur calls its "irreducible" nature or its ontological nature (83-87). The notion of "ascription," as in H. L. A. Hart, provides a useful advance, but remains only a limited one (99).

These four avenues of approach are all too limited. From the fifth essay, Ricoeur introduces *narrative identity*, which introduces his own more positive contribution. He sums up the problem: "Looking back, the greatest lacuna in these earlier studies most obviously concerns the *temporal* dimension of the self" (115). Ricoeur repeats: "*Personal* identity can be articulated only in the temporal dimensions of human existences" (114). This convincing observation owes much in the first instance to Hegel, Heidegger, and Dilthey. Indeed, Ricoeur approves of Dilthey's basic theme of *connectedness* of life (115). Gadamer and Pannenberg also stress this. Ricoeur refers back to his writing of *The Voluntary and the Involuntary*. Time may nurture habit, disposition, and *"acquired identifications"* (121). *Such experiences as "keeping one's word" and "promising" point to a stable self* (123-24). The paradoxes of self-identity are apparent in the philosophy of Locke and Hume, especially if (with Hume) we can perceive only strings of isolated perceptions. As C. A. Campbell observes, Hume's approach would be like listening to Big Ben striking nine o'clock and perceiving it as striking one o'clock nine times. Hume was seeking "what he could not hope to find" (128). Ricoeur takes up Heidegger's concept of "mineness," which he claims does not adequately feature in the discussions of Derek Parfit (129-39).

Ricoeur's reference to "interconnectedness" brings him back to a discussion of "plot" in his sixth study. Here we also find a correlation between act and character, which are intentionally related to concordance and discordance. Moreover, the functions of narrative, as he argued in volume 3, have *ethical* implications. The ethical aim of the self is discussed further in the seventh study. Ricoeur engages with three or perhaps four traditions of philosophy: with Aristotle on friendship; with Hume on the Is/Ought question; with Husserl and Levinas on reciprocity; and with Heidegger on "solicitude," if this differs from Husserl and Levinas. His eighth study considers "the good life," with reference, first, to Kant's categorical imperative of "duty," which allows for universalization, and second, to "virtue ethics." "Virtue" in Aristotle and MacIntyre transcends mere "duty." Justice remains a philosophical concept, even if only Christian theology can speak of love (223). The ninth study provides a discussion of practical wisdom or *phronēsis* in relation to the self. There is an interlude on tragedy. Ricoeur considers Hegel's perspective on Sophocles' *Antigone,* and *Sittlichkeit* in Hegel. In the light of such diverse ethical goals as "liberty," "equality," "solidarity," "security," and so on, Ricoeur insists on "the irreducible plurality of the ends of good government" (259).

The tenth study embodies Ricoeur's conclusions. His ontology demands dialectic with otherness. He concludes, "Otherness is not added on to selfhood from outside, as though to prevent its solipsistic drift" (317). It belongs to the "ontological constitution of selfhood" (317). The other must not be reduced, but it is "polysemic." Otherness is "inherent in the relation of intersubjectivity" (318). Ricoeur states the aphorism "Existing is resisting" (322); and also, "the other is presupposed" (332). Yet in moral issues "the ultimate equivalency with respect to the structure of the Other in the phenomenon of conscience is perhaps what needs to be pressured" (353). The role of selfhood is concerned with *sameness, continuity, and stability. This implies accountability.* A self remains *responsible* for its attitude and actions *even through change and difference.* This principle is far more convincing than anything that Locke suggested about continuity of mind or body. Our ethical accountability survives through bodily and mental changes. To offer a mundane example, a particular person may justifiably expect a given pension or superannuation, whatever career changes may have occurred. So also the law, by analogy, may call someone to account for long-past actions as the same person as the one who committed the misdemeanor.

Ricoeur later produced works on justice and institutional responsibility. His earlier work on the self, finitude, and guilt has traveled full circle through work on symbol, metaphor, and hermeneutics. All this work demonstrates the interdisciplinary character of hermeneutics, and the complex character of "reading," whether reading texts or human subjects. Even in his earlier work *The Rule of Metaphor,* he wrote that his phenomenology "tries to exact from lived experience the essential meanings and structures of purpose, project, motive, wanting, trying and so on" ([Toronto: Toronto University Press, 1977; London: Routledge Kegan Paul, 1978], 316). The problem of evil is brought into the field of research, as well as new linguistic perplexities. Ricoeur seeks always to write as a philosopher, and much more rarely as a biblical interpreter or as a theologian. However, in the early 1970s he produced several essays on biblical hermeneutics, some of which are presented as a single volume in Ricoeur, *Essays on Biblical Interpretations* (London: SPCK, 1982; Philadelphia: Fortress, 1980). In his important essay "Toward a Hermeneutic of the Idea of Revelation" (73-118), he distinguishes between the five kinds of biblical texts. (i) *Prophetic discourse,* the mode of discourse most familiar to people, is one in which the prophet speaks in the name of God (25-77). (ii) *Narrative texts* especially underline plot and the role of a person or of characters (77-81). (iii) *Prescriptive discourse* contains utterances of law or covenant (51-85). (iv) *Wisdom discourse* often expresses the incomparability of God, as, for example, in Job (85-88). (v) *Hymnic discourse* can best be seen in many of the Psalms. These are often written in the first person, but nonetheless remain part of Scripture (88-90). *Each of these requires a different approach and hermeneutical method.* Ricoeur has also written in *Semeia* 4 on the interpretation of Job, and also several more recent essays.

Biblical and theological scholars will find in all of Ricoeur's writings a treasury of suggestive thoughts and themes, in spite of his insistence that he writes primarily as a philosopher who has interdisciplinary interests. He is one of the most creative and seminal minds of the late twentieth century, and always repays study. (*See also* **Hermeneutics; Metaphor; Narrative; Other, Otherness; Symbol.**)

Reading: W. C. Dowling, *Ricoeur on Time and Narrative* (Notre Dame, Ind.: University of Notre Dame Press, 2011); Lewis E. Hahn, ed., *The Philosophy of Paul Ricoeur* (Chicago: Open Court, 1995); R. Kearney, *On Paul Ricoeur* (Burlington, Vt., and Aldershot, U.K.: Ashgate, 2004); D. Klemm, *The Hermeneutical Theory of Paul Ricoeur* (Toronto: Associated University Press, 1983); Paul Ricoeur, *Freud and Philosophy* (New Haven: Yale University Press, 1970); Paul Ricoeur, *Time and Narrative*, 3 vols. (Chicago: University of Chicago Press, 1984, 1985, 1988); Paul Ricoeur, *Oneself as Another* (Chicago: University of Chicago Press, 1992).

Righteousness
Righteousness is denoted in the OT by the Hebrew *ts-d-q,* which can occur in its verbal form or in the noun form, *ts^{e}dāqâ*. Together, they occur with great frequency, that is, 525 times in the OT alone. The term denotes *being in accordance with a norm, fundamentally with the character of God,* although secondarily in accordance with expected ethical conduct. Most uses occur in the Psalms, Prophets, and Wisdom literature, but the term occurs throughout the OT. Noah is described as a righteous man (Gen. 6:9; 7:1); Abraham believed God, and the Lord "reckoned it to him as righteousness" (Gen. 15:6). In Gen. 30:33 Jacob claims to be righteous (NRSV, "honest"). Significantly, however, the basis of Israel's entry into the Promised Land was God's promise, not their righteousness (Deut. 9:4-6). In Lev. 19:36 and Deut. 25:15 righteousness entails using the right weights and measures. Deut. 4:8 declares that the Lord is righteous.

The eighth-century prophets, especially Amos and Isaiah, attack injustice and demand righteousness. Amos makes unfavorable comparisons with reliance on offerings and sacrifices (Amos 5:22-24), especially condemning the exploitation of the poor (8:4-6). Similarly in Hosea, God desires "steadfast love and not sacrifice" (Hos. 6:6). Isaiah begins to see righteousness as derived from God's righteousness, and often equates righteousness with justice (Isa. 5:8-13; 10:1; 33:5; 59:17). Luther drew his contrast between "my" righteousness and "God's" righteousness from his lectures on the OT as well as from Rom. 1:17. God "brings" holiness, righteousness, and truth to Israel. God reveals himself as the One who is "absolute in righteousness and truth" (T. C. Vriezen, *Outline of Old Testament Theology* [Oxford: Blackwell, 1962], 162; Ps. 7:8-11). In relation to the poor, needy, and oppressed, God vindicates them in his righteousness (Ps. 112:9). The term occurs in Isaiah at least eighty times. In Jer. 9:24, God acts with justice and righteousness. In due time, he will raise up for David a righteous branch (23:5). He will send a future ruler who will be characterized by righteousness (Isa. 11:4-5; 16:5). In Ps. 36:5-6 the psalmist declares, "Your righteousness is like the mighty mountains"; and in Ps. 51:14, "My tongue shall sing aloud of thy righteousness" (KJV). In Ps. 97:2, "Righteousness and justice are the foundation of his throne."

The supposed distinction in historical theology, then, between the *gift* of righteousness as *derived from God,* and *behavioral or ethical righteousness* in *human* conduct, clearly *comes from the OT.* The OT background to Rom. 1:17, pinpointed by Luther, remains a genuine one.

Both streams find expression in the Greek *dikaiosunē* (noun), *dikaios* (adjective), and *dikaioō* (verb). J. Ziesler's claim that behavioral or ethical righteousness is mainly denoted by the adjective and noun, and "putting things right" is indicated by the verb, may have some substance, but it runs against some exceptions and is generally felt to be an exaggeration (*The Meaning of Righteousness in Paul* [Cambridge: CUP, 1972]). BDAG translates *dikaiosunē* as (i) "the quality, state, or practice of judicial responsibility . . . justice, equitableness, fairness"; (ii) "quality as state of judicial correctness with focus on redemptive action, righteousness"; (iii) "the quality or characteristic of upright behaviour . . . righteousness" (247-49). It translates the verb *dikaioō* as (i) "to take up a legal cause, show justice, do justice"; (ii) "to render a favourable verdict, vindicate"; (iii) "to cause someone to be released from personal or institutional claims"; and (iv) "to demonstrate to be morally right, prove to be right" (249). *Dikaiōma* may mean "a regulation relating to right action" or "an action that meets expectations as to what is right or just" (249-50). F. Danker provides NT passages that illustrate each of these nine meanings. Under (ii) of the verb, he cites Rom. 1:17, 3:21-26, 2 Cor. 3:9, 2 Cor. 5:21, and 1 Cor. 1:30, which he says "refer to righteousness bestowed by God" (247). Certainly at first sight this suggests that Luther was not on exegetical and lexical shaky ground in his exposition of Rom. 1:17, when he at first "hated" the notion of righteousness, and then learned to love the concept of *God's* gift of righteousness (*see* **Luther, Martin,** esp. his "Tower experience").

This does not imply, however, that Luther had said the last word about the subject. J. Weiss stressed the *eschatological* nature of righteousness, as in Gal. 5:5, "We eagerly wait for the hope of righteousness." Righteousness, when seen within a *historical* frame ("all have sinned"), does not "contradict" righteousness when seen within an *eschatological* frame (*see* **Justification**). E. Sanders, J. D. G. Dunn, and to some extent N. T. Wright stress the *communal* or *corporate* sense of the term. C. K. Barrett and others stress its covenantal character as vindication. Wright rightly wishes to broaden the Reformation interpretation. Sanders and Dunn stress the equal status of Jews and Gentiles in the church. Within an apocalyptic framework, E. Käsemann holds together God's action in salvation history with a Reformation approach. The behavioral or ethical aspect is found more continuously in the Synoptic Gospels, for example, "Unless your righteousness exceeds that of the scribes and Pharisees, you will never enter the kingdom of heaven" (Matt. 5:20), and "Blessed are those who are persecuted for righteousness' sake, for theirs is the kingdom of heaven" (5:10). Similarly, "the word of righteousness" in Heb. 5:13 seems to constitute part of basic Christian instruction. But the two themes come together in Matt. 6:33: "Strive first for the kingdom of God and his righteousness, and all these things will be given to you as well."

We may conclude by looking more closely at Wright's approach to the term. First, he sees it as part of God's covenant theology (*Justification* [London: SPCK, 2009], 222). It entails "putting the whole world right," where *righteous* is one useful metaphor among others. He begins with the account of Abraham in Genesis 15–18. Second, the purpose of a theological exposition of "righteousness of God" is to provide assurance (223), both in the present through faith, and in the future. Third, although he is sympathetic with John Piper's approach, Wright gives five arguments for rejecting his equation of "God's righteousness" with "God's concern for God's own glory." He writes that God's overflowing, generous, creative love is "In the flourishing and well-being of everything else" (51). Fourth, he rejects the older debate about whether God's righteousness in Rom. 1:17 is "subjective" or "objective"; it is "possessive" (46-47). Thus Wright retains much of the Lutheran emphasis, but interprets it explicitly in a communal and covenantal context. He takes account of Sanders's "new perspective" by stressing the Jew/Gentile context, without allowing it to dominate his entire interpretation. Seyoon Kim claims that this occurs in his critique of Sanders and Dunn. None of this detracts from contexts where righteousness denotes an ethical quality; but this nevertheless derives, as the OT implies, from the righteousness of God. (*See also* **Justification; Luther, Martin; Wright, N. Thomas.**)

Reading: D. Hill, "The Background and Meaning of *Dikaiosunē* and Cognate Words," in *Greek Words and Hebrew Meanings* (Cambridge: CUP, 1967), 82-162; R. W. L. Moberly, "*Abraham's Righteousness* (Gen. 15:6)," in *Studies in the Pentateuch*, ed. J. A. Emerton, Vetus Testamentum Supplements 41 (Leiden: Brill, 1990), 103-30; Graf Henning Reventlow and Y. Hoffmann, eds., *Justice and Righteousness* (Sheffield: Sheffield Academic Press, 1992); N. T. Wright, *Justification* (London: SPCK, 2009); J. Ziesler, *The Meaning of Righteousness of Paul* (Cambridge: CUP, 1972).

Risk

Risk is said to have been introduced into theology by Kierkegaard. He wrote, "Without risk there is no faith" (*Concluding Unscientific Postscript* [Princeton: Princeton University Press, 1941], 182). Although reason may have a role, eventually a paradox emerges, when faith must take a risk to decide to believe. The idea is anticipated in Blaise Pascal, who also stressed faith as a decision, which may be compared with a "wager" for or against God.

Ritschl, Albrecht

Born in Berlin the son of a Lutheran preacher and bishop, Albrecht Ritschl (1822-1889) had probably more influence than any other theologian over the last quarter of the nineteenth century. He studied at Bonn, Halle, and Heidelberg, but became an ardent disciple of F. C. Baur at Tübingen. He lectured mainly on the NT as a professor at Bonn, where he wrote on Luke (1846) and the rise of the early Catholic Church (1850). However, in 1864 he was called to succeed I. A. Dorner as professor of dogmatics at Göttingen, where he published his major work, *The Christian Doctrine of Justification and Reconciliation* (3 vols., 1870-1874). Also discussed in this work were other issues such as the knowledge of God and Kant's philosophy.

From 1874 to 1880 he gathered a group of disciples around him, including A. Harnack and W. Herrmann. He began to arouse the hostility of conservative Lutherans and Pietists. He wrote his *History of Pietism* (Ger. *Geschichte des Pietismus*, 3 vols. [Bonn: Marcus, 1880-1886]). J. Weiss was his son-in-law, and Häring his successor on his death in 1889. He called Schleiermacher his predecessor, and bequeathed what is often called "the Ritschlian School," which is characterized by its emphasis on the community and on ethics. Ritschl saw justification as "the acceptance of sinners into communion with God," based on the work of Christ, but effective within the context of community. This is the ethical community of the kingdom of God. He perpetuated Kant's contrast between fact and value, which later did so much to shape Bultmann's theology. Through Harnack and Herrmann many see Ritschl as transmitting the liberal tradition. But J. Richmond wrote a reappraisal of Ritschl to counteract Barth's "uncompromising hostility towards . . . Ritschl" (*Ritschl* [London: Collins, 1978], 35). "The attempt is made to throw off neo-orthodox preconceptions and prejudices" (38), and "distorting stereotypes" (39). In the light of Barth's comments, it may be ironic that Ritschl opposed natural theology and metaphysics, resisted the notion that God can be known as an abstract concept, and is often called christocentric. He is constantly concerned with the work of Christ, although he rejects the traditional "two-natures" Christology, and concludes, "The conception of the emotion of the wrath of God has no religious value for Christians." Barth is right, however, about his inadequate conception of the kingdom of God.

Ritschl has often been attacked or misrepresented, Richmond claims, from two opposite sides. The more conservative side criticized his deference to "religion" as a universal trait; his dependence upon human consciousness in Schleiermacher; and his equating of "God" with human faith and trust in God. The more liberal side accused him of an overnarrow Christocentricity, personalism, and building too specifically on the Bible. (*See also* **God, Trinity: Historical Development.**)

Reading: J. Richmond, *Ritschl: A Reappraisal* (London: Collins, 1978); A. Ritschl, *The Christian Doctrine of Justification and Reconciliation* (Edinburgh: T. & T. Clark, 1902).

Robinson, John A. T.

John A. T. Robinson (1919-1983) was an influential, sometime revolutionary NT scholar and churchman. He served as curate in Bristol under Mervyn Stockwood, who later became bishop of Southwark. Robinson became a lecturer at Trinity College, Cambridge, and later, dean, and was appointed bishop of Woolwich, by Mervyn Stockwood. In 1950 Robinson published *In the End, God . . .* ; in 1952, *The Body: A Study in Pauline Theology;* in 1959, *Jesus and His Coming;* in 1963, *Honest to God;* in 1973, *The Human Face of God;* in 1976, *Redating the New Testament;* in

1981, *The Roots of a Radical*; in 1984, *The Priority of John*; as well as other works. In his thought and in his writings his radical views have been compared with those of Harvey Cox, but in other respects his view of the NT could at times be conservative, and he never lost the capacity to surprise.

Robinson's book *In the End, God...* stressed a cosmic view of eschatology, but tended toward universalism. *Honest to God* was a popular book that sold millions of copies, and expressed deep doubts about prayer and traditional doctrines of God. Ian Ramsey and Michael Ramsey (the archbishop of Canterbury) criticized his work for conveying a simplistic view of religious language. Like the later work of Don Cupitt, Robinson attacked the notion of a God "out there," drawing on Tillich's notion of God as the ground of our being, on Bultmann's view of myth, and on Bonhoeffer's notion of "secular" religion. The *Human Face of God* attacked the Christology of Chalcedon. Its positive contribution was to take with utmost seriousness the humanity of Jesus: the "sinlessness" of Jesus did not mean "the static perfection of flawless porcelain" ([London: SCM, 1973], 77). His temptations meant "really to feel the pull of evil" (91). But in negative terms some would say that he exaggerated the difficulties of belief in the virgin birth and a two-nature Christology. But he stressed that "The Christ is God with a human face" (229). In *Redating the New Testament* Robinson criticized the traditional dating of the NT writings and argued that the NT was completed much earlier than is generally recognized. Indeed, it was virtually all written before A.D. 70. The Gospel of John, he concluded, is a reliable and early historical tradition.

Romanticism
Romanticism flourished from the very end of the eighteenth century through the first half of the nineteenth century, although it is often defined differently in accordance with whether literature, philosophy, art, or music is in question. Broadly, it constituted a reaction against the dry rationalism and formalism of much of the eighteenth century. It reacted against mechanical and mechanistic models of life and reality, and the domination of the physical or natural sciences. It highly valued creativity, organic approaches, conflict, and "storm and stress" *(Sturm und Drang)*. Examples can be found in literature, poetry, art, music, painting, and to a lesser extent in theology.

William Blake (1757-1827), William Wordsworth (1771-1850), Samuel T. Coleridge (1772-1834), and George Byron (1788-1824) represent English Romanticism. Blake reacted against the mechanism of the Industrial Revolution, expressing nostalgia for the rural life based on the soil, in contrast to industry's "dark satanic mills." Wordsworth defined poetry as "emotion recollected in tranquility." Both Blake and Wordsworth argued that "meddling intellect" misshapes the beauteous form of things. Analysis, Wordsworth believed, sees only difference; vision perceives wholeness and nurtures creativity. Coleridge moved away from rationalism to stress "creative imagination." This is expressed in his poetry and theology. Byron drew on German, Italian, and Greek mythology also. In German

Romanticism the earliest or central figure is probably J. G. Herder (1744-1803). He worked in many fields of philosophy, urging a vitalist pantheism, which influenced Goethe, Schelling, and even Hegel. His interest extended to art, language, literature, and religion. F. von Schlegel (1772-1829) influenced Schleiermacher in a Romanticist direction. J. W. Goethe (1749-1832) ranks as the greatest Romantic poet. He believed that God was within the vibrancy of nature, not its mechanistic "external" cause. In 1794 he formed a friendship with J. C. F. Schiller (1759-1805), a major dramatist, artist, and poet.

The Romantic Movement also influenced music and painting. Ludwig van Beethoven (1770-1827) is often said to have reflected the transition to Romanticism between his first two symphonies and the Third ("Eroica") of 1804, although hints appear in the "Moonlight Sonata" of 1801. His music from 1804 is often seen as "a prodigious assertion of the human will," often out of "storm and stress." The Fifth Symphony of 1807 brought him to the attention of other Romanticists. Carl Weber (1787-1826) began in the classical tradition, but in his later period produced a Romantic opera, which paved the way for Wagner. Richard Wagner (1813-1883) is fully Romanticist in every sense, especially in such works as *The Flying Dutchman* (1841) and *Tannhäuser* (1845). Many would also include Berlioz (1803-1869) in France; Mendelssohn (1809-1847) and Schumann (1810-1856); Chopin (1810-1849) from Poland; and the Hungarian Franz Liszt (1811-1886). In painting the later work of John Constable (1776-1837) began to reflect Romanticist influence after about 1815. E. Delacroix (1798-1863) provides an example from French painting.

In Christian theology Schleiermacher's feeling of utter dependence on God reflects the tendency toward the Romantics, but this constitutes only one of three or four strong influences on him, and mainly concerns immediacy of experience of God (*see* **Schleiermacher, Friedrich D. E.**). The theology of Coleridge is no less pronounced. Like Schleiermacher, he suspected the inadequacy of metaphysical approaches to Christian faith, and expounded the role of creative imagination. Commenting on practical immediate experience, he asserted: "The Bible *finds* me at a deeper level than any other book."

Reading: B. M. G. Reardon, *Religion in the Age of Romanticism* (Cambridge: CUP, 1985).

Rupert of Deutz

Rupert of Deutz (c. 1075-1129) was abbot of Deutz, near Cologne (c. 1120), and a prolific writer. He forms a bridge between the death of Anselm and the emergence of Bernard of Clairvaux and Peter Abelard. He produced biblical commentaries on Matthew, John, the Apocalypse, and the Minor Prophets, and a treatise *On the Trinity* (c. 1114). He ascribed creation especially to the Father; redemption, to the Son; and renewal, to the Holy Spirit. Many of the Fathers regarded each as a work of the whole Trinity. He defended the Western "double procession" of the Holy Spirit.

S

Sachkritik

Sachkritik is the German term regularly translated as "content criticism" in English. But Robert Morgan warns us that in the special context of Bultmann's NT studies, this translation is only partially correct. He argues that it is "not totally wrong," but nevertheless misses much of the point of Bultmann's use of the term. Bultmann uses the term to criticize what is said in a text "in the light of the *Sache* (or content) that the New Testament author intended to speak" (i.e., what he meant; "Thiselton on *Sachkritik*," in *Horizons in Hermeneutics,* ed. S. E. Porter and M. R. Malcolm [Grand Rapids: Eerdmans, 2013], 39). Bultmann's program to interpret myth did indeed presuppose that the content of the NT can sometimes, in his view, run counter to its purpose. If we translate *Sachkritik* as "content criticism," this assumption should be borne in mind in understanding the term. Whether this distinction is tenable remains a separate question.

Sacraments

The term "sacrament" does not appear in the biblical writings. The word first entered Christian currency at the end of the second century in Tertullian's treatise *On Baptism*. In 1.1, he writes, "Here is our sacrament of water." Elsewhere he enjoins all who are presbyters to undertake the duty of administering the sacraments at all times (*On Exhortation to Chastity* 7). The Greek equivalent to the Latin *sacramentum* (sacrament, symbol, rite) is *mustērion,* although the earliest use in this specific sense seems to be in the fourth century with Eusebius. It is well known that the Roman Catholic Church traditionally followed Thomas Aquinas in enumerating seven sacraments, while the major Reformers and Protestant churches in that tradition spoke only of two "dominical" sacraments, baptism and the Lord's Supper, Holy Communion, or the Eucharist.

Questions about the "proper" number of sacraments cannot be answered in isolation from determining their character and function. In practice, the term "sacrament" is used in any of three distinct ways. (i) In the Reformation tradition "dominical" sacraments are restricted to the *two* that Jesus explicitly instituted (Matt. 26:26-29; 28:19; Mark 14:22-25; Luke 22:15-20; Rom. 6:3-4; 1 Cor. 11:23-26). (ii) At the opposite end of the spectrum, almost *any* physical object or event can become an outward and visible sign of an inward and spiritual grace or reality. For example, washing may become a symbol of cleansing and forgiveness; waking up in the morning may be a tactile and visible foretaste of resurrection or renewal. The Fourth Gospel has an abundance of "sacraments" in this sense, and such wider symbols are used for devotional purposes in all traditions, notably by the medieval mystics. (iii) Roman Catholic and Eastern Orthodox traditions use the term "sacrament" to denote not only baptism and Holy Communion, but also (at least traditionally) five other visible signs of inward grace that the church has supposedly validated: ordination (where the outward sign is the laying on of hands); marriage (where the wedding ring and oral vows constitute a visible sign); confirmation; penance; and extreme unction, for which Vatican II recommended the title "Anointing of the Sick." To these three distinct meanings should be added the most basic of all, namely, the incarnation of Jesus Christ, which becomes the greatest visible, public, and tangible expression of the love of God for the world.

Once we develop this approach, it is easy to see why Vatican II approved the notion that the church is also a sacrament, in several senses. W. Pannenberg also approves of this idea. In Col. 1:26 the word "mystery" is used of the public manifestation of the word of God. Augustine left an indelible influence on Christian thought by defining the term as a "visible form of invisible grace," which is also enshrined in the Church of England's *Book of Common Prayer*. Historically, Pseudo-Dionysius distinguished baptism, the Eucharist, and unction, as three sacraments, to which he then added ordination and monastic consecration. The traditional seven then appeared in Peter Lombard (*Sentences* 4.1.2), and were affirmed by Thomas Aquinas (*Su Th* 3, qu. 60-65; Blackfriars ed., vol. 56, if it is authentic to Thomas) and the Council of Trent (1545-1563).

Sacraments are "effective signs" of the covenant (*see* **Covenant**), as Reformation theology urges. Luther, Melanchthon, and Calvin all understood them as pledges, promises, or effective signs of divine promise. This helps to account for two themes in the major Reformers: the sacrament of baptism could be administered to infants as a sign of promise; and the sacraments were regarded as of equal importance to (not greater importance than) the Word. Melanchthon insisted: "the gospel is the promise of grace. This section on signs is very closely related to promises as seals which remind us of the promise. . . . They are certain witnesses to the Divine will" (Melanchthon, *Loci Communes,* in *Melanchthon and Bucer,* ed. W. Pauck [Philadelphia: Westminster, 1969], 133). John Calvin defines a sacrament as "an external sign, by which the Lord seals on our consciences his promises of good-will toward us . . . to sustain the weakness of our faith" (*Institutes* 4.14.1; Beveridge, 2:491-92). For Calvin, they are parallel with OT covenantal signs such as circumcision, which he calls "symbols of the covenant" (*Institutes* 4.7).

Martin Bucer and Peter Martyr called the sacraments "visible words," and with Thomas Cranmer stressed their parity as such with the oral or aural words of preaching and the Liturgy of the Word. They remain not "bare signs," but they "offer what they show" (quoted by D. F. Wright, *Martin Bucer: Reforming the Church and Community* [Cambridge: CUP, 1994], 59). However, it is selective to stress *only* visibility, when each of the five senses is involved: seeing, hearing, touching, tasting, even perhaps smelling. They are especially significant in relation to *weakness* of faith. They do not tell more of the gospel than the Word; but as tangible and effective signs of covenant assurance, they reinforce the validity of a two-way pledge and promise: God's commitment to us and ours to God. Thus Pannenberg rightly stresses the "not-yet" character of sacraments, or their eschatological dimension. We need sacraments in this interim period of faith and doubt; one day in the future faith will vanish from sight, and promise will become obsolete in the fulfillment of that which has been promised. Hence Paul asserts that they *"proclaim"* Christ, like the Word (1 Cor. 11:26). Moreover, if they are signs, they should draw attention not to themselves, but to that to which they point, namely, the gospel and Christ. Often a desire to stress the dignity of the sacraments can unwittingly allow the signs to point only to themselves. Today, however, we do not need to reduce the importance of the sacraments; the task today is to reinstate the momentous eventfulness of the Word, with which the sacraments function in common. In the church today, the only large bodies not to observe and participate in the dominical sacraments are the Quakers and the Salvation Army. (*See also* **Baptism; Lord's Supper.**)

Reading: D. M. Bailey, *The Theology of the Sacraments* (New York: Scribner, 1957); C. K. Barrett, *Church, Ministry, and Sacraments* (Eugene, Ore.: Wipf and Stock, 2005); L.-M. Chauvet, *Symbol and Sacrament* (Collegeville, Minn.: Liturgical Press, 1995); J. Calvin, *Institutes* (London: James Clarke, 1957), 4.14 (Beveridge, 2:491-511); G. Rowell and C. Hall, *The Gestures of God* (London and New York: Continuum, 2004). (*See also bibliographies under* **Baptism** *and* **Lord's Supper.**)

Sacrifice

The prophets of the OT attacked exclusive dependence on sacrifice as a mechanical or exclusively liturgical means of obtaining salvation. Sacrifices constituted symbols of worship pleasing to God, provided they were expressions of appropriate conduct and attitudes. The prophets could assert the ineffectiveness and pointlessness of sacrifice unless it expressed a corresponding attitude of heart. If there is no integration between liturgy and life, Amos in the eighth century depicts God as declaring:

> I hate, I despise your festivals....
> Even though you offer me your burnt offerings and grain offerings,
> I will not accept them. (Amos 5:21-22)

Jeremiah even claims that in the era of the exodus "I did not . . . command them concerning burnt offerings and sacrifices. But this command I gave them, 'Obey my voice, and I will be your God' " (Jer. 7:22-23). H. H. Rowley suggests that this is not to be understood in an absolute sense, but concerns sacrifice that was not the expression of obedience to God. The well-known Hos. 6:6, "I desire steadfast love and not sacrifice," is usually understood as focusing on contrast. Walther

Eichrodt questions those who draw an oversharp line between opposing sources in "P" (the Priestly Code), which attaches importance to God's command to sacrifice, and others. He pointedly comments: "This is not just a post-exilic theory" (*Theology of the Old Testament,* vol. 1 [London: SCM, 1961], 163).

Broadly, four types of sacrifices functioned to express three types of inward and outward attitude. (i) The *minchah,* or meal offering, signified donated *gifts* offered to God, usually in thanksgiving, gratitude, or joy. It was basically a bloodless gift. (ii) The *'olâ,* or burnt offering, expressed dedication and *devotion,* and was part of the *regular* morning and evening sacrifices of each day, often in the form of a lamb. (iii) The *shᵉlāmîm,* or peace offering, essentially expressed *communion* with God, in which the worshiper gave a part to God and a part to the priest, and took the remaining part for himself. It was eaten in the sanctuary in the presence of God, as a sign of *fellowship.* (iv) The *'āshām,* or guilt offering, mentioned only in this so-called P strata, expressed anticipatory *expiation,* or *compensation* for sin or guilt.

These four types or categories are not clear-cut and self-contained, and each has related variants that attach to it. The *minchah,* or gift, can be given from one human being to another, and the bloodless sacrifice may be combined with another type of sacrifice. There may be many different motives behind the gift: from *spontaneous joy and gratitude* at a special deliverance or mercy, to motives that are less worthy. An outstanding "good" example is the gift of a *tithe* or *first fruits.* The offering of the first fruits was a joyful sacrificial occasion, usually for the autumn harvest, as evidenced especially in Deuteronomy. The *shᵉlāmîm,* or peace offering, strengthened sacral communion, often expressed in the ancient world in the sharing of a meal. In Hebrew technical terms, the context of the *zebach* was often that of the covenant. God declares that he will "give them a share of his own life" (Eichrodt, 1:157). The fourth category is especially associated with redemption, and expresses the idea of atonement or expiation. It is possible that what is sacrificed in the *'āshām* symbolically substitutes for the sinner or guilty. Some would argue that it foreshadows Anselm's notion of satisfaction, or of what is due, especially due to God. Sometimes the word *chaṭṭā'th,* "sin offering," is used. It is made in conjunction with confession and supplication.

The Day of Atonement is in effect a unique extension of the regular sacrificial system. The Day of Atonement arises from a concern that the sacrificial system might not cover every sin, including unconscious ones. Any offense that has been overlooked needs expiation or atonement. The sacrificial theology in the Epistle to the Hebrews becomes poignant at this point. Only in the work of Christ, the author argues, is a full, perfect, and sufficient or complete sacrifice, as the Day of Atonement might suggest. We also find a full integration between the prophetic demand for obedience and the priestly requirement of sacrifice. Hence only Jesus, unlike the Aaronic priests, fulfills all the requirements of a perfect sacrifice.

In Heb. 4:14–10:8 four marks of the perfect priesthood of Christ are identified. (i) As High Priest he shares fully the humanity of humankind, and so can represent humankind to God. (ii) As High Priest, he is duly appointed for the task by God. (iii) Offering sacrifices on behalf of others is not compromised by the need to offer sacrifices for himself or his own sins, for Jesus is sinless. (iv) The sacrifice must be so transparently *complete* that Jesus Christ can "sit down" after his completed work. The Aaronic priests can claim only the first two of these four. On the third point, Jesus is not only "without sin" (Heb. 4:15), "unlike the other high priests, he has no need to offer sacrifices day after day" for his own sins (7:27). On the fourth point, Jesus is High Priest "forever" (7:17), not in a succession of incomplete ministries. Indeed, "God finds fault" with the old system (8:8); Christ "entered once for all into the Holy Place ... with his own blood ... obtaining eternal redemption" (9:12); not "to offer himself again and again, as the high priest ... year after year" (9:25). The author continues: "in these sacrifices there is a reminder of sin year after year" (10:3); and "Every priest stands day after day ... offering again and again the same sacrifices that can never take away sins. But when Christ had offered for all time a single sacrifice for sins, 'he sat down at the right hand of God' " (10:11-12). Older theologians used to speak of "the heavenly session," the title of a book by Tait. (*See also* Expiation; Redeem, Redemption; Scapegoat.)

Reading: G. A. Anderson, *Sacrifices and Offerings in Ancient Israel* (Atlanta: Scholars, 1987); R. E. Averbeck, "Minchah," in *NIDOTTE* 2:978-90; W. Eichrodt, *Theology of the Old Testament*, vol. 1 (London: SCM, 1961), 141-77; F. Young, *Sacrifice and the Death of Christ* (London: SPCK, 1975).

Sanctification

When God or the Holy Spirit is the subject of the verb, "to sanctify" denotes "to make holy" (Gk. *hagiazō;* cognate from *hagios,* "holy," *hagiōsunē,* "holiness"). When it denotes a human condition, the word means either "made holy" or "being made holy." The Hebrew *q-d-sh* may mean to dedicate or separate for God's use, since God is the source of all holiness. The adjective "holy" may mean what is separate from common use in the OT. It is broadly like the English "sacred" in contrast to "secular" or "profane." Objects as well as people may be set apart as holy to God, for example, the gold of the sanctuary (Matt. 23:17); "holy ground" (Exod. 3:5; Acts 7:33); "the holy city" (Matt. 4:5; Rev. 21:2); a holy mountain (Ezek. 20:40); and God's holy name (Ezek. 43:8; Luke 1:49). But in the NT it more often applied to people: a holy person (Mark 6:20); "holy prophets" (Luke 1:70); "Holy Father" (John 17:11); a living and holy sacrifice (Rom. 12:1); the people of God as a holy temple (1 Cor. 3:17); and "holy apostles" (Eph. 3:5).

The problem for many in theology is whether these terms denote a *status conferred in an event* or a disposition of life that *involves process, struggle, and growth.* Most would agree that in the former sense all Christians are holy in that they belong to God. But in practice only those in the Holiness Movement, many Pentecostals, and some in the Renewal Movement would conceive of sanctification conferred as an event. In normal parlance, sanctification denotes a process that involves struggle and growth. Luther insisted that testing or temptation normally or often constitutes a means of encouraging Christian growth in holiness *(Anfechtung)*. There are some, however, who see "sanctification" as complete already in some such event as "a second blessing" or "baptism in the Holy Spirit." Notoriously, Wesley's position is debated and controversial.

In scholarly terms, this debate is bound up with an appreciation of the "now" and "not yet" of eschatology. Those who fail to distinguish between the kingdom of God and the church might well claim that "sinless perfection," as it has been called, has already been given. But the strong assertion "If we say that we have no sin, we deceive ourselves, and the truth is not in us" (1 John 1:8) contradicts such a notion. As Oscar Cullmann has stated, "Christians still sin and still die." Total obedience to God (as King over his kingdom) is only *in process of* arrival (*see* **Kingdom of God**). Nevertheless, 1 John causes understandable difficulty. It also says, "Those who have been born of God do not sin ... cannot sin" (3:9). Stephen Smalley well sums up this verse: "The true child of God is opposed to sin. Whereas the determined sinner (like the heretic in John's church, as opposed to the orthodox Christian) belongs to the devil (v. 8), the spiritually reborn believer, being a member of God's family, cannot *as a settled policy* act lawlessly (cf. v. 4)" (C. S. Smalley, *1, 2, 3 John* [Waco, Tex.: Word, 1984], 171, italics mine).

A "gradual" or progressive view of sanctification is held by the Eastern Orthodox Church, which cites the Eastern Church Fathers. It prefers to use "deification," often citing Anselm's words "God became man that we might become God," not in the sense of assuming a divine status, but in that of participating in a gradual process of becoming more like God. It corresponds to the Western Church's "sanctification," being made holy, or like God. After comparing Anselm's dictum, Vladimir Lossky writes, "Our Saviour opens to us anew the way of deification, which is the *final end* of man. The work of Christ calls out to the work of the Holy Spirit" (*The Mystical Theology of the Eastern Church* [Cambridge: James Clarke, 1957, 1991], 134, italics mine).

In the Western Protestant Church sanctification is clearly distinguishable from justification by grace through faith, which is the gift of Christ. Luther, who stressed justification, nevertheless saw the Christian as *simul iustus et peccator:* at the same time righteous and a sinner. Calvin calls this doctrine "the principal ground on which religion must be supported," and comments, "We simply interpret justification, as the acceptance with which God receives us into his favour as if we were righteous" (Calvin, *Institutes* 3.11.1, 2; Beveridge, 2:37, 38). Tillich calls this "Accepting that we are accepted." The Holy Spirit implements this conferred status to make actual what God has already accounted us as, in his ministry of sanctification. All Christians would acknowledge that "faith by itself, if it has no works, is dead" (James 2:17); genuine faith leads to transformation into the image of God or Christ. In Paul's words, it is "being transformed into the same image from one degree of glory to another; for this comes from the Lord, the Spirit" (2 Cor. 3:18). Succinctly put, justification relates to status; sanctification to state (*see* **Justification**).

Sanctification is an aspect of union with God in Christ, for God is the source of holiness. The roots of this theme can be found in Lev. 11:44: "I am the LORD your God; sanctify yourselves therefore, and be holy, for I am holy." Calvin relates to election: "God elected us that we might be holy" (*Institutes* 3.22.3). James Arminius equally insisted that humankind needed grace "to will and perform what is truly good" (*The Free Will of Man* 1.5.2). In his earliest epistle, Paul enjoins: "This is the will of God, your sanctification" (1 Thess. 4:3). John Chrysostom notes the context of the call to purity, in contrast to living among mire, which might spread (*Homily on 1 Thess.* 5). Quoting this verse, Luther exclaims, "Follow holiness without which no man shall see the Lord" (*Luther: Early Theological Works* [London: SCM; Philadelphia: Westminster, 1962], 235). Jeremy Taylor expounds the practical aspects of sanctification in his *Holy Living* (1650), with much practical advice. This was followed more than a century later by William Law in *A Serious Call to a Devout and Holy Life*. Here he invites us to compare the lives of the earliest Christians and the Bible: we see that "watching and prayer, self-denial and mortification was the common business of their lives" ([London: Dent, 1906], chap. 14, p. 167).

John Wesley was influenced by William Law, and many (but certainly not all) see him as the ultimate father of the Holiness Movement and Pentecostalism. It is understandable that he reacted against much eighteenth-century formalism and rationalism (just as the Reformers did to contemporary Roman Catholicism in the sixteenth century). He therefore laid great emphasis upon sanctification. But whether he saw it as an "event," not a process, and whether he believed in "sinless perfection" are still the subject of passionate debate. Rightly, he perceived sanctification as a gift from God. Wesley and many Roman Catholics would stress the alignment of justification and sanctification, as in Paul's words "you were washed, you were sanctified, you were justified" (1 Cor. 6:11). But whether "sanctified" is used here in the sense of "become part of God's own people," or in the popular, widespread sense of "sanctification," is still debated, and reveals the roots of much of this controversy.

Many regard the medieval mystics and perhaps the Desert Fathers as a distinctive source of a way of sanctification. Bernard of Clairvaux wrote about "the four degrees of love" (*On the Love of God* 8-10), and about humility and pride. These are processes, but they are still "a gift of the Holy Spirit." Hildegard of Bingen was inclined to use "visions" and "pictures," but also, like many later Protestants, she attacked laxity among clergy. Richard of St. Victor acknowledged more explicitly the sovereignty of the Holy Spirit in the process. Bonaventura stressed the journey of the mind into God. Catherine of Siena gave herself to the service of the poor and sick, and wrote of pictures, images, and metaphors, especially of the bridge "from heaven to earth ... moistened with the blood of Christ." Julian of Norwich was an anchoress and Benedictine nun who focused on the cross and passion of Christ. Teresa of Ávila depicted the journey of the soul in her interior castle, working toward "a supreme state of ecstasy." Walter Hilton wrote *The Scale of Perfection,* which had considerable influence. He valued humility but attacked a number of features of mysticism as insufficiently self-critical. These mystics offer a distinctive approach of their own to sanctification. Biblical and Reformation traditions, however, represent the main classical and orthodox approaches to the subject, even if insights are also found in other traditions. (*See also* **Justification; Holy, Holiness; Wesley, John.**)

Reading: D. L. Alexander, *The Pursuit of Godliness* (Lanham, Md.: University Press of America, 1999); Karl Barth, *Church Dogmatics* IV/2 (Edinburgh: T. & T. Clark, 1958), 499-613; John Calvin, *Institutes of the Christian Religion* (London: James Clarke, 1957), 3.6-8; Beveridge, 2:1-24; R. N. Flew, *The Idea of Perfection in Christian Theology* (London: OUP, 1934); W. E. Hulme, *The Dynamics of Sanctification* (Minneapolis: Augsburg, 1966); J. Wesley, *The Works of John Wesley* (Nashville: Abingdon, 1986), vol. 3, *Sermons*.

Sartre, Jean-Paul

Jean-Paul Sartre (1905-1980) attempted to combine atheistic existentialism with Marxism. He was born in Paris, and taught philosophy there and elsewhere. He published a philosophical novel, *La Nausée,* in 1938, and a collection of stories, *Le Mur,* in 1939. W. Kaufman has described "The Wall" as "one of the classics of existentialism," and it is available in English in his *Existentialism from Dostoevsky to Sartre* (New York: World Publishing, 1956), 223-41. It involves the interrogation and fear of prisoners. His major philosophical work is *Being and Nothingness* (1943; Eng. New York: Citadel Press, 1966). He distinguished between human consciousness and all other things. Consciousness is "for itself" *(pour-soi);* everything else is "in itself" *(en-soi)* (*Being and Nothingness,* 49-147). Consciousness has both freedom and relationship of conflict; objects do not. Sartre here explores the existentialist themes of "facticity" and "situatedness." A human being's personal history determines his choice. In theology Bultmann expounds this theme. In the 1950s Sartre became embroiled in radically "left-wing" politics, writing his *Critique of Dialectical Reason* in 1960. The witty but pessimistic tone of Sartre's writings is conveyed by the well-known quotation from *La Nausée:* "Three o'clock is always too late or too early for anything you want to do."

Scapegoat

Aaron's ritual or ceremony on the Day of Atonement in Lev. 16:1-28 involved five animals, of which two were goats. One goat was to be sacrificed; the other (vv. 20-22) was kept alive and presented to the Lord: "Then Aaron shall lay both his hands on the head of the live goat, and confess over it all the iniquities of the people of Israel . . . putting them on the head of the goat, and sending it away into the wilderness by means of someone designated for the task" (v. 21). Symbolically these sins are "lost" in the wilderness, or according to another tradition, "destroyed" by the goat's being driven over a rocky cliff. This act suggests expiation and purification by means of substitution or representation. (*See also* **Azazel; Day of Atonement.**)

Schelling, Friedrich W. J. von

Friedrich W. J. von Schelling (1775-1854) was influenced from the first by Kant, Fichte, and Hegel. He followed Fichte's "radical" Kantianism, rather than Kant, however, and before 1804 most of his contemporaries saw him as close to Hegel. Indeed, he published most of his works before 1804: *On the Ego as a Philosophical Principle* (1795); *On the True Idea of a Nature Philosophy* (1801); *A System of Transcendental Idealism* (1800); and *Philosophy of Art* (1803). Hegel did not appreciate the perceived identification with his work and observed, "Schelling carried on his philosophical education before the public, and signalled each fresh stage with a new treatise" (G. Hegel, *Sämtliche Werke,* 22 vols. [reprint, Stuttgart: Frommann, 1965], 19:647). From 1810 onward he worked on *The Ages of the World,* which paralleled aspects of Hegel's thought.

For Christian theologians, four aspects of his work may have particular significance. First, his early work was on the nature and language of myth. No doubt this had some influence on Strauss, and ultimately Bultmann. Second, his emphasis on preconceptual thinking (in contrast to Hegel's stress on critical concepts) constituted an early discussion of how to overcome the subject-object divide, which has concerned so much theology. Third, Schelling is concerned with how consciousness emerged as consciousness of the self. He begins the discussion of alterity or otherness, which later features in Ricoeur, Jauss, and hermeneutics. He is sometimes viewed as an exponent of subjective idealism, in contrast to the objective ideology of Hegel, although even then with qualifications. Fourth, his view of God raises questions about pantheism, the personality of God, and whether God can be a "presupposition" of the world order.

Reading: A. Bowie, *Schelling and European Philosophy* (London: Routledge, 1993).

Schillebeeckx, Edward

Edward Schillebeeckx (1914-2009) was a Belgian Roman Catholic theologian and member of the Dominican Order. After Rahner, Küng, Balthasar, and Congar, he was very influential in Catholic theology, and was a progressive, antihierarchical voice at Vatican II. He was born at Antwerp, was educated by the Jesuits at Turnhout, and studied theology at the Catholic University of Louvain. Early influences upon him included Hegel, Husserl, and Merleau-Ponty, as well as Aquinas and Dominic De Petter (1905-1971). In 1946 Schillebeeckx went to live in France, and did postgraduate study at the Sorbonne and the College de France, especially in philosophy. In 1947 he became professor of theology at Louvain, mainly to prepare Dominican candidates for the priesthood. He taught creation, Christology, the sacraments, and eschatology. From 1957 to 1966 he was professor of dogmatic theology at Nijmegen in the Netherlands. In 1966 he visited North America, and began to teach hermeneutics, and briefly visited England in 1970. By 1976, Rome had become concerned about his christological views, and 1976-1981 witnessed three investigations of his theology. Yet during the 1980s Philip Kennedy writes, "Schillebeeckx received widespread acclaim"

(*Schillebeeckx* [London: Chapman, 1993], 27). He retired in 1982, and lived into the new century.

Schillebeeckx was one of the most active theologians during Vatican II, but he had already become suspect for his "progressive" views, especially on the papacy and episcopal collegiality. With Congar, Kuhn, and Rahner, he launched *Concilium*. But the most serious source of controversy was his book *Jesus: An Experiment in Christology* (Dutch 1974; Eng. London: Collins, 1979). This was soon followed by *Christ: The Christian Experience in the Modern World* (Dutch 1972; Eng. London: Sheed and Ward, 1974), and *The Church: The Human Story of God* (London: SCM, 1990). Like many others, he explored "the intelligibility for man of Christological belief in Jesus, [and what it] can intelligibly signify for people today" (*Jesus*, 37). He argued, "Every period has its own way of representing Jesus" (64). He looked especially at the "praxis" of Jesus and his parables, that is, his lived action (179, 229, 310). But what troubled authorities in Rome was mainly his view of the resurrection. Schillebeeckx had argued that Christ's being taken up into heaven "in no way" depended on "a possible empty tomb or on appearances" (558). It is said that Schillebeeckx had reflected on J. A. T. Robinson's writings about related issues. Kennedy comments, "The period . . . 1966 to 1974 was a time of considerable intellectual ferment in Schillebeeckx's life" (*Schillebeeckx*, 43). This began with an interest in hermeneutics and sociology. On hermeneutics he studied Gadamer and Ricoeur, as well as Bultmann and the New Hermeneutic. On sociology and critical theory he studied Habermas, while on language he studied Wittgenstein, Ryle, and Strawson. Meanwhile in his 1978 volume *Christ* he argued, "There is no experience without 'theorizing,' without queries, hypothesis and theories" (34). The experience of grace occupied the large part 2 of the volume, including some exegesis of the Hebrew word *chēn* and the Greek word *charis*. Viewed from outside the Catholic tradition, much in these volumes seems a suggestive, but sometimes puzzling, mixture of biblical seriousness and hints of the largely "liberal" climate of the 1960s and 1970s.

Schleiermacher, Friedrich D. E.

Friedrich D. E. Schleiermacher (1768-1834) is often called "the father of modern Protestant theology" and "the founder of modern hermeneutics." His initial education was among the Moravians. He never entirely lost his evangelical or Pietist roots. His sense of vocation as a preacher never left him. He declared that "preaching to the congregation to awaken faith" constituted "the sweetest desire" of his life. When he entered the University of Halle, however, he felt liberated from his conservative background by Enlightenment scholarship and by his introduction to Kant. He was also deeply influenced by Romanticism and the philosophy of Kant. Hence B. A. Gerrish has described him as a liberal evangelical, and K. Barth, often a severe critic, acknowledged, "He did not found a school, but an era" (*Protestant Theology in the Nineteenth Century* [London: SCM, 1972], 425).

The influence of Romanticism and the church can be seen in his very early work *Speeches on Religion* (1799; New York: Harper, 1958). This was aimed at "cultural despisers" of the Christian faith. Claude Welch calls this book "a new mapping of theology's place in... intellectual terrain." Theology must be intelligible to the outsider (hence his concern from 1805 for hermeneutics). "Cultural despisers" included "the educated, artistic, and philosophical habitués of the Berlin salons" (K. Clements). Schleiermacher called his first speech "A Defence" in the tradition of apologetics. He argues, "Millions have been satisfied to juggle with its [religion's] trappings; few have discerned religion itself" (*Speeches*, 1). Religion concerns "the innermost springs of my being" (3). This concerns our dependence on God, and the immediacy of our awareness of this. In his address to the people of Berlin and Germany he criticizes the British preoccupation with trade, wealth, and power, and French "witty frivolity." Germans are more capable of "holy awe," but thoughtlessly "destroy the tenderest blossoms of the human heart."

Schleiermacher develops this in his second speech. He urges the "immediate sense of utter dependence on God *(Gefühl schechthinniger Abhängigkeit)*." He states: "Piety cannot be... a craving for a mess of metaphysical and ethical crumbs" (31). On the contrary, "True religion is a sense and taste for the infinite" (39). It is not just "a moral life" (45). It is not primarily a system of doctrine. "Miserable love of system" misses the transcendent otherness of religion (55). Religion is an expression of "longing for love" (72). All this reflects Romantic influences, and contrasts with Hegel, who would be his colleague at Berlin University. Hegel was not backward in his criticisms of this approach. In his third speech Schleiermacher considers the cultivation of religion, extols the place of art, and attacks abstract rationalism (119-46). The fourth speech turns to the place of community and interaction between people. Finally, the fifth speech examines "higher" existence. God seeks to reconcile all things to himself (241). Other religions may reflect consciousness of God, but this is maximal in Christianity (242). Critics argue that the five speeches veer too far toward pantheism. But Schleiermacher spoke of transcendent otherness, and might have admitted only to panentheism, and more importantly to his notion of an immediate relation to God.

In 1800 Schleiermacher published *Soliloquies*, on his relation to Romanticism. In 1805 he produced his early aphorisms on hermeneutics and his *Christmas Eve: A Dialogue*. Again, it includes a Romanticist theme. After Holy Communion, members of the congregation return home. The women celebrate the birth of Jesus by singing hymns to him; the men discuss the conceptual difficulties of the incarnation. The women, Schleiermacher urges, capture "the mood of our festival" better than the men. This distinction will feature in his 1810 *Hermeneutics*.

In 1810 Schleiermacher became professor of theology at Berlin, where he continued his regular preaching at Trinity Church. That year he also produced his *Hermeneutics* (Missoula, Mont.: Scholars, 1977). Rudolf Otto calls his earlier work "a veritable manifest of the Romantics," and he stresses "divinatory" *(divinatorisch)* understanding in his hermeneutics. He had also shared rooms with F. Schlegel in Berlin. But M. Redeker urges us not to overestimate this Romanticist influence. First, like Kant, he approaches hermeneutics with transcendental questions: How is understanding possible (not simply, how do we understand)? Schleiermacher's first great contribution was to see hermeneutics not as a series of "how to" *rules,* but as the *art of understanding.* The subject is not merely to support an understanding supposedly already reached. "Hermeneutics is part of the art of thinking" (*Hermeneutics,* 97). NT hermeneutics must also address "the rootedness of the New Testament authors in their time and place" (104). Second, we should draw on *both* the "feminine" approach of "divinatory," intuitive, or perceptive understanding, *and* the "masculine" or "comparative" approach of language, history, context, and critical rational reflection. He is not simply or exclusively "Romanticist." He sees both approaches as complementary. He writes, "The divinatory method seeks to gain an immediate comprehension of the author.... The comparative method proceeds by subsuming the author under a general type.... Divinatory knowledge is the feminine strength in knowing people; comparative knowledge, the masculine. Each method refers back to the other" (150). The third major contribution of Schleiermacher is to develop F. Ast's concept of the hermeneutical circle. He explains, "One must already know a man to understand what he says" (56). "The understanding of a given statement is always based on something prior ... a preliminary knowledge" (59). It is like slotting in a piece of jigsaw puzzle. Only when we can identify the context or bigger picture does a specific piece come to make sense. This positive principle has become known as the hermeneutical circle, and is broadly endorsed by Heidegger, Bultmann, and Gadamer (*see* **Hermeneutical Circle; Hermeneutics** for various versions of this principle).

In 1811 Schleiermacher published *A Brief Outline of Theology,* and in 1821-1822 his major work, *The Christian Faith* (2nd ed. 1830-1831; reprint, Edinburgh: T. & T. Clark, 1989). In his introduction he first considers the method of theology as a "science." Predictably he then expounds "piety" as the corporate givenness of religion. As in *The Speeches,* he repeats that this is not simply a "knowing" or a "doing," but an experience of immediacy (5). God, he urges, "is in all that lives" (*see* **Immanence**). Everything depends on relation with God (12). We must seek "the highest grade of human self-consciousness" (18). However, in Christianity this is focused in Jesus of Nazareth (57). Jesus is a model or paradigm of human nature's "taking up the divine into itself" (64). He states, "There is no other way of obtaining participation in the Christian communion than through faith in Jesus as the Redeemer" (68). Although he dislikes abstract doctrine, Schleiermacher concedes that "Christian doctrines are accounts of Christian religious affections set forth in speech" (76).

Part 1 proper begins at section 32. Again Schleiermacher urges: "The immediate feeling of absolute dependence is presupposed ... in every ... Christian self-consciousness" (131). But "godlessness ... has its cause simply in defective or arrested development" (134; *see* **Sin: Historical**). This is "the lowest grade of development" (135). His strength is to urge that creation is not self-sufficient: "A world exists only in absolute dependence upon God" (142). Partly because of the problem of dualism, he comments, "We should abandon the idea of the absolutely supernatural" (183). This has consequences for his Christology.

Part 2 of *The Christian Faith* is longer, and addresses consciousness of sin, consciousness of grace, and Christ. Much work appears promising as *Christian* theology. Schleiermacher asserts: "We have fellowship with God only in a living fellowship with the Redeemer, such that in it His absolutely sinless perfection and blessedness represent a free, spontaneous activity... [and] a free assimilative receptivity" (371). Nevertheless, Schleiermacher asserts, "His influence is only of the same kind as others" (374). Partly under the influence of Kant's idealism, he concludes, "Ideality is the only appropriate expression for the exclusive dignity of Christ" (379). Schleiermacher's Christology has been criticized from both sides. D. F. Strauss calls it "a last attempt to make the Churchly Christ acceptable to the modern mind." On the other side, A. McGrath contends that "the divine state of Christ" is understood "within the realm of natural causality" (*The Making of German Christology* [Oxford: Blackwell, 1986], 23). J. Macquarrie also criticizes the extent of his indebtedness to Kant, which makes Christ's difference from ordinary humans merely one of degree, not of kind. Yet Schleiermacher seeks to avoid both Docetism (381) and an Ebionite approach (396-98).

Perhaps the strongest insight of Schleiermacher's Christology is his insistence on the mutuality of Christ's person and work. He argues that the activity of Jesus Christ and "the exclusive dignity of the Redeemer imply each other, and are inseparably one in the self-consciousness of believers" (374). He urges: "The Redeemer, then, is like all men in virtue of the identity of his human nature, but is distinguished from them by the constant potency of this God-consciousness, which was a veritable existence of God in Him" (385). Macquarrie expresses concern about whether "ideality" *(Urbildlichkeit)* sufficiently avoids Docetism. He considers that this is ultimately a "humanist" Christology. Schleiermacher endorses John's "The Word was made flesh," but not the Church Fathers' Chalcedonian formulations. The concluding sections of *The Christian Faith* concern the Holy Trinity. Some see this as the climax of the work. But it is equally possible, and perhaps more convincing, to see this as a short appendix to the work, added almost as an afterthought.

Schleiermacher's *Christian Faith* has been compared with Calvin's *Institutes* and Barth's *Church Dogmatics* as a landmark in Christian theology, but many will regard this as an exaggeration. Certainly it introduces a new theology for the nineteenth century. Kant, Romanticism, and evolutionary theory are seldom out of view. One key problem is that "the self-consciousness of the Christian believer" prepares the way for "subjectivity" in R. Bultmann. But any disappointment with *The Christian Faith* cannot obscure the brilliant insights, ahead of his time, of his *Hermeneutics*. This work alone would mark him out as a creative and original thinker. Parts of his *Speeches* also still serve apologetics.

Reading: J. Marina, ed., *The Cambridge Companion to Friedrich Schleiermacher*

(Cambridge: CUP, 2005); F. D. E. Schleiermacher, *On Religion: Speeches to Its Cultured Despisers* (New York: Harper, 1958; London: Kegan Paul, 1893); F. D. E. Schleiermacher, *Hermeneutics: The Handwritten Manuscripts* (Missoula, Mont.: Scholars, 1977); F. D. E. Schleiermacher, *The Christian Faith* (Edinburgh: T. & T. Clark, 1989); T. N. Tice, *Schleiermacher* (Nashville: Abingdon, 2006).

Scholasticism

Scholasticism flourished from the eleventh century until the sixteenth century. Abelard and Peter Lombard compiled anthologies of opposing or contradictory texts from the Church Fathers, which they called "Sentences." These formed a framework of questions, and presented puzzles to students, to make them think through the problem presented. Scholasticism presupposed that questioning is the way to truth. To resolve conflicting claims, logic became the primary tool. By the late twelfth century the texts of Aristotle often provided a point of departure, questioning, and debate. With the founding of the universities in the thirteenth century, this method became widely used. Thomas Aquinas became a model of establishing a series of questions, to which he provided objections and conclusions. Often biblical passages, or extracts from Aristotle and Augustine, were quoted in these exercises. After Thomas, Duns Scotus developed the scholastic technique further. Often in practice this method was used to defend orthodoxy in the schools.

Science and Religion

This subject is vast, producing a massive amount of literature, and touching on many issues that are considered under separate entries (*see* Atheism; Cause, Causality; Cosmological Argument; Creation; Darwin, Charles R.; Empiricism; Evolution; Hume, David; Incommensurability; Materialism; Miracles; Skepticism; Teleological Argument). One possible starting point is to compare Ian G. Barbour's contrast of four possible relationships between science and religion: conflict, independence, dialogue, and integration (*Religion and Science* [London: SCM; New York: Harper, 1998], 77-105).

The era of *conflict* was partly due to mythologies from the past, but it is also partly alive today. The past still reverberates with echoes of the notorious debate following the era of Galileo and Copernicus that moved thinking from a geocentric universe to a sun-centered solar system, and the instant reaction to Darwin's formulation of evolutionary theory. Since those times we have seen the emergence of scientific materialism, especially in the French Enlightenment, and the empiricism and skepticism of David Hume. In the twentieth century there emerged the view that only science was objective, and this was developed and discussed as if it were a theory of language in logical positivism. These movements cast the present debate in a particular form: Is scientific *method* as a way of approaching scientific data the same as a scientific *worldview*? Is science a *method of inquiring* about appropriate data, or a metaphysical belief about *reality*?

It is easy for the first to slide into the second, and it frequently does. Some would argue that this is even legitimate and necessary. While many theists insist on there being different *levels* of reality, many scientists believe that "higher" levels, which involve art, religion, or consciousness, can be collapsed into one minimal, quasi-physical level. Barbour (*Religion,* 77) cites Francis Crick, the co-discoverer of DNA in genetics, and his belief that *all* biology can be reduced to physics and chemistry (*Of Molecules and Men* [Seattle: University of Washington Press, 1966], 10). Similarly Jacques Menod reduces everything to mechanical interactions, claiming, "The animal is a machine. Man is a machine" (in his *Chance and Necessity*). The philosopher Daniel Dennett claims that evolution is a mindless, purposeless process. He is aware of the charge of reductionism, but claims that consciousness is an illusion.

Today a group associated with Richard Dawkins promotes a similar view (*see* **Atheism**). Barbour comments, "These authors have failed to distinguish between *scientific* and *philosophical* questions" (*Religion,* 81). Barbour does not lay the blame for conflict with theism wholly on such "scientists," however. He also attacks those theists who use the Bible to address questions of science. Admittedly he rightly argues that Luther, Calvin, and the medieval church cannot be accused of consistently treating the Bible as a textbook of science. But he suggests circles that we discuss under the entry on fundamentalism too often make this mistake.

The second suggested relation is *independence,* as if science and religion represented wholly autonomous domains. What is done or claimed in one area, it is suggested, is irrelevant to the other. This category may seem to suggest a straw man. Barbour's appeal to existentialists might not necessarily include Bultmann's appeal to neo-Kantian models, and his exaggerated concern about the perils of "modern science" for "modern believing." However, the one plausible part of this section relates to those few thinkers who misinterpret Wittgenstein as if to say that a pluralism of "language games" concerns many hermetically sealed or isolated "forms of life." We find such an approach in the later period of Paul van Buren and perhaps William Hordern. Richard Rorty tends to move in this direction, but he does recognize that language games are more like an "archipelago" than separate, self-contained islands. Wittgenstein spoke of "human life," or "being human," in a way that implied that language games normally overlap, except in eccentric or hypothetical situations.

Barbour's third category is *dialogue.* He cites both T. F. Torrance and Wolfhart Pannenberg as making coherent and testably "public" claims for theology, while seeing theology, at least in Pannenberg's case, as concerned with a "larger," more comprehensive sphere than the natural sciences. He uses "universal rational criteria," but because theological reality transcends the world, he recognizes that "the parallels eventually break down" (91). Pannenberg's method is subtle and complex, not least in his *Theology and the Philosophy of Science* (Philadelphia: Westminster; London: DLT, 1976) (*see* **Pannenberg, Wolfhart**). Barbour also appeals to the work of the Catholic theologians Karl Rahner and David Tracy and alludes to Michael Polanyi (91-94).

Barbour's fourth category is *integration*. Clearly Thomas Aquinas is a good example of this, even if he also made room for faith. His positive view of the teleological argument sees purpose in the world, just as William Paley does, and F. R. Tennant after him. Reformulations of the argument have occurred since Tennant. Richard Swinburne, John Polkinghorne, and several others have formulated and reformulated "the anthropic principle," which believes that life on earth could have emerged only with the exact duration of time and expanding size of the universe, which prevailed in research in astrophysics. Barbour even suggestively cites Stephen Hawking: "If the rate of expansion one second after the big bang had been smaller by even one part in a hundred thousand million, the universe would have recollapsed before it even reached its present size" (Hawking, *A Brief History of Time* [New York: Bantam Books, 1988], 291; Barbour, 99). John Polkinghorne makes an almost identical point in *The Way the World Is* ([London: SPCK, 1984, 1992], 7-16). Barbour considers Arthur Peacocke and Teilhard de Chardin under "Theologies of Nature." They stress the role of human stewardship, hold a sacramental view of nature, and see the Holy Spirit as animating nature. Barbour expresses his own agreement with this approach (101-5).

The integration view, coupled with the dialogue view, seems to be the most promising. This is so, especially since highly respected scientists who are also respected theologians adopt these approaches. Ian Barbour was a professor of physics and received a Templeton book award; John Polkinghorne was professor of mathematical physics at Cambridge and is an ordained Anglican who is president of Queens' College, Cambridge; Arthur Peacocke is a physical biochemist, and dean of Clare College, Cambridge. Others who follow this path are Malcolm Jeeves, former president of the Royal Society, and emeritus professor of psychology and neuroscience at St. Andrews University; R. J. Berry, professor of genetics at London University, who also received the Templeton Individual Award; A. E. McGrath, formerly professor of theology at King's College, London, and currently Andreas Idreas Professor of Science and Religion at the University of Oxford. He holds a doctorate in quantum theory and molecular biology. To the best of my knowledge, all follow this fourth pathway, as well as the third, and all have multiple books on the present subject.

The one modifying or additional comment that requires emphasis is to stress the complementary roles of science and religion in this "integration" approach. Polkinghorne is among the many who rightly stress that physicists properly ask, "*How* was the universe created?," and call this a big question. Theologians, however, also ask, "*Why* was the universe created?" This, in any showing, is an even "bigger" question (Polkinghorne, *Quarks, Chaos, and Christianity* [London: SPCK/Triangle, 1994], and Ian Barbour, *Issues in Science and Religion* [London: SCM, 1966], 23-26). Truth in science and religion is complementary, not competitive or contradictory. They do not address different self-contained segments of reality. This complementary view is no newcomer to theism. For example, although Sir Isaac Newton (1642-1727) was not fully orthodox in terms of Christian faith, he was nearer to theism than to Deism, and had no difficulty in holding together his scientific discoveries with a devout theism. God, he believed, sustained the rational order of the universe, which Newton explored.

The old-fashioned notion that scientists work only with "objective," value-neutral questions has long been challenged. Again, to quote Polkinghorne, it is not just *what* scientists see, "but *the way that they see it* that counts" (*Quarks,* 5). Karl Heim makes similar points. Alister McGrath painstakingly sifts through a number of different fields within "science," and concludes: "It will be clear from the analysis thus far that there is no generalised scientific methodology which can be applied without variance and uncritically to all sciences" (*A Scientific Theology,* vol. 2, *Reality* [London and New York: T. & T. Clark/Continuum, 2002], 283). He then evaluates the significance of quantum theory and Heisenberg's "uncertainty principle." He refers to Brian Appleyard. Appleyard cites this principle as "evidence that science *has abandoned the quest for objective knowledge*" (*Understanding the Present* [New York: Doubleday, 1994], 157-59, italics mine).

Once this is fully recognized, we may move on to "levels" of explanation and interpretation. One cannot "interpret" the form and structure of a musical symphony, for example, by reducing it to the production of wavelengths or visual patterns seen on an oscilloscope. A purely empirical approach would reduce the music of Beethoven or Mozart to acoustic vibrations of varying wavelengths and wave shapes. But could this be a comprehensive account of the world? Is painting to be reduced to varying patterns of light waves within the color spectrum? Polkinghorne sets out these "levels of explanation" with reference to Bach's *Mass in B Minor,* the figures of Michelangelo, moral obligation, and other examples (*The Way the World Is,* 17-19). Polkinghorne also considers the explanation of human beings as machines, or systems of "elementary particles" (21). How is the brain of neurophysiology related to the stream of conscious thought? Polkinghorne writes: "Most reductionist of all is physics. Above that are levels of chemistry, biochemistry, biology, psychology, sociology and so on. At each level, new concepts appear which are not reducible to elements found at lower levels, and that gives to each mode of description its own validity and autonomy. The whole is more than the sum of its parts" (22). The principle stands, even if some of the divisions may be permeable. In biology, for example, it used to be thought that lawlike behavior at the macrolevel rested on statistical analysis at a microlevel. But nowadays more attention is given to "dynamic newness," not just to the interplay between chance and causal uniformity (Peacocke, *Creation and the World of Science* [Oxford: OUP, 1979], 62). Polkinghorne concludes, "The clockwork universe is dead."

Responses to criticisms of the teleological argument for the existence of God are discussed under the entry for the teleological argument, including the reformulations by Tennant, Swinburne, and others. These writers insist on "the orderedness of the universe." Polkinghorne, Barbour, and many others insist that our universe as it is, required *time* for its creation. Again, Polkinghorne urges that the sustaining of carbon-based life by brute possibility would be "one in a trillion" (*Quarks*, 27). In the end, much depends on an evaluation of selfhood. If an identical twin shares exactly the same genetic makeup as the other twin, is there no difference in character or personality? What about an animal clone and its donor? Even genetic developments may on occasion be cocreated with God. Pannenberg appears to hint at such a possibility.

Within the space here, we cannot provide a systematic or comprehensive account of relations between science and religion. We have aimed to provide a sample of the kinds of questions that those major writers who are both scientists and theologians have formulated. In addition to the cross-references listed at the beginning of this entry, *see* **Image of God; Logical Positivism**.

Reading: Ian G. Barbour, *Religion and Science* (London: SCM; New York: Harper, 1998); Malcolm A. Jeeves and R. J. Berry, *Science, Life, and Christian Belief* (Leicester: Apollos, 1998); A. E. McGrath, *The Foundations of Dialogue in Science and Religion* (Oxford: Blackwell, 1998); A. E. McGrath, *A Scientific Theology*, vol. 2, *Reality* (London and New York: T. & T. Clark/Continuum, 2002); A. R. Peacocke, *Creation and the World of Science* (Oxford: Clarendon, 1979); John Polkinghorne, *The Way the World Is* (London: SPCK, 1992); John Polkinghorne, *Scientists as Theologians: A Comparison of Ian Barbour, Arthur Peacocke, and John Polkinghorne* (London: SPCK, 1996).

Scofield Reference Bible

The Scofield Reference Bible (1909) is an annotated version of the KJV/AV edited by Cyrus Scofield, and dependent on J. N. Darby's view of the "rapture" and two returns of Christ, allegedly in 1 Thess. 4:13-17. Darby originated "dispensationalism." In the nineteenth century William Miller, the Mormons, and many in America were said to be, in E. Sandeen's words, "drunk on the millennium" (*Roots of Fundamentalism* [Chicago: University of Chicago Press, 1970], 42). The so-called rapture would take place allegedly at the first coming of Christ, where 1 Thess. 4:17 reads "caught up" or "snatched." Few, if any, mainline NT scholars accept this reading of 1 Thess. 4:13-17. (*See also* **Darby, John Nelson.**)

Scotus of Erigena

Scotus of Erigena (c. 810-c. 877), otherwise known as John the Scot, was an Irish philosophical scholar under the patronage of Charles the Bald. He sought to reconcile the Neoplatonist notion of divine emanations with the Christian teaching about creation.

Scriptural Reasoning

"Scriptural reasoning" was coined as a technical term in 1995 by D. F. Ford, D. Hardy of Cambridge, and P. Ochs of the University of Virginia. In Ford's words, respect and hospitality are maintained between Jewish, Christian, and Muslim believers, who gather to study passages of Scripture together. Scripture is studied corporately by adherents of the three Abrahamic faiths. Normally participants read the text aloud, meet together in small groups, and share their thoughts about the passage selected. They usually begin with the plain meaning of the text in its historical and linguistic context; second, they may consider the canonical meaning (*see* **Canon; Childs, Brevard**); and third, they discuss its theological meaning through the lens of each faith community. Members of this group work in a nonjudgmental way. Some others may suggest that many churches and other groups have already practiced such activity regularly, and sometimes it has encouraged unduly subjective readings. But Ochs and Ford are aware of such dangers and seek mutual understanding. The most distinctive feature of scriptural reasoning is the nonjudgmental approach of Jewish-Christian-Muslim dialogue. The term is also distinguished from "textual reasoning," used by Ochs of Jewish groups studying the Talmud together (*see* **Ochs, Peter**). On other aspects, see John Webster, *The Domain of the Word* (New York and London: T. & T. Clark, 2012).

Self-Involvement

The importance of this term for Christian theological language can scarcely be overestimated. Yet theological writers have used the actual term for little over fifty years. The breakthrough came with D. D. Evans, *The Logic of Self-Involvement* (London: SCM, 1963). He defines it as, in effect, showing "the logical connections between a man's utterances and his practical commitments, attitudes, and feelings" (11). Admittedly, earlier writers were aware of, and used, this *concept*, but seldom the actual *word*. Many preferred the term "existential," which brought its own pitfalls and differences, as well as positive insights. The reason why 1963 constitutes the earliest date of the term's serious application to religious language is that it was only first used orally in 1955; in published work in 1962 by J. L. Austin, *How to Do Things with Words* (Oxford: Clarendon). This was the most striking and memorable example of self-involving utterances in early speech act theory. Admittedly in NT studies it had long been recognized that, in the words of J. Weiss, "What it means (to call Christ 'Lord') in a practical religious sense will best be made clear through the correlative concept of 'servant' or 'slave' of Christ" (Rom. 1:1; 1 Cor. 7:22-23; Gal. 1:10; Phil. 1:1; Col. 4:12) (*Earliest Christianity* [New York: Harper, 1959], 2:458 [originally 1937]). R. Bultmann similarly argues that to confess Christ as Lord means to *belong* to him; hence the Christian "lets this care [for his own life] go, yielding himself entirely to the grace of God; he recognizes himself to be the property of God or of the Lord" (*Theology of the New Testament*, vol. 1 [London: SCM, 1952], 331). The point here is that to call Christ "Lord" involves having "practical commitments, attitudes, feelings" on the part of the self.

The problem with Bultmann's use of "existential" is that although the self-involving dimension comes to the fore, it tends to be regarded as an *alternative* to *God's* appointing Christ "Lord" at the resurrection at the level of ontology (Rom. 1:4). As I have pointed out in numerous publications, quoting Austin, a self-involving utterance becomes operative only when certain *facts* or situations are *true*. Evans applies self-involving logic especially to the language of creation. When God created humankind, this gave to humans a role to perform, an attitude of thanksgiving, and so on. Genesis 1 and 2 is not simply a history of the beginning of the world; it depicts "God's action in an appointing of creatures to a status and role; and an impressive-expressive revelation of His glory" (*Logic of Self-Involvement* [London: SCM, 1963], 13). To express this adequately, he asserts, modern theology needs a new logic (13-14). To be God's creature involves taking responsibility as a steward of the earth, who exercises dominion over the animals without exploiting them. As beings made in God's image, humankind is to represent God's being and character to the world (*see* **Image of God**). Appropriate human behavior comes under Austin's word "behabitives," which includes thanking, glorifying, and worshiping. Accepting commitments may come under his term (also used by Austin and J. R. Searle) "commissives," as when one promises, undertakes, and so on (30). Exercising authority comes under Austin's term "exercitives" (33). The key point remains that the relationship between the utterances and attitudes or behavior is *not a brute, physical* cause, but an *"institutional"* one (33). Evans states, "Most human language concerning God is Behabitive or Commissive; but this does not automatically eliminate the relevance of facts — factual presuppositions."

Evans suggests many further parallels in everyday life, for example, those of king, legal guardian, husband, creditor, all of which carry with them appropriate attitudes and roles (66-78). At this point, however, the practical thrust of self-involvement has become clear. After Evans, Searle, F. Recanati, and others explored speech act theory in more detail (*see* **Speech Act Theory**). A. C. Thiselton, N. Wolterstorff, R. S. Briggs, and others apply it to hermeneutics, exegesis, and Christian theology.

Reading: J. L. Austin, *How to Do Things with Words* (Oxford: Clarendon, 1962); R. S. Briggs, *Words in Action* (Edinburgh: T. & T. Clark, 2001); D. D. Evans, *The Logic of Self-Involvement* (London: SCM, 1963); A. C. Thiselton. *Thiselton on Hermeneutics* (Grand Rapids: Eerdmans; Aldershot: Ashgate, 2006), 53-150.

Silence

Silence lets go of all thoughts of self-evaluation and evaluations of life by placing the worshiper in the hands of God, to think only about God. It represents an acceptance of what God has given and done, especially in reconciliation and atonement. It points to the recognition that God is all. Silence also releases the worshiper from any need to say the right thing. It makes room for God, and responds to God's presence when words might be too clumsy. Above all, it constitutes *waiting upon God*. Paul declares, "[The] Spirit intercedes for us with sighs too deep for words" (Rom. 8:26). Silence is not simply negative. In music, in preaching, or in rhetoric, the pregnant pause may contribute more than another note or another word. It is a response to God's overwhelming transcendence. In Habakkuk's words,

> The LORD is in his holy temple;
>   let all the earth keep silence before him! (Hab. 2:20)

When the Lamb opened the seals and released God's mysterious and surprising work, "There was silence in heaven" (Rev. 8:1). In the exchange of love, God is closer than a heartbeat. In reverent attentiveness, as Fuchs declares, "Love does not just blurt out."

The historical witness to the role of silence is impressive. Gregory of Rome writes, "To speak to God is . . . of great value. But there is one that is more, to purify oneself before God in silence." Thomas Merton writes, "The secret of prayer is hunger for God and for vision of God, a hunger that lies far deeper than the level of language or affection" (*Seeds of Contemplation* [New York: New Directions, 1949], 140, 143). Dietrich Bonhoeffer writes, "Being silent before God means making room for God so that He may speak the first and last word about us. . . . It means not wanting to justify ourselves" (*Meditating in the Word* [Cambridge, Mass.: Cowley, 1986], 59). He continues, "We are so afraid of silence that we chase ourselves from one event to the next in order not to have to spend a moment alone with ourselves" (60). He explains, "That is why even our silence before God takes practice and work" (61). "The silence of the soul," he says, is "the soul that waits for God" (58).

John Dalrymple attacks verbosity in liturgy. He laments that innovative young men and garrulous old men put themselves, rather than God, at the center of the stage, by a ceaseless commentary on liturgical acts such as "we sit to hear the Word of God"; "we stand for the Gospel"; "now comes the offertory; the offertory is . . ." They may imagine that this is helpful to visitors, but it may also be intrusive, and perhaps approval seeking. K. Rahner indicates that there is no room and no need for self-defensiveness, self-assertion, or illusion. The whole worshiping community wishes to wait on God without distraction. One of the most damning criticisms of much in Christian faith and worship is summed up in Edward Muir's well-known quip: "the word made flesh here has been made word again." (On the history see D. MacCulloch, *Silence: A Christian History* [London: Allen Tate, 2013].)

Sin

Biblical

Although the biblical foundations and historical interpretations of human sin quickly become intermingled, it seemed clearer and more effective to treat these two areas as separate, shorter articles. We cannot, however, refrain from mentioning some historical examples in this biblical section. "Sin" is one of the few theological terms that people hesitate to use in everyday speech. Indeed, it is clearly reductive to substitute the word "wrongdoing," widely used in the media, for it presupposes that sin is an act which is "done," in contrast to the biblical notion of an *attitude* or *state of being*. It would be more accurate to speak of *misdirected desire, alienation*, or *self-imposed bondage*, or all three. The shallowest of all is *failure*, which includes only sins of omission. It is crucial that for the biblical writers the term has little to do with mere ethics or moralism, but denotes *a turning away from God to self.* Even the terms "narcissism" and "egocentricity" convey more of the biblical idea.

Biblical vocabulary, especially in Hebrew, conveys three distinct ideas. (i) The verb *chāṭā'* (noun *chaṭṭā'th*) conveys the notion of straying from the commands of the Lord (Leviticus 4–5). If this term stood alone, the notion of sin as disobedience or failure might be said to stand, but it is part of a trio of terms. The *Book of Common Prayer* picks up the term in the General Confession: "we have erred and strayed from Thy ways." In Num. 5:22-31 it is distinguished from a defiant sin, suggesting carelessness or unintentional sin, in contrast to "sin with a raised hand." But often it is associated with defilement. The term is also used in Gen. 4:7, 18:20, Exod. 10:17, 32:32, Lev. 4:23, 5:6, Num. 5:6, 12:11, Deut. 9:18, 19:15, 1 Sam. 2:17, 15:23, 1 Kings 8:34, 14:16, Neh. 1:6, Ps. 38:3, Isa. 6:7, and so on. Sometimes the term may denote sin offering. In the NT, Hebrews connects this tradition with the issues of purification (Heb. 9:14).

(ii) The second term in Hebrew is *pāsha'*, meaning "rebellion," "offense," "revolt," or "become alienated." It essentially denotes a deliberate breach of relationship. When the ordinary secular person disclaims wrongdoing, this merits the response: "What of your relationship with God?" The verb occurs forty-one times in the OT, and the noun ninety-three times. This term relates, among other things, to the covenant. The KJV/AV often translates this as "transgression," for example, in Exod. 23:21; 34:7; Lev. 16:16, 21; Num. 14:18; 1 Kings 8:50; Job 7:21; Pss. 5:10; 19:13; 39:8; 51:3; Isa. 53:5, 8; and so on. In Ps. 19:13 Coverdale translates it "offence." It is used not only in relation to God, but also of breaches in political alliances, social relations, and interpersonal friendships. It can denote covenant *treachery* (Ezek. 14:11) or *betrayal* of loyalty or the breaking of a commitment. Amos and Ezekiel use the term of disrupting the covenant relation to God. Nationally Israel can become "a rebellious nation" (Ezek. 2:3 NIV) or "a brood of rebels" (Isa. 57:4 NIV). The LXX translators often use *asebeō* for the verbal term, although it also uses other terms.

(iii) The *resultant condition* that follows *pāsha'* is often conveyed by *'āwen*, "iniquity," "wicked person," or sometimes "deception" or "distortion"; or *'wh* ("pervert" or "perversion"). The noun occurs about seventy-four times in the OT, but the verbal form is absent. It often occurs in poetry, especially in the Psalms (twenty-nine times). *'Āwen* has unsettling effects that bring harm, destruction, distortion, deception, or calamity. It may sometimes be associated with *chāmās,* "violence" (Isa. 59:6; Hab. 1:3), or *rā'â,* "wickedness" (Pss. 64:2; 94:16; Prov. 17:4; Isa. 31:2). This word certainly does not denote what is unintentional or accidental. God will banish those who commit *'āwen* from his presence (Ps. 125:5). The OT speaks of the evil of idolatry (*'āwen ūtᵉrāpīm,* 1 Sam. 15:23). Idols speak only wickedness (*'āwen,* Zech. 10:2). It is the most terrifying and deep-seated of the three groups of terms.

In the NT numerous words denote sin, not least because of its many aspects or dimensions. Paul, for example, speaks of *anomia*, "lawlessness"; *akatharsia*, "impurity"; *asebeia*, "impiety" or "transgression"; *adikia*, "injustice"; *planē*, "error"; *paraptōma*, "disobedience"; *parabasis*, "transgression"; *hamartēma* and *hamartia*, "sin." Paul, however, is more concerned with the corporate and individual *condition* of sin in its multiple aspects, than with particular individual *acts* of sin. This partly reflects his legacy from apocalyptic, denoting the misery and bondage of humankind apart from grace and new creation. The universality of sin (Rom. 3:23) underlines human corporate solidarity under sin, sometimes referred to as "this body of death" (Rom. 7:24).

D. E. H. Whiteley has suggested that Paul sets out three versions of "the Fall": Rom 1:18-32, Rom. 5:12-21, and Rom. 7:11-25. Admittedly Rom. 1:18-32 is probably borrowed from the typical form used in Jewish homily on the drastic consequences of idolatry and immorality. Wis. 14:8-31 is one of several parallels. But the main thrust will be that Jews and Gentiles alike are characterized by fallenness. Rom. 5:12-21 demonstrates human corporate liability. W. D. Davies comments that these verses do "not aim at explaining the existence of sin" but assert "a connexion between the first man Adam's transgression and the sinfulness of the world" (*Paul and Rabbinic Judaism* [London: SPCK, 1955], 31). Humankind, in effect, daily endorses Adam's attitude of sin, and shares in his liability. This is not Adam's "fault," for everyone sins on his or her own account. Unlike the Apocalypse of Ezra (Esdras), he does not "blame" Adam, but like 2 *Baruch*, he sees everyone as the Adam of oneself. In Rom. 7:11-25 Paul expounds the seriousness of the human plight as rendering the Law powerless as a remedy. The references to "sin deceived me" (7:11) and "I do not do what I want" are *not* biographical or autobiographical accounts, but Paul's reflection on the plight of the Jews and the whole of humanity.

Indeed, in a highly influential article Krister Stendahl has shown that there is much widespread misunderstanding about Paul's personal sense of sin or guilt (cited below). He readily admits: "No one could ever deny that *hamartia*, sin, is a crucial word in Paul's terminology, especially in . . . Romans. Romans 1–3 sets out to show that *all* — both Jews and Gentiles — have sinned." But he adds, "It is much harder to gauge how Paul experienced the power of sin in his life." When we consider his genuinely autobiographical statements, he asserts: "I know nothing against myself" (1 Cor. 4:4 ASV), that is, he has nothing on his conscience about his ministry; and "as to righteousness under the law, blameless" (Phil. 3:6). Indeed, Stendahl claims that Paul has a "robust" conscience.

One difficult passage in Paul (Rom. 8:19-23) seems to suggest a "fall" of the whole creation. It was "subjected to futility" (8:20, 21). This may perhaps refer to the "cursing" of the ground in Gen. 3:17-18; Jürgen Moltmann writes of the renewal, restoration, and transformation of the world at the last time. G. B. Caird speaks of "the solidarity of man with the rest of creation." The "Fall," however, is not related to the rabbinic *yester-hārā'*, or inclination to evil, for the rabbis believed that the *yester*, for good or ill, was a driving force in humankind before sin entered the world.

To return to the three "Pauline versions" of the "Fall," it is well known that C. H. Dodd described Rom. 1:18-32 as a process of cause and effect in a moral universe, although many have rejected this as an unduly "impersonal" interpretation in relation to Paul's phrase "the wrath of God." It is probably more accurate to speak of sin as bringing *"internal"* consequences, or as bringing its own penalty. Similarly Rom. 5:12-21 provides an account of the corporate, transindividual consequences of sin, in the context of explaining how grace through the cross of Christ can likewise be extended to humankind in a parallel but greater way. The generosity of solidarity with Christ far outweighs any issue of "unfairness" by virtue of our solidarity with Adam. It also indicates the possibility of *structural* evil, rather than simply corporate or individual guilt. On Rom. 7:11-25, a multitude of writers agree that this is not a personal autobiography. So-called original sin is better expressed as humankind's being "under the power of sin" (Rom. 3:9) than any genetic theory. Rom. 7:14 speaks of our being "sold under sin," and Rom. 6:6 and 6:20 as our being "slaves of sin." When the Reformers spoke of "total depravity," they were expressing Paul's theme that "nothing good dwells within me" (Rom. 7:18), that is, the bondage of sin taints every aspect of human life, even if we seek to do "good."

Oscar Cullmann argued that although Christ has in principle destroyed sin, sin still mars the life of the Christian. In the years immediately after World War II he borrowed military terminology then familiar to everyone. D-Day denoted the decisive Normandy landing of the Allies: it constituted a decisive victory; while V-Day denoted total and final victory at the end of the war. Cullmann writes: "The hope of the final victory is so much the more vivid because of the unshakably firm conviction that the battle that decided the victory has already taken place" (*Christ and Time* [London: SCM, 1951], 87). But meanwhile, Christians still sin, just as they still die: "the time tension is manifest in the Church through the continuances of sin, which nevertheless has already been defeated by the Spirit" (155).

The Gospels and Johannine writings confirm this. The prologue of John affirms that light shines in the darkness, and "the darkness did not overcome it" (John 1:5). The light illumines everyone, or sheds light upon them *(phōtizō)* in judgment, as well as grace (1:9). Before the discovery of Qumran in 1948, Bultmann and others claimed that the dualisms of light and darkness, truth and falsehood, Spirit and flesh, and so on reflected Greek or Gnostic sources of a relatively late date. But with the discovery of the same dualisms in the Dead Sea Scrolls, this view is no longer tenable.

In John, humankind stood in need of new birth (or birth from above; John 3:3-6); stood in need of salvation (3:16); needed living water, which was ever-fresh and ongoing (4:14); needed to be transformed from death to life (5:24); and needed the living bread (6:35). Sin is a quality of life that leads to death, slavery, and blindness (8:24, 34; 9:25). Above all, sin in John is distinctively lack of trust or faith in the person of Christ (16:9; cf. 15:21-22). The First Epistle of John asserts, "If we say that we have no sin, we deceive ourselves, and the truth is not in us" (1 John 1:8). 1 John 3:4 also declares, "Everyone who commits sin is guilty of lawlessness; sin is lawlessness." Christians still sin, but they do not habitually sin as an expression of their new life.

In the Synoptic Gospels John the Baptist baptizes for the forgiveness of sins (Mark 1:4-5). Jesus' proclamation of the kingdom of God involves repentance or "turning" (Mark 1:15). Parables often depict the rescue of sinners through everyday imagery (Luke 15:7, 10). In Acts, early Christian preaching calls for repentance (Acts 2:38; 3:19). It also proclaims the need for "universal restoration" (3:21). The "Lord's Prayer," enjoined by Jesus, includes "forgive us our debts" (Matt. 6:12), "forgive us our sins" (Luke 11:4), and "may your kingdom come." In the Epistle to the Hebrews, Jesus is the High Priest who "made purification for sins" (Heb. 1:3), makes "atonement for sins" (2:17), and "offers gifts and sacrifices for sins" (5:1; cf. 7:27).

In the light of these themes from the OT, from Paul, from John, and from other parts of the NT, it is astonishing that some approaches to the subject in historical thought have been frankly moralistic, or have reduced sin to conscious acts of commission or omission rather than to conditions of the heart that relate to God.

Reading: G. J. Botterweck and H. Ringgren, eds., *TDOT* 1:140-46; 4:309-19; J. D. G. Dunn, *The Theology of Paul the Apostle* (Edinburgh: T. & T. Clark; Grand Rapids: Eerdmans, 1998), 79-127; C. Ryder Smith, *The Bible Doctrine of Sin* (London: Epworth, 1953); K. Stendahl, "Paul and the Introspective Conscience of the West," *HTR* 56 (1963): 199-215; reprinted in *Paul among Jews and Gentiles* (Philadelphia: Fortress, 1976), 78-96; A. C. Thiselton, *The Hermeneutics of Doctrine* (Grand Rapids: Eerdmans, 2007), 257-73 and 283-88; W. A. Vangemeren, ed., *New International Dictionary of Old Testament Theology and Exegesis* (Carlisle: Paternoster, 1997), 1:309-15; 2:87-93; and 3:706-10.

Historical

(i) Irenaeus (c. 130–c. 200) has roots in both Asia Minor and the West. He viewed human sin as a challenge to growth and maturity. On Adam, he writes: "Humankind was little, being but a child. It had to grow and reach full maturity.... Its mind was not yet fully mature, and thus humanity was easily led astray by the deceiver" (*Demonstration of the Apostolic Teaching* 12). This view may invite the critical question of whether the "image of God" could represent God to the world (as Athanasius would point out), although Irenaeus distinguished *image* from *likeness*. Likeness, he argued, was *yet* to be acquired (*Against Heresies* 5.6.1). Both image and likeness were lost at the "Fall" (3.18.1). In effect, what distinguishes humankind is free will. The Fall, in effect, achieves an *educational* purpose, and is not an unmixed evil. John Hick will apply this "educational" approach that he calls an "Irenaean theodicy" in his *Evil and the God of Love* (1966 and 1977). Irenaeus, he claims, sees pain as assuming a positive role in leading humankind from naïve innocence to maturity. Hick also identifies this approach with Schleiermacher. Harnack calls this a "teleological" account of the Fall. In his theology of redemption from sin, Irenaeus perceives Christ as recapitulating all the stages of human life from innocence to perfection. The Latin *recapitulatio* (Gk. *anakephaiōsis*) was derived from Paul's use of the term in Eph. 1:10, which the NRSV translates as "to gather up all things in him" (*Against Heresies* 1.10.11; 3.16.6; 5.20.2). (*See* **Recapitulation.**)

(ii) Clement of Alexandria (c. 150–c. 215) saw sin primarily as ignorance and irrationality, much as Socrates did. "Adam" was not created perfect, but was seduced by lust. Ignorance and weakness gave rise to sin, because they could allow humankind to see the sinful as good (*Stromata* 2.14). Clement declared, "The sources of all sin are but two, ignorance and inability. Both depended on ourselves, inasmuch as we will not learn" (7.16.101; *ANF* 2:553). Anticipating Rudolf Bultmann, he denied any connection between sin and physical death, which to him was a natural necessity. His approach has been compared with that of Pelagius, and owes much to Greek philosophy.

(iii) Tertullian (c. 150–c. 225) belongs to a different world. He is the classic advocate of Traducianism, the notion that humankind inherits their "soul" from Adam. Allegedly this derived from such passages as Rom. 5:12-20 and 1 Cor. 15:22: "As all die in Adam." But it may owe more to the Stoic view of the soul (Lat. *anima*) as a corporeal or quasi-material substance. Tertullian is curiously self-contradictory, for he insists on following only the Bible and the apostolic rule of faith, but in practice borrows extensively from Stoic thought. He writes: "I call on the Stoics to help me.... The soul *(anima)* is a corporeal substance ... [it] shares the pain of the body" (*On the Soul* 5; *ANF* 3:184-85). On this basis Tertullian argues for the transmission of original sin. Each generation, he claims, is an offshoot *(tradux)* of the previous one. Sin is hereditary, transmitting the qualities of fallen Adam to all his descendants *(tradux animae tradux peccati)*. He declares, "The soul which in the beginning was associated with Adam's body ... proved to be the germ ... of the entire substance [of the soul] and of creation" (9; *ANF* 3:189).

(iv) Like his teacher Clement, Origen (c. 185–c. 254) stressed freedom of the will, and interpreted the account of Adam's sin and expulsion from Eden as purely allegorical (*De principiis* 4.1.16; *ANF* 4:365). The Fall occurred before the creation of the world. Like Plato, he believed that "bodily" existence was second best, implying a prior fall. Through bearing the image of God, by grace and their own efforts, humankind can practice virtue. Origen wrote, "Every rational creature is capable of earning praise and censure" (1.5.2; *ANF* 4:256). He vehemently opposed a Gnostic doctrine of predestination.

(v) Athanasius (c. 296-373) showed caution about how much we can infer from biblical texts, which primarily concern Christ and the gospel. He explicitly rejected the view of Irenaeus that Adam before the Fall was like a child, innocent but immature. After all, he then had intercourse with God and bore his image. He almost reached a doctrine of "original righteousness," but did not formulate it. Sin brings corruption (Gk. *phthora*), which N. P. Williams interprets as "disintegration" in this context (*The Ideas of the Fall and of Original Sin* [London and New York: Longmans, Green, 1929], 260-61). Originally human beings had a "capacity" for perfection, but the Fall constituted a relapse into the condition of nature (partly anticipating Lossky). Only the endowment of the image of God can point the way out beyond the natural state. The sense in which "death" intervened was overcome by Jesus Christ. Christ did not merely "reverse" humanity's plight, but improved it.

(vi) Ambrose (c. 338-397) provided a stepping-stone in the Western Church to Augustine. It is crucial, as we saw in the biblical section, and as Pannenberg later stressed, that sin is viewed *as a state or condition, not simply as an act.* For Ambrose, sin is a state of human nature. On Rom. 5:12 he stressed, as Paul did, the solidarity and unity of humankind; but R. S. Moxon claims that, like Augustine, he stressed that humankind existed *in* Adam (*The Doctrine of Sin* [London: Allen and Unwin, 1922], 44). Certainly Ambrose reflects Paul's notion of exchange. He quotes Paul: "For as by one man's disobedience many were made sinners, so by the obedience of one shall many be made righteous" (Rom. 5:19; *On the Christian Faith* 5.8.109; *NPNF*, ser. 2, 10:298). He also states: "Death is alike to all ... although through the sin of one alone, yet it passed upon all" (*On the Belief in the Resurrection* 2.6; *NPNF*, ser. 2, 10:175). He regards free will as weakened by the Fall.

(vii) Augustine of Hippo (354-430) speculated about the state of humankind before the Fall, ascribing to "Adam" *possibilitas peccandi*. Any equipoise of choice between good and evil was lost at the Fall. In his *Confessions* (8.10.11) Augustine stated, "The enemy held me and thence made a chain for me, and bound me." Sin and the sinful state have become universal. Commenting on Rom. 7:7-25, Augustine argued that sin has become ingrained in human nature (*To Simplician* 20). According to Williams, in 397 "for the first time in the history of Christian thought we meet the epoch-making phrase *originale peccatum*, meaning sinful quality which is born with us and is inherent in our constitution" (*Ideas of the Fall*, 327). Humankind as such constitutes a single corporate *massa peccati*, or "lump of sin." Williams calls this "the fully rounded ... 'African' or 'twice born' type of the Fall-doctrine" (329); but Williams is as hostile to Augustine as Pannenberg is supportive of Augustine.

Augustine himself, however, would not have wished to isolate his view of sin from his doctrine of grace. His well-known declaration "Give what you command, and command what you will" *(da quod iubes, et iube quod vis)* stung Pelagius as badly overstated (*Confessions* 10.29; cf. *On the Merits and Remission of Sins* 2.5, *NPNF*, ser. 2, 5:46; *On the Spirit and the Letter* 22). H. Chadwick calls this "the start of the Pelagian controversy, Pelagius being the unqualified advocate of an ethical perfectionism as a requirement of the gospel" (Chadwick, *Confessions* [Oxford: OUP, 1992], 202-3), Williams nevertheless insists that Pelagius believed himself to be an orthodox Christian. However, the African church condemned Pelagius and his collaborator Caelestius at the Synod of Carthage in 411-412 (*see* **Grace**). Augustine insisted that without divine grace the human race was morally corrupt. Pannenberg wishes to preserve "the classical significance of Augustine," and thereby to resist the "reduction" of sin "to the individual act ... [or] moralism, stressing the reality of evil and the universality of sin, and understanding its destructive effects" (*ST* 2:234-44).

Debate continued, however, over Augustine's definition of freedom, his notion of "original righteousness," and his view of predestination. There is also the notorious problem of Augustine's reading of Rom. 5:12, "because all have sinned" (Gk. *eph' hō pantes hēmarton*), on the basis of the Latin *in quo*, "in whom" (*On the Merits and Remission of Sin* 1.10; *NPNF,* ser. 2, 5:9). In Pelagian terms and often modern liberal terms, freedom brings responsibility and blame only when it brings an equal opportunity to choose good or evil. For Augustine it denotes freedom to express the desire of the will, without external compulsion. Hence if the heart is corrupted, sin may become an unconscious expression of the will. Many liberals and perhaps many in the Eastern Church hesitate to accept this. But in Augustine's eyes, any supposed unevenness is overcome by the extravagant generosity of grace. What applies to one (being "in Adam"), also applies to the other (being "in Christ"). The matter is different on the subject of Adam's supposed "original righteousness" before the Fall. Many argue that original fellowship with God, as well as the image and likeness of God, would suggest this. But the vast majority of biblical scholars nowadays insist that such speculation goes beyond the concern of biblical writers, and remains speculative (*see* **Election and Predestination**). More significant is Augustine's notion of prevenient grace. He concludes that God commands humankind to do nothing that he does not make possible or give (*Against Two Letters of the Pelagians* 2.23; 4.15; *NPNF,* ser. 2, 5:401, 423). The Pelagian controversy dragged on until Pope Innocent I excommunicated Pelagius in 417. John Cassian later opposed Augustine's supposed "fatalism," and a number from southern Gaul came to be known as "semi-Pelagians." The name, however, does not justly describe a movement whose aim was simply to moderate the extremes of Augustinian doctrine.

(viii) The dominant thinker of the Middle Ages was Thomas Aquinas (1225-1274). Much of his work constitutes a reinterpretation of Augustine. In the *Summa Theologiae* 1.2 he discusses sin (qu. 71-80), original sin (81-85), and the effects of sin (86-89). Aquinas asserts: "Sin cannot entirely take away from the fact that he is a rational being" (qu. 85, art. 2). He explicitly appeals to Augustine (*On Nature and Grace* 67.67) that sin brings its own punishments internally, namely, ignorance and error or vexation (qu. 85, art. 3, obj. 5). He adds, "The soul, through sinning once, is more easily inclined to sin again" (qu. 85, art. 3, reply to obj. 1). He concludes: "Death is the punishment of sin" (art. 6).

If we move from effect to cause, Thomas states that the three causes of sin are ignorance, passion, and malice (qu. 76-78). Sin is "committed by habit" (qu. 78, art. 2, reply). "This corrupt disposition is either a habit acquired by custom, or a sickly condition. . . . The will, of its own accord, may tend toward evil" (art. 3). The most grievous sin is committed through malice (art. 4, reply). But these are largely "internal" causes. Questions 79-81 consider "external" causes. These may include the devil "unless he is restrained by God" (qu. 80, art. 3, reply) or "a human corruption pertaining to nature" (qu. 81, art. 3, reply). He repeats Augustine's point: "Original sin is transmitted from the first parent to his posterity" (art. 4, reply). Yet, as long as humans *want* God's grace, sin becomes no longer an absolute, unmodified necessity. Grace, like sin, can build a "habit." Moxon, for one, argues that Aquinas is "softer" than Augustine.

(ix) In the later Middle Ages, Duns Scotus (c. 1266-1308) was Franciscan regent master of the University of Paris, and further modified Aquinas's view of sin, in a direction leading away from Augustine. Williams argues that he returned to Irenaeus's notion of sin as immaturity, and Adam as "a starting point for progress" (*Ideas of the Fall,* 409). In Franciscan thought, the Fall again becomes a crowning moment, which makes redemption possible. It is even described as *"felix culpa."* But Duns Scotus is more interested in philosophical problems. The Dominicans, for their part, continued to support the views of Aquinas.

(x) Martin Luther (1483-1546) and John Calvin (1509-1564) underlined Augustine's doctrine. On the consequences of the Fall, Calvin writes: "This is the hereditary corruption to which early Christian writers gave the name of Original Sin, meaning by the term the depravation of a nature formerly good and pure" (*Institutes* 2.1.5; Beveridge, 1:214). Calvin recognizes the degree of controversy that surrounds this issue, calling the view of Pelagius "his profane fiction." He continues, "The orthodox, therefore, and more especially Augustine, laboured to show, that we . . . bring an innate corruption from the very womb. . . . 'I was shapen in iniquity . . .' (Ps. 51:5). . . . All of us . . . come into the world tainted with the contagion of sin . . . in God's sight defiled" (*Institutes* 2.1.5; 1:214). Indeed, "All the parts of the soul were possessed by sin, ever since Adam revolted from the fountain of righteousness" (*Institutes* 2.1.9; 1:218). "All the parts of the soul" explains what the Reformers mean by "total depravity." It means not the impossibility of ever aiming at good, but that *every* part of humanity as a totality was somehow tainted by sin. But it would be a mistake to interpret this primarily as about past history. As the Reformed theologians G. C. Berkouwer and H. Bavinck stress, the main concern was the reality and universality of human guilt and the need for grace.

(xi) Friedrich Schleiermacher (1768-1834) is often characterized as the father of modern theology. He saw sin primarily as an inadequacy of God-consciousness. In a positive sense, he still related sin to awareness of God, not to mere moralism. In a negative sense, he moved away from "orthodox" Western tradition in Augustine, Aquinas, and Calvin. Pannenberg accuses him of "oversimplifying" the problem (*Anthropology in Theological Perspective* [London and New York: T. & T. Clark/Continuum, 1985], 252-53). The deepest problem is his typical nineteenth-century concern with "development." John Hick closely associates him with Irenaeus, for whom sin remains a matter of "arrested development." Indeed, Emil Brunner calls this "idealistic evolutionism" (*Man in Revolt* [London:

Lutterworth, 1939], 123-24). In Schleiermacher's words, "Sin ... has arrested the free development of the God-consciousness" (*The Christian Faith* [Edinburgh: T. & T. Clark, 1989], 271). Sin is "a result of the unequal development of insight and will-power" (275), and "in general exists only in so far as there is a consciousness of it" (277). Original sin is only "the personal guilt of every individual who shares in it" (285). Again, his era coincides with the rise of individualism.

(xii) A. Ritschl (1822-1889), however, sought to reinstate the corporate and communal character of sin. Sin is whatever is contrary to the kingdom of God, which "cannot be completely represented ... within the framework of individual life" (*The Christian Doctrine of Justification* [Clifton, N.J.: Reference Book Publishers, 1966], 10-11). Nevertheless, whether Ritschl's liberalism leads to a "Pelagian" view of sin remains controversial. R. S. Moxon asserts, "Ritschl repudiates the old doctrine of Original Sin, and seeks to explain sinfulness by a development of the Pelagian idea of the 'influence of example,' and finds its origin entirely in man's environment" (*Doctrine of Sin,* 200). On the other hand, James Richmond decisively rejects this "stereotype" of Ritschl. Like Origen, he sees "punishment" for sin as internal, generated by the destructive consequences of sin, not by some divine intervention.

(xiii) Frederick R. Tennant (1866-1957) provides a philosophical, empirical, and individualist account of sin, which is unduly influenced by naturalist theories of evolution. "Adam" becomes a wholly mythological or symbolic figure. In essence, sin is described in exclusively *moralistic* or *ethical* terms. Whereas Athanasius had identified sin as lack of contemplation of God, Tennant sees it as *moral* culpability. E. J. Bicknell points out that he writes primarily as a philosopher, not as a theologian (*The Christian Idea of Sin* [1923], 32-34). After the horrors of a world war, he comments, Tennant is curiously out of date.

(xiv) Karl Barth (1886-1968) regarded human sin as pride, in the sense of trust in the self, in contrast to finding one's security in God. Further, what sin amounts to must be assessed in the light of Jesus Christ: "Jesus is man as God willed and created Him" (*CD* III/2, 50). To be truly human as God wills is to be like Christ. There can be no question "Was Jesus truly human?" It is rather: "Are we truly human?" in the light of the humanness of Christ. In the light of Christ, Barth continued, sin is revealed as "a [man's] personal act and guilt, his aberration from the grace of God and its command, his refusal of the gratitude he owes to God ... his arrogant attempt to be his own master, provider and comforter, his unhallowed lust for what is not his own, the falsehood, hatred and pride in which he is enmeshed in relation to his neighbour, the stupidity to which he is self-condemned" (III/3, 305). He added: "The fall of man ... corresponds exactly to ... the essence of sin — the pride of man. 'Pride goes before a fall' — The proverb is true" (IV/1, 478). This becomes "self-alienation from ... the majesty of God" (478). Humankind is created to be "open to God"; sin is a rejection of this (421). (*See* **Barth, Karl.**)

(xv) Like Barth, Emil Brunner (1889-1966) considered sin in relation to the purpose for which God created humankind. He writes: "Through sin man has lost ... his God-given nature" (*Man in Revolt,* 94). Like Barth, he perceived sin as "the assertion of human independence over against God, the declaration of rights ... as independent of God's will" (129). Brunner continued: "Presumption, arrogance" is the "primal sin" (130). He also urges the corporate nature of sin: "we are a unity bound together in solidarity. ... Sin ... is the destruction of communion with God" (139-41).

(xvi) Paul Tillich (1886-1965) identified sin with hubris, namely, "the self-elevation of man into the sphere of the divine" (*Systematic Theology,* vol. 2 [London: Nisbet, 1957], 57). It leads to tragic self-destruction, and attributes the divine to finite human culture. The "fall of Adam" remains entirely symbolic; it is not about "what happened" (33). However, "when man turns away from God ... [he] turns towards himself ... the separation of man's will from the will of God" (54). Sin especially leads to fragmentation, in place of integration. It treats parts as if they were the whole, and treats the penultimate as if it were the ultimate. Carl Gustav Jung influences Tillich here. The constant theme in volume 2 of *Systematic Theology* is existential alienation, which only God in Christ can restore to wholeness (*see* **Tillich, Paul**).

(xvii) Reinhold Niebuhr (1892-1971) showed concern equally for sin as pride before God and as socially disruptive and exploitative. In his powerful but small book *Moral Man and Immoral Society* (London: SCM, 1932), he showed that human sin is more pernicious in groups than individually, involving self-deception of a corporate nature. For example, "The family may become a means of self-aggrandisement" (47), as when we seek promotion at the expense of others supposedly "for the sake of the family." Niebuhr wrote, "The selfishness of nations is proverbial" (84). Patriotic action is often "self-deception and hypocrisy" (95). In *The Nature and Destiny of Man* (2 vols. [London: Nisbet, 1941-1943]), sin takes the form of either sensuality or pride. "It is the essence of man to love himself" (1:113). Of these two, like Barth, Brunner, and Tillich, he saw pride as the more fundamental. (*See* **Niebuhr, Reinhold**).

(xviii) Karl Rahner (1904-1984) perceived the essence of sin as "rejection of God" (*FCF* 115). He had hesitations about judicial imputation and biological heredity as an explanation for the transmission of sin. He did not reject the *term* "original sin," but sought to retain the basic *idea* without its unfortunate baggage. Rahner insisted that sin should not be restricted to a wholly private sphere. This diminishes its coercive power, and risks reducing it to moralism. Sin marks social institutions. Rahner's theology took account of many other issues, including revelation and the theory of knowledge. As a Roman Catholic thinker, he stressed that sinners are members of the church, as against the Donatists and others. Further, he comes near to the Reformation principle of humans being both sinners and justified at the same time (*TI* 6:227-30, 258-63).

(xix) Among feminist writers, Valerie Saiving (1921-1992), in 1960, criticized the emphasis of sin as pride in Barth and Niebuhr on the ground that this represented a distinctively "masculine" sin. She suggested that distraction and triviality were more relevant to women (*JR* 40 [1960]: 100-112). Judith Plaskow (b. 1947) built on this in *Sex, Sin, and Grace* in 1980, attacking Niebuhr and Tillich, arguing that competitiveness represented a "male" sin, while she saw "wanting to be rid of herself" as a female one. It is doubtful, however, whether either fully captures the theological dimension of seeking security by human means. They tend to speak of sin*s*, rather than sin.

(xx) Wolfhart Pannenberg (b. 1928) devotes 100 pages of volume 2 of his *Systematic Theology* to this subject (175-275). Humankind loses its engagement and communication with the source of all that is good: life, grace, and blessing. Hence he realistically uses the term "misery" rather than "lostness" or other terms to denote humankind's sinful condition. Sin can be understood only in the light of the human "destiny of fellowship with God," and "only in the light of the incarnation of the eternal Son as a man" (175). Hence: "Misery, then, is the lot of those who are deprived of the fellowship with God that is the destiny of human life" (178). He writes: "The term 'misery' sums up our detachment from God.... The term 'alienation' has a similar breadth" (179). Pannenberg also corrects the Platonic view of a dualism of spirit and body. Creaturely life, he writes, has "an ec-centric character." We do not exercise dominion over the earth, as Ps. 8:6-8 envisages. One result is that we do not see ourselves as "there for others as well as [ourselves]" (194). "Little is left of the traditional dogma of a perfect first estate" before the Fall (214). It is still true, however, that "Through sin there was an increasing distortion in individuals." He concludes, "Only in Jesus ... did the image of God appear with full clarity" (216). Christ-likeness becomes our destiny; we must become aware of "a horizon that transcends [our] finitude" (229). Very emphatically, he states: "The decay of the doctrine of original sin led to the anchoring of the concept of sin in acts of sin, and finally the concept was reduced to the individual act" (234). The Bible and Augustine, however, remind us of sin's structural, corporate, and destructive effects (241-44). The misery of sin means that "we are caught fast in the self" (251). "Absolute self-willing ... alienates us from God" (261). "We achieve liberation from sin and death only where the image of the Son takes shape in human life through the operation of the Spirit of God" (275). (*See* **Pannenberg, Wolfhart.**)

(xxi) Hans Küng (b. 1928) offers a Catholic response to Barth's theology of justification. He discusses sin and death, the wretchedness of sin, and the ruin of man in a way not incompatible with Barth and Pannenberg, and places divine grace at the center of his concerns (*Justification* [London: Burns and Oates, 1964], 141-80).

(xxii) John Zizioulas (b. 1931) reinterprets the Eastern Church Fathers for Greek Orthodoxy today. His theme is communion with God, which sin can disrupt and break. Above all, he sees sin as elevating the self into the place of God, and making the self "the ultimate reference-point of existence" (*Being as Communion* [New York: St. Vladimir's Seminary Press, 1985], 102).

Reading: Karl Barth, *Church Dogmatics* III/2, III/3, IV/1 (Edinburgh: T. & T.

Clark, 1957-1975); R. S. Moxon, *The Doctrine of Sin* (London: Allen and Unwin, 1922); Reinhold Niebuhr, *Moral Man and Immoral Society* (London: SCM, 1932, 1963); W. Pannenberg, *Anthropology in Theological Perspective* (London and New York: T. & T. Clark/Continuum, 1985), 80-156; W. Pannenberg, *Systematic Theology*, vol. 2 (Edinburgh: T. & T. Clark; Grand Rapids: Eerdmans, 1994), 175-275; N. P. Williams, *The Ideas of the Fall and of Original Sin* (London and New York: Longmans, Green, 1929).

Sinaiticus. *See* **Codex Sinaiticus**

Sinless Perfection
Sinless perfection is often based on those biblical passages that appear to command being "perfect," of which probably the best known is the reference in the Sermon on the Mount: "Be perfect, therefore, as your heavenly Father is perfect" (Matt. 5:48). This command arises from the need to "love your enemies" (v. 44), for God "makes his sun rise on the evil and on the good" (v. 45). It is not enough to love only "those who love you" (v. 46). Historically the injunction is also applied to lax or careless eras in the life and history of the church. This may partly explain Wesley's genuine or alleged concern for perfection. Yet Jesus is using the main NT word for "perfect," Greek *teleios*. Danker translates this as (i) "meeting the harshest standard"; (ii) "being mature, full-grown, adult"; (iii) "being initiated"; and (iv) "being fully developed in a moral sense" (BDAG 995-96). The adjective has a cognate verb *teleioō*, which has the primary meaning of "to complete," or "bring to full measure," and only in very few cases "make perfect." Danker places Matt. 5:48 under the heading "being fully developed." Similarly Newton Flew considers Phil. 3:12-15, where NRSV translates "goal" (v. 14) and "who are mature" (v. 15) as closely following "Not that I have already obtained this or have already reached the goal" (v. 12), to show that this cannot be "sinless" perfection. There are numerous passages the NRSV translates "mature," while only KJV/AV translates "perfect" (e.g., NRSV "adults," 1 Cor. 14:20; "mature," 1 Cor. 2:6; "maturity," Eph. 4:13; "complete," 1 Cor. 13:10); although it retains "perfect" in Heb. 9:11 and Rom. 12:2, where not moral growth but eschatological fulfillment is in question. Matt. 19:21 is also translated "perfect" because this emphasizes going beyond the call of normal duty, and may address the hubris of the question that parades the questioner's self-value, "I have kept all these." In any case, Newton Flew renders it, "If you want to be full grown in the spiritual life."

The comments on this subject by Robert Newton Flew have special value for two reasons. First, together with some seven or more other books, he wrote *The Idea of Perfection in Christian Theology: A Historical Study* (London: OUP, 1934). Second, he was a Wesleyan Methodist, and the doctrine of sinless perfection is rightly or wrongly attributed to John Wesley. If Wesley did indeed hold such a view, Flew is one of the few Methodists to have roundly criticized him on this point. He regarded this view as overoptimistic and offering an "instantaneous" notion of sanctification. He was professor of NT at Wesley House, Cambridge, and was awarded the Oxford D.D. The book is a meticulous piece of scholarship. He considers the lexicographical evidence for *teleios* in the NT and among Stoics and Epictetus, in which it clearly means "full grown." Flew concludes, "The full Christian perfection is only attainable in the other life beyond the grave." Admittedly no limits can be set to the grace of God, but sin always remains this side of the grave. Wesley's view was controversial. He appears to promote "sinless perfection," but in what sense he did this and under what provocation remain unclear.

Skepticism

Skepticism regards human beliefs as an expression of mere opinion, not as an expression of truth. It assumes that human knowledge cannot be supported by justified or reasonable criteria. Radical skepticism demands suspension of belief; moderate skepticism denies the possibility of human certainty. Skepticism as a philosophical system is often attributed to Pyrrho of Elis (c. 360-270 B.C.). He called for suspension of judgment (Gk. *epochē*) and the practice of silence *(aphasia)*, on the ground that our beliefs are no more reasonable than their denial. Skepticism seems to have faded until the revival of ancient studies in Renaissance humanism, when Pyrrho and Sextus Empiricus underwent a brief revival. R. H. Popkin has expounded the history of skepticism in *The History of Scepticism* (1979) and (with C. B. Schmitt) *Scepticism from the Renaissance to the Enlightenment* (1987). Popkin argues that Erasmus inherited from Pyrrho the claim that divided opinions may make knowledge obscure, and that this lay behind Luther's controversy with him about the perspicuity of Scripture. After Erasmus, we see more basic skepticism in M. Montaigne (1533-1592). In broader terms, D. Hume declared himself a skeptic. One standard reply to skeptics is: How do I know that I cannot know? Wittgenstein claimed that doubt comes only *after certainty.*

Sobornost

Sobornost is a virtually untranslatable Russian term that characterizes much of the theology of the Russian Orthodox Church. Some consider that the nearest equivalent is "catholicity," but most argue that it is a deep and emotional sense of *solidarity*. The Eucharist is said to be the foundation of ecclesial *sobornost;* this might imply that the Greek *koinonia* is a near equivalent.

Social Gospel

The term "Social Gospel" strictly denotes a movement that flourished in America and Canada in the late nineteenth and early twentieth centuries. In an earlier generation F. D. Maurice and C. Kingsley had represented "Christian Socialism" in England. It was largely a movement of protest against injustice for the working classes. Washington Gladden (1836-1918) is sometimes called "the father of the movement." He was a Congregationalist minister. But the key founder and leader of the movement was Walter Rauschenbusch, who published *A Theology for the*

Social Gospel in 1919. He argued that in the teaching of Jesus the kingdom of God had nothing to do with founding an institution, the church, but was directed to the transformation of society. In his view it combined ethical teaching with social reform and political action.

The greatest problem with Rauschenbusch's theology was a lack of careful exegesis of the Gospels. While some, such as Shailer Mathews, still saw the kingdom of God as a term for "the supreme good to be enjoyed by humanity" (1921), NT scholarship had rapidly been coming to the conclusion that "kingdom of God" meant the "rule" or "reign" of God. The work of such scholars as G. Dalman and J. Weiss had understood the kingdom of God in a different way. Dalman stressed "kingly rule," while Weiss stressed an apocalyptic rather than an ethical understanding. The Social Gospel movement was linked with liberal theology, including Harnack's emphasis on "the brotherhood of man." With the outbreak of the First World War and with the rise of Barth's theology, the movement declined after about 1920.

Socinianism

Socinianism was an alternative name for anti-Trinitarian Unitarianism, at least until the late nineteenth century. There is no single individual called Socinus; the term refers to two Italian humanists whose surnames were combined to form the Latin name Socinus (strictly, Lelio Sozini, 1526-1562; Lat. Laelius Socinus, and his nephew Fausto Sozzini [with a double *z*], 1539-1604; Lat. Faustus Socinus). The latter formed the Minor Reformed Church of Poland, and in 1594 published a theology of the work of Christ akin to Abelard's. He suffered harassment from the Jesuits. Socinian influence temporarily reached the Church of England, and John Riddle became known as "the Father of English Unitarianism."

Soteriology

Soteriology (from Gk. *sōtēria*, "salvation") usually has as its essential concern the saving work of Christ, which we have discussed in our entries on **Atonement; Blood; Christology; Covenant; Grace; Holy Spirit; Reconciliation; Redemption; Sacrifice**, not to mention such historical theologians as Abelard, Anselm, and Calvin. Humankind is in need of salvation as set out under our entries on **Anthropology** and **Sin**. Under **Grace**, it is stressed that the work of Christ is the fruit of grace, not the root of grace, and entails the initiative of the triune God. God's purposes of salvation also include sanctification by the Holy Spirit. They also embrace the covenant, election, and salvation history, or **Heilsgeschichte**, and relate to **Eternity** as well as **Time**. In Paul grace also stands in contrast with the law, and finds expression in **Justification** and **Sanctification**. The process of sanctification involves **Perseverance, Assurance**, struggle, and even **Temptation**. Salvation through **Faith** involves fellow believers in the church and the resources of **Ministry**. Finally, salvation leads to **Glory** and to the **Beatific Vision**. All this explains why we have written no single comprehensive article on soteriology; *it* *is covered in a multiplicity of separate articles.* Soteriology involves almost everything that has been written *under these separate entries.* A useful general survey is J. Davidson and M. A. Rae, *God of Salvation* (Aldershot: Ashgate, 2010).

Soul
(Heb. *nephesh;* Gk. *psuchē* or *psychē*). Because the meaning of this term is still hotly debated, we must consider the varied Hebrew and Greek meanings in detail, labored though this may seem. It appears to denote a variety of meanings according to context, but most biblical scholars do not see a one-to-one correspondence between the English "soul" and the Hebrew or Greek terms that have sometimes been translated as "soul." According to BDB, *nephesh* is translated not only as "soul," but also as "living being," "life," "self," "person," "desire," "appetite," "emotion," and "passion." It is then subdivided into "that which breathes, the breathing being," and "the inner being"; "a living being"; "a living being whose life resides in the blood"; "a human being, the seat of the appetites"; "the seat of the passions"; "mental acts"; and "acts of will" (659-61). C. Ryder Smith writes that *nephesh* occurs in the OT 756 times, of which the KJV/AV uses forty-two different translations, including "life" (117 times) and "soul" (428 times). But he insists, "English has no one word for *nephesh* because we have no wholly corresponding ideas" (*The Bible Doctrine of Man* [London: Epworth, 1951], 6). *Nephesh of life* is used of animals (Gen 2:7, 19). "Living creatures," Smith suggests, would be better. If we must classify, Smith suggests three categories: (i) uses meaning "life as against death" (Exod. 4:19; Deut. 19:21, 1 Sam. 19:11; Job 2:4); (ii) uses meaning "person," "people," or "human beings" (Gen. 46:27), or where *nephesh* is a synonym for "me" (Pss. 6:4; 16:10; 33:20). In Lev. 19:28 and in Num. 6:6 a dead *nephesh* denotes a corpse. (iii) *Nephesh* can denote everything in the realm of feeling, knowing, or willing (Deut. 12:20; Judg. 18:25; Ps. 103:1).

H. W. Wolff insists that *nephesh* does not denote a part or component of human beings that they "have"; a person *"is nephesh,* he lives as *nephesh*" (*Anthropology of the Old Testament* [London: SCM; Philadelphia: Fortress, 1974], 10). The Hebrew uses include "throat," "neck," "desire," "soul," "life," and "person," or substitute for a pronoun (11-25). "Soul" constitutes a *minority* of translations. It may be despondent or exhausted (Job 42:5-6; Jon. 2:7; Jer. 4:31; Isa. 53:11). E. Jacob shows the varied and problematic uses of *nephesh* in volume 9 of Kittel, *TDNT* (617-31). As we should expect, the Hebrew is often translated by *psychē.* He argues that *n-ph-sh* originally meant to "breathe," but became connected with blood, person, corpse, expression of will, and a human being in contrast to body or flesh. Very often, as Wolff and Smith argue, *nephesh* merely denotes "me," as in Ps. 35:9-10: "My *nephesh* shall be joyful in Yahweh." When the OT writer wants to speak of the inner or hidden core or depths of a person, usually the chosen word is *not "soul" but "heart"* (*lebh,* 626-28). E. Lohse argues that in postbiblical Judaism "*nephesh* denotes the living man in thought, decision, and action" (*TDNT* 9:636).

In NT uses of *psuchē* (or *psychē*), E. Schweizer provides a similar picture

(*TDNT* 9:637-65). In the Gospels and Acts it denotes natural physical life (Matt. 6:25); the giving of life (Mark 10:45, as a ransom for many); the whole person or the whole human being, especially as threatened by death (Acts 2:43; 7:14); even the place of feeling (Matt. 12:18, of God; Luke 12:19); or in the sense of "heart." One of the very *few* instances in which we should think of "soul" is when it stands in contrast to "body" (Matt. 10:28). Schweizer insists that Paul's use of *psuchē* is "rare ... in comparison with the Old Testament" (648). He cannot adopt the Greek or Hellenistic idea of "soul." *Psuchē* usually denotes natural life (1 Thess. 2:8; Rom. 11:3; 16:4), or person (Rom. 2:9; 13:1). Hebrews and the Catholic Epistles do not normally use *psuchē* to denote "soul." Certainly "*psuchē* and spirit" in Heb. 4:12 means simply "all of you, through and through." As in 1 Thess. 5:23, it means "in every action" or "through and through," like the English "put your heart and soul into it."

R. Jewett has researched every anthropological term in the Pauline Epistles thoroughly. He concedes that *psuchē* has often "been at the centre of controversies" (*Paul's Anthropological Terms* [Leiden: Brill, 1971], 334). Paul can use the adjective *psuchikos* to denote natural or animal life or unspiritual life (340). It is used three times in Romans, usually to denote "person" or "life" (e.g., Rom. 11:3; 16:4; Jewett, 356-57). In 1 Corinthians *psuchikos* becomes a key term for describing one who cannot receive the Spirit of God (1 Cor. 2:14). In 2 Cor. 12:15 it probably means "lives," as in Paul spent himself the the lives *(psuchai)* of the Corinthians (355). In Philippians it denotes the church as a living organism (Phil. 1:27), or simply life (2:30). In his conclusion, Jewett states that *psuchē* often denotes one of three meanings: "*earthly life* as it is publicly observable" (448); *life that can be lost at death;* and *an individual person.* The "Gnostic" use is entirely different.

F. W. Danker calls *psuchē* a "multivalent word" (BDAG 1098). He lists its English meanings as (i) *life on earth* or *earthly life:* (ii) seat and *center of inner human life;* (iii) *a person.* But (ii) overlaps strongly with *heart.* One modern writer insists that this is a "colourless term." D. E. H. Whiteley crusades on behalf of a "unitary" and "aspective" view of the human being in Paul: "each individual man is a unity"; so is "mankind as a whole" (*The Theology of St. Paul* [Oxford: Blackwell, 1971], 44). J. D. G. Dunn also rejects a dualist view, maintaining that *psuchē* is clearly "person" in several passages (*The Theology of Paul the Apostle* [Grand Rapids: Eerdmans, 1998], 76). This is no mere new-fangled fashion. The conservative J. Laidlaw made this point in 1895 (*The Bible Doctrine of Man* [Edinburgh: Clark, 1895], 54-56, 320-23).

For Christian theologians the problem lies not with the Bible but with an ambiguous Christian tradition. The Roman Catholic theologian Edmund Hill reviews *A Catechism of Christian Doctrine* (1971), which still reflects Augustine on "soul." It unfortunately asserts, "The likeness to God is chiefly in my soul.... My soul is like God because it is a spirit and is immortal." Hill comments that this, sadly, "irrevocably commits" the user of the Catholic catechism "to the view of man satirized by Ryle as the ghost-in-the-machine view.... It is very sad to find it still in a catechism revised *after* the Second Vatican Council" (*Being Human* [London: Chapman, 1984], 209). Plato certainly held a dualist view of body and soul, in which the body was a mere prison-house of the soul. Aristotle was less radically dualist, but a dualist view found its way to Aquinas. In *Summa Theologiae* 1, questions 75-78, the questions cover "The Soul's Nature," "The Soul's Union with the Body," and "The Power of the Soul" (Eng. and Lat., 11:3-143).

First, Aquinas denies the view of second-century Stoics and Tertullian that the soul is corporeal. He appeals to Augustine: the soul "is not extended quantitatively through . . . the body" (qu. 75, art. 1). In article 4 he quotes Augustine again, "Man is neither the soul alone nor the body alone, but body and soul together *(animam simul et corpus esse arbitratur)*." Aquinas declares, "The human soul *(anima)* . . . must of necessity be held to be incorruptible" (art. 5, reply). The soul is not an accident. In question 76, however, Thomas seems to compound the problem because, like Plato, he seems to regard "the soul" as the rational part or "intellective principle" *(intellectivum principium)* of a human being. Later, he seems to regard a human person as "a compound unity, matter [body] plus form [soul]" (art. 1, reply). He asserts: "The intellective soul *(anima)*, like an angel, is not constituted out of matter" (art. 2, reply). He concludes, "Aristotle is . . . saying that it (the soul) is the activating part of an organic physical body that has the power to live. . . . Such power to live does not exist apart from the soul" (art. 4, reply). Aquinas adds, "Man is constituted of two substantial elements, the soul and the reasoning power, the flesh with its senses" (qu. 77, art. 8). He depends here on Augustine, but admits that "Augustine is speaking inquiringly rather than definitively" (art. 8, reply).

Although Aquinas appeals often to Augustine, Augustine is frequently hesitant on this subject. He does indeed appear to assert that the soul is created by God in human beings (*On the Soul and Its Origin* 1.25-28). Yet Aquinas clearly takes a new departure. Admittedly Tertullian was strongly influenced by Stoic views of the soul. But Athenagoras and many others argued for the resurrection of the body on the ground that body and soul form a unity. Origen affirmed the preexistence of the soul, largely in the light of borrowings from Plato. The patristic tradition is ambiguous. Yet after Aquinas the tradition regularly taught the existence of the soul. Calvin addresses the subject in *Institutes* 1.15.2: "There can be no question that man consists of a body and a soul; meaning by soul, an immortal though created essence, which is his nobler part. Sometimes he is called a spirit" (Beveridge, 1:160). He then connects the idea with humankind made in the image of God. The trend became exaggerated by the dualism of Descartes (1596-1650), and was regularly held until after Harnack, with his talk of "the infinite value of the human soul." In idealism it was often confused with the human spirit. But by the early twentieth century a Reformed theologian such as G. C. Berkouwer could comment on Harnack, "It is certainly incorrect to think that the words themselves imply an anthropology which contrasts higher (soul) and lower (body), and this was surely not Harnack's intention" (*Man* [Grand Rapids: Eerdmans,

1962], 226). The Anglican theologian J. Macquarrie writes, "The view that the soul is an independently existing substantial entity that somehow 'inhabits' the body and interacts with it" does not imply face-value acceptance of "the soul" (*In Search of Humanity* [London: SCM, 1982], 49).

It is not surprising, however, that in the light of Aquinas, the "official" Roman Catholic view, as expressed in *The Catechism of the Catholic Church,* defines the soul as "the innermost aspect of humans. . . . 'Soul' signifies the spiritual principle in man" (363). Eastern Orthodox views are "officially" not dissimilar. But this does *not* mean that individual Roman Catholics necessarily hold this view. One of the most distinguished Catholic philosophers, Peter Geach, writes, "The existence of a disembodied soul would not be a survival of the person"; he does not follow Aquinas at substantial points (*God and the Soul* [London: Routledge and Kegan Paul, 1969], 24). He concedes that the biblical and traditional Christian belief is not in "the immortality of the soul," but in God's creative act of resurrection. Moltmann and Pannenberg stress this point. The Catholic K. Rahner wants to retain the notion of a "soul," but admits that the resurrection of the body constitutes "final perfection"; this cannot be "a purely spiritual union with God" (*TI* 4:351). (*See also* **Body**.)

Reading: P. Geach, *God and the Soul* (London: Routledge and Kegan Paul, 1969); J. B. Green, *Body, Soul, and Human Life* (Grand Rapids: Baker Academic, 2008); R. Jewett, *Paul's Anthropological Terms* (Leiden: Brill, 1971); N. Murphy, *Bodies and Souls or Spiritual Bodies?* (Cambridge: CUP, 2006); R. Swinburne, *The Evolution of the Soul* (Oxford: OUP, 1997); H. W. Wolff, *Anthropology of the Old Testament* (Philadelphia: Fortress, 1974).

Speech Act Theory
Otherwise known as performative language or illocutionary language, speech act theory owes its origin in the modern era to J. L. Austin, whose 1955 lectures on the subject were published in 1962 as *How to Do Things with Words* (Oxford: Clarendon). Strictly, a speech act constitutes an *illocutionary* utterance, which Austin defined as "the performance of an act *in* saying something, as opposed to performance of an act *of* saying something" (99). An act *of* speaking can be called a "locutionary" act; the performance of an act *by* saying something can be called "a perlocutionary act or perlocution" (101). After Austin, the philosopher of language who most influentially developed speech act theory further in the 1960s and 1970s was John R. Searle, especially in *Speech Acts* (Cambridge: CUP, 1969) and in *Expression and Meaning* (Cambridge: CUP, 1979).

A rudimentary version of speech acts was anticipated by the Reformer William Tyndale in his short treatise *A Pathway into the Holy Scripture* (in his *Doctrinal Treatises* [Cambridge: CUP, 1848], 7-29). His central point was that Scripture was not only mere "words" of information, but also *conveyed "the promises* of God." Luther had influenced his approach. Hence the Bible *did* things, or *performed actions:* "it maketh a man's heart glad"; it proclaims "joyful tidings"; it "nameth to be"

(God's) heirs. Tyndale lists eighteen speech acts within a dozen pages. Scripture, he said, "appoints," "gives," "condemns," "curses," "blesses," "cures," and so on. Wittgenstein had already noted that such language as "we mourn" constitutes an *act* of mourning, not usually a description of the act. In the 1930s and 1940s several theologians, including Barth, argued that the Bible *performed acts,* and during the 1950s and 1960s E. Fuchs in Germany and R. Funk in America spoke of biblical language as "eventful" *(Sprachereignis),* or "performative." But the word "performative" was used here too loosely. In 1963 D. D. Evans showed that performative language or speech acts strictly depended not on *causal* force, but on a complex of *institutional* causes and conditions, as Austin sets out (*see* **Self-Involvement**).

In the first of his 1955 lectures Austin gave numerous examples of performative utterances. He suggested: "I do (take this woman as my lawful wedded wife)" in a marriage; "I name this ship the *Queen Elizabeth,*" uttered by the appropriate person when smashing a bottle against the stern; "I give and bequeath my watch to my brother" in a duly valid will; or "I bet you . . ." (5). All these *do* something: make someone a married person; give a name to a ship; transfer property; convey money (or lose money). After this explanation of performatives, Austin sets out conditions for a "happy" (i.e., effective) performative utterance. He writes: "An accepted conventional procedure must have a certain conventional effect" (14, 17, 26). The person who speaks must have been appointed to perform the act. Any or every individual could not "name" a rowing boat simply by smashing a ginger beer bottle against it. Austin gives hilarious examples of "misfires" or "infelicities." What if the archbishop of Canterbury declares a library open, but then the key snaps in the lock (37)? What if the clergyperson declares, "I baptize you infant No. 2704"?

Further conditions follow in lectures 3 and 4. The procedure must be complete. What happens if a team captain selects George, but George mutters, "not playing" (28)? Suppose I declare, "My seconds will call on you," but you reply, "This is the twenty-first century! We don't decide issues by dueling nowadays!" The utterance could be insincere. Could I effectively say, "I bid you welcome," when I am not glad to see you at all (59)? The key statement is reached in the next lecture, which expounds the principle largely ignored by Fuchs and German theologians. Austin declares, "For a certain performative utterance to be happy, *certain statements have to be true*" (45). The truth or falsehood of the process does not apply directly to the utterance: we do not speak of a "false" baptism. But always *some truth or state of affairs is presupposed.* I cannot "bequeath" a watch that is not mine; or marry a bride if I am already married (51).

Of special significance for theology is the example of *promising.* Austin asks us to imagine a boy who sends his cricket ball through the greenhouse next door. It is not effective if his mother calls on the neighbor and says, "He promises he won't do it again, don't you, Willie?" It is effective only if Willie makes the promise himself as a commitment (63). Indeed, in lectures 7 and 11, Austin draws up a classification of performatives (83-94, 152-63). He classifies *"behabitives,"* which relate to behavior, such as "I apologize," "I am sorry"; *"verdictives,"* which express verdicts, such as "acquitted" or "I pronounce" (89), and which relate to justification by grace; *"exercitives,"* which exercise power, such as promising, and "commit you to doing something" (150-51). In theology, we argue, if God makes a promise, it commits him to a certain course of action, and makes some alternative impossible. Promises voluntarily tie our hands. All this underlines the point Evans will make in 1963: performative utterances depend on *institutions,* not causal force. In Christian theology these will probably include the covenant.

In 1963 Evans expounded this approach in terms of the logic of self-involvement, as we note in that entry. However, the next widely influential exponent of speech act theory is John Searle. He presupposes much of what Austin has argued, but with two reservations. First, he renames and reclassifies Austin's performatives for a particular reason. Second, he rightly fears that we may move too quickly from the use of a given *vocabulary* to identifying a *type or category* of performatives. He is a more professional philosopher of language than Austin claimed to be. In *Speech Acts* he speaks of language as a "rule-governed form of behaviour" (17); of speech units as sentences rather than words (16); and of stretches of language that have a given context. He distinguishes between a propositional content (P) and its force (F; 31-33). He discusses the "background of certain kinds of institutions" in contrast to "brute facts" (51-52). He expounds "background" more fully in his later book *Intentionality* (1986).

To replace Austin's word "exercitive," Searle proposes the word "directive." François Recanati, Stephen Levinson, and Geoffrey Leech follow Searle here. In theological terms, we suggest, "the Word of the Lord" has power to appoint, to direct, to authorize, and to command. All this presupposes the relationship established between God and Israel or the church. The purpose of this becomes clear in Searle's exposition of "the direction of fit" between words and the world. This is clearly expounded in *Expression and Meaning* (1979). The purpose of most simple descriptions or propositions is "to get the words (more strictly their propositional content) to match the world" (3). This is one "direction of fit." But for commands, promises, and most directives, the purpose is "to get the world to match the words. Assertions are in the former category; promises and requests are in the latter" (3). Searle borrows E. Anscombe's illustration of the difference between two ways of looking at the homely example of shopping in stores. If the store detective records a series of thefts, he or she is using descriptive propositions. However, if a spouse takes items from the shelves to match the spouse's shopping list, this reflects a directive speech-act, of a descriptive proposition. In Searle's language, the first lets words fit or reflect the world through propositions. The second example uses directives to make the world match the word. In this respect it is a transformative speech act. Recanati similarly talks about this as a "direction of correspondence" between words and the world (*Meaning and Force* [Cambridge: CUP, 1987], 150; cf. 150-63).

Searle's classifications substitute well for Austin's assertives, directives, expressives, and declaratives, while he accepts "commissives" in the sense used by Austin. Expressives presuppose either of the two directions of fit: declaratives bring about a change in the world. When we come to apply this to biblical and theological language, the significance for Christology is clear. If the utterance "Your sins are forgiven you" was effective, this presupposes that Christ was appointed to be One empowered to forgive sins in the place of God. Theological language is explored in this context by A. C. Thiselton, *New Horizons in Hermeneutics* (London: HarperCollins; Grand Rapids: Zondervan, 1992, 2013), 283-312, and by Richard S. Briggs, *Words in Action* (Edinburgh: T. & T. Clark, 2001). In a theological context we should also mention N. Wolterstorff, *Divine Discourse* (Cambridge: CUP, 1995). Again, he stresses that performative utterances do not depend on "causal efficacy" (78). An ordinary stretch of language, he argues, may *"count as"* an illocutionary utterance in appropriate circumstances (84). Utterances may also constitute delegated speech (95-129). Briggs discusses speech acts in the first part of his book. Then he examines the performative force of confessions of faith (183-216) and forgiveness of sins (217-56). He concludes with further implications for the hermeneutics of the Bible. In 2006 J. W. Adams applied speech act theory to Isaiah 40–55. Many other linguisticians and philosophers of language have written further on speech act theory. These include F. Kiefer and M. Dietwisch (1980); D. Vanderveken (1985); and S. L. Tsohatzidis (1994). On speech acts in 1 John, D. Neufeld has written *Reconceiving Texts as Speech-Acts* (Leiden: Brill, 1994); and there are half a dozen essays in *Thiselton on Hermeneutics* (Grand Rapids: Eerdmans; Aldershot: Ashgate, 2006), 53-150.

Reading: J. W. Adams, *The Performative Nature and Function of Isaiah 40–55* (New York and London: T. & T. Clark, 2006); J. L. Austin, *How to Do Things with Words* (Oxford: Clarendon, 1962); R. S. Briggs, *Words in Action* (Edinburgh: T. & T. Clark, 2001); J. R. Searle, *Expression and Meaning* (Cambridge: CUP, 1979); A. C. Thiselton, *New Horizons in Hermeneutics* (Grand Rapids: Zondervan, 1992, 2013), 272-312; A. C. Thiselton, *Thiselton on Hermeneutics* (Grand Rapids: Eerdmans, 2006), 51-150; N. Wolterstorff, *Divine Discourse* (Cambridge: CUP, 1995).

Spener, Philipp Jakob

Philipp Jakob Spener (1635-1705) is often ranked as the first of the Pietists, who indirectly influenced John Wesley and Jonathan Edwards through Count Nikolaus von Zinzendorf. He owes much to Luther, but also reflects the Radical Reformers, and partly anticipates Pentecostalism and the Renewal Movement. His most important work is *Pia Desideria* (1675). He argued that Lutheran orthodoxy should be extended by a more comprehensive and less selective use of Scripture. He urged: "All Scripture, without exception, should be known by the congregation." He argued that a congregation should use a wider range of the "gifts of the Spirit" in 1 Corinthians 12–14, but did not support those who placed the Spirit above Scripture. He urged the priesthood of all believers. In many ways he advocated a middle position between Luther and the Radical Reformers.

Spinoza, Baruch

Baruch Spinoza (1632-1677) was a complicated thinker. He is generally thought of as a pantheist or monist. But at one extreme he is regarded as an atheist; at the other extreme he has been called "God-intoxicated." The reason for this is that, on the one hand, he derived from Descartes the conviction that "substance" is the underlying ground of Being, while on the other hand he regarded "God" as coextensive with all reality. Hence he believed that "God is all"; but God is also "substance," which excludes personhood and theism. His slogan *Deus, sive Natura* suggests that "God" is another name for nature.

Spinoza was born in Amsterdam of Portuguese Jewish parents. It is scarcely surprising that he was expelled from the synagogue on a charge of atheism (1656). He promptly changed his Jewish name Baruch to the Latin form, Benedict. He completed his major work *Ethics Demonstrated in a Geometrical Manner* in 1675, but it was published only posthumously in 1677. He was an ardent advocate of "free thought," especially in his *Tractatus Theologica-Politicus* (1670), as can also be seen from his theories of biblical criticism. Since he regarded the human will as part of the divine mind, he denied absolute free will. He advocated a rationalistic, naturalistic, and "scientific" approach to political theory. Again, it is no surprise to find that Thomas Hobbes retained a particular influence on him.

Spirituality

Spirituality can be defined in many ways, even in both positive and negative terms. In positive terms Paul defines the Greek adjective *pneumatikos* (the Greek adjective "spiritual" has no abstract noun deriving from it) fundamentally as *pertaining to the Holy Spirit,* and to his presence, power, and activity. It is not usually used in the "Greek" way to denote *spiritual in contrast to material.* In 1 Cor. 2:6–3:4 "spiritual" *(pneumatikos)* clearly refers to revelation through the Holy Spirit who is "from God" (in contrast to the quasi-Stoic "spirit of the world," 2:12). "Unspiritual" (2:14) refers to those without gifts from the Holy Spirit, and "spiritual people" in 3:1 refers to those open to the transforming action of the Holy Spirit. The same contrast marks the resurrection mode of being. A "spiritual body" means a public (or less happily, "bodily") mode of life bestowed by the Holy Spirit (1 Cor. 15:44). Everywhere in Paul "the Spirit" denotes the person of the Holy Spirit, with rare exceptions.

Yet the term "spirituality" has come into vogue over the last fifty years to denote a concern for the realm beyond the world, sometimes in the most ambiguous and vague terms. From the point of view of the major Reformers, this use more than hints at "human religious aspiration," to the utter dismay of such theologians as Karl Barth. If we want to use this term, the Reformers and Barth might say, it has nothing to do with what humans may construct, but with God's self-revelation and action, as Paul indicates. Often the term is not specific to Christianity, but suggests some interreligious common ground. Pastorally, on the other hand, there may be a case for describing those who are aware that life involves more than material things under this term. Thus "spirituality" in the latter sense may well conflict with the biblical uses, but this does not mean that this use of the term is valueless.

Contrary to the popular view, however, even specialists in "spirituality" recognize that over the centuries respected theologians have expressed hostility to the term. In one classic on spirituality, *The Rule and Exercise of Holy Living*, Jeremy Taylor expressed a preference for the term "piety," although today this often has negative overtones. Many associated the term with mysticism. Sir Edwyn Hoskyns's translation of Barth's *Romans* deplored any involvement with either "spirituality" or "piety," especially by the Oxford Anglo-Catholics, arguing for the better term "devotion." A contemporary Australian archbishop lamented the fashion of speaking of "spirituality," commenting, "why not speak of *walk with God?*" Traditionally many Protestants have expressed suspicion with the mainly Catholic and medieval notion of an upward "journey," insisting that the grace of God "descends" in the reverse direction. Yet in *Pilgrim's Progress*, John Bunyan, the Baptist writer, undertakes a journey to the Celestial City. It seems that the issue is mainly one of definition, rather than of theological disagreement. The important caveat remains that the biblical use should not be flooded out by more recent and current popular attitudes. Most "objections" to the term could be anticipated by a strong emphasis on grace, and a more thoroughgoing intellectual critique of self-deception and any attempt to earn "merit." "Spirituality" must involve the whole person: intellect, emotions, and will.

The formation of all spirituality consists of prayer, and recognition that this is prompted not solely by the self but by the Holy Spirit (Rom. 8:15-17, 26-27). The role of mediation through Christ may be controversial, but is stressed in all "classics" of spirituality. The Word of God in some form must have a role. After this, spiritual classics may be found in all traditions of the church. Renewal literature offers many ways of overcoming spiritual dryness and liturgical formalism and routine. Evangelical spirituality can be found in William Law, who seeks to relativize "the bustle and hurry of the world." He stresses the difference between "saying prayers" and *praying,* in his *Serious Call to a Devout and Holy Life* (1729). John Wesley's *Journal* and Charles Wesley's hymns constitute another major aid to devotion. George Whitefield, Henry Venn, John Newton, and William Cowper are superb further examples, not least in their hymns.

At the Catholic end of the spectrum, the many devotional books of John Dalrymple are exceedingly useful aids to "spirituality," including *The Christian Affirmation* (London: Darton, Longman, Todd, 1971), on saying "yes" to God, and other works. He speaks of giving and receiving, prayer, constraints in life, fellowship, illness, and much else. Thomas Merton was a Catholic and a mystic who had been a Trappist monk; he wrote some seventy books. In 1944 he was accepted into the Franciscan Order, and became a priest in 1949. Many value his autobiographies *The Seven Story Mountain* (1948), *The Sign of Jonah* (1953), and *Day of a Stranger* (1981), while his biblical reflections include *Bread in the Wilderness* (1956) and *He*

Is Risen (1973). His meditations include *The Ascent to Truth* (1951) and *Contemplative Prayer* (1969). Some find these useful as "spirituality" books; others regret his hospitality to Buddhism. Many have found Brother Lawrence (c. 1605-1691), *The Practice of the Presence of God,* and the thought of many medieval mystics helpful.

Among other pre-Reformation works, many value Athanasius and the Desert Fathers. Some note that Walter Hilton was not only a mystic, but laid down practical cautions about mysticism, including the threat of self-deception. Julian of Norwich and Catherine of Siena have sometimes been found useful aids to devotion, although many have serious reservations about mysticism. It would be a pity if "spirituality" were monopolized by a single tradition, and the biblical meaning of the term should be given priority.

Reading: Louis Bouyer and Jean LeClercq, eds., *A History of Christian Spirituality,* 3 vols. (London: Burns and Oates, 1968-1982); William Law, *A Serious Call to a Devout and Holy life* (London: Dent; New York: Dutton, 1906); Robin Maas and Gabriel O. Donnell, O.P., eds., *Spiritual Traditions of the Contemporary Church* (Nashville: Abingdon, 1990); David MacCulloch, *Silence: A Christian History* (London: Allen Lane, 2013); Anthony C. Thiselton, *The Holy Spirit* (Grand Rapids: Eerdmans, 2013); Gordon S. Wakefield, ed., *A Dictionary of Christian Spirituality* (London: SCM, 1983), esp. 361-63; Rowan Williams, *The Wound of Knowledge* (London: Darton, Longman and Todd, 1990).

Stoics, Stoicism

The name is derived from Greek *stoa,* "porch" or "colonnade," where the Stoics of Athens used to meet. Zeno of Citium (c. 334-262 B.C.) is credited with being the founder of Stoicism. He was followed by Cleanthes and Chrysippus in the middle period (150-50 B.C.). The later Stoics were contemporaneous with the NT and the early Fathers. Divine reason *(logos)* gave order to the world, although a circular view of time suggested repeated universal conflagrations, and a repeated regeneration (Gk. *apokatastasis*) of all things. Humankind is a microcosm of divine reason, whose vocation is "to live in harmony with nature." The Stoic world-soul is pantheistic, and Paul dissociates the Spirit of God from world-soul, especially in 1 Cor. 2:11-13, where the Spirit is *from God* (Gk. *ek tou Theou*), not from the world. The popular version of Stoicism today is drawn from the Stoic ideal of self-sufficiency. Whereas biblical thought is largely communal, the Stoics were individualistic, as is much of the modern world. Their morals were often austere, giving an active role to conscience. Later Stoicism ranged from Seneca to Marcus Aurelius. The Epicureans constituted a rival school of philosophy and thought.

Strauss, David F.

David F. Strauss (1808-1874) was a pupil of F. C. Baur, and went to Berlin to study under Hegel. But Hegel died in the year of his arrival, and he reluctantly studied under Schleiermacher, whose work he regarded as too "churchly." When he was as young as twenty-seven, he published the first edition of *The Life of Jesus.* In this he expounded his celebrated (or notorious) notion of myth as ideas conveyed in the form of narrative. He denied any "supernatural" causality or dimension in the life of Jesus, and rejected the tradition of the unique figure of Jesus Christ. He severely attacked the miracle narratives, explaining them as contrived myths. His book shocked the church at the time, but also had a powerful effect on readers. In effect, it drove apart the notion of a "Christ of faith" from "the Jesus of history." Baur, however, criticized his work as a historian. As it did for Baur (at a later stage), Hegel's philosophy influenced the background of his work.

Strauss published a number of editions of his work, and in 1846 George Eliot translated into English the fourth edition of 1840. It thus brought an English readership, largely unfamiliar with German scholarship, into interaction with the Continent. In 1865 Strauss explicitly attacked Schleiermacher's work, and in 1872 produced *The Old Faith and the New,* which virtually denies and rejects the Christian faith.

Reading: H. Frei, "David Friedrich Strauss," in *Nineteenth Century Religious Thought in the West,* ed. N. Smart et al., vol. 1 (Cambridge: CUP, 1985), 215-60; Strauss, *The Life of Jesus, Critically Examined* (Philadelphia: Future Press, 1972).

Strawson, Peter F.

Peter F. Strawson (1919-2006) was Waynflete Professor of Metaphysical Philosophy in the University of Oxford from 1968 to 1987. His article "On Referring" (1950) criticized B. Russell's theory of descriptions, and used existential quantifiers that could bracket out Russell's descriptions. In 1952 he published his *Introduction to Logical Theory.* From the standpoint of theology, his *Individuals* (London: Matthew, 1959) is significant. He argues for the irreducible concept of "person" by an overlapping of "M" (material, bodily) predicates and "P" (supramaterial or personal) predicates. P. Ricoeur considers his work a modest but inadequate advance on questions of personhood, which lacked the ethical dimension of accountability.

Structuralism

Structuralism has no general, easily accepted definition. Its context in linguistics differs from its significance in social anthropology. However, most begin with its meaning in linguistics and the work of Ferdinand de Saussure (1857-1913). Saussure saw language *(la langue)* as a structure or system from which words of speech utterances were selected for use *(la parole).* The "whole" gives a word its meaning, whether by substitution or choice. The color word "orange," for example, derives its currency from being adjacent to red on one side and yellow on another. In social anthropology, there are parallels in the work of Claude Lévi-Strauss. Kinship terms derive their meaning or significance from an implied clan structure, or a total system of clan relations. Both contexts suggest that "meaning is difference," for example, between *sister* and *wife.* J. Trier states that, in his field of semantics, "Only as part of a whole . . . does a text yield a meaning, and only within a field." In literature the principle was taken up to suggest a "narrative grammar," gathered around binary oppositions. A. J. Greimas postulated the roles of hero and villain, helper and opponent, task and victory.

Biblical and theological scholars became enthusiastic about uncovering so-called deep structures in language and narrative. From a wider perspective, Roland Barthes revealed the significance of conventions and surprises in examples of biblical narrative. His work was even more successful in showing that systems of clothes or furniture did not simply serve comfort or convenience, but constituted disguised systems of social aspiration or class consciousness. His book *Mythologies* (London: Cape, 1972) readily shows the disguised but "deep" purpose of many myths and even advertisements. In the 1970s and 1980s, "structural analysis" became fashionable among academics, not least in the journal *Semeia*. David Patte, J. D. Crossan, Jean Calloud, Dan O. Via, and many others worked on this approach. But the energy and length of writings turned out to be disproportionate to the results. This may have happened because identifying "deep structures" behind language did not always elucidate meaning itself. Indeed, structural analysis was not intended to illuminate historical context or meaning directed from an author. In spite of a few spectacular successes, initial enthusiasm has died down. The movement is too disengaged from history to continue to attract many biblical scholars. Nor can structuralism claim the "objectivity" those disillusioned by the subjectivism of existentialism had tended to seek.

Subjectivity, Subject-Object Relation

Traditionally the subject-object relation stood at the heart of epistemology, or the theory of knowledge. Both the rationalists, Descartes and Leibniz, and the empiricists, Locke and Hume, presuppose a knowing subject who perceived or observed a passive object. This changed with the terminology and concerns of Kierkegaard. For him, subjectivity denoted being an active human being at every level. He defined subjectivity as "inner transformation . . . infinite passionate interest" (*Concluding Unscientific Postscript* [Princeton: Princeton University Press, 1974], 51). He continues, "Passion is subjectivity" (117). One of his best-known aphorisms is "Subjectivity is truth, subjectivity is reality" (306). He is utterly opposed to the notion that the elimination of the subjective is a virtue because it gives us an "objective" depiction of reality. Even before Kierkegaard, Kant showed that the human subject shapes and conditions cognition and what we count as "experience." Such categories as causation, he argued, are imposed upon phenomena by the human mind. With Kant, we pass beyond the simpler world of traditional rationalists and empiricists. With Kierkegaard, subjectivity implies self-involvement, or being sharpened into an "I."

Following Kierkegaard, a long line of theologians and philosophers develop and modify his notion of subjectivity, leaving the world of "objective" knowledge to the natural sciences only, if at all. In practice, Martin Buber, Martin Heidegger, Karl Jaspers, Rudolf Bultmann, and H.-G. Gadamer all modify but basically follow

Kierkegaard, although Barth has his own reasons for stressing God as Subject. Many reject Descartes's notion of an active subject scrutinizing a passive object. This has revolutionized hermeneutics and the reading of Scripture, where "analysis" and scrutiny alone have been largely replaced by *listening*. E. Fuchs declares, "The text has us as its object." Buber stresses both God and humankind as subject in his *I and Thou* (1923). In personal address two "subjects" address and respond to each other as subjects, not as things or objects. The human self must retain its status as an "I" and "Thou." Jaspers emphasizes human beings as fully conscious "subjects," free for actualizing possibilities. Heidegger prefers to speak of human beings as *Dasein*, being-there, situated in history and in time. Hence knowledge that is "objective" produces distortion. Even objects can be seen as what they are only in the light of *human* uses and purposes. A subjective understanding of time tells us more than mere chronological sequence and measurement.

In their earlier period of dialectical theology, Barth and Bultmann both stressed that theology and faith were not *about* God (as if God were a mere object of inquiry) but *from* God, especially as address, revelation, and response to such address. In his *Church Dogmatics* I/1, Barth asserts that God is "indissolubly Subject." Since all knowledge of God is through God alone, God is always active in initiating revelation (*see* **Barth, Karl**). Bultmann becomes his most emphatic in his work on hermeneutics. He declares, "The 'most subjective' *(subjectiviste)* interpretation is . . . the most objective *(objectiviste)*, that is, only those who are stirred by the question of their own existence can hear the claim which the text makes" ("Hermeneutics," in *Essays Philosophical and Theological* [London: SCM, 1955], 238; cf. 234-61; Ger. *Glauben und Verstehen*, 2:215). The understanding of a musical or mathematical text is not a purely "objective" matter; it involves a reader's prior knowledge of the subject. This outlook reveals itself in other works. In *The History of the Synoptic Tradition* and in *Kerygma and Myth*, Bultmann does not merely seek to reconstruct "objective" history, but takes account of the interests and concerns of readers in the first century and today. Gadamer attacks the whole project of Descartes and the Enlightenment. He is followed more moderately by Paul Ricoeur, who also stresses criticism. Paul Tillich seeks to move *beyond* any subject-object dichotomy, chiefly through his use of symbol. (*See also* **Kierkegaard, Søren; Tillich, Paul.**)

Reading: J. Brown, *Subject and Object in Modern Theology* (London: SCM, 1955); J. M. Robinson and J. B. Cobb, eds., *New Frontiers in Theology*, vol. 2, *The New Hermeneutic* (New York: Harper and Row, 1964), 22-39.

Subordinationism

Subordinationism in effect is said to regard the Son, or the Son and the Holy Spirit, as subordinate to God the Father. Some see trends toward this in Paul, where he says, "God is the head of Christ" (1 Cor. 11:3), and Christ "hands over the kingdom to God the Father . . . that God may be all in all" (1 Cor. 15:24, 28). But both of these passages are in 1 Corinthians; the Corinthians may well have made more of a familiar "cult Lord" *(Kurios)* Jesus Christ than a supposedly more shadowy and remote "God." In Romans and 1 Thessalonians, however, *God* remains prominent. Paul, the author of Hebrews, and John assert that Christ and the Holy Spirit alone with the Father belong to the *uncreated order* of beings. They are not "creatures." The Church Fathers soon stressed the coequality and codignity of Father, Son, and Spirit, and especially the inseparability of their work in creation and redemption. While one or two passages may appear to reflect hints of subordinationism, this is often to emphasize the transcendence and uniqueness of God as Father. (*See also* **God**.)

Substitution

Substitution becomes a large issue in theology especially in the context of the atonement. At first sight it may seem puzzling that the role of substitution is often so fiercely debated in this context. We can cite three reasons why it meets sometimes with fierce opposition, and four reasons why, whatever the understandable hesitations, the concept must be retained in a comprehensive account of the atonement.

(i) **Objections to the Concept.** (a) The strongest criticism is that "substitution" may lead to *lack of participation* in Christ's death. This may be understood as lack of adequate *identification* with Christ in the atonement, or even an undervaluing of "being in Christ," as if the beneficiary of Christ's atonement simply stands by and watches Christ standing in his or her place. This is the burden of the otherwise moderate writer D. E. H. Whiteley, who regards the atonement as operative "by virtue of our solidarity with him" (*The Theology of St. Paul* [Oxford: Blackwell, 1970], 130). His account of the atonement is "participatory" (132), and he criticizes the use of three classic "substitutionary" biblical passages: Rom. 8:3, 2 Cor. 5:21, and especially Gal. 3:13-14. He argues that they cannot sustain a doctrine of vicarious substitution. He challenges various exegetical details.

(b) On the basis sometimes of alleged parallels with child abuse, some see God the Father as "sending" Jesus to become a suffering substitute for others, while he gazes, almost uninvolved, at the substitutionary sacrifice. Supposedly he even turns his back when Jesus exclaims, "My God, my God, why have you forsaken me?" (Mark 15:34). This is a minority view, for J. Moltmann denies that the Father was free from active suffering (*The Trinity and the Kingdom of God* [London: SCM, 1981], 23-24). In the cross, he urges, God suffered "self-humiliation" (27). God gives himself (33). Moltmann writes, "A God who cannot suffer cannot love either" (38); "'God' is forsaken by God" (80).

(c) Much of the objection and criticism concerns the attempt to make substitution an *exclusive* model of the atonement. But as J. Jeremias argues, Paul and others use an increasing number of images to convey the truth of the atonement (*The Central Message of the New Testament* [London: SCM, 1965], 36). This objection remains valid only if the "substitution" approach is isolated as the only one.

(ii) **Retaining the Concept.** (a) The first reason to retain "substitution" in models of the atonement concerns the use of prepositions in the NT that help to explain the atonement. Greek usually uses one or more of three: *anti,* "instead of" (Mark 10:45; Matt. 20:28; cf. BDAG 87-88); *hyper* (or *huper*), "in or on behalf of, for the sake of" (1 Cor. 5:7; John 11:50-52; 18:14; Rom. 5:7; BDAG 1030-31); and *peri,* "concerning," or "for," especially in the phrase "atone for" (Rom. 8:3; 1 Pet. 3:18; Heb. 5:3; 10:8, 18, 26; cf. BDAG 798). *Anti* certainly means "instead of" in everyday Hellenistic Greek, and Mark 10:45, "The Son of Man came ... to give his life a ransom for *(anti)* many," can signify only substitution. *Hyper* may have a broader meaning, but "for the benefit of" often *includes* substitution implicitly. *Peri* is broadest of all in lexicographical terms, but has a narrower history when it functions in relation to an atoning sacrifice.

(b) One of the strongest arguments put forward in favor of retaining substitution is offered by J. K. S. Reid, in *Our Life in Christ* (London: SCM, 1963), 89-91. He first quotes P. T. Forsyth as saying, "He saved us by his difference from us." He then adds that in the atonement there is a *rule of correspondence:* "because he lives, we shall live also." But there is also "*a rule of contrariety:* Christ wins those benefits for us who had himself no need of them," that is, forgiveness, acquittal, and so on (90-91). This implies substitution.

(c) If Christ has substituted himself for us, this offers a clear assurance of salvation to a greater degree than participation. This is stressed especially in Luther and Calvin.

(d) Substitution concerns not only the death of Christ, but also his life (Jeremias, *Central Message,* 38). Jesus experienced special constraints in his life, which formed part of his sacrifice or offering. Further, it is not only an allegedly "past" historical act, but it initiates the eschatological situation of the believer.

All seven points cumulatively point to the importance of substitution as a major category that should not be underrated in studying the atonement. (*See also* **Atonement; Blood; Christology; Day of Atonement; Grace; Mediator, Mediation; Sacrifice.**)

Reading: Relevant books are listed under **Atonement**, and the entries cited above.

Supralapsarianism

Supralapsarianism relates predestination to the Fall *(lapsus)* of humankind. It holds that God predestined the elect and humankind *before* the Fall, in contrast to infralapsarianism, which holds that God's decree occurred *after* the Fall. Outside Calvinism, it is thought to be "harsher" than the second doctrine. But Calvin wished to exclude any idea of foreseen merit, and against accusations of injustice, insisted that God's will is eternal and inscrutable.

Symbol

Like metaphors, symbols point beyond themselves. But so do signs and sacraments, and Paul Tillich firmly distinguished symbols from signs. One particular understanding of symbols was mediated through C. G. Jung, K. Jaspers, and Tillich, and more recently developed through the sounder linguistic work of Paul Ricoeur. These writers do not use "symbol" as it is used in logic, often to denote a variable within a logical proposition. Sometimes in sociology and philosophy symbol has been linked with G. M. Mead and fellow American pragmatists. It may be correct that, as Tillich claimed, they resonate with the unconscious, but theologians are not committed to Jung's theories of the collective unconscious in the way that Tillich was. In Ernst Cassirer symbol may be associated with art. In Jung, symbol is a perpetual challenge to our thoughts and feelings, and grips us intensely. We use symbols, he wrote, "Because there are innumerable things beyond the range of human understanding" (*Man and His Symbols* [New York: Doubleday, 1971], 21). His own belief was that archetypal patterns generated them, and mediated them through humankind's collective unconscious.

If we seek to extract hard fact from speculative theory, Jung, Jaspers, and Tillich all seem to be correct in assigning integrative power to symbol. They can often integrate conscious and unconscious levels of the mind. Biblical symbols are more than explanatory metaphors. Symbolic uses of father, shepherd, savior, rock, redemption, or freedom resonate with deep longings hidden within the human heart. Jung and Ricoeur both stress the "double meaning" of symbols, which they share with the distinction between vehicle and tenor in metaphor. Tillich argued that they allow us to see the transcendent. He spoke of the symbol's "innate power . . . a power inherent within it that distinguishes it from a mere sign" ("The Religious Symbol," in *Religious Experience and Truth,* ed. S. Hook [Edinburgh: Oliver and Boyd, 1961], 3-11). He asserted, "Every symbol is two-edged. It opens up reality, and it opens the soul. . . . It opens up hidden depths of our own being" (*Theology of Culture* [New York: OUP, 1964], 57).

One of Ricoeur's most memorable sayings is "The symbol gives rise to thought" (*Freud and Philosophy* [New Haven: Yale University Press, 1970], 543). Like Tillich, Ricoeur took account of the *power* of symbols, but he also recognized the problem of an unbalanced *preoccupation* with *given* symbols. Hence he declared, "In our time we have not finished doing away with idols, and we have barely begun to listen to symbols" (27). In theology Ricoeur cited examples from the symbolism of evil: spot and stain, deviation and sin, burden and fault. In all these there is analogy between the symbol and the everyday or conventional meaning (17). Symbols, he insisted, are "not a non-language," but an enrichment of language (19). Like Tillich, he regarded symbols as *creative* (504).

Ricoeur admitted that metaphor has had a longer history than symbol. Hence the study of double meaning is better seen in the nature of metaphor. Yet in the history of religions, as M. Eliade argued, concrete entities such as trees, ladders, labyrinths, and mountains readily acquire significance as symbols (*Interpretation Theology* [Fort Worth: Texas Christian University Press, 1976], 53). Psychoanalysts often link these with psychic conflicts. But these "extensions of meaning" should only be used with care. People differ. A sunrise in a Wordsworth poem is more than a meteorological phenomenon. But to place weight on God as *Father* without balancing or complementary symbols may damage those who have experience of parental abuse. Symbols usually carry with them a "surplus of meaning" (55). Hence symbols "give rise to an endless exegesis" (57). Since they are rooted in people's experience, they require sensitivity and care. The hermeneutical issue turns on the *use* that we make of symbol, rather than simply on the symbol itself. Ricoeur was right to call attention to hymnic discourse in the Bible, which is a major source of symbolism (*Essays on Biblical Interpretation* [London: SPCK, 1981], 88-95). But apocalyptic, including the book of Revelation, should not be neglected. The seer writes, "The angel showed me the river of the water of life, bright as crystal. . . . On either side of the river is the tree of life . . . and the leaves of the tree are for the healing of the nations" (Rev. 22:1-2).

Synergism

Synergism (from Gk. *sunergeō*, "to engage in cooperative endeavor, to work together with") denotes the cooperation of the human will with divine grace. Loosely it is used in contrast to Augustine, Luther, and Calvin, who stress that humankind contributes nothing to their salvation. More strictly it denotes the less rigid position of Melanchthon that the human will cooperates with the Holy Spirit and with grace, although he still stressed that God's grace was the primary power, and thereby escaped the charge of Pelagianism.

Systematic Theology

Systematic theology draws on biblical studies (OT and NT), historical theology (from the Fathers to the modern era), church history, and philosophy of religion to present an ordered, coherent, and systematic theology, which has been carefully assessed and evaluated. It differs from dogma or dogmatic theology only in the explicit church context of dogmatics. In place of dogmatics systematic theology has become a more appropriate title for university or academic studies. It came into vogue in the eighteenth century. But many today suspect it of being tied to a given philosophical framework. Hence many proponents of the subdiscipline defend an "open" system, which is still capable of expansion and modification, while it still retains its ordered and ideally comprehensive status. An admirable model is W. Pannenberg, *Systematic Theology* (3 vols., 1991-1998), which demonstrates meticulous engagement with biblical and historical texts, as well as with relevant philosophy.

T

Tanner, Kathryn
Kathryn Tanner (b. 1957) is Frederick Marquand Professor of Systematic Theology at Yale Divinity School. She grew up in Pennsylvania, took her M.A. and Ph.D. from Yale, and has also been professor of theology at the University of Chicago. She serves on the theological committee of the House of Bishops in America, so it is understandable that, like the English thinkers P. Selby, D. F. Ford, and J. Welby, she is passionate about the relation between Christian theology and the current crisis in economics and financial markets.

In addition to her interests in the social sciences and economics, Tanner has written on other central themes in Christian theology. Her first major book, *God and Creation in Christian Theology* (Oxford: Blackwell, 1998), mainly explored a noncompetitive relation between God and his creatures. Her next book, *The Politics of God* (Philadelphia: Fortress, 1992), applied this noncompetitive relationship to the sphere of politics. She has also written *Theories of Culture* (1997) and, more especially, *Economies of Grace* (Philadelphia: Fortress, 2005). It is in this book that she passionately explores the relationship between the grace of God and financial markets and economic systems. Her latest book is *Christ the Key* (Cambridge: CUP, 2010), in which she argues for the centrality of Christ. She urges that the hypostatic union of Christ's natures invites all of humanity to participate in, and to share, the divine life. God's relation to the world, the Holy Trinity, and the atonement are addressed in her exposition of Christology. God and the world remain distinct, but through the incarnation and through Christ as the Word of God, participation in God becomes possible. She does not shrink from declaring Christ's divinity (56).

Taylor, Jeremy
Jeremy Taylor (1613-1667) is best remembered for his books *The Rule and Exercises of Holy Dying* and *The Rule and Exercises of Holy Living* (1650). He graduated from Gonville and Caius College, Cambridge, in 1630, where he became a fellow. Under the patronage of Archbishop Laud, he became chaplain to Charles I and in the royalist army. He suffered imprisonment under Cromwell, and after the Restoration became vice-chancellor of the University of Dublin. Taylor argues, "God is everywhere present by His power.... He guides all creatures with His eye.... God is present at your breathings and hearty sighings of prayer." He made practical observations in holiness of life and humility.

Reading: C. H. Sisson, ed., *Jeremy Taylor: Selected Writings* (Manchester: Carcanet Press, 1990).

Teilhard de Chardin, Pierre

Pierre Teilhard de Chardin (1881-1955) was a French Jesuit theologian and scientist. He also worked in China and the USA. His most influential book was *The Phenomenon of Man* (Fr. 1955; Eng. New York: Harper; London: Collins, 1959). He was an original thinker who cannot be fitted into any predetermined category. On one side, his book depicts the surging evolution of the world and the universe; on the other side, it is a visionary speculation about the End. It seeks to combine the physical world with a vision concerning spirit. He uses the notion of *convergence* to denote the upward tendency of humankind. But he also speaks of *"complexification,"* that is, increasingly elaborate organizational structures. This process involves "cellular organisation" and chromosomes (95-96), but also consciousness (329). Convergence may result in "Omega," or an "Omega Point" (316-20), which is the ultimate at the end of ever-higher levels of consciousness. The end of a "materially exhausted planet" will be "the liberation of that percentage of the universe which . . . will have succeeded in synthesising itself to the very end" (317). This is clearly a speculative, rather than conventional, eschatology. Teilhard also wrote *The Future of Man* (Fr. 1959; Eng. 1964).

Teleological Argument

The teleological argument for the existence of God is one of the three such classic arguments, together with the cosmological and ontological arguments. A fourth approach uses the moral argument. The teleological argument is known as the argument from design or purpose (Gk. *telos*), and is often said to depend on the validity of the cosmological argument, as Hume argued. Kant did not accept the validity of the argument as such, because he believed that the human mind imposes "order" onto the world. But he asserted that it deserves respect, because it is the oldest, clearest, and most accordant with the common reason of humankind (*Critique of Pure Reason* [1788; Eng. London: Macmillan, 1933], chap. 3, sect. 6). Many trace it possibly to Anaxagoras (c. 499-422 B.C.), and certainly to Plato (428-348 B.C.) and Aristotle (384-322 B.C.). Thence it features in Augustine and especially in Thomas Aquinas as the fifth of his "Five Ways."

William Paley established the most basic form of the argument. His anecdotal analogy is well known: "In crossing a heath . . . I found a watch upon the ground. . . . When we came to inspect the watch, we perceive that its several parts are formed and put together for a purpose, e.g. that they are so formed and adjusted as to produce motion, and the motion so regulated as to point out the hour of the day" (*Natural Theology, or Evidences of the Existence and Attributes of the Deity* [1802; Oxford: OUP, 2006], chap. 1, sect. 2). He draws parallel conclusions from the complexity of the human eye. This, it can be argued, depends on Aristotle's notion of final cause, and on Aquinas's argument known as his "fifth way," from "the guidedness of nature" (Lat. *ex gubernatione rerum*). Aquinas uses another traditional analogy, namely, the archer. An archer directs an arrow toward the target; it does not reach the target by accident. Such mechanisms abound in nature. Paley suggests that the argument remains convincing even if the watch is faulty, or if we have never seen the watchmaker. Paley was educated at Christ's College, Cambridge, and became fellow and tutor there. He lectured on Joseph Butler and John Locke. In 1782 he became archdeacon of Carlisle. The bishops of London, Durham, and Lincoln gave him cathedral stalls or benefices, which provided together a very large income, as a reward for his *Evidences*.

David Hume had died before the publication of Paley's *Evidences,* but his work *The Dialogue concerning Natural Religion* (1779) virtually anticipated Paley's argument, and attacked it. In the *Dialogue* Hume's character "Cleanthes" represents Paley's type of argument; "Demea" represents an orthodox theist; while "Philo" represents a skeptic, whose position is probably akin to Hume's. Philo argues that if Cleanthes infers a Designer, he could equally infer a plurality of designers. Moreover, the notion of a "watch" or any mechanism offers no more than an analogy to the creation of the world. We *observe* not cause, but constant conjunction. Although he did not share Hume's view in general, Kant agreed with Hume that the teleological argument depends on the cosmological "proof," and insisted that order or design is read "into" nature by the human mind.

A more serious attack on Paley's argument, however, came with Charles Darwin's theory of evolution by natural selection. *The Origin of Species* appeared in 1859. Hegel had prepared the way for a "developmental" approach to the world, and later Herbert Spencer would urge "the survival of the fittest" in biology and ethics. Romanticism also replaced a mechanistic model of the world by a more organic one. After those changes, many no longer argued that the eye was designed to give sight; rather, because the eye developed in an evolutionary process, organisms that could see survived over those that could not. Rather than arguing that "God filled all things living with plenteousness," it was argued that creatures that could not find "plenteousness" were those that died. "Plenteousness" was a condition of life. Today the evolutionary principle is evidenced in genetic mutation. We must also take some account of certain processes that seem to have no purpose (*see* **Dysteleology**). Nature is often "Red in tooth and claw." Analogies such as the beehive could be countered by the "cruelty" of predators in nature.

F. R. Tennant, although he wrote in 1930, is often credited as one of the most sophisticated teleologists of the early twentieth century. He wrote, "The sting of Darwinianism . . . lay in the suggestion that proximate and 'mechanical' causes were sufficient to produce the adaptations from which the theology of the eighteenth century had argued to God" (*Philosophical Theology,* 2 vols. [Cambridge: CUP, 1930], 2:84). However, theists today do not seem to mind rejecting Paley's specific argument, as long as they may retain his conclusions. We need not set out from the particular adaptations in individual organisms. Tennant writes: "The survival of the fittest presupposes the arrival of the fit, and throws no light thereupon.... Room is left for the possibility that variation is externally predetermined or guided" (85). Theism, he insists, is "indifferent to the banishment of the Paleyan types of teleology" (85). R. Swinburne seems similarly to exchange an argument from micro-adaptation to a more general notion of order (*The Existence of God* [Oxford: Clarendon, 1979], 134-40). We can do better, Swinburne claims, "than to rely on the older arguments. We need to appeal only to regularities of succession. This would be wiser than the men of the eighteenth century." This "better" appeals to "order in the world." Scientific inquiry and theology are *complementary, rather than competitive.* This is the argument of Malcolm Jeeves, *Minds, Brains, Souls, and Gods* (Downers Grove, Ill.: IVP Academic, 2013).

More recently John Polkinghorne, among many others, has considered Maxwell's equations, quantum theory, electromagnetism, and the replication of molecules, and in that light concludes, "For me, the beauty that is revealed in the structure of the world was like a rehabilitation of the argument from design — not as a knockdown argument for the existence of God . . . but as an insight into the way the world is" (*The Way the World Is* [London: SPCK/Triangle, 1992], 12). Earlier Polkinghorne wrote, "The essential character of the objective world is not sensibility but intelligibility" (11). We are capable of *understanding* the world. We can speak of the interplay of chance and necessity only because new things can happen within the frame of regular laws of nature. Polkinghorne also addresses the "delicate and intricate balance in its [the world's] structure necessary for the emergence of life" (12). The vastness of the universe provides one such condition; a long duration of time provides another. Like Tennant, Swinburne, and Jeeves, Polkinghorne expounds the *different levels* of descriptions of the world. Explorations in physics may operate on one level, but the melody produced by an orchestra operates on another level. We must look for the *preconditions* of purpose and order that lie behind "scientific" explanations of certain processes.

Reading: Brian Davies, ed., *Philosophy of Religion* (Oxford: OUP, 2000), 245-303; John Polkinghorne, *The Way the World Is* (London: SPCK, 1992); John Polkinghorne, *Science and Theology* (Philadelphia: Fortress; London: SPCK, 1998); Eleonore Stump and M. J. Murray, eds., *Philosophy of Religion* (Malden, Mass., and Oxford: Blackwell, 1999), 61-65, 94-138; R. Swinburne, *The Existence of God* (Oxford: Clarendon, 1979; rev. ed. 1991); David Wilkinson, *Christian Eschatology and the Physical Universe* (London: Continuum and T. & T. Clark, 2010).

Temple. *See* Judaism

Temptation

"Temptation" (Heb. *massah;* Gk. *peirasmos;* verb, *peirazō*) raises at least two problems. First, does it refer to *trial* or *testing,* especially the eschatological trial, or to the regular, virtually daily experience of *temptation?* Greek *peirazō* can mean either of these. Second, is testing or temptation *positive* or *negative?* James 1:2 declares, "Whenever you face trials of any kind, consider it nothing but joy" (NRSV), and "Count it all joy when you fall into divers temptations" (KJV/AV). Such "testing," James continues, "produces endurance" (1:3 NRSV). 1 Peter asserts that "trials" and "testing" show "the genuineness of your faith ... more precious than gold" (1 Pet. 1:6-7). Similarly, the Holy Spirit "drives" (Gk. *ekballei*) Jesus into the wilderness to be tempted by Satan (Mark 1:12; with parallels Matt. 4:1 and Luke 4:1). Paul declares that "testing" (NRSV) or "temptation" (KJV/AV) is common to being human, as God will provide a way forward (1 Cor. 10:13). Ernst Käsemann, the NT scholar, calls it "the locus of faith" (*New Testament Questions of Today* [London: SCM, 1969], 117). Luther makes much of the role of struggle (*Anfechtung*) for faith. Yet on the negative side, Jesus teaches, "Do not bring us to the time of trial" (NRSV) or "Lead us not into temptation" (KJV/AV; Matt. 6:13; Luke 11:4; Gk. *mē eisenenkēs hēmas eis perasmon*, in both parallels). He urges the disciples, "Pray that you may not come into the time of trial" (NRSV), or "Pray that ye enter not into temptation" (KJV/AV, Matt. 26:41). Hebrews seems to cover both senses (Heb. 2:18; 3:9; 11:37).

The meaning of *peirazō* cannot be determined for all contexts on the basis of lexicography alone. Danker (BDAG 79-93) suggests four meanings for *peirazō*: (i) "to make an effort to do something," "try," "attempt"; (ii) "to endeavour to discover the nature or character of something by testing"; (iii) "to put to the test"; and (iv) "to entice to improper behaviour." The latter sometimes recurs with *ho peirazōn*, "the tempter," for example, in Matt. 4:3 and 1 Thess. 3:5. Ernst Lohmeyer, *The Lord's Prayer* (London: Collins; New York: Harper and Row, 1965) favors "temptation" in the context of the Lord's Prayer (193-208). He finds other references for "temptation" in Matt. 26:41, James 1:13, Ecclus. 44:20, and elsewhere. Yet he acknowledges that the concept of temptation is "varied," and reflects on "the numerous themes which appear in Old Testament and Jewish writings" (197). Heinrich Seesemann also appears to accept "temptation" as appropriate in many contexts, especially the temptations of Jesus (Matt. 4:1-11 and parallels), in Gethsemane (Mark 14:32-42), and in James and 1 Peter (*TDNT* 6:28-36). He also understands the Lord's Prayer to signify "temptation," and regards it as a "mistake" to interpret it in the light of the imminent expectation of the End. "A more general application to all affliction yields a better sense" (31). On the other hand, it is a mistake to invoke God's omniscience as an argument against "testing," for if this is a *disposition*, the response to testing emerges *only* when it is *actualized* in a response to testing.

In the petition in the Lord's Prayer, Jesus is not advocating a withdrawal from the world, or what Alex Richardson called "cloistered virtue." He agrees with James and others that blessing comes from struggle. This is intimately connected with whether sanctification is regarded as involving a long process, often with prolonged struggle, or alternatively as an instantaneous "event." It was against this assumption by the Radical Reformers that Luther (and later Käsemann) insisted that temptation or *Anfechtung* builds a sanctified character. The Holy Spirit "drives" (Mark) or "leads" (Matthew) Jesus into the wilderness to be tempted or tested. Each temptation (Matt. 4:3, 5-6, 8-9) admittedly concerned messianic ends, but the issue was whether these were to be fulfilled in the way that God purposed. This was to be through obedience and suffering, not through spectacular populist miracles, or divided loyalties. Hebrews indicates that these three were not the only messianic temptations or trials: Jesus needed to "trust" God (Heb. 2:13), and was "in every respect . . . tested (or tempted) as we are, yet without sin" (4:15). Nevertheless, in Richardson's language, we are urged to pray, "Keep us away from situations fraught with moral peril, where our resistance might be broken down." It is a prayer against overconfidence and arrogance. In most circumstances, Luther and Käsemann are right: "Temptation is the locus of faith" (117).

Teresa of Ávila

Teresa of Ávila (1515-1582) was a Spanish Carmelite nun who was a mystic. She speaks of the journey of the soul, often in symbols and pictures. In 1555 she experienced something like a second conversion, which led to a radically ascetic life, and contributed to her writing *The Way of Perfection* (begun in 1562). Her most famous work is *Interior Castle,* in which the soul rises through "assaults of the devils" (1.13). Eventually it reaches "a supreme state of ecstasy" (4.18). In the seventh stage the Holy Trinity reveals itself. Teresa elaborates the imagery of the castle: it has rooms, garden fountains, and labyrinths. Her writings, however, remain Christ-centered. She collaborated with John of the Cross. Many Reformers understood the "upward" journey of mystics as undermining the "downward" grace of God, but Teresa maintains a Christ-centered theology.

Tertullian

Tertullian (c. 150–c. 225) was born and educated in Carthage, where he also practiced law. By at least 197, when he was in middle life, he had undergone a conversion from paganism to Christianity. Much of his subsequent work attacked Gnosticism, Marcion, and Praxeas. He produced probably more works than any other Christian writer of the third century, of which more than thirty survive. He is the first Christian thinker to write extensively in Latin. His more philosophical works include his treatise *On the Soul,* which was strongly influenced by Stoicism, and his treatise *Against Praxeas.* He comments, "Reason has taught us its [the soul's] corporeal nature" (*On the Soul* 9). However, Tertullian did not reject all philosophy. As we have noted, he was influenced by Stoicism, but made the point that the biblical and apostolic tradition must not be compromised. One of his most memorable sayings was "What has Jerusalem to do with Athens?" (*Prescriptions against Heretics* 7). He was a rigorous ascetic. He wrote various apologetic works, and some polemical ones, as in his work *Against Marcion.* Marcion had rejected the unity of the two Testaments, and postulated a dualism between the God of Jesus Christ and the God of the Old Testament. Tertullian also wrote ethical treatises, including *On Idolatry, On Repentance,* and *On the Veiling of Women.*

Sometime between 203 and 207 Tertullian espoused Montanism. At that time he had written about half of his writings. These included works on baptism, on the rule of faith, on creation, and on the Holy Spirit. With reference to the Trinity, he formulated the sentence "The Holy Spirit proceeds from no other source than from the Father through the Son" (*Against Praxeas* 4). To many his asceticism seemed to border on perfectionism and the notion of a "pure" church, like the later Donatists. He wrote with passion, especially in his polemical works, and in his Montanist period he expected a speedy outpouring of the Holy Spirit on the church. Also during his Montanist period, he attracted two women disciples, Prisca and Maximilla, who gathered a movement that expanded from Phrygia to North Africa, and called themselves "Spirit-filled." On the other hand, they described mainline Christians as "psychicals," or "ordinary" Christians. Maximilla declared, "After me, [there is] no prophet more, but the End" (R. E. Heine, *The Montanist Oracles* [Macon: Mercer University Press, 1989], 163-69). Others referred to the movement as "the New Prophecy." Eusebius claimed this movement had an "arrogant" spirit, which "reviles the entire universal Church" with "false prophecy" (*Church History* 5.16). Some stress the connection between Montanism and the positive face of feminism. S. Burgess calls the movement the first Pentecostal theology (*The Holy Spirit* [Peabody, Mass.: Hendrickson, 1984], 63). Attitudes range from highly critical to cautiously sympathetic. J. Wesley was at first critical, then became sympathetic to it.

Theism
Theism stands in contrast to Deism and pantheism. In theism God is both transcendent and immanent. Theism did not arise, however, as a reaction *against* Deism or pantheism, but from God's revelation of himself to Abraham and to Israel. Judaism, Christianity, and Islam are all theistic faiths. Unlike Deists, most theists believe that God created the world because he loves it, and that he therefore also engages with the world. Theism is also distinguished from atheism, which denies the existence of God, and agnosticism, which regards the question of God's existence as unanswerable. Typically the term is used in philosophy of religion rather than in religion or theology.

Theodore of Mopsuestia
Theodore of Mopsuestia (350-428) was a biblical exegete and theologian from the Antiochene School. He was a friend of John Chrysostom, and studied with him under Diodore in Antioch. He became bishop of Mopsuestia in 392, and established a reputation for learning and for producing commentaries.

Theodoret
Theodoret (393-458) was primarily an exegete. He was born in Syrian Antioch, gave away his property to serve the poor, and entered the monastic life. In 423 he was made bishop of Cyrrhus, against his personal inclination. He became involved in the christological controversy between Nestorius and Cyril of Alexandria, de-

fending "Antiochene" Christology. He did not go as far as Nestorius, but he attacked Cyril, insisting on a clear distinction between the two natures of Christ, and even suggesting a "mixed union" of natures. The Council of Ephesus (449) sought to exile him. His OT exegesis was highly valued, and he was a capable administrator of his diocese.

Theological Positivism
Theological positivism is almost equivalent to fideism. It rejects any claim to be built upon metaphysics or philosophy as a foundation. Karl Barth, for example, insisted on basing his dogmatic theology exclusively on God's self-revelation through his Word as Christ, Scripture, and the church's kerygma, but he would reject the name fideism.

Theology of Crisis
Theology of crisis describes dialectic theology during the period of the Weimar Republic between the end of the First World War (1919) and the beginning of the rise of Hitler (1933). It was initiated by the early writings of Barth, including his *Commentary on Romans,* his essays published in *The Word of God and the Word of Man,* and *The Resurrection of the Dead.* For a limited period Bultmann shared this approach, which was shared by E. Thurneysen. K. J. Kuschel ascribes the phenomenon to the social, religious, and political context of the times. God comes "vertically from above" without continuity with humankind. The movement shares Kierkegaard's view of reason in his *Either/Or.* Christianity, Kierkegaard argues, presents humans with a decision. The Word of God comes to humankind without human preparation or human readiness. Kuschel compares this with the development of quantum theory between 1924 and 1927 by Niels Bohr and W. Heisenberg. We cannot predict outcomes with certainty. Classical physics and liberal theology were being shattered during this period. Even in literature and music we see "the disintegration of the self and destruction of reality," and in physics and in theology "the recognition of non-objectifiability" (Kuschel, *Born Before All Time?* [London: SCM, 1992], 79). Barth saw only a "no" of judgment on the old creation, and "yes" on the new.

Tillich, Paul
Paul Tillich (1886-1965) resists easy labeling or categorization. He attacks "the cheap and clumsy way of dividing theologians into ... liberal or orthodox as an easy way of shelving somebody" (*The Protestant Era* [Chicago: University of Chicago Press, 1948; London: Nisbet, 1951], ix-x). He sees himself as an apologist, whose theology constitutes an "answering theology" (*Systematic Theology,* 3 vols. [Chicago: University of Chicago Press; London: Nisbet, 1953, 1957, 1963], 1:6). He writes, "Most of my writings ... try to define the way in which Christianity is related to secular culture" (*Theology of Culture* [Oxford: OUP, 1964], vi). He was a controversial figure, inviting T. M. Greene's description of him as the most

enlightening and therapeutic theologian of our time, or J. H. Randall's evaluation of him as the ablest Protestant theologian of the time; and, equally, Kenneth Hamilton's denunciation of him as teaching little more than atheism. He was open to many influences: to Romanticism and Schleiermacher; to Christianity and art; but above all to Carl Jung and his depth psychology of the symbol.

Tillich was born and bred in Prussia, and became professor in Frankfurt. But his opposition to Hitler led to his dismissal from his chair. Reinhold Niebuhr, however, secured for him an invitation to the USA, where he spent sixteen years at Union Theological Seminary, New York, subsequently moving to Harvard from 1955 to 1962. He eventually retired to Chicago, where he remained until his death. His publications are numerous. The most important is his *Systematic Theology*. A popular book for unbelievers was *The Courage to Be* (1952), while *The Shaking of the Foundations* (1948) comprised sermons mainly for believers. Other theological works included *The Protestant Era* (1957), *Dynamics of Faith* (1957), *The Theology of Culture* (1964), *Ultimate Concern* (1965), and *On the Boundary* (1967).

Tillich's *"answering theology"* is also known as a *theology of correlation*. His *Systematic Theology* seeks to offer a correlation between five fundamental questions and five "answers." The first volume begins with questions about human reason, and seeks answers in terms of revelation. Then he raises questions about "Being," and answers them in terms of symbols that point to God. In the second volume he asks questions about concrete existence, or the existential situation of humankind, and offers answers that relate to Jesus Christ as the New Being. In the third volume, Tillich asks questions about the ambiguities of human life, and finds "answers" in terms of the action of the Holy Spirit, or the Spirit. Finally, he asks questions about the meaning of history and suggests a correlative "answer" in terms of the kingdom of God. Sometimes we have put "answers" in quotation marks, because whether these genuinely rank as open questions and real answers has been disputed by those who see the relation between question and answer as too heavily one of mutual influence. But Tillich insists that "the method of correlation... makes an analysis of the human situation... and it demonstrates that the symbols used in the Christian message are the answers to these questions" (*Systematic Theology*, 1:70).

There is no doubt that in analyzing the human situation Tillich captures human anxieties about fate and death, emptiness and meaninglessness, guilt and condemnation. But do these attitudes reach beyond the 1940s, and do they pervade America as well as Europe and Germany (*The Courage to Be* [London: Collins, 1977], 37-59)? Perhaps more far-reaching is his work on "answering" symbol, which points beyond itself and beyond the penultimate, to the genuine Ultimate, which we call God. Because the ultimate "God" lies beyond the "god" of our human formulations, Tillich sees a call for "Protestantism" to become "a new form of Christianity... not yet named" ("Autobiographical Reflections," in *The Theology of Paul Tillich*, ed. Charles W. Kegley and R. W. Bretall [New York: Macmillan, 1964], 8). The ultimate is to be located only in God, not in a book (the Bible), not in formulations of doctrine, not in the church or its sacraments. These are *pen*ultimates. Where many other theologians would have spoken of *faith,* Tillich speaks of *Ultimate Concern.* "God" is the name for what concerns us ultimately. "It means that whatever concerns a man ultimately becomes god for him" (*Systematic Theology,* 1:42). "Protestant theology protests in the name of the Protestant principle against the identification of our ultimate concern with any creation of the church, including the Biblical writings" (42). Hence, Tillich concludes, *"The object of theology is what concerns us ultimately"* (15). This has an immediate pastoral, evangelistic, or apologetic application. Tillich bids the inquirer who seeks God to seek this Ultimate beyond "god" of the penultimate. If we imagine that we have hurled "him out of our consciousness . . . ultimately we know that it is not he whom we reject and forget, but that it is rather some distorted picture of him" (*The Shaking of the Foundations* [New York: Scribner, 1948], 49).

This brings us to Tillich's central concern about symbols, which owes much to the psychology of Carl Jung. He writes that religious symbols are "a representation of that which is unconditionally beyond the conceptual sphere" ("The Religious Symbol," in *Religious Experience and Truth,* ed. S. Hook [Edinburgh, 1962], 303). Like Jung, Tillich believes that humanity suffers from a decay of images and symbols. For symbols integrate the conscious and unconscious. He writes, "The centre of my theological doctrine of knowledge is the concept of the symbol" (in Hook, 3). Symbols, however, point beyond themselves, as Jesus Christ pointed away from himself to God. Symbols also "participate in" that to which they point. This makes them different from mere signs. They also open up levels of reality, as well as the human mind. He appeals to poetry and to art to make this point, as Heidegger did in his later thought. Symbols grow out of the collective unconscious and can operate with enormous power.

Hence symbols may point to "God," who is "beyond god." They enable us to emphasize God's transcendence or otherness. Like Dietrich Bonhoeffer, he asserts: "A god whom we can easily bear, a god from whom we do not have to hide, a god whom we do not hate in moments . . . is not God at all" (*Shaking,* 50). "God" is bound up with "Ultimate Concern," which can refer both to the attitude of faith and to the divine object of faith. Like Schleiermacher on "consciousness of dependence," and like Rudolf Otto on the holy or numinous, this human attitude of ultimate concern is always directed *toward* the Ultimate.

This possible ambiguity brings us back to Tillich's work as an apologist. He sees himself as producing a theology of mediation. In his book *On the Boundary* he seeks to stand on the boundary between philosophy and theology, between culture and religion, between socialism and Lutheranism, between German and American thought, between village and city, and so on. Indeed, for him compartmentalism and fragmentation are symbols of the fallenness of humankind, and are "demonic." But again, some question whether this is genuine mediation. He writes, "Every theologian is committed and alienated; he is always in faith and doubt; he is inside and outside the theological circle" (*Systematic Theology,* 1:13).

Moreover, his "philosophy" is largely that of Heidegger and existentialism. The contribution of Anglo-American philosophy is relatively small. Many would see his early years in Germany as decisive for his thought, including his defense of socialism (e.g., *The Socialist Decision* [1933]).

In volume 2 of *Systematic Theology* Tillich's existential questions about emptiness and meaninglessness seem to point to *Christ* as the *New Being*. Apart from Christ "there is no point in time and space in which created goodness was actualised" (2:50). The world can be characterized by "estrangement," in which "man in the totality of his being turns away from God. . . . He turns toward himself and his world" (54). This "tragic self-destruction followed *hubris*. . . . Man identifies his cultural creativity with divine creativity" (58). Disruption and fragmentation follow, and lead to doubt and meaninglessness (83). Finally, humanity experiences insecurity and despair. The use of "the" historical method to arrive at a picture of Jesus, however, introduces "a dangerous insecurity . . . complete scepticism" (130). Tillich introduces "the New Being" but cannot guarantee that his name is Jesus of Nazareth (131). Here we enter the realm of "the risk of faith" (134). What is important to Tillich is the symbolic value of "existence," including Christ's subjection to it, and "the relation of the Christ to . . . his conquest of it" (176). There is great uncertainty about the historical Jesus.

In the third volume of his *Systematic Theology*, Tillich considers the multidimensional nature of human life, and therefore also its ambiguities. This applies no less to religion. In relation to this ambiguity, even the divine self-manifestation "becomes not only great, but also small, not only divine, but also demonic" (3:117). But the Spirit makes possible "self-transcendence," in which the ultimate and unconditional grasps the self (119). The Spirit may bring "ecstasy," in the sense of standing out of, or above, oneself. God does not become an "object," but "we can only pray to the God who prays to himself through us" (127). This is effected by the Spirit, who was given to Jesus Christ. The Eastern Church allows for "a theocentric mysticism"; the Western Church insists on a "Christocentric criterion" of the Spirit (158-59). But in all this, "Doubt is unavoidable as long as there is separation of subject and object" (254).

In the second part of volume 3 Tillich turns to life and history, and to the quest for the kingdom of God. Jesus Christ is the center of history only in a *metaphorical* sense. The "preexistence" of Christ points only to his potential presence in all periods of history (390). The *kairos*, or moment of opportunity, brought by Christ relates to all moments of personal involvement (395). But the kingdom of God represents the struggle against polarization and demonization. The churches, with all their ambiguities, are in a sense part of "the world" (409). On the other hand, God's kingdom brings integration, the *Telos*, and the glory of God (419). Tillich looks for "the dynamic-creative interpretation of the symbol 'Kingdom of God'" (423). He adds: "Eternal blessedness is not a state of immovable perfection . . . the Divine Life is blessedness through fight and victory" (431). But, once again, we have only the language of symbols to express it.

It is understandable that Tillich had admirers but also many critics. On one side, he is original, distinctive, and thought-provoking, and presents a view of God that is compatible with his apologetics. On the other hand, because he removes "God" from the realm of contingent existence (or engagement with the world), he comes out with such statements as "To argue that God exists is to deny him" (*Systematic Theology*, 1:227), and he has been accused of atheism. Tillich is so concerned to show solidarity with a variety of standpoints that some conclude that he has sacrificed too much, and that he departs too radically from Christian tradition. In pastoral terms, some find his concern for a God "beyond god" very helpful, and many find insights in his sermons, *The Shaking of the Foundations*. Tillich does write differently for different readerships.

Reading: Thomas J. Heywood, *Paul Tillich: An Appraisal* (Philadelphia: Westminster; London: SCM, 1963); Charles W. Kegley and R. W. Bretall, eds., *The Theology of Paul Tillich* (New York: Macmillan, 1964); P. Tillich, *The Protestant Era* (Chicago: University of Chicago Press, 1948; London: Nisbet, 1951); P. Tillich, *Systematic Theology*, 3 vols. (Chicago: University of Chicago Press; London: Nisbet, 1953, 1957, 1963); P. Tillich, *Dynamics of Faith* (New York: Harper and Row, 1957); P. Tillich, *On the Boundary* (New York: Scribner, 1966); P. Tillich, *The Courage to Be* (London: Collins, 1977).

Time

In everyday life we are entirely familiar with chronological time, otherwise known as clock time, or as astronomical time, measured by the rotation of the earth and other celestial bodies. Philosophers often call this objective time. It can be measured by instruments. The philosopher Martin Heidegger, however, pointed out that objective time is very different from our perception of time as a subjective experience. We may speak of "time for a leisured walk," or "time for a conversation," or "time to perform a task," and these may vary objectively, but fit certain human purposes.

Gérald Genette, the literary critic, went further and spoke of "narrative time." It is well known that in a detective story, the narrator often uses such devices as "flashbacks," slow motion, and rapid time to shape a plot. If we began chronologically with the crime, and proceeded as events unfolded, there would be no suspense, and the story would become impossible. The Gospel of Mark uses narrative time of three different speeds. It begins by rapidly rushing on until Peter's confession of Sonship and Messiahship, then slows down, and finally portrays the passion and the cross in slow motion. Thereby it shows that the aim and meaning of the whole narrative concern the passion and cross.

In addition to the contrast between clock time, subjective time, and narrative time, another version of subjective time has usually been called "sociological time," "social" time, or human time. The sociologists Robert Lauer and Alvin Troffler point out that a measure of social rank or control arises from the human time-tabling of time, and the use of appointments and diaries. Units of time, or periodicity, may be allocated for tasks, for leisure, and for rest, together with the speed at which tasks reach completion. Employers and trade unions may debate which organization of human time may benefit whom. An employee "waits" for the time of appointment with a boss. "The right time" for a discussion is seldom a matter of clock time or chronology.

The immediate point to be drawn is that time in the Bible is not always chronological time. It is sometimes naïve and gauche to describe different timings, for example, in the four Gospels, as "inconsistent," as if some failed to portray chronological time accurately. Time is not a "thing"; it concerns the relation between chronology and human perceptions and purposes.

In philosophy it has long been debated whether time is "real." Immanuel Kant saw time as a device that made it possible for the human mind to assign order and intelligibility to what humans perceive. Some took this to an extreme, as when the philosopher F. H. Bradley claimed that time was unreal. In response, G. E. Moore asked why, in that case, it should matter if we take lunch before breakfast. Many post-Einsteinian scientists point out that the speed of time, in human experience, varies in accord with the speed of travel of the observer. Stephen Hawking argues that as we come closer to the origin of the universe, the nature of time changes. Indeed, time may melt away until we reach a point where there is no time. In this light, it becomes unduly simplistic to talk about what might precede "the beginning of time," or what might follow the "end" of time. As long ago as the fifth century, Augustine declared that God did not create the world "in" time, but created it "with" time. Quantum theory adds great complexity to more naïve theories of time.

Among biblical scholars and various religions, debates have occurred about the linear and cyclical nature of time. Oscar Cullmann struck a keynote in his book *Christ and Time* (1951) in stressing that the Bible largely presupposed linear time, to allow room for divine purpose, and a redemptive divine plan that entailed "stages of the redemptive history." He argues both for a continuous linear time *(chronos)* and for special moments of opportunity *(kairos)*. Nevertheless, it is too simple to suggest that this is an *alternative* to cyclical time. For within the unfolding of linear time there occurs the cyclical experience of nature around the year. Christians celebrate the great festivals of Christmas, Easter, the Ascension, and Pentecost, even if some dates are contrived. Jesus celebrated the Passover, and Christians, Jews, and Muslims celebrate the Sabbath, even if the chronological day of the week varies. The combination of linear time (great overall purposes) and cyclical time (festivals and remembrances) provides both purposive order and times of review and refreshment. In physics the phenomenon of entropy (loss of total energy) seems to confirm the irreversible and unidirectional nature of time.

For Christians the experience that makes sense of this draws on prophecy and promise, accountability and faithfulness. These become vital links of continuity between past, present, and future. Sometimes, as Pannenberg stresses, the future, or the realization of promise, may take unexpected and surprising forms. Human identity, especially in terms of accountability (as in Paul Ricoeur), depends on the relation between past and future. There is every reason to believe that the next stage "beyond" time will not be "timelessness," but a new experience of a new kind of time (*see* **Eternity**).

Reading: O. Cullmann, *Christ and Time* (London: SCM, 1951); C. Sherover, *The Human Experience of Time* (New York: New York University Press, 1975); A. C. Thiselton and others, *The Hermeneutics of Promise* (Grand Rapids: Eerdmans, 1999), 183-91.

Tongues, Speaking in. *See* **Glossolalia**

Torrance, Thomas Forsyth
Thomas Forsyth Torrance (1913-2007) was born in China of missionary parents, educated at the University of Edinburgh, and ordained to the Church of Scotland ministry in 1940. He undertook doctoral studies under Karl Barth, and entered parish ministry in Aberdeen. He became professor of church history in Edinburgh in 1950, and was professor of Christian dogmatics there from 1952 until 1979. He was appointed moderator of the Church of Scotland in 1976, and was awarded the Templeton Prize for Progress in Religion in 1979. For nearly thirty years he coedited the *Scottish Journal of Theology,* and he translated Calvin's NT commentaries as well as Barth's multivolume *Church Dogmatics.*

The 1960s and early 1970s were a period of theological controversy. Writers such as J. A. T. Robinson were calling for a "new reformation" on behalf of neoliberalism, while Torrance called for "a new reformation" on behalf of Reformed theology. In his major work, *Theology in Reconstruction* (London: SCM, 1965; Grand Rapids: Eerdmans, 1966), he expounded the central themes of Reformed theology: revelation and knowledge of God, the atonement, the Holy Spirit, and a central theme of Christian orthodoxy, Nicene Christology. In his introductory chapter he discusses the problems of scientific evidentialism (14-17), language and reality (17-21), and interpretation, or hermeneutics, and history (21-29). He then turns to the role of analogy in the Church Fathers, and its significance for Christology (30-45). The rest of the book expounds orthodox theology, Calvin, Barth, justification, and the doctrine of grace (150-92). The final chapter discusses the issue of a new reformation (259-83).

Among his remarkably numerous publications, Torrance's *Theological Science* (London and New York: OUP, 1969) stands as a masterpiece. Theological science, he argues, differs from natural science, not least because God is no mere object within the universe. Following Barth, he warns us in his preface, "Whenever religion is substituted in the place of God [we should be cautious. For] *in religion we are concerned with the behaviour of religious people*" (viii), so this is bound to focus on humankind rather than on God. Barth, he urges, is to be understood as "a rethinking and re-stating of Reformed Theology" (8). Knowledge of God, whatever our misunderstanding of Barth may be, remains "a rational event" (11). Knowledge of God is conceptual (13); but these concepts are "open," not closed, and can be "clipped onto propositional ideas" (15). Theological statements relate to hearing, objectivity, and possibility (22-26, 35-39). God makes himself known "in his divine otherness" (53). Torrance compares the primacy of God as object with "scientific objectivity," which entails simply "disinterested truth" (75). There is a parallel with the Reformers' "repentant readiness to rethink all preconceptions and presuppositions" (75). Yet the Reformation emphasis on "for me" too readily became a preoccupation with "me" (81). By contrast, theological knowledge shows submission to the mastery of the truth. Torrance discusses the massive change that has come through "the theory of relativity and quantum mechanics" (92). For example, as A. Eddington and M. Polanyi show, a personal factor now inevitably enters into scientific knowledge. In Heisenberg we see "the interplay between nature and ourselves" (95).

This leads to a discussion of scientific method. He expresses reservations about Descartes and dualism, and respect for Einstein and Oppenheimer on chaotic diversity and complementarity (110-11). Like Gadamer and Collingwood, Torrance expounds the value of questions for opening the way to new knowledge. But where natural science stresses discovery, theology stresses revelation (131). Torrance also advocates the value of dialogue. But again, in theology, what is all-determinative is Christ (138). Torrance then discusses the nature of truth with particular reference to Christ. There is an interconnection between propositions and judgments (163). Experience statements must be related to coherence statements. We must "wait upon the Truth" (195). Problems of logic require questions and the use of analogy (228). Torrance engages with Wittgenstein and Waismann. His final chapter discusses special sciences and theology. In both areas inquiry is important (286), but we cannot impose concepts drawn from one field onto the other. In both, "objectivity and relativity fall together" (297). Theology expresses the covenantal relationship of the community of believers with God (350).

Torrance explores many of these issues further in his *God and Rationality* (London and New York: OUP, 1971). He addresses theological rationality and the call for "objective" knowledge and for care in uses of language; explains "the eclipse of God" in much modern theology; and discusses the "disastrous consequences" of cutting away "the intervention of God with the world" (49). He compares cheap grace and costly grace, especially with reference to Bonhoeffer (73-79). The central chapter returns to theology and science, and additionally to hermeneutics. In other contexts Torrance also addresses ecumenism. These themes focus on further specialization in the thought of Torrance. He has a remarkable knowledge of advances in the natural sciences, and also addresses questions of ecumenism. He had demonstrated the former especially in his book *Space, Time, and Incarnation* (1969), and would write further in *Christian Theology and Scientific Culture* (1988). The latter was addressed in his *Theology of Reconciliation: Essays toward Evangelical and Catholic Unity in East and West* (Grand Rapids:

Eerdmans, 1976). Among his later writings, *The Trinitarian Faith* (Edinburgh: T. & T. Clark, 1995) traces the formulation of Trinitarian theology especially in the Fathers, relating "the Almighty Creator," "the Incarnate Saviour," and "the Eternal Spirit" as the one God.

Torrance has been extraordinarily influential not only in defending orthodoxy and Reformed theology, but also in exploring issues of method, and the relationship between Christian theology and the natural sciences. He also did much to rescue the reputation of Karl Barth in an era when Barth was, largely through misunderstanding, becoming unfashionable. Like Barth, his theology centers especially in God, Christ, and the Trinity. Daniel Hardy in his essay "Thomas Torrance," in *The Modern Theologians*, ed. D. F. Ford, 3rd ed. (Oxford: Blackwell, 2005), observes: "We await someone who can, as Torrance did with Barth, stand on Torrance's shoulders and promote a cognitive account of the basis of Christian Theology ... in response to the changing understanding both of the sciences and theology" (176). (*See also* **Christology; God, Trinity; Hermeneutics; Reformed Theology; Science and Religion.**)

Reading: Daniel Hardy, "Thomas Torrance," in *The Modern Theologians*, ed. D. F. Ford, 3rd ed. (Oxford: Blackwell, 2005), 163-78; A. E. McGrath, *T. F. Torrance: An Intellectual Biography* (New York and London: T. & T. Clark, 2006); T. F. Torrance, *Theology in Reconstruction* (London: SCM, 1965; Grand Rapids: Eerdmans, 1966); T. F. Torrance, *Theological Science* (London and New York: OUP, 1969); T. F. Torrance, *Theology and Reconciliation* (Grand Rapids: Eerdmans, 1976); T. F. Torrance, *The Trinitarian Faith* (Edinburgh: T. & T. Clark, 1995).

Tractarianism

The term denotes the earliest stage of the Oxford Movement from 1833 to 1841. The movement began with J. Keble's sermon on "national apostasy," which attacked the government's decision to suppress ten Irish bishoprics. This was seen as political interference, an attempt to shape the church of the apostles. A series of tracts were then written entitled *Tracts for the Time*, of which J. H. Newman wrote three in 1833 in defense of apostolic succession. Other writers included Keble and R. H. Froude. What began as brief pamphlets became theological treatises. Newman's famous tract 90 on parts of the Thirty-nine Articles and his conversion to Roman Catholicism ended the series in 1841. (*See also* **Anglo-Catholic.**)

Tracy, David

David Tracy (b. 1939) is widely noted for his three major books, *Blessed Rage for Order* (New York: Seabury Press, 1975), *The Analogical Imagination* (London: SCM, 1981), and *Plurality and Ambiguity* (San Francisco: Harper and Row, 1987). Currently he is Distinguished Service Emeritus Professor of Catholic Studies and Professor of Theology and Philosophy of Religion in the University of Chicago. He has also written *Christianity, Theology, and the Culture of Pluralism,* and other works. He has taught a wide range of subjects in theology, but especially systematic theology and hermeneutics. It is significant that the term "pluralism" occurs in the subtitles or titles of these four books. Whether or not he would use the term "liberal Catholic," he aims at liberating an older Catholic tradition to address the contemporary age.

In *Blessed Rage for Order,* Tracy first addresses "the pluralist context of contemporary theology" (3-21). He then surveys five "basic models" in contemporary theology, including orthodox, liberal, neoorthodox, radical, and revisionist models. Like so many books and lectures, he chooses the last, and approves "the method of correlation," as used by Tillich and others. The rest of the book largely concerns religious language, God, and hermeneutics. *The Analogical Imagination* promisingly considers the thesis of systematic theology as hermeneutical (99-187), and picks out Gadamer's notion of the hermeneutical role of "the classic." For "classics" we "recognise nothing less than the disclosure of a reality we cannot but name truth" (108). We "enter a 'game' where truth is at stake" (113, Gadamer's analogy). As a revisionist, he suggests, he is compelled to think again (117). "A claim that transcends any context forms my pre-understanding" (119). Like Jauss, he speaks of "provoking expectations and questions in the readers" (179). Like Gadamer, he speaks of "effective history" (155). *Plurality and Ambiguity* has been called "a brief, clear explanation of postmodern hermeneutics," and a practical application of hermeneutics. Again, like Gadamer and Jauss, he finds *questions* to be of the utmost importance.

Some may argue that important hermeneutical questions from Germany have simply been transmitted to America in "radical" or "revisionist" forms. That part of Tracy's work seems to convey a now dated ethos, compared with a more vigorous and confident theology today.

Tradition

"Tradition" (Gk. *paradosis*) can be used to denote everything that is handed down from the beginning in Christianity, including gospel, doctrine, ethics, church order, and practice. In the Church Fathers it characteristically denotes what is handed down from apostles publicly. The term was sometimes used to denote an alternative source to Scripture, but virtually all sides recognize today that this is not the use of the early church. It simply did not set the two sources in opposition or contrast, as has sometimes been the case in specific periods of church history.

Paradosis occurs thirteen times in the NT, nine of which refer to halakha, or rabbinic elaboration of the Law. Three denote Christian traditions, for example, the tradition Paul received *(parelabon)* and transmitted *(paredōka)* about the Lord's Supper (1 Cor. 11:23) and the resurrection (1 Cor. 15:3). Other NT passages refer to the idea without explicitly using the term *paradosis* (Luke 1:2; Rom. 6:17; 2 Pet. 1:21; Jude 3). Four classic modern treatments include R. P. C. Hanson, *Tradition in the Early Church* (London: SCM, 1962), and C. H. Dodd, *The Apostolic Preaching and Its Developments* (London, 1936); and from a Catholic viewpoint

J. P. Mackey, *The Modern Theology of Tradition* (New York: Herder, 1962), and Y. Congar, *Tradition and Traditions* (Fr. Paris, 1960). O. Cullmann sees an analogy between Christian tradition and halakha in Judaism (*The Earliest Church* [1956] and *The Earliest Christian Confessions* [1949]). He also emphasizes the role of the apostles in originating and mediating the tradition.

By the time of the early Church Fathers, the concept of the apostolic tradition or "the rule of faith" had become prominent in Irenaeus, Tertullian, Hippolytus, and Origen. Irenaeus gives an account of the rule of faith in *Against Heresies* 1.2, 3.4.1, and 4.53.1, that is, at least three times. These include belief in the one God as Creator; belief in Jesus Christ and his becoming man for us and suffering crucifixion for us; and in 4.53.1 belief in the Spirit of God, who gives us knowledge of the truth. In 3.4.1 creation also occurs "through" the Son. In Irenaeus, in contrast to the Gnostic notion of a "secret" tradition, this tradition remains *public,* and open to rational discussion. Tertullian also conveys a similar tradition or "rule of faith," at least three times (*Against Praxeas* 2; *On the Prescription of Heresies* 13.1-6; and *On the Veiling of Virgins* 1.3). The first two "rules of faith" are Trinitarian. Hippolytus includes the tradition of the apostles in *Against Noetus* 17 and 18. During the third century, Hanson writes, "tradition" *(paradosis)* meant three things: the teaching of the apostles; the doctrine handed down by succession in the churches; and ecclesiastical practices handed on by custom (94).

Since the 1970s the reliability of oral tradition in NT times was first stressed by G. N. Stanton, *Jesus in New Testament Preaching,* in contrast to Bultmann's claims about its fluidity. More recently Richard Bauckham has done much to establish the validity of early oral tradition in *Jesus and the Eyewitnesses* (Grand Rapids: Eerdmans, 2006) and in *The Testimony of the Beloved Disciple* (2007). He also calls attention to oral tradition in B. Gerdhardsson, *Memory and Manuscript* (Uppsala: Almqvist & Wiksell, 1961), and in W. H. Kelber's work on orality.

Traducianism

Traducianism is the theory or doctrine that the soul is transmitted down the generations from parents to children. It is most famously connected with Tertullian. Among the Church Fathers, it stands in contrast to the dominant view that is usually called creationism, and to Origen's belief in the preexistence of the soul. Tertullian expounds it in *On the Soul* 23-41, esp. 37 (*ANF* 3:218). Augustine considered it an explanation for original sin (*Epistle to Jerome* 166; chaps. 1–17). But some suggest that it perhaps rests on an unbiblical dualism of body and soul, rather than on their unity. Some Lutherans have held it, and it had a brief revival in the nineteenth century. A. H. Strong commended it (*Systematic Theology* [London: Pickering and Inglis, 1907], 493-97), and C. Hodge discusses it (*Systematic Theology,* vol. 2 [Grand Rapids: Eerdmans; New York: Scribner, 1871], 68-70). It was condemned by Pope Anastasius II in 498, and is rejected by the majority of Protestants.

Transcendence

"Transcendence" must not be confused with the term "transcendental." "Transcendence" usually applies to God to denote that God is beyond or above the universe. He is not to be equated with the universe, which would be the case in pantheism. Transcendence is usually contrasted with the immanence of God (*see* **God, Trinity: God Creates, Speaks, or Reveals; Acts in Transcendence and Immanence**). "Transcendental," by contrast, is a philosophical term deriving from Kant's exploration of the *possibility* of knowledge, and its grounds or basis. Among theologians of the nineteenth and twentieth century, Kierkegaard and Barth stress divine transcendence. The famous vision in Isaiah 6 provides a good example: the seraphim call God "Holy, holy, holy" and cover their faces; Isaiah sees himself "lost, for I am a man of unclean lips" (Isa. 6:2, 3, 5). Abraham declares that he hesitates to make a request to God: "Who am I but dust and ashes?" In the words of Barth and Otto, God is "wholly other." Transcendence is secondarily used of self-transcendence, when a person rises above, or transcends, the ordinary or natural. Jaspers and Tillich use the term in this way. The transcendence of God also excludes the world from being an emanation of God. Although it stands in contrast to immanence, it is not incompatible with it. Indeed, in the Bible the transcendent and holy God not only sustains the world but also loves his creatures, and has communion with them.

Transcendental

The term must not be confused with "transcendent." The two terms are different. Transcendental philosophy was mainly introduced by Kant and concerns the *possibility* of knowledge. Whereas the rationalists and empiricists had asked, "What do we know?" Kant asked, "What *conditions* are necessary for the *possibility* of knowledge, thought, or reason?" "Transcendental" denotes what human experience presupposed, not what is derived from experience. Aristotle had hinted at such a concept; Fichte and Hegel developed it further. Schleiermacher utilized it, and more recently it has an importance for Rahner and others.

Trent, Council of

The Council of Trent (1545-1563) was an attempt to express, shape, or control the Roman Catholic Counter-Reformation. In early sessions (1545-1547) the council affirmed the sole right of the church to interpret the Bible and asserted the authority of the Vulgate. It also affirmed that all seven sacraments were instituted by Christ. But political tension between Charles V and the pope hindered progress. The second session (1551-1552) reaffirmed transubstantiation and rejected the views of Luther, Calvin, and Zwingli on eucharistic theology (*see* **Lord's Supper**). The third session (1562-1563) was largely dominated by the Jesuits. The eucharistic presence of Christ in the elements was asserted, and the Mass, baptism, confirmation, marriage, ordination, penance, and the last rites were reaffirmed as the seven sacraments. In general, the council strengthened the theological tradition of Aquinas. Clerical seminaries were established, and purgatory and other issues received attention.

Trinity, the Holy

It is unnecessary to repeat the biblical and historical material that is set out in the entry **God, Trinity**. However, we may emphasize three points that emerge from that article. First, a narrative approach to the Holy Trinity, especially in terms of the biblical material, has proved to be an intelligible way to present the doctrine of the Trinity to a congregation or class. As Pannenberg, Moltmann, and Rogers point out, at every critical point in the narrative of Jesus all three persons of the Trinity are involved. This is evident above all in the baptism of Jesus: the Son is obedient to the Father; the Father commissions and blesses the Son; the Holy Spirit visibly descends and equips him for the messianic temptations. Second, as Gregory of Nazianzus and Gregory of Nyssa insist, "three" has nothing to do with numerals or numbers, which apply only to created beings or things. Analogies designed to explain "three" are mistaken and misleading. Third, as Athanasius, Basil, Gregory of Nyssa, Gregory of Nazianzus, Hilary, and Ambrose all argue, *all persons of the Trinity* work together in every act of creation, redemption, and salvation, even if one appears the most prominent in different events. This saves a misunderstanding about the atonement. "In Christ God was reconciling the world to himself" (2 Cor. 5:19). There is nothing theoretical about the doctrine of the Trinity. It is at the heart of Christian doctrine, life, and faith, and is intensely pastoral and practical. (*See also* **God, Trinity**. G. Emory has also edited the *Oxford Handbook to the Trinity* [Oxford: OUP, 2011], with numerous articles.)

Troeltsch, Ernst

Ernst Troeltsch (1865-1923) was a German liberal theologian, and a leading figure in the history of religions school. Adopting a strictly historical approach to theology and religion, he paid special attention to the social forms and contexts of Christianity, working closely with Max Weber. This resulted in his substantial work *The Social Teaching of the Christian Churches* (1912; Eng., 2 vols., 1931). His theological outlook was influenced by A. Ritschl, and his hermeneutics and sociology by W. Dilthey. He tended to relativize the Christian religion, especially in *Christian Thought: Its History and Application* (1923). In effect, he applied sociological theory to theology.

Tutu, Desmond

Desmond Tutu (b. 1931) was born in South Africa and educated at St. Peter's Theological College, Rosettenville, and Kings College, London. In 1975 he became the first black Anglican dean of Johannesburg, and became bishop of Johannesburg in 1985. He was appointed archbishop of Cape Town in 1986. In 1989 he led a protest march against apartheid, and conferred with Nelson Mandela and F. W. de Klerk. In 1995 he was appointed chair of the Truth and Reconciliation Commission. In 2009 he received the Presidential Medal of Freedom from President Obama, and in 2013 the Templeton Prize.

Desmond Tutu strongly supports the concept of *Ubuntu,* usually defined in South Africa as stressing community, redemption, civil order, and humanism. Tutu believes that only through their relation to others do people achieve full humanity. He wrote, "A person with *Ubuntu* is open and available to others, does not feel threatened that others are able and good" (*No Future without Forgiveness* [1999]). He stated, "You can't exist as a human being in isolation." In Christian theology, Zizioulas, Lossky, and Ricoeur, among others, have similarly defined human personhood in terms of relationality and accountability.

Tyconius

Tyconius (d. c. 390-400) was mainly significant for his influence on Augustine, especially through his *Book of Rules* on biblical interpretation, and his commentary on Revelation. He was also a Donatist, embroiled in the controversies of Cyprian and Carthage. Augustine sums up his principle of biblical interpretation in *On Christian Doctrine.* Tyconius was especially interested in symbolic numerology and apocalyptic.

Tyndale, William

William Tyndale (c. 1494-1536) was one of the major Reformers and translators of the Bible. He was born in Gloucestershire and studied at Oxford and Cambridge. About 1522 he began to translate the Bible. He had a lifelong passion that ordinary people should be able to read the Bible in their own tongue, which had hitherto been impossible. But with the opposition of Bishop Tunstall of London, he traveled to do his work in Hamburg. He continued to translate at Antwerp, frequently revising his translation. Much of his thought followed Luther, especially on the authority of the Bible. On the Lord's Supper he tended to follow Zwingli. He wrote on Romans (1526) and on Christian obedience (1528). He also wrote against Wolsey and Henry VIII's divorce. He was a first-class linguist, using the Greek text of Erasmus. He completed his translation of the NT from Greek, and most of the OT from Hebrew. His work is strongly reflected in the KJV/AV and the RV. Many of his standard phrases have entered the English language. We are indebted to Tyndale, for example, for "let there be light, and there was light"; "my brother's keeper"; "the Lord bless thee, and keep thee: the Lord make his face shine upon thee"; "the salt of the earth"; "the powers that be"; "filthy lucre"; and "fight the good fight." On the authority of the Bible he stressed the effects of Scripture, and anticipated what we call speech act theory, setting out at least fourteen actions the reading of the Bible performed. For example, it appointed, it liberated, it blessed, it enacted promises, and so on. Like Luther, he emphasized the Word of God as promise. Henry VIII remained hostile to Luther and Tyndale, and at that early stage to the translation of the Bible. Ultimately Henry ensured that Tyndale never returned to England, and that he suffered martyrdom in Belgium by being burned at the stake.

Typology

Typology "is the interpreting of an *event* belonging to the present or recent past as the fulfilment of a similar situation recorded or prophesied in Scripture" (R. P. C. Hanson, *Allegory and Event* [London: SCM, 1959], 7). It is difficult to improve on this definition. Hanson emphasizes the role of an "event" or "object or person" in typology with that of ideas in allegory. In an allegory, Hanson argues, the contrast or comparison is not between events, but between *"ideas."* Events involve historical occurrences. Given this definition, Leonhard Goppelt is correct to assert: "Typology is the method of biblical interpretation that is characteristic of the New Testament.... Typology and typological method have been part of the church's exegesis and hermeneutics from the very beginning" (*Typos* [Grand Rapids: Eerdmans, 1982], 4). Paul was the first to use the Greek *typos*, "type," or the adverb *typikōs* (or *tupikōs*) of the events of Israel's wanderings in the wilderness and the church's current experiences in 1 Cor. 10:6, 11. This usage thereafter became firmly established in Barnabas, Hermas, and Justin. But the word *typos* was not used in the LXX or in Philo with this particular meaning, although it meant more generally a pattern or model (BDAG 1019-20, second meaning). It primarily meant "a mark made as the result of a blow or pressure," from *typtō*, "to inflict a blow," to "strike."

Certainly Jewish writers, including Philo, had used *allegorical* interpretation, and after the subapostolic era, Alexandrian writers, including Clement and Origen, used allegory freely. Heb. 7:1-3 appears to apply the unique status of Melchizedek to Christ in this way, which Hanson attributes to its Alexandrian context (83). The *Epistle of Barnabas* uses allegorizations of ceremonial law, and allegorizations of the 318 persons circumcised by Abraham as a prediction of the cross (99). Hanson argues, however, that there are instances of allegory in the *Didachē*, but perhaps traces of typology in the eucharistic prayer of *Did.* 9.2. Justin has abundant examples of allegorical interpretation (Hanson, *Allegory*, 105-10), followed by Irenaeus (110-13), Clement (113-20), and Origen (133-86). Andrew Louth stoutly defends the use of allegory in his essay "Return to Allegory," in *Discerning the Mystery* (Oxford: Clarendon, 1983), 96-131. Allegory is certainly not "dishonest" (97), nor "a way of obfuscation" (111), but is profoundly theological (122-31). Louth rightly cites de Lubac as an ally, especially in his *Medieval Exegesis* (Edinburgh: T. & T. Clark; Grand Rapids: Eerdmans, 2000). More open to controversy, however, is the blurring of the distinction between allegory and typology. Louth calls typology a word "of very recent coinage from about 1840," and argues that "types" are "not simply events, but the stories of events" (118). This opposes the verdict of Hanson and Goppelt.

Hanson, Goppelt, and F. F. Bruce take care to distinguish the two, and the historical dimension of typology is not so easily dismissed, mainly on the strength of an appeal to de Lubac and Daniélou. Goppelt may well agree about the "deeper meaning" of both, but the historical dimension does provide limits to what the OT is believed to presage, or the NT and the church to expound. (*See also* **Allegory, Allegorical Interpretation; Analogy; Hermeneutics; Symbol.**)

U

Ubuntu. See **Tutu, Desmond**

Ultramontanism
Ultramontanism aims at the centralization of the authority of the papacy and papal Curia. It derives from the Latin "beyond the mountains," when Catholics north of the Alps disputed the scope of the pope's authority. The term was originally used pejoratively in the seventeenth and eighteenth centuries. But in the nineteenth century it was used as a positive term by those who sought more power for the papacy, as opposed to the local authority of bishops or nations. The Jesuits, Pope Pius IX, and the First Vatican Council supported papal infallibility, influence, and power. In reaction against this, some northern Catholics broke with Rome.

Unitarianism
Unitarianism denotes a form of Christian or religious belief that rejects the doctrine of the Trinity (*see* **God, Trinity**). Some anticipated it even before Socinianism and the Minor Reformed Church in Poland. The *Racovian Catechism* (1605) was the first formal statement of Unitarian doctrine. The movement was suppressed in Poland but spread to parts of Europe, especially Britain. In the seventeenth century John Riddle published *Against the Deity of the Holy Spirit,* and Stephen Nye wrote *A Brief History of Unitarians* in 1687. Many General Baptists (*see* **Baptist Theology**) became Unitarians in the eighteenth century, and the first Unitarian Chapel in Britain was founded in London. An early theological thinker was James Martineau (1805-1900). W. E. Channing (1780-1842) in effect led the movement in America. Unitarians stress the unity of God, rejecting the status of the Son and the Spirit as separate persons from God. They usually regard Jesus as completely human, and the Spirit as a subpersonal force.

Universalism
Today it has become increasingly frequent not to defend "dogmatic universalism" but to defend "hoped-for universalism." The former asserts that "we know" that all will be saved. The latter declares, "We do not know, but we *hope* that all will be saved." It is well known that in the nineteenth century F. D. Maurice was ejected from his chair of theology at King's College, London, on the ground of

his universalism. But Maurice had expressed universalism as a *possibility*, not as a *certainty*. Today Roman Catholic theologians Hans Urs von Balthasar and Karl Rahner, among others, have formulated universalism as a hope. Among Protestant theologians, N. T. Wright, former bishop of Durham, rejects the two extreme positions of everlasting torment and "dogmatic universalism" (*Surprised by Hope* [London: SPCK, 2007], 177-98).

In the patristic era three views were dominant. (i) Origen and Gregory of Nyssa believed in the restoration of all things. B. E. Daley comments, "For Origen universal salvation is an indispensable part of the 'end' promises by Paul in 1 Cor. 15:24-28, when Christ will destroy all his enemies, even death" (*The Hope of the Early Church* [Cambridge: CUP, 1991], 58; cf. *De principiis* 2.3.7). Gregory declares, "Error may be corrected, and what was dead [is] restored to life" (*Catechism* 25). (ii) Irenaeus argues that life is a gift from God. Hence, "Those who separate themselves from God face loss of the gift of life" (*Against Heresies* 5.18.1). (iii) John Chrysostom and Augustine believe that hell is "not temporary" (Chrysostom, *Homilies on 2 Thessalonians,* hom. 2 and 3). Augustine writes, "The soul . . . is tormented. In that penal and everlasting punishment . . . the soul is justly said to die" (*City of God* 13.2).

Today the first and second views are widely represented among theologians. The Church of England Doctrine Commission asserted in 1995 that hell is an affirmation of the reality of freedom. The commission declared, "Dogmatic universalism contradicts the very nature of love. . . . Love cannot compel the surrender of a simple heart that holds out against it" (*The Mystery of Salvation* [London: Church House, 1995], 198). On the other hand, Jürgen Moltmann regards anything less than universalism as a defeat for the sovereign grace of God. If this possibility occurred, "God would not be God" (*Sun of Righteousness, Arise!* [London: SCM, 2010], 141). The universal glorification of God, he asserts, necessitates "universal reconciliation" (141). (*See also* **Eschatology; Hell; Resurrection of the Dead.**)

Universals

Universals are generalized abstractions such as "redness," "whiteness," or "roundness." Plato spoke not of "universals," but of forms or ideas. Those who support "universals" argue that individual particulars are only instantiations of universals in time and space.

V

Vatican I
The First Vatican Council (1869-1870) was called by Pope Pius IX in 1868, and held in Rome. It was the period of the "Ultramontanites," who pressed for the centralization and influence of the papal Curia, and opposed liberalism, semi-independent orders in the Roman Church, and trends toward the independence of nations, especially from the pope. This majority group sought to strengthen the power of the pope and the definition of papal infallibility. A strong supporter of this group was H. E. Cardinal Manning of Westminster. A supposedly more "liberal" or progressive group, however, was represented by J. I. von Döllinger in Bavaria, and J. H. Newman in England. Between 700 and 800 bishops attended. The draft *(schema) De Fide* attacked rationalism, naturalism, and materialism. The *schema Dei Filius* expounded traditional teaching on revelation, faith, creation, and other doctrines. *Pastor Aeternus* underlined papal infallibility, in spite of some explicit opposition. A debate on papal infallibility lasted for some time, concluding with 451 *"placets"* and 88 *"non-placets"*; but in the end it was formally affirmed for those occasions when the pope speaks *ex cathedra*. Further debate was interrupted by the Franco-Prussian War. A minority in Germany and Austria rejected some conclusions and formed the "Old Catholic" Church.

Vatican II
The Second Vatican Council constituted a watershed in Roman Catholic thought, and ushered in a new era. It was held from October 1962 to December 1965, and was convened at the initiative of Pope John XXIII (1958-1963). John announced this intention in July 1959, and held preparatory commissions beginning in June 1960. It aimed to renew the church and its vision, and to initiate a dialogue with other churches to promote Christian unity. About 2,600 bishops attended the congregation of the council. Over 200 theologians served as consultants, including Karl Rahner, Yves Congar, and Hans Küng. After the death of Pope John in September 1963, Pope Paul VI presided over proceedings. About a third of the delegates came from Europe, about a third from the Americas, and a third from Africa, Asia, and Australasia. Much of the outcome was due to meticulous preparation and global representation. Pope John urged the council at the beginning not merely to reaffirm traditional teaching, but to proclaim the faith afresh to a new generation. In the event, the council was both pastoral

and doctrinal. The debates and findings of the council were divided into four "constitutions" as follows.

(1) *The Constitution on the Sacred Liturgies (Sacrosanctum Concilium)* reflected profoundly on the nature of liturgy, worship, and the sacraments, especially the Eucharist. Its conclusions advocated concelebration (copresidency or cocelebration) and the administration of both bread and wine (A. P. Flannery, ed., *Documents of Vatican II* [Grand Rapids: Eerdmans, 1975], 1-282, esp. 57-60, dated March 1965). Its work included sacred liturgy (3.2), the Mass (2.3.2), worship (2.2), and pastoral directions about the use of music in Catholic worship. Music in worship might now be not in *Latin only* but in the *vernacular* (80-87). But the documents still asserted *transubstantiation* (104; *see* **Lord's Supper**), although the constitution also stressed the *priesthood of all the faithful* and the "ministerial priesthood" (110). Predictably the council affirmed the *reserved sacrament* (130) and the wearing by the presiding priest of the chasuble and stole (197). *Masses for the dead* were also authorized (205). It also considered "social communication," and stressed attention to public opinion, and the intelligible preaching of the gospel, including the use of films and other means of communication. Part 2 focused on the media (301-29).

(2) A second constitution was called *Dogmatic Constitution in the Church* (350-440), or *Lumen Gentium,* after the first words of this section (November 1964; 3.3.2, 1-5). In this the church was described as a "sacrament — a sign and instrument... of communion with God" (350). This signified a great breakthrough, as Pannenberg and others saw it, suggesting that the church was not an end in itself, but a pointer to communion with God, although, as all Christians would affirm, it can also convey grace. *Lumen Gentium* also affirms "the collegiate character and structure of Episcopal order" (374), thus substituting the college of bishops for a single monarchical bishop, working, in effect, alone. The bishops (plural) also live and work "in communion with one another and the Roman Pontiff, in a bond of unity, charity, and peace" (374). The bishops are to teach and to preach (378). Moreover, this constitution urges, "the bishops, taken individually, do not enjoy the privilege of infallibility" (379), but proclaim the doctrine of Christ. Chapter 4 of this section turns to the laity, who share "the call to holiness" (396). The church as a whole is the "Pilgrim church" (402-13). Under the section "Our Lady," her obedience to the plan of God is stressed (413-21), and the document affirms that she is "rightly honoured" (421). Nevertheless, "It strongly urges theologians and preachers of the word of God to be careful to refrain as much from all false exaggeration as from too summary [or arbitrary?] an attitude" (422). We recall that the term "Mother of God" is used in Christology of Christ's manhood; in the Fathers it is not primarily about the status of Mary. This section also considers "Catholic Eastern Churches." The council expresses respect for the term "patriarch," as implying jurisdiction over diocesan bishops, "without prejudice to the primacy of the Roman Pontiff" (444). It affirms the validity of the sacraments of the Eastern churches (445), and "wishes the institution of the permanent diaconate to be restored" (447).

(3) The third constitution was *Dei Verbum, On Divine Revelation*. This includes dogma (3.3), exegesis (2.1.6), salvation history (4.2), the teaching office (1.3), and the Word of God (3). *Dei Verbum* defines revelation in terms to which the majority of Christians of all traditions would assent. It speaks of "hearing the Word of God with reverence and proclaiming it with faith" (750); it urges that "God addresses men as his friends. . . . Revelation is realized by deeds and words . . . in the history of salvation" (751). The OT is included and the passages from Heb. 1:1-2 fully cited. Privilege is accorded to "apostolic preaching" (754), and to "the Tradition that comes from the apostles . . . with the help of the Holy Spirit" (754). It comments, "Sacred Tradition and sacred Scripture are bound closely together, and communicate one with the other" (755; *see* **Tradition**). It declares: "Sacred Scripture is the speech of God, as it is put down in writing under the breath of the Holy Spirit" (755). Two chapters are devoted to the OT and NT (758-62). It concludes: "Sacred theology relies on the written Word of God" (763). Bishops must instruct the faithful "in the correct use of the divine books" (764). On exegesis, the constitution declares, "Students should receive a most careful training in holy Scripture, which should be the soul, as it were, of all theology. . . . They should receive an accurate initiation in exegetical method" (719). They should study the themes of divine revelation. In dogmatic theology, it urges, "Biblical themes should have the first place" (719). Clearly the advice of Küng, Rahner, and Congar has been at work, and most Protestants would also endorse and welcome these sections.

(4) The fourth constitution is *Gaudium et Spes, On the Church in the Modern World*. Section 2.1 concerns human dignity; 2.3.3 concerns peace; and 4 concerns the Roman Catholic Church. "Contemporary man is becoming increasingly conscious of the dignity of the human person; more and more people are demanding that men should exercise fully their own judgment and a responsible freedom in their actions" (199). This council is urged to pay careful attention to these "spiritual aspirations." This provides a radical change in the attitudes of the hierarchy down through the generations. The constitution recognizes "these obligations that bind man's conscience" (800). Further, it is urged, "the human person has a right to religious freedom" (800). This has often been far from the case in history. The constitution commends "freedom or immunity from coercion in religious matters, which is the right of individuals" (802). To some Catholics this seems to open a Pandora's box to issues ranging from contraception and abortion to politics, liberation theology, and the place of women in the church. The constitution presses home the issue of religious liberty in a variety of ways (799-812). *Gaudium et Spes* (joy and hope) begins with a comment that resonates with liberation theology. The document begins: "The joy and hope, the grief and anguish of the men of our time, especially of those who are poor or afflicted in any way, are the joy and hope, the grief and anguish, of the followers of Christ as well" (903). It calls for *change in the social order*. Urbanization, emigration, rural settings, and mass media are considered. Hence, it is urged, "A change in attitudes and structures

frequently calls accepted values into question" (907). International aid must be supported (997-99). There is to be dialogue with unbelievers (1002-14).

(5) Nine decrees were adopted. They concerned social communication, Eastern Orthodox relations, ecumenism, the pastoral office of bishops, the training of priests, religious renewal, lay apostleship, missionary activity, and the life of priests. The net result is more pastoral than dogmatic. But it placed the papacy in the wider context of the whole church, gave a special place and priority to preaching, recognized the aspirations of people in the modern world, saw the oneness of Scripture and tradition, and thus changed the face of the Roman Catholic Church in our day. Pope John Paul II (1978-2005) addressed many of the issues that Vatican II raised, and Pope Benedict XVI (2005-2013) especially stressed evangelization of the secular world, and what he called "the hermeneutic of reform" to follow "a hermeneutic of discontinuity and rupture." In the twenty-first century a counterreaction to liberation theology and minor aspects of the council has set in, but the general trend of Vatican II cannot easily be reversed.

Reading: G. Alberigo and J. A. Komonchak, eds., *History of Vatican II*, 5 vols. (Maryknoll, N.Y.: Orbis, 1995-2006); Austin P. Flannery, ed., *Documents of Vatican II* (Grand Rapids: Eerdmans, 1975); A. Hastings, ed., *A Concise Guide to the Documents of Vatican II*, 2 vols. (London: Darton, Longman and Todd, 1968-1969); George Lindbeck, *The Future of Roman Catholic Theology: Vatican II* (Philadelphia: Fortress, 1970).

Virgin Birth

Virgin birth is a loose, popular name for the virginal conception of Jesus. The fullest biblical witness is the account of the message by the angel Gabriel "to a virgin (Gk. *pros parthenon*) engaged to a man whose name was Joseph, of the house of David. The virgin's name was Mary" (Luke 1:27). Luke does not explicitly cite Isa. 7:14, but his phrases reflect the language of Isa. 7:10-17. Matt. 1:23, however, does explicitly cite Isa. 7:14. The LXX version of Isaiah 7 uses Greek *parthenos*, but the Hebrew Masoretic Text uses ʿ*almāh*, "young woman or maid" (BDB 761). John Walton concludes, "Applied to a female, the term refers to one who has not yet borne a child [but] . . . is full of childbearing potential" (*NIDOTTE* 3:418). He also declares, "Though Matthew cites Isa. 7:14 in support of the virgin birth of Christ, he does not depend on the meaning of ʿ*almâ* to establish that doctrine. Likewise, *parthenos*, as with ʿ*almâ*, does not refer specifically to a virgin" (418). Joel Green concurs that the primary meaning of the passage in Isaiah 7, and in Matthew, is christological, denoting "God with us," although it is "congruent" with the virginal conception. Luke, however, declares, "The Holy Spirit will come upon you" in direct response to Mary's question, "How can this be, since I am a virgin?" (Luke 1:34-35). The phrases "come upon" and "overshadow" have a prehistory in Israel's narrative, probably of God's creative power. The rest of the NT, including Paul, does not explicitly refer to the virgin birth, although the phrase "son of Mary" (Mark 6:3) may have significance in this direction. Gal. 4:4 uses the phrase "born of a woman."

The Apostles' Creed includes the phrases "Conceived by the Holy Spirit, born of the Virgin Mary," and the Nicene-Constantinopolitan Creed also has "was incarnate by (or of) [Gk. *ek*] the Holy Spirit and the Virgin Mary" (fourth century). Statements to this effect are formed at the end of the first century or the beginning of the second in Ignatius (*To the Ephesians* 18.1; 19.1; *To the Smyrnaeans* 1.1-2). The *Protevangelium of James* includes a more legendary account of Mary's piety and miraculous conception.

The theological significance of the virgin birth has more to do with Christology than with the status of Mary in the Church Fathers. It points to God's creative activity and purposes. Matthew and Luke are not making genetic or biological comments, but christological ones. The Christian faith, as Robinson and others claim, does not stand or fall by belief in the virgin birth as such. Nevertheless, it is firmly embedded in biblical and Christian tradition. An older conservative classic is J. Gresham Machen, *The Virgin Birth of Christ* (1930); the "scientific" questions are addressed by R. J. Berry, "The Virgin Birth of Christ," *Science and Christian Belief* 8 (1996): 101-6.

Reading: C. E. B. Cranfield, "Some Reflections on the Subject of the Virgin Birth," *SJT* 41 (1988): 177-89; J. B. Green, "Virgin Birth," in *NIDB* 5:786-90; and G. J. Wenham, "*Betulah,* 'A Girl of Marriageable Age,'" *VT* 22 (1972): 326-48.

Volf, Miroslav

Miroslav Volf (b. 1956) was born in Osijek, Croatia, and brought up in Novi Sad, Serbia, both in the former Yugoslavia. The son of a Pentecostal minister, he found himself, as a boy, "on the margins" in a Marxist, largely atheist state. He studied philosophy and Greek at the University of Zagreb. In 1977 he wrote a thesis on Feuerbach, and graduated from Fuller Theological Seminary with an M.A. From 1980 to 1985 he pursued doctoral studies at Tübingen under Jürgen Moltmann, gaining a Ph.D. on Marx; his *Habilitation* was on the Holy Trinity. For a while he taught at Osijek, but became a professor at Fuller (1991-1997), and then at Yale Divinity School (from 1998).

Rowan Williams describes Volf in Volf's book *Free of Charge* (Grand Rapids: Zondervan, 2003) as "one of the most celebrated theologians of our day." This book expounds the central theme of grace, giving, and forgiving. The Trinitarian God gives creation as a gift; gives Jesus Christ to die upon the cross for our sin; grants justification through faith, and community. Prior to this book, Volf published *Work in the Spirit* (Oxford: OUP, 1991) and his well-known book *Exclusion and Embrace* (Nashville: Abingdon, 1996). This won the Grawemeyer Award for religion in 2002. Its theme is reconciliation, and Volf proposes that the term "embrace" provides a better alternative to the well-worn "liberation." Estranged parties must act with generosity toward the other.

Volf's theology is always applied to practical situations in life. Like Moltmann, he regards theology as a practical path of life, which has implications for political theology, society, and economics. He stresses the need for a theological interpretation of Scripture as the basis for all theology, especially in his book *Captive to the Word of God* (Grand Rapids: Eerdmans, 2010). His book *A Public Faith* (Grand Rapids: Brazos, 2011) illustrates his concern to eliminate any division between public and private spheres in theology. He has done much to set up constructive dialogue with Muslims, especially in *Allah: A Christian Response* (New York: HarperOne, 2011). Christians and Muslims, he concludes, worship the same, common God, albeit understood in very different ways.

Vulgate

The Vulgate is the Latin translation of the Bible *(Editio vulgata)* most widely used in the West. It was largely the work of Jerome, and was begun in 382, partly to reconcile textual differences with the Old Latin manuscripts. Jerome's Greek original was similar to the Codex Sinaiticus. At first the Vulgate encountered some hostility because of associations with certain earlier texts, and it embodied corruptions and inaccuracies. In 1546 the Council of Trent declared it the only valid Latin translation, and in 1590 Pope Sixtus V made it definitive for the Roman Catholic Church. In spite of its errors (*see* **Annunciation**), there were papal prohibitions against its revision.

W

Warfield, Benjamin B.
Benjamin B. Warfield (1851-1921) was Charles Hodge Professor at Princeton Theological Seminary from 1887 to 1921. In Germany he studied under E. Luthardt and F. Delitzsch. He was ordained in the Presbyterian ministry in 1879. In 1881 he wrote on biblical inerrancy with A. A. Hodge. In his theology he attacked modernism and defended the principle of "Scripture alone." He was loyal to the Westminster Confession of Faith and to Reformed theology. Some considered him strongly conservative, and yet progressive on evolution; certainly he was wholly conservative on biblical inspiration and inerrancy. On this issue he adopted a more extreme position than James Orr and others.

Webster, John
John Webster (b. 1955) is one of the world's leading thinkers in systematic theology. He was born in Mansfield, England, and educated in the University of Cambridge (Ph.D., 1982), and later received a D.D. and F.R.S.E. He was chaplain and tutor at St. John's College, Durham (1982-1986); professor at Wycliffe College, Toronto (1986-1996); Lady Margaret Professor of Divinity, University of Oxford, and Canon of Christ Church (1996-2003); and professor of systematic theology, University of Aberdeen (2003-2013). He is now professor of divinity at the University of St. Andrews (from 2013). With Colin Gunton, he edited the *International Journal of Systematic Theology*. He has published more than twenty significant books on systematic theology.

Webster's first book was a two-volume translation of, and introduction to, Eberhard Jüngel: *Theological Essays* (Edinburgh: T. & T. Clark, 1989). These volumes focus on "the priority of grace" and "language about God" (1:1). This theology, he argued, worked "with a dogmatic framework of Trinitarian and Christological theory." This shows constant resonances with Karl Barth. It also relates to hermeneutics, including the New Hermeneutic of G. Ebeling and E. Fuchs, and also metaphorical truth. Metaphor brings together "two horizons of meaning" (5), and may creatively expand our horizons. Webster notes and expounds Jüngel in speech event. A second edition was published by Cambridge University Press in 1995. Webster published a study of Jüngel in *Eberhard Jüngel: An Introduction* (Cambridge: CUP, 1991). In 2006 Webster published *The Possibilities of Theology* (Edinburgh: T. & T. Clark), also on Jüngel. He also published *Barth's Ethics of*

Reconciliation (Cambridge: CUP, 1995) and *Barth's Moral Theology: Human Action in Barth's Thought* (New York and London: T. & T. Clark, 1998). This reexamines Barth's earlier work in the late 1920s; considers sin, hope, and freedom; and argues that Barth's work on grace enhances the role of human response. Indeed, all of Barth's theology may be called moral theology in this sense. J. D. Godsey commended this work "without hesitation."

Webster edited *The Cambridge Companion to Karl Barth* (Cambridge: CUP, 2000). He further wrote *Barth's Early Theology* (2004); *Word and Church* (2002); and *Holiness* (2003). In his book *Confessing God* (2005) he discusses the clarity of Scripture, the nature of confession, ecclesiology, hope, and freedom. *The Domain of the Word of God* (New York and London: T. & T. Clark, 2012) developed themes central to systematic theology further. These include the nature of Scripture, especially in Barth and Torrance, and the task and methods of systematic theology. He is currently working on a projected five-volume systematic theology.

Weil, Simone

Simone Weil (1909-1943) was born and educated in Paris, and was qualified to lecture in philosophy, but was most noted for her life of utterly selfless devotion. After the summer of 1941, she was also noted for her profound Christian integrity and Christian perspective on suffering. She abandoned secondary school teaching to experience at first hand "oppression" in factory work and heavy industry. Oppression is more than suffering, she argued; it involves "humiliation" and slavery. In 1941 she labored in the fields of southern France, and when she was asked to help the war effort in England, refused to eat more than oppressed compatriots in France, in spite of headaches and fragile health. A key point came in 1941 with her introduction to the Dominican Father Perrin. In May 1942 she wrote to him what is now printed as "Letter IV: Spiritual Autobiography" in *Waiting on God* (London: Routledge, 1951), 15-36. Here she speaks of her "bottomless despair" in adolescence, when she "preferred to die rather than live without the truth" (17). She recalls her choice to work "in the factory, indistinguishable ... from the anonymous mass," when "the affliction of others entered into my flesh and soul" (19).

A turning point began when she read George Herbert's poem "Love bade me welcome, yet my soul drew back" (21). She states that before September 1941 "I had never once prayed in all my life," but in 1941 she "went through the 'Our Father' word for word in Greek," and recalls that "the infinite sweetness of the Greek text took hold of me" (23). She then said it each day with absolute attention. "At times the very first words tear my thoughts from my body" (24). She reflects: "God likes to use cast-away objects, waste, rejects" (24). She now saw "intellectual honesty" in a new light. Christianity is to become incarnate in a collective body. She was attracted to Christianity partly through its affirmation of, and sympathy with, slaves. She later wrote, "A man loses half his soul the day he becomes a slave. ... Affliction is an uprooting of life" (63, 64). Elsewhere she writes, "We can be thankful for fragility ... to be 'nailed to the very centre of the cross'" (*Gateway to God* [London: Collins, 1952], 88). In 1943 she was admitted to Maddison Hospital, and died in Ashford, Kent, suffering malnourishment and near-starvation, which were contributing factors to her death at thirty-four.

Welker, Michael

Michael Welker (b. 1947) was ordained in the Protestant church and graduated with a Ph.D. under J. Moltmann. In 1980 he completed his *Habilitation* in Tübingen on Whitehead and process thought. He has been successively professor of systematic theology at Tübingen (1983-1987), professor of Reformed theology at Münster, and professor of dogmatics at Heidelberg (from 1991). He has also lectured in America, China, Canada, Hungary, Korea, and elsewhere. He has written *God the Spirit* (Ger. 1992; Eng. Minneapolis: Fortress, 1994); *Creation and Reality* (Minneapolis: Fortress, 1999); *The End of the World and the Ends of God* (Harrisburg, Pa.: Trinity, 2000); and edited *Resurrection — Theological and Scientific Assessments* (Grand Rapids: Eerdmans, 2002) and *The Work of the Spirit* (Grand Rapids: Eerdmans, 2006). This last includes essays by James Dunn, Frank Macchia, John Polkinghorne, and others.

In *God the Spirit,* Welker draws on process thought, as associated with A. N. Whitehead, and stresses the value and importance of change. He rightly focuses more on action and effect in God's work than on "things," and explores interconnections between phenomena. More questionable, however, is his defense of a pluralist and postmodern approach to the doctrine of the Holy Spirit. Postmodernism has healthy elements, but its tendency to fragmentation becomes problematic in this area on the Holy Spirit. Welker tends to prioritize paradox over continuity. Nevertheless, he shows sympathy with Pentecostals and the importance of self-criticism. But he offers some creative interpretations of biblical passages, and also rightly speaks of the Holy Spirit's "selflessness."

Wesley, John

John Wesley (1703-1791) was the son of Samuel Wesley (1662-1735), rector of Epworth, Humberside. He was educated at Charterhouse and Christ Church, Oxford. In 1726 he was elected fellow of Lincoln College, Oxford, and from 1727 to 1729 served as curate to his father at Epworth. At Oxford he and his group of friends, who included his brother Charles and George Whitefield, were nicknamed "the Holy Club" and "the Methodists" because of their attempts to duplicate what they believed to be the devotional practices of earliest Christianity. Wesley was influenced both by Jeremy Taylor's *Holy Living* and William Law's *A Serious Call to a Devout and Holy Life* (1728). Law had distinguished, for example, between "saying prayers" and genuinely praying.

In 1735 John and Charles set out for Savannah, Georgia, on a missionary enterprise under the auspices of the Society for the Propagation of the Gospel. During the voyage they were impressed by the devotion to God of some Moravians. But in spite of his first conversion, events fell out badly, both in his Christian work and in an unsuccessful love affair with Sophia Hopkey, which ended in legal action. In 1737 he returned to England (*Wesley's Journal* [London: Isbister, 1902], 3-28). Wesley now doubted whether indeed he had "saving faith," and began long conversations with Peter Böhler, a Moravian, about his spiritual state (33-41). On 24 May 1738 he awoke at 5 A.M. and read in his NT of God's "exceeding great and precious promises" (2 Pet. 1:4). In the afternoon he went to St. Paul's Cathedral, and heard the anthem "Out of the Depths Have I Called You." In the evening he went "very unwillingly" to a Moravian meeting in Aldersgate Street, London, where "one was reading Luther's Preface to the Epistle to the Romans." He recounts: "I felt my heart strangely warmed. I felt I did trust in Christ, Christ alone, for salvation; and an assurance was given me that he had taken away my sin" (*Journal*, 43). Next morning he was "buffeted with temptations," but cried, "Jesus, Master" (44). In the afternoon he returned to St. Paul's, where he could "taste the good word of God." Afterward he believed that he had "peace with God."

On 7 June Wesley traveled to Germany to meet with Moravians for about three months (69). He returned to England, and found many churches closed to him. But at the urging of Whitefield he began evangelistic work at Bristol. He preached "to about a thousand persons at Bristol," and then to fifteen hundred colliers at Kingswood, Bristol (48). His audience increased to five thousand, and he became an itinerant preacher in London, Bristol, and Newcastle. In 1739 he uttered his famous dictum: "All the world is my parish" (54-56). At Moorfields, London, he addressed ten thousand, and "described the difference between what is generally called 'Christianity' and the true, old Christianity, which under the new name of Methodism, is everywhere spoken against" (61). During this period he may be said to have founded "Methodism," provided it is seen at that particular time as a reform movement within the Church of England. Wesley never wanted to leave the Church of England, or in fact did so, and his brother Charles remained an Anglican even more firmly. But the authorities of the Church of England did not (or perhaps could not) recognize the lay preachers whom Wesley gathered and commissioned as true ministers or priests of the church. Episcopal ordination has long remained a bone of contention in England, and Wesley's preachers, in effect, formed a new denomination.

In America Wesley ordained Francis Asbury (1745-1816) and his colleague Thomas Coke (1747-1814). Asbury and Coke performed in practice the roles of Methodist bishops (called "general superintendents"), and ordained others. In fairness, we may note that Wesley had requested the bishop of London to ordain someone among his American Methodists, but the bishop declined. A new Methodist Episcopal Church was formed in America, for which Wesley edited parts of the *Book of Common Prayer*. There are currently no Methodist bishops in Britain. By 1784 a strain arose between the brothers John and Charles, the hymn writer, because Charles found that John's insistence on ordinations would separate "Methodists" from the Church of England, in which Charles remained with greater and deeper conviction than John. Charles wrote, "With all her blemishes

[Anglicanism is] nearer the scriptural plans than any other in Europe." However, in the light of reading Edward Stillingfleet, John believed that ordination could be valid whether by a bishop or by a presbyter.

Although he is often regarded as a Pietist, John Wesley was always cautious about claims to mediate the voice of the Holy Spirit. He wrote, "How many have mistaken the voice of their own imagination for this witness of the Spirit of God" (Wesley, *Sermon 10,* "The Witness of the Spirit"). His sermons also demonstrate his Trinitarian orthodoxy. He regularly appealed, like Hooker, to Scripture, patristic tradition, and reason, to which he added the fourth component of Christian experience and the witness of the Holy Spirit. A. Outler and others have described this as "Wesley's Quadrilateral." Yet during his lifetime the cold "age of reason" often misunderstood his zeal for God. Bishop Butler told him, "Sir, the pretending to extraordinary revelations and gifts of the Holy Ghost is a horrid thing, a very horrid thing." In 1750 Wesley became "fully convinced that the Montanists . . . were real, scriptural Christians." On the subject of doctrine, it is recognized that he was broadly Arminian, together with Fletcher, his successor. Whitefield, Harris, and Cennick, however, tended toward Calvinism. Ronald Knox claimed that Wesley had an overreliance on "feelings," and regularly referred to "dreams" (*Enthusiasm* [Oxford: Clarendon, 1950], 536; 422-548). The Calvinist-Arminian debate broke out more seriously later. Augustus Toplady and Richard Hill belonged to the Calvinist side; Wesley and Fletcher, to the Arminian side.

It is still widely debated today whether Wesley held to "sinless perfection." In view of his many references to struggle and temptation, most people (including this writer) have strong doubts, but it remains a live question. Moreover, "perfection" is not used in an absolutist way. This was perhaps not a central issue for Wesley. He is said to have traveled over 200,000 miles, to have preached over 40,000 sermons, and to have written thousands of letters. The Methodist Church has steadily grown in America. Wesley never deviated in his emphasis on justification by grace. Whatever his particular points of doctrine, it is for his preaching and his passionate warmth that he will be most remembered. (*See also* **Methodism.**)

Reading: R. P. Heitzenrater, *Wesley and the People Called Methodists* (Nashville: Abingdon, 1995); A. C. Outler, ed., *John Wesley* (New York: OUP, 1964); John Wesley, *Wesley's Journal,* abridged by P. L. Parker (London: Isbister, 1902); John Wesley, *Journals of John Wesley,* ed. N. Curnock, 8 vols. (London: Epworth, 1909-1916); John Wesley, *The Works of John Wesley* (1771-1774), ed. R. P. Heitzenrater and F. Baker, 26 vols. (Nashville: Abingdon, 1975-1982); K. Wilson, *Methodist Theology* (London: T. & T. Clark, 2011).

Westcott, Brooke Foss
Brooke Foss Westcott (1825-1901) studied at Trinity College, Cambridge, and became Regius Professor at Cambridge from 1870 to 1890 (D.D. 1870). He succeeded J. B. Lightfoot as bishop of Durham in 1890 and served until his death.

Although most of his published work was that of an NT scholar, he wrote also as a theologian. He is grouped with Lightfoot and Hort in what William Baird describes as the "Cambridge Triumvirate," as being "not like grasshoppers, but giants in their own right — equal in stature to the tallest of the Germans . . . servants of the Church, dedicated to the relevance of the Bible for faith and life" (Baird, *History of New Testament Research*, vol. 2 [Minneapolis: Fortress, 2003], 83).

Westcott confessed to a special interest in the Epistle to the Hebrews. He rejected Pauline authorship, and highly valued both the language and spiritual power of this anonymous but canonical writing. He dated it before A.D. 70. In 1889 he published his commentary on Hebrews, based on oral lectures. It includes historical, linguistic, textual, and theological details and notes, especially on Christology and on Christ's work as High Priest. He sees the gospel as the fulfillment of the Jewish Law and Jewish priesthood. In Christ, he argues, "the essence of God is made distinct; in Christ . . . God's character is seen." In contrast to more skeptical debates on Christology in the 1870s, Westcott saw Hebrews as combining coherently a firm emphasis on the manhood of Christ with a firm emphasis on his deity.

Between 1870 and 1881 Westcott was continually engaged with textual criticism of the NT, working with Lightfoot and Hort to produce a new text of the NT. Their Greek text especially used Sinaiticus, Vaticanus, Codex Bezae, and the Old Latin. In 1881 he published his commentary on John, and two years later his commentary on the Johannine Epistles. Both followed public lectures on these books. Altogether he published more than twenty-five books. When he became bishop of Durham, he entered fully into the practical problems of the diocese and everyday life, including successfully mediating a bitter strike of the Durham miners. His career was a public witness to the mutual relevance of learning, NT scholarship, Christian theology, and daily life.

Reading: William Baird, "Brooke Foss Westcott," in Baird, *History of New Testament Research*, vol. 2 (Minneapolis: Fortress, 2003), 73-84.

Westminster Confession

The Westminster Confession (1646) is a Calvinist exposition of the Christian faith, which was adopted by the Church of Scotland in 1647, and became the confession of most Presbyterian churches. It originates from the Westminster Assembly's instruction to revise the Thirty-nine Articles of the Church of England in a Puritan direction. It was approved by Parliament in 1648. It consists of thirty-three articles of Christian Faith, from creation to the Last Judgment, and stresses the doctrines of election and grace.

William of Ockham

William of Ockham (c. 1285-1349) was born in Ockham, Surrey, England, and taught at Oxford and London. He was a member of the Franciscan Order, and a late Scholastic philosopher. He was a thoroughgoing nominalist, arguing that language always denotes particular objects, qualities, or events. Universals, he urged, are artificial linguistic and semantic constructions. He taught both Aristotelian logic and Christian theology. "Ockham's Razor" resists undue multiplication of explanatory hypotheses. He argued, "Multiplicity is not to be assumed without necessity." Ockham was a major figure in later medieval thought, and he was sometimes passionately discussed in universities throughout Europe from the 1320s. His academic work was interrupted by a summons to Rome to become involved in a debate between Pope John XXII and the minister general of his Franciscan Order. He was eventually excommunicated by this pope in 1328, upon which he fled to Bavaria under the protection of Emperor Ludwig. According to his nominalist views, general concepts always signify the particular objects that suggest the concepts. The concept "red" simply denotes all particular red objects.

Williams, Rowan D.
Rowan D. Williams (Baron Williams of Oystermouth, b. 1950), former archbishop of Canterbury (2002-2012), and currently master of Magdalene College, Cambridge University, and chancellor of the University of South Wales (from 2013), was born in Swansea into a Welsh-speaking family. He studied at Christ's College, Cambridge, and received his D.Phil. in 1975 from Wadham College, Oxford. He first lectured at two Anglican theological colleges, and was ordained priest in 1978. He became dean and chaplain of Clare College, Cambridge, in 1984, and Lady Margaret Professor of Divinity at Oxford in 1986, at the unusual age of thirty-six. Oxford awarded him the D.D. in 1989, and he was elected a Fellow of the British Academy (F.B.A.) in 1990, and a Fellow of the Royal Society of Literature (F.R.S.L.) in 2003. He became bishop of Monmouth in 1992, archbishop of Wales in 1999, and archbishop of Canterbury and primate of All England in 2002.

Williams has published more than twenty books, and is known internationally as a theologian, poet, and translator. He has specialized largely in patristics, but also in moral theology, ethics, spirituality, Anglicanism, and social change. He is said to read eleven languages, and to have learned Russian to appreciate Dostoevsky in the original language. Some have described him as a "liberal Catholic," but his thought is far too complex for him to be pigeonholed in some generalized category. While archbishop of Canterbury, he did his utmost to listen carefully to traditionalists and liberals to preserve the unity of the Anglican Communion, ranging, for example, from the conservative primates, Peter Akinola of Nigeria and David Drexel Gomez of the West Indies, to liberal primates such as Frank Griswold of the Episcopal Church of the United States of America. Attempts to provide unifying tools find expression in the so-called Windsor Report of 2004 and the "Anglican Covenant," which allowed for different levels of unity and autonomy. But this covenant was rejected in England by a majority of dioceses, and in other provinces. Williams was immensely irenical and sympathetic in trying to negotiate between different attitudes toward gay clergy. He suggested that two apparently incompatible narratives could be transcended, but the debate remained polarized.

The first edition of *The Wound of Knowledge: Christian Spirituality from the New Testament to St. John of the Cross* appeared in 1979 (Cambridge, Mass.: Cowley), with the second edition in 1990 (London: DLT). It grew out of seminary lectures on spirituality given at the College of the Resurrection, Mirfield, and Westcott House, Cambridge. In it Williams expressed his debt to Prof. Donald MacKinnon. The title comes from a poem by R. S. Thomas. "Spirituality" arises, he urged, from one's appropriation of questioning that lies at the heart of the Christian faith. Every human story is marked by ambivalence, not least in terms of a conflict between the family, the state, the psyche, and "pure" realities such as "the soul" (12). The exploration begins with "New Testament Foundations" (14-24). In Paul and elsewhere Christ is Lord. The resurrection of Christ sets free the mission of the church to reconcile, while Calvary uncovers "inexhaustible" truth (15). Yet the acknowledgment of God in the ministry of Jesus brought division. Living by the law can be misleading. The NT shows the "uncompromising reality of God over against our patterns of 'religious control' " (17). Williams cites a number of passages from the major Pauline Epistles that make this clear. Yet he also opposes "event sanctification"; there is no "all-conquering fulness in a single moment" (18). The new life is not a possession or achievement. We must resist "a desire for immediacy" (21).

Williams comments that the unity of the NT is "a unity of direction and vision, not of formulation" (24). Ignatius turns all his polemical vigor against the notion that God in Christ should not share "wholly in the vulnerability of humanity." As a martyr, Ignatius knew both the closeness of God and the reality of his bonds. Martyrdom is the "culmination of a far more prosaic process of unselfing" (27). Only in the second century, however, did something like a "systematic theology" appear, in Irenaeus and Tertullian. They were provoked to write primarily by the system of Gnosticism, with its claims to "enlightenment" and "knowledge." Theirs was "a flight from the particular" (33). Irenaeus stressed that salvation was not "natural" to humankind (35; *Against Heresies* 2.44), while history is real and "bodily." Saving knowledge is not detached from this.

The Word of God is "visible" in Jesus and in history (39). Humankind's destiny is communion with God. Clement of Alexandria and others may speak of "gnosis," but this differs from what the Gnostics teach (43-48). Similarly, Origen moves between the corporate and the individual, especially in his work *On Prayer*. Again the Christian life is an imitation of Christ. Our present life does not wholly enter the brightness of God: "We are in shadow" (51), as the title of this chapter, "The Shadow of the Flesh" indicates. Williams concludes by stressing the complexity of Origen's thought.

Williams explores "the Arian crisis" and Athanasius (57-61). Arius agreed with the Fathers that God is "without a source" *(agennētos)*. But he regarded Jesus, or the Logos, more as a matter of God's election and grace than in terms of a Christology. Athanasius replied that if Christ is a creature, he cannot reconcile God with man. He cannot convey *theōsis* to humanity. In Christ God communicates *something of himself* in history. As the fourth century developed, the debate became increasingly polarized. Knowledge of God, many urged, transcended definition. Gregory of Nyssa expounded participation in God, not in terms of what he is, but in terms of what God does (63). The medieval notion of pilgrimage, it is argued, stems from Gregory's notion of participation, together with Paul's idea of "reaching for what is ahead" in Philippians, and with "going ahead" in Hebrews. This merges into "the celestial journey of the soul" (71). Hence Gregory sees human nature as "self-transcending" (77).

The chapter entitled "The Clamour of the Heart" is largely about Augustine, with the twin themes, especially in *The Confessions,* of struggle and homecoming. God waits for "the soul to come back to its home with him" (79). This is "to rediscover the eternal, patient, faithful love of our Creator" (80). God heals our wounds. A third element in Augustine is desire. The heart is tossed about by desire, but eventually finds its fulfillment in God. Pannenberg, we may note, similarly found this a too-easily neglected resource in Augustine. Augustine's view of suffering is certainly not "moralistic," but is a sharing in the cross. God's love springs entirely from his grace (93). Williams considers Antony, monasticism, and the Desert Fathers, and their theme of "growth-through-conflict" (105). They valued "the limited routine of trivial tasks, the sheer tedium and loneliness" that provided a background for this. Yet the love of one's neighbor remains fundamental. Williams explores Cassian and Eastern monasticism. Reverence must be given to all, especially to the poor. Then Bernard of Clairvaux enters the scene, together with Benedict. Then follow Maximus the Confessor and his work on Dionysius, and Thomas Aquinas, who is "cautious about complex analysis of the contemplative experience" (136). Aquinas provides "the first philosophical exposition" of the struggle involved in the contemplation of God. Finally in this chapter comes Meister Eckhart. Then Williams discusses Luther's inner struggle at the Reformation. Luther, he argues, "looked, with rare simplicity, into the face of God" (155). He notes Luther's substitution of "repent" for the Vulgate's "penitence," and examines in depth "the pivotal statement of the Heidelberg Disputation," especially theses 21 to 24 (157). He stresses the centrality of the cross in Luther (*see* **Luther, Martin**). He rightly notes Luther's theology of the Holy Spirit. In the last chapter he turns to St. John of the Cross and Teresa of Ávila. He calls John "a prophetic figure" (171). John echoes Augustine's attitude toward the beauty of creation, and his theme of "Christ is the Way." Some reviews expressed regret that this book finishes with John of the Cross. Nevertheless, this early book illustrated Williams's broad concern for various aspects of traditional and historical spirituality. It also signaled his constant concern about *struggle, ambiguity, and vulnerability in daily life.*

Williams published *Resurrection: Interpreting the Easter Gospel* (London: DLT, 1982). It arose from Lenten lectures that should not be "completely irrelevant to a divided, complex, and deprived community," especially in Docklands of the East End of London (preface). He acknowledged his indebtedness to V. Lossky and

E. Schillebeeckx. He began with the first preaching of the resurrection of Christ in the early chapters of Acts. The resurrection proclaimed a "startling reversal: the exaltation of the condemned Jesus" (9). Christ is exalted to be judge, and to share the ultimate authority of God. God's act was "faithful to his character as creator" (23). Williams endorsed Augustine's identification of memory with the self. Williams wrote, "On the far side of the resurrection, vocation and forgiveness occur together, always and inseparably" (35). The church must place its own structures and life under judgment: "Only a penitent Church can manifest forgiveness" (53). The church must address all human violence. The church is "the voice of the voiceless" (69). But we should be cautious, he observed, about reading Christ's sufferings as "mine" in a more self-centered way. Christ suffered in a unique sense: his sufferings are experienced not only as mine, but as *a stranger's* (79). Finally, Williams explored the regular issue about the nature of the resurrection. Although the body of Christ was not "a resuscitated body," it is seen in "recognizably bodily ways. He [Christ] speaks and is heard; it is possible to touch him" (100). Williams rejected "vision" as a "clumsy category," thereby separating his view from those of Bultmann, Conzelmann, and Marxsen. In a later paper he also distances himself from Spong. All this placed a question mark against his categorization as liberal, even if his careful choice of words is always sensitive and fair, and never harshly polemic. If he is "liberal," this is only in the classic sense of scholarly and fair-minded, with an eye to the modern situation.

We must endeavor to treat more shortly five more representative books, from 1987, 2000, and 2007. Williams published *Arius: History and Tradition* in 1987 (London: DLT), with a second edition in 2001 (Grand Rapids: Eerdmans). We considered his verdict briefly under the entry for Arius. He first traced the "image" of Arius as an arch-heretic. In Williams's words, "The 'demonizing' of Arius is extraordinarily powerful" (2). Newman saw him as too near to Antiochene Christianity, and as giving a humanitarian and "Judaizing" view of Christ. Harnack regarded him as reflecting "Aristotelian rationalism" (6). Gwatkin saw Arianism as "other" (11). In his book Williams gives a more sensitive, balanced assessment, in the light of his particular historical context and more recent research. He cites, for example, W. R. Telfer, T. Barnes, and especially Christopher Stead, Ely Professor at Cambridge. As usual, Williams stresses ambiguities and complexities, and Arius's rehabilitation in 327, and in 335, by bishops from Jerusalem (79). He concedes that we must live with uncertainties about Arius, but that the controversy with Athanasius was not as sharp and polarized as the Nicene party at times claimed. Indeed, the "Catholic" model of the church comes to be seen as more "monolithic" than it probably was (87). We have in any case only a handful of texts that we can confidently treat as from Arius himself (95). Williams adds a theological postscript on modern scholarship, which he entitles "Arius since 1987," in his second edition. This volume shows Rowan Williams as a meticulous patristic scholar. But it also reveals his wide sympathies and suspicion of "polarization," which was to stand him in good stead as a force for unity as archbishop of Canterbury. He also regarded the controversy as artificially inflamed by emperors, bishops, and "charismatic" teachers.

In 2000 Williams published *Christ on Trial* (Grand Rapids: Zondervan) and *On Christian Theology* (Oxford: Blackwell). The first is published by a conservative evangelical publisher; the second, by a "mainstream" or theologically neutral publisher. *Christ on Trial* considers Christ's trials through the eyes of the four Evangelists. George Carey, his predecessor, commended it warmly as a Lent book. Again Williams focuses on the experience of weakness and vulnerability. He comments, "A trial is an attempt to find out the truth" (ix), and traces the role of "temptation" or "trial" *(peirasmos)* through Job and in the NT. He regards the double meaning as fruitful. In Mark Jesus was "stripped and bound before the court," and was "outside the system of the world's power" (7). Mark invited us to reflect on the nature of "transcendence." Matthew read the OT in his distinctive way. He was "a theologian of God's wisdom" (29), and "trial" tests our whole system of religious language and concepts. If we are freed from our system, we might become attuned to God (44-46). Luke spoke of the God who "turns away the powerful" (51), and gives voice to the voiceless, and to those who are made "outsiders." Luke challenged us to ask: "Who are the important people in your 'map' of the world?" (71). John examined the *identity* of Jesus, and raised questions of authority, truth, and reality. George Carey comments, this book "repays careful study" (viii). It is biblical exposition in the light of today's world, and challenges the assumption of the term "liberal" in many senses of the term to Williams.

Williams dedicates *On Christian Theology* to his wife Jane, who is also a theologian. In his prologue he shows how critical theology may be celebratory as well as sometimes more negative. He cites, for example, the theology of Balthasar. Critical theology questions the "freezing" of theological thought, and can be "as easily conservative as revisionist" (xv). His first chapter explores theological integrity. Reflection may entail "giving our language to God" (9). Praise answers to a reality not already embedded in the conventions of our speech. Williams next explores the unity of truth. As D. Ritschl observed in *The Logic of Theology,* we may seek either a "monothematic" theology with a single focus, or a coherent summary of various topics. The author has suggested examples of each. But each has its dangers, including the distortion of biblical exegesis and perhaps a relative neglect of historical context. But the search for the unity of truth is "required by a commitment to the unity of God" (23), as Pannenberg, we may note, also argues. Theological unity also demands constant conversation with others. This may include "reclaiming the insights of 'pre-critical' exegesis" (44), and observing the discipline of Scripture. The truth of the incarnation and the finality of Christ are involved, and Word and Spirit must be held together. The function of revelation, including poetry, plays a full part in Trinitarian theology (133). Resurrection, ethics, and daily life are also part of the equation.

It is not surprising that Gregory Jones calls Williams creative and profound, and that Fergus Kerr refers to Williams's excellent documentation and generosity to the views of others. He provides running conversations with such thinkers as Bonhoeffer, Luther, Ricoeur, and Aquinas. This admirably introduces his more recent work, *Wrestling with Angels: Conversations in Modern Theology,* ed. M. Higton (London: SCM, 2007). Here Williams begins with his special interest in Lossky. He refers to Lossky's study of Eckhart and the *via negativa*. He brackets this with Dionysius and Gregory of Nyssa, and discusses the research of Daniélou and Puech. The goals of his apophatic theology are "personal confrontation between man and God in love, and the importance of *ekstasis*" (or self-transcendence; 13). This essay is a reprint from 1979. Williams's second chapter is a reprint of "Hegel and the Gods of Postmodernity" in *Shadow of Spirit* (1992). He critically assesses J. Derrida, J. Caputo, and K. Hart. He is reluctant to resort to negative theology, which is "along Derridean lines" (33). The third chapter concerns Hegel again, from a 1998 essay. Williams has at least two chapters on Balthasar, including his work on analogy, or lack of it, between God and humankind (79-83). Williams then discusses Barth on the Holy Trinity. This may relate to Barth on God's self-revelation, but everything is carefully and cautiously framed. Barth's starting point is not a dogma, but the *event of God's speaking* (115). Williams corrects popular misunderstandings of Barth. This, again, comes from an essay in 1979. Other essays consider Simone Weil, D. Z. Phillips, and Wittgenstein and Bonhoeffer. The whole book is marked by a careful and meticulous concern not to oversimplify.

Our last sample from Williams's works is his *Tokens of Trust: An Introduction to Christian Belief* (Norwich: Canterbury Press, 2007). This leads us through the creeds, inviting trust in God the Creator, who is always doing new things, as we might trust a loving parent. He suggests that belief may be helped a little by intellectual discussion, but "is seldom, if ever, settled by it" (28). There are counterarguments, such as the problem of evil and human pain. A world of perpetual safety, he observes, would be artificial. God is interested not only in the "acceptable" parts of our lives. We must "live in Jesus' company" (58). He considers the claim of Calvin and Balthasar that "the cross is the enduring hell itself, the experience of alienation from God" (89). But he also comments, "This is a difficult speculation." Many modern theologians and poets take part in the conversation. Believing in the church, he urges, is "believing in the unique gift of the *other* that God has given you to live with" (106). The gentle and persuasive reasoning of the book is both profoundly accessible and profoundly devotional.

This sample drawn from some twenty books helps us to appreciate Williams's concerns as archbishop of Canterbury. He has always resisted polarization, polemics, and oversimplification. He has been deeply concerned with the unity of the church and the biblical gospel. The charge that he is "liberal" probably depends on his personal conviction of generosity toward "gay" clergy. But he has been scrupulously fair in listening to both sides of this debate. His sympathy for ecumenism and Eastern Orthodoxy is not unconnected with his special respect for Lossky. He is also sympathetic with much Russian thought, as exemplified in his more recent work, *Dostoevsky: Language, Faith, and Fiction*. He attended the inauguration of Benedict XVI, and led a service with him during the papal visit to England in 2010. He has consistently opposed violence, including the Iraq war. He is also deeply concerned with such social issues as homelessness, and interfaith relations with Jews and Muslims. My enduring memory personally has been as a member of the Crown Nominations Commission, which recommends the nomination of diocesan bishops to the prime minister and the Queen. Williams was always a scrupulously fair chairman, and an inspiring preacher and biblical expositor, and president of the Lord's Supper. He is now in his early sixties, and we may confidently await further theological thinking from him, this time without his also carrying the burdens of Canterbury.

Reading: R. D. Williams, *Resurrection* (London: DLT, 1982); R. D. Williams, *The Wound of Knowledge*, 2nd ed. (Cambridge, Mass.: Cowley, 1990); R. D. Williams, *On Christian Theology* (Oxford: Blackwell, 2000); R. D. Williams, *Arius,* 2nd ed. (Grand Rapids: Eerdmans, 2001); R. D. Williams, *Wrestling with Angels* (London: SCM, 2007).

Wisdom

Wisdom in the Bible and in history is clearly to be distinguished from knowledge. H.-G. Gadamer has expounded this distinction more sharply than most others. Wisdom is generally practical, exploratory, creative, and has its roots in the *community*. It stands in contrast with the more *individualist* quest for knowledge, which may deteriorate into a search for mere information. Gadamer cites the parallel contrast between Giambattista Vico and René Descartes, for whom the growth of knowledge began with the lone individual (Gadamer, *Truth and Method* [London: Sheed and Ward, 1989], 19-30; Vico, *On the Study of Methods* [Indianapolis: Bobbs-Merrill, 1965]). William Temple was so appalled at Descartes's assumption that the individual is the starting point of knowledge that he described the formulation of his method as "perhaps the most disastrous moment in the history of Europe" (*Nature, Man, and God* [London: Macmillan, 1940], 57). Vico traces the role of community and tradition from the Roman *sensus communis* and classical wisdom. The Greek *sophia* and *phronēsis* are invoked. U. Wilckens declares, "For Aristotle . . . wisdom *(sophia)* is a purely theoretical virtue . . . not, like *phronēsis,* a practical virtue (*"Sophia,"* in *TDNT* 7:472; cf. 465-528). Gadamer traces the communal concept of wisdom from Vico to Thomas Reid, and even to Oetinger's Pietism. He makes a full-scale onslaught on Enlightenment rationalism, which he sees as shallow and deceptive, and on the pretensions of science to offer a model of all human knowledge. He sees wisdom as relating to all practical human life (*see* **Hermeneutics**).

In the OT there are nearly 200 occurrences of *chokmâ,* "wisdom." Among individual books, the Wisdom literature, as we might expect, carries the highest proportion of references. Proverbs offers on the whole an optimistic view of providence and the practical and educational role of wisdom. Job and Ecclesiastes anticipate more limitations and difficulties. In the Apocrypha, the Wisdom of Ben Sirach shares the general optimism of Proverbs and Deuteronomy, while the Wisdom of Solomon shares the cautious and questioning approach of Job and Ecclesiastes. In the NT "wisdom" or "wise" *(sophia* or *sophos)* occurs twenty times in the Gospels and Acts, and over forty times in the Epistles. Sometimes the OT also uses *bînâ* and *tebûnâ,* "understanding," often in contrast to "knowledge." By contrast, our twenty-first century often misses the contrast, often replacing traditions of wisdom by "information technology," which construes arts, humanities, and human relations as if all could be reduced to "scientific information." Wisdom takes time and patience, and is often transgenerational. "Information technology" can be supplied at the click of a computer. The biblical concept of wisdom replaces the potential arrogance of the self-sufficient individual with a humble willingness to learn from others. Hence: "The fear of the LORD is the beginning of wisdom" (Prov. 9:10); and "My child, be attentive to my wisdom" (5:1). Wisdom is explicitly associated with humility (11:2), willingness to learn (22:4), and patience (14:29). Wisdom concerns practical education and formation of character.

Often wisdom discourse involves indirect communication, rather than confrontation. In Kierkegaard's language it explores the *way.* As he asserts, he who has not the way has not the truth. As in Socrates and Wittgenstein, often "wisdom" asks questions, and seldom, if ever, does it offer neatly packaged, systematic "answers." Sometimes it offers aphorisms: "When pride comes, then comes disgrace" (Prov. 11:2). At other times it may offer paradoxes: "Some give freely, yet grow all the richer" (11:24). Often it uses similes, metaphors, or comparisons:

> Like clouds and wind without rain
> is one who boasts of a gift never given. (25:14)

Sometimes it will use antithetic parallelism:

> Better is a dry morsel with quiet
> than a house full of feasting with strife. (17:1)

> It is better to live in a corner of the housetop
> than in a house shared with a contentious wife. (21:9)

"Wisdom" also varies in its scope in different passages. Brown, Driver, and Briggs distinguish a number (BDB 314-15). For example, "wisdom" may denote skill in craftsmanship (Exod. 35:25); or wisdom in administration (Gen. 41:33, 39; Deut. 1:13, 15); prudence or shrewdness; or various gifts for the complexities of life. Much is said in Proverbs about character, temperament, and habit. This may include truthfulness and integrity (23:23); patience (19:11); self-control and discretion (18:21); and financial responsibility and keeping out of debt (22:27). Yet through all this, God's role in human affairs must have the last word (16:2; 21:30-31). Gerhard von Rad makes this point admirably (*Wisdom in Israel* [London: SCM, 1972], 100-101).

During the intertestamental period, Ben Sirach perpetuates the wisdom tradition:

> Do not slight the discourse of the sages,
> but busy yourself with their maxims. (8:8)

By contrast, the Wisdom of Solomon is later, probably in the first century B.C. It is a time of disillusion. In common with many synagogue sermons of the period, it condemns idolatry (14:8, 12). Yet it preserves some aphoristic maxims about wisdom. In the main, however, it is more akin to Ecclesiastes than to Proverbs.

In terms of style and form, many utterances of Jesus sound like Wisdom sayings. In the 1990s the well-known "Jesus Seminar" of the Society of Biblical Literature proposed a new understanding of Jesus as a "sage" with an allegedly Cynic-style background, based on certain sayings in Q (the hypothetical source of the double tradition in Matthew and Luke), pithy and aphoristic pronouncements. N. T. Wright, B. Witherington, and others have questioned how far such a hypothesis can be pressed (Witherington, *Jesus the Sage* [Minneapolis: Fortress, 1994], 155-208). Nevertheless, it cannot be doubted that some of the sayings of Jesus in the Sermon on the Mount reflect the *style* of "wisdom" pronouncements: "Blessed are the poor in spirit, for theirs is the kingdom of God" (Matt. 5:3-12 and parallel Luke 6:20-23); or "Ask, and it will be given you; search, and you will find; knock, and the door will be opened for you" (Matt. 7:7; Luke 11:9). The parables of Jesus are often standard examples of "indirect communication." Often a story draws the hearer into the "world" of the parable. While the hearer is engrossed in the plot, suddenly a transcendent word or pronouncement catches the listener unawares. The communication has been effective, if unexpected.

The Epistle of James is a prime source of wisdom material in the NT. J. B. Mayor calls wisdom "the principal thing" to which James draws attention, comparable to faith in Paul and love in John. Like Job, James mentions trials to be overcome, and declares, "If any of you is lacking in wisdom, ask God, who gives to all generously and ungrudgingly, and it will be given you" (1:5). 1:5-8 relates to trials; 1:12-18 relates to wisdom, trials, and truth; and 3:13-18 sets out wisdom qualities needed for teachers, for example, gentleness (v. 13), humility (v. 14), self-discipline (v. 16), and integrity (v. 17). Wisdom is not merely intellectual cleverness. Much of James shares the same emphasis as the teaching of Jesus on practical conduct.

Paul sets out a consistent contrast between the wisdom of God, which finds expression in the cross, and purely human wisdom, which is always in danger of arrogance, self-confidence, and presumption. This is especially the case in 1 Corinthians: "If you think that you are wise . . . you should become fools so that you may become wise" (3:18). This also would echo the teaching of some Greek philosophers, notably Socrates. But it is especially centered in Christ and the cross in 1 Cor. 1:18-2:5. Paul writes: "The message about the cross is foolishness to those who are perishing, but to us who are being saved it is the power of God. For it is written, 'I will destroy the wisdom of the wise, and the discernment of the discerning I will thwart.' Where is the one who is wise? . . . Has not God made foolish the wisdom of the world?" (1:18-20). On the other hand, "Christ [is] the power of God and the wisdom of God" (1:24). God has brought about a reversal of human and divine wisdom in the cross. "Yet among the mature we do speak wisdom . . . God's wisdom" (2:6-7). This brings us back to Proverbs: "The fear of the LORD is the beginning of wisdom." (*See also* **Gadamer, Hans-Georg; Hermeneutics.**)

Reading: H.-G. Gadamer, *Truth and Method* (London: Sheed and Ward, 1989), 19-30; S. M. Pogoloff, *Logos and Sophia* (Atlanta: Scholars, 1992); G. von Rad, *Wisdom in Israel* (London: SCM, 1972); A. C. Thiselton, "Wisdom," *Theology* 114 (2011): 163-72 and 260-68; U. Wilckens, *"Sophia,"* in *TDNT* 7:465-528; B. Witherington, *Jesus the Sage* (Minneapolis: Fortress, 1994).

Wittgenstein, Ludwig J. J.

Ludwig J. J. Wittgenstein (1889-1951) was without doubt one of the most brilliant and creative philosophers of the twentieth century. There is not space to do justice to his fascinating life; it is recounted in part in Norman Malcolm and G. H. von Wright, *Ludwig Wittgenstein: A Memoir* (Oxford: OUP, 1966). He was born in Vienna into a musical home, but in 1908 undertook research into aeronautics at Manchester University. By 1912 his interest had shifted to pure mathematics, which he studied under B. Russell at Trinity College, Cambridge. With the outbreak of the First World War (1914), he joined the Austrian army, carrying material for his *Notebooks* in his knapsack during war service, which finally emerged as the *Tractatus Logico-Philosophicus* (1921). This was organized around seven major propositions, with numerous subdivisions. The work may be described as one of "logical atomism," that is, as an atomistic picture of the world and language. Independent "facts" are correlated with propositions, which may either be descriptive or purely logical or formal. His third proposition is "A logical picture of facts is a thought." His so-called picture theory of language accounted for all the propositions of the natural world. Some, including Russell, regarded this as excluding God and theism, but Wittgenstein, on the contrary, believed that on some valid questions we could only remain silent. These may be the more important. In proposition 4.1212 he declared, "What *can* be shown *(gezeigt) cannot* be said *(gesagt).*" In secondary literature, A. Janik and S. Toulmin, *Wittgenstein's Vienna* (London: Nicholson, 1973), demonstrate this in Wittgenstein. His concluding proposition is "What we cannot speak about we must pass over in silence" (7).

Russell secured the publication of the *Tractatus,* even though Wittgenstein disowned a positivist interpretation. Even in this early period he admired the indirect communication of Kierkegaard and Dostoevsky and had met Brahms and Ravel in his home. It is possible to see the *Tractatus* in Kantian terms, as a study of the limits of thought and reason, leaving a "beyond" that transcends the limits of conceptual thought. From 1919 until nearly 1929 Wittgenstein genuinely believed that he had "solved" the main problem of philosophy, and in *logical* terms the *Tractatus* was a masterpiece. But dissatisfaction began to surface. After nearly ten years as a schoolmaster in Austria, he returned to Cambridge as a fellow of Trinity College. Malcolm recounts, "He drove himself fiercely with absolute, relentless honesty [and] ruthless integrity" (27). He produced works between 1929 and 1933 that revealed a new exploration of concepts and logic. Around 1933 he came to see language as infinitely complex and multilayered, and as serving many "ordinary" functions in everyday life.

While his thinking was developing, Wittgenstein produced thoughts that were later published as *The Blue and Brown Books* (Oxford: Blackwell, 1958). *The Blue Book* comprised Cambridge class notes made in 1933-1934, and *The Brown Book*, notes to two pupils dictated in 1934-1935. Even Wittgenstein acknowledged, "It's very difficult to understand them, as so many points are just hinted at" (v). Already he wrote, first, "Language games are forms of language in which a child begins to make use of words" that relate to "activities, reactions" (17). Second, he wrote, "Our craving for generality . . . or preoccupation with the method of science . . . leads the philosopher into complete darkness. . . . I could also have said, 'the contemptuous attitude towards the particular case'" (18). Third, he rejected "an ideal language, as opposed to an ordinary one. . . . Our method is not merely to enumerate actual usages of words but deliberately to invent new ones" (28). Fourth, he examined especially such words as "to wish, to expect, to long for" (30) and their logical "grammar."

These four remarks lay the foundation for Wittgenstein's most famous work, *Philosophical Investigations* (Oxford: Blackwell, 1958). Part 1 was complete by 1944; part 2 was written between 1947 and 1949, and edited by Rush Rhees and G. E. M. Anscombe. First, he rejects "this general notion of the meaning of a word" (sect. 5). We must take account of context-to-life or of "language and the actions into which it is woven, [i.e.,] the 'language game'" (sect. 7). What is important is how words are *used* and *applied* (sect. 11). Second, there are "*countless kinds*" of sentences, for "the *speaking* of language is part of an activity, or of a form of life," as the term "language game" indicates (sect. 23). Wittgenstein writes, "Compare the multiplicity of the tools in language . . . with what logicians have said about the structure of language" (including the author of the *Tractatus*; sect. 23). Third, "an ostensive definition can be variously interpreted in *every case*" (sect. 28). This applies to a name or a picture. A picture of a boxer, for example, may mean "fight like this," or "don't fight like this," or "this is how *x* fought." He remarks: "point to a piece of paper. And now point to its shape — now its colour — now to its number. . . . How did you do it?" (sect. 33). This is the context of his famous observation, "Philosophical problems arise when language *goes on holiday,*" that is, when it is abstracted from its context or purpose or function in life (sect. 38). Hence he makes the comment "For a *large* class of cases, though not for all, . . . the meaning of a word is its use in the language" (sect. 43). In other words, we cannot ask about meaning in language "*outside* a particular language-game" (sect. 47). "Naming" is not an operative move in a language game "any more than putting a piece in its place on the board is a move in chess" (sect. 49). To stress language-in-action or use, Wittgenstein writes, "One learns the game by watching how others play" (sect. 54).

Even these basic comments show Wittgenstein's value for theology. We do not evangelize an outsider, or convey theological meaning to the world, simply by discovering and changing words into a trendy or secular *vocabulary,* as some in the 1960s seemed to think. Second, *"pictures,"* often prized by mystics and charismatics, tell us nothing in themselves, but in as far as they are reflectively *interpreted.* Too often, in Wittgenstein's words, "A picture held us captive. And we could not get outside it" (sect. 115). Third, the principle has begun to emerge that the *language and life* are bound together as a unity, not only for the sake of integrity, but for *credibility* and *communication.* People learn Christianity by "watching" how people *act* as well as speak.

As *Philosophical Investigations* proceeds, Wittgenstein turns increasingly to specific examples of conceptual grammar, which he explores further in *Zettel* and other works. In all cases, he writes, "There is not *a* philosophical method, though there are indeed methods, like different therapies" (sect. 133). Most of his selected concepts are relevant to theology. He explores the grammar of "understanding" (sects. 138-55), which is relevant to hermeneutics. Like Gadamer, he observes, "The application is still a criterion of understanding" (sect. 146). He compares "understanding" with "knowing," and "knowing how to go on" (sects. 179-205). He examines "private language" and "common behaviour" (sects. 206-42). He especially explores "pain" and "pain language" (sects. 243-317). "Giving" presupposes action and public criteria; for example, "Why can't my right hand give my left hand money?" This relates to "body" in theology. He returns to "thinking" and "saying" (sects. 318-69).

Wittgenstein pursues this in *Zettel* (Oxford: Blackwell, 1967). The grammar of "love" and the grammar of "pain" relate to *life,* and are hugely different. He writes, "Love is not a feeling. . . . One does not say 'That was not true pain, or it would not have gone off so quickly'" (*Zettel,* sect. 504). But could some say, "I love you so deeply," and add, "Oh, it's all right; it's gone off now"? Wittgenstein also develops this in part 2 of *Investigations.* Over many pages he explores what it is to "see . . . as . . ." (part 2, XI, 193-229). I have applied this to justification by grace through faith in several studies (*see* **Justification**, and *The Two Horizons* [Grand Rapids: Eerdmans, 1980], 415-22). "Seeing as" takes place within a system or framework: God sees the believer as sinful within the framework of history; he sees the believer as righteous within the framework of eschatology. Wittgenstein shows how "I believe . . ." relates to behavior, as a disposition: "my own relation to my words is wholly different from other people's" (II, X, 192); belief has consequences for behavior. Reflection on "to expect" began in *The Blue Book,* 20-21, 36-40, and continues in *Investigations* sects. 444-60. Expectation is not just a mental or "inner state." To expect someone for tea means laying the table, buying food, perhaps tidying the room (*The Blue Book,* 20). To expect the parousia or return of Christ is to act appropriately, not to nurture an emotion or state of mind (discussed in A. C. Thiselton, *Life after Death* [Grand Rapids: Eerdmans, 2012], 58-67). I have argued that it even shed light on Paul's notorious passage "We who are alive, who are left" (1 Thess. 4:17; *Life after Death,* 68-69, and elsewhere). Wittgenstein specifically observes that *Investigations* serves "to stimulate someone to thoughts of his own" (x). This is one of his great understatements.

Reading: D. M. High, *Language, Persons, and Belief* (New York: OUP, 1967); A. Janik and S. Toulmin, *Wittgenstein's Vienna* (London: Nicholson, 1973); N. Malcolm and G. H. von Wright, *Wittgenstein: A Memoir* (Oxford: OUP, 1966); A. C. Thiselton, *The Two Horizons* (Grand Rapids: Eerdmans, 1980), 24-33, 357-431; L. Wittgenstein, *Philosophical Investigations* (Oxford: Blackwell, 1958, 1967); L. Wittgenstein, *Tractatus Logico-Philosophicus* (New York: Humanities Press; London: Routledge, 1961); L. Wittgenstein, *Zettel* (Eng. Oxford: Blackwell, 1967).

Wolterstorff, Nicholas
Nicholas Wolterstorff (b. 1932) has made outstanding contributions as a Christian philosopher to epistemology, metaphysics, speech act theory, aesthetics, and the philosophy of religion. He was educated in the Christian Reformed tradition at Calvin College, Grand Rapids, where he also taught. He also studied at Harvard, and taught at the Free University of Amsterdam and at Yale. In the period up to 1980 he published *On Universals* (1970), *Reason within the Bounds of Religion* (1976), *Works and Worlds of Art* (1980), and *Art in Action* (1980). Wolterstorff broadly defends realism, but with the added concerns characteristic of critical realism. His work in art leads him to engage with speech act theory. Wolterstorff writes, "By performing one and another action with or on his work of art, the artist generates a variety of other, distinct, actions. Some of those . . . are count-generated" (*Art in Action* [Grand Rapids: Eerdmans, 1980, 1994], 14). One action "counts as" another, whether this be the artist's paint, or a motorist's hand signal. The latter may "count as" indicating a right or left turn.

This principle is developed in Wolterstorff's *Divine Discourse* (Cambridge: CUP, 1995). He comments, "Speech-action theory opens up the possibility of a whole new way of thinking about God's speaking" (13). God may elect a deputy to speak on his behalf, so that the speech of the deputy (or biblical writer or agent) may "count as" God's speech. On belief in the content of religion, Wolterstorff discusses "entitled" belief in his work *John Locke and the Ethics of Belief* (Cambridge: CUP, 1996). His new appreciation of Locke focuses on the "reasonableness" of belief in the hitherto neglected fourth book of Locke's *Essay concerning Human Understanding* (1690). Wolterstorff has continued to contribute philosophically to Christian theology through his *Religion in the Public Square* (with R. Audi; Rowman and Littlefield, 1997), and *Thomas Reid and the Story of Epistemology* (Cambridge: CUP, 2001). He has provided (with A. Plantinga) a unique blend of very wide philosophical thought and what is in essence a Reformed theology.

Womanism

Womanism expresses the concerns of a diverse network of Afro-American women and other racial minorities, who broadly support feminism, but see their own experience and problems as not at all represented by the feminist protests of white, mainly professional women. In 1970 F. Beale drew attention to the "double jeopardy" of black women both as a racial minority and as women. She criticized the failure of white feminists to address racism and colonialism. As the movement grew, womanists criticized what they perceived as the narrow focus of feminism, especially with the concerns about career, promotion, and largely middle-class life. Womanism broadened its concerns to include a variety of serious social, sociological, and sexual issues. The term "womanist" may perhaps be derived from A. Walker's book *In Search of Our Mothers' Gardens* (1983). Whereas some feminists speak of "an *ecclesia* of women," womanism shows less readiness to set black women against black men. Defining the movement is still in progress.

Word of God

"Word of God" has three or perhaps four distinct uses in the Bible. (i) First, "word" (Heb. *dābār*) occurs nearly 1,500 times as a noun, and over 1,100 times as a verb, excluding the very numerous uses of *'āmar,* "to say" and "speak." God's Word in this first sense is his self-communication, or self-revelation. It is *God* who is addressing or commanding humankind. (ii) Second, in the NT John explicitly declares that not only is the Word God, but "the Word became flesh" in Jesus Christ. Jesus Christ is the Word of God both in speech and in action. All that Jesus did, including his incarnation, ministry, suffering and death, and resurrection, constitutes the Word of God. (iii) Third, God speaks his Word through agents or mediators such as the prophets. Hence the message that has concrete form in the Scriptures may be viewed as the Word of God, especially when mediated through the Holy Spirit as well as human agents. (iv) It might be possible to add a fourth meaning. The Greek *logos* denotes not only God's speech and the person of Christ, but also the "Logos" of Hellenistic speculation, who is often viewed as a semi-independent hypostasis of God. Many argued that John's prologue also offered a bridge to Hellenistic thought. Christ, John suggests, more than fulfills any notion in Philo's thought about Wisdom or the Word.

The three primary notions of Word of God, however, have a significant history in theology. From the earliest church until the Reformation, all three senses of the term were universally affirmed, although the Roman Catholic tradition placed the "tradition" of the church alongside Scripture. The Reformers stressed the three primary meanings, but post-Reformation Protestant orthodoxy tended to narrow the definition to give special prominence to the third. "The Word of God" became synonymous with "Scripture alone," partly to guard against increasing emphasis in Catholicism on tradition not as a supplement but almost as a rival source. In much evangelical theology today, this view still prevails at a more popular level. Partly in reaction to this, Karl Barth insists on the threefold nature of the Word of God as God's self-revelation: (i) as Jesus Christ himself (the proper sense of "Word of God"); (ii) as written in Scripture; and (iii) as preached in the church. Further, Scripture is strictly a witness to revelation, rather than revelation itself, and is interpreted through preaching. For Barth, the Word of God is always a living Word, represented by *revelatio* rather than *revelatum,* the past record or deposit of revelation. Emil Brunner tends to share the emphasis on Christ as the Word of God. W. Pannenberg stresses the intertwining of Word and event as one "Word" *together,* in which each interprets the other. Thus language and history together express God's Word of grace and judgment. (*See also* **Authority of the Bible; Revelation; Speech Act Theory.**)

Wrath of God
Two characteristics of divine wrath are often overlooked. Whereas his love, righteousness, and holiness are features of God's character that are *eternally intrinsic* to his Being, divine wrath remains time-bound in the sense of being reactive to external people or situations in history. Love remains a *permanent* quality that *characterizes* God; wrath does not. Second, we often imagine that wrath is the opposite of love. But *it is the opposite not of love but of indifference.* To illustrate the point by a human analogy, parents may show wrath when a child is bent on self-destruction, self-harm, or harm to others, because they care so much about their child. Grandparents may still care, but less intense love may invite less intense wrath; they may feel more relaxed than parents about a situation that may bring harm to the child, even to the point of sometimes being more indulgent, and being accused of "spoiling" the child. A. Nygren observes, "As long as God is God, He cannot behold with indifference that His creation is destroyed" (*Commentary on Romans* [London: SCM, 1952], 98).

The OT contains several Hebrew words for wrath or anger. One frequent Hebrew word is '*aph* (e.g., Exod. 22:24; Job 16:9; 19:11; Pss. 2:5; 95:11). It occurs at the very least 200 times. The Hebrew *chēmâ* may sometimes denote "fury" (Deut. 29:23, 28; 2 Kings 22:13, 17; Ps. 59:13; Ezek. 13:15). It occurs at least 35 times. *Chārôn* is sometimes translated as "fierce wrath" (Exod. 15:7; Pss. 69:24; 88:16; Ezek. 7:12, 14). A fourth Hebrew term is *'ebrâ,* usually simply translated as "wrath" (Pss. 78:49; 85:3; Prov. 14:35; Isa. 9:19; 14:6); and a fifth Hebrew word is *qetseph* (Num. 16:46; Josh. 22:20; Pss. 38:1; 102:10), which occurs some 25 times.

Chēmâ is often associated with fire or burning (Jer. 21:12; Isa. 42:25). K. D. Schunck argues that it suggests divine emotion. "*Chēmâ* probably . . . lent expression to the hot inward excitement accompanying anger" (*TDOT* 4:463). Hence *chēmâ* can be "kindled" (2 Kings 22:13, 17). But *chēmâ* can also be "turned away," and not be permanent (Prov. 15:1; 21:14). When God's wrath is provoked by oppressors, it can lead to vindication of the oppressed. In the OT idolatry (Exod. 32:22-24) and social injustice are prime causes of divine anger. Self-willing and self-centeredness invite not only anger, but alienation (*see* **Reconciliation**). Both Augustine and Athanasius recognized this.

The Greek NT uses only two words in general, *orgē* and *thumos*. *Orgē* occurs about 35 times, 11 times in Romans; and *thumos* about 18 times, although some do not refer to the wrath of God. Hatch and Redpath list 300-500 uses of *orgē* in the LXX, and some 300 occurrences of *thumos* in their *Concordance to the Septuagint*. *Orgē* usually applies to God, especially in Romans and Revelation. C. H. Dodd, as is well known, saw wrath as immanent in the world as a self-chosen effect of sin. No doubt "internal" processes are involved, as when many sins bring their own punishment. To cite a mundane analogy, if someone is consistently lazy and disobedient at school, that person's job prospects will diminish. But Dodd is generally criticized for making "wrath" appear too subpersonal. This would also reduce the force of the work of Christ as bringing reconciliation and deliverance from the wrath of God (1 Thess. 2:16). Charles Cranfield criticizes Dodd, but with sensitivity, pointing to the apocalyptic background of Rom. 1:18-32, which speaks of wrath as "revealed from heaven." Similarly the Law brings wrath upon disobedience. Indeed, Rom. 9:22 even speaks of "vessels of wrath."

We cannot claim that the wrath of God is *always* remedial, although it very often has this purpose. "Wrath" in the book of Revelation mainly concerns oppressors who have killed the martyrs or oppressed the church. At all events, the old-fashioned liberal notion that the OT portrays a wrathful God whereas the NT portrays a God of love is thoroughly misguided. It is a subject on which we must beware of glib generalizations. The subject is a serious one, but it is not readily packaged into neat answers.

Reading: B. E. Baloian, *Anger in the Old Testament* (Grand Rapids: Zondervan, 1997); A. T. Hanson, *The Wrath of the Lamb* (London: SPCK, 1957); C. D. Marshall, *Beyond Retribution* (Grand Rapids: Eerdmans, 2001); G. Stählin et al., *"Orgē,"* in *TDNT* 5:382-447; S. H. Travis, *Christ and the Judgment of God* (Milton Keynes: Paternoster; Peabody, Mass.: Hendrickson, 2008).

Wright, N. Thomas

N. Thomas Wright (b. 1948) is a leading international NT scholar, who is currently research professor at St. Andrews University, Scotland, and was bishop of Durham from 2003 to 2010. Wright has the proven ability to write at a profound intellectual and theological level, and also to produce popular reflections on biblical passages that are easy to read at any level. He also speaks regularly in various parts of the world.

Wright was born in Morpeth, Northumberland. In 1968 he entered Exeter College, Oxford, gaining a first-class honors degree in classics, and in 1973 also graduated in theology. He was ordained in the Church of England, and was chaplain and fellow at Downing College, Cambridge (1978-1981). He received his Oxford D.Phil. in 1981 for the thesis "The Messiah and the People of God," which was especially on Pauline theology, with reference to Romans. He then served five years as assistant professor at McGill University, Montreal (1981-1986), and became chaplain, fellow, and tutor at Worcester College, Oxford (1986-1993), and briefly fellow at Merton College (1993-1994). He became dean of Lichfield Cathedral (1994-1999), and canon theologian of Westminster Abbey (2000-2003). He was then appointed bishop of Durham, and finally research professor at St. Andrews.

Wright is a long-term strategist concerning publications. As a preliminary to a projected five-volume series on Christian origins and God, he published *The Climax of the Covenant* (Minneapolis: Fortress, 1991), a collection of essays on Paul, and then *The New Testament and the People of God* (London: SPCK; Minneapolis: Fortress, 1992). Here he discusses historical method, event and meaning, and worldviews. He places Jesus firmly in the context of the OT, the covenant, and "Palestinian" Judaism. The second volume of the projected series, for which the overall title was Christian Origins and the Question of God, was *Jesus and the Victory of God* (London: SPCK, 1996). Here he reviewed the work of the "Jesus Seminar" of SBL, which included especially the work of John Dominic Crossan as well as Burton Mack and Marcus Borg. He addressed the notion of Jesus as a peasant cynic teacher-philosopher in the Wisdom tradition, and the so-called Third Quest. He constantly asks, "What was Jesus seeking to *do* within Judaism?" (99). The "Old" and "New" Quests tended to stress the work of Jesus as a teacher, often following the work of Geza Vermes. The so-called Third Quest is much broader, asking a host of varied questions about the aims of Jesus. Brandon argued that Jesus advocated revolution, but this is corrected by the language of Hengel and Borg about the kingdom of God. Wright patiently and carefully considers the diverse approaches. The real question, "Did he intend to 'found' a church?" Wright argued, is a simplistic one. It is more accurate to say that Jesus envisaged a "restored Israel," beginning symbolically with the twelve disciples. He stands with Sanders and Meyer in this.

It might be regretted that Wright follows the publisher's marketing device of speaking of an Old, a New, and a Third Quest, although this has become a convention. But he succeeds in showing that little holds together in the Third Quest, except its diversity. It does, however, take seriously the deeply *Jewish* setting of the ministry of Jesus, which is exactly the point urged by Wright. Given this viewpoint from within Judaism, many things fall into place. Conflict was caused not by the Pharisees as such, but by language about the temple and "the most cherished boundary-markers of Israel" (179). Jesus used parables, and like other Jewish teachers, used "Jewish apocalyptic and subversive literature" (177). Particularly interesting, to my mind, is the refreshing extrication of Mark 9:1 and much of Mark 13 from long-standing assumptions about the imminence of the end of the world, rather than *also* referring to the fall of Jerusalem. This argument was first forcefully stated by G. B. Caird (Wright, *Jesus and the Victory,* 362 and 470).

The third volume of the projected five is *The Resurrection of the Son of God* (London: SPCK; Minneapolis: Fortress, 2003). Part 1 considers death and resurrection in the broadest sense. Part 2 focuses on resurrection in Paul, and expands 1 Corinthians 15. 1 Thess. 4:16-17 and 1 Cor. 15:51-52, Wright argues, are "functionally equivalent" (215). In Romans Paul considers "faith in God the life-giver, who ... calls non-existent things into existence" (286), and in Romans 8 looks back to liberation as promised in the exodus (258). Wright is one of the few writers who (rightly) explains "spiritual body" in 1 Corinthians as one "energized by the Divine Spirit" (286, 348-54). Such a "body" is "animated by, enlivened by, the Spirit of the true God" (354). Paul's "seeing" postresurrection Jesus Christ was not merely " 'seeing' with the eye of the heart," as Bultmann, Marxsen, and Conzelmann have argued (382). Part 3 expounds the resurrection in Mark and the other Gospels, and moves on to the apologists and others. Resurrection is God's "gift of new bodily life to all his people" (448). Part 4 is on the story of Easter, and takes account of Mary Magdalene (607), Matthew's earthquake (632-36), and other phenomena. Wright sums up much of this at a popular level in his excellent book *Surprised by Hope* (London: HarperCollins, 2008).

The fourth volume, *Paul and the Faithfulness of God* (London: SPCK; Minneapolis: Fortress, 2013), has just appeared at the time of writing. It is in two parts of 1,700 pages. This explores Paul and his context in detail, including his Jewish, Greek, and Roman background. Paul's letters and theological themes are examined in detail. It is too early to pursue this content further. The companion-part is entitled *Paul and His Recent Interpreters.* Wright has long been known as a scholar who, *in broad terms,* approves of Sanders and Dunn in their "New Perspective on Paul," but also has some reservations about it. He sympathizes with their approach but has too much Reformation blood in his veins to accept the notion that it outdates Luther's approach, rather than modifies or supplements it.

Rowan Williams calls the third volume "a worthy succession to his earlier magisterial studies," and Joel Green calls it "Breath-taking, mind-expanding, ground-breaking.... The fourth volume ... is a game-changer."

Wright's huge production of popular literature should not be forgotten, but neither should it eclipse his scholarly research. Like those previous former Cambridge professors and bishops of Durham, Westcott and Lightfoot, he serves both the academic world and the church. His shorter popular books include *Paul: Fresh Perspectives* (2005); *What Paul Really Said* (1997); *Matthew for Everyone* (2004); *Mark for Everyone* (2004); *Luke for Everyone* (2004); and similarly titled volumes throughout most of the NT.

Reading: See titles listed above.

Wycliffe, John

John Wycliffe (c. 1330-1384) was in effect a Reformer before the Reformation. He was a fellow of Merton College, Oxford, and master of Balliol College. His earliest reputation was as a philosopher who reacted against widespread skepticism in

Oxford at that time. In theology he stressed the inspiration and authority of the Bible, and looked to the Fathers rather than primarily to medieval thought. He attacked the doctrine of transubstantiation on both philosophical and theological grounds, although he venerated the sacrament. His book *On the Eucharist* aroused hostility at Oxford, and he was condemned by the university in 1381. He also challenged the authority of the pope, and in his book *On the Truth of Sacred Scripture* he defended the truth and authority of Scripture. He was a well-informed preacher, and when he was rejected by the university, he retired to a pastoral ministry at Lutterworth, tirelessly preaching and writing sermons for publication.

Y

Young, Frances M.
Frances M. Young (b. 1939), Emeritus Cadbury Professor in Theology in the University of Birmingham, is a well-known scholar in historical theology, especially in the patristic period. She became lecturer in Birmingham in 1971, Cadbury Professor in 1986, and Pro-Vice-Chancellor (1997-2002). In 1998 she was awarded the O.B.E. for services to theology, and was elected a fellow of the British Academy in 2004. She edited five volumes of *Studia Patristica*. She was ordained as a Methodist minister in 1984. She also has a special interest in biblical interpretation, and in those persons, like her son, who have disabilities. She has connections with Jean Vanier and his L'Arche community, which provides Christian support, social care, and medical services for the disabled and others.

Young's first book was *Sacrifice and the Death of Christ* (London: SPCK, 1975; London: SCM, 1994), which examines the theology of the patristic church. She then contributed to *The Myth of God Incarnate* in 1977, expressing differences from its more reductionist conceptions of Christology, and parting company especially with Michael Goulder. In 1985, her book *Face to Face* provided essays on the theology of suffering. Cojointly with David Ford, she produced *Meaning and Truth in 2 Corinthians* (Cambridge: CUP, 1988), but she is especially well known for her book *The Making of the Creeds* (with G. Jones; London: SCM, 1991, 2002). This considers the Nicene and Apostles' Creeds, and is exceptionally readable and clear as an ideal textbook for students. The period from the fourth to the sixth century cannot easily be presented better than she does in her book *From Nicaea to Chalcedon: A Guide to the Literature and Background* (London: SCM, 1983, 2011), which examines such thinkers as Eusebius, Arius, Athanasius, Basil, Gregory of Nyssa, Chrysostom, and others. She turned to biblical interpretation in *The Art of Performance* (London: DLT, 1990). This carries the subtitle *Towards a Theology of Holy Scripture* and follows Kelsey and Lindbeck in stating that the Bible shapes people's identities so decisively as to transform them (173).

Young also developed this theme in *Biblical Exegesis and the Formation of Christian Culture* (Cambridge: CUP, 1997). She continued her interest in the NT in *The Theology of the Pastoral Letters* (1994, 2003). In *Brokenness and Blessing* (2007), she wrote on spirituality, as well as in *God's Presence: A Recapitulation of Early Christianity*, based on her Bampton Lectures delivered at Oxford in 2011, and published by Cambridge University Press in 2013.

Z

Zizioulas, John D.
John D. Zizioulas (b. 1931) is the Eastern Orthodox metropolitan of Pergamon, chairman of the Academy of Athens, and a noted and influential theologian of the Greek Orthodox Church. He studied at Thessalonica and Athens, and undertook research on G. Florovsky. In 1970-1973 he was professor of patristics at the University of Edinburgh, and then of systematic theology, first at Glasgow (1983-1987) and then at King's College, London. While he was metropolitan of Pergamon, he became professor of dogmatics at Thessalonica. His main interest is in ecclesiology, and also relationality, the Holy Spirit, and ontology. His three best-known works are *Eucharist, Bishop, and Church* (2001), *Communion and Otherness* (2006), and *Being as Communion* (Eng. New York: St. Vladimir's Seminary Press, 1985). The church, he argues, is founded on a twofold economy, of Christ and of the Holy Spirit. "There is, so to say, *no Christ until the Spirit is at work*, not only as forerunner announcing his coming, but also as the one *who constitutes his very identity as Christ*, either at his baptism (Mark) or at his biological conception" (Matthew and Luke; *Being as Communion*, 127-28).

On relationality, Zizioulas writes, "God is a relational being: without the concept of communion it would not be possible to speak of the being of God.... 'God' has no ontological content, no true being, apart from communion" (17). Hence "Ecclesial being is bound to the very being of God. From the fact that a human being is a member of the Church, he becomes an 'image of God' ... he takes on God's 'way of being'" (15). This mode of being is from the Holy Spirit. He criticizes Vatican II for not allowing "pneumatology" to play a more adequate role. We must relate the institutional in the church to the pneumatological or charismatic. The Spirit also ensures the place of the *local* church in ecclesiology (132). Zizioulas's theology is a creative injection into Greek Orthodoxy today, holding much in common with Lossky's Russian Orthodox theology. (*See also* Ecclesiology; Holy Spirit: The Spirit in Historical Theology; Intersubjectivity; Other, Otherness.)

Zwingli, Ulrich
Ulrich (strictly, Huldreich) Zwingli (1484-1531) studied at Basel and Berne and became a leading Swiss Reformer. He became an exegete of the Pauline Epistles and John. In 1518 he moved from Einsiedeln to the Great Minster at Zurich as

pastor or "peoples' preacher." By 1525 he had preached through the NT. From 1519 onward he attacked the idea of purgatory, monasticism, and the invocation of saints. In 1522 he urged freedom from the control of the papacy and the bishops, and the following year freedom from observance of the Catholic Mass, seasons of fasting, and clerical celibacy. He accepted the authority of the Bible in its original languages, and rejected that of the Roman Catholic Church. His fullest exposition of this principle was his *True and False Religion* (1525).

In 1529 Zwingli engaged in disputation with Luther at the Colloquy of Marburg. He opposed any notion of a quasi-physical presence of Jesus Christ at the Eucharist (*see* **Lord's Supper**). He argued that "This is my body" means "signifies" or "represents" the body. Christ is present, not in the Eucharist, but at the right hand of God. He also claimed that his view of justification by grace through faith was independent of Luther's, although some dispute this claim. An indirect dependence is possible. Together with Luther, however, he opposed the Radical Reformers A. Carlstadt and T. Müntzer, not least on their view of the role of the state, where he also sided with Luther. Further, both Luther and Zwingli saw the role of the godly ruler as positive, in contrast to many or most Anabaptists, although Zwingli did not share Luther's theology of the two kingdoms. Like Luther, he defended infant baptism, and emphasized in this context the unity of the two covenants. The relation between church and state was the subject of Zwingli's *Divine and Human Righteousness* (1523). His *Defence of the Reformed Faith* remains a classic of Reformation theology. In his work *On Baptism* he declares, concerning the nature of signs, "Some have taught that signs are given for the confirmation of an assisting faith . . . but this is not so . . . we are speaking of seals and pledges . . . like circumcision under the old covenant . . . a covenant sign" (reprinted in G. W. Bromiley, ed., *Zwingli and Bullinger* [London: SCM, 1963], 138). Zwingli's reforms received state support, but some factions in the Swiss Confederation resisted them, and Zwingli was killed in the second battle of Kappel in 1531. His successor in Switzerland was H. Bullinger, who also influenced the production of the 1552 prayer book in England.

Reading: G. W. Bromiley, ed., *Zwingli and Bullinger* (London: SCM; Louisville: Westminster, 1963, 1979); W. P. Stephens, *The Theology of Huldrych Zwingli* (Oxford: OUP, 1986).

www.ingramcontent.com/pod-product-compliance
Lightning Source LLC
Chambersburg PA
CBHW032125010526
44111CB00033B/77